Classical Islam and the Naqshbandi Sufi Tradition

Shaykh Muhammad Hisham Kabbani

INTRODUCTION BY
Shaykh Nazim Adil al-Haqqani

FOREWORD BY
Seyyed Hossein Nasr

Islamic Supreme Council of America

 Published 2004. Second edition

Library of Congress Publication Control Number: 2004104760
ISBN: 1-930409-23-0

The first edition of this book was originally published as *The Naqshbandi Sufi Way: History and Guidebook of the Saints of the Golden Chain.*

Published and Distributed by:
Islamic Supreme Council of America (ISCA)
4200 Wisconsin Ave. NW
Washington, DC 20002 USA
Tel: (202) 939-3400
Fax: (202) 939-3410
Email: staff@islamicsupremecouncil.org
Web: http://www.islamicsupremecouncil.org

Publishing Office:
17195 Silver Parkway, #201
Fenton, MI 48430 USA
Tel: (888) 278-6624
Fax: (810) 815-0518

Printed in Canada

بسم الله الرحمن الرحيم

وَاتَّقُواْ اللّهَ وَيُعَلِّمُكُمُ اللّهُ

Observe your duty to God and God will teach you. (2:283)

يَا أَيُّهَا الَّذِينَ آمَنُواْ اتَّقُواْ اللّهَ وَكُونُواْ مَعَ الصَّادِقِينَ

O ye who believe! Fear God and be with those who are true (in word and deed). (9:119)

أَلَمْ تَرَ كَيْفَ ضَرَبَ اللّهُ مَثَلاً كَلِمَةً طَيِّبَةً كَشَجَرةٍ طَيِّبَةٍ أَصْلُهَا ثَابِتٌ وَفَرْعُهَا فِي السَّمَاءِ تُؤْتِي أُكُلَهَا كُلَّ حِينٍ بِإِذْنِ رَبِّهَا وَيَضْرِبُ اللّهُ الأَمْثَالَ لِلنَّاسِ لَعَلَّهُمْ يَتَذَكَّرُونَ

Seest thou not how God sets forth a parable? A goodly word like a goodly tree, whose root is firmly fixed, and its branches (reach) to the heavens - of its Lord. It brings forth its fruit at all times, by the leave of its Lord. So God sets forth parables for men, in order that they may receive admonition. (14:24)

فَوَجَدَا عَبْداً مِّنْ عِبَادِنَا آتَيْنَاهُ رَحْمَةً مِنْ عِندِنَا وَعَلَّمْنَاهُ مِن لَّدُنَّا عِلْماً

So they found one of Our servants, on whom We had bestowed Mercy from Ourselves and whom We had taught knowledge from Our own Presence. (18:65)

اللَّهُ نُورُ السَّمَاوَاتِ وَالْأَرْضِ مَثَلُ نُورِهِ كَمِشْكَاةٍ فِيهَا مِصْبَاحٌ الْمِصْبَاحُ فِي زُجَاجَةٍ الزُّجَاجَةُ كَأَنَّهَا كَوْكَبٌ دُرِّيٌّ يُوقَدُ مِن شَجَرَةٍ مُّبَارَكَةٍ زَيْتُونِةٍ لَّا شَرْقِيَّةٍ وَلَا غَرْبِيَّةٍ يَكَادُ زَيْتُهَا يُضِيءُ وَلَوْ لَمْ تَمْسَسْهُ نَارٌ نُّورٌ عَلَى نُورٍ يَهْدِي اللَّهُ لِنُورِهِ مَن يَشَاءُ وَيَضْرِبُ اللَّهُ الْأَمْثَالَ لِلنَّاسِ وَاللَّهُ بِكُلِّ شَيْءٍ عَلِيمٌ

God is the Light of the heavens and the earth. The Parable of His Light is as if there were a Niche and within it a Lamp: the Lamp enclosed in Glass: the glass as it were a brilliant star: Lit from a blessed Tree, an Olive, neither of the east nor of the west, whose oil is well-nigh luminous, though fire scarce touched it: Light upon Light! God doth guide whom He will to His Light: God doth set forth Parables for men: and God doth know all things. (24:35)

إِنَّمَا يَخْشَى اللَّهَ مِنْ عِبَادِهِ الْعُلَمَاءُ

Those truly fear God, among His Servants, who have knowledge. (35:28)

Shaykh Nazim Adil al-Haqqani (left) is the fortieth and current head of the internationally renowned Golden Chain, and the first to spread Naqshbandi teachings throughout the world. Shaykh Muhammad Hisham Kabbani (right) is Shaykh Nazim's son-in-law and the author of this book. The Golden Chain dates back to early seventh century.

Shaykh Jamaluddin al-Ghumuqi al-Husayni 35th master of the Golden Chain.

Shaykh Abu Muhammad al-Madani, 37th master of the Golden Chain.

Shaykh Sharafuddin ad-Daghestani, 38th master of the Golden Chain.

Shaykh Muhammad Nazim Adil al-Haqqani 40th master of the Golden Chain.

Shaykh Muhammad Nazim Adil al-Haqqani with his son-in-law, Shaykh Muhammad Hisham Kabbani (right), and his brother, Shaykh Muhammad Adnan Kabbani (left).

I
Dedicate
this book to the
Perfect Man
in this time,
the Knower of Knowers,
the Master of Saints
and the Saint of Masters,
my beloved shaykh,
the Red Sulphur,
the Rare Jewel,
the Pearl for Every Heart,
the Beacon of my way,
the Guide of my life,
the Sultan of
Internal and External
Knowledge
in the Most Distinguished
Naqshbandi Order
of this time,
Shaykh Muhammad Nazim Adil
Al-Qubrusi an-Naqshbandi al-Haqqani.
Through him I have been guided
to this Sufi Path,
which illuminated
the light of my heart,
and through him thousands and thousands of people
throughout the world have been guided to this Most
Distinguished Naqshbandi Order; and to all those who worked
hard on this book,
especially our brother Mateen Siddiqui and our sister Dr.
Hedieh Mirahmadi; and to all those who denounced the evil of
terrorism in all its forms, political, ideological, cultural and
eligious; and especially to the people of Bukhara, from whence
this holy tradition was established and refined under its masters
of learning, Shaykh Ismail al-Bukhari and Shah Bahauddin
Naqshband.

Contents

Exordium I
Foreword III
Preface VII
Introduction XIII
About the Author XV
Acknowledgement XVII
Publisher's Notes 21

INTRODUCTION TO THE SPIRITUAL PATH 23

The Naqshbandi Sufi Way 25
Searching for the True Inheritor of the Secret of the Prophet ﷺ 31
The Principles and Transmission of the Naqshbandi Order 57

HISTORY OF THE SAINTS OF THE GOLDEN CHAIN 63

1. The Messenger of God, Prophet Muhammad ibn Abd Allah ﷺ 69
2. Abu Bakr as-Siddiq ؓ 89
3. Salman al-Farsi ؓ 99
4. Qasim ibn Muhammad ibn Abu Bakr ؓ 105
5. Jafar as-Sadiq ؓ 111
6. Tayfur Abu Yazid al-Bistami ق 117
7. Abul Hasan al-Kharqani ق 125
8. Abu Ali al-Farmadi ق 129
9. Abu Yaqub Yusuf al-Hamadani ق 133
10. Abul Abbas al-Khidr ؑ 139
11. Abd al-Khaliq al-Ghujdawani ق 145
12. Arif ar-Riwakri ق 159
13. Khwaja Mahmud al-Injir al-Faghnawi ق 163
14. Ali ar-Ramitani ق 167
15. Muhammad Baba as-Samasi ق 173
16. Sayyid Amir Kulal ق 179
17. Muhammad Bahauddin Shah Naqshband ق 183
18. Alauddin al-Attar ق 217
19. Yaqub al-Charkhi ق 225
20. Ubayd Allah al-Ahrar ق 231
21. Muhammad az-Zahid ق 247

22. Darwish Muhammad ق 253
23. Muhammad Khwaja al-Amkanaki ق 257
24. Muhammad al-Baqi Billah ق 261
25. Ahmad al-Faruqi as-Sirhindi ق 265
26. Muhammad Masum ق 275
27. Muhammad Sayfuddin ق 281
28. Nur Muhammad al-Badawani ق 285
29. Shamsuddin Habib Allah ق 289
30. Abd Allah ad-Dahlawi (Shah Ghulam Ali) ق 297
31. Khalid al-Baghdadi ق 307
32. Ismail ash-Shirwani ق 321
33. Khas Muhammad ash-Shirwani ق 331
34. Muhammad Effendi al-Yaraghi ق 337
35. Jamaluddin al-Ghumuqi al-Husayni ق 347
36. Abu Ahmad as-Sughuri ق 359
37. Abu Muhammad al-Madani ق 365
38. Sharafuddin ad-Daghestani ق 375
39. Abd Allah al-Faiz ad-Daghestani ق 391
40. Muhammad Nazim Adil al-Haqqani ق 425
Burial Places of the Masters of the Golden Chain 473

ACADEMIC RESEARCH ON THE NAQSHBANDIYYA-HAQQANIYYA ORDER 475

The Scientific Observation of Spirituality 477
Harvard University 479
The Haqqaniyya 480
The Charisma of the Shaykh 481
The Structure of the Order 482
The Structure of the Organization in the United States 485
The Political Message 488
University of Birmingham 489
Description of the the Project 489
Methodology/study design 490
Academic and policy implications 490
Focuses of Research 493
Howard University 495
Literature Review 495

Theoretical Framework 497
Methodology 498
Hypotheses 498
Research Design 499
Results and Discussion 500
Summary of Findings 503
UNIVERSITY OF BERNE 507
Introduction to the Study 508
Subjectivity 508
Spiritual Methodology of the Order in Historical Context 509
Historical Outline and Development of Spiritual Methodology 512
Principles of Transmission and Uwaysi Initiation 514
Conformity to *Shariah* 515
Absolute Transcendence and the End in the Beginning 520
Adab, or Proper Conduct 526
Conduct with One's Shaykh 527
Suhbah, or the Gathering with the Saints 529
Rabitah, Binding One's Heart with the Shaykh 530
Visualizing the Shaykh - *Tasawwur-i-shaykh,* 530
Meeting with Shaykh Hisham Kabbani 535
Interview with Shaykh Hisham Kabbani 542
Association with Shaykh Nazim 547
Second Association with Shaykh Nazim 560
Another Association with Shaykh Nazim 562
Association with Shaykh Hisham Kabbani 569
The New *Tajalliyyat* 570
Attraction Through Love 574
Diagnosis: *Bayah* and Beyond 576
Treatment and Healing 577
Treatment and Application 580
Training the *Murid* in the Relativism of All Knowledge 583
Overcoming the Ego and Levels of Sainthood 588
The Six Realities of the Saints 590
Tawajjuh, or the Spiritual Transmission of the Shaykh 592
On the Reality of *Suhbah* 594

DOCTRINAL FOUNDATIONS OF THE SPIRITUAL PATH 601

TAZKIYYAT AN-NAFS (PURIFYING THE SELF) 603
SUFISM: DEFINITIONS, TERMINOLOGY, AND HISTORICAL OVERVIEW 607
Tasawwuf among the Pious Predecessors 607
Tariqah: The Spiritual Path 609
Sufi Leaders Who Established Thriving Communities 610
Contemporary Misconceptions 611
Development of Islamic Sciences after the Time of the Prophet ﷺ 612
Linguistic Roots of the Term *Tasawwuf* 614
The Primacy of the Heart over All Other Organs 614
Evidence from the Quran 618
The Superiority of Love in Worship 620
Classical Teachings on Purifying the Ego 623
Classical Teachings on the State of Perfected Character (*Ihsan*) 623
The *Hadith* of Gabriel عليه السلام 625
Behind the Prophet's House: The People of the Bench(*Ahl as-Suffa*) 632
The Relationship Between One's Deeds and Spiritual Evolution 637
Jihad an-Nafs: The Greater Struggle Is against the Ego 638
Traditions on the Jihad against the Ego 640
SCHOLARLY OPINIONS ON THE PRECEDENCE OF INTERNAL KNOWLEDGE 643
DHIKR: REMEMBRANCE OF GOD 659
Dhikr is the Greatest Obligation and a Divine Command 659
Meanings of *Dhikr* 663
Loudness in *Dhikr* 666
Gatherings of Collective, Loud *Dhikr* 667
Types and Frequency of *Dhikr* 671
Meditate as Often as Possible 673
The Importance of Silent Remembrance 675
Spiritual Retreat, or Seclusion (*khalwah, uzla*) 678
Empowering *Dhikr* with the Divine Name "Allah" 680
Dhikr with *"Hu," "Hayy,"* and *"Haqq"* 682
Dhikr in Dimly lit Surroundings 683
Movement During *Dhikr* 684
More Traditions on the Virtues of *Dhikr* 685
Istighfar—Asking God's Forgiveness 687
Use of *Dhikr* Beads (*Masbaha, Sibha, Tasbih*) 689
Weak Report on Collective *Dhikr* in Darimi's *Sunan* 693
Benefit of Invoking Blessings on the Prophet ﷺ 696

Specific Benefits of *Salawat* 698
Excerpts on the Remembrance of God 700
On the *Dhikr* of Inanimate Objects 703
Six Benefits of Remembrance of God 705

GUIDEBOOK OF THE SAINTS OF THE GOLDEN CHAIN 715

THE NAQSHBANDI WAY OF *DHIKR* 717
THE SPIRITUAL PRACTICES 722
Daily Spiritual Practices for Initiates 722
Spiritual Practices for the Prepared 724
Spiritual Practices for People of Determination 724
NOTES TO THE SPIRITUAL PRACTICES 725
Prayers 725
Testification of Faith 725
Allahu Allahu Allahu Haqq 726
The Verse "*The Messenger believeth...*" (2:285-286) 726
Suratu-l-Fatiha (1) 727
Chief of prayers on the Prophet 728
Suratu-l-Ikhlas (112) 730
Suratu-l-Inshirah (94) 730
Suratu-l-Falaq (113) and Suratu-n-Nas (114) 730
Muhasabah – Accounting 732
DHIKR IN CONGREGATION: KHATMU-L-KHWAJAGAN 734
INVOKING THE MASTERS 742
INVOCATION OF IMAM AL-MAHDI AND HIS DEPUTIES 744
SALATU-L-MAGHRIB 746
Adhan (call to prayer) 746
Salatu-l-Janazah 750
Salatu-l-Awwabin 752
SALATU-L-ISHA 755
SALATU-L-FAJR 757
Salatu munajiyyah 760
99 Beautiful Names of God 771
SALATU-Z-ZUHR 775
SALATU-L-ASR 776
PRACTICES DURING RAJAB, SHABAN AND RAMADAN 777
Practice of the Month of Rajab 777

Daily Practices Between Maghrib and Isha in Rajab 783
Invocation of Rajab 784
Practices on the Blessed Night of Desires 786
Practices on Night of Ascension 787
Daily Practice Between Maghrib and Isha in Shaban 789
Practices of the 15th of Shaban 791
The Grand Transmitted Supplication 793
Ramadan Salatu-t-Tarawih 804
NOTES TO THE GUIDEBOOK 805
Salatu-l-Maghrib 805
Salatu-l-Janazah 805
Salatu-l-Awabin 805
Salatu-l-Witr 806
Salatu-l-Fajr 806
EXPLANATIONS AND PROCEDURES 807
Salatu-n-Najat 807
Salatu-t-Tasabih 810
CONDUCT OF PILGRIMAGE - HAJJ 811
Obligations of Hajj According to the Four Schools 812
Restrictions of *Ihram* 812
Summarized Steps of Hajj 813
Umrah – Summary of Steps 815
Hajj and *Umrah* - Detailed Steps 815
Ihram 817
Tawaf al-Qudum 823
Sai 825
Standing at Arafah 826
Stoning the *Jamarat* 827
Stay at Mina 828
Zamzam 829
Significance of the Black Stone 830
Significance of *Sai* 831
Holy Places of Visitation in Makkah 832
VISITING MADINAT AL-MUNAWWARAH 835
Significance of the Prophet's Mosque and Grave 835
Etiquette in the *Rawdah* 838
Greeting the Prophet ﷺ 842

Exordium

All praise belongs to God Almighty Who created the universe from absolute nothingness; Who brought the creations into existence and illuminated them with His Light, adorning them with His Names and Attributes; and Who reflects them in the mirror of His Reality. He honored His special servants by letting them behold the splendor of His Light and manifested to them His abiding Presence by raising them to an exalted station.

Praise be to God, Who lavished His Divine Love on the people of ecstasy, and adorned them with His acceptance and satisfaction, and blessed those who are seeking the most distinguished path to Him. He allows whomsoever He likes to enter into His Presence and to receive from His Words, which are the Origin of Origins, the Reality of Realities, the Light of Lights. Praise belongs to Him, and through this Praise, I am asking Him to open to us the doors of His heavenly Goodness and thanking Him with thanks scented with the perfume of the roses of His Names.

I bear testimony that He is the Only One to be worshipped, and He is the Only Source of Goodness. I bear witness that His Messenger, our supporter, Muhammad ﷺ, is His sincere and loyal Servant whom He chose to be the Heart of His Divine Essence. May God bestow His blessings on His beloved Prophet ﷺ, on his family, on his companions, on all those who follow in his footsteps and on all saints and masters of the most distinguished Naqshbandi Order and of all other orders.

May God's blessings and greetings of peace be on our beloved Prophet Muhammad ﷺ, who is a sun from the unseen Light of the Divine Presence, who came forth and outshone the light of the sun. As he perceived he informed, and as he discovered he described. With his light, the Light of Prophecy shone forth, and the lights of prophets thereby appeared. You cannot find one among lights more luminous than his. Who can be brighter than the one who shines upon all creation? His fervor precedes all fervors, his existence preceded Absolute Nothingness, and his name preceded the Pen, because he was before all that is. He is the Master of this creation.

His name is Muhammad ﷺ. He is unique. His word is confirmed. His attributes are most honored. O wonder at his appearance, at his visions, at his greatness, at his fame, at his light, at his purity, at his godliness, at his power, at his visions, at his reality, at his essence.

He was, and he is, from pre-Eternity to post-Eternity. He was known before the universes. He was known before Creation. He was known in God's Divine Presence as the Heart of the Essence, where the Essence manifests itself through him. He was the sincere servant to his Lord from that time. He was mentioned before there was a before, and he will be after there is an after. He is the Sign for all signs. He is the pearl of all jewels. He is the rainbow of all colors. He is connected with God, and neither is he nor can he ever be disconnected. All knowledge is but a drop in his ocean. All centuries are but one moment in his time. He is the truth and reality of existence. He is the first in connection. He is the last in prophethood. He is the internal in truth and the external in knowledge.

God sent him as His representative from His Light and as a sincere servant for His Creation, raising him up to His Divine Presence and putting his name next to His Name. He was a prophet when Adam عليه السلام was between water and clay. Greetings of peace be on his Family and illustrious Companions—God be pleased with them all—who were guided by the greatness of his deeds, the clarity of his speech, the light of his being, and the perfection of his religion; who drank from the oceans of his good manners, of his ethics, and of his perfect state; who bathed themselves in the spring of his secrets in the attainment of knowledge and truth.

Foreword

Sufism has penetrated into the Western world at two far removed periods of history, if we exclude the Muslim population of Europe in such lands as Albania and Bosnia. The first was what in the West is called the Medieval period and in such lands as Spain and Sicily where Sufi orders flourished and even influenced certain esoteric currents of both Judaism and Christianity elsewhere in Europe. The second is the present century when Sufism has expanded much more widely into the Occident, including both Europe and America. During this second period, it was first of all the Shadhiliyyah Order which sank its roots seriously into the soil of the West and created a "space" for Sufism in that world. We can put aside Sufi movements which divorced their teachings from Islam and turn to other orthodox and traditional orders which soon followed the Shadhiliyyah Order in creating branches in the West, including the Chishtis, Rifais, Qadiris, Nimatullahis, and Khalwati-Jerrahis.

Finally, one of the most widespread of Sufi orders, the Naqshbandi, has come to Europe and America and begun to spread its teachings extensively especially during the past two decades. Furthermore, it continues to grow appreciably on both sides of the Atlantic. It is, therefore, appropriate that the present book should now appear from within the Order to explain its doctrines, practices, and history from the traditional point of view for the Western and especially American audience.

The Naqshbandi Order was founded by Shaykh Bahauddin Shah Naqshband born in the eighth/fourteenth century near Bukhara in what is now called Central Asia, but which, at that time, was culturally a part of the Persian-speaking world. The Order spread rapidly from its original home into the Eastern areas of Persia and present-day Afghanistan, and from there into India, which became the home of some of its greatest later figures. Also, it spread eastward to China, where it remains strong to this day, and westward to the Ottoman Empire expanding rapidly into the Balkans as well, where it survives to this day in Macedonia, Kosovo, Albania, and Bosnia. It therefore covers most of the Islamic world except for Islamic

At the same time, the Naqshbandi Order has been one of the main conduits for the propagation of Sufi metaphysic and esoteric doctrines. Some of the foremost expositors of the teachings of Ibn Arabi and his school have been members of this Order including Abd al-Rahman Jami, one of the greatest expositors of Ibn Arabi's teachings. The Order has also included major theological and philosophical figures such as Shaykh Ahmad Sirhindi and Shah Wali Allah of Delhi. And while being strictly orthodox, it has produced masters interested in discourse and dialogue with other religions including not only Christianity and Judaism but also Hinduism as the teachings and interests of the twelfth/eighteenth century Indian Naqshbandi master, Mirza Mazhar Jan-i-Janan make clear.

While not given as much to Sufi musical concerts (*sama*) as some of the other Sufi orders, the Naqshbandi Order has also been directly involved in Islamic art including literature. Some well-known miniaturists were associated with the Order while Jami, already mentioned as one of the foremost expositors of Ibn Arabi, is also one of the greatest of Persian poets given the title of "Seal of Poets." There are also notable Naqshbandi poets who have composed verses in Arabic, Turkish, Urdu and other Islamic languages.

But, of course, at the heart of the Naqshbandi teachings, as that of other Sufi orders, lies the practice of the remembrance and invocation of God (*dhikr Allah*). The goal of the whole of the spiritual life is to remember God, a remembrance which transforms, consumes, annihilates, and finally resurrects the followers of the Sufi path in the Divine Reality. It is the virtue of the present book to present the centrality of *dhikr* on the basis of the most respected sources of the Naqshbandi Path and in the context of the Islamic Tradition and the authentic teachings of masters who alone are competent to guide the adept upon the path of spiritual perfection based upon dhikr and the meditation (*fikr*) which accompanies it.

Shaykh Kabbani must be congratulated for making available this first account in the English language of the history and teachings of the Naqshbandi Order. At a time when there is so much distortion in the presentation of Sufism, the present volume is a precious reminder of the traditional and orthodox understanding of Sufism as represented by one of its major orders. Both those in quest of an authentic spiritual life and serious scholars of Sufism must be grateful to Shaykh Kabbani for this work.

May God shower His blessings upon him and give him strength to continue to present the authentic voice of Sufism, which is none other than the heart of Islam and which seeks to enable man to surrender himself fully to God with all his mind and will through the remembrance of His Blessed Name as taught by the Prophet ﷺ and transmitted over the centuries by various traditional chains of Sufism and masters of the path that leads to the realization of the One.

Seyyed Hossein Nasr
Jumada al-Thaniyah 1415 AH/November 1994 CE
Bethesda, Maryland

Preface

By order of our shaykh, Shaykh Muhammad Nazim Adil al-Haqqani, fortieth in the Golden Chain of Naqshbandi masters, we present this humble volume filled with the Light of these noble masters, their aphorisms, teachings, way of life, and exemplary saintliness. Our goal is to introduce a taste of the lives of these precious gems who light our way to the knowledge of Reality and Truth, to love of the beloved Prophet ﷺ, and to the ultimate goal: to reach the Divine Presence of our Creator.

From its advent, religion has been beset with enemies—both from inside and outside its ranks—whose goal is to destroy its very foundations. While atheism has played a key role in challenging the faithful, more often free thought and socio-political corruption have been the greater perpetrators. Today, there is a vast absence of capable advisors and teachers for the spiritually minded, from whom they receive guidance, counsel, training, and learn the teachings of the prophets and saints. Nowadays one is nearly at a complete loss to find guides proficient in classical Islamic teachings, in the higher disciplines of morality and ethics that constitute Islam's essential character.

On the contrary, today we see ample cases of would-be, self-proclaimed religious "scholars" who are not only unscholarly, but grossly ignorant of the faith. In some cases, these misrepresentative, unworthy leaders indulge in corruption, buying seats of religious authority. This practice renders a harsh injustice to the faith and its sincere, God-fearing adherents, as such leaders abandon Divine guidance for worldly gain, displacing Truth with Falsehood for a paltry price. Sunk in lives of pleasure, they dabble in the role of guiding, advising and preaching, but in reality they scorn the simple lifestyle of Prophet Muhammad ﷺ, his companions ؓ and the generation of Successors ؓ.

Current events have led the world community to ask, what does Islam teach? What do Muslims believe? Do they really condemn injustice, tyranny, and terrorism? While Islam has been thrust onto the world stage, the world observes and learns about Islam, and Muslims everywhere have been put under a kind of microscope. People everywhere are wondering if Muslims truly practice what they preach. Do Muslims really believe men and women and people of all ethnicities are equal? Do Muslims really believe in peace, tolerance, and the love and unity of God as the beloved Prophet ﷺ taught?

In these times of global turmoil it is appropriate to ask, in which direction is our Community headed? Timely measures could have been taken to develop well-trained, wise scholars, whose unstained lives would have promoted them as role models. They would have undertaken the mission of reminding the Community of the Prophet ﷺ of the Divine message brought forth in the Quran and the *Sunnah* (way of life of the Prophet ﷺ). Our condition as a people would have improved; we would have been rewarded and brought closer to God, achieving higher spiritual stations.

The situation was not always like this. On the contrary, as formerly this sacred mission, this great service of calling the Community to remembrance of its proper heritage framed by the Quran and set out in the Prophet's *Sunnah*, was performed by devoted and sincere scholars of spirituality. In time, these individuals came to be known as "Sufis," a word derived from the Arabic *safa'a* which means "to purify," because of the assiduousness with which they applied themselves to holding firmly to the *Sunnah* and employing it to purify their character from all defects in behavior and morality.

For example, we know that in the early second century of Islam, renunciation of the world (*zuhd*) grew as a reaction against worldliness in society. Derived in principle from the order of God to His Prophet to purify people (Quran 2:129, 2:151, 3:164, 9:103, 62:2)[1], the practitioners of this way held firmly to the Prophetic way of life as it was reflected in the lives of his Companions and their Successors, in the ways they employed to purify their hearts and character from moral imbalances and to inculcate in themselves

---

[1] The Quranic verses referred to are: "*A Messenger who shall instruct them in Scripture and Wisdom and sanctify them.*" (2:129); "*We have sent among you a Messenger of your own, rehearsing Our Signs and purifying you and instructing you in Scripture and Wisdom.*" (2:151); "*A Messenger from among themselves, rehearsing unto them the Signs of God, sanctifying them and instructing them in Scripture and Wisdom.*" (3:164); "*Purify and sanctify them and pray on their behalf. Verily your prayers are a source of security for them.*" (9:103); "*A Messenger from among themselves to rehearse to them His Signs, to sanctify them and to instruct them in Scripture and Wisdom.*" (62:2).

and in those around them the manners and upright moral stature of the best of humanity, the Prophet Muhammad ﷺ.

Through slow evolution, this Way ended up as a school of practical thought and moral action endowed with its own structure of rules and principles. This became the basis used by Sufi scholars to direct people on the Straight Path. As a result, the world soon witnessed the development of a variety of schools of purification of the ego. Sufi thought, as it spread everywhere, served as a dynamic force behind the growth and fabric of Islamic education. This tremendous advance occurred from Islam's first century to the seventh, in parallel with the following developments:

- ❖ Development of the bases of the Divine Law and jurisprudence through the Imams of the Divine Law.
- ❖ Development of the bases of the system of belief through Imam Abul Hasan al-Ashari and others.
- ❖ Development of the Science of Traditions (*hadith*) resulting in the six authentic collections and innumerable others.
- ❖ Development of the arts of speaking and writing Arabic.

We see in the verse of Holy Quran, *"Had they kept straight on the path (*tariqah*), We would have made them drink of a most limpid water."* (72:16). The term *tariqah* literally means "path" or "way." It is derived from the *Sunnah* of the Prophet ﷺ, ordering his followers to adhere to his *Sunnah* and that of his Successors. *Sunnah* also means "path" or "way." *Tariqah* thus came to be a term applied to groups of individuals belonging to the school of thought pursued by a particular scholar or shaykh, as such a person was often known.

Although these shaykhs applied different methods in training their followers, the core of each one's program was identical, not unlike what we find today in faculties of medicine and law. The approach in different faculties may differ, but the body of law, the state of art in medicine remains essentially the same everywhere. When students graduate from these faculties, each student bears the stamp of its character. Yet, none are considered any less a lawyer or doctor because their respective affiliations differ.

Similarly, the student product of a particular shaykh will bear the stamp of that shaykh's teaching and character. Consequently, the names given to various schools of Sufi thought differ according to the names and the perspectives of their founders. This variation manifests itself in a more concrete fashion, in the different supererogatory spiritual practices or devotions used as the practical methodology of spiritual formation. Such differences, however, have nothing to do with the religious principle. In basic principle, the Sufi schools are essentially the same.

The Sufi Way, under which individuals undertook the path to God, was an itinerary which charted the course of inward and outward progress in religious faith and practice. Following the tradition of the Companions of the Prophet ﷺ who used to frequent his company—those called "the People of the Bench" or "porch"—practitioners of the Way lived a communal life. Their dwelling places were the mosque-schools, border forts and guest houses where they gathered together on specific occasions, dedicated to the traditional festivals of the Islamic calendar. They also gathered on a regular basis in associations for conveying knowledge, assemblies to invoke the name of God and recite the remembrances inherited from the prophetic Tradition, and circles of study in the Divine Law. Yet another reason for their gathering was to hear inspired preaching and moral exhortations.

The Shaykhs exhorted their students to actively respond to God and His Messenger ﷺ, to cleanse their hearts and purify their souls from the lower desires prompted by the ego, and to reform erroneous beliefs. All this was accomplished by cleaving to the prophetic *Sunnah*. The methods of remembering God, which they instilled in their students, were the very same methods passed down from the Prophet ﷺ. In this way, they propagated upright behavior both through word and deed, while they encouraged the believers to devote themselves to God Almighty with their whole hearts. The aim of their endeavor, then, was nothing less than obtaining God's satisfaction and inspiring love for His Prophet ﷺ. In short, what they aimed for was a state where God would be pleased with them even as they were pleased with God.

These shaykhs, therefore, were the radiant beacons that dispelled darkness from a believer's path as well as the solid cornerstones upon which the Community could build the foundations of an ideal society. The ideal here was the spirit of sacrifice and selflessness that characterized their very effort. These values, in time, imbued the entire social fabric of Islam. The guesthouses, for example, were more often than not found in the neighborhoods of the poor and economically disadvantaged. Needless to say, for this reason they became remedies for many social ills.

As a result of such teaching and training, we find that many students of Sufi shaykhs became fully empowered to carry burdens of others, even as they strove to illuminate the way of Truth. Furthermore, through training and self-discipline they had developed the manifest and decisive will to do so. Genuine scholars and teachers of the Sufi Way leave no stone unturned in conducting their personal jihad (literally "struggle," referring to both the physical struggle against unbelief and the spiritual struggle against the unseen allurements that trap the soul).

History books are filled with the names of Sufis who struggled in the Way of God, some of whom were martyrs, who devoted their lives to confronting the enemies of the faith and calling mankind to the Divine Presence of God, as well as calling back those who had deviated from the true path and the *Sunnah* of the Prophet ﷺ. They accomplished this with wisdom, and they were overwhelmingly effective. Their names and stories are too numerous to list in the span of a single book, even if it had hundreds of volumes.

It suffices to say that the lives of these Sufi shaykhs are overwhelming evidence that Sufism, far from encouraging quietism and retirement from the world that impedes social progress, upheld the highest values of social consciousness as well as religious inquiry and science. In fact, they provide adequate testimony to an unremitting struggle against social injustice and social inaction that took place over the centuries.

It is our opinion that among the various Sufi Ways, the Naqshbandi Way is the easiest and simplest way for the student to understand monotheism (the Oneness of God). It urges its followers to seek a state of complete worship of God, both publicly and privately, by keeping the complete code of conduct of the prophetic *Sunnah*. It encourages people to keep to the strictest modes of worship and to abandon exemptions. It is also free from all innovations and deviations. It does not demand of its followers perpetual hunger or wakefulness. That is how the Naqshbandi Way has managed to remain free from the excesses of the ignorant and the charlatans. In sum, we say that our way is the mother of all Ways and the guardian of all spiritual trusts. It is the safest, wisest, and clearest Way. It is the purest drinking station, the most distilled essence. The Naqshbandi Way is exempt from any attack because it keeps the *Sunnah* of the beloved Prophet ﷺ.

The Naqshbandi Way has two sources. If someone receives from both, he or she will gain everything in this life. The first draws completely from the example of the Prophet ﷺ and the second draws from the example of the perfected shaykh who will take the seeker to the Presence of the Prophet ﷺ. To these shaykhs the reality of remembrance of God (*dhikr*) is to banish heedlessness and to exist in the Divine Presence.

There are two ways for the seeker—whether male or female—to practice *dhikr,* for the Sufi Path offers the Way to anyone without discrimination of gender or race. The seeker may, first of all, recite *dhikr* with the tongue. Second, the seeker may also recite the silent *dhikr* in the heart. Both practices are mentioned often in the Quran and in the *Sunnah* of the Prophet ﷺ[2]. By their means one can reach and be honored in the Divine Presence.

It is a great honor for an individual to taste the honey of a master of the Naqshbandi Order. If God grants that you meet one of them, you will have been granted the most precious jewel to adorn your heart, and you will smell the sweet fragrance of the Way, a Way of which you never conceived, the Way to love and happiness. The Naqshbandi Way is the easiest way to God, Almighty and Exalted, because in it there is no exaggeration in fasting or other excesses. Rather, it is a moderate line in which one can enter worship and be with people, training the heart always to be present with the Almighty Lord.

[2] Example of silent *dhikr*: "*Call on your Lord humbly and silently.*" (7:55) Example of the loud *dhikr*: the Traditions of Abu Mabad and Ibn Abbas, "In the lifetime of the Prophet ﷺ it was the custom to celebrate God's praise aloud after the obligatory congregational prayers." [Bukhari]

Introduction

Our praise and thanks be to God, and our salutations to his beloved Prophet ﷺ. I congratulate my son-in-law and deputy, Shaykh Hisham Kabbani, for compiling this luminous volume on the miraculous lives of the great Sufi Masters, the Saints of the Golden Chain. May he be granted the best of heavenly rewards.

The impetus behind this book is twofold. Our goal has been to introduce to English-speaking people the history of the Naqshbandi Sufi Order, a history imbued with classical Islamic teachings, with deep roots throughout the Middle East, Central Asia, and the Pacific Rim. For fifteen centuries their lives have inspired the masses to God's service. They encouraged entire nations to stand for religious freedom and struggle against tyranny and oppression. Their teachings perfected the spiritual evolution of their followers, lifting millions men and women to heavenly stations, illuminating their daily lives with the remembrance of God and an understanding of life's higher purpose.

As the world around us further erodes into the darkest chapters of its history, in an era when the sheer force of evil relentlessly challenges faith, many seek the beacon of light that will lead them to the Divine shelter of peace and protection. We, therefore, wanted to present the spiritual discipline dating back to Prophet Muhammad ﷺ in the early seventh century, preserved by these Masters over the course of forty generations. We have included the guidebook of spiritual practices, replete with instructions, notes, and transliterations, which are designed to overcome doubt and other negative attributes that bind one to the physical world, thereby opening the heart to spiritual elevation.

In these times when Islam has been thrust onto the world stage, it is sincerely hoped through this humble work that readers will come to better understand the core teachings of Islam, namely, the universal endorsement to practice moderation and follow the middle course, to hold patience, to uphold tolerance and respect for others, to approach conflict resolution in peaceful ways, to condemn all forms of terrorism, and above all, to love

God, appreciate His Divine favors, and strive in His service. The greatest Islamic teaching is that there is no higher station than to serve the Lord Almighty.

I would like to particularly thank my daughter, Hajjah Naziha Adil, and those who labored hard with Shaykh Hisham to bring this volume to print.

As my spiritual heir and deputy, who is entrusted with the secrets of the Golden Chain and the support of the Naqshbandi Masters, I pray for Shaykh Hisham's success in quickly bringing a second volume to print, which will further elaborate the miracles, discipline, and Divine powers inherent in the Naqshbandi Sufi Way, whose access is guaranteed through sincerity, devotion, and the purification of hearts.

May God Almighty bless our efforts and those who are on the Straight Path as we move towards the Last Days.

Shaykh Muhammad Nazim Adil al-Haqqani
Fortieth Master of the Naqshbandi Golden Chain
Worldwide Leader of the Naqshbandi-Haqqani Sufi Order
27 Rajab 1424 AH/September 24, 2003 CE
Lefke, Cyprus

About the Author

Shaykh Muhammad Hisham Kabbani is a world-renowned author and religious scholar, who has dedicated his life to promoting the traditional Islamic principles of peace and tolerance and opposing extremism in all its forms. The shaykh is a member of a respected family of traditional Islamic scholars that includes the former head of the Association of Muslim Scholars of Lebanon and the present Grand Mufti (highest Islamic authority) of Lebanon.

Shaykh Kabbani himself serves as: Chairman, Islamic Supreme Council of America; Founder, Naqshbandi Sufi Order of America; Chairman, As-Sunnah Foundation of America; Chairman, Kamilat Muslim Women's Organization; and Founder and President, *The Muslim Magazine.*

Shaykh Kabbani is highly trained, both as a Western scientist and as a classical Islamic scholar. He received a bachelor's degree in Chemistry from the American University of Beirut and studied medicine in Louvain, Belgium. He holds a degree in Islamic Divine Law from Damascus, Syria, under the tutelage of Shaykh Abd Allah ad-Daghestani. He received a license to teach, guide, and counsel religious students in Islamic spirituality from Shaykh Muhammad Nazim Adil, the world leader of the Naqshbandi-Haqqani Sufi Order.

Shaykh Kabbani is the author of numerous published articles and books. His books, which have been translated into many different languages, include the *Encyclopedia of Islamic Doctrine* (seven volumes), *Angels Unveiled, The Naqshbandi Sufi Way, Encyclopedia of Muhammad's Women Companions and the Traditions They Related* (with Dr. Laleh Bakhtiar), *Remembrance of God Liturgy of the Sufi Naqshbandi Masters, Liberating the Soul: A Guide for Spiritual Growth,* and *The Approach of Armageddon? An Islamic Perspective.*

In an effort to promote a better understanding of classical Islam, Shaykh Kabbani meets constantly with heads-of-state, leading men and women of Muslim and non-Muslim nations, scholars, religious leaders, clergy and officials of all faiths.

Shaykh Kabbani has hosted two international conferences in the United States, both of which attracted scholars from throughout the world in his efforts to promote spirituality, understanding and compassion within the family of mankind. The shaykh has also participated in many international conferences and has lectured at colleges and universities throughout the world. As a resounding voice for traditional Islam, Shaykh Kabbani's counsel is sought by journalists, academics and government leaders.

Acknowledgement

My deepest gratitude goes to my shaykh, Mawlana Shaykh Nazim Adil al-Haqqani; the fortieth in the Naqshbandi Golden Chain. My special thanks go to my wife, Naziha Muhammad Nazim Adil, and to all the women who have lent a patient hand in the making of this book, especially Dr. Hedieh Mirahmadi, whose dedication to the Naqshbandi Tradition, far-reaching efforts and inexhaustible striving have been the means by which the moderate image of Islam's authentic teachings have been brought to prominence in this time.

Women are honored to carry in themselves the greatest secret—that of human life.

Jalaluddin Rumi wrote:

The Prophet, to whose speech the whole world was enslaved,
used to say, "Speak to me, O Aisha!"
The Prophet said that women dominate men of intellect
and Possessors of hearts,
but ignorant men dominate women,
for they are shackled by the ferocity of animals.
They have no kindness, gentleness, or love,
since animality dominates their nature.
Love and kindness are human attributes,
anger and sensuality belong to the animals.
She is not your "sweetheart"—she is the radiance of God!

What better example of a woman is there than the daughter of the Prophet ﷺ, Fatimah az-Zahrah ؑ? When she saw that her father was constantly saying, "O my Community," she wanted to do something herself for the benefit of this Community. When God ordered the Prophet ﷺ to find a husband for his daughter, the Prophet ﷺ called all the Companions without discrimination and said to them, "God has ordered me to say that whoever recites the Quran from beginning to end tonight may marry my daughter Fatimah, if she consents."

Again, the angel Gabriel came to the Prophet ﷺ saying, "God is ordering you to ask her what her condition is." Now look at what God had put into her heart and consider the benefit and station of women in spirituality.

The Prophet ﷺ said, "O Fatimah, what is your condition?"

She said, "I hear you continuously, day and night, praying for your Community. You say, 'O my Lord! Give me permission to lead my Community to you! Forgive them! Purify them! Take away their sins and difficulties and burdens!' I hear you, and know how much you suffer for your Community. I know from what you have said that when you pass away, you will still be saying, 'My Community!' before your Lord, in your grave, and on the Judgment Day.

"My father, I see you suffering so much for your Community. Since that love of your Community is also in my heart, I want your Community as my dowry. If you accept, I will marry Ali."

She asked for all of the Prophet's Community, everyone without discrimination. What was the Prophet ﷺ going to say? It was not in his hand to give such a dowry. He waited for Gabriel, but Gabriel did not come quickly. He kept him waiting for some time, then came and said, "God sends you His greetings and accepts Fatimah's request. He gives her what she asked for as her dowry to marry Ali." The Prophet ﷺ immediately stood up and performed two *rakats* of prostrations of thankfulness to his Lord.

Fatimah was only concerned for the salvation of the Community of the Prophet ﷺ. No one is going to be outside of her dowry because if God removes one person from the dowry, it will be as if her marriage to Ali had been invalid. Therefore, she is going to take the entire Community under her wing and they shall enter with her into Paradise. This is from the power of one Muslim woman. She will take everyone with her into Paradise.

What about other such women in Islam? What will their power be? What about saints? What about prophets? God has created human beings pure. He keeps them pure with such power as that of the Prophet ﷺ, Abu Bakr, Umar, Uthman, Ali, and especially our grandmother, Fatimah al-Zahrah, as well as our Grandshaykh, our Shaykh, and the masters of the Naqshbandi Order and other orders.

May God guide us and all seekers in the Way of Divine Love and the Divine Presence.

Shaykh Muhammad Hisham Kabbani
Chairman, Islamic Supreme Council of America
Washington, D.C.

Publisher's Notes

References from the Quran and the *hadith* (holy traditions) are most commonly italicized and offset. References from the Quran are noted in parenthesis, i.e. (3:127), indicating the third chapter, verse 127. References from *hadith* are attributed to their transmitter, i.e. Bukhari, Muslim, Ahmed, etc. Quotes from other sources are offset without italics.

Dates of events are characterized as "AH/CE," which infers "after Hijrah (migration)" on which the Islamic calendar is based, and "Christian Era," respectively. A table of Islamic months and holy days is provided.

Muslims around the world typically offer praise upon speaking, hearing, or reading the name "*Allah*" and any of the Islamic names of God. Muslims also offer salutation and/or invoke blessing upon speaking, hearing or reading the names of Prophet Muhammad, other prophets, his family, his companions, and saints. We have applied the following international standards, using Arabic calligraphy and lettering:

ﷺ *sall-Allahu 'alayhi wa sallam* (God's blessings and greetings of peace be upon him) following the names of the Prophet.

عليه السلام *'alayhi 's-salām* (peace be upon him) following the names of other prophets, angels, and Khidr.

عليها السلام *'alayhā s-salām* (peace be upon her) following the name of Mary, Mother of Jesus.

رضي الله عنه/رضي الله عنها *rady-Allahu 'anhu/'anhā* (may God be pleased with him/her) following the name of a male or female companion of the Prophet.

ق *qaḍḍas-Allāhu sirrah* (may God sanctify his secret) following the name of a saint.

Transliteration

To simplify reading the Arabic names, places and terms are not transliterated in the main text. Transliteration is provided in the glossaries and in the section on the spiritual practices to facilitate correct pronunciation and is based on the following system:

Symbol	Transliteration	Symbol	Transliteration	Long vowels	
ء	ʼ	ط	ṭ	آ ى	ā
ب	b	ظ	ẓ	و	ū
ت	t	ع	ʻ	ي	ī
ث	th	غ	gh	**Short vowels**	
ج	j	ف	f	َ	a
ح	ḥ	ق	q	ُ	u
خ	kh	ك	k	ِ	i
د	d	ل	l	**Dipthongs**	
ذ	dh	م	m	ـَو	au
ر	r	ن	n	ـَي	ay/ai
ز	z	ه	h	ـِيّ	iy
س	s	و	w	ـُوّ	uww
ش	sh	ي	y		
ص	ṣ	ة	ah; at		
ض	ḍ	ال	al-/'l-		

Introduction to the Spiritual Path

The Naqshbandi Sufi Way

The most distinguished Naqshbandi Way is a school of thought and practice that stood in the vanguard of those groups which disseminated truth and fought against evil and injustice, especially in Central Asia and India in the past, in China and the Soviet Union in modern times, and in Europe and North America today. I specifically mean the Naqshbandi shaykhs who took up political, social, educational, and spiritual roles in their communities, acting according to the Holy Quran and the *Sunnah* of the Prophet ﷺ.

The most distinguished Naqshbandi Order is the way of the Companions of the Prophet ﷺ and those who follow them. This Way consists of continuous worship in every action, both external and internal, with complete and perfect discipline according to the *Sunnah* of the Prophet ﷺ. It consists in maintaining the highest level of conduct and leaving absolutely all innovations and all free interpretations in public customs and private behavior. It consists in keeping awareness of the Presence of God, Almighty and Exalted, on the way to self-effacement and complete experience of the Divine Presence. It is the Way of complete reflection of the highest degree of perfection. It is the Way of sanctifying the self by means of the most difficult struggle, the struggle against the self. It begins where the other orders end, in the attraction of complete Divine Love, which was granted to the first friend of the Prophet ﷺ, Abu Bakr as-Siddiq ؓ.

The First Spiritual Inheritors of the Prophet ﷺ

Historically speaking, the Naqshbandi Way can be traced back directly to the first of the rightly-guided caliphs, Abu Bakr as-Siddiq ؓ, who succeeded the Prophet ﷺ in his knowledge and in his role of guiding the Muslim community, and indirectly to the fourth rightly-guided caliph, Ali ibn Abi Talib ؓ.

Imam Ahmad relates in his *Musnad* the following Tradition with a reliable, authentic chain of transmission: "Abu Bakr does not surpass you by virtue of much fasting or prayer, but by virtue of a secret that took root in his heart." The Prophet ﷺ alluded to this secret when he said, in the following Traditions mentioned respectively by Suyuti,[3] "Whatever God poured into my breast, I have poured into the breast of Abu Bakr as-Siddiq," and by Bukhari,[4] "God has expanded my breast to receive what He has expanded the breast of Abu Bakr and Umar to receive." This knowledge is again alluded to in the following authentic Tradition related by Tirmidhi, *"I am the City of Knowledge and Ali is the Door."*

This knowledge is the heavenly knowledge possessed only by prophets and their inheritors, the saints. The latter are defined thus by Ali ibn Abi Talib ﵁:

> *They are the fewest in number, the greatest in rank in the sight of God. By them does God protect His creation. They are His proof on earth, until they bequeath it to their likes, and plant it firmly in their hearts. By them knowledge has taken the reality of things by assault so that they found easy what those given to comfort found hard, and found intimacy in what the ignorant found desolate. They accompanied the world with bodies whose spirits were attached to the highest regard. They are the vice-regents of God, the Exalted, in His land. How one yearns, how one yearns to see them!*[5]

God said in the Holy Quran referring to Abu Bakr as-Siddiq ﵁:

> *He was the second of two in the cave, and he said to his friend (Abu Bakr), "Do not be afraid for God is with us."* (9:40)

Of Abu Bakr as-Siddiq ﵁, the Prophet ﷺ said:

> *If I had taken to myself a beloved friend, I would have taken Abu Bakr as my beloved friend; but he is my brother and my companion.*

The Naqshbandi School is distinguished from other Sufi orders by virtue of its having taken its foundations and principles from the teachings and example of six bright stars in the firmament of the Prophet ﷺ. These great figures were: Abu Bakr as-Siddiq ﵁, Salman al-Farsi ﵁, Jafar as-Sadiq ﵁, Bayazid Tayfur al-Bistami, Abd al-Khaliq al-Ghujdawani and Muhammad Bahauddin Uwaysi al-Bukhari, known as Shah Naqshband, from whose name this Order takes its title.

---

[3] See *al-Hawi li-l-fatawi.*

[4] See *Sahih al-Bukhari.*

[5] See Habib Ahmad Mashhur al-Haddad, *Key to the Garden.* Translated by Mostafa al-Badawi.

Behind the word *naqshband* stand two ideas: *naqsh,* which means engraving and suggests engraving the name of God in the heart, and *band,* which means "bond" and indicates the link between the individual and his Creator. This means that the Naqshbandi follower has to practice his prayers and obligations according to the Holy Quran and the *Sunnah* of the Prophet ﷺ and to keep the Presence and Love of God alive in his heart through a personal experience of the connection between himself and his Lord.

Besides Abu Bakr as-Siddiq ؓ, one of the stars in the firmament of the Prophet ﷺ was Salman al-Farsi ؓ. His origin was Isfahan, Persia, and he was the one who advised the Muslims to dig a trench in the Battle of Ahzab. After the Muslims seized al-Madain, the capital city of Persia, he was made governor of that city and remained there until his death.

Another star was Jafar as-Sadiq ؓ. Although a descendant of the Prophet ﷺ on his father's side and of Abu Bakr ؓ on his mother's, he rejected all positions of honor in favor of retreat and spiritual learning and practice. He was called "the inheritor of the Prophetic Station" and the "inheritor of the truthful station." The oldest recorded occurrence of the term "Sufi" was in reference to his student, Jabir ibn Hayyan, in the middle of the second century after *hijra* (the migration). He was a master in exegesis, a scholar of Traditions, and one of the greatest scholars qualified to give legal decisions in Madinah. His commentary upon the Quran is partially preserved in Sulami's *Haqaiq at-tafsir*. Layth ibn Saad, one of the most reliable transmitters of Traditions, witnessed Jafar's ؑ miraculous powers as the latter was able to ask for anything and God would grant it to him on the spot.

Another star was Bayazid Tayfur al-Bistami, whose grandfather was a Zoroastrian. Bayazid made a detailed study of the statutes of Islamic Law and practiced self-denial. All his life he was assiduous in the practice of his religious obligations. He urged his students to put their efforts in the hands of God, and he encouraged them to accept a sincere and pure doctrine of knowledge of the Oneness of God. This doctrine, he said, imposes five obligations on the sincere:

- Keep obligations according to the Quran and *Sunnah*
- Always speak the truth
- Keep the heart free from hatred
- Avoid the forbidden food

- Shun innovation

Bayazid said that the ultimate goal of Sufis is to know God in this world, to reach His Divine Presence, and to see Him in the hereafter. To that effect he added, "There are special servants of God who, if God veiled them from His vision in Paradise, would have implored Him to bring them out of paradise as the inhabitants of the fire implore Him to escape from Hell."

Yet another star in the firmament of the Prophet ﷺ was Abd al-Khaliq al-Ghujdawani, who was born in the village of Ghujdawan, near Bukhara in present-day Uzbekistan. He studied the Quran and the Islamic sciences of both external and internal knowledge until he reached a high station of purity. He then traveled to Damascus, where he established a school from which many students graduated and went on to become masters of jurisprudence, the Traditions, and spirituality in their time, both in the regions of Central Asia and in the Middle East.

Abd al-Khaliq continued the work of his predecessors by formulating the *dhikr* (remembrance of God) passed down from the Prophet ﷺ according to the *Sunnah*. In his letters he set down the code of conduct that the students of the Naqshbandiyya were expected to follow.

Imam of the Naqshbandi Way: Shah Bahauddin Naqshband

In this constellation, we come finally to Muhammad Bahauddin Uwaysi al-Bukhari, known as Shah Naqshband, the Imam of the Naqshbandi Way. He was born in the year 717 AH/1317 CE in the village of Qasr al-Arifan, near Bukhara. After he mastered the sciences of the Divine Law at the young age of eighteen, he kept company with Shaykh Muhammad Baba as-Samasi, who was an authority on the Traditions in Central Asia. After the latter's death, he followed Shaykh Amir Kulal, who continued and perfected his training in the external and the internal knowledge.

The students of Shaykh Amir Kulal recited *dhikr* aloud when sitting together in a group and silent *dhikr* when alone. Although Shah Naqshband never criticized nor objected to the loud *dhikr*, he preferred the silent *dhikr*. Concerning this he says, "There are two methods of *dhikr*. One is silent and one is loud. I chose the silent one because it is stronger and therefore more preferable." The silent *dhikr* thus became the distinguishing feature of the Naqshbandi among other Sufi orders.

Shah Naqshband performed the prescribed pilgrimage three times, after which he resided in Merv and Bukhara. Towards the end of his life, he went back to settle in his native city of Qasr al-Arifan. His teachings became quoted everywhere, and his name was on every tongue. Visitors from far and wide came to see him and to seek his advice. They received teaching in his school and mosque, a complex which once accommodated more than 5,000 people. This school is the largest Islamic center of learning in Central Asia and still exists in our day. It was recently renovated and reopened after surviving seventy years of Communist rule.

Shah Naqshband's teachings changed the hearts of seekers from darkness to light. He continued to teach his students the knowledge of the Oneness of God in which his predecessors had specialized, emphasizing the realization of the state of excellence for his followers according to the Tradition of the Prophet ﷺ, *"Excellence is to worship God as if you see Him."* When Shah Naqshband died, he was buried in his garden as he requested. The succeeding kings of Bukhara took care of his school and mosque, expanding them and increasing their religious endowments.

Later shaykhs of the Naqshbandi Way wrote many biographies of Shah Naqshband. Among them are Masud al-Bukhari and Sharif al-Jarjani who composed the *Awrad Bahauddin,* which narrates his life's works, including his legal decisions. Shaykh Muhammad Parsa, who died in Madinah in 822 AH/1419 CE, wrote *Risala Qudsiyya,* in which he talks of Shah Naqshband's life, his virtues, and his teachings.

Shah Naqshband's literary legacy included many books. Among them are: *Awrad an-Naqshbandiyyah, Tanbih al-ghafilin, Maslak al-anwar,* and *Hadiyyatu as-salikin wa tuhfat at-talibin.* He left numerous noble expressions praising the Prophet ﷺ and he gave many legal rulings. One of his opinions was that all the different acts and kinds of worship, whether obligatory or voluntary, were permitted for the seeker in order to reach Reality. Prayer, fasting, paying the poor-due, striving, and self-denial were emphasized as ways to reach God Almighty.

Shah Naqshband built his school on the renewal of the teachings of Islam. He insisted on the necessity of keeping the Quran and the teachings of the *Sunnah.* When they asked him, "What are the requirements of one who follows your way?" he said, "To follow the *Sunnah* of the Prophet ﷺ." He continued saying: "Our way is a rare one. It keeps the unbreakable bond. It asks nothing else of its followers but to take hold of the pure *Sunnah* of the

Prophet ﷺ and follow the way of the Companions of the Prophet ﷺ in their efforts for God."

Before speaking about the principles and transmission of the Naqshbandi Order, let us provide a brief explanation of *tasawwuf* (Sufism).

Searching for the True Inheritor of the Secret of the Prophet ﷺ

The Shaykh

The shaykh must be deeply imbued with the knowledge of the religion, externally and spiritually. He must inherit from the Prophet ﷺ and all his predecessors the ability and blessing to guide the followers in the externals of the religion and its inner realities. He must be able to guide them according to their needs to the Divine Presence and the Presence of the Prophet ﷺ.

Importance of Finding a Shaykh

God said in the Holy Quran:

O ye who believe, fear God and keep company with those who are truthful. (9:119)

God's Word is for all time, for every era and for every century. It is an ongoing order, from which we understand the importance of keeping company with the trustworthy. God orders all human beings to accompany them, because by keeping their company, one will see how they live their lives, how they deal with people, how they address their companions, how they eat, how they sleep, and how they worship. By accompanying them, one will learn all their good manners and their ways of life.

Another way to understand this verse is that one should accompany a trustworthy person, because to be trustworthy is very rare and not many people achieve it. Everyone, however, can find a trustworthy person and accompany him, in order to be guided. Following a trustworthy person is essential to our spiritual path. Such a person is needed to lead us, to guide us, and to be a beacon for us on that way. In the Naqshbandi Order, the living presence of a connected shaykh is essential. Through his physical and spiritual linkage to the Prophet ﷺ, he establishes the disciple's connection. The disciple's obligation is to maintain his connection to his shaykh, to hold tightly to the hand of the one within his reach. The shaykh maintains the further connection to the previous shaykhs and to the Prophet ﷺ.

A KNOWER

To be a knower means the master must have the knowledge of the conditions of the state of excellence, as mentioned by the Prophet ﷺ in the Tradition:

Worship God as if you see Him, and if you do not see him, know that He sees you.[6]

A knower must bear witness in his heart that God is the Unique One in His Essence, in His Attributes, and in His Actions. He must know about His Attributes through vision and taste, by experiencing self-effacement in the Divine Presence.

SANCTIFIED

The master must have already purified or sanctified himself as a seeker under a master of his own. He will have come to know the different stages of the ego, its illnesses and its defects. The master must be fully aware of all the methods Satan uses to enter the breast. He must know all the ways to sanctify others and the methods to heal his followers in order to raise them up to reach the state of perfection.

If a seeker comes to the shaykh with perfect sincerity and truthfulness, asking to be initiated in the Order, the shaykh must not hurry to initiate him, until he knows that he will remain trustworthy when he reaches the goal. He must look at his capability. If his capability corresponds to the capability of the near ones, then he will show him the way, as it is the way of the trustworthy.

That way is built on effacing one's own will and connecting and submitting oneself to the will of one's shaykh. The seeker must do as the Prophet ﷺ said, "*Die before you die!*" He must leave his natural will, which causes him to move according to his mind, and leave all his affairs to the will of his shaykh. The shaykh will lift him up through a path filled with difficulties, train him through worship, and guide him to a state of complete self-effacement. Only this will elevate him to the Divine Presence.

That is why Khwaja Ubayd Allah al-Ahrar said:

Who is the shaykh? The shaykh is the one who can know, through the vision that God has granted him, the capability of his disciple. From the

---

[6] Muslim.

day he meets him to the day of his death, he will know which state the disciple will attain, in which way he will taste, and in which way he will reach the Divine Presence. If the shaykh cannot summon that knowledge, it is forbidden for him to give the seeker initiation. The shaykh must avoid the wealth of his disciple. If the disciple wishes to help the shaykh it, is his choice. The states of guidance are above all states, and the master must not ask except from the Divine Presence.

It is said that once a disciple of Junayd came to him and wanted to give him all his money. Junayd refused and said, "No." When that same disciple reached the state of perfection and was lifted up to the Divine Presence, he came to Junayd and again offered to give all his money to him. At that time Junayd said, "Yes. Now, I accept, because when you give now, you will not regret later."

We do not like our disciples to give money to the shaykh before they have reached the state of perfection because they might regret later and be in doubt. This will harm them. When the disciple reaches that state, he will give sincerely and will never regret it later. The evidence of this is that Abu Bakr ﵁ and Umar ﵁ came to the Prophet ﷺ and from the first Abu Bakr ﵁ gave all his money. The Prophet ﷺ asked, "What have you left for your family?" He replied, "I have left them God and His Prophet ﷺ." When the disciple reaches the state of real generosity and real perfection, then the shaykh may accept what he gives. If he has not reached that state, his gift must not be accepted.[7]

The shaykh must not order any of his followers to do something he himself cannot do or would not do. He must know all the obligatory and forbidden actions according to the Divine Law. Similarly, he must know all the states of spirituality, and must have tasted all tastes, so that he is an example, and when he speaks he speaks with real knowledge.

An example of this is a lady who came to a perfect shaykh with her son, saying, "My son is always asking for sweets. Please pray for him to leave that desire, as I do not always have sweets to give him." He said, "Be patient for three days and then bring him back to me." After three days, she brought him back and the shaykh told him, "O my son, do not eat candies,

---

[7] See the biography of Ubayd Allah al-Ahrar later in this volume.

because it is harmful for your stomach." From that day the child never ate sweets again. Sometime later someone asked the shaykh, "Why did you wait three days to give the child that advice?" That shaykh replied, "When the lady came to me, she asked me to prevent her child from eating sweets. I could not do that for him because I myself was under that temptation of eating sweets. So I stopped eating sweets for three days. When I had stopped, I was able to supplicate for him, and that supplication was accepted."

Qushayri relates in his *Letters* that Hallaj was once asked to talk about poverty. He said, "Wait a minute." He entered his house, went out somewhere, and came back. Then he sat and spoke, saying poverty consists of this and that. One disciple asked him, "O my shaykh, why did you not speak like this from the beginning?" He said, "When I was asked, I had one *dirham* in my house. I could not speak about poverty while I still had something. So I went and took that *dirham*, spent it in God's way, and then I could speak on poverty."

HAVING AUTHORIZATION

The shaykh must have authorization from his master to train his followers and to show the Way of this Path. That permission must reach him through the chain of the grandshaykhs from one to another, all the way back to the Prophet ﷺ. As the wise person will not go to a doctor who has no license in healing, so the seeker in this way must find a perfect guide who has received the license, the permission, from his shaykh.

Imam Muslim said, "This great knowledge (the knowledge of the self) is by itself the religion. So you have to know from whom you take your religion." In the book of Hafiz ibn Ali, *Kanz al-ummal,* the following Tradition is found:

> *The Prophet ﷺ said, "O Umar, your religion is your flesh and blood. Look at those from whom you take your religion. Take it from those who are on the right path and do not take from those who have deviated." A knower said, "Knowledge is a spirit which is blown into the hearts, not philosophy or pretty tales to be written. So be very careful from whom you take it."*

The Signs of Mastery

The main indication of mastery is that when you sit with a master you feel a breeze of faith, spiritual pleasure. He does not speak except about

God. He is always advising the good. You will benefit from being in his company as you benefit from his words. You will benefit when you are far from him as you benefit when you are near him. You must see among his disciples the picture of faith, sincerity, humbleness, and piety (God-consciousness), and you must remember, when you are mixing with them, the highest state of love, truth, and deference to others. You must see that his followers represent all different kinds of people in the community. That is how the Companions of the Prophet ﷺ were.

Initiation

The seeker must follow a perfect master able to guide him to the way of God, Almighty and Exalted, and to illuminate for him that way until he reaches the state of annihilation. The seeker must give his oath and his promise to his guide, to learn from him how to put aside his bad manners and to lift himself to better conduct in order to reach the perfect knowledge of spirituality. The meaning of initiation and its conditions has been mentioned in the Holy Quran, in the *Sunnah* of the Prophet ﷺ, and in the lives of the Companions:

> *Verily those who swear allegiance to thee indeed swear allegiance to God. The Hand of God is over their hands. So whoever breaks his oath, breaks it to his own loss; and whoever fulfills the covenant that he has made with God, He will surely give him a great reward.* (48:10)
>
> *And fulfill the Covenant of God when you have made it. Break not your oaths after making them firm, while you have made God your surety. Certainly, God knows what you do.* (16:91)
>
> *And fulfill the covenant, for the covenant shall be questioned about.* (17:34)

We see the Quran encouraging people to give their oath and to keep their oath to the Prophet ﷺ, who leads them to the Presence of God, Almighty and Exalted. That initiation was done in the time of the Prophet ﷺ and after the time of the Prophet ﷺ.

According to the *Sunnah* of the Prophet ﷺ, the oath was taken from men, as a group or as individuals; from women, as a group or as individuals; and even from children.

Bukhari and Muslim narrate that Ubada ibn Samit ؓ said:

The Prophet ﷺ said, "Give me your pledge and oath not to associate anything with God, not to steal, not to commit adultery, not to kill your children, not to backbite, not to fall into sin. And who keeps his promise, then his reward is from God, Almighty and Exalted." And then we gave our pledge to the Prophet ﷺ and our oath.

The Prophet ﷺ gave initiation to all people and urged them to take it. Bukhari and Muslim narrated in their books that Abd Allah ibn Umar ؓ said:

When we pledged to the Prophet ﷺ to listen and obey, the Prophet ﷺ said, "To the limit that you can bear."

INITIATION OF WOMEN

The Prophet ﷺ accepted the allegiance of women many times. It is narrated by Imam Ahmad in the *Musnad* that Salma bint Qays ؓ said:

I came to the Prophet ﷺ with many people from the Helpers. We gave him our pledge that we would not associate anyone with God, we would not steal, we would not commit adultery, we would not kill our children, we would not backbite, and we would not disobey. We gave him our pledge and we went.

INITIATION OF CHILDREN

The Prophet ﷺ, according to the books of Nisai and Tirmidhi, accepted allegiance from Umaymah bint Ruqiyyah ؓ. It was narrated by Tabarani that Izza bint Khayyil ؓ gave her allegiance to the Prophet ﷺ when she was not yet seven. It was also narrated by Tabarani in an authentic Tradition that the Prophet ﷺ accepted the allegiance of al-Hasan ؓ, al-Husayn ؓ, Abd Allah ibn Abbas ؓ, and Abd Allah ibn Jafar ؓ when they were seven years of age.

INITIATION WITH THE CALIPHS

The Companions of the Prophet ﷺ gave their pledge to the caliphs of the Prophet ﷺ after his passing. It is narrated through the biographies of the Companions that they gave their pledge to Abu Bakr as-Siddiq, to Umar ibn al-Khattab, to Uthman ibn Affan, to Ali ؓ, to Muawiya ؓ, and to all the caliphs who came later, as they had given it to the Prophet ﷺ.

The Prophet ﷺ said in a Tradition related by Abu Dawud and Ahmad: Whoever imitates a group of people will be of them.

Therefore, the inheritors of the master of the Sufi orders, especially the Naqshbandi Sufi Order, inherited the initiation in every century. Just as it was an obligation in the times of the Prophet ﷺ, the Companions, the Successors, the Successors of the Successors, and in the times of the Umayyads, Abbasids, Seljuks, and Ottomans, so it is also an obligation to give our pledge to a perfect guide who leads us to the Way of God, Almighty and Exalted. And who is a better guide than the Sufi masters who are inheritors of the Prophet ﷺ and inheritors of the Divine Presence?

The scholar, Abul Hasan Ali Nadwi, said:

> Abd al-Qadir Gilani, the Arch-Intercessor of the Sufi Orders, Shaykh Muhyiddin ibn Arabi, and all the Masters of the Naqshbandi Golden Chain, opened the door of initiation as wide as possible, for every individual who has good and true belief, to find something that will be of value to him spiritually, and for everyone to renew his covenant with God, Almighty and Exalted. These Sufi Masters of the Naqshbandi Golden Chain and all Sufi orders lifted their followers to a station of truthfulness, to feel the responsibility of their initiation and to renew their faith.[8]

Thus we see that it is an important factor in every Sufi order for one to give one's allegiance to the shaykh in order to sanctify oneself and to be lifted up to the Divine Presence. These guides are the revivers in every century to connect our hearts with the heart of the Prophet ﷺ, who in turn connects our heart to the Divine Presence. These guides are the beacon of the light of the Prophet ﷺ and the Light of the Divine Presence. They are the true examples for all people to follow.

Conduct of the Disciple with the Shaykh

There are two categories of conduct of the disciple with his shaykh: internal and external.

INTERNAL CONDUCT OF THE DISCIPLE

- ❖ The seeker (*murid*) must submit to the will of the shaykh and obey him in all his orders and advice, because the shaykh has more experience and more knowledge in Truth, in the Way, and in the

---

[8] Abul Hasan Ali Nadwi. *Rijal al-fikr wad-dawah*, p. 253.

Divine Law. As the sick person gives himself to his doctor to be cured, so too does the disciple, sick in his conduct and behavior, submit to the shaykh's experience in order to be healed.

- The seeker must not object to the way the shaykh instructs and controls the disciples. Each shaykh has his own way that he has been permitted by his own shaykh to use. Imam Ibn Hajar al-Haythami said, "Whoever opens the door of criticism against shaykhs and their behavior with their disciples and their actions will be punished and will be isolated from receiving spiritual knowledge. Whoever says to his shaykh, 'Why?' will never succeed."[9]
- The seeker must know that the shaykh might make some mistakes, but that these will not prevent him from lifting the disciple up to the Divine Presence. So the disciple must excuse the shaykh, as the shaykh is not the Prophet ﷺ. Only the Prophet ﷺ was free of error. Although it is rare, just as the doctor might make a mistake in treating a patient, so too might the shaykh make a mistake in treating his disciple's spiritual illness, and that must be excused.
- The seeker must respect and honor the shaykh in his presence and in his absence, if only because the shaykh can see with the eye of the heart. It is said that whoever is not happy with the orders of the shaykh, and does not keep good conduct and manners with him, will never keep good conduct with the Quran and with the *Sunnah* of the Prophet ﷺ. Shaykh Abd al-Qadir Gilani said, "Whoever criticized a saint, God will cause his heart to wither."
- The seeker must be sincere and loyal to the companions of his shaykh.
- The seeker must love the shaykh with an extraordinary love. He or she must know that the shaykh is going to take him the Presence of God, Almighty and Exalted, and to the presence of the Prophet ﷺ.
- The seeker must not look to any other than his shaykh, though he must keep respect for all other shaykhs.

---

[9] Ibn Hajar al-Haytami, *Fatawa hadithiyya*, p. 55.

EXTERNAL CONDUCT OF THE DISCIPLE

- The seeker must agree with the opinion of the shaykh completely, as the patient agrees with the physician.
- The seeker must behave well in the association of the shaykh, by avoiding yawning, laughing, raising the voice, talking without authorization, extending the feet, and by always sitting in a respectful manner.
- The seeker must serve his shaykh and make oneself as useful as possible.
- The seeker must not mention from the speeches of the shaykh what listeners cannot understand. This might harm the shaykh in a way of which the disciple is unaware. Ali ﷺ said, in a Tradition narrated in Bukhari: "Speak to people at a level they can understand, because you do not want them to deny God and His Prophet ﷺ."
- The seeker must attend the company of the shaykh. Even if living far away, the seeker must make an effort to go as often as possible.

Ibn Hajar al-Haythami said:

Many people, when they see their guide is firm on the matter of obligations and the *Sunnah* of the Prophet ﷺ, accuse him of being strict. They say that he is praying too much or keeping the *Sunnah* too firmly. These people do not realize that they are falling to their own destruction. Beware of believing your ego's complaints about the firmness of the shaykh's adherence to the Divine Law.[10]

Abu Hafs an-Nishaburi is quoted as saying:

Sufism is composed of manners and good conduct. For every state and station there is an appropriate manner. For every time there is a proper conduct. Whoever keeps the manners will reach the station of moral goodness and whoever discards manners is very far from acceptance into God's Divine Presence.[11]

CONDUCT WITH FELLOW DISCIPLES

- To keep respect for them in their presence and in their absence, not backbiting anyone.

---

[10] *Ibid.*

[11] *Tabaqat as-sufiyya*, p. 119.

- To advise them when necessary, with the intention of strengthening them. Advice must be offered in private, with leniency, and free of judgment or arrogance. The one advised must accept the advice, be thankful, and practice it.
- To think only good about fellow disciples and not search out their bad manners.
- To accept their apology if they apologize.
- To make peace between them.
- To support them when they are attacked.
- To not ask to lead them, but to consider them as equals.
- To show humility towards them as much as possible, for the Prophet ﷺ said, *"The master of a people is the one who serves them."*

The good conduct of the disciple has no end. He or she must always strive for spiritual progress with the shaykh, with fellow disciples and within the community, because God, the Prophet ﷺ, the shaykh, and the previous spiritual masters observe each disciple. With constant improvement, day by day, and with the shaykh's guidance and support, disciples will reach the state of perfection.

Remembrance of God

Remembrance of God (*dhikr*) is the means by which stations yield their fruit, until the seeker reaches the Divine Presence. On the journey to the Divine Presence, the seed of remembrance is planted in the heart and nourished with the water of praise and the food of glorification until the tree of *dhikr* becomes deeply rooted and bears its fruit. It is the power of all journeying and the foundation of all success. It is the reviver from the sleep of heedlessness, the bridge to the One remembered.

The shaykhs strive to remember their Lord with every breath, as the angels are always in the state of *dhikr*, praising God. One of our shaykhs said, "I remembered You because I forgot You for a moment, and the easiest way for me is to remember You on my tongue." If the disciple will mention his Lord in every moment, he will find peace and satisfaction in his heart, he will uplift his spirit and his soul, and he will sit in the Presence of his Lord. The Prophet ﷺ said in an authentic Tradition mentioned in Ahmad's *Musnad*, *"The people of* dhikr *are the people of My Presence."* So the Gnostic is the one who keeps the *dhikr* in his heart, and leaves behind the attachments of the world.

Mention of *Dhikr* in the Quran

Dhikr is mentioned in many places in the Holy Quran. In most verses what was meant by the word *dhikr* is glorifying, exalting, and praising God, and sending salutations upon the Prophet ﷺ:

> *Remember Me and I will remember you* (2:152)
>
> *...and remember your Lord much and glorify Him in the evening and in the early morning.* (3:41)
>
> *Those who remember God while standing, sitting, and lying on their sides...* (3:191)
>
> *Those who believe, and whose hearts find their rest in the remembrance of God—for, verily, in the remembrance of God hearts do find their rest.* (13:28) *...and men who remember God much and women who remember Him...* (33:35)
>
> *O you who believe! Remember God with much remembrance; and glorify Him morning and evening.* (33:41-42)

There are many other verses of Quran mentioning *dhikr*. Imam Nawawi said:

> All scholars of Islam have agreed on the acceptance and permissibility of *dhikr* by heart and by tongue, for adult men and women, for children, for the one who has ablution, and for the one without ablution, and even for the woman during her menses. Moreover, *dhikr* is allowed by all scholars in the form of glorification, exhalting, praising, and sending salutations to the Prophet ﷺ.[12]

Dhikr polishes the heart and is the source of the Divine breath that revives the dead spirits by filling them with the blessings of God, decorating them with His Attributes, and bringing them from a state of heedlessness to the state of complete wakefulness. If we keep busy with *dhikr Allah*, happiness and peace will be granted to us. *Dhikr* is the key to happiness, the key to joy, and the key to Divine Love.

---

[12] Imam Nawawi, *al-Futuhat ar-rabbaniyyat ala-l-adhkar an-nawawiyya*, vol. 1, pp. 106-109.

Mention of *Dhikr* in the *Sunnah*

According to Bukhari, Abu Musa al-Ashari ﵁ related that the Prophet ﷺ said:

The difference between one who recites dhikr and one who does not recite dhikr is like the difference between the living and the dead.

Tirmidhi narrated from Anas ﵁ that the Prophet ﷺ said:

If you pass by the gardens of paradise, stay there." They asked, "O Messenger of God, what are the gardens of paradise?" He said, "The groups who recite dhikr!

Bukhari narrated in his book from Abu Hurayra ﵁ that the Prophet ﷺ said:

God, Almighty and Exalted, has angels who seek the people of dhikr. If they find the people of dhikr, they encompass them until they reach the first heaven. And God asks his angels, "What are my servants doing?" The angels say, "O God, they are praising You, and glorifying You, and they are reciting dhikr." God says, "Did they see Me?" The angels answer, "No, they did not see You." Then God asks, "How would it be if they were to see Me?" The angels reply, "O God, if they were to see You, they would offer more praise of You, more glorification of You, and more remembrance of You." And God asks "What are they asking for?" The angels say, "They are asking for Your Paradise." God asks, "Did they see My Paradise?" The angels answer, "No, our Lord." God continues, "How would it be if they saw My Paradise?" The angels reply, "They would be more attracted and more eager to reach it." Then God asks them, "Of what are they afraid?" And the angels say, "They are afraid of Hellfire," and God asks, "How would it be if they saw my Hellfire?" and they reply, "They would flee all the more from it and ask more protection from it." Then God said, "All of you bear witness that I forgive them of all their sins." Then one angel asked, "O our Lord, there is among these people one who is not from them. He came only to ask for something from one of them." God said, "Those are my beloved ones who are remembering Me. Anyone who comes into their circle will be forgiven."

In both *Sahih Bukhari* and *Sahih Muslim*, it is narrated from Abu Hurayra ﵁ that the Prophet ﷺ said:

God says, "I am as my servant thinks of Me so will I be for him. I am with him if he will remember Me. If he calls on Me in himself, I will call him in Myself, and if he calls on Me in a group of people, I mention him in a better group in My Presence. If he approaches Me one hand span, I will approach him one arm's length; if he approaches Me one arm's length, I will approach him by a cubit; if he comes to Me walking, I will come to him running."[13]

Tirmidhi and Ibn Majah narrated on the authority of Abu ad-Darda that:

The Prophet said, "Do you want me to tell you of your best deeds—the most honored and praised and sanctified to Your Lord—and the highest in its reward—better than spending gold, better than meeting your enemy and fighting them?" They said, "Yes, O Messenger of God." He said, "Dhikr Allah."

The Prophet said:

Everything has a polish and the polish of hearts is dhikr Allah.

Muadh ibn Jabal said:

Nothing saves you from God's punishment except dhikr Allah.

Ibn Abbas said:

God, Almighty and Exalted, put a limit on all the obligations that He ordered human beings except for dhikr. For it there is no limit.

There are numerous other Traditions about the benefits and blessings of *dhikr*, such that it is impossible to quote all of them here.

Imams' and Scholars' Opinions Regarding *Dhikr*

Ibn Qayyim al-Jawziyya said:

There is no doubt that the heart oxidizes, just as copper and silver oxidize. Its polishing is the *dhikr*, which will make it like a white mirror. The oxidation of the heart is due to heedlessness and sin. Its polishing is by means of two actions: repentance and *dhikr*. If someone's heart is cloudy, the reflections of images will be unclear. He will see falsehood as truth and truth in the image of falsehood. When

---

[13] See *Sahih Bukhari* and *Sahih Muslim*.

there is too much oxidization on the heart, the heart will be darkened, and in the darkness the images of the Truth and Reality never appear. The best way to polish it is through *dhikr Allah*.

Ibn Ata Allah said:

By *dhikr* you leave behind heedlessness and forgetfulness. You keep your heart present with God, Almighty and Exalted. The best way to approach His Presence is by reciting the name *"Allah,"* in the heart or on the tongue, or by reciting any of His Names.[14]

Abul Qasim al-Qushayri said:

Dhikr is the strongest support in the way of God, Almighty and Exalted. No one can reach the Divine Presence except by continuing to recite *dhikr*.[15]

Mulay al-Arabi ad-Darqawi said:

Do not say, "I am nothing." Neither say, "I am something." Do not say, "I need such and such a thing" nor yet, "I need nothing." But say, "*Allah*," and you will see marvels.[16]

We see from what has been mentioned that all guides and perfect shaykhs advised the seeker in the Way of God to recite continuous *dhikr* in all states of their lives and to join the company of people in groups who practice thankfulness. We see that the Holy Quran and the *Sunnah* of the Prophet ﷺ and the scholars are all in accordance on this matter.

Types of *Dhikr*

Dhikr can be done both silently or aloud. The Prophet ﷺ encouraged people to do both kinds. Among the scholars of the Divine Law and the Sufi shaykhs, some preferred the loud *dhikr* and some preferred the silent *dhikr*.

---

14 Ibn Qayyim al-Jawziyya, *al-Wabil as-saib*, p. 52.

15 Ibn Ataillah as-Sakandari, *Miftah al-falah*, p. 4.

16 Abul Qasim al-Qushayri, *Risalat al-Qushayriyya*.

say it three times and I will listen to you." Then the Prophet ﷺ said it and I repeated it in a loud voice.

In the narration of Imam Ahmad and Tabarani, this Tradition continues, describing how the Prophet ﷺ taught his Companions the *dhikr*.

Ubada ibn Samit ؓ said that the Prophet ﷺ said, "Is there any stranger among you?" And we said, "No, Messenger of God." He said, "Close the door." Then he said, "Raise your hand and repeat after me 'la ilaha ill-Allah.'" We raised our hand and said, "la ilaha ill-Allah." Then the Prophet ﷺ said, "Praise be to God that He sent me to this world with these words, He commanded me to it, He promised me Paradise with it, and He never changes His Promise." Then the Prophet ﷺ said, "Be happy! God has forgiven you."[17]

Jalaluddin as-Suyuti mentioned the benefits of the loud *dhikr* in an article called *Natijat al-fikr fi jahr adh-dhikr*. He cites twenty-five authentic Traditions that mention doing loud *dhikr*.

SILENT *DHIKR*

God mentioned in the Quran:

And remember thy Lord in thyself with humility and fear, and without loudness of speech, in the mornings and evenings, and be not of the neglectful. (7:205)

Imam Ahmad narrated that Abu Hurayra ؓ reported from the Prophet ﷺ that God said:

I am with My servant when he remembers Me and by his remembrance of Me, his lips move.

Commenting on this Tradition, Imam Nawawi said:

God is with the one who remembers Him and calls Him in his heart, and calls Him on his tongue, but we must realize that the *dhikr* of the heart is more perfect. The rememberer recites *dhikr* of the tongue in order to reflect the occurrence of the *dhikr* in his heart. When the love of God and His remembrance overwhelms the heart and the spirit, the tongue is moved and the seeker is brought near.

---

[17] Mulay al-Arabi ad-Darqawi, *Letters of a Sufi Master*. *Hadith* narrated by Imam Ahmad.

Shaykh Amin al-Kurdi said in *Tanwir al-qulub*:

> The *dhikr* by the tongue, which combines sounds and letters, is not easy to perform at all times, because buying and selling and other such activities altogether divert one's attention from such *dhikr*. The contrary is true of the *dhikr* with the heart, which is named thusly in order to signify its freedom from letters and sounds. In that way nothing distracts one from his *dhikr*, as the poet says, "With the heart remember God, secretly from creation, wordlessly and speechlessly. That remembrance is best of all: out of it flowed the sayings of the saints."

That is why our Naqshbandi masters have chosen the *dhikr* of the heart. Moreover, the heart is the place where the Forgiver casts His Gaze, the seat of belief, the receptacle of secrets, and the source of lights. If it is sound the whole body is sound, and if it is unsound, the whole body is unsound, as was made clear for us by the chosen Prophet ﷺ.

A Tradition that confirms this was narrated on the authority of Aisha ﵂:

> *God favors dhikr above dhikr seventy-fold (meaning, silent dhikr over loud dhikr). On the Day of Resurrection, God will bring back human beings to His account, and the recording angels will bring what they have recorded and written. God Almighty will say, "See if something that belongs to my servant was left out?" The angels will say, "We left nothing out concerning what we have learned and recorded, except that we have assessed it and written it." God will say, "O my servant, I have something good of yours for which I alone will reward you. It is your hidden remembrance of Me."*

Also on the authority of Aisha ﵂:

> *The dhikr not heard by the recording angels equals seventy times the one they hear.*[18]

Stages of *Dhikr* and Its Fulfillment

People of Sufism understand *dhikr* is essential because it is the primary means for conveying the seeker to the Presence of God. It is of three gradations reflecting the stages of the journey to the Divine Presence:

- The *dhikr* of common people with the tongue.

---

[18] Amin al-Kurdi, *Tanwir al-qulub*, p. 522. Bayhaqi narrates it.

- The *dhikr* of special people with the heart.
- The *dhikr* of elect of the special people by their annihilation in their *dhikr;* when they see the One they are remembering and are annihilated in His Presence.

Imam Ghazali said:

> You must know that God removed all the veils of ignorance and brought people to the state of vision through their continuous *dhikr*. The first stage is *dhikr* of the tongue, then the *dhikr* of the heart, then the appearance of the Divine Presence in the reciter of *dhikr*, making him no longer need to do *dhikr*.[19]

Shaykh al-Munawi said:

> For the seeker in God's Way, the thing of highest benefit to him is *dhikr* with the Name "*Allah*" whereby he will taste and see the Love of the Divine Presence.[20]

Imam Junayd said:

> Whoever recited *dhikr* with the all-encompassing Name "*Allah*" is the one who left himself behind, connecting to His Lord, existing in His Presence, looking at Him through his heart, where the Light of God has burned away his physical body.[21]

Therefore, it is the practice of the grandshaykhs of the Naqshbandi Order to initiate their disciples in *dhikr* with the unique Name encompassing all Attributes, *Allah*, and by negation and affirmation with the sacred words "*la ilaha ill-Allah*." Through these two forms they will be able to reach the state of excellence, which was mentioned by the Prophet ﷺ in the Tradition narrated by Bukhari and Muslim:

> *Excellence is to worship God as if you see Him.*

Ibn Qayyim al-Jawziyya said:

> If a person wants to be guided, he must look for a person who is from the people of *dhikr*. If he finds one who is from the people of *dhikr*,

---

[19] Imam Ghazali, *Kitab al-arbain fi usul ad-din*, pp. 52-55.

[20] Shaykh al-Munawi, *Faydul-qadir*, vol. 2, p. 309.

[21] See Farid ad-Din Attar, *Mystics and Saints*, p. 102.

keeping *dhikr* continuously, and following the *Sunnah* of the Prophet ﷺ, he must stick to him.[22]

Ibn Hajar al-Haythami said:

The seeker in the first stages, before reaching to the stage of knower, must obey the orders of his shaykh, who is carrying both kinds of knowledge—Divine knowledge and knowledge of the Divine Law, because he is the great physician who has tasted and sensed all the heavenly wisdom through keeping the *dhikr* in his heart.

Seclusion

Seclusion is better than isolation. It is a kind of isolation that can only be prescribed by the shaykh. Its shortest duration is forty days, as mentioned in the Holy Quran about Prophet Moses ﵇:

And remember We appointed forty nights for Moses. (2:51)

Muslim narrated that the Prophet ﷺ secluded himself in the cave of Hira. The aim of such seclusion is to free the heart from connection to this world of material pleasures and to bring it to a state of remembrance of God, Almighty and Exalted. In it countless visions occur. It elevates the disciple to a state of knowing the self, and from there to a state of knowing God. Seclusion requires the seeker to disconnect from people and to disengage from all material interactions for a set period of time. His heart must be engaged only in God's remembrance, and his mind relaxed from daily concerns. All this must take place under the guidance of a Gnostic shaykh, to teach him if he forgets, to remind him if he is heedless, and to throw out of the heart all gossip and whispers of the ego.

The shaykh orders the disciple to seclude himself in a room where he will be served every day only with what is necessary for survival. Then he will teach his tongue the way of reciting *dhikr*, until he will be engaged with that recitation. The shaykh will support his disciple in opening the vision of the Divine Presence in the heart. Whatever happens to the disciple during the seclusion, he must tell his shaykh, and he must conceal it from anyone other than the shaykh.

---

[22] Ibn Qayyim al-Jawziyya, *al-Wabil as-saib*, p. 53.

Seclusion is not an innovation, but is an order of God, Almighty and Exalted, in His Holy Book and in the example of the Prophet ﷺ. The Prophet ﷺ secluded himself in the cave of Hira in the mountains of Makkah, remembering God, Almighty and Exalted.

> *So remember the name of thy Lord, and devote thyself to Him with full devotion.* (73:8)

Allama Abu Saud in his commentary on the explanation of the Quran by Fakhr ad-Din al-Razi says:

> The meaning of this verse is to keep secluding yourself from anyone other than God, Almighty and Exalted, remembering Him day and night, by glorification, praising, and negation and affirmation, and to disconnect yourself, by all the power you have, and approach Him through the meditative stations such that you will not see anyone except Him, and be away from connections to other than Him through that meditation.[23]

The Islamic form of meditation is founded on seclusion. The proof for this in the Quran can be found in the story of Mary عليها السلام, the mother of Jesus عليه السلام:

> *So her Lord accepted her with a gracious acceptance, and caused her to grow an excellent growth, and made Zachariah her guardian. Whenever Zachariah visited her in her seclusion he found with her provision. He said, "O Mary, whence hast thou this?" She replied, "It is from God. Surely, God gives to whomsoever He pleases without measure."* (3:37)

Mentioning the story of the Companions of the Cave, God said in the Quran that they were ordered:

> *Betake yourself to the cave: Your Lord will shower His mercies on you and dispose of your affair towards comfort and ease.* (18:16)

Similarly, seclusion has a proof in the *Sunnah*. Bukhari reports that Aisha رضي الله عنها said:

> *The Prophet ﷺ loved to seclude himself. He secluded himself in the Cave of Hira.*

---

[23] Allama Abu Said's commentary on Fakhr ad-Din ar-Razi's commentary on the Quran, vol. 8, p. 388.

Imam Nawawi, explained the Tradition of Aisha رضي الله عنها:

> To be alone with the One you love is real seclusion. It is the way of the pious, and it is the way of knowers.

He said, in his explanation in *Sahih Muslim*:

> The Prophet ﷺ said, *"I was made to love seclusion,"* because with it the heart will be empty of all this materialistic life. It will be at peace. It helps to deepen the meditation on God's Divine Presence. With it, one's attachments to the world will decrease. With it, his reverence will increase.

Imam Zuhri said:

> I wonder at people, that they do not practice seclusion. The Prophet ﷺ did things and then left them, yet he never stopped the practice of seclusion until he died.

Abu Jamra said in explanation of this Tradition of Aisha رضي الله عنها:

> When the Prophet ﷺ secluded himself, left people behind and disconnected himself from this world, he received revelation from Gabriel عليه السلام in the Cave of Hira. Anyone who will imitate the Prophet ﷺ in doing seclusion, under the order of his shaykh, will be lifted to the state of sainthood.

The proof of seclusion is that the Prophet ﷺ, through his seclusion in the Cave of Hira, was lifted up to the state in which he received revelation. During his seclusions the first fruit was true dreams, and from that state he was elevated to the state in which he received revelation, the state where he could receive revelation from the angel Gabriel عليه السلام. Then he was lifted up during the Night of Ascension, until he reached the Divine Presence to the station of *"two bows' length or nearer."* (53:9)

All these stations were the fruit of his seclusion in the Cave of Hira. We learn from this, if we follow the footsteps of the Prophet ﷺ, we will be lifted from one state to another until we reach the high states of sainthood, and we will find ourselves in the Divine Presence.

Shaykh Abd al-Qadir said:

> From the Cave of Hira, where the Prophet ﷺ secluded himself, the light emanated, the dawn shone forth, and sunrise came. The first sparks of the luminescence of Islamic Sufism were struck. Never did the Prophet

leave his seclusion, even when he left the Cave of Hira. All his life he continued the practice of seclusion during the last ten days of Ramadan.[24]

This demonstrates that, throughout his life, the Prophet ﷺ continued his practice of seclusion on a regular basis. Of course, the enormous tasks of delivering God's Message to humanity and establishing the Community of Believers required him to reduce the amount of time he spent alone. For his followers, however, forty days remained—and remains—the minimum.

Imam Qastallani, in explaining this Tradition says:

> Seclusion will put the heart at peace and open in it fountains of wisdom, because it will disconnect the disciple from the materialistic life and enable him to remember God, Almighty and Exalted. In his seclusion he must also isolate himself and seclude himself from himself, to see only God, Almighty and Exalted. At that time only will he receive unseen knowledge, and his heart will be a foundation for it.[25]

Ibn Hajar al-Asqalani, in explaining the Tradition of Aisha, said: "Seclusion is emptying the heart of everything except God."[26]

In regard to seclusion, Abul Hasan ash-Shadhili said:
There are ten benefits from seclusion:

- ❖ Safety from all misconduct of the tongue, because there is no one to talk to in seclusion.
- ❖ Safety from all misconduct of the eyes, because there are no human beings to see.
- ❖ Safety of the heart from all kinds of show, and other like illnesses.
- ❖ It will lift you to the state of asceticism.
- ❖ It will save you from accompanying evil people.
- ❖ It will give you free time to do *dhikr*.
- ❖ It will give you the sweet taste of worship, prayers and supplication to the Divine Presence.
- ❖ It will give satisfaction and peace to the heart.

---

[24] See *Endowment of Grace*.
[25] Imam Qastallani, *Rashad us-sari*, vol. 1 p. 62.
[26] Ibn Hajar al-Asqalani, *Fath al-Bari*, vol. 1, p. 18.

- It will keep your ego from falling into bad manners.
- It will give you time to meditate, to take account of yourself and to make your goal the Divine Presence.

That is what the Prophet ﷺ mentioned in his Tradition, narrated by Bukhari, in the book of *Riqaq*:

> *Abu Hurayra ؓ reported that the Prophet ﷺ said, "There are seven who will be kept under God's Shadow on the Day when there is no shadow other than God's Shadow. One of them is a man who recites dhikr in seclusion and tears flow from his eyes."*[27]

EXPLANATION OF SECLUSION BY SHAYKH ABD ALLAH AD-DAGHESTANI

Once, a famous French orientalist came to visit Shaykh Abd Allah ad-Daghestani in Damascus and said:

> O my master, I come to you after studying the Psalms, the Torah, the Bible, and the Holy Quran. I have studied philosophy, the religions, and many systems of knowledge. But still, I feel nothing in my heart. I feel no satisfaction. On the contrary, it is as if I was standing on the edge of a cliff and was about to fall. I have become so shaky that I am going from one center to another, seeking what is Real. Where can I reach that Reality and gain satisfaction in my heart? Where can I find my Lord? I have been everywhere. I have asked famous philosophers, orientalists, people whom I considered saints. I have read everything I could. Yet, when I have asked any scholar a question, I felt as if they were giving me an answer I already knew. They were not giving me anything new. I am confused. I heard your name and I have finally come to you. After you I am not going anywhere. Will you give me an answer to my question? Whatever you say I will follow and believe. But if you do not give me an answer, I shall remain, as I am, confused and uncertain for the rest of my life.
>
> Grandshaykh said:
>
> My son, if you take the seed of an apple, or any fruit, and leave it there dry, for hundreds of years it will remain dry. But if you take that seed, and put it in a field, and plant it, then come back after one month, you

---

[27] See *Sahih Bukhari*.

will find that a green sprout has come out. If you dig and try to find that seed, you will not find it anymore. It has vanished, replaced by something new. If you continue to water that plant, it will become a tree and that tree will bear fruit. But where is the original seed? It has disappeared. There is no original seed anymore. The seed has become a large tree now, with fruit coming forth, giving people fruit to eat. Similarly, if you take an egg and place it under a chicken, after exactly twenty-one days that egg disappears and a new chick comes. Something new comes into being. If you look under the chicken you will no longer find the egg there. The egg has vanished. It was the twenty-one days under that chicken that turned it into a new generation.

Something similar happens with human beings when they are in their mother's womb for about nine months and ten days. Inside that womb they are without any connection to anything outside, alone. Yet after those nine months and ten days of loneliness there will come forth a new generation, a new creation.

My son, in every one of these three examples there was something that went into seclusion. The seed cut itself off from the material world above the ground and went into seclusion for several weeks. Then a new plant emerged. The egg went into seclusion under its mother, with no connection to the material life outside its shell, and came out a new generation. The sperm went into seclusion in the egg within the mother's womb for nine months, without connection to the external world of this materialistic life, but after the seclusion, it emerged a new generation.

My son, if you do not enter into seclusion, then never say to yourself, as the seed says to itself, "I want to cut myself off from the materialistic life of this world and vanish from it for the love of God and for the benefit of other human beings." For the seed begets fruit. If you do not experience a retreat like this, if you do not cut yourself off from the materialistic life, forsake your ego, and vanish into nothingness to exist only in God, never will you find your ultimate reality, your true self. Never will you be like that tree that gives fruit for people to eat. If you will not be like that egg and sever yourself from materialism, retreating into the shell of seclusion and existing only in the presence of your Lord, meditating, concentrating on Him, worshipping Him in your heart, keeping His Presence always in your heart, never will you find that satisfaction and happiness you seek.

Why must you imitate that seed that enters into seclusion for nine months? The embryonic covering consists of three layers. This was mentioned 1,400 years ago in the Holy Quran in *Surat az-Zumar* (39:6) at a time when no microscopes existed. The Prophet ﷺ also said, *"The womb of a mother is composed of (layers of) darknesses."* You must enter into this loneliness, severing your bond to everything external, cutting yourself off from the material layers of this world, to be alone with your Lord, and thus make connection to your ultimate reality, by fitting that image you wear here to its original in the Divine Presence. Never will you know satisfaction, no matter how many books you read, for when you read, you only hear the books. The knowledge they contain is only hearsay knowledge, and not Real. Yet in seclusion, you not only hear, but you feel. You will not only see, but you will smell. It is then that the eyes of the heart open. My son, if you do not enter into seclusion, your heart will never feel the contentment you have been so long seeking.

Immediately the scholar said, "You have given me an answer to my question and a solution to my problem that I have never before received from anyone. My heart is open. Show me the way." Grandshaykh gave him permission to enter into seclusion in a designated place, cutting himself off from everything. He entered that place an ordinary man, but after one year he left it a saint.

The Principles and Transmission of the Naqshbandi Order

The designation of the Naqshbandi Golden Chain has changed from century to century. From the time of Abu Bakr as-Siddiq ﷺ to the time of Bayazid al-Bistami it was called *as-Siddiqiyya*. From the time of Bayazid to the time of Abd al-Khaliq al-Ghujdawani it was called *at-Tayfuriyya*. From the time of Abdul-Khaliq al-Ghujdawani to the time of Shah Naqshband it was called the *Khwajaganiyya*. From the time of Shah Naqshband through the time of Ubayd Allah al-Ahrar and Ahmad Faruqi, it was called *Naqshbandiyya*.

Naqshbandiyya means to "tie the *naqsh* very well." The *naqsh* is the perfect engraving of God's Name in the heart of the seeker, follower, student or disciple. From the time of Ahmad al-Faruqi to the time of Shaykh Khalid al-Baghdadi it was called *Naqshbandiyya-Mujaddidiyya*. From the time of Khalid al-Baghdadi until the time of Shaykh Ismail ash-Shirwani it was called the *Naqshbandiyya-Khalidiyya*. From the time of Ismail ash-Shirwani until the time of Shaykh Abd Allah ad-Daghestani, it was called *Naqshbandiyya-Daghestaniyya*. And today it is known by the name *Naqshbandiyya-Haqqaniyya*.

The 'Uwaysi' Transmission of Spiritual Knowledge

Shah Bahauddin Naqshband al-Uwaysi al-Bukhari received the silent *dhikr* from the spiritual presence of Khwaja Abd al-Khaliq al-Ghujdawani. He did not meet with him physically because there were five shaykhs between them in the Golden Chain. Similarly, Abul Hasan al-Kharqani took spiritual guidance and initiation in the Naqshbandi Order from the spiritual presence of Bayazid Bistami. In this form of spiritual transmission, the spirits met in the world of spirits, which is beyond the material plane. Whoever takes knowledge through spirituality from a deceased master in the Naqshbandi Way is called both Uwaysi and Naqshbandi. That spiritual connection is as powerful and effective as the physical connection.

The sign of the favor of God, Almighty and Exalted, on His servant is to authorize one of His saints to lift that servant up to the Divine Presence. That is why many saints who came in previous times were guides for those who came after through this spiritual (Uwaysi) connection. It is known that many saints have been under the guidance and training of prophets and other saints who lifted them up.

As we mentioned, Abd al-Khaliq al-Ghujdawani was raised up by Khidr عليه السلام, Uways al-Qarani رضي الله عنه, and the spiritual presences of Ali ibn Abi Talib رضي الله عنه and Abu Bakr as-Siddiq رضي الله عنه. Then Abd al-Khaliq raised Shah Naqshband, who also received guidance from Uways al-Qarani, Ali رضي الله عنه, Abu Bakr رضي الله عنه, and the Prophet ﷺ. Jafar as-Sadiq رضي الله عنه raised up Bayazid al-Bistami. Bayazid al-Bistami raised up Abul Hasan al-Kharqani. Ubayd Allah al-Ahrar was raised up by the spiritual connection to Jesus عليه السلام and to Shah Naqshband. It is known that Ahmad al-Faruqi, in addition to the spiritual power he received from Shah Naqshband, also received spiritual support and power from Ali رضي الله عنه.

Shaykh Sharafuddin ad-Daghestani was raised through spirituality by Abu Bakr as-Siddiq رضي الله عنه and by Muhammad ﷺ. Shaykh Abd Allah ad-Daghestani was under the spiritual guidance of Ali رضي الله عنه, of Uways al-Qarani رضي الله عنه, of Abd al-Khaliq al-Ghujdawani, and of Shah Naqshband. Shaykh Nazim received, in addition to the guidance received from Shaykh Abd Allah and Shaykh Sharafuddin, guidance from Jalaluddin Rumi and Abd al-Qadir Gilani, who were his paternal and maternal grandfathers, respectively.

These are the shaykhs of the Naqshbandi Order mentioned by Shaykh Abd Allah ad-Daghestani, who have, in addition to their physical connection, received the Uwaysi connection. They are known as the "Shaykhs of the Two Wings," meaning that both the physical lineage and the spiritual lineage are combined in them. These saints are only nine in number. Each one represents one of the nine spiritual points on the chest of the human being. Through these points these saints can reach their followers at any time. Because they have the authority of these Nine Points, they consider all of humankind to be their followers, whether they are aware of their spiritual connection to them or not. Through these points, which are of Uwaysi nature, they can reach and affect any human being, intercede for them, and inspire their hearts in order to direct them to the Divine Love, although they have never met physically.

Shaykh Abd Allah ad-Daghestani's Vision of Uways al-Qarani ﷺ

Our grandshaykh, Abd Allah ad-Daghestani, said:

After Shaykh Sharafuddin passed away and I was awaiting an opening to emigrate from Turkey, I was in seclusion in the mosque next to the tomb of my shaykh, praying one night before the dawn prayer. It was a cold and snowy night. I could feel the coldness in my bones. I could hear the quiet falling of the snow on the trees and the howling of wolves in the woods. I heard a voice calling my name, "Abd Allah Effendi." I looked around but saw no one. Then I heard the voice again calling out, "Abd Allah!" I looked again, but again could not see anyone. I knew it was the voice of my shaykh. The warmth of that voice energized me, and I ran outside, without even putting on my shoes or my woolen cloak. I saw my shaykh in a brilliant vision, standing on the hill. He called to me and said, "Abd Allah Effendi, come." I did not even think to put on shoes. I walked on the snow and could feel warmth from Divine Love emanating from his spirit. As I reached him he said, "My son, tonight I have been ordered to take you to the presence of Uways al-Qarani ﷺ by the order of the Prophet ﷺ."

Then he said, "My son, take my hand." I was very happy to take the hand of my shaykh. As soon as I took his hand I found myself in a group of saints, in the presence of the Prophet ﷺ. Uways al-Qarani ﷺ was sitting there. We entered, and found there were two places reserved for us. We offered our respects and took our seats. Then Ali ﷺ stood up and said, "For the first time we are revealing this secret to the company of saints. Only now have we received the permission from the Prophet ﷺ for that secret to appear."

I saw present in the gathering the 7,007 Naqshbandi saints, together with the 313 Naqshbandi saints who are on the footsteps of the 313 great messengers, and the grandshaykhs of the Golden Chain. Ali ﷺ said, addressing the group, and especially me, "When the Prophet ﷺ was dying, he called Umar and myself to his presence and he said, "After I die, you take the clothes I am wearing when I pass away, as a trust from me to Uways al-Qarani. You will find Uways al-Qarani in such and such a place."

heavens. From his neck and up, I was unable to see, but it was above the Lote-Tree of the Furthermost Boundary. Then he told me, 'Look from my navel and down.' I looked and I saw all these universes, all these worlds, stars and planets had disappeared and all that I saw was the Prophet ﷺ, from his waist to his knees, filling up that entire space. And from his knees down to his feet I was unable to see. Then he ﷺ said, 'Look at all of me, from top to bottom.' I looked at him, and the Lote-Tree of the Furthermost Boundary and all the universes disappeared. All I saw was Muhammad ﷺ everywhere. At that time I knew that Muhammad ﷺ is the heart of the Divine Presence.'

"Then Uways looked at me and said, 'You really saw the Prophet ﷺ once. That is why he said about you, 'I am the City of Knowledge, and Ali is its Door. ' God has also given this Divine Knowledge to Abu Bakr as-Siddiq, as the Prophet ﷺ mentioned, 'Whatever God poured into my heart, I poured into the heart of Abu Bakr as-Siddiq.'

"In this state of wonderment, Umar asked Uways, 'What is the significance of that robe we brought to you?' He said, 'O Umar, that is one of the greatest secrets which will not be revealed to people until the Last Days of his Community. While the Prophet ﷺ was dying, he was asking for intercession for his Community.'

"Then he said, 'His Community includes all human beings. And that is why God said, *'Say (O Prophet): O humanity! I am a Messenger to you all from God, to Whom belongs the kingdom of the heavens and the earth.'* (7:158) The Prophet ﷺ asked for intercession and God gave permission. He interceded for every individual that God created. As he was asking he was sweating, and each drop of sweat represented one human being. He took on the burden of each person until he was satisfied that God had forgiven everyone. Then he left this world. And the symbols of that forgiveness are the drops of sweat, which soaked this robe. This robe was given to me because the Prophet ﷺ wanted to tell me, 'O Uways, I am passing the Divine Knowledge to you to purify the Community after they commit sins or wrongdoings. You must pass that power to your successors, from me to you and from you to them.'"

Ali ؓ said, "Uways al-Qarani ؓ said, 'I did not see the Prophet ﷺ physically, but in every moment of every day, I was with him during his life. I received from him every matter of importance for his Community. I am going to transmit this secret to the many successors and inheritors among God's saints. They will receive the secret of the purifying power without a physical connection but through a spiritual connection and revive it in every century, until the Day of Judgment.'"

Then Ali ؓ said to the group of saints, but directing his speech to me, "What is passed to you and to many saints before you is from that Uwaysi power. This is the first time that this secret has been revealed, by permission of the Prophet ﷺ."

Then my shaykh said to me, "O my son, now you can go back to your seclusion." As soon as he said that, I found myself entering the mosque and feeling the cold again.

From time to time, saints experience such inspirations and visions through the spiritual power of their exalted predecessors.

History of the Saints of the Golden Chain

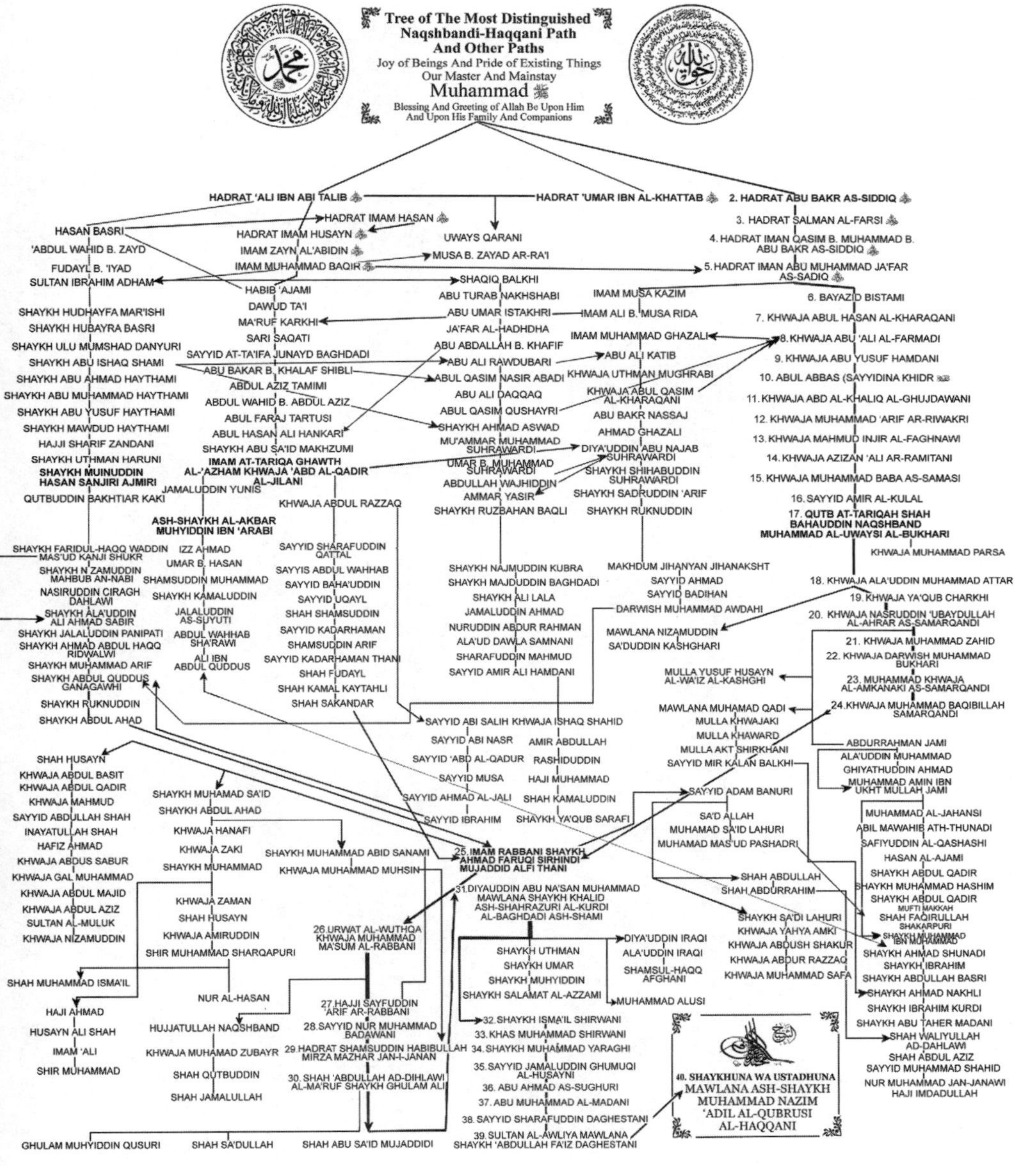
Tree of The Most Distinguished
Naqshbandi-Haqqani Path
And Other Paths
Joy of Beings And Pride of Existing Things
Our Master And Mainstay
Muhammad ﷺ
Blessing And Greeting of Allah Be Upon Him
And Upon His Family And Companions
HADRAT 'ALI IBN ABI TALIB
HADRAT 'UMAR IBN AL-KHATTAB
2. HADRAT ABU BAKR AS-SIDDIQ
HASAN BASRI
HADRAT IMAM HASAN
HADRAT IMAM HUSAYN
UWAYS QARANI
3. HADRAT SALMAN AL-FARSI
'ABDUL WAHID B. ZAYD
IMAM ZAYN AL'ABIDIN
MUSA B. ZAYAD AR-RA'I
4. HADRAT IMAN QASIM B. MUHAMMAD B. ABU BAKR AS-SIDDIQ
FUDAYL B. 'IYAD
IMAM MUHAMMAD BAQIR
5. HADRAT IMAN ABU MUHAMMAD JA'FAR AS-SADIQ
SULTAN IBRAHIM ADHAM
SHAQIQ BALKHI
HABIB 'AJAMI
ABU TURAB NAKHSHABI
IMAM MUSA KAZIM
6. BAYAZID BISTAMI
SHAYKH HUDHAYFA MAR'ISHI
DAWUD TA'I
ABU UMAR ISTAKHRI
IMAM ALI B. MUSA RIDA
7. KHWAJA ABUL HASAN AL-KHARAQANI
SHAYKH HUBAYRA BASRI
MA'RUF KARKHI
JA'FAR AL-HADHDHA
IMAM MUHAMMAD GHAZALI
8. KHWAJA ABU 'ALI AL-FARMADI
SHAYKH ULU MUMSHAD DANYURI
SARI SAQATI
ABU ABDALLAH B. KHAFIF
SAYYID AT-TA'IFA JUNAYD BAGHDADI
ABU ALI KATIB
9. KHWAJA ABU YUSUF HAMDANI
SHAYKH ABU ISHAQ SHAMI
ABU ALI RAWDUBARI
ABU BAKAR B. KHALAF SHIBLI
ABUL QASIM NASIR ABADI
KHWAJA UTHMAN MUGHRABI
10. ABUL ABBAS (SAYYIDINA KHIDR)
SHAYKH ABU AHMAD HAYTHAMI
ABDUL AZIZ TAMIMI
ABU ALI DAQQAQ
KHWAJA ABUL QASIM AL-KHARAQANI
SHAYKH ABU MUHAMMAD HAYTHAMI
ABDUL WAHID B. ABDUL AZIZ
ABUL QASIM QUSHAYRI
11. KHWAJA ABD AL-KHALIQ AL-GHUJDAWANI
SHAYKH ABU YUSUF HAYTHAMI
ABUL FARAJ TARTUSI
ABU BAKR NASSAJ
SHAYKH AHMAD ASWAD
12. KHWAJA MUHAMMAD 'ARIF AR-RIWAKRI
SHAYKH MAWDUD HAYTHAMI
ABUL HASAN ALI HANKARI
AHMAD GHAZALI
13. KHWAJA MAHMUD INJIR AL-FAGHNAWI
HAJJI SHARIF ZANDANI
SHAYKH ABU SA'ID MAKHZUMI
MU'AMMAR MUHAMMAD SUHRAWARDI
DIYA'UDDIN ABU NAJAB SUHRAWARDI
14. KHWAJA AZIZAN 'ALI AR-RAMITANI
SHAYKH UTHMAN HARUNI
IMAM AT-TARIQA GHAWTH AL-'AZHAM KHWAJA 'ABD AL-QADIR AL-JILANI
UMAR B. MUHAMMAD SUHRAWARDI
SHAYKH SHIHABUDDIN SUHRAWARDI
15. KHWAJA MUHAMMAD BABA AS-SAMASI
SHAYKH MUINUDDIN HASAN SANJIRI AJMIRI
JAMALUDDIN YUNIS
ABDULLAH WAJHIDDIN
AMMAR YASIR
SHAYKH SADRUDDIN 'ARIF
16. SAYYID AMIR AL-KULAL
QUTBUDDIN BAKHTIAR KAKI
KHWAJA ABDUL RAZZAQ
SHAYKH RUZBAHAN BAQLI
SHAYKH RUKNUDDIN
17. QUTB AT-TARIQAH SHAH BAHAUDDIN NAQSHBAND MUHAMMAD AL-UWAYSI AL-BUKHARI
ASH-SHAYKH AL-AKBAR MUHYIDDIN IBN 'ARABI
KHWAJA MUHAMMAD PARSA
SHAYKH FARIDUL-HAQQ WADDIN MAS'UD KANJI SHUKR
IZZ AHMAD
SAYYID SHARAFUDDIN QATTAL
SHAYKH NAJMUDDIN KUBRA
MAKHDUM JIHANYAN JIHANAKSHT
SHAYKH NIZAMUDDIN MAHBUB AN-NABI
UMAR B. HASAN
SAYYIS ABDUL WAHHAB
SHAYKH MAJDUDDIN BAGHDADI
SAYYID AHMAD
18. KHWAJA ALA'UDDIN MUHAMMAD ATTAR
NASIRUDDIN CIRAGH DAHLAWI
SHAMSUDDIN MUHAMMAD
SAYYID BAHA'UDDIN
SHAYKH ALI LALA
SAYYID BADIHAN
19. KHWAJA YA'QUB CHARKHI
SHAYKH ALA'UDDIN ALI AHMAD SABIR
SHAYKH KAMALUDDIN
SAYYID UQAYL
JAMALUDDIN AHMAD
DARWISH MUHAMMAD AWDAHI
20. KHWAJA NASRUDDIN 'UBAYDULLAH AL-AHRAR AS-SAMARQANDI
SHAYKH JALALUDDIN PANIPATI
JALALUDDIN AS-SUYUTI
SHAH SHAMSUDDIN
NURUDDIN ABDUR RAHMAN
MAWLANA NIZAMUDDIN
SHAYKH AHMAD ABDUL HAQQ RIDWALWI
ABDUL WAHHAB SHA'RAWI
SAYYID KADARHAMAN
ALA'UD DAWLA SAMNANI
SA'DUDDIN KASHGHARI
21. KHWAJA MUHAMMAD ZAHID
SHAYKH MUHAMMAD ARIF
ALI IBN ABDUL QUDDUS
SHAMSUDDIN ARIF
SHARAFUDDIN MAHMUD
22. KHWAJA DARWISH MUHAMMAD BUKHARI
SHAYKH ABDUL QUDDUS GANAGAWHI
SAYYID KADARHAMAN THANI
SAYYID AMIR ALI HAMDANI
MULLA YUSUF HUSAYN AL-WA'IZ AL-KASHGHI
23. MUHAMMAD KHWAJA AL-AMKANAKI AS-SAMARQANDI
SHAH FUDAYL
SHAH KAMAL KAYTAHLI
SHAYKH RUKNUDDIN
SHAH SAKANDAR
MAWLANA MUHAMAD QADI
24. KHWAJA MUHAMMAD BAQIBILLAH SAMARQANDI
SHAYKH ABDUL AHAD
SAYYID ABI SALIH KHWAJA ISHAQ SHAHID
MULLA KHWAJAKI
MULLA KHAWARD
SAYYID ABI NASR
AMIR ABDULLAH
MULLA AKT SHIRKHANI
ABDURRAHMAN JAMI
ALA'UDDIN MUHAMMAD
SHAH HUSAYN
SAYYID 'ABD AL-QADUR
RASHIDUDDIN
SAYYID MIR KALAN BALKHI
GHIYATHUDDIN AHMAD
KHWAJA ABDUL BASIT
KHWAJA ABDUL QADIR
SAYYID MUSA
MUHAMMAD AMIN IBN UKHT MULLAH JAMI
SHAYKH MUHAMAD SA'ID
HAJI MUHAMMAD
SAYYID ADAM BANURI
KHWAJA MAHMUD
SAYYID AHMAD AL-JALI
SHAH KAMALUDDIN
SAYYID ABDULLAH SHAH
SHAYKH ABDUL AHAD
SA'D ALLAH
MUHAMMAD AL-JAHANSI
INAYATULLAH SHAH
SAYYID IBRAHIM
SHAYKH YA'QUB SARAFI
KHWAJA HANAFI
MUHAMAD SA'ID LAHURI
ABIL MAWAHIB ATH-THUNADI
HAFIZ AHMAD
KHWAJA ZAKI
SHAYKH MUHAMMAD ABID SANAMI
25. IMAM RABBANI SHAYKH AHMAD FARUQI SIRHINDI MUJADDID ALFI THANI
MUHAMAD MAS'UD PASHADRI
SAFIYUDDIN AL-QASHASHI
KHWAJA ABDUS SABUR
SHAYKH MUHAMMAD
KHWAJA MUHAMMAD MUHSIN
HASAN AL-AJAMI
KHWAJA GAL MUHAMMAD
SHAYKH ABDUL QADIR
31. DIYAUDDIN ABU NA'SAN MUHAMMAD MAWLANA SHAYKH KHALID ASH-SHAHRAZURI AL-KURDI AL-BAGHDADI ASH-SHAMI
SHAH ABDULLAH
KHWAJA ABDUL MAJID
SHAH ABDURRAHIM
SHAYKH MUHAMMAD HASHIM
KHWAJA ZAMAN
KHWAJA ABDUL AZIZ
SHAYKH ABDUL QADIR
SULTAN AL-MULUK
SHAH HUSAYN
26. URWAT AL-WUTHQA KHWAJA MUHAMMAD MA'SUM AL-RABBANI
SHAYKH SA'DI LAHURI
MUFTI MAKKAH SHAH FAQIRULLAH SHAKARPURI
KHWAJA NIZAMUDDIN
KHWAJA AMIRUDDIN
DIYA'UDDIN IRAQI
KHWAJA YAHYA AMKI
SHAYKH MUHAMMAD IBN MUHAMMAD
SHAYKH UTHMAN
KHWAJA ABDUSH SHAKUR
SHAYKH AHMAD SHUNADI
SHIR MUHAMMAD SHARQAPURI
ALA'UDDIN IRAQI
SHAYKH UMAR
KHWAJA ABDUR RAZZAQ
SHAYKH IBRAHIM
SHAMSUL-HAQQ AFGHANI
SHAYKH MUHYIDDIN
KHWAJA MUHAMMAD SAFA
SHAYKH ABDULLAH BASRI
SHAH MUHAMMAD ISMA'IL
SHAYKH SALAMAT AL-AZZAMI
SHAYKH AHMAD NAKHLI
NUR AL-HASAN
MUHAMMAD ALUSI
27. HAJJI SAYFUDDIN 'ARIF AR-RABBANI
SHAYKH IBRAHIM KURDI
HAJI AHMAD
32. SHAYKH ISMA'IL SHIRWANI
SHAYKH ABU TAHER MADANI
HUJJATULLAH NAQSHBAND
28. SAYYID NUR MUHAMMAD BADAWANI
HUSAYN ALI SHAH
33. KHAS MUHAMMAD SHIRWANI
SHAH WALIYULLAH AD-DAHLAWI
KHWAJA MUHAMAD ZUBAYR
29. HADRAT SHAMSUDDIN HABIBULLAH MIRZA MAZHAR JAN-I-JANAN
34. SHAYKH MUHAMMAD YARAGHI
SHAH ABDUL AZIZ
IMAM 'ALI
SAYYID MUHAMMAD SHAHID
35. SAYYID JAMALUDDIN GHUMUQI AL-HUSAYNI
SHIR MUHAMMAD
SHAH QUTBUDDIN
NUR MUHAMMAD JAN-JANAWI
40. SHAYKHUNA WA USTADHUNA MAWLANA ASH-SHAYKH MUHAMMAD NAZIM 'ADIL AL-QUBRUSI AL-HAQQANI
36. ABU AHMAD AS-SUGHURI
HAJI IMDADULLAH
SHAH JAMALULLAH
30. SHAH 'ABDULLAH AD-DIHLAWI AL-MA'RUF SHAYKH GHULAM ALI
37. ABU MUHAMMAD AL-MADANI
38. SAYYID SHARAFUDDIN DAGHESTANI
39. SULTAN AL-AWLIYA MAWLANA SHAYKH 'ABDULLAH FA'IZ DAGHESTANI
GHULAM MUHYIDDIN QUSURI
SHAH SA'DULLAH
SHAH ABU SA'ID MUJADDIDI

Tree of The Most Distinguished Naqshbandi-Haqqani Path And Other Paths

Joy of Beings And Pride of Existing Things
Our Master And Mainstay
Muhammad ﷺ
Blessing And Greeting of Allah Be Upon Him
And Upon His Family And Companions

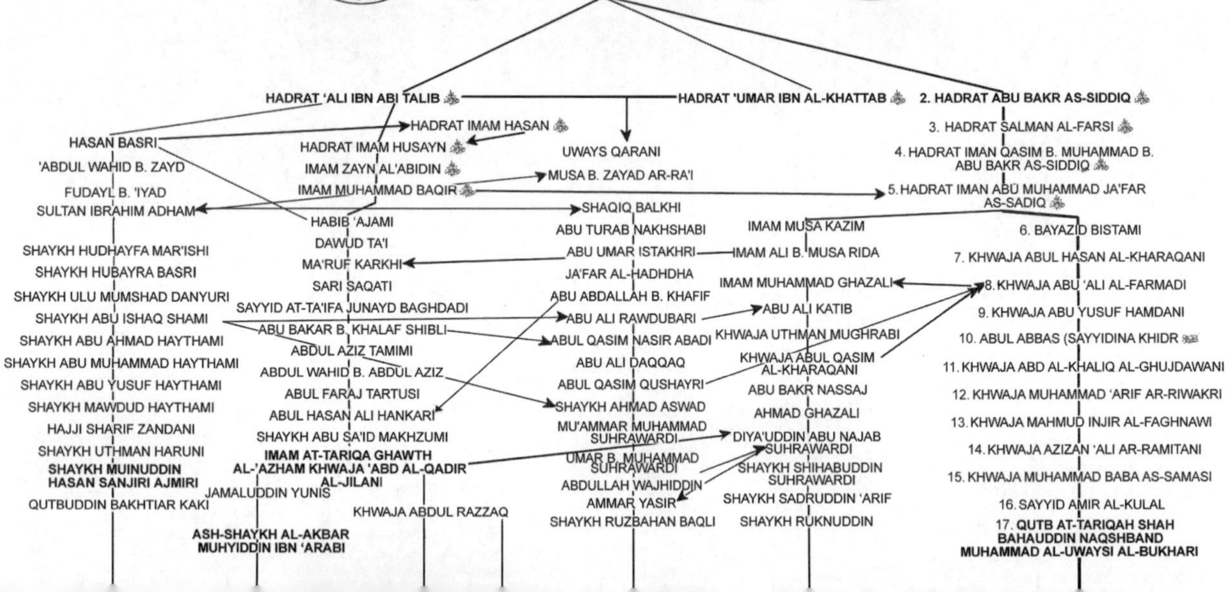

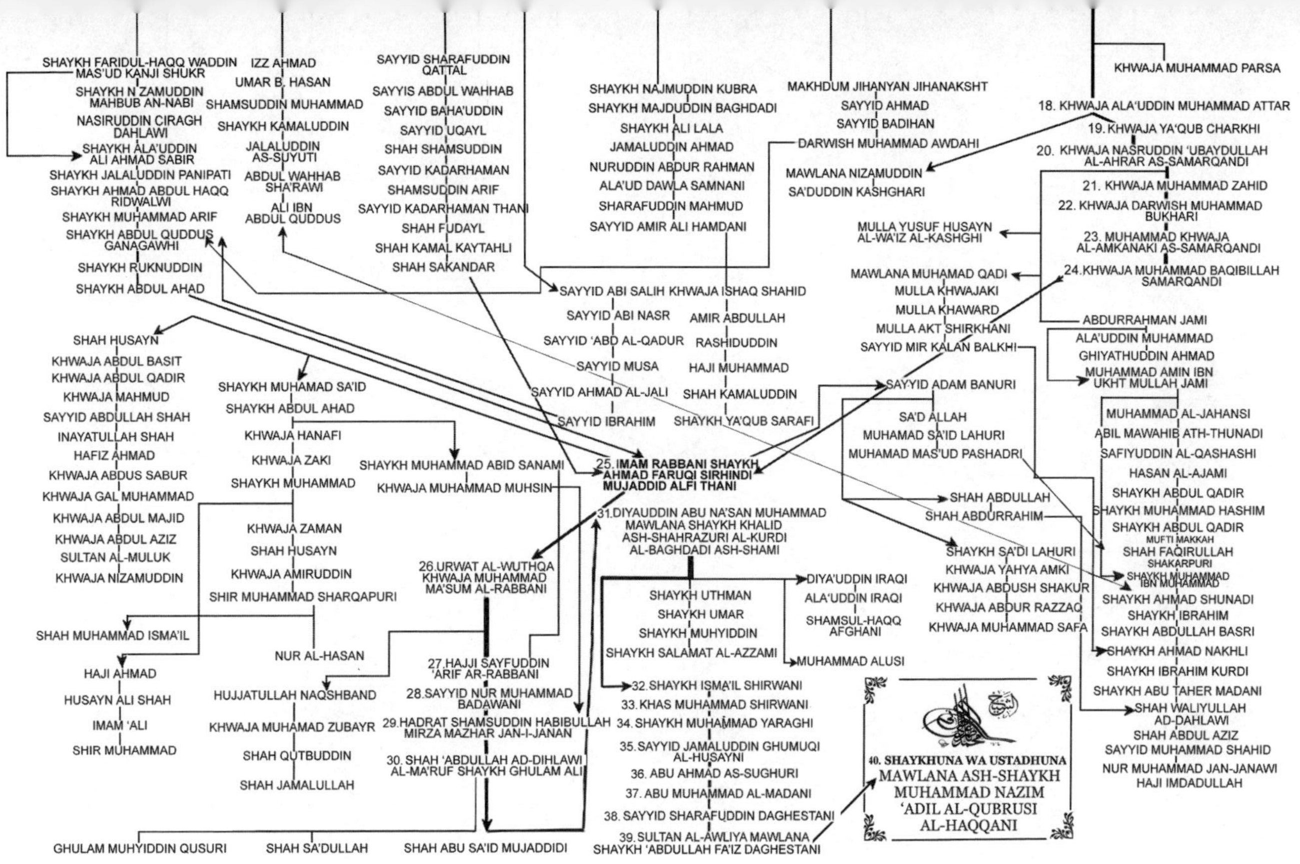
SHAYKH FARIDUL-HAQQ WADDIN MAS'UD KANJI SHUKR
SHAYKH N ZAMUDDIN MAHBUB AN-NABI
NASIRUDDIN CIRAGH DAHLAWI
SHAYKH ALA'UDDIN ALI AHMAD SABIR
SHAYKH JALALUDDIN PANIPATI
SHAYKH AHMAD ABDUL HAQQ RIDWALWI
SHAYKH MUHAMMAD ARIF
SHAYKH ABDUL QUDDUS GANAGAWHI
SHAYKH RUKNUDDIN
SHAYKH ABDUL AHAD
IZZ AHMAD
UMAR B. HASAN
SHAMSUDDIN MUHAMMAD
SHAYKH KAMALUDDIN
JALALUDDIN AS-SUYUTI
ABDUL WAHHAB SHA'RAWI
ALI IBN ABDUL QUDDUS
SAYYID SHARAFUDDIN QATTAL
SAYYIS ABDUL WAHHAB
SAYYID BAHA'UDDIN
SAYYID UQAYL
SHAH SHAMSUDDIN
SAYYID KADARHAMAN
SHAMSUDDIN ARIF
SAYYID KADARHAMAN THANI
SHAH FUDAYL
SHAH KAMAL KAYTAHLI
SHAH SAKANDAR
SHAYKH NAJMUDDIN KUBRA
SHAYKH MAJDUDDIN BAGHDADI
SHAYKH ALI LALA
JAMALUDDIN AHMAD
NURUDDIN ABDUR RAHMAN
ALA'UD DAWLA SAMNANI
SHARAFUDDIN MAHMUD
SAYYID AMIR ALI HAMDANI
MAKHDUM JIHANYAN JIHANAKSHT
SAYYID AHMAD
SAYYID BADIHAN
DARWISH MUHAMMAD AWDAHI
MAWLANA NIZAMUDDIN
SA'DUDDIN KASHGHARI
KHWAJA MUHAMMAD PARSA
18. KHWAJA ALA'UDDIN MUHAMMAD ATTAR
19. KHWAJA YA'QUB CHARKHI
20. KHWAJA NASRUDDIN 'UBAYDULLAH AL-AHRAR AS-SAMARQANDI
21. KHWAJA MUHAMMAD ZAHID
22. KHWAJA DARWISH MUHAMMAD BUKHARI
23. MUHAMMAD KHWAJA AL-AMKANAKI AS-SAMARQANDI
24. KHWAJA MUHAMMAD BAQIBILLAH SAMARQANDI
MULLA YUSUF HUSAYN AL-WA'IZ AL-KASHGHI
MAWLANA MUHAMAD QADI
MULLA KHWAJAKI
MULLA KHAWARD
MULLA AKT SHIRKHANI
SAYYID MIR KALAN BALKHI
ABDURRAHMAN JAMI
ALA'UDDIN MUHAMMAD
GHIYATHUDDIN AHMAD
MUHAMMAD AMIN IBN UKHT MULLAH JAMI
SAYYID ABI SALIH KHWAJA ISHAQ SHAHID
SAYYID ABI NASR
SAYYID 'ABD AL-QADUR
SAYYID MUSA
SAYYID AHMAD AL-JALI
SAYYID IBRAHIM
AMIR ABDULLAH
RASHIDUDDIN
HAJI MUHAMMAD
SHAH KAMALUDDIN
SHAYKH YA'QUB SARAFI
SHAH HUSAYN
KHWAJA ABDUL BASIT
KHWAJA ABDUL QADIR
KHWAJA MAHMUD
SAYYID ABDULLAH SHAH
INAYATULLAH SHAH
HAFIZ AHMAD
KHWAJA ABDUS SABUR
KHWAJA GAL MUHAMMAD
KHWAJA ABDUL MAJID
KHWAJA ABDUL AZIZ
SULTAN AL-MULUK
KHWAJA NIZAMUDDIN
SHAYKH MUHAMAD SA'ID
SHAYKH ABDUL AHAD
KHWAJA HANAFI
KHWAJA ZAKI
SHAYKH MUHAMMAD
KHWAJA ZAMAN
SHAH HUSAYN
KHWAJA AMIRUDDIN
SHIR MUHAMMAD SHARQAPURI
SHAYKH MUHAMMAD ABID SANAMI
KHWAJA MUHAMMAD MUHSIN
25. IMAM RABBANI SHAYKH AHMAD FARUQI SIRHINDI MUJADDID ALFI THANI
SAYYID ADAM BANURI
SA'D ALLAH
MUHAMAD SA'ID LAHURI
MUHAMAD MAS'UD PASHADRI
SHAH ABDULLAH
SHAH ABDURRAHIM
SHAYKH SA'DI LAHURI
KHWAJA YAHYA AMKI
KHWAJA ABDUSH SHAKUR
KHWAJA ABDUR RAZZAQ
KHWAJA MUHAMMAD SAFA
MUHAMMAD AL-JAHANSI
ABIL MAWAHIB ATH-THUNADI
SAFIYUDDIN AL-QASHASHI
HASAN AL-AJAMI
SHAYKH ABDUL QADIR
SHAYKH MUHAMMAD HASHIM
SHAYKH ABDUL QADIR
MUFTI MAKKAH
SHAH FAQIRULLAH
SHAKARPURI
SHAYKH MUHAMMAD IBN MUHAMMAD
SHAYKH AHMAD SHUNADI
SHAYKH IBRAHIM
SHAYKH ABDULLAH BASRI
SHAYKH AHMAD NAKHLI
SHAYKH IBRAHIM KURDI
SHAYKH ABU TAHER MADANI
SHAH WALIYULLAH AD-DAHLAWI
SHAH ABDUL AZIZ
SAYYID MUHAMMAD SHAHID
NUR MUHAMMAD JAN-JANAWI
HAJI IMDADULLAH
31. DIYAUDDIN ABU NA'SAN MUHAMMAD MAWLANA SHAYKH KHALID ASH-SHAHRAZURI AL-KURDI AL-BAGHDADI ASH-SHAMI
SHAYKH UTHMAN
SHAYKH UMAR
SHAYKH MUHYIDDIN
SHAYKH SALAMAT AL-AZZAMI
DIYA'UDDIN IRAQI
ALA'UDDIN IRAQI
SHAMSUL-HAQQ AFGHANI
MUHAMMAD ALUSI
32. SHAYKH ISMA'IL SHIRWANI
33. KHAS MUHAMMAD SHIRWANI
34. SHAYKH MUHAMMAD YARAGHI
35. SAYYID JAMALUDDIN GHUMUQI AL-HUSAYNI
36. ABU AHMAD AS-SUGHURI
37. ABU MUHAMMAD AL-MADANI
38. SAYYID SHARAFUDDIN DAGHESTANI
39. SULTAN AL-AWLIYA MAWLANA SHAYKH 'ABDULLAH FA'IZ DAGHESTANI
40. SHAYKHUNA WA USTADHUNA
MAWLANA ASH-SHAYKH MUHAMMAD NAZIM 'ADIL AL-QUBRUSI AL-HAQQANI
26. URWAT AL-WUTHQA KHWAJA MUHAMMAD MA'SUM AL-RABBANI
27. HAJJI SAYFUDDIN 'ARIF AR-RABBANI
28. SAYYID NUR MUHAMMAD BADAWANI
29. HADRAT SHAMSUDDIN HABIBULLAH MIRZA MAZHAR JAN-I-JANAN
30. SHAH 'ABDULLAH AD-DIHLAWI AL-MA'RUF SHAYKH GHULAM ALI
SHAH MUHAMMAD ISMA'IL
HAJI AHMAD
HUSAYN ALI SHAH
IMAM 'ALI
SHIR MUHAMMAD
NUR AL-HASAN
HUJJATULLAH NAQSHBAND
KHWAJA MUHAMAD ZUBAYR
SHAH QUTBUDDIN
SHAH JAMALULLAH
GHULAM MUHYIDDIN QUSURI
SHAH SA'DULLAH
SHAH ABU SA'ID MUJADDIDI

1. The Messenger of God, Prophet Muhammad Ibn Abd Allah ﷺ

The Shaykhs of the Naqshbandi Order are known as "the Golden Chain" because of their connection to the highest, most perfect human being, Muhammad ﷺ: the First to be created, the First to be mentioned, the First to be honored.

How can people in this world grasp his reality?
They, who are asleep and pleased by dreams from him.
How beautiful, what has been said about his reality!
"Your light is everything and everything else is particles."
O Prophet, your soldiers in any time are your Companions.
—Imam Busayri, *al-Burda*[28]

[28] Quoted and translated in Shaykh al-Alawi, *Knowledge of God*, p. 354.

When did God order the Pen to write? When did the Pen write? When did that writing of *la ilaha ill-Allah Muhammadun Rasul Allah* occur? No one knows. The mention of the name of the Prophet ﷺ by God, Almighty and Exalted, is something that happened before the creation of anything, and its reality occurred in pre-Eternity. That is the reason the Prophet ﷺ mentioned, *"I was a Prophet when Adam was between water and clay."*

When God ordered the Pen to write, it asked, "What shall I write?" And God said, "Write '*la ilaha ill-Allah*.'" The Pen wrote "*la ilaha ill-Allah*" for 70,000 of God's years and then it stopped. One of God's days is equal to 1,000 of our years. Then God ordered it to write again, and the Pen asked, "What shall I write?" and God answered, "Write '*Muhammadun Rasul Allah*.'" And the Pen said, "O God, who is this Muhammad that You have put Your Name next to his name?" God said, "You must know that if it were not for Muhammad ﷺ I would not have created anything in Creation." So the Pen wrote "*Muhammadun Rasul Allah*" for another 70,000 years.

The Beloved of God, Prophet Muhammad ibn Abd Allah ﷺ, is the perfect human being. He is the seal of all prophets and messengers. What can a weak servant say in order to honor the Master of Messengers? If it were not for him, no one would ever have known God, Almighty and Exalted. Never would the fabric of the universe have been woven into existence as it has been woven. Therefore, the pen cannot describe the most perfect of the perfect human beings, the Master of Masters, the King of Kings, the Sultan of Sultans of the Divine Presence. He is the heart of the Divine Presence. He is the heart of the Unique Essence. He is the Sign for Oneness and the Sign of Oneness. He is known as the Secret of All Secrets. He is the only one addressed by God, Almighty and Exalted, because he is the only one considered responsible in the Presence of God who said, "Were it not for him I would not have created any of My creation." All of the creation was given to the Prophet ﷺ as a divine gesture of honor from God, Almighty and Exalted. Therefore the Prophet ﷺ is responsible for that creation which is his honor and his trust. For that reason, he is the only one to be addressed in the Divine Presence.

The singular status of the Prophet ﷺ is the heart and the essence of the phrase of monotheism, namely, "There is no god but God, Muhammad is the Messenger of God" and the foundation of Sufism. The Prophet ﷺ is the "one soul" mentioned in the Quranic verse:

"(O humanity) Your creation and your resurrection is in no wise but as an individual soul." (31:28)

It is also the Prophet ﷺ who is the "single life" represented in the verse:

"If anyone slew a person ... it would be as if he slew the whole of humanity. And if anyone saved a life, it would be as if he saved the life of the whole of humanity." (5:32)

The Prophet ﷺ, moreover, referred to his responsibility in the Tradition, "All your actions are shown to me every day. If they are good, I pray for you. If they are bad, I ask God's forgiveness for you." That means that the Prophet ﷺ is the one who is responsible towards God for his Community. That is why, as we said, he is "the only one to be spoken to." It is the basis of intercession. God refers to this intercession in the verse:

If they had only, when they were unjust to themselves, come unto thee and asked God's forgiveness, and the Messenger had asked forgiveness for them, they would have found God indeed Oft-Returning, Most Merciful. (4:64)

His honorable biography and his blessed speeches and actions can never be encompassed in a book. But we can say that he is Muhammad ibn Abd Allah ibn Abd al-Muttalib ibn Hashim and that his lineage goes back to Abraham عليه السلام. He was born in Blessed Makkah on a Monday, the 12th of *Rabi al-Awwal*, 570 CE, in the Year of the Elephant. His father died before he was born. His mother, Amina رضي الله عنها , when she gave birth to him, saw a light coming from her that turned all darkness into light as far as Persia. When he was born, the first thing he did after coming from his mother's womb was to fall into prostration. He was nursed by Thuayba رضي الله عنها and then by Halima as-Saadiyya رضي الله عنها, with whom he stayed for four years.

While returning with him from a visit to his uncles in Madinah (at that time known as "Yathrib"), his mother fell sick and died. He was six years old. His grandfather raised him for two years, until his grandfather also died. Orphaned three times, he went to live with his uncle, Abu Talib. God, Almighty and Exalted, ordered the Angel of the Trumpet, Israfil عليه السلام to accompany him at all times until the age of eleven years. Then God ordered Gabriel عليه السلام to accompany him, to look after him, to keep him in his safekeeping and to send to his heart the heavenly and spiritual powers.

He traveled with his uncle to Damascus. On their way they passed by Bostra where a monk named Bahira, living in a monastery nearby, recognized him as a prophet and told Muhammad's ﷺ uncle, "Take him back, it will be safer for him. Great things are in store for him." At that time he was twelve years old. Years later he traveled again to Sham with Maysara ؓ, to trade on behalf of the Lady Khadija ؓ. They were very successful. Maysara ؓ told Khadija ؓ about his miraculous powers and his business acumen. She became interested in him. She proposed marriage and he accepted her offer. He married her when he was twenty-five years of age and she was forty.

He was known throughout his tribe as the truthful and trustworthy one (*as-sadiq al-amin*). When he was thirty-five years old, the Quraysh tribe was renovating the House of God, the Kabah. They disputed among themselves as to who should place the sacred Black Stone in its place. They finally came to an agreement that the most trustworthy person should replace it, and that person was the Prophet ﷺ.

HIS SECLUSION

At that time inspirations came to his heart. He was always in a state of spiritual vision and insight, but he was not authorized to speak about it. He preferred to be alone. He used a cave in a mountain called al-Hira for contemplation and meditation. He sought seclusion as the means to reach the Divine Presence of God, Almighty and Exalted.

He avoided all kinds of attachment, even with his family. He was always in meditation and contemplation, afloat on the ocean of the *dhikr* of the heart. He disconnected himself completely from everything until there appeared to him the Light of God, Almighty and Exalted, which graced him with the condition of complete intimacy and happiness. That intimacy allowed the mirror of revelation to increase in purity and brightness until he attained to the highest state of perfection where he observed the dawning of a new creation. The primordial signs of beauty shone forth to spread and decorate the universe. Trees, stones, earth, the stars, the sun, the moon, the clouds, wind, rain and animals would greet him in perfect Arabic speech and say, "*as-salam alayka ya Rasul Allah,*" "Peace be upon you, O Prophet of God."

REVELATION

At forty years of age, when standing on the Mountain of Hira, there appeared on the horizon a figure he did not recognize, who said to him, "O

Muhammad, I am Gabriel and you are the Prophet of God whom He has sent to this Community." Then he handed him a piece of silk that was decorated with jewels. He put it in his hand and told him, "Recite." He asked, "What should I recite?" He hugged the Prophet ﷺ and told him, "Recite." He again said, "What should I recite?" He hugged him again and said:

> *Recite, in the name of your Lord, who created, created the human being out of a blood clot, recite, and your Lord is most bountiful Who has taught with the Pen, taught the human being what he knew not!* (96:1-5)

Then he ordered him to climb down the mountain to the plains below. He placed him on a large white stone and gave him two green robes. Gabriel ﵇ hit the earth with his feet. Immediately a spring poured forth. The angel made ablutions with it and ordered him to do the same. Gabriel ﵇ took a handful of water and threw it on the face of the Prophet ﷺ. Sufi saints say that the water he threw was a sign that the Prophet ﷺ was granted authority to spread the knowledge of the secrets of God's Divine Presence to human beings, either by physical or by spiritual means. He prayed two *rakats* of prayer and told the Prophet ﷺ, "This is the way to worship," and he disappeared.

The Prophet ﷺ returned to Makkah and told his wife ؓ all that had occurred. She believed him and became the first Muslim. She went with the Prophet ﷺ to Waraqah ibn Nawfal ؓ, her uncle, who was considered a knowledgeable person in spirituality. The Prophet ﷺ told him what happened. Waraqah ibn Nawfal ؓ said, "This is the Holy Spirit which descended on Moses ﵇." He said, "Would that I be alive when your people expel you from Makkah!" The Prophet ﷺ asked, "Are my people going to put me out of Makkah?" He said, "Yes, that is what is written."

Ali ibn Abi Talib ؓ, who was a young boy at that time living with the Prophet ﷺ, accepted Islam and Abu Bakr ؓ became the first adult male believer. In public, the Prophet ﷺ gave guidance needed for daily life. In private, he would give the special advice needed for attaining the state of excellence or perfect, good character. That is why Abu Hurayra ؓ said in an authentic Tradition mentioned in *Sahih Bukhari*:

> *The Prophet ﷺ has poured into my heart two kinds of knowledge: one I have spread to people and the other, if I were to share it, they would cut my throat.*

Divine Presence, closer and closer, until Gabriel ﷺ said to him, "O Messenger of God, I cannot continue further, or I will be extinguished."

The Prophet ﷺ said, "O Gabriel, accompany me!" He said, "I cannot, or I will be burned in God's Light." So Muhammad ﷺ, the most perfect of the perfect, continued alone. Driven by his love for God's Divine Presence, he approached closer and closer, achieving the state of complete annihilation in five different stages.

The Prophet ﷺ moved from one stage to another into God's Divine Secrets. Between each stage was 500,000 years. He passed through these vast Divine oceans of knowledge, which God, Almighty and Exalted, has created, until he was completely dissolved in God's Existence, seeing nothing except Him. Then God called him to return to existence after he had reached the state of annihilation. He returned and God told him, "O Muhammad, approach closer." From this it is understood that the Prophet ﷺ, having reached the state of complete annihilation, was called by God by his name, indicating that he was appearing anew with God's appearance. He reached so near to the Divine Light, that he was *"two bow-lengths or nearer"* (53:9). God asked him, "Who are you, O Muhammad?" At that time the Prophet ﷺ was not conscious of himself and he replied, "You, O my Lord." This is the perfection of the state of not associating anyone with God. It is the perfect sign of monotheism (Oneness), when nothing exists except His Glory, His Essence, Himself.

Shaykh Nazim al-Haqqani has related from the hidden knowledge of the Sufi saints some of the events that occurred on that incredible journey of the Prophet ﷺ. This is the knowledge from the Prophet that Abu Hurayra ؓ referred to in his Tradition, knowledge passed down from the heart of Abu Bakr as-Siddiq ؓ. The Prophet ﷺ said, *"Whatever God poured into my heart I poured into the heart of as-Siddiq."* This knowledge was then passed to the Naqshbandi Sufi saints and constitutes their spiritual inheritance.

Shaykh Nazim al-Haqqani said:

> God, Almighty and Exalted, said to the Prophet ﷺ on the Night of Ascension, "O Muhammad, I have created all of creation for your sake, and I am giving it all to you." At that moment God granted the Prophet ﷺ power to see all that He had created, with all of their lights and favors that God had granted His creatures by decorating them with His Attributes and with His Divine Love and Beauty.

Muhammad ﷺ was enthralled and enraptured because God had given him the gift of such a creation. God said to him, "O Muhammad, are you happy with this creation?" He said, "Yes, My Lord." He said, "I am giving them to you in trust to keep, to be responsible for, and to return to Me just as I gave them to you." Muhammad ﷺ looked at them in delight because they were illuminated with beautiful lights. He said, "O My Lord, I accept." God said, "Do you accept?" He replied, "I accept, I accept." As he finished replying the third time, God granted him a vision of the sins and the many forms of misery, darkness, and ignorance into which they were going to fall.

When Muhammad ﷺ saw this he was dismayed, wondering how he would be able to return them to His Lord as pure as in their original state. He said, "O My Lord, what is this?" God replied, "O My beloved, this is your responsibility. You have to return them to Me as pure as I gave them to you." Then Muhammad ﷺ said, "O my Lord, give me helpers to help me purify them, to sanctify their spirits, and to take them from darkness and ignorance to the state of knowledge, of piety, of peace and love."

Then God, Almighty and Exalted, granted him a vision in which he informed him that, out of this creation, He had chosen for him 7,007 Naqshbandi Saints. He told him, "O My beloved, O Muhammad, these saints are from the most distinguished saints that I created to help you in keeping this creation pure. Out of them are 313 who are in the highest, most perfect state in the Divine Presence. They are the inheritors of the secrets of 313 messengers.[29] Then I am giving you forty who are carrying the most distinguished powers. They are considered the pillars of all saints. They are going to be the masters of their times. They are going to be the inheritors of the secrets of Reality."

---

[29] Ahmad ibn Anas bin Malik ؓ narrated that Abu Dharr (al-Ghifari) ؓ in a long *hadith* narrated that he asked the Prophet ﷺ, "O Messenger of Allah, how many prophets are there?" He ﷺ replied, "One hundred and twenty-four thousand prophets." I asked, "How many messengers are there?" He ﷺ replied, "a large crowd of three hundred and thirteen messengers." *The Beauty of the Righteous and Accounts of the Elite,* translation of Abu Nuaym al-Isfahani's *Hilyat al-awliya* by Shaykh Muhammad al-Akili, 1:379, p 155.

"At the hands of these saints everyone will be healed from his wounds, both externally and internally. These saints will be able to carry the whole Community and the whole of creation without any sign of tiring. Every one of them will be the Arch-Intercessor (*Ghawth*) in his time, under whom will be the five spiritual poles (*Aqtab*)."

The Prophet ﷺ was happy and he said, "O my Lord, give me more!" Then God showed him 124,000 saints. He said, "These saints are the inheritors of the 124,000 prophets. Each one is an inheritor from one prophet. They also will be there to help you purify this Community."

While the Prophet ﷺ was ascending to the Divine Presence, God made him hear a human voice. The voice was that of his friend and closest Companion, Abu Bakr as-Siddiq ؓ. The Prophet ﷺ was told by God Almighty to order Abu Bakr as-Siddiq ؓ to call all the Naqshbandi saints: the 40, the 313, and the 7,007, and all their followers, in their spiritual forms, into the Divine Presence. All were to receive those distinguished lights and blessings.

Then God ordered the Prophet ﷺ, who ordered Abu Bakr ؓ, to call the 124,000 saints of the other forty Sufi Ways and their followers to be given that light in the Divine Presence. All of the shaykhs began to appear in that gathering with all of their followers. God then asked the Prophet ﷺ to look at them with his Prophetic power and light, and to lift them all to the station of the trustworthy and the truthful. God, Almighty and Exalted, said to the Prophet ﷺ, and the Prophet ﷺ said to the saints, "All of you and all of your followers are going to be stars shining among human beings, to spread that light which I gave you in pre-Eternity to all human beings on earth."

Shaykh Muhammad Nazim al-Haqqani says:

That is only one of the secrets that has been revealed about the Night of Ascension to the hearts of the saints through the transmission of the Golden Chain of the Naqshbandi Order.

Many more visions were given to the Prophet ﷺ, but there is no permission to unveil them.

That Night, the Prophet ﷺ was ordered by God to perform fifty prescribed prayers a day. He asked that God shorten it to five prescribed prayers a day on the advice of the Prophet Moses ﷺ. He returned from that Night Journey, and the first one to believe him was Abu Bakr as-Siddiq ؓ. The unbelievers, hoping to ridicule him, asked him to describe Jerusalem. He described it in all its details. The unbelievers were humiliated.

Persecution against the Prophet ﷺ and his Companions escalated. Then God sent him the Helpers from Madinah. Islam had begun to spread among the tribes of this small oasis not far from Makkah. God gave the believers permission to emigrate to Madinah, the home of the Helpers. Abu Bakr ؓ wanted to emigrate, but Muhammad ﷺ told him, "Do not leave yet. Wait and maybe you will travel with me. There is a very important event which must take place."

THE PROPHET'S ﷺ MIGRATION

The Prophet ﷺ departed at night with Abu Bakr ؓ and left behind him Ali ؓ to impersonate him in his bed. On the way he stopped to hide in the Cave of Thawr. Abu Bakr ؓ said, "O Prophet ﷺ, do not enter, I will enter first." In his heart he thought that there might be something harmful inside. He chose to encounter it first. He found a hole in the cave. He called the Prophet ﷺ to come in while he put his foot over the hole. The Prophet ﷺ came in and lay down with his head on Abu Bakr's ؓ thigh.

A snake inside the hold began to bite the foot of Abu Bakr ؓ He tried not to move although he was in great pain. Tears flowed down his cheeks. One warm tear dropped on the blessed face of the Prophet ﷺ. At this, as was mentioned in the Quran:

He said to his friend, "Grieve not, for verily God is with us." (9:40)

The Prophet ﷺ also said, "What do you think of two when God is their third?"[30] Abu Bakr ؓ said to the Prophet ﷺ, "O Prophet of God, I am not sad, but I am in pain. A snake is biting my foot and I am worried that it might bite you. I am crying because my heart is burning for you and for your safety." The Prophet ﷺ was so pleased with the reply from his beloved Companion that he hugged Abu Bakr as-Siddiq ؓ, put his hand on his heart and poured the knowledge that God had given him into the heart of Abu Bakr as-Siddiq ؓ. That is why he said in a Tradition, "Whatever God poured into my heart, I poured into the heart of Abu Bakr."

---

[30] *Sahih Bukhari.*

Shaykh Muhammad Nazim al-Haqqani, describing some of the secrets given to the Naqshbandi saints, says:

> Following this the Prophet ﷺ put his other hand on the foot of Abu Bakr as-Siddiq ؓ and recited, "In the Name of God, the Merciful, the Compassionate," and the foot was immediately healed. Then he ordered the snake to come out and the snake came out, coiling itself in front of the Prophet ﷺ. Then the Prophet ﷺ said to the snake, "Do you not know that the flesh of a *siddiq* is forbidden to you? Why are you eating the flesh of my Companion?" He replied to the Prophet ﷺ in a perfect and pure Arabic, "O Prophet of God, were not all things created for your sake and for your love? O Prophet, I too love you. When I heard that God, Almighty and Exalted, said that the best Community is your Community, I asked Him to prolong my life, to grant me the honor of being from your Community, and to look at your face. God granted me that wish and that honor. When Abu Bakr put his foot in that hole, it blocked my sight. I wanted him to move his foot to enable me to see you." The Prophet ﷺ said, "Look at me now and fulfill your wish." The snake looked and looked. After a while, it died. The Prophet ﷺ ordered the jinn to carry the snake away and bury it.
>
> Then the Prophet ﷺ said to Abu Bakr ؓ, "There was no need to stop in this cave, except that a significant event will happen here. The Light of the root of the spiritual Tree that is going to spread over all humanity, the Light coming directly from the Divine Presence, will appear here. God has ordered me to transmit it to you and to all the Naqshbandi Sufi followers."
>
> This lineage was not called the Naqshbandi at that time, but was known as the children of Abu Bakr as-Siddiq ؓ, and he was known to saints as the "father" of this line. God asked the Prophet ﷺ to order Abu Bakr as-Siddiq ؓ to call all the masters of the Golden Chain who are the inheritors of Abu Bakr ؓ. The latter called the grandshaykhs of this Golden Chain, all of them, from his time down to the time of the Mahdi ؑ. All of them were called through their spirits from the world of souls. Then he was ordered to call the 7,007 Naqshbandi saints. Then the Prophet ﷺ called the 124,000 prophets.

Abu Bakr as-Siddiq ﷺ, by order of the Prophet ﷺ, ordered every grandshaykh to summon all his followers to appear spiritually. Then Abu Bakr as-Siddiq ﷺ ordered all the shaykhs to take the hands of their followers to receive initiation. He put his hand above them all. Muhammad ﷺ put his hand above all of them. God put His Hand, the Hand of Power, over them all. God by Himself put on the tongue of everyone present His recitation. He told the Prophet ﷺ to order Abu Bakr as-Siddiq ﷺ to order all the saints present with their followers to recite what they were hearing from the Voice of Power.

Allahu Allahu Allahu Haqq

Allahu Allahu Allahu Haqq

Allahu Allahu Allahu Haqq

All of those present followed their shaykhs. The shaykhs followed what they heard the Prophet ﷺ reciting. God, Almighty and Exalted, taught the secret of the *dhikr*, known as *Khatm al-Khwajagan* (recitation of the masters) to Abd al-Khaliq al-Ghujdawani, who led the first *dhikr* among the saints of this Order. The Prophet ﷺ announced to Abu Bakr ﷺ, who announced to all saints, that Abd al-Khaliq al-Ghujdawani is the leader of the *Khatm al-Khwajagan*. Everyone was honored to receive that secret and light from Khwaja Abd al-Khaliq al-Ghujdawani, in the presence of all saints, in the presence of Abu Bakr as-Siddiq ﷺ, in the presence of the Prophet ﷺ, in the Presence of God, Almighty and Exalted.

Anyone who accepts initiation from us or attends our *dhikr* must know that he was in the cave at that blessed time, in the Presence of the Prophet ﷺ, and that he received all of these secrets then. These secrets have been transmitted to us from the masters of the Golden Chain, through Abu Bakr as-Siddiq ﷺ.

Abu Bakr as-Siddiq ﷺ was overjoyed and astounded with what took place in the cave. He understood why the Prophet ﷺ had chosen him to be the Companion of his Emigration. The Naqshbandi shaykhs consider the events in the cave as the foundation of the spiritual Way. Not only is it the source of the daily devotion, but also the souls of all members of the Order were present together at that time.

After the events in the cave they continued on to Madinah. When they reached Quba, a village near Madinah, on a Monday in *Rabi al-Awwal,* they stopped for several days. There the Prophet ﷺ built the first mosque. They continued on their way on a Friday, after praying the first Friday congregational prayer at Quba. He entered Madinah with his friend, amid shouts of "*Allahu Akbar*" and "Praise belongs to God," and the excited, joyful happiness of everyone. He moved to the place his camel stopped. It is there that he built his mosque and his home. He stayed as a guest in the home of Abu Ayyub al-Ansari رضي الله عنه until his mosque was built.

When the Prophet ﷺ went to Madinah, disease was rampant. As soon as he arrived, the diseases disappeared.

Chronology of the Prophet's ﷺ Years in Madinah

YEAR ONE

The Prophet ﷺ was inspired to call the people to prayer by means of the human voice (*adhan*).

YEAR TWO

He was ordered to institute the monthly fast of Ramadan. He was directed to face the Kabah in Makkah during prayers, instead of towards Jerusalem as they had done previously. It was the year that he fought the unbelievers in the decisive Battle of Badr.

YEAR THREE

The Prophet ﷺ fought the unbelievers at Uhud.

YEAR FOUR

The Battle of Bani Nadhir took place, and permission was given for shortening the prayer during traveling and fighting. Alcohol was forbidden. Dry ablution when water is not available (*tayammum*) was allowed, and the "prayer of fear" was authorized.

YEAR FIVE

The Battle of Khandaq took place and the defection of the Banu Qurayzah and Mustaliq occurred.

YEAR SIX

The Treaty of Hudaybiyya took place, as did the Pledge of Loyalty—the model of Sufi initiation—under the Tree. The fifth pillar of the religion, the obligation of the prescribed pilgrimage, also came in this year.

YEAR SEVEN

The Battle of Khaybar took place.

YEAR EIGHT

The events of Muta, the peaceful conquest of Makkah and the Battle of Hunayn occurred.

YEAR NINE

The Battle of Tabuk occurred and the pilgrimage of as-Siddiq ﵁. It was called the Year of Delegations.

YEAR TEN

The Prophet ﷺ made what is known as the Farewell Pilgrimage.

YEAR ELEVEN

The Prophet ﷺ passed on to the other life.

Description of the Holy Prophet's ﷺ Features

God Almighty and Exalted adorned the Prophet ﷺ with His Divine Lights and Manners. Then He added more by saying to him:

Truly you are of a sublime nature. (68:4)

The Prophet ﷺ was neither tall nor short, but he was of middle height. He had broad shoulders. His color was light, neither dark nor white. He had a broad forehead, with heavy eyebrows, not connected but with a blaze shining like silver in the middle of them. His eyes were large. His teeth were very white, like pearls. His hair was not curly nor was it straight, but in between. His neck was long. His chest was broad, without much flesh. The color of his chest was light, and between his sternum and his navel was a line of hair. He had no hair on his chest other than that line. His shoulders were wide and had hair on them. On his shoulders were two seals of prophecy. All his Companions looked at them. The right shoulder had a black beauty mark, and around it were a few hairs, like the hairs of a horse. His forearms were large. His wrists were long. His fingers were also long. His palm was smoother than silk. Whenever he put his hand on the head of a child or a man, the beautiful scent of musk came from it. Wherever he moved, a cloud moved with him that shaded him from the heat of the sun. His sweat was like white pearls, and its smell was like amber and musk. The Companions said they had never seen anything like it before.

The Holy Prophet ﷺ characteristically looked down more than he raised his head. He amazed whoever saw him from afar. Whoever knew him intimately loved him. He was the most handsome, both in his external and internal appearance.

Amr ibn al-As ؓ said:

> *No one was dearer to me than the Holy Prophet ﷺ, nor was anyone more glorious than him in my eyes. So bright was his glory that I could not look at his face for any length of time, so that if I were asked to describe him I would not be able to do so as I had not looked at him long enough.*

The Prophet ﷺ was the bravest among people, the most just and the most generous. He walked alone among his enemies at night without a guard. He was never afraid of anything in this world. He was the most modest of men, the most sincere, and the most pious. He never spoke just to spend time. He preferred silence to speech and never showed pride, although he was the most eloquent speaker.

God gave the Prophet ﷺ mastery in politics and mastery in private conduct. Although he did not read or write, God raised him from the land of ignorance, taught him the best of manners and the best of ethics.

He was the gentlest of men, the most tolerant, and as God Himself called him "*...the kindest and most merciful.*" (9:128) He smiled at everyone and joked with everyone in a decent way. Alone, he cried and entreated God for forgiveness for his Community. He was continuously in a state of meditation and contemplation. He often sat and remembered God by reciting *dhikr*.

He was known to the widow and orphan and was often approached by them. He showed humility to unbelievers, praying for faith to enter their hearts. Someone asked him to "Pray for God to curse the unbelievers." He said, "I was not sent to curse, but as a mercy. I will ask for them to be guided because they do not know."

He called everyone to God. He never humiliated the poor. He was never afraid of a king. He always chose the easy way, according to God's wish. ("*God wants ease for you*." 2:185; 20:2)

He laughed without making a sound, not out loud. He always said, "Serve your people." He milked his own goats, served his family, and mended his clothes. He walked barefooted to visit the sick, even if they were unbelievers or hypocrites. He visited the graves of believers and greeted them. He trained with the sword, the bow and arrow, and rode the horse, the camel, and the donkey. He ate with the poor. He always accepted a gift graciously, even if it was a spoonful of yogurt, and rewarded whoever gave it. He never ate from charity, but immediately passed it on to the poor. He never kept one *dinar* or one *dirham* in his house except to give it to the poor. He never came home until he spent all that God had given him.

He was very good to his family and to his friends. He urged his friends to walk in front of him and he walked behind them. He said, "Leave my back for angels." His companionship was the companionship of patience and modesty. Whoever argued with him saw patience from him. He did not reply to those who insulted him. He never came against anyone in anger nor ever used bad language. He was never angry for himself and was only angry for his Lord's sake. He was often known to eat with his servants. He never slapped anyone with his hand. He never punished for a mistake, but always forgave.

His servant Anas ﷺ said:

In all my life, he never asked me once, "Why did you do this, or why did you not do that?"

The Clothes of the Holy Prophet ﷺ

He wore whatever he found, cotton or wool, but mostly he wore cotton. He liked green clothes. Abu Hurayra ﷺ says, "He wore long, loose shirts, the cloaks, the wrap and the robe. He wore the turban with a face-veil and loose-ended, the waist wrapper (sarong) and the gown."

Jabir ibn Samurah ﷺ said:

I saw the Prophet ﷺ on a moonlit night. He had a red cloak over his body. I looked attentively in turn towards him and the moon. Certainly, he appeared to me more beautiful than the moon itself. He wore a white turban, a black turban and sometimes a red turban. He left a tail at the back of his turban.

Imam Tabari said:

He had a turban of seven arms' lengths. He had a turban called "The Clouds" which he gave to Ali ؓ. He wore a silver ring on his right hand, engraved with the words, "Muhammadun Rasul Allah." He wore leather socks on his feet. He liked perfumes and fragrant scents.

He never sought ease and comfort. He never possessed even a bed, as he wished to make his abode in the next world. His mattress was made from tree leaves. He had a big cloak that he spread on the floor and sat on. He most often slept on a reed mat or directly on the floor.

The Miracles of the Holy Prophet ﷺ

He was a healer for himself and for others, primarily by reciting the Quran for whoever was ill. He warned people to avoid overeating. He performed countless miracles. He prayed that Ali ؓ not feel the hot and cold weather, and thereafter, he never felt them. He prayed for Ibn Abbas ؓ to be a genius in religion, jurisprudence, and explanation of the Quran, which came to pass. When Qutada's ؓ eye fell out of its socket, he restored it, and Qutada ؓ was able to see with it better than he ever had before. He rubbed the foot of Ibn Abi Atiq ؓ when it was broken and it was healed immediately.

The moon split on his order as a sign to the unbelievers. Water sprang forth from his fingers from which a whole army drank and made ablution. Water poured forth from a small cup of water, converting the desert into an oasis. The branch of a tree under which he sat, bowed in a gesture of love as he stood up to leave. The *minbar*, from which he preached, used to give a moaning sound, as if crying for him. The stones in his hand praised God, so that everyone heard them.

The animals complained to him. The deer and the wolf witnessed his prophethood. He predicted that his daughter Fatimah ؓ would be the first to follow him in death. He foretold that Uthman Dhun Nurayn ؓ, his third rightly-guided caliph and son-in-law, would be assassinated. He announced the murder of al-Aswad ibn Anas ؓ on the night of his death in Sana, in far-off Yemen. He mentioned the death of the king of Persia to his Companions at the exact moment it occurred. He ate meat full of poison, but nothing happened to him, although the one who ate with him died immediately. Countless other miracles could be mentioned.

The Sayings of the Holy Prophet ﷺ

No one can make a complete account of his sayings. Even if the seas of this world were ink and the trees were pens, no one could encompass all the wisdom of the Prophet Muhammad ﷺ. Hundreds of thousands of his Traditions (narrated sayings) have been compiled. It is known as *ulum al-hadith*, the science of the Holy Traditions. He said:

> *God rewards people according to what they achieve.*
>
> *God said, "Whoever comes against one of My saints, I will declare war against him."*
>
> *God's saints are under His domes. No one knows them except Him.*
>
> *Be near the poor (meaning the spiritual poor) because they have a government of their own.*
>
> *Be in this world as a stranger and a guest. Make the mosques your homes. Teach your heart leniency. Recite the remembrance of God much and cry much.*
>
> *How many people welcome a day whose end they will not live to see and expect a tomorrow that they will not reach?*
>
> *Speak the truth, even if it be to your detriment.*
>
> *Make everything easy. Do not make it difficult. Give good tidings and do not cause people to run away.*
>
> *God said, "O Son of Adam, you will get what you have intended and you will be with the one whom you love more."*
>
> *Keep God and He will keep you. Keep God before you. If you need help, ask His Help.*
>
> *Be austere in this lower world and God will love you. Be austere with what is in the hands of people and the people will love you.*
>
> *The one who has the most perfect mind is the one who is most fearful of God.*

Beware of the lower world because it is black magic.

Refrain from speaking except what is good.

Give back the trust and do not betray it.

When God loves someone, He will put him in difficulties.

When God wants good for His servant, He will guide him to someone that shows him the way.

Forgive others and God will forgive you.

Be merciful and God will be merciful towards you.

The one under the heaviest punishment on the Day of Judgment is a scholar devoid of compassion.

The one under the heaviest punishment on the Day of Judgment is a scholar whose knowledge did not benefit him.

Ask God forgiveness and health.

Keep what you are doing secret.

The most sinful person is the one whose tongue is always lying.

All of creation is a servant of God. The most beloved to Him among them is the one that helped his brothers.

The best deed is when people will be safe from your tongue and your hand.

As long as you say, "There is no god but God," it will lift God's punishment from you and change you for the good.

O people, are you not ashamed that you collect more than you can eat and that you build more houses than you need to live in?

The Holy Prophet's ﷺ Passing from this World

When God, Almighty and Exalted, perfected the community of His Prophet ﷺ and completed His favor on him, He transferred him to a house better than his house, and to a Friend better than his friends. God called his soul in his last days. As a result, his final sickness began in the last ten days of the month of *Safar*, in the house of his wife Maimuna ﵂. When his sickness intensified, he moved to the house of Aisha ﵂. He was sick for

2. Abu Bakr as-Siddiq رضي الله عنه

Abu Bakr as-Siddiq رضي الله عنه was the best friend and most beloved Companion of the Holy Prophet ﷺ. Although God honored Abu Bakr رضي الله عنه by making him first in innumerable ways, his dearest title was probably, *"The second of two when they were in the cave."* (9:40)

The moon traverses the constellations of the zodiac in a single night,
So why do you deny the Miraj (Ascension)?
That wondrous, unique Pearl (the Prophet) is like a hundred moons—for when he made one gesture, the moon was split in two.
And the marvel that he displayed in splitting the moon
was in keeping with the weakness of the creatures' perception.
The work and business of the prophets and messengers
is beyond the spheres and the stars.
Transcend the spheres and their revolution!
Then you will see that work and business.
—Rumi, *Mathnavi*[31]

---

[31] Jalaluddin Rumi, *Mathnavi,* translated by William Chittick, p. 75.

God granted him even more honor when he chose him to be second, for Abu Bakr ؓ was the only Companion of the Holy Prophet ﷺ on his migration from persecution in Makkah to shelter in Madinah. Umar ؓ said, "I wish all the deeds of my life were equal to his deed of that one day."

Ibn Abbas ؓ said that one day the Prophet ﷺ was sick. He went to the mosque, wrapped his head with a cloth, sat on the minbar, and said, "If I were to take anyone as my intimate friend, I would take Abu Bakr, but the best friend to me is the friendship of Islam." He then ordered all doors of the neighboring houses that opened into the mosque of the Prophet ﷺ to be closed except the one of Abu Bakr ؓ. And that door is still open to this day.

The four Imams and the Shaykhs of the Naqshbandi Order understand from this Tradition that anyone who approaches God through the teachings and example of Abu Bakr ؓ will find himself passing through the only door left open to the Presence of the Prophet ﷺ.

The secret of the Golden Chain was transmitted and flowed from the Messenger of God ﷺ to the first rightly guided caliph, Imam of Imams, Abu Bakr as-Siddiq ؓ. Through him the religion was supported and the Truth protected. God mentions and praises him in His Holy Quran in many verses:

As for him who gives and keeps his duty, we facilitate for him the way to ease. (92:5-7)

And (away from the Fire) shall be kept the most faithful who gives his wealth, thereby purifying himself, and seeks to gain no pleasure or reward other than the Presence of his Lord, the Most High. (92:17-21)

Ibn al-Jawzi states that all Muslim scholars and the Companions were certain that these verses referred to Abu Bakr ؓ. Among all the people he was called "al-Atiq," the most pious, delivered from the punishments of the Fire.

When the Quranic verse 33:56 was revealed, namely, "*God and His angels bless the Holy Prophet,*" Abu Bakr ؓ asked if he also was included in this blessing. The verse was then revealed:

He it is who sends His blessings on you and so do His angels, that He may bring you forth out of darkness into light. And He is merciful to the believers. (33:43)

Ibn Abi Hatim explained that a verse came in reference to Abu Bakr as-Siddiq ﷺ:

And for him who fears to stand before his Lord there are two gardens. (55:46)

Referring to Abu Bakr as-Siddiq ﷺ, God said:

We have enjoined on the human being kindness to his parents: in pain did his mother bear him, and in pain did she give him birth. The carrying of the (child) to his weaning is thirty months. At length, when he reaches the age of full strength and attains forty years, he says, "O my Lord! Grant me that I may be grateful for Thy favor which Thou has bestowed upon me, and upon both my parents, and that I may work righteousness such as Thou mayest approve; and be gracious to me in my issue. Truly have I turned to Thee and truly do I bow (to Thee) in submission." Such are they from whom We shall accept the best of their deeds and pass by their ill deeds. (They shall be) among the Companions of the Garden: a promise of truth, which was made to them (in this life). (45:15-16)

Ibn Abbas ﷺ says that these verses came as a description of Abu Bakr as-Siddiq ﷺ, God honoring and elevating his state among all the Companions of the Prophet ﷺ. Ibn Abbas ﷺ notes further that verse 3:159 was revealed in reference to Abu Bakr ﷺ and Umar ﷺ:

And take counsel with them on important matters.

Finally, the great honor accorded to Abu Bakr ﷺ in accompanying the Holy Prophet ﷺ on his flight from Makkah to Madinah, is referred to in the verse:

When the unbelievers drove him out, he had no more than one companion. The two were in the cave, and he said to his companion, "Fear not, for God is with us." (9:40)

In addition to the praise of God, Abu Bakr as-Siddiq ﷺ received the praise of the Holy Prophet ﷺ and of his Companions. This is recorded in many well-known Traditions:

God will show His glory to the people in a general way, but He will show it to Abu Bakr in a special way.

Never has the sun risen or set on a person, other than a prophet, greater than Abu Bakr.

> Never was anything revealed to me that I did not pour into the heart of Abu Bakr.
>
> There is no one to whom I am obligated and have not repaid my debt except Abu Bakr, for I owe him much for which God will compensate him on the Day of Judgment.
>
> If I were to take an intimate friend other than my Lord, I would have chosen Abu Bakr.
>
> Abu Bakr does not precede you because of much prayer or fasting, but because of a secret that is in his heart.

Bukhari narrates from Ibn Umar :

> In the time of the Prophet ﷺ we did not recognize anyone higher than Abu Bakr as-Siddiq, then Umar, then Uthman.

Bukhari also narrates from Muhammad ibn al-Hanafiyya (Ali's son):

> I asked my father, "Who is the best person after God's Apostle ﷺ?" He said, "Abu Bakr." I asked, "Who then?" He said, "Then Umar." I was afraid he would say Uthman next, so I said, "Then you?" He replied, "I am only an ordinary person."

Tabarani narrated through Muadh that the Prophet ﷺ said:

> I had a vision that I was put on one side of the scale and my Community was put on the other side and I was heavier. Then Abu Bakr was put on one side and my Community was put on one side and Abu Bakr was heavier. Then Umar was put on one side and my Community was put on the other and Umar was heavier. Then Uthman was put on one side and my Community on the other and Uthman was heavier. Then the scale was raised up.

Hakim narrated that Ali was asked, "O Commander of the Faithful, tell us about Abu Bakr." He said, "He is a person whom God called as-Siddiq from the tongue of the Prophet ﷺ and he is the caliph of the Prophet ﷺ. We accept him for our religion and for this world."

There are many other Traditions indicating the great attainment of Abu Bakr as-Siddiq with respect to all the other Companions.

Abu Bakr was the best friend and most beloved Companion of the Holy Prophet ﷺ. He had never joined in the worship of idols practiced by his contemporaries. He came to Islam without any trace of doubt or hesitation. Many years later, the Holy Prophet ﷺ recalled, "Whenever I offered Islam to anyone, he always showed some reluctance and hesitation and tried to enter into an argument. Abu Bakr was the only person who accepted Islam without any doubt or hesitation, and without any argument."

He was first in his spiritual support. He remained steadfast in his support throughout the difficult years in Makkah. He was the first to speak out when events passed beyond the understanding even of the new Muslims themselves, as in the case of the Night Journey. Later in Madinah, when the Treaty of Hudaybiyya was signed, only Abu Bakr رضي الله عنه remained absolutely faithful. He counseled his companions, "Do not be critical, but hold fast to the stirrup of the Holy Prophet ﷺ."

He was first in his material support. While others of the Muslims gave large fortunes in support of their faith, Abu Bakr رضي الله عنه was the first to give everything he had. When asked what he had left for his children, he answered, "God and His Prophet ﷺ." On hearing this Umar رضي الله عنه said, "None can surpass Abu Bakr in serving the cause of Islam."

He was first in kindness to, and compassion for, his fellow believers. A very wealthy merchant, he always watched out for the poor and the weak. He freed seven slaves before leaving Makkah, among them Bilal رضي الله عنه. He not only spent large amounts to buy their freedom, but he then took them into his own household and educated them.

When he assumed the role of caliph, he said:

> Help me, if I am in the right. Set me right if I am in the wrong. The weak among you shall be strong with me until, God willing, his rights have been vindicated. The strong among you shall be weak with me until, if God wills, I have taken what is due from him. Obey me as long as I obey God and His Prophet ﷺ. When I disobey Him and His Prophet ﷺ, obey me not.

In early Islam interpretation of dreams was considered a spiritual exercise. Only those with pure hearts and spiritual vision could have meaningful dreams, and only those with pure hearts and spiritual vision could interpret them. Abu Bakr رضي الله عنه was an acknowledged interpreter of dreams. The Prophet ﷺ himself would consult only him in search for clarity of his prophetic dreams. Before the Battle of Uhud, the Holy Prophet ﷺ saw in a dream that he was herding animals. Some of them were being slaughtered. The sword that he held had a piece broken off. Abu Bakr ؓ interpreted the slaughtered animals to prophesize the death of many Muslims and the broken sword to signify the death of one of the Prophet's ﷺ relatives. Unfortunately, both these predictions were realized at the Battle of Uhud.

Abu Bakr ؓ was also a poet before he became Muslim. He was known for his exceptional recitation and his excellent memory of the long poems in which the Arabs took great pride. These qualities served him well in Islam. His recitation of the Quran was so lyrical and charged with emotion that many people came to Islam simply after hearing him pray. The Quraysh tried to forbid his praying in the courtyard of his house in order to prevent the people from hearing him.

It is due to his memory that many of the most important Traditions come to us today. Among them are those indicating the proper form of prayer and those specifying the proper proportions of the poor-due. Yet out of the many thousands of Traditions verified and recorded, only 142 come through Abu Bakr ؓ. His daughter, Aisha ؓ, related that her father kept a book of over 500 Traditions, but that one day he destroyed it. The knowledge that Abu Bakr ؓ chose to keep hidden related to the heavenly knowledge, the source of all saintly knowledge, a knowledge that can only be transmitted from heart to heart.

Although a quiet and gentle man, he was also first on the battlefield. He supported the Holy Prophet ﷺ in all of his campaigns both with his sword and with his counsel. When others failed or ran, he remained at the side of his beloved Prophet ﷺ. It is stated that once Ali ؓ asked his companions who they considered to be the bravest. They replied that Ali ؓ was the bravest. But he answered: "No. Abu Bakr is the bravest. On the day of the Battle of Badr, when there was no one to stand guard where the Holy Prophet ﷺ prayed, Abu Bakr stood with his sword and did not allow the enemy to come near."

He was of course the first to follow the Holy Prophet ﷺ as caliph and leader of the faithful. He instituted the public treasury to take care of the poor and needy. He was the first to compile the entire Quran and called it *mushaf*.

Regarding spiritual transmission, he was the first person to give instruction in the method of reciting the sacred words *"la ilaha ill-Allah"* for purifying the heart by *dhikr*.

TRADITION OF INTERCESSION

Bukhari relates from Mabad ibn Hilal al-Anzi ؓ the famous Tradition of Intercession through *"la ilaha ill-Allah."*

We [i.e., some people from Basra] gathered and went to Anas ibn Malik. We went in company with Thabit al-Bunnani so that he might ask him about the Tradition of Intercession on our behalf. Behold, Anas was in his house and our arrival coincided with his noon prayer. We asked permission to enter and he admitted us while he was sitting on his bed. We said to Thabit, "Do not ask him about anything else first but the Tradition of Intercession." He said, "O Abu Hamzah! There are your brethren from Basra coming to ask you about the Tradition of Intercession."

Anas then said, "Muhammad ﷺ talked to us saying, 'On the Day of Resurrection, the people will surge with each other like waves. Then they will come to Adam and say, "Please intercede for us with your Lord." He will say, "I am not fit for that, but you had better go to Abraham as he is the intimate Friend of the Beneficent." They will go to Abraham and he will say, "I am not fit for that, so you had better go to Moses as he is the one to whom God spoke directly." So they will go to Moses and he will say, "I am not fit for that, but you had better go to Jesus as he is the spirit of God and His Word." They will go to Jesus and he will say, "I am not fit for that but you had better go to Muhammad."

"'They will come to me and I will say, "I am fit for that." Then I will ask for my Lord's permission and it will be given. Then He will inspire me to praise Him with such praises as I do not know now. I will praise Him with those praises and will fall down prostrate before Him. Then it will be said, "O Muhammad, raise your head and speak, for you will be heard. Ask, for you will be granted your request. Intercede, for your intercession will be accepted." I will say, "O Lord, my Community, my Community!" Then it will be said, "Go and take out of the Fire all those who have faith in their hearts equal to the weight of a grain of barley..."

"'I will go and do so and return to praise Him with the same praises, and fall down prostrate before Him. Then it will be said, "O Muhammad, raise your head and speak, for you will be heard; and ask, for you will be granted your request; and intercede, for your intercession will be accepted." I will say, "O Lord, my Community! my Community!" And then it will be said, "Go and take out all those in whose hearts there is faith even to the lightest, lightest mustard-seed."'"

When we left Anas I said to some of my Companions, "Let us pass by Hasan who is hiding himself in the house of Abu Khalifa and request him to tell us what Anas ibn Malik has told us." We went to him and we greeted him. He admitted us. We said to him, "O Abu Saeed! We came to you from your brother Anas ibn Malik. He related to us a Tradition about the intercession the like of which I have never heard." He said, "What is that?" Then we told him of the Tradition and said, "He stopped at this point." He said, "What then?" We said, "He did not add anything to that."

He said, "Anas related the Tradition to me twenty years ago when he was a young fellow. I do not know whether he forgot or if he did not want to let you depend on what he might have said." We said, "O Abu Saeed! Narrate it to us." He smiled and said, "The human being was created hastily. I mentioned it precisely because I wanted to narrate it to you. Anas told me the same as he told you and then added [that the Prophet ﷺ, said], 'I will then return for a fourth time and praise Him similarly and prostrate before Him. It will be said, "O Muhammad, raise your head and speak, for you will be heard. Ask, for you will be granted your request. Intercede, for your intercession will be accepted." I will say, "O Lord, allow me to intercede for whoever said, 'La ilaha ill-Allah.'" Then God will say, "By My Power and Majesty, Greatness and Magnificence, I will take out of Hell whoever said, 'La ilaha ill-Allah.'"'"

From His Sayings

No speech is good if it is not directed toward the pleasure of God. There is no good in a person if his ignorance overcomes his patience. And if a person becomes attracted by the charms of this lower world, God will dislike him as long as he keeps this in his heart.

We have found generosity in piety (God-consciousness), wealth in certainty, and honor in humbleness.

Beware of pride because you will be returning to the earth and your body will be eaten up by the worms.

When he was praised by people, he would pray to God saying, "O God, You know me better than I know myself. I know myself better than these people who praise me. Make me better than what they think of me. Forgive those sins of mine of which they have no knowledge. Do not hold me responsible for what they say."

If you expect the blessings of God, be kind to His people.

One day he called Umar ﷺ and counseled him until Umar ﷺ cried. Abu Bakr ﷺ told him, "If you keep my counsel, you will be safe. My counsel is, 'Expect death always and live accordingly.'"

Glory be to God who has not given to his creatures any way to attain knowledge of Him except by means of their helplessness and their hopelessness of ever reaching such attainment.

Abu Bakr ﷺ returned to God on a Monday, as did the Prophet ﷺ, between the evening and night prayers on the 22nd of *Jumada al-Akhir*, 13 AH/634 CE. May God bless him and give him peace. The Holy Prophet ﷺ once said to him, "Abu Bakr, you will be the first of my people to enter Paradise."

The Prophet's ﷺ secret passed from Abu Bakr as-Siddiq ﷺ to his successor, Salman al-Farsi ﷺ. ۞

3. Salman al-Farsi رضي الله عنه

Salman al-Farsi رضي الله عنه is known as "the Imam," "the Inheritor of Islam," "the Wise Judge," "the Knowledgeable Scholar" and "One of the House of the Prophet ﷺ." These were all titles the Prophet ﷺ gave him.

My heart has become capable of all forms:
A pasture for gazelles, a monastery for monks,
A temple for idols, the Kabah of the pilgrims,
The tablets of Torah, the Book of Quran.
I profess the religion of Love.
Whatever direction love's camels take,
That is my religion and my faith.
—Ibn Arabi, Tarjuman al-ashwaq [32]

---

[32] Ibn Arabi, *Tarjuman al-ashwaq*, pp. 43-44.

Salman al-Farsi stood fast in the face of extreme difficulties and hardships, to carry the Light of Lights and to spread the secrets of hearts, to lift people from darkness to light. He was a noble Companion of the Prophet ﷺ who reported sixty of the Prophet's Traditions.

He came from a highly respected Zoroastrian family from a town near Isfahan. One day while passing by a church, he was attracted by the voices of men praying. Drawn by their worship, he ventured in and found it better than the religion of his upbringing. On learning that the religion originated in Syria, he left home, against his father's wishes, went to Syria and associated himself with a succession of Christian anchorites. He came to know from them the coming of the Last Prophet ﷺ and the signs accompanying his advent.

He then traveled to the Hijaz where he was seized, sold into slavery, and taken to Madinah, where he eventually met the Prophet ﷺ. When he found in the Prophet ﷺ the fulfillment of all the signs of which he had been informed by his Christian teachers, he accepted Islam. Servitude prevented Salman ؓ from being at the battles of Badr and Uhud. The Messenger ﷺ helped him gain his release from slavery by planting, with his own hand, 300 palm trees and giving him a large piece of gold. Once a free man, he took part in every subsequent battle with the Prophet ﷺ.

In Ibn Ishaq's *Sirat Rasul Allah,* we find the following in Salman's ؓ account to the Prophet ﷺ of his journey in search of the true religion:

Asim ibn Umar ibn Qatada said that he was told that Salman the Persian ؓ told the Prophet ﷺ that his master in Ammuriya told him to go to a certain place in Syria where there was a man who lived between two thickets. Every year as he went from one to the other, the sick stood along his way and everyone he prayed for was healed. He said, "Ask him about this religion which you seek, for he can tell you of it." So I went on until I came to the place of which I had been told. I found that people had gathered there with their sick until he came out to them that night passing from one thicket to the other. The people came to him with their sick. Everyone he prayed for was healed. They prevented me from getting to him. I could not approach him until he entered the thicket to which he was headed. I took hold of his shoulder. He asked me who I was as he turned to me and I said, "God have mercy on you, tell me about the Hanafiya, the religion of Abraham ؑ." He replied, "You are asking about something men do not inquire of today. The time has come near when a prophet will be sent with this religion from the people of the sacred area. Go to him, for he will bring you to it." Then he went into the thicket. The Prophet ﷺ said to Salman ؓ, "If you have told me the truth, you met Jesus ؑ the son of Mary ؑ."

In one of the Prophet's ﷺ battles called al-Ahzab or al-Khandaq, Salman ؓ advised the Prophet ﷺ to dig trenches around Madinah in defense of the city, a suggestion that the Prophet ﷺ happily accepted. He then went ahead and helped the digging with his own hands. During this excavation, Salman ؓ struck upon a rock that he was unable to break. The Prophet ﷺ took an axe and hit it. The first strike brought forth a spark. He then hit it a second time and brought forth a second spark. He then struck for the third time and brought forth a third spark.

He then asked Salman ؓ, "O Salman, did you see those sparks?" Salman ؓ replied, "Yes, O Prophet ﷺ, indeed I did." The Prophet ﷺ said, "The first spark gave me a vision in which God has opened Yemen for me. With the second spark, God opened Damascus and al-Maghrib (the West). And with the third one, God opened for me the East." Salman ؓ reported that the Prophet ﷺ said: *"Nothing but supplication averts the Decree. Nothing but righteousness increases life,"* and *"Your Lord is Munificent and Generous and is ashamed to turn away empty the hands of a servant when he raises them to him."*[33]

At-Tabari recounts that in the year 16 AH/637 CE the Muslim army turned to the Persian front. In order to confront the Persian king at one point, the Muslim army found itself on the opposite bank of the great Tigris River. The commander of the army, Saad ibn Abi Waqqas ؓ, following a dream, ordered the entire army to plunge into the rushing river. Many people were afraid and hung back. Saad ؓ, with Salman ؓ by his side, prayed first, "May God grant us victory and defeat His enemy." Then Salman ؓ prayed, "Islam generates good fortune. By God, crossing rivers has become as easy for the Muslims as crossing deserts. By Him in whose hand lies Salman's soul, may the soldiers emerge from the water in the same numbers in which they entered it." Saad ؓ and Salman ؓ then plunged into the Tigris. It is reported that the river was covered with horses and men. The horses swam and when they tired the river floor seemed to rise up and

---

[33] Tirmidhi transmitted them.

Abu Hurayra ؓ relates:

While we were sitting with the Holy Prophet ﷺ, Surat al-Jumuah was revealed to him. When the Prophet ﷺ recited the verse, "And He (God) has sent him (Muhammad) also to others (than the Arabs)" (62:3), I said, "Who are they, O God's Messenger?" the Prophet ﷺ did not reply until I repeated my question three times. At that time Salman al-Farsi was with us. God's Messenger ﷺ put his hand on Salman, saying, "If faith were at the Pleiades, even then some men from these people (i.e. Salman's folk) would attain it."

Abu Juhayfa ؓ relates:

The Prophet ﷺ made a bond of brotherhood between Salman and Abu ad-Darda al-Ansari. Salman paid a visit to Abu ad-Darda and found Umm Darda (his wife) dressed in shabby clothes. He asked her why she was in that state. She said, "Your brother Abu ad-Darda is not interested in the luxuries of this world." In the meantime Abu ad-Darda came and prepared a meal for Salman. Salman requested Abu ad-Darda to eat with him, but Abu ad-Darda said, "I am fasting." Salman said, "I am not going to eat unless you eat." So Abu ad-Darda ate with Salman. When it was night and a part of the night had passed, Abu ad-Darda got up (to offer the supererogatory night prayer), but Salman told him to sleep and Abu ad-Darda slept. After some time Abu ad-Darda again got up but Salman told him to sleep. When it was the last hours of the night, Salman told him to get up then, and both of them offered the prayer. Salman told Abu ad-Darda, "Your Lord has a right over you, your soul has a right over you, and your family has a right over you." Abu ad-Darda narrated the whole story to the Prophet ﷺ. The Prophet ﷺ said, "Salman has spoken the truth."

From His Sayings

Sulaiman al-Teemi ؓ narrated that Salman al-Farsi ؓ said:

Nimrod starved out two lions, and then released them to devour God's bosom friend, Abraham. But when the lions reached him and by God's leave, they stood before him in reverence, and they both lovingly licked him all over and prostrated themselves at his feet.[34]

[34] Abu Nuaym al-Isfahani, *Hilyat al-awliya, The Beauty of the Righteous and Accounts of the Elite*, translated by Shaykh Muhammad al-Akili, 1:474, p 204.

Abi al-Bakhtari narrated that Salman al-Farsi ؓ had a female servant of Persian descent and he once spoke to her in her Persian tongue saying, "Prostrate yourself even once before God." She replied with disdain, "I do not prostrate to anyone!" Someone asked Salman, "O Abu Abd Allah, what would she benefit from a single prostration?" Salman replied, "Each link is an important part of a chain, and perhaps should this woman accept to offer a single prostration before God Almighty, then this may lead her to regularly engage in offering the five times prayers. In fact, one who has a share in the blessings of Islam is not equal to someone who has naught of it."[35]

Sulaiman al-Teemi narrated that Salman al-Farsi ؓ said:

If a man spends his entire night freeing slaves from bondage and another man spends his night reading the Quran and invoking the remembrance of God (*dhikr*), the second man would be in a higher state.[36]

His Passing

Beloved Salman al-Farsi ؓ passed away in 33 AH/654 CE during the reign of Uthman ؓ. He passed his secret on to Abu Bakr's grandson, Imam Abu Abd ar-Rahman Qasim ibn Muhammad ibn Abu Bakr as-Siddiq ؓ. ✿

---

[35] *Ibid.*
[36] *Ibid.*, p 202.

4. Qasim ibn Muhammad ibn Abu Bakr

Qasim ibn Muhammad ibn Abu Bakr as-Siddiq was one of the seven most famous jurists in Madinah, being the most knowledgeable among them. When he approached death it is related that the Kabah said, "O Qasim! I am going to miss you and I am not going to see you again in this *dunya*." Then the Kabah made five hundred circumambulations around Qasim out of respect for him.

So long as you have not contemplated the Creator,
You belong to created beings.
But when you have contemplated Him,
Created beings belong to you.
—Ibn Ata Allah, Hikam[37]

[37] Ibn Ataillah, *Sufi Aphorisms*, p. 57.

Shaykh Qasim ibn Muhammad ibn Abu Bakr as-Siddiq ؓ descended from Abu Bakr as-Siddiq on his father's side and from Ali ibn Abi Talib ؓ on his mother's side. He was born on a Thursday, in the holy month of Ramadan.

It is narrated that he said, "My grandfather, Abu Bakr as-Siddiq ؓ, was alone with the Prophet ﷺ in the Cave of Thawr during migration from Makkah to Madinah, and the Prophet said to him, 'You have been with me all your life and you have carried all sorts of difficulties. And now I want you to make a supplication to invoke God's favor on you.' Abu Bakr ؓ then said, 'O Prophet of God, you are the secret of my soul and the secret of my heart. You know better what I need.'"

The Prophet ﷺ raised his hands and said, "O God, as long as my Divine Law proceeds to Judgment Day [38] may God grant that among your descendants are those who carry it and those who inherit its inner secrets, and grant that among your descendants are those who are on the Straight Path and those who guide to it."

The first answer to that supplication and the first one to receive that blessing was Sayyidina Qasim ؓ. In his time he was known in Madina as Abu Muhammad. People came to listen to his guidance, his lectures (*suhbah*) and his disclosures of the hidden meanings of the Quran. Qasim ibn Muhammad ibn Abu Bakr as-Siddiq ؓ was one of the seven most famous jurists in Madinah, being the most knowledgeable among them. It was through these seven great Imams that the Traditions, early jurisprudence, and Quranic commentaries were disseminated to the people.

He met some of the Successors of the Companions, including Salim ibn Abd Allah ibn Umar ؓ.

He was a pious imam and was very knowledgeable in the narration of the Traditions. Abu Zannad said, "I never saw anyone better than him in following the *Sunnah* of the Prophet ﷺ. In our time no one is considered perfect until he is perfect in following the *Sunnah* of the Prophet ﷺ, and Qasim is one of the perfected men."

Abd ar-Rahman ibn Abi Zannad said that his father said, "I did not see anyone who knew the *Sunnah* better than al-Qasim."

---

[38] God said, *"We have, without doubt, sent down the Message; and We will assuredly guard it (from corruption)."* (15:9) This means the Divine Law is protected up to Judgment Day.

Abu Nuaym said of him in his book *Hilyat al-Awliya*: "He was able to extract the deepest juristic rulings and he was supreme in manners and ethics."

Imam Malik narrated that Umar ibn Abd al-Aziz ﵁, considered the fifth rightly-guided caliph, said, "If it were in my hands, I would have made al-Qasim the caliph in my time."

Sufyan said, "Some people came to al-Qasim with charity which he distributed. After he distributed it, he went to pray. While he was praying, the people began to speak negatively about him. His son said to them, 'You are speaking behind the back of a man who distributed your charity and did not take one *dirham* from it for himself.' Quickly his father scolded him saying, 'Do not speak, but keep quiet.'" He wanted to teach his son not to defend him, as his only desire was to please God. He had no concern for the opinion of people.

Yahya ibn Sayyid said, "We never found, in our time in Madinah, anyone better than al-Qasim." Ayyub as-Saqityani ﵁ said, "I have not seen anyone better than Imam Qasim. He left 100,000 *dinars* behind for the poor when he passed away, and it was all from his lawful earnings."

One of His Miracles

Grandshaykh Sharafuddin ad-Daghestani narrated the following story:

> The year in which Abu Muhammad Qasim ﵁ was to leave this world, he set out on the pilgrimage on the third of Ramadan. When he arrived at al-Qudayd, where pilgrims usually sojourn, God opened to his vision to behold angels descending from heaven and ascending in countless numbers. They would come down, visit the place, and then go back up. And while he watched these angels carrying the blessings with which God was sending them, it was as if that light and concentrated power was being poured into his heart directly, filling it with sincerity and God-consciousness.
>
> As soon as this vision occurred, he fell asleep. In a dream he saw Abu Bakr as-Siddiq ﵁ coming to him. He said, "O my grandfather, who are these heavenly beings that are descending and ascending and who have filled my heart with God-consciousness?"
>
> Abu Bakr as-Siddiq ﵁ answered, "Those angels you see ascending and descending have been assigned to your grave by God the Most High.

They are constantly visiting it. They are obtaining blessings from where your body is going to be buried in the earth. To reverence you, God ordered them to come down and to solicit blessings for you. O my grandson, don't be heedless about your death; it is coming soon. You are going to leave this world and be raised to the Divine Presence."

Qasim ﵁ immediately opened his eyes and saw his grandfather before him. He said, "I just saw you in a dream." Abu Bakr as-Siddiq ﵁ replied, "Yes, I was ordered to meet you." "That means I am about to leave this world," said Qasim ﵁. "Yes, you are going to leave the world and accompany us to the hereafter," said our master Abu Bakr as-Siddiq ﵁.

"What kind of deed do you advise me to do in my last moments on earth?" Qasim ﵁ asked his grandfather. Abu Bakr as-Siddiq ﵁ answered, "O my son, keep your tongue moist with *dhikr Allah* and keep your heart ready and present with *dhikr Allah*. That is the best you can ever achieve in this world."

Then Abu Bakr ﵁ disappeared and Qasim ﵁ began *dhikr* on his tongue and in his heart. He continued his journey to Makkah where he stayed until the time of Hajj. Then he witnessed the standing at Arafah (which occurs each year on the 9th of Dhul-Hijja). In that year many saints, both men and women, were spiritually present at Arafah, and Qasim bin Muhammad bin Abu Bakr as-Siddiq ﵁ met with them.

As they were standing, they all heard the Plain of Arafah and its mountain crying mournfully. They asked Mount Arafah, "Why are you crying this way?" and Mount Arafah replied, "I and all the angels are crying, because today this earth is going to lose one of its pillars."

They asked, "Who is that pillar that the earth is about to lose?" Mount Arafah replied, "Abu Muhammad Qasim is going to leave this world, and the world will no longer be honored with his steps, and I will no longer see him on my plain, where all pilgrims come, and I will miss him. That is why I am crying in this way. Not only from myself, but his grandfather Muhammad, and his grandfather Abu Bakr, and his grandfather Ali, and the whole world is crying. They say the death of a scholar is the death of the world."

At that moment the Prophet ﷺ and Abu Bakr as-Siddiq ؓ were spiritually present on Arafah, where they were crying. Prophet ﷺ said, "With the death of Qasim great corruption will appear on earth, for he was one of the pillars able to prevent it."

Previously, that mournful crying of Mount Arafah only occurred when the Prophet ﷺ passed away from this world, then when Abu Bakr ؓ passed, then when Salman ؓ passed, and when Qasim ؓ passed. One of the saints, Rabia al-Adawiyya, met Qasim ؓ in the spiritual assembly of saints and he said, "Every dry thing and living thing, I heard them crying. Why, Oh Rabia, did this happen? I never experienced such crying in my life. Do you know its cause?" She replied, "O Abu Muhammad, I also was not able to discern the nature of that crying, so you must ask your grandfather, Abu Bakr."

Abu Bakr ؓ appeared to them spiritually saying, "That crying from every point on this earth is because you are leaving this worldly life, as I informed you on your pilgrimage." Then Qasim ؓ raised his hands and prayed to God, "Since I am passing away from this life now, forgive whoever stood with me on Mount Arafah." Then they heard a voice saying, "For your sake, God has forgiven whoever stood with you on Mount Arafah on this Hajj." At that moment God revealed to Qasim's heart unlimited Gnostic knowledge.

Then he departed from Mount Arafah and said, "O Mount Arafah, don't forget me on Judgment Day. All saints and all prophets stood here and so I ask you not to forget me on Judgment Day." That huge mountain replied, "O Qasim," in a loud voice which everyone could hear, "Don't forget me on the Judgment Day. Don't forget me. Let me be part of the intercession of the Prophet."

At that moment Qasim ؓ left Mount Arafah and arrived at Makkah al-Mukarrama, at the Kabah . There he heard the sound of crying coming from the House of God and it kept increasing as he approached, until everyone could hear it. That was the voice of the Kabah, crying for the passing of Qasim ؓ from this world. At the same time a flood of tears poured forth from the Kabah, flooding the entire area with water.

> The House of God said, "O Qasim! I am going to miss you for I will never again see you in this world." Then the House of God made five hundred circumambulations around Qasim ؓ out of respect for him.

It must be known that whenever a saint visits the Kabah and greets it, the Kabah responds to that greetings saying, *"Wa alayka as-salam ya wali-Allah,"* "and upon you be peace, O friend of God."

Al-Qasim ؓ then said farewell to the *Hajar al-Aswad* (Black Stone), then to *Jannat al-Mualla,* the cemetery in which Khadija al-Kubra ؓ, first wife of the Prophet ﷺ, is buried, and then to all of Makkah.

He then left and went to al-Qudayd, between Makkah and Madinah, on the 9th of Muharram, where he passed on to the next life. The year was 108 (or 109) AH/726 CE, and he was seventy years old. He passed the secret of the Naqshbandi Golden Chain to his successor, his grandson, Imam Jafar as-Sadiq ؓ.

5. Jafar as-Sadiq ﵁

He was a master in exegesis of the Quran, a scholar of jurisprudence, and one of the greatest scholars qualified to give legal decisions in Madinah. Jafar ﵁ acquired both the external religious knowledge, as well as the internal confirmation of its reality in the heart. The latter was reflected in his many visions and miraculous powers, too numerous to tell.

I have discovered—and exaggeration is not in my nature—
That He who is my sustenance will come to me.
I run to Him, and my quest for Him is agony for me.
Were I to sit still, He would come to me without distress.
—Urwa ibn Adhina [39]

---

[39] Urwa ibn Adhina, quoted in Jalaluddin Rumi, *Signs of the Unseen: The Discourses of Jalaluddin Rumi* (*Fihi ma Fihi*), translated by W.M. Thackston, p. 192.

The son of Imam Muhammad al-Baqir ﵁, son of al-Imam Zain al-Abidin ﵁, son of Husayn ﵁, son of Ali ibn Abi Talib ﵁, ibn Muhammad ﵁ was born on the eighth of Ramadan in the year 83 AH/702 CE. His mother was the daughter of al-Qasim, great granddaughter of Abu Bakr as-Siddiq ﵁.

He spent his life in worship and acts of piety for the sake of God. He rejected all positions of fame in favor of isolation from the mundane world. One of his contemporaries, Umar ibn Abil-Muqdam, said, "When I look at Jafar ibn Muhammad I see the lineage and the secret of the Prophet Muhammad ﷺ united in him."

Jafar ibn Muhammad ﵁ received from the Prophet ﷺ two lines of inheritance: the secret of the Prophet ﷺ through Ali ﵁ and through Abu Bakr ﵁. In him the two lineages met and for that reason he was called "Inheritor of the Prophetic Station and of the Truthful Station." In him was reflected the light of the knowledge of Truth and Reality. That light shone forth and that knowledge was spread widely through him during his lifetime.

Jafar ﵁ narrated from his father, Muhammad al-Baqir ﵁, that a man came to his grandfather, Zain al-Abidin ﵁, and said:

> "Tell me about Abu Bakr!" He said, "You mean as-Siddiq?" The man said, "How do you call him as-Siddiq when he is against you, the family of the Prophet ﷺ?" He replied, "Woe to you. The Prophet ﷺ called him 'as-Siddiq' and God accepted his title of as-Siddiq. If you want to come to me, keep the love of Abu Bakr and Umar in your heart."

> Jafar ﵁ said:

> The best intercession that I hope for is the intercession of Abu Bakr as-Siddiq."

> The following invocation is reported from Jafar as-Sadiq ﵁:

> O God, You are my witness that I love Abu Bakr and I love Umar and if what I am saying is not true may God cut me off from the intercession of Muhammad ﷺ.

He took the knowledge of the Traditions from two sources: from his father, through Ali ﵁, and from his maternal grandfather, al-Qasim. Then he increased his knowledge of the Traditions by sitting with Urwa, Aata,

Nafi, and Zuhri. The two Sufyans, Sufyan al-Thawri and Sufyan bin Ayinah, Imam Malik, Imam Abu Hanifa, and al-Qattan all narrated Traditions through him, as did many others from later scholars of the Traditions.

Once, someone complained to Mansur, the governor of Madinah, about Jafar ﷺ. They brought him before Mansur and asked the man who had complained, "Do you swear that Jafar did as you say?" He said, "I swear that he did that." Jafar ﷺ said, "Let him swear that I did what he accused me of and let him swear that God punish him if he is lying." The man insisted on his complaint, and Jafar ﷺ insisted that he take the oath. Finally, the man accepted to take the oath. No sooner were the words of the oath out of his mouth than he fell down dead.

Once he heard that Hakim ibn al-Abbas al-Kalbi crucified his own uncle Zaid on a date palm. He was so unhappy about this that he raised his hands and said, "O God send him one of your dogs to teach him a lesson." Only a brief time passed before a lion in the desert ate Hakim. Imam at-Tabari narrates that Wahb said:

> I heard Layth ibn Saad say, "I went on pilgrimage in the year 113 AH/731 CE. After I performed the afternoon prayer, I was reading some verses of the Holy Quran when I saw someone sitting beside me invoking God saying, '*Ya Allah, Ya Allah...*' repeatedly until he lost his breath. He then continued by saying, '*Ya Hayy, Ya Hayy...*' until his breath was again lost. He then raised his hands and said, 'O God, I have the desire to eat grapes, O God give me some. And my robe is becoming so old and tattered. Please, O God, grant me a new one.'
>
> "He had hardly finished his words before a basket of grapes appeared in front of him while at that time there were no grapes in season. Beside the basket of grapes there appeared two cloaks more beautiful than I had ever seen before. I said, 'O my partner let me share with you.' He said, 'How are you a partner?' I replied, 'You were praying and I was saying '*amin*'.' Then Imam Jafar ﷺ said, 'Then come and eat with me,' and he gave me one of the two cloaks. Then he walked off until he met a man who said, 'O son of the Prophet ﷺ, cover me because I have nothing but these tattered garments to cover me.' He immediately gave him the cloak that he had just received. I asked that man, 'Who is that?' He replied, 'That is the great imam, Jafar as-Sadiq.' I ran after him to find him but he had disappeared."

This is only a sample of the many anecdotes and stories of the miraculous powers of Jafar as-Sadiq ﷺ. From his knowledge he said to Sufyan al-Thawri, "If God bestows on you a favor, and you wish to keep that favor, then you must praise and thank Him excessively, because He said, *'If you are thankful, God will increase for you.'* (14:7)" He also said, "If the door of provision is closed for you, then make a great deal of begging for forgiveness because God said, *'Seek forgiveness of your Lord, certainly Your Lord is oft-Forgiving.'* (11:52)" And he said to Sufyan, "If you are upset by the tyranny of a Sultan or other oppression that you witness, say: *'There is no change and no power except with God,'* (18:39) because it is the key to relief and one of the treasures of Paradise."

From His Sayings

The letter of the Arabic alphabet, *nun*,(ن) at the beginning of *Surah Qalam* (Chapter 68 of Quran) represents the light of pre-Eternity, out of which God created all creations, and which is Muhammad ﷺ. That is why He said in the same verse, *"Truly you are of a sublime nature."* (68:4)—that is, you were privileged with that light from pre-Eternity.

God, Almighty and Exalted, told the lower world, "Serve the one who serves Me and tire the one who serves you."

Prayer is the pillar of every pious person. Pilgrimage is the sacred struggle of every weak one. The poor-due of the body is fasting. The one who asks for God's blessings without performing good deeds is like one trying to shoot an arrow without a bow.

Open the door of provision by giving donations. Fence in your money with the payment of the poor-due.

The best is he who wastes not.

Planning is the foundation of your life. To act prudently is the basis of intellect.

Whoever makes his parents sad has denied their rights on him.

The jurists are the trustees of the Prophet ﷺ. If you find the jurists sticking to the company of the sultans, say to them, "This is forbidden," as the jurist cannot express his honest opinion under the pressure of the sultan's proximity.

No food is better than piety and there is nothing better than silence. No enemy is more powerful than ignorance. No illness is greater than lying.

If you see something you do not like in your brother, try to find from one to seventy excuses for him. If you cannot find an excuse, say, "There might be an excuse, but I do not know it."

If you hear a word from a Muslim that is offensive, try to find a good meaning for it. If you do not find a good meaning for it, say to yourself, "I do not understand what he said," in order to keep harmony between Muslims.

Jafar as-Sadiq ؏ passed away in 148 AH/765 CE. He was buried in *Jannat al-Baqi*, in the same graveyard as that of his father, Muhammad al-Baqir ؏, his grandfather, Zain al-Abidin ؏, and the uncle of his grandfather, Hasan ibn Ali ؏. He passed the secret of the Golden Chain to his successor, Grandshaykh Tayfur Abu Yazid al-Bistami, more commonly known as Bayazid al-Bistami. ✺

6. Tayfur Abu Yazid al-Bistami ق

"I made four mistakes in my preliminary steps in this way: I thought that I remember Him, that I know Him, that I love Him, and that I seek Him; but when I reached Him, I saw that His remembering of me preceded my remembrance of Him, that His knowledge about me preceded my knowledge of Him, that His love towards me was more ancient than my love towards Him, and that He sought me in order that I would begin to seek Him."

I have planted love in my heart
And shall not be distracted until Judgment Day.
You have wounded my heart when You came near me.
My desire grows, my love is bursting.
He has poured me a sip to drink.
He has quickened my heart with the cup of love
Which He has filled at the ocean of friendship.
—Bayazid al-Bistami [40]

[40] Quoted in Emile Dermenghem, *Vie des saints musulmans,* p.169.

Bayazid al-Bistami's grandfather was a Zoroastrian from Persia. Bayazid made a detailed study of the statutes of Islamic Law and practiced self-denial. All his life he was assiduous in the practice of his religious obligations and in observing voluntary worship.

He urged his disciples to put their affairs in the hands of God. He encouraged them to accept sincerely the pure doctrine of the Oneness of God. This doctrine consisted of five essentials: to keep the obligations according to the Quran and *Sunnah*, to always speak the truth, to keep the heart free from hatred, to avoid forbidden food, and to shun innovations.

From His Sayings

One of his sayings was, "I have come to God through God. I have come to know what is other than God with the Light of God." He said, "God has granted His servants favors for the purpose of bringing them closer to Him. Instead, they are fascinated with the favors and are drifting further from Him." And he said, praying to God, "O Lord, You have created this creation without its knowledge. You have placed on it a trust without its will. If You do not help it, who will?"

Bayazid said the ultimate goal of the Sufi is to experience the vision of God in the hereafter. To that effect he said, "There are special servants of God who, if God veiled Himself from their sight in Paradise, would implore Him to take them out of Paradise just as the inhabitants of the Fire implore Him to release them from Hell."

He said about God's love for His servant, "If God loves His servant, He will grant three attributes that are the proofs of His Love: generosity like the generosity of the ocean, favor like the favor of the sun in its giving of light, and modesty like the modesty of the earth. The true lover never considers any affliction too great and never decreases his worship because of his pure faith."

A man asked Bayazid, "Show me a deed by which I will approach my Lord." He said:

> Love the Friends of God in order that they will love you. Love His saints until they love you. Because God looks at the hearts of His saints, and He will see your name engraved in the heart of His saints, and He will forgive you.

For this reason, the Naqshbandi followers have been elevated by their love for their shaykhs. This love lifts them to a station of continuous pleasure and continuous presence in the heart of their beloved.

Many Muslim scholars in his time, and many after his time, said that Bayazid al-Bistami was the first one to spread the reality of annihilation. Even that strictest of scholars, Ibn Taymiyya, who lived in the seventh *Hijri* century, admired Bayazid for this and considered him to be one of his masters. Ibn Taymiyya said about him:

> There are two categories of annihilation: one is for the perfect prophets and saints and one is for seekers from among the saints and pious people. Bayazid al-Bistami is from the first category of those who experience annihilation, which means the complete renunciation of anything other than God. He accepts none except God. He worships none except Him. He asks from none except Him.

He continues, quoting Bayazid saying, "I want not to want except what He wants."

It was reported that Bayazid said:

> I divorced the lower world three times in order that I would not have to return to it, and I moved to my Lord alone, without anyone, and I called on Him alone for help by saying, "O God, O God, no one remains for me except You." At that time I came to know the sincerity of my supplication in my heart and the reality of the helplessness of my ego. Immediately the acceptance of that supplication was perceived by my heart. This opened to me a vision that I was no longer in existence, and I vanished completely from myself into Him. He brought up all that I had divorced before in front of me, dressed me with light, and with His Attributes.

Bayazid said, "Praise to me, for my greatest Glory!" And he continued saying, "I set forth on an ocean when the prophets were still by the shore." And he said, "O My Lord, Your obedience to me is greater than my obedience to You," meaning, "O God, You are granting my request and I have yet to obey You."

When Bayazid al-Bistami had been persecuted and stoned by his tribe, he went on a ship and said, "O My Lord take me to a place where I will feel happy." Then the ship began to toss about on the high waves. The captain of the ship said, "There must be a great sinner on board who is causing this calamity." He said, "I am that sinner; throw me in the ocean."

He said to himself, "I am going into that ocean and I am going to seek the presence of God." As soon as he was thrown in, the water stopped tossing about, and Bayazid—without thinking of any other purpose and using his utmost spiritual power—began to plunge into that ocean at a speed greater than that of light, and he reached a place where it was complete darkness and complete void. There he heard a voice, described as, "*Huuuuuuuuuuuuuuuuuu.*"

God had granted Bayazid extraordinary spiritual powers, similar to those given to Shah Naqshband. Using his spiritual power, he was trying to count the number of all the people saying "*Hu*" at that location. Despite applying all his power he could not count them. He realized it was a presence he could not reach, and he knew it was that of Shah Naqshband with his followers. Although Shah Naqshband appeared many centuries after Shaykh Bayazid al-Bistami, on this occasion Bayazid was able to reach his spiritual presence, along with Shah Naqshband's *murids*.

Adh-Dhahabi further relates that he said:

> O God, what is your fire? It is nothing. Let me be the one person to go into your fire and everyone else will be saved. What is your paradise? It is a toy for children. Who are those unbelievers whom you want to torture? They are your servants. Forgive them.

Ibn Hajar said in reference to Bayazid's famous utterances:

> God knows the secret and God knows the heart. Whatever Abu Yazid spoke from the knowledge of Realities the people of his time did not understand. They condemned him and exiled him seven times from his city. Every time he was exiled, terrible afflictions would strike the city until the people would call him back, pledge allegiance to him, and accept him as a real saint.

Attar and Alusi related that Bayazid said when he was exiled from his city, Bistam:

> O blessed city, whose refuse is Bayazid!

Bayazid said:

God, the Most Just, called me into His Presence and said to me, "O Bayazid, how did you arrive in My Presence?" I replied, "Through self-denial, by renouncing the world." He said, "The value of the lower world is like the wing of a mosquito. What kind of renunciation have you come with?" I said, "O God, forgive me. I came to You by dependence on You." He said, "Did you ever betray the trust which I promised you?" I said, "O God, forgive me. I came to You through You." At that time God said, "Now We accept you."

I stood with the pious but I did not progress with them. I stood with the warriors in the cause but I did not progress a single step with them. I stood with those who pray excessively and those who fast excessively, but I did not progress a footstep. Then I said, "O God, what is the way to You?" and God said, "Leave yourself and come."

Ibrahim Khawwas said:

The way that God showed to him, with the most delicate word and the simplest explanation, was to leave self-interest in the two worlds, this world and the hereafter. "Leave everything other than Me behind." That is the best and easiest way to come to God, Almighty and Exalted. The most perfect and highest state of affirming Oneness is not to accept anything or anyone except God, the Most High.

Adh-Dhahabi quoted him in many great matters, among which were "Praise to Me, for My greatest Glory!" and "There is nothing in this robe I am wearing except God."

Adh-Dhahabi's teacher, Ibn Taymiyya, explained, "He did not see himself as existing any longer, but only saw the existence of God, due to his self-denial."

One of the followers of Dhun Nun al-Misri was a follower of Bayazid. Bayazid asked him, "Whom do you want?" He replied, "I want Bayazid." He said, "O my son, Bayazid has wanted Bayazid for forty years and has still not found him." That disciple of Dhun Nun then went to him and narrated this incident to him. On hearing it, Dhun Nun fainted. He explained later saying, "My master Bayazid has lost himself in God's Love. That causes him to try to find himself again."

They asked him, "Teach us about how you reached true Reality." He said, "By training myself, by seclusion." They said, "How?" He said, "I summoned myself to accept God, Almighty and Exalted, and it resisted. I took an oath that I would not drink water and I would not taste sleep until I brought my self under my control."

He also said, "O God! It is not strange that I love You because I am a weak servant, but it is strange that You love me when You are the King of Kings."

He said, "For thirty years, when I wanted to remember God and do *dhikr*, I washed my tongue and my mouth for His glorification."

He said, "As long as the servant thinks that there is among the Muslims someone lower than himself, that servant still has pride."

They asked him, "Describe your day and describe your night." He said, "I do not have a day and I do not have a night, because day and night are for those who have characteristics of creation. I have shed my self the way the snake sheds its skin."

Of Sufism, Bayazid said:

> It is to give up rest and to accept suffering.

Of the obligation to follow a guide, he said:

> Who does not have a shaykh, his shaykh is Satan.

Of seeking God he said:

> Hunger is a rain cloud: If a servant becomes hungry, God will shower his heart with wisdom.

Of his intercession he said:

> If God will give me permission to intercede for all the people of my time I will not be proud, because I am only interceding for a piece of clay.
>
> If God gave me permission for intercession, first I would intercede for those who harmed me and those who denied me.

To a young man who wanted a piece of his old cloak for blessing, Bayazid said:

> Should you take all Bayazid's skin and wear it as yours, it would avail you nothing unless you followed his example.

They said to him, "The key to Paradise is bearing witness that there is no god but God." He said:

> It is true, but a key is to open a lock. The key of such witnessing can only operate with the following conditions: a tongue that does not lie or backbite; a heart without betrayal; a stomach without unlawful or doubtful provision; and deeds without desire or innovation.

> The ego or self always looks at the world, and the spirit always looks at the next life. Spiritual knowledge always looks at God, Almighty and Exalted. He whose self defeats him is from those who are destroyed. He whose spirit is victorious over his "self" is of the pious, and he whose spiritual knowledge enlightens his spirit is of the God-conscious.

Ad-Daylami said:

> Once I asked Abd ar-Rahman ibn Yahya about the state of trust in God. He said, "If you put your hand in the mouth of a lion, do not be afraid of other than God." I went in my heart to visit and ask Bayazid about this matter. I knocked and I heard from inside, "Was not what Abd ar-Rahman said to you enough? You came only to ask and not with the intention of visiting me." I understood, and I came again another time one year later and knocked at his door. This time he answered, "Welcome my son, this time you came to me as a visitor and not as a questioner."

They asked him, "When does a man become a man?" He said:

> When he knows the mistakes of his self and he busies himself in correcting them.

> For twelve years I was the blacksmith of my self. For five years I was the polisher of the mirror of my heart. For one year I looked in that mirror and I saw on my belly the girdle of unbelief. I tried hard to cut it. I spent twelve years in that effort. Then I looked in that mirror and I saw that girdle inside my body. I spent five years cutting it. Then I spent one year looking at what I had done. God opened for me the vision of all creations. I saw all of them dead. I prayed four exaltations of the funeral prayer for them.

If the Throne, what is around It, and what is in It were placed in the corner of the heart of a knower, they would be lost completely inside it.

Of Bayazid's state, al-Abbas ibn Hamza related the following:

I prayed behind Bayazid the noon prayer. When he raised his hands to say *Allahu akbar* he was unable to pronounce the words, fearing from God's Holy Name. His entire body trembled. Sounds of breaking bones could be heard. I was seized by fear and awe.

Munawi relates:

One day Bayazid attended the class of a jurisprudent who was explaining the laws of inheritance, "When a man dies and leaves such-and-such, his son will have such-and-such, etc." Bayazid exclaimed, "O *faqih*, O *faqih*! What would you say of a man who died leaving nothing but God?"

People began to cry. Bayazid continued, "The slave possesses nothing. When he dies, he leaves nothing but his own Master. He is such as God created him in the beginning." He recited, *"You shall return to us alone, as We created you the first time."* (6:94)

Sahl at-Tustari sent a letter to Bayazid that read, "Here is a man who drank a drink which leaves him forever refreshed." Bayazid replied, "Here is a man who has drunk all existences, but whose mouth is dry and burns with thirst."

When Bayazid died, he was over seventy years old. Before he died, someone asked him his age. He said, "I am four years old. For seventy years I was veiled. I got rid of my veils only four years ago."

The thirty-ninth shaykh of the Golden Chain, Sultan al-Awliya Shaykh Abd Allah ad-Daghestani, referred to this saying in his encounter with Khidr عليه السلام, who told him, as he was pointing to the graves of some great scholars in a Muslim cemetery, "This one is three years old. That one, seven. That one, twelve."

Grandshaykh Bayazid died in 261 AH/875 CE. It is said that he is buried in two places; in Damascus and Bistam, in Iran.

The secret of the Golden Chain was passed from Mawlana Bayazid al-Bistami to Shaykh Abul Hasan al-Kharqani.

7. Abul Hasan al-Kharqani ق

Abul Hasan Ali ibn Jafar al-Kharqani was the Arch-Intercessor of his time and unique in his station. He was the focus of attention of his people and an ocean of knowledge from which saints still receive waves of light and spiritual knowledge.

Mayest Thou deign to be sweetness and let life be bitter!
If Thou art content, what matter that men be angry.
Let everything between me and Thee be cultivated,
Between the worlds and me let all be desert!
If Thy love be assured, all is then easy,
For everything on earth is but earth.
—Anonymous [41]

[41] Quoted in Shaykh al-Arabi ad-Darqawi, *Letters of a Sufi Master,* p. 23.

Abul Hasan Ali ibn Jafar al-Kharqani proved a deep well of knowledge for his followers and supporters. He emptied himself of everything except God's Oneness, refusing for himself all titles and aspirations. He would not be known as a follower of any science, even a spiritual science, and he said:

> I am not a hermit. I am not an ascetic. I am not a speaker. I am not a Sufi. O God, You are One, and I am one in Your Oneness.

Of knowledge and practice he said:

> Scholars and servants in the lower world are numerous but they don't benefit you unless you are engaged in the satisfaction of God's desire and from morning to night are occupied with the deeds that God accepts.

About being a Sufi he said:

> The Sufi is not the one who is always carrying the prayer rug, nor the one who is wearing patched clothes, nor the one who keeps certain customs and appearances, but the Sufi is the one to whom everyone's focus is drawn, although he is hiding himself.
>
> The Sufi is the one who in the daylight does not need the sun, in the night does not need the moon. The essence of Sufism is absolute nonexistence that has no need of existence because there is no existence besides God's existence.

He was asked about truthfulness. He said:

> Truthfulness is to speak your conscience.

Of the heart he said:

> What is the best thing? The heart that is always in remembrance of God (*dhikr Allah*).
>
> The best of hearts is the heart that contains nothing but the Presence of God, Almighty and Exalted.
>
> Today it will have been forty years that God has been looking in my heart and has seen nothing except Himself. I have had nothing in my heart except God for forty years. While my ego is asking for cold water and a drink of milk, I have not allowed it that for forty years in order to control myself.

The vision with the eyes of the head does not bring happiness, but the vision with the eyes of the heart and the secret that God gives to the soul will bring out that happiness.

Of Bayazid he said:

When Abu Yazid said, "I want not to want" that is exactly the wanting that is real desire.

He was asked, "Who is the appropriate person to speak about annihilation and subsistence?" He answered:

That is knowledge for the one who is as one suspended by a silk thread from the heavens to the earth when a big cyclone comes and takes all trees, houses, and mountains and throws them in the ocean until it fills the ocean. If that cyclone is unable to move the one who is hanging by the silk thread, then he is the one who can speak on annihilation and subsistence.

Once Sultan Mahmud al-Ghazni visited Abul Hasan and asked his opinion of Bayazid al-Bistami. He said, "Whoever follows Bayazid is going to be guided. Whoever saw him and felt love towards him in his heart will reach a happy ending." At that Sultan Mahmud said, "How is that possible when Abu Jahl saw the Prophet ﷺ and he was unable to reach a happy ending but rather ended up in misery?" He answered, "It is because Abu Jahl did not see the Prophet ﷺ but he saw Muhammad ibn Abd Allah ﷺ. And if he saw the Messenger of God ﷺ he would have moved out of misery into happiness. As God said, "*You see them looking at you but without clear vision.* (7:198)" He continued with the saying already quoted, "The vision with the eyes of the head..."

Others of his sayings:

Ask for difficulties in order for tears to appear because God loves those who cry (referring to the advice of the Prophet ﷺ to cry much).

In whatever way you ask God for anything, still the Quran is the best way. Do not ask God except through the Quran.

The inheritor of the Prophet ﷺ is the one who follows his footsteps and never puts black marks in his Book of Deeds.

Grandshaykh Abul Hasan al-Kharqani died on Tuesday, 10th of Muharram in 425 AH/1033 CE. He was buried in Kharqan, a village of the city of Bistam in Iran. He passed on the secret of the Golden Chain to Abu Ali al-Fadl ibn Muhammad al-Farmadi at-Tusi. ۞

8. Abu Ali al-Farmadi ق

Abu Ali al-Farmadi is called "the Knower," "the Merciful," and "the Custodian of Divine Love." He said, "For the (Knower) a time will come wherein the light of knowledge will reach him and his eyes will see the incredible unseen."

"O child!" said Luqman the Wise,
"Do not let the rooster be more watchful than you,
calling God at dawn while you are sleeping."
He is right, he who said:
"The turtledove wept on her branch in the night
And I slept on—what lying, false love is mine?
If I were a true lover, never would turtledoves overtake me.
I am the dry-eyed lover of his Lord,
While animals weep!"
—Ghazali, Ayyuhal-walad[42]

[42] Imam Ghazali, *Ayyuhal-walad*, pp. 20-21.

On behavior towards one's master, he said:

If you are true in your love of your shaykh, you have to be respectful towards him.

On spiritual vision, he said:

For the Gnostic (Knower), a time will come wherein the light of knowledge will reach him and his eyes will see the incredible unseen.

Whoever pretends he can hear, yet cannot hear the glorification of birds, trees, and the wind, is a liar.

The hearts of the people of Truth are open, and their hearing is open.

God gives happiness to His servants when they see His saints. This is because the Prophet ﷺ said, *"Whoever sees the face of a knower of God, sees me."* And also, *"Whoever sees me, has seen Reality."*

Sufi Masters have thus employed the practice of concentrating on the face of the shaykh, for the purpose of attaining a vision of Reality.

Shaykh al-Farmadi also said:

Whoever looks after the actions of people will lose his way.

Who prefers the company of the rich over the company of the poor, God will send to him death of the heart.

Imam Ghazali reports:

I heard that Abul Hasan al-Farmadi said, "The ninety-nine Attributes of God will become attributes and descriptions of the seeker in the way of God."

Mawlana Abul Hasan al-Farmadi died in 447 AH/1084 CE. He was buried in the village Farmad, a suburb of the city of Tus. He passed on the secrets of the Golden Chain to Grandshaykh Abu Yaqub Yusuf ibn Ayyub ibn Yusuf ibn al-Husayn al-Hamadani. ۞

9. Abu Yaqub Yusuf al-Hamadani ق

Yusuf of Hamadani was one of the rarest knowers of God, a pillar in the *Sunnah* of the Prophet ﷺ, and a unique saint. He was a religious leader, a religious scholar, and a Gnostic. He made progress in self-denial and contemplation until he became the Arch-Intercessor (*Ghawth*) of his time.

Think not that there are no travelers on the road,
Or that those of perfect attribute leave no trace.
Just because you are not privy to the secrets,
Do you think that no one else is either?
—Rumi, *Fihi ma fihi*[43]

[43] Jalaluddin Rumi, *Signs of the Unseen: The Discourses of Jalaluddin Rumi* (*Fihi ma Fihi*), translated by W.M. Thackston.

Born in Buzanjird near Hamadan in 440 AH/1048 CE, Abu Yaqub Yusuf al-Hamadani moved from Hamadan to Baghdad when he was eighteen years old. He studied the Shafii school of jurisprudence under the supervision of the master of his time, Shaykh Ibrahim ibn Ali ibn Yusuf al-Firuzabadi. He kept association in Baghdad with the great scholar, Abu Ishaq ash-Shirazi, who gave him greater deference than to any of his other students, although he was the youngest.

He was the master of his time in raising the stations of his followers. Scholars and pious people flooded in huge numbers into his center in the city of Merv, in present-day Turkmenistan, to listen to him. Later in his life, he secluded himself and left the world behind. He became an ascetic and engaged in constant worship and spiritual struggle. He associated with Shaykh Abd Allah Ghuwayni and Shaykh Hasan Simnani, but his secret was given him by Shaykh Abu Ali al-Farmadi.

He was so brilliant a jurisprudent that he became the most knowledgeable reference of his time for all scholars in the field. He was known in Baghdad, the center of Islamic knowledge, in Isfahan, Bukhara, Samarqand, Khwarazm, and throughout Central Asia.

He was known as the rain of realities and truth and spiritual knowledge. He finally settled in Merv. Through him countless miraculous events occurred.

From His Miracles

He reflected the Divine Attribute of Severity (*al-Qahhar*) with those who opposed the dissemination of spirituality. The following are two accounts of his miraculous deeds in that respect.

One day he was enlightening a group of the listeners with heavenly knowledge. Two literalist scholars who were present said, "Keep quiet because you are innovating." He said to them, "Do not talk about matters that you do not understand. It is better for you to die than to stay." As he spoke these words they immediately fell dead.

Ibn Hajar al-Haythami records in his book *al-Fatawa al-Hadithiyya*, that Abu Saeed Abd Allah ibn Abi Asrun, the Imam of the Shafii school, said:

> When I began a search for religious knowledge I accompanied my friend, Ibn as-Saqa, who was a student in the Nizamiyya School, and it

was our custom to visit the pious. We heard that there was in Baghdad a man named Yusuf al-Hamadani who was known as the Arch-Intercessor and that he was able to appear whenever he liked and was able to disappear whenever he liked.

So I decided to visit him along with Ibn as-Saqa and Shaykh Abd al-Qadir Gilani, who was a young man at that time. Ibn as-Saqa said, "When we visit Shaykh Yusuf al-Hamadani I am going to ask him a question the answer to which he will not know." I said, "I am also going to ask him a question, and I want to see what he is going to say." Shaykh Abd al-Qadir Gilani said, "O God, protect me from asking a saint like Yusuf al-Hamadani a question, but I will go into his presence asking for his blessings and Divine knowledge."

We entered his group. He veiled himself from us and we did not see him until after one hour had passed. He looked at Ibn as-Saqa angrily and said, without having been informed of his name, "O Ibn as-Saqa, how dare you ask me a question when your intention is to confound me? Your question is this and your answer is this!" Then he said to Ibn Saqa, "I am seeing the fire of disbelief burning in your heart." He looked at me and said, "O Abd Allah, are you asking me a question and awaiting my answer? Your question is this and your answer is this. Let the people be sad for you, because they are losing as a result of your disrespect for me."

Then he looked at Shaykh Abd al-Qadir Gilani and said to him, "Approach, my son. I am going to bless you. O Abd al-Qadir, you have satisfied God and His Prophet ﷺ with your proper respect for me. I see you in the future sitting on the highest place in Baghdad, and speaking, and guiding people, and saying to them that your feet are on the neck of every saint. And I see every saint of your time bowing to you because of your great station and honor."

Abd al-Qadir was raised and all that Shaykh al-Hamadani said about him came to pass. There came a time when he did say, "My feet are on the necks of all the saints." He was a reference and a beacon guiding all people in his time to their destinations.

The fate of Ibn as-Saqa was something else. He was brilliant in his knowledge of the Divine Law. He surpassed all the scholars in his time. He debated with the scholars and prevailed over them, until the caliph called him to be in his company. One day the caliph sent him as a messenger to the king of Byzantium, who in his turn called all his priests and the scholars of the Christian religion to debate with him. Ibn as-Saqa defeated all of them in debate. They were unable to give answers in his presence. He was giving answers that made them look like children and mere students in his presence.

His brilliance so fascinated the king of Byzantium that he invited him to his private family meeting. There he saw the daughter of the king. He immediately fell in love with her, and he asked her father, the king, for her hand in marriage. She refused except on condition that he accept her religion. He left Islam and accepted the Christian religion of the princess. After his marriage, he became seriously ill. They threw him out of the palace. He became a town beggar, asking everyone for food, yet no one would provide for him. Darkness had come over his face.

One day I saw him again and I asked, "What happened to you?" He replied, "I fell into a temptation." I asked him, "Do you remember anything from the Holy Quran?" He replied, "I only remember, '*Again and again will those who disbelieve wish that they were Muslims* (15:2).'" He was trembling as if he was giving up his last breath. I turned him towards the Kabah (the West), but he kept turning towards the East. Then I turned him back towards the Kabah, but he turned himself to the East. I turned him a third time, but he turned himself to the East. Then as his soul was passing from him, he said, "O God, that is the result of my disrespect to Your Arch-Intercessor, Yusuf al-Hamadani."

I went to Damascus and the king there, Nuridin ash-Shahid, appointed me head of the religious department and I accepted. As a result, the world came from every side: provision, sustenance, fame, money, and position, for the rest of my life. That is what the Arch-Intercessor, Yusuf al-Hamadani, had predicted for me.

Yusuf al-Hamadani's words illustrate his high station among the saints. He said:

> The opening of the faculty of spiritual hearing in the friends of God is like a message from Reality, a chapter in the Book of God, a blessing from the knowledge of the unseen. It is the beginning of the opening of the heart and its unveiling—good tidings from the heavenly stations! It is the dawn of understanding of Divine meanings. This hearing is sustenance for the spirit and life for the heart. It is the subsistence of the secret. God makes Himself Witness for the visions of His chosen servants, and adorns them with His blessed acts and decorates them with his Attributes.
>
> Of his saints, he makes one group hear through His Exalted Witnessing. He makes others hear through His Unique Oneness. He makes another group of them hear through His Mercy. And He makes some hear through His Power.
>
> Let it be known to you, O human being, that God has created, from the Light of His manifestations, 70,000 angels and assigned them to various stations between the Throne and the Chair. In the Presence of Intimacy, their dress is green wool, their faces are like the full moon, they stand in His Presence in awe, fainting, drunk with His Love, running endlessly from the Throne to the Chair and back because of the emotion and the mercy which is burning in their hearts. Those are the Sufis of the heavens and Israfil عليه السلام (the angel who will blow the Trumpet on the Judgment Day) is their leader and their guide, and Gabriel عليه السلام is their president and their speaker, and *al-Haqq* (God, the Truth) is their King. God's blessings are upon them.

This is how Mawlana Yusuf al-Hamadani, the shadow of God on earth, described the heavenly reality and exalted stations of the Sufis. May God bless his soul and sanctify him. He died in Khurasan, between Herat and Bakshur, on the 12th of Rabi al-Awwal, 535 AH/1140 CE and was buried in Merv. Near his tomb a large mosque and a large school were built. He passed his secret to Abul Abbas who in turn passed it on to Grandshaykh Abd al-Khaliq al-Ghujdawani, who received it directly from Yusuf al-Hamadani as well. ۞

10. Abul Abbas al-Khidr عليه السلام

Abul Abbas, Khidr عليه السلام, whom God mentioned in the Holy Quran (18:65), is the one who met with the Prophet Moses عليه السلام. He preserved and maintained the Reality of the Golden Chain until the next link in the Chain, Abd al-Khaliq al-Ghujdawani, could assume his destined station. The important role of Khidr عليه السلام as the initiator of saints may be illustrated by the importance of his role as the initiator of prophets, particularly of the Prophet Moses عليه السلام.

Whoever enters the Way without a Guide
will take a hundred years to travel a two-day journey.
The Prophet ﷺ said, "In this Way, you have no more
faithful companions than your works."
How can these works and this earning in the way of righteousness
be accomplished without a master, O father?
Can you practice the meanest profession in the world
without a Master's guidance?
Whoever undertakes a profession without a master
Becomes the laughingstock of city and town.
—Rumi, *Mathnavi*[44]

---

[44] Jalaluddin Rumi, *Mathnavi*. Translated by William Chittick, pp. 122-123.

Bukhari relates in the *Book of Prophets* that the Prophet ﷺ said:

Khidr (the Green Man) was so named because he sat on a barren white land once, after which it turned luxuriantly green with vegetation.

Moses عليه السلام was a powerful prophet, one of the five greatest God sent to this world, including Noah عليه السلام, Abraham عليه السلام, Jesus عليه السلام, and Muhammad ﷺ. Yet even with his depth of knowledge, God caused him to be in need of Khidr عليه السلام, even though Khidr عليه السلام was not a prophet. This is to teach us, as God said in the Holy Quran:

Above every knower there is a greater knower. (12:76)

The story of Moses' عليه السلام encounter with Khidr عليه السلام is related in the Quran (18:65-82). The following is a paraphrased commentary of the story:

> Moses عليه السلام and his servant found one of God's servants whom God had honored uniquely and had taught knowledge from His Own Presence. Moses عليه السلام asked him, "May I accompany you?" He answered him, "You cannot bear to accompany me." Moses عليه السلام was surprised and insisted he could. Khidr عليه السلام said, "You cannot, but if you do, do not ask about what I am doing until I speak to you about it." This means that Khidr عليه السلام was going to do something that Moses عليه السلام would not understand. Although he was the Messenger of a great religion, he was in need of Khidr عليه السلام to teach him something.
>
> They took a boat to cross a river. When they were in the middle of the river, Khidr عليه السلام made a hole in the boat. Moses عليه السلام was unable to keep quiet, and asked, "Why are you doing this strange thing? Those people gave you the boat, are you now scuttling it?" Khidr عليه السلام replied, "Did I not tell you that you were unable to bear with me patiently?" Moses عليه السلام had not yet understood, even though he was a prophet and could read hearts, that there was something he did not know.
>
> They continued and found a young boy. As soon as they saw him, Khidr عليه السلام killed him. Moses عليه السلام said, "What are you doing? Have you slain an innocent child? This is against all laws!" Again Khidr عليه السلام said, "Did I not tell you that you could not keep company with me? The third time you ask me, we will part ways." Then they reached a city where they asked for food. No one gave them any food or hospitality. On their way out, they found a wall about to fall down. Khidr عليه السلام

> rebuilt the wall and made it straight. Moses عليه السلام said, "Surely you could have exacted some recompense for this work?"
>
> Khidr عليه السلام said, "This is the point where we separate, for you did not understand the wisdom of what I was doing. O Moses عليه السلام, what we do is what God tells us to do. First, I rendered the boat useless because there is a tyrant who is taking every boat from the poor people on this side of the river. That tyrant is going to die tomorrow, and tomorrow, they can repair their boat and use it safely. I killed the child because God did not want that child to cause his parents, who believe in you, to despair and leave your religion. God will give them better children than him. I repaired the wall that belonged to a man who was in life very generous to the poor. When he passed away, he left a treasure buried under the wall for his two orphans. Were that wall to come down, people would see the treasure and take it. I rebuilt it in order that the two children get their treasure later. You did not understand God's wisdom."

Here we see that even Moses عليه السلام, with all the honor bestowed on him by God, found himself ignorant before Khidr عليه السلام. How can we, who know so little in comparison to Moses عليه السلام, consider ourselves knowledgeable? Moses عليه السلام himself, with all his knowledge in the Divine Presence, was unable to understand certain things. This is a lesson in humility for human beings, and particularly for scholars and religious leaders. It means our knowledge is not worth mentioning. There are always others more knowledgeable than we. As high or as deep as we travel into knowledge, there is a deeper depth and a higher height than where we stand. For this reason, when someone sits to give advice, he must sit with complete humbleness and complete respect for the listeners, and he cannot consider himself higher than them, otherwise light will never come to their hearts. Everyone is in need of a guide, as was shown by the Guided of guides himself, the Prophet ﷺ, when he took Gabriel عليه السلام as a guide for Revelation, and when he took a guide in traveling to Madinah.

This is how Ibn Arabi in *Fusus al-Hikam* explains the three acts of Khidr عليه السلام witnessed by Moses عليه السلام:

> Moses عليه السلام was tested *"by many ordeals"* (20:40), the first of which was the murder of the Egyptian (28:15), an act which he committed by

Divine impulsion and with the approbation of God deep inside him, without however, his perceiving it; nevertheless, he felt no affliction in his soul for having killed the Egyptian, although he himself was not acquitted until he had received a Divine revelation on the subject. For all prophets are interiorly preserved from sin without their being conscious of it, even before they are warned by inspiration. It is for that reason that Khidr ؑ showed him the putting to death of the boy, an action for which Moses ؑ reproached him, without remembering his murder of the Egyptian, upon which Khidr ؑ said to him: "I have not done it of my own initiative," recalling thus to Moses ؑ the state in which he, the latter, found himself when he did not yet know that he was essentially preserved from all action contrary to the Divine Order.

He showed him also the perforation of the boat, apparently made to destroy the people, but which has, however, the hidden sense of saving them from the hand of a "violent man." He showed this to him as an analogy to the ark that hid Moses ؑ when he was thrown into the Nile. According to appearances his act was equally to destroy him, but according to the hidden sense, it was to save him. Again his mother had done that for fear of the "violent man," in this case Pharaoh, so that he would not cruelly kill the child.

Moses ؑ arrived then at Madian. There he met the two girls and for them drew water from the well, without asking from them a salary. Then he *"withdrew to the shade,"* that is to the Divine shadow, and said: *"O my Lord! Truly am I in need of any good that Thou dost send me!"* (28:24) He attributed, then, to God alone the essence of the good that he did and qualified himself as poor towards God. It was for that reason that Khidr ؑ reconstructed before him the crumbling wall without asking a salary for his work, for which Moses reprimanded him, until Khidr ؑ reminded him of his action of drawing water without asking for reward, and other things, too, of which there is no mention in the Quran. The Prophet ﷺ regretted that Moses ؑ did not keep quiet and did not remain with Khidr ؑ, so that God could tell him more of their actions.[45]

---

[45] Ibn Arabi, from the chapter on Moses in *Wisdom of the Prophets*, translated by Titus Burckhardt and Angela Culme-Seymour with slight alterations, pp. 102-103, 107-108. Imam

According to Ibn Arabi, Khidr ﷺ said to Sahl at-Tustari:

> God created the Light of Muhammad ﷺ from His Light. This Light stayed before God for 100,000 years. God directed His Gaze upon it 70,000 times every day and night, adding to it a new light from His Light every time. Then, from that Light, He created all creations.[46]

When the Prophet ﷺ left this world and condolence came, they heard a voice from the corner of the house saying, "Peace, God's mercy and blessings be upon you, members of the Family of the Prophet ﷺ!" It was Khidr ﷺ.[47] ۞

Bukhari (*Book of the Prophets*) narrates the Tradition of the Prophet ﷺ, "May God have mercy on Moses! If only he had remained patient, more of their story (Moses and Khidr's) would have been related to us."

[46] *al-Futuhat al-Makkiyyah* 2:60, 663; 3:41, 86, 395; 4:249, 376 etc. Quoted in Michel Chodkiewicz, *Le Sceau des saints: Prophetie et saintete dans la doctrine d'Ibn Arabi*, p. 85.

[47] Bayhaqi, *Dalail an-nubuwwa*.

11. Abd al-Khaliq al-Ghujdawani ق

Abd al-Khaliq al-Ghujdawani was known as the shaykh of miracles, one who shone like the sun. He was the master of the high stations of spirituality of his time. He was a perfect knower in Sufism and accomplished in asceticism. He is considered the fountainhead of the Naqshbandi Sufi Order and the wellspring of the masters of Central Asia.

The lights of some people precede their dhikr,
While the dhikr of some people precede their lights.
There is the one who does (loud) dhikr
So that his heart be illumined;
And there is the one whose heart has been illumined
And he does (silent) dhikr.
—Ibn Ata Allah [48]

---

[48] Ibn Ata Allah, *Sufi Aphorisms (Kitab al-hikam),* trans. Victor Danner (Leiden: E.J. Brill, 1984), p. 59.

Abd al-Khaliq was born in Ghujdawan, a town near Bukhara in present-day Uzbekistan. There he lived and passed his life and was buried. He was a descendant of Imam Malik. His father was Shaykh Abd al-Jamil, one of the most famous scholars in Byzantine times in both external and internal knowledge. His mother was a princess, the daughter of the king of Seljuk Anatolia.

In his childhood, Abd al-Khaliq al-Ghujdawani studied the Quran and its exegesis, the science of the Traditions, the sciences of the Arabic language, and jurisprudence with Shaykh Sadruddin. After mastering the Divine Law, he moved on to spiritual struggle, until he reached a high station of purity. He then moved to Damascus where he established a school from which many students graduated. Each became a master of jurisprudence and the Traditions as well as spirituality, both in the regions of Central Asia as well as in the Middle East. The author of the book *al-Hadaiq al-wardiyya* tells us how he reached his high station within the Golden Chain:

> He met Khidr ﷺ and accompanied him. He took from him heavenly knowledge and added it to the spiritual knowledge he had obtained from his shaykh, Yusuf al-Hamadani. One day when he was reading the Quran in the presence of Shaykh Sadruddin, he came upon the following verse:
>
> *Call unto your Sustainer humbly, and in the secrecy of your hearts. Verily, He loves not those who transgress the bounds of what is right.* (7:55)
>
> This verse prompted him to inquire of Shaykh Sadruddin about the reality of silent *dhikr* and its method. Abd al-Khaliq put his question thus, "In loud *dhikr* you have to use your tongue. People might listen to you and see you, whereas in the silent *dhikr* of the heart, Satan might listen to you and hear you, since the Prophet ﷺ said in his holy Tradition: '*Satan moves freely in the veins and arteries of the children of Adam.*' What, then, O my Shaykh Sadruddin, is the reality of 'Call unto your Sustainer humbly, and in the secrecy of your hearts?'" His shaykh replied, "O my son, this is a hidden, heavenly knowledge, and I wish that God Exalted and Almighty send you one of his saints to inspire on your tongue and in your heart the reality of secret *dhikr*."

From that time Shaykh Abd al-Khaliq al-Ghujdawani waited for that prayer to be fulfilled. One day he met Khidr ﷺ who told him, "Now, my son, I have permission from the Prophet ﷺ to inspire on your tongue and in your heart the hidden *dhikr* with its numbers." He ordered him to submerge himself under water and to begin making *dhikr* in his heart *"la ilaha ill-Allah, Muhammadun Rasul Allah."* He did this form of *dhikr* every day, until the Light of the Divine, the Wisdom of the Divine, the Love of the Divine, and the Attraction of the Divine were opened to his heart. Because of those gifts, people began to be drawn to Abd al-Khaliq and sought to follow in his footsteps. He took them to follow in the footsteps of the Prophet ﷺ.

He was the first one in this honorable Sufi order to use the silent *dhikr*. He was considered the master of that form of *dhikr*. When his spiritual shaykh, Yusuf al-Hamadani, the Arch-Intercessor came to Bukhara, he spent his time in serving him. He said about him, "When I was twenty-two years old, Shaykh Yusuf al-Hamadani asked Khidr to continue raising me and to keep an eye on me until my death."

From His Miracles

There is a renowned water well at his tomb in Uzbekistan, and it is commonly believed that if one drinks from that well, he will be cured of illness. If you visit it today, you will find that hundreds of people are visiting that tomb and the well, which has only one cup from which to drink, although none of the visitors get contaminated from the other, and many are cured.

Grandshaykh Sharafuddin ad-Daghestani, the thirty-eighth shaykh of the Golden Chain, said:

> There was an event that happened on the night known as *Laylat al-Raghaib*, the Night of Desires, which takes place on the evening of the first Thursday of the Islamic month of Rajab. It is related in the life story of the Prophet ﷺ that it was the night that the Prophet's ﷺ light passed from his father to his mother, Lady Amina ﵂, that he passed from his father to his mother's womb. And that is why Muslims around the world respect that night. It occurred on Thursday night, the night before Friday.
>
> That day the mother of Abd al-Khaliq al-Ghujdawani had to do her laundry at the bank of the river. She took her son and was looking after

him very well because her son was playing on the side of the river bank. Suddenly, she saw a man standing there, speaking with her son. She did not know who the man was, although he was making her son laugh, entertaining him. Then suddenly she looked and they had both disappeared.

She became frantic, searching along the river bank for her son, but he was gone. She began to cry. At that moment, she saw a pious man coming towards her. He said, "Why are you crying?" She said, "My only child, my son, on account of whom I saw many miracles in my life, has now disappeared, and I don't know what happened to him." He said to her, "Why are you worried? Do you not know that God takes care of pious people? If you are patient you will derive a lot of goodness. Where you are (your spiritual station) no one can become frustrated."

She asked, "Who are you?" He said, "I am the Prophet Elijah (Ilyas)." She said, "May God have mercy on you and us; again, who are you?" He replied, "God prohibited the earth to eat the flesh of the prophets. We are alive, not dead. We can move about where we like."

She asked, "Can you tell me where my son is?" He said, "Do you know what night this is?" She answered, "No." He said, "This is the night of the sixth of Rajab—the night in which good desires come. On that night, God sends on the Nation such mercy that angels of seven heavens are carrying, blessings on human beings so numerous that no one can count them other than God."

"On that night the the pure atom of the Prophet ﷺ passed from his father to his mother's womb. On that night, God orders all angels, all prophets and all saints to meet in the House of God. They meet in that place in order to get the blessings of the Prophet ﷺ. Your son, although he is still young, is one of the great saints of his time. Khidr عليه السلام is who you saw speaking to him, and he took him and carried him to Makkah. From Merv to Makkah he was transferred in the blink of an eye. There he is going to see all these prophets, angels, and saints and he is going to inherit his share of sainthood from them. Be happy."

She asked, "When will he come back?" He said, "After the pre-dawn meal before fasting the day he will return." With this news, she left and went home.

Then Sayyidina Abd al-Khaliq al-Ghujdawani was carried by Khidr ﷺ, and he was given in turn from one saint to another, and after that from one prophet to another until he reached the presence of the Prophet Muhammad ﷺ. Each saint was building up his spirituality, building up the light of his heart until he was prepared to meet the Prophet ﷺ.

Then the Prophet ﷺ hugged him in his arms and ordered all the spirits of the Companions ؓ to come forth. As soon as they appeared, the child was carried from one to another, one to another, until he reached the hands of Malik bin Sinan al-Ansari ؓ, who carried him to Prophet Muhammad ﷺ. The Prophet ﷺ said, "We are very happy and honored that this son is from our descendants." So our master Abd al-Khaliq al-Ghujdawani was a descendant on one side from Malik bin Sinan al-Ansari.

Then the child was being passed around, from the hand of one Companion to another, until daytime appeared, and then, by means of the spiritual power of conveyance of Sayyidina Khidr ﷺ, he was returned home.

His mother saw him and said, "O my son. I asked Prophet Elijah to get me a blessing and he said to me, 'On that night there are many groups of angels, no one knows their number except God the Exalted, and they are constantly busy in worship in every moment. They commit no sins and they are each in different aspects of *salat* (ritual prayer). Some bowing, some standing, some in *prostration,* some sitting, and some are reciting the Testification of Faith. For the sake of your son, God is going to share the worship of all these angels, and it will be written by the scribe-angels on your shoulders. Anyone who follows the path of your son, (the Naqshbandi Way) a share of the glorification and praise (supplication) of these angels up to Judgment Day will be written as a gift to them, and God will grant to them from their prayers from today up to Judgment Day."

Abd al-Khaliq, who was quite young, replied, "Mother, what he said is but a drop of an ocean, and what God opened to me from the blessing of the Prophet ﷺ is but a drop of an ocean."

Shaykh Muhammad Parsa, a friend and biographer of Shah Naqshband, said in his book *Faslul Kitab* that the method of Khwaja Abd al-Khaliq al-Ghujdawani in *dhikr* and the teachings of his eight principles were embraced and hailed by all of the Sufi Orders as the way of truth and loyalty, the way of consciousness in following the *Sunnah* of the Prophet ﷺ, by leaving innovation and by scrupulously opposing low desires. Because of that he became the master of his time and the first in this line of spirituality. His reputation as an accomplished spiritual master became widespread. Visitors flocked to see him from every land. He gathered around him the loyal and sincere disciples for training and teaching. In this regard, he wrote a letter to his son, al-Qalb al-Mubarak Shaykh Awliya al-Kabir, to specify the conduct of followers of this Order. In it he says:

> O my son, I urge you to acquire knowledge and righteous conduct and the fear of God. Follow the steps of the pious early generation of Muslims. Hold fast to the *Sunnah* of the Prophet ﷺ, and keep company with sincere believers. Study jurisprudence, the Traditions and Quranic commentary. Avoid ignorant charlatans, and maintain the prescribed prayers in congregation.
>
> Beware of fame and its danger. Be among the ordinary people and do not seek positions. Do not enter into friendship with kings and their children nor with the innovators. Keep silent, don't eat excessively and don't sleep excessively. Run away from people as you would run from lions. Keep seclusion. Eat lawful food and leave doubtful actions except in dire necessity. Keep away from love of the lower world, because it might fascinate you.
>
> Do not laugh too much, because too much laughter will be the death of the heart. Do not humiliate anyone. Do not praise yourself. Do not argue with people. Do not ask anyone for anything except God. Do not ask anyone to serve you. Serve your shaykhs with your money and abilities. Do not criticize their actions. Anyone who criticizes them will not be safe, because he does not understand them. Make your deeds sincere by intending them only for God. Pray to Him with humility.

> Make your business jurisprudence, your mosque your house, and your Friend your Lord.

The Principles of the Naqshbandi Way

Abd al-Khaliq al-Ghujdawani coined the following phrases that are now considered the principles of the Naqshbandi Sufi Order:

CONSCIOUS BREATHING

Conscious breathing (*hosh dar dam*) means "mind" (*hosh*) and "breath" (*dam*). According to Abd al-Khaliq al-Ghujdawani, it means:

> The wise seeker must safeguard his breath from heedlessness, coming in and going out, thereby keeping his heart always in the Divine Presence. He must revive his breath with worship and servitude and dispatch this worship to His Lord full of life, for every breath, which is inhaled and exhaled with Presence, is alive and connected with the Divine Presence. Every breath inhaled and exhaled with heedlessness is dead, disconnected from the Divine Presence.

Ubayd Allah al-Ahrar said:

> The most important mission for the seeker in this Order is to safeguard his breath, and he who cannot safeguard his breath, it would be said of him, "he lost himself."

Shah Naqshband said:

> This Order is built on breath. So it is a must for everyone to safeguard his breath in the time of his inhalation and exhalation, and further, to safeguard his breath in the interval between the inhalation and exhalation.

Shaykh Abul Janab Najmuddin al-Kubra said in his book, *Fawatih al-Jamal*:

> *Dhikr* is flowing in the body of every single living creature by the necessity of their breath—even without will—as a sign of obedience, which is part of their creation. Through their breathing, the sound of "*Huwa*" of the Divine Name of God is made with every exhalation and inhalation and it is a sign of the Unseen Essence serving to emphasize the Uniqueness of God. Therefore, it is necessary to be present with that breathing, in order to realize the Essence of the Creator.

The name *"Allah"* which encompasses the Ninety-Nine Names and Attributes consists of four letters: *alif, lam, lam* and *ha* (*Allah*). The people of Sufism say that the Absolute Unseen Essence of God, Exalted and Almighty, is expressed by the last letter as vowelized by the *alif, "Huwa."* The first *lam* is for the sake of emphasis. Safeguarding your breath from heedlessness will lead you to complete Presence.

Complete Presence will lead you to complete vision. Complete vision will lead you to complete manifestation of God's Ninety-Nine Names and Attributes. God leads you to the manifestation of His Ninety-Nine Names and Attributes and all His other Attributes, because it is said, "God's Attributes are as numerous as the breaths of human beings." It must be known by everyone that securing the breath from heedlessness is difficult for seekers. Therefore, they must safeguard it by seeking forgiveness, because seeking forgiveness will purify it and sanctify it and prepare the seeker for the real manifestation of God everywhere.

WATCH YOUR STEP

It means that the seeker, while walking, must keep his eyes on his feet (*nazar bar qadam*). Wherever he is about to place his feet, his eyes must be there. He is not allowed to cast his glance here or there, to look right or left or in front of him, because unnecessary sights will veil the heart. Most veils on the heart are created by the images that are transmitted from your eyes to your mind during your daily living. These may disturb your heart with turbulence because of the different kinds of desire that have been imprinted on your mind. These images are like veils on the heart. They block the Light of the Divine Presence. This is why Sufi saints do not allow their followers, who have purified their hearts through constant *dhikr*, to look at other than their feet. Their hearts are like mirrors, reflecting and receiving every image easily. Looking about might distract them and bring impurities to their hearts.

So the seeker is ordered to lower his gaze in order not to be assailed by the arrows of devils. Lowering the gaze is also a sign of humility. Proud and arrogant people never look at their feet. It is also an indication that one is following the footsteps of the Prophet ﷺ who, when he walked never looked right or left, but looked only at his feet, moving steadfastly towards his destination. It is also the sign of a high state when the seeker looks nowhere except towards his Lord. Like one who intends to reach a destination quickly, so too the seeker of God's Divine Presence is single-minded, not looking to his right or his left, not looking at the desires of this world, but looking only for the Divine Presence.

Imam ar-Rabbani Ahmad al-Faruqi said:

> The gaze precedes the step and the step follows the gaze. The ascension to the high state is first by the vision, followed by the step. When the step reaches the level of the ascension of the gaze, then the gaze will be lifted up to another state, to which the step follows in turn. Then the gaze will be lifted even higher and the step will follow in its turn. And so on until the gaze reaches a state of perfection to which it will pull the step. We say, when the step follows the gaze, the disciple has reached the state of readiness in approaching the footsteps of the Prophet, peace be upon him. So the footsteps of the Prophet ﷺ are considered the origin of all steps.

Shah Naqshband said:

> If we look at the mistakes of our friends, we will be left friendless, because no one is perfect.

JOURNEY HOMEWARD

The journey homeward (*safar dar watan*) means that the seeker travels from the world of creation to the world of the Creator. It is related that the Prophet ﷺ said, "*I am going to my Lord from one state to a better state and from one station to a higher station.*" It is said that the seeker must travel from the desire for the forbidden to the desire for the Divine Presence.

The Naqshbandi Sufi Order divides that travel into two categories. The first is external journeying and the second is internal journeying. External travel is to travel from one land to another searching for a perfect guide to take and direct you to your destination. This enables you to move to the second category, the internal journey. Seekers, once they have found a perfect guide, are forbidden to go on another external journey. In the external journey, there are many difficulties that beginners cannot endure without falling into forbidden actions, because they are weak in their worship.

The second category, internal journeying, requires the seeker to leave his coarse manners, move to praiseworthy manners, and to throw out of his heart all worldly desires. He will be lifted from a state of impurity to a state of purity. At that time he will no longer be in need of more internal journeying. He will have cleansed his heart, making it pure like water, transparent like crystal, polished like a mirror, showing the realities of all matters essential for his daily life, without any need for external action on his part. In his heart will appear everything that is needed for his life and for the life of those around him.

SOLITUDE IN THE CROWD

Seclusion, *khalwah*, means to be outwardly with people while remaining inwardly with God. There are also two categories of seclusion. The first is external and the second is internal seclusion.

External seclusion requires the seeker to seclude himself in a private place that is empty of people. Staying there by himself, he concentrates and meditates on *dhikr Allah*, the remembrance of God, in order to reach a state in which the heavenly realm becomes manifest. When he chains the external senses, his internal senses will be free to reach the heavenly realm. This will bring him to the second, more intense form of seclusion.

Internal seclusion (*khalwat dar anjuman*) means seclusion among people. Therein the heart of the seeker must be present with his Lord and absent from His creation while remaining physically present among them.

It is said the seeker will be so deeply involved in the silent *dhikr* in his heart that, even if he enters a crowd of people, he will not hear their voices. The state of *dhikr* overcomes him. The manifestation of the Divine Presence envelops him, making him unaware of all but his Lord. This is the highest state of seclusion, and is considered true seclusion, as mentioned in the Holy Quran:

> *People whom neither business nor profit distract from the remembrance of God.* (24:37)

This is the way of the Naqshbandi Order. The primary seclusion of the shaykhs of the Naqshbandi Order is internal seclusion. They are with their Lord, and simultaneously, they are with the people. As the Prophet ﷺ said, *"I have two sides: one faces my Creator and one faces creation."*

Shah Naqshband emphasized the goodness of gatherings when he said, "Our Way is companionship, and goodness is in the gathering."[49]

Shah Naqshband said:

> The basic principle of our spiritual path is fellowship (*suhbah*). Aloofness from other people involves the desire for fame, while disaster resides in celebrity. Goodness resides in society and society in gathering. Each of the two aspects must be given its proper due, and they must not be confused with one another.

It is said that the believer who can mingle with people and carry their difficulties is better than the believer who keeps away from people. On that delicate point, Imam Rabbani said:

> It must be known that the seeker at the beginning might use external seclusion to isolate himself from people, worshipping and concentrating on God, Almighty and Exalted, until he reaches a higher state. At that time he will be advised by his shaykh, in the words of Sayyid al-Kharraz, "Perfection is not in exhibitions of miraculous powers, but perfection is to sit among people, sell and buy, marry and have children, and yet never leave the presence of God even for one moment."

ESSENTIAL REMEMBRANCE

Abd al-Khaliq's term was *yad kard. Yad* (remembrance) is *dhikr* and *kard* is the doing of the *dhikr*. It is the doing of *dhikr*, which is the essence, or heart of remembrance. The seeker must recite *dhikr* by negation and affirmation on his tongue until he reaches the state of the contemplation of his heart. That state will be achieved by reciting every day the negation *(la ilaha)* and affirmation *(ill-Allah)* on the tongue, between 5,000 and 10,000 times, removing from his heart the elements that rust and tarnish it. This *dhikr* polishes the heart and takes the seeker into the state of manifestation. He must keep that daily *dhikr*, either by heart or by tongue, repeating *"Allah,"* the Name of God's Essence that encompasses all other names and Attributes, or by negation and affirmation through the saying of *"la ilaha ill-Allah."* This daily *dhikr* will bring the seeker into the perfect presence of the One who is glorified.

---

[49] Arabic: *Tariqatuna as-suhbat wal-khayru fil-jamiyya.*

The *dhikr* by negation and affirmation, in the manner of the Naqshbandi Sufi masters, demands that the seeker close his eyes, close his mouth, clench his teeth, press his tongue to the roof of his mouth, and hold his breath. He must recite the *dhikr* through the heart, by negation and affirmation, beginning with the word *"la"* (no). He lifts this *"la"* from under his navel up to his brain. Upon reaching his brain the word *"la"* brings out the word *"ilaha"* (God), moves from the brain to the left shoulder, and hits the heart with *"ill-Allah"* (except God). When that word hits the heart its energy and heat spreads to all the parts of the body.

The seeker who has denied all that exists in this world with the words *"la ilaha,"* affirms with the words *"ill-Allah"* that all that exists has been annihilated in the Divine Presence. The seeker repeats this with every breath, inhaling and exhaling, always making it come to the heart, according to the number of times prescribed to him by his shaykh. The seeker will eventually reach the state where in one breath he can repeat *"la ilaha ill-Allah"* twenty-three times. A perfect shaykh can repeat *"la ilaha ill-Allah"* an infinite number of times in every breath. The meaning of this practice is that the only goal is God and that there is no other goal for us. The understanding of the Divine Presence as the Only Existence awakens in the heart of the disciple the love of the Prophet ﷺ, and at that time he says, *"Muhammadun Rasul Allah"* ("Muhammad is the Prophet of God"), which is the heart of the Divine Presence.

RETURNING

"Returning" (*baz gasht*) is a state in which the seeker, who recites *dhikr* by negation and affirmation, comes to understand the Holy Prophet's ﷺ phrase, "O my God, You are my Goal and Your Good Pleasure is my aim."[50] The recitation of this phrase will increase in the seeker the awareness of the Oneness of God, until he reaches the state in which the existence of all creation vanishes from his eyes. All that he sees, wherever he looks, is the Absolute One. The Naqshbandi disciples recite this sort of *dhikr* in order to extract from their hearts the secret of Oneness, and to open themselves to the Reality of the Unique Divine Presence. The beginner has no right to leave this *dhikr* if he does not find its power appearing in his heart. He must keep on reciting it in imitation of his shaykh, because the Prophet ﷺ has

---

[50] Arabic: *Allahum anta maqsudi wa ridaka matlubi.*

said, *"Whoever imitates a group of people will belong to them."* And whoever imitates his teacher will some day find this secret opened to his heart.

The meaning of the word "returning" (*baz gasht*) is the return to God, Exalted and Almighty, by showing complete surrender and submission to His Will, and complete humbleness in giving Him all due praise. That is the reason the Holy Prophet ﷺ mentioned in his invocation, *"We did not remember You as You deserve to be remembered, O God."* The seeker cannot come to the Presence of God in his *dhikr*, and cannot manifest the secrets and attributes of God in his *dhikr*, if he does not recite *dhikr* with God's Support and with God's Remembrance of him. As Bayazid said, "When I reached Him I saw that His remembering of me preceded my remembrance of Him." The seeker cannot recite *dhikr* by himself. He must recognize that God is the one reciting *dhikr* through him.

ATTENTIVENESS

Attentiveness (*nigah dasht*) means that the seeker must watch his heart and safeguard it by preventing bad thoughts from entering. Bad inclinations keep the heart from joining with the Divine. It is acknowledged in the Naqshbandi Order that for a seeker to safeguard his heart from bad inclinations for fifteen minutes is a great achievement. For this he would be considered a real Sufi.

Sufism is the power to safeguard the heart from bad thoughts and protect it from low inclinations. Whoever accomplishes these two goals will know his heart, and whoever knows his heart will know his Lord. The Holy Prophet ﷺ has said, *"Whoever knows himself knows His Lord."* One Sufi shaykh said, "Because I safeguarded my heart for ten nights, my heart has safeguarded me for twenty years."

Abu Bakr al-Qittani said, "I was the guard at the door of my heart for forty years, and I never opened it for anyone except God, Almighty and Exalted, until my heart did not know anyone except God, Almighty and Exalted." Abul Hasan al-Kharqani said, "It has been forty years that God has been looking at my heart and has seen no one except Himself. And there is no room in my heart for other than God."

RECOLLECTION

Recollection (*yad dasht*) refers to when the reciter of *dhikr* safeguards his heart with negation and affirmation in every breath without leaving the

12. Arif ar-Riwakri ق

Shaykh Arif ar-Riwakri was a knower whose inner Truth appeared to him in all its brightness and light. He was a sun of knowledge that illuminated the dark sky of his age. He was called "the Light in the Garden of Reality" and "the Light in the Garden of the Prophet ﷺ."

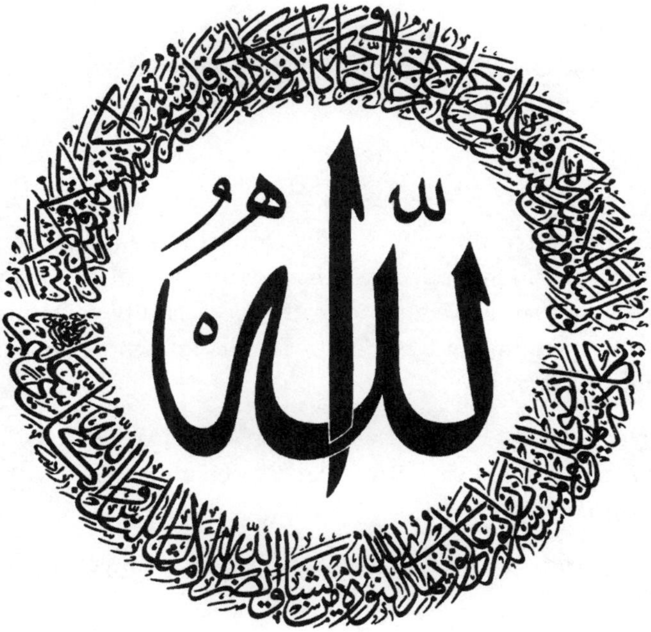

Is there any place our King is not?
But His sorcery has blindfolded the viewer.
He blindfolds your eyes, such that you see a dust mote at midday,
but not the greatest Sun, a ship at sea, but not the ocean's waves.
The ships' bobbing tells you about the sea, just as the movement
of people tells the blind man that it is daytime.
Have you not read the verse, "God has set a seal." (2:7)
It is God who sets the seal,
and "it is He who removes it and lifts up the coverings." (50:22)
—Rumi, *Divan*

Shaykh Arif ar-Riwakri was born in the village of Riwakar, six miles from Bukhara and one mile from Ghujdawan. He stood at the door of his shaykh, Abd al-Khaliq, and served him until the shaykh gave him permission to give guidance to others. He took the secret of the Order from his shaykh, who witnessed his attainment to the state of perfection. He filled the countries around Bukhara with the scent of his blessings. He opened the minds and the hearts of the people of his time to the secrets of his knowledge. His students recorded many of his sayings.

From His Sayings

Trust in God until He becomes your Teacher. Make the remembrance of death your partner.

Too much hope in the future veils you from the good found in God's Way.

Whoever says ten times in a day, "Oh God! Guide the Community of Muhammad ﷺ. Oh God! Bless the Community of Muhammad ﷺ. Oh God! Remove all afflictions from the Community of Muhammad ﷺ," will be written among the group of saints known as the substitutes or transformed ones.

Whoever asks for Paradise without any good deeds it will be written for him as the sin of sins. Whoever awaits intercession without a cause has a form of pride.

It is surprising to see so many righteous, and yet so few truthful, believers.

To achieve healing from any affliction keep your affliction secret from people, because they can be of no benefit to you. They can neither help you nor can they keep it from reaching you.

There are three kinds of hearts: the heart like a mountain, which nothing can move; the heart like a palm-tree, its roots firm, but its branches in motion; and the heart like a feather, which the wind blows from right to left.

Whoever hopes to protect his religion must avoid the company of people.

O God, whenever you want to punish me, do it, but do not keep me away from your Presence.

Mawlana Arif ar-Riwakri died in the same city he was born, Riwakar, and he was buried there in 636 AH/1239 CE. He passed his secret of the Golden Chain to Grandshaykh Khwaja Mahmud al-Injir al-Faghnawi. ۞

13. Khwaja Mahmud al-Injir al-Faghnawi ق

Khwaja Mahmud was a Master from whose heart the water of knowledge and wisdom gushed forth. His heart was polished by the Divine Effulgence, making him one of the best of the chosen ones, purified from all darkness and misery, and translucent as crystal.

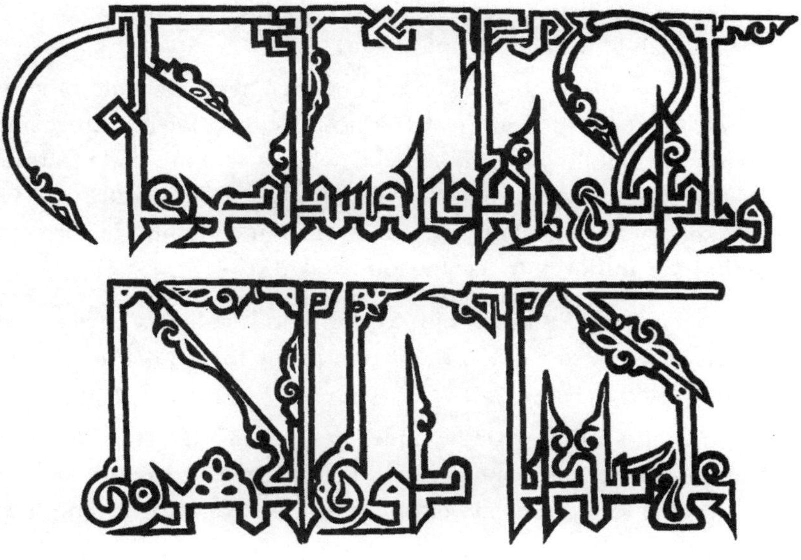

If I repeat Your Name, it is not because I fear forgetfulness.
But the mention of it on my tongue is the happiness of dhikr.
—Abul-Hasan Sumnun [51]

---

[51] Abul-Hasan Sumnun, quoted in *Diwan al-Hallaj*, p. 151.

He was born in the village of Anjir Faghna, three miles from Bukhara. In his youth, he worked in construction. He devoted his life to the guidance of people to God's Presence. He was the first in the line of the masters of wisdom (*khwajagan*) to introduce the method of loud *dhikr* in accordance with the needs of the time and as required by the conditions of the seekers. When he was asked why he used the loud *dhikr*, he replied, "To awaken the sleeper."

The Acceptability of Loud Dhikr

One day Khwaja Mahmud attended a scholarly gathering and Shaykh Shams al-Halwani requested the Shaykh Hafiz ad-Din, an authority in external knowledge, ask Shaykh Mahmud Faghnawi why he was doing loud *dhikr*. Shaykh Mahmud Faghnawi said:

> ...it is the best *dhikr* to awaken an outsider from his state of slumber and to attract the attention of the heedless so that he direct himself towards God, following the shaykh who is making *dhikr*, straighten himself on the Way, and make his repentance to God a pure one, which is the key to all good and happiness. If your intention is correct, you will find the authority to use the loud *dhikr*.

Shaykh Hafiz ad-Din asked him to clarify to him just who is permitted and allowed to practice the loud *dhikr*, in order to justify the practice to those who opposed it. He said:

> The loud *dhikr* is for anyone who wishes to reach the state of purifying his tongue from lying and backbiting, and freeing his private actions from what is forbidden, and cleaning his heart from pride and the love of fame.

One day Shaykh Ali Ramitani said that a man saw Khidr عليه السلام and asked him, "Tell me where I can find someone who practices the Divine Law of the Prophet ﷺ and the straight Path, in order that I may follow him." He said, "The one whom you are seeking is Shaykh Mahmud al-Injir al-Faghnawi."

It is said that Shaykh Mahmud walked on the footsteps of the Prophet Muhammad ﷺ in the station of knowledge of God. He also walked on the footsteps of Moses عليه السلام in the station of the Word of God, the station of one who speaks with God. Shaykh Mahmud radiated his knowledge from his mosque, which he built in the village of Wabiqni, close to Bukhara. He passed away in the village of Qilit, near Bukhara, on the 17th of Rabi al-Awwal, in the year 717 AH/1317 CE. He passed the secret of the Naqshbandi Sufi Order to his caliph, Shaykh Ali ar-Ramitani.

14. Ali ar-Ramitani ق

Shaykh Ali ar-Ramitani was a noble flag of Islam and a great scholar who opened the locks to the treasures of the heart and explained secrets from the unseen. He received, from the kingdom of knowers, bounties and prizes and honors.

No such thing as a broken heart turning me to You;
In truth, from me to You, all the cells in my body are hearts.
—Abu Bakr ash-Shibli [52]

52 Abu Bakr ash-Shibli. Quoted in *Hilyat al-awliya*, 10:372.

Shaykh Ali ar-Ramitani was born in the village of Ramitan, two miles from Bukhara. He lived there, and was an avid student of the knowledge of the Divine Law until he achieved fame in the study of the Traditions, the Quran, jurisprudence, and the *Sunnah.* He was already a reference for anyone asking for legal decisions when he contacted Shaykh Mahmud al-Injir al-Faghnawi for spiritual guidance.

In the shaykh's presence, he was lifted up to the high stations of the manifestation of Divine Love and the Divine Presence. He became known and famous under the name *"Azizan,"* a word in Persian used for one of elevated station. He guided the needy to the station of spiritual knowledge. His name flew high in the skies of guidance, and there are no words to express his knowledge nor his state. To us he may be described, like the Mother of Books (the Holy Quran), as "one written in an elevated state."

From His Many Sayings

Do and do not count.

Confess your shortcomings and continue work.

Attain to the Presence of the Divine, especially when you are eating and when you are talking.

God Almighty and Exalted said in His Holy Quran, *"O Believers, repent to God with a pure repentance."* (66:8) This verse brings us good tidings. Since God asks for repentance, it means He will accept it, because if He were not going to accept your repentance, He would not tell you to repent.

The Prophet ﷺ said, *"God looks at the heart of the Believer every night and day 360 times."* This means that the heart has 360 entrances. And every organ has 360 roots, all of them connected to the heart. So if the heart, under the influence of *dhikr Allah,* is led to the station of God's gaze, this will lead all organs of the body to the gaze of God. As a result, every organ will be obedient to God and from the light of that obedience every organ will be connected to the Divine outpouring. This is what draws the gaze of mercy from God to the heart of the rememberer.

More Concerning Loud *Dhikr*

Mawlana Sayfuddin Fidda, a great scholar in his time, asked him, "Why do you raise your voice in *dhikr*?" Shaykh Ali said:

> O my brother, Muslim scholars throughout the centuries, from the time of the generation following the Companions up until today, have permitted the loud *dhikr* in the last moments of life. At this time those who are near the dying one encourage him to repeat the testimony of faith. The Prophet ﷺ said, *"Make your dying ones say, 'There is no god but God.'"* In the science of Sufism, the scholars have emphasized that each moment may be your last. This leads to the conclusion that you may say *"la ilaha ill-Allah"* in a loud voice at every moment of your life.

He was asked by Shaykh Mawlana Badruddin al-Midani, who was a great scholar in his time, "God has ordered us in the Quran to do excessive *dhikr* by His saying, *'Remember God excessively.'* (33:41) Is that *dhikr* to be by the tongue or by the heart?" Shaykh Ali Ramitani answered:

> For the beginner it is best that it be by the tongue, and for the adept it is best that it be by the heart. This is because, for the beginner to remember God, he must apply a great deal of effort. Since his heart is distracted and unstable and his efforts are scattered, it is better for him to do it with the tongue. But the adept has already polished his heart and is easily affected by *dhikr*. All of his organs become rememberers so that the whole body of the adept, both externally and internally, remembers God in every moment. The equivalence of this is that one day's *dhikr* of the adept is equal to one year's *dhikr* of a beginner.
>
> The duty of a guide is first to know the capability of the seeker. Then he will put on his tongue the most perfect method of *dhikr* to raise him to the highest station.
>
> If there had been on earth one of the followers of Abd al-Khaliq al-Ghujdawani at the time of Hallaj, Hallaj would never have been crucified, because there would have been someone capable of defending him from the accusations of the ignorant.

Shaykh Fakhruddin an-Nuri, another famous scholar in his time, asked him, "God mentioned in the Holy Quran that on the Day of Promises He asked, *'Am I not your Lord?' They said, 'Yes!'* (7:172), whereas on the

Judgment Day He will ask '*To whom belongs the Kingdom on this day?*' (40:16) And no one will answer. Why is it that they answered the question, '*Am I not your Lord?*' whereas on the Judgment Day they will not answer?"

In his answer, Shaykh Ali Ramitani demonstrated the incredible depth of understanding of Quran and Traditions possessed by the Naqshbandi Masters. He said:

> When the first question, "Am I not your Lord?" was put to humankind, it was the day God had placed the obligations of the Sacred Law on all human beings. To reply when asked a question is an obligation under the Law. That is why they answered the question. However, on the Judgment Day, all obligations have come to an end, and at that time, awareness of the Truth and the spiritual world begins. In spirituality there is no utterance better than silence, because spirituality is a flow from and to the heart unrelated to the tongue. That is why to the second question there is no need to give an answer. God Himself answers His own question, "To whom belongs the Kingdom this Day?" by saying, "It belongs to God, the Unique, the Irresistible."

Upon receiving a Divine command he moved from Bukhara to Khwarazm. When he reached Khwarazm, he did not enter the city, but stayed at its gate and sent his messenger to the king to tell him, "A poor weaver has come to enter your kingdom and to stay in it. Do you give permission or not? If you give permission, he will enter. If not, he will go back." He asked the messenger to obtain a written letter, signed by the king, granting his permission. When he received that letter, the shaykh moved inside the city and began to spread the Naqshbandi Way. Every day he went to the town center, speaking with the people, asking them to come to his gatherings and paying their wages for that day. He made the entire city his followers, pious worshippers, and dedicated keepers of remembrance. He became very famous in the city. People from far and wide visited him. His good reputation made the king and his ministers afraid of his influence on the people. They tried to remove him from the city. Having foreseen this event, he sent the letter back to the king. At that, the king came to the shaykh and apologized, asking for his forgiveness. He became one of his foremost disciples.

Shaykh Ali died on Monday, 18th Dhul-Qida in the year 715 AH/1315 CE or 721 AH/1321 CE, at the age of 130 years. He had two sons who were very well known for following in the footsteps of their father. However, he did not pass the secret on to them. Instead, he passed it to Shaykh Muhammad Baba as-Samasi. ۞

15. Muhammad Baba as-Samasi ق

Shaykh Muhammad Baba as-Samasi, the distinguished student of al-Azizan, was the scholar of the saints and the saint of the scholars. He was unique in the two kinds of knowledge, the inner and the outer. His blessings permeated every nation in his time. From his desire to learn, he caused untold, unseen knowledge and secrets to appear.

We went down to a sea,
And stood upon the station of the seashore.
Above that station was a sun rising in our horizon.
Its setting is in us and from us rises its dawn.
Our hands touched its jewels, from which came forth our souls.
At that time we, too, became jewels.
Tell us what is that sun, its meaning and secret.
What is that pearl which came out from the sea?
We went down to a universe whose name in our book is the Void.
It is too narrow to contain us, but can be contained in us.
We left behind the stormy seas.
How can the people know what we have reached?
—Attributed to Abu Madyan

Shaykh Muhammad Baba as-Samasi was born in Sammas, a village in the suburbs of Ramitan, three miles from Bukhara. He was the pinnacle of the suns of external and internal knowledge of the eighth *Hijri* century. One of his miraculous signs was his ascension from the Dome of the Rock, which was his heart, to the station of the knower of the knowers.

From everywhere those versed in spiritual wisdom made the pilgrimage to his garden of knowledge and circumambulated the Kabah of his guidance.

He progressed in his journey by reading from the sciences of the Quran, memorizing the Quran and the Traditions, and becoming a great scholar in jurisprudence. Then he began to study speculative theology, logic, and philosophy, as well as history, until he was a walking encyclopedia of every kind of art and science.

He followed Shaykh Ali Ramitani al-Azizan, and he was constantly engaged in struggling against his *nafs* (self). He secluded himself on a daily basis, until he reached such a state of purity that his shaykh was permitted to transmit to his heart from the unseen heavenly knowledge. He became very famous for his miraculous powers and his high state of sainthood. Shaykh Ali Ramitani chose him before his death as his successor and ordered all his students to follow him. He said, as he passed the village of Qasr al-Arifan, "I smell the scent of a spiritual knower who is going to appear and after whose name this entire Order will be known."

One day he passed the village and said, "I smell the scent so strongly that it is as if the knower has now been born." Three days passed, and the grandfather of a child came to Shaykh Muhammad Baba as-Samasi saying, "This is my grandson." He said to his followers:

> This baby is the knower that I was telling you about. I see in his future that he is to be a guide of all humanity. His secrets are going to reach every sincere and pious person. The heavenly knowledge that God is going to shower on him will reach every house in Central Asia. God's name is going to be engraved (*naqsh*) on his heart. And the Order will take its name from this engraving.

From His Sayings

> The seeker must always stand on his keeping God's Divine Orders. He must be continuously in the state of purity. He must first have a pure

heart that never looks towards anything but God, Almighty and Exalted. Then he must keep pure that inner self, which is never revealed to anyone, and which perceives the true vision. The purity of the breast consists of hope and contentment with His Will. The purity of the spirit consists of modesty and reverence. The purity of the stomach depends on only eating permitted food and abstinence. This is followed by purity of the body, which is to leave desire. This is followed by purity of the hands, which consists of piety and endeavor. Then comes purity from sins, which is regret and heartbreak for past wrongdoing. After this is purity of the tongue, which consists of *dhikr* and asking forgiveness. Then he must purify himself from neglect and slackness, by developing fear of the Hereafter.

We must continuously be asking for wisdom, being careful in all our affairs, following in the footsteps of the good and pious, following their internal teachings, and safeguarding the heart from all whisperings.

Be guided by the teachings of your shaykhs, because they are a more direct cure for you than reading books.

You must keep the company of saints. In that company, you must keep your heart from gossiping and you must not speak in their presence in a loud voice, nor should you be busy in their company with prayers and voluntary worship. Keep their company in everything. Do not talk when they are speaking. Listen to what they say. Do not look in their homes at what they have, especially in their rooms and their kitchens.

Never look towards another shaykh but keep the belief that your shaykh will help you arrive. And do not ever connect your heart to another shaykh, as that might harm you. Leave behind whatever you have been raised on in your childhood.

In keeping your shaykh, you must not keep in your heart anything but God and His Name.

The meaning of 'in the Name of God' (*Bismillah*), is 'in the name of the perfect human being' (*bism al-insan al-kamil*), meaning the Messenger of God ﷺ.

Explaining this the poet and scholar Abd al-Rahman Jami said, "that is the interpretation of the term 'name' (*ism*). It is nto the interpretation of the word *Allah*.

Know that the holy words of the saints are collected from the light of the Reality of the Prophet ﷺ and therefore deserves to be treated with high respect due to the Quran and the traditions of the Prophet ﷺ (*hadith*).

ON ASCENSION

Once I went to see my shaykh, Shaykh Ali ar-Ramitani. When I entered his presence, he said to me, "O my son, I see in your heart the desire for ascension." As soon as he said that he placed me in the state of vision, where I saw myself walking day and night from my country to reach the mosque of the Dome of the Rock, Masjid al-Aqsa. When I reached there, I entered the mosque and I saw a man, clothed all in green. He said to me "Welcome, we have been waiting for you for a long time." I said, "O my shaykh, I left my country on such-and-such date. What is today's date?" He answered, "Today is the 27th of Rajab." I realized I had taken three months to reach the mosque, and to my surprise, I had arrived on the same night as the night of the Prophet's Ascension.

He told me, "Your shaykh, Sayyid Ali ar-Ramitani, has been waiting for you here for a long time." I went inside, and my shaykh was ready to lead the prayer. He led the prescribed night prayer. After completing the prayer, he looked at me and said, "O my son, I have been ordered by the Prophet ﷺ to accompany you from the Dome of the Rock Mosque to the Lote-Tree of the Furthermost Boundary, the same place to which the Prophet ﷺ ascended." When he finished speaking the green man brought two creatures the like of which I had never seen before. We mounted these creatures and we were lifted up. Wherever we ascended, we acquired knowledge of those stations that were between earth and heavens.

It is impossible to describe what we saw and learned in that ascension, because words cannot express what relates to the heart. It cannot be conveyed except by taste and experience. We continued until we reached the state of the Reality of the Prophet ﷺ, which is in the Divine

Presence. As soon as we entered this state, my shaykh vanished and I vanished. We saw that there is nothing in existence in this universe except the Prophet ﷺ. We perceived that there is nothing beyond that except God, Almighty and Exalted.

Then I heard the Prophet's ﷺ voice saying to me, "O Muhammad Baba as-Samasi, O my son, the path you are on is one of the most distinguished ones. Those who have been chosen to be stars and beacons for human beings will be accepted in that path. Return and I will support you with all my power, just as God supports me with His Power. And keep in the service of your shaykh."

As the voice of the Prophet ﷺ came to an end, I found myself standing in the presence of my shaykh. It is a great blessing, to be in the company of such powerful shaykhs who can take you to the Divine Presence.

Shaykh Muhammad Baba as-Samasi died in Samas on the 10th of Jumada 'l-Akhir, in the year 755 AH/1354 CE. He had four caliphs. He passed the secret of the Golden Chain to Shaykh Sayyid Amir Kulal ibn as-Sayyid Hamza. ۞

16. Sayyid Amir Kulal ق

Sayyid Amir Kulal is known as "the Rose of the Characteristics and Attributes of the Prophet," "the Furthest Lote Tree of Desire for the Ultimate Stations," "the Owner of the Throne of Guidance," "the Attractor of Heavenly Blessings," and "the Teacher with His Holy Breath of the Secrets of the Divine."

We have a way from this visible world to the Unseen,
For we are the companions of Religion's Messenger.
We have a way from the house to the garden,
We are the neighbor of cypress and jasmine.
Every day we come to the garden
And see a hundred blossoms.
In order to scatter them among the lovers,
We fill our robes to overflowing. Behold our words!
They are the fragrance of those roses—
We are the rosebush of certainty's rose garden.
—Rumi, *Divan*[53]

---

[53] Jalaluddin Rumi. *Divan,* translated by William Chittick, p. 341.

Sayyid Amir Kulal was born in the village of Sukhar, two miles from Bukhara. He is a renewer of the Divine Law, a master of the Way, a builder of Reality, and a guide for creation. He was distinguished for mastery among the saints of his time, who applied the following saying to him, "The Saints of Mastery are the masters of all saints."

His family was descended from the Holy Prophet ﷺ. His mother said:

> When I was pregnant with him, whenever my hand went towards doubtful food, I would be unable to convey it to my mouth. This happened to me many times. I knew that I had someone special in my womb. I was careful and chose my food from the best and assuredly lawful food.

He was a wrestler in his childhood. He practiced all of its arts until he became one of the most famous wrestlers in his time. All the wrestlers would gather around him to learn from him. One day, a man watching him wrestle had the following thought come to his heart, "How is it that a person who is the descendant of the Prophet ﷺ and who is deeply knowledgeable in the Divine Law and Way, is practicing this sport?" He immediately fell into a deep sleep and dreamt that it was Judgment Day. He felt that he was in great difficulty and that he was drowning. Then Shaykh Sayyid Amir Kulal appeared to him and rescued him from the water. He woke up and Sayyid Amir Kulal looked at him and said, "Did you witness my power in wrestling and my power in intercession?"

Once his shaykh-to-be, Muhammad Baba as-Samasi, was passing by his wrestling arena, accompanied by his followers. He stopped and stood there. An evil whisper came to the heart of one of his followers saying, "How is it that the shaykh is standing here in this wrestling arena?" The shaykh looked at his follower immediately and said, "I am standing here for the sake of one person. He is going to be a great knower. Everyone will come to him for guidance and through him people will reach the highest states of Divine Love and the Divine Presence. My intention is to bring this person under my wing."

At that moment Amir Kulal gazed at him, was attracted, and abandoned the sport of wrestling. He followed Shaykh Muhammad Baba As-Samasi to his house. Shaykh Baba Samasi taught him the *dhikr* and the principles of this most distinguished Way. He told him, "You are now my son." Shaykh Amir Kulal followed Shaykh Baba Samasi for twenty years, spending all his time in *dhikr*, seclusion, worship, and self-denial. No one saw him in these twenty years except in the company of his shaykh. He would come to see his shaykh in Samas every Monday and Thursday, although the distance was five miles and the journey difficult, until he reached a state of unveiling. At that time, his fame began to spread everywhere until he left this world.

He had four children, Sayyid al-Amir Burhanuddin, Sayyid al-Amir Hamza, Sayyid al-Amir Shah, and Sayyid al-Amir Umar. He also had four caliphs, but he passed his secrets to only one of them, the master of masters, the knower of knowers, the greatest of Arch-Intercessors, the sultan of the saints, Shaykh Muhammad Bahauddin Shah Naqshband.

Shaykh Sayyid Amir Kulal died in the same village in which he was born, Sukhar, the 8th of Jumada al-Awwal, 772 AH/1370 CE.

17. Muhammad Bahauddin Shah Naqshband ق

Muhammad Bahauddin Shah Naqshband is the imam of the Naqshbandi Sufi Order and was a rare scholar of *ilm ash-Shariah,* the science of Islamic Divine Law, and of *ilm al-Haqiqat,* the science of Reality. He was known as *Dhu-Janahayn,* "Possessor of Two Wings," keeping two sorts of knowledge: one shared with all, and one reserved for his followers. He was also known as *Sultan al-Arifeen,* "King of the Gnostics."

The turtledove sings its lament at dawn, and weeps.
My tears disturb her sleep and her tears disturb mine.
When she and I complain, we understand not each other.
But I know her grief and she knows mine.
—Abul Hasan an-Nuri.[54]

---

[54] Quoted in Sarraj, *Kitab al-luma,* edited by R. Nicholson, p. 305.

Shah Naqshband was an ocean of knowledge that has no shore. Its waves were woven with the pearls of heavenly knowledge. He cleansed humanity with his ocean of innocence and piety. He quenched the thirst of souls with the water of his spiritual support. The whole world, including its oceans and continents, were within his grasp. He was a star decorated with the crown of guidance. He sanctified all human souls, without exception, with his holy breath. He adorned even the remotest corner with the secrets of "*Muhammadun Rasul Allah* ﷺ."

His light penetrated every dark lair of ignorance. His outstanding proofs cast away the least whisper of doubt from the hearts of humanity. His powerful miracles brought life to hearts after their deaths and provided souls with their provision for the spiritual realm. He was nursed in the station of the Arch-Intercessor when he was a child in the cradle. He sipped the nectar of unseen knowledge from the cup of Reality. If Muhammad ﷺ were not the last of the prophets, he would have been a prophet. All praise to God for sending such a reviver of religion. He uplifted the hearts of humanity causing them to soar in the sky of spirituality.

He made kings stand waiting at his door. He spread his guidance from north to south and from east to west. He left no one without heavenly support—even the wild beasts in the jungles. He was the greatest Arch-Intercessor, the sultan of saints, the necklace of all the spiritual pearls that were bestowed on this world by the Divine Presence. By the light of his guidance, God caused the good to be the best and transformed evil into goodness. He was the master of this Way, the Shaykh of the Golden Chain, and the best of those who carried this lineage from the Khwajagan.

He was born in the month of Muharram, in 717 AH/1317 CE, in the village of Qasr al-Arifan, near Bukhara. God granted him miraculous powers in his childhood. His first teacher, Sayyid Muhammad Baba as-Samasi, taught him about the secret of this Way. Then he was given the secret and the mastery of the Order by his shaykh, Sayyid Amir Kulal. He was also Uwaysi in his connection to the Prophet ﷺ, as he was raised in the spiritual presence of Abd al-Khaliq al-Ghujdawani, who preceded him by 200 years.

Questioning by Prophet Moses عليه السلام

Shaykh Sharafuddin ad-Daghestani narrated the *hadith, "Whenever God's saints are mentioned, His mercy descends on that group."* The source of that mercy is one of the secrets revealed by the Prophet ﷺ to Grandshaykh Sharafuddin ad-Daghestani and Grandshaykh Abd Allah al-Faiz ad-Daghestani (the thirty-eighth and thirty-ninth in the Naqshbandi Golden Chain, respectively) during their seclusions. Explaining this, Shaykh Sharafuddin ad-Daghestani said, "When the stories of the saints and details of their lives are mentioned, the sins of the listeners will be shattered away as the shattering of a glass,"

The great scholar, ibn Hajar al-Haytami, would travel one or two days only to listen to the stories of Naqshbandi shaykhs. One such story is about Shah Naqshband.

It is narrated that, when he reached the age of seven years, Shah Naqshband was spiritually brought to meet with the spirits of all the messengers of God, including Prophet Muhammad ﷺ. In the spiritual presence of the Prophet ﷺ, there is no age, as it has no significance; only the spirit is significant. That is why he was able to be in their presence at such a young age.

Shah Naqshband was unique, for no one among all the Naqshbandis of that time could match his high spiritual station. In the presence of Prophet Muhammad ﷺ, Prophet Moses عليه السلام asked him, "O *fard al-alam*! (Shah Naqshband's title, meaning "Unique Saint of the World") When were you chosen (or granted) as a guide for mankind?"

Shah Naqshband replied, "I was an initiating guide (*murshid*) when the saints were in complete non-existence." What he meant was, "I was a guide before God created the saints." He was not referring to his physical creation, but to the Secret of the Prophet ﷺ which was passed to him. So Prophet Moses عليه السلام said, "Explain; we want to know more."

In deference to Abu Bakr as-Siddiq رضي الله عنه and out of good manners towards the Prophet Moses عليه السلام, Shah Naqshband remained silent as the former answered for him, "O Moses, when he spoke to you, he spoke to you from the level he inherited from Prophet Muhammad ﷺ. He answered you from the secret of that level." Then Abu Bakr رضي الله عنه looked at Shah Naqshband, indicating permission to respond to the questions.

Shah Naqshband continued, "I was a guide when there were no saints, before God granted the saints their position, on the Day of Promises, when God asked, *'Am I not Your Lord?'* (7:172) and God allowed me to look after my followers and their sustenance, and to guide them when the saints were yet in the void."

He asked for the sake of Prophet Muhammad ﷺ, and when he asked, the Prophet ﷺ looked at him, and the Prophet ﷺ raised him for every letter of Quran multiplied by the 12,000 knowledges given on each letter to these *awliya*, and for each of these 7,007 saints he was raised that many levels.

We say there are 70,000 veils of darkness between us and the Presence of the Prophet ﷺ. The nearer you approach the Prophet ﷺ, the last remaining veil will cause you to feel you are ever more distant from his blessed reality. For as much as you approach the presence of the Prophet ﷺ, the intensity of your love (*ishq*) will cause you to feel even further away from him.

From that knowledge Shah Naqshband revealed this great matter:

> When saints destroy those veils, and approach the Presence of the Prophet ﷺ, then there are 700,000 additional veils to reach the essence of the Presence of the Prophet ﷺ. I crossed where no one reached before.

The Beginning of His Guidance and the Guidance of His Beginning

Shah Naqshband was eighteen years of age when he was sent by his grandfather to the village of Samas to serve the Shaykh of the Way, Muhammad Baba as-Samasi, who had asked for him. From the beginning of his companionship with the shaykh, he perceived within himself countless blessings and the urge for great sincerity and devotion. Of his youth he relates:

> I would arise early, three hours before the prescribed dawn prayer, take ablution, and after performing the *Sunnah* prayers, I would go into prostration, supplicating God with the following prayer: "O my Lord, give me the power to carry the difficulties and the pain of Your love." Then I would pray the dawn prescribed prayer with the shaykh.
>
> One day on his way out, he looked at me and said, as if he had been with me when I made that supplication, "O my son, you have to change the method of your supplication. Instead say, 'O God, grant Your pleasure to this weak servant.' God does not like His servants to be in difficulties. Although God in His Wisdom might give some difficulties to His servants to test them, the servant must not ask to be in difficulties, for this would not be respectful to your Lord."

When Shaykh Muhammad Baba as-Samasi died, my grandfather took me to Bukhara and I married there. I lived in Qasr al-Arifan, which was God's special care to me because I was near Sayyid Amir Kulal. I stayed in his service, and he told me that Shaykh Muhammad Baba as-Samasi had told him a long time before that, "I will not be happy with you if you will not take good care of him."

One day, I was sitting with a friend in seclusion when the heavens opened and a grand vision came to me, and I heard a voice saying, "Is it not enough for you to leave everyone and to come to Our Presence Alone?" This voice reduced me to a state of trembling, causing me to run away from that house. I ran to a river. I threw myself in it. I washed my clothes and prayed two *rakats* in a way that I had never prayed before, feeling as if I was praying in the Divine Presence. Everything was opened to my heart in a state of unveiling. The entire universe disappeared and I was not aware of anything other than praying in His Presence.

At the beginning of my state of attraction, I had been asked, "Why are you going to enter on this Path?" I answered, "In order that whatever I say and whatever I want will happen." I was answered, "That will not be. Whatever We say and whatever We want is what will happen." I said, "I cannot do that. I must be permitted to say and to do whatever I like, or I do not want this Way." Then I received the answer, "No, it is whatever We want to be said and whatever We want to be done that must be said and done." I said again, "Whatever I say and whatever I do is what must be." Then I was left alone for fifteen days, until I was overwhelmed with a tremendous depression. Finally I heard a voice, "O Bahauddin, whatever you want, We will grant." I was overjoyed. I said, "I want to be given a Path that will lead anyone who travels on it straight to the Divine Presence." I experienced a great vision and heard a voice saying, "You are granted what you have asked."

On His Progress and Struggle on the Way

Shah Naqshband relates:

Once I was in a state of Divine attraction and in a state of absent-mindedness, moving from here to there, not aware of what I was doing. My feet were torn and bleeding from thorns when darkness fell.

I felt myself attracted to the house of my shaykh, Sayyid Amir Kulal. It was a pitch-black night with no moon or stars showing. The air was very cold and I had nothing on but an old leather cloak. When I arrived at his house, I found him sitting with his friends. When he saw me he told his followers, "Take him out; I do not want him in my house."

They put me out, and I felt that my ego was trying to overcome me and that it was taking over my heart and my feelings, trying to poison my trust in my shaykh. At that point God's Divine Care and His Mercy were my only support in carrying this humiliation in the cause of God and the cause of my shaykh. I said to my ego, "I will not allow you to poison my trust in my shaykh."

I felt so tired and so depressed that I put the state of humbleness at the door of pride, placed my head on the threshold of the door of my teacher, and took an oath that I would not remove it until he accepted me again. The snow was beginning to fall and the frigid air penetrated my bones causing me to tremble in the dark night. There was not even the warmth of the moon to comfort me. I remained in that state until I nearly froze. But the love that was inside my heart, the love for the Divine and the love for the door of the Divine, my shaykh, kept me warm.

Dawn came and my shaykh stepped out of his door without seeing me physically. He put his foot on my head, which was still on his threshold. On sensing my head, he immediately withdrew his foot, took me inside his house and said to me, "O my son you have been adorned with the dress of happiness. You have been adorned with the dress of Divine Love. You have been adorned with a dress with which neither my shaykh nor myself has been adorned. God is happy with you. The Prophet ﷺ is happy with you. All the shaykhs of the Golden Chain are happy with you."

Then, with great care and delicacy, he pulled the thorns from my feet and washed my wounds. At the same time he poured into my heart such knowledge that I had never experienced before. This opened for me a vision in which I saw myself entering into the secret of "*Muhammadun Rasul Allah.*" I saw myself entering into the secret of the verse that is the Reality of Muhammad ﷺ. This led me to enter the secret of *"la ilaha ill-Allah"* which is the secret of the Uniqueness of God. This then led me to enter the secrets of God's Names and Attributes that are expressed by the secret of Oneness of God. Those states cannot be put into words, but can only be known through taste that is experienced in the heart.

In the beginning of my travel on the Way, I wandered at night from one place to another in the suburbs of Bukhara. I visited cemeteries by myself in the darkness of the night, especially in the wintertime, to learn a lesson from the dead. One night I was led to visit the grave of Shaykh Ahmad al-Kashghari and to recite *Surat al-Fatiha* for him. When I arrived, I found two men, whom I had never met before, waiting for me with a horse. They put me on the horse and they tied two swords on my belt. They directed the horse to the grave of Shaykh Mazdakhin.

When we arrived, we all dismounted and entered the tomb and mosque of the shaykh. I sat facing the *qiblah,* meditating and connecting my heart to the heart of that shaykh. During this meditation, a vision was opened to me and I saw the wall facing *qiblah* come tumbling down. A huge throne appeared. A gigantic man, whom no words can describe, was sitting on that throne. I felt that I knew him. Wherever I turned my face in this universe I saw that man. Around him was a large crowd in which were my shaykhs, Shaykh Muhammad Baba as-Samasi and Sayyid Amir Kulal. I felt afraid of the gigantic man while at the same time I felt love for him. I had fear of his exalted presence and love for his beauty and attraction. I said to myself, "Who is that great man?"

I heard a voice among the people in the crowd saying, "This great man who nurtured you on your spiritual path is your shaykh. He looked at your soul when it was still an atom in the Divine Presence. You have been under his training. He is Shaykh Abd al-Khaliq al-Ghujdawani, and the crowd you see are the caliphs who carry his great secret, the secret of the Golden Chain."

Then the shaykh began to point to each shaykh and say, "This is Shaykh Ahmad. This is Kabir al-Awliya. This is Arif Riwakri. This is Shaykh Ali Ramitani. This is your shaykh, Muhammad Baba as-Samasi, who in his life gave you his cloak. Do you know him?" I said, "Yes."

Then he said to me, "That cloak which he gave you such a long time ago is still in your house, and with its blessing God has removed from your life many afflictions." Then another voice came and said, "The shaykh who is on the Throne is going to teach you something you need while traveling on this way." I asked if they would allow me to shake hands with him. They allowed this and took the veil away and I took his hand. Then he began to tell me about wayfaring, its beginning, middle, and end. He said, "You have to adjust the wick of your self in order that the light of the unseen can be strengthened in you and its secrets can be seen. You have to show constancy, and you have to be firm in the Divine Law of the Prophet ﷺ in all your states. You have to '*enjoin the right and forbid the wrong*' (3:110, 114) and keep to the highest standard of the Divine Law."

He continued, "You have to leave the dispensations of ease, throw away innovation in all its forms, and make your *qiblah* the Prophet's ﷺ Traditions. You have to investigate his life and the life of his Companions. Urge people to follow and to read the Quran both day and night, and to perform the prescribed prayers with all their supererogatory worship. Do not ignore even the smallest thing from what the Prophet ﷺ has shown us of deeds and good works."

As soon as Abd al-Khaliq finished, his caliph told me, "In order to be assured of the certainty of this vision, he is sending you a sign. Tomorrow go and visit Mawlana Shamsuddin al-Ambikuti, who will be judging between two people. Tell him that the one called 'at-Turki' is right and the other, called 'as-Saqqa,' is wrong. Say to him, 'You are trying to help as-Saqqa, but you are mistaken. Correct yourself and help at-Turki.' If as-Saqqa denies what you say, and the judge continues in helping as-Saqqa, tell him, 'I have two proofs.' The first requires you to tell as-Saqqa, 'O as-Saqqa, you are thirsty.' He will know what that thirst means. As for the second proof, you must tell as-Saqqa, 'You slept in adultery with a woman. She became pregnant. You had the baby she was carrying aborted. You buried the baby under the grapevines.' On your way from Mawlana Shamsuddin, take with you three dry raisins and pass by your shaykh, Sayyid Amir Kulal. On your way to him you will find a shaykh who will give you a loaf of bread. Take the bread and do not speak to him. Continue until you meet a caravan. A horseman will approach you. Advise and reproach him. He is going to repent and become one of your followers. Wear your hat and take the cloak of Azizan to Sayyid Amir Kulal."

After that they moved me and the vision ended. I came back to myself. The next day, I went to my house and I asked my family about the cloak that had been mentioned in the vision. They brought it to me and told me, "It has been sitting there for a long time." When I saw the cloak a state of internal weeping overcame me. I took the cloak and went to the village of Ambikata, in the suburbs of Bukhara, to the mosque of Mawlana Shamsuddin. I prayed the dawn prayer with him and then I told him about the sign that astonished him. As-Saqqa was present and he denied that at-Turki was right. Then I told him about the proofs. He accepted the first and he denied the second. Then I asked the people in the mosque to go to the grapevine that was near the mosque. They did and found the child who was buried there. As-Saqqa came crying and apologized for what he had done, but it was over. Mawlana Shamsuddin and the others in the mosque were in a state of great astonishment.

I prepared to travel the next day to the city of Naskh and had with me the three dry grapes. Mawlana Shamsuddin tried to detain me by telling me, "I see in you the pain of longing for us and the burning desire to reach the Divine. Your healing is in our hands." I answered him, "O my shaykh, I am the son of someone else and I am his follower. Even if you offer to nurse me from the breast of the highest station, I cannot take it, except from the one to whom I gave my life and from whom I took my initiation." Then he kept quiet and permitted me to travel.

I moved on as I had been instructed until I met the shaykh, and he gave me a loaf of bread. I did not speak to him. I took the loaf from him, as I had been ordered. Then I met a caravan. They asked me where I was coming from. I said, "Ambikata." They asked me when I had left. I said, "At sunrise." They were surprised and said, "That village is miles away and crossing that distance would take you a long time. We left that village last night and you left at sunrise and yet you have reached us." I continued on until I met a horseman. He asked me, "Who are you? I am afraid of you!" I told him, "I am the one on whose hand will be your repentance." He dismounted his horse, showing complete humbleness to me and repented and threw away all the wine that he was carrying. He accompanied me to my Shaykh, Sayyid Amir Kulal. When I saw him, I gave him the cloak.

He remained silent for some time and then he said, "This is the cloak of Azizan. I was informed last night that you would be bringing it to me, and I have been ordered to keep it in ten different layers of covering." Then he ordered me to enter his private room. He taught me and placed in my heart the silent *dhikr*. He ordered me to keep that *dhikr* day and night. As I had been ordered in the vision of Shaykh Abd al-Khaliq al-Ghujdawani to keep to the difficult way, I kept that silent *dhikr* which is the highest form of *dhikr*. In addition, I attended the company of the external scholars to learn the sciences of the Divine Law and the Traditions and to learn about the character of the Prophet ﷺ and his Companions. I did as the vision told me, and this resulted in a big change in my life. All that Shaykh Abd al-Khaliq al-Ghujdawani taught me in that vision bore its blessed fruits in my life. His spirit was always accompanying me and teaching me.

On Loud and Silent *Dhikr*

It is mentioned in the book *al-Bahjat as-saniyya* that from the time of Mahmud al-Faghnawi to the time of Sayyid Amir Kulal they kept the way of the loud *dhikr* when in association and the silent *dhikr* when alone. However, when Shah Bahauddin Naqshband received his secret, he kept only the silent *dhikr*. Even in the associations of Sayyid Amir Kulal, when they began to do the loud *dhikr*, he retired to his room to do silent *dhikr*. This made the disciples somewhat upset. While his shaykh was doing the loud *dhikr*, he was doing the silent *dhikr*. Yet he stood in the service of his shaykh all his life.

One day, as Shah Bahauddin and all the followers of Sayyid Amir Kulal were taking a rest from building a new mosque, Sayyid Amir Kulal said, "Whoever was keeping bad thoughts about my son Bahauddin was wrong. God has given him a secret that no one was given before. Even I was unable to know it." And he told him:

O my son, I have fulfilled the will and advice of Shaykh Muhammad Baba as-Samasi when he ordered me to raise you and nurse you in my way of training until you surpassed me. This I have done, and you have capacity to continue yet higher. So, my dear son, I am now giving you complete permission to go wherever you like and to obtain knowledge from whomever you find.

On Subsequent Shaykhs

Once I followed Mawlana Arif ad-Din Karrani for seven years. Then I followed Mawlana Kuthum Shaykh for many years. One night I slept in the presence of my shaykh and I saw Shaykh al-Hakim Attar, who was one of the famous shaykhs of the Turks, telling something to a dervish named Khalil Ghirani. When I awoke, the picture of the dervish stayed in my mind. I had a pious grandmother to whom I mentioned the dream. She told me, "O my son, you are also going to follow many Turkish shaykhs." So I looked in my travels for Turkish shaykhs and I never forgot the picture of that one dervish.

Then one day, in my own country of Bukhara, I saw a dervish, and I recognized him as the one in my dream. I asked him his name and he told me, "I am Khalil Ghirani." I had to leave him, but I felt terrible to do so. At the time of the evening prescribed prayer, someone knocked at my door. I answered and a stranger told me, "Dervish Khalil Ghirani is waiting for you." I was so surprised. How had that person found me? I took a gift and went with him.

When I reached his presence I began to tell him the dream. He said, "No need to tell me that dream, I know it already." This moved my heart to be more attached to him. In his company, new unseen knowledge was opened to my heart. He always looked after me, praised me, and lifted me up. The people of Transoxiana put him as a king over them. I continued to keep his company, even in the time of his sultanate, and my heart grew in love for him even more, and his heart lifted me ever higher in knowledge. He taught me how to be in the service of the shaykh. I stayed in his company six years. In his presence and in my seclusion I kept my connection with him.

In the beginning of my travel on this Way, I met a lover of God and he said to me, "It seems as if you are from us." I told him, "I hope you are from us and I hope to be a friend to you." Once he asked me, "How do you treat yourself?" I said to him, "If I find something I thank God, and if not I am patient." He smiled and said, "This is easy. The way for you is to burden your ego and to test it. If it loses food for one week, you must be able to keep it from disobeying you." I was very happy with his answer and I asked his support.

He ordered me to help the needy, and to serve the weak, and to motivate the heart of the broken-hearted. He ordered me to keep humbleness and humility and tolerance. I kept his orders and I spent many days of my life in that manner. Then he ordered me to take care of animals, to cure their sicknesses, to clean their wounds, and to assist them in finding their provision. I kept on that way until I reached the state that, when I saw an animal in the street, I would stop and make way for it.

He ordered me to look after the dogs[55] of this group with truthfulness and humility and to ask them for support. He said to me, "Because of your service to one of them, you will reach great happiness." I took that order in the hope that I would find that one dog, and through service to him, I would find that happiness. One day I was in the company of one of them and I felt a great state of happiness overcome me. I began crying in front of him until he fell on his back and raised his forepaws to the skies. I heard a very sad voice emanating from him, and so I raised my hands in supplication and began to say "*amin*" in support of him until he became silent. What then opened for me was a vision that brought me to a state in which I felt that I was part of every human being and part of every creation on this earth.

After Wearing the Cloak

One day I was in my garden in Qasr al-Arifan (where his mosque and tomb are located), wearing the cloak of Azizan, and around me were my followers. I was suddenly overwhelmed by the heavenly attractions and blessings, and I felt I was being dressed and adorned with His

---

[55] Dogs represent the characteristics of sincerity and loyalty.

Attributes. I trembled in a way that I had never experienced before, and I could not remain standing. I faced the *qiblah* and I entered into a great vision. I found myself completely annihilated, and I did not see any existence except my Lord's. Then I saw myself coming out from His Divine Presence reflected through the Mirror of *"Muhammad Rasul Allah,"* in the image of a star in an ocean of Light without beginning or end. My external life ended, and I saw only the meaning of *"la ilaha ill-Allah, Muhammadun Rasul Allah"*.

This led me to the meaning of the Essence of the name *"Allah,"* which led me to the Absolute Unseen, which is the essence of the Name *"Huwa"* (He). When I entered that ocean, my heart stopped pumping and my life ended, putting me in a state of death. My soul left my body, and all those around thought I had died and were crying. Then, after six hours, I was ordered to return to my body. I perceived my soul slowly re-entering my body and the vision ended.

To deny your existence and to neglect and disregard your ego is the currency of this order. In this state, I entered into every level of existence, which made me a part of all creations and which developed in me a certainty that everyone is better than I. I saw that everyone provides a benefit and that only I give no benefit. One day a surprising state came upon me. I heard the Divine voice saying, "Ask whatever you like from Us."

So I said, with humility, "O God, grant me one drop of Your Oceans of Mercy and Blessings." The answer came, "You are asking from Our Great Generosity for only one drop?" This was like a tremendous slap on my face, and the sting of it lasted on my cheek for days. Then one day I said, "O God grant me from Your Oceans of Mercy and Blessings and the power to bear it." At that moment, a vision was opened to me wherein I was seated on a throne and that throne was over an ocean of mercy. And a voice said to me, "This Ocean of Mercy is for you. Give it to My servants."

I received secrets from every side, especially from Uways al-Qarani ﷺ, who greatly influenced me to depart from all worldly matters and to attach myself exclusively to spiritual matters. I did this by firmly keeping the Divine Law and the orders of the Prophet ﷺ, until I began spreading the unseen knowledge and the granted secrets from the Unique Oneness that no one before had ever shared.

The Miracles of His Sayings and the Differences among Imams

In an assembly of great scholars in Baghdad, Shah Naqshband was asked about the differences in the sayings of the four caliphs of the Holy Prophet ﷺ. He said:

> Once as-Siddiq ؓ said, "I never saw anything except that God was before it," and Umar al-Faruq ؓ said, "I never saw anything except that God was behind it." And Uthman ؓ said, "I never saw anything except that God was within it." The differences in these sayings are based on the differences in the circumstances at the times they were spoken and not on differences in belief or understanding.

Traveling on the Path

> What is the meaning of Prophet's ﷺ narration, "Part of faith is to remove what is harmful from the Way?" What he meant by "harmful" is the ego, and what he meant by "the Way" is the Way of God, as He said to Bayazid al Bistami, "Leave your ego and come to Us."

Shah Naqshband was once asked, "What is meant by traveling the path?" He said, "The details in spiritual knowledge." They asked him, "What are the details in spiritual knowledge?" He said:

> The one who knows and accepts what he knows will be raised from the state of evidence and proof to the state of vision... Whoever asks to be in the Way of God has asked for the way of affliction. It was narrated by the Prophet ﷺ, "Whoever loves me, I will burden him." One person came to the Prophet ﷺ and said, "O Prophet I love you," and the Prophet ﷺ said, "Then prepare yourself to be poor." Another time a person came to the Prophet ﷺ and said, "O Prophet I love God," and the Prophet ﷺ said, "Then prepare yourself for affliction."

It is reported by his successor, Alauddin al-Attar, that when Shah Naqshband got new clothes he would give them to someone else to wear, and after they were used he would borrow them back.

He recited the verses:

Everyone desires the good,

But no one has attained the ascension,

Except by loving

The One who created the good.

He said:

Everyone who likes himself must deny himself. Whoever wants other than himself, wants in reality only himself.

On Spiritual Training, Stations and Poverty

There are three ways that knowers reach their knowledge: contemplation; vision; reckoning. In the state of contemplation, the seeker forgets the created and remembers only the Creator. In the state of vision, inspirations from the unseen come to the heart of the seeker accompanied by two states: contraction and expansion. In the condition of contraction, the vision is of Majesty, and in the state of expansion, the vision is of Beauty. In the state of reckoning, the seeker evaluates every hour that has passed: was he in complete Presence with God or in complete presence with the world?

The seeker in this way must be busy in rejecting evil whisperings and the ego's insinuations. He might reject them before they reach him; or he might reject them after they reach him, but before they control him. Another seeker, however, might not reject them until after they reach him and control him. He cannot get any fruit, because at that time it is impossible to take the whisperings out of the heart.

Shah Naqshband was asked, "How do the people of God perceive the hidden actions and the whispers in the chest?" He said:

By the light of the vision that God granted them, as mentioned in the Holy Tradition, "Beware of the vision of the believer, because he looks with the Light of God."

Shah Naqshband was asked about showing miraculous powers. He said:

What more miraculous powers do you want than that we are still walking this earth with all these sins upon us and around us.

He was asked, "Who is the reciter and who is the Sufi in the saying of Junayd, 'Disconnect yourself from the reciters of books, and accompany the Sufis?'" He said, "The reciter is the one busy with the words and names, and the Sufi is the one who is busy with the essence of the names."

He warned, "If a disciple, a shaykh or anyone speaks about a state that he has not attained, God will forbid him to reach that state." He said, "The mirror of every shaykh has two directions. But our mirror has six directions."

> What is meant by the Holy Tradition, "I am with the one who remembers Me," is clear evidence and a proof supporting the people of the heart who remember Him always. And the other saying of the Prophet ﷺ, speaking on behalf of God, *"The fast is for Me"* is an affirmation that the true fast is to abstain from all that is other than God.

Shah Naqshband was asked, "Why are the seekers called the poor?" He said:

> Because they are poor, but they do not need to supplicate. Just as Prophet Abraham ﷺ, when he was thrown into the fire and Gabriel ﷺ came and asked him, "Do you need any help?" He replied, "I have no need to ask. He is well-aware of my state."
>
> Poverty is a sign of annihilation and the erasure of the attributes of existence.

He once asked, "Who is the poor one?" No one answered him. He said, "The poor one is the one whose inside is always in struggle and whose external is always at peace."

On Proper Manners with One's Shaykh

> It is necessary for the follower, if he is confused about something his shaykh has said or done and is unable to understand his reasons, to be patient and carry it, and not to become suspicious. If he is a beginner, he might ask, but if he is a disciple, he has no reason to ask and should remain patient with what he does not yet understand.
>
> It is impossible to reach the love of the people of God until you come out of yourself.

represents *Yad Allah,* the Hand of God; and *Ha,* which represents *Hidayat Allah,* the Guidance of God. Intention is the breeze of the soul.

On the Duties of the Saints

God created me to destroy the materialistic life, but people want me to build their materialistic life.

The people of God carry the burden of creation for creation to learn from them. God looks at the heart of His saints with His Lights, and whoever is around that saint will get the blessing of that Light.

The shaykh must know the state of his disciple—in the past, the present, and the future—in order for him to raise the disciple up.

Whoever is initiated by us and follows us and loves us, whether he is near or far, wherever he is, even if he is in the East and we are in the West, we nourish him from the stream of love and give him light in his daily life.

On Loud and Silent *Dhikr*

From the presence of Azizan there are two methods of *dhikr*: the silent and the audible. I preferred the silent because it is stronger and more advisable.

The perfected one must give the permission for the *dhikr,* in order to influence the one who is using it, just as the arrow from a master of archery is better than the arrow thrown from the bow of an ordinary person.

Shah Naqshband added three principles to Shaykh Abd al-Khaliq's eight: awareness of time, numbers and the heart.

Awareness of Time

Awareness of time means to watch one's composure and check one's tendency to heedlessness. The seeker must know how much time he has spent in moving towards spiritual maturity and must recognize at what place he has arrived in his journey towards the Divine Presence. The seeker must make progress with all his efforts. He must spend all his time making his one and only goal the arrival at the station of

> Divine Love and Divine Presence. He must become aware that, in all his efforts and in all his actions, God witnesses the smallest detail. The seeker must make an account of his actions and his intentions every day and every night and analyze his actions each hour, each second, and each moment. If they are good, he thanks God for it. If they are bad, he must repent and ask God's forgiveness.
>
> Yaqub al-Charkhi said that his shaykh, Alauddin al-Attar, said:
>
> In the state of depression, you must seek forgiveness excessively, and in the state of elation, praise God excessively.

To take into consideration these two states, contraction and expansion, is the meaning of awareness of time. Shah Naqshband explained that state by saying:

> You have to be aware of yourself. If you were following the Divine Law then you have to thank God, or else you must ask forgiveness.
>
> What is important for the seeker in this state is to keep secure the smallest period of time. He has to stand guard on his self and judge if he was in the Presence of God or if he was in the presence of his ego, at every moment of his life.
>
> You have to evaluate how you spend every moment: with Presence or in Negligence.

Awareness of Numbers

Awareness of numbers means that the seeker who is reciting *dhikr* must observe the exact number of repetitions comprising the silent *dhikr* of the heart. To keep an account of the *dhikr* is not for the sake of the account itself, but is for the sake of securing the heart from bad thoughts and to cause it to concentrate more in the effort to achieve the repetition prescribed by the shaykh as quickly as possible. The pillar of *dhikr* through counting is to bring the heart into the Presence of the One who is mentioned in that *dhikr* and to keep counting, one by one, in order to bring one's attention to the realization that everyone is in need of that One whose Signs appear in every creation.

Shah Naqshband said, "Observance of the numbers in *dhikr* is the first step in the state of acquiring heavenly knowledge." This means that counting leads one to recognize that only One is necessary for life. All mathematical equations are in need of the number One. All creation is in need of the Only One.

Awareness of the Heart

Awareness of the heart means to direct the heart of the seeker towards the Divine Presence, where he will not see other than his Beloved One. It means to experience His manifestation in all states. Ubayd Allah al-Ahrar said, "The state of awareness of the heart is the state of being present in the Divine Presence in such a way that you cannot look to anyone other than Him." In such a state, one concentrates the place of *dhikr* inside the heart because this is the center of power. All thoughts and inspirations, good and bad, are felt and appear one after another, circling and alternating, moving between light and dark, in constant revolution, inside the heart. *Dhikr* is required in order to control and reduce that turbulence of the heart.

The Meaning of the Community of Muhammad ﷺ

Shah Naqshband said:

When the Prophet ﷺ said, *"The portion of my Community destined for the Hellfire is like the portion of Abraham destined for the fire of Nimrod,"* he gave the good news of salvation for his Community just as God had written salvation for Abraham عليه السلام: *"O fire, be cool and safe for Abraham."* (21:69) This is because the Prophet ﷺ said, *"My Community will never agree on error,"* affirming that the Community will never accept wrongdoing, and thus God will save the Community of Muhammad ﷺ from the Fire.

Shaykh Ahmad al-Faruqi reported that Shah Naqshband said:

The Community of Muhammad ﷺ includes whoever comes after the Prophet ﷺ. It is composed of three types: *Ummat ad-dawah, Ummat al-ijaba,* and *Ummat al-mutabaa.*

Ummat ad-dawah: Absolutely everyone who came after the Prophet and simply heard his message. That the Prophet ﷺ came to all people without exception is clear from many verses in the Quran [56]; furthermore, his Community is the moderating witness over all other

[56] God said, *"My Mercy extends to all things."* (7:156) He called the Prophet ﷺ by the name of *"Mercy for the worlds."* (21:107); *"Say: O people! I am sent unto you all."* (7:158).

Communities, and the Prophet ﷺ is the one witness over everybody, including the other Communities and their own respective witnesses.[57]

Ummat al-ijaba: Those who accepted the message.

Ummat al-mutabaa: Those who accepted the message and followed the footsteps of the Prophet ﷺ.

All of these categories of the Prophet's ﷺ Community are saved. If they are not saved by their deeds, then they are saved by the intercession of the Prophet ﷺ, according to his saying, "My intercession is for the sinners of my Community."

On Reaching the Divine Presence

Shah Naqshband said:

What is meant by the Tradition of the Prophet ﷺ, "Prayer is the ascension of the believer," is a clear indication of the levels of Real Prayer, in which the worshipper ascends to the Divine Presence and there is manifest in him awe, and reverence, and obedience, and humility, such that his heart reaches a state of contemplation through his prayer. This will lead him to a vision of the Divine Secrets. That was the description of the Holy Prophet's ﷺ prayer in the biographies. It is said that, when the Prophet ﷺ would reach that state, even the people outside the city could hear coming from his chest a sound that resembled the humming of bees.

One of the scholars of Bukhara asked Shah Naqshband, "How can a worshipper reach the Divine Presence in his prayer?" He replied: "By eating from the hard-earned sweat of your brow and by remembering God, Almighty and Exalted, inside your prescribed prayer and outside your prescribed prayer, in every ablution and in every moment of your life."

---

[57] *"We have made of you a Community justly balanced that you might be witnesses over the Communities and the Messenger a Witness over yourselves."* (2:143) and *"How then if We brought from each people a witness and We brought thee as a witness over them!"* (4:41)

On Hidden Polytheism[58]

Shaykh Salah, his servant, reported:

Shah Naqshband once said to his followers, "Any connection of your heart with other than God is the greatest veil for the seeker," after which he recited this verse of poetry:

The connection with other than God
Is the strongest veil,
And to be done with it,
Is the Opening of Attainment.

Immediately after he recited this verse, it came to my heart that he was referring to the connection between faith and submission to the Will of God. He looked at me and laughed and said, "Did you not hear what Hallaj said? 'I rejected the religion of God, and rejection is obligatory on me even though that is hideous to Muslims.' O Shaykh Salah, what came to your heart—that the connection is with belief and Islam—is not the important point. What is important is real faith, and real faith for the People of the Truth is to make the heart deny anything and everything other than God. That is what made Hallaj say, 'I denied your religion and denial is obligatory on me, although that is hideous to Muslims.' His heart wanted nothing except God."

He continued, "Hallaj, of course, was not denying his faith in Islam, but was emphasizing the attachment of his heart to God Alone. If Hallaj was not accepting anything except God, how could one say that he was actually denying the religion of God? His testimony of the reality of his witnessing encompassed and made as child's play the ordinary witnessing of the common Muslim."

Shaykh Salah continued:

Shah Naqshband said, "The people of God do not admire what they are doing; they act only out of the love of God.

"Rabia al-Adawiyya said, 'O God I do not worship seeking the reward of Your Paradise nor fearing Your punishment, but I worship You for Your Love alone.' If your worship is to save yourself or to gain some

---

[58] Polytheism is the worshipping of God together with other than Him.

reward for yourself, it is a hidden polytheism, because you have associated something with God, either the reward or the punishment. This is what Hallaj meant."

Shaykh Arslan ad-Dismashqi said, as Shah Naqshband reported:

O God, Your religion is nothing but hidden polytheism and to disbelieve in it is obligatory on every true servant. The people of religion do not worship You, but are only worshipping to attain Paradise or to escape from Hell. They worship these two as idols, and that is the worst idolatry. You have said, "*Whoever disbelieves in idols and believes in God has grasped the Firm Handhold.*" (2:256) To disbelieve in those idols and to believe in You is obligatory on the people of Truth.

Shaykh Abul Hasan ash-Shadhili, one of the greatest Sufi shaykhs, was asked by his shaykh, "O my son, with what are you going to meet your Lord?" He said, "I am coming to Him with my poverty." His shaykh replied:

> O my son, do not ever repeat this again. This is the biggest idol, because you are still coming to Him with something. Free yourself of everything and then come to Him. The people of laws and external knowledge hold fast to their deeds, and on that basis, they establish the concept of reward and punishment. If they are good, they find good, and if they are bad, they find bad; what benefits the servant is his deeds and what harms him is his deeds. To the People of the Way, this is the hidden polytheism, because one is associating something with God. Although this is an obligation to do (good deeds), yet the heart must not be attached to those deeds. They should only be done for His sake and for His love, without expectation of anything in return.

On the Naqshbandi Way

Shah Naqshband said:

Our Way is very rare and very precious. It is the "Firm Handhold," the way of keeping firm and steadfast in the footsteps of the Prophet ﷺ and of his Companions. They brought me to this Way from the door of Favors, because at its beginning and at its end, I witnessed nothing but the Favors of God. In this Way, great doors of heavenly knowledge will be opened up to the seeker who follows in the footsteps of the Prophet ﷺ.

To follow the *Sunnah* of the Prophet ﷺ is the most important means by which the door will be opened to you.

Whoever is not coming to our Way, his religion is in danger.

He was asked, "How does someone come to your Way?" He replied, "By following the *Sunnah* of the Prophet ﷺ."

We have carried in this Way humiliation, and in return God has blessed us with His Honor.

Some people said about him that he was sometimes arrogant. Shah Naqshband answered, "We are proud because of Him, because He is our Lord, giving us His Support!"

He said:

To reach the Secrets of Oneness is sometimes possible, but to reach the secrets of spiritual knowledge is extremely difficult.

Spiritual knowledge is like water, it takes the color and shape of the cup. God's Knowledge is so great, that however much we take; it is like a drop of a huge ocean. It is like a vast garden, however much we have cut, it is as if we had cut but one flower.

His Attitude Towards Food

Shah Naqshband, may God sanctify his soul, was in the highest states of the denial of desire for this world. He followed the way of piety, especially in the act of eating. He took all kinds of precautions in regard to his food. He would only eat from the barley he had grown himself. He would harvest it, grind it, make the dough, knead it, and bake it himself. All the scholars and seekers of his time made their way to his house in order to eat from his table and to partake of the blessings of his food.

He reached such a perfection of austerity that in winter he only put old and worn carpets on the floor of his house, which gave no protection from the bitter cold. In summer he put very thin woven mats on the ground. He loved the poor and the needy. He urged his followers to earn money through lawful means, that is, by the sweat of their brows. He urged them to spend that money on the poor. He cooked for the poor and invited them to his table. He served them with his own holy hands and urged them to remain always in the Presence of God, Almighty and Exalted. If they put a bite of food in their mouth in a heedless way, he would inform them, through his state of vision, what they had done and urge them to keep remembrance of God while eating.

He taught that one of the most important doors to the Presence of God is to eat with awareness. The food gives the body strength, and to eat with consciousness gives the body purity.

Once he was invited to the city of Ghaziut where one of his followers had prepared a dinner for him. When they sat for dinner, he did not eat. His host was surprised. Shah Naqshband said, "O my son, I am wondering how you prepared this food. From the time you kneaded the dough and cooked it, until you served it, you were in a state of anger. The food is mixed with that anger. If we eat that food, Satan will find a way to enter through it and to spread his evil throughout our bodies."

Another time he was invited to the city of Herat by King Husayn. The king was very happy at the visit of Shah Naqshband and prepared a great feast for him. He invited all his ministers, the shaykhs of his kingdom, and all his noblemen. He said, "Eat from this food. It is pure food. I made it from the lawful earnings which I inherited from my father." Everyone ate except Shah Naqshband, prompting the Shaykh al-Islam of that time, Qutb ad-Din, to ask, "O our shaykh, why are you not eating?" Shah Naqshband said, "I have a judge to whom I go for counsel. I asked him and that judge told me, 'O my son, about this food there are two possibilities. If this food is not lawful and you do not eat, when you are questioned, you may say I came to the table of the king, but I did not eat. Then you are safe because you did not eat. But if you eat and you are asked, then what are you going to say? Then you are not safe.'"

At that time, Qutb ad-Din was so overcome by these words that he began to shake. He had to ask the king's permission to stop eating. The King was very confused and asked, "What shall we do with all this food?" Shah Naqshband said, "If there is any doubt about the lawfulness of the food, it is better to send it to the poor. Their need will make it lawful for them. If, as you say, it is lawful, then there is more blessing in giving it as charity to those who need than in feasting those who do not."

He fasted most of his days. If a guest came to him and he had something to offer him, he would sit with him, break his fast and eat. He told his followers that the Companions of the Prophet ﷺ did the same. Shaykh Abul Hasan al-Kharqani said in his book, *The Principles of the Way and the Principles of Reaching Reality*:

> Keep harmony with friends, but not in sinning. This means that if you were fasting and someone comes to you as a friend, you must sit with him and eat with him in order to keep proper company with him. One of the principles of fasting, or of any worship, is to conceal what one is doing. If one reveals it, for example by saying to the guest, "I am fasting," then pride may enter and ruin the fast. This is the reason behind the principle.

One day he was given a cooked fish as a gift. There were in his presence many poor people, among them a very pious boy who was fasting. Shah Naqshband gave the fish to the poor and told them, "Sit and eat," and he told the boy who was fasting, "Sit and eat." The boy refused. He told him again, "Break your fast and eat," but he refused. He asked him, "What if I give you one of my days of Ramadan? Will you sit and eat?" Again he refused. He told him, "What if I give you my whole Ramadan?" Still he refused. He said, "Bayazid al-Bistami was once burdened with a person similar to you." After that the boy was seen running after the worldly life, never fasting and never worshipping.

The incident to which Shah Naqshband was referring occurred one day when Shaykh Abu Turab an-Naqshabi visited Bayazid al-Bistami. His servant offered him food. Abu Turab said to the servant, "Come, and sit with me, and eat." The servant said, "No. I am fasting." He said, "Eat, and God will give you the reward of fasting for one year." He refused. He said, "Come and eat, I will pray to God that He give you the reward of two years of fasting." Then Shaykh Bayazid said, "Leave him. He has been dropped from God's care." Later his life degenerated, and he became a thief.

His Miracles and Generosity

Shah Naqshband's state is beyond description and the extent of his knowledge cannot be described. One of the greatest miracles was his very existence. He often hid his actions in order not to display miraculous power. Many of his miracles, however, were recorded.

Shah Naqshband, may God bless his soul, said:

One day I went out with Muhammad Zahid to the desert. He was a truthful disciple, and we had a pick axe with which we were digging. As we were working with the pick, we were discussing such deep states of knowledge that we threw aside the pick and entered deeper into spiritual knowledge. We were going deeper and deeper until the conversation led us to the nature of worship. He asked me, "O my shaykh, to what limit does worship reach?" I said, "Worship reaches such perfection that the worshipper can say to someone 'die,' and that person will die." Without thinking, I pointed at Muhammad Zahid. Immediately he fell down dead. He was in the state of death from sunrise until the midday. It was very hot. I was very anxious because his body was deteriorating from the excessive heat. I pulled him under the shade of a tree, and I sat there contemplating the matter. As I was contemplating, an inspiration came to my heart from the Divine Presence telling me to say to him, "O Muhammad, live!" I said it to him three times. In response, his soul slowly began to enter his body, and life slowly began to return to him. He gradually returned to his original state. I went to my shaykh and told him what had happened. He said, "O my son, God gave you a secret that He has given to no one else."

Shaykh Alauddin al-Attar said:

Once the king of Transoxiana, Sultan Abd Allah Kazgan, came to Bukhara. He decided to go hunting around Bukhara, and many people accompanied him. Shah Bahauddin Naqshband was in a nearby village. When the people went out hunting, Shah Naqshband went to the top of a hill and sat there. While sitting there, it came to his heart that God gave much honor to saints. Because of that honor, all kings of this world *should* bow to them. That thought had not yet passed from his heart before a horseman with a crown on his head, like a king, came into his presence and dismounted from his horse. With great humility he greeted Shah Naqshband and stood in his presence in the most polite manner. He bowed to the shaykh but the shaykh did not look at him. He kept him standing one hour. Finally, Shah Naqshband looked up and said, "What are you doing here?" He said, "I am the king, Sultan Kazgan. I was out hunting, and I smelled a very beautiful smell. I followed it here and I found you sitting in the midst of a powerful light." His very thought, "All kings of this world should bow to the saints," had instantly become reality. That is how God honors the thoughts of his saints.

One of his followers who was serving him in the city of Merv reported:

One day I wished to go see my family in Bukhara, having received news that my brother Shamsuddin had died. I needed to take permission from my shaykh to go. I spoke with Amir Husayn, the Prince of Herat, to ask permission on my behalf from Shah Naqshband. On their way back from the Friday congregational prayer, Amir Husayn told him about the death of my brother and that I wanted permission to go to my family. He said, "No, it is impossible. How can you say he is dead when I can see him alive? More than that, I can even smell his smell. I am going to bring him here now." He had hardly finished his words before my brother appeared. He approached the shaykh, kissed his hand and greeted Amir Husayn. I hugged my brother and there was great happiness among us.

Shaykh Alauddin Attar said:

Shaykh Shah Naqshband was once sitting in a large association in Bukhara speaking about the unveiling of the state of vision. He said, "My best friend, Mawla Arif, who lives in Khwarazm, (400 miles from Bukhara) has left Khwarazm for the government building, and he reached the station of the horse-carriages. When he reached that station, he stayed there for a moment and now he is going back to his house in Khwarazm. He is not continuing on to Saray. This is how a saint can see in his station of gnosis." Everyone was surprised at this story, but we all knew that he was a great saint, so we recorded the time and the day. One day Mawla Arif came from Khwarazm to Bukhara and we told him about that incident. He was very surprised, and he said, "In truth, that is exactly what happened."

Some scholars from Bukhara traveled to Iraq with some followers of Shah Naqshband and they reached the city of Simnan. They heard that there was a blessed man named Sayyid Mahmud, who was a disciple of the shaykh. They went to visit his house and asked him, "How did you become connected with the shaykh?" He said:

One night I saw the Prophet ﷺ in a dream, sitting in a very nice place, and beside him sat a man of majestic appearance. I said to the Prophet ﷺ, with complete respect and humbleness, "O Messenger of God, I was not honored to be your companion in your lifetime. What can I do in my lifetime that will approximate that honor?" He told me, "O my son, if you want to be honored by being our friend and to sit with us and be blessed, you have to follow my son, Shah Bahauddin Naqshband." I then asked, "Who is Shah Bahauddin Naqshband?" He said to me, "Do you see that person sitting next to me? This is the one. Keep company with him." I had never seen him before. When I awoke, I wrote his name and his description in a book that I have in my library.

Much time passed after that dream, until one day, while I was standing in a shop, I saw a man with a luminous and majestic appearance come into the shop and sit on a chair. When I saw him, I remembered what happened in the dream. Immediately, I asked him if he would honor me by coming to my house and staying with me. He accepted and began to walk in front of me while I followed. I was shy to walk in front of him, even to lead the way to my house. He did not look at me once, but took the path directly to my house. I was about to say, "This is my house," when he said, "This is your house." He walked inside and went straight to my special room. He said, "This is your room." He went into the closet and he took one book from among hundreds of books. He gave me the book and asked me, "What did you write in this?"

It was what I had seen in the dream. Immediately a state of unconsciousness overtook me, and I fainted from the light that poured into my heart. When I awoke, I asked him if he would accept me. He was Shah Bahauddin Naqshband.

Shaykh Muhammad Zahid said:

In the beginning of my traveling on the Path, I was sitting beside him one day, in the spring season. A craving for watermelon entered my heart. He looked at me and said, "Muhammad Zahid, go to that river near us, and bring us what you see, and we will eat it." Immediately, I went to the river. The water was very cold. I reached into it and found a watermelon under the water, very fresh, as if it had just been cut from the vine. I was very happy and I took the watermelon and said, "O my shaykh, please accept me."

One of his followers reported the following about a visit to him:

Before the visit, I asked Shaykh Shadi, one of the senior disciples, to advise me. He said to me, "O my brother, when you go to visit the shaykh or when you are sitting in the presence of the shaykh, be careful not to place your legs so that your feet face him." As soon as I left Ghaziut on my way to Qasr al-Arifan, I found a tree and lay down under it with my legs extended. Unfortunately, an animal came and bit me on the leg. Later I fell back asleep in pain. As I was sleeping again, an animal bit me. Suddenly I realized that I had made a great mistake. I had extended my feet in the direction of the shaykh. I immediately repented, and the animal stopped biting me.

Once Shah Naqshband was pushed to show miraculous power in order to defend one of his successors in Bukhara, Shaykh Muhammad Parsa. This occurred at the time when Shaykh Muhammad Shamsuddin al-Jazairi came to Samarkand, in the time of King Mirza Aleg Beg, to determine the correctness of the chains of transmission in Traditions of the Prophet ﷺ. Some of the jealous and corrupt scholars had complained that Shaykh Muhammad Parsa was giving narrations of Traditions whose chains of transmission were not known. They told Shamsuddin, "If you try to correct that problem, God will give you a great reward." Shaykh Muhammad Shamsuddin asked the Sultan to order Shaykh Muhammad Parsa to appear before him. The Shaykh al-Islam of Bukhara, Husamuddin an-Nahawi, was there, along with many scholars and imams from the area.

Shah Naqshband came with Muhammad Parsa to the meeting. Shaykh Husamuddin asked Muhammad Parsa about a Tradition. Muhammad Parsa narrated the Tradition along with its chain of transmission. Shaykh al-Jazairi said, "There is no error in the Tradition, but the chain is incorrect. Upon hearing this, the jealous scholars were happy. They asked Muhammad Parsa to give another chain for the tradition. He did, and it was again said that it was not correct. They asked for another chain, and he gave it, and still they found fault with it.

Shah Naqshband interfered, because he knew that whatever chain he gave they would say it was incorrect. He inspired Muhammad Parsa to

Bukhara took care of his prestigious school and mosque, expanding them and increasing their religious endowments. After the fall of Communism in Central Asia, the center of learning he established has once again been restored to prominence.

Abd al-Wahhab ash-Shaarani, the spiritual pole of his time said, "When the shaykh was buried in his grave, a window to Paradise was opened for him, making his grave a Paradise from Heaven. Two beautiful spiritual beings entered his presence and greeted him and said, 'From the time that God created us until now, we have waited for this moment to serve you.' He replied, 'I do not look to anything other than Him. I do not need you, but I need my Lord.'"

Shah Naqshband left behind many successors, the two most honorable among them being Shaykh Muhammad ibn Muhammad Alauddin al-Khwarazmi al-Bukhari al-Attar and Shaykh Muhammad ibn Muhammad ibn Mahmud al-Hafizi, known as Muhammad Parsa, the author of *Risala Qudsiyya*. It is to the first that Shah Naqshband passed on the secret of the Golden Chain. ۞

18. Alauddin al-Attar ق

Alauddin al-Attar was a star from among the perfect saints. He was one of the scholars who act on what they know. He was known as "the Fruit of the Tree of Divine Knowledge," "the Life of Spiritual Knowledge," "the Eraser of Darkness," "the Guide of the Noble and Common People Alike," "the Fountain that Never Dries Up," and "the Best Guide to Enlightenment on the Path to the Lord."

Your image is constantly before my eyes,
Your remembrance always upon my lips;
The thought of You forever in my heart.
Where can You hide from me?
—Attributed to Mansur al-Hallaj [59]

---

[59] Mansur al-Hallaj, world-renowned tenth-century Sufi mystic and martyr.

Alauddin al-Attar left everything that he had inherited from his family and devoted himself to study in the religious schools of Bukhara. He became accomplished in all Islamic arts, especially in the knowledge of Sufism and the Islamic sciences.

He was foremost in removing the thorns of falsehood from the path of Truth. He stood in the center of the realm of the spiritual poles. He carried the burden of the spiritual caliphate. He raised the souls of his brothers until the whole universe was calling him and remembering him. The external and internal knowledge of religion flourished because of his truthfulness.

He asked Shah Naqshband for his daughter's hand in marriage. Shah Naqshband's answer came one day after midnight, when awakening from his sleep in Qasr al-Arifan, he went quickly to the school in Bukhara where Alauddin lived. There he found everyone asleep except Alauddin, who was up reading the Holy Quran by the light of a tiny oil lamp. He came up behind him and tapped him on the shoulder, but Alauddin did not respond. He prodded him more, but still he did not react. Then, through his spiritual vision, Shah Naqshband perceived that Alauddin was not present, but was in the Divine Presence. He then called him spiritually, and Alauddin immediately looked up and said, "O my shaykh." Shah Naqshband said, "I had a dream in which the Prophet ﷺ accepted your proposal for my daughter. For that reason I have come to you by myself, late at night, to inform you of the good news."

Alauddin said, "O my shaykh, I have nothing to spend on your daughter or myself, because I am very poor, having given all my inheritance to my brothers." Shah Naqshband replied, "O my son, whatever God has written for you on the Day of Promises will accrue to you. So do not worry, God will provide."

He said:

> One day a shaykh asked me, "How is your heart?" I said, "I do not know how my heart is." He said, "I know my heart, and it is like the moon in the third night." I related this story to Shah Naqshband who said, "He answered according to his heart." When he said this, he stepped on my foot and pressed on it. Immediately, I left myself and I saw that everything in this world and this universe was in my heart. When I awoke from that state of unconsciousness, he was still standing on my foot. He said, "If the heart is like that, then no one can describe

it. What do you think now about the holy Tradition, 'Neither My earth nor My Heavens can contain Me, but the heart of the Believer contains Me.' This is one of the hidden secrets you must come to understand."

Then Shah Naqshband took full responsibility for him. He raised him from one state to another, and prepared him to appear in the Divine Presence, and to ascend the lofty towers of spiritual knowledge, and leave behind all kinds of ignorance in order to reach the state of Reality. He became unique among the many followers of Bahauddin Naqshband. The Shaykh ordered him, during his lifetime, to enlighten some of the Shaykh's followers also. Thus Shaykh Muhammad Parsa followed him as well. Shaykh Muhammad Parsa wrote that he heard from Shaykh Alauddin, "I was given such power by my shaykh, Shah Naqshband, that if I were to focus on everyone in this universe, I would raise all of them to the state of perfection."

Once the scholars of Bukhara had a disagreement concerning the possibility of seeing God in this world. Some of them denied the possibility and some of them affirmed it. All of them were followers of Shaykh Alauddin. They came to him and said, "We are asking you to be judge in this matter." He answered, "Those of you who have denied the possibility of seeing God in this life, stay with me three days, keeping ablution at all times and remaining silent." He kept them in his presence for three days, directing his spiritual power on them, until they all beheld a very powerful state, causing them to faint. When they regained consciousness, they came to him crying out, "We believe and we confirm that it is true!" and kissed his feet. They told him, "We accept what you said, that it is possible to see God in this life." They devoted themselves to him, never leaving him and making it their custom to kiss the threshold of his door. They composed the following verse:

Out of blindness they asked,

"How can we reach the Divine?"

Put in their hands the candles of purity.

They will know that the possibility

Of seeing is not impossible.

Shaykh Alauddin was very dear and special to Shah Naqshband, just as Joseph عليه السلام had been dear to the heart of his father, Jacob عليه السلام.

From the Light of His Sayings

The intention of seclusion is to leave the earthly connection and to direct the self to the heavenly Truth.

It is said that the seeker of external knowledge must hold tight to the Rope of God, and the seeker of internal knowledge must hold tight to God.

LEVELS OF ANNIHILATION

When God makes you forget both worldly power and the heavenly kingdom, this is absolute annihilation. If He makes you forget absolute annihilation, it is the essence of absolute annihilation.

PROPER CONDUCT

You have to be at the level of the people around you and to hide your state from them, because the Prophet ﷺ said, *"I have been ordered to speak with people according to what their hearts can contain."*

Beware of hurting the hearts of Sufis. If you want their company, you must first learn how to behave in their presence or you are going to harm yourself, for their way is a very delicate way. It is said, "There is no place in Our Way for one who does not have good manners."

If you think you are behaving well then you are wrong, because seeing your own behavior as good is itself a form of pride.

ON VISITING GRAVES

The benefit of visiting the graves of your shaykhs depends on the knowledge you have of them.

To be near the graves of pious people has a good influence, but it is better to direct yourself to their souls. This carries with it a higher spiritual influence. The Prophet ﷺ said, *"Send prayers for me wherever you are."* This means that you can reach him wherever you are. It applies to His saints also, because they take their power from him. The proper way of visiting graves is to direct yourself to God and to make these souls your means to God, humbling yourself to His Creation. You humble yourself externally to them and internally to God. To bow before human beings is not allowed unless you look on them as appearances of God. Then that humbleness will not be directed to them, but it will be directed to the One Who is appearing in them, and that is God.

THE BEST *DHIKR*

The way of contemplation and meditation is higher and more perfect than the way of *dhikr* by *"la ilaha ill-Allah."* The seeker, through contemplation and meditation, can reach the internal knowledge and will be able to enter the heavenly kingdom. He will be authorized to look at God's Creation and he will know what is passing in their hearts, even the slightest gossip or whispering. He will be authorized to enlighten their hearts with the light from the essence of the essence of the state of Oneness.

PROTECTING THE HEART

Silence is the best state, except under three conditions: you must not keep silent in the face of bad gossip attacking your heart; you must not keep silent in directing your heart to the remembrance of God; and you must not keep silent when the vision inside your heart orders you to speak.

To protect your heart from evil thoughts is very difficult, and I protected my heart for twenty years without letting in a single whisper.

The best deed in this Way is to punish the whispering and gossip in the chest.

I was unhappy with some of my followers, because they did not try to keep the state of vision that appeared to them.

LOVE OF THE SHAYKH

If the heart of the follower is full of the love of the shaykh, this love replacing all other loves of the heart, then the heart will be able to receive the transmission of the heavenly knowledge, which has no beginning and no end.

The disciple has to tell all his states to his shaykh. He has to believe that he will never reach his goal except through the satisfaction and love of his shaykh. He must seek that satisfaction and he must know that all

> doors are blocked, internal and external, except the one door, which is his shaykh. He has to sacrifice himself for the sake of his shaykh. Even if he has the highest knowledge and the highest capacity for struggle, he must leave all that and feel as though he has nothing before his shaykh. The seeker must give the shaykh authority in all his affairs, religious and worldly, in such a way that he has no will before the will of his shaykh. The duty of the shaykh is to look at the daily activities of the disciple and to advise and correct him, his living and his religion, to help him find the best way to reach his reality.
>
> To visit saints is an obligatory *Sunnah*, a duty on every seeker, at least every day, or every other day, while keeping the limits of respect for the shaykh. If the distance is great between you and your shaykh, visit him at least every one or two months. Do not rely only on your connection with his heart, lest you become disconnected.
>
> I guarantee to anyone who seeks this Way, if he imitates the shaykh with sincerity, he will eventually find its reality. Shah Naqshband ordered me to imitate him, and whatever I did in imitation of him immediately brought its results.

However, he also warned:

> The masters of our Way cannot be known except in the station of colors and changes. Whoever imitates their behavior in that station will succeed. Whoever imitates their behavior in their station of perfection, however, will be corrupted. He will be safe from corruption only if his master has mercy on him and reveals to him the reality of that station.

What he means, and God knows best, is that the seeker cannot reach perfection until he has been perfected. The station of color and changes (*maqam at-talwin*) is the one in which the seeker struggles hard by fasting, by worshipping, by seclusion, and by maintaining steadfastness in his love and respect for his master from one difficulty to another. Imitating his master in this manner will bring him success, because his master excels in all these efforts. However, if he imitates the master when the latter is in his state of Perfection, he will be in danger, just as if he tried to fly without first growing wings. It is necessary for the seeker to climb the mountain first before he enjoys the view at the top.

To climb the mountain, the seeker must journey from the lower world to the Divine Presence. He must travel from the ego's world of sensual reality to the soul's consciousness of the Divine Reality. To make progress on this journey, the seeker must bring into his heart the picture of his shaykh, as it is the most powerful means of detaching himself from the hold of the senses. The shaykh becomes, in his heart, the mirror of the Absolute Essence. If he is successful, the state of self-effacement or absence from the world of the senses appears in him. To the degree that this state increases in him, his attachment to the world of the senses will weaken and disappear, and the station of the absolute void of sensing other-than-God will dawn on him. The highest degree of this station is called annihilation. Thus Shah Naqshband counseled his disciples, "When that state of self-effacement comes on me, leave me alone and give yourself also to that state and accept its rights on us."

Of this journey, Shaykh Alauddin said to his disciples:

> The shortest path to our goal, which is God, Almighty and Exalted, is for God to lift the veil from the Essence of the Face of His Oneness that appears in all creation. He does this with the state of erasure and annihilation in His Absolute Oneness, until His Majestic Essence dawns upon and eliminates consciousness of anything other than Him. This is the end of the journey of seeking God and the beginning of another journey.
>
> At the end of the journey of seeking and the state of attraction comes the state of self-effacement and annihilation. This is the goal of all mankind as God mentioned in the Quran. *"I did not create jinn and mankind except to worship me."* (51:56) Worship here means perfect knowledge.

On the 2nd of the month of Rajab, 802 AH/1400 CE, Alauddin said, "I am going to leave you to go to the other life, and no one can stop me." He died on the 20th of Rajab, 802 AH/1400 CE. He was buried in the city of Jaganyan, one of the suburbs of Bukhara. He passed his secret of the Golden Chain to one of his many caliphs, Grandshaykh Yaqub al-Charkhi. ۞

19. Yaqub al-Charkhi ق

Shaykh Yaqub al-Charkhi appeared among human beings dressed in the two kinds of knowledge: the external and the internal. People followed him because his way was the best, for he had inherited knowledge of the unseen from the Prophet ﷺ.

I have known God and I see none other than Him
So that the 'other' in us is shut out.
Since I realized unity, I no longer fear separation;
This day I have arrived and am united.
—Anonymous [60]

---

[60] Quoted in Shaykh al-Arabi ad-Darqawi, *Letters of a Sufi Master*.

Shaykh Yaqub al-Charkhi revived spirituality within the Divine Law, and he revived the Divine Law within spirituality. His conduct and character were so refined that he reflected the attributes of God to all people.

He was born in the city of Charkh, a suburb of Garnin, between the two cities of Kandahar and Kabul, in Transoxiana. In his youth, he went to the city of Herat to educate himself. He then went to Egypt, where he learned the sciences of the Divine Law and logic. He memorized the Quran as well as 500,000 Traditions, both the correct and the false.

One of his teachers was Shihabuddin ash-Shirwani, known as the Encyclopedia of the Age. He continued his education until he reached the level where he could give legal decisions on any matter that faced Muslims. He was capable of independent legal reasoning in both kinds of knowledge, external and internal. He returned to his country and followed Bahauddin Naqshband and then Alauddin al-Attar to educate himself in the hidden knowledge.

A Scholar of Saints and a Saint of Scholars

Of his teacher in spiritual knowledge and of his initiation, he said:

> I was sincere and loyal in my love for Shaykh Bahauddin before I even knew him. When I received permission to employ independent reasoning and to issue edicts, I went back to my country, and I went to visit him and pay my respects. I said to him, with complete humbleness and obedience, "Please keep me always in the essence of your vision." He said, "You came to me on your way back to your country of Charkh?" I said to him, "I love you and I am your servant, because you have the greatest fame and you are accepted by everyone." He said, "That is not a good enough reason for me to accept you."
>
> Then I replied, "O my shaykh, the Prophet ﷺ said in an authentic Tradition, if God loves someone, he will influence the hearts of people to love that person as well." Then Bahauddin smiled and said, "I am the spiritual inheritor of Azizan. What you say is true." When he said this phrase, I was so surprised, because I had heard in a dream, one month before, a voice saying to me, "Be the disciple of Azizan." At the time, I didn't know who Azizan was. But he mentioned the word as if

he had been aware of the dream. Then I took his leave. He said, "You may go, but let me give you a gift by which you will remember me." He gave me his turban. He said, "When you see this or use it you will remember me, and when you remember me you will find me, and when you find me you will find your Way to God."

He told me, "On your way back to your country of Balkh, if you meet Mawlana Tajuddin al-Kawlaki, keep your heart from gossiping in his presence, because he is a great saint and he will scold you." I said to myself, "I am going back to Herat by way of Balkh, but I am not going through Kawlak, where Mawlana Tajuddin is living. So I do not think that I will see him." But, on the way, the caravan with whom I was traveling was obliged to change course and to go by way of Kawlak. I remembered the words of Shaykh Bahauddin, "If you pass by Kawlak, then visit Shaykh Tajuddin al-Kawlaki." It came to my heart that Shaykh Bahauddin caused the event to occur so that I would go to visit the shaykh. When we arrived in Kawlak, it was very dark, with no stars in the sky. I went to the mosque to ask about Mawlana Tajuddin Kawlaki. One person came to me from behind a pillar and said to me, "Are you Yaqub al-Charkhi?" I was astonished. He said, "Do not be surprised. I knew you before you came here. My shaykh, Shaykh Bahauddin, sent me to take you to Shaykh Tajuddin al-Kawlaki."

On the way to see him, we met an old man, who said, "O my son, our way is full of surprises. Whoever enters it cannot understand it. The seeker must leave his mind behind." We then entered the presence of Mawlana Tajuddin, and it was very difficult to keep my heart free from any gossip. Mawlana Tajuddin gave me a piece of spiritual knowledge that he possessed and which I had never heard before. All that I had learned was nothing compared to this knowledge. I was so happy with my shaykh, Shaykh Bahauddin, and the way in which he arranged for me to meet with Mawlana Tajuddin, that my love for him increased greatly.

After I reached my country, from time to time, I would go to Bukhara to visit Shaykh Bahauddin. In Bukhara, there was a person lost in the Divine Love who was very well known and to whom people went for blessing. One day when I intended to visit Shaykh Bahauddin, I

Shaykh Bahauddin continued, "I have been ordered by God, Almighty and Exalted, and by the Prophet ﷺ, and by my shaykh, not to accept anyone in my way unless God, the Prophet ﷺ, and my shaykh accept that person. So I will look tonight to see if you are accepted." This was the most difficult day of my life. I felt I would melt from the fear that they would not accept me on this Way. I performed the dawn prescribed prayer behind him, and I was so afraid. When he looked into my heart, everything disappeared and he was appearing everywhere. I heard his voice saying, "May God bless you. He accepts you and I accept you."

Then he began to recite the names of the Masters of the Golden Chain from the Prophet ﷺ to Abu Bakr ؓ, Salman ؓ, Qasim ؓ, Jafar ؓ, Tayfur, Abul Hasan, Abu Ali, Yusuf, Abul Abbas, Abd al-Khaliq. Every shaykh he mentioned appeared in front of him. When he mentioned Abd al-Khaliq, he stopped and Abd al-Khaliq appeared in front of me. He said, "Give him to me now," and he taught me more of the awareness of numbers. He told me that knowledge came to him through Khidr ؑ. Then my shaykh continued reciting the chain: Arif, Mahmud, Ali Ramitani, Muhammad Baba as-Samasi, Sayyid Amir Kulal. They each appeared to me by turn and gave me initiation. I continued serving him, standing at his door, learning from him, until he gave me permission to be a guide to people on this Way. He said to me, "This Way is going to be the greatest happiness for you."

Ubayd Allah al-Ahrar reported that Yaqub had said to him, "O my son, I received an order from Shah Naqshband to accompany Shaykh Alauddin al-Attar. By the order of my shaykh, I was in his company as his disciple until Alauddin's death in Jaganyan in Bukhara. By the blessing of his companionship, my state was elevated and my training completed."

Ubayd Allah al-Ahrar said that Shaykh Yaqub al-Charkhi and Shaykh Zainuddin al-Khawafi were like brothers when they studied together in Egypt under the teaching of the scholar, Shaykh Shihabuddin ash-Shirwani. Shaykh Zainuddin said that Shaykh Yaqub al-Charkhi disappeared and reappeared during his lectures. This miracle was the result of the state of complete self-effacement in the Presence of God Almighty. This was his state in Egypt, until he came and followed Shah Naqshband and Shaykh Alauddin, and then he reached a state of perfection.

Shaykh Yaqub al-Charkhi died in the village of Hulgatu, on the 5th of Safar, 851 AH/1447 CE. He had many caliphs. He passed the secret of the Naqshbandi Order to Shaykh Ubayd Allah al-Ahrar, may God bless his secret. ۞

20. Ubayd Allah al-Ahrar ق

Shaykh Ubayd Allah al-Ahrar was the pole of the circle of the knowers of God, an ocean of knowledge that would never be exhausted, even though all of creation was to drink from it to quench its spiritual thirst.

As soon as I remember You—my Secret, my Heart,
And my spirit starts to disturb me during Your remembrance.
Until an observer from You called to me,
"Beware, beware—of remembrance beware."
Do you not see the Real? His proofs appeared.
The meaning of totality joined Your meaning.
The rememberers when remembering Him
Are more forgetful than the ones who forget to remember Him.
The Prophet ﷺ said, "The one who knows God,
His tongue is paralysed."
—Anonymous[61]

---

[61] Quoted in Shaykh al-Alawi, *Knowledge of God*, pp. 174-175.

Shaykh Ubayd Allah al-Ahrar was a king who owned the pure light of the Unique Essence and released it from its captivity in the hidden to spread it among all knowers. He unveiled the hidden side of the moons of the Attributes of the Lord from the cradle until he reached his perfected state. He was given authority as a youth and set to work to receive the secret of secrets and to unveil the veils. He never looked at a worldly desire.

He progressed until he reached the highest states of sainthood, where knowledge of the Essence of the unseen is bestowed and the secret of Absolute nothingness becomes revealed. Then he traveled on from Absolute Nothingness to Absolute Light. God revived this Order through him during his time, and He supported him with His Favor. He made him a golden link in this Golden Chain, and He made him one of the most elevated inheritors of the Prophet ﷺ. Shaykh Ubayd Allah tried his best to wash from the hearts of people the dirt and darkness that had covered them. He became a sun to light the way of the seekers to the state of certainty and the hidden treasure of spiritual knowledge.

He was born in the village of Shash in the year 806 AH/1404 CE, in the month of Ramadan. It was related that, before he was born, his father began to exhibit a tremendous state of renunciation, which made him leave all worldly actions and enter seclusion. He nearly gave up sleep and food, disconnected himself from people, and took to practicing the spiritual way of the Sufi Path. While in this spiritual state, his wife became pregnant with Ubayd Allah. That is one reason for the latter's high station; his spiritual training began while in his mother's womb. When his mother became pregnant, his father's unusual spiritual state ended and he returned to his normal life.

Before Ubayd Allah was born, the following took place in which his great station was foretold. Shaykh Muhammad as-Sirbili said:

> When Shaykh Nizamuddin al-Khamush as-Samarqandi was sitting in my father's house, meditating, he suddenly screamed in a tremendous voice. This made everyone afraid. He said, "I saw a vision of an enormous man coming to me from the east, and I could see nothing in the world except for him. That person is named Ubayd Allah, and he is going to be the greatest shaykh of his time. God is going to make the whole world subject to him, and I hope I will be among his followers."

The Beginning of His State and the State of His Beginning

The signs of happiness were visible on him in his childhood. The light of guidance appeared in his face. One of his relatives said, "He did not accept the breast of his mother for nursing until she was clean of any post-partum bleeding and discharge."

Ubayd Allah reported:

> I still recall what I heard when I was one year of age. From the age of three years, I was in the Presence of God. When I studied the Quran with my teacher, my heart was in God's Presence. I thought that all people were this way.
>
> One day during the winter, I went out while it was raining and my feet and shoes sank into the mud. It was very cold. I tried to pull my feet out of the mud. I realized that my heart was in big danger, because for that moment I had forgotten to remember God. I immediately began to ask for forgiveness.

He was raised in the home of his uncle, Ibrahim ash-Shashi, who was the greatest scholar of his time. He taught Ubayd Allah very well and when the latter completed his training, his uncle sent him from Tashkent to Samarqand.

He said to his uncle, "Whenever I go to study I feel sick." He replied, "O my son, I know the state you are now in. So I am not going to force you to do anything. Do as you like. You are free."

Ubayd Allah narrates:

> One day while in that state, I went to visit the grave of Shaykh Abi Bakr al-Kaffal. I took a nap and I had a vision. I saw Jesus عليه السلام in the vision. I rushed to bow down and kiss his feet. He raised my head and said, "O my son, do not become sad, I am taking the responsibility of raising you and educating you." That vision ended. I related the vision to many people. One of them was an expert in the interpretation of spiritual states.
>
> He explained it this way: "You are going to be very high in the science of medicine." I did not like his explanation. I told him, "I know better what the vision represents: Jesus عليه السلام in spiritual knowledge represents the state of the Living Ones. Anyone who reaches that state among the saints will be given the title the Living One. God mentioned in the Holy

Quran a verse describing them: *'Truly, they are alive with their Lord, receiving sustenance.'* (3:169) Since he promised to raise me in that line, it means I am going to reach the state of the Living-Hearted." It was not much longer before I received that state from the Living One in my heart.

I saw Prophet Muhammad ﷺ in a grand vision. A very large crowd accompanied him, standing at the foot of a mountain. He looked at me and he said, "O Ubayd Allah, lift up this mountain and take it up to that other mountain." I knew that no one can carry a mountain, but it was a direct order from the Prophet ﷺ. I lifted the mountain, and I carried it to the place he asked me. Then the Prophet ﷺ looked at me and said, "I knew that this power was in you. I wanted people to know about it and to see the power you are carrying." From this I knew that I would be the means of guiding a great many people to this Way.

When I was young I once sought the spiritual aid of a roaming Turk pleading, "Please take notice of me and send a glance of care in my direction!" The man was astonished at my request. He said, "I am a simple desert nomad who barely knows how to clean myself." I said, "I have learned that one must give respect to every person one meets: he may be Khidr; and to give attention to devotion every night for any night may be the Night of Power." He raised his hand and implored God on my behalf on account of which I received many Divine graces.

One night I saw Shah Naqshband come to me and work on my internal state. When he went, I followed him. He stopped and looked at me. He said, "May God bless you, my son. You are going to have a very high position."

I followed the spiritual pole, Nizamuddin al-Khamush, in Samarqand. Then when I was twenty-two years old, I went to Bukhara where I met the great Knower, Shaykh Sirajuddin al-Birmisi. He lives four miles from Bukhara. When I visited him, he looked at me intensely, and he wanted me to stay with him. But my heart was telling me to travel to Bukhara. I only stayed with him briefly. He worked in the day making clay pots, and at night he sat in his prayer room, on the floor. After finishing his night prayer, he would sit until the dawn prayer. I never saw him sleep during the day or the night. I stayed with him seven days, and never did I see him sleep. He was one of the most advanced in both external and internal knowledge.

Then I moved to Bukhara, where I kept company with Shaykh Jamaluddin ash-Shashi and with Shaykh Alauddin al-Ghujdawani. They were among the followers of Shah Naqshband, Alauddin al-Attar, and Yaqub al-Charkhi. Shaykh Alauddin al-Ghujdawani would sometimes disappear completely while lecturing, and then he would reappear. He had an excellent way of speaking. He never stopped making *dhikr* and struggling with his self. I met him when he was ninety years old. I frequented his company. One day I went for a walk to the grave of Shah Naqshband. When I came back I saw Shaykh Alauddin al-Ghujdawani coming halfway to meet me. He said, "I think it is better that you stay with us tonight."

We prayed the night prayer. He offered me dinner. Then he said to me, "O my son, let us keep this night alive." He sat cross-legged, and I sat behind him. He was in perfect meditation and *dhikr*. He never moved right or left. I know through my spiritual knowledge that people in that state must be in complete Presence and vision of the Divine. I was surprised that at his age of ninety years, he did not feel tired. By midnight, I myself began to feel exhausted.

I began to make little sounds, hoping he would give me permission to stop. He ignored me. Then I stood up to attract his attention, but he still ignored me. I felt ashamed and went back to my place and sat again. At that time I experienced a vision in which he was pouring into my heart the secret of the knowledge of firmness and constancy. From that time on, I felt that whatever difficulty came my way, I would be able to carry it without any disturbance. I realized that this Order is based completely on the support of the disciple by the shaykh. He taught me a lesson that one must struggle to keep firm and constant in the *dhikr*, because whatever you acquire easily, without difficulty, will not stay with you. Whatever you earn by the sweat of your brow, however, will stay with you.

On another occasion he narrated:

Once I went to visit Shaykh Sayyid Qasim at-Tabrizi in Herat. There I followed an ascetic life leaving everything of the world. When he ate, he would give me the remains. I would eat them without saying anything. One day he looked at me and said, "You are going to be very rich. I am predicting this for you." At that time I had nothing. When I returned to my country, I was a farmer. I had one acre of land on which I kept some cows. In a very short time, his prediction came true. My land increased until I had many farms and herds of cattle. All this wealth did not affect my heart. I dedicated it all for the sake of God."

The Superiority of Service and Conduct

His benevolence, in private and in public, marked his way. He said:

Once I went to the school of Qutb ad-Din as-Sadr in Samar. I found four people there with very high fevers. I began to serve them, cleaning their clothes and feeding them, until I too became infected with the same fever. This did not stop me from serving them. The fever in me increased and increased until I felt that I was going to die. I made an oath to myself, "Let me die, but let these four people be served." The next day I found myself completely cured, while they were still sick.

To help and serve people, in the understanding of this Way, is better than *dhikr* and meditation. Some people think that to do the supererogatory *Sunnah* prayers is better than serving and helping those in need. It is our view, however, that to take care of people and to help them and to show them love is better than anything else.

In this regard, Shah Naqshband often said:

We love to serve, not to be served. When we serve, God is happy with us, and this brings more attraction to the Divine Presence and God opens that state more for us. However, to be served brings pride and weakness to the heart and causes us to recede from the Divine Presence.

Shaykh Ubayd Allah said:

I did not take this spiritual path from books, but I pursued this way through service to people.

Everyone enters through a different door. I entered this spiritual order through the door of service.

He was extremely strict in keeping the right conduct of both external and internal behavior, in his seclusion and among the people. Abu Saad al-Awbahi said:

> I accompanied him for thirty-five years. I was with him continuously. In all that time, I never saw him remove the skin or the seeds of fruit from his mouth, so as not to open his mouth with food inside. When he was sleepy, he would never yawn. I never saw him spit. I never saw him do something that would disgust people. I never even saw him sitting cross-legged; he sat only on his knees, in perfect good conduct.

From His Miraculous Knowledge of the Glorious Quran

Shaykh Ubayd Allah has been often quoted:

> I will tell you a secret from among the many secrets of "*Praise belongs to God, Lord of the Worlds.*" (1:2) The perfect praise is to God, from God. The perfection of praise is when the servant praising Him knows that he is nothing. The servant must know that he is completely empty, no body or form exists for him, no name and no action belongs to him, but he is happy because God, Almighty and Exalted, made His Attributes to appear in him.
>
> What is the meaning of God's saying in the Quran, "*And few of My servants are thankful*?" (34:13) The servant who is truly "thankful" is the one who can see the Grantor of favors to human beings.
>
> What is the meaning of the verse, "*And leave the one who turns away from Our Remembrance*"? (53:29) It indicates that for the one who is in deep contemplation of His Divine Presence and has reached the state of seeing nothing except Him, there is no need for acts of remembrance. If he is in the state of complete vision, do not order him to recite *dhikr* as it might cause coldness in his heart. While he is totally preoccupied with his state of vision, anything else is a distraction and might interrupt the state.
>
> Muhyiddin ibn Arabi said regarding this matter: "By remembrance of God (*dhikr Allah*) sins increase, and visions and hearts will be veiled. To perform *dhikr* is a better state because the sun never sets."
>
> What he means here is that, when the knower is in the Divine Presence and in the state of absolute vision of the Oneness of God, at that time

everything is annihilated in God. For him *dhikr* would be a distraction. The knower exists in His Existence and appears in His Appearance. He is in a state of annihilation in the Divine Presence, whereas in *dhikr Allah* he would be in a state of absence, in need of reminding himself that God is there.

What is the meaning of the verse, *"Be with the trustworthy ones"*? (9:119) This means to keep both their physical and their spiritual company. The seeker may sit in the physical company of the people of Truth, watch them, listen to them, and God will enlighten his heart and will teach him to be like them. To keep the spiritual company of the people of Truth, the seeker must direct his heart toward their spiritual heart. The seeker must keep their company always in his heart until they reflect all their secrets and all their stations on him. He must not turn his face to anything in this world except to the master who will take him to the Presence of God. Love and follow Lovers. Then you will be like them, and their love will reflect on you.

About the *dhikr* with *"la ilaha ill-Allah,"* some of the masters say that *"la ilaha ill-Allah"* is the *dhikr* of the common people, *"Allah"* is the *dhikr* of the preferred people, and *"Huwa"* is the *dhikr* of the preferred of the preferred. But to me *"la ilaha ill-Allah"* is the *dhikr* of the preferred of the preferred, because it has no end. Just as God is the Creator in every moment, so in every moment knowledge increases for the knower. For the knower, his previous state is as nothing once he enters a new, higher state. The knower negates one state as he discards it and affirms a new state as he enters it. This is the manifestation of *"la ilaha ill-Allah"* in the servant of God.

What is meant by the verse, *"O you who believe, Believe!"* (4:136) is, *"O Believers, you are safe."*[62] You are safe because you have connected your heart with God, Almighty and Exalted, and anyone who connects his heart with God is guaranteed safety.

What is the meaning of the verse, *"To whom belongs the Kingdom on this day? To God, the One, the Irresistible?"* (40:16) This verse has had many

---

[62] A reference to the double meaning of the word *aminu* in the verse, which can mean respectively, "Believe!" and "Be safe!"

explanations, but the key is to understand that the kingdom referred to is the heart of the seeker. If God looks at the heart of the seeker with the light of His vision, then He erases the existence of everything except God in his heart. That is what caused Bayazid to say, "Glory to Me for my Greatness!" and Hallaj, "I am the Truth." In that state, the heart is speaking, the heart from which God has erased everything but Himself.

What is the meaning of the verse, *"Every day (moment) He manifests Himself in yet another wondrous way"*? (55:29) This verse relates to two aspects of subsistence after annihilation.

First, the seeker, after he realizes the Truth through his heart and is firmly established in his vision of the Unique Essence of God, Almighty and Exalted, returns from the station of self-effacement to the station of complete presence. His senses become the place of appearances of God's Names and Actions. He finds in himself traces of both the heavenly Attributes and the worldly attributes. He is now able to distinguish between the two different levels of attributes. He is able to obtain benefit from every Attribute and Knowledge.

The second meaning of the verse is that the spiritual traveler finds in himself, in every moment and in every miniscule particle of time, a trace of the Unique Essence of God, which cannot be found outside the state of annihilation in the vision of the One. From one fractional moment to another, he will visualize the parts of the states of the Unique Divine Essence and understand the "connectedness" of everything in the Divine Unity. This connectedness varies in its colors and effects on the person, because it will thus be distinguished according to the time in which it appeared. This state is a very rare state and few saints attain it. Those few in each century who reach it are in a state of great honor, and they observe the meaning of the verse, *"Every day He manifests Himself in yet another wondrous way."* (55:29)

What is the meaning of the Tradition, "Close all doors which face my mosque except the door of Abu Bakr?" Abu Bakr as-Siddiq ؓ existed in a state of perfect love toward the Prophet ﷺ. All doors to the Prophet ﷺ are closed except the door of love, as represented by the open door of Abu Bakr as-Siddiq ؓ. The way of the masters of the Naqshbandi

Order is connected through Abu Bakr as-Siddiq ؓ to the Prophet ﷺ. Love for the master brings the seeker to the door of Abu Bakr ؓ which leads him to the love of the Prophet ﷺ, and from the love of the Prophet ﷺ to love of God, Almighty and Exalted.

The Meaning of *Siddiq*

Shaykh Ubayd Allah narrated:

If a truthful saint (*siddiq*), progressing in the Way of God, is heedless for one moment, he loses in that one moment more than the attainment of a thousand years. Our Order is a Way in which all states are multiplied quickly in every moment. One second may be multiplied to the value of a thousand years.

There was a group of my followers who were reported to the caliph as hypocrites. He was advised, "If you kill them you will be rewarded, because people will be saved from their misguidance." When they were brought before the caliph, he ordered them to be killed. The executioner approached to kill the first one. His companion called out and said, "Leave him and kill me first." When the executioner approached the second, a third one called him and said, "Kill me first." This was repeated for all four of them.

The executioner was very surprised. He asked, "What group do you belong to? It is as if you like to die." They said, "We are the group that prefers others to ourselves. We have reached a state in which for every action we perform, our rewards are doubled and we are increased in spiritual knowledge. Each of us tries his best to do good for someone else, even if only for a brief moment, in order to be raised higher and higher in the eyes of God." The executioner began to shake and could not take their lives. He went to the caliph and explained their state. The caliph immediately had them released and said, "If these are hypocrites, then there are no more People of Truth (*siddiqeen*) left on the earth."

Essential Remembrance

Khaja Ahrar said:

If someone devotes himself totally to remembrance, he will reach such a level, in five or six days, that shouting and quarrelling among people will all seem like remembrance. The same will apply to his own conversation.

The Conduct of the Shaykh and Disciple

One great religious scholar wrote to Shaykh Ubayd Allah, "If you would like to educate any of your disciples, please send me one and I will teach him." He replied, "I do not have any disciples, but if you need a shaykh, I have many."

Sufism requires you to carry everyone's burdens and not to put yours on anyone.

The best time of the day is one hour after the afternoon prescribed prayer. At that time, the disciple must make progress in his worship. One of the best forms of worship at this time is to sit and evaluate the good deeds of the day. If the seeker finds what he has done to be good, he must praise God. If he finds anything wrong, he must ask forgiveness.

One of the best deeds is to follow a perfect shaykh. To follow him and to keep his company will enable the seeker to reach the Divine Presence of God, Almighty and Exalted.

Keeping the company of people of different mentalities causes the people to fall into differences.

Once Bayazid al-Bistami was sitting in association. He found disagreement within the group. He said, "Look carefully among yourselves. Is there anyone who is not from us?" They looked and did not find anyone. He said, "Look again for there is someone who is not from us." They looked again and found the walking stick of someone not from the group. He said, "Throw that away quickly, because it is reflecting its owner and that reflection is causing disagreement."

One day a Sufi joined the group of the scholar, Mawlana Zainuddin at-Tibabi. The Sufi was asked, "Who do you love more, your shaykh or Imam Abu Hanifa?" He answered, "For a long time, I followed the Way of Imam Abu Hanifa very carefully. Yet for all those years, the bad manners that were in my heart would not leave me. After I had followed my shaykh for only a few days, all my bad manners

Once King Abu Saeed had a dream in which he saw the great Imam Ahmad al-Yasawi, one of the caliphs of Yusuf al-Hamadani, asking Ubayd Allah al-Ahrar to read the first chapter of the Quran, *al-Fatiha,* with the intention that God give support to Abu Saeed. In the dream Abu Saeed asked, "Who is that shaykh," and was told, "Ubayd Allah al-Ahrar." When he awoke, he still had the image of the shaykh in his mind. He called his advisor in Tashkent and asked him, "Is there anyone by the name of Ubayd Allah?" He said, "Yes." Then the sultan went to Tashkent to meet him, and he found him in the village of Farqa.

The shaykh came out to meet him. The Sultan recognized him right away. Immediately his heart was attracted. He dismounted and ran to the shaykh, kissing his hands and feet. He asked the shaykh to recite *al-Fatiha* for him. The shaykh said, "O my son, when we need something we recite *Fatiha* once and that is enough. We already did that as you saw in your dream." The king was astonished that the shaykh knew the content of his dream. He then asked permission to move to Samarqand and the shaykh said, "If your intention is to support the Divine Law of the Prophet ﷺ, then I am with you and God will support you." The king said, "This is my intention." The shaykh said, "When you see the enemy coming against you, be patient and do not attack immediately. Wait until you see the crows coming from behind you, then attack." When this came to pass and the two armies were facing each other, Abu Saeed waited while the larger army of Abd Allah Mirza was attacking. The generals urged Abu Saeed to attack. He said, "No. Not until we see the blackbirds coming, as my shaykh foretold. Then we will attack." When he saw the crows coming, he ordered the army to attack. The horse of Abd Allah Mirza became stuck in the mud. He was captured and imprisoned. Then Abu Saeed was able to take all the territories.

He then called Ubayd Allah al-Ahrar to move to Tashkent from Samarqand. Ubayd Allah accepted and moved there with all his followers. He became the advisor to the king. After some years, Sultan Abu Saeed received the news that Mirza Babar, nephew of Abd Allah Mirza, was moving towards Khurasan with 100,000 warriors in order to avenge his uncle and take back his kingdom. Sultan Abu Saeed went to Ubayd Allah and told him about this, saying, "We do not have enough soldiers." The shaykh said, "Don't worry." When Mirza Babar arrived in Samarqand, Sultan Abu Saeed consulted his advisors. They advised him to retreat to Turkestan. He prepared to return to Turkestan. The shaykh came to him, and said, "How is it that you are disobeying my orders? I told you not to fear. By myself I am enough for all the 100,000 soldiers." The next day plague attacked the army of Sultan Mirza Babar, causing them to die by the thousands. Sultan Mirza Babar made a peace treaty with Abu Saeed. Then Mirza Babar left Samarqand in defeat with the remains of his army.

About His Own Station

Had I taken on the role of shaykh, none of my contemporaries would have found one follower – but that is not our affair. Our concern lies in protecting the people from tyranny. Thus it is our duty to connect with the worldly rulers and capture their hearts; by this means we turn their hearts in the direction we wish.

He said:

God gave me great power to influence anyone I like. Even if I send a letter to King Khata, who proclaimed that he was God, he would come crawling barefoot to me. I have never used that power, however, because in this Order, the will must follow the Will of God, Almighty and Exalted.

His Passing

Shaykh Ubayd Allah died after the prescribed night prayer on Saturday, 12th of Rabi al-Awwal, 895 AH/1490 CE in the city of Kaman Kashan, in Samarqand. Through his books, he left us many rare jewels of wisdom, including *Anas as-salikin fi-t-tasawwuf* and *al-Urwatu-l-wuthqa li arbaba-l-itiqad*. He established a highly respected Islamic university and mosque that are still in use today.

His son, Muhammad Yahya, and many of the people present at his deathbed saw a light so brilliant shine from his eyes that it made the candles appear dim. All of Samarqand, including the sultan, were shaken and grief-stricken at his passing. Sultan Ahmad attended the funeral with all his army. The Sultan himself was a pallbearer, who carried the great shaykh's coffin to its final resting place in this physical world.

Shaykh Ubayd Allah al-Ahrar passed the secret of the Golden Chain to Shaykh Muhammad az-Zahid al-Qadi as-Samarqandi. ۞

21. Muhammad az-Zahid ق

Shaykh Muhammad az-Zahid was the perfection of the pious, the genius of the guides, the essence of sainthood. Upon him was bestowed the Divine Caliphate, and the spiritual kingdom was his shelter. He combined in his person the heavenly knowledge and the Divine Law.

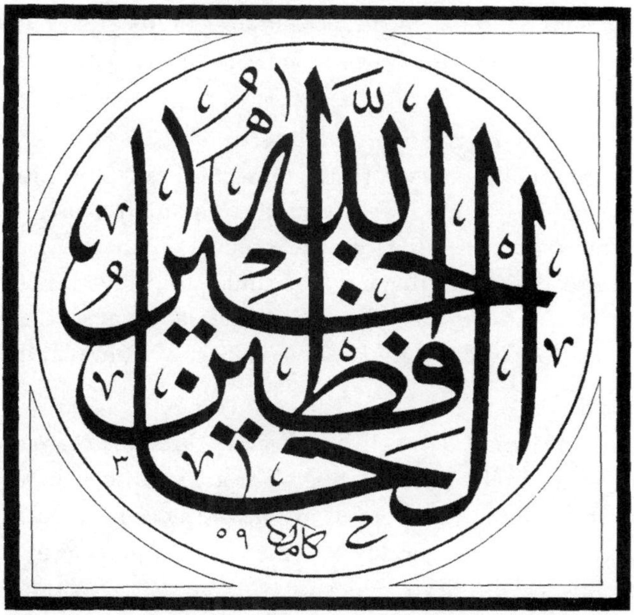

My illness is that I no longer care about my illness.
O Remedy of my illness—it is You Who are my illness.
For a time, I repented; but since I've known You,
My repentance became lost in You.
Your coming near is now like Your growing distant.
When shall rest come?
—Abu Bakr ash-Shibli [63]

---

[63] Abu Bakr ash-Shibli, quoted in *Hilyat al-awliya,* 10:252.

Shaykh Muhammad az-Zahid grasped the best of the Way and Truth, until he became the locus of all heavenly inspirations. In him appeared the knowledge of spiritual knowers. He is known as the unique one in knowledge and in the use of the pen. He carried in his heart the secrets of attracting the hearts of people. All praise belongs to God who established in him heavenly inspiration and who gave him miraculous powers in every important matter. He adorned him with the perfect light of Muhammad ﷺ in the beginning of his ascent to the state of spiritual knowledge. He was the secret of his shaykh, the *qiblah* for his shaykh's people, the inheritor of his shaykh's knowledge.

He wrote a book on the spiritual hallmarks of his great mentor, Shaykh Ubayd Allah, called *Silsilat al-Arifin wa Tadhkirat as-Siddiqeen* wherein he said:

> I served my shaykh for twelve years (from 883-895 AH/1478-1490 CE) until his death. The cause of my connection and my initiation to him occurred one day when I went with a companion, Shaykh Nimatullah, from Samarqand to Herat for the sake of furthering our education. When we reached the village of Shadiman, we stayed there many days to rest because it was the hot season. One day Shaykh Ubayd Allah al-Ahrar came to the same city, and we went to visit him at the time of the afternoon prayer.
>
> He asked me where I was from. I said, "From Samarqand." He was speaking to us in the finest manner. Through his speech, he revealed all the private matters that were in my heart, piece by piece, until he told me why I was traveling to Herat. That was so amazing that it made my heart connect with him. He said to me, "If your goal is to seek education and knowledge, you can find it here. There is no need to go to Herat." I acknowledged that every petty gossip and every inspiration that was in my heart was as open to him as the pages of a book. Even so, I was still intending to go to Herat.
>
> A little while later, one of his followers who was unhappy with my intention said, "The shaykh is busy writing. You can go." I did not go, but waited until the shaykh came back again. The shaykh came back and said to me, "Now tell me your real story. Why are you going to Herat? Are you going in search of the spiritual path or are you going

there to seek external knowledge?" My friend replied on my behalf, "He is seeking spiritual knowledge, but he is using the pursuit of external learning as a cover." He said, "If that is the case, that is good." Then he took me in his private garden, and we walked together until we disappeared from the sight of the people. He took hold of my hand, and I immediately entered the state of self-effacement for a long time. I understood he was connecting me to his shaykh, and from him to his shaykh, and from him to his shaykh, all the way to the Prophet ﷺ, and from the Prophet ﷺ up to God, Glorious and Exalted.

He then told me that I would be able to read and understand his writings. He wrapped them up, gave them to me, and told me, "In them is the reality of worship through obedience and piety and humbleness. By means of this paper, if you follow it, you will realize a vision of God, Almighty and Exalted.

"This Way is based on the love of God, which is based on following the footsteps of the Prophet ﷺ, which is based on knowledge of his *Sunnah*. The Prophet ﷺ said, '*You have to follow my way, and the way of my caliphs after me.*' For this, you must accompany the righteous scholars who are the inheritors of the knowledge of the religion and the inheritors of the knowledge of heaven; the inheritors of the unseen knowledge and the knowledge of the holy attributes; the Inheritors of the Love of the Divine Presence. Their company will lead you to manifest the Divine Knowledge and to follow the pure way of the Prophet ﷺ.

"You must keep away from corrupt scholars who use religion as a means to collect the pleasure of this world and to acquire fame and position. Do not listen to those who speak without understanding about all kinds of nonsense, about the lawful and the unlawful, without ever speaking of the importance of not deviating from the beliefs of the Community of the Way of the Prophet ﷺ.

"Do not listen to the arguments of the philosophers and the people who understand nothing of Sufism except its name, and yet pretend to be Sufis. May God, my son, greet you with the greetings of Islam."

He then went back to his group, recited *Surah Fatiha* for me and gave me permission to go to Herat. I left his presence, directing myself to

Bukhara. He sent after me a messenger with a letter addressed to the Shaykh Kallan, son of Mawlana Saad ad-Din al-Kashgari. In it was written, "You have to look after my son who is carrying my letter and to keep him from mixing with bad scholars." When I saw that lovely gesture from him, my love for him deepened in my heart. Yet I did not go back to him, but continued on to Herat.

The way to Bukhara took a long time, because my mount was weak. I had to stop every one or two miles. I had gone through six donkeys by the time I reached Bukhara. When I finally arrived, my eyes became afflicted, and I was unable to see for many days. When my condition improved and I was prepared to leave for Herat, I came down with a high fever. I was so sick that it came to my heart that if I continued I might die. I decided not to travel further but to go back and serve the shaykh.

After I reached Tashkent, I decided to visit Shaykh Ilyas al-Ashaqi. I left my books, my clothes, and my animal with a caretaker. One of Shaykh Ubayd Allah's servants saw me on the way. I said, "Let us visit Shaykh Ilyas." He asked, "Where is your animal? Bring it to my house, and then we will go to visit." As I was going to retrieve my animal, a voice came to me saying, "Your animal is dead, and all that is on it has disappeared."A great confusion came over me. I realized that the shaykh was not happy with my planned visit to Shaykh Ilyas. The thought came to my heart, "Look how my shaykh is directing all his power to lift me up, while I have decided to visit someone else."

I decided not to visit Shaykh Ilyas al-Ashaqi, but instead to go directly to Shaykh Ubayd Allah al-Ahrar. When this came to my heart, a man came to me and said, "We have found your animal with all your possessions on it." I returned to the person with whom I had left the animal and he told me, "I tied your animal here, and when I looked up, it had disappeared. I looked everywhere. It was as if the earth had swallowed it up. Then I returned again, and there was the animal, right where I had tethered it in the first place." I took my animal and set off to Samarqand to Shaykh Ubayd Allah al-Ahrar. When I arrived he came out saying, "Welcome, welcome." I stayed with the shaykh and never left him until he left this world.

He had perfect belief. He accepted whatever his shaykh taught him and nothing anyone could say would change that belief. He said:

> My shaykh spoke about spirituality and secret knowledge. He would always direct his speech towards me and ask, "When you hear me speak about Divine Realities, does it cause any conflict in you with regard to the beliefs which you got from your parents and your teachers and scholars?" I said, "No, my shaykh." He said, "Then you are one to whom we can speak."
>
> One day my shaykh was sick and he ordered me to get a doctor from Herat. Mawlana Qasim came to me and said, "O Muhammad, make your traveling very quick coming and going, because I cannot stand for the shaykh to be sick for long." I traveled quickly and returned with the doctor, but I found that the shaykh was well and Mawlana Qasim had died. My trip had taken me thirty-five days. I asked my shaykh, "How did Mawlana Qasim die when he was so young?" He said, "When you left, Mawlana Qasim came to me and said, 'I am giving my life for your life.' I told him, 'O my son, do not do that, because so many people love you.' He said, 'O my shaykh! I did not come here to consult you; I have made the decision, and God has accepted it from me.' No matter what I said, I couldn't change his mind. The next day he became sick with the sickness I had, which was reflected on him. He died on the 6th of Rabi al-Awwal and I was immediately well, without the need of a doctor."

Shaykh Muhammad as-Zahid died on the 12th of Rabi al-Awwal, 936 AH/1529 CE in Samarqand. He passed his secret to his nephew, Shaykh Darwish Muhammad as-Samarqandi. ۞

22. Darwish Muhammad ق

Muhammad az-Zahid Darwish Muhammad as-Samarqandi was the Arch-Intercessor of the famous saints and the blessing of the scholars of Islam. He was the dawn and the light of both the East and the West. He was the master of the kingdom of guidance.

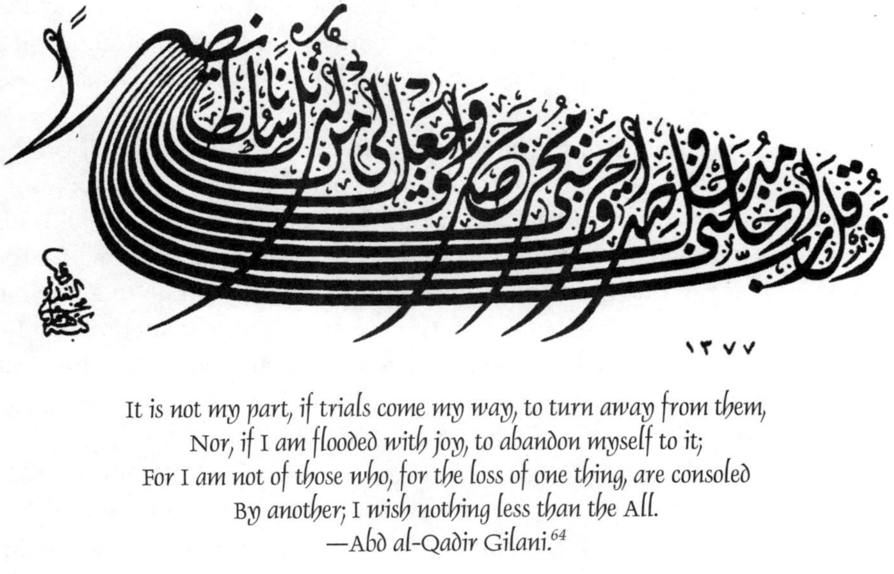

It is not my part, if trials come my way, to turn away from them,
Nor, if I am flooded with joy, to abandon myself to it;
For I am not of those who, for the loss of one thing, are consoled
By another; I wish nothing less than the All.
—Abd al-Qadir Gilani.[64]

[64] Abdul Qadir Gilani, quoted in Shaykh al-Arabi ad-Darqawi, *Letters of a Sufi Master*, translated by Titus Burckhardt, p. 26.

Darwish Muhammad as-Samarqandi grew up in the house of his uncle who taught him the best manners, educated him in spiritual and religious knowledge, and nursed him from the fount of morality and ethics. He quenched his thirst with the heavenly realities and unseen knowledge, until his heart became a house of inspiration, as God said in the Holy Tradition, "Neither My heaven nor My earth could contain Me, but the heart of My believing Servant contains Me."

He was known in his time as "Darwish Wali." He grasped all kinds of understanding of the religion. He was able to undo the misguidance of many of the false teachers of his time. He revived languishing hearts. He mended broken hearts, until he became the blessing of his time and the human essence of guidance. He had many followers throughout the country. His house and his mosque were filled with visitors asking and seeking his guidance.

Once, after a gathering, Shaykh Muhammad az-Zahid told him to go up a certain hill at some distance and wait for him there. The shaykh told him he would be coming later. Darwish Muhammad obediently went as his shaykh had instructed. His conduct was perfect. He went and waited for the shaykh to come, without using his mind to ask: How shall I go there? What shall I do when I get there? And so forth. He moved immediately. Time for the afternoon prayer came and the shaykh did not show up. Then the time of the evening prayer came and went. His ego told him, "Your shaykh is not coming. You have to go back. Maybe the shaykh forgot." His true self, however, told him, "O Darwish Muhammad, believe in your shaykh. Believe that he is certainly coming, as he said. You have to wait."

How was Darwish Muhammad's heart to believe his ego when his heart was being lifted into the presence of his shaykh? He braced himself and waited. Night came and it was very cold on the hill. He spent all night awake. His only source of warmth was his *dhikr* of *"la ilaha ill-Allah."* Dawn came and the shaykh had still not come. He was hungry and started looking for something to eat. He found some fruit trees, ate, and continued to wait for the shaykh. The day went, and then the next day. He was again in confrontation with his ego, but he kept thinking, "If my shaykh is a real shaykh, he knows what he is doing."

A week went and then a month. The shaykh did not come. The only distraction Darwish Muhammad had from waiting was *dhikr Allah* and his daily prayers that were his only other activity. He continued until the power of his *dhikr* made the animals come and sit around him to make *dhikr* with him. He realized that this miraculous power had come to him from his shaykh.

Winter came and the shaykh still did not come. It began to snow. It was extremely cold. There was no more food. He began to cut the bark of the trees and feed himself on the moisture inside. He ate from roots and whatever green leaves he could find. Deer came to him. He began to milk the ewes. This was another miracle that appeared to him. He was lifted to higher and higher spiritual levels. His teacher sent him spiritual knowledge through these miracles and visions. Khidr عليه السلام appeared to him and taught him.

A year passed, then another, then a third, and then a fourth year. The shaykh did not come. Darwish Muhammad was in a complete state of patience. He kept thinking, "My shaykh knows." At the end of the seventh year he began to smell the fragrance of his shaykh filling all the space around him. He ran to meet the shaykh. All the wild animals trailed behind him. He was completely covered with hair.

Shaykh Muhammad az-Zahid arrived. When Darwish Muhammad saw him, he felt intense joy in his heart and an immense love for his shaykh. He ran to him and kissed his shaykh's hand, as he cried out, "Peace be upon you, O my shaykh! How I love you, O my shaykh!"

His shaykh said, "What are you doing here? Why did you not come down?" He said, "O my shaykh, you said to come here and wait for you. So I waited for you." The shaykh said, "What if I had died, or perhaps I forgot?" Darwish Muhammad said, "Oh my shaykh, how are you going to forget when you are the representative of the Prophet ﷺ?" He said, "What if something had happened to me?" Darwish Muhammad said, "O my shaykh, if I had not stayed here and waited for you and obeyed, you would have never come to me by permission of the Prophet ﷺ!" Darwish Muhammad had detected in his heart that his shaykh was coming by order of the Prophet ﷺ.

The shaykh laughed and said, "Come with me." At that moment he poured into him the secret and the power of this Golden Chain of the Naqshbandi Order that he had in his heart. He then ordered him to be the shaykh of the disciples. Darwish Muhammad remained in his shaykh's service until Shaykh Muhammad az-Zahid passed away.

23. Muhammad Khwaja al-Amkanaki ق

Shaykh Muhammad Khwaja al-Amkanaki was the inheritor of the secrets of the Prophet ﷺ and the ultimate of the preferred saints. He was the Imam whose majestic position everyone acknowledged and whose blessings reached far and wide.

O perfect, full moon!
The house of the heart is Thine!
The intellect—which was once
The master—has become Thy slave and doorman.
From the day of Alast ("Am I not") the spirit has been drunk with
Thee, though for a Time it was distracted by water and clay.
Since the clay has now settled to the bottom, the water is clear—
no more do I say, 'This is mine, that is Thine.'
—Rumi, Divan [65]

---

[65] Jalaluddin Rumi, *Divan*, translated by William Chittick, p. 300.

Shaykh Muhammad Khwaja al-Amkanaki was born in Amkana, a village of Bukhara. His father and his uncle raised him. During his childhood, he was well guided, until he became like one beneath an exalted dome, protected from every shame. He never discovered any good characteristic except that he acquired it. He discarded even the smallest mistakes and errors. He never encountered a high station without encompassing it, nor a valuable secret without keeping it, nor a delicious spiritual taste without savoring it.

He followed his father like the sun on a bright day and like the full moon on a dark night. He sat on the throne of succession. He tried his best to lift up the hearts of people. He wore the cloak of the spiritual poles. Every atom in this world, whether human or animal, plant or inanimate object, was supported by his spirituality. The light of his power enlightened the Way of this Order, so that his fame spread far and wide. People ran to him to receive his knowledge, to be guided by his light, and to be enlightened by his guidance. His door became the aim of ever knower and the *qiblah* (focus of spiritual attention) of the hearts of the pious. He was dressed and decorated with the attributes of the Divine, attesting to his high position in the heavenly realm.

These are some of his blessed remarks:

> Everyone must know that for the seeker to progress in this Way, he must first sear into his heart the image of his shaykh, until the traces of that connection become visible. He must direct that heat to the essential, universal heart. This is the level of the heart in which exist the combined realities of all humanity and all creation, worldly and heavenly. Although there is no physical incarnation, all ancestors, and eventually, all creation, exist in the essential heart. The seeker must not be distracted by the details of the creation, but must direct the power of the heart towards the One whose Reality encompasses everything. He must be free of any doubt regarding the manifestation of the One who is always present, and must know that nothing exists except God, Almighty and Exalted. He must see with the eye of Truth that all creation appears and exists through God alone.

> The demand of this Way is to direct yourself to the state of erasure and annihilation, which is the first state of bewilderment. This will lead you to the state of receiving the pure light of the Essence. In that state, there

will be no other element existing except that Pure Essence. Even the Names and the Attributes cannot exist in that state of the Pure Essence. The one who can reach the state of the Pure Essence is higher than the one who is in the state of the Names and Attributes.

Shaykh Muhammad Khwaja al-Amkanaki died in 1008 AH/1599 CE. He passed his secret to Shaykh Muhammad al-Baqi Billah. ۞

24. Muhammad al-Baqi Billah ق

Shaykh Muhammad al-Baqi Billah was the knower, annihilated in God, existing through His Existence, who was lifted to the highest station of vision. He was a secret of God's secrets and a miracle of God's miracles.

O Sayyid! A Gnostic of high degree said,
"Being a *darwish* is to correct the imagination."
In other words, nothing other than the Real
Should remain in the heart. In truth, he spoke well.
O Sayyid! Since the veil is nothing but imagination,
The veil must be lifted through imagination.
Night and day you must dwell in imagining Oneness.
—Shaykh Baqi's son, Khwaja Khurd.[66]

[66] Shaykh Baqi's son, Khwaja Khurd, quoted in *Nur i-wahdat*, translated by William Chittick, Khwaja Khurd's "Light of Oneness," in *God is Beautiful and He Loves Beauty*, pp. 138-139.

Shaykh Muhammad al-Baqi Billah was born in 972 AH/1564 CE in the city of Kabul, in the land of Ajam that was a colony of the Sultanate of India. His father was the judge, Abd as-Salam. He first went to India on personal business. God awakened in him spiritual thirst. He left this physical world behind and sought spiritual knowledge. He kept company with masters and saints, until he himself became an ocean of intellect and a saint of spirituality. He combined in his person the two types of knowledge: the outer knowledge and the heavenly knowledge. God gave him from the two oceans and conferred on him authority in the two worlds of humanity and jinn.

Imam Rabbani Ahmad al-Faruqi said:

> Muhammad al-Baqi Billah was the one sitting on the throne of all shaykhs. He was the deputy of all masters of the Naqshbandi Golden Chain who reached the end of the infinite, who achieved the highest states of being a friend of God. He was the spiritual pole who supported every creature on this earth. He unveiled the secrets of Reality. He was the verifier of the station of the Reality of Muhammad ﷺ. He was the pillar of the people of guidance. He was the essence of the knowers and the guide of the verifiers.

Muhammad al-Baqi Billah traveled continuously, until he reached the city of Samarqand. There he connected himself to the master of his time, Muhammad Khwaja al-Amkanaki. He received from him the Way of the Naqshbandi Order. In a very short time, he received what most seekers require a lifetime to receive. He was elevated also through the spiritual care of Ubayd Allah al-Ahrar. His honor became known everywhere. His shaykh, Muhammad Khwaja al-Amkanaki, authorized him to take followers and to train them in the conduct of the Order. He ordered him to go back to India. He predicted, "You are going to have a follower who will be like the sun," in anticipation of Imam Rabbani Ahmad al-Faruqi.

He moved back to India and stayed in the city of Delhi-Jahanabad, which he filled with faith and knowledge, secrets and lights. Through him, the Naqshbandi Order spread with great swiftness throughout the Indian subcontinent. Millions of people were connected to him through his deputies. All nations in the subcontinent were attracted to his knowledge and his heavenly power, and to the prophetic characteristics with which he was adorned. It became known throughout Hindustan that anyone coming to him and looking in his eyes or sitting in his company doing *dhikr* would enter a state of self-effacement, through which he could reach a state of annihilation, in a single meeting. By this miraculous power, he attracted millions of people, until teachings of this Naqshbandi Order were on the tongue of every person in his time.

Shaykh Muhammad al-Baqi Billah died on Wednesday, the 14th of Jumada 'l-Akhir, 1014 AH/1605 CE, in the city of Delhi at the age of forty years and four months. His grave is on the west side of Delhi.

He passed the secret to his successor, the reviver of the second millennium, al-Imam ar-Rabbani Mujaddid Alf ath-Thani, Shaykh Ahmad al-Faruqi as-Sirhindi.

25. Ahmad al-Faruqi as-Sirhindi ق

Shaykh Ahmad al-Faruqi was the pearl of the crown of the knowledgeable saints. He was the treasure of those who came before and of those who came after. In him were combined all their favors and generosity.

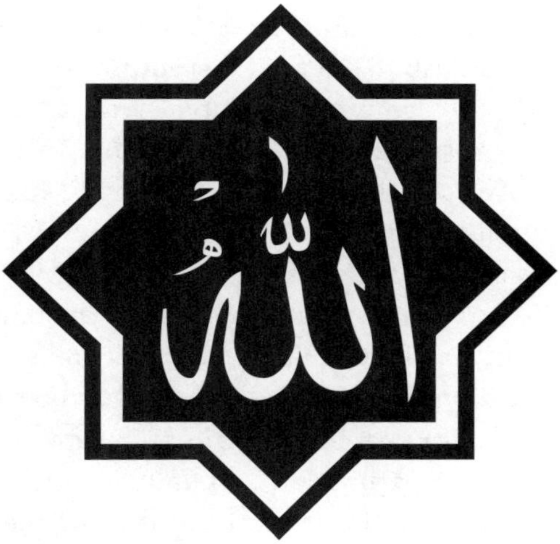

If God causes one to approach Him, He reveals Himself to him
as the object of his Desire, without his knowing,
As the fire of Moses, which he saw through the eye of his need,
And who is the Divinity that he did not recognize.
If thou understandeth my words thou knowest
That thou hast need of the apparent form:
If Moses had searched for something other than the fire
He would have seen Him in that, and not inversely.
—Ibn Arabi, *Fusus al-Hikam*[67]

---

[67] Ibn Arabi, *Fusus al-Hikam*. From the chapters on Moses and Jesus in Ibn Arabi's *Wisdom of the Prophets*, pp. 77, 115.

Shaykh Ahmad al-Faruqi as-Sirhindi was the Sinai of Divine Manifestation, the Furthermost Lote Tree of the unique knowledge, and the fountain of the hidden prophetic knowledge. He was the genius of scholars and the sultan of the earth, which smiled when he was born and was honored by his existence. He was the perfect perfected guide. He was the caller to God's presence, the one pole and the unique heavenly Imam.

Shaykh Ahmad was the reviver of the second millennium, our leader and master, son of Shaykh Abd al-Ahad son of Zain al-Abidin, son of Abd al-Hayy, son of Muhammad, son of Habib Allah, son of Rafiuddin, son of Nur, son of Sulayman, son of Yusuf, son of Abd Allah, son of Ishaq, son of Abd Allah, son of Shuayb, son of Ahad, son of Yusuf, son of Shihabuddin, known as Farq Shah al-Qabidi, son of Nasruddin, son of Mahmud, son of Sulayman, son of Masud, son of Abd Allah al-Waiz al-Asghari, son of Abd Allah al-Waiz al-Akbar, son of Abdu-l-Fattah, son of Ishaq, son of Ibrahim, son of Nasir, son of Abd Allah ﵁, the son of Amir al-Muminin, the caliph of the Prophet ﷺ, Umar al-Faruq ﵁.

He was born on the day of Ashura, the 10th of Muharram in the year 971 AH/1564 CE in the village of Sihar Nidbasin. In some translations it is called Sirhind in the city of Lahore, in present day Pakistan. He received his knowledge and education through his father and through many shaykhs in his time. He made progress in three spiritual orders: Suhrawardi, Qadiri, and Chishti. He was given permission to train followers in all three spiritual orders at the age of seventeen. He was busy spreading the teachings of these orders and guiding his followers; yet he felt that something was missing in himself, and he searched continuously for it.

He felt an interest in the Naqshbandi Order, because he could see by means of the secrets of the other three Sufi orders that it was the highest. His spiritual progress eventually brought him to the presence of the Arch-Intercessor and spiritual pole of his time, ash-Shaykh Muhammad al-Baqi, who had been sent from Samarqand to India by the order of his shaykh, Muhammad al-Amkanaki. He studied teachings of the Naqshbandi Order from the shaykh and stayed with him for two months and some days, until Muhammad al-Baqi opened to his heart the secret of this spiritual Order, and gave him authorization to train his disciples in the Order. Shaykh Muhammad al-Baqi said about him, "He is the highest spiritual pole in this time."

Predictions of His Advent

The Prophet ﷺ predicted his advent in one of his Traditions when he said, *"There will be among my Community a man called Silah (connection). By his intercession many people will be saved."* It was mentioned in the collection of Suyuti, *Jam al-Jawami*. What confirmed the truth of this Tradition is what Shaykh Ahmad al-Faruqi wrote about himself: "God has made me the *silah* (connection) between the two oceans," meaning that God had made him a connection between the two kinds of knowledge, external and internal.

Shaykh Mir Husamuddin said:

> I saw the Prophet ﷺ in one of my dreams standing on the *minbar* and praising Shaykh Ahmad as-Sirhindi. The Prophet ﷺ was saying, "I am proud and happy with his presence within my Community. God has made him a reviver of the religion."

Many saints predicted his advent. One of them was Shaykh Ahmad al-Jami, who said:

> After me will appear seventeen men of the people of God, all of whom are named Ahmad, and the last one among them will be at the head of the millennium. He is going to be the highest of them, and he is going to receive the state of unveiling. He is going to revive this religion.

Another to predict his advent was Muhammad Khwaja al-Amkanaki, who told his caliph:

> A man from India is going to appear. He will be the Imam of his century. He will be trained by you, so hurry to meet him, because the people of God are awaiting his arrival.

Muhammad al-Baqi said, "That is why I moved from Bukhara to India." When they met, he told Ahmad al-Faruqi:

> You are the one whose appearance Shaykh Muhammad Khwaja al-Amkanaki predicted. When I saw you, I knew you were the spiritual pole of your time. When I entered the region of Sirhind in India, I found a lamp that was so big and so bright that its light reached up to the heavens. Everyone took from that lamp's light. You are that lamp.

It is said that the shaykh of his father, Shaykh Abd al-Ahad, who was a shaykh of the Qadiri Order, had been given a cloak from his shaykh which had been passed down from the Arch-Intercessor, Abd al-Qadir Gilani. Abd al-Qadir had said about it to his successors:

> Keep it for that one who is going to appear at the end of the first millennium. His name is Ahmad. He is going to revive this religion. I have dressed him with all my secrets. He combines in himself both the internal and external knowledge.

The Seeking of the King and the King of Seeking

HIS VISIONS AND ASCENSION

Shaykh Ahmad al-Faruqi said:

> Let it be known to you that the heavenly guardians attracted me because they wanted me to be attracted. They facilitated for me the passage through time and space in all the different states of the seeker. I found that God is the Essence of all matter, as the people of Sufism have said it. Then I found God in all matter without incarnation. I found God together with all matter. I saw Him ahead of everything. Then I saw Him and I saw nothing else. This is what is meant by the term, witnessing the Oneness, which is also the state of annihilation. That is the first step in sainthood, and the highest state in the beginning of the Way. This vision appears first on the horizons, then secondly in the self. Then I was lifted to the station of subsistence that is the second step in sainthood.
>
> This is a station that many saints did not speak about because they did not reach it. All of them speak about the station of annihilation, but following that state is subsistence. In that state, I found all creation another time, but I found that the Essence of all these creations is God, and God's Essence is the Essence of myself. I found God in everything, but in reality in myself. I was raised to a higher state, to find God with everything, but in reality He was with myself.
>
> I was lifted to see Him preceding everything, but in reality He preceded myself. I was lifted to a state where He followed everything, but in reality He followed myself. I saw Him in everything, but in reality He was in myself. Then I saw everything and I did not see God. And this is the end of the stations by which they had brought me back to the beginning. In sum, they lifted me to the station of annihilation,

then to the station of Existence, then they brought me back to be with people, in the station of the common people. This is the highest state in guiding people to the Presence of God. It is the perfect state of guidance, because it matches the understanding of human beings ...

I accompanied today one who has reached the end of ends, the spiritual pole of all creatures, the perfect human being, Shaykh Muhammad al-Baqi. Through him I received incredible blessings. By his blessing I was granted a power of attraction that allowed me to reach every human being that God had created. I was honored to attain a station that combines the state of the ending with the state of the beginning.

I achieved all the states of seeking and I reached the ending, which is the meaning of "reaching the name of *ar-Rabb* (the Sustainer)," by the support of the Lion of God (*asad Allah*), Ali ibn Abi Talib ؓ, may God ennoble his face. I was raised up to the state of the throne, which is the Reality of the Truth of Muhammad ﷺ, by the support of Shaykh Shah Bahauddin Naqshband. Then I was lifted even higher, to the state of Beauty, which is the state of the Truth of the Muhammadan spiritual poles, by the support of the prophetic holy spirit.

I was supported by Shaykh Alauddin al-Attar, from whom I received the states of the greatest spiritual poles from the Presence of Muhammad ﷺ. Then God's heavenly care attracted me, and I ascended to a state that is beyond that of the spiritual poles, the special, original state. Here the support of the Arch-Intercessor, Abd al-Qadir Gilani, pushed me up to the state of the origin of origins.

Then I was ordered to come back down. As I was descending, I passed by all thirty-nine spiritual Ways other than the Naqshbandi and the Qadiri. I looked at the states of their shaykhs. They greeted me and saluted me. They threw on me all their treasures and all their private knowledge, which unveiled to me realities that had never been unveiled to any person in my time. Then, on my descent, I met Khidr ؑ, and he adorned me with the heavenly knowledge before I reached the state of the spiritual poles.

I ascended on many occasions. Once I ascended above the Throne. I was raised above the Throne a distance equal to that between the earth and the Throne. There I saw the station of Shah Naqshband. Then I saw under his station the station of many shaykhs. I saw above him the station of the Imams of the family of the Prophet ﷺ and the rightly-guided caliphs. I saw above them the stations of all prophets on one side and on the other side the station of our Prophet ﷺ. I saw angels around them all. Such ascensions happened to me many times.

ON HIS DESTINY

Abu Dawud, in an authentic Tradition related that the Prophet ﷺ said, "At the beginning of every century, God will send someone by whom the religion will be revive." However, there is a difference between the reviver of the century and the reviver of the millennium. It is like the difference between one hundred and one thousand.

Ahmad al-Faruqi said:

In a vision, the Prophet ﷺ gave me good tidings: "You are going to be a spiritual inheritor and God is going to give you the authority to intercede on behalf of hundreds of thousands on the Day of Judgment." He bestowed on me with his holy hand the authority to guide people, and he said to me, "Never before have I given that authority to guide people."

The knowledge that emerges from me comes from the state of sainthood. I receive it from the Light of the Prophet Muhammad ﷺ. Saints are unable to bring forth such knowledge, because it is beyond the knowledge of saints. It is the knowledge of the essence of this religion and the essence of the knowledge of God's Essence and Attributes. No one before has spoken about it and God has granted me to be the one to revived the religion in its second millennium.

God unveiled to me the secrets of the unique Oneness. He poured into my heart all kinds of spiritual knowledge and its refinement. He unveiled to me the secrets of the verses of the Quran so that I found beneath every letter of the Quran an ocean of knowledge all pointing to the high Essence of God, Almighty and Exalted. If I were to reveal one word of the meaning of it he would cut off my head, as they did with

Hallaj and Ibn Arabi. This is the meaning of the Tradition of the Prophet ﷺ, in Bukhari, narrated by Abu Hurayra ؓ, "The Prophet ﷺ poured into my heart two kinds of knowledge, one of which I have revealed another which if I were to reveal they would cut my throat."

God, Almighty and Exalted, has shown me all the names of those who enter our Way, from the day of Abu Bakr ؓ to the Day of Judgment, both men and women, and all of them are going to enter Paradise, with the intercession of the shaykhs of the Way.

Al-Mahdi ؑ will be one of the followers of this Way.

One day I was in a gathering with my followers reciting *dhikr*. It came to my heart that I had done something wrong. Then God opened to my eyes, "I have forgiven anyone who sits with you and anyone asking intercession by means of you."

God has created me from the light remaining from the creation of His Prophet ﷺ.

The Kabah often came and circumambulated around me.

God, Almighty and Exalted, said to me, "Anyone for whom you pray the funeral prayer will be forgiven. If anyone mixes earth from your grave with the earth of their grave, they will be forgiven."

God said, "I have given you special gifts and perfections which no one will receive other than you until the time of the Mahdi ؑ."

God gave me an incredible power of guidance. Even if I direct my guidance to a dead tree, it will become green.

HIS WONDERS

One great shaykh wrote to him asking, "Did the Companions receive the states that you reached and you speak about? If so, did they receive them at once or did they receive them at separate times?" Ahmad al-Faruqi answered, "I cannot give you an answer unless you come into my presence." When the shaykh came, he immediately unveiled to him his spiritual reality and cleansed the darkness of his heart until the shaykh fell prostrate at his feet and said, "I believe, I believe! I see now that these states were all revealed to the Companions simply by looking at the Messenger ﷺ."

Once Ahmad al-Faruqi was invited in the month of fasting, Ramadan, by ten of his disciples to break fast with them. He accepted the invitation of each of them. When it came time to break the fast, he was present at each of their houses, breaking the fast, and they saw him in each of their houses at the same time.

He looked at the sky and it was raining. He said, "O rain, stop until such-and-such hour." It stopped until the exact time he had said, after which it started raining again.

The king ordered a certain man to be executed. That man came to Shaykh Ahmad al-Faruqi and said, "Please write a stay of execution for me." He wrote to the Sultan, "Do not execute this man." The Sultan was fearful and pardoned the man.

Shaykh Ahmad al-Faruqi said:

> I have met with the spiritual presence of Imam Abu Hanifa, and all his teachers, and all his students. I have met them, and I learned from him and from them the Hanafi school. I met spiritually with Imam Shafii and all his teachers and followers, and learned the Shafii school from them. From this learning, I became an expert in both these schools, and I can give edicts in them both.
>
> I was authorized to initiate in three Sufi orders: Naqshbandi, Suhrawardi and Chishti.

He was so famous that the scholars of external knowledge in his time became jealous of him. They went to the king and told him, "He is saying things that are not accepted in the religion." They pushed the king until he put him in jail. He stayed in jail for three years. His son, Shaykh Sayyid, said, "He was under very intense security in jail. Guards surrounded his room on every side. Yet every Friday he would be seen in the big mosque. No matter how much security he was under, he would disappear from prison and appear in the mosque." From this, they knew they could not put him behind bars, and therefore, they released him.

FROM HIS BOOKS

Shaykh Ahmad al-Faruqi wrote many books, one of the most famous of which is the *Maktubat*. In it he said:

It must be known that God has placed us under His obligations and His prohibitions. God said, *"Whatever the Prophet gives you, take it, and whatever he withholds from you, leave it."* (59:7) If we are going to be sincere in this, we have to attain to annihilation and the love of the Essence. Without these, we cannot reach this degree of obedience. Thus, we are under another obligation, which is to seek the Way of Sufism, because this Way will lead us to the state of annihilation and the love of the Essence. Each order differs from the other in its states of perfection; so, too, does each order keep the *Sunnah* of the Prophet ﷺ and have its own definition of what that entails. Every order has its own way of keeping the *Sunnah* of the Prophet ﷺ. Our Order, through its shaykhs, requires us to keep all the commands of the Prophet ﷺ and to leave aside all the things he prohibited. Our shaykhs do not follow the easy ways but insist on keeping the difficult ways. In all their seeking, they keep in mind the verse of Quran, *"People whom neither business nor trade will divert from the Remembrance of God."* (24:37)

In the journey leading to the unveiling of the Divine Realities, the seeker moves through various stages of knowledge of and proximity to his Lord. Moving to God is a vertical movement from the lower stations to the higher stations until the movement surpasses time and space and all the states dissolve into what is called "the Necessary Knowledge of God." This is also called annihilation. Moving in God is the stage in which the seeker moves from the station of Names and Attributes to a state that neither word nor sign can describe. This is the state of subsistence in God.

Moving from God is the stage in which the seeker returns from the heavenly world to the world of cause and effect, descending from the highest station of knowledge to the lowest. Here he forgets God by God, and he knows God with God, and he returns from God to God. This is called the state of the farthest and the nearest.

Moving in things is a movement within creation. This involves knowing intimately all elements and states in this world after having vanished in annihilation. Here the seeker can achieve the state of guidance, which is the state of the prophets and the people following the footsteps of the Prophet ﷺ. It brings the Divine Knowledge into the world of creation in order to establish guidance.

The entire process is like threading a needle. The thread seeks the eye of the needle, passes through, and then proceeds down to where it began. There the two ends meet, form a knot, and secure the entire thread. They form a whole, thread, eye, and needle, and any material they catch is sewn into the fabric of the unity.

The Naqshbandi shaykhs choose to guide their disciples first through the movement from God, traveling from the higher states to the lower. For this reason they maintain the common veils over the spiritual vision of the disciple, removing the veil of ordinary consciousness only at the final step. All other Ways begin with the movement to God, moving from the lowest states to the highest, and removing the common veils first.

It is mentioned in the Traditions of the Prophet ﷺ, "Scholars are the inheritors of the prophets." The knowledge of prophets is of two kinds: knowledge of laws and knowledge of secrets. The scholar cannot be called an inheritor if he does not inherit both kinds of knowledge. If he takes only one kind of knowledge, he is incomplete. Thus the real inheritors are the ones who take the knowledge of the laws and the knowledge of the secrets, and only the saints have truly received and protected this inheritance.

Shaykh Ahmad al-Faruqi left behind many books. He died on the 17th of Safar 1034 AH/1624 CE at the age of 63. He was buried in the village of Sirhind. He was a shaykh in four Sufi orders: Naqshbandi, Qadiri, Chishti and Suhrawardi. He preferred the Naqshbandi, because he said, "It is the mother of all Sufi orders." He passed the secret of the revered Golden Chain to Shaykh Muhammad Masum. ۞

26. Muhammad Masum ق

Shaykh Muhammad Masum was the rope of God, the pious guide who combined in himself the Divine Law and Reality. He showed the difference between ignorance and true guidance.

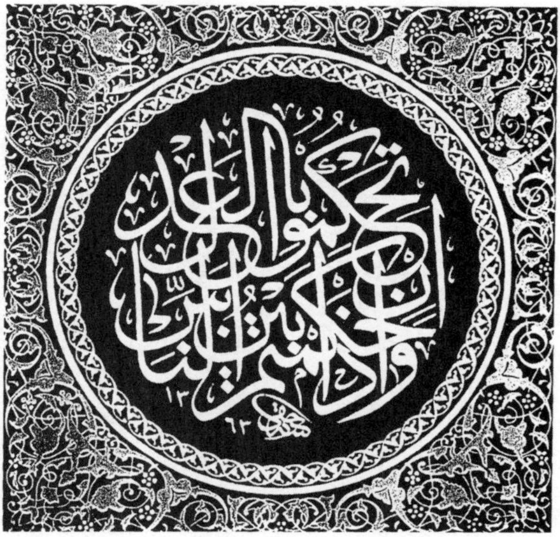

In the place of refuge my heart sought refuge, shot with enmity's arrows.
O Mercy of God for His slaves, God placed His trust in you
Among all inanimate forms. O House of my Lord,
O light of my heart, O coolness of my eyes, O my heart within!
O true secret of the heart of existence, my sacred trust, My purest love!
O direction to which I turn from every quarter and valley,
From subsistence in the Real, then from on high, from self-extinction,
then from the depths! O Kabah of God, O my life, O path of good fortune,
O my guidance! God sheds His light on your court,
and something of His light appears in the heart.
—Ibn Arabi, *al-Futuhat al-Makkiyyah*[68]

[68] Ibn Arabi, *Futuhat al-makkiyyah,* 1:701.

Shaykh Muhammad Masum was born in the year 1007 AH/1599 CE. He was educated by his father from the special knowledge of saints. He sat on the throne of guidance in the Naqshbandi Way at the age of twenty-six after the passing of his shaykh. He became famous everywhere. His name was known on every tongue. Kings acknowledged his greatness in his time. People flocked to him from everywhere.

He was a saint from his childhood. He refused to nurse during the day in Ramadan. He spoke on the knowledge of Oneness at the age of three by saying, "I am the earth, I am the heavens, I am God ...I am this, I am that." He memorized the Quran in three months at the age of six. He tried to learn true knowledge, the Divine Law, and Reality through his heart. He attained a high state in them. At the age of seventeen, he was considered to be the greatest scholar of his time. He was very truthful in all his legal decisions. He accepted neither innovation nor easy dispensations.

His father, Ahmad al-Faruqi, testified when he was young that a very great power would appear in him. Once he said to his father, "I see myself as a life that is moving in every atom of the atoms of these universes. And these universes are taking light from it as the earth takes light from the sun." His father said, "O my son, that means you are going to be the spiritual pole of your time. Remember that from me."

His father also said:

> You have been molded from the residue of my residue, which was the residue of the Prophet's ﷺ clay.
>
> I have poured into my son, Muhammad Masum, everything that I have been given.
>
> The perfect knower that is honored to exist in the state of the complete existence will witness and observe the beauty of God in the mirror of this universe, and he will see himself in everything. This universe will be him, and he will be this universe. He will see himself moving in every individual of this universe, encompassing the whole in the part and the part in the whole.

From His Miracles

Once one of his deputies, Khwaja Muhammad as-Siddiq, was riding on a horse. His foot slipped from the stirrup, and he was dangling from one side. The horse was running so fast that everyone expected him to be killed.

He remembered at once to say, "O my shaykh support me." As soon as he said, "O my shaykh, support me," he saw his shaykh appear, take the reins of the horse and stop it.

One of his followers said, "I fell into the sea and I did not know how to swim. I called out his name, and he came and took me out."

Once he was sitting with his followers in his retreat. They began to see water pouring from his hands and his sleeves. They were surprised. They asked him, "What is this, O our shaykh?" He said, "One of my disciples was just now on a ship. That ship was in a storm and was sinking. He called me. I immediately reached out my hand and saved him from drowning." They recorded the time of that event and some months later a merchant visited them. They asked him about that event and he said, "Yes, at that time my shaykh came and saved me."

It happened at that time that a magician built a fire, entered it, and it did not burn him. There arose a great confusion among people. It made a great dissension. The shaykh started a huge fire in the city, and he told the magician, "Enter my fire!" The magician was afraid. The shaykh then told one of his disciples, "Enter my fire, and while you are walking into it say '*la ilaha ill-Allah*.'" The disciple entered. It was cool and peaceful for him, as it had been for Abraham عليه السلام (21:69) when he was thrown in the fire. When the magician saw this, he immediately converted and recited, "I bear witness that there is no god but God and that Muhammad is the Messenger of God."

Once Shaykh Abd ar-Rahman at-Tirmidhi said:

> I came with my brother to visit Shaykh Muhammad Masum. He gave everyone a gift from his clothes except me. When we returned to our country I was very sad, because I did not receive anything from him. After a while, a rumor spread throughout the city that the shaykh was coming to visit the city. All the people went to welcome him. I went with them. I saw the shaykh coming on a white horse. He looked at me and said, "Abd ar-Rahman, do not be sad. I have tested you. I have saved my special robe for you which I inherited from my father, Ahmad al-Faruqi." I took it from him and put it on. Immediately, everything disappeared, and my shaykh appeared in front of me in every atom and every particle, he was appearing. I reached a state of immense happiness, and I entered the Divine Presence.

One day a blind man came to him and asked him, "Please pray for me that God restore my vision to me." He rubbed his saliva on his eyes and told him, "Go to your house and do not open your eyes until you get there." He reached his home and opened his eyes, and he could see.

They told him, "There is someone who is cursing the caliphs of the Prophet ﷺ." He became upset. There was a knife in his hand with which he was cutting a watermelon. As he cut the watermelon, he said, "As I cut this watermelon, I am cutting the neck of that one who is cursing the caliphs of the Prophet ﷺ." Immediately that man died.

He said:

> When I was on pilgrimage, I saw the Kabah hugging me and kissing me with great compassion and emotion. Then in a vision, God unveiled to me lights and blessings coming out of myself, and increasing and increasing, until they filled up all the deserts, then all the mountains, then the oceans; they then filled up all the universes, and they entered every atom of these universes. Then all these atoms were drawn back to the love of the Essence of the Kabah. I saw many spiritual beings, among them angels and saints, all of them standing in my presence as if I was their sultan. Then I received a letter, delivered to me by an angel, and on it was written, "From the God of heavens, universes and all creation, I accept your pilgrimage."
>
> Then I continued my travel to visit Blessed Madinah, the City of the Prophet ﷺ. I entered the City of the Prophet ﷺ. I went to visit him at his tomb. When I directed my face to his face, I saw the Prophet ﷺ coming out of his grave. He hugged me and kissed me. Then I saw myself in a state where my heart was as if combining with his heart, my tongue with his tongue, my ears with his ears, until I no longer saw myself; I saw the Prophet ﷺ. When I looked at the Prophet ﷺ, I saw myself. That vision took me to the station of ascending to where the Prophet ﷺ had ascended in the Night of Ascension. I received there all the knowledge that the Prophet ﷺ wanted me to receive. I moved toward the two grand caliphs of the Prophet ﷺ. As soon as I was in the presence of Abu Bakr ؓ, I saw on my shoulders a red robe. Then when I moved on to Umar ؓ, I saw a yellow robe on my shoulders. When I was leaving, I saw a green robe dressed on my shoulders, which I knew was from the Prophet ﷺ. Then I saw a vision that God removed from me all the veils

that were on my heart, and I saw that all that God had created from the station of the Throne to the station of the earth was in need of the beloved Muhammad ﷺ. He was the center of all light that moves in every atom.

What the Prophet ﷺ gave me at that moment, if I were to say it, they would cut my throat. Then I found that every prayer for the Prophet ﷺ, all praise of the Prophet ﷺ, and all poetry that was written for the sake of the Prophet ﷺ were as if they were for me. Then I saw all these universes, from the station of the Throne to the station of the world, had been enlightened and were shining with my light. When the time came to go back to my country, I was on my last visit to the Prophet ﷺ, and I was crying in the farewell state, and I saw the Prophet ﷺ come out of his station.

He dressed me with robes of light that have never been seen before, and he put on my head a crown. That crown came from the King of Kings, from the Divine Presence, decorated with every kind of jewel, whose description cannot be described in this world. And I knew that crown and those robes of light had been given to me from the robes of light that God, Almighty and Exalted, gave to His Prophet ﷺ on the Night of Ascension, and which the Prophet ﷺ had kept for me and adorned me with on that night.

Shaykh Muhammad Masum was a miracle of God's miracles and a light that God showered down on this world in order to guide humanity. It is said that he gave initiation into this Sufi Way to more than 900,000 people and that he had 7,000 deputies, and each of them was a saint. That is because, in one week's association, he could bring his follower to the state of annihilation, and in one month, to the state of subsistence. It is also said that he could bring some followers to the state of subsistence in one single sitting in his association. He died on the 9th of Rabi al-Awwal 1079/1668 CE. He passed the secret of this Order to Sayfuddin al-Faruqi al-Mujaddidi.

27. Muhammad Sayfuddin ق

Shaykh Muhammad Sayfuddin was a reviver of this Order and a reviver of the true path of the *Sunnah*. He derived great spiritual benefit from his great ancestor, Umar al-Faruq رضي الله عنه, and from his grandfather, Ahmad al-Faruqi. With the blessings of the Prophet ﷺ, he was able to spread this Order far and wide.

The sound of the flute is the image of God's call to man.
We were all part of Adam and heard those melodies in Paradise.
Though water and clay have covered us with doubt,
We still remember something of those sounds.
But since they are mixed with the dust of sorrows,
How should these high and low notes produce that joy?
—Rumi, *Mathnavi*[69]

[69] Jalaluddin Rumi, *Mathnavi*.

Shaykh Muhammad Sayfuddin was born in 1055 AH/1645 CE. He was raised in the home of his father, Muhammad Masum, and he was nursed with the milk of the knowledge of his father, his grandfather and his blessed ancestors. During his father's life he sat on the throne of guidance, and he followed the footsteps of his predecessors. His house became a light for the scholars of the religion, who came like moths from all around. As his subtle knowledge grew, his fame rose ever higher in the heavens, reaching the orbits of the knowers, until he was able to decipher the symbols of hidden knowledge and to open the treasure of heavenly affairs. He spread the external and internal knowledge, and he joined together the beginners and the adepts, and he taught the knowledge of taste.

On the orders of his father, he moved to the city of Delhi to spread the knowledge of the Divine Law and the light of the Way. The Sultan himself, Muhammad Alamagir, became his student. Consequently, the people of the Court, the Sultan's ministers, and all the princes became his followers. With the support of the Sultan, it was not long before the entire kingdom accepted him. He embodied the *Sunnah* of the Prophet ﷺ and inspired love for the Divine Law throughout the nation. By means of the deep knowledge that filled his heart, he hoisted high the flag of Islam and removed the traces of ignorance and tyranny from the kingdom.

Through the blessings of Shaykh Sayfuddin's companionship, God made the sultan succeed in all his affairs and prevented harmful and unlawful conduct from occurring in the realm. The sultan banished tyrants and oppressors. He kept the company of the shaykh, following him as a student. Through the shaykh's encouragement, he was able to memorize the Holy Quran. He spent his late night hours fulfilling the obligations of the Way, reciting the *dhikr,* while his daylight hours he spent looking after the affairs of his kingdom.

The shaykh endeavored to eliminate all forms of misery and tyranny from the kingdom by means of the sultan. He achieved tremendous success, until the whole of India was living in peace. He achieved such a position of reverence that all sultans and princes would stand in his presence out of respect for him.

One day, a man was standing with the other princes and sultans in the presence of the shaykh. An insinuating whisper came to his heart, saying, "That shaykh is so arrogant." The shaykh looked at him and said, "You are right, because my pride is from God's Pride."

Once a man denied the truth of the shaykh's words. That night he saw a dream in which a group of men came and attacked him. They beat him and beat him, asking, "How dare you deny the speech of the shaykh when he is the Lover of God?" He awoke to find himself in severe pain. He hastened to the presence of the shaykh and asked his forgiveness.

Every day in his retreat, around 6,000 seekers slept and ate from the food he was providing.

One day, he heard from his neighbor's house the sound of the reed flute. He was so enchanted by the sound of it that he fainted. When he came to he said, "Do you think that I am empty of compassion and emotion? No, those who listen to the reed flute and feel no compassion and emotion are empty. But when we hear something beautiful, we are so touched that we are immediately transported to the Divine Presence." To the saints, God's call is heard without any admixture of the "dust of sorrows," and this is why they faint when they hear it.

One day, a leper came and asked him for his supplication that he be healed. He blew on him and immediately the disease disappeared.

Shaykh Muhammad Sayfuddin died in 1095 AH/1684 CE and he was buried in the city of Sirhind. He passed on the secret of the Golden Chain to Grandshaykh Nur Muhammad al-Badawani. ۞

28. Nur Muhammad al-Badawani ق

Shaykh Nur Muhammad al-Badawani was a descendant of the Prophet ﷺ. The heavenly station powered his light. He poured peace and happiness into the confused hearts, until he became the appearance of every favor and a means to God, Almighty and Exalted, for every person in his time.

Hear, O faqir: Every time I was lacking something,
great or small, and turned away from it
in turning towards my Lord,
I found it there in front of me, thanks to the power of Him
who hears and knows.
We see that the needs of ordinary people are filled
by paying attention to them,
whereas the needs of the elect are filled by the very fact
that they turn away from them and concentrate upon God.
He, who by remembering Me is distracted from his petition,
will receive more than those who ask.
—Mulay al-Arabi ad-Darqawi [70]

---

[70] Mulay al-Arabi ad-Darqawi, *Letters of a Sufi Master*, p. 17.

Shaykh Nur Muhammad al-Badawani was born in 1075 AH/1664 CE. He was raised in a blessed house, quenching his thirst for external and internal knowledge at the fountain of the Naqshbandi Order from his early childhood. He received the blessings of his shaykhs, and they were proud of his progress. He continued to advance his state until, in the country of India, he became a shining lamp. Visitors came to him from everywhere, receiving from him both the blessing of his secrets and the blessings of his ancestors.

He sat on the Throne of the Way, following his master, and he was like a beacon guiding by his light all those seeking in the Way. He left behind him a celebrated name, and how could it be otherwise when the Prophet Muhammad ﷺ was his ancestor? He was a branch of the tree of prophetic knowledge and a descendant of the pure family of the Prophet ﷺ. It is no wonder that he became the *qiblah* of the saints and his threshold became the goal of all people of God.

Through him God, renewed the Divine Law and the spiritual reality, like the full moon on a dark night. He is known to have revived countless *Sunnah* and for having removed many innovations that had crept into religious practice.

He was so pious that he spent most of his time reading and studying the ethics and character of the Prophet ﷺ and the character and good conduct of saints. His strict adherence to the form and intent of the Prophet ﷺ in all his actions is illustrated by the following incident. One day he entered the bathroom with his right foot, which is contrary to the practice of the Prophet ﷺ. It resulted in his being constipated for three days, because he had strayed from the propriety of the *Sunnah* in that single step. He asked God's forgiveness, and God relieved him of his distress.

Nur Muhammad al-Badawani began his life in a state of self-effacement. He remained in that state for fifteen years. During this period, he was always in the state of self-effacement. He was never out of that state, except during the prayers. When he prayed, he would return to self-awareness and perform the daily prayers. He would then return to that state. He was careful to eat only from earnings made by the sweat of his brow. He ate only bread he baked himself, and he ate it only in very small amounts. He spent all his time in meditation and contemplation. When the bread was finished, he would return to prepare more, and then he would return to contemplation and meditation. From his excessive contemplation, his back became bowed. He was in the service of his shaykh for many years. He also served Shaykh Muhammad Muhsin, son of the great narrator of Tradition of his time, and Shaykh Abd al-Haqq, one of the caliphs of Muhammad Masum, until, by means of his service, he reached a high state of perfection.

He said, "For the past thirty years the thought, 'How am I going to make a living?' never came to my heart. The subject of provision never came to my heart, but I ate when I felt the need." He never ate from the food of a proud person. He said, "The food of proud, rich people contains darkness."

If he borrowed a book, he would read it in three days, because he said, "The reflection of the darkness and ignorance of the owner of the book will be reflected on me." He was very careful in such matters. His caliph, Habib Allah, used to cry when he remembered him, and he would say to his followers, "You did not see that holy person. If you had been in his time it would have renewed your faith in God's power that He had created such a person."

Habib Allah also said, "Shaykh Nur Muhammad al-Badawani's visions were extremely detailed and incredibly precise. He saw with his heart better than anyone can see with their eyes. He once told me when I was in his presence, 'O my son I see in you the traces of adultery. What have you done today?' I said, 'O my shaykh, when I was coming to you my eyes saw a woman on the street.' He said, 'Next time take care to protect your eyes.'"

Shaykh Habib Allah said, "Once as I was on my way to the shaykh, I saw an alcoholic on the street. When I came to the shaykh he told me, 'I am seeing in you the traces of alcohol.' I realized from this that everything in this life is reflected from one person to another, and the character of one person is reflected on another. That is why we have to keep ourselves very clean at all times, and always keep company with the people of God."

Shaykh Habib Allah said, "One day, a lady came to Shaykh Nur Muhammad and said, 'O my shaykh, a spiritual being (*jinn*) kidnapped my daughter. I have tried by every means to get her back, but it has been to no avail!' He meditated on that matter for about an hour. Then he said, 'Your daughter will come tomorrow around the time for the afternoon prayer so now go and rest.' The lady reported later, 'I was so eager for that time to come and for my daughter to appear, that I could hardly rest. At the exact time the shaykh had mentioned, I heard a knock at the door. In walked my daughter. I asked her what had happened. She said, "I had been kidnapped and taken to the desert by a jinn. I was there in the desert and just now a shaykh came and took me by the hand and brought me here."'"

Shaykh Nur Muhammad al-Badawani died in the year 1135 AH/1722-23 CE. He passed the secret of the Golden Chain to his successor, Shaykh Shamsuddin Habib Allah Jan-i-Janan al-Mazhar.

29. Shamsuddin Habib Allah ق

Shaykh Shamsuddin Habib Allah Jan-i-Janan al-Mazhar was the sun of eternal happiness. He was the beloved of God, Almighty and Exalted. He was the spirit of the people of Truth, and the essence of the spirit of the people of Taste. He was the Kabah of the pious and one of the flags of the Noble Messenger ﷺ. He elevated the knowledge of the religion of Muhammad ﷺ and revived the way of the Naqshbandi Order.

My eyes never beheld anyone more beautiful than you;
No woman gave birth to one more handsome,
Born faultless, as if created as you wished.
—Hassan ibn Thabit ؓ, speaking to the Prophet ﷺ

Shaykh Shamsuddin Habib Allah Jan-i-Janan al-Mazhar was born in 1113 AH/1701 CE in India. From his childhood the light of guidance and the traces of piety shone from his forehead. His features were molded with the manifestation of heavenly Beauty. He was famous, like the Prophet Yusuf عليه السلام, for his beauty. It is also the attribute of the Prophet ﷺ, about whom Anas رضي الله عنه said, "Your Prophet ﷺ was the most beautiful in appearance and had the best voice of all prophets." Because of this, Shaykh Abd ar-Rauf al-Munawi said, "The Prophet ﷺ has no partner in his beauty."

When Shaykh Mazhar was nine years of age, he saw Abraham عليه السلام, who gave him miraculous powers through spiritual transmission. At this age, if anyone mentioned Abu Bakr as-Siddiq رضي الله عنه in his presence, he would see him appear with his physical eyes. He was also able to see the Prophet ﷺ and all the Companions, as well as all the shaykhs of the Naqshbandi Order, especially Shaykh Ahmad al-Faruqi.

His father raised him and educated him in all branches of religious knowledge. At a young age his heart was attracted to the spiritual light coming from his shaykh, Sayyid Nur Muhammad. His shaykh opened the eyes of his heart and fed him from the nectar of the flower of the hidden knowledge. The shaykh took him out of the state of self-awareness and lifted him up to the highest stations, which produced in him great astonishment and caused him to faint. When he awoke, he accompanied Shaykh Nur Muhammad in further ascension. The shaykh allowed him to observe the mysteries of the hidden world and gave him gifts from his miraculous powers and stations.

One look of his shaykh opened in him the Nine Points, the loci of the Naqshbandi secrets. From the knowledge of the Nine Points, he delved into the secrets contained in the five more powerful points, until his shaykh authorized him to "activate" the Nine Points at any time and to use them. Then he brought him back down to be in his presence, and only in his presence. He brought him from one stage to another, enveloped him with his light, and protected him with his gaze until he achieved the ultimate perfection and awakened himself from ignorance.

Jan-i-Janan was steadfast in serving his shaykh with complete truthfulness. He continued to progress by entering seclusions in the desert and in the jungle on the orders of his shaykh. In these seclusions, his only food was wild herbs and roots. During his period of asceticism, he wore only what would cover his nakedness. One day, after many of these seclusions, he looked in the mirror but did not see himself. He saw his shaykh.

At this state, the shaykh authorized him to guide God's servants to their destinies and to the Straight Path. He put him on the throne of succession, and by him the sun of guidance ascended the tower of happiness.

When his teacher passed away, he continued to visit his grave. For two years he received whatever lights and knowledge his master was able to transmit to him from his grave. Then he was ordered through his spiritual connection to his shaykh to connect himself with a living master.

He reached the door of the perfect saints of his time, Shaykh Muhammad Afdal, Shaykh Hafiz Saad Allah, and Shaykh Muhammad Abid. He attached himself to Shaykh Shah Kalshan and to another shaykh by the name of Muhammad az-Zubayr. He attended the session of Shaykh Muhammad Afdal, one of the caliphs of the son of Muhammad Masum. He visited and studied with shaykh Abd al-Ahad and received from him knowledge of the Prophetic Traditions. During this class, whenever the shaykh would mention a Tradition, he would disappear through self-effacement, and a vision would come to him in which he would find himself sitting with the Prophet ﷺ and hearing the Tradition directly from the Prophet ﷺ. He would correct any mistakes that might occur in the shaykh's narration of the Tradition and was acknowledged as a genius in the science of the Traditions.

Shaykh Jan-i-Janan kept the company of these shaykhs for twenty years. He progressed further and further in the states of perfection until he became an ocean of knowledge. He rose in the firmament of the spiritual poles until he became the spiritual pole of his time, shining like the sun at high noon. Shaykh Muhammad Afdal said, "Shaykh Mazhar Habib Allah was given the state of the spiritual pole, and he is the central pivot of this Sufi order in this time."

His spiritual perfection attracted people from all reaches of the subcontinent. In his presence, each seeker would find what he needed until, through his blessing, the Indian subcontinent became like a Kabah encircled by flocks of angelic beings.

This attractive power influenced everyone, even students of other Naqshbandi shaykhs. One of these was Shah Wali Allah of Delhi, who grew very fond of Shaykh Jan-i-Janan. He said in reference to him:

> He was a beacon lighting the way for me to the Divine Presence and through him I received a great deal of guidance. Although he was no older than I, I consider him as my master, like my own shaykhs, my father, Shaykh Shah Abd ar-Rahim, and Shaykh Abu Taher Madani.

Shah Wali Allah was referring to Jan-i-Janan and to his other two teachers when he said, in his book *Altaf al-Quds:*

> The second category of teachers of the path consist of persons of such perfection that the Divine Wisdom has appointed them to be guides to the people. Through their agency the community is united and disciplined, and God's purpose is made manifest... Spiritual guides such as these have mapped out the way correctly. They have prescribed a cure for every disease and suggested a remedy for every hardship.

In his noble person were combined the power of four Sufi orders. He was a master of the Naqshbandi, Qadiri, Suhrawardi, and Chishti Orders. He said, "I received the secrets and knowledge of these orders from my shaykh, Sayyid Nur Muhammad al-Badawani, until I attained a very distinguished power in these orders. He lifted me from the Abrahamic stage to the Muhammadan stage, which caused me to see the Prophet ﷺ sitting in my place, while I was sitting in his. Then I disappeared, and I saw him sitting in both places. Then I saw him disappearing, and I was myself sitting in both places."

Shaykh Mazhar said:

> Once I was sitting in the presence of Shaykh Muhammad Abid, and the shaykh said, "The two suns at the two ends met, and if their lights were combined and spread throughout this universe, they would have burned everything."
>
> Shaykh Muhammad Afdal was much older than I, but he stood for me when I entered. He said to me, "I am standing in deference to the high lineage that you possess."
>
> This whole world and the entire universe are in my hand. I can see everything in them, just as clearly as I can see my hand.

He had innumerable miraculous experiences and numberless visions about the heavenly world, as well as the lower world. Once he traveled with some of his followers without any food or provision. They walked, and whenever they got tired they sat. The shaykh would call them and say, "This food is for you," and tables of food would appear in front of them.

One day during the trip, there was a terrible storm. The wind was blowing everything in its path. It was freezing. Everyone was shivering because of the cold. Their situation worsened until it appeared that they were going to die in that frozen desert. Then Shaykh Mazhar raised his hands and said, "O God make it surround us but not be upon us." Immediately, the clouds lifted from around them, and though the freezing rain continued to fall one mile away, around them the temperature rose to a comfortable level.

He said:

> Once I visited the grave of Shaykh Muhammad Hafiz Muhsin. I disappeared from myself, and in a vision, I saw his body. It had suffered no decomposition and his shroud was still perfectly clean except for a patch of dirt on one part by his feet. Through my spiritual power I asked him about that. He said, "O my son I will tell you a story. One day I took a stone from the garden of my neighbor and put it in a hole in my garden. I said to myself, 'In the morning I will return it to him,' but I forgot. As a result of that action, the dirt has appeared on my shroud. That one action has tainted my shroud."

He said:

> As long as you are lifted upward in piety, you will be lifted up in sainthood.

Once, he became angry with a tyrant. He said, "A vision came to me in which I saw that all shaykhs, from Abu Bakr as-Siddiq ﷺ up to the shaykhs of today, were unhappy with that tyrant." The next day the tyrant died.

A man came to him and said, "O my master, my brother has been jailed in another village. Please pray to God to save him." He said, "O my son, your brother has not been jailed, but he has done something wrong and tomorrow you will receive a letter from him." It turned out to be just as he described.

Shaykh Jan-i-Janan informed his followers of great tidings and some jealous people refused to accept what he said. He answered, "If you do not believe me let us bring a judge. We will each tell him our point of view and let him judge between us." They said, "We do not accept any judge except the Prophet ﷺ, and on Judgment Day we will ask for his judgment in this matter." Then he said, "There is no need to wait until the Judgment Day. We will ask the Prophet ﷺ to give his Judgment now." He entered a deep state of contemplation in his heart and was told to recite the *Fatiha*. This he did, and immediately the Prophet ﷺ appeared to everyone and said, "Shamsuddin Habib Allah Jan-i-Janan al-Mazhar is right, and all of you are wrong."

About Creation

Existence is an Attribute of God alone. This world is a mere shadow of realities existing in the Divine Presence. The reality of all possible creations results from the action of the Divine Attributes and Qualities on the void. The Real Existence of all that manifests in physical creation is confirmed as a light in the Divine Presence.

Everything that appears in the physical creation is but a shadow of the luminous reality projected by the Divine Qualities upon the void of non-existence. The World of the Divine Attributes is the origin of the wellsprings of the created universes. Because all physical creation arises from a combination of God's Divine Qualities and the void, creation thus partakes of two origins of opposite nature. From the nature of the void of non-existence and "nothingness" arise the dense qualities of physical substance that in the sphere of human action produce darkness, ignorance, and evil. From the Divine Attributes come light, knowledge, and good. Thus the Sufi, when he looks at himself, sees all that is good in him as a light from the Divine that is reflected on him, but that is not of him. A simile for it would be a borrowed suit of fine clothes with which the seeker is beautifully dressed but that does not truly belong to him and for which he deserves no credit. Conversely, he sees himself as base substance, full of darkness and ignorance, with a nature worse than that of an animal. With this dual perception he loosens his attachment to the attractions of the self and effaces himself, and turns in repentance towards the Divine Source of all Good. With this turning, God fills his heart with love and yearning for the Divine Presence. As God said in a Holy Tradition, "If My servant approaches Me by one hand's length, I will approach him by one arm's length. If he comes to Me walking, I will come to him running."

His State upon Leaving this World

Shortly before his death, Shaykh Jan-i-Janan was in a state of great emotion and intense love of God. He experienced a great unhappiness at having spent so long in this transient world. He spent his last days in intense contemplation. When asked, he would always say that his state was that of annihilation and subsistence in God, Almighty and Exalted. He increased his *dhikr* in his final days. As a result of the intense light of attraction generated thereby, thousands and thousands of seekers entered into the Way. Each new day would bring 3,000 new people to his door. He would not let one of them go without meeting him. Finally, he became so exhausted that he scheduled only two times a day to meet with people.

One day, one of his followers, Shaykh Mullah Nazim, asked permission to travel and visit his parents in his homeland. He said, "My son, if you want to go you may, but I may not be here when you return." This reply went from one mouth to another, shaking the hearts of people, as it indicated that his era was ending. With tearful eyes and broken hearts, people all around the Punjab began wailing and crying. His house was full, and no one knew what was going to happen when he was gone. Then he took a paper and wrote to one of his successors, Mullah Abdur-Razzaq, "O my son, I am now over eighty. My life is coming to an end. Remember me in your prayers." He sent him that letter, and he sent many others the same letter.

Thanking God for His Favors, he said:

> There is nothing left in my heart of anything that I have wished to achieve or to reach that remains to be accomplished. There is nothing for which I have asked God that I did not receive. My only remaining desire is to leave this world and be in His Presence continuously. God gave me everything, except permission to go to Him. I ask God to take me to Him today, before tomorrow. But I do not want to go to Him as an ordinary person. I want to go to him as God described in the Holy Quran, as a martyr who is always alive. So, O God, make me a martyr in this world and take me to you as a martyr. This kind of death will bring happiness to my heart and will cause me to be in the presence of

Your Prophet ﷺ and that of Abraham ؏, and of Moses ؏, and with all your 124,000 prophets. I will be with all the Companions of the Prophet ﷺ, and with Junayd, and the master of this Order, Shah Naqshband, and with all the masters of the Sufi Way. O God, I want to combine the witnessing of physical martyrdom with spiritual death in the state of witnessing, in the state of annihilation.

On Wednesday evening, the seventh of Muharram, of the year 1195 AH/1781 CE, his servant came to him and said, "There are three men at your door. They want to visit you." He said, "Let them enter." When they entered, he came out of his bedroom and greeted them. One of them said to him, "Are you Mirza Jan-i-Janan Habib Allah?" He answered, "Yes." The two said to the third, "Yes, he is the one." One of the men took a knife from his pocket and stabbed him in the back, piercing his kidney. Because of his age, he was unable to withstand the severity of the blow. He fell to the ground. When it was time for the dawn prayer, the king sent him a doctor. He sent back the doctor and said, "I do not need him. As for the men who stabbed me, I forgive them, because I am glad to die as a martyr, and they came as an answer to my prayer."

He passed from this life on Friday. When the day reached its middle, he recited *al-Fatiha* and *Surah YaSin* until the time of the afternoon prayer. He asked his followers how many hours were left until sunset. They told him, "Four hours." He said, "It is still long until the meeting with my Lord." He said, "I have missed ten prayers in my life, all in these past two days, because my body is full of blood and I have been unable to raise my head." They asked him, "If a sick person is in such a weak condition, is he obliged to pray with movements of his eyes and his forehead, or to postpone his prayer?" He answered, "Both ways are correct."

Shaykh Jan-i-Janan waited with patience for the sunset and he died. It was the night of Ashura, 1195 AH/1781 CE. He passed his secret of the Golden Chain to his successor, Shaykh Abd Allah ad-Dahlawi.

30. Abd Allah ad-Dahlawi (Shah Ghulam Ali) ق

Shaykh Abd Allah ad-Dahlawi was the summit of knowers, the king of the perfect guides, the revealer of the knowledge of the religion, the revealer of the secret of certainty; the verifier of the state of perfection, shaykh of all shaykhs of the Indian subcontinent, the inheritor of the knowledge and secrets of the Naqshbandi Order.

Is it not sad enough that I beg You ceaselessly,
As if I were far from You, as if You were absent?
I ask for Your charity without greed, and I see none
Who is as poor as I, and who desires You like I desire You.
—Abul Hasan Nuri

Shaykh Abd Allah ad-Dahlawi is known as "the Unique Diver and Swimmer in the Ocean of Oneness," "the Traveler in the Desert of the Ascetic State," "the Spiritual Pole of all Orders," and "the Red Sulfur ("rarest of the rare") of all Truth."

He perfected himself and adorned himself with the best ethics and manners. He lifted himself up to the high heavens of spiritual knowledge and adorned himself with its stars. He became the foremost in every science. He grew to be a full moon. He saw his light coming from the sun of his teacher until his teacher accepted to train him formally and to care for him.

The shaykh supported him by means of his spiritual power and raised him to the highest blessing until he attained the station of the certainty of Truth and the station of the Furthermost Lote Tree. Then he sent him back to this world until he became, as we said before, the guide for every human being. He was given permission to give initiation in the Naqshbandi Order. He supported the Divine Law, upheld the *Sunnah,* and revived the Truth of five Sufi orders: Qadiri, Suhrawardi, Kubrawi, Chishti, and Naqshbandi. He passed the secrets and authority of all five Sufi orders to his successor, and through him, to all subsequent shaykhs of the Golden Chain. He raised all of his disciples to the exalted stations of the highest saints.

Shaykh Abd Allah ad-Dahlawi was born in 1158 AH/1745 CE in the village of Bitala in the Punjab. He was a descendant of the family of the Prophet ﷺ. His father was a great scholar and ascetic trained in the Qadiri Order by Shaykh Nasir ad-Din al-Qadiri, who had been trained by Khidr عليه السلام. Before he was born, his father saw Ali رضي الله عنه, the fourth rightly guided caliph, in a dream telling him, "Call him by my name." His mother saw in a dream a pious man telling her, "You are going to have a boy. Call him Abd al-Qadir." Then his father and mother saw the same dream in which the Prophet ﷺ told them, "Call him Abd Allah." Because the Prophet's ﷺ order took precedence over any other suggestion, he was named Abd Allah Shah Ghulam Ali.

He memorized the Quran in one month due to his genius. He educated himself in external and spiritual knowledge until he became the highest of the scholars. As a youth, he went many times to the desert, reciting *dhikr* there for months at a time, subsisting on whatever food he could find. Once, he stayed forty days without sleeping and without eating a morsel of food. His *dhikr* did not stop. His father's shaykh ordered his father to bring his son to him to initiate him in the Qadiri Order. The same night that he reached the shaykh's house, the shaykh died. His father told him, "We would have gladly given you the Qadiri Order, but now you are free to find whatever way suits you."

He kept company with the shaykhs of the Chishti Order in Delhi, among them Shaykh Dia Allah, Shaykh Abd al-Addad, caliph of Shaykh Muhammad Zubayr, Shaykh Mirdad, Mawlana Fakhruddin, and many others, until he reached the age of twenty-two. He came by himself to the *khaniqah* of Shaykh Jan-i-Janan Habib Allah.

He asked his permission to enter the Naqshbandi-Mujaddidi Order. Shaykh Habib Allah said to him, "It is better for you to be with those orders that have taste and compassion, for in our Order there is nothing except to lick the stone without any salt." He said, "That is my highest goal." Shaykh Habib Allah accepted him and said, "May God bless you. Stay here."

He said:

> After I received the knowledge of the Traditions, memorized the Quran, and learned its interpretation, I stood in the presence of my shaykh. He gave me initiation into the Qadiri Order with his holy hand. He also gave me initiation into the Naqshbandi-Mujaddidi Order. I was in the presence of the circles of *dhikr* and in his company for fifteen years. Then he gave me the authorization to guide and train disciples.
>
> I was hesitant at first, because I was afraid that Abd al-Qadir Gilani would not give me permission to teach in the Naqshbandi Order. One day, during my period of hesitation, I saw him in a vision sitting on a throne. Shah Naqshband entered. Immediately, he stood up and put Shah Naqshband on the throne. He remained standing in his presence. It came to my heart that this was a sign of respect for Shah Naqshband. He said to me, "Go to Shah Naqshband. The goal is God. Whatever Path you choose, you can reach Him."
>
> I was living on income from a piece of property that I owned. I gave it away for God's sake. After that I faced many difficulties because I had no income. I was left with only an old mat to sleep on in cold weather and a small old pillow on which I rested my head. I became very weak. I locked myself in my room and said to myself, "O self, this is your grave. I am not going to open that door for you. Whatever God

> provides for you, you may take. You are going to live here without food and without anything but that mat and that pillow. Your food is going to be water. O my spirit, your food is going to be *dhikr Allah.*" I stayed in that state for forty days, growing very weak, until God sent someone knocking at my door. He served me with food and provided me with clothes for fifty years thereafter.
>
> When I locked the door of my room and I said what I said, God's care reached me. One day a person came to me and said, "Open the door." I said, "I do not want to open it." He said, "Do you not need me?" I said, "No, I need God, Almighty and Exalted." At that moment I experienced a vision in which I was raised up to God's Presence. It was as if I had spent 1,000 years in His Presence. Then I returned and He told me, "Open that door." After that I never experienced any difficulty.

People came to him from everywhere. His fame reached to Byzantium, Iraq, Khurasan, Transoxiana, and Syria. It even went as far as North Africa. He sent his caliphs and deputies everywhere on the spiritual order of Prophet Muhammad ﷺ. Among them was Khalid Baghdadi. He reached people through dreams and guided people in far countries. They traveled to him from great distances, telling him, "You called me to you through my dreams."

Characteristically, his *khaniqah* fed 2,000 persons every day. It was always full. He never kept any food for the next day. Out of modesty, he never slept extending his feet, because he was afraid of extending his feet towards the Prophet ﷺ or any saint or the Divine Presence. He never looked in a mirror.

If a dog entered his house to eat, he would say:

> O God, who am I to be a means between You and Your Lover? And who am I to feed them when You are feeding them and me? O God, I am asking for the sake of Your creation, this one and everyone who comes asking me for mercy, send me Mercy for their sake, bring me nearer to You, help me to hold fast to the *Sunnah* of the Prophet ﷺ, and to accept what You have prescribed, and to leave what You have prohibited.

On another occasion, he said:

> Once Ismail al-Madani came to visit me by the order of the Prophet ﷺ. He had traveled thousands of miles from his country in the Hijaz. He had brought with him some of the relics of the Prophet ﷺ. He gave them to me as a gift. I put them in the Great Mosque in Delhi.

The King of Nabdilkahand came to him once. He was wearing the clothes of the unbelievers. When the shaykh saw him, he was angry with him and said to him, "You cannot sit in my presence in such clothes." The king said, "If you are condemning me so much, I will not come to your group." The shaykh said, "That is better." He stood up angrily to go. When he reached the door, something happened to him, no one knew what. He threw off the clothes of the unbelievers and came running back and kissed the hand of the shaykh. He gave his allegiance to him and became one of his loyal followers. They asked him later what happened. He said, "When I was going out, I saw the shaykh coming in through the door with the Prophet ﷺ, while he was inside! That is what made me run back to him."

He slept very little. When he awoke for the supererogatory night prayer, he would awaken everyone to sit with him to contemplate and recite the Quran.

It was his practice every day to read one-third of the Quran and then pray the dawn prayer with the group. Then he would sit in the circle of *dhikr* and contemplation until sunrise. He would pray two *rakats* of voluntary prayer just after sunrise and then he would give a talk. He would sit to recite the Traditions and read commentaries on the Quran. He would pray late morning prayer and then sit to eat with all his followers. He ate little. After he ate he would read religious and spiritual books and write letters. After the noon prayer he would sit and recite commentaries on the Quran and Traditions until time for the afternoon prayer. After the afternoon prayer, he would speak about Sufism and its distinguished luminaries, such as al-Qushayri, or Ibn Arabi, or Shah Naqshband. Then he would sit in a circle of *dhikr* until time for the evening (sunset) prayer. After the evening prayer, he would sit in the private circle of his followers. Then he would eat dinner and pray the night prayer. After the night prayer, he would spend the night in *dhikr* and contemplation. He would sleep for only one or two hours, and then he would wake once again for the supererogatory night prayer.

His mosque was too small for his followers, as it would only hold 2,000 worshippers, so he often recited *dhikr* with his followers by turns, each time filling the mosque. Whenever someone gave him a donation he would first pay the poor-due from it, according to the school of Imam Abu Hanifa, without waiting for the passage of a year, because to give the poor-due immediately is better than to give voluntary charity. He would use what remained for preparing food and sweets for the poor, for the needs of his center, and finally, for his own needs.

Some people would steal from that money and he would not reprimand them, but would leave them for God. One day a man stole a book from him and then returned to sell it back. He praised him and gave him the money. One of his followers said, "O my master, this is from your own library and it has your signature in it." He said, "Do not backbite. That is between him and God."

He always sat on his knees, never cross-legged or with legs extended, out of respect for the Prophet ﷺ. He died in this posture. He concealed what he gave in charity. He never showed how much he gave nor to whom. He wore old clothes. If he was given new clothes, he would sell them and buy many old clothes with its price. He said, "Better for many to have some clothes than for one to have fine clothes."

Being in his company was like being in the company of Sufyan al-Thawri. Never was a loud voice raised, nor did backbiting occur, nor were worldly affairs discussed. Nothing was heard in it except spirituality and religion. One day, the shaykh was fasting and one of his followers spoke harshly about the king of India. He told him, "What a pity for me. I lost my fast." They said to him, "O our master, you did not do anything. The one who spoke is responsible." He said, "No, the speaker and the listener partake of that sin equally."

He loved the Prophet ﷺ so much that whenever he heard his holy name he would shake, and at times, faint. He was meticulous in following the Prophet ﷺ in his actions and in keeping his *Sunnah*.

The Words of His Perfection and the Perfection of His Words

The Naqshbandi Order is built on four principles: Keeping the Presence of God; divine inspirations; attraction; and disregarding whispers.

Whoever asks for taste and yearning is not really asking for the Reality of the Divine Presence.

The seeker must be fully aware of how he passes every single moment. He must know how he prayed. He must know how he recited the Quran. He must know how he read the Traditions. He must know how he recited the *dhikr*. He must know how much darkness he received from doubtful food.

Food is of two kinds. One is to satisfy the self and the second is to nourish the self. The first kind is not acceptable, but the other is accepted because it provides the strength needed to fulfill your obligations and to keep the *Sunnah* of the Prophet ﷺ.

Just as asking for permitted things is an obligation on every believer, so too, is the rejecting of permitted things an obligation on every knower: the knower, the Sufi, is the one who rejects this world and the next world, even though they are permitted. He accepts nothing but God, Almighty and Exalted.

It must be understood by everyone that the Prophet ﷺ is the summation of all perfections. The appearance of his perfection in every different century and time has been according to the preparedness and state of that century and that time. That is why the appearance of his perfection in his lifetime and the time of his Companions was in the form of jihad, struggle, and calling to religion. His appearance to the saints in later centuries through his holy Presence was in the form of self-effacement, annihilation, taste, compassion, emotion, secrets of Oneness, and all other spiritual states. That is what has appeared to the hearts and on the tongues of saints.

For us, the night of hunger is the night of Ascension. The night of hunger is the night of desire for God.

Initiation is of three categories: the first is for the intercession of the shaykhs; the second is to repent from sins; the third is to adhere to, to connect with, and receive the lineage.

All the perfections of a human being, including the prophetic, appeared in Ahmad al-Faruqi, and the prophetic perfection appeared in Shah Naqshband also.

Men are of four categories: those who are barely human because all they ask for is this world; those who ask for the hereafter; mature humans who ask for the hereafter and for God; special humans who ask only for God.

The angel of death will take the souls of human beings, but the souls of the elect cannot be approached by any angel; God Himself takes them with His Holy Hand.

The Divine Mind is the mind that knows its way to its goal without a mediator, and the earthly mind is the mind that needs to see its way by means of a guide and a saint.

Whoever wants to serve, he must serve his shaykh.

His Visions

I had a vision in which I saw al-Mir Ruh Allah, one of the followers of Jan-i-Janan Habib Allah, saying to me, "The Prophet ﷺ is waiting for you." I moved in that vision to the place where the Prophet ﷺ was waiting. He hugged me, and by means of that embrace, I changed to be like him. Then I changed to be like the image of my shaykh, Jan-i-Janan Habib Allah. Then I changed to be like Amir Kulal. I then changed to be like Shah Naqshband, and then I changed to be like Abd al-Khaliq al-Ghujdawani. Then I changed to be like Abu Bakr as-Siddiq ؓ, the Friend of the Prophet ﷺ.

I had a vision near the time of night prayer in which I saw the Prophet ﷺ coming to me and telling me, "I have advice for you and your followers: Never sleep before the night prayer."

I had a vision that I was asking the Prophet ﷺ, "You said, *'Whoever sees Me sees the Truth.'*" He said, "Yes, and he will see God, Almighty and Exalted."

I had a vision in which I saw the Prophet ﷺ coming to me. He said to me, "You and your followers should never stop reciting the Quran and reciting *dhikr*. Always send its reward as a gift to me. In this way, you will derive a great reward."

> I had a vision in which I said to the Prophet ﷺ, "I am very afraid of Hellfire." He said to me, "Whoever loves us never enters the Fire."
>
> I had a vision and I saw God, Almighty and Exalted, speaking to me. He said to me, "Your face is the face of the sultan of saints, and you are that one."
>
> I saw in a vision Shah Naqshband come to me, hug me, and merge with me. We were one. I asked him, "Who are you?" He answered, "Shah Bahauddin Naqshband, and you are me, and I am you."

From His Miracles

Once he was by the sea. The waves were raging. He saw a ship sailing in the tempest. It was in danger of foundering, but as soon as he looked at it, the ship stopped tossing and the sea became calm.

One of his followers, Shaykh Ahmad Yar, was traveling for business in a caravan. The caravan stopped to rest. He slept and saw his shaykh in a dream saying, "Go immediately away from here. There are thieves who are about to attack." He awoke and told the people, but they refused to believe him. He left by himself, and the highwaymen came and killed everyone.

Shaykh Zul Shah set out to visit Shaykh Abd Allah from very far away. He got lost on the way. A man came to him and pointed him in the right direction. He asked the man who he was. He answered, "I am the one you are going to visit."

Shaykh Ahmad Yar said:

> Once, Shaykh Abd Allah went to give his condolences to a pious woman whose daughter had died. She and her husband were serving him. He told the woman and her husband, "God is going to give you a son in the place of your daughter." She said, "I am sixty years old. I have passed childbearing age. My husband is eighty. How is it possible that we could have a child?" He said, "Do not ask how God can do that! It is His blessings to you and my blessings to you." Then he went out and made ablution and came to the mosque and prayed two *rakats*. Then he raised his hands in supplication and said, "O God, grant them the child as You promised me." Then he turned to me and said, "That supplication has been accepted." Later, the woman gave birth to a son.

A woman who was a relative of Mir Akbar Ali and a follower of the shaykh became ill. Mir Akbar Ali came to the shaykh and asked him to pray to God to take the sickness away, but the shaykh refused to make that supplication. Mir Akbar Ali insisted. The shaykh said, "It is impossible, because that lady is going to die in fifteen days." Mir Ali went back and two weeks later the woman died.

There was a drought in the region around Delhi. No crops were able to grow. The people were desperate. On one particularly hot day Shaykh Abd Allah went out to the yard of the mosque. With the sun beating down, he said, "O God! I will not move from here until You shower us with rain." He had not finished his supplication before the sky filled with clouds and it began to rain. That rain continued for forty days.

He said:

I would like to die like my shaykh, Mazhar Jan-i-Janan Habib Allah, as a martyr, but I remember that after he passed away, the people suffered a drought for three years. There was much killing and troubles because God was angry with those who had killed him. Therefore, O God, I do not ask to die that way, though I would like it, but I ask You to take me to You.

Shaykh Abd Allah ad-Dahlawi passed away on the 12th of Safar in the year 1241 AH/1825 CE. He died with the book of the Traditions of the Prophet ﷺ of at-Tirmidhi in his hands. He was buried next to his shaykh in Jan Janan Habib Allah's *khaniqah* in Delhi.

He left many books, including *Maqamat an-Naqshbandiyya, Risalat al-Ishtighal bi ismi-l-jalal, Manahij at-Tahqiq,* and *Minatu-r-Rahman*. He passed the secret of the Golden Chain to Shaykh Khalid al-Baghdadi al-Uthmani as-Sulaymani. ۞

31. Khalid al-Baghdadi ق

Shaykh Khalid al-Baghdadi al-Uthmani as-Sulaymani was the keeper of the secrets of Realities and the reality of the secrets. He was the scholar of the perfect saints and the saint of the perfect scholars.

He praises me, and I praise Him;
He serves me, and I serve Him;
By my existence I affirm Him;
And by my determination I deny Him;
It is He who knows me, when I deny Him;
Then I discover Him and contemplate Him.
—Ibn Arabi, *Fusus al-Hikam*[71]

[71] Ibn Arabi, *Fusus al-hikam*. From the chapter on Abraham in Ibn Arabi's *Wisdom of the Prophets*, p. 44.

Shaykh Khalid al-Baghdadi al-Uthmani as-Sulaymani was the scholar of scholars, the saint of saints, the knower of knowers, and the light and the full moon of this Order in his time. His secrets moved into every human being just as the soul moves into the body. If the Prophet ﷺ had not been the Seal of Prophecy, his words would have been revelation. He spread the knowledge of both Islamic Law and Sufism. He was an authority in both the Divine Law and the Way.

He achieved all the spiritual and the worldly knowledge. He was the center of the circle of the spiritual poles in his time. He was the means of merging the ends with the beginnings and the beginnings with the ends. Shaykh Khalid al-Baghdadi was the reviver of the thirteenth *Hijri* century. The universe was proud of his existence.

He was born in the year 1193 AH/1779 CE in the village of Karada, of the city of Sulaymaniyyah, in Iraq. He was raised and trained in that city where there were many schools and mosques. It was considered the primary educational city of his time. His grandfather was Pir Mikail Chis Anchit, which means Michael, the saint of the six fingers. His title is Uthmani because he is a descendant of Uthman ibn Affan ؓ, the third caliph of the Prophet ﷺ. He studied the Quran and the explanation of Imam Rifai according to the Shafii school. He was famous for his poetry. When he was fifteen years of age, he took asceticism as his creed, hunger as his horse, wakefulness as his means, seclusion as his friend, and energy as his light.

He was a traveler in God's world. He attained all the kinds of knowledge available in his time. He studied with the two great scholars of his time, Shaykh Abd al-Karim al-Barzinji and Shaykh Abd ar-Rahim al-Barzinji. He read with Mullah Muhammad Salih. He returned to Sulaymaniyyah, and there studied the sciences of mathematics, philosophy, and logic. Then he came to Baghdad where he studied the *Mukhtasar al-muntaha fi-l-usul*, an encyclopedia of the principles of jurisprudence.

Then he studied the works of Ibn Hajar, Suyuti, and Haythami. He memorized the commentary of the Quran of Baydawi. He was able to find solutions for even the most difficult questions in jurisprudence. He memorized the Quran according to the fourteen different ways of recitation and became very famous everywhere for this. Prince Ihsan Ibrahim Pasha, the governor of Baban, tried to persuade him to look after the schools in his kingdom. However, he refused and moved to the city of Sanandaj, where he studied the sciences of mathematics, engineering, astronomy, and chemistry. His teacher in these disciplines was Muhammad al-Qasim as-Sanandaji. After completing the study of the secular sciences, he returned to the city of Sulaymaniyyah. Following the plague of 1213 AH/1798 CE, he took over the school of his shaykh, Abd al-Karim Barzinji. He taught the modern sciences, verifying the most delicate equations of astronomy and chemistry.

He then entered seclusion, leaving everything he had studied behind, coming to God's door with all kinds of pious actions and much *dhikr*, both loud and silent. He no longer visited the sultans, but kept to himself and to his disciples until the year 1220 AH/1806 CE when he decided to make the pilgrimage and to visit the Prophet ﷺ. He left everything and went to the Hijaz through the cities of Mosul, Yarbikir, ar-Raha, Aleppo, and Damascus where he met its scholars and followed its shaykh, the master of both ancient and modern knowledge and the teacher of Traditions, Shaykh Muhammad al-Kuzbari. He received authorization in the Qadiri Order from Shaykh al-Kuzbari and his deputy, Shaykh Mustafa al-Kurdi, who traveled with him until he reached the city of the Prophet ﷺ.

He praised the Prophet ﷺ in Persian poetry in such a way that people were astonished at his eloquence. He spent a long time in the city of the Prophet ﷺ. He reported:

> I was looking for someone of rare piety in order to take some advice when I saw a shaykh on the right-hand side of the *Rawdatu sh-sharifa*.[72] I asked him to give me advice, counsel from a wise scholar to an ignorant person. He advised me not to object when I enter Makkah to matters which might appear to be counter to the Divine Law, but to keep quiet. I reached Makkah, and keeping in my heart that advice, I went to the Holy Mosque early on the morning of Friday. I sat near the Kabah reading *Dalail al-Khayrat*,[73] when I saw a man with a black beard leaning on a pillar and looking at me. It came to my heart that the man was not showing the proper respect to the Kabah, but I did not say anything to him about the matter.

---

[72] *Rawdatu 'sh-sharifa* refers to the space between the Prophet's ﷺ *minbar* and his tomb which he identified as a garden from the Gardens of Paradise.

[73] A book of prayers on the Prophet ﷺ by Muhammad al-Jazuli (d. 870 H).

He looked at me and scolded me, saying, "O ignorant one, do you not know that the honor of the heart of a believer is far more than the privilege of the Kabah? Why do you criticize me in your heart for standing with my back to the Kabah and my face to you? Did you not hear the advice of my shaykh in Madinah who told you not to criticize?" I ran to him and asked his forgiveness, kissing his hands and feet and asking him for his guidance to God. He told me, "O my son, your treasures and the keys to your heart are not in these parts, but in India. Your shaykh is there. Go there, and he will show you what you have to do." I did not see anyone better than him in all the sacred area. He did not tell me where to go in India, so I went back to Sham and associated with its scholars.

He then returned to Sulaymaniyyah and continued his teachings of self-denial. He was always looking for someone to show him the way. Finally, there came to Sulaymaniyyah the Shaykh Mawlana Mirza Rahim Allah Beg al-Maruf, known by the name of Muhammad ad-Darwish Abd al-Azim al-Abadi, one of the caliphs of the spiritual pole, Abd Allah ad-Dahlawi. He met with him and gave him respect and asked him about the perfect guide to show him the way. He told him, "There is one perfect shaykh, a scholar and a knower, showing the seeker the way to the King of Kings, expert in this delicate matter, following the Naqshbandi Way, carrying the character of the Prophet ﷺ, a guide in the knowledge of spirituality. Come back with me to his service in Jahanabad. He had told me before I left, 'You are going to meet someone, bring him back with you.'"

Shaykh Khalid moved to India in 1224 AH/1809 CE through the city of Ray, then Tehran, and then some provinces of Iran, where he met the great scholar Ismail al-Kashi. Then he traveled to Kharqan, Simnan, and Nishapur. He visited the master of the mother of all Sufi orders in Bistam, Shaykh Bayazid al-Bistami, and he praised him in his grave and with a very eloquent poem in Persian. Then he moved on to Tus where he visited Sayyid al-Jalil al-Manus Imam Ali Rida. He praised him with another Persian poem that caused all the poets of Tus to accept him. Then he entered the city of Jam, and he visited Shaykh Ahmad an-Namiqi al-Jami and praised him with another Persian poem. He then passed through the city of Herat in Afghanistan, then Kandahar, Kabul, and Peshawar. In all these cities, the great scholars with whom he met would test his knowledge in the sciences of the Divine Law and Sufism, and those of logic, mathematics, and astronomy. They found him like a wide river, flowing with knowledge, or like an ocean without a shore.

He moved from there to Lahore, where he met with Shaykh Thanaullah an-Naqshbandi and asked for his prayers and his supplications. He recalled:

> That night I slept in Lahore. I had a dream in which Shaykh Thanaullah an-Naqshbandi pulled me with his teeth. When I awoke I wanted to tell him the dream but he said, "Do not tell me the dream. We know it already. That is a sign to move on to my brother and shaykh, Abd Allah ad-Dahlawi. The opening of your heart will be by his hands. You will take initiation in the Naqshbandi Order." Then I began to feel the shaykh's spiritual attraction. I left Lahore, crossing mountains and valleys, forests, and deserts until I reached the Sultanate of Delhi known as Jahanabad. It took me one year to reach his city. Forty days before I arrived he told his followers, "My successor is coming."

The night he entered the city of Jahanabad, he wrote a poem in Arabic, recounting his year of travel and praising his shaykh. Then he praised him with a Persian poem, which surprised everyone with its eloquence. He gave everything that he was carrying with him and all that was in his pocket to the poor. Then he was initiated by his shaykh, Abd Allah ad-Dahlawi. He served in the mosque-school of the shaykh and made rapid progress in the struggle against his self. Five months had not passed when he became one of the people of the Divine Presence and the Divine Vision.

He took permission from Shaykh Abd Allah to return to Iraq. The shaykh gave him written authority in five Sufi orders. The first was the Naqshbandi Order, or the Golden Chain. The second was the Qadiri Order through Ahmad al-Faruqi's shaykh, Shah Sakandar and thence to Abd al-Qadir Gilani, al-Junayd, as-Sari as-Saqati, Musa al-Kazim ﵁, Jafar as-Sadiq ﵁, Imam al-Baqir ﵁, Zain al-Abidin ﵁, Husayn ﵁, Hasan ﵁, Ali ibn Abi Talib ﵁, and Prophet Muhammad ﷺ. The third Sufi order, as-Suhrawardi, traced its chain of transmission similarly to the Qadiriyya until al-Junayd, who went back to Hasan al-Basri, and then to Ali ﵁ and the Prophet ﷺ. He also gave him authority in the Kubrawi Order, which had the same lineage as the Qadiri but through Shaykh Najmuddin al-Kubra. Finally, he was granted authority in the Chishti Order through a line that went back from Abd Allah ad-Dahlawi and Jan Janan to Ahmad al-Faruqi and then through many shaykhs to Shaykh Mawrud Chishti, Nasir Chishti, Muhammad Chishti, and Ahmad Chishti to Ibrahim ibn Adham, Fudayl ibn al-Iyad, Hasan al-Basri, Ali ؓ, and the Prophet ﷺ.

The shaykh gave him authorization to teach all the sciences of the Traditions, commentary upon the Quran, Sufism, and the daily practices. He memorized the books of the Twelve Imams, the sourcebooks for the knowledge of the descendants of Ali ؓ.

He moved to Baghdad in the year 1228 AH/1813 CE for the second time. He stayed in the school of Ahsaiyya Isfahaniyyah. He filled it up with the knowledge of God and His Remembrance. Then some of the jealous people wrote against him to the Sultan, Said Pasha, governor of Baghdad, criticizing him. They accused him of unbelief and other things that cannot be repeated. When the governor read the letter, he said, "If Shaykh Khalid al-Baghdadi is not a believer, then who is a believer?" He had his envious enemies thrown out of his presence and jailed.

The shaykh left Baghdad for some time and then returned again for a third time. He returned to the same school that had been renovated to welcome him. He began anew to spread all kinds of spiritual and heavenly knowledge. He unveiled the secrets of the Divine Presence, illuminating the hearts of the people with the lights that God gave to his heart, until the governor, the scholars, the teachers, the workers, and people from every walk of life counted themselves among his followers. Baghdad was so famous in his time for his knowledge that it was called, "the Place of the Two Knowledges," and "the Place of the Two Suns." Similarly, he came to be known as "He of the Two Wings," an allusion to his complete mastery of the external and the internal knowledge. He sent his caliphs everywhere, from the Hijaz to Iraq, from Sham (Syria) to Turkey, from Iran to India and Transoxiana, to spread the way of his forerunners in the Naqshbandi Order.

People would invite him to their homes wherever he went. Whatever home he entered, that home would become prosperous. One day, he visited the Dome of the Rock in Jerusalem with many of his followers. He reached the Dome of the Rock and his caliph, Abd Allah al-Fardi, came out to meet him with a large crowd of people. Some of the Christians asked him to enter the Church of Kumama to bless it with his presence. Then he continued on his way to al-Khalil (Hebron), the City of Abraham ؑ, the Father of all

Prophets ﷺ. He was welcomed by all people. He entered the mosque of Abraham ﷺ, the Friend of God and he took the blessings of its walls.

He went again to the Hijaz to visit the House of God, the Holy Kabah in the year 1241 AH/1826 CE. A large crowd of his caliphs and disciples accompanied him. The city of the Holy Mosque with all its scholars and saints came out to meet him and all took initiation from him. They gave him the keys of the two Holy Cities. They considered him to be the spiritual shaykh of the two holy cities. He circled around the House, but in Reality the Kabah was circling him.

The visit to the Holy Cities strengthened the shaykh's position in the eyes of the scholars of the community and the common folk. In *Taste of Modernity: Sufism, Salafiyya, & Arabism in Late Ottoman Damascus,* Itzchak Weismann observes:

> Many among the ulama and notables ...regarded Shaykh Khalid as the renovator (*mujaddid*) of the thirteenth century of Islam... the religious awakening he headed was indeed the last major effort... to generate a religious renewal in the traditional sense of the term—*tajdid.*[74]

Shaykh Khalid came back from his visit to the Holy Cities with a deepened concern at the danger he saw coming from that region—the Wahabi movement. His letters of that time convey this concern with their advance. He designated them as Khawarij—a heretical sect from Islam's first century who created immense schism by opposing the Companions of the Prophet ﷺ. He saw them, Weismann writes, as "an even greater menace to the Ottoman Empire" than its external enemies.

After his pilgrimage and visit to the Holy Prophet ﷺ, he went back to Blessed Syria. He was so well respected by the Ottoman Sultan, Mahmud Khan, that when he entered Damascus, a huge celebration was held and 250,000 people welcomed him at the gate of the city. All the scholars, ministers, and shaykhs, the poor and the rich, came to receive his blessing and to ask for his prayers. It was a day of celebration. The poets sang its praises. The rich fed the poor. Everyone was equal before him when he entered the city. He revived the spiritual knowledge as well as the external

---

[74] Itzchak Weismann, *Taste of Modernity: Sufism, Salafiyya, & Arabism in Late Ottoman Damascus,* Brill, p. 55.

knowledge. He spread that light for which people, both Arabs and non-Arabs, came and accepted the Naqshbandi Order at his hand.

Shaykh Khalid displayed the traditional Naqshbandi focus on activism, scholarship and working among the people. Shaykh Khalid developed new methods of spiritual practice as well modified traditional ones. In particular in his teachings emphasized renewal of the society (*tajdid*). Shaykh Khalid built his teachings on firm theological foundations, stressing that *"there is nothing for man but what he strives to acquire"* (53:39) emphasizing the Sunni doctrines that while God is Creator of man's actions, it is man who is the "actor" and thus responsible for the choices he makes. Shaykh Khalid, writing on man's "particular will," stressed that the way of the Companions, of which the Naqshbandiyya is the apex, strikes the middle path between predestination with its inescapable fatalism, and free will with its implied restriction of God's Knowledge of His creation.

One of the manifestations of this "middle path" is seen in the Naqshbandiyya in its emphasis on *khalwah fi jalwah,* the importance of the seeker maintaining his public duties and associating with people, while in fact, his heart is with God. Weismann remarks:

> As we have seen, many of ...[the Naqshbandi] masters have been involved in the social and political affairs of their countries, leaving their mark on their histories. This legacy was reinforced by Shaykh Khalid and consequently became an important trait of... the Khalidiyya. For him, the *alim amil,* the Naqshbandi definition of the genuine master, was one that combined not only legal and theological knowledge with the mystic path, but also religious knowledge in general with practical life. This was, after all, the *sunnah* of the Prophet, whose strict following is the external definition of the Naqshbandiyya. [75]

Weismann defines how this concept manifested in daily life:

> Thus the adherents of the Naqshbandiyya.. . can be magnificently dressed and well fed, reflecting the wealth that God has bestowed on them. Leaving no discernible indications as to their real identity, it is

[75] *Ibid.*, p. 46-47.

only their hearts that are permanently engaged in recollecting God's name.[76]

Working with Rulers

This principle was shown as well in the way Naqshbandi masters sought to work with the rulers, despite their often manifest corruption and deviance from the path of Islam. Often this was seen by critics as association with the worldly, but in fact nothing could be further from the truth. Regarding this, Weismann writes:

> The purpose of his work was to reinforce the wielders of political power, as a means to improve the state of the umma in general. Thus in his letters to his deputies, Khalid emphasizes mainly their duty to treat rulers with respect and pray on their behalf... His eagerness to attract to his order the local governors in the regions in which he was active derived from his aspiration to guide them back to the straight path of the *Shariah*... [his] emphasis on the obligation to work among rulers, however, must not lead us to infer that in his opinion the *ulama amilun* should be on intimate terms with them. On the contrary, the very task that the Naqshbandiyya assigned to these religious men to guide the rulers implied a position of distance based on superiority over them.[77]

For this reason Shaykh Khalid would often recite the verse *"O ye who believe! Obey God, obey the Prophet and those in authority among you,"* (4:59) explaining those in authority among you as the scholars (*ulama*) of Islam. He would explain that "nothing is more precious than knowledge of the religion; therefore while the kings rule the people, true scholars rule the kings."

His Esteem among Scholars

Of the enormous esteem in which Shaykh Khalid was held by the scholars of Damascus, Weismann says:

> The movement of religious renewal aroused by Shaykh Khalid... reflected the characteristic Naqshbandi combination of adherence to the *Shariah* and following the *tariqah*. In propagating this reformist

---

[76] *Ibid.*, p. 48.

[77] *Ibid.*, p. 54.

combination ...[he] could not have been successful, however, without ready acceptance of his authority by the Damascene men of religion. Many established *ulama* in the city, who held senior posts in its religious administration and in its central mosques, as well as the younger *ulama* who acquired their religious status by their own merit, were among his supporters. The various positions adopted by the Damascene *ulama* towards Shaykh Khalid, and toward the orthodox principles that he came to represent, were to last after his death, shaping their attitudes towards religious reform under the regimes of Ibrahim Pasha and the early *Tanzimat*, when the traditional character of the city remained basically intact.[78]

On Humility

Shaykh Khalid said:

The seeker must see himself as the most lowly of all creatures, not to see that he has any right imposed on anybody, and to discharge his responsibilities concerning his obligations to others by fulfilling or paying them and by severing all attachments to anything other than his aim, which is none other than God's Pleasure.

The corollary of this is that one must not despise anybody. Rather whomever one sees, assume he is Khidr, or one among the honored among God's saints and seek his prayers on your behalf. Indeed our Prophet ﷺ mentioned in an authentic hadith that a disheveled and dusty man, pushed away from all doors, and to whom no one gives heed, if he asks by swearing an oath by God, He will answer him.

On Watchfulness (*Muraqabah*)

Watchfulness (*muraqabah*) is an independent way for arrival. Thus the seeker must have the knowledge that God is overseeing him. Turning the heart towards God (*tawajjuh*) and watchfulness (*muraqabah*) are higher and superior than "denial and affirmation," and closer to Divine Attraction (*jadhba*). By persisting in watchfulness and turning the heart towards God, the level of Ministry results, administering in the physical (*mulk*) and spiritual realms (*malakut*) becomes possible as well

---

[78] *Ibid.*, p. 56.

as clairvoyance of others'' thoughts, and it will be made possible for him to enlighten the inner being of those accepting it with the light of guidance by the sole Power by God. Whoever persists in watchfulness reaches continuous gathering of his thoughts (as opposed to involuntary scattering) and continuous acceptance by the sincere hearts, which is called in the convention of Sufis gathering (*jam*) and acceptance (*qubul*).

It was related that al-Junayd said: "My teacher in the Way of watchfulness is the cat: One day, I was passing in the street, I saw a cat sitting and watching the hole of a mouse, so absorbed in its hole that not one of its hairs was moving. I was bemused by its concentration and watchfulness, and I was called in my innermost: 'O you with the lowly determination! Do not let me be in your purpose less than the mouse, and you, do not be in the seeking less than the cat.' So I awoke, adhered to the Way of watchfulness (*muraqabah*), and achieved the results that I did."

His Passing

In the last ten days of Ramadan of the year 1242 AH/1827 CE, Shaykh Khalid decided to travel to Jerusalem (Quds) from Damascus. His followers were very happy and he said, "Praise belongs to God, we will do it after Ramadan at the beginning of Shawwal, if God gives us life." That was an indication that he might be leaving this world.

In the first days of Shawwal, the plague began to spread quickly in the city of Damascus. One of his followers asked him to pray for him to be saved from the plague, and added, "And for you also my shaykh." He said, "I feel shy before my Lord, because my intention in coming to Damascus was to die in this holy land."

The first one to die from the plague was his son, Bahauddin, on the night of Friday, and he said, "Praise belongs to God, this is our way," and he buried him on the Mount of Qasiyun. He was five years and some days old. That child was fluent in three languages, Persian, Arabic, and Kurdish, and he read the Quran.

Then, on the 9th of Dhul-Qida, another son, Abd ar-Rahman, passed away. He was older than his brother by one year. Mawlana Khalid ordered his disciples to reopen the grave to bury his second son. He said, "From my followers many are going to die." He ordered them to dig many graves for the many followers, including his wife and his daughter. He ordered them to water the area. Then he said, "I am giving the authority to succeed me in the Naqshbandi Order to Shaykh Ismail ash-Shirwani." He said this the year of his death, 1242 AH/1827 CE.

One day he said:

> I had a great vision yesterday: I saw Uthman Dhun-Nurayn ﷺ as if he were dead, and I was praying for him. He opened his eyes and said, "This one is from my children." He took me by the hand, brought me to the Prophet ﷺ, and told me to bring all the Naqshbandi followers of my time and after my time up to the time of the Mahdi ﷺ, and he blessed them. Then I came out of that vision, and I performed the evening prayer with my followers and my children.
>
> Whatever I have of secrets I have given to my deputy Ismail ash-Shirwani. Whoever does not accept him is not from me. Do not argue, but be of one mind. Follow the opinion of Shaykh Ismail. I guarantee that anyone of you who accepts and follows him will be with me and with the Prophet ﷺ.

He ordered them not to cry on his behalf. He asked them to slaughter animals and feed the poor for the love of God and for the honor of the shaykh. He asked them to send him gifts of reading from the Quran and recitations of prayers. He ordered them not to write anything on his grave except, "This is the grave of the stranger Khalid."

After the night prayer he entered his house, called his family, and advised them, "I am going to pass away on Friday." They stayed with him all night. He arose before dawn, made ablution, and prayed for a while. Then he entered his room and said, "No one may enter my room except those I order to do so." He lay on his right side, facing the *qiblah*, and said, "I have been struck by the plague. I am carrying all the plague which has descended on Damascus." He raised his hands and prayed, "Whoever the plague touches, let it strike me instead and spare everyone in Damascus."

Thursday came and all his caliphs entered. Ismail ash-Shirwani asked him, "How are you feeling?" He said, "God has answered my prayer. I will take all the plague from the people of Damascus, and I alone will die on Friday." They offered him water, but he refused and said, "I left the world behind to meet my Lord. I have accepted to carry the plague and relieve those in Damascus who are infected. I will pass away on Friday."

He opened his eyes and said, *"Allahu, Allahu, Allahu Haqq,"* the oath of initiation into the Naqshbandi Order. He then read the Quran:

O soul in complete rest and satisfaction! Come back to thy Lord—well pleased and well pleasing. Enter thou among My devotees! Enter thou My heaven! (89: 27-30)

Then he gave his soul to His Lord as he had predicted, on the 13th of Dhul-Qida, 1242 AH/1827 CE. They carried him to his school and they washed him with water full of light. They shrouded him while all of them recited *dhikr*, especially Shaykh Ismail ash-Shirwani, Shaykh Muhammad, and Shaykh Amin. They recited the Quran around him, and in the morning, they carried him to the mosque in Yulbagha.

Shaykh Ismail ash-Shirwani asked Shaykh Amin Abidin to pray the funeral prayer for him. The mosque was unable to accommodate all the people who attended. It is said that more than 300,000 people prayed behind him. Shaykh Ismail promised those who could not pray in the mosque that he would pray the funeral prayer a second time at the grave. Those who washed him took him down into the grave. The next day, Saturday, it was as if a miracle had happened in Damascus, the plague immediately stopped and there were no further deaths.

Mawlana Khalid passed his secret of the Golden Chain to his successor, Grandshaykh Ismail ash-Shirwani. ۞

32. Ismail ash-Shirwani ق

Shaykh Ismail ash-Shirwani was an imam of spiritual power. He was one of the masters of Sufism, the owner of the throne of guidance, the focus of Divine outpouring, and a tower of the unseen secrets of the Divine Essence.

I spoke about Myself.
Those who heard me said: "See how he boasts!"
How could I compare the Real to the other-than-Real,
When one drop, one atom of Him fills the two worlds?
The part is the All, and the All is here.
In Him the two worlds are lost—
the soul and the one she quickens.
There is the Sun, here, the ray.
Whoever saw a ray separated from the Sun?
The Sufi is entirely there, only his trace is here.
And the trace is never separated from the All.
—al-Ansari al-Harawi, *Munajat*

Through Shaykh Ismail ash-Shirwani, humanity was guided on the Path of heavenly knowledge. By means of him, they became distinguished. He was a beacon for his time. He was the imam for whose elevated knowledge the people bore witness. In his century, he was the Sufi to whom all eyes turned.

Shaykh Ismail ash-Shirwani was the one to take the Naqshbandi Order to Caucasia, to encourage jihad against the cruel Russian occupation, and to revive the religion of Islam in his country after it had been nearly eradicated.

He was born on a Tuesday, the 7th of Dhul-Qida of the year 1201 AH/1787 CE in Kurdemir, in the Khanate of Shirwan, in Caucasia. He had a very strong and well-built body and he was tall. He had a very light complexion. His eyes and beard were black. He had a high-pitched voice.

He received his education in Shirwan through his father, who was one of the greatest scholars of his time, Shaykh Anwar ash-Shirwani. He educated young Ismail in the memorization of the Quran, which he completed by the age of seven. He then spent time memorizing the seven different readings. At the age of nine, he began learning jurisprudence and the science of Traditions from Shaykh Abd ar-Rahman ad-Daghestani. At that young age, he was able to give the evidences from the Quran and Traditions for almost any question of jurisprudence.

One day, he was struck by a powerful heavenly influence which made him lose awareness of himself completely and took him into a state of self-effacement. This state, in which he was lost to himself, impelled him to wander in search of the Reality he could see in his heart. Then one day he had a vision, in which a voice told him, "You must direct yourself towards Delhi where you will learn from its scholars and its shaykhs. God may grant you the good fortune to meet with the successors of Shaykh Abd Allah ad-Dahlawi."

That vision kept appearing to him until he reached the age of seventeen. He said to his father, "I want to go become one of the followers of Abd Allah ad-Dahlawi." His father was very fearful to let him go to such a far-off country, but he finally relented and gave permission for his son to travel. Ismail set out on foot for Delhi, walking day and night without conveyance. It took one year to reach Abd Allah ad-Dahlawi in Delhi.

He stayed in the shaykh's *khaniqah*, learning from him. He was in his service for several years. In 1224 AH/1809 CE, he met Mawlana Khalid, when the latter came to India to meet Shaykh Abd Allah ad-Dahlawi and to take the Order from his hand. Shaykh Ismail carefully observed the behavior of Mawlana Khalid with Shaykh Abd Allah. He was very impressed by the manner and sincerity with which Mawlana Khalid served the shaykh. Shaykh Abd Allah once looked at Ismail and said, "Your secrets are with Shaykh Khalid. When he returns to his country you will follow him."

When Mawlana Khalid returned to Damascus in 1225 AH, Shaykh Ismail ash-Shirwani went back to Caucasia to say farewell to his parents. On his journey back to Shirwan, he stopped in a city where he found the people standing in the desert with their hands raised in supplication, asking God to send them rain. They had had no rain for a whole year. When they saw him and glimpsed the piety in his face, they asked him, "Can you ask God to shower rain on us?" He raised his hands in supplication. The clouds gathered and the wind began to blow. It started to rain and continued to rain for seven days without stopping.

When he reached Shirwan, he asked his parents' permission to move to Damascus. However, he stayed there for several years. While he was there people came to him constantly to learn from his teachings. During this time he planted the seeds of the ideology that would surface several decades later in the armed struggle against Russian tyranny in the Caucasus known as the Murid Wars.

In *Muslim Resistance to the Tsar: Shamil and the Conquest of Chechnia and Daghestan,* Gammer writes:

> Shaykh Mansur did not establish the (Naqshbandi) Order in the Caucasus. This was done, in fact, by the Naqshbandiyya Khalidiyya, a branch of the order named after Shaykh Diya al-Din Khalid al-Shahrazuri (Khalid al-Baghdadi). One of his disciples, Shaykh Ismail al-Kurdumiri (Ismail ash-Shirani) was active for many years in Shirwan as Shaykh Khalid's caliph (deputy) in the late 1810s. Following the annexation of the Khanate in 1820 Russian authorities started to persecute the movement...[79]

---

[79] Moshe Gammer, *Muslim Resistance to the Tsar: Shamil and the Conquest of Chechnia and Daghestan,* p. 39.

From His Sayings

If a person devotes himself to God, Almighty and Exalted, the first benefit he will receive will be that he will no longer be in need of people.

The sweet smell of the lovers of God will arise from them and spread. Even if they try to conceal it, they will not be able to, from wherever they come and to wherever they go.

Whoever hears wisdom and does not apply it is a hypocrite.

The company of the heretics is an illness and the medicine for it is to leave them.

God, Almighty and Exalted, has said that whoever is patient with Us will reach Us.

God provides his servants with the sweetness of His *dhikr*. If one thanks God and is happy with that, He will provide him familiarity with Him. If he is not thankful and happy with that, He will take the sweetness from the *dhikr* and leave it only on his tongue.

God expresses familiarity with His servants by means of showing them His saints.

Sufism is purity. It is not a description. It is a Truth without an end, like a river of red roses.

Sufism is to walk with the secrets of God.

Whoever prefers the company of the rich over that of the poor, God will make his heart to be dead.

For the knower, there is a time when the light of knowledge will shine on him. It makes him see the wonders of the unseen.

Whoever proclaims he is hearing, and yet he does not hear the *dhikr* in the song of the birds and in the sounds of the woods and in the applause of the wind, is a liar.

Ismail ash-Shirwani was asked about human beings. He said, "There are four kinds of people and jinn. On them, God's Will is pouring forth."

He spent a few years in Shirwan. Then he had a vision in which Shaykh Abd Allah ad-Dahlawi ordered him to move to Damascus to serve Shaykh Khalid al-Baghdadi. He traveled to Damascus, walking in an indirect route, all the while spreading the teachings, from Shirwan to Kuman, from Kuman to Azerbaijan, and on to Tiflis. From there he went to Tabriz, then to Amad, Aleppo, Hama, and Homs. He finally arrived in Damascus, the center of Sham, after one year of travel.

In Sham, he immediately went to meet his shaykh. From Marja in the city center where he had arrived, there was no easy way to go up the mountain, which overlooks all of Damascus, where his shaykh's *khaniqah* was located. He walked from Marja to that mountain in two hours, until he arrived at his shaykh's door. As he entered his shaykh was waiting for him. He said, "We received the news of your arrival. Welcome."

Shaykh Khalid immediately placed him in seclusion for a long period of time. In that seclusion he taught him what he needed in order to reach perfection, then he gave him the power of this Order. He told all his followers to listen to him. He said:

> This is my caliph. He is like the dome of a mosque, the dome of the mosque of the Prophet ﷺ. From him the secret of this Order is going to spread to Daghestan. From there, I can see its light shining forth through seven generations of shaykhs. Every one of these seven shaykhs will represent the highest powers of the Divine Presence. Through them, there will be great support against the army of ignorance which is going to overwhelm the area of Daghestan.
>
> From among the people of Daghestan, there will be one warrior who will be living in the time of three great shaykhs of this Order. He will be supported by them. He will lead the fight against this army of ignorance.
>
> Shaykh Ismail ash-Shirwani is the best of all scholars in this time. I raised him up to be one of the perfected saints. He will guide you and guide everyone after me. He is going to be the knower that spreads the secret of this Order in the territories of the Caucasus. This imam is going to be the first to sit on my throne. He is going to be the trustee of whatever I have to spend in God's Way. And his duty is to look after my children.

Shaykh Ismail served his shaykh and kept his company whenever he was not in his home country of Shirwan. He traveled with Shaykh Khalid and lived with him in his house for several years. He was given the absolute caliphate. He was given permission to guide seekers. He directed people to the best of his knowledge, until his fame spread throughout Sham, Iraq, Persia, Turkey, Armenia, and Caucasia.

Shaykh Khalid assigned him to teach and train people. He observed and evaluated the actions of every seeker, one-by-one, and presented it to his shaykh, Mawlana Khalid. Whatever question he was asked by the disciples he presented to the shaykh. Then the shaykh would either give an answer or ask Shaykh Ismail to issue an edict.

It was reported:

> Shaykh Ismail often said to us, "I am a polished mirror. Whatever Mawlana Khalid has engraved on me I have reflected it to you." And he never saw himself higher than us.

When Shaykh Khalid passed away, Shaykh Ismail cried. He was shaking, but despite this, he was firm, like a mountain, steadfast. He made all the followers of the shaykh come together and testify in unison that they would hold fast to the rope of God. He renewed their energies and took the sadness from their hearts. He gave them respect. He praised them and blessed them. He taught them the best way of worship and prepared them to receive elevated spiritual knowledge. He took control of guiding the seekers in place of his shaykh. He kept it as it had been. He said, "Do you not know that Mawlana Khalid was of the people of God and that those people never die? They are with us in every moment and in every second."

He left for Shirwan after some time and reached there very quickly. In his *zawiya* in Shirwan, he trained Khas Muhammad. Seeing in him the light of this Order, he told him, "You are going to be one of my successors." Eventually he passed the secret of the Order to him, as well as to two other great saints of Daghestan, Shaykh Muhammad Effendi al-Yaraghi and Sayyid Jamaluddin al-Ghumuqi al-Husayni.

During his travel in his homeland, Shaykh Ismail spread the Order and encouraged his people to fight the Russians, who were opposed to religion and the spiritual life. His followers were soon everywhere. Many of them became active in the Murid Wars against the Russians. They were tireless in spreading the Naqshbandi Order in Daghestan, until every village and every house was known to be Naqshbandi.

Imam Shamil ad-Daghestani and Ghazi Muhammad, the leaders of the movement against the Russians, were among the followers of his deputies.[80] For thirty-six years under the directorship of his immediate successors in the lineage, they defended their country from the oppressive Russian onslaught.

From His Miraculous Powers

It is said that, one day, Shaykh Ismail was in a mosque. He observed a poor person who appeared destitute. He approached him and asked, "What do you desire?" He said, "I desire hot bread and some food." Shaykh Ismail raised his hands in supplication and said, "O God, here is your servant who has not eaten in three days. Please send him what food You would like for him." He had not finished the supplication before a man entered the mosque saying, "My wife became ill and I made an oath that I would feed the poor so that she might be blessed. I have brought some hot bread and some food to feed the hungry."

One of his followers in Daghestan narrates:

> Shaykh Ismail said to himself one day, "O my ego, I am angry with you. I am going to throw you into difficulties." He went into the mountains of Shirwan and lay down at the mouth of a cave in which there were two lions. They did not move and we, who had followed him, were very surprised. The male lion had a big piece of meat in his mouth and sat down, far away, watching him. The lioness approached with some meat in her mouth. She began to cry and roar. The male approached the female and made her stop her crying. They sat for a while watching the shaykh. Then the male lion took his two young cubs and gave them to the mother, after which he approached Shaykh Ismail. He sat down quietly beside him, staying until the shaykh left.

One day Shaykh Ismail passed by a village. When some people of the village saw him and recognized him, all the people came running out to

80 According to the book, *Mystics and Comissars,* it was Shaykh al-Ghumuqi al-Husayni who initiated Mullah Fawzi (or Ghazi) Muhammad, first Imam, and Shamil, third Imam of Daghestan. See Alexandre Benningsen and S. Enders Wimbush, *Mystics and Commissars: Sufism in the Soviet Union.*

meet him. The shaykh of the village came and said, "O Shaykh Ismail, please come and teach us." He said, "O Abu Saeed, God has two ways of teaching: the common way and the special way. The common way is the way you and your companions are on. As for the special way, come with me and I will show you." They followed him until he came to a river. He said, "This is the Way of God," and he walked across the water to the other side. Walking away, he disappeared.

Shaykh Abd ar-Rahman ad-Daghestani related:

> One day I was sitting amongst a large group of people. We saw Shaykh Ismail approaching wearing a woolen cloak and on his feet were new shoes. I said to myself, "That Shaykh Ismail is a real Sufi shaykh. I am going to go to him and ask him a difficult question to see if he can answer it or not." I approached him and he saw me. As I drew near he said, "O Abd ar-Rahman, God said in the Holy Quran to avoid bad thoughts. Do not try to question me. That is not good behavior." I said in my heart, "What a miracle! That is a great miracle! How did he know my question, and how did he know my name? I must follow him and ask him more." I ran after him but I could not find him.
>
> One day I saw him in a village. He was standing and praying. His eyes were full of tears. When he had finished, I ran towards him. It came to my heart to ask his forgiveness for what I had done the last time. He looked at me and said, "Recite for me the Quranic verse, '*Without doubt, I am He that forgives again and again, to those who repent, believe, and do right; who are ready to receive true guidance.*'" (20:82)
>
> Then he left. I thought to myself, "Surely he is one of the deputies of the spiritual pole. This is the second time he has addressed the thoughts in my heart."
>
> Later that same day, on my way home, I passed by that village again and I saw him standing by a well with a cup in his hand. He wanted to drink from the well. While I was watching him, the cup fell into the well. Then I saw him raise his hands and recite this supplication, "O God, I am thirsty for water and water is my only food. O God, You know my heart and You know that I am thirsty." By God, not a second had passed before the water in the well rose up until it reached the top. It flooded out of the well and with it the cup. He took the cup and

> drank. Then he performed ablution and prayed four *rakats* of prayer. He put sand in the cup, put some water in with the sand and stirred it with his finger. He then sat and ate from the mixture. I came and said, "O Shaykh Ismail, let me eat with you. What are you eating, dirt?" He replied, "O Abd ar-Rahman, keep good thoughts of God." He gave me the cup. I put it to my mouth. It was water and honey. I swear by God that I never in my life drank anything so delicious. Many days passed after that, and I did not need to eat or drink, I felt so satisfied from the sweetness of that single cup.

Shaykh Muhammad ad-Daghestani said:

> Once I went out to see Shaykh Ismail ash-Shirwani. I kissed his hand, and I asked to accompany him on his travels. I traveled with him for two days. In that time, I never saw him drink or eat. I became extremely hungry and thirsty. I became very weak from continuous walking without food or drink. I said, "O my shaykh, I am so weak." He said, "Are you thirsty or hungry?" I said, "Yes, both." He said, "Then you are not worthy of my company. Close your eyes." I closed my eyes, and when I opened them, I found myself at my home.

His Death and Succession

Shaykh Ismail ash-Shirwani died on the 10th of Dhul-Hijjah, a Wednesday, 1255 AH/1840 CE. He was buried in Amasya.

He passed his secret of the Golden Chain to his three caliphs. This multiple succession was similar to that in the time of Shah Naqshband when he passed the secret of the Order to many caliphs. However, it differs in that Shah Naqshband passed the main secret to only one, Alauddin al-Attar, whereas Shaykh Ismail passed it to Shaykh Khas Muhammad ash-Shirwani, Shaykh Muhammad Effendi al-Yaraghi al-Kurali, and Sayyid Jamaluddin al-Ghumuqi al-Husayni.

Shaykh Ismail Shirwani informed his three caliphs of a prediction for their futures:

> I am passing to each of you the secret of the Order, at the same time, by order of the Prophet ﷺ, by the orders of Abd al-Khaliq al-Ghujdawani, and the Imam of the order, Shah Naqshband, and my shaykh, Khalid al-Baghdadi, and through the spiritual presence of Uways al-Qarani □. Each one of you will carry the secret of this Golden Chain with the

> same power, but your ascension to the throne of guidance will be in sequence. Each of you will keep the relations with the other as I say now: directly after me the authority of that secret will be in the hands of Shaykh Khas Muhammad ash-Shirwani. Then it will be in the hands of Muhammad Effendi al-Yaraghi al-Kurali. Finally, it will be put in the hands of Sayyid Jamaluddin al-Ghumuqi al-Husayni.

The wonder of this prediction of Shaykh Ismail was that he told his caliphs the order of their passing away, which occurred just as he had predicted. ۞

33. Khas Muhammad ash-Shirwani ق

Shaykh Khas Muhammad ash-Shirwani was the wisest scholar of his time, adorned with the arts of science, dressed in the robes of piety and patience, enlightened with the essence of certainty, and supported with the firmness of faith.

I weep and He makes me happy.
I become sober and He makes me drunk.
I am rescued and He drowns me.
Once He befriends me, another time He lifts me.
Another time He fights me until I become angry.
Once I am playful with Him, one time I accompany Him,
Another time I avoid Him, another time I speak to Him.
If you say He is happy you will find Him angry,
Or if you say He is obligated, you will find He decides.
—Abd al-Karim Jili [81]

---

[81] Abd al-Karim Jili, quoted in Shaykh al-Alawi, *Knowledge of God*, p. 16.

Shaykh Khas Muhammad ash-Shirwani knew Truth from Falsehood. He was unsurpassed in eloquence and clarification. He was a master of this Way and the first in this group. He was the champion of the knowers and the signpost for the seekers. His speeches were exemplary and exquisite in their eloquence. His proofs and examples were metaphors that clarified elevated concepts to make them accessible to the people. All were overwhelmed by his eloquence. If he passed through a city in Daghestan, the people would line the streets to see him. Writers attended his group for the sake of his eloquence, jurists for his legal rulings, philosophers for his logic, speakers for his clarity, and Sufis for his manifestation of the Truth.

He was born in Kulal, in a district of Shirwan, south of Daghestan, on the 1st of Muharram, a Monday, in the year 1201 AH/1786 CE. He was tall and very fair. His beard was of mixed color, black and white. His eyes were black. His voice was high-pitched. He was one of the pious jurists, following and teaching the Shafii school of Divine Law. He memorized Imam Shafii's *Kitab al-Umm* (The Mother of Books). He was able to give judicial decisions at the age of twenty. He was respected by all in his city. He received his first teachings in Sufism from his family.

From His Sayings

> Our way is controlled by the Quran and the *Sunnah*.
>
> I have met four types from the Naqshbandi Order and of each type, thirty perfect exemplars; but in the end I chose to follow Shaykh Ismail ash-Shirwani.
>
> God did not send anything to this earth except as a lesson for His servants to learn from.

They asked him, "Who is the Knower?" He answered, "The Knower is the one who knows your secret without you even speaking."

> We did not take Sufism through speeches and flashy words or by saying, "Our shaykh said this and our shaykh said that." We took Sufism by being hungry, by leaving attachment to this world behind and by disconnecting ourselves from reliance upon creatures.

He was asked, "What is the difference between the seeker and the sought?" He replied:

> The seeker is the one who acquired knowledge through his activities and this learning. The sought is the one who receives knowledge through inspiration. The seekers move and walk, but the sought flies, and what a great difference between the one who walks and the one who flies.
>
> Sincerity between God and His servants is not witnessed by anyone, neither the angels to write it, nor the devil to corrupt it, nor desire to destroy it.
>
> Even the trustworthy changes his opinion more than forty times during a single night, although he is trustworthy. The witness, however, is firm in his view for forty years. The one who is in the "state of witnessing" of the Divine Presence sees Reality. He will achieve the three states of witnessing: Knowledge of Certainty (*Ilm al-Yaqin*), Vision of Certainty (*Ayn al-Yaqin)* and the Reality of Certainty (*Haqq al-Yaqin*). The knowledge that he attains will be received directly from the Divine Presence, which never changes. Therefore, the people of witnessing are firm in their decisions, which come from Reality and not from the opinion of the mind.
>
> A person cannot be called a wise servant until nothing appears in him that God dislikes.
>
> The Naqshbandi Sufi Order is based on four rules of behavior:
>
> do not speak except when asked;
>
> do not eat except when weak with hunger;
>
> do not sleep except when overcome by fatigue;
>
> do not keep quiet when you are in His Presence (i.e. ask incessantly from God).
>
> The purity of the heart depends on the purity of the *dhikr* and the *dhikr*'s purity depends on the absence of any hidden worship of another with God.

> The speech of prophets is from the Divine Presence. The speech of Sufis is from witnessing.
>
> The path of the Sufi to God is by struggling against the self.
>
> The state of unique and sincere Oneness is reached when the servant goes back from the end to the beginning, and becomes as he was before he existed.
>
> The knowledge of Oneness has been veiled from the eyes of the external scholars for a long time. They can only talk about its outer shape.
>
> What causes the heart to feel happiness and peace when it hears a beautiful sound? It is a consequence of God's having spoken to the spirits when they were atoms in His Presence and having asked them, "Am I not Your Lord?" The sweetness of His speech became imprinted on them. Thus in this world, whenever the heart hears anything of *dhikr* or music, it experiences happiness and peace, because these are a reflection of that sweetness.

His Miracles

For twenty years Shaykh Khas Muhammad ash-Shirwani did not eat except once a week. His daily practice of remembrance consisted of 350 *rakats* of prayer. Shaykh Ahmad al-Kawkasi said:

> Once I was traveling from the city across the forest to another city on important business. On my way, snow was falling heavily and a great wind was blowing. The snowfall cleared, and in its stead, rain poured down, making all the roads like rivers. I had no choice but to pass through that forest. I entered it as night was approaching and got lost in the middle.
>
> The skies were pouring rain, night was overtaking me, the flood was increasing, and I did not know where to go. I came to a river running through the woods. The flood made that river like an ocean, full of waves. The bridge over it was wrecked, but I had to cross. The river was raging, rising higher and higher, until it reached up the legs of my horse to my legs. I feared drowning for myself and my horse. I raised my hands and asked my Lord, "O God, help me in this difficulty."

Immediately I heard a voice behind me saying, "O Ahmad, why are you calling me and bringing me from my house?" I looked and I saw Shaykh Khas Muhammad behind me, but he was huge. He said, "Hold my hand and cross the river with me." I felt fear. He said, "When you are with us, you must not feel fear." Then we crossed the river. He walked on the river, and I was walking with him on the water. We crossed to the other side. He said, "Now you are safe," and he disappeared. When I reached my destination and went to the mosque, I saw him sitting there. I asked, "How did you come?" He said, "O Ahmad, for us there are no boundaries; we can be anywhere and everywhere at any time."

Gammer in *Muslim Resistance to the Tsar: Shamil and the Conquest of Chechnia and Daghestan*, has this to say about Shaykh Khas Muhammad:

> The seed sown by Shaykh Ismail found a fertile ground in Daghestan where it was transferred by another of his disciples, al-Shaykh Khas Muhammad ash-Shirwani. He ordained al-Shaykh Muhammad al-Yaraghi who, in turn, ordained Jamal al-Din al-Ghazi Ghumuqi.[82]

Benningsen and Wimbush describe the influence of Shaykh Ismail ash-Shirwani and his caliphs in Daghestan in this way:

> The Naqshbandi Order was to play a very important role in Caucasian history. Iron discipline, total dedication to its ideals, and the strict hierarchy on which it was based explain the epic resistance of the Caucasian mountaineers to Russian conquest—a resistance that lasted from 1824 to 1855—in which not only all the leaders of the movement, but also the local authorities (*na'ibs*) and the majority of the fighters were Naqshbandis. It can be said that the nearly fifty-year-long Caucasian wars made an important contribution to the material and moral ruin of the Tsarist Empire and hastened the downfall of the Russian monarchy.
>
> The brotherhood achieved another deep and long-lasting result: it transformed the half-pagan mountaineers into strict orthodox Muslims

[82] Moshe Gammer, *Muslim Resistance to the Tsar: Shamil and the Conquest of Chechnia and Daghestan*, p. 39.

> and introduced Islam into the animist areas of upper Chechnia and among the Circassian tribes of the western Caucasus...
>
> The subsequent massive migration of the Caucasian Muslims to Turkey did not destroy the Naqshbandiyya in Daghestan and Chechnia; its roots had spread too wide and too deep.[83]

Shaykh Khas Muhammad died on the 3rd of Ramadan, a Sunday, in the year 1260 AH/1844 CE while returning to Daghestan from pilgrimage to Makkah. He was buried in Damascus. He passed the authority of the order and the secret of the Golden Chain to his successor, Shaykh Muhammad Effendi al-Yaraghi, according to the will of their common shaykh, Ismail ash-Shirwani. ۞

---

[83] Alexandre Benningsen and S. Enders Wimbush, *Mystics and Commissars: Sufism in the Soviet Union*.

34. Muhammad Effendi al-Yaraghi ق

Shaykh Muhammad Effendi al-Yaraghi was a pious imam respected by everyone. He brought out the treasures of knowledge and its delicate code of behavior and rules. He bore the signs of perfection, having put his ego under his control. From his forehead, the light of heavenly knowledge shone forth.

I never ceased to stand, because of Your love,
On a station where minds are bewildered.
—Abul Hasan an-Nuri [84]

[84] Abul Hasan an-Nuri, quoted in Sarraj, *Kitab al-Luma*, p. 210.

Shaykh Muhammad Effendi al-Yaraghi was a sign of miraculous power in knowing the secrets of the hearts of his followers, and in showing them the way to reach the perfect state of Divine Love. He was a great Sufi, a Knower known in all the nations surrounding Daghestan. His fame spread to Turkey, Persia, and throughout the countries of the Arab world. His heart was filled with sincerity and a spirit of the greatest ease and purity. He studied the external—in addition to the internal—knowledge. He was a scholar of the Quran and the Traditions. He mastered the science of jurisprudence. He was learned in chemistry, astronomy, and logic. He was a reference in every science.

His many sayings were a guidebook to the ways of the seekers. He was very brave in the fight against the Russian imperialists in his time. He had true piety and a very pure faith. He was humble towards everyone. He encouraged people to follow the Naqshbandi Sufi Way and to support it on their tongues, and with their actions, and in their hearts. He was a garden full of roses from which the bees would gather the nectar and produce the finest honey. People ran to his threshold to attain the happiness of this world and the hereafter.

Shaykh Muhammad Effendi al-Yaraghi trained his disciples who numbered in the thousands. During the day, he taught them military strategy for fighting the Russians. During the night, he taught them spirituality. He rarely slept more than two hours a day. His food was often only water. His clothes consisted of a single woolen robe. He was familiar to all throughout Daghestan. He lived in the time of the infamous tyrant Shah Shawus, governor of Daghestan.

He was born in Kural, in Shirwan, Caucasia, on Tuesday, the 2nd of Dhul-Qida, in the year 1191 AH/1777 CE. He was tall and fair-complexioned; his beard white, his eyes green, and his voice soft.

From His Sayings

> If the lovers of the One were to speak about their love for Him, every lover would die from that description.
>
> The seeker does not want anything for himself except what God desires for him. He does not need anything from the universe except his Lord.
>
> If a seeker says after five days of fasting, "I am hungry," he is not fit for our Way.

Depression in the heart is from three sicknesses: loss of harmony with nature; keeping the customs with which one has been raised that are contrary to the ways of the *Sunnah*; and keeping the company of corrupt people.

When the hearts despaired of visualizing the Essence of God, He sent them His Attributes. They were calmed, and quieted, and they were happy.

Examining is from the eyes. Witnessing is from the heart. Unveiling is from the secrets of vision.

When is God not happy with His servant? It is when His servant becomes annoyed at the length of the gathering of *dhikr*. If his love for God were true, it would be like the blink of an eye.

Death denied happiness to the one who is attached to this world.

God never elevated anyone who loved money.

The love of the believer is a light in his heart.

Islam is to surrender your heart to your Lord and not to harm anyone.

As a sign of his humbleness he said:

If someone were to call out in the mosque, "Let the most corrupted person leave," I would be the first to go.

Whoever comes to God with his heart, God will send the hearts of all His servants to him.

I see in human beings God's handiwork, but their false idea of themselves makes them blind to this vision. I hear from them an endless *dhikr* praising the Creator, but their ears are deaf to it.

Not everyone is able to wear the woolen clothes.[85] To wear the woolen clothes requires purity of the heart.

Whoever wears the woolen clothes (of Sufis) in humbleness, God will raise him up and shine light on his heart. Whoever wears the woolen clothes in arrogance and pride, God will put him down.

---

[85] A play on the word *suf* which in Arabic means "wool."

From His Miracles

His custom was to put his disciples in seclusion in stages. He would put the experienced disciples, those who had already undergone many seclusions, in a very intense seclusion in special underground rooms. He accepted both men and women to come to him for advice, and he put in seclusion both male and female disciples, each in their own separate seclusion.

A scholar who was jealous of Shaykh al-Yaraghi's fame and wished to destroy his reputation went to the governor of Daghestan, Shah Shawus, and claimed that Shaykh al-Yaraghi was actually mixing the sexes. The scholar told the governor, "That man is destroying the Divine Law," even though Shaykh al-Yaraghi was well known in his time for his strictness in maintaining the Law and the *Sunnah*. That scholar tried to pressure the governor to put him in jail. The governor sent the shaykh a messenger with a letter. The shaykh read the letter and then he said to the messenger, "Wait! I am sending a gift to the governor on the condition that he does not open it until the day of my appearance before him." He went into his room and came out with a box which he gave to the courier.

The governor received the box. He felt fear at the thought of opening it. On the day of the hearing, Muhammad Effendi al-Yaraghi arrived with all his followers. When he entered, the governor stood up. The people saw him standing and knew that something had happened, as he was not in the habit of standing for anyone.

The shaykh said, "Open the box!" Shah Shawus opened the box and he found a letter in it. Under the letter was charcoal, burning intensely. Under the charcoal was a piece of cloth, completely unaffected by the coals. Under the cloth, there was gunpowder. The shaykh said, "Read the letter!" The governor opened the letter and began to read it out loud. "To the governor. Although the charge brought against us is untrue, nevertheless we ask: Can the one who is keeping a box full of burning charcoal which has been lying on gunpowder for one week—," at which point the governor began to shake. The shaykh told him, "Do not tremble. Read on." The governor continued, "...which has been lying on gunpowder for one week without any harm or explosion, is he not able to keep his disciples, men and women, from exploding with the fire of passion?"

Muhammad Effendi often predicted the future for his followers, and it always came true. When the blind and handicapped came to him and he prayed for them, they would be healed. If the poor came and he prayed for them, they would become rich.

Once a woman brought her son to him. He was four months old. He called the child, and to everyone's astonishment, the child walked to him. He told the child, "Recite after me," and he repeated the Chapter of Sincerity (*Surah* 112) after the shaykh. He told him, "Recite it by yourself," and the child recited it by himself. The one reporting the incident said, "I saw that child thirty years later, and he showed the same great intelligence at that time as he had in front of the shaykh."

His Defense of Religious Freedom

J. F. Baddeley, in his book, *The Russian Conquest of the Caucasus,* distinguishes Shaykh Muhammad Effendi al-Yaraghi:

> ...as the founder of the politico-religious movement which... united for a time in the great struggle for freedom a majority of the Muslim inhabitants of Daghestan and Chechnia, but he never took upon himself the actual leadership, and is wrongly counted by some as the first imam.[86]

> While the glittering circle of Russian bayonets closed in on every side, Mullah Muhammad (al-Yaraghi)'s influence had been growing steadily year by year. Intangible, immaterial, it passed surely and silently through the hedge of bristling steel as a miraged ship through opposing cliffs, or as a moss-bog fire creeps up against the wind. The two forces, material and moral, moving in concentric rings of opposite direction, kept equal pace, and just when to outward seeming the last spark of liberty was trampled under foot in Central Daghestan by the soldiers of the tsar, the sacred flame was ready to burst forth and illuminate the land on every side, even to its outermost borders.[87]

Gammer, in *Muslim Resistance to the Tsar: Shamil and the Conquest of Chechnia and Daghestan,* says about Shaykh Muhammad Effendi al-Yaraghi:

> The Russian sources claim unanimously that Muhammad al-Yaraghi and his disciples preached jihad against the Russians from the very

---

[86] John F. Baddeley, *The Russian Conquest of the Caucasus,* p. 234.

[87] *Ibid.,* p. 242.

beginning. This would not be surprising (due) to the influence of Muhammad al-Yaraghi's preaching.

The first concern of Muhammad al-Yaraghi and his disciples was to establish and enforce the *Shariah* and eradicate the *adat.*

(Shaykh Muhammad Effendi al-Yaraghi said:) "O people... you are neither Muslims, nor Christians, nor pagans... The Prophet ﷺ said, '*He is a true Muslim who obeys the Quran and spreads my* Shariah. *He who acts according to my commandments will stand in heaven higher than all the saints who preceded me.*' Vow, O people, to stop all your vices and henceforth to stay away from sin. Spend your days and nights in the mosque. Pray to God with zeal. Weep and ask Him for forgiveness."[88]

Leslie Blanch affirms in her book *Sabres of Paradise* that Shaykh Muhammad Effendi al-Yaraghi was the shaykh of Imam Shamil an-Naqshbandi. During their war against the Russians, he directed Imam Shamil in strategy and tactics, as did Jamaluddin al-Ghumuqi al-Husayni after him.

The first Imam of Daghestan and first leader of the jihad against the Russians was Ghazi Muhammad ibn Ismail ad-Daghestani, also known as Kazi Mulla. He took initiation into the Naqshbandi Order from Shaykh Jamaluddin al-Ghumuqi, the caliph of Shaykh Muhammad Effendi al-Yaraghi. Gammer says about him:

> ...(Sayyid) Jamal al-Din then took Ghazi Muhammad to his murshid, Shaykh Muhammad al-Yaraghi, "to complete his instruction in the *Shariah*... Muhammad Effendi allowed (him) to spread... (*tariqah*) in Daghestan and gave Ghazi Muhammad his (own) daughter in marriage... Ghazi Muhammad, thus, became one of Jamal al-Din's *khalifas* and acted very energetically and successfully.[89]

Shaykh Abd Allah ad-Daghestani mentioned that Shaykh Muhammad Effendi al-Yaraghi had a vision of Shaykh Ismail ash-Shirwani, ordering him to carry out, by the permission of the Prophet ﷺ, the jihad against the

---

[88] Moshe Gammer, *Muslim Resistance to the Tsar: Shamil and the Conquest of Chechnia and Daghestan*, pp. 43-44.
[89] *Ibid.*, p. 49.

oppressor. He mentions what Shaykh Muhammad Effendi said about that vision.

> Once, after the prescribed dawn prayer, I lay down for a nap in my mosque. I saw Shaykh Ismail ash-Shirwani coming to me, accompanied by the Prophet ﷺ and Salman al-Farsi ؓ. Salman al-Farsi ؓ said to me, "Be to your shaykh as I was to the Prophet ﷺ. I was digging the trench for the battle of Khandaq, which saved the Emigrants and the Helpers from the attack of the unbelievers and the oppressors." He pointed to Shaykh Ismail ash-Shirwani and said, "For a long time Ismail ash-Shirwani encouraged you and Khas Muhammad to establish a front against the invader. So now is the time." Then Shaykh Ismail looked at me and said, "My son, you now have my permission to go ahead and you will be supported. Declare the jihad (struggle against religious oppression)."

> Gammer mentions this story in the following manner:

> Inside Daghestan, there was now a general movement towards a united stand against the Russians. No less important, Shaykh Muhammad al-Yaraghi moved now from tacit to open support of Ghazi Muhammad and in September 1830 declared jihad against the Russians.[90]

Shaykh Abd Allah said about Shaykh Muhammad Effendi al-Yaraghi's connection to the jihad against the Russians, who were attempting to take control of Daghestan:

> When Shaykh Muhammad Effendi al-Yaraghi received permission for jihad in that vision, he was ordered to raise the *mujahidin* and to support them. One day, in his supplication, he said, 'O God, as You sent to the Prophet ﷺ one of the two Umars, send to me imams for the *mujahidin*, to train them in the spirituality of the Naqshbandi Sufi Way, and to support them through the shaykhs of the Golden Chain, especially the living shaykh of their time."

The first Imam, Ghazi Muhammad, was martyred in a Russian attack in 1832. He was succeeded by the second Imam of Daghestan, Hamza Bek

---

[90] *Ibid.*, p. 51.

ibn Ali al-Hutsali. Gammer describes his appointment to the leadership of Daghestan:

> After the (first) imam's death, "the *'ulama* and dignitaries appointed Hamza Bek in his place." The gathering and the appointment of the new imam were the initiative of Shaykh Muhammad al-Yaraghi... Muhammad al-Yaraghi, understanding well the negative effects of Ghazi Muhammad's death would become stronger with the passage of time, prevented them at the very beginning by the swift appointment of a new imam.[91]

About Imam Shamil (1212-1289 AH/1796-1871 CE) who, as the Imam of Daghestan, led the jihad against the Russians for twenty-five years, Gammer says:

> ...Shamil followed his elder friend (the first Imam of Daghestan, Ghazi Muhammad)... to be initiated into the Naqshbandiyya by Shaykh al-Sayyid Jamal al-Din and to be ordained as a *khalifa* by Shaykh Muhammad al-Yaraghi...[92]

About his selection to be third Imam of Daghestan, after the assassination of the second Imam, Hamza Bek, Gammer says:

> ...He summoned a meeting of *'ulama* and other dignitaries... to choose a new imam... Indeed, the participants unanimously chose Shamil... In this they were influenced by the strong support given to Shamil's nomination by Sayyid Jamal al-Din—the only *murshid* [spiritual guide] in Daghestan after the death of Muhammad al-Yaraghi—no less than by Shamil's strong personality...[93]

Shaykh Abd Allah said about Imam Shamil:

> The success of Imam Shamil against the oppressor was due to the spiritual support that he received from Shaykh Khas Muhammad, Shaykh Muhammad Effendi al-Yaraghi and Sayyid Jamaluddin al-Ghumuqi, through the support of the Prophet ﷺ. No single force was able to defeat him as long as he was granted that spiritual support. Once Shaykh Muhammad Effendi al-Yaraghi sent a message to Imam

---

[91] *Ibid.*, p. 60-61.

[92] *Ibid.*, p. 69.

[93] *Ibid.*, p. 71.

Shamil via Sayyid Jamaluddin al-Ghumuqi: "Always keep your connection with us; you will defeat everyone. Otherwise, you will be defeated."

Shaykh Muhammad Effendi al-Yaraghi died on the 17th of Muharram, a Wednesday, in 1265 AH/1848 CE. He authorized his successor, Sayyid Jamaluddin al-Ghumuqi al-Husayni, to carry on as the master of the Way with the secret of the Golden Chain he had been given by their common shaykh, Ismail ash-Shirwani, as he had been ordered. ۞

35. Jamaluddin al-Ghumuqi al-Husayni ق

Shaykh Jamaluddin al-Ghumuqi al-Husayni was one of the perfect human beings whom God graced with His Divine Names and Attributes. He represented His Lord as His shadow in this world, his heart adorned with the pearls and diamonds of the Essence of the Unique Oneness.

How can I find You, with sciences or with ecstasy?
Who can find You without apparent existence?
You awoke me with knowledge, then You left me bewildered.
I tasted, then I saw nothing.
Ecstatically I meditate upon existence, and yet remain
In anguish, sometimes present, sometimes passing out.
—Abul Hasan Sumnun ibn Hamza-l-Khawwas [94]

---

[94] Abul Hasan Sumnun ibn Hamza-l-Khawwas, quoted in Sarraj, *Kitab al-Luma,* p. 250.

God made Shaykh Jamaluddin al-Ghumuqi al-Husayni the central pillar of Divine inspiration of the hidden secrets and the key for the lock of the throne of knowledge. He made him the house of His Light. He was the sustenance for the hearts of the seekers, and he was the means for those wishing to hear directly the Divine Words. He was the red sulfur, weighed in the Divine Scales, the guarantor for unveiling the deep secrets of worship. He was the dictionary of the language of the special knowledge; in him resided the green emerald and the red ruby of the divers in that ocean, to whom came the massive heritage of reviving the knowledge of spirituality and religion.

Shaykh Jamaluddin comprehended the speech of birds. He was the translator of the passion of Divine Love. He was distinguished by the revelations of this Order. He was the appearance of the prophetic state of the Truth of Muhammad ﷺ. He was a master of masters, a light of lights, and a knower of knowers. He was a guide of this order who took his power through his purest of blood lineages to the Prophet ﷺ, being Hasani and Husayni by ancestry. He took the spiritual power of the Order from the Prophet ﷺ, through Abu Bakr as-Siddiq ؓ and Ali ibn Abi Talib ؓ.

Shaykh Jamaluddin al-Ghumuqi al-Husayni was born in the district of Kubu, in Ghazikumuk, Daghestan, in the year 1203 AH/1788 CE, on Thursday, the 16th of Muharram. From the first day he came into this world, he was in a state of witnessing, and lived his whole life in an unveiled state.

He was a scholar in both exoteric knowledge and esoteric knowledge. He was known to speak more than fifteen languages, including Arabic, Persian, Urdu, Pashtu, Hindi, Russian, Turkish, the Daghestani and Circassian dialects, and Armenian. He had memorized the Quran by heart and 775,000 Traditions, both the correct and the false.

He was an encyclopedia of the Holy Traditions and a reference in the explanation of the Holy Quran. He mastered the sciences of jurisprudence and logic. He was a scientist and a mathematician and had a particular mastery of the science of physics. He was a renowned homeopathic physician. In fact, there was not any branch of science known at that time that he had not studied deeply. He was a very great Sufi and authored a book entitled *Adab al-muridiyya fi-t-tariqat an-Naqshbandiyya* (The Rules of Conduct of the Disciples in the Naqshbandi Order).

He was already a saint and a spiritual pole in the time of his shaykh. He held that station for forty years. His shaykh, Shaykh Ismail, showed him all kinds of secret knowledge important for the training and raising of his followers. During the lives of the two other great saints of Daghestan and caliphs of his shaykh, Khas Muhammad and Shaykh Muhammad Effendi al-Yaraghi, he continued to be the saint carrying the main secret of the Naqshbandi Order. However, only when his shaykh, Shaykh Muhammad Effendi al-Yaraghi, passed away, was he given permission to become the master of the Order.

He was tall and thin. His complexion was very white. His beard was very long and wide. His eyes were red. His voice was very soft and sweet. When he was young, he was a student of scholars and Sufis in Daghestan. For a while, he was the private secretary of the governor of the state of Ghazikumuk. He decided to leave that position because he said, "God gave me power to see with two special eyes, the power to see into the seven heavens and to see through the earth. I cannot work for an oppressor." After leaving, he directed himself to the Naqshbandi Order, which was flourishing at that time, preparing the people to fight the Russians. Later, when he was a shaykh, he was the advisor and inspiration behind Imam Shamil's armed resistance against the Russians, and also his father-in-law.

Shaykh Jamaluddin al-Ghumuqi's knowledge of the Naqshbandi Order made people come from all around to listen to him. When people asked him why he left his high government position, he answered with the words quoted above. They were overwhelmed at his answer. In a short period of time, he became very famous.

During the time of Imam Shamil, another governor by the name of Arlar Khan asked him to accept the position of religious authority. He refused, saying, "I will not work for oppressors." Then the governor ordered him to take the position, but he ignored him and simply walked away. The governor then ordered that he be hung. Shaykh Jamaluddin stood with the rope around his neck and was about to be executed, when the governor came running to the balcony shouting, "Stop! Stop! Don't hang him!" In full view of the people he then threw himself off the balcony and died in the street below. They immediately removed the noose from Jamaluddin's neck and let him go. This was one of his miracles.

From His Teachings

You must use your knowledge. If you do not use it, it will be used against you.

The first step in the station of Unique Oneness is to keep the saying of the Prophet ﷺ, *"To worship God as if you are seeing Him."*

The worship of the knower is better than the crowns on the heads of kings.

If the knowledge about which I am talking to you were from me, it would have vanished. But it is from Him, and since it is from Him, it never vanishes.

Among the deeds whose rewards no angel can see is *dhikr Allah.*

The best and the highest association is to sit with God in the state of Oneness.

Keep track of your hours, because they are going, never to return. Pity the one who is heedless. Connect your daily practices of *dhikr* one to another, like links in a chain. You will find a benefit from it. Do not make your heart busy with attachment to this world because it will take the importance of the hereafter from your heart.

The stories of pious people and saints are like battalions from God's Army, by means of which the states of disciples are revived and the secret knowledge of knowers is known. The proof of this is in His Holy Book, the Quran, when He said to the Prophet ﷺ, *"We will tell you stories of the prophets who came before you, to make your heart firm."* (11:120)

Be in your heart with God, Almighty and Exalted, and be in your body with the people, because he who leaves people will leave the group. He who leaves the group will fall into ignorance. The one who would use his secret to be exalted among people will fall into tests and temptations, and he will be veiled from the Presence of His Lord.

God has unveiled for His servants the extent of their defects when He revealed that they had been created from clay. He showed them their lowliness when He said that they come from a sperm-drop. And He made them witness their helplessness and their weakness when He created the need to go to the bathroom.

Pride is the gravest danger for human beings.

The knowledge of Oneness is the specialty of the Sufis, allowing them to differentiate between the eternal and the transient.

From His Miracles

It is said that God granted him two additional physical eyes and thereby gave him added vision. One eye was below his navel, the other one above his navel. When he was an infant, the women of Ghazikumuk came to see those two eyes, which God gave spiritual power by which He would unveil whatever hidden knowledge was to be known: either heavenly knowledge or that related to the spiritual beings of this world.

With the eye above his navel he could see the heavenly knowledge and was given the spiritual power to transport himself into the Divine Presence with complete vision, without any self-effacement. He was able to look at the Divine Secrets with complete self-awareness and speak about them to his followers. Whenever any question was asked by his disciples about heavenly stations, he answered by first looking with perfect vision at the stations and then giving the answer.

The eye below the navel he used for any question concerning this world and the spiritual beings known as jinn. He was very famous for telling his followers all that was needed about their future, their present, and their past. The lineages and the relationships between his followers and their ancestors were unveiled to him like a book. He could satisfy anyone asking about his lineage because he was able to recall his ancestors one by one.

Once, he was sitting with his followers eating apples. Suddenly, he took the apples from the plate and threw them up in the air. The disciples were surprised at this seemingly childish action, especially in light of the Sufi principle of strict avoidance of all that qualifies as needless or blameworthy actions. He looked at them and said, "Do not look at actions and misinterpret them, that would be a big error on your part. The meaning of what I have done will be known after four hours when a disciple will come from another village. Then you will have the explanation."

As predicted, a man came and said, "O my shaykh, my brother died a short while ago." The shaykh said, "That is what happened. Now tell them exactly when he died." He said, "He died four hours ago." The shaykh explained, "I saw the angel of death, Izrail عليه السلام, coming to take my follower's soul with anger and punishment. I threw that apple up and with that action I stopped Izrail عليه السلام. I told him to go back to God, Almighty and Exalted, and tell Him that Sayyid Jamaluddin is asking that He change the death of that servant from a bad ending to a good ending. On Izrail's عليه السلام way back down with the answer that God had changed the destiny from punishment to mercy, I threw the second apple up and told Izrail عليه السلام that he should go and that I would take the soul of my disciple myself. I was the one who took the soul out of his body in the last seven breaths."

Some visitors were on their way from Kazan to visit Jamaluddin. On the way they passed by the home of an old lady named Salahuddin Aisha. She said, "When you pass by the shaykh, ask him to give me initiation, as I am not able to go to him myself." At the conclusion of their meeting with Shaykh Jamaluddin, they asked him for a daily devotion for Salahuddin Aisha. He said, "Take her this piece of cloth." They brought her the piece of cloth which the shaykh had given them. She took the piece of cloth, opened it and looked at it saying, "I understand, I understand!" and she put it on top of her head. Then she left and some time later came back with a pitcher of milk. She said, "Take this back to the shaykh."

When they returned to the shaykh and gave him the milk, he was in severe pain, because he had been tortured by the governor. He drank the milk and said, "Praise belongs to God, I am healed by means of this milk, which the lady has milked from deer. She is very wise. She understood me immediately. I had put a burning coal in the piece of cloth and the cloth did not burn. When I sent it to her, she understood that to hold this Order is to hold a burning coal. She took the coal, and she sent me the milk. The milk is a sign of purity of the heart. So she sent me an answer saying, "I accept the difficulty of this Way. I dedicate the purity of my heart to you."

Then the people of the village went back to the woman and told her what the shaykh had said. She related, "When I received the charcoal, two deer appeared at my door. Never before had I seen such a thing. I immediately knew that I should milk them and send the milk to the shaykh."

One night, Sayyid Jamaluddin al-Ghumuqi was with his followers in the big mosque of the city praying in congregation. When the prayers were finished, everyone went out. They locked the mosque from the outside. One person remained behind inside the mosque, hiding behind a pillar. His name was Orkallisa Muhammad, one of the best disciples of Sayyid Jamaluddin. He was talking to himself and saying, "O Orkallisa Muhammad, now there is no one with you. You are alone. Defend yourself." And he answered himself, "How can I defend myself? I am the worst person that God has created on the face of the earth. To prove it, I swear an oath that if what I say is not what I honestly believe, then may my own wife become forbidden to me!" He did not know that his shaykh was also hiding himself in the mosque and observing him. The shaykh looked into his heart. He saw that in his heart he truly believed himself to be the worst person in creation.

Sayyid Jamaluddin revealed himself, laughing and saying, "Orkallisa, come here." The latter was very surprised to see his shaykh because he thought he was alone. The shaykh told him, "You are right, and you are also loyal and sincere." As soon as he heard this, Orkallisa Muhammad floated up and hit his head on the ceiling of the mosque. He came down and floated up and came down again. This happened seven times. When the disciple is cleansed of attachment to this world, his soul will lift him up and he will fly like a bird.

Then Shaykh Jamaluddin told him, "Sit," and he sat. The shaykh was pointing with his index finger to the heart of Orkallisa Muhammad with a circular motion. As he was rotating his finger he was opening his heart, not to the Divine Presence, but to the secrets hidden already in his own heart. What he opened up to him were the six levels that must be opened to the seeker in order to set foot on the first step on the Way. These are: the reality of attraction, the reality of receiving heavenly revelation, the reality of directing the heart's power to someone, the reality of intercession, the reality of guidance, and the ability to move in space and time in one moment.

These six powers that he opened to him are the first major step on the Sufi Path. As he opened these six powers, he was able to take him to the state of witnessing. In that state of vision, he saw himself sitting with 124,000 white birds encircling him. One large green bird flew to the middle. After that vision the white birds disappeared and in their places appeared the spirituality of 124,000 saints. Then the green bird disappeared and there appeared the spiritual form of the Prophet ﷺ. The Prophet ﷺ said, "I bear witness that he has reached the state of perfection and now you can depend on him. Give him the secret of the Naqshbandi Order. Then Shaykh Jamaluddin poured from his heart into the heart of Orkallisa Muhammad secrets and knowledge of which he had never dreamed. He said to his shaykh, "O my shaykh, do these things exist in the Way?" He replied, "Yes, my son, and that is only the beginning of the Way."

It is said that the secret of his shaykh could be seen in Orkallisa Muhammad. He would go up on the *minbar* on Friday and he would clap his hands and say, "O people cry!" and they would all begin crying. Then he would clap his hands and say, "Laugh!" and they would laugh. Then he would make a supplication, saying, "O God, they are crying in repentance and asking forgiveness. Forgive them. And they are laughing at the pleasure of Your Mercy!" Then he would clap a third time and say, "Do you accept the Naqshbandi Sufi Order to be your Order?" and they would say, "Yes." Then he would ask them, "Do you accept to repeat 5,000 times, 'Allah,' with the tongue and 5,000 times 'Allah,' in the heart?" and they would answer, "Yes." By this method he spread he Naqshbandi Order all over the land of Daghestan, Kazan, southern Russia, and among the soldiers of Imam Shamil.

Shaykh Jamaluddin al-Ghumuqi al-Husayni was deeply involved in directing the war against the Russians. He fought to keep the teaching of spirituality strong in Caucasia. He supported Imam Shamil in his fight against Russia for nearly forty years. The Imam's ranks consisted solely of Naqshbandi disciples, as he allowed no other affiliation in his army.

Leslie Blanch writes the following about their relationship in her book *Sabres of Paradise*:

> Shamil obeyed him (Shaykh Jamaluddin) long after he (Shamil) had become the imperious ruler who would brook no word of criticism elsewhere. With his tutor, Shamil was from the first disciplined and studious. He learned Arabic and studied Arabic literature, philosophy and theology, progressing towards the complicated Sufi doctrines which, since religious evolution is a fundamental principle of Sufism, included a comparative study of Adam, Abraham, Moses, Jesus and Muhammad. It was apparent that this was no ordinary student, and

> Jamaluddin sought to prepare his charge for that great destiny which, according to some, was already written on his brow... However much (he) planned action, a Holy War, still (he) drew (his) spiritual inspiration from the Sufi teachings of (Jamaluddin)...[95]

Gammer describes his relationship with his shaykh, saying:

> As mentioned above, Shamil was a *khalifa* in the Naqshbandi-Khalidi Order. His position as imam, though, did not leave him time to act as a Sufi shaykh. Yet no matter how high his rank, he was, as a murid, bound to complete obedience to his murshid, Jamal al-Din al-Ghazi-Ghumuqi. Indeed, during his entire reign, Shamil treated Jamal al-Din with respect and veneration as his *Murshid* and as a *Sayyid*... The imam treated each wish of his murshid as a command... Jamal al-Din demonstrated his support for Shamil also by giving his daughter Zahida in marriage to the imam... Jamal al-Din's support contributes greatly to Shamil's prestige and authority.
>
> ...He also had a growing number of troops at his disposal to carry out his policy. This ability, and readiness, to enforce his will coupled with his title, legitimacy and the support of the spiritual head, Sayyid Jamal al-Din, made any opposition futile... The foundations of a state had begun to emerge.[96]

When Imam Shamil was defeated and taken prisoner by the Russians in 1279 AH/1859 CE, Shaykh Jamaluddin decided that the people of Daghestan should emigrate en masse from Daghestan to Istanbul in Turkey. Once the decision was made, the people of Daghestan, Kazan, Chechnya, Armenia, Azarbaijan, and other areas, all began to prepare for migration out of Russian held lands. They went to Turkey and Arab countries among other places.

Shaykh Shamil was released by the Russians on condition that he would swear never to resume fighting against them. He went on pilgrimage, and was given a hero's welcome at Makkah, where it is said that he was made to pray on top of the Kabah in order for everyone to benefit

---

[95] Moshe Gammer, *Muslim Resistance to the Tsar: Shamil and the Conquest of Chechnia and Daghestan*, p. 75.

[96] *Ibid.*, p. 77-81.

from seeing him. He died in Madinah and was buried in the cemetery of the Companions, al-Baqi.

Shaykh Jamaluddin moved to Istanbul, accompanied by his family and the family of Shaykh Shamil. There they lived in the district of Uskudar, on the Asian side of Istanbul. From there he spread the Naqshbandi Sufi teachings all over Turkey.

At that time all the houses were made of wood. One day a great fire swept through the district of Uskudar. People fled their houses to save themselves. They came to him, urging him to leave. Shaykh Jamaluddin said very calmly, "There is no way that I will leave, because my house will not burn up. This house was built from money which was earned by my own hands. Never will a house burn which was built with pure, lawful money." The entire district burnt, but his house remained untouched by flames. That house has been preserved until today, and is very famous.

His behavior with his family and with his disciples was always impeccable. He kept the best of manners with them. He never reacted to the complaints or objections of his family. He never objected to or criticized his disciples. He always tried to make them happy.

One day, shortly before his death, Shaykh Jamaluddin called his wife and daughter. He said, "Today I have done a great work, and it has taken all my power and left me very weak. When you read the newspaper, you will see that a big ship ran aground in the Bosporus. No one died, and they were saved by an unknown person. I was that unknown person, and you will hear about it." Then he passed away. The next day his daughter, with astonishment and tears, read the story in the newspapers, about how a great ship had grounded and how an unknown person had saved all the people on board. That newspaper is still kept by his descendants.

Shaykh Jamaluddin al-Ghumuqi al-Husayni died in 1285 AH/1869 CE on the 5th of Shawwal, at the age of eighty. He was buried in Istanbul, near the family of Imam Shamil, in Uskudar. Some time after his death and burial, the location of his grave was lost. No one was able to find it. It was not discovered again for many years.

Shaykh Sharafuddin, who came forty years after Shaykh Jamaluddin had passed away, was the one who rediscovered his grave. When he was living in Rashadiyya, 150 miles from Istanbul, he saw in a vision that he was being brought to Uskudar, to a cemetery. A person appeared to him dressed in a green cloak. He said, "I am Shaykh Jamaluddin. You have to reveal the location of my grave." Shaykh Sharafuddin asked, "How will I know your grave?" He said, "This is the graveyard of Karaja Ahmad, a saint who is buried here," pointing to a place a short distance away. Then he said, "My son, try your best to discover the location of my grave."

The next day Shaykh Sharafuddin wrote to people in Istanbul, and told them to dig in such-and-such a place. They dug and found the grave, and they found the headstone, marked with his name.

Shaykh Jamaluddin passed the secret of the Golden Chain of the Naqshbandi Order to Grandshaykh Abu Ahmad as-Sughuri.

36. Abu Ahmad as-Sughuri ق

Shaykh Abu Ahmad as-Sughuri was the inheritor of the knowledge of prophets, the imam of the spiritual poles, and the advisor of the kingdom of guidance. He was the summit of ascetic saints, addressed by the heavenly kingdom as the caliph of this kingdom on earth.

The "Sword of Religion" is he who enters combat
for religion's sake and whose efforts are totally for God.
He discerns correct from incorrect and truth from falsehood.
But he first struggles with himself
and rectifies his own character traits.
As the Prophet said, "Begin with your own self!"
—Rumi, *Fihi ma fihi*[97]

---

[97] Jalaluddin Rumi, *Fihi ma fihi*, translated by William Chittick, p. 148.

Shaykh Ahmad as-Sughuri quenched his spiritual thirst by drinking from the fountain of heavenly knowledge. He reached a stage of annihilation at the age of thirty.

In his person were combined both kinds of knowledge, and he acquired and grasped all the benefit of the Way and the Truth. He became the center of all heavenly inspirations. He was a secret from God's secrets and a miracle from God's miracles. He was the unique banner of the knowledge of spirituality and the knowledge of the pen. He was like the pole star giving direction and illuminating the way for the people of his time. He revived dead hearts and he wore the cloak of the great saints. He did not leave an atom in this world unsupported by his spiritual power.

He was born in Sughur, a village in Daghestan on Wednesday, the 3rd of Rajab in 1207 AH/1793 CE. He sat on the throne of the spiritual poles for forty years. His fame spread everywhere. He trained his followers and lifted them by means of his spiritual power. If anyone appeared in his presence, even for one hour, he was raised to the state of hearing and the state of vision.

He said:

> I do not depend on the effort of the disciple, but I depend on the light that God has given to me for that disciple. I raise him by means of that light, because I know that it is not possible for a person to reach the state of unveiling by his own effort alone. That is the meaning of the supplication of the Prophet ﷺ, *"O God, do not leave me to my ego for the blink of an eye."*

From His Sayings

> God has provided every servant with his provision. Whoever does not acquire knowledge of the daily provision that God has granted him, will be considered ignorant in our Way.

> Those who achieve the Reality of this Way are very few. With the power of that Reality, one can reach all the saints in this world, and with the Divine Power conferred when you attain the Reality of this Way, you can reach all angels, one by one.

> The spiritual light that God gives to you on your way in this order is the beacon that lights the Way to His Divine Presence, without fear.

In this Way, to distinguish other than God is unbelief.

The Sufi is the one who has left the world behind, the hereafter behind, the Divine Presence behind, and who subsists in Him Alone.

I achieved the three levels of sainthood: annihilation, subsistence, and spiritual knowledge. I received these from the presence of the light of the Prophet Muhammad ﷺ, and I received the three states of perfection and the seven realities from my teacher, Jamaluddin al-Ghumuqi al-Husayni.

Pride never entered the heart of a person but that his mind decreased to the degree that the pride had increased in his heart.

Difficulties might touch a believer, but they would not affect the one who recites *dhikr*.

Abu Ahmad as-Sughuri spent most of his life in seclusion. He liked seclusion. He liked to be away from people. For that reason, he was quite happy when he was put under house arrest by the Russians, which happened to him many times.

One day I was in my seclusion and the room was filled with a beautiful scent. I did not raise my eyes, but kept meditating in my seclusion. Then a spiritual sword, shining with more light than that of the sun, descended toward my head. I was wondering what it was that I felt descending on me. A vision appeared to me, in which the Prophet ﷺ enveloped me with his spirit, and I entered in him, and I saw myself in him.

Once I entered the presence of my shaykh, Jamaluddin al-Ghumuqi al-Husayni. He said, "My son, you have attained the highest state of the Muhammadan perfection." I said, "O my shaykh, I would like to reach the lineage of your state." As soon as I said that, I saw him disappearing from his place and appearing in me, and I saw myself disappearing and appearing in his place and with his form.

From His Miraculous Power

He was granted miraculous powers unprecedented among the saints. Of his unveiling of the hidden in this universe, and of his grant from the Divine spiritual knowledge of the states of people after their death, the extent was so boundless and vast that no book can encompass its description.

It is said that when he was young, he often beheld the name of God written in light between heaven and earth. That generated in him great modesty and humbleness. No one was able to take a photograph of him. When anyone tried, the camera would break apart. Whenever they tried to draw his likeness on paper the pen would not write, or the next day the picture would disappear. He said:

> I do not want to be known in this world after I die, because I do not wish for myself any form of existence.

He often prayed the dawn prayer with the same ablution as the night prayer, indicating that he had not slept. Once as he was traveling with his family, they found themselves without water in the desert on the way to Hijaz. His family was very thirsty. He told his servant, "Go and get some water." He said, "O my shaykh, how will I find water in this desert?"

He asked the people in their caravan if anyone had water, but no one did and all their waterskins were dry. The shaykh then took an empty waterskin and went off into the desert for ten minutes. When he returned, the skin was full and with it he quenched his family's thirst and that of the people of the caravan. Then he filled all the water bags of the caravan from that one bag and returned to his family with it still full as if it had never been used.

His Defense of Religious Freedom

He was the reviver of the Way and the Truth in his time. He attracted thousands and thousands of people to Islam and to the Naqshbandi Order. In Daghestan, he was considered both a spiritual shaykh, carrying the teachings of the Naqshbandi Order, and at the same time, a great warrior like Imam Shamil, because he fought the religious persecution of the Russians. He was the main religious authority after Sayyid Jamaluddin's departure.

The Russian army took him prisoner many times. Once they put him in a carriage to take him away. All the people of his village came to him to bid him farewell. They cried as if they were losing their hearts. He sat in the carriage quietly searching the crowd for someone. The man who was driving the carriage whipped the horses to get them to move but they would not move. Abu Ahmad as-Sughuri said, "Why are you beating the horses?" He said, "I am beating the horses to make them move." He said, "They are not going to move until I give the order. They are under my command. And I am waiting for someone."

They sat like that for several hours, until a man came running through the crowd. He was a Russian officer. Abu Ahmad asked him, "Are you not the son of my friend, Ahmad? Why are you in the Russian army? You are Daghestani. You must not be with their army while they are killing Muslims. You have to leave them and listen to us." He said, "Yes, my shaykh, I will listen to you." He said, "Of course you will listen to us, because even the wild animals in the forest listen to us when we go there to recite *dhikr*. Even these horses listen to us and will not move except by our order. Your father is a great shaykh, and I say you must leave them. You are going to be a saint. O my son, do not leave the people of exoteric knowledge and do not leave the people of esoteric knowledge. Look at that cemetery and do not forget that one day you and I are going to be buried there."

Immediately, that young officer took off his uniform and took initiation from the shaykh. The soldiers took him prisoner as well. Then Abu Ahmad as-Sughuri said, "Now you have permission to move," and the horses began to move.

God and the Prophet ﷺ loved him for his sincerity and loyalty. His shaykh was very happy with him, and his village cherished him. Each time he was released from imprisonment, his house filled with provision and guests. They asked him, "You are not working, the Russians are against you and you are fighting. How is it that your house is always full with provision?" He said, "Anyone who is struggling in the way of God, God will provide for him. That is what God said in Quran, *'Every time that Zachariah entered her chamber, he found her supplied with sustenance.'*" (3:37)

He died in Sughur on the 17th of Rabi al-Awwal in the year 1299 AH/1882 CE at the age of ninety-two. Many years after he had passed away his daughter saw him in a dream. He told her, "O my daughter, the stone of my grave has fallen down and is laying on my chest, pressing on me and hurting me." The next day his daughter went quickly to the shaykhs of the city and told them that dream. Indeed, she told the dream to everyone she met. The people believed the dream and went quickly to open the grave. They found that the stone that covered his body had fallen down, and the walls of the grave had tumbled in around him. They found his body clean and unchanged. His shroud was still white, as if he had just been buried that same day.

They removed his body, again dug the grave and replaced his body. Everyone was surprised and astonished at how he had come to her in the dream and told her about the situation in his grave. More surprising, however, was the perfect condition of his body. After seeing this, they all were initiated by his successor, Shaykh Abu Muhammad al-Madani.

Shaykh Abu Ahmad as-Sughuri had two caliphs: Abu Muhammad al-Madani and Shaykh Sharafuddin ad-Daghestani. The secret of the Golden Chain was passed to the first, and upon his death, to the second. ۞

37. Abu Muhammad al-Madani ق

The blessings of Shaykh Abu Muhammad al-Madani reached everyone in his time. He was a special one, carrying the secrets of the prophetic descriptions. He had great, miraculous power that was visible wherever he went.

The man of God is quenched without water,
The man of God is full without roast meat.
The man of God is all confused, distraught,
The man of God needs neither food nor sleep.
The man of God, he is a boundless sea,
The man of God rains pearls without a cloud.
The man of God knows not of wrong, but right.
—Rumi [98]

---

[98] Jalaluddin Rumi, quoted in Annemarie Schimmel's, *Deciphering the Signs of God: A Phenomenological Approach to Islam*, p. 193.

Shaykh Abu Muhammad al-Madani was born in Kikunu, a district of Ghanib, in the state of Timurhansuro, Daghestan in the year 1251 AH/1835 CE. He emigrated fifty-five years later with his family from Daghestan to Turkey, finally settling in the village of Rashadiya, between Bursa and Istanbul.

He was a true inheritor of the physical appearance of the Prophet ﷺ. He was very handsome. He resembled the Prophet ﷺ according to the description of the Prophet ﷺ in his biographies. He authored a book entitled *Ya waladi*, "My Son," in the tradition of Imam Ghazali, who wrote *Ayyuhal walad*, "O My Son."

The village of Kikunu, in which he grew up, was a spiritual place. The villagers kept the Divine Law and all of them followed shaykhs. One day before his birth, Shaykh Abu Ahmad as-Sughuri passed by the village and he said, "From this village an enlightened child is going to appear. His light will shine from earth to heaven. He is going to be a great saint." He was predicting the birth and high station of Abu Muhammad al-Madani.

Daghestan in his time was known as "the Land of Saints." During his early years, two great shaykhs lived there: Shaykh Muhammad Effendi al-Yaraghi and Sayyid Jamaluddin al-Ghumuqi. He received the power of guidance in six Sufi orders: Qadiri, Rifai, Shadhili, Chishti, Khalwati and Naqshbandi. He was famous as a shaykh in all six orders.

He sat on the throne of guidance, spreading external and internal knowledge, especially from the Divine Presence. He was a master of this Order. He was distinguished among the Knowers. He was a supporter of the weak.

From His Miracles

Before Shaykh Abu Muhammad al-Madani was initiated in the Naqshbandi Order, Hajji Nuri and Hajji Murtaza passed by his village. They told him, "We are going to visit Ahmad as-Sughuri to be initiated by him. Would you like to come with us?" He said, "Yes," and all three of them made the intention to join the Order at the hand of Shaykh Abu Ahmad as-Sughuri.

Shaykh Abu Ahmadas-Sughuri gave them advice and then he called Abu Muhammad al-Madani, initiated him in the Naqshbandi Order and planted the *dhikr* on his tongue. He did not give anything to Hajji Murtaza and Hajji Nuri. He told them, "I gave the secret to Abu Muhammad al-

Madani. There is no need to take the secret from me. Take it from him. Anyone who wishes to follow my Way may take it though Abu Muhammad al-Madani." They complained in their hearts, "Why did Abu Ahmad as-Sughuri put Abu Muhammad al-Madani as an intermediary between us?"

A drought came to their village. The people of the village asked them to pass by the village of Abu Muhammad al-Madani to ask him to pray to God for rain. On their way to see him, they said to each other, "We will know now if he is truly a saint and why Abu Ahmad as-Sughuri put him ahead of us." On their way they passed a house and saw a beautiful woman inside. They were so attracted to that woman's beauty that they stood looking at her for a long time. Finally they arrived at Abu Muhammad's house and they knocked at the door.

He said from inside the house, "Who is at the door?" They were speaking with each other in low voices saying, "How could he be a shaykh when he does not know who is at his door?" They knocked again, but there was no answer. Then from behind the door came his voice, "Hajji Murtaza and Hajji Nuri, it is easy for someone to become a shaykh and a guide without knowing who is behind the door, but it is very difficult for someone to become a shaykh and a guide who is following his desires in a way that is not acceptable, looking at naked women." He said to them, "I cannot allow you inside my house."

In their hurry to leave, they forgot to tell him that they had come to ask him to pray for rain. After five minutes he came running behind them and told them, "As for what you came for, as soon as you reach your village it will be raining." As soon as they reached the village, the clouds gathered and it began to pour down rain.

His Struggle

The people of Daghestan remember well how hard he fought the Russians, both physically and spiritually. Even the Russians cited his courage and his spiritual miracles. Many of the events that are known about him were recorded by his enemies.

Once, he was fighting the Russians. They came in overwhelming strength against him. He escaped to an abandoned house. No one knew he was there. A woman saw him from the roof of her house. She told the Russians, "Abu Muhammad al-Madani is in that house." They came to capture him. They found that the house he was hiding in was surrounded with green grass because of the blessings of his presence, although due to the heat of summer there was no green vegetation to be seen anywhere else. Due to the information given by the woman, they were able to capture him. That night the woman became very ill, and the next day she was dead. As God, Almighty and Exalted, revealed to the Prophet ﷺ in the holy Tradition, *"Whoever comes against one of My saints, I will declare war against him."*[99]

They put him under house arrest and told him he could go to a nearby restaurant to eat. He refused to eat in their restaurant. He never ate their food, saying, "You are my enemy and I will never eat your food." He did not eat their food for months. They did not know how he was surviving. Finally, someone from a Tartar region near Kazan came to the governor and said, "If he is not eating from your food, give him to me, I will take him to my village of Sartar to care for him." They sent him there.

There was a boy from Kikunu studying in Bukhara who was engaged to a girl from Sartar. He was studying the Divine Law. He had been gone for many years and had not returned. In the meantime, the girl had decided to marry someone else. The news of this reached Bukhara, where the boy heard it. He was very upset. That night before he fell asleep he heard a voice saying, "Come back to Sartar. Come back to Sartar." He heard that voice the next night and the following day. He decided to go back. He had a very long journey, nearly to Moscow, to reach Sartar. He walked and walked until he finally reached the village.

He found the people all gathered in one place, carrying food. They told him, "A great shaykh has come to Sartar from Kikunu, and he is healing people and feeding the poor. We were so attracted to his spiritual power that we have all become his followers. Come with us to see him." He went with them. The people of the village said to the shaykh, who was Abu Muhammad al-Madani, "You might be taken away by the Russians. Please leave someone here who will be authorized to guide us on the Way." When that boy arrived at the house of the shaykh, the shaykh told him, in the same voice he had heard in Bukhara, "O my son, you heard our message, and you heard our voice. Come! You are going to be my deputy, and you are going to teach these people what they need of spirituality and of the obligations of religion. And you are going to marry your fiancé." The boy was very happy. He took initiation from the shaykh in the Naqshbandi

[99]Narrated by Abu Hurayra in Bukhari's *Sahih* and Ahmad's *Musnad.*

Order and the five other Sufi orders. Shaykh Abu Muhammad al-Madani then married him to his fiancé.

This was a miraculous gift for the people of Sartar, from Abu Muhammad al-Madani. It was also a sign that his days in Sartar were ending. The next day, the Russians came and took him to Siberia. He was locked inside a high-security prison. Although they locked him in his room, they would often find him in the yard, praying, sitting, or reading. The guards were surprised and took him back. Then after a few hours they would find him outside again. So they chained him to the wall. Still they found him outside the room, walking with someone. Later he would tell people, "I was walking with Khidr عليه السلام." They again chained him up, and again, they found him outside his cell.

They were so upset by their inability to imprison him that they wrote to Moscow asking advice on how to hold him. Moscow told them, "Put him underground in a dungeon." They tried to do that, but no matter how far down they put him he would always be found outside his cell. Finally they were so frustrated in their attempts to incarcerate him that they allowed him to go free within the borders of Russia. His intention, however, was to escape to Turkey.

When they left him free in Siberia, he saw an officer and told him, "My son, I will see you in Istanbul, Turkey. We will meet you there." Later that young man tired of serving in the Russian army and deserted. He fled to Turkey with his family and ended up in Istanbul. There he later met Shaykh Abu Muhammad al-Madani, as the shaykh had foretold.

Shaykh Abu Muhammad al-Madani decided to pass through his homeland in the Caucasus to visit his parents and family on his way to Turkey. One day before he was to arrive, he appeared to his sister in a dream, telling her that he was coming. She told her mother the next day, "O my mother, increase the food a little, because my brother is coming today." Her mother said, "What are you saying? No one even knows if he is alive in Siberia, and you are saying he will come here?" At that moment there was a knock on the door and Shaykh Abu Muhammad al-Madani appeared. As he was eating with his family he told them, "I must hurry, because there is a ship waiting to take me to Trabzon across the Black Sea." They told him in surprise, "We are in Caucasia, and you are talking of Trabzon?"

Shaykh Abu Muhammad al-Madani directed himself to the coast on the Russian side of the Black Sea. When he arrived there, the ship he expected was waiting to take him to Turkey. He went to the captain and told him, "Take me to Turkey on your ship." The captain replied, "I have been trying to go for twenty days, but the ship is not running properly." He said, "Now it will run. Take this money as my passage, and take me to Turkey." The captain took him and put him near the engine room. Then the captain went to sleep while the crew sailed the ship. The captain saw in a dream that the engine had changed into the shape of the shaykh and that the ship had grown wings and was flying, arriving at Trabzon. He awoke and ran outside. The crew told him, "We have arrived in Trabzon." He ran down to the shaykh's room and the shaykh asked him, "Have we arrived?" He said, "Yes, my shaykh, I am coming to tell you that I want to take initiation from you. This trip normally takes three days, and we have arrived in one." He took initiation from him in the Naqshbandi Order and the five other Sufi orders.

The shaykh left the ship and went to a coffee shop. There he saw a man who had been imprisoned with him in Siberia, by the name of Muhammad at-Tawil. Muhammad at-Tawil said, "Praise belongs to God, my shaykh, you have arrived here safely. You will be my guest in my home." For a year the shaykh remained as a guest in the house of Muhammad at-Tawil. As long as Shaykh Abu Muhammad al-Madani was a guest in his home, Muhammad at-Tawil would find two golden coins under his pillow every day. He was so astonished that after five days he went to the shaykh, who said, "As long as I am here and as long as you keep this secret, you will find these coins under your pillow every day. If you do not tell anyone, these coins will continue to come."

The following year, Sultan Abul Hamid II heard that Shaykh Abu Muhammad al-Madani had arrived safely in Trabzon, and he sent a ship to carry him from Trabzon to Istanbul. One day after the shaykh had gone on to Istanbul, the wife of Muhammad at-Tawil was cleaning the bed and she found two coins. She began to make a fuss asking her husband from where he got the coins. Finally he told her that it was the blessing of the shaykh. Immediately she went and told the neighbors. As soon as she told them, the miracle stopped.

That incident happened in 1308 AH/1890 CE. However, the story was never told until the son of Abu Muhammad al-Madani was visiting his father's friend, Muhammad at-Tawil, sometime after his father had passed away. Muhammad at-Tawil told him the story at that time, and showed him the coins he had received so miraculously.

Sultan Abd al-Hamid, the emperor of the Ottoman Empire, was a follower of the Naqshbandi Order. He had been initiated by Abu Muhammad al-Madani. In 1314 AH/1896 CE, the sultan gave him the choice of any piece of land in Istanbul on which to build a *zawiya* for the Order and a house for himself. He replied, "That choice is not ours, but a matter of Divine Decree." So he waited until the next day. Sultan Abd al-Hamid eagerly came to him to hear the answer. Shaykh Abu Muhammad al-Madani told him, "O my son, God has directed me to a place from which the Naqshbandi Order is going to flourish. That is where the sincere Daghestani followers will be and is where the Naqshbandi Order will grow, and where my nephew will take authority of the order."

The sultan said, "Whatever you have decided, I will obey your decisions." The next day Abu Muhammad al-Madani told the sultan, "Send me to Yalova. Between Yalova and Bursa is the place I am going." The sultan arranged a horse carriage for him to take him wherever he wanted to go. When he reached the area of Yalova, he directed the horses to go as they like. They stopped in a place near Orhanghazi. There in the forest, he built the first house out of wood. After a short while 680 houses had sprung up in the forest. And that place was named Rashadiya, after Sultan Rashad, and is now known as Gunekoy.

All emigrants who came from Siberia and from the Caucasus moved to that village, where Shaykh Abu Muhammad al-Madani, as well as Shaykh Sharafuddin and Shaykh Abd Allah were present. Once, the people came to Shaykh Abu Muhammad al-Madani complaining, "How are we going to eat? There is nothing here." He stamped his foot on the ground. Where he stamped his foot, mines of iron and clay were found. At the same time a tree fell down. From these signs he showed them that they would earn a living by mining clay and iron, and harvesting wood. There were soon 750 houses, two mosques and one school for children.

Years later, during the Balkan War, the Greeks and Serbians who were fighting the Turks came to this village. Many homes were destroyed and many villagers fled. There remained 220 homes after that attack. Nothing happened to the mosque, however, and all the prayers continued to be held.

No evil or corruption could be found in that village. No drinking, no gambling, no wrongdoing occurred. From early childhood, everyone was raised reciting *dhikr*. It was a piece of Paradise. Everyone lived in harmony, reciting *dhikr* every night. It was an ideal village, a heavenly community. That is why the shaykh had told Sultan Abd al-Hamid, "Light is going to stream out of that village."

The village was full of blessings. They needed no provisions from outside. They had wood for cooking and heat, livestock for labor, dairy, and meat, and lush fields ripe with crops. Every action of its citizens was accompanied with *dhikr*. Mothers nursed their children with *dhikr*; their menfolk labored to the sound of *dhikr*. The entire village was filled with *dhikr*. This was how Shaykh Abu Muhammad al-Madani, Shaykh Sharafuddin, and later Shaykh Abd Allah ad-Daghestani raised the people of the village. It became known throughout Turkey as the "Village of *Dhikr*."

Turkey was involved in the Balkan War. Once Shaykh Abu Muhammad al-Madani's neighbor, Hasan Muhammad Effendi, came to him and said, "I want to go fight and die as a martyr." He told him, "There is no need for you to go outside the village to become a martyr. You are going to be a martyr here."

Soon the armies of the Greeks and Serbs approached, shooting into the village. In one of these attacks Hasan Muhammad Effendi was shot and killed. He died as a martyr, as he had wished, and in the way the shaykh had predicted.

Shaykh Abu Muhammad had been married for years and all his children were girls. One day he said to the people, "I am seeing three boys coming to me." The people were very surprised, because his wife was old and past childbearing age. Shortly after this, his wife fell ill and passed away. Later he remarried, and with his new wife, he had three boys.

Once on the 27th of Ramadan, *Laylat al-Qadr*, he was leading the *dhikr* with the whole village. He said, "Everyone is engaged in *dhikr*. All the animals are doing *dhikr* with us. The worms are doing *dhikr* with us. The birds are doing *dhikr*. Every being in this village is doing *dhikr* with us except one animal that is disconnected from his father and is depressed. God is not happy. The Prophet ﷺ is not happy and the saints are not happy. And this is all because of a childish prank!"

He spoke to the owner of the house in which they were doing *dhikr*, "Go to your son and ask him what he has in the box." He went to his son and asked him, "What do you have in the box? What animal have you captured?" The boy was confused, "What box? I only have a little matchbox, in which I put one little worm." He was told, "Take that worm and put it back in the earth." From that, the people of the village understood and raised their children with an understanding that harming any creature, no matter how small, causes unhappiness and earns the displeasure of God, of the Prophet ﷺ, and of saints. Because of such deep teachings, the village was pure and innocent of any wrongdoing.

Shaykh Abu Muhammad al-Madani died on the 3rd of Rabi al-Awwal, a Sunday, 1331 AH/1913 CE. He was buried in Rashadiya (Gunekoy). His grave is visited until this day by the people of the Daghestani community and especially by the family of Shaykh Shamil.

He passed the secret of the five Sufi orders that he was holding and gave authorization in them to his nephew, Shaykh Sharafuddin ad-Daghestani, completing what Shaykh Abu Ahmad as-Sughuri had passed to Shaykh Sharafuddin from the secret of the Naqshbandi Order. ۞

38. Sharafuddin ad-Daghestani ق

Shaykh Sharafuddin ad-Daghestani was a perfect Knower in the Divine Presence. He was a Knower whose face shone like a diamond and whose heart was transparent like a crystal. Sufism was his house, his nest, his heart. Islam was his body, his faith, his belief. Reality was his path, his way, and his destiny. The Divine Presence was his cave, his refuge. Spirituality was his vessel. He was the tongue of the people of Daghestan.

I have no power save to knock at Thy door,
And if I be turned away, at what door shall I knock?
In full abandon I put my trust in Thee,
Stretching out my hands to Thee, a pleading beggar.
—Imam Shafii, Munajat

Shaykh Sharafuddin ad-Daghestani was an ocean of knowledge, a whirlwind of spirituality, a waterfall of inspirations, a volcano of Divine Love, a whirlpool of attraction, a rainbow of Divine Attributes. He was overflowing with knowledge like the Nile when it floods. He was the carrier of the secret of *sultan adh-dhikr*, which no one had carried before his time. He was the key to the most inaccessible Divine Knowledge. He was a true scholar, decorated with the lights of the Divine Attributes. He was supported by true faith. He was a warrior in the way of God, Almighty and Exalted. He was the voice for the Divine Presence in his time. He was the shaykh of shaykhs in Islamic knowledge. He was the authority for the most specialized, the most precise, and the most difficult matters in every area of knowledge.

Shaykh Sharafuddin was the master of wisdom in the beginning of the twentieth century, and its reviver. He was a genius in the science of the Divine Law, a scholar in the knowledge of jurisprudence, and a narrator of Traditions. Hundreds of scholars attended his lectures. He was the mufti of his time. He was also one of the finest calligraphers to copy the Quran.

He was the advisor to Sultan Abd al-Hamid II. He held the position of Shaykh al-Islam, the highest religious authority in the Ottoman Empire. He was respected even by the government of the new Turkish regime at the time of Ataturk. Shaykh Sharafuddin and his caliph, Shaykh Abd Allah, were the only two shaykhs allowed to wear their turbans in the entire secular Turkish Republic established by Ataturk. Others were imprisoned for wearing the head covering of the Prophet ﷺ. Practicing Islam in its outward forms was utterly banned.

Shaykh Sharafuddin reached a state of vision in which he was dressed with the manifestation of Divine Majesty. At that time, no one could look into his eyes, for if they did, they would faint or be powerfully attracted to him. For this reason, when he entered that state, he would cover his eyes with a veil.

He was light-skinned. His eyes were blue and his beard was black. In his old age, his beard was very white, like cotton. He came into this world with open eyes and an open heart.

He was born in Kikunu, in the District of Ganep, in the state of Timurhansuro, in Daghestan, on the 3rd of Dhul-Qida, a Wednesday, 1292 AH/December 1st, 1875 CE. Shaykh Abu Muhammad al-Madani was his uncle and father-in-law. He gave him the power of the six Sufi orders long before his own death. He bequeathed to him all his disciples while he was still living. Shaykh Abu Muhammad al-Madani accepted the opinion of Shaykh Sharafuddin in all matters.

He was born at a very difficult time, a time in which religion was banned and spirituality had all but disappeared. Nonetheless, his mother said, "While I was giving birth, he was speaking, reciting *'la ilaha ill-Allah.'* Every time I nursed him he said: *'Allah, Allah.'*" He was so famous for this miracle during his infancy, that every nursing mother in his district came to see him reciting the Name of God. The index finger of his right hand was always extended in the position of the affirmation of the Divine Unity. From his childhood, he could hear trees, stones, animals, birds, and even the mountains—all reciting *dhikr*.

He was raised very well by his parents, and was under the supervision of his uncle. His supplication was always accepted. He was always in an inner state of seclusion. He started attending the gatherings of Abu Ahmad as-Sughuri when he was five years old. He was very intelligent and he was immediately able to grasp the Sufi teachings that Abu Ahmad as-Sughuri delivered from the Divine Presence.

At the age of six years, he told his mother, "Give me the newborn calf of that ox when it is born." She said, "If it is female I will keep it, and if it is male I will give it to you." He said, "Do not bother yourself my mother, because that ox is going to give birth to a male." She said, "How do you know that?" He said, "I can see what is in her womb." An hour later, the ox gave birth to a male calf. He took the baby ox and sold it and bought a male and a female sheep intending to bring them to Shaykh Abu Ahmad as-Sughuri as a gift. On his way to the shaykh, the two sheep escaped from him. He continued on to his shaykh's home, and sat next to him, feeling sadness in his heart because he had lost the sheep. The shaykh asked him, "What is the matter?" He said, "I had two sheep I was bringing for you, but they escaped." A short time later a shepherd appeared and said, "I found these two sheep among my lambs." They were the two sheep that had escaped from him.

When he was young, he went with his friends to collect wood. He did not cut the wood from the trees like his friends, but would only collect dry wood from the ground. This made his father very upset with him. He went to Shaykh Abu Ahmad as-Sughuri and complained that the boy was only collecting dry and useless wood. Shaykh Abu Ahmad as-Sughuri told him,

"Why do you not ask him why he does that?" The young Sharafuddin said, "How can I cut the green tree when it is reciting *dhikr* of *'la ilaha ill-Allah*?' I prefer to collect the dead branches, not to burn the branches that are reciting *dhikr*."

He left Daghestan as a result of the incessant incursions of the Russian military against the villages of his district. He moved with his family and his sister's family to Turkey. They walked overland for a period of five months through the worst of the winter season. They would walk during the night and hide during the day. They went first to Bursa, and then they moved to Yalova on the Marmara Sea, about 150 kilometers from Istanbul. There he established himself with his family and relatives in the village of Rashadiya, where his uncle had recently settled, having carried the Naqshbandi Order from Daghestan to Turkey.

In Daghestan, he had been trained under Shaykh Abu Ahmad as-Sughuri, who gave him the Naqshbandi Order when he was very young. In Rashadiya, Turkey, he was trained further by Abu Muhammad al-Madani, his uncle and future father-in-law, whom he helped in establishing a school and building the village's first mosques and *khaniqah*. His uncle welcomed all immigrants escaping from the tyranny of the imperialist and ruthless Russian rule. In addition, many students came to his uncle's school from all parts of Turkey. They quickly built new homes in Rashadiya and the surrounding area between Bursa and Yalova.

In addition to the Naqshbandi, his uncle connected him to the five other Sufi orders he was carrying: Qadiri, Rifai, Shadhili, Chishti and Khalwati. He became a master in all six of these orders at the age of twenty-seven.

He was highly respected in Rashadiya, especially after he had married the daughter of Shaykh Muhammad al-Madani. He was known as a person of miraculous powers among his people. Stories of his wonders began to spread throughout Turkey. In addition, he was so renowned for his knowledge of the externals of religion that many great scholars came to hear him lecture.

He had undergone several seclusions while in Daghestan, the longest for three years. He secluded himself in the mountains of Rashadiya for up to six months on the order of Shaykh Abu Muhammad al-Madani. He was always in a state of seclusion in the crowd.

One day during a six-month seclusion, as he was standing and about to go into prostration, he found a large snake in his place of prostration, poised to bite him. He said to himself, "I do not fear anyone but God," and he placed his head down directly on the head of that snake. Immediately the snake disappeared.

During that seclusion, many states of Divine Love appeared to him. As soon as he emerged from the seclusion, his shaykh withdrew and gave all the responsibility of directing and guiding people to Shaykh Sharafuddin. Shaykh Abu Muhammad thereafter sat in the company of his son-in-law as his disciple, and was the first shaykh to become a disciple of his disciple. Out of obedience to his shaykh's insistence that he sit in the highest chair, Shaykh Sharafuddin would then be the one to dispense the teachings of the Golden Chain even in his shaykh's presence.

Shaykh Sharafuddin was supported spiritually by the power of Shaykh Jamaluddin al-Ghumuqi al-Husayni and Shaykh Abu Ahmad as-Sughuri, his shaykh as a young child in Daghestan. He attained the state of pure love for God. In that state, he felt as though his body was on fire with the love of the Divine Presence. He would run out from his seclusion, take off all his clothes, and dive into the ice cold water of the river during the winter. Whenever he did that, all the villagers could hear the sound of steam coming from the river, like the sound of hot iron being quenched in water. There were still old disciples of Shaykh Sharafuddin alive in 1994 who remembered hearing the sound of the water hissing and steaming from hundreds of yards away.

Shaykh Sharafuddin was a spiritual inheritor of the Prophet ﷺ. Through that spiritual connection, he reached the state of perfection. He was a descendant of the family of Miqdad ibn al-Aswad ؓ, one of the greatest of the Companions of the Prophet ﷺ, who was left to represent him whenever the Prophet ﷺ would travel from Madinah. He reported forty-two Traditions, among which is:

> *God's Messenger ﷺ said, "On the day of resurrection the sun will come near created beings until it is about a mile from them. Humanity will sweat according to what they have done, the sweat reaching the ankles of some, the knees of others, the waists of others, while some will have their mouths covered by the sweat," and God's Messenger ﷺ pointed his hand at his mouth.*

Shaykh Sharafuddin had the mark of the hand of the Prophet ﷺ on his back. He inherited this birthmark from his ancestor, Miqdad ibn al-Aswad ؓ, in the place where the Prophet ﷺ had put his hand on his back and made a supplication for him and his descendants. That mark on the back of Shaykh Sharafuddin always gave out light, just as his face shone radiantly. He received a secret from the Prophet ﷺ: the ability to see behind him as clearly as he could see in front of him.

His uncle, Shaykh Abu Muhammad al-Madani, bestowed on him the caliphate (successorship) of the Sufi Order and leadership of his village. He enlarged the village to take more emigrants, expanded the roads and brought water into the city. He welcomed every emigrant coming from Russia, offering them whatever they needed in the way of food and shelter and asking nothing in return. As a result, the Daghestani people found a new home in place of the home they had left to the Russians. They found happiness and peace in the new land. The emigrants were especially happy to be in the company of a living shaykh carrying on the teaching which had flourished in Daghestan, as it had flourished in Central Asia hundreds of years earlier. With him in their village, blessed by his presence with the Divine bounty pouring from his blessed person, they found the love and happiness which they had lost under the tyranny of Russian soldiers.

From His Sayings

ON THE STATION OF THE HEART

> Whoever enters this station will experience and reach the Essence of God's Name. It is the sultan of all Names, because it encompasses all their meanings and to it all Attributes return. It is the Word that encompasses all these Attributes and that is why it is called the Most Majestic Name, for He is the Highest, and He is the Glorified, and He is the Greatest.
>
> It is impossible, through the understanding of the mind, to harvest the fruit of these secrets. The human body cannot encompass the realities of the meaning of God. It is impossible for human bodies to reach the hidden kingdom of the Unique One. For the people of the essence, there is only wonder and astonishment. Once they enter these stations of hidden knowledge, they are lost, wandering. What then about the

people of attributes, those people who are of such high quality that there appears on every one of them an Attribute of God, dressing and decorating them? Yet they cannot be decorated by the Essence of the Name which encompasses all of the Names, except by entering into the hidden secrets of all ninety-nine Attributes. At that time they will be allowed to reach a state of unveiling of the light of the Name encompassing all Names and Attributes, the name "*Allah*."

If the seeker continues reciting *dhikr* with the Most Glorified Name, *Allah*, he will begin to walk in the stages of that *dhikr*, of which there are seven. Every seeker that continues in doing *dhikr* of God silently, from 5,000 to 48,000 times a day, will reach a state of perfection in which he becomes impeccable in the *dhikr*. At that time, he will find his heart reciting the name "*Allah, Allah*" without any need to move the tongue. He will build up his internal power by burning up all the filth within, because the fire of the *dhikr* leaves no impurity behind. Nothing will be left, except jewels shining with the power of that spiritual fire.

As the *dhikr* enters and strengthens in his heart, he will ascend until he reaches the state in which he perceives the *dhikr* of everything in creation. He will hear everything reciting *dhikr* with him in the manner that God destined for it. He hears each of God's creations, its own tone and melody distinct from any other. His hearing of one does not affect his hearing of another, but he hears them all simultaneously, and distinctly, and he is able to differentiate between each different kind of *dhikr*.

As the seeker passes through that state, increasing ever more in *dhikr*, he will see that everyone that God created is reciting the same *dhikr* as himself. At that time, he will realize he has reached the perfect Unique Oneness. Everything is reciting the same *dhikr* and using the same word. Any kind of differences will be erased from his vision, and he will see everyone with him at the same level with the same *dhikr*. This is the state of unification of everyone in the One. Here he will completely root out all forms of hidden polytheism (*shirk*) and all creation will appear as One in the One. This is the first of seven steps on his journey.

From the state of unification, he will travel to the state of the essence of unification, in which everyone who existed will be annihilated, and the Oneness of God Alone will appear.

Then he will travel to the primordial state of perfect simplicity, where he will be able to appear in any image.

From there he will travel to the state of the keys of the secrets, known as the state of Names, in which the archetypes of the creations are made to appear from the unseen into the world of manifestation. This will make him swim in the orbit of Names and Attributes and he will know all its hidden knowledge.

Then he will travel to the state of the hidden of the hidden, the essence of all that is hidden. He will know all that is hidden through the Unique Oneness of the Essence. He will see all its powers and all its forms.

From there he travels to the state of the perfect realities of the Essence of the Names and Actions. He will appear in them all, in their atoms and in their totality. He will be dressed with the Most Glorified Name, and he will be glorified by being crowned with the state of Greatness.

Then he travels to the state of God's descent from His glorified state to the states of the worldly heaven. He arrives at that state, nearest the worldly station, beyond which the reciter of the *dhikr* has no state to reach through his recitation. Dawn comes to his inner self and the sun of perfection appears through himself and in his body, as it has appeared through *dhikr* in his heart and in his spirit. As a result, when the sun of perfection appears in his body and his limbs, he will be in the state mentioned in the prophetic Tradition, "God will be the ears with which he hears, the eyes with which he sees, the tongue with which he talks, the hand with which he grasps, the feet with which he walks." Then he will find himself and declare to himself, "I am helpless and abjectly weak," because at that time, he understands the Divine Power.

Whenever he was consulted, if he said, "Do whatever you like," that person would never succeed. But when he said, "Do this and do that," then that person would succeed.

It was said about him that he never liked to mention anything which had passed. He never accepted any backbiting and would banish the backbiter from his gatherings.

It was reported that whenever people sat in his association, love for the world would disappear from their hearts.

He said:

> Never sit without doing recitation or *dhikr*, because death is following you.
>
> The happiest moment for a human being is when he dies, because when he dies, his sins die with him.
>
> Every seeker who does not accustom and train himself to fast during the day and wake for worship at night and serve his brothers, will achieve no good in this Way.

Shah Naqshband's Disclosure Concerning Shaykh Sharafuddin

His successor, our grandshaykh, Shaykh Abd Allah ad-Daghestani, related the following during one of his gatherings:

> Once, during one of my seclusions, Shaykh Sharafuddin came to me and spoke to me about the greatness and specialties of Shah Naqshband. He praised him and told me how Shah Naqshband would intercede on the Day of Judgment. He said, "If anyone should look at Shah Naqshband's eyes, he would see them rotating, the white on the black and the black on the white. He aimed to save his spiritual power for the Day of Judgment and not to use it in this life.
>
> "On the Day of Judgment, he will send light from his right eye which will go out and circle back to his left eye, encircling in the process a vast number of people at the gathering. Whoever is embraced by that light will be saved from Hell and will enter Paradise. He will fill four paradises with that intercession."
>
> As he was describing that great event, I experienced a powerful vision, in which I witnessed the Judgment Day. I saw Shah Naqshband sending out the light of his vision, saving the people. As I was observing that vision, I felt a great love for Shah Naqshband. I ran to him and kissed his hands. Then that vision finished and my shaykh

left. I continued my seclusion of that day by reciting *dhikr*, and the Quran, and praying. At night, after I had prayed the night prayer, a state of self-effacement came over me which put me in a state of vision. I saw Shah Naqshband enter the room. He said to me, "My son, come with me." Then my spirit left my body and I saw my body motionless below me. I accompanied Shah Naqshband.

We traveled through space and time, not by the power of looking and reaching the place looked at, but by using a power in which we would think about a place and we would reach it. For three nights and four days non-stop, we continued this mode of travel.

It was my custom in my seclusion, when I wanted my daily food and drink, to knock on the floor of my room. Hearing the knocking from downstairs, my wife would bring me my provision. The first day she did not hear any knocking. The second day she again did not hear any knocking. Finally, she became so worried she opened the door and found me lying there without movement. She went to Shaykh Sharafuddin and said, "Come and see your son. He looks like he has died." He said to her, "He is not dead. Go back and do not tell anyone. He will return."

After three days and four nights of traveling with that tremendous power, Shah Naqshband stopped. He said, "Do you know who that is appearing on the horizon?" Of course, I knew, but out of respect for the master I said, "O my master, you know best." Then as the person approached and came closer he said, "Now do you recognize that person?" I said, again out of respect, "You know better, O my shaykh," even though I saw it was my shaykh. He said, "That is your shaykh, Shaykh Sharafuddin."

He said, "Do you know who that creature is behind him?" pointing to a huge creature bigger than the highest mountain on this earth which he was pulling with a rope. Out of respect I said again, "You know best, O my shaykh." He said, "That is Satan, and your shaykh is authorized as no other person was authorized before him. As every saint is authorized in a specialty, so is your shaykh authorized. His specialty is that in every day and every night, on behalf of every person who has committed sins because of Satan's influence, your shaykh is authorized to purify those people of all their sins, to cast these sins back on Satan, and to present all those people to the Prophet ﷺ clean. Then with his spiritual power, he elevates their hearts, preparing them for salvation, to be within the circle of light which I will spread on the Judgment Day. I will fill four paradises by this means. This intercession is the specialty of Shaykh Sharafuddin. In addition, those who have been left out of these four paradises will enter in Shaykh Sharafuddin's intercession, by permission of the Prophet ﷺ, who has been given this power by God Almighty. This is the tremendous authority Shaykh Sharafuddin has been given. As he is chaining the neck of Satan, he is limiting the influence of sins on this earth."

Then he said, "O my son, you are cultivating the love that is in your heart. Just like the waterwheel that irrigates one field but cannot irrigate two fields, the love that you are growing for your shaykh must be for your shaykh. If you split it between two shaykhs it may be inadequate, just like the waterwheel that is not able to adequately irrigate two fields. Do not give your heart freedom to go here and there. That love of yours will reach me through the Golden Chain and will continue to the Prophet ﷺ. Don't split it in half between the two of us. What your shaykh is doing for the Community of Muhammad ﷺ, for human beings, no one saint has ever been authorized to do before him."

Then Shah Naqshband brought me back, again traveling in that powerful manner, for four days and three nights. I came back to my body again. I felt my soul entering my body, and I watched it enter my body piece-by-piece, and cell-by-cell. Then the vision ceased, and I knocked for my wife to bring food and tea to give my body energy. That was Shah Naqshband's disclosure about Shaykh Sharafuddin.

One of Shaykh Sharafuddin's disciples, Eskici Ali Usta, who was 120 years old in 1994 and lived in Bursa, reported:

My shaykh was a wondrous shaykh. Once, when I was a young man, I was in Istanbul. I had just taken initiation in the Order from Shaykh Sharafuddin. I met one of my friends from Daghestan, but he was stubborn and did not believe in Sufism. I thought that I would speak to him and soften his heart and tell him of my shaykh's miraculous power. Instead, he was able to convince me and change my beliefs. I put my beads on the wall and stopped reciting *dhikr*. Almost immediately, I was overcome by my desires and twice I committed major sins.

After one week, I went to Sirkici, and I saw the shaykh on the way. He was also walking in that district, on his way to Rashadiya. When I saw him coming from one side, I ran to the other side to try to avoid him. When I hid myself on the other road, I felt a hand on my back and the shaykh was addressing me, "Where are you going, O Ali?" I returned with him and on the way I was thinking, "I cannot hide myself from the shaykh anymore and the shaykh cannot bring me back anymore."

We continued until we met someone named Husayn Effendi. The shaykh told me, "When you first came to me, I looked at you and I saw bad character in you. Everyone has good character mixed with bad character. When you took initiation, all the bad actions you had done previously I changed into good actions, except two: sexual desire and anger. Last week we removed from you those two bad characters, desire and anger." When he mentioned these two things, I knew he had been sitting with me, seeing my sexual desire and my anger, and I began to cry and cry and cry. As I was crying, Shaykh Sharafuddin began speaking with that person, Husayn, in a language that I had never heard before, even though I was from Daghestan, and I know all the languages of my area. Later, I found out that Shaykh Sharafuddin was speaking in Syriac, a very rare language.

After two hours of crying, he said, "Enough crying! God has forgiven you and the Prophet ﷺ has forgiven you." I said, "O my shaykh, have you really forgiven me? Has the Prophet ﷺ forgiven me? Has God forgiven me? Have the open-eyed shaykhs really forgiven me? I thought I was doing something all by myself, but now I have found that all of you are seeing me." He said, "O my son, we are servants at the door of the Prophet ﷺ and the door of God. Whatever we ask of them, they accept, as we are in their presence and we are One." I said, "As a good gesture from my side, since I have been forgiven, what is the proper way to give thanks to God and to honor you and the Prophet ﷺ? By celebrating the Prophet's ﷺ birth, or donating a lamb, or some other charity?" He said, "What we want from you is only this: that you keep constant in the *dhikr* of the Naqshbandi Order."

One of Eskici Ali Usta's friends who had migrated with him from Daghestan had received a letter, while still in Daghestan, from Shaykh Sharafuddin saying, "Leave Daghestan. There is no longer any spirituality there. It is no longer under Divine Protection because there is too much tyranny. Come here to Turkey and to Rashadiya." That man had taken the letter of Shaykh Sharafuddin and put it aside, ignoring it and thinking, "How can I leave all my property and all that I have here?" Soon the Russians conquered his town and took everything from him. Then he remembered the letter that the shaykh had sent. He finally managed to escape to Turkey and to Rashadiya. He had lost his family and his property as a result of his delay.

Once, Shaykh Sharafuddin came to Istanbul. He stayed at the Hotel Massarat. He was asked by a person named Shaykh Zia, "How are you going to die?" He said, "Is that an important question to you, how I am going to die?" He said, "It came to my heart to ask that question." He said, "I will die when we have an invasion from Armenia, and there will be a great deal of oppression at that time." Then Shaykh Zia that night made ablution and prayed two *rakats* and asked God, "O God, take away that difficulty from us, the invasion of the Armenians, and spare our beloved shaykh." The next day Shaykh Sharafuddin said to him, "O Shaykh Zia, what have you been doing all night, praying? Your prayer has been accepted. That difficulty has been taken from me, but you will suffer instead of me and die as a martyr." Eight years after that incident in the hotel, the Armenians and Greeks entered Rashadiya, Zia Effendi was shot dead, and the prediction of Shaykh Sharafuddin came to pass.

Yusuf Effendi, a man who in 1994 was about 100 years old, tells the following story:

> Once Shaykh Sharafuddin was jailed in Eskisehir, and I was his guard. In that jail was another great personality, the famous shaykh, Said Nursi. Shaykh Sharafuddin was jailed along with his caliph, Shaykh Abd Allah, and other disciples, and Said Nursi was jailed along with his disciples. When Said Nursi became aware of Shaykh Sharafuddin's imprisonment in the same prison, he sent his disciples to ask him if he

needed anything and offered their help. Shaykh Sharafuddin replied, "Thank you, but we have nothing and we are in need of nothing."

The disciples of Said Nursi kept coming to Shaykh Sharafuddin, asking him if he needed anything. He would always reply in the negative. One day, Shaykh Sharafuddin told the disciples of Said Nursi to ask their shaykh, "Why are we here?" The disciples of Said Nursi went and asked him. He answered, "We are here to reach the station of Yusuf ﷺ, the station of silent choice." After he asked that question and Shaykh Said Nursi gave his reply, that was the end of the discussion.

This exchange made me very perplexed, and I began to ponder deeply. Then I asked the shaykh, "What is the secret of your being here?" Finally, at my insistence, Shaykh Sharafuddin replied, "I was sent here to carry the secrets of many people, these people who have been jailed without cause. I am supporting these people. God sent me here, because you are all gathered here, and it is difficult to gather you. I am here to say farewell to you, because soon we are leaving this world. We are going to deliver to you your secrets. For us there is no jail, we are always in the Divine Presence and we are never affected by a jail. All of you, after a while, are going to leave, but you will meet again, when an important person is going to pass away and you will all meet together then." The disciples of Said Nursi heard this, as well as the other prisoners and the jailers who were all listening intently.

After about three months, he was released from the jail. He told Shaykh Abd Allah, "I am going to pass away soon, because I spent too much of my power extracting the secrets of *Surat al-Anam* (the sixth chapter of Holy Quran)." He wrote his will, assigning Shaykh Abd Allah to be his successor on the throne of guidance.

Three days before he died, he called Sultan al-Awliya Mawlana Shaykh Abd Allah al-Faiz ad-Daghestani and some of his other disciples, and said, "For three months I have been diving into the ocean of *Surat al-Anam* to bring out from one of its verses the names of all the saints of the Naqshbandi Order, whose number is 7,007. Praise belongs to God, I was able to obtain their names with all their titles and I have recorded them in my private notebook, which I am giving to my successor, Shaykh Abd

Allah. It contains the names of all the different groups of saints who are going to be present in the time of Mahdi ﷺ."

The next day, he called his caliph, Shaykh Abd Allah ad-Daghestani and said:

> O my son, this is my will. I am going to die in two days. On the order of the Prophet Muhammad ﷺ, I am assigning you as my successor in the Naqshbandi Order, together with the five other Sufi orders that I have received from my uncle. All the secrets that were given to me and all the powers that were bestowed on me from my predecessors in the Naqshbandi Order and the other five Sufi orders, I am bestowing on you. All the disciples to whom you give initiation in the Naqshbandi Order, are also going to be initiated in the other five orders and to receive their secrets as well. Soon there will be an opening for you to leave Turkey and to move to Damascus. Watch for it and seize that opportunity.

Shaykh Abd Allah said, "He gave me that will, and I tried to hide it as I wished to hide myself."

Grandshaykh Sharafuddin died on the 27th of Jumada al-Awwal, a Sunday, 1355 AH/1936 CE in Rashadiya. He was buried in the cemetery in Rashadiya on the top of a hill. Until today, his mosque and *zawiya* are still open. Many people go there to visit and obtain his blessings. The same beads that Shaykh Sharafuddin used to conduct the *Khatm al-Khwajagan* (*dhikr* of the masters) are still there, hanging on the wall.

Our Grandshaykh, Shaykh Abd Allah, the caliph and successor of Shaykh Sharafuddin, said:

> When the news of his death was made known, everyone came to his house to receive his blessings. Even Ataturk, the president of the new Republic of Turkey, sent a delegation out of respect. We washed his body. When we laid him down to wash him, he moved his hands towards his thigh to cup the water that poured off him. All his disciples came and drank from the water of that ritual purification, as had been done by Ali ؓ with the water used for the washing of the Prophet's ﷺ blessed body. When every disciple had passed to drink, he moved his hand back to its original place. That was a miracle from his ocean of miracles, and that happened after his death.

When we buried him the next day, more than 300,000 people came to his funeral. The city could not accommodate that crowd of people. They came from Yalova, Bursa, and Istanbul. It was an enormous crowd and a huge mass of sobbing people. Men were crying, women wailed, and children were crying as well. May God Almighty raise up His saints in every century.

One of his disciples, Yusuf Effendi, said:

It is true that we never found ourselves in the same place with all of his disciples—there were too many—but at the time of his death, all the cities of Bursa, Adapazar, Yalova, Istanbul, Eskisehir, Orhanghazi and Izmir, heard about his passing, and all of the citizens of these towns gathered to recite the funeral prayer for him.

Grandshaykh Sharafuddin has written many books, but they were all lost during the Balkan War. Nevertheless, many manuscripts remain with his family containing the secrets of the Naqshbandi Order. The disciples go to them to read these books. He passed the secret of the Golden Chain to his successor, Sultan al-Awliya, Grandshaykh Abd Allah al-Faiz ad-Daghestani. ۞

39. Abd Allah al-Faiz ad-Daghestani ق

The red sulphur among the saints, the crystal lamp of this universe and its foundation, Shaykh Abd Allah al-Faiz ad-Daghestani was supported by steadfast faith. He was nursed from the breast of the station of the Arch-Intercessor, whose throne he ascended later in life. He was a reviver of religion in his time.

You are something inseparable from the heart.
My eyelids never close
But that You are between them and my eyes.
Your love is part of me like the soul's internal speech.
I cannot breathe except You are in my breath
And I find You coursing through each of my senses.
—Abul Hasan Sumnun [100]

---

[100] Abul Hasan Sumnun, quoted in *Hilyat al-awliya*, 10:310.

The earth shone with a brilliant new light when Shaykh Abd Allah al-Faiz ad-Daghestani was born. A knower of the hidden meanings of the Holy Quran, he was the key to its secret, enlightened with the pure essence of the Truth. He had enormous experience in the Way of his predecessors. Sufism was his blood. Prophet Muhammad ﷺ was his heart. The Divine Presence was his soul. He was the Luminary of Knowledge for human beings in his time, owner of the perfect characteristics and controller of his active self. He was the ocean of wisdom for all human beings to sail upon and reach their appointed shore unscathed.

His reputation for wise counsel and guidance spread over the earth. Kings stood at his door. Scholars sought his disclosures. In his time, no one was left who did not receive nourishment from his spirituality. By means of his light, darkness disappeared and the secrets of blessings shone from the people. He was the perfect saint and the pillar of the knowers.

People ran to his door to find through him the happiness of this life and the hereafter. He was an ocean of instruction whose waves crashed roaring on the Divine shore. He left the erudite perplexed with his superior knowledge, and he was the greatest of all ascetics ever seen or read about. He gave selflessly from his spirit to quench the thirst of the spiritual and the physical worlds. He was a galaxy by himself, garlanded with suns and stars of varied size and color, bringing a different light to each individual. He wore the crown of God's Divine Love, and from him, people sipped the longed-for honey of Divine Secrets. He never left a person without reaching and raising him with his spiritual breath. The darkness of ignorance disappeared in the illumination of his knowledge.

He was born in Daghestan in the year 1309 AH/1891 CE to a family of doctors. His father was a general practitioner and his brother was surgeon general in the Russian army. He was raised and trained by his uncle, Shaykh Sharafuddin ad-Daghestani, the master of the Naqshbandi Order at that time, who took special care of him from his early youth.

During his sister's pregnancy, Shaykh Sharafuddin told her:

> The son you are carrying has no veils on his heart. He will be able to see events that have passed or that are coming. He is one of those who can read the unseen knowledge from the Preserved Tablets directly. He is going to be *"Sultan al-Awliya"* in his time. He is going to be called, among the saints, "the Leader of the Community of Muhammad ﷺ."

He is going to perfect the ability of being with God and being, at the same time, with people. He will inherit the secret from the Prophet ﷺ which he referred to when he said, "I have one face looking at the Creator and I have one face looking at creation," and "I have one hour with the Creator and I have one hour with the creation."

When you give birth to him, call him Abd Allah, because he will be carrying the secret of servanthood. He will spread the Order back to the Arab countries. Through him, his successor will spread the Order in Western countries and in the Far East. You must be careful with him. I am asking that, when he reaches the age of seven, you give him to me to raise and to be under my guardianship.

On the 12th of Rabi al-Awwal, a Thursday, his mother Amina gave birth to her son, whom she named Abd Allah. When she gave birth to him at around midnight, no one was with her. His father was busy and his brother was away. She said that, when she was delivering him, she saw a vision in which two ladies came to her. One was Rabia al-Adawiyya and the other was Asiya (Pharaoh's wife, who believed in Moses ﷺ). They helped her in giving birth. After a while the vision disappeared, and she saw a baby come forth. At that moment, her husband arrived and helped her deliver her son.

His parents never heard him cry. In his childhood, at the age of one year, they often saw him with his head on the floor in prostration. His mother, family, and neighbors were astonished at this. He spoke at the age of seven months and was able to make himself understood clearly. He was unlike most children in other respects as well. He would often be seen moving his head from right to left while speaking the Divine Name. At the age of three, he was known to tell visitors about their future. He would know their name without being familiar with them or being told. He astonished the people of his country. People came to visit his parents' home in order to see this remarkable child and to hear him speak.

By the age of seven, he was learned in the Quran. He often sat with his uncle, Shaykh Sharafuddin, and answered questions people put to him. His answers were always very clear on matters of the Divine Law, although he had never studied jurisprudence. He would recite the supporting evidences from the Quran and the Traditions without ever having studied their sciences. This caused people to be ever more attracted to him.

His father's house was always full of visitors coming to ask him about their problems, difficulties, and daily affairs. He would answer them and predict their outcomes. He became so famous at the age of seven that if anyone in his village wanted to marry, they would first go to him and ask if the marriage was destined to succeed. More than that, they would ask if the marriage was according to the Will of God as mentioned in the Preserved Tablets.

The scholars of his time verified his decisions and accepted his jurisdiction. Knowers in his time were so fascinated with his knowledge, although he was only seven years of age, that they would come from afar to hear the spiritual knowledge that flowed from him like a fountain. His uncle asked him how he was able to speak so effortlessly and endlessly. He answered, "O my uncle, it comes to me as words written right in front of me from the Divine Presence. I only have to look and read what is written." He discussed subjects of deep knowledge that were at the time unknown. At the age of seven, he said to the spiritual masters of wisdom of his time, "If I speak what has been put into my heart of Divine Knowledge, even saints will cut my throat."

He was extremely meticulous in keeping the prescriptions of the Divine Law. He was the first to appear for prayer in the mosque five times a day. He was the first to be present for *dhikr*. He was the first to be present in the meetings of scholars. He was the first to be present in the spiritual gatherings.

He acquired fame for healing sick people by recitation of *Surat al-Fatiha*. Many people were brought to him with different kinds of sicknesses. He would read *Surat al-Fatiha,* and blow on them, and they would be healed. He had a tremendous power for healing even people who were far away. People would come to him and ask for help for parents, or a wife, or someone else who was sick and unable to come to him. He would read one *Fatiha* and send it for them. They would be instantly cured, from any distance. Healing was one specialty from among his endless specialties.

Speaking of Himself

I am a descendant of Miqdad ibn al-Aswad ﵁, whom the Prophet ﷺ appointed as his deputy whenever he left Madinah on an expedition. I inherited, like my uncle, the five marks of the Blessed Hand of the

Prophet ﷺ which he had placed on the back of my blessed grandfather, Miqdad ibn al-Aswad ☗. From that birthmark shines a special light.

At this time in the late 1890s, Daghestan was under the severe oppression and tyranny of the Russian occupying armies. His uncle, who was the spiritual head of the village, and his father, who was a well-known doctor, decided to migrate from Daghestan to Turkey. After reaching this decision, they asked Shaykh Abd Allah to make spiritual consultation on the appropriateness of migrating at that time. Shaykh Abd Allah described the event:

> That night I prayed the night prayer. I renewed my ablution. I prayed two *rakats*. I sat in meditation, connecting myself through my shaykh, my uncle, to the Prophet ﷺ. I saw the Prophet ﷺ coming to me with 124,000 Companions, saying to me, "O my son, I release all my powers and those of my 124,000 Companions from my heart. Tell your uncle and the caretakers of the village to migrate immediately to Turkey."
>
> Then I saw the Prophet ﷺ embracing me and I saw myself disappearing in him. As soon as I disappeared in him, I saw myself ascending from the Dome of the Rock from which the Prophet ﷺ ascended in the Night Journey. I saw myself astride the same Buraq which carried the Prophet ﷺ. I saw myself carried up in a true vision, to the station of *"two bows' length"* (53:9), where I could see the Prophet ﷺ, but not myself.
>
> I felt myself to be a part of the entirety of the Prophet ﷺ. Through that ascension, I received the realities that the Prophet ﷺ poured into my heart from what he had received on the Night of Ascension. All these different kinds of knowledge came to my heart in words of light, which began as green and changed to purple, and the understandings were poured into my heart in a quantity that is immeasurable.
>
> I heard a voice coming from the Divine Presence saying, "Approach, O my servant, to My Presence." As I approached through the Prophet ﷺ, everything disappeared; even the spiritual reality of the Prophet ﷺ disappeared. Nothing existed except God, Almighty and Exalted.
>
> Then I heard a voice from all His Lights and Attributes that were shining in His Presence, "O My servant, now come to the state of

subsistence within this Light." I felt myself come into subsistence through the Prophet ﷺ, after having been annihilated, appearing, and subsisting in the Divine Presence, decorated with the Ninety-Nine Names and Attributes. Then I saw myself inside the Prophet ﷺ, appearing inside every creation that was existing by God's Power. That took us to a state in which we were able to realize that there are universes other than this universe, that there are endless creations of God, Almighty and Exalted. Then I felt my uncle shaking my shoulder, saying, "O my son, it is time for the dawn prayer."

I prayed the dawn prayer behind him, and more than 300 people from the village prayed in congregation with us. After the dawn prayer, my uncle stood and said, "We asked my nephew to do a spiritual consultation." Everyone was eagerly waiting to hear what I had seen. My uncle immediately said, "He was brought to the presence of the Prophet ﷺ by my power. The Prophet ﷺ gave everyone permission to move to Turkey. Then he took him through states up to the station of *'the distance of two bows' length.'* (53:9) Then he took him to a station in which he opened to him a vision of knowledge that has never been opened to any saint before, including myself. His ascension was a means of instruction for past and present saints, and a key to open a gigantic ocean of knowledge and wisdom."

I said to myself, "My uncle was with me in that vision, and it was with his power that I received that vision."

Everyone in the village began to prepare for the emigration. We moved from Daghestan to Turkey on a trip that was full of difficulties caused both by Russian soldiers and by highwaymen who killed without the slightest provocation. Near the border with Turkey, we were traveling through a forest which was known to be filled with Russian soldiers. It was time for the dawn prayer. My uncle said, "We will perform the dawn prayer and then we will cross the forest." We offered the dawn prayer and began moving. Shaykh Sharafuddin said to everyone, "Stop!" He asked for a cup of water. Someone handed him a cup of water and he read on it from *Surah YaSin*, *"And We have set a barrier in front of them and a barrier behind them, and We have enshrouded them in veils so that they cannot see."* (36:9) Then he recited, *"God is the best Protector, and He is the Most Merciful of those who show mercy."* (12:64)

As he was reciting these verses, everyone felt something come to their hearts. I saw all the emigrants trembling. God gave me a vision at that moment so that I could see that we were surrounded by the Russian Army on every side. I saw that they were shooting at anything that moved, even a bird. Then I saw that we passed by and that we were safe. We were crossing the forest, and they heard no sound of our footsteps or our animals. We arrived safely at the other side of the border.

The vision ended as Shaykh Sharafuddin finished reciting. He cast the water ahead of us and he said, "Move now! But do not look behind." As we moved on, we could see the Russian soldiers on every side, yet it was as if we were invisible. We moved for twenty miles through that forest. It took us from morning until after the night prayer. We did not stop except to pray and we were invisible to everyone. We heard the Russian army shooting at people, birds, animals, and anything that moved, but we passed undetected and unscathed. We were the only people who were safe. We exited the forest and crossed over into Turkey.

We traveled first to Bursa, where Shaykh Sharafuddin established his home for one year. After that he moved to Rashadiya, joining his uncle, Shaykh Abu Muhammad al-Madani, where they established a village for Daghestani emigrants. It was located thirty miles from Yalova, which is on the Marmara Coast, around fifty miles from Bursa and about sixty miles from Adapazar. There he built the first mosque in that village. Next to it, he built his own house. All the emigrants busied themselves with building their houses. My father and mother built a house adjacent to the house of Shaykh Sharafuddin.

When I reached the age of thirteen, Turkey was under the attack of the British, French, and Greek armies. The Turkish army was conscripting everyone, even the children. They wanted me to go join the army, but my uncle, who had a good relationship with Sultan Abd al-Hamid, refused to send me. My father died and my mother was alone, so I had to work to support my mother. When I reached fifteen years of age,

> Shaykh Sharafuddin told me, "Now, my son, you are mature, and an adult, and you have to marry." I married at the very young age of fifteen years and lived with my mother and my wife.

His First Seclusion and Spiritual Training

Shaykh Sharafuddin raised and trained Shaykh Abd Allah with intensive spiritual discipline and long hours of *dhikr*. Six months after his marriage, he was ordered to enter seclusion for five years. He said:

> I was a newlywed of only six months when my shaykh ordered me to enter seclusion for five years. My mother was so unhappy she went to complain about it to my shaykh, who was her brother. My wife was also unhappy, but my heart never complained. On the contrary, my heart was completely happy to enter the seclusion I desired so intensely.
>
> I entered the seclusion though my mother was crying and saying, "I have no one except you. Your brother is still in Russia and your father has passed on." I felt pity for my mother, but I knew it was an order of my shaykh and that it was coming directly from the Prophet ﷺ. I entered that seclusion with orders to take six showers every day with cold water, and to keep all my obligations and daily devotional practices (*wird*). In addition, I was ordered to recite at least seven—and up to fifteen—sections of the Quran and to repeat the Holy Name of *Allah* 148,000 times and salutations upon the Prophet ﷺ 24,000 times daily.
>
> There were many other practices as well, all to be performed in a focused and meditative state. I was in a cave, deep in a large forest, high on a snow-covered mountain. One person was assigned to serve me with seven olives and two ounces of bread every day. I entered that seclusion when I was fifteen-and-a-half years old. When I emerged from that seclusion at twenty years of age, I was very thin, weighing only one hundred pounds.
>
> What was unveiled to me of experiences and visions cannot be expressed in words. When I entered the seclusion I said to my ego, "O my ego, even if I am going to die, I am not going to leave this seclusion. You must know that. Do not try to change my mind or to cheat me."

There was an opening in the roof of the cave to the outside and when I entered the seclusion I stopped up the hole with a piece of cloth.

I slept very little in that seclusion. I never felt any need to sleep, because I had such strong heavenly support. Once, I had a vision of the Prophet ﷺ in seclusion in the Cave of Hira. For forty days, I sat behind him and never slept but continued in that state.

As I was reciting *dhikr* one night after midnight, a huge storm raged on the mountain. I could hear that storm felling trees, pouring rain, and finally, snow. It was very cold and nothing made me warm except the heat of my *dhikr*. My heart almost stopped. Then it occurred to me to close the hole again. As soon as that thought came to me, I saw the vision of my shaykh shouting, "O my son! Are you busy with yourself, or are you busy with the One who created you? If you die from the cold it is better for you than allowing your heart one moment of heedlessness." That vision gave me warmth in my heart and determination to restart the *dhikr* immediately. As I continued the *dhikr*, more wind came, and with it, more snow. I struggled with myself, finally telling myself, "Let me die, even so I am continuing my *dhikr*." As soon as I said that, the wind stopped and the snow stopped. Then a tree fell, and covered that hole in the cave.

One day after I prayed the last prayer of the night, while I was busy with *dhikr* and my heart was connected with its Origin, I saw a vision of myself reciting *dhikr* in the Divine Presence. At the same time, I felt something encircling me. I knew it was not something heavenly, that it was something physical. I remembered the saying of the Prophet ﷺ, "*Nothing puts fear in my heart except the fear of God.*" Although I felt something around me wrapping me up, my heart remained undisturbed in the Divine Presence.

In that state, I reached a place in the station of the awareness of numbers at 777,777 repetitions of the Divine Name. I was going to 777,778 when I heard the Divine Presence addressing me, "O my servant! You have reached the secret of awareness of numbers tonight. You have gained the key for that station. Enter into Our Presence in the state of the one who speaks with God, the state of Moses عليه السلام, *kaleemullah*, when he spoke directly with God." I saw that I was

> speaking with the Divine Presence. I received answers to questions that saints had never been able to reach before. I took the opportunity to ask God, "O *Allah,* what is Your Greatest Name?" And I heard, "O my servant, you will be given that later." Then that vision disappeared and it was time for the dawn prayer.
>
> Before each prayer, I was obliged to take a cold shower. There was, of course, no running water, so I had to use melted snow to shower. As I was about to stand up to wash for prayer, I found that facing me was the head of a snake, which had encircled me completely. Its head was poised so that any movement out of fear would cause him to strike me. I did not give that snake any importance. I knew if I felt any fear, it would attack. So, in my mind, I made it to be nonexistent. I could not take a shower with the snake wrapped around me, but the shaykh's order had to be followed. So I poured the water over my clothes and over the snake. For forty days that snake remained wrapped around me. When I was praying, it would move its head to allow for my prostrations. For forty days, that snake kept watch, looking for any mistake or fear, to attack me. This test from my shaykh, to see if I had fear of any but God, finally ended and that snake began to unwind itself from around me. It sat for a while in front of me. Then it disappeared.

Shaykh Abd Allah spent five years in that particular seclusion, which ended when he was twenty. When he emerged, he was eligible for military conscription.

His Ascension

He describes an incident that occured during his service in the Ottoman Army:

> I saw my mother for only one or two weeks. Then they took me to the battle known as Safar Barlik in the Dardanelles. One day, there was an attack from the enemy and about 100 of us were left behind to defend a frontier. I was an excellent marksman, able to hit a thread from a great distance. We were unable to defend our position and were under fierce attack. I felt a bullet strike my heart, and I fell to the ground mortally wounded.

As I lay dying, I saw the Prophet ﷺ coming to me. He said, "O my son, you were destined to die here, but we still need you on this earth in both your spiritual and physical form. I am coming to you to show you how a person dies and how the Angel of Death takes the soul." He presented me with a vision in which I saw my soul leaving my body, cell by cell, beginning from the toes. As the life was withdrawing, I could see how many cells are in my body, and the function of every cell, and the cure for every sickness of each cell, and I heard the *dhikr* of every cell.

As my soul was passing away, I experienced what a person feels when he dies. I was brought to see the different states of death: painful states of death, easy states of death, and the most blissful states of death. The Prophet ﷺ told me, "You are from those who pass in a blissful state of death." I was enjoying that passing so much because I was going back to my origin, which made me comprehend the secret of the Quranic verse, *"To God we belong, and to Him is our return."* (2:156)

That vision continued until I experienced my soul departing on the last breath. I saw the Angel of Death come and heard the questions he would ask. All the kinds of visions that appear to the dying I experienced, yet I was alive during that experience and this enabled me to understand the secret of that state.

I saw in that vision my soul looking down on my body, and the Prophet ﷺ was telling me, "Come with me!" I accompanied the Prophet ﷺ. He took me to a vision of the Seven Heavens. I saw everything he wished me to see in the Seven Heavens. He raised me to the station of truthfulness where I met all the prophets, all the saints, all the martyrs, and all the righteous.

He said, "O my son, now I am going to take you to see the tortures of Hell." There I saw everything that the Prophet ﷺ had mentioned in the Traditions about the tortures and punishments of that place. I said, "O Prophet ﷺ, you who were sent as a Mercy for human beings, is there not any way for these people to be saved?" He replied to me, "Yes, my son, with my intercession they can be saved. I am showing you the fate of those people if I did not have the power to intercede for them."

The Prophet ﷺ said, "O my son, now I will return you to earth and to your body." As soon as the Prophet ﷺ said that, I looked down and saw my body, looking somewhat swollen. I looked at that and said, "O Prophet of God, it is better to be here with you. I do not want to go back. I am happy with you in the Divine Presence. Look at that world. I have already been there and now I have left. Why must I go back? Look, my body is swollen."

He said, "O my son, you must go back. That is your duty." By the order of the Prophet ﷺ, I went back to my body, even though I did not want to. As I entered my body I saw the bullet in my heart had been encased in flesh and the bleeding had stopped. As I smoothly entered into my body, the vision ended. When it ended, I saw the medics on the field of battle looking for the survivors among the dead. Then one of them said, "That one is alive, that one is alive." I had no power to speak or to move, and I realized that it had been seven days that my body had been lying there.

They took me and treated me, until I recovered and my health was restored. Then they sent me back to my uncle. As soon as I reached him he asked me, "O my son, did you enjoy your visit?" I did not say, "Yes," and I did not say, "No," as I wanted to know if he meant the visit to the army or the visit in the company of the Prophet ﷺ. Then he asked me again, "O my son, did you enjoy your visit with the Prophet ﷺ?" Then I realized that he knew everything that had happened to me. So I ran to him and kissed his hand and I told him, "O my shaykh, I went with the Prophet ﷺ, and I must admit that I did not want to come back. But he told me that it is my duty."

Shaykh Abd Allah's Total Surrender

Shaykh Abd Allah continued his life under the watchful eyes of his uncle, Shaykh Sharafuddin. He advanced ever higher in spiritual knowledge. One day, Shaykh Sharafuddin was sitting in a gathering of 300 scholars, both religious and spiritual. They were there to discuss matters of importance to their spiritual life. They were sitting on a hill near his mosque.

Shaykh Abd Allah came up the hill towards the gathering. Some of the scholars said to Shaykh Sharafuddin, "We are astonished at the great importance you give to that child." The Shaykh replied:

> Look at him. He is coming to see me. If a little child of seven were to come to him and say, "Your shaykh is sending you a message that you must go to Makkah," even if I had not sent that child, Abd Allah would immediately accept and do what that child says. This is because he relates everything to me, and he knows that whatever comes to him comes from me, regardless of the means. He knows that if it comes from me, the order is from the Prophet ﷺ, because my heart is connected to his heart, and that its origin is from God. Now if that were to happen, without going back to his wife or his mother to say goodbye, nor to pack any provisions, he would immediately direct his steps toward Makkah. That is why I give him such importance; and also because I know what kind of station he is in.
>
> The state that he is now in, no one before him, including myself, has ever been able to enter or to see. He has reached a state higher than my state and higher than that of my masters in this Way. As the Order continues from one master to another, it moves upward. As the secret is passed from one shaykh to another, the rank will be increased by the addition of the successor's secret to the secret that he receives. At the same time, the rank of the Prophet ﷺ is always increasing, in every moment, and as he is raised ever higher, so too are the saints of his Community. That is the meaning of the verse, "*And above every possessor of knowledge there is a greater knower*." (12:76)

A Meeting with Gurdjieff

Grandshaykh Abd Allah served in his master's *khaniqah*. Every day, hundreds of visitors arrived to visit the shaykh, most of them coming from Daghestan. Among the many visitors to the shaykh was the Russian teacher George Gurdjieff. Having recently arrived in Turkey, after a long and arduous escape from Russia at the time of the Communist revolution, Gurdjieff came to visit Shaykh Sharafuddin. He had had many contacts with Sufis of various orders and had been raised in, and had traveled extensively throughout, the region of the Caucasus. He was pleased to find the inheritors of the distinguished Daghestani Naqshbandi lineage.

Shaykh Sharafuddin asked Shaykh Abd Allah to host their guest. Shaykh Abd Allah recounted the events of the meeting to several of his disciples many years later. As soon as they met, Shaykh Abd Allah said, "You are interested in the knowledge of the Nine Points. We can speak on it in the morning after the dawn prayer. Now you eat something and rest." At the time of the dawn prayer, Shaykh Abd Allah called Gurdjieff to come and pray with him. As soon as the prayer finished, the shaykh began to recite *Surah YaSin* from the Holy Quran. As he finished reading, Gurdjieff approached him and asked if he could speak of what he had just experienced. Gurdjieff said:

> As soon as you finished the prayer and began to recite, I saw you come to me and take my hand. We were transported to a beautiful rose garden. You told me that this garden is your garden and these roses are your disciples, each with his own color and perfume. You directed me to one particular red rose and said, "That one is yours. Go smell it." As I did, I saw the rose open and I disappeared within it and became the rose. I entered its roots, and they led me to your presence. I found myself entering into your heart and becoming a part of you.
>
> Through your spiritual power I was able to ascend to the knowledge of the power of the Nine Points. Then a voice, addressing me as Abd an-Nur, said, "This light and knowledge have been granted to you from the Divine Presence of God to bring peace to your heart. However, you must not use the power of this knowledge." The voice bid me farewell with the salutation of peace and the vision ended as you were finishing the recitation from the Quran.

Shaykh Abd Allah replied:

> *Surah YaSin* was called "the Heart of the Quran" by the Holy Prophet ﷺ and the knowledge of these Nine Points was opened to you through it. The vision was by the blessings of the verse, *"Peace! A Word (of salutation) from a Lord Most Merciful."* (36:58)
>
> Each of the Nine Points is represented by one of nine saints who are at the highest level in the Divine Presence. They are the keys to untold powers within the human being, but there is no permission to use these keys. This is a secret that, in general, will not be opened until the Last Days when the Mahdi عليه السلام appears and Jesus عليه السلام returns.

This meeting of ours has been blessed. Keep it as a secret in your heart and do not speak of it in this life. Abd an-Nur, for that is your name with us, you are free to stay or go as your responsibilities allow. You are always welcome with us. You have attained safety in the Divine Presence. May God bless you and strengthen you in your work.

His States and Discourses after His Second Seclusion

At thirty years of age, Shaykh Abd Allah was ordered to enter a second long seclusion for five years. During that seclusion, many visions and states were granted to him which are impossible to describe within the scope of this book. After he completed this second seclusion, the power of his spiritual attraction increased. He became so renowned that even during his shaykh's lifetime, people came from everywhere to learn from him.

Selected Discourses

FIVE STATIONS OF THE HEART

I do not speak to you about any station, manifestation, or rank without my having already entered that station or position and experienced that manifestation. I am not like many others. I do not speak separating my sight from my heart, enumerating the stations for you without my knowing their Reality. No! First of all I followed that path and saw what it was. I learned those realities and secrets which may be found along it. I worked my way along it until I obtained the knowledge of certainty, the eye of certainty, and the truth of certainty. Only then do I speak to you, giving you a tiny taste of what I have tasted until I am able to make you reach that station without tiring you and without difficulties.

There are five Stations of the Heart: *qalb, sirr, sirr as-sirr, khafa,* and *akhfa*. *Qalb* is the heart, *sirr* is the secret, *sirr as-sirr* is the secret of the secret, *khafa* is the hidden, and *akhfa* the most hidden. The secret of this order is based on these five subtle Stations of the Heart (*lataif*).

Latifat al-qalb, the stage of the heart, is under the authority of Adam عليه السلام, because it represents the physical aspect of the heart. *Latifat as-sirr,* the station of the secret, is under Noah عليه السلام, because it is the vessel which is saved from the ocean of darkness, from the flood of ignorance. *Latifat sirr as-sirr*, the station of the secret of the secret, is under two prophets: Abraham ﷺ and Moses ﷺ, who represent God's Divine Presence on earth. God made Abraham ﷺ the symbol of all His caliphs on this earth, as mentioned in the verse of the creation of mankind (2:30).[101] Moses ﷺ was blessed with hearing and speaking to God which are the two essential attributes of knowledge.

Latifat al-khafa, the hidden station, is under Jesus ﷺ because of his relationship with hidden knowledge. He represents spiritual understanding. *Latifat al-akhfa*, the most hidden station, is under the Reality of Muhammad ﷺ, because he was granted a station high above that of all other prophets and messengers. He was the one who was raised up on the Night of Ascension to the Divine Presence. This is represented by the sacred phrase of the testimony of faith in which, "There is no God but God" is joined with "Muhammad is the Messenger of God."

The lights of these stations have been shown to me. The light of the heart is a yellow hue. The light of the secret is red. The light of the secret of the secret is white. The light of the hidden station is green. The light of the most hidden station is black.

NINE POINTS

These five stations are the center of the Nine Points which represent the locus of inspiration of the Divine Presence in the heart of the human being. These Nine Points are located on the chest of each person and they represent nine different hidden states in every human being. Every state is connected to a saint, who has the authority to control that point.

If the seeker in the Naqshbandi Way is able to unveil and to make spiritual contact with the authorized master controlling theses points, he may be given knowledge of, and power to use, these Nine Points.

---

[101] *Behold, thy Lord said to the angels: "I will create a vicegerent on earth." They said: "Wilt Thou place therein one who will make mischief therein and shed blood?—whilst we do celebrate Thy praises and glorify Thy holy (name)?" He said: "I know what ye know not."*

The conditions related to opening these Nine Points can only be alluded to obliquely. The first station involves the power of imprisoning the ego.

The key to the second state is *dhikr* with *"la ilaha ill-Allah."*

The third state consists in witnessing the engraving of God's Name on the heart *(naqsh)*. The fourth state relates to the meaning of that engraving on the heart.

The fifth state is to imprint the engraving with your *dhikr*. In the sixth state, the heart is made to stop pumping at will and to start pumping at will.

The seventh state is to be aware of the number of times one stops the heart from pumping and the number of times one restores the pumping of the heart.

In the eighth, state one mentions the phrase *"Muhammadun Rasul Allah"* ﷺ in every cessation of the heart and every restoration of its pumping.

The ninth stage is to return to your cave, as God mentioned in *Surat al-Kahf*, *"When ye turn away from them and the things they worship other than God, betake yourself to the Cave. Your Lord will shower His mercies on you..."* (18:16)

The Cave is the Divine Presence. Here one utters the cherished prayer of the Prophet ﷺ, "O God, You are my destination and Your Pleasure is what I seek." The heart, as it cycles between the cessation and restoration of its pumping, is existing at the level of the Essence of the Divine Presence. Because that Divine Essence is the source of all created being, that heart will be at one with even the most minute creation in this universe. The heart which has reached the secrets of the Nine Points will be able to see everything, hear everything, know everything, taste everything, sense everything, *"until He will be the ears with which he hears, the eyes with which he sees, the tongue with which he speaks, the hand with which he grasps, and the feet with which he walks. He will be Lordly, he only need say to a thing Be! and it will be."*

IF YOU ENTER, DO NOT BACK OUT

This means if you start a deed, complete it and excel in it for the sake of God. Your deeds should not be like Iblis', done for a certain objective, or in order to obtain miraculous powers, or to obtain a title or rank, or for a reward or a wage, deviating from your goal and your aim, that is the cause of your existence and your final ambition. Hence we proclaim, "O Lord! Thou art my destiny, and Thy satisfaction is my objective!"[102]

THE DETERMINATION OF 'MEN' CAN ROOT OUT MOUNTAINS

The power of the determination is from faith. "Men" is *rijal* in Arabic, meaning not the male gender but those who are manly in fighting their egoes. Thus "men" in the Tradition of the Sufis means those who defeated their egoes in mortal combat and "died before they died."

This principle means you must maintain unstoppable determination in your struggle to reach to Knowledge of Certainty (*Ilm al-Yaqin*), Vision of Certainty (*Ayn al-Yaqin*) and to the Reality of Certainty (*Haqq al-Yaqin*). Challenge the adversities of the world, such as hunger, struggle, thirst, cold and hot, in the name of your goal and aim. Most importantly, cut the down the mountain of your ego (*nafs*) with the pick and shovel of fasting from whatever it may crave. Hence we proclaim, "O Lord! Thou art my destiny, and Thy satisfaction is my objective!"

THERE IS NO REST IN RELIGION[103]

This means that you should fold up your rest, and the rest of your ego, and throw them to the bottom of the great ocean of spiritual struggle (*mujahadah*) for good, and you should maintain patience:

Those who patiently persevere will truly receive a reward without measure! (39:10)

---

[102] Arabic: *Allahuma anta maqsudi wa ridaka matlubi.*

[103] Arabic: *la rahata fid-din.*

Shaykh Sharafuddin's Will

In the last days of Shaykh Sharafuddin's life, he wrote his will and gave it to Shaykh Abd Allah. He predicted at that time, "After I die, an opportunity will come for you to leave Turkey. When that opportunity comes you must take it, because your duty does not lie here, but outside Turkey."

Shaykh Abd Allah had two daughters from his wife Halima; the eldest was named Rabia and the younger Madiha. Nine other of his children had not survived. After his shaykh passed away, a delegation came to him from King Faruq of Egypt to convey the condolences of the king, as Shaykh Sharafuddin had many followers in Egypt. One of the princes who came with the delegation saw his daughter Madiha. He felt attracted to her and asked to marry her.

Shaykh Abd Allah realized that this was the opportunity to leave Turkey that his shaykh had foretold. He immediately accepted the proposal, and with his daughter's acceptance, the marriage quickly took place. Soon after that he received an invitation from his daughter's new husband to come to Egypt. He said:

> I went to Egypt and stayed with my daughter. The relationship between her and her husband was not good. After some time the marriage failed and ended in divorce. I took my shaykh's advice to use that opportunity. I boarded a ship with my wife and daughters in Alexandria and sailed to Latakia. From Latakia I went to Aleppo, where I landed with only ten piastres (about ten cents) in my pocket, and no other worldly possessions with me. I went to the mosque to pray the evening prayer with my daughters and my wife. There a man approached me and said to me, "O my shaykh, please be my guest." He took me and my family and he hosted us. I consider this to be one of my shaykh's miracles, which took us from Turkey to Egypt to Aleppo, where God opened a door for us.

He stayed some time in Aleppo where people were honored to have him. Scholars came to sit and listen to him, and they were fascinated with his speeches and his knowledge. They called him "the Reviver of the Religion." From there he moved to Homs, where he visited the mosque and tomb of the Companion of the Prophet ﷺ, Khalid ibn Walid ﵁. He stayed briefly in Homs. He moved to Damascus, in the Maidan District, near the tomb of Saad ad-Din Jibawi, a saint from the family of the Prophet ﷺ. There he established the first *zawiya* for the branch of the Naqshbandi Order which had gone to Daghestan. With him, the Golden Chain of the Naqshbandi Order which had gone from Damascus under Shaykh Khalid to Daghestan with Shaykh Ismail and his caliphs, now returned to Damascus. His two daughters were married. Rabia had four children, three girls and one boy. Madiha was married to Shaykh Tawfiq al-Hibri, one of the great Islamic scholars of Lebanon.

Soon people began to crowd into his *zawiya*. They arrived there from all over the city: Sufis, government people, businessmen, and common people. Disciples were coming every day to sit at the door of his *khaniqah*. Daily, food was served to hundreds, many of whom also slept there.

Then he received a spiritual order to move to the Mountain of Qasiyun. It is the highest point in Damascus, from whose vantage the entire city can be viewed. With the help of his two senior disciples, Shaykh Muhammad Nazim Adil and Shaykh Husayn Ali, he built a house. This house and the mosque next to it still stand, and the mosque is the site of his tomb. He saw in a vision, while he was building the mosque, that the Prophet ﷺ, with Abu Bakr as-Siddiq ؓ, Ali ؓ, Shah Naqshband, and Ahmad al-Faruqi, came and put posts to mark the shape and location of the walls of the mosque. As soon as the vision ended, the markers were visible and everyone present saw them. At that mosque, over the years, hundreds of thousands of visitors were received: for healing, for prayers, for training, coming to learn all kinds of external and internal knowledge.

Many times he was ordered by the Prophet ﷺ to go into more seclusions, which varied in length from forty days to one year. He went into over twenty seclusions during his lifetime. Some of these seclusions were made in Damascus, some in Jordan, some in Baghdad at the tomb of Abd al-Qadir Gilani, and many were in Madinah. With each seclusion, his spiritual power and rank were amplified.

Once, he sent a message via Mawlana Shaykh Nazim to Sharif Abd Allah, who was the King of Jordan and one of his disciples, telling him, "Do not go and pray in congregation, especially on a Friday, because I had a vision that you will be killed." That message was given to Sharif Abd Allah, but he did not heed the warning. The next week he was killed as he left from the Friday congregational prayers.

OUR FIRST TRAINING

When my brother and I first came to Grandshaykh he immediately put us under training (*tarbiyyah*). Knowing that we hail from a prominent and wealthy Lebanese family he looked into our faces and said, "How did you come here, you and your brother?" We had come to Damascus in a new and very expensive car. "Give me the keys," he ordered. Taking the keys he called one of his deputies and said, "Take this car and sell it in the market!" He then said to us, "You want me to guide you? Very well, I am guiding you! I had a helper who used to assist me. He died when he was 107 years old." Pointing he said, "His clothes are down in one of those baskets. Go and put them on, you and your brother."

That was crushing. Grandshaykh was teaching us, "Don't come to our door while you have pride in yourself, thinking you are something special." Grandshaykh continued, "Give me your clothes for I am selling them also."

As soon as we put those old clothes on, we were instantly covered with fleas, biting us all over. He looked us up and down and said, "Alright, now I am guiding you! Go to the Mosque of Muhyiddin ibn Arabi, the greatest saint of Damascus, put a cloth on the ground and sit down in front of his shrine. Stay there—people will throw food and money at you." While we said, "Yes sir!" the words did not come easily. All the while Grandshaykh was examining our hearts. We set out for the mosque. It was a twenty-minute walk down the steep mountainside. We had walked no more than a few steps than a deputy came running after us saying, "Stop! Come back. It is enough."

These are the methods the shaykhs of this order used to polish the hearts of their followers.

A MIRACULOUS OPERATION

Years later, a cousin of ours was caught by accident in gunfire in Beirut. He was taken for emergency surgery. We went to visit our grandshaykh, terrified for our cousin's condition. As soon as we walked in, and before we could speak, he said to us, "Go back! It was written that he would die, but with my prayers he will live. The operation he is going through will succeed." When we returned, our cousin was in a coma and they were taking him to surgery. We informed his mother of what grandshaykh had said to give her hope. The next day our cousin regained consciousness. He said, "I saw grandshaykh coming to me and doing surgery on me. That is what saved me."

ON DESTINY

Shaykh Abd Allah often talked about foreordained things. He said:

It is known that there are two types of destiny. The first kind of destiny is termed suspended, or mutable, destiny. It is written on the Preserved Tablets. This will vary according to will and behaviour, cause and effect. All saints can change this kind of destiny for their disciples, in order to train them and to influence their destiny by changing their actions and behaviour. The authority to change the mutable destiny is given to the shaykhs for their disciples because they are connected to each other by Divine Will.

The second type of destiny is contained in the Mother of the Book as mentioned in the verse, *"God blots out or confirms what He pleases: with Him is the Mother of the Book* (13:39)," and is called fixed destiny. Saints never interfere in that fixed destiny, which is in the hand of the Creator.[104]

God gave the authority to change the fixed destiny only to the nine saints who are at the highest level in the Divine Presence, by permission from the Prophet ﷺ who is first to take that power from God. They control the Nine Points of human consciousness related to the different stages of the ascent of an individual on his path to the

---

[104] The proof that the Decree in the Preserved Tablet may be changed is when God said:
God erases what He will, and He consolidates what He will, and with Him is the Mother of the Book. (13:39).

We know that Ibn Umar ؓ said in his invocations, "O God, if You have foreordained hardship for me, erase it and write felicity for me."

God the Exalted said: *"Say: I seek refuge in the Lord of the Cleaving from the evil of what He has created."* (113:1)

The reading of that oath at the time something good befalls God's servant will repel (foreordained) evil before it reaches him. Also:

Good deeds and upholding family ties repel a bad death and eventually turn it into a good one. (Tirmidhi, *Zakat* #28.)

Invocation and affliction are suspended between heaven and earth, vying, and invocation repels affliction before the latter is able to come down. (Cf. Ibn Majah, *Muqaddima* #10, *Fitan* #66; Tirmidhi, *Witr* #21, *Qadar* #6; Ahmad 5:277, 280, 282; Ibn Hibban.)

Divine Presence. God gave these nine saints, whose number has not changed from the time of the Prophet ﷺ until today, the power to use *Sultan adh-Dhikr,* the Greatest Remembrance.

Everyone knows that *dhikr* is primarily the repetition of *"la ilaha ill-Allah"* and that is what is practiced by all Sufi orders, including the Naqshbandi. But the *Sultan adh-Dhikr* is a completely different type of *dhikr.*

God said, *"We have revealed the* dhikr, *and we are the One to protect that* dhikr *in you."* (15:9) The *dhikr* mentioned here is the Holy Quran. The *dhikr* of these nine saints, besides *"la ilaha ill-Allah,"* is the secret of the Holy Quran. They recite the Quran, not as we recite it reading from beginning to end, but they recite it with all its secrets and inner realities.

Because God said, *"Nor is there anything fresh or dry but it is inscribed in a clear Record."* (6:59) there is not one of God's creatures in all the created universes that have not been mentioned already, with all its secrets, in the Clear Book, the Quran.

The saint reciting the Quran in *Sultan adh-Dhikr* is, therefore, reciting it with all the secrets of every creation, from beginning to end. God gave every letter of the Quran, according to the nine highest masters of the Naqshbandi Order (this was the first time the shaykh ever mentioned this secret), twelve thousand knowledges. The Quran contains around 600,000 letters, so for every letter, these saints are able to take 12,000 knowledges!

Each of these nine saints differs from the other in his level as well. We may see that one of them, for example, was able to recite the Holy Quran by the power of *Sultan adh-Dhikr,* which is to grasp 12,000 meanings on every letter, only once in his life. Another was able to recite it three times in his life. The third was able to do it nine times in his life. Another was able to recite it ninety-nine times in his life.

This secret differed from one saint to another. Shah Naqshband was able to do it 999 times in his life. Ahmad al-Faruqi was able to recite it 9,999 times in his life. Shaykh Sharafuddin was able to recite it 19,999 times.

Here Shaykh Abd Allah stopped. Shaykh Nazim said, "In every breath, Grandshaykh Abd Allah Daghestani was exhaling with *Sultan adh-Dhikr* and inhaling with *Sultan adh-Dhikr*. He completed the secret of the Quran twice in every breath."

Saint of the Scholars

Grandshaykh Abd Allah was a wonder of his time. When he spoke great scholars, inflated with the knowledge of letters and words (*ilm al-huruf*) would sit in his presence like children, not saying a word. Some of the chief scholars of Damascus would attend his associations and some would attend secretly, sitting in the back rows of his association for fear of being spotted in another scholar's circle.

One of our uncles was the president of the Muslim scholars association of Lebanon. He was a brilliant scholar surpassing by far other great jurists of the day. He was known as the "walking encyclopedia" of jurisprudence (*fiqh*), Quranic exegesis (*tafsir*), and the life history of the Prophet (*sirah*). His library held close to 30,000 books and he had read all of them.

Every time a president or prime minister from the Middle East would visit Lebanon he would visit my uncle. My uncle would write many of the op-eds for the Arab newspapers. Everyone sought his opinion on difficult issues of jurisprudence—even the scholars of al-Azhar would forward knotty issues to him.

Once my brother and I asked him to come with us to meet Grandshaykh. He said, "Why do I need to meet another teacher? Is he more well-read more than I?" We pressured him until he finally agreed, and for such an erudite scholar the decision was not easy.

We set off from Beirut to Damascus and arrived at the blessed house of Grandshaykh in three hours. As soon as we arrived at the door he pulled it open saying, "Welcome! I have been waiting for you." This unexpected action melted my uncle's conceit. We went inside and sat down. Shaykh Abd Allah said to my uncle, "You are a scholar, and I must say that you are a substantial scholar and very well known. However in an association, only one may speak, not two. Do you want to speak or shall I? You decide."

My uncle, keeping impeccable conduct, said, "No, I am a guest. If you were the guest I would speak." Grandshaykh then said to him, "Would you like to use the bathroom before I begin?" This was his way of saying, "Once

I begin speaking do not interrupt me." He said, "Yes I need to renew my ablution." That was the second clear miraculous sign for my uncle.

Grandshaykh began by reciting the verse, *"Obey God, obey the Prophet and those in authority among you."* (4:59) He then began to speak without stopping. Each of us was moving around right and left, in discomfort, yet Grandshaykh spoke on and on, and I made sure to take detailed notes. He finished after four hours. My uncle, who had been listening with rapt attention, rushed forward to kiss his hand. Not once before had I ever seen my uncle kiss the hand of anyone, not even that of his wife, so we were extremely surprised. After praying the afternoon prayer, Grandshaykh served us dinner, and after eating we left for the return trip to Lebanon.

As soon as he sat down in the car my uncle began to weep. That was another wonder for before that day I had never seen my uncle cry. As tears streamed from his eyes, he said:

> If I am going to write a book on what the Shaykh said, I could write one volume on every sentence. What he explained today were issues that have bewildered the minds of scholars—not only average ones, but great scholars and philosophers; they have even confounded the minds of saints. There are seven questions that have to date puzzled everyone and before we left Beirut I put them in my mind. To date no one has been able to bring forth an answer to any of these seven questions. And without me even mentioning the questions, he answered all seven of them!

Grandshaykh had addressed the subject of the reality of human beings (*haqiqat al-insan*), and the Perfect Human (*al-insan al-Kamil*): What is his reality and from where does his reality come?

It is mentioned in a hadith of the Prophet ﷺ that every human being has seven heavenly names in God's Presence: one for each level in paradise. Therefore a person will be named according to the level and station he attains. Each of these names begins with "Servant of" (*abd*) such as Abd al-Karim or Abd ar-Razzaq. Each name is related to a different Divine Attribute, and each name is unlike any other. In this world countless people have the same name. But in heavenly realities, names are unique and there is no possibility that a name be repeated. Yet each begins with "Abd" and ends with a Divine Attribute. Some say that there are only ninety-nine Divine Names and Attributes. Those are the essential Names, but in reality there are an infinite number of Names for God. Each is different and so God is the Source of an infinite number of Attributes whose manifestation He bestows on endless creations. Reflect therefore on the greatness of God!

More importantly, the question that has puzzled scholars even more from before the time of the Prophet ﷺ until now is "what is the Greatest Name of God (*ismullah al-adham*)?" All prophets sought to know that and yet God only hinted at the answer to them. The Prophet Moses عليه السلام had asked to learn that name. Scholars sought eagerly to know that name. My uncle continued, "I had that question in my mind and he addressed it as someone relating a story for a child! I was unable to see that any of my knowledge had any value whatsoever when he spoke to me about that name and how we know it."

Grandshaykh had explained that God's Greatest Name is hidden within the human being, *al-insan*. It means that God created the human being as the recipient of a great honor, for within his heart, His Greatest Name exists. If one will dig inside the heart, he or she will come to know that Name. More that that cannot be mentioned in this book.

After that, my uncle never tired of saying, "The greatest moment in my life was that meeting with Shaykh Abd Allah."

A Meeting with John Bennett

Among the many visitors and seekers at the door of Grandshaykh was the Englishman, John G. Bennett. In several of his books, he recounts his meetings with Shaykh Abd Allah. The following is part of his accounts compiled from *Concerning Subud* and *Witness*.[105]

Bennett writes in *Concerning Subud*, "Shaykh Abd Allah is a true saint in whom one feels an immediate complete trust." He elaborates in more detail about their meeting in *Witness*:

> The shaykh was waiting for me on the roof of his house. It was high up above the city, commanding a superb panorama... I felt at ease from the start, and very soon I experienced a great happiness that seemed to fill the place. I knew that I was in the presence of a really good man.
>
> After the usual salutations, and compliments of the excellence of my Turkish, he astonished me by saying, "Why did you not bring the lady

[105] *Concerning Subud*, p. 45; *Witness*, pp. 308-310.

sister who is with you? I have a message for her as well as you." It seemed unlikely that anyone could have told him about Elizabeth. We had walked straight to his house, and the Dadji, my guide, had left me at the door without speaking to anyone. I replied that as he was a Muslim, I did not think he would wish to speak with a woman. He said very simply: "Why Not? Rules and customs are for the protection of the foolish; they do not concern me. Next time you pass through Damascus, will you bring her to me?" I promised to do so if the opportunity came.

We sat for a long time in silence, watching the ancient city. When he began to speak, I found it hard to come out of the deep reverie into which I had fallen. He was saying: "I was expecting someone today, but I did not know it would be you. A few nights ago an angel came to my room and told me that you would come to visit me and I was to give you three messages. You have asked God of guidance about your wife. She is in God's keeping. You have tried to help her, but this was wrong. You disturb the work that God is doing in her soul. There is no cause for anxiety about her, but it is useless for you to try to understand.

"The second message concerns your house. You have asked God for guidance as to whether you should go your way or follow others. You must trust yourself. You will be persecuted by the Armenians, but you must not be afraid. You have to attract many people to you and you must not hesitate even if other people are angry."

He fell silent again. I was astonished at the two messages, for it was true that I had prayed for guidance on just those two questions..."The most important message is the last. You must know that there is great wickedness in the world. People have given themselves over to the worship of material things, and they have lost the will and the power to worship God. God has always sent Messengers to show the way out of such situations, and He has again done so in our present age. A Messenger is already on earth, and his identity known to many. Before long he will come to the West. Men have been chosen to prepare the way for him... It was shown to me that you are one of those chosen to prepare the way... The Messenger will come to your country and even to your house…

"You should never cease to worship God, only you must not show it. Outwardly you must behave as others do. God has appointed two angels to take care of you. One will guide and direct you so that you will no longer make mistakes as before. The other will perform the religious duties that you cannot do for yourself. I advise you frequently to repeat in your heart the words, *'la ilaha ill-Allah,'* which means surrender to God alone."

When I said that this was the Muslim profession of faith, he replied that it is as much Christian as Muslim, for the foundation of all religion is that man should not follow his own will, but the Will of God.

His Passing from this Life

We observed many wondrous events with our Grandshaykh. His life was full of beneficent activity. He was always smiling, and never angry. He had no income, yet the food was always abundant in his house. How was he supported was the question in the mind of everyone. People would show up unannounced until they sometimes numbered up to two hundred, but they would find food prepared and ready for them. We often wondered, "Where did that rice, and bread, and meat come from?"

I rarely saw him sleep at night. During the day he was always receiving people, and at night he was always sitting in his special room, reading Quran, reading *Dalail al-Khayrat*, doing his personal *dhikr*, or reading praises on the Prophet ﷺ. It was his habit to pray after midnight until the dawn. He helped the needy as much as he was able and sheltered many homeless in his mosque. He served humanity. The tongue is helpless to describe his good manners and good characteristics.

One day, in 1973, he said, "The Prophet ﷺ is calling me. I have to go and see him. He told me, 'You will come to me after you have had an operation on your eye,'" referring to the short-sightedness in his left eye. He was hinting to us that he was going to pass on, but we were not able to accept that hint. He was alive in us and alive in all those who knew him, even the cats that were always around him.

After he went for the eye surgery, he stopped eating. We begged him to eat, but he refused saying, "I am in complete seclusion, because the Prophet

ﷺ is calling me." He would only accept dry bread soaked in water, once a day. He said, "I do not want to live any longer, I want to go to join my Prophet ﷺ and to be with him. He is calling me, God is calling me." This was like a thunderbolt for us, but still we could not believe it. Then he wrote his will and said, "Next Sunday, I am going to pass on." It would be the 30th of September, 1973 CE, the 4th of Ramadan, 1393 AH. Everyone was shocked and fearful, awaiting that day to see if his prediction would come to pass.

It was ten o'clock on the Sunday that he had predicted, and we were sitting in his room. He said to me, "Feel my pulse." I felt his pulse, and it was over 150 beats per minute. Then he said, "O my son, these are the last seconds of my life. I do not want anyone here. Everyone must leave and go to the big meeting room." There were only ten of us inside the room. At that moment two doctors arrived: one was my brother and the other a friend. Both were surgeons. Grandshaykh did not allow anyone other than family in the room.

We heard his daughter cry out, "My father has died, my father has died." We all ran into the room and we saw that Grandshaykh was not moving. Quickly, my brother took his pulse and his blood pressure, but they were not detectable. He ran hysterically to the car to get a syringe with medicine, returning minutes later. He re-entered in the same manner, wanting to inject the shaykh in his heart to try to restart its pumping. The other doctor said, "What are you doing? The Shaykh has been dead for over seven minutes. Stop your foolishness." But he would not stop and insisted on going ahead with the injection.

Then Grandshaykh opened his eyes, put his hand up and said in Turkish, "*Burak*," which means, "Stop!"

Everyone was shocked. They had never heard the dead speak before. I will never forget this in all my life. All those present, professors and doctors, will never forget either. After that, my brother put his instruments away. We stood there in shock, not knowing what to say. Was he dead or not? Was he simply veiling himself to return shortly? That is the secret God gives to His lovers and saints who travel in His Kingdom, in His Love, in His Secrets. It was an unforgettable day.

The news of his passing was like a tremendous tornado, whirling through Damascus, Aleppo, Jordan, Beirut. People came from everywhere to him for one last look. We washed him, and from his holy body came a very beautiful smell. We prepared him for the funeral prayers and for burial the next day. All the scholars of Damascus attended his funeral. Four hundred thousand people came to his funeral prayers. People were lined up from his house to the Mosque of Muhyiddin Ibn Arabi, where his body lay in state.

When we returned to his home after the funeral prayer, we saw the coffin gliding over the heads of people without any help from anyone, moving to his mosque for its burial. Because of the huge crowd in the streets, it had taken us three hours to walk back from the Mosque of Muhyiddin Ibn Arabi to Grandshaykh's mosque, a trip which normally takes twenty minutes.

Everyone was crying. They did not want the shaykh to be buried. No one could believe it and no one could accept it. It was enough to make us remember the state of the Companions when the Prophet ﷺ passed away. We understood why Umar ؓ, Uthman ؓ, and Ali ؓ could not accept that the Prophet ﷺ had passed away. We underwent that same state and wondered how Abu Bakr ؓ could have borne those feelings.

All the government officials and scholars were at the mosque waiting to bury him. A message was delivered to the imam from out of the blue saying, "Do not bury Grandshaykh until Shaykh Nazim arrives." No one could believe it, as there had been no way to contact Shaykh Nazim, who was in Cyprus. There was no phone, no fax machine, and even a telegram would have taken two days. No one accepted that the message was real. But for the love of our Shaykh, we were happy to postpone his burial and insisted to wait until Shaykh Nazim arrived.

It was Ramadan; everyone was fasting. The scholars and the crowd grew restless. People said they wanted to go. We told them they were free to go if they wanted, but that we must wait. After some time most of the people left, and only the most sincere followers of the shaykh remained. Shortly before sunset, Shaykh Nazim was seen climbing the stairs. How he arrived so quickly no one knows. It remains a mystery to this day.

Shaykh Nazim brought Grandshaykh's body back into the mosque and prayed the funeral prayer for him again. He buried him with his own hands. When he lifted the shroud from his face, we smelled the sweet perfume of sandalwood, amber, and musk, the likes of which we had never smelled before. Then Shaykh Nazim asked us all to go out and prepare to break the fast. Only my brother and I stayed, watching from the window to see what was happening inside.

He stood at the head of the grave, as if in prayer. Then in the blink of an eye, Shaykh Nazim disappeared. This event added an extraordinary surprise to our previous surprises. There were no words to express our feelings. Fifteen minutes passed, and suddenly we saw Shaykh Nazim appear in the same place from which he had disappeared. Then we ran to the door as he came out. He said, "What! Still here? You didn't break your fast? Never mind, my company is better!" We went down to break our fast with him. Shaykh Nazim returned that night to Beirut, and took a plane back to Cyprus.

His Predictions

Grandshaykh Abd Allah ad-Daghestani, *naqib al-ummah,* may God bless his soul, predicted many events, some of which have come to pass and some of which we still await.

In 1966, he said, "Next year there will be a war between the Israelis and the Arabs. The Arabs will be defeated." He predicted that another war between Israel and the Arabs would occur. Shortly before he passed away he said, "There will be a big war within one month between the Israelis and Arabs." This came to pass. On the 3rd of October, three days after his passing, the Arabs and Israelis entered another war.

Once Grandshaykh's daughter, Madiha, was considering buying a house with her husband in Beirut and Grandshaykh said, "No." She insisted, but still he said, "No." She continued to insist, but he was adamant and said: "Beirut is going to be full of bloodshed. Every house is going to be effected by that bloodshed, and no one will escape its touch." He mentioned this in 1972, and it began to happen in 1975. He told us before he passed away, "I see you in Tripoli, in the north of Lebanon." This was his way of suggesting that we move away from Beirut.

He said, "I see England entering Islam." He predicted that a royal family in Europe is going to support Islam, because in their bloodline is the blood of Arabs. "This will draw them into spirituality, and arouse in them an interest in many faiths, and draw them towards the Divine Presence."

On a related matter he said:

> When John Bennett met me and bore witness that God is One and Muhammad is the Messenger of God, he asked what he could do. I told him to keep his testimony secret. Thereby, he was able to bring many

people in his homeland of England to bear witness, and to interest them in spirituality.

He said:

China is under the authority of a great saint, who will be one of the greatest saints in the time of Mahdi ﷺ and Jesus ﷺ. His name is Abd ar-Rauf al-Yamani. Through his influence China will sign an agreement with the West not to use its nuclear weapons. China will split into many different small countries. There will be problems in the Far East, in the Korean Peninsula, and a great power will intervene to stop that conflict.

He said:

A non-Arab Middle Eastern country will attack the Persian Gulf area, which will put the whole world into fear that the source of petroleum will be cut off.

He said:

Cairo is going to sink underwater. Later the Russians built the Aswan Dam; it contains an enormous amount of water and has recently been found to contain loose underpinnings which are eroding.

He said:

Cyprus will sink underwater, and Mount Olympus, near Bursa, will erupt. Under it are two elements, gas and fire, which have until now been kept separate, and saints have always prayed that these elements would not combine. From its explosion, hundreds of thousands of people will be wounded and become homeless.

He also said:

There will be a war in the Gulf Area where a huge fire will arise and involve the rest of the world.

Germany and England will lead the whole of Europe. In Germany there is a saint, assigned by Mahdi ﷺ and Jesus ﷺ, who is to raise and train the people in spirituality. That saint is hidden, but he is among them.

> There will be a big change in the approach of Arabs to politics, and one powerful regime is going to change to a better way of government.

Before he passed away, in a private meeting with some of his closest disciples, he said:

> There will be peace, and America will be the one leading the talks for peace, which will end the war between the Arabs and Israel. This is going to happen. The sign of it is the collapse of Communism and the splitting of the Russian Empire into many parts. There will be no power in this world, except for America. Most Arab governments will turn to the Americans. The conflict will completely quiet down, and Arabs and Israelis will live in peace. Slowly every conflict on the earth will be put to an end, and everywhere there will be peace. America will lead that. Everyone will be happy, and no one will expect war to ever occur again.
>
> Suddenly, in the midst of peace, an attack will be made on Turkey from a neighboring country and a war will start, followed by an invasion of Turkey by a close neighboring country. This will threaten the U.S. bases in Turkey and will cause a greater battle to ensue. This will result in a great disaster on earth and a horrible war. During the course of the war, Mahdi عليه السلام will come forth and Jesus عليه السلام will return. His purpose will be to bring spirituality, peace and justice, and to overcome tyranny, fear and terror. Love and happiness and peace will fill this earth, with the power of Mahdi عليه السلام and Jesus عليه السلام, by the Will of God Almighty.

The Secret of the Golden Chain was passed to the sun of suns, the leader of those brought near, the discoverer of secrets, Shaykh Muhammad Nazim Adil al-Qubrusi ar-Rabbani an-Naqshbandi al-Haqqani. ۞

40. Muhammad Nazim Adil al-Haqqani ق

Shaykh Muhammad Nazim Adil al-Haqqani is the imam of the people of sincerity, the secret of sainthood, who revived the Naqshbandi Order at the end of the twentieth century with heavenly guidance and prophetic ethics. He infused into the Community and the planet, love of God and love of the lovers of God, after they had been darkened with the fire and smoke of tribulation and terror, anger and grief.

O you who've gone on pilgrimage
Where are you? Where, O where?
Here, here is the Beloved
O come now, come, O come!
Your friend, He is your neighbor,
He is next to your house—
You, erring in the desert!
What air of love is this?
—Rumi, Divan.[106]

---

[106] Jalaluddin Rumi, *Divan*, quoted in Annemarie Schimmel, *Deciphering the Signs*, p. 64.

Shaykh Muhammad Nazim Adil al-Haqqani is the unveiler of secrets, the keeper of light, the shaykh of shaykhs, the sultan of ascetics, the sultan of the pious, and the leader of the people of the Truth. He was the chief master without peer of the Divine Knowledge in the late twentieth century, and he has carried the flame of that Knowledge into the new millennium. He is the rain from the ocean of knowledge of this Order, which is reviving spirits in all parts of this world. He is the saint of the seven continents, his light having attracted disciples from all quarters of the globe. He wears the cloak of the Light of the Divine Presence. He is unique in his time. He is the orchid planted in the earth of Divine Love. He is the sun for all the universes. He is known as "the Saint of the Two Wings:" the external knowledge and the internal knowledge.

Shaykh Nazim is a miracle of God's miracles, walking on the earth and soaring in the heavens. He is a secret of God's Secrets, appearing in His Divinity and existing in His Existence. He is the owner of the throne of guidance, the reviver of the Divine Law, the master of the Sufi Way, the builder of the Truth, the guide of the circle, and the lyric poem of all the secrets. He is the master of saints and the saint of the masters. Seekers circle the Kabah of his light. He is a fountain always flowing, a waterfall continuously cascading, a river always flooding, an ocean endlessly cresting and breaking on infinite shores.

With full support of all the blessed saints of the Golden Chain, and at the command of his shaykh, Grandshaykh Abd Allah al-Faiz ad-Daghestani, Shaykh Nazim Adil al-Haqqani has spread the teachings of the Naqshbandi Sufi Order throughout the world. God has granted him miraculous power through a constant, uninterrupted reception of energy from the Golden Chain, with which he continuously penetrates the entire world, reaching every region with his spiritual power and message of divine peace and harmony.

Thanks to his enlightened leadership, the teachings of the Golden Chain remain as attractive to seekers of the Truth today as they were a thousand years ago. The Naqshbandi Sufi Order remains an oasis of peace in a world of suffering and conflict. Its members are pacifist in nature and have always been champions of religious tolerance. Followers of the Naqshbandi Way are community builders who aspire to establish a higher quality of life based on the consciousness of God. As a beloved Friend of God (*wali*), Shaykh Nazim epitomizes this philosophy. He is known throughout the world for his unceasing efforts to build goodwill and unify diverse peoples and groups in the Oneness of God.

Shaykh Nazim Adil al-Haqqani was born in Larnaca, Cyprus, on the 23rd of April 1922, a Sunday, the 26th of Shaban, 1340 AH. His lineage from his father's side traces its roots to Abd al-Qadir Gilani, founder of the Qadiri Order. His lineage from his mother goes back to Jalaluddin Rumi, founder of the Mevlevi Order. He is Hasani-Husayni, related to the Prophet ﷺ through the lineages of his grandfathers to the Family of the Prophet ﷺ. From his father's side, he received the Qadiri Sufi Order, and from his mother's side, the Mevlevi Sufi Order.

During his childhood in Cyprus, he sat with his paternal grandfather, who was a shaykh of the Qadiri Order, to learn its discipline and its spirituality. Extraordinary signs appeared early in him. His conduct was perfect. He never fought nor argued with anyone. He was always smiling and patient. Both his paternal and maternal grandfathers trained him for the spiritual path.

As a youth, Shaykh Nazim was given great consideration because of his unusually high spiritual station. Everyone in Larnaca knew about him, because at a young age he was able to advise people, to predict the future, and to reveal it spontaneously. From the age of five, there were times when his mother could not find him. After searching, she would find him either in the mosque or at the grave of Umm Hiram ﵂, a Companion of the Prophet ﷺ whose grave has a mosque built next to it. Tourists came to her grave in large numbers, attracted by the spectacle of a rock suspended in space above her grave. When his mother would try to bring him home, he would say, "Leave me here with Umm Hiram ﵂, she is one of our ancestors." He was often seen speaking to Umm Hiram ﵂, who was buried fourteen centuries ago, listening and then speaking, listening and answering, having a conversation with her. Whenever anyone would disturb him, he would say, "Leave me, I am speaking with my grandmother who is in this grave."

His father sent him to study secular knowledge during the day, and in the evening, he studied the religious sciences. He was a genius among his fellow students. After completing his high school studies, he would devote his time every night to study teachings of the Mevlevi and Qadiri Orders. In addition, he conducted the Qadiri and Mevlevi *dhikr* circles on Thursday and Friday evenings.

Everyone in Cyprus knew him as an intensely spiritual person. He learned the Divine Law, jurisprudence, the science of the Traditions, the science of logic, the commentary of the Quran, and he was able to give legal rulings on the whole range of Islamic subjects. He was able to speak from all spiritual levels. He had a gift for explaining difficult realities in clear, easy-to-understand aphorisms.

After completing high school in Cyprus, he moved to Istanbul in 1940, where his two brothers and one sister lived. He studied chemical engineering at the University of Istanbul, in the Bayazit District. At the same time, he studied the Divine Law and the Arabic language with Shaykh Jamaluddin al-Lasuni (d. 1955). He received his degree in chemical engineering and excelled among his colleagues. When his university professors encouraged him to go into research, young Nazim replied, "I feel no attraction to modern sciences; my heart is always drawn to the spiritual sciences."

During his first year in Istanbul, Shaykh Nazim met his first spiritual master, Shaykh Sulayman Arzurumi, a shaykh of the Naqshbandi Order (d. 1948). While he studied chemical engineering, he also attended meetings of Shaykh Sulayman to learn the discipline of the Naqshbandi Way, in addition to the Qadiri and the Mevlevi methods of spiritual development.

As a student, Shaykh Nazim was often seen in Sultan Ahmad's Mosque, meditating by himself throughout the night. About this he states:

> There I received great blessings and great peace in my heart. I always prayed the dawn prayer in that mosque with my two guides, Shaykh Jamaluddin al-Lasuni and Shaykh Sulayman Arzurumi. They educated me and put spiritual knowledge in my heart. I had many visions during that time, drawing me to go to Damascus, but I did not yet have permission from my shaykh. Many times in my visions, through self-effacement, I saw the Prophet Muhammad ﷺ calling me to his presence. There was a deep yearning in my heart to leave everything and to migrate to the Holy City of the Prophet ﷺ.
>
> One day, when this longing in my heart was particularly intense, I saw a vision in which Shaykh Sulayman shook me by the shoulder and told me, "Now the permission has come. Your secrets, your trust, and your spiritual guidance are not with me. I only held you as a trust until you were ready for your real shaykh who is also my master, Shaykh Abd

Allah ad-Daghestani. He holds your keys. Go to him in Damascus. This permission comes from me and from the Prophet ﷺ."

(Shaykh Sulayman Arzurumi was one of the 313 saints of the Naqshbandi Order who stand in the footsteps of and represent the 313 messengers.)

That vision ended, and with it, I had received the permission to move to Damascus. For the next two hours, I looked for my shaykh to tell him about that vision. He opened his arms and said to me, "My son, are you happy with your vision?" Then I knew that he knew everything that had happened. He said, "Do not wait. Direct yourself to Damascus." He did not give me an address or any other information, except the name, Shaykh Abd Allah ad-Daghestani in Damascus. I traveled from Istanbul to Aleppo by train, where I stayed some time. While there I went from one mosque to another, praying, sitting with scholars, and spending time in worship and meditation.

Then I traveled to Hama, which, like Aleppo, is a very ancient city. I tried to move on to Damascus, but it was impossible. The French, who occupied Damascus, were preparing for an attack by the English. So I traveled to Homs to the grave of Khalid ibn Walid ؓ, a companion of the Prophet ﷺ, then I went into the mosque and prayed. A servant came to me and said, "I saw a dream last night in which the Prophet ﷺ came to me. He said, 'One of my grandsons is coming here tomorrow. Take care of him for me.' He showed me how you look, and I see you are that person."

I was so taken by what he said that I accepted his invitation. He gave me a room in that mosque, where I stayed for one year. I did not go out except to pray and to sit in the company of two eminent scholars of Homs who were teaching Quranic recitation and exegesis, the Traditions, and jurisprudence. They were Shaykh Muhammad Ali Uyun as-Sud and Shaykh Abd al-Aziz Uyun as-Sud, the mufti of Homs. I also attended the spiritual teachings of two Naqshbandi shaykhs, Shaykh Abd al-Jalil Murad and Shaykh Said as-Suba'i. My heart was yearning to go to Damascus, but because the war was so intense, I decided to go by a safer route to Tripoli, then on to Beirut, and then Damascus.

In the year 1364 AH/1944 CE, Shaykh Nazim traveled to Tripoli by bus. He was a stranger there, not knowing anyone. As he wandered around, he saw Shaykh Munir al-Malek, the mufti of Tripoli and the shaykh of all Sufi orders in the city. He approached and said, "Are you Shaykh Nazim? I saw a dream in which the Prophet ﷺ told me, 'One of my grandsons is coming to Tripoli.' He showed me your appearance and told me to look for you in this area. He told me to take care of you."

Shaykh Nazim relates:

> I stayed with Shaykh Munir al-Malek for a month. He arranged for me to go to Homs and from Homs to Damascus. I arrived in Damascus on a Friday, at the beginning of the *Hijri* year 1365 AH (1945). I knew that Shaykh Abd Allah was living in the district of Hayy al-Maidan, near the tomb of Bilal al-Habashi ؓ and many descendants of the Prophet ﷺ, an ancient area full of monuments from long ago.
>
> I did not know which house was the shaykh's. A vision appeared to me at that moment, while standing in the street, that the shaykh was coming out of his house and calling me inside. That vision ended, but I could see no one in the streets. It was empty because of the bombardment by the French and the English. Everyone was afraid, hiding in their houses. I was alone in the streets. I contemplated in my heart to know which house was the shaykh's. Then in a vision I saw a specific house with a specific door. I looked until I found that door. As I approached to knock, the shaykh opened the door. He said, "Welcome, my son, Nazim Effendi."
>
> His unusual appearance immediately attracted me. I have never seen such a shaykh before. Light poured from his face and forehead. Warmth was coming from his heart and from the brilliant smile on his face. He took me upstairs, climbing up to his room telling me, "We have been waiting for you."
>
> In my heart, I was completely happy to be with him, but I also had a yearning to visit the city of the Holy Prophet ﷺ. I asked him, "What shall I do?" He said, "Tomorrow I will give you your answer. For now, rest." He offered me dinner, and I prayed the night prayer with him and slept. In the early morning, he woke me for the supererogatory night prayer. Never in my life had I felt such power as that in his

prayer. I felt myself in the Divine Presence and my heart was even more attracted to him.

A vision came to me. I saw myself climbing a ladder from our prayer place to the *Bayt al-Mamur,* the Kabah of the heavens, step by step. Every step was a state in which he put me. In each state, I received knowledge in my heart that I had never before learned or heard about. Words, phrases, and sentences were put together in such a magnificent way, transmitted inside my heart in every state that I had been lifted to, until we reached the *Bayt al-Mamur.* There I saw 124,000 prophets standing in rows for prayers, with the Prophet Muhammad ﷺ as imam. I saw 124,000 Companions of the Prophet Muhammad ﷺ standing in rows behind them. I saw the 7,007 saints of the Naqshbandi Order standing behind them for prayer. I saw 124,000 saints of the other orders, standing in rows for prayers.

There was a space left for two people directly on the right side of Abu Bakr as-Siddiq ؓ. Grandshaykh went to that open space, and he took me with him, and we performed the dawn prayer. Never in my life had I experienced the sweetness of that prayer. When the Holy Prophet Muhammad ﷺ led the prayer, the beauty of his recitation was indescribable. It was an experience that no words can describe, because it was a Divine matter. As the prayer ended, the vision ended, and I heard the shaykh telling me to make the call for the dawn prayer.

He prayed the dawn prayer, and I prayed behind him. Outside I could hear the bombardment of the two armies. He gave me initiation in the Naqshbandi Order and he said to me, "O my son, we have power that in one second we can make our disciple reach his station." As soon as he said that he looked into my heart with his eyes. As he did so, they turned from yellow to red, then to white, then to green and black. The color of his eyes changed as he poured into my heart the knowledge associated with each color.

The yellow light was the first and corresponded to the state of the heart. He poured into my heart all kinds of the external knowledge which is necessary for the daily life of people. Then he poured from the stage of the secret, the knowledge of all forty orders which came from Ali ibn Abi Talib ؓ. I found myself a master in all these orders. While transmitting the knowledge of this stage, his eyes were red. The third stage, which is the secret of the secret, is only permitted for shaykhs of the Naqshbandi Order, whose imam is Abu Bakr ؓ. As he poured into my heart from this stage, his eyes were white in color. Then he took me into the stage of the hidden, the station of hidden spiritual knowledge, where his eyes changed to green. Then he took me to the station of complete annihilation, the station of the most hidden where nothing appeared. The color of his eyes was black. Here he brought me into the Presence of God. Then he brought me back to existence.

My love for him at that moment was so intense that I could not imagine being away from him. I desired nothing more than to stay with him forever and serve him. Then the storm arrived, the tornado descended, and turbulence threatened the calm. The test was gigantic. My heart was in despair when he told me, "My son, your people are in need of you. I have given you enough for now. Go to Cyprus today." I had spent one year and a half to reach him, and had spent one night with him. Now he was ordering me to go back to Cyprus, a place I had not seen in five years. It was a terrible order for me, but in the Sufi Way, the disciple must surrender and submit to the will of his shaykh.

After kissing his hands and feet and taking his permission, I tried to find a way to travel to Cyprus. World War II was reaching its end. There was no transportation. As I was in the street thinking these thoughts, a person came to me and said, "O shaykh, do you need a ride?" I said, "Yes! Where are you going?" He said, "To Tripoli." He took me in his truck and after two days we reached Tripoli. When we arrived there I said, "Take me to the seaport." He said, "What for?" I said, "To find a ship to Cyprus." He said, "How? No one is traveling by sea with this great war going on." I said, "Never mind that. Just take me there." He took me to the seaport and dropped me off. I was again surprised when I saw Shaykh Munir al-Malek coming towards me. He said, "What is that love your grandfather has for you? The Prophet ﷺ came again to me in my dream and said, 'My son Nazim is coming. Take care of him.'"

I stayed with him three days. I asked him to help me arrange passage to Cyprus. He tried, but it was impossible at that time because of the war and the shortage of fuel. He could find nothing except a sailboat. He told me, "You can go, but it is dangerous." I said, "I must go, because that is the order of my shaykh." Shaykh Munir paid the owner a heavy price to get him to take me. We set sail. It took us seven days to reach Cyprus, a trip which normally takes four hours by motorboat.

As soon as I landed and put my foot on the soil of Cyprus, immediately a spiritual vision was opened to my heart. I saw Grandshaykh Abd Allah ad-Daghestani saying to me, "O my son, nothing was able to keep you from carrying out my order. You have achieved a lot by listening and accepting. From this moment I will always be visible to you. Anytime you direct your heart towards me, I will be there. Any question you have, you will receive an answer directly from the Divine Presence. Any spiritual state you wish to achieve, it will be granted to you because of your complete submission. The saints are all happy with you; the Prophet ﷺ is happy with you." As soon as he said that I felt him beside me, and since then he has never left me. He is always beside me.

His Early Success in the Spread of Naqshbandi Teachings

Shaykh Nazim began to spread spiritual guidance and Islamic teachings in Cyprus. Many followers came to him and accepted the Naqshbandi Order. Unfortunately, it was a time when all religion was banned in Turkey, and as he was in the Turkish community of Cyprus, religion was entirely banned there as well. Even the reciting of the *adhan*, the call to prayer, was prohibited.

His first action after reaching his birthplace was to go to the mosque and call the people to prayer in Arabic. He was immediately jailed. He stayed in jail for one week. As soon as he was released, he went to the big mosque of Nicosia and called the people to prayer from its minaret. This made the officials very angry. They filed a lawsuit against him. While he awaited the lawsuit, he went all over Nicosia and nearby villages calling the people to prayer from the minarets. As a result, many more lawsuits were raised. Eventually there were 114 cases pending against him. Lawyers advised him to stop calling the people to prayer, but he said, "No, I cannot. People must hear the call to prayer."

The day of the hearing arrived for the 114 cases. If prosecuted and convicted he could have received over 100 years in jail. The same day, the election results came in from Turkey. A man named Adnan Menderes had been voted into power. His first action as president was to open all mosques and to permit the call to prayer to be made in Arabic. That was a miracle of our Grandshaykh.

During his years there, Shaykh Nazim traveled all over Cyprus. He also visited Lebanon, Egypt, Saudi Arabia, and many other places to teach the Sufi Way. He moved back to Damascus in 1952 when he married one of the disciples of Grandshaykh, Hajjah Amina Adil. From that time, he lived in Damascus and he visited Cyprus every year for the three holy months of Rajab, Shaban and Ramadan. His family lived in Damascus with him and would travel with him to Cyprus when he went there. He had two daughters and two sons.

His Early Travels to Spread the Light of God

For twenty-seven successive years, Shaykh Nazim led delegations of Cypriot Muslims on the Islamic pilgrimage in Makkah (the Hajj). On these occasions, he looked after the disciples and followers of Grandshaykh Abd Allah. In later years, he organized international groups of Muslims to attend the pilgrimage, which continues to this day. Characteristically, many of these groups, containing pilgrims numbering in the dozens, paid visits to Shaykh Nazim at his home in Cyprus immediately following the Hajj.

SYRIA

Once Grandshaykh told him to go from Damascus to Aleppo on foot and to stop at every village on the way to spread the Naqshbandi teachings, the knowledge of Sufism, and the knowledge of religion. The distance between Damascus and Aleppo is about 400 kilometers. It took him more than a year to go and return. He walked one or two days, reached a village, spent one week spreading the Naqshbandi Order, leading *dhikr*, training the people, then he would move on down the road to the next village. Soon his name was on every tongue, from the border of Jordan to the border of Turkey near Aleppo.

CYPRUS

Similarly, Grandshaykh once told Shaykh Nazim to walk through Cyprus. He walked from one village to another, calling people to Islam, to leave atheism, secularism, materialism, and to come back to God. He became so well known throughout Cyprus, and so beloved, that the color of his turban and cloak, both a dark green, became known throughout the island as the "Shaykh Nazim green head" (Shaykh Nazim *yeşilbas*).

LEBANON

He visited Lebanon many times, where we came to know him. In 1955, I was in the office of my uncle, who was the General Secretary for Religious Affairs in Lebanon, a high-ranking government position. It was time for the afternoon prayer which my uncle, Shaykh Mukhtar Alayli, prayed daily in the Masjid al-Umari al-Kabir in Beirut. It was a church at the time of Umar ibn al-Khattab ﷺ, converted into a mosque during his time. Beneath the mosque there remain the foundations of the church. My uncle led the prayer and two of my brothers and I prayed behind him. A shaykh came and prayed beside us. He looked at my brother and said to him, "Are you so-and-so?" and mentioned his name. He looked at my other brother and mentioned his name. He looked at me and called me by name also. We were very surprised at this, as we had never seen him before. My uncle was also drawn to him. This was our first contact with Shaykh Nazim.

My eldest brother insisted on hosting the venerable shaykh in our house and my uncle came with us. Our guest said, "I have been sent by Shaykh Abd Allah. He told me, 'The one on your right side after the afternoon prayer is named such-and-such, and the other is named such-and-such, and the other is named such-and-such. Initiate them into the Naqshbandi Order. They are going to be among our followers.'" His knowing all our names astonished us and drew us to him. Being quite young, I was particularly attracted to him.

From that time on, he made it a practice to visit Beirut regularly. We also visited Damascus every week to see Grandshaykh Abd Allah and Shaykh Nazim. We received a lot of spiritual knowledge and witnessed the miraculous powers that they were spreading to the hearts of seekers. We were so drawn to them that we were always begging our father to let us go see them every Sunday.

Shaykh Nazim's house was never empty of visitors. At least a hundred visitors would pass through his house each day. He served each and every one of them. His house was near Grandshaykh's on Jabal Qasiyun, a mountain overlooking the city, on the southeastern side of Damascus. He lived in a modest stucco house in which everything was simple, made by hand out of wood or some other natural material.

His Seclusions

His first seclusion by the order of Shaykh Abd Allah ad-Daghestani was in the year 1955, in Sueileh, Jordan. There he spent six months in seclusion. The power and purity of his presence attracted thousands of disciples, so that Sueileh and its surrounding villages, Ramta and Amman became full of disciples. Scholars, officials, and so many people were attracted to his light and his personality.

When he had only two children, a daughter and a son, he was called by our grandshaykh, Shaykh Abd Allah ad-Daghestani. He told him, "I have received an Order from the Prophet ﷺ for you to observe seclusion in the mosque of Abd al-Qadir Gilani in Baghdad. Go there and make seclusion for six months."

> Describing that event, Shaykh Nazim says:
>
> I did not ask the shaykh any questions. I did not even go back to my house. I directed my steps immediately to Marja in the downtown. I did not think, "I need clothes, I need money, I need provisions." When he said, "Go!" I went. I was drawn to do seclusion with Abd al-Qadir Gilani. When I reached the downtown, I saw a man looking at me. He looked at me and recognized me. He said, "Where are you going?" I said, "To Baghdad." He was a disciple of Grandshaykh. He said, "I am going to Baghdad myself!" He had a truckload of goods to deliver in Baghdad. So he took me with him.
>
> When I entered the mosque of Shaykh Abd al-Qadir Gilani, there was a giant man closing the door of the mosque, holding it shut. He said, "Shaykh Nazim!" "Yes," I answered. He said, "I am the one assigned to be your servant during your stay here. Come with me." I was surprised at this, but in my heart there was no surprise because we know in *tariqah* that everything is always arranged by the Divine Presence. I followed him as he approached the grave of the Arch-Intercessor, *al-Ghawth*. I gave greetings to my great-great-grandfather, Shaykh Abd al-Qadir Gilani. Then he took me to a room and told me, "Every day, I will serve you one bowl of lentil soup with one piece of bread."
>
> I only emerged from my room for the five prayers. Other than that I spent my whole time in that room. I was able to reach such a state that I could recite the whole Quran in nine hours. I recited *"la ilaha ill-Allah"*

124,000 times and 124,000 salutations on the Prophet ﷺ, in addition to reading the entire *Dalail al-Khayrat*. Added to that, I was regularly reciting 313,000 *"Allah, Allah, Allah..."* every day, as well as all the prayers that were assigned to me. Vision after vision appeared to me. These visions took me from one state to another until I was annihilated in the Divine Presence.

One day, I had a vision that Shaykh Abd al-Qadir Gilani called me to his grave. He said, "O my son, I am waiting for you at my grave. Come!" Immediately, I took a shower, prayed two *rakats* and walked to his grave which was only some few feet from my room. When I got there I began contemplating, and I said, *"as-salam alayka ya jaddi"* ("peace be upon you, O my grandfather"). Immediately, I saw him come out of the grave and stand beside me. Behind him was a great throne decorated with rare stones. He said to me, "Come with me and sit with me on that throne."

We sat like a grandfather with his grandson. He smiled and said, "I am happy with you. The station of your shaykh, Abd Allah al-Faiz ad-Daghestani is very high in the Naqshbandi Order. I am your grandfather. I now pass to you—directly from me—the power that I carry as the Arch-Intercessor. I initiate you now directly into the Qadiri Order."

Immediately after that, Grandshaykh appeared, the Prophet ﷺ appeared, and Shah Naqshband appeared. Shaykh Abd al-Qadir Gilani stood up in respect for the Prophet ﷺ and for the shaykhs, as did I. He said, "O my Prophet, O Messenger of God, I am the grandfather of this grandson of mine. I am so happy with his progress in the Naqshbandi Order, and I would like to add the Naqshbandi Order to my powers." The Prophet ﷺ was smiling, and he looked to Shah Naqshband, and Shah Naqshband looked to Grandshaykh. This was the proper conduct, because Shaykh Abd Allah was the living shaykh at that time. Grandshaykh passed the secret of the Naqshbandi Order received from Shah Naqshband through the lineage to the Prophet ﷺ from Abu Bakr as-Siddiq رضي الله عنه, adding to the state of Shaykh Abd al-Qadir Gilani the power of the Naqshbandi Order.

When Shaykh Nazim had finished his seclusion and was about to leave, he went to Shaykh Abd al-Qadir Gilani's grave to say good-bye. Shaykh Abd al-Qadir Gilani appeared in the flesh to him and said, "O my son. I am very happy with the states you have reached in the Naqshbandi Order. I am renewing your initiation to me through the Qadiri Order." Shaykh Abd al-Qadir Gilani then said, "O my grandson, I am going to give you a token of your visit." He hugged him and gave him ten coins. Those coins were from the time he was living in, not from our time. Up until today, Shaykh Nazim has kept those coins.

Before he left, Shaykh Nazim gave his cloak as a remembrance to the shaykh who had served him. He told him, "I used that cloak during all of my seclusion, either as a mat to sleep on or as a dress when praying and reciting *dhikr*. Keep it, and God will bless you and the Prophet ﷺ will bless you. All the masters of this Order will bless you." The shaykh took the cloak, kissed it, and wore it. Shaykh Nazim left Baghdad and went back to Damascus, Syria.

In 1992, when he visited Lahore, Pakistan, he went to the tomb of Shaykh Ali al-Hujwiri. The shaykh of the Qadiri Order invited him to his house, where Shaykh Nazim spent the night. At the time of the dawn prayer, his host said:

> O my shaykh, I kept you here tonight to show you a very precious cloak that we inherited twenty-seven years ago. It was passed from one great shaykh of the Qadiri Order to another from Baghdad. Finally, it reached us. All our shaykhs have kept it and preserved it, because it was the personal cloak of the Arch-Intercessor of his time.
>
> A Turkish shaykh of the Naqshbandi Order kept seclusion in the mosque and tomb of Shaykh Abd al-Qadir Gilani. When that shaykh finished his seclusion he gave the cloak as a present to a Qadiri shaykh who had served him during his seclusion. That Qadiri shaykh, before he passed away, told his successors to take great care of that cloak, because if anyone wears it, he will be healed of any illness. Any seeker wearing that cloak, in his path to the Divine Presence, will be lifted easily to high states of vision.

He opened the closet and revealed the cloak preserved in a glass case. He opened the case and took the cloak out. Shaykh Nazim was smiling. The shaykh asked him, "What is it my shaykh?" Shaykh Nazim said, "This brings me great happiness. This is the cloak I gave to the Qadiri shaykh at the conclusion of my seclusion." When the shaykh heard this, he kissed the hand of Shaykh Nazim, asked to renew his initiation in the Qadiri Order and to take initiation in the Naqshbandi Order. God takes good care of His saints, wherever they go, by means of his sincere and beloved servants.

SECLUSION IN MADINAH

Many times Shaykh Nazim was told to go into seclusion, which varied in length from forty days to one year. The seclusions also varied in the degree of isolation from outside contact: sometimes there was no contact; sometimes there was the small amount necessitated by performing the daily prayers in congregation; and sometimes more contact was permitted for attendance at circles gathering for lectures or *dhikr*. He observed many seclusions in the city of the Prophet ﷺ. He said:

> No one ever had the privilege of performing seclusion with his shaykh. I had this privilege in the same room with my shaykh in Madinah. It was in an ancient room near the Prophet's ﷺ Holy Mosque. It had one door and one window. As soon as I entered the room with my shaykh, he blocked the window by boarding it up. He gave me authorization to leave the room only for the five daily prayers in the Holy Mosque of the Prophet ﷺ.
>
> I was told by my shaykh to keep the practice "watching the step," when I walked to the prayers. By disciplining and controlling the sight, this practice is a means to disconnect oneself from everything except God, Almighty and Exalted, and His Prophet ﷺ.
>
> My shaykh never slept during that seclusion. For one year, I never saw him sleep. He never touched food. We were given one bowl of lentil soup and one piece of bread each day. He would always give his share to me. He only drank water. He never left that room.
>
> Day-after-day and night-after-night, my shaykh sat reading Quran by the light of a candle, reciting *dhikr,* and raising his hands in supplication. For hours he would supplicate and one supplication never resembled another. Each one was different from the other. Throughout the whole year he never repeated the same supplication.

Sometimes I was not able to understand the language he was using in the supplication, because it was a heavenly language. I could only understand these supplications by means of the visions and inspirations that came to my heart.

I did not know when night left and day arrived except by the prayers. Grandshaykh Abd Allah never saw the light of day for one whole year, only the light of the candle. I would see the daylight only when I went out for the prayers.

Through that seclusion I was raised to different levels of spirituality. One day I heard him saying, "O God give me the power of intercession, from the power of intercession You have granted Your Prophet ﷺ, to intercede for all human beings on the Day of Judgment, to lift them up to be in Your Divine Presence." As he said this I was in a vision experiencing the Judgment Day. God, Almighty and Exalted, descended on His Throne and judged people. The Prophet ﷺ was on the right side of the Divine Presence. Grandshaykh was on the right side of the Prophet ﷺ, and I was on Grandshaykh's right side.

After God had judged the people, he authorized the Prophet ﷺ to intercede. When the Prophet ﷺ had interceded and finished, he told Grandshaykh to give his blessings and to lift the people up with the spiritual power that he had been given. That vision ended as I heard my shaykh saying, "*Alhamdulillah, Alhamdulillah,* Nazim Effendi, I got the answer."

These visions continued. One day he told me, after I returned from the dawn prayer, "Nazim Effendi, look!" Where should I look, up, down, right or left! It came to me to look at his heart. As soon as I looked at his heart, a great unveiling occurred to me and I saw Abd al-Khaliq al-Ghujdawani appear in his physical body and tell me, "O my son, your shaykh is unique. No one like him has ever come before." Then he invited Grandshaykh and me to come with him.

Immediately, we saw ourselves with Abd al-Khaliq in another place on this earth. He said, "God, Almighty and Exalted, has told me to go to that rock." We followed him to a rock. He said, "God has told me to hit that rock." When he hit the rock an incredibly powerful stream of water came gushing forth from that rock, the like of which I had never seen before. Shaykh Abd al-Khaliq said, "That water is coming out today and is going to continue to pour out like this until Judgment Day."

Then he said, "God, the Exalted, has told me that He is creating from every drop of this water an angel of light, which will be praising Him until Judgment Day. And He has told me by saying, 'O My servant Abd al-Khaliq al-Ghujdawani, your job is to give every angel its name. You cannot use any name twice. You must name each one with a different name and count their praises. You will divide the rewards of their praises among the followers of the Naqshbandi Order. That responsibility is on you.'" Then that vision ended. I was so attracted to Shaykh Abd al-Khaliq al-Ghujdawani and amazed by his incredible task.

Visions continued to rain on me in similar fashion. In the last day of our seclusion, after the dawn prayer, I heard a voice outside the room crying. I heard one great voice and many smaller voices like the voices of many children crying. That crying did not stop, but I was unable to go and see who was crying, because I had no permission. The sound of crying kept increasing and continued for hours.

Then Grandshaykh looked at me and said, "Nazim Effendi, do you know who is crying?" Though I knew that it was not the cries of human beings, I said, "O my shaykh, you know better." Immediately, he told me, "This is Iblis (Satan) and his soldiers. Do you know why they are crying?" I said, "O my shaykh, you know better." He said, "Satan announced to his devils that two people on this earth have escaped their control."

Then I saw a vision that Satan and his soldiers were encircled with a heavenly chain that prevented them from reaching my shaykh and me. That vision ended. Then Grandshaykh said, "Praise belongs to God, the Prophet ﷺ is happy with you, and I am happy with you." He put his hand on my heart, and I immediately saw the Prophet Muhammad ﷺ and all of the other prophets, 124,000 Companions, 7,007 Naqshbandi Saints, 313 exalted saints, the five spiritual poles, and the Arch-Intercessor. All of them congratulated me. They each poured into my heart their Divine Knowledge. I inherited from them the secrets of the Naqshbandi Order and the secrets of the other orders.

From His Miracles

MY FATHER'S DEATH

In 1971, Shaykh Nazim was in Cyprus for the three months of Rajab, Shaban, and Ramadan, as was his custom. One day in Shaban, we received a call from the airport in Beirut. It was the shaykh telling us to come and get him. We were surprised that he had come, as we were not expecting him, but we quickly went to pick him up. He told us, "I have been told by the Prophet ﷺ to come to you today, because your father is going to die. I am to wash him, shroud him, and bury him, and then go back to Cyprus." We said, "O our shaykh, our father is healthy, nothing is wrong with him." He said, "That is what I have been told." He was absolutely certain, and since we had been taught to accept what the shaykh says, we submitted to him.

He told us to gather the family and to bring them to see my father one last time. We believed him, and we called all the family to come. Everyone was surprised, and some did not believe us when we called them. Some came and some did not come. My father knew nothing about that matter, but only saw the relatives coming to see him as something ordinary. It was a quarter to seven in the evening. The shaykh said, "Now I have to go up to your father's apartment to recite *Surah YaSin* as he passes away." He went up to my father's flat from our flat below. He was greeted by my father at the door. My father said, "O Shaykh Nazim, it has been a long time since we heard you recite the Quran. Will you read it for us?" Then Shaykh Nazim began to recite *Surah YaSin*. Just as he was finishing the *surah*, the clock struck seven. Just then my father cried out, "My heart, my heart!" We lay him down, and my brother and sister, who are both doctors, came to check him. They found his heart racing out of control and within minutes he breathed his last.

Everyone looked at Shaykh Nazim with awe and astonishment. "How did he know?" we were wondering. "How did he come from Cyprus just for this? What kind of saint is he? How did he know that time so precisely? What kind of secret was he carrying in his heart? What kind of perfect saint is he who knows things that people cannot know?"

The secret he carries is a result of God's love and mercy to him. God authorized him with that power and prescience because he maintained his sincerity and piety and loyalty to God's religion. He kept his obligations and his prayers. He honored His Holy Quran. He is like all saints of the Naqshbandi Order before him, like all saints of other orders before him, like his ancestors, Shaykh Abd al-Qadir Gilani and Jalaluddin Rumi, and like Muhyiddin Ibn Arabi, who followed and preserved the tradition of Islam for 1,400 years.

We were caught between two emotions. On the one hand, we cried for our father's passing away, and on the other, we were happy with our master and what he had done for our father. His coming to take care of our father at his last breath was a gesture we will never forget. It was a blessed miracle written with words of light. He washed his body, covered him with a shroud, and buried him with his holy hands. Having accomplished this task he took a flight back to Cyprus without delay.

What kind of emotions and feelings enter the heart of a person when he sees such events before his eyes, events which the material mind cannot encompass or even imagine? The pen cannot express these feelings. We can only say one thing: this is the Truth. This is what happened. It is a reality that happens with a mystical power, an unbelievable power that can be given to a person when he has been granted love from the Divine. With that love he will be granted knowledge, wisdom, and spirituality from the Divine. He will be granted everything. He will be a knower of the past, a knower of the present, and a knower of the future.

BEING PRESENT ON HAJJ

Once, Shaykh Nazim was visiting Lebanon for a period of two months during the pilgrimage season. The governor of the city of Tripoli, Lebanon, Ashur ad-Daya, was head of the official convoy to the pilgrimage. He invited Shaykh Nazim to go with him on the pilgrimage. The shaykh said, "I cannot go with you, but God willing, I will meet you there." The governor insisted, "If you are going, please go with me. Do not go with anyone else." Shaykh Nazim replied, "I do not yet know if I will go or not." After the season of the pilgrimage finished and the governor had returned, he rushed to the house where Shaykh Nazim was staying. In front of 100 people, while we were watching, he said, "O Shaykh Nazim, why did you go with someone else, why did you not come with me?" We said, "The shaykh did not go on pilgrimage. He has been here with us for two months traveling around Lebanon."

He said, "No! He was on the Hajj! I have witnesses. One day I was making the ritual circumambulation of the Kabah, and Shaykh Nazim came to me and said, 'O Ashur, are you here?' I said, 'Yes, my shaykh.' Then he circumambulated with me. We spent the night together in our hotel in Makkah. He spent the day with us on Arafah, in our tent. He spent the night with me in Mina. He stayed with us in Mina for three days. Then he told me, 'I have to go to Madinah to visit the Prophet ﷺ.'"

As he told this story, we were carefully observing Shaykh Nazim, as we knew that he had never left our presence in Lebanon. We saw that unique, hidden smile, as if he meant to say, "That is the power that God grants to His saints. When they are on His Way, when they reach His Divine Love and His Divine Presence, God will grant them everything."

When he saw that, the governor said, "O my shaykh, what is this miraculous ability that you showed us? It is incredible. That is something I never saw in all my life. I am a politician. I rely on my mind and my logic. Yet I must say that you are not an ordinary person. You have superhuman powers. It must be something with which God Himself has adorned you!" He kissed the hand of the shaykh and asked him for initiation in the Naqshbandi Order. Whenever Shaykh Nazim would visit Lebanon, that governor and the prime minister of Lebanon would sit in the shaykh's company. Up until today, their families and many of the Lebanese people are his followers.

From His Sayings

About the State of Unique Oneness he said:

It means the impossibility of the existence of multiplicity, and it is of three categories:

- The Unique Oneness of the Essence (*Tawhid adh-dhat*): This means that His Essence is not compounded nor combined from two or more parts, and there is nothing which resembles His Divine Essence.
- The Unique Oneness of His Attributes (*Tawhid as-siffat*): This means that God, Almighty and Exalted, does not possess two kinds of

Attributes which represent the same thing. For example, He does not have two Wills nor two Intentions; He is One in every attribute.

- The Unique Oneness of His Actions (*Tawhid al-afal*): It means that He is the Creator, by His Own Wish and His Own Will, of everything that appears in this universe. All creations are either a substance, or a description, or an action. Thus, all His Actions are created by Him for His servants.

If the love is true, then the lover must keep respect for the Beloved and proper manners with Him.

The highest certainty of truth is when the shaykh glorifies the Divine Presence in your eye and diminishes everything other than God.

There are three big snakes that harm human beings: to be intolerant and impatient with the people around you; to be habituated to something you cannot leave; and to be controlled by your ego.

To achieve honors in this world is humiliation. To achieve the next life is honor. I am amazed at those who prefer humiliation to honor.

If God, Almighty and Exalted, opened the Essence of His Divine Love, everyone on earth would die from that love.

We must always be engaged in the following: pondering God's verses in the Holy Quran and His signs which cause love to evolve in us; thinking about His Promise to reward us, which will generate and bring forth in us yearning; and thinking about His Warning of punishment, which will generate in us shyness of God.

God said, "Whoever will be patient with Us will reach Us."

If fear of God is grounded in the heart, the tongue will never speak what is of no purpose.

Once Junayd saw Iblis (Satan) in a vision. He was naked. He told him, "O accursed one, are you not ashamed to appear naked before people?" He said, "O Junayd, why should I be ashamed when they are not ashamed themselves?"

When you meet a seeker in the way of God, approach him with sincerity and loyalty and with lenience. Do not approach him with knowledge. Knowledge might make him wild at the beginning, but leniency will bring him quickly to you.

A seeker should be someone who has left himself and connected his heart with the Divine Presence. He stands in His presence performing his obligations while visualizing the Divine with his heart. God's Light has burned his heart, giving him a thirst for the nectar of roses and withdrawing the curtains from his eyes, allowing him to see His Lord. If he opens his mouth, it is by order of the Divine Presence. If he moves, it is by the order of God, and if he becomes tranquil, it is by the action of the Divine Attributes. He is in the Divine Presence and with God.

SUFISM (*TASAWWUF*)

The Sufi is the one who keeps the obligations that God has conveyed by the Holy Prophet ﷺ and strives to raise himself to the state of perfection, which is the Knowledge of God, Almighty and Exalted.

Sufism is the purity of progressing to God's Divine Presence. Its essence is to leave this materialistic life.

Sufism is a knowledge from which one learns the state of the human soul, praiseworthy or blameworthy. If it is blameworthy, he learns how to purify it and enable it, by becoming praiseworthy, to journey to God's Divine Presence. Its fruits are the heart's development: Knowledge of God, Almighty and Exalted, through direct experience; salvation in the next world; triumph through gaining God's pleasure; the attainment of eternal happiness; and illumination and purification so that noble matters disclose themselves, extraordinary states are revealed, and one perceives what others are blind to.

Sufism is not a particular type of worship, but is rather the attachment of the heart to God. Such attachment demands that, whenever something is preferred according to the standards of the Divine Law for someone in one's circumstances, then one does it. This is why we find that Sufis have served Islam in a wide variety of capacities. Islamic scholars must acquire the higher education of Sufism.

Each defined *tasawwuf* according to his experience and according to the time. Shah Naqshband said "Our Path is companionship, and good is in the collective." Grandshaykh Bayazid al-Bistami said, "It is to bear with opposites." Grandshaykh Abd Allah ad-Daghestani said, "It is the abandonment of anger." He also said, with regard to the beginner, "It is leaving 'Why?' with one's teacher." Then someone asked Shaykh Nazim for his own definition but, out of modesty and good manners, he would not give one. Instead, he said, "We are servants and followers of these men and hope they will accept us as such!"

He once defined *tasawwuf* as, "The foot in the shoe" (meaning, the placing of each thing in its precise place, in all humbleness and simplicity). Shaykh Nazim defined injustice as "placing something other than in its right place." Thus, *tasawwuf* is the pinnacle of justice. Imam al-Qushayri said in his Tafsir titled *Lataif al-Maarif*, "Whoever trains his sight in its right place shall attain knowledge of God Most High."

ONENESS OF BEING (*WAHDAT AL-WUJUD*)

None of the Sufi Paths made this doctrine (of oneness of being—*wahdat al-wujud)* an essential tenet of theirs; they fought and argued without result. Those who claim oneness of being with Absolute Being *(al-wujud al-mutlaq)* are only trying to affirm their own existence together with Absolute Existence, and this is *shirk*—partnership with God!

DIVINE NAMES AND ATTRIBUTES

The Manifestations *(tajalliyyat)* are of four types: Divine Essence, Divine Attributes, Divine Names, and Divine Acts. The Name of the Pure Essence *(al-dhat al-baht)* is *Hu* (He) while *Allah* is the comprehensive *(jami)* Name for all the Names and Attributes. Every created being is a manifestation of a Name or under the tutelage of one of the Divine Names, which that being reveals. Hence, there is no created being, nor glimpse of a second in time, that equals another. From the Pure Essence appear the Attributes and Names, while the worlds appear from the Acts. As for Hu, He never appears, for He is *as-Samad*—the Self-Sufficient, Impregnable, Eternally Besought of all, Everlasting Sovereign Who has no interior, nor is circumscribed in a place or direction, and everything in creation subsists through this quality of His *(samadiyya)*. Therefore, it is impossible for even an atom to exist outside of this quality of His. If it were attributed to other than Him, it would be *shirk*.

DISTINCTION OF THE CREATOR FROM THE CREATED

Creation is all from the ocean of the Attribute of Power *(al-qudrah)* and under the heading of the manifestation of the acts. Creation is not "of God" in the sense of being a part from or parcel of Him—never![107] *"He begets not nor was begotten."* (112:3) This means, He never gives anything from His Essence, nor from Himself (*min dhatihi*), and is never given anything from someone else. *"But His command, when He intends a thing, is only that he says unto it: Be! and it is."* (36:82) Therefore, the existence of all things belong to the World of the Divine Command. They appear out of the Ocean of Power according to His determination, designation, and timing. Whenever He wishes, they go back to the Ocean of Power and disappear—then where is "Oneness of Being" and where is "incarnation?" Never! God is our refuge.

THE PRE-EMINENCE OF HUMAN BEINGS OVER ALL CREATION

Human beings were allowed to observe huge creations and understand something of their extent and infinity. The secret of the Divine Caliphate (*al-khilafa al-rabbaniyya)* was placed in the human being, by which his soul goes to the farthest extent of the cosmos and comes back, above the angels! And also, God said, *"Verily We have honored the children of Adam. We carry them on the land and the sea, and have made provision of good things for them, and have preferred them above many of those whom We created with a marked preferment."* (17:70)

THE LIGHT OF FAITH: INFORMED REASON IN THE HEART

Science has reached the point of proving that the smallest particle can carry in it the hugest power, like atomic power. And in the human mind *('aql),* there is a small atom-*point*. Some say it is in the head and some say it is in the heart; the latter is the correct view, because the sultan is the heart. That atom-point of light is able to encompass all that we have said and is able to know God. But if we were to gather together the intelligence of all the wisest philosophers and sages, they would be unable to know this, and the worlds cannot carry it.

---

[107] A reference to the mistake of Christians who misconstrue the preposition "of" to mean part and parcel in attributions such as "Spirit of God."

THE GOLDEN CHAIN CONVEYS THE LEGACY OF ALL THE SUFI CHAINS

Shaykh Nazim narrated that, once, someone expressed *surprise* at the light which he saw on the faces of the Naqshbandis and asked Grandshaykh, "From where does one obtain that light?" Shaykh Nazim explained, "It is the light of their shaykhs and their legacy which was poured into the hands of *Sayyidi al-Shaykh*. They worked and we inherited. So it is correct to say this (light) is from your blessings."

THE POWER OF *SHAHADA* AND SURATU-L-FATIHA

It is impossible that a servant of God, even a disbeliever, reads the *Fatiha* and will not benefit from it in the next life. Whoever says *"la ilaha ill-Allah"* once, even in jest, receives reward because of the saying of the Prophet ﷺ, *"Whenever the servant says the testimony of faith, God Most High creates an angel that makes mention of His Highest Majesty until the Day of Judgment, and the reward for all this* dhikr *goes to that servant!"*[108]

When asked if there are pre-conditions for its utterance and for the servant's reward, and is the one who speaks in jest rewarded nevertheless, Shaykh Nazim replied:

> What about the one who swallows poison unintentionally? Is he not affected by it? It is the same with the one who does *dhikr*—intentionally or in jest. And if this is the case for the *Shahada*, then what do you think is the case for the *Fatiha*—the Mother of the Book and the essence of the Noble Quran?

THE GREATNESS OF GOD IN HIS CREATION

The greatness of God! God *is* great. But the word "great"—that is going to be unable to convey anything from the reality of God's greatness. He

[108] It was narrated from al-Numan ibn Bashir that the Prophet ﷺ said: *"Whatever you mention in reverence of the Divine Majesty such as* Tasbih, Tahlil, *and* Tahmid, *rally around the Throne with a sound like the sound of bees, a reminder of whoever uttered them. Does not each and everyone of you love for himself to have a perpetual reminder (at the Throne)?"* Al-Mundhiri said in *al-Targhib*: "Ibn Abi al-Dunya, Ibn Majah, and al-Hakim narrated it, the latter grading it sound per Muslim's criterion." Another proof is the *hadith* of Malik ibn Dukhshum, who was considered a hypocrite, yet the Prophet ﷺ said: *"None testifies that there is no god but God, and that I am the Messenger of God, and then enters the Fire."* Anas was so pleased when he heard this *hadith* that he told his son to write it down. It is in *Sahih Muslim*.

is great, and He is only One. There cannot be a second "one" in existence.

It is said that there are 10,000,000 galaxies in this universe. They may say 100,000,000 galaxies. Do you think that space contains 100,000,000 galaxies? What do you think? Even more? One billion? That is only space, and space is not God. God is Allah. And this space—do you imagine that you can fill it with galaxies? If I ask you to fill it, can you?

How about one ocean? If the Mediterranean Sea just went dry, do you think that you could fill it with a bucket? How many buckets do you need to fill the Mediterranean Sea? I am not saying the Atlantic Ocean, or the Indian Ocean, or the Pacific Ocean. Do you think that you can fill it? Not empty it, fill it. Do you think that you can do that?

Do you think that billions, or trillions, or a quadrillion times a quadrillion of galaxies—each one gigantic in itself—can fill space? I am speaking to you about unlimited numbers of galaxies that may be swimming through this huge space, and at the end, it is so dark. Through that depthless darkness, do you think that trillions of quadrillion of galaxies give any more than a small spot of light?

It is a grant for the children of Adam عليه السلام to be able to think about that point. That is an honor that we have been granted. God, the Exalted, is saying, *"We have honored the children of Adam."* (17:70) Only to think about it gives honor to you!

MAN'S CALIPHATE

The caliphate is a grant from God, the Exalted, adorning Adam عليه السلام. If God, the Exalted, showed Adam عليه السلام in the true raiment with which He, the Almighty, dressed him as His Deputy, Satan would have been the first to prostrate before him. But, because this world cannot bear that divine appearance, Adam's عليه السلام true appearance, God made it less and less, in the end adorning his physical being with only one ray from that light. By means of that single ray, our master Adam عليه السلام, was shining like the sun. But it was not enough to make Satan surrender. May God forgive us.

They are speaking now of God and His Deputy, Man. Who are you? How is it that you are claiming, "I am something." How are you going to speak on the Oneness of Existence (*wahdat al-wujud*)? That is ignorance. Where is Existence—true, real Existence—*Wujud Haqqani*? Where is your existence? But people cannot be blamed for saying about themselves, "I am something. I am someone." God, the Exalted, was giving Greatness to people when He said, *"And when your Lord said unto the angels: Lo! I am about to place a viceroy (*khalifa*) in the earth."* (2:30) And no one knows the real position of being Viceroy of God, the Exalted.

IGNORANCE IS WITHOUT LIMITS

What is not known is without end, while what is known is within limits.[109]

The perfections of Man are true wonders![110]

Outwardly, Man is disconnected, but in reality he is connected.[111]

THE SOURCES OF IBN ARABI'S KNOWLEDGE

Shaykh Muhyiddin wrote out of spiritual openings, but he did not understand all that he wrote. He spoke according to three Presences (*hadarat*). The first was the Divine Presence—and this is the type of knowledge that he did not understand, but he told of it so that the great saints would scoop from it at a later stage. The second was the Prophetic Presence, and the third was from the Presence of the great saints. At times, he wrote in a state of near-unconsciousness and reported types of knowledge of concern to later authorities that understood that knowledge exclusively of others.

REVERING THE DIVINE SECRET OF CREATION

Once, I was walking with Grandshaykh Abd Allah. We were going home on Mount Qasiyun, upwards from the Shaykh Muhyiddin Ibn Arabi Mosque. I kicked aside a stone that was in the middle of the road and might have caused harm. Grandshaykh said: "Do not do this again. This stone is one of the creatures of God, and every single

---

109 Arabic: *al-majhul bila nihaya wal-malum ila nihaya.*

110 Arabic: *kamalatu-l-insan ajaib.*

111 Arabic: *al-insanu zahiruhu munfasil wahuwa haqiqatan muttasil.*

creature subsists through the Light of God. Therefore, bow out of respect for that light and move it with your hand."

Then Grandshaykh told us the story of the famous Sufi poet and spiritual master, Jalaluddin Rumi, who was walking with his disciples in Konya, when a monk approached from the opposite direction. The monk bowed down as a sign of humility before Rumi, but Rumi bowed to the monk even lower. His disciples wondered, how can he bow in such fashion before the monk? Rumi answered them: "We also surpass them in humility." This explanation is for common seekers. For the elite, its meaning is: "He bowed down only in reverence for the light that was stored in him by God, the Most High, Who said: 'W*e have honored the children of Adam.*' (17:70)

THE FOLLOWERS AND THE MASTER

They told Rumi, "You are a remarkable man, but your students are unworthy," to which he replied, "Who do you see at the physician's door, the healthy or the sick?"

People carry unlit torches and come to the sun in order to light them. The followers of the Prophet ﷺ lived in the Time of Ignorance; then they became the best of human beings and the models of perfection. It is for this that the great guides came: to render people beautiful and perfect.

Our master, Ahmad al-Rifai al-Kabir, told his followers, "If you see anything wrong in me, do not hide it from me, but tell me of it immediately." He made them promise. One of them said, "O my master, I saw one thing wrong in you." He asked, "What?" The student replied, "Your one wrong is that you have such as ourselves for disciples."[112] They kept *adab* (good manners) with their shaykh.

DISCERNMENT IS THROUGH SECLUSION

Shaykh Nazim narrated:

An Englishman sent by J.G. Bennett came to Grandshaykh, one who had accepted Islam at the hand of Grandshaykh and named himself Muhammad Ali. He was a man with many questions, which he began

[112] Narrated in al-Munawi's *Tabaqat al-sufiyy*.

posing around mid-morning and did not finish until after the night prayer! Among other things, he asked about the science of physiognomy (*al-qiyafa aw al-firasa*) so that he could find out which among his students was suitable for certain things and what the best orientation was for such students. Grandshaykh mentioned the *hadith* of Bukhari and Muslim, "Each is facilitated for that for which he was created." Then he said, "Seclusion is crucial so that the heart-apparatus (*jihaz al-qalb)* will work. There is no egg without the rooster. If the shaykh is other than a shaykh of education (*shaykh at-tarbiyyah),* then, yes, there will be an egg without a rooster—in which case he would be only a shaykh of blessing."

When he was asked whether the seclusion will bear fruit if entered into upon the request of the disciple, rather than the shaykh's own order, Shaykh Nazim replied, "No." Then he added, "Except in the way of training and self-control."

When asked, "What is the way to kill the ego?" he joked, "The Arabs use the sword while the English have the axe, the French the guillotine, and the Barbarians hanging!" In other words, the only way to kill the ego is through physical death.

Once a disciple exclaimed, "O my master, I never saw in my life a teacher more eloquent or knowledgeable than you!" Shaykh Nazim replied, *"Whoever dedicates purely to God* (akhlasa lillah*) forty mornings, the wellsprings of wisdom break forth from his tongue."*[113]

GRANDSHAYKH'S SECLUSION IN MADINAH

The order came from the Prophetic Presence that Grandshaykh should enter seclusion in Madinah al-Munawwara, and that he should take with him a shaykh from Aleppo. When the latter heard the news, he said, "This is for beginners! As for ourselves, O Shaykh, we are beyond seclusion." He refused to accompany Grandshaykh or respond to his call. So, Grandshaykh then entered the forty day seclusion with Shaykh Nazim and no one else except God and His Prophet ﷺ.

We heard in Sham from the noble Sayyid Shaykh Abd al-Qadir al-Jili al-Madani al-Qadiri, the son of Shaykh Muhammad Ahmad al-Mahi al-

---

[113] An authentic *hadith* narrated by Imam Ahmad in *The Book of Simple Living (al-Zuhd)*, Ibn Abi Shayba in his *Musannaf*, and others through many narrative chains.

Bukhari (who was 140 years old when he died), that Shaykh al-Mahi saw Grandshaykh in Madina when the latter came out of that seclusion, shook his hand, and supplicated for him.

LEVITY

Shaykh Nazim makes a point not only during communal meals but also in almost all his interactions to maintain a tremendous sense of humor. This is in keeping with the *Sunnah* of the Prophet ﷺ as related in the following hadith:

> Al-Husayn ibn Zayd said to Jafar ibn Muhammad, "Tell me, did our beloved Prophet ﷺ ever joke?" He answered, "God bestowed on him the best of manner of joyfulness. God sent other prophets who had suffering and distress, but he sent Muhammad ﷺ for mercy and compassion. One of the signs of his kindness was that he joked with them. He did this so that they would not stay away from him out of awe."[114]

TODAY'S SPIRITUAL ILLNESSES

Shaykh Nazim said that there are two great spiritual illnesses that afflict the people in this time: the first is to rejects shaykhs and that is manifest in the advent of Wahabi beliefs in many places in the world; the second is that each person imagines that he is in fact a shaykh. Both are in fact one and the same illness, manifest in two different forms: to consider oneself self-sufficient and above all others.

THE ADVENT OF AL-MAHDI عليه السلام

Scholars have debated when the Mahdi عليه السلام will appear and return justice to the world. Shaykh Nazim said:

> We do not accept that God be disobeyed, and that the Nation be tormented, and that the flag of Satan continue to be raised for one, two, or four more years, nor for one day more. Therefore, every morning we say, "Tonight he will appear;" and every night we say, "Tomorrow he will appear."

---

[114] Cited by Ibn Al-Husayn Al-Sulami, *The Book of Sufi Chivalry Futuwwah,* trans. by Sheikh Tosun Bayrak al-Jerrahi al-Halveti, (New York, Inner Traditions International, 1983) p. 43.

Regarding the saying of some of the people of Maghrib that the Mahdi عليه السلام shall come out of the Maghrib, Shaykh Nazim remarked, "It is not as they said. The one who knows is not like the one who does not know."

TYRANTS

The method of tyrants is to show contempt and belittle the people until they are obeyed. Sick souls accept and submit to this. *"Thus did he* (Pharaoh) *make fools of his people, and they obeyed him. Lo! they were a wanton folk."* (43:54)

SILENCE AND INQUIRY

The shaykh was asked which was better: the disciple who queries his shaykh, or the disciple that does not query, but receives his answers from the shaykh through the heart. Shaykh Nazim replied, "The shaykh might cast the question into the heart of the disciple so that the latter will ask him with his tongue, for entertainment."

FOLLOWING THE QURAN AND TRADITIONS WITHOUT A SPIRITUAL GUIDE

How can the Book, and the *Sunnah,* and the Arabic dictionary be one's spiritual guide? Even if there are too many impostors, the genuine spiritual guide is like the red sulphur: very rare, and almost unobtainable. One must search in earnest. Whoever strives, finds.

LOOKING WITHOUT LEARNING IS A CAPITAL OFFENSE

I was with Grandshaykh, crossing the Asruniyya Souk in Damascus. We passed by a certain shop. Grandshaykh looked at the window, so I looked too. When I looked, he turned to me and said: "Nazim Effendi, looking without wisdom is a capital offense." This means to look at the variegations of the world without specific order nor necessity is harmful to the light of the heart and forbidden to the saints. But if it is for wisdom, then it is not harmful.

DIVINE ATTRIBUTES ARE SIGNPOSTS OF THE ESSENCE

Grandshaykh Abd Allah ad-Daghestani said, "Were it not for the Attributes, the absolute Divine Identity would never be known, for it is in a 'heavy cloud.' *'He was in a heavy cloud above which there was air and*

> *below which there was air.'*[115] Then God's Attributes appeared and He became known. The Names are indicators of the Attributes. Were it not for the Names, the Attributes could not be known."
>
> God also said, *"And landmarks, and by the stars they find a way."* (16:16) So the Attributes are the landmarks of the Essence, the Names are the landmarks of the Attributes, the Acts are the landmarks of the Names, and all creatures are subsumed in the Acts.

His World Travels

As Shah Naqshband was the reviver in Bukhara and Central Asia, as Ahmad as-Sirhindi al-Mujaddidi was the reviver of the second Islamic millennium, as Khalid al-Baghdadi was the reviver of Islam, the Divine Law, and the Way in the Middle East, now Shaykh Muhammad Nazim Adil al-Haqqani is the reviver, the renewer, and the caller to God in this age, the age of technology and material progress.

He possesses a light-hearted demeanor and an ability to touch the hearts of people from all walks of life. Spiritually guided and supported by his shaykh and all of the previous shaykhs of the Naqshbandi Golden Chain, Shaykh Nazim has been blessed with an unprecedented spiritual power and responsibility to reach all around the world on his mission of enlightenment. His goal is always the same: to restore the consciousness of God among all peoples and invite them to sincere belief and worship.

Wherever Shaykh Nazim visits, people are swept away by his personality, reminded of their spiritual traditions and given the opportunity to soar with him to the Divine Presence. He carries with him the noble practices and good manners taught by generations of Sufi masters. At each stop on his journeys, Shaykh Nazim leads the people in *dhikr,* conducts the night vigil *(tahajjud),* and leads the daily prayers, often with several hundred worshippers accompanying him. The shaykh showers pearls from his wisdom and gems from his years of experience on the gathered crowds, reviving their hearts and uplifting their souls.

Since his early travels through Turkey, Lebanon, and Syria six decades ago, Shaykh Nazim continues to meet with people from all walks of life, and from diverse religious and cultural backgrounds. He is sought out by heads

---

[115] *Hadith* of the Prophet ﷺ narrated by al-Tirmidhi, Ibn Majah, and Ahmad.

of state and monarchs, by policymakers and activists, by academics and elite industrialists. He has visited the Vatican and met with the leaders of many faiths, as well as the heads of small churches, monasteries, synagogues and temples. Audiences with the shaykh are sought by writers, publishers, and documentary filmmakers—even by celebrities who seek his guidance and spiritual blessing. However, Shaykh Nazim has never lost his fondness for the common folk. Indeed, every day and every night finds him surrounded by people earnestly seeking his guidance and he is renowned for his unlimited patience in hearing their stories, resolving their problems, and alleviating their suffering. Today, his followers number in the hundreds of thousands, and they can be found in every region of the world.

TURKEY

In 1974, the year after Grandshaykh Abd Allah ad-Daghestani passed away, Shaykh Nazim made his first trip back to Turkey, visiting Bursa. For the next twenty years, he made an annual walking tour of the Turkish countryside, typically spending three or four months traveling through one specific region of the country.

One year he visited the area of Istanbul, Yalova, Bursa, Eskisehir and Ankara; another year he traveled to Konya, Isparta, and Kirsehir; and later trips took him along the southern sea coast, through the Eastern region and to the Black Sea. On each of these journeys, the shaykh moved from one district to another, from one town to another, from one mosque to the next, spreading the word of God, spirituality and light wherever he went. In each location, he was welcomed by crowds of common citizens and honored by local officials, all of whom knew him by the affectionate nickname of "al-Qubrusi" (the Cypriot).

Shaykh Nazim maintains his affection for Turkey, and his face and name are still known virtually everywhere through extensive media coverage and by word-of-mouth. He has often been consulted on current and world events. He walks the middle path recommended by the Prophet ﷺ,[116] enabling him to address issues with balance and due consideration, keeping the best interest of all parties in mind.

---

[116] Based on the Tradition, '*The best matters are the middle ones.*'

WESTERN EUROPE

In 1973, Shaykh Nazim visited London for the first time. When he arrived, many young people, particularly the followers of John Bennett, came to meet him. The shaykh realized that there was a tremendous thirst for the authentic spirituality of the Naqshbandi teachings in the West, and he agreed to return the following year, beginning an annual tradition of journeying to Britain and the Continent.

During the next year, the first Naqshbandi centers were established in England and Germany. The audiences for these annual trips grew rapidly, and soon thousands of seekers from across Europe and North America were making their own journeys to those centers to meet with Shaykh Nazim. These gatherings, generally held during the holy month of Ramadan, soon became a tradition within the Order.

As a result, the Naqshbandi Order spread quickly, reaching every region of Europe, together with the United States, Canada, South America, Australia and Southeast Asia. Soon Shaykh Nazim inaugurated three popular centers in London, each devoted to training seekers in the ways of Islamic spirituality, removing their depression and spiritual afflictions, and lifting them to a state of inner peace. Addressing the needs of Muslims in London, he established the first large Islamic prayer hall, Shacklewell Lane Mosque, in addition to a large Muslim cemetery twenty-five miles southwest of London in the historic borough of Woking.

His radiant, smiling face quickly became known throughout the United Kingdom, Germany, France, Italy, Austria, Belgium, Holland, and Spain. Shaykh Nazim is deeply loved and respected by tens of thousands of his European followers—and now their children—for bringing the true taste of spirituality into their lives.

Through the miracle of his blessed mission, Naqshbandi centers are thriving in each of these countries and his numerous books have been translated most European languages. With each successive visit to Europe, the ranks of Shaykh Nazim's followers continue to grow at an astounding rate. He has been greeted with similar success in the United States and Canada. The shaykh has often attributed this phenomenon to the West's craving for spirituality, but those who follow him attribute it to the Divine inspiration that permeates his every word, action, glance and breath.

SPAIN

In 1997, Shaykh Nazim traveled to Spain. In this former Muslim land, the shaykh was hosted by his followers there, Spanish converts to Islam. His travels included stops in the once-Muslim cities of Granada, Cordoba and Valencia, as well as visits to the island of Ibiza and Barcelona. Arriving at this northern Spanish port of Barcelona, the shaykh and his entourage, traveled high into the mountains to an ancient Catholic monastery that now hosts Buddhist devotees.

As the keynote speaker at several large events attended by Christians, Jews, Buddhists and Muslims, Shaykh Nazim pointed out the commonality of all faiths and called on those present to devote themselves to a more intense worship of God and a finer expression of love for all human beings, for this worldly habitat, and for all creation.

In the venerable shaykh's travels throughout Spain, more than five hundred individuals accepted Islam, while hundreds more opened their hearts to belief in God, abandoning the darkness of atheism. Still others were simply refreshed by their encounters with our master—knowingly or unknowingly taking from his light and his wisdom. Disciples who already had a connection with the shaykh renewed it and were given the enthusiasm (*himmat*) to perform ever-greater Divine service.

BOSNIA

In 1997 and 1998, Shaykh Nazim, accompanied by an entourage of disciples from around the world, visited Bosnia-Herzegovina as that nation was emerging from the ashes of a terrible war.

During his first visit after many years absence, the shaykh was hosted in Sarajevo by Chief of Islamic Scholars, Grand Mufti Mustafa Ceric. Later, traveling throughout the war-ravaged nation by bus, he was accompanied by the muftis of the many towns he visited. Shaykh Nazim was much aggrieved to see the horrific results of the war and, wherever he went, would spend much time at the new graves, praying for those who had fallen victim to its savagery. At the location of one particularly horrendous event, he noted with poignancy that Bosnia had been like a child who, under the oppression of a harsh master, cries a flood of tears. Shaykh Nazim explained that such tears were the cause for Divine Mercy to descend and relieve the suffering of the tortured and oppressed. That Mercy, he said, would suffice to draw all of Europe towards the Divine Light of faith.

Wherever the shaykh traveled in Bosnia, he was greeted by disciples, well-wishers, common folk and scholars. His presence revived the Sufi tradition in this former Ottoman land where the Naqshbandi Order had once flourished and spread Islam's spiritual teachings far and wide.

In 1998, he returned again to re-established several traditional *tekkes*, or centers of the Naqshbandi Order, and assigned local imams to lead *dhikr* and teach the good conduct and practices of the Way.

MIDDLE EAST

Since the end of the last century, Shaykh Nazim has traveled twice each year to his spiritual homeland in Sham, modern day Syria and Lebanon. This is where he now spends most of each Ramadan, surrounded by thousands of disciples from all over the world.

During his trips through the region, Shaykh Nazim is hosted in the homes of high officials, religious leaders and scholars. Wherever he goes, he is welcomed at mosques and other holy sites. He meets with other Sufi shaykhs, religious scholars, government leaders and businessmen, but the common man is always welcome at his gatherings. Where the shaykh stops, God's Bounty flows. The poor are fed in droves and charity is distributed to those in need.

The scholar Leif Stenberg in the article "Naqshbandiyya in Damascus" reports:

> Shaykh Nazim still has his own house in Syria—the one he and his family inhabited for many years. On his visits to Syria it is Shaykh Nazim's custom to visit with Shaykh Ahmad Koftaro, who is Syria's Grand Mufti.[117]

---

[117]Stenberg writes, "in 1946 at the age of 31, Shaykh Koftaro was a founding member of the League of Muslim Scholars. He was appointed a mufti of Damascus in 1951 and in 1958 he became the top mufti of Damascus and a member of the Supreme Council of *Fatwa, Majlis al-Ifta*. Shaykh Koftaro was elected Grand Mufti in 1964. He is also a member of the Supreme Council of *Awqaf*.

"The Grand Mufti holds the highest religious official position in the country and it should be noted that he can be described both as a traditional religious authority and as a leader of a Sufi order. ...

"Another contemporary and neighboring example from the Naqshbandiyya is Shaykh Muhammad Nazim Adil al-Haqqani an-Naqshbandi. He is a Naqshbandi shaykh but also a scholar of *Shariah*...

Many throughout the region consider him to be the "Reviver of the Age." Leif Sternberg writes:

> ...the young men I communicate with often return to the term *mujaddid* or renewer when they describe their ideas of Islam ...something that they have been taught by Shaykh Koftaro [who] often refers to this term. Shaykh Nazim al-Haqqani is often referred to as the *mujaddid* of this century...[118]

The shaykh always brings with him the sound of *dhikr,* often reviving the traditional remembrance of God in places where His Holy Names have been all but forgotten. Thanks to him, the Prophetic *Sunnah* rises once more in the land which Shaykh Nazim has foretold will be the center of spirituality and blessings in this new millennium. His compassionate approach to people, opening the way of Islam to people from all walks and styles of life, has made him beloved among rich and poor, educated and illiterate, young and old, for as he treats each person as an individual without distinction, giving unconditionally of his heartfelt love, so all treat him as their wise guide, support and spiritual father.

In 1986, Shaykh Nazim traveled to the Far East, where he visited Brunei, Malaysia, Indonesia, Singapore, Pakistan, and Sri Lanka.

"Shaykh Nazim Haqqani spent some time in Syria, and both of them are very active in presenting themselves on the Internet and both have started institutes ...in the US."

Leif Stenberg, "Naqshbandiyya in Damascus: Strategies to establish and strengthen the order in a changing society," published in *Naqshbandis in Western and Central Asia,* Edited by Elisabeth Ozdalga (Curzon Press, 1997) p. 106.

[118] Explaining the term *mujaddid,* Stenberg writes:

As conceptualized by him and his disciples the term means to return to the Quran and *Sunnah*... however in Shaykh Koftaro's understanding, the term relates not only to a renewer but it refers to the person who reactivates and authenticates the truth in conformity with the contemporary world. Islam cannot be connected to a specific time or place in history but must develop in accordance with the society. This can be seen as a critique of the opinion of many religious scholars (*ulama*) that Shaykh Koftaro is considered to be firmly riveted in a particular interpretation of Islam. The method of carrying out this interpretation of Islam, *ijtihad,* means to reread the Quran and the *Sunnah,* that is, to go back to the authentic sources of islam. The use of *ijtihad* also enables Shaykh Koftaro to influence his followers' understanding of Islam... he interprets Islam in a flexible manner that servers to show that Islam is the ultimate order of the human being... his general idea of Sufism is to go back to the term *tazkiyya,* purification... means the purification of hearts and he states that this is the original term denoting the practices that are usually described as Sufism."

Ibid., p. 114.

Everywhere he went, he was welcomed by sultans, presidents, members of parliament, and other government officials, as well as, of course, by the common people. Since that initial visit, the shaykh has returned many times to this region, where many hail him as the "Saint of the Age."

MALAYSIA

Shaykh Nazim is considered the great shaykh of the Naqshbandi Order in Malaysia. Since his initial visit in 1986, Shaykh Nazim has returned each year to Malaysia or has sent his representative. As recently as 2001, I was blessed to accompany Shaykh Nazim throughout Malaysia and the entire Pacific Rim. As his representative, I visit the region annually, but this was his first return visit after several years.

In April 2001, he arrived in the capitol of Kuala Lumpur, where Shaykh Nazim was the guest-of-honor of Sultan Azlan Shah of Perak, Malaysia's then-reining monarch. The sultan's son, His Royal Highness Raja Ashman Shah, has been a devoted follower since Shaykh Nazim's early days in London. Hosted at the Palace, Shaykh Nazim and his entourage were treated like visiting heads-of-state. Shaykh Nazim was also hosted by the Deputy Prime Minister, the Minister of Defense, the Minister of Youth, the former Chief Minister and Governor of Sarawak State, and many other leaders.

Of course, as a renowned religious leader, Shaykh Nazim was asked to lead the Friday prayers in Kuala Lumpur's largest mosque, which were attended by thousands of worshippers.

INDONESIA

In April 2001, the shaykh also returned to Indonesia, the world's largest Muslim country. During his brief stay in the country, Shaykh Nazim met with more than 100,000 disciples. Over the previous years, his fame had spread throughout Indonesia. Having taken initiation through his deputies, many disciples spoke of their spiritual visions and of having seen the shaykh on the island weeks before his physical arrival. In fact, when Shaykh Nazim was still in Kuala Lumpur, reports mentioned seeing him in the center of Jakarta, in the area called Menteng Pulo, two days before his arrival.

Shaykh Nazim's visit was a non-stop reception of government officials, Islamic scholars, Sufi shaykhs, and disciples. Assembly halls were often filled to capacity, as people from all walks of life came to glimpse this great Master, of whom they had heard so much over the years.

Then-President K.H. Abdurrahman Wahid, an Islamic scholar who had quickly and unexpectedly risen to power, sent an eager request to meet the shaykh. During the visit, Shaykh Nazim gave him initiation into the Order and told him to be patient in what he predicted would be a coming storm of adversity. Later, the president appeared unannounced as an ordinary citizen at a dinner hosted by the Haqqani Foundation of Indonesia in Jakarta in order to pay his respects to the shaykh.

During his time in Indonesia, Shaykh Nazim gave several television, radio, and newspapers interviews. He was the highlight of the national news for an entire month, even after his departure. During his historic stay, the shaykh addressed two Friday congregations at At-Taqwa Mosque in Jakarta and Daarut Tauhid in Bandung, each time speaking to congregations numbering in the tens of thousands. Shaykh Nazim's shining countenance appeared on billboards and posters throughout the nation and its hundreds of constituent islands.

Indonesia is a country with a rich tradition of Islamic spirituality. During his visit, Shaykh Nazim met with many of the nation's leading Sufi shaykhs and religious authorities, among them Habib Luthfi ibn Ali Yahya, chairman elect of all the recognized Sufi orders of Indonesia and president of the national board of traditional scholars (the *Jamiah Thariqah al Mutabaroh*); Dr. Hj. Tutty Alawiyya, a member of parliament, former minister for women's affairs and founder of the Islamic University of As-Syafiiyah, where the shaykh was welcomed by 20,000 women and girls, all students of *tasawwuf*; and Shaykh Thahir Bin Abd al-Fatah, master of the *Dalail Khayrat Jamaah Ki Thohir*, an important mosque in the heart of the spiritual village of Pekalongan. This mosque is renowned for its 10,000-member congregation, which for the past 150 years has maintained the tradition of reciting the *Dalail al-Khayrat* in praise of the Prophet ﷺ every afternoon. In Pekalongan, Shaykh Nazim also visited the *maqam* of Sayyid Abd Allah Al-Khani, a student of Shaykh Khalid al-Baghdadi of the Golden Chain, who came to Indonesia in the early nineteenth-century to spread the light of Naqshbandi Order.

On the island of Java, Shaykh Nazim was hosted at the Al-Falah Pesantren of Nagrek, a special *zawiya* established for the memorization of the Quran. There, as a guest of Shaykh Ahmad Syahid, Shaykh Nazim was honored to address an association *(suhbah)* of 15,000 disciples and renew their initiation to the Order. Shaykh Nazim met with K. H. Abd Allah Gymnastiar, famous for teaching the spiritual doctrine of *Manajemen Qalbu*, who was initiated by the shaykh into the Naqshbandi Order along with hundreds of his students. He also met with the renowned Indonesian Sufi master K.H. Shohibul Wafa Tadjul Arifin, known as "*Abah Anom*" (Young Master). The most famous Qadiriyah wa Naqshbandiya shaykh in Indonesia, Abah Anom has over 20,000,000 students throughout Asia and Australia. Great joy was apparent in the faces of these two shaykhs when they met. Abah Anom, crippled by intense pain and normally unable to speak, was suddenly animated and raised his hands in prayer. His followers were moved to tears at this manifest miracle and joined with him as he accepted initiation from our master, Shaykh Nazim.

JAPAN

In May 2001, Shaykh Nazim visited Japan for the first time. Those accompanying the shaykh were surprised when he was greeted by a thriving community of Naqshbandi disciples in Tokyo and other cities. Most of these disciples had never met the shaykh in person, but had been granted dreams and visions of him. Others had learned about the shaykh and the Naqshbandi teachings through his books, the Internet, and from fellow disciples from other countries. Together, they have established mosques and retreat centers throughout Japan, spreading the light of the Naqshbandi Sufi Order among the people of that nation.

During his visit, Shaykh Nazim was invited to visit the Sharp Corporation's headquarters as a guest-of-honor. There, he met with the company's chief executive officer and board of directors, explaining to them the spiritual significance of Japan's role in the world today. Many Japanese entered Islam during the shaykh's visit, and many also accepted initiation into the Naqshbandi Order.

SRI LANKA

Shaykh Nazim also visited Sri Lanka in 2001, the island nation where, according to his teachings, Adam عليه السلام first set foot on earth after leaving Paradise. The shaykh's followers there number more than 100,000.

There, he met with ministers and statesmen and was granted a major honor by the Sri Lanka United Nations affiliate organization, which named him an international "Goodwill Ambassador" as world leader of the Naqshbandi-Haqqani Sufi Order. The shaykh visited the grave of Shaykh Uthman, the grand *wali* of the island, and delivered a Friday sermon to a crowd of more than 5,000 disciples. During his stay, Shaykh Nazim also visited many Islamic universities and schools, where he was invariably greeted by long lines of students singing traditional songs praising the Prophet ﷺ *(salawat)*. He also addressed various interfaith groups comprised of Muslims, Buddhists, and Hindus. At each occasion, Shaykh Nazim spoke on the importance of Sufism and traditional learning, warning against the Wahhabi innovations and their erroneous opposition to commemorating the birth of the Prophet ﷺ, known as *Mawlid ash-Sharif.*

PAKISTAN

In Pakistan, where he has tens of thousands of disciples, Shaykh Nazim is acknowledged as the reviver of the Sufi Path. Since 1988, he has made regular visits to Pakistan, each one bringing thousands of new followers into the Order.

He has conducted the classical Naqshbandi *dhikr* for audiences as large as 15,000 and has been welcomed in Karachi, Lahore, and Islamabad by throngs of well-wishers, from common citizens to government officials. Before his tragic death in 1988, General Ziau 'l-Haq met with Shaykh Nazim to seek his prayers and blessing. In 2001, Shaykh Nazim met with then-President Rafiq Tarar, and was hosted in the homes of the governors of Sindh and Punjab provinces. Traveling north, he met with Afghan refugees, many of whom had made Pakistan their home after fleeing the terrible turmoil in their strife-torn nation.

SOUTH AFRICA

In 2000, Shaykh Nazim made his first visit to South Africa. It was particularly momentous occasion for the author of this book, for in 1998 when I had visited, the first person to take initiation with our master was now leading a group of more than 11,000 disciples. During his travels there, the shaykh was escorted by the muftis of South Africa and its most prestigious Islamic scholars. Shaykh Nazim prayed in local mosques and visited homes all over the country. These events were often attended by crowds numbering in the thousands, and at the end of each, he gave initiation to those gathered and lead them in the *Khatm al-Khwajagan*.

Officials of South Africa came to meet and welcome the shaykh, including the Minister of Transport, the *Majlis Ulama* (board of scholars) of Cape Town, and other dignitaries. Shaykh Nazim's physical presence reminded them of the original teachings of Islam, which their ancestors had brought centuries ago from Indonesia, India and Yemen. His spiritual presence was like the showering spring rain, pouring forth God's Mercy and Blessings on everyone who set their eyes upon his holy face, or touched his holy hand. Those who saw our master for the first time were moved to tears and those who heard his magnificent teachings on the Greatness of the Lord and the importance of the afterlife were overwhelmed by the Divine manifestations which accompanied his sweet words.

During this auspicious trip Shaykh Nazim touched the lives of many of the indigenous peoples of South Africa, reminding the immigrant Muslims of their duty not only to spread the faith, but to open their hearts and hands to help the poor and struggling in their local communities. He inaugurated several centers in Cape Town, Durban, and Johannesburg. During this brief sojourn, our master implemented practical measures to develop greater cooperation between South African Muslims and other religious groups. Most importantly, he revived Islam's traditional spiritual teachings and practices after years of dominance by radical Islamic sects.

He served as *Hujjat as-sunnah*, proof of the *Sunnah*, to many who had lost the traditional practices to this Wahhabi influence, and he served as the Reviver of Faith to those who had forgotten the Sufi traditions of respect, good conduct, and seeking a means of approach to God's Divine Presence. His visits to the shrines of dozens of saints, who had brought the Islamic faith to that land, served to revive this important practice in the hearts of the people who had been beset by doubt under an onslaught of Wahhabi sectarian attacks.

RUSSIA AND THE CAUCASUS

In 1997, Shaykh Nazim honored Russia, Daghestan, and then-newly-independent Chechnya with his blessed presence. Finally free to practice Islam after ninety years under the atheistic communist yoke, the Muslim scholars of the former U.S.S.R. were eager to host the world leader of the most distinguished Naqshbandi Order as their guest-of-honor and acknowledge him as the reviver of the faith.

Shaykh Nazim traveled to the first Quranic conference in Russia, where he met with many Naqshbandi scholars who had secretly maintained their faith during the Soviet era by means of the Order's spiritual training and discipline. He called on these scholars to unite under one flag, to restore the true teachings of classical Islam (*Ahl as-Sunnah wal-Jamaah*), and to repel the invasion of the Wahhabi sect, whose teachers had already begun to flood the mosques and Muslim communities of the former Soviet Union.

From Moscow, the shaykh traveled to Derbent in Daghestan, where so much of the history of this Order unfolded. There he visited many Naqshbandi and Qadiri Sufi groups that had preserved their faith and traditions against all odds. He then made a brief visit to Grozny and other towns in Chechnya, calling the people to moderation and tolerance in religion and urging them to reject the calls of the militant Wahhabis who were then trying to turn the Chechen people away from their traditional Sufi practices and beliefs.

In big cities and tiny villages, Shaykh Nazim met with the local shaykhs and initiated countless believers into the Naqshbandi Order. Those who had lost their faith were called by the venerable shaykh to belief in The One True God and His Prophet ﷺ, while those who had held fast were given a living reminder of the *Sunnah* of the Prophet ﷺ and the traditions of the Sufi orders that have always been the foundation of Islam in that region.

UZBEKISTAN AND CENTRAL ASIA

In 1993, Shaykh Nazim, as the fortieth grandshaykh and current head of the Golden Chain, attended the rededication of the mosque and school of Imam Bukhari in Bukhara, Uzbekistan. He was the first in many generations of shaykhs of this line to be able to return to the heartland of the great Central Asian masters who had so powerfully imprinted their Way and names upon the Naqshbandi Order.

Since his first visit to Uzbekistan, Shaykh Nazim has lent strong support to the restoration of religious institutions and classical Islam within Uzbekistan. He has enlisted the support of the Uzbek government in this effort, which has contributed greatly to the revival of traditional Islam in post-Soviet Uzbekistan.

Shaykh Nazim returned to Uzbekistan in 2001 at the start of the Naqshbandi-Haqqani Eastern World Tour, which I was privileged to organize. We decided to begin our journey in Uzbekistan to honor our great

Naqshbandi forefathers and their teachings. As official guests President Islam Karimov, Shaykh Nazim and the entire entourage—which consisted of Islamic scholars from various parts of the world, academics, professionals and new Muslims seeking the sources of the Naqshbandi way—were hosted in a most generous manner. Our delegation visited many of the holiest sites in Uzbekistan, such as the tombs of Imam Bukhari, Shah Naqshband, and the Prophet's ﷺ companion and cousin Quthum ibn al-Abbas ؓ. We also visited the tombs of seven other grandshaykhs of the Naqshbandi Golden Chain who were born in, lived in, and taught in this land rich in religious scholarship and love for God and His Prophet ﷺ.

Wherever we went, Shaykh Nazim was warmly welcomed by the Uzbek people. Hosted by the local muftis, we were often privileged to enter locations reserved only for dignitaries of foreign nations, including the underground tomb of famous Amir Timur, the renowned ruler of Bukhara. We were extremely impressed by the religious fervor of the Uzbek people and officials.

Our delegation also met with high government leaders, including the ministers of religious affairs, trade, tourism and security, as well as the governors of the provinces we toured. Our most favorable impression was of Uzbekistan's President Karimov. In a meeting at the presidential palace in Tashkent, Shaykh Nazim informed him, "You are descended from a long line of sultans of this holy land." He praised the president's extensive programs for reviving Islam and Uzbek traditional culture, and for denying militant Islamist radicals a foothold in that sacred land. President Karimov presented us with elegant gilt-edged robes reserved for champions of the nation, acknowledging Shaykh Nazim as a champion of truth in the battle against falsehood, extremism, and terror.

NORTH AMERICA

Shaykh Nazim first journeyed to North America in 1991. Though already approaching seventy, the energetic shaykh traveled to more than fifteen states, meeting with people of different religious beliefs and ethnic backgrounds, including Muslims, Christians, Jews, Sikhs, Buddhists, Hindus, Native Americans, and New Age believers. The huge outpouring of interest generated by this visit prompted the establishment of more than a dozen spiritual centers of the Naqshbandi Sufi Order across North America.

Shaykh Nazim made subsequent visits to the United States and Canada in 1993, 1996, and 1998. During each, he inaugurate many new Naqshbandi centers—a testament to the miraculous growth of the Order in the West. He also hosted two highly successful international Islamic unity conferences, the first in Los Angeles, California, and the second in Washington, D.C.

At his blessed direction, both of these events were my distinct honor to develop and oversee. Both conferences brought together an unprecedented array of religious scholars and regional leaders from all over the Muslim world who adhere to and promote classical Islam, as it was taught by Prophet Muhammad ﷺ. Moreover, these were the first Islamic conferences to introduce the traditional practices of *dhikr* and *Mawlid an-Nabi* (the celebration of the birth of Prophet Muhammad's ﷺ) to an American audience.

To each of these conferences, as to all gatherings which he attends, Shaykh Nazim brought his unique insights on current and world events, always encouraging the establishment of peace between nations and "tribes." The Washington conference opened on August 7, 1998—the day the U.S. embassies in Tanzania and Kenya were bombed. Shaykh Nazim immediately led the entire conference in publicly condemning the terrorist acts as a declaration of war against the teachings of God. At the time, his condemnation was unprecedented throughout the Muslim community in North America. His unflinching stand against terrorism was hailed in the Western media and throughout the mainstream Muslim community. To date, Shaykh Nazim remains one of the most vociferous opponents of terrorism, in all its forms, whether political, cultural, intellectual, or ideological.

The two conferences introduced Shaykh Nazim to people from all strata of American society. Some came to know him by attending these events, others through the unprecedented media coverage they received. Major news networks like CNN, BBC, C-Span and Voice of America provided in-depth coverage of these events, along with most of the nation's leading newspapers. This gave Shaykh Nazim the opportunity to share the traditional principles of classical Islam with Americans—the teachings of moderation, peace and love for all of God's creation that are at the heart of the Islamic faith. These stand in stark contrast to the way that Islam is too often portrayed in the American media.

While attending the conference in Los Angeles in 1996, the shaykh also worked to build bridges with other faith communities and draw attention to the plight of the world's suffering children by launching the "International Day of the Orphan"—an event that drew broad support from people of diverse faiths, celebrities and government representatives. That event culminated in a parade through downtown Los Angeles that was attended by thousands of people from all walks of life.

Through these and other efforts, thousands of Americans have embraced Islam and the teachings of the Naqshbandi Order.

ON THE WORLD STAGE

In 1999, Shaykh Nazim was elected to a five-year term as co-president of the World Conference on Religion and Peace (WCRP), a world body that addresses issues of religious leadership, interfaith initiatives, and collaborative efforts towards peaceful conflict resolution. Through his role at WCRP, Shaykh Nazim has been consulted on matters of Islamic Law and its various applications in contemporary society. He has also been the Muslim voice at a variety of WCRP-sponsored events.

In 2000, Shaykh Nazim was honored to represent a large segment of the Muslim community at the United Nations Millennium Peace Summit in New York. Shaykh Nazim led an impressive delegation to the three-day summit, where he addressed several issues critical to building strong societies and the spread of traditional, peace-loving Islam. He also led participants in the traditional Naqshbandi *dhikr*.

Modernity and globalization

In the paper "Naqshbandiyya in Damascus" Leif Stenberg writes about how followers of Shaykh Nazim use modern technology to spread his teachings:

> Many educated people leave the Muslim world to study and often eventually to settle in the West. As a result of this, and the ease with which information is conveyed globally today, western concepts of organization, use of technology and the modern work ethic are now entering the Muslim world at a faster rate than in the past. Shaykh Nazim, in his role as leader of the order, has given the ijtihad that the adoption of western methodologies and technology is useful, particularly in the area of religious teaching and propagation.

Given that many of Shaykh Nazim's followers are Westerners this has resulted in a tremendous leveraging of information technology and Western methods of teaching and transmittal by the *tariqah* in spreading the shaykh's teachings. This can be seen in the proliferation of videotapes, audio tapes, CDs, DVDs, magazines, brochures and books by Shaykh Nazim with translations into nearly every language of the western world, as well as the adaption of conventions, conferences, seminars and training workshops to the spiritual teachings of the Naqshbandiyya. [119]

Grandshaykh's Predictions Concerning Shaykh Nazim

Before Grandshaykh Abd Allah ad-Daghestani passed away, he finalized his will, which he entrusted to the author and his brother, Shaykh Adnan:

> By the order of the Prophet ﷺ, I have trained and lifted up my successor, Nazim Effendi, and put him through many seclusions, and trained him in severe training, and I am assigning him to be my successor. I see that in the future he will spread this Order through the East and the West. God will make all kinds of people, rich and poor, scholars and politicians, come to him, learn from him and take the Naqshbandi Order, at the end of the twentieth century and the beginning of the twenty-first century. It will spread all over the world, such that not one continent will be devoid of its sweet scent.
>
> I see him establishing and founding a huge headquarters in London, through which he will spread the Naqshbandi Way to Europe, the Far East, and America. He will spread sincerity, love, piety, harmony, and happiness among people. All shall leave behind ugliness, terrorism, and politics. He will spread the knowledge of peace within the heart, the knowledge of peace within communities, the knowledge of peace between nations, in order that wars and struggles will be taken away from this world and peace will become the dominating factor. I am seeing young people running to him from everywhere, asking for his blessings. He will show them the way to keep their obligations in the

---

119 Leif Stenberg, "Naqshbandiyya in Damascus: Strategies to establish and strengthen the order in a changing society," published in *Naqshbandis in Western and Central Asia*, Edited by Elisabeth Ozdalga (Curzon Press, 1997) p. 106.

Islamic tradition, to be moderate, to live in peace with everyone of every religion, to leave hatred and enmity. Religion is for God and God is the judge of His servants.

That prediction has come to pass, just as Grandshaykh Abd Allah described it. His teachings continue to spread to all parts of Europe, North Africa, Southern Africa, the Gulf countries, the Americas— both North and South—the Indian subcontinent, Southeast Asia, Russia and parts of China, Japan, Malaysia, Indonesia, Singapore, Australia, and New Zealand.

His Followers

You cannot find in the countries we have named and countries we have not named a place where the touch of Shaykh Nazim is not felt. This is what differentiates him from all saints that are living now and all saints that came before. You find all languages spoken in his presence. Every year, in the month of Ramadan, a huge gathering of his followers convenes in London, with more than 5,000 people attend from all over the world. As God said, *"We made you nations and tribes that you might know one another."* (49:13)

His followers come from all walks of life. You find the poor, the middle class, the wealthy, the businessman, the doctor, the lawyer, the psychiatrist, the astronomer, the plumber, the carpenter, ministers of government, politicians, senators, parliament members, prime ministers, presidents, kings, sultans, and royalty of all ranks—each attracted to his simplicity, his smile, his light, and to his spirituality. That is why he is known as the multi-colored, universal shaykh.

Shaykh Nazim's sayings and associations have been collected and published in many books, including the "Sufi Wisdom" series, and number more than thirty-five titles. They have been translated into many languages and are distributed throughout the world. His spiritual lectures and gatherings are preserved on hundreds of audio and video tapes, and each year brings new talks, new books, new tapes and new videos. ۞

Burial Places of the Masters of the Golden Chain

Prophet Muhammad Ibn Abd Allah ﷺ	Madinah
Abu Bakr As-Siddiq ؓ	Madinah
Salman Al-Farsi ؓ	Jerusalem
Qasim ibn Muhammad ibn Abu Bakr ق	Qudayd (near Madinah)
Jafar As-Sadiq ؑ	Madinah
Tayfur Abu Yazid al-Bistami ق	Damascus or Bistam
Abul Hasan Ali Al-Kharqani ق	Kharqan (near Bistam)
Abu Ali Al-Farmadi at-Tusi ق	Farmad (near Tus)
Abu Yaqub Yusuf al-Hamadani ق	Merv
Abul Abbas al-Khidr ؑ	
Abd al-Khaliq al-Ghujdawani ق	Ghujdawan (near Bukhara)
Arif Ar-Riwakri ق	Riwakar (near Ghujdawan)
Khwaja Mahmud Al-Injir Al-Faghnawi ق	Qilit (near Bukhara)
Ali Ar-Ramitani ق	Khwarazm (near Bukhara)
Muhammad Baba As-Samasi ق	Samas (near Bukhara)
Sayyid Amir Kulal ق	Sukhar (near Bukhara)
Muhammad Bahauddin Shah Naqshband ق	Bukhara
Alauddin Al-Attar ق	Jaganyan (near Bukhara)
Yaqub Al-Charkhi ق	Hulgatun
Nasir Ad-Din Ubayd Allah Al-Ahrar ق	Kaman Kashan (near Samarqand)
Muhammad Az-Zahid ق	Samarqand
Darwish Muhammad ق	Samarqand
Muhammad Khwaja Al-Amkanaki ق	Shash
Muhammad Al-Baqi Billah ق	Delhi
Ahmad Al-Faruqi As-Sirhindi ق	Sirhind
Muhammad Al-Masum ق	Sirhind
M. Sayfuddin Al-Faruqi Al-Mujaddidi ق	Sirhind
Sayyid Nur Muhammad Al-Badawani ق	Lahore
Shamsuddin Habib Allah ق	Cafevyan
Abd Allah Ad-Dahlawi ق	Delhi
Khalid Al-Baghdadi ق	Damascus
Ismail Muhammad Shirwani ق	Amasya
Khas Muhammad Shirwani ق	Damascus
Muhammad Effendi Al-Yaraghi ق	Sughur (Daghestan)
Jamaluddin Al-Ghumuqi Al-Husayni ق	Istanbul
Abu Ahmad As-Sughuri ق	Sughur (Daghestan)
Abu Muhammad Al-Madani ق	Rashadiya (Gunekoy)
Sharafuddin Ad-Daghestani ق	Rashadiya (Gunekoy)
Abd Allah Al-Faiz Ad-Daghestani ق	Damascus

Academic Research on the Naqshbandiyya-Haqqaniyya Order

The Scientific Observation of Spirituality

Shaykh Nazim and the Haqqani branch of the Naqshbandiyya have been the subject of many research studies by Western academics from a variety of perspectives—not the least of them being the shaykh's emphasis on traditional Islamic teachings of love, compassion, tolerance, respect and peace which are sharply at odds with the many other Islamic figures of renown today.

In this section we will present excerpts from a number of research studies of Shaykh Nazim and the Naqshbandiyya-Haqqaniyya order without comment. This represents only a sampling of papers written about the shaykh and his *tariqah,* and many others are available for the assiduous researcher. Unless highlighted in **bold**, footnotes are the authors' own. For brevity, some footnotes have been eliminated or shortened. In order to maintain consistency we have conformed the spellings of names and transliterations to the standard used throughout this book and we have added informative headings in addition to those provided by the author, where appropriate.

Harvard University

The Naqshbandiyya in the United States

Dr. Annabelle Bottcher, has written several papers which discuss the Naqshbandi Order and its role in Islamic renewal in the Middle East as well as its growing influence in the West. In a talk delivered at the Sorbonne[120], and later at the Middle Eastern Studies Department of Harvard University in the year 2000, Dr. Bottcher, presented her research into the Naqshbandi-Haqqaniyya Order under Shaykh Nazim, with a particular focus on the order's work in the United States. We present excerpts from the article here:

> The activities and the structures of the Order of the Naqshbandis in United States are inseparable from the situation of Muslims in the country. In 1997, the number of Muslims living in the United States was estimated at between 5 and 8 million persons. The descendants of black slaves constituted the first layer of American Muslims.
>
> Between 1950 and 1960, foreign students who stayed in the United States after studying there have composed the essence of the second layer. Since the 1970's, immigration for the sake of a better living, from the Middle and Far East, Morocco, and Asia has expanded the number of Muslims on American soil. Research on Islam in the United States is relatively young, and research into the Sufis is practically nonexistent except for some brotherhoods which have begun to distribute their own research and to publish from their own publishing houses. Certain Sufi circles and orders were created by people who came to the United States to study and then chose to stay. In other cases, it was Americans who studied in the Islamic world and accepted the *tariqah* of a shaykh and then came back to the United States...

---

[120] **Bottcher, Annabelle, "La Naqshbandiyya aux États-Unis," (paper presented at a seminar, at l'Ecole Pratique des Hautes Etudes, Section Religieuse, Sorbonne, Paris, March 28 2000).**

The adaptation of Sufi Islam on American soil is a strange phenomenon, and very interesting. It seems to me, although it is only a hypothesis, that spiritual Islam in the United States is more intellectual than in the "old" Islamic world. I use this term to describe a rational approach rather than pure experience. American Sufism seems to lack a popular base for spreading through the population. Americans who adopt spiritual Islam are frequently white Americans—academics of the Middle Class.

It is necessary to draw a distinction between spirituality inspired by Sufism and Islamic spirituality. In certain groups, the conversion to Islam is not mandatory. The flexibility of Sufism seems more attractive to new converts than the Salafi Islam inspired by Wahhabism.

There is a large variety of *tariqahs* (*turuq*) originating in Pakistan, the Middle East, Indonesia, China, Turkey, etc. I propose to examine a case study from the Naqshbandiyya of the United States: the Haqqani-Naqshbandi of Shaykh Nazim al-Qubrusi al-Haqqani, of which you must certainly have heard...

The Haqqaniyya

Surely you have all heard talk of the Haqqaniyya of Shaykh Nazim al-Qubrusi al-Haqqani, a Cypriot Shaykh whose central point is in Lefke, close to the border between the North and the South of the island. For several decades, this *tariqah* has enjoyed an immense success on the international level. In the town of Freiburg in Breisgau, where I have performed most of my study, we are accustomed to the turbaned disciples of this Shaykh. It was not only in Lebanon and later in the United States that I was made to realize that this *tariqah* could make an excellent case study for those who seek to understand the order's global Islamic revival. I mean by this the growth of an order that surpasses its regional and national origin.

The Haqqaniyya is a branch of the Naqshbandiyya-Mojaddidiyya-Khalidiyya.[121]

Its manner of presenting Sufism attracts a large audience everywhere in the world and notably in the West. When one asks these shaykhs about the secret of their success, they always respond that it is the Grace and *Barakah* of Allah, the Grace of God. It's certain that Microsoft's Bill Gates or CNN's Ted Turner owe equally a part of their success to the *barakah* of Allah, but this is not a sufficient explanation. Apart from intangible factors at the sociological and psychological level, we can distinguish three other closely-related aspects which explain this success:

- the charisma of the Shaykh
- the structure of the orders and their capacity for absorbing diverse nationalities, ethnicities, and beliefs, and
- the message of the Shaykh, which creates cohesion of the order

...The order is very firmly entrenched in the Near East and includes several thousand disciples in India and in England.

The Charisma of the Shaykh

...Even if Shaykh Nazim is a Cypriot Shaykh with a limited experience of Cyprus and the Near East, more than half of his disciples come from Europe, Asia (notably from Malaysia and Sri Lanka) or from the United States. Gradually, the order took an international dimension, with great success and millions of *muhibbun* (adherents – lit. "lovers").

...Women are a part of the Haqqaniyya *tariqah,* but unfortunately their role is still a little bit in the shadow of what it is presented in historiography as the past. However, Hajji Anne, the wife of Shaykh

---

[121] For more information on the Naqshbandiyya, see for example: Muhammad Ahmad al-Durnaiqa, *Al-tariqa al-naqshbandiyya wa-alamuha,* (Beirut 1987); Marc Gaborieau, Alexandre Popovic, Thierry Zarcone, eds. *Naqshbandis* (Istanbul: ISIS, 1990).

Nazim, plays an important role in *dawah.*[122] She is the head of a considerable women's movement. It is said that in England, her disciples number even more than her husband's. The German branch of the Haqqaniyya has a Gorski & Spohr publication house situated at Bonndorf in the Black Forest. They published, in 1997, a book of Amina Adil's, titled, *Gaben des Lichts. Geschichten aus dem Leben des Propheten*. The success of this Naqshbandi order in the West is therefore founded also on the capacity to integrate female disciples by offering them an attractive and charismatic model.

The Structure of the Order

The Haqqaniyya has a pyramid, hierarchical structure. The influence of the Shaykh on the life of his disciples depends on the intensity of their affiliation. For the students (*muridun*) who have taken *bayah* with the Shaykh, the relationship is much more intimate than for the "*muhibbun,*" who remain at the periphery of the brotherhood. For a *murid,* his shaykh is a spiritual father. His spiritual affiliation becomes more important than the biological relation with his parents. The charisma and the message of the Shaykh play an eminent role in *dawah,* the mission-work of Islam. The structure of a brotherly order reflects this mix of charisma and message... For me, the relation between the Shaykh and the disciple is based on this exchange of loyalty of the disciple against the "religious product or message" of the Shaykh. If, as is the case with Shaykh Nazim, the disciples are from multiple ethnic, national, and confessional backgrounds, his personality and his presentation of Islam correspond to their needs. If a Malaysian prince and an Oxford professor find the Haqqaniyya equally attractive, the attraction of this "Islamic product," has a global appeal.

It is definitely risky to make a comparison with the satisfaction of pleasure that can follow the consumption of a pair of Levis, a Prada purse, a bottle of Coca-Cola, or the music of Nuzrat Fatih Ali Khan, but it is of the same type. I do not consider whether there was a

---

[122] Hoda Boyer, "From Azhar to Oak Park," in: Steven Barboza, *American Jihad: Islam after Malcolm* X (New York/London: Doubleday, 1994) p.26.

period of "adaptation to the international market" for Shaykh Nazim, but he has succeeded in presenting his Sufi message to a very varied audience. The message and its presentation apart, the structure of the order plays an essential role for the integration of the disciples. *Dawah* attracts the curiosity of people, who come sporadically to listen, watch, and participate. In his *dawah*, Shaykh Nazim has in his relationships what Larry Posten in his book, *Islamic Dawah in the West*" has called the "lifestyle approach," an indirect form of spreading the message by his way of life.[123] At the same time, his method also represents a direct approach by verbal and written communication of his message. At the beginning one attracts individuals by attracting their curiosity. Then there is a dynamic in the order which has as its goal the solid inclusion of all the elements of the periphery. For this, the authority of the Shaykh has to be accepted. Sufism is not necessarily based on strong exoteric expertise. It is possible that an unlettered shaykh like Grandshaykh Abd Allah al-Faizi ad-Daghestani attracts disciples based on his esoteric knowledge and his "*karamat*," his ability to produce miracles. The miracles seem to play a decisive role in the motivation of a potential disciple.

Another characteristic that contributes to the success of an order is the capacity of the shaykh to direct the order and its components, that is to say his ability to manage human resources. Shaykh Nazim has a great deal of experience in *irshad*, knows how to put together, intelligently and with great finesse, the intellectual and spiritual resources of his disciples. The leadership in each country is based on the team of a shaykh and his wife, the two cooperating in *dawah*, something not necessarily visible from the exterior.

The existence of a large variety of talents and ideas makes of this enterprise a veritable think-tank. There is among the Haqqaniyya an entire organization of very well-educated technocrats. If one sees the national branches of the Haqqaniyya one will readily admit that they are very active in the domain of publication. In Germany, the

---

[123] Larry Posten, *Islamic Dawah in the West: Muslim Missionary Activity and the Dynamics of Conversion to Islam* (New York/Oxford: Oxford University Press, 1992) p.4.

Publishing House, "Gorski & Spohr" publishes a review Der Morgenstern and a large number of books of very high quality. In the United States, The Muslim Magazine has been published quarterly since 1998.

Another highly developed strategy is the involvement of individuals possessing financial and political resources, who often are accompanied by their families and clans. So Shaykh Nazim has guarded the loyalty of a group from the Kabbani family of Tripoli, Lebanon, and has been able thereby to establish the *tariqah* in that city. The Kabbani family is very well-anchored in the Sunni and Sufi milieu of the Near East, and plays an important role in the top management of the order. I want to just mention two prominent members of this clan, who are not disciples of Shaykh Nazim; Shaykh Rashid Kabbani, the Mufti of Lebanon, and Marwan Kabbani, the director of the Sunni *awqaf* (religious foundations) in the administration of *Dar al-Fatwa*.

After the death of Shaykh Abd Allah , the brothers Adnan and Hisham Kabbani decided to follow the leadership of Shaykh Nazim . The rest of the family, disciples of Ibrahim al-Ghalayini[124] and of Abul Khayr al-Midani[125] rejoined (the lineage of) Abd Allah Daghestani later. The family turned from the Kurdish Shafii Naqshbandiyya to the Caucasian Shafii Naqshbandiyya.

The Kabbani brothers' mother was a disciple of Shaykh Salih Koftaro, the uncle of the current Grand Mufti of Syria. It was probably also with the Kabbani family that the Haqqaniyya was established in

---

[124] Born 1300/1882 in Damascus to a poor family; worked in the market; began to study; took tariqa from Shaykh Isa al-Kurdi; became *khatib, imam,* and *Mufti* of Qatana in 1330/1911; died 1377/1958. See: Muti al-Hafiz, Nizar Abaza, *Tarikh ulama Dimashq fil-qarn al-rabi ashr al-hijri* (Damascus: Dar al-Fikr, 1361-1405) vol. 2, p. 687-692.

[125] Born in Midan in 1293/1875 to a poor family, studied with the Rashidiyya and Anbar, then in Istanbul; student of Shaykh Salim al-Masuti, then of Shaykh Abd al-Hakim al-Afghani, and then of Shaykh Isa al-Kurdi; married the daughter of Shaykh Isa; died 1380/1961. See: Muti al-Hafiz, Nizar Abaza, *Tarikh ulama Dimashq fil qarn al-rabi ashr al-hijri* (Damascus: Dar al-Fikr, 1361-1405) vol. 2, p. 720-732. A more detailed biography by Muhammad Riyad al-Malih, precedes the text of Khalid al-Mujaddidi al-Naqshbandi, *Jaliyat al-akdar wal-sayf al-battar fil-salat ala al-Mukhtar* (ed. Muhammad Abul-Khayr al-Midani, Damascus 1967) p. 5-13.

Tripoli. And it was from Lebanon that the Haqqaniyya have been able to establish themselves in the US.

When I did my field-research between 1998 and 1999 in Lebanon, the situation was as follows: Shaykh Adnan Kabbani and Shaykh Mustafa Alayli were the major Naqshbandi shaykhs in Lebanon. The latter comes from a family of *ulama* with a strong reputation in Lebanon. Shaykh Hisham Kabbani, the brother of Shaykh Adnan, became the deputy of Shaykh Nazim in the United States. While Shaykh Nazim has a discreet and indirect approach in his *dawah*, the American Haqqani Shaykh prefers the direct approach, using the media, print, and audio-visual materials. For his *dawah* he has adopted modern marketing strategies following the rules of American *capitalism*, redistributing some of his resources within the order.

The Structure of the Organization in the United States

The leader of the American branch, Shaykh Hisham, has a double background in Natural Sciences and Islamic Sciences. He studied chemistry at the American University in Beirut and medicine at Louvain in Belgium. He also studied in Damascus…

He married Naziha Adil al-Haqqani al-Qubrusi, the eldest daughter of Shaykh Nazim. In 1991 the couple received green cards to emigrate to the United States where Shaykh Hisham was named *khalifah* for leading Islamic *dawah*.

They began with an ambitious project of constructing a Sufi religious enterprise, well-structured around several different foundations, and with the help of a strong presence on the Internet. We will discuss it next week during a seminar course on Sufis and the Internet. This American branch made remarkable progress over the years with development and foundation of 23 Sufi centers in the United States and Canada.[126] The head office located near a large farm, is located in Fenton, Michigan. The residence of the couple is in Los Altos in

---

[126] For Montreal see: Mark Abley, "Sufi's Choice, a mystical tradition in Islam is finding wide appeal," The Gazette (Montreal, 22 October, 1994) online.

California; and in the capitol, Washington DC the organization has a lobbying office.

I will try to describe the structure of this religious enterprise, according to the presentation that is made on the Internet and in its publications, not all of which I have read. I have not had the opportunity to have direct contact except for a short visit in Washington, DC, where Shaykh Hisham received me....

One branch of the Haqqani Foundation in California with Shaykh Nazim as its leader, serves as an official headquarters. The blueprint for this structure are in fact classical in origin and comparable to movements in the Middle East. These last are based legally on a *jamiyya khairiyya* with diverse *dawah* activities. The different activities are distributed among education, charity work, and the distribution of the traditional Islamic message. They are of course very well imbricated. The presentation on the Internet of the *tariqah* is that of an international didactic foundation, whose vocation is the promotion of peace, tolerance, and respect as foundations of the Islamic faith. According to the website, the mission of the foundation is the diffusion of Sufi teachings. The Haqqanis engage themselves in this domain using modern methods like the Internet and the radio, along with traditional methods such as circles of *dhikr* and the spiritual development of *muridun* and *muhibbun* (students and seekers). The *tariqah* attempts to inform and influence both the Muslim and non-Muslim public. Its interest in regional politics in states and towns and in national and international American politics is, I think, a novelty in the milieu of American Muslims, and follows the strategies of other ethnic and religious groups. The interest in political affairs is a characteristic of the Naqshbandis, who have always in the past been involved in politics, and also in the present as we have seen in Syria and Lebanon and elsewhere.

The Haqqaniyya are at the same time an economic organization. They sell books, audio-visual materials like videos and CD's, rosaries, and perfume. Recently they began to sell products like waterproof socks (*khuffs*). We are seeing that the Haqqaniyya are trying to profit from their Internet presence by making links to large organizations like CVS.

According to their own descriptions, the Haqqani enterprise is subdivided into many "branches:"

- As-Sunna Foundation of America (ASFA)
- Kamilat (for women and families)
- Islamic Supreme Council of America (ISCA)

...According to their description, As-Sunna Foundation of America (ASFA) occupies itself primarily with the promotion of knowledge of the different schools of *fiqh* (*madhahib*). According to ASFA, the stability of these *madhahib* guarantees at the same time the stability and the cohesion of the *Ummah*. ASFA has published a number of books on fiqh, like the very well-made seven-volume *The Encyclopedia of Islamic Doctrine*. Several institutions, like al-Azhar in Egypt, the Supreme Council of Singapore (Majlis al-Ugama Singapura), ...a university in London and one in Lahore, Pakistan, ...are all affiliated with ASFA. On the As-Sunna Foundation website, one finds a biography of Shaykh Hisham Kabbani and a list of biographies of ulama and saints which we will discuss later during the seminar on Sufis on the Internet.

Kamilat is the organization of women under the Haqqani umbrella formed in 1997 by Shaykh Hisham, whose main center is in Fenton, Michigan. Kamilat works in various towns and treats questions relating to the family, children, their health, schools, marriage in Islam, and problems of domestic violence. These are the classic female subjects, which face a traditional public. Kamilat even provides information on the political campaign which intends to introduce a stamp for the commemoration of the month of Ramadan in the United States. Kamilat offers cultural sensitivity training seminars for private and public institutions. It works with families and refugees—for example people (refugees) from Bosnia.

This type of work is also done by another branch of the Haqqaniyya, ... an organization which helps refugees and orphans. This organization works with fundraising, which is done in the traditional fashion – by letter and email. The magazine The Muslim Magazine is published four times per year.... [of which] Shaykh Hisham is the president...

Shaykh Hisham also founded the Islamic Supreme Council of America (ISCA), to "put into practice and to structure the understanding in the United States of the revealed Islamic law according to officially accepted doctrine." In effect, this is the political branch of the American Haqqaniyya.

The Political Message

The Haqqaniyya have made themselves known in North America by their tense relations with those known as the Wahhabis. Even if Sufism and the "Salafi" Islam of Wahhabi inspiration only rarely maintain cordial relations, the polemic against Wahhabism is presented everywhere in the writings of the American branch. In January 1999, this culminated in a declaration by Shaykh Hisham Kabbani at the State Department in Washington, DC. In the course of this debate, organized by the State Department on the theme, "The Evolution of Extremism: a Viable Threat to US National Security," Shaykh Hisham criticized the degree of influence of Wahhabis in the mosques and in American institutions. ۞

University of Birmingham

A Study of an International Sufi Order of Naqshbandi Shaykh Nazim al-Haqqani

The United Kingdom's Economic and Social Research Council has funded a project entitled "A Study of an International Sufi Order of Naqshbandi Shaykh Nazim al-Haqqani", spanning the years 1998-2001. The 1.5 million dollar study of Shaykh Nazim and the *tariqah* that he leads was conducted over the three-year period by four research professors from the University of Birmingham's Department of Theology and the Center for Study of Islam and Muslim-Christian Relations. We quote portions here from the study's description.[127]

Description of the the Project

> The main aim of this project is to broaden our understanding of how Islam functions across boundaries of states, communities and ethnic groups. While contemporary research attention on Islam has concentrated on its political expressions, the Sufi tradition continues to be important for the majority of Muslims. Through a hierarchical chain of adherence to the spiritual leader, or shaykh, the Sufi orders (*tariqas*) link local communities across many different regions. One of the more ubiquitous of such contemporary tariqas is that led by Shaykh Nazim al-Qubrusi al-Haqqani. With roots in the Ottoman empire and especially in the Caucasus, it now has centres in North America, Britain and most of western Europe, the Middle East and South and Southeast Asia. The *tariqah* has had particular success in attracting converts from outside Islam and among young educated professionals in the Muslim world. Communications play a significant role in maintaining the

---

[127] Website: "Transnational Sufism: Ethnicity, politics and transnational Islam: A study of an international Sufi Order", Economic and Social Research Council; Selly Oak Colleges; Centre for the Study of Islam & Christian-Muslim Relations at the Department of Theology University of Birmingham, URL: http://www.transcomm.ox.ac.uk/wwwroot/nielsen.htm and http://artsweb.bham.ac.uk/mdraper/transnatsufi/.

cohesion of this transnational network and the *tariqah* makes extensive use of all forms of media publication including a notable presence on the Internet managed from the U.S. Through fieldwork and a detailed analysis of texts the project aims to develop an understanding of how and with what degree of success a form of Muslim organisation, which is central to traditional Islam, is able to adjust to rapidly changing contemporary environments, to establish the significance of modern electronic communications relative to more traditional media, and to up-date and refine our knowledge of how Sufi forms of Islam function locally and transnationally.

Methodology/study design

The project will be based on ethnographic and anthropological fieldwork running concurrently in three locations. In parts of the northern Caucasus, the *tariqah* exists in a more or less traditional form, which is now relating actively to the post-Soviet weakening of the central state and general economic and political instability. In Lebanon, the *tariqah* has grown significantly in the years following the end of the civil war and, with fast-growing telecommunications links, could be seen as being in a state of transition. In Britain, the *tariqah* has a number of centres some with a mainly ethnic minority following, others with a multi-ethnic composition including significant numbers of converts. Texts in a variety of media forms will also be gathered in the three locations together with a regular survey and recording of materials on the Internet. These will be analysed in terms of content, audience and the circumstances of their production and in relation to the fieldwork results.

Academic and policy implications

The interdisciplinary nature of such study of religious organisation is likely to raise a number of theoretical issues to do with the interaction between ideas and organisation and how far a shared community can function with different discourses. The project will contribute to a broadening of our understanding of contemporary transnational Islamic organisations and thus assist policy makers, the media, and agencies working with Muslim communities in reaching better informed policies and practices.

The Sufi *tariqahs* have historically been one of the most important channels for the social expression of the transregional nature of Islam. Through a hierarchical chain of adherence to the Shaykh, they constituted a network linking local communities across geographical, political and ethnic boundaries. Having traditionally found their membership through social networks of trade, profession and clan, the *tariqas* went into apparently irreversible decline with the economic and social upheavals associated with colonialism and global economic integration. However, during the last two to three decades it has become clear that the decline has been reversed. *Tariqahs* have re-established themselves and are thriving both in traditionally Muslim regions and among the more recently settled Muslim communities of western Europe and North America. In the process they have changed and are continuing to do so. They have adapted to new state structures constructed over the last century and, in that sense, have become transnational. They are redefining their relationships with the communities in which they live, possibly redefining communities with reference to themselves, as well as creating new communities which are sometimes radically different in constitution and structure from the traditional ones. They are in some areas making use of modern communications technologies, which impacts on the lines and nature of authority within the *tariqah*. Throughout they appear to be able to preserve roots in the communities of believers, distinguishing themselves from the more publicly visible 'fundamentalist' movements whose programmes tend to be heavily political in character.

One of the more widespread *tariqahs* is the one led by Shaykh Nazim al-Qubrusi al-Haqqani (born 1922). Part of the larger Naqshbandi tradition it differs from the mainstream, which traces its antecedents to Central Asia, by finding its roots via the eastern parts of the Ottoman empire, especially the Caucasus. Shaykh Nazim was sent by his shaykh, Abd Allah ad-Daghestani, to London in the early 1970s to establish the *tariqah* in the West. His active following is now among the largest and most international of the Sufi *tariqahs*, with centres in North America, Britain and most of western Europe, the Middle East, South and South East Asia. The *tariqah* has had particular success in attracting converts from outside Islam and among educated professionals, men and women, within the Muslim world.

The *tariqah* is organized in the form of local or regional centres, each led by a *khalifah*, or deputy to the Shaykh. However, the organizational structure is loose with varying levels of active membership, and individual khalifas have been known to exceed the bounds of their authority. Doctrinally, Shaykh Nazim particularly emphasizes the personal struggle with the ego, which may account for some of his appeal to a western audience which has been familiar with the mystical discourses of theosophical traditions. Shaykh Nazim lays great emphasis on the coming of the Mahdi as a warning of the imminence of the last days, a theme which has regularly provoked controversy within the *tariqah* and with its opponents. The legal tradition (*madhhab*) of the movement is an unusual integration of the two main traditional law schools, so followers regularly have to look to the Shaykh for guidance. There are implications here for a comparative sociology of religion in terms of the tensions between an individual commitment and a collective commitment to a religious community.

The coherence of such a *tariqah* would be expected to depend on a number of elements. These should include adherence to the authority of the Shaykh and the shared teaching and rite. On the other hand, Sufi *tariqahs* have survived major changes over the centuries by being flexible and able to adapt. The extreme variety among the following of Shaykh Nazim is evidence of this. Communications play a significant role in maintaining this cohesion, and the *tariqah* makes extensive use of all media possibilities, including audio- and videotapes, leaflets, posters, magazines and books. Some parts of the *tariqah* maintain an internet presence which is regularly attacked by opponents.

The project plans to seek answers to the key questions by researching the *tariqah* in three of its centres of activity:

In the northern Caucasus Islam has been dominated by Sufi *tariqahs* since the 15th century. The Naqshbandis became pre-eminent in a society which continues to exhibit the characteristics of traditional segmentary ethnic and kinship networks. Before and after the Soviet era, the *tariqahs* have played a significant role in defending local interests against Russian intrusion, whether by resistance or by co-operative manipulation. *Tariqahs* today are closely associated with the revival of local ethnic politics in a region where the centralized state has become weak and where alternative trends of Islam are being actively propagated.

In Lebanon Sufi *tariqahs* traditionally played a significant role in linking the urban commercial and rural landowning sectors with particularly strong bases in the coastal cities. With increasing integration into an interregional cash economy and the growth of the financial and service sectors, especially in Beirut, the orders lost much of their influence. The collapse of the Lebanese state during fifteen years of civil war, coinciding with the regional resurgence of Islam, gave the *tariqas* a new lease of life as a focus of order and stability. Post-war developments have encouraged further growth in which Shaykh Nazim's *tariqah* has also taken part, and one of the shaykh's sons-in-law are Lebanese. With the modernisation of telecommunications, Lebanese participation in the *tariqah*'s internet presence is growing.

The *tariqah* is relatively new in Britain dating from Shaykh Nazim's arrival here in the early 1970s. It has a strong presence in London, Birmingham and Sheffield, with smaller centres elsewhere. The London centres have attracted a multi-ethnic following with significant numbers of converts, including many women. The Birmingham centre is primarily an ethnically based group attracting a Pakistani British following.

Focuses of Research

In each of these areas the project will need to investigate how the *tariqah* manifests itself. This will involve relating its history and membership. Local research will need to determine how the *tariqah* defines itself and is defined in relationship to its environment and to other Muslim groups locally as well as more widely. How does the *tariqah*, itself experiencing significant growth, relate to the phenomenon of international Islamic resurgence and 'political' Islam? This is a question which needs to be viewed from both a local and an overall perspective. The research team expects to be working with the local fieldwork evidence and the textual evidence of published materials, including that published electronically, to find answers to further questions. How do the internal communications work? How do practices differ from theories of organisation and structures of authority? What is the meaning and content of membership of the *tariqah* for its adherents?

The project will be concerned with content, context, and process, so the methods for collection and use of data will be qualitative rather than quantitative. Data collection will take three forms. Field work involving in-depth interviews with representative participants, key personalities and observers, will be supplemented by analysis of texts and recording of contemporary events. The interdisciplinary nature of the research and the experience of applying this to a religious group will raise issues of theory and methodology.

The research team has been constituted so as to facilitate access and combine the various skills required both for the field work and for the theoretical parts of the project. Apart from the principal researchers, the team includes two people responsible for the field work in Britain, one of them on a full-time basis, while two part-time researchers have been recruited locally for the research in the northern Caucasus and in Lebanon. As part of the management of a complex project, an advisory group has been appointed selected to represent the main academic interests, religious organizations, the press, international cultural and development policy as a well as a member nominated by Shaykh Nazim.

Howard University

Relationship Between Religious Practices and Adaptation of Immigrant Sufi Muslims in the United States

In 2003, Zulkarnain Ahmad Hatta, a student at Howard University, wrote his PhD dissertation on "Relationship Between Religious Practices and Adaptation of Immigrant Sufi Muslims in the United States" and chose as the subject of his study members of the Naqshbandi-Haqqani *tariqah*. We present portions of this research in following pages.[128]

Literature Review

> ...in reviewing the literature on adaptation, assimilation, and integration, there is a glaring absence of one particular factor – the influence of religion. Cox noted that researchers are generally reluctant to focus on general cultural background, of which religion is a subset.[129] Alkhazraji made a similar observation in his study on immigrants' cultural adaptation in the American workplace, i.e., stressing the need to investigate the effect of religion on the adaptation process.[130] Since religion is a significant aspect of the lives of immigrants, it is imperative to look into religion as a variable when trying to understand the migration phenomenon...
>
> Haddad and Lumms in their research found that some Muslims feared that assimilation would jeopardize the maintenance of their Islamic values...[131] The literature reviewed illustrates that the question for

---

[128] **Hatta, Zulkarnain Ahmad, "Relationship Between Religious Practices and Adaptation of Immigrant Sufi Muslims in the United States," PhD Dissertation (Howard University, 2003) p. 41.**

[129] Cox, D. R. *Religion and Welfare* (Department of Social Studies, University of Melbourne, 1982).

[130] Alkhazraji, K. M. *Immigrants and cultural adaptation in the American workplace. A study of Muslim employees* (New York and London: Garland Publishing, Inc., 1997).

[131] Haddad, Y. Y. & Lummis, A. T. *Islamic values in the United States* (New York: Oxford University Press, 1987).

immigrant Muslims is to what extent one should adapt to American society without losing Islamic values. As has been discussed above, if Islam is a religion that does not confine its practice to one part of the world, then the fear of losing one's values in a new land should not be a major issue because the religion allows for a harmonious co-existence with other cultures, norms and values.[132] Based on Islamic world view, the issue of losing one's faith, culture and values because of exposure to new cultures and values is unwarranted[133].[134]

...In a comparative study of Hindus, Sikhs and Muslims who assimilated in the United Kingdom, Muslims showed the most resistance to assimilation.[135] The resistance is in part influenced by the perception among them that for every degree of cultural and structural assimilation they undertake, something from their old ways of lifestyle will erode[136].[137]

Muslim immigrants in the U.S. are faced with tremendous ambivalence. Generally they are happy with the new-found freedom; nonetheless, they are not too sure how to negotiate that freedom with their inherited values. The anxiety of losing inherited values seems to be a consuming preoccupation that would impede their adaptation process[138].[139]

---

[132] Denny, Frederick M. "Islamic theology in the New World: Some issues and prospects." *Journal of the American Academy of Religion, 62,* no.4 (Winter 1994), pp. 1069-1084.

[133] Nazim, M. *Pure hearts* (London: Healing Hearts/Zero Productions, 1998).

[134] **Hatta, *Op. cit.,* p. 44.**

[135] Stopes-Roe, M. and Cochrane, R. "The process of assimilation in Asians in Britain: a study of Hindu, Muslim and Sikh immigrants and their young children." *International Journal of Comparative Sociology, 28,* (1987) pp. 43-56.

[136] Kovacs, M. L. & Cropley, A. J. "Alienation and assimilation of immigrants." Australian Journal of Social Issues, 10, (1975) pp. 221-230.

[137] **Hatta, *Op. cit.,* p. 45.**

[138] Harris, J., *Identity: A study of the concept in education for a multicultural Australia.* Canberra: AGPS, (1980).

[139] **Hatta, *Op. cit.,* p. 46.**

Theoretical Framework

In the American context, assimilation is commonly known as "Americanization".[140] Notwithstanding the dictionary definition, there could be confusion as to the exact meaning of "assimilation." [141]

Religion fits into the framework of cultural context because the former is a pervasive component of culture.[142] According to Cox, religious systems are broader than any cultural system. Adherents of many religions argue that their concepts and dogma are beyond culture, most of them at the same time acknowledge that their belief systems and religious organizational life in any place and at any time are usually extremely culture-bound. As stated by Tillich, religion is the substance of culture, culture is the form of religion.[143] This is a most important proposition to consider when discussing the transplantation of a religious system into a new environment as a result of migration...

Most religions can function in almost any given society because of their adaptative qualities. This is especially true for Islam, as has been explained by the concept of *urf* (culture). Islam can assimilate some elements of any given culture as long as they do not contradict the Islamic laws (*Shariah*). In other words, the Shariah is able to embrace a variety of cultures even though they do not originate from an Islamic tradition. Certain traditions and values are universal and do cross paths. [144]

To place this study into the context of the broader American culture, one has to look at the concept of cultural pluralism. Cultural pluralism or multiculturalism is a theory most relevant for this research. Of the three theories, this one takes the path of tolerance and inclusiveness. It does not assume that all non-English immigrants who come to America would want to discard their cultural patterns just to be

---

[140] Borrie, W. D., *Italians and Germans in Australia* (Cheshire: Melbourne, 1954).

[141] **Hatta, *Op. cit.*, p. 51.**

[142] Cox, D. Migration/integration as a process: welfare services for migrants: can they be better planned? *International Migration Review, 23,* (1987) p. 17.

[143] Tillich, P., *Theology of culture* (New York: Oxford University Press, 1959).

[144] **Hatta, *Op. cit.*, p. 56-57.**

"Americanized".[145] It is safe to assume that all ethnic groups wish to maintain some, if not all, of their native cultural patterns... "acculturation" should be a two-way process, accomplishing the twin goals of cultural pluralism. Both the immigrants and the host learn from each other's cultural richness.[146]

Methodology

This chapter presents the methodology that was used in the investigation of this research study. It includes a review of the hypotheses, variables, research design, selection of the study population, sampling method, study instrument, methods of data collection, and finally data analysis procedures.

A theoretical framework which describes the adaptation outcome of the Naqshbandi Muslim immigrants was employed to examine: (a) the relationship between religious practice and adaptation outcome, and (b) relationships between gender, age, marital status, level of education, employment status, country/region of origin, length of stay in the United States, and number of children and adaptation outcome. The hypotheses for the study are presented as follows.

Hypotheses

Null Hypothesis 1.

There is no statistically significant relationship between the level of religious practice and the adaptation outcome of immigrant Naqshbandis in the United States.

Hypothesis 1.1.

There is a statistically significant positive relationship between religious practice and integration and separation;

- the higher the practice, the higher the integration and
- the higher the separation.

---

[145] Berry, J. W., *Understanding the process of acculturation for primaryintervention* (Kingston, Ontario: Queens College, Department of Psychology, 1987).

[146] **Hatta, *Op. cit.*, p. 63.**

Hypothesis 1.2.

There is an inverse relationship between religious practice and assimilation and marginalization; the higher the practice, the lower the assimilation and the lower the marginalization.

Null Hypothesis 2.

There is no statistically significant relationship between background characteristics as gender, employment status, education level, marital status, country/region of origin, age, length of stay in the United States and number of children and adaptation outcome.

Research Design

This study is based on the cross-sectional design. By definition, a cross-sectional study is based on observations representing a single point in time.[147] It is also a correlational study. The study attempts to describe and examine the relationship between the phenomena of religious practices and adaptation outcomes of the Naqshbandi Muslim immigrants.

STUDY POPULATION

The Muslim population in the United States is estimated at six million.[148] Within this population, the Naqshbandi immigrant population (a subset) is the focus of this study. According to the Haqqani Foundation (2000)—the parent organization of the Naqshbandi Muslims in the United States—about twenty thousand Naqshbandis live in the United States. Preliminary investigation has shown that Naqshbandi Muslims are either immigrants who have come from various countries such as Pakistan, India, Syria, Turkey, Ivory Coast, Senegal, Malaysia, Morocco and Iran, or are American converts...

---

147 Rubin, A. & Babbie, E., *Research methods for social work* (Pacific Grove, CA: Brooks/Cole Publishing Company, 2001).

148 Nyang, Sulayman S., *Islam in the United States of America* (Chicago: ABC International Group, Inc, 1999).

SAMPLING METHOD

The Haqqani Foundation, located in Fenton, Michigan, has a database of the Naqshbandi followers of Shaykh Muhammad Nazim. An extensive screening of the database was conducted based on three criteria regarding the immigrants: (a) lived in the United States for at least five years, (b) age range between 25-60 years old, and (c) from different countries and non-Americans (American converts were excluded from the sample). Only those who migrated to the United States were included. About five hundred fit the criteria. Three hundred and fifty were randomly selected from the five hundred who met the criteria for the study.[149]

THE STUDY INSTRUMENT

To measure the levels of religious practice and attitude of the subjects toward Islam and Islamic traditions, a Religious Scale (RS) designed by the Islamic Resource Institute was used with some modifications.150 The original scale had twenty-three items, measured on an ordinal Likert scale (Appendix A)... The modified scale had a reliability coefficient of .80 (Appendix B). High scores indicated high degree of religious practice and positive attitude towards the religion. [151]

Results and Discussion

This chapter presents the findings of the study from data gathered through the use of the survey instruments. Survey instruments were distributed to 350 individual Muslim immigrants belonging to the Naqshbandi *tariqah* in the United States. 204 (58.3%) of the surveys were completed and used in this study. The data obtained from these surveys were processed using the Statistical Package for Social Sciences (SPSS).

---

[149] **Hatta, *Op. cit.*, p. 81-83.**

[150] Islamic Resource Institute. (Indiana: ISNA, 1992).

[151] **Hatta, *Op. cit.*, p. 81-83.**

Summary of Research Questions, Independent Variables and Dependent Variable, and Statistical Tests

Research Questions	Indepen-dent Variables	Dependent Variable	Measurements	Statistics
1. What is the relationship between religious practice and adaptation outcome among immigrant Muslims?	Level of religious practice	Adaptation Outcome Preferred Mode of Adaptation	1. Religious Scale (RS) 2. Adaptation Scale (AS) 3. Direct Question on the Preferred Mode of Adaptation	1. Pearson r or Spearman rho 2. ANOVA or Kruskal-Wallis
2. What is the relationship between demographic variables - gender, age, education, marital status, employment, # of children, country of origin, and # of years in the U.S. and adaptation outcome?	1. Gender 2. Age 3. Level of education 4. Marital status 5. Employ ment status 6. Children 7. Country of origin 8. # of years in the U.S.		Demographic questionnaire Direct Question on the Preferred Mode of Adaptation	1. T-test or Mann-Whitney U 2. Chi-square test 3. ANOVA or Kruskal-Wallis 4. Pearson r or Spearman rho
3. What are the set of variables that best predict the adaptation outcome?	1. Level of religious practice 2. Gender 3. Age 4. Level of education 5. Marital status 6. Employ ment status 7. Children 8. Country of origin 9. # of years in the U.S.	Adaptation Outcome	Adaptation Scale	Multiple Regression

The mean age of the participants is 36 years old with a standard deviation of 8.8. The mean of their stay in the United States is 12 years with a standard deviation of 8. Of the 204 respondents, 65% were males. Seventy-seven percent (77%) of them are employed, and the vast majority (93%) have a college education. Out of those with college education, 66% had at least a bachelor's degree. In terms of marital status, 55% of the participants were married. A majority of the respondents had one child.

These findings imply that this study included both male and female respondents. While 77% were employed, that was not necessarily at 23% unemployment rate because majority of these 23% were housewives. They may had elected not to work outside their homes despite the fact that a very high percentage had college degrees.[152]

The participants came from fifty-four countries, grouped into four main regions: Sub-Continent, Middle East, Africa, and other (which included the Far East, the Americas and Europe). The Sub-Continent and Middle Eastern countries represented 50% of the participants. Twenty-five percent (25%) came from the African continent and the remaining came from either the Far East (12%), the Americas (5%) or Europe (8%).

One country within each of the six regions that had the largest group of immigrants – from the Sub-Continent most were from Pakistan (13%); from the Middle East most were from Turkey (7%); from Africa most were from Morocco (4%); from the Far East most came from Indonesia (4%); from the American continent most came from Canada (3%) and from Europe most were from Bosnia (3%). Thus, this group of respondents represented Naqshbandis from all over the world, almost equally distributed among the four regions.

LOCATION OF PARTICIPANTS IN THE UNITED STATES

The majority of the participants are concentrated in four large metropolitan—Chicago metro (30%), San Francisco Bay Area (21%), Greater Washington D.C. metro (16%), and the New York City—

[152] **Hatta, *Op. cit.*, p. 93-94.**

Newark metro (12%). Thus, this group of immigrants live predominantly in large metropolitan areas.[153]

About fifty-seven percent of the immigrants were practicing their religious duties less in their country of origin than they are now. This indicates that coming to the United States has increased their level of religious practice. The mean score of 62.3 reported for level of religious practice is above the mid-point of 49. This suggests that participants are religious in their behavior. The scores also show that the mean for the participants' adaptation outcome (65.3), is very close to the mid-point of 66. The score which is close to the mid-point, suggests that the participants have neither assimilated nor are they segregated. They tend to integrate into the host society.

MODES OF ADAPTATION

The respondents' willingness both to accept American culture and retain their original culture is reflected in their adaptation scale score. Most of the respondents gravitate around the median (65), indicating that they are in the continuum of Marginalization and Integration... The mean and mode are 65.3 and 64, respectively.

Summary of Findings

DEMOGRAPHIC PROFILE

The following is a summary of the demographic profile of the study sample. More than half of the participants were males with a mean age of 36 years old. Over half of the participants were married, averaging one child in the family. Their average stay in the United States was twelve years. More than half came from the Sub-Continent and the Middle East. While the participants for this study came from more than fifty countries, those who came from Pakistan represented the largest bloc. Their place of residence in the United States were around the metropolitan areas of major cities such as Chicago and San Francisco. A vast majority (93%) of the respondents had a college degree.

---

[153] **Hatta, *Op. cit.*, p. 95.**

RELIGIOUS PRACTICE AND ADAPTATION OUTCOME

Prior to coming to the United States, about 57 percent of Naqshbandi Muslim immigrants were not practicing their religion as much as they did at the time of the study. This study indicated that after coming to the United States, they may have started to practice their religion more assiduously. Their mean score of 62.4 on the religious scale, well above the mid-point score of 49, suggests that the participants may have rediscovered their religion. This finding confirms the observation made by de Jong, in which he noted that an individual can grow in his/her faith through migration. The experience of migration creates for some a greater and richer concept of God and a deeper insight of oneself through religion...[154]

In general, most of the participants in this study do take their religion seriously. It is postulated that being in the *tariqah* implies that one is serious about one's religion. The finding of this study does suggest that assumption, which should be tested through future research.[155]

...Finally, the findings of this study affirm the theory of cultural pluralism. To place this study into the context of the broader American culture, one has to look at the concept of cultural pluralism. This theory takes the path of tolerance and inclusiveness. It does not assume that all immigrants who come to America would want to discard their cultural patterns just to be "Americanized." It is safe to assume that all ethnic groups like to maintain some, if not all, of their native cultural patterns. The choice of Marginalization or Separation for some of these Naqshbandis do not necessarily mean that they are hostile to the dominant society's norms, mores and values. It simply espouses that "acculturation" should be a two-way process, accomplishing the twin goals of cultural pluralism. Both the immigrants and the host learn from each other's cultural richness.[156]

---

[154] de Jong, P., *Migration and the Christian faith*. Research Group for European Migration Problems. Bulletin Supp, (Hague, 1964).

[155] **Hatta, *Op. cit.*, p. 116.**

[156] **Hatta, *Op. cit.*, p. 124.**

Third, future research should examine the influence of the *tariqah's* teachings in the life of Naqshbandi Muslims. Three aspects that can be examined are as follows:

1. the influence of the shaykh in the life of the Naqshbandi Muslims in providing the guidance for life in the United States, including the adaptation process,
2. the influence of the shaykh on the level of religious practice, and
3. explore the religiosity/spirituality aspects of the Naqshbandi Muslims.[157]

[157] **Hatta, *Op. cit.,* p. 125.**

University of Berne

A Living Sufi Saint: Shaykh Muhammad Nazim Adil al-Haqqani and the Naqshbandi Method of Self-Transformation

In 1999 a PhD researcher at the University of Berne approached us, asking for a meeting to discuss the Naqshandi Order. He had a large number of questions, many based on his studies of the spiritual methods for self-development in other religious and spiritual traditions.

After answering his questions, the student Andrew Vidich, expressed the wish to meet and interview Shaykh Nazim. This request was unusual in that the person making it was coming not as a seeker, but as an impartial observer, seeking to write his PhD dissertation on the Naqshbandi Order and the methods of spiritual development for seekers in the order. As a student of world faiths, he had heard much about the order and especially the large number of westerners who were entering it, and often willingly changing their lifestyles in order to conform with a life of dedicated spiritual purpose and religious conviction. What he had heard from numerous academic sources, convinced him that a study of the order was essential in order to provide the academic world with some idea of how the order has been so successful in the west.

Andrew Vidich set out on his task with great poise and determination. He took a list from us of a number of followers of our master and proceeded to interview them, one by one. After collating this sequence of interviews, he again approached us with questions of clarification and this time we arranged for him to meet with Shaykh Nazim. The end result was a dissertation of 652 pages titled *A Living Sufi Saint: Shaykh Muhammad Nazim Adil al-Haqqani and the Naqshbandi Method of Self-Transformation.*

Due to the excellent quality of Vidich's methodology, interviews, observations and extensive analysis, we are presenting here a large section devoted to excerpts from his thesis. All footnotes belong to the thesis except those designated in **bold** which are our own.

Introduction to the Study

This study examines the Haqqani branch of the Naqshbandiyya Haqqani order under the direction of Shaykh Muhammad Nazim Adil al-Haqqani. It provides a broad historical outline of the history of the order and the development of its methodology over the course of the last seven hundred years. It then isolates and examines the various methodologies employed by the Sufi teacher to create spiritual change in the disciples, in the process exploring the function, purpose, and scope of each specific technique.

Since the concept of a spiritual teacher may have a variety of meanings within a given order, one of the research goals has been to identify those different meanings and their implications for learning from the perspective of the student.[158]

Preliminary research suggests that Sufi teachers have access to other realms of knowledge inherently different from ordinary knowledge. Existing research suggests that these realms of knowledge can be accessed through altered states of consciousness.[159] We are concerned with how this takes place and the effect these states of knowledge have on the teaching process.[160]

Subjectivity

Like Michaela Ozelsel, I do not approach Sufism as a distant observer with skepticism or fear. My experience with Sufism dates back over twenty-five years and has involved me informally with a number of different Sufi orders. Along with my informal study of Sufism, I have made a more formal study of the literature over the course of the last fifteen years.

...third concern that surfaced was the need to taste the spiritual experience that the disciple was actually going through. This concern

---

[158] **Vidich, Andrew Wicks, "A Living Sufi Saint: Shaykh Muhammad Nazim Adil al-Haqqani and the Naqshbandiyya Method of Self-Transformation," PhD dissertation, (Berne University, 2000) p. 3.**

[159] Csikszentmihalyi, M. Flow, *The psychology of optimal experience* (New York: Harper and Row, 1990).

[160] **Vidich, *Op. cit.*, p. 19.**

was underscored in my first meeting with Shaykh Hisham, who immediately said, "The problem with all books about Sufism is that the authors have not 'tasted' Sufism itself." He compared it to someone who studies the texture of a plum, its size, its color, and where it came from, but never actually tastes it. "What," he said, "was the good of this kind of work?"[161]

Spiritual Methodology of the Order in Historical Context

The heart and core of the Sufi path rest upon the cardinal pillars of the teaching shaykh and the methodology of spiritual advancement. The two are inextricably intertwined, for the shaykh at the deepest level cannot be separated from his methodology. Not only is the teaching shaykh the living exponent and prophetic model within the *silsila,* but he is the authorized interpreter of the tradition for his *murids*. In him rests the power to increase the faith of his *murids* as well as advance the cause of his order and of Islam according to the dictates of the era.

...Our purpose is to situate the order, specifically the present-day Haqqani order, within the historical context of Sufism. We begin by dividing the Haqqani methodology into the tripartite formula of *Shariah, dhikr,* and *rabitah*. In the category of *Shariah* we include all practices proscribed in the Quran and required of all Muslims. These include doing good deeds, moral conduct outwardly and inwardly *(adab*), and following the *Sunnah* (example) of the Prophet. In the second category, *dhikr,* are all practices unique to the Naqshbandi Haqqani order. These include the long *khatm* done in silence, the short *khatm* done aloud at *dhikr* ceremonies, and the basic litany or *awrad* done throughout the day. This section also includes the eleven central practices and principles of the order established by Abd al-Khaliq al-Ghujdawani and Bahauddin Naqshband and the Naqshbandi method of *dhikr* in correlation to the theory of the subtle centers (*lataif).*

In the final section, we include the practices of bonding with the shaykh (*rabitah*) and keeping the association with the shaykh (*suhbah),* which ultimately lead to intense love and total surrender (*islam*) to the shaykh. Also included are the practices of visualizing the shaykh

---

[161] **Vidich, *Op. cit.*, p. 251.**

(*tasawwur*), connecting to the shaykh or *rabitat-u-sharifah,* [162] and receiving the shaykh's spiritual transmission (*tawajjuh*).[163 164]

CURRENT SCHOLARSHIP

Until fairly recently, serious research into the Naqshbandi *tariqah* has been scant and sporadic, but this picture has begun to change quite dramatically. Annemarie Schimmel notes in her introduction to Arthur Buehler's Book, *Sufi Heirs of the Prophet,* the recent surge in interest in the Naqshbandi order and particularly its contribution to Sufi methodology and theology.[165] Of particular interest to both scholars and the general Muslim community is the work of Fritz Meir of Basel, who has devoted several articles and an important book to the inner

---

[162] The practice of *rabitat-u-sharifah* is, as far as I can determine, identical to what earlier Naqshbandi manuals referred to as *muraqabah.*

[163] Buehler encapsulates the Naqshbandi methodology in a tripartite formula: (1) *dhikr, fikr*, and *rabitah.* See Ahmad Said, *Arba anhar,* p. 2, and Zawwar Husayn, *Umadat al-suluk,* p. 279. "Ubaydullah Ahrar (d. 895/1490), a contemporary of Jami, outlined three possibilities: (1) doing good deeds and spiritual exercises; (2) realizing one's weaknesses and surrendering to God; and (3) depending on the influence of a master's power (*himmat*). The third method is the fastest and most sure, for a seeker realizing his weakness can use the means (*wasila*) of his *pir*'s spiritual power to arrive near God. Kashifi, *Rashahat,* pp. 500-01, cited in Fritz Meier, *Zwei Abhandlungen uber die Naqshbandiyya,* p. 256" (Buehler, 1998, p. 131). It seems that in actual practice, the Naqshbandi *murid*s of Shaykh Nazim would conceive of surrendering to God and relying upon the shaykh's spiritual power as identical. The tripartite system seems rather to be a choice between relying on one's own efforts in doing *dhikr* and good deeds, and completely surrendering to the shaykh and relying on his power entirely. This important distinction is at the heart of the Haqqani self-identity. Scholars of comparative religion will be interested in comparing both the Hindu Bath tradition of the 16th century poet-saint Tulsa Sahib (1543/1623) as well as the founders of the Sant Tradition beginning with Kabir and Nanak in the late 15th and early 16th centuries. See *Kavitavali* by Tulsi Das, translated by Raymond Allchin, London: Allen and Unwin, 1964, p. 34. See also Kirpal Singh, *A Great Saint: Baba* Jaimal *Singh, His Life and Teachings* (Delhi, India: Ruhani Satsang, 1971) p. 113.

[164] **Vidich, *Op. cit.,* p. 106.**

[165] Annemarie Schimmel notes the recent interest in the Naqshbandi order in her foreword to Arthur Buehler's *Sufi Heirs to the Prophet*: *The Indian Naqshbandiyya and the* Rise *of the Mediating Shaykh* (South Carolina: South Carolina Press, 1998) p. xi. She mentions several other scholars' works, including M. Gaborieau, A. Popovic, and T. Zarcone, whose work was published after the 1989 conference devoted to the study of the Naqshbandi order.

life, theology, and psychology of the Naqshbandiyya.[166] Hamid Algar has also published some significant articles and titles on the Naqshbandiyya order. The work of J.T. Haar, Yohanan Friedman, and Albert Hourani, and to a lesser extent Warren Fusfeld and J.M.S. Baljon, should also be mentioned. Recent scholarly research about the Naqshbandi order is relatively scarce. Arthur Buehler's recent book, *Sufi Heirs to the Prophet: The Indian Naqshbandiyya and the Rise of the Mediating Shaykh,* is significant in two respects. First, it opens a new chapter in the theoretical and practical aspects of the Naqshbandiyya and their status in the present-day Punjab. Second, while touching on the entire history of the order, it provides a closer view of the Central Asian developments in the subcontinent.

Other academic articles on this movement include Semra Galip, *Un Gourou Nakshbendi: Sheyh Nazim Kibrisi...* Most recently, the Selly Oaks Institute is now engaged in studying the Naqshbandi Haqqani branch of Shaykh Nazim from the perspective of its rapid internationalization and methods of attracting membership. This work, although still in its infancy, should provide a more global view of the order.[167]

OTHER SOURCES OF DATA

Shaykh Muhammad Hisham's *The Naqshbandi Sufi Way: The History and Guidebook of the Saints of the Golden Chain* provides an insider's account of the history and methodology of the Golden Chain order of the Naqshbandiyya. Written in the style of earlier classical Sufi manuals[168]

---

166 We have tried to refer to Arthur Buehler's recent work as both a gauge and point of reference to compare current Naqshbandi teachings of the Haqqani branch with the Mujaddidiyya historical tradition portrayed by Buehler.

167 **Vidich, *Op. cit.*, p. 106-109.**

168 Shaykh Hisham's book is not unlike the work of Nizam ad-din Awliya's *Morals for the Heart (Fawaid al-fuad)* and Sharaf ad-din Maneri's *Table Laden with Good Things (Khawan-i-our nimat).* John Renard describes the distinctive features of this work in his *Seven Doors to Islam:* "Nizam ad-din *Awliya*'s early fourteenth-century *Morals for the Heart* was one of many of a genre, especially among members of the Chishti *tariqa,* serving as a primary means of passing on the order's distinctive manner of dealing with everyday issues. Compiled by the disciple Amir Hasan Sijzi, the collection became a model for similar works by members of virtually all the other major Sufi fraternities of the Indian subcontinent. Like Rumi, Nizam ad-din uses parable and anecdote to address concerns indirectly rather than head-on." Renard, J., *Seven doors to*

by the appointed *Khalifa* of Shaykh Nazim, it provides fascinating biographical sketches of the most distinguished saints of the Naqshbandi order as well as first-hand accounts of both Shaykh Abd Allah ad-Daghestani and Shaykh Nazim al-Haqqani. It also presents a detailed explanation of the order's methodology and history. We also draw heavily upon the extensive informal recorded talks and books of Shaykh Nazim going back to the early 1960s, as well as the recorded sayings of his Grandshaykh, Abd Allah ad-Daghestani. Included in this category is a soon-to-be-released book of his most recent talks (April and May of 1999) entitled *Bridge to Eternity*. Finally, we include a number of important interviews with shaykhs of the order gathered over the course of this study.

All these sources, but particularly the latter two, play a significant part in outlining the historical background of the Naqshbandiyya-Haqqani methodology. However, we draw upon a number of other Naqshbandiyya biographical, autobiographical, and scholarly works that have a direct bearing on Naqshbandi methodology.[169]

Historical Outline and Development of Spiritual Methodology

According to historical tradition, the shaykhs of the Naqshbandi order trace their initiatic lineage directly back to the Prophet through Abu Bakr as-Siddiq, one of the four rightly guided caliphs and companions of the Prophet. In contrast, all the other Sufi orders trace their lineage back to the Prophet through Ali bin Abu Talib (d. 40/661), the son-in-law of the Prophet. This distinction is of great significance for the Naqshbandiyya because of the exalted position that Abu Bakr as-

---

Islam: Spirituality and the religious life of Muslims (Berkeley and Los Angeles: University of California Press, 1996) p. 190.

[169] Some of the more scholarly works cited include Warren Fusfeld, "The Shaping of Sufi Leadership in Delhi: The Naqshbandi-Mujaddidiyya, 1750-1920," Ph.D. dissertation (University of Pennsylvania, 1981); J.G.T. Haar, *Follower and Heir of the Prophet: Shaykh Ahmad Sirhindi (1564-1624) as Mystic* (Leiden: Het Oosters Instituut, 1992); Marcia Hermansen, "Shah Wali Allah's Theory of Subtle Centers (*lataif*): A Sufi Model of Personhood and Self-transformation," *Journal of Near Eastern Studies* (vol. 47, no. 1, 1988) pp. 1-25; Dina Le Gall, *The Ottoman Naqshbandiyya in the Pre-Mujaddidi Phase: A Study in Islamic Religious Culture and Its Transmission,* Ph.D. dissertation (Princeton University, 1992); Athar Rivzi, *A History of Sufism in India,* in two volumes (New Delhi: Munshiram Manoharlal, 1983); and Albert Hourani, *Shaikh Khalid and the Naqshbandi Order* (Charlotte: University of South Carolina Press, 1972).

Siddiq holds in Sufi genealogy and spiritual status. Since Abu Bakr is considered the most perfect of humans, second only to the Prophet, any *silsila* traced directly through him to the Prophet would have superiority over other orders.[170] According to Shaykh Hisham, the superiority of the Abu Bakr as-Siddiq's lineage is supported by a number of well-known traditions. The first is mentioned by al-Suyuti: "Whatever God poured into my breast, I have poured into the breast of Abu Bakr as-Siddiq." The second is supported by Bukhari: "God has expanded my breast to receive what He has expanded the breast of Abu Bakr and Umar to receive."[171] This formulation, Buehler notes, took place during the life of Ahmad Sirhindi, considered by the Naqshbandis one of the most distinguished and exalted shaykhs.[172] ...

The controversy over the initiatic chains (*silsilas*) leading directly back to the Prophet is important to Sufi orders for a number of reasons. At issue is not just the superiority of one companion's (those who had a close physical relationship) connection to the Prophet over another, but the specific nature of that connection as well. Since each companion had his own particular relationship to the Prophet, each received a different kind of blessing (*barakah*) and spiritual influence (*fayd*) from the Prophet.[173] These differences in spiritual affiliation to the Prophet, according to some sources, accounted for the differences in approach

---

[170] It is for this reason that Naqshbandis regard the Naqshbandiyya *tariqat* as the "mother of all *tariqahs*" Kabbani, Hisham. Interview in Saddle River, N.J., by Andrew Vidich, June 21, 1999.

[171] Kabbani, Muhammad Hisham. *Mercy Oceans' Shore of Safety*. Fenton, Michigan: Haqqani Islamic Trust, 1993, p. 4.

Shaykh Hisham, in his introduction to *The Naqshbandi Sufi Way*, mentions no less than ten traditions supporting the claim of Abu Bakr as the closest spiritually to the Prophet. See Kabbani, Muhammad Hisham, *The Naqshbandi Sufi Way: The History and Guidebook of the Saints of the Golden Chain*, Chicago: Kazi Publications, 1995.

[172] See Arthur Buehler's *Sufi Heirs to the Prophet: The Indian Naqshbandiyya and the Rise of the Mediating Shaykh* (North Carolina: North Carolina Press, 1998, p. 90). Buehler notes that according to Dina Le Gall, "more often Naqshbandi *silsilas* of the sixteenth and seventeenth centuries consist of several parallel derivations, 'Bakri' as well as 'Alid.'" See Dina Le Gall, *The Ottoman Naqshbandiyya in the Pre-Mujaddidi Phase: A Study in Islamic Religious Culture and Its Transmission* (Ph.D. dissertation, Princeton University, 1992) p. 137.

[173] Buehler notes that at issue for Bahauddin "was not which companion transmitted God's divine grace through Muhammad but that each connection (*nisbah*) to the Prophet had its own unique blessings." A. Buehler, *Sufi Heirs to the Prophet: The Indian Naqshbandiyya and the Rise of the Mediating Shaykh* (North Carolina: North Carolina Press, 1998) p. 92.

and methodology of each order. The special character of Abu Bakr as-Siddiqi, is said to account for the special quality of "sobriety" and the strict adherence to the Sunna of the Prophet characteristic of the Naqshbandi Golden Chain order of Shaykh Nazim al-Haqqani.[174] A review of the Naqshbandi principles of transmission and initiation will be helpful in understanding this distinction.[175][176]

Principles of Transmission and Uwaysi Initiation

At the basis of the concept of initiatic chain (*silsila*) is the notion of spiritual transmission, known in Sufi orders as the "passing of the secret." Thus, the spiritual secret of Muhammad was passed directly to Abu Bakr as-Siddiq, and he in turn passed it on to his successor until it reached the present living shaykh of this era. In theory, each initiatic chain is directly connected spiritually to the Prophet. Without this spiritual link back to the Prophet, the authenticity and power of the order would be in question. Verifying these chains through extensive genealogies becomes an important task, for it legitimizes each order's claim to authentic spiritual authority. The closer the link with the Prophet, the more exalted the status of the order.

It is important to understand that the "passing of the secret" from one successor to another is not merely a ritual formality but the transmission of the essence of the teaching directly to the next living exponent. The prophetic light originally embodied by Muhammad is therefore never extinguished but passed on from generation to generation. Using the analogy of a light bulb which, when burned out, is replaced by a new bulb, the light of the eternal never leaves the world but is continuous and unbroken while the individual

---

[174] Buehler notes that both sobriety and silent recollection of God (*dhikr*) were inherited directly from Abu Bakr as-Siddiq.

[175] All Sufi orders claimed at least one or more of the first eight Shii *imam*s among their spiritual ancestors, referred to as the "Golden Chain" by the Naqshbandi order. In the case of the Naqshbandi, these usually included either Jafar as-Sadiq, Ali ar-Rida (d. 203/818), the eighth *imam,* or Ali b. Abu Talib. In the case of the Golden Chain order of Shaykh Nazim, it includes Hadrat Imam Abu Muhammad Jafar as-Sadiq A. Buehler, *Sufi Heirs to the Prophet: The Indian Naqshbandiyya and the Rise of the Mediating Shaykh* (North Carolina: North Carolina Press, 1998, pp. 92-93).

[176] **Vidich, *Op. cit.,* pp. 115 - 116.**

manifestations of that divine light change from one human pole to another.

According to Sufi tradition, this exchange of spiritual knowledge can be accomplished in two ways. First, the shaykh can communicate it directly on a physical level to the successor through the eyes or any other physical means chosen by the successor. Second, it can be transferred through spiritual means, in which case it is known as Uwaysi. In this second form of spiritual transmission, Shaykh Hisham explains, "The spirits meet in the world of spirits which is beyond the material plane. Whoever takes knowledge through spirituality from a deceased master in the Naqshbandi Way is called both Uwaysi and Naqshbandi."[177] The Uwaysi transmission is a "sign of the favor of God, Almighty and Exalted, on His servant"[178] for it indicates that those who had an Uwaysi connection had been lifted up into the divine presence.[179]

Conformity to *Shariah*

The Naqshbandi Haqqani methodology is grounded and deeply rooted in the daily performance of the five prescribed prayers as well as conforming to the essential beliefs of Sunni Islam. The daily life of each *murid* begins and ends in the performance of these prayers and sacred rituals. It is only after the fulfillment of these components[180] of the faith that the supererogatory works actually come into play. If the *murid*'s conformity to the *Sunnah* of the Prophet is flawed, his supererogatory works will also be flawed, for the quality of the latter is contingent upon the quality of the former. Perfection is defined as someone who "is careful to keep *Sunnah*." The insistence on practicing the prescribed prayers, which may for an outsider appear at times to be mechanical,

---

[177] Kabbani, Muhammad *Hisham. Mercy Oceans' Shore of Safety* (Fenton, Michigan: Haqqani Islamic Trust, 1993) p. 10.

[178] *Ibid.*, p. *10.*

[179] **Vidich, *Op. cit.*, pp. 114-118.**

[180] The use of loud *dhikr* on Friday evening *dhikr* ceremonies is permitted, even encouraged, *among* new *murids* because of the efficacy of the loud *dhikr* in purifying the heart of novices. More advanced *murids* are encouraged to recite the silent *dhikr* throughout the day as much as possible.

even tedious, is the lifeblood for a *murid* of Shaykh Nazim.[181] Prayer (*salat*) is the dominant note in the music of the Haqqani devotions, and, indeed, for most of Sunni Islam. No treatment of the order would be accurate if this fact were not duly emphasized. An excellent explanation of the significance of prayers is given in a Muslim devotional manual entitled *The Light*:

> It is not a mechanical drill but the various postures of humility in *salat* indicate complete external or bodily submission to God which conforms with the spiritual submission, and this is a necessity since man has a body as well as a soul which exercise great influence on each other through their movements. The submissive movements of the body in this prayer produce equivalent submissive movements in the soul.[182] [183]

Having situated Haqqani methodology within the performance of the prayer-rite, we can then apply its practical corollary, which is its method of individual application. The essential principle is that the entire teaching is given *according to the capacity and readiness of each disciple*. This is based on the axiom of the Prophet, who said, "The ways to God are as numerous as the breaths of human beings" (*hadith*). Since each soul is a reflection of a unique name of God or names of God, each soul's path through the *Shariah* is slightly different. In practical terms, while *murids* are encouraged to perform the prescribed prayers as well as the superogatory work (*dhikr*, *tawajjuh*, etc.), I noticed little if any formal pressure put on new *murids* to conform to the *Shariah*.[184] Each

---

[181] During my stay at the *dergah* in Cyprus, I observed that the spiritual, biological, and even psychological rhythms of the *murids* are conditioned by the daily performance of the prescribed prayers. In this is the secret of the order. Shaykh Nazim, *even* at 80 years of age, continues to perform every aspect of the daily prayers, exhibiting a rigor and devotion that cannot go unnoticed by even a casual observer (Cyprus, August, 1999).

[182] *Padwick, C.E., Muslim devotions: A study of* prayer-manuals in common use. Oxford, England: One World Publications, 1996, p. 8.

[183] For an excellent review of the beneficial effects of the various postures on the body, their exact positions, and relative length, see Shaykh Hakim Moinuddin Chishti's *The Book of Sufi Healing* (New York: Inner Traditions Press, 1985) pp. 98-107.

[184] I concluded from *my* interviews with *murids* that a great deal of allowance is made for new murids in conforming to the *Shariah*. …Shaykh Hisham both confirmed this and indicated that some *murids* may never fully comply with the outer requirements. Others will not only fulfill

disciple progresses at his or her own pace and according to his or her own level of attraction *(jadhba)* to God. As with almost every aspect of Naqshbandi methodology, this practice is traced back to the life of the Prophet, who according to tradition, took 23 years to fully reveal the divine law *(Shariah)* to his people. Shaykh Nazim explains the foundations of the methodology:

> A real shaykh speaks to people in accordance to their ranks and levels of understanding; as such shaykhs are inheritors of the Prophet Muhammad, who said, "Whosoever wants to teach people must be careful to notice the level of understanding of his audience and to address them accordingly."[185]

The same principle applies to the performance of religious actions. Each *murid* is guided according to his level of attainment and rank. Some *murids* are asked to recite more *dhikr* or even to go into seclusion, while others may never be given any specific guidance at all. The ideal *murid* will come to trust his shaykh and therefore leave everything in the shaykh's hands.[186]

If *suhbah* is the central pillar of the Naqshbandi *tariqah,* then its outer corollary and Quranic basis resides in perfect life of the Prophet, and "modeling the way of the Prophet" in every aspect.

SHARIAH: THE PATH OF THE PROPHET AND PERFECTION OF PROPHETHOOD

The concept of "following in the footsteps of the Prophet" has become for the Naqshbandi Haqqani *tariqah* of Shaykh Nazim a kind of litmus test against which they see themselves in contrast to other orders. It is safe to say that the Naqshbandi Haqqani *tariqat* of Shaykh Nazim may

---

the requirements of the *Shariah,* but also go on to make rapid progress in the *dhikr* and other aspects of the *tariqat*. In this sense, there is no compulsion in the development of the *murid*. I found this refreshing, given the sometimes fanatical approach of certain orthodox elements of Islam. Sincere newcomers are welcome at the *dhikr* ceremonies and are treated with deference and respect.

185 Nazim, Shaykh Muhammad, *Mercy Oceans' Hidden Treasures* (Konya: Sebat Offset Printers, 1987) p. 52.

186 **Vidich, *Op. cit.,* pp. .223-225.**

be unsurpassed in its emphasis on strict reliance upon religious duties *(Shariah)* and modeling the Prophet's actions in all things.[187][188] The insistence and strict reliance on following the *Shariah* is based both on the belief in the superiority of Prophethood (*wirathat al-Nubuwwa*) over sainthood (*al-wilayat al-Kubra*) and the superiority of strict reliance on religious law over superogatory works.[189] Hence, the most important duty of every Muslim is that he "faithfully comply with the prescriptions of Sunni Islam, in the first place with regard to its teaching and in the second place with regard to practice"[190] [191] It is for

---

[187] Schimmel, A. *Mystical dimensions of Islam* (Chapel Hill, N.C.: University of North Carolina Press. 1975)

[188] It was precisely this belief which Sirhindi is credited with reviving during a time when the universalistic tendencies in Islam had become increasingly popular during the reign of Akbar. The Naqshbandiyya-Mujadidiyya not only survived the universalistic tendencies but also was able to consolidate power and become the best-known *tariqat* in India within 100 years after Sirhindi's death. See Hamid Algar's "A Brief History of the Naqshbandi Order" in Marc Gaborieau, Alexandre Popovic, and Thierry Zarcone, eds., *Naqshbandis: Historical Development and Present Day Situation of a Muslim Mystical Order* (Istanbul: Editions Isis, 1990).

[189] For a discussion of the difference between the path of the greater saintship (*al-wilayat al kubra*) versus the path of the prophetic inheritance, see Marcia Hermansen's article "Shah Wali Allah's Theory of the Subtle Spiritual Centers (*lataif*): A Sufi Model of Personhood and Self-transformation" (Hermansen, 1988, p. 1). In her article, she purposes to show how Shah Wali Allah's recasting of certain elements of the model "embodies" his position on several theological issues as well as his understanding of spiritual transformation (p.1). One critical issue argued by Sirhindi and other scholars and mystics of the Indian subcontinent was the notion that the path of prophetic inheritance is superior to the path of saintship. As she notes, "Those who held that the path of saintship, associated with the annihilation of self in the Divine Essence, was superior believed that the saint remained close to his divine origin, and they tended to support the philosophy of *wahdat al-wujud*, or the unity of existence. Those who followed Sirhindi in emphasizing the superiority of the prophetic path, on the basis that the Prophet descends further into the world so that in his ascent he can perform a significant transformative function, supported the philosophy of *wahdat al-shuhud*, or unity of experience" (p. 14). Shah Wali Allah attempted to mediate these two positions, affirming that on a more profound level they were in actual agreement. In terms of practical application today, Sirhindi's view of the superiority of the prophetic inheritance seems to have the upper hand, although no one I interviewed was willing to venture an opinion on the subject. However, the methodology of the *tariqat* views the path of the Prophet as superior to the path of the lesser saintship, because it emphasized the ultimate transcendence of God. This is most clearly revealed in the Naqshbandi Haqqani *tariqat's* overwhelming stress on avoiding the distractions and temptations of inner "revelation" (*kashf*) in favor of the absolute transcendence of God.

[190] Haar, J.G.J., *Follower and heir of the Prophet: Shaykh Ahmad Sirhindi (1564-1624) as mystic* (Leiden, Netherlands: Hetoosters Instituut, 1992) p.47.

this reason that the practice of *sama,* dance, and other innovative *(bidah)* techniques have been strictly forbidden. The foundation of the *tariqah* is based on the singular importance of adhering to the duties of *Shariah,* not only as a kind of prerequisite for spiritual training, but as an ongoing support and nourishment throughout the journey. The ideal follower will not only bring his actions in line with the requirements of Islamic *Sunnah* but continue to follow the *Shariah* regardless of his level of attainment. In addition he will try to imitate in every detail the habits and actions of the Prophet. Shaykh Nazim explains:

> Now we have been ordered to follow his ways because in the ways of the Prophet we can find lights that make our ways clear for us, as the sun makes clear for people their ways. Therefore the more you can be a real follower of the Prophet, the more lights you may acquire, and to the extant that you acquire more lights, your future is going to be more clear for you."[192]

In practice, followers of Shaykh Nazim are encouraged to adhere as closely as possible to the habits of the Prophet, including his manner of dress, eating, and personal hygiene. In short, the imitation of the customs of the Prophet is itself a form of worship, for what the Prophet disliked Allah made him dislike, and what the Prophet liked Allah made him like. Therefore, what customs could be better to follow than the Prophet's?[193]

HOW SHAYKH NAZIM PERFORMS THE PRAYER:

Shaykh Nazim entered the *dergah* from the side, and without any fuss or delay immediately engaged himself in the Isha prayer. The rest of the *murids* followed his lead in reverent silence. It became clear that not only did he not spare himself in the performance of the prayer rite, despite his eighty years age, he was profoundly engaged as well. The

---

[191] For Shaykh Nazim, mysticism not based on Sunni orthodoxy, and orthopraxy is not genuine mysticism.

[192] Nazim, Shaykh Muhammad, *Toward the divine presence* (Karachi, Pakistan: Jamil Wahab (Trust) Foundation., 1984) p. 132

[193] *Hubbiba ilayya,* or "It was made beloved to me" (*hadith*).

level of his concentration could easily seen from even a casual observer's perspective. I was particularly fascinated by the magnetism he seemed to bring to the prayer. One sensed the sublimity of his personal spirituality and the magnitude of his piety.[194]

...Later in the evening, Shaykh Nazim returned to lead the final evening prayer. This evening the small room, which was already crowded with fifty people, was now bursting on all sides with new arrivals. Since Thursday evening was "*dhikr* night," *murids*, Muslims, and seekers from all over the island came to participate and be in Shaykh Nazim's presence. The room, which once seemed full with fifty people, now contained over one hundred people. It was so tight that while I was doing my prostrations I could not fully bow down, or the person behind me would not have had enough room to make prostrations (*sajda*). The term communal prayer here becomes both literally and symbolically true. The *murids* were so close to one another that one could not move in either direction more than a few inches. Yet I was amazed that despite the sardinelike conditions and blistering heat, a sweet fragrance and coolness permeated the room. Again paradoxically, the outer closeness only seemed to enhance the inner spiritual communion that permeated the room. It was effortless and fluid like the slow churning of milk that produces butter. Surprisingly, Shaykh Nazim seemed unaffected by either the extreme heat or close quarters. To be present in this room was to witness the reality of the *Shariah* as a living component in Islam and as an integral element of the Naqshbandi practice.[195]

Absolute Transcendence and the End in the Beginning

One of the most important aspects of Naqshbandi methodology is the belief in the absolute transcendence of God. The basic belief is that God's Essence (*dhat*) is transcendent and unknowable in itself. All that can be said is that God is One and that He is real existence. As Ruzbihan Baqli summarizes:

---

[194] **Vidich, *Op. cit.*, p. 329.**

[195] **Vidich, *Op. cit.*, p. 364.**

> He exists eternally without beginning or end. He is existent, not like the existence of things that depend on something else; his existence depends on itself, without body, substance, or accident, for substance is the locus of accidents... The essence of him who is exalted does not enter things or depart from them, nor is it a state inhering in something or imposed on it. Rather, he transcends any relation with temporality, for he is one in every respect.[196]

Ruzbihan, like other Sufis, realized that only God in His ultimate essence (*dhat*) was Lasting and Perfect, and therefore everything else was contingent and perishing. To become overly concerned with or attached to the various visions, lights, or stages of the path was extremely dangerous. Since each stage of the journey is more beautiful and enrapturing than the previous, it is easy for the disciple to become fixated and stuck along the way. The ultimate goal of the mystics is God and God alone, and therefore anything less than the achievement of that goal is a form of self-deception. Abu Yazid's description of his *miraj* (ascent) to God following the archetypal "night journey of the Prophet" gives us an indication of the subtle deception of even his most exalted visionary experiences.

Abu Yazid also said:

> At first I went to unicity and became a bird whose body was of oneness and whose wings were of everlastingness. I kept flying in the atmosphere of quality for ten years until I went to an atmosphere like that a hundred million times. I kept flying until I went to the plains of pre-eternity. In it I saw the tree of oneness... I looked, and I knew that this was all deceit.[197]

Notwithstanding the great heights of realization that Abu Yazid attained, the ultimate concern of the mystic surpasses any concern for

---

[196] Ernst, C.W., *Sufism:* An *essential introduction to the philosophy and practice of the mystical tradition of Islam* (Boston: Shambhala, 1996) p. 29.

[197] Ernst, C.W., Sufism*: An essential introduction to the philosophy and practice of the mystical tradition of Islam (*Boston: Shambhala, 1996) pp. 161-162.

or "attention to and occupation with the observation of existence and the Kingdom."[198]

In other words, the men of God who have reached the final station, which is neither a station or state, know that heeding anything but God is deception...

According to Naqshbandi methodology, there are seventy thousand veils between us and the station of the Prophet. The Naqshbandi Haqqani order, for the forgoing reasons, reverses the order of the removal of the inner veils covering the *murid*'s inner vision. Instead of slowly removing the veils from the bottom up by means of mystical practices, the veils are lifted from the top down...

The insistence on protecting the *murid* from the deceptions along the path is consistent with the Naqshbandi belief in controlling the ego at all costs. If a seeker attains certain stations and states, he may be tempted to seek recognition and fame in the world.[199] The ego, according to Naqshbandi methodology, will never neglect to demand "its share of the excitement and admiration, and by so doing taint the whole process of spiritual endeavor."[200] To combat the ego and secure the future of the *murid*, the shaykh prevents the disciple from witnessing these states until he has achieved moral perfection and control over the ego. The ego, it should be noted, is not destroyed but

---

[198] Sviri, S., *The taste of things hidden* (Inverness, Calif.: Golden Sufi Center, 1997), p. 130.

[199] Quite early in the history of Sufism, Sufi teachers realized the necessity of controlling the *murid*'s ego in order for the disciple to make rapid progress. Since the ego was the predominant obstacle, every measure was taken to subvert and control its evil tendencies. Sviri notes that a particular Sufi order, later called the Malamatis, were "concerned with the fact that the lower self, the *nafs*, wants to own every human experience, and thus claims ownership of any accomplishment, including mystical states. When this happens, they maintained, and it happens virtually all the time, a one to one relationship with God is blocked" (Sviri, S., *The taste of things hidden* (Inverness, Calif.: Golden Sufi Center, 1997) p. 133). Thus, the *murid* begins loving God for the experiences and not for God's own sake. To combat this universal tendency, the Malamatis tried to eliminate every exposure to external honor that might bring about conceit or inflate the ego. It is very possible that the Naqshbandis may have adopted certain aspects of this general practice and applied it to the methodology of ascension. See also Rumi, *Diwan*, 1647, quoted in Chittick, *The Sufi Path of Love*, p. 327.

[200] Kabbani, Muhammad Hisham. *Naqshbandi Sufi Way: History and guidebookof the saints of the Golden Chain* (Chicago: Kazi Publications. 1995) pp. 413-414.

put under the foot of the shaykh, thereby rendering it useful for the shaykh and useless for the *murid*'s personal gratification.

A second reason given for the use of this methodology is that it teaches the murid that the highest path of ascension is that of perfect servanthood. As we mentioned earlier, the true *murid* should love God and the Prophet alone and not for any other reason. To worship God for his gifts is a sacrilege and a fall from grace for the true murid. Neither the longing for paradise nor the fear of hell has anything to do with the true aspiration of the lover for God. His only duty is that of being a true servant. He is to follow the divine law as prescribed by the *Sunnah,* do what is prescribed, and avoid what is forbidden. It is in this context that performance of the outer divine laws and the inner hidden esoteric rules converge.

THE END IN THE BEGINNING AND THE BEGINNING IN THE END

The Naqshbandi belief in the ultimate transcendence of God and the insistence on following the *Sunnah* of the Prophet are both couched in the concept of the "end in the beginning." According to Naqshbandi cosmology, most Sufi *tariqahs* end in the stage of "lesser intimacy" *(wilayat-i sughra),* which is a degree lower than the "greater intimacy" (*wilayat-i kubra),* and significantly lower than the "highest intimacy" or the *perfection of messengership*. The ultimate station is the "reality of servitude" co-existing in the "reality of Ahmad,"[201] which is the "*reality of realities.*" [202] Naqshbandi shaykhs begin the process of spiritual advancement by removing the veils of light and darkness at the stage

---

[201] The notion that there could be a rank higher than the "reality of Muhammad" was quite a controversial proposition during Sirhindi's time. In essence, he asserted that there was a reality above *wahdat-al-wajud*, proposed by Ibn Arabi, to which he did not give a name but that later mystics termed *wahdat-i-shuhud* or the "unity of appearance." Sirhindi held that the "experience of *wahdat-i-wujud* or unityism is a stage in the mystic evolution. If the mystic outgrows this stage, and attains to still higher stages, he comes to realize that the experience of *wahdat-i-wujud* or unityism was simply a subjective experience—that the *wahdat* or unity he experienced was merely *shuhud* or appearance; and that *wahdat-i-wujud* or unityism is not an objectively real fact." The "reality of Ahmad" was a station in which the mystic came to see his essential servanthood, and the station of "praise" (*ahamad*) evolved from the essential transcendence of God in relation to his servant (Faruqi, 1940, p. 116-117).

[202] For a detailed discussion of the higher stages on the path of the Mujaddidiyya see Dhawqi, *Sirr-i-dilbaran*, 4th ed., Karachi: Mashhur Offset Press, 1985, p. 201a.

of the greater intimacy (*wilayat-i kubra*), skipping over the lesser intimacy also known as the path of *wahdat al-wujud*. Hence, what is considered the end for most Sufi *tariqahs* is only the beginning for the Naqshbandi path—a path that will lead ultimately far beyond the domain of *wahdat al-wujud* to the domain of *wahdat al-shuhud* articulated by Ahmad Sirhindi.[203] [204] In the last phase, only a few chosen individuals "begin the third portion of the journey, returning to the world of creation for God and by means of God" (*sayr an Allah billah*).[205] Here the seeker is in the stage of "moving from God," that is, a descent in which:

> the seeker returns from the heavenly world to the world of cause and effect, descending from the highest knowledge to the lowest. Here he forgets God by God, he knows God with God, and he returns from God to God. This is called the state of the farthest and the nearest.[206]

---

[203] Buehler, A., *Sufi heirs of the Prophet: The Indian Naqshbandiyya order and the rise of the mediating Sufi Shaykh* (Columbia, S.C.: University of South Carolina Press, 1998) pp. 123-124. Buehler seems to indicate that the second *baqa* is associated with the phase of *wahdat al-shuhud,* but from my reading of the text the second *baqa* does not start until after the phase of *wahdat al-shuhud* has been completed. Warren Fusfeld, in his analysis of the Naqshbandi Mujaddidiyya path, tells us, "This return to the world is part of the final goal in this tradition, while the starting point for this, which comes after the relatively early phases associated with *tauhidi i-wajudi and thud i-shuhudi,* is believed to be beyond the final stages that Sufis in other traditions even hope to attain." See Fusfeld, W. "The shaping of Sufi leadership in Delhi: The Naqshbandi Mujaddidiyya, 1750 to 1920." Ph.D. dissertation (University of Pennsylvania, 1986) pp. 105-106.

[204] For an excellent overview of why Ahmad Sirhindi believed the final stage was beyond *wahdat al-wujud,* see Faruqi, Burhan Ahmad, *The Mujaddid's Conception of Tauhid* (Lahore: Sh. Muhammad Ashraf Publications, 1979) p. 36-56. It is interesting to note that Ahmad Sirhindi's belief that he had achieved a higher level of attainment than any previous shaykh was disturbing at the time but today seems of almost no consequence. To be sure, he did not deny the stage of *wahdat al-wujud,* but realized through years of contemplative struggle a higher level in which the seeker perceives "the next sphere in the structure of reality which leads him to maintain a restored belief in the duality of God and the created world" (Fusfeld, *Op. cit.*, p. 97).

[205] Buehler, A., *Sufi heirs of the Prophet: The Indian Naqshbandiyya order and the rise of the mediating Sufi Shaykh* (Columbia, S.C.: University of South Carolina Press, 1998) p. 123.

[206] Kabbani, Muhammad Hisham, Naqshbandi *Sufi Way: History and guidebookof the saints of the Golden Chain* (Chicago: Kazi Publications.1995) p. 239.

The last phase, achieved by only the Prophets and perfect individuals—called "moving in things"—is the movement of the seeker within creation itself. Sirhindi explains:

> This involves knowing intimately all elements and states in this world after having vanished in annihilation. Here the seeker can achieve that state of guidance, which is the state of the Prophets and the people following the footsteps of the Prophet.[207]

Summarizing the method of guidance, Shaykh Hisham explains this process:

> The Naqshbandi shaykhs choose to guide their disciples first through the movement from God, traveling from the higher states to the lower. For this reason, they maintain the common veils over the spiritual vision of the disciple, removing the veil of ordinary consciousness only at the final step. All other Ways begin with the movement to God, moving from the lowest states to the highest, and removing the common veils first.[208]

But in all their seeking, the fundamental principle which both underpins and guides Naqshbandi methodology is found in the Quranic verse that states, *"People whom neither business nor trade will divert from the remembrance of God"* (24:37). It requires no imagination to see why following the *Sunnah* of the Prophet and proper conduct (*adab*)

---

[207] *Op. cit.*, p. 129.

[208] *Op. cit.*, p. 241.

One of the unique features of following this methodology is that it effectively eliminates passing through the stages of attraction, or *tariq-i jadhba,* associated with the stage of lesser intimacy. In my interviews, murids told me seekers who take *bayah* from Shaykh Nazim who previously may have been out of control or experiencing various states of ecstasy become grounded and "sober" very quickly. It was for this reason that the Naqshbandi were often dubbed the "sober Sufis." Throughout my period of observation, I saw only one instance of any outward signs of spiritual intoxication or states of uncontrolled ecstasy by murids (*majdhubiyyah*).

as prescribed by the Prophet is so central to Naqshbandi thinking and orthopraxy.[209]

Adab, or Proper Conduct

The word *adab,* strictly translated, means conduct or behavior, but it has come to mean not only the correct performance of one's religious duties but also the entire way of living of the *murid*. The goals of Sufi etiquette are summarized as follows:

1. proper attitude to the shaykh outwardly and inwardly,
2. controlling the student's ego, and
3. perfection of moral character. [210]

An interesting anecdote from the life of Khwajah Ahrar, one of the earlier Central Asian Naqshbandi shaykhs (806/1403-896/1490), suggests the degree to which a Naqshbandi shaykh strove to achieve perfect manners in his disciples:

---

[209] For a general overview of the concept of *adab,* see Metcalf, Barbara, *Moral Conduct and Authority: The Place of Adab in South Asian Islam,* Los Angeles: University of California Press, 1983. Her book examines the many facets and nuances of the concept of *adab* and its moral expectations not only for the king and saint, but for the teacher, master craftsman, and family head alike. One conclusion drawn from the many articles was that unlike "the theory in Hinduism that one can reach salvation through different paths—of action, knowledge, or devotion—here one can define three domains, *Shariah* (Law), *tariqah* (the way of the Sufis), and *adab,* that are analytically distinguishable, that have their respective specialists that can be seen in tension with each other. Yet all emerge, at core, as attempts to codify and embody the practice of the Prophet; they are ultimately the same in mainstream Islam." In essence, *adab* was based upon the teachings of the other two domains. In the final analysis, although *adab* may mean correct outer behavior, "it is understood as cause of and then reciprocally, fruit of one's inner self." With inner realization comes the perfection of moral conduct and with the perfection of moral conduct the flowering of spiritual vision and ascent to God. It is this relentless struggle to overcome one's lower self, to refine the *nafs,* that gives life its ultimate meaning and value. It is this unceasing effort to perfect our animal nature that is the unique gift of human beings. This is the greater *jihad* and why in the final analysis *adab* or good manners is Islam (Metcalf, *Op. cit.,* pp. 9-10).

[210] See Qaimuddin Qanungui, *Dhikr-i mubarak: mashaikh-i sadat-i Makan Sharif,* Lahore: Muazzam Printers, n.d. p. 161; cited in Buehler, A., *Sufi heirs of the Prophet: The Indian Naqshbandiyya order and the rise of the mediating Sufi Shaykh* (Columbia, S.C.: University of South Carolina Press, 1998) p. 148.

> He considered pride an obnoxious habit and cited an incident from the life of Abu Yazid to highlight its evil effect on a mystic. While walking in a street, he came across a dog with a wet body and tried to save his skirt from being polluted. The dog said, "If your skirt had touched my body, a little water would have cleaned it, but what about the filth that you have put on your skirt by considering yourself purer than myself. Which water would clean this."[211]

Conduct with One's Shaykh

> The protocol of behavior in relation to the shaykh consists of a number of rules of etiquette concerning one's outward actions and inward thoughts while in the shaykh's company. For example, everyone, including the newcomer, sits on the floor lower than the elevation of the shaykh.
>
> ...The same rules apply to women, except that they also remain separate from the men, both as a group and individually. Fraternization between the sexes is discouraged... Women usually gather as a group in the back of the room during the informal talks, formal prayers, and during *dhikr*.[212]

---

[211] Nizami, 1997, p. 170. Nizami mentions two aspects of Khawaja Ahrar's thought that provide interesting parallels with other religious traditions. First, that the development of the soul continues after the death of the outer body (*taraqqi bad al-mawt*); and second, that even rocks and fossils have life and respond to human action. He referred to Ibn Arabi's researches in this area and believed that even stones accept the influence of man (Nizami, 1997, p. 171). Scholars of comparative religion should look at the work of Raimon Panikkar (Joseph Prabhu, ed.), *The Intercultural Challenge of Raimon Panikkar* (New York: Orbis Books, 1996) pp. 91-106. Also see the work of Sri Aurobindo and that of Sant Kirpal Singh, *The Crown of Life* (Delhi: Ruhani Satsang, 1974) pp. 12-18.

[212] A strict code of conduct is practiced in regard to the dress and appearance of women. I found little deviation except in the case of young women. It was also apparent from my interviews that adapting to the dress code was harder for women than men because of the cultural stigma attached to wearing scarves in Western society. However, most women *murids* I interviewed did not struggle with it very long. They considered it a relatively easy sacrifice and could see its inner significance in terms of controlling the sexual urges of both men and women. Women coming from Eastern backgrounds (Middle East or India) had little problem adapting to the dress code.

Whenever the shaykh arrives or leaves, everyone in the room immediately stands and remains standing until the shaykh has seated himself, or has left. If any *murid* has to leave, he first asks permission of the shaykh, and is then careful not to turn his back to the shaykh while leaving. According to Naqshbandi *adab,* one should leave the presence of the shaykh (whether living or deceased) by backing up, until one reaches the door and puts one's shoes on.

While in the shaykh's presence, the soles of the feet should never be pointed toward the shaykh, and in no circumstances does anyone dare go to sleep. *Murids* should refrain from using the shaykh's personal belongings and always maintain a reverential and soft tone in addressing the shaykh.[213] Buehler notes that *murids* are forbidden to look the shaykh in the face, but my observations revealed the opposite. Devoted *murids* gaze steadfastly into the shaykh's face as well as directly into his eyes to receive his spiritual transmission (*fayd*).

Inward Conduct or the "Conduct of Anticipation"

The outer behavior of the disciple should mirror the inner attitude of trust and submission toward the shaykh. After the disciple has taken initiation *(bayah)* and placed himself in the hands of an authorized shaykh, he must be willing to proceed as authorized by him. He must be willing at all times to "receive the orders of the shaykh, just as the Prophet awaited the coming of Gabriel with revelation for God Almighty and Exalted" He must have as Hisham notes, "the conduct of anticipation,"[214] which means that the *murid* is at all times awaiting the orders of the shaykh. He must adopt the attitude of a humble household servant ready to perform even the most menial task at the drop of the hat. The disciple's readiness to act and carry out orders is a barometer of his degree of submission and progress. Hence, inattention or lack of compliance is considered a fall from grace for an advanced *murid* and a disgrace upon him. An example from one of my observations is worth noting here.

---

[213] Buehler, A., *Sufi heirs of the Prophet: The Indian Naqshbandiyya order and the rise of the mediating Sufi Shaykh* (Columbia, S.C.: University of South Carolina Press, 1998).

[214] Kabbani, Muhammad Hisham. Naqshbandi Sufi Way: *History and guidebookof the saints of the Golden Chain* (Chicago: Kazi Publications, 1995) p. 414.

THE IMPORTANCE OF OBEDIENCE

In the short space of the two or three days that I spent with Shaykh Hisham, he returned again and again to the theme of learning to become a true and obedient servant to one's shaykh. Indeed, the entire order, as Shaykh Nazim had so eloquently pointed out, is dependent on a living shaykh who has that spiritual connection to the Prophet. This teacher-disciple relationship is ultimately justified, according to Shaykh Hisham, in the relationship between Gabriel and the Prophet. Shaykh Hisham explains:

> Moreover, who is the teacher of Prophet? It was Gabriel. Why did not the Prophet say, I took wisdom directly from God? Why do you need a Prophet? The Prophet did not say, "Gabriel, I don't need you." He needed Gabriel. He was asking him what he has to say and what he has to do. Correct. So Gabriel was his teacher, and he was teaching him. Why did not the Prophet say he did not need Gabriel? Why did he insist he was his teacher? He was teaching us we need a teacher. Allah does not need Gabriel to go to the Prophet because Allah called the Prophet to his presence. He said he is *"the distance of just two bows' length,"* (53:9) from the Divine Presence. There was no need for Gabriel. However, he was teaching us, all *mumins*, all Muslims, all humans beings. Without a teacher, you cannot reach anywhere.[215]

Suhbah, or the Gathering with the Saints

The *suhbah* of the shaykhs has the function of softening the hearts of the followers to become able to experience a deep bonding and affection for others. The real sign of spiritual progress is a sense of open-heartedness and concern for one's fellow beings. Again, Shaykh Nazim tells us:

> You aren't a real believer until you want for others what you would like for yourself, until you can put yourself in the shoes even of those with whom you find yourself in conflict. Until you can feel affection and familiarity towards a group of

[215] Kabbani, Hisham. Interview in Saddle River, N.J., by Andrew Vidich, June 27, 1999.

> fellow seekers, it is impossible to imagine sympathy for people inimical to yourself.[216]

Rabitah, Binding One's Heart with the Shaykh

In this methodology is the secret of *rabitah* and the essence of the Naqshbandi *tariqah* itself. Indeed, one cannot develop familiarity unless the hearts of the *murids* first meet in the heart of one of Allah's saints. For only in the heart of saints is the divine attraction capable of being a medium for the divine transmission (*fayd*). It is in the divine ground of the saint's heart that everyone's true affinity is developed and sustained. For the Naqshbandi *murids,* the words of the shaykh become secondary to the actual transmission the *murid* is receiving. Shaykh Nazim clarifies this point: "This familiarity is a transmission from heart to heart. Don't bother with my words, just receive my transmission." [217] The process of receiving transmission is not an intellectual process but a question of directed attention and attunement to the shaykh.[218] Through this attunement, Buehler notes, "the *murid* unites with the 'lights of his lofty attributes and beautiful character,' creating continual *rabitah,* independent of physical proximity."[219]

Visualizing the Shaykh - *Tasawwur-i-shaykh,*

One method of receiving the spiritual transmission from the heart of the shaykh is visualizing the face of the shaykh (*tasawwur-i-shaykh*) and seems to have developed over a period. J. Haar mentions a Naqshbandi source dating back to the beginning of the 16th century A.D., in which the practice of *rabitah* meant "that a novice constantly keeps the 'face of

---

[216] Nazim, Shaykh *Muhammad, Oceans ofUnity* (Konya: Sebat Offset Printers. 1987) p. 70.

[217] *Op. cit.,* p. 71.

[218] The diaries of Irina Tweedie reinforce this point from a scientific perspective. She quotes her Naqshbandi shaykh: "Why do we insist on *Satsang*? Because it is a quickening. We do not teach; we quicken. I am stronger than you are so your current adjusts themselves to mine. This is a simple law of nature. The stronger magnetic current will affect, quicken, the weaker. If you let flow an electric current through two wires, side by side, one a strong one and the other a weak one, the stronger will affect the weaker. It will increase its potency. It is so simple" (Tweedie, *The Chasm of Fire: A Woman's Experience of Liberation Through a Sufi Master,* Worcester, Great Britain: Element Books, Ltd., 1979, p. 103).

[219] Buehler, A., *Sufi heirs of the Prophet: The Indian Naqshbandiyya order and the rise of the mediating Sufi Shaykh.* Columbia, S.C.: University of South Carolina Press, 1998, p. 135.

the shaykh' (*surat-i-shaykh*) in his mind, in order to attain not only total submission to the will of the shaykh but a kind of identification with him."[220] Sirhindi also had apparently incorporated this practice into the Mujaddidi system, especially for aspirants who had not gained sufficient control over their egos.[221] It was later developed and used by a succession of Naqshbandi shaykhs over the centuries, but particularly those who followed the line of Ala al-Din Attar (*taifa-i-alaiyya* or the Ala al-Din Attar order).[222]

The practice of *tasawwur-i-shaykh* continues in the Haqqani branch of Shaykh Nazim, but not in the form mentioned in the writings of earlier Naqshbandi shaykhs. We must, however, draw a clear distinction between gazing steadfastly at the outer face of the shaykh and inwardly recollecting the face of the shaykh while not in his presence. The former practice of looking at the outward form of the shaykh is currently in wide use, while the practice of inwardly recollecting the form of the shaykh does not appear to have widespread, if any, application. It is currently referred to as *muraqabah*, or "contemplation of the shaykh's form." It is worth examining this critical difference in more detail.

---

[220] Haar, J.G.J., *Follower and heir of the Prophet: Shaykh Ahmad Sirhindi (1564-1624) as mystic.* Leiden, Netherlands: Hetoosters Instituut, 1992, p.320.

[221] Both Buehler and J.G.T. Haar cite several instances in the recorded sayings of Sirhindi, Abd al-Rahman Jami, Khwaja Ala al-din Attar, and Bahauddin Naqshband of the use of *tasawwur-i-shaykh* in their instructions to novices. In one of the stories, Bahauddin advises one of his novices to concentrate on him, that is, to call to mind the face of his shaykh, and to say, "It is not me, it is the Khwaja." Haar, J.G.J., *Follower and heir of the Prophet: Shaykh Ahmad Sirhindi (1564-1624) as mystic* (Leiden, Netherlands: Hetoosters Instituut, 1992) p. 321. See also Buehler, A., *Sufi heirs of the Prophet: The Indian Naqshbandiyya order and the rise of the mediating Sufi Shaykh* (Columbia, S.C.: University of South Carolina Press, 1998) p. 135, for a similar description of the practice of visualizing the shaykh.

[222] According to Haar, the techniques of *rabita* and *tawajjuh* as understood by later generations of Naqshbandis "appears to be an elaboration and refinement of the idea of *tawajjuh* put forward by Bahauddin Naqshband and his disciple Alauddin Attar." Haar, J.G.J.,*Follower and heir of the Prophet: Shaykh Ahmad Sirhindi (1564-1624) as mystic* (Leiden, Netherlands: Hetoosters Instituut, 1992) p. 321.

VISUALIZING THE SHAYKH'S FORM OUTWARDLY

The practice of gazing steadfastly and with full attention upon the physical form of the shaykh, especially his eyes, seems to be in widespread use within the Haqqani branch today. By riveting the attention upon the face and forehead of the shaykh, the disciple opens the spiritual doors to direct transmission from the shaykh.[223]

SHAYKH NAZIM'S APPEARANCE

After about one hour or so Shaykh Nazim emerged with little fanfare from behind an enclosed staircase into the courtyard. Shaykh Nazim appeared dressed in traditional Sufi robes with a tall white and green turban and walking cane in his right hand. His long perfectly white beard reached nearly halfway down his chest. He is by sight calculation about 5′ 5″ in height but appears much larger from a distance because of his regal bearing. His high forehead, diamond-shaped chiseled face, and deeply set eyes immediately set him apart from everyone else.

I immediately noticed his beautiful sky-blue eyes peering, or should I say darting, all around. Certainly, his most striking feature is his eyes. They appear I think even to a casual observer to be strangely luminous with a warm and tender simplicity to them. His smile too impressed me as disarmingly fragile and innocent.

CONNECTING WITH THE SHAYKH (*MURAQABAH*)

The practice of visualizing the shaykh's face inwardly appears in a number of Naqshbandi treatises. As-Sanusi, while not a Naqshbandi, describes one of the techniques prevalent during his time:

> In order to attain this he must visualize interiorly the image of his shaykh. He imagines his image as though on his *right* shoulder. Then picturing from the right shoulder to his heart a line, which can act as a passage whereby the spirit of the shaykh can take possession of that organ. This process

[223] **Vidich, *Op. cit.*, p. 206.**

> maintained continuously will ensure his attaining absorption in the shaykh (*al-fana fi-sh-shaykh*).[224]

In more conservative Naqshbandi orders, the practice was not advocated; instead, the *murid* was asked to "picture the Name Allah as engraved in his heart and continuously put his mind to it as a means to be in God's presence."[225] A similar method was apparently employed by disciples of Sher Muhammad, who asked his disciples to "visualize the written forms of 'Allah' and '*Hu*,' which he drew with his fingers." [226] The use of visualization appears widespread over the centuries, and other orders seem to have established similar practices.[227]

In my conversations with shaykhs in the Haqqani order, I learned that the practice of "visualizing the shaykh's face" was not advocated. ...Instead, shaykhs encourage their *murids* to simply recollect the master sweetly and lovingly without attempting to actually bring the image of the shaykh's faces to one's conscious mind. In an unpublished manuscript, the following description appears:

> Make *ghusl* or *wudu* and put on clean clothes if possible. Pray two *rakat "Tahiyatu-l-wudu."* Then sit down in a silent private place and face the *qiblah*. Close your eyes and try to stop all movements, thinking and wishing. Imagine yourself in the presence of your shaykh and him sitting in front of you. For that purpose you can try to remember a moment you had with the shaykh which was pleasant or impressive to you, or use a picture of him to remember his face. Connect with him through your heart, turning in love towards him. "Sincerity is to worship Allah as if you were seeing Him; and even if you don't see Him, he is always looking to you." The shaykh is the

---

[224] Trimingham, *Sufi Orders of Islam*, 3rd ed. (Oxford, England: Oxford University Press, 1998) p. 212.

[225] Haar, J.G.J., *Follower and heir of the* Prophet*: Shaykh Ahmad Sirhindi (1564-1624) as mystic* (Leiden, Netherlands: Hetoosters Instituut, 1992) p. 320.

[226] Buehler, A., *Sufi heirs of the Prophet:* The *Indian Naqshbandiyya order and the rise of the mediating Sufi Shaykh.* Columbia, S.C.: University of South Carolina Press, 1998, p. 138.

[227] Trimingham mentions the use of a similar practice, termed *ar-rabita* in a Qadiri book by Ismaiil ibn M. Said, *Al-Fuyudat ar-Rabbaniyya*, p. 26. See Trimingham, *Sufi Orders of Islam*, 1998, p. 213.

> representative of the Holy Prophet who is the *Caliphatullah*. Remember that the Shaykh is always looking to us, that he is always with us, even though we may not be able to see, hear or feel him. This is why we are not with him and forget him. Imagine yourself always in his presence, he being at your side, no matter what you do.

The *murid* should then connect with the shaykh by doing the following practice.

> To connect with the shaykh, read three times (the Quranic chapter) *Suratu-l Ikhlas* and one time *Suratu-l-Fatiha*. Dedicate them to the Holy Prophet Muhammad and to the soul of our Grandshaykh Abd Allah ad-Daghestani. Then ask for Mawlana Shaykh Nazim.[228]

The danger, according to the current methodology, lies in recollecting an imagined image and not the reality of the shaykh's face as it appears in the shaykh's luminous body or in the world of divine command (*jism-i mithali*)... many [*murids*] were aware of the more general practice known as *rabitatu sh-sharifah*, mentioned above, for connecting to the shaykh's spiritual form in dreams, waking visions, and during prayer.[229] [230]

---

[228] Nazim, Shaykh Muhammad, Interviews in Lefke, Cyprus, by Andrew Vidich, August 11-19, 1999, p. 101.

[229] In personal interviews with *murid*s of Shaykh Nazim, December 1-15, 1998, and May 1-15, 1999.

[230] Buehler notes that not all Mujaddidis "enthusiastically endorsed visualization of the shaykh. Apparently Sher Muhammad did prohibit even the spontaneous visualization of the shaykh though not for the same reasons given by current Naqshbandi shaykhs. Later, after we assume some degree of advancement, "the shaykh's heart spurs the seeker's heart via the chain of masters leading to the Prophet's presence. The novice having the picture of his shaykh's face in his heart at this point is assisted by Muhammad to arrive at God." Buehler, A., *Sufi heirs of the Prophet: The Indian Naqshbandiyya order and the rise of the mediating Sufi Shaykh* (Columbia, S.C.: University of South Carolina Press, 1998) pp. 137-138.

Meeting with Shaykh Hisham Kabbani

From the outset, I was extremely conscious of the need to interview Shaykh Hisham Kabbani,[231] who is the duly appointed *khalifah* (successor) to Shaykh Nazim in North and South America, responsible in a literal and spiritual sense for everything that goes on in these areas. It was also clear that without his tacit approval, I would not have had access either to the *murids* or to other important information.

A word about Shaykh Hisham is in order here. He is the son-in-law of Shaykh Nazim and has spent most of his life as a *murid* of both Shaykh Abd Allah al-Faiz ad-Daghestani[232] and Shaykh Nazim. He was appointed by Shaykh Abd Allah ad-Daghestani to be his *khalifa* for the United States before his passing. In 1991, under the direct orders of Grandshaykh Nazim al-Haqqani, he came to the United States to further the work of the Haqqani order. Since then, he has been extremely active in spreading the Haqqani teachings throughout the United States. He has convened two large conferences and opened a large retreat center in Fenton, Michigan. He is the author of five books all or most about the Naqshbandis, founded the Naqshbandi The Muslim Magazine, and is credited with initiating thousands of people to Islam and to the Naqshbandi order.[233]

My first interview with Shaykh Hisham Kabbani took place nearly six months into my research study. However, on several previous

---

[231] Shaykh Muhammad Hisham Kabbani is Shaykh Nazim's duly authorized deputy in America and his son-in-law. Shaykh Hisham Kabbani settled in Los Altos Hills near San Francisco in 1991, under the direction of Shaykh Nazim. In the last year (1999), he has moved to the Fenton retreat center because of Shaykh Nazim's predictions concerning future catastrophic events in California. It is important to note that Shaykh Hisham was appointed *khalifa* for the West directly by Grandshaykh Abd Allah ad-Daghestani before he passed on. His status within the order is therefore unquestioned.

[232] Please see page 271 for a photograph of the orders "tree" of spiritual descent with photographs of all the most recent shaykhs. For a complete lineage see Appendix 4. Moving from the top left to right and top to bottom the figures are Shaykh Nazim Adil al-Haqqani, Shaykh Abd Allah al-Faiz ad-Daghestani, Shaykh Jamaluddin al-Ghumuqi al-Husayni, Sharafuddin ad-Daghestani, Shaykh Muhummad al-Madani, another photo of Shaykh Muhammad al-Madani, Shaykh Adnan and Shaykh Nazim and his two *khalifas* Shaykh Hisham Kabbani and Shaykh Adnan in the lower right hand corner.

[233] For up-to-date information about the activities of Shaykh Hisham and the order, see the Naqshbandi Web site at http://www.naqshbandi.org/.

occasions, I had tried to arrange a meeting with Shaykh Hisham. His schedule is so busy that *murids* consider it a blessing just to speak him on the telephone. Finally, in the second week of June I was informed by my contact that Shaykh Hisham was coming to New York. On the previous night, my contact left a message that Shaykh Nazim would give a talk at a New Jersey Mosque on the *mawlid* (birthday) of the Prophet. I was pleased that the opportunity for which I had been waiting so long had materialized before my very eyes without any effort on my part. I was informed I should come and meet him at the Newark airport at 2:30 P.M. My first meeting with him is worth describing in detail.

I knew next to nothing about Shaykh Hisham before meeting him at Newark airport except that he was the son-in-law of Shaykh Nazim. I had just finished parking my car and had entered the pavilion when I saw a group of red-white-and-green-turbaned Naqshbandis greeting him on the next level up. I approached the group, and Yasin Sefu immediately grabbed me by the hand and introduced me to Shaykh Hisham.

Shaykh Hisham has a cherubic face with a very long white beard extending down to the middle of his chest. He stands about five feet six or seven inches tall but appears somewhat larger because he carries himself with a regal bearing. I found his manner extremely deliberate and refined. As I introduced myself, he looked at me with a kind of double-take. As our eyes met, for a brief instant there was an immediate recognition on both our parts. It is difficult to describe the sense of familiarity that I felt in this first encounter. It was almost as if I was meeting a long-lost relative. It is not a physical recognition but spiritual. The Naqshbandis explain this by saying Sufis "believe that God gathered our spirits together on the day of the Primordial Covenant, when, according to the Quran, *"He drew forth from the children of Adam, from their loins, their descendants, and made them testify against themselves: 'Am I not your Lord?' They said, 'Yes, we testify'"* (7:171) According to Naqshbandis, spirits were able to meet one another on that day, and any immediate recognition is interpreted as a sign that the spirits recognized that meeting in pre-eternity.[234] From my perspective, it is the recognition of the soul or light of God residing in each of us that the soul perceives and honors.

As he led the group out toward the parking lot, the *murids* kept a respectful distance of about five paces. As I followed, he turned around and engaged me in conversation. He asked, "Are you aware that a research group in England has recently been given over a million pounds to study the Naqshbandi order?"[235] I replied, "Yes, I am aware of the group. In fact, one of the Naqshbandi *murids* had told me about it while I was staying in England. They have even given me their address for me to contact." I think he was somewhat surprised I had already heard about the project. I then said, "Are you aware that Shaykh Nazim actually visited the researcher institute to ask some questions about the project?" He did not reply but raised his eyebrows slightly, indicating he was not aware of this. Our conversation ended abruptly as his attention turned toward getting in the car and giving directions to his *murids*.

The others immediately jumped into their cars to follow Shaykh Hisham as closely as possible to where he would be staying. In the ensuing confusion, some of us got lost, but after an hour or so, we managed to find our way to Brother Roz's house where Shaykh Hisham was staying. When we arrived, we entered the living room of a ranch-style suburban home with several photos of Grandshaykh Nazim and Shaykh Hisham on the wall. I also noticed several other pictures of Islamic calligraphy and a photo of the Prophet's tomb. Except for one large, luxurious couch in the center and a carpet on the floor, there was only one other large chair. I assumed much of the furniture had been removed to accommodate all the *murids*.

---

[234] Valerie Hoffman makes the further point that a "shaykh and his disciple should always have such a pre-formed affinity; a natural attraction is considered a prerequisite for a proper shaykh-disciple relationship." Hoffman, V.J., *Sufism, mystics, and saints in modern Egypt* (Columbia, S.C.: University of South Carolina Press 1995) p. 36). In many of the interviews I conducted with *murids*, this attraction appeared to be quite strong and at times even overwhelming—I would say even a common feature of the bond between shaykh and *murid*.

[235] The institution doing the research is the Selly Oak Foundation at the University of Birmingham... The Web site is at http://www.sellyoak.ac.uk/csic; it is part of the CSIC site.

When I walked in the room, everyone was already seated on the floor cross-legged or on their knees, crowded around Shaykh Hisham who was seated on the couch. The women were seated to the right and to the back, where the dining room connected with the living room. All the women, as far as I could see, were wearing a *hijab* or scarf covering the head. However, except for the scarves for women and turbans and *kufis* for most men, the dress of both women and men varied greatly. Some were in casual summer dress, others in traditional Pakistani *kurtas* and long pants, and still others in business attire. The various colored turbans worn to indicate the different races and the variety of dress all created an atmosphere of multiculturalism. The one link in this sea of diversity was Shaykh Hisham. All eyes were respectfully riveted on Shaykh Hisham, who appeared totally relaxed and at home.

Shaykh Hisham asked a few questions, and a conversation ensued about the details of the program and other issues. During this short interlude it was clear Shaykh Hisham wielded all the authority—not, however, in a traditional sense, but spiritually. No one spoke unless questioned by Shaykh Hisham, and a reverential silence pervaded the entire room. If anyone had to leave, they asked the Shaykh's permission to leave and walked backward toward the door, careful to keep their face always toward the shaykh.

Soon Shaykh Hisham asked his host, Roz, "Where is it best to conduct the evening prayers?" Roz, a tall, middle-aged man dressed in Western clothing but obviously from Pakistan, replied with great deference, "What you think best, Mawlana." His reply, in keeping with the proper *adab* surrounding the shaykh, was intended to indicate he was allowing the shaykh to make all the decisions, even apparently insignificant ones. Clearly, as it was Roz's house, he was probably the more knowledgeable party. These subtle exchanges between *murid* and shaykh on the outside may appear, from the point of view of efficiency, a waste of time. Nevertheless, they are at the essence of the proper *adab* between shaykh and *murid*. The *murid*'s job is to place everything in the shaykh's hands and to become "a corpse in the hands of a body washer"[236]. Shaykh Hisham replied nonchalantly, "I think we should all go downstairs." Glancing around the room briefly, Shaykh Hisham got up and then went downstairs to lead the evening prayers. As soon as Shaykh Hisham had left, everyone followed in single file behind him to a larger basement area converted for the use of prayers. Within minutes, everyone was seated in straight rows and ready to begin prayers.

The procedure for performing evening prayers has become so ingrained that everyone lines up in rows without wasting any time. The clearly defined protocol is second nature to most of these *murids* and is a staging ground for both the communal and simultaneously the deeply private world of each *murid*'s relationship to Allah. For a newcomer, the routine has a combined quality of both discipline and reverence. Each *murid* is careful to align himself or herself appropriately and at the same time keep a reverential attitude. Talking is clearly discouraged except by the shaykh or his deputy, who will lead the prayer. Once the prayer begins, it develops a force of its own.

After the Asr prayers, the celebration of the *mawlid* of the Prophet commenced. The Naqshbandi *tariqah* not only advocates the celebration of the Prophet's birth but also openly defends this position against the Wahhabis.[237] Shaykh Hisham in recent months has become somewhat of a controversial figure for his position in regard to a number of traditional Sufi practices. However, this is the subject of a later

---

[236] During a private interview in Cyprus, I learned that Shaykh Nazim always conducts himself as a normal person. He does not want the *murid* to think, "Oh, the shaykh knows everything; therefore I have no need to say anything." In this sense, the shaykh exhibits the *adab* of acting in a normal way in conformity with the culture and times he lives in.

[237] "Wahhabism" is a puritanical Islamic movement that originated in 18th-century Arabia under the leader Muhammad Abd al-Wahhab (1703-1787). Ira Lapidus notes, "Wahhabi reformism took the extreme position of totally rejecting belief in and veneration of saints or any human in any form as *shirk* or polytheism. It also rejected the common pantheistic types of Sufi theology" Lapidus, I.M., *A history of Islamic societies* (Cambridge, England: Cambridge University Press, 1988) p. 673. Present-day scripturalist movements among Muslims, while not "wahhabis" in a literal historical sense, share the movement's agenda of denial of the role of Muslim saints (Sufis) and the function of the Prophet Muhammad as an intercessor and "super-human" example. They also disapprove of practices such as commemorating the Prophet's birthday.

discussion.[238] The *mawlid* began with a recitation of the Quran sung in Arabic by several different *murids*. The songs were read from a traditional source and described the wonderful qualities and attributes of the Prophet. Although I did not understand much, the Quranic singing had a deep and resonant quality that moved me deeply. After the reading, Shaykh Hisham led us in the final evening prayer, and then everyone was invited for the traditional evening meal.

A MEAL IS SERVED

The meal is served on the floor in traditional Indo-Pakistan style. *Murids* sat cross-legged on the floor and were served their food by others as they sat. Everyone is served until satiated. The food, prepared in Indo-Pakistani style, consists of rice, salad, and a simple meat and vegetable dish. It is by most Western standards somewhat spicy, but I was quite accustomed to it.

TALK AT A LOCAL MOSQUE

After the evening meal, everyone was invited to the local mosque, where Shaykh Hisham was to give a talk about the Prophet followed by a short question-and-answer period.

Although his 45-minute talk did not cover any issues of Sufi methodology, it was important for another reason. Shaykh Hisham spent most of his talk refuting the claims of the Wahhabis and defending the Sufi practice of celebrating the birth of the Prophet. I was a little surprised by this, as it seemed an inappropriate venue to defend Naqshbandi doctrine. Politics seemed to have usurped the real celebration of the Prophet. It was difficult to comprehend from my position why he was so concerned with this. About twenty minutes into his talk, he looked over at me in a crowd of about two hundred people and said, "This is not a Sufi talk," as if replying to my question.

---

[238] Shaykh Hisham has written extensively in defense of the Naqshbandi position regarding the celebration of the Prophet's birth, but also on more substantial concerns of methodology and epistemology. For a detailed exposition see al-Zahawi's, *The Doctrine of Ahl-Sunna Versus the "Salafi" Movement: A Complete Refutation and Translation in English with Introduction and Notes* by Shaykh Muhammad Hisham Kabbani (Chicago: As-Sunna Foundation of America, 1996) pp. 22-51.

Since my concern was with understanding, the inner workings of the order, political concerns, and the internal geopolitical struggles between different branches of Islam seemed off-putting.

Later in the talk I came to realize that the struggle to defend the Naqshbandi position and thereby exert influence on the larger Muslim community was very much a part of Naqshbandi concerns. Although strictly speaking it does not directly affect the inner disciplines of the *murids*, it does have a broad generalized effect by making them aware of their relationship to the larger world of Islam. It has also grown out of, in a very organic sense, the practice of *khalwat dar anjuman,* or "solitude in the crowd," which historically has been the reason the Naqshbandis have taken such a keen interest in the politics of their times.[239] In their belief, they cannot avoid these struggles because they also have the task of caring for and guiding the larger Muslim community.

Looked at from this perspective, it is a constant reminder of each *murid*'s responsibility to play a role in guiding the Muslim doctrine and in bringing a greater sense of unity. There are many ways the *murids* reflect the internalization of this practice. It is also clear that the Naqshbandi see themselves as part of the larger community not only of Muslims but also of the community of Muhammad and the community of God.[240]

---

[239] Shaykh Hisham has made extensive efforts to bring about a greater sense of unity among Muslims. The two conferences convened by the Naqshbandi order in 1993 and 1996 were testaments to this effort, and as far as I can tell were well received within the Muslim community. Most recently, however, Shaykh Hisham Kabbani has outspokenly challenged the religious practices of American Muslims' established leadership. According to an article in *The Los Angeles Times,* "...Kabbani's allegations about Muslim American extremism, delivered at a State Department forum this year, have, in particular, turned what began as a theological debate into a political war. In an unprecedented joint statement, major Muslim American groups condemned Kabbani and demanded an apology" (Watanabe, April 25, 1999). While Shaykh Hisham has not backed down, he clarified his statement by saying that the "Muslim community as a whole was not extremist but that they were controlled by funds from extremists groups abroad" (Kabbani, Hisham. Interview in Saddle River, N.J., by Andrew Vidich, June 1999, private interview).

[240] According to Shaykh Hisham, simply by saying the *Fatiha* once one becomes part of the community of Muhammad and will be saved on the Day of Judgment. The community of God

Interview with Shaykh Hisham Kabbani

The following day I scheduled an interview with Shaykh Hisham at 10:00 A.M. ...[241]

After I introduced myself, I gave a brief synoposis of the purpose and intent of the thesis. I explained in some detail that this was a work about a living shaykh and a living order. I was interested in understanding the Naqshbandi method of self-transformation and the "charismatic" presence of the shaykh.

He replied, "You will have two problems in your study. First, when you study the *murids*, you are studying the perceptions of people who are in a hospital. Everyone who comes to the order has some sickness. Therefore how can they give you an accurate assesment of the order or its teachings? Only the shaykh knows their condition, and only the shaykh can give the correct pill to alleviate it. Second, to understand Sufism one must experience it. One must have a taste of it. You may study a plum, its size, shape, color, etc., but unless you taste it, how can you know anything about it?" I replied, "Exactly, I agree entirely with your diagnosis. However, I am not so much concerned with why each *murid* is the hospital but what 'pill' the shaykh gives to them to alleviate their condition." He paused and thought for a moment, perhaps realizing the direction I was interested in. Then he replied, with a slight smile on his face, "Oh, you are interested in the 'pill' which the shaykh gives." I nodded affirmativeily. "Yes, yes; I am also interested in what experiences the *murid* undergoes along the way. How does the 'pill' affect and transform the *murid*'s life?" Shaykh Hisham nodded his head several times and then gathered himself for a moment.

I should mention that by this time, the whole room was filled with *murids*, and everyone was listening with pin-drop silence. I was sitting about three feet from the shaykh's face, and at times it became only two feet or even less as he pivoted back and forth in his chair. He then

---

is in fact the community of Muhammad because Muhammad's light is the Light of God and is intended for everyone.

[241] **Vidich, *Op. cit.*, p. 283 – 288.**

began to speak in a very animated and powerful way without a break for about four and half hours.

It is difficult to articuate what I experienced. I felt inwardly and outwardly in contact with his soul. Throughout his talk, my attention was fixed on his face, and his attention was entirely on me.[242] As he spoke, he was fully engaged and appeared fully concentrated. His facial expressions varied from intense focus to childlike humor. Each word he infused with a quality of exultation. There was a sweetness and playful delight that made him all the more easy to listen to and enjoy.

It is significant here because it underscores the Naqshbandi style of discourse and the methods of *attunement,* to use a word applied by Francis Trix.[243] The shaykh is always communicating in at least two ways, first through his spiritual radiation *(fayd)* and secondarily through his use of words.[244] In this instance, enthnographic observation is framed and conducted within the context of this highly specialized environment mediated by the shaykh. Everything the shaykh says takes on a new meaning because of the nature of the medium in which knowledge is conveyed. Marshall McLuhan was right when he said "the medium is the message." The transmssion is felt by the *murid* in direct relationship to his receptivity to the shaykh. Even if the shaykh says nothing, his *fayd* or radiation continues unabated. This wordless transmission is at the heart of the *suhbat* and is the essence of companionship with the shaykh. Rumi's description of the silent transmission of the third Caliph, Uthman, is a excellent example of this.

---

242 The substance of the talk was completely new to me, and as far as I know has never before been written about in any Naqshbandi literature.

243 Trix, F., Spiritual *discourse: Learning with an Islamic master.* Conduct and Communication series. Philadelphia: University of Philadelphia Press. 1995.

244 Shaykh Hisham mentions six secrets that are revealed by the shaykh in order that the seeker can take his first major step on the Way. These six powers are "the reality of attraction, the reality of receiving heavenly revelation, the reality of directing the heart's power to someone, the reality of intercession, the reality of guidance, and the ability to move in space and time in one moment" Kabbani, Hisham, *The Naqshbandi Sufi way: History and Guidebook of the Saints of the Golden Chain* (Chicago: Kazi Publications. 1995) p. 314.

> When Uthman became Caliph he went to the pulpit (*minbar*) [to give a sermon]. People waited for him to say something, [but] he did not say anything. He [just] kept looking so intently at the people that they could not leave nor have any idea where each other were sitting. Never with a hundred admonishments, preachings, and sermons would they have had such an excellent state. [Nor] would they have received [such] benefits and have [had such] secrets revealed with so much effort and preaching. Until the end of the session he kept looking at them like this without uttering a word. When he wanted to descend from the pulpit he said, "It is better that you have an effective imam [leader] rather than a prattling imam[245] [246]

My choice to interact in the role of a *murid* was an unplanned decision which in retrospect greatly influenced the results of the interview. Frances Trix, in her study of learning with a Bektashi master, noted significant differences between a "typical interactionist" relationship between a student and teacher, interviewer and interviewee, or doctor and patient, and the *murid*-shaykh relationship. "Previous Islamic studies," she notes, "have preserved the poetry of *murshid*s and certain biographical details but have tended to take for granted the process of their teaching."[247][248] However, since the *murid*-shaykh relationship is almost entirely dependent upon process, the relationship itself becomes central to the learning journey.

Two of the central features of the relationship are that of continual scrutiny on the part of the shaykh and his nurturing, even motherly,

---

[245] Rumi, Jalaluddin, *Discourses of Rumi (Fihi ma fihi)* (New York: Samuel Weiser, 1961) p. 129.

[246] Buehler notes that Badiuzzaman Furzanfar documents how this story related by Rumi changed considerably from the shorter version he had located in the *hadith* literature (Buehler, *Op. cit.*, 1998, p. 134).

[247] Trix, F., *Spiritual discourse: Learning with an Islamic master.* Conduct and Communication series (Philadelphia: University of Philadelphia Press.1997) p.147.

[248] One important exception is Martin Ling's *A Sufi Saint of the Twentieth Century: Shaikh Ahmad Al-Alwawi, His Spiritual Heritage and Legacy* (Cambridge: Islamic Texts Society, 1993). In the first section of his book, pp. 13-33, he gives a vivid account of Dr. Marcel Carret's meeting with Shaikh Alawi. His account gives some indication of the "power" of the shaykh's presence that is central to the understanding of a shaykh.

concern for his *murids*. Because of these twin characteristics, the *murid*-shaykh relationship can resemble the mother-child or the lover-beloved relationship.[249] Trix notes that in contrast, using the methodological stance of an interviewer coming from a secular institution tends "to be choppier, both in terms of frequency of questioning and number of episodes." More significantly, "Baba's [her shaykh] responses in the interview became shorter and shorter and his irritation grew until all verbal interaction ceased."[250]

I realized that by playing the role of a *murid* I was learning how a *murid* learns. I was entering into a "relationship of nurturance" and participating in the "process of attunement." I found that this process demanded at least three conditions on my part. First, it required a willingness to assume a deferential stance with the shaykh, never questioning or challenging his authority. Second, it necessitated a gradual adoption of a shared "reference system."[251] Put differently, it was important for me accept, on a conditional basis, the doctrines and teachings of Islam from the perspective of the Naqshbandi framework. Third, I had to try to anticipate and inwardly "attune myself" to the internal dialogue of the shaykh, removing as much as possible the walls of my own mindset.

Since much of what the *murid* is receiving is in fact nonverbal attention from the shaykh's presence *(fayd)*, as the excerpt from Rumi so well illustrates, the *murid* is really attuning himself to the vibration of the

---

[249] Margaret Malamud, in her article "Gender and Spiritual Self-Fashioning: The Master-disciple Relationship in Classical Sufism," points out, "Medieval male Sufis often used gendered imagery to describe the relationship between a Sufi Master (shaykh or *murshid*) and his disciple (*murid*)." She quotes from Fakhr al-din Iraqi's *Divine Flashes*, "I have drunk from the breasts of two mothers" (Sadr ad-Din Qunawi). Cited in the *Journal of American Academy of Religion*, LXIV/1, p. 89.

[250] Trix, F., *Spiritual discourse: Learning with an Islamic master.* Conduct and Communication series. Philadelphia: University of Philadelphia Press, 1997, p.150.

[251] Harriet Feinberg notes, in her study of teaching and learning in Martin Buber's *Hasidic Tales,* that sudden illumination depends on a "shared reference system" of student and teacher and on spiritual strength built up over long periods of interaction (Feinberg, 1972). Francis Trix, in her study *Spiritual Discourse: Learning with an Islamic Master,* recounts that her sudden understanding of the special contextualized meaning of the word *hu* was not fully understood until after many repeated interactions with her teacher. This reflects the continual "attunement" of the *murshid*'s heart with the heart of the *murid* (1996).

shaykh. The *murid* achieves this by focusing fully on the shaykh, with as little mental inference as possible. My experience of the shaykh was that he was consciously directing his energy toward me as he was speaking. I experienced this powerful current, infused with peace and exhilaration...

In all, the interview lasted almost five hours. When I looked around the room, I noticed most of the *murids* were in a similar state of enjoyment and were obviously appreciative of the opportunity. Shaykh Hisham got up at about 2:30, and everyone proceeded downstairs for lunch and afternoon prayers... In general, Shaykh Hisham has a very gentle and unassuming disposition; on occasion, however, he became quite forceful. This was particularly true when he was defending his position against the Wahhabis or when reprimanding a *murid* for some reason. But for the most part I found him very affable, light-hearted, and deferential with everyone.

Conduct of the Interview

During my first interview with Shaykh Hisham Kabbani, he frequently asked people to do small tasks while he was being interviewed. At one point, I told him I was interested in collecting stories from the *murid*'s perspective on the path. I explained that since this book was about a living order, it was important to give some indication of what the *murids* were experiencing. Shaykh Hisham replied that the *murids*' experience was of someone who was in the hospital and therefore did not reflect a true understanding of the spiritual path. If that were understood, then the experience of the *murids* would be valuable for other seekers.

At that point Shaykh Hisham immediately glanced around the room and called out the name of one *murid*. I was a bit surprised, and I am sure the *murid* was as well—first because he was put on the spot, and second because he might feel shy in revealing any personal stories in front a large group. Yet the *murid* began without hesitation to tell the story of how he came to take *bayah* from Shaykh Hisham. It was a moving story and brought tears to people's eyes. I was impressed with the readiness of this *murid* to comply with Shaykh Hisham's request.

Other *murids* did not fare as well as the first and had a hard time expressing themselves in a public forum.[252]

A real shaykh speaks to people in accordance to their ranks and levels of understanding; as such shaykhs are inheritors of the Prophet Muhammad, who said, "Whosoever wants to teach people must be careful to notice the level of understanding of his audience and to address them accordingly."[253]

Many of the *murids* emphasize the importance of maintaining the Islamic law (*Shariah*) but do not necessarily comply with all aspects of it. Their perception of the self-identity of the order is based on the practice of Islamic law (*Shariah*). The Islamic scriptural texts and the living words of Shaykh Nazim al-Haqqani further support this rule. However, the reality of most *murids'* practice is at variance with their perception of their order. Shaykh Hisham mentioned that some *murids* do make rapid progress and comply with all aspects of the *Shariah,* but most *murids* are at the beginning stages of adherence to the *Shariah.*

Shaykh Hisham elucidated this point by saying that if you "study the *murids,* you are studying those who are in the hospital. How can a sick person give you an adequate understanding of the order? In reality, only the shaykh has the correct view." It is at the razor edge of these discrepancies between the *murid*'s perception of himself and the reality perceived by the shaykh that the real work of the shaykh occurs.

Association with Shaykh Nazim

My wife and I arrived in Cyprus via Istanbul on August 10 [1999] at about 12:30 in the morning. We decided to spend the first night in a small town called Bellapais, which was only about an hour from Shaykh Nazim's *dergah.* The next day we decided to stay at a lovely hotel situated directly adjacent to a 12th-century abbey known to be one of the earliest and most beautiful Gothic churches not only in Cyprus, but in the entire Middle East. From this town, I decided to

---

[252] Kabbani, Hisham. Interview in Saddle River, N.J., by Andrew Vidich, 1999, June 26.

[253] Nazim, Shaykh Muhammad, *Mercy Oceans'Hidden Treasures* (Konya: Sebat Offset Printers, 1987) p. 52.

travel back and forth to Shaykh Nazim's *dergah* in the small town of Lefke about an hour away by taxi.

Lefke is a small rural town situated on a small hillside overlooking the Mediterranean Sea. It boasts only a small central square with a few dozen shops and cafes sporadically lining the streets. It is remarkably close to the Greek border and apparently had been a battleground between Turks and Greeks nearly thirty years ago when the island was partitioned. Today, most of the people work in shops or in the outlying areas either in agriculture-related industries or in the tourist business. Although Cyprus has some beautiful cedar forests and scenic mountain areas, Lefke is largely a semi-arid land with few trees and no large standing forests. It is quite common for residents to maintain small gardens, which do a great deal to beautify the landscape, but the area was originally a great deal more fertile and cultivated. When the country was partitioned in 1974, most of the Greeks left behind beautiful gardens and fruit orchards. The Greeks were skilled gardeners and had cultivated the land quite extensively. On the other hand, the Turks who settled the area had no experience with gardening, and most of the land was left to waste away unattended.[254]

I arrived in the town of Lefke late Wednesday, August 11, at about 3:00 in the afternoon. The taxi driver dropped me off near the entrance to Shaykh Nazim's *dergah* and instructed me to proceed down a path. I was surprised by how well hidden it was from the average person. There were no signs, no directions, and no indication of any special activity going on. I then noticed several *murids* walking up a road from a distance of about twenty meters. I inquired of them where Shaykh Nazim lived. They greeted me warmly and then pointed, saying, "It is just down the road about onehundred yards." I thanked them and proceeded as they had directed.

---

[254] The day I arrived, I had an extensive conversation with a murid of Shaykh Nazim who was visiting from Palestine. He was extremely well versed in the history and politics of the local area as well as of the Middle East in general. He indicated to me that most of the Turks who settled the region after the occupation had come from central Turkey and were primarily sheep herders. They had little knowledge or interest in the land, and it slowly deteriorated over the years.

Within a few minutes, I encountered a large house and a number of *murids* talking and conversing. I immediately recognized the house from pictures I had seen in several of the books. I introduced myself to the *murids*, and we exchanged greetings. There was a genuine openness in the *murids'* attitude toward me, and I was relieved to be welcomed so warmly. Within minutes, I encountered a *murid* I had interviewed in London in February named Safiud-din. We embraced and began speaking. I asked him why he had come to Cyprus. He indicated to me that his plans had changed quite suddenly because of the recent predictions of Shaykh Nazim.[255] I was happy to see him in any case, because he had been so helpful and kind while I was in London.

We spoke briefly, and then he invited me to join him for the afternoon at the house where he was staying, which was located only a few hundreds yards down the road. I readily accepted. Safiud-din is a charming English *murid* with a delightful if sometimes irreverent sense of humor. We spent the next several hours talking informally with a German *murid* named Ahmad who was renting the house. The conversation was light and congenial and covered a wide range of subjects and issues, from Shaykh Nazim's predictions to life in the *dergah*. As we spoke, Safiud-din was cutting and squeezing lemons for lemon juice for Shaykh Nazim's kitchen. Both of these *murids* would later become wonderful sources of anecdotal information as well as assisting me in acclimating myself to the workings of Shaykh Nazim's *dergah*.

At about 6:00, we heard the call to prayer and stood up to face the *qiblah*. Safiud-din mentioned we should all get ready to go, as Shaykh Nazim would be leading the evening prayer [Asr] shortly. As we returned to the *dergah*, the room was already filled with *murids*, and Shaykh Nazim had just begun the evening prayer. There were about fifty or so *murids* packed in a small square room that could not have been more than thirty feet square. The room was decorated with

---

[255] Shaykh Nazim has increasingly been predicting major changes before the next millennium begins. He has indicated in many writings, as well as in his informal talks for *murids*, to leave big cities and go to the countryside where water supplies are more readily available. He has advised his *murids* to become less reliant on technology and "return to a more natural way of living" (Cyprus, August 17, 1999, informal talk).

Islamic calligraphy and covered with simple woolen carpets, mostly quite worn and threadbare. Red pillows decorated with Bokhara design octagonal medallions lined the outside of the walls. A very simple prayer niche was located in the center of the wall facing east. It was decorated with a green machine-made prayer rug hanging from the wall. Outside of these unsophisticated decorations, the room was rustic and unadorned.

As soon as I arrived, I joined all the other *murids* in what was my first real association with Shaykh Nazim. Immediately after completing the evening prayer (which took about twenty-five minutes), Shaykh Nazim prepared to leave the room through the side entrance. I realized this was as good a time as any to introduce myself to him in a more formal way. I approached from the left-hand side, presented myself before him, and bowed my head reverentially. I said, "My name is Andrew Vidich, and I am writing a book about the Naqshbandis." He stopped in his tracks, glanced at me with a somewhat serious look, and then said, "Welcome. You are welcome. Where are you from?" I replied, "New York City." Suddenly, without any warning, he demanded, "What will happen when the electricity goes?" Somewhat off-guard, I replied, "What do you mean?" He continued, "What are people going to do when the water goes?" Still unclear what he was referring to, I said, "Shaykh, you know best." He seemed somewhat nonplused by my reply. He surveyed the room briefly and then said more pointedly, "No, what do you think?" At this point, I was baffled and confused. I looked around the room for some help. Then it dawned on me: Perhaps he is asking about the Y2K problem. So I looked at another *murid* who was standing close by and asked, "Does he mean will there be a computer problem in Y2K?" Several *murids* immediately nodded their heads, confirming my suspicion. I then replied, "I believe the problem is mostly fixed, but not everywhere." Shaykh Nazim looked at me with some annoyance, and then said, "And what are they saying they are going to do? If they say they have fixed it, they are liars". With that comment he abruptly turned his head and began walking toward the side entrance. I was baffled and perplexed. I was not sure exactly what had happened.

I later learned in a conversation with other *murids* that Shaykh Nazim is predicting major technology problems in the big cities around the world.[256] According to Naqshbandi theology, the saints (*awliya*) have control of electricity, which is a lower aspect of the soul power. If they withdraw their power, the electricity will break down or experience some kind of problem. I later surmised his question was a way of checking me out as well as letting me know where he stood. For the next two hours, I remained in a small entrance adjacent to the prayer room where *murids*, both male and female, often greet Shaykh Nazim. It was not long before I was engaged in several conversations about the nature of my visit and other related issues of my research. The time fled as I introduced myself to numerous people from all over the world.

In the first hour, I saw clearly the multicultural tapestry of personalities, nationalities, and cultures that surrounded this enigmatic figure. There were Germans, French, English, Spanish, Americans, Pakistanis, Lebanese, Turks, Syrians, and many other nationalities represented. I was amazed by the breadth of representation in such an out-of-the-way place. While speaking with several *murids*, I was invited to stay at the *dergah* if I wished. What that meant, in reality, was that I would share a small room directly adjacent to the *dergah* with five to seven other people with absolutely no privacy. I later learned it was also the room where the women pray together and where Shaykh Nazim conducted interviews when it was not being used as sleeping quarters. This meant, among other things, that all the men who were staying there had to vacate during prayer times, as it became the women's domain then. I consulted Safiud-din, who informed me that I had a choice between this room and the more comfortable Western quarters about a half-mile from the *dergah*. The difference was that at the *dergah* there was no charge, whereas at the Western quarters there was a small weekly fee of about $70 U.S. In addition, he explained, while the Western quarters afforded a more comfortable living environment, if I really wanted "to see what is going on," I should stay

256 I was not able to ascertain exactly what reactions *murids* had in response to these predictions. Each *murid* must interpret them according to his or her own level of understanding.

at the *dergah*. I decided to take his advice and stay at the *dergah*, as it seemed a better vantage point from which to conduct my research.

Asr Prayer

...Shaykh Nazim leisurely strolled out from his house to lead the Asr prayer. His house is directly adjacent to the *dergah* and therefore only minutes away. Despite the fact that the house is so close, there is a strict prohibition against going into his house unless specifically invited by the shaykh. As far as I could discern, this rule is rigorously followed, and his family is able to maintain at least some modicum of privacy.[257] Shaykh Nazim entered the *dergah* from the side, and without any fuss or delay immediately engaged himself in the Asr prayer.

...

After he completed the Asr prayer, he turned around and sat down facing the *murids*. This became an occasion for an informal *suhbah*.

As it turned out, a number of *murids* were leaving the *dergah* that evening and presented themselves in front of him. Each in turn kissed Shaykh Nazim's hand and then said goodbye and left. Then Shaykh Nazim turned his attention to several Turkish *murids*. It was not entirely clear whether they were, in fact, *murids*, because they were dressed in Western clothing and were not wearing the Naqshbandi turbans. In any case, they were Muslims.

He looked at one of them and asked a direct question with a penetrating glance, strong enough to make them aware of his displeasure about something. The three young men then moved within a few feet of Shaykh Nazim. He continued to converse with them in a very animated fashion, laughing and sometimes poking fun and making jokes, while simultaneously obviously giving some kind of lesson. As he did this, I continued to look very directly at Shaykh Nazim, never taking my eyes off him. He occasionally looked over and

---

[257] By Western standards, Shaykh Nazim lives an almost totally communal lifestyle. Everyone who comes to the *dergah* is, in fact, Shaykh Nazim's personal guest. There is probably not a moment of his day, except perhaps during prayers, that he is not involved with his *murids*. Living in association with Shaykh Nazim is not merely communal, it is intimate by most normal standards—a point that needs to be reexamined in the light of our current understanding of the concept of association with a saint.

acknowledged my presence. When he finished speaking with them, he dismissed everyone. As soon as he moved to get himself up, two *murids* rushed to assist him.[258] He then made his way slowly to the side entrance. As he did so, *murids* approached him and asked questions. He gave various directions and instructions in very terse and simple English or Turkish. Sometimes a nod of the head or a simple gesture was enough to convey his meaning. As he moved out of the *dergah,* he entered the small corridor where female *murids* had a chance to interact with and ask questions of Shaykh Nazim.[259] The behavior of the female *murids* was remarkably similar to that of the males, except they maintained a certain distance from him. He was quite deferential with the female *murids*...

Preparing Dinner

In the meantime, all the male *murids* returned to the *dergah,* where preparations were underway for the evening communal meal. I immediately took a seat on the floor around two large green plastic mats that stretched the length of the *dergah*. I watched as several *murids* broke stale crusty pieces of bread into small pieces and placed them in several large metal trays. By Western standards, these pieces of stale bread would be considered inedible. However, as I learned, nothing is wasted at the *dergah*. An integral part of the *murids'* training is to learn to recycle everything. It is a message of simplicity and respect for nature.

Serving the Murids

Not long after, Shaykh Nazim returned and took a seat at the head of one of the green mats. Each *murid* received a single large spoon with which to eat. As far as I could see, no other utensils, including paper or Styrofoam plates, were ever used. As the cooks brought in a number of different trays of food, Shaykh Nazim personally poured a simple soup dish over each of the trays of broken bread. As soon as he had done this, the trays were passed around the room for everyone to eat from.

---

[258] *Murids* consider it a special blessing to be able to assist Shaykh Nazim in this way. In fact, any contact with Shaykh Nazim is an occasion for receiving his *barakah*.

[259] The women do not enter the *dergah* but pray in an adjoining room. After the prayers, they greet Shaykh Nazim in a corridor that is used by both male and female murids.

When all the food was eaten, the tray was passed back to Shaykh Nazim to be replenished with other dishes. Finally, after several courses circulated in this fashion, a sweet dish consisting of *halwa* made of cream of wheat, sugar, and milk concluded the meal. Each *murid* partook until he was completely satiated; although the food was simple, there was always plenty of it.

Throughout the meal *murids* engaged in light and jovial conversation. Shaykh Nazim was silent most of time but did engage in conversation at times and made occasional jokes. He not only directed the manner of the food preparation and distribution but orchestrated the entire meal from start to finish. He was keenly aware of everyone and occasionally would look over to see if a *murid* was eating enough. I felt his motherly presence watching over his *murids* with an inward as well as an outward eye.

Being a vegetarian, I faced the difficult task of navigating my way through a meal in which almost every dish had either meat flavoring or meat in it. I did not want to alienate Shaykh Nazim or draw attention to myself, so I politely refused most of the dishes except the salad and *halwa*. I realized later that at some point I would have to explain my dietary view more clearly. In the meantime, I tried to blend into the environment as best I could given the circumstances. I later learned that most of Shaykh Nazim's *murids*, while they have nothing against vegetarians, do not restrict themselves beyond following the dietary requirements dictated by the *Shariah*.[260]

After the meal was over, Shaykh Nazim gave a brief blessing and then got up and left. As he was leaving, *murids* huddled close to him, asking his blessings and questioning him on various issues. His answers again were short and terse, often no more than a simple gesture. Within minutes, he was gone. As I was standing around wondering what to

---

[260] The Quranic verse translated says, "*He hath only forbidden you dead meat, and blood and the flesh of swine, and that which any other name of hath been invoked besides Allah*" (2:173). It also specifically enjoins to eat "*what is on earth, lawful and good*" (2:168). Good: *tayyib*, meaning pure, wholesome, nourishing, pleasing to the taste. Therefore, clearly vegetarians by these injunctions follow the *Shariah* to a greater, not lesser, degree.

do, a *murid* came over and said, "Don't go anywhere; Shaykh Nazim will be back to lead the Maghrib prayer this evening."

Maghrib Prayer

When he finally returned it was nearly 8:00 P.M. The ritual commenced, and Shaykh Nazim lead everyone in the Maghrib prayer. After the prayer was completed and the *murids* were slowly dispersing for the evening, he turned directly toward me and without warning said, "You have a double. He looks just like you. Go outside and see." He gestured strongly, indicating that I should go outside and see whom he was talking about. So without hesitation I got up and went to the back of the *dergah*. As I walked out, I saw a man speaking fluent English with a Scottish accent. I introduced myself and said, "Hi my name is Andrew. Shaykh Nazim asked me to come out and meet you." The man replied, "My name is Patrick." I then asked, "What do you do here?" He responded, "I sell vegetables to the local people in the village." Although his appearance was a bit slovenly, for a farmer he would have appeared quite normal. He seemed a perfectly nice person, although somewhat on the simple side. By appearance, however, he was more than a little unkempt, and his hair was quite disheveled. A number of missing teeth and an extremely thin figure only added to the impression that he was either very poor or unconcerned with his physical attire. Had I not found out that he spoke such good English, I would have thought him to have fallen on hard times. He was obviously not a *murid*, nor did he have any particular interest in Islam that I could discern. Apparently he came every evening to sell vegetables to the *dergah*. I said, "Shaykh Nazim sent me out here to meet you. He said I looked just like you." It was obvious to both of us that not only did I not look anything like him physically, but there seemed little else that we shared in common. Patrick looked at me incredulously, wondering why this was happening. In fact, on a purely outer level we seemed to have little to discuss—except, perhaps, our love for organic vegetables. I replied, in leaving, "Thank you, and nice to meet you." We then went our separate ways. A few minutes later I began to put the picture together slowly.

By this time, Shaykh Nazim had finished speaking with the other *murids* and was making his way to the corridor before retiring for the evening. I quickly decided to follow him and meet him in the corridor. Throughout the evening, I had made a point of gazing at him at every opportunity. I did this not with any intent to be disrespectful, but only to make sure I did not miss a single move or action he made. Ironically, as Shaykh Nazim rounded the corner into the meeting room, he immediately fixed his gaze directly at me. He then proceeded to walk closer and closer while continuing to gaze intently into my eyes until he was less than a few inches away from my face. Then with a most mischievous smile said, "You are a very clever professor." Then, abruptly turning around to another *murid* who was behind him handing out information about an upcoming event, he took one flyer and presented it to me. I bowed down in recognition of the gift while simultaneously keeping my eyes below his and then said, "Thank you" as submissively as I could. Incidentally, the handout he had given me was in Turkish, so I had no way of knowing what it said.

In reflecting back, I realized I was for the few minutes of our dialogue completely unaware of what he had said. For those fleeting moments, I was experiencing a delicately subtle and exhilarating sweetness. I was happy but had no particular reason to be so. As he left the corridor, I began to think about what had just transpired. I realized that I had not said anything about my being a professor, nor to my knowledge had anyone informed Shaykh Nazim of my background. The likelihood of such a guess was extremely remote. He had in fact not only correctly identified who I was, but simultaneously had revealed a small portion of his own spiritual powers. I did not react negatively but instead took his remark as a playful method of establishing a deeper rapport while simultaneously providing an avenue for testing *(bala)* the fragility of my ego and sincerity. The practice of testing newcomers is a general practice employed in many Sufi *tariqahs* and goes back many centuries.[261]

---

[261] Shaykh Nazim goes into considerable detail in describing the various methods his grandshaykh used in greeting visitors and newcomers. He says that he would treat those who had very big egos with extreme deference, as they could be dangerous to the *tariqah* and to the

Clearly, he must have perceived my inward state through his spiritual perception, though that was not his entire purpose. I realized in that instant that the teaching was a *living organism*. It was neither irrational nor planned but evolved out of the shaykh's continuous well of divine inspiration. I understood something about Sufi methodology in a few moments that no book could ever fully impart. Outwardly, I placed very little importance on the title of "professor," as both my parents had been professors all their lives. However, on some level, he had hit the nail on the head, as there was somewhere deep in my subconscious an investment in being known as a professor. I continued ruminating over the word "clever" and finally concluded that his intention was to indicate that official titles meant nothing and intellectuality was of no concern here. Nevertheless, he had opened a door, giving me a glimpse of the subtle places my ego was fixated. More importantly, he established a new context for our relationship, freeing me of any preconceptions and delusions.

These kinds of anecdotes are recorded throughout the annals of Sufism.[262] One enlightening example is found in the Muhyi al-Din ibn Abi al-Wafa, *Al-Jawahir al-Mudia fi Tabaqat al-Hanafiya,* about the meeting with the poet Jalal-al-din Rumi and Qutb al-Din.

When Qutb al-Din came into Rumi's presence, the old poet ignored him for a long time and then told a story. The scholar Sadr-i Jahan of Bukhara used to pass a beggar on the street each day but never gave him anything. One day after this happened, the beggar said to his friends, "Tomorrow I will lie down, and you cover me with my cloak and act as though I were dead." They did so, and when Sadri-i Jahan came by, he gave some money. The beggar abruptly sat up. Sadr-i Jahan said, "If you hadn't been dead, I wouldn't have given you

---

murids. His purpose was to entertain them and send them away as soon as possible, as they were not ready for the teaching (Nazim, Shaykh Muhammad, *Toward the Divine Presence*. Karachi, Pakistan: Jamil Wahab (Trust) Foundation, 1984).

262 Of particular interest in this connection is the story entitled "The Nature of Discipleship," from Idries Shah's *Tales of the Dervishes* (New York: Dutton, 1970). It reveals in a "dramatic manner the difference between what the would be disciple thinks his relationship with a teaching master would be; and what it actually would be" (p. 147).

anything." From this, Qutb al-Din understood that until he died to his self, Rumi could give him nothing. He was silent and left.[263]

I was grateful for Shaykh Nazim's interest, as even "negative attention" is still attention and would be helpful in developing some rapport with him. My experiences with my own spiritual teachers have led me to understand that any form of attention can be a vehicle for receiving the teacher's blessings (*fayd*). After this incident, I was aware of his powerful penetrating gaze and his sudden changes in facial expression. One moment he would have an angelic look, the next a very serious or compassionate one. As I left I bowed again, smiled, and said, "Thank you." He did not reply nor look back at all! As he turned his face, I observed his expression quickly change again.[264]

Dhikr with the Shaykh

We returned at 11 P.M. for the final Isha prayer. A group of forty to fifty murids performed the prayer and then immediately formed a circle for the Thursday evening *dhikr*. Before beginning the *dhikr,* everyone took a seat against the wall of the *dergah*. A large *tasbih* with large wooden balls perhaps fifty to sixty feet long was passed around the room. Each murid grabbed one segment. At this point, one murid got up and turned the light very low, so only flickers of light the size of a small candle lighted the room. Shaykh Nazim was sitting with his back to the *qiblah*[265] and then began the recitation of affirmation and negation, *La ilaha illa Allah*. All the murids followed him and began reciting the same in silence. The large *tasbih* contains one thousand beads, and by completing one rotation of the *tasbih*, each murid will have completed one thousand recitations of the dhikr of affirmation

---

[263] Aflaki, Rumi's biographer, gives a version in which Qutb al-Din becomes a follower of Rumi. See Walbridge, *The Science of Mystic Lights: Qutb al-Din Shirazi and the Illuminist Tradition in Islamic Philosophy* (Cambridge, Mass.: Harvard University Press, 1992) pp. 14-15.

[264] The gaze or glance of an authentic shaykh is the source of great power and spiritual upliftment. Shaykh Nazim mentions one Sufi who, having attained to a very high rank, always wore a veil over his face. It was said his glance was so powerful that if anyone looked into his eyes, he would fall down dead. See Shaykh Nazim's *Mercy Oceans' Hidden Treasures* (Konya: Sebat Offset Printers, 1987).

[265] This is the direction of Mecca, toward which Muslims orient themselves in prayer.

and negation. The *dhikr* ended with a final round of affirmation by Shaykh Nazim.[266]

At about 11:50 or so, Shaykh Nazim began to speak. Immediately all the murids clustered as close as they could get around him. About six or seven small recording machines were placed at his feet. He then closed his eyes and tilted his head backward a bit before beginning. As he spoke, his hands involuntarily gestured up and down and right and left. They seemed pulled by a divine puppeteer. I find no way of accurately describing his movements. Every so often, his eyes would open and a very, very far-away look appeared in them. He seemed immersed in a world of divine beauty and bliss. He occasionally repeated a word or two, as if describing the reality he saw before his inward eye. His words were forceful and commanding but filled with a subliminal sweetness and humility. He seemed merely a conduit for the outpouring of divine knowledge that passed through him.[267] The murids hung on each word he spoke and remained in rapt silence throughout the *suhbah*. Every so often, an occasional "Allah Allah" spontaneously escaped from a spiritually intoxicated murid who could not contain his delight.

---

[266] This evening of *dhikr* was not to be confused with the recitation of the *Khatam-i-khwajagan*, which is also used at regular Friday *dhikr* meetings. I had the experience of both... in Cyprus, Shaykh Nazim lead the *dhikr* of affirmation and negation. According to Hasan Shushud Khwaja, Mahmud Faghnawi first introduced the public *dhikr* in the Naqshbandi order. See Hasan Lufti Shushud's *Masters of Wisdom of Central Asia* (trans. by Muhtar Holland, Oxford: Coombe Springs Press, 1983) p.29-30.

[267] It was extremely difficult to find parallels with the experience I had while in Shaykh Nazim's company. The effect of his *suhbats* and his delivery were mesmerizing and enigmatic. Martin Lings quotes Rahimahu Llah in one of the best descriptions I have found of the presence of authentic shaykh: "His eyes, like two sepulchral lamps, seemed to pierce through all objects, seeing in their outer shell merely one and the same nothingness, beyond which they saw always one and the same reality—Infinite. His head would sometimes rock rhythmically to and fro while his soul was plunged in the unfathomable mysteries of the Divine Name, hidden in the *dhikr*, the reality of remembrance... He gave out an impression of unreality, so remote was he, so inaccessible, so difficult to take in on account of his altogether abstract simplicity. He was surrounded, at one and the same time, with all the veneration that is due to saints, to the old and to the dying'" Lings, M., *A Sufi Saint of the Twentieth Century* (reprint, Cambridge: Islamic Texts Society, 1993) p. 117, cited in *Cahiers du Sud* by Frithjof Schuon, (Aout-September 1935).

Second Association with Shaykh Nazim

> We are seeking Your protection and we belong to You. We are declaring that You are our Lord. You are granting to us everything, You are never giving to any other creature and we are sinners seeking Your forgiveness and blessings. We are coming from the East and the West and You are sending us blessings. We are servants, we are seeking Your blessings. But Your orders must be obeyed. Your orders must be obeyed. Everyone must be Your obedient servant. You are our Lord, the Lord of heavens and earth, Lord of here and hereafter. We are not happy with our actions and ourselves.
>
> You are the most high, most powerful. You are our Lord. What You like must be, must be followed and must be obeyed. Instead of writing on our egos, our egos are writing on us. Moreover, we are praying to Your Divine Presence saying, "O our Lord, save us from our egos, we are happy with You. O our Lord, You Most High, please send from Your new endless treasures. Only You may give what we are seeking. And Your endless treasure oceans are never getting less... Your endless treasure oceans, Your endless blessing oceans, are never getting less. If they were to become less it means that one day they would be finished. If they were to become less by the smallest amount in creation they would still one day be finished. But, they cannot be lessened at all even by the tiniest amount.
>
> O Allah, Your endless oceans are never emptied, they are always full of pleasure. [Shaykh Nazim struggles to find words to describe Allah's Mercy Oceans, O Allah who created man, we thank You, our Lord *shukr* Rabbi. You created us and we are the most wicked of creatures. However, there is good news for mankind always, the mercy oceans, they are never spent, never emptied.[268]

---

[268] Shaykh Nazim's use of the word ocean appears in not less than six of his book titles and throughout his writings, as well as his *suhbats.* His usage appears similar not only to the usage of other Naqshbandi saints but also to that in earlier Sufi mystical treatises. Shaykh Nazim, in

> Show us Your beloved servants, because they are following You. We want to follow the followers of Allah. If we follow them, we will reach our destination. Follow them and reach them and then every step follow them in your heart.[269] If we do this, no more trouble will reach your heart. Our hearts will always be full with pleasure, full with light. We must let them fill our hearts with You, O Lord. To be with them, that is our request, but we are not with Him. We are Your servants, please take our hearts and mind and bodies to You.[270]

As soon as he finished, he made a slight effort to lift himself as if he was going to get up. As soon as he did so, several *murids* ran to his side to aid him. His legs seemed too weak to hold him, and for a moment I thought he would collapse under his own weight. However, he suddenly regained his balance. He then sat down on a small stool. Immediately all the *murids* formed a long line and proceeded in turn to kiss the hand of their shaykh. As each *murid* approached Shaykh Nazim, he knelt down, kissed his hand on the left and right side, and then placed his forehead upon Shaykh Nazim's hand to receive his

---

his use of *ocean* or *mercy oceans*, indicates the divine realms of *sirr, sirr al sirr,* and *ahkafa.* Since Shaykh Nazim, according to Naqshbandi theology, rests continually in these realms, *ocean* or *mercy oceans* indicate the "wellspring of vision and revelation of Truth from which all Saintliness arises." The visionary writings of the great Persian mystic Ruzbihan Baqli provide a remarkably analogous usage: "I saw one night a *great ocean,* and the sea was of red wine. I saw the Prophet sitting cross-legged in the midst of the *deep ocean,* drunk, and in his hand he had a cup of wine from that *ocean,* which he drank. When he saw me, he ladled out a cup of wine and gave it to me to drink. After that something was revealed to me, and I knew he was above all the rest of creation, since they die thirsty and he is drunk in the midst of the ocean of beauty" (cited in Carl Ernst's *Ruzbihan Baqli: Mysticism and the Rhetoric of Sainthood in Persian Sufism,* Surrey, England: Curzon Press, 1996, p. 61).

269 The particular and specific meaning behind the word *follow* or *following* (*ittiba*) in Naqshbandi theology has a generally much wider scope than its traditional sense of simply outwardly following a saint. Here it refers to a state in which the *murid* fully complies with every order of the shaykh. Shaykh Nazim quotes his own shaykh in explaining this concept more completely: "O my son, to carry out orders is more important and of greater value than performing the devotions of all mankind and Genie [*Jinn*]; for performing all these devotions is not possible, but carrying out orders is possible and this is what is important in the Divine Presence." To comply fully with every order of the shaykh is to win the greatest of Holy wars (*jihad al-akbar*). Nazim, Shaykh Muhammad, *Mercy Oceans, Rising Sun* (Konya: Sebat Offset Printers. 1985) pp. 154-155.

270 Nazim, Shaykh Muhammad, Cyprus, August 11, 1999, evening *suhbat.*

blessings *(barakah)* directly. As this ritualized greeting continued, the other *murids* devotedly sang songs in praise of the Prophet and the order.[271] Shaykh Nazim in turn responded fully and directly to their love by acknowledging each *murid* with a loving glance and blessings with his hand. As soon as all the *murids* had kissed Shaykh Nazim's hand, they greeted each other with the traditional Islamic handshake and sometimes with a kiss on each cheek. As I watched, I could see the love the *murids* had for their shaykh as well as the love he had for them. After this ritual of loving greetings, Shaykh Nazim left and retired at about 12:30 A.M. I also left to retire for the evening.

Before I went to bed, I recorded all my experiences, including my inner experiences while performing *dhikr*.[272] That night I slept on a rickety old metal bed with wire springs along with six other people in a small room. I was unable to fall asleep, as I was transfixed in a whirlpool of images, thoughts, and sounds circulating relentlessly within my mind. Finally, at about 2 in the morning I succumbed to sleep.

Another Association with Shaykh Nazim

Shaykh Nazim arrived at the *dergah* at about 11:45 in the morning to lead the *Duha* prayer. I was the first to enter the prayer space. I walked up behind him, and unexpectedly he turned around to greet me. He looked at me as if to see if I had obeyed his request the previous day and then said, "Did you meet that man, your double?" I replied "Yes, I did, shaykh." He replied, "He has no mind like you," and then abruptly turned his face away from me. His intention was completely

---

[271] Although the Naqshbandis are traditionally known for their silent practice of *dhikr,* they also sing and recite various liturgies aloud. The most important liturgy is known as the *Khwajagan,* which has been more fully described in chapter 2. This particular *awrad,* which is unique to the Naqshbandis, has also been adapted to a musical score and even recorded on CD. Portions of it were recited on occasions like the above, as well as in its complete form during *dhikr* ceremonies along with the silent *awrad*. However, portions of it may be recited to meet the need of the occasion. Shaykh Hisham has published in small pamphlet form the entire *awrad* for those interested in this aspect. See *The Remembrance of God: Liturgy of the Sufi Naqshbandi Masters* (Chicago, Ill.: ABC International group) 1997.

[272] Although I recorded all my inner experiences while at the *dergah* and originally intended to relate some of them to give the reader a fuller picture of my stay, I later changed my decision. In retrospect, I felt that it would not add anything to the reader's understanding of the *tariqat* and might, in fact, needlessly draw attention to myself.

clear and without equivocation. He wanted to bring my ego down a few notches. His words were not intended as a Zen-like reference connoting "emptiness" or "spiritual clarity." This remark was a further prick if not direct stab directly into my ego. It was neither off-handed nor uttered in jovial fashion but pointed, powerful, and meant to humiliate.[273]

The moment after he made his remark, my thoughts were clouded. I felt a disturbance in my heart and my inner thoughts stopped. Something had reached me in a deep place this time. I could feel a sensation of pain in my heart. Not because of the words per se nor because I believed I was an idiot, which in his jargon was synonymous with "no mind," but because of the spiritual energy (*fayd*) with which he had invested the words. Upon reflection, I surmised his intention was to reach deep into my essence and test what was there. Was it sweet or sour, bitter or honey? At that instant, I momentarily stopped breathing. The utter simplicity and beauty of his teaching struck me. From that moment on I realized I did not have to ask a single question but just be willing to place myself on the surgeon's table. Submitting meant allowing Shaykh Nazim to operate as he choose and according to his divine knowledge.[274] When I realized what had just happened, I was inwardly stunned. This was much more than I had expected, and now I found myself both the researcher and the researched. The mirror had been turned and was now facing myself.[275]

---

[273] **Vidich, *Op. cit.,* p. 347 - 354.**

[274] Of course, I could have decided to leave and therefore end the relationship altogether. However, this would have been too easy and certainly the least productive. Staying, on the other hand, meant a certain willingness to continue the process. Murat Yagan explains in his book *I Came from Behind Kaf Mountain* that if the *murid* perseveres, the shaykh will give him more. "If the dervish is not dissuaded and does not give up, more will be given him and he will awaken more, and when this awakening is activated, there will be two things to which this person will be awakened. In the mind of the *Baba* all along is his task to teach the *murid* love and humility" Yagan, Murat, *I Came from Behind Kaf Mountain* (Vermont: Kebzeh Productions, 1997) p. 164.

[275] According to Shaykh Hisham, there are two stages to this process. First, the shaykh shows us our faults by becoming a mirror in which to see ourselves. Second, he breaks the mirror, which is our ego, so we can enter ourselves completely. So long as we are still seeing ourselves through the mirror of the ego, we can never proceed to the divine presence (Kabbani, Hisham. Interview in Saddle River, N.J., by Andrew Vidich, June 21, 1999).

After this incident, Shaykh Nazim continued and completed the Duha prayer. Then he moved to the corridor, where I was informed he often conducts interviews. He made his way slowly into the corridor and sat down in the corner on a simple bench with only a small cushion on it. I entered the corridor from the other entrance and sat down at the opposite side of the room. He began speaking in Turkish with several *murids* who had apparently just arrived. A few moments passed, and then he glanced over in my direction and indicated to me that he wanted me to come closer. I looked around the room to confirm that he was referring to me and when other *murids* nodded, I immediately went over. As I took a seat on the floor next to him, he shook his head and indicated to me that I should sit on the couch opposite him. Therefore, I did so without hesitation.

Then in a very direct and yet simple manner he asked, "What is your mission?" I replied, "I am writing a book about the Naqshbandiyya *tariqah*. About who the shaykh is and his method of transforming disciples spiritually." Shaykh Nazim thought for a moment and then asked me, "Have you written about what we are eating?" Slightly dumbfounded by his question, I was unsure how to respond. Was he really asking me whether I was researching what the *murids* eat at the *dergah*? If this was the case, why was he asking me such an apparently trivial question? In either case, the answer seemed to me no. I actually had not even considered the question. So I replied, "No, I haven't." He disapprovingly shook his head, indicating I had missed the entire point of the shaykh's role. Perhaps I had been too intellectual after all. My "clever professorial" stance had missed the most obvious of points. Life with the shaykh is communal in nature, and the communal meal is a reaffirmation of the bonds of love between the shaykh and his *murids*.[276]

---

[276] In Ibn Al Husayn Al-Sulami's *The Book of Sufi Chivalry*, he instructs, "Care for your brethren more than you care for your own family. Through Ismail ibn Ahmad al-Khallali we hear that Fatimah, daughter of the Messenger of Allah, asked her husband, Ali for a servant. Ali answered, 'Do you wish me to abandon those who have given up everything for Allah so that their bellies contract from hunger while I get you a servant?'" Al-Sulami, Ibn Al Husayn, *The Book of Sufi Chivalry* (New York: Inner Traditions, 1983) p. 40).

He then began to speak in English, which, though often grammatically incorrect, was never difficult to understand. In fact, I was surprised by how precise his words were, despite the limitations of his English:

> What does the shaykh do first? What is the first thing the shaykh does? He feeds the people. The horse, the oxen, the donkeys are weak and they need food from their long journey. So the shaykh must feed them and make them strong again. This is the way of the shaykh. Then he asks the oxen, the donkeys, and the horses, Where is your rider going? Which direction are you going? However, they do not know. Therefore, he directs them to the Divine Presence. Because the horse must know where they are going. Therefore, he gives them directions to the Divine King.[277]
>
> May Allah forgive us. We are asking His forgiveness and blessing. That is our main target. Nothing else. If we are asking something, more that person must be a fool, or no-mind person or foolish one, stupid, idiot, or crazy one. There cannot be anything to be asked for our Lord except His blessings and forgiveness because we are always doing wrong things.
>
> You may say, What is wrong with me? I am not harming anyone through my hands or through my tongue and I am keeping respect to everyone of our people, people at my work and my family and my community. You may say I am a good man. What is wrong that I am asking forgiveness?
>
> The biggest sin for a servant is to forget that he is always with his Lord. In addition, I do not think that one person in one hundred or one person in one thousand or even one person in a hundred thousand persons is keeping the presence of his Lord. You may imagine if you are going into huge palace and taking a seat in front of that emperor, to come into his majestic

[277] The first two or three minutes of this *suhbah* were recorded from memory immediately after this talk. Shaykh Nazim asked me at this point if I wanted to record it. I nodded and went to get my recorder. The remainder of this talk was recorded live and transcribed from audiotape, as were all the rest of his talks and *suhbats*.

presence and instead of looking to him we are looking up and down. At the very least, the sultan is going to say, "What is he looking at? I am such a majestic person. I am accepting him in my majestic presence." Look what he is doing. If we are saying to God, This is our servant, we will do everything for you, excellent. That emperor may say, "Now I am inviting you into my majestic presence," but then look what he is doing. A person, a believer, his value is coming down quickly when he occupies his heart with everything around himself except for his Lord. That person is not a good servant. He must ask forgiveness. That person must ask the emperor for forgiveness, "Oh, your majesty, our biggest sin is to be heedless of our Lord Almighty Allah." It is not so easy. To be heedless of His Dvine Pesence, this is the biggest sin, as I said to you.

Therefore, the whole *tariqahs* are asking to prepare servants so they should always reach their Lord's Divine Presence, and then they should keep themselves in Allah's Divine Presence. That is the main purpose of the most distinguished Naqshbandi order. What I am saying is true for all religions. No one can object on that point. Jesus Christ, Moses, Abraham, Adam, John, Zachariah, and all the Prophets called their people to be with their Lord in such a way. To pay respect, the most high respect, to their Lord. To be with their Lord eye to eye and not to make their eyes like this [he gestures up and down]. The Old Testament and up through the New Testament and then through the Quran, it is mentioned as a summary what I am saying now.

In addition, through all the *tariqahs* this is mentioned, particularly in the most distinguished Naqshbandi *tariqah*. They are calling people to be with their Lord eye to eye—to be present with their Lord forever, forever. I think this is a forward or preface, you may say. And those who are accepting this are the lucky ones. Those who are not accepting this, it means he is under the level of man and human nature. You can write this in the beginning of your book, and then whatever you are saying more must be under that title.

Observations

Although the length of this short *suhbah* was not more than thirty minutes, by the time he had finished, I felt it had been hours. The normal limitations imposed by time seemed to evaporate and disappear. As Shaykh Nazim spoke, I again tried to concentrate totally on his face. Since I knew I was recording the talk, I did not really listen to the words as much as try and absorb myself into his being, a technique that is central to the Naqshbandi *tariqah* and the essence of *suhbah*.[278] I found myself saying *Alhamdulillah* many times over, almost like a refrain to a piece of choral music.

It is difficult to describe the difference in the experience of listening when one's attention is placed on the "being" of the shaykh rather than just his words. The mind stops "loading up" and begins to enter the "flow of energy" (*fayd*) being transmitted by him. Instead of digesting the talk at an intellectual level, one enters the *experience of the shaykh* while he talks. The spiritual method of "learning through becoming" or "learning by absorbing oneself" in the object of concentration is in practice today in most esoteric mystery schools as well as within the mystical traditions of many great religions.[279]

---

[278] The Naqshbandi practice of *tasawwur i-shaykh,* while not unique to the Naqshbandis, is unique in being central to their practice. Apparently, "Bahauddin, on his second trip to the Hijaz, ordered his companion and disciple Muhammad Parsa to fix his face in his imagination." See Muhammad Parsa, *Risala-yi Qudisyya,* cited in Ahmad Said's *Bil-fawaid al-rabita* (N.p.: Matba-i Husna, 1875) pp. 41-42, cited in Buehler, *Op. cit.* p. 135. Buehler notes there were many other saints within the Naqshbandi lineage who also mentioned this practice.

[279] For a fascinating discussion of similar methods of concentration exercises within esoteric Christianity, see K.C. Markides's *Homage to the Sun: The Wisdom of The Magus of Strovolus* (New York: Arkana Books, 1987) p. 169. Daskolus, the Christian Cypriot healer, explains the results of these concentration exercises: "You begin to express to a greater extent these virtues (tolerance, patience) and in addition your psychic powers begin to expand. You develop greater abilities of concentration, of thought, of understanding and of will power. Let me explain what I mean. On the material plane, through my eyesight, I have the ability to concentrate over a landscape. I absorb certain impressions but only a small portion of them will be retained in my consciousness. After the first initiation, I am able, through psychonoetic exercises, to retain in my memory experiences derived from the gross material plane. During the first stages of the second initiation, on the other hand, while in exomatosis (leaving the body), I cover a greater field of vision and begin to receive more experiences and impressions. I am not limited to the five senses. I also have a greater awareness of existing conditions." For an overview of the different types of concentration exercises within different mystical traditions, see *On the*

This experience indicated for me that Shaykh Nazim is not operating solely on an intellectual level. Naqshbandi saints explain this by saying the saint speaks through the intellect but acts through the higher emanations and stations of *sirr,* and *sirr as-sirr,* or what Sirhindi referred to as the higher intimacy.[280] I found it difficult to listen on an intellectual level while also trying to "absorb him spiritually," and therefore abandoned the former idea. In fact, it seemed that Shaykh Nazim deliberately tried to confound the mind or dislodge the rational mind. The intellectual mind thinks in terms of causal relationships, time and space, and is necessarily limited by its preconceived ideas and points of view. According to Naqshbandi theory, Shaykh Nazim's divine presence emanates from the realms above the physical in the regions of *maqam i-jabrut* and *maqam i-lahut*. Therefore, his spiritual emanations (*tajalli*) bear the stamp of these realms. To attempt to analyze his actions from a purely intellectual context is self-defeating. Outwardly he is puzzling, perplexing, funny when one least expects it, and the next moment self-absorbed and serious. The intellectual paradigm has its limitations here. Instead, I found it useful to simply observe his sudden shifts in moods and enjoy his "presence," which provided me with ongoing insights and realizations as well as much delight and entertainment.

As soon as Shaykh Nazim had finished, I thanked him for his willingness to address my research needs. He nodded and then got up and left. He seemed pleased and now quite accepting of me. I was somewhat surprised by the sudden turnaround, and even more so because it had happened within such a short period. As I reflected back, I could see that the normal cause-and-effect relationship that we assume in our dealings with others is absent in relating to Shaykh Nazim. He operates by divine intuition, and therefore causal links are often not available for the *murid* to see. I was grateful for his

---

Psychology of Meditation by C. Naranjo and R. Ornstein, New York: Viking Press, 1971. Incidentally, Robert Ornstein is said to be Idries Shah's deputy in the West since 1974. Significant controversy still surrounds the claims of Idries Shah to be an authorized Naqshbandi shaykh. See David Nicolson Friedberg, "The Naqshbandis in America" (Master's thesis, University of Colorado, 1994) p. 26-27.

280 The Quranic support for this is found in the following passage, "*then God sent down his security* [*sakinah*]..." (9:40).

generosity, although I did not know why he had changed his mind so quickly. I spent the next few hours catching up with my observations and resting until the evening prayer.

After the afternoon prayer, *murids* return to their places of residence and have lunch on their own, as there is no communal meal in the afternoon. Because of the extreme heat during this season, many *murids* will go to the seashore, which is only a mile or so away, and relax on the beach. *Murids* informed me that after the Dhuhr prayer, Shaykh Nazim often remarks "Take rest either at the seaside or bedside." Many *murids*, especially those with small children, go to the sea for the afternoon. This time is also utilized in catching up on errands like washing clothes or buying necessities at the local market. Nevertheless, because of the extreme heat, which soars to over one hundred degrees F., it was not wise to spend too much time in the direct sunlight. I was quite content to just sit in my small room, rest, and spend some time in solitude. On occasion, however, my thoughts turned to my wife and the beautiful hotel she was staying in. Later, in the afternoon, inspired by that thought, I took a short walk exploring the local environs. After a bit of exploration I could see that Shaykh Nazim's residence was completely surrounded and isolated from the rest of the community by large orange groves, vegetable gardens, and other fruit trees. The trees and gardens not only provide cool shade and seclusion but also produce a large amount of produce for use in the *dergah* kitchen.

From several conversations with people on the island, I learned that Shaykh Nazim was well known for his generosity in assisting people in difficult or dire circumstances. Even those who were nonreligious or anti-Sufi often expressed their appreciation for Shaykh Nazim's generosity and assistance that he had provided for either their friends or relatives[281]

Association with Shaykh Hisham Kabbani

Naqshbandi shaykhs place a high priority on the guidance and spiritual power (*tawajjuh*) of the shaykh on the mystical path. They

---

[281] **Vidich, *Op. cit.,* p. 391.**

have gone so far as to say, as did Ubayd Allah Ahrar, that "the shadow of the guide is better that the [rite of] remembrance of God."[282] From Ubayd Allah Ahrar's statement, we see the extreme importance that companionship with the shaykh (*suhbah*) has in the Naqshbandi *tariqah*. If even *dhikr* is subordinate to companionship with the saints, the shaykh's *tawajjuh* becomes the preeminent means by which spiritual growth is achieved. In short, the *murid* progresses with the shaykhs, by the shaykhs, and ultimately through the shaykhs.

The experience of *fana* has been variously described by different mystics as a gradual "ripening of love in which the lover comes to realize that the Beloved, the goal, cannot be reached as long as he remains locked into the world of opposites, as long as he himself remains himself."[283] Throughout my interview with Shaykh Hisham, reflections of this kind of fusion presented themselves. In fact, the most astounding feature of Shaykh Hisham is the degree to which he defers to Shaykh Nazim in everything he says. I believe it is impossible to understand Shaykh Hisham's role without clarifying this point.[284]

The New *Tajalliyyat*

I begin my interview with Shaykh Hisham where he deals specifically with the changes that the *tariqah* has undergone. These changes provide some of the background context from which to comprehend the order historically. In fact, some of these changes represent a departure from the methodology of the "teaching shaykh" during previous eras:

---

[282] Haar, J.G.J. *Follower and heir of the Prophet: Shaykh Ahmad Sirhindi (1564-1624) as mystic* (Leiden, Netherlands: Hetoosters Instituut, 1992) p. 84.

[283] Rumi's famous story of a man who knocks at a door illustrates this clearly:

"Who's there?" asks a voice from within. "It's me," says the man. "Go away then," answers the voice. "There's no room here for 'me.'"The man goes away and wanders in the desert until he realizes his error. He returns and knocks again at the door. "Who's there?" asks the voice. "Thou," answers the man. "Then come in," the voice replies.

See *The Drunken Universe*, trans. by Wilson and Pourjavady (Grand Rapids, Mich.: Phanes Press, 1987) p. 72.

[284] **Vidich, *Op. Cit.*, p. 414.**

In past times, the living Sufi shaykh and saints never accepted a *murid* or follower before completing his Islamic law and jurisprudence, memorizing the entire Quran, and knowing the *Shariah* from beginning to end. Then and only then would they give them *bayah* or initiation. Because they know they are sound. At that time, everyone had to study Islamic knowledge. This was going on until recently. In the past, wherever a parent raised a child—whether on the subcontinent, the Middle East, or the East, where most of the saints are living—their focus was that their children grow up and study the basic structure of Islam. This was their higher education. If you look into history, this was the educational system and whatever other subjects or sciences that were directly related to it. So these people were given a complete understanding before they took *bayah* from a shaykh.

All of the people who were coming into the *tariqah*, they knew what the Sufi saints had stated and they were coming to the shaykh after they had graduated. Then they wanted to have the spiritual aspect as well. After they finished the physical dimension, now they wanted the *haqiqah* dimension. By the way, now they are stronger because the knowledge of Reality does not change the external (*Shariah*) knowledge. No, it simply gives it a boost.

Today no one is looking for such knowledge. Now, everyone is seeking the knowledge of science. In this era, in this century, the educational system is focusing on science, computers, and so on. Although both parties are going to die and they will not take that science with them to the grave, the party that took the knowledge of Reality, they will receive something beneficial because they took something that is eternal.

Today the people's focus is scattered. So now, the Naqshbandis and especially the Haqqani Naqshbandi, which is a direct chain to the Prophet through the lineage of the grandshaykh—because since the time of shaykhs we know that in spirituality, knowledge is always rising. Knowledge is

> always growing. It is impossible, like in any science, for knowledge to stop; it is always getting higher and higher.
>
> Therefore, in the Naqshbandi knowledge, spirituality is always ascending, because the Prophet's knowledge is continuously ascending. Moreover, as the Prophet is ascending, all other prophets are ascending, all *awliya* are ascending, because scholars and saints are inheritors of the prophets. So you move with them. Therefore, that knowledge is growing. Therefore, from one century to another century, knowledge is always increasing and more new things are coming.
>
> Therefore, in understanding the spirituality of Islam, our grandshaykh used to say that in the past the *tariqah* meant obedience. But today the *tariqah* is love, because not everyone can obey today, because our grandshaykh said nobody has the ability to obey or listen. Therefore, what would be the benefit in our *tariqah*? Therefore, that is why the *tajalliyyat* has changed.

I was not surprised by Shaykh Hisham's explanation of the changes undergone in the *tariqah* today, as it parallels in some respects the conclusions indicated by Buehler in his study of the Naqshbandi on the subcontinent.[285] However, there are some critical differences as well. The role of the shaykh and his personal authority remain as they have in past times, that is, to directly connect the *murid* to his eternal Lord. This differs significantly from Buehler's conclusion that individual *murids* are no longer taught how to connect directly with

---

[285] According to Buehler, "the mediating-shaykh reflects a new form of Naqshbandi personal authority, a mediational Sufism radically departing from the symbols and practices of directing-shaykhs and indicating a paradigm shift which fundamentally alters what earlier Naqshbandis conceived to be Sufism. The mediating shaykh as the sole intermediary between the Prophet and believers dramatically contrasts with Naqshbandi directing-shaykhs, who taught disciples how they themselves could arrive near God and manipulate supernatural power." Buehler, A., *Sufi heirs of the Prophet: The Indian Naqshbandiyya order and the rise of the mediating Sufi Shaykh* (Columbia, S.C.: University of South Carolina Press, 1998) p. 191.

the Prophet and Allah Almighty.[286] What seems to be similar to Buehler's conclusion is the explicit nature of the relationship between the shaykh and his *murids*. Buehler notes, "Naqshbandi mediating-shaykhs reformulated spiritual practices to emphasize love; the goal itself became love. With love of the *pir*, everything else, including salvation, followed. Only love could traverse the ever-increasing hierarchical distance between a seeker and an ever-remote shaykh."[287] For Shaykh Hisham, it was not the shaykh who was becoming remote, but the increasing difficulty the *murids* had in "obeying," which caused the chasm. The shaykh was ready as always to prepare the way and teach, but the *murids* were not prepared or ready to receive.[288]

---

[286] In both my informal and depth interviews with disciples, I found significant evidence to support the assumption that *murid*s are still being taught the fundamental principles of the *tariqah* methodology. In addition, I also found evidence in both Shaykh Nazim's and Shaykhs Hisham's *suhbats* that the mystical practices continue to be articulated to those who are "ready" to receive the higher practices.

[287] Buehler, A., *Sufi heirs of the Prophet: The Indian Naqshbandiyya order and the rise of the mediating Sufi Shaykh* (Columbia, S.C.: University of South Carolina Press, 1998) p. 191.

[288] Shah Wali Allah, an 18th century Naqshbandi from India, in his work *Hamaat* outlines the broad stages of spiritual emanations (*tajalliyyat*) into four phases. These four basic stages are pervasive themes in Shah Wali Allah's understanding of the historical process of the rise and fall of Sufi *tariqah*s. His depiction is particularly useful here in understanding the dynamic nature of Sufism as it has evolved over the centuries. I am particularly grateful to Dr. Marcia *Hermansen* for providing these excerpts and translations.

"1) The first phase is sober Sufism, characterized by following the Islamic law *(Shariah),* the absence of ecstatic states (*wajd*), and the fear of Hell and desire for paradise.

"2) The second phase, epitomized by the figure of Junayd (910), is, "in the time of the master of the Sufi sect, Junayd, and slightly earlier, another tendency emerged. The generality of people involved maintained the same attitudes, but some of the elite ones obtained a special spiritual state after making great efforts, performing austerities, completely cutting themselves off from the world and continuous practice... It is truer of this state of Sufism to say they only expressed what they had experienced personally... They separated themselves from the masses and went to the mountains and wilderness. Their sincerity was that they worshiped God neither out of fear of hell nor ambition for paradise, but rather out of love for Him.

"3) Then came the phase of eradicating the lower soul or ego (*nafs*), represented for Shah Wali Allah by the Sufis, Abu Said ibn Abul-Khayr (1049) and Kharaqani (1034). Their total concern was with perfecting that focus. All of these other spiritual experiences (*nisbats*) they termed 'veils of Light.' At this time, they distinguished between unity of witnessing (*tauhid i-shuhudi*), and the unity of essence (*tauhid i-wujudi*). However, their essential goal was achieving or extinguishing the individual ego.

Attraction Through Love

In Shaykh Hisham's mind, the teaching has adapted to the changing needs of the times. As he explains:

> It is enough in this century for the *murids* to love, because the times are harder. The darkness is more and sinning is more. Therefore, mercy is higher, so as mercy is greater now, only a very thin wire is needed to pull, and it is enough. If you keep that connection, you do not need a big rope now. You need love, because everyone is running and not doing the practices. When you do it, you will get that benefit if you are holding the rope. [Shaykh Hisham pauses pensively, wanting to make his point clearer.] Let us say in this house there is a treasure of one hundred gold coins. If anyone comes to pray, these one hundred gold coins are going to be distributed among whomever comes to pray.
>
> Therefore, if one hundred people come, each person can take away one. If fifty people come, each person can take two. If only one person comes, he takes all one hundred. [Everyone begins to laugh.] Therefore, Allah, God is generous. Whatever He has given, He does not take back. When He gave to His "*Ummah*"—His humanity—on the Day of Promises, Allah asked His servants, "Who am I and who are you?" They said, "We are your servants; you are our Lord." He took from them a promise to worship him, to accept him. When they said "Yes," He threw on everyone that money. So that money is so huge that it encompasses everyone. So all the servants, when

"4) In the fourth phase, the mystic Ibn Arabi (1240) represents a culminating figure who is said to have penetrated the descending emanations (*tanziliyyat*) of the One. In this phase 'they went from states of psychological ecstasy (*wajdan nafsaniyya*) to investigating the realities of the higher commanding self (*nafs al-amriyya*) as it really is, and to understanding the descending manifestations of the Necessary Being. They came to recognize the identity of the first emanator, the process of emanation, and matters of this type."

These four broad phases provide the historical background from which to understand Shah Wali Allah's own formulation of the seven cycles (*dauran* or *adwar*) of the Naqshbandi *tariqah*, and what *tariqah* meant to him. We will present these in the pages that follow. In providing the passages, we hope to shed some light on Shaykh Hisham's understanding of the direction of the *Naqshbandi tariqah* and its evolution into the next millennium.

> they are not doing their prayers and are not practicing, those who are doing it take it, because it is coming down.
>
> So now he said if you keep a bridge or a connection to the living shaykh, it is enough, you will be saved. And that *hikmah* [wisdom] that I want to describe in this time is that Mawlana Shaykh (may Allah bless him), he is giving bayah without restriction, because he knows no one knows *Shariah* or Islamic jurisprudence.
>
> At that time they did not have a choice; they had to study the main curriculum of the educational system. Now it is not religion anymore. Religion is being thrown away like a bone. No one is teaching religion anymore even in Muslim countries, unless you really want to study religion. It might be one in one thousand in the total population that desire to study religion.
>
> So the wisdom of Allah was that He did not want to leave the *Ummah* [community] without any connection. So an order came from the *awliya* to give *bayah* to anyone who asks for it. Even if he only goes one time, it is enough; you have hooked him.[289]

Once the seeker has been drawn into the order and has taken *bayah* from Shaykh Nazim or Shaykh Hisham or any acting deputy of Shaykh Hisham, the process of bringing the person into the *Shariah*

---

[289] According to Shah Wali Allah's formulation, the seven cycles of the *tariqah* are as follows:

(1) True faith (*iman tariqah*), which consists of purifying the original nature (*fitrah*) with which every person is endowed. This is described as the sphere of reason for which prophet Adam is the exemplary model.

(2) He terms the second stage that of "opening the Breast" (*sharh al-sadr*). It is considered the first stage of "annihilation."

(3) The third stage is that of "drawing near (to Allah) through supererogatory actions (*Qurb al-nawafil*)."

(4) The fourth stage is wisdom (*Hikmah*): "*Whoever is given the Hikmah is given the greatest good*" (2:269).

(5) *Qurb al-faraid,* or "nearness through the Obligatory acts of worship."

(6) *Qurb al-malakuti,* or "drawing near to Allah through the angelic influences."

(7)*Al-Kamal,* the perfected. This is referred to as the stage in which the Prophet said, "Many men have been perfected, and among women only Khadija bint Khawailid, Miriam bint Imran, Asiya the wife of Pharaoh, and Fatimah daughter of Muhammad."

commences. This was, as Shaykh Hisham said on several occasions, a gradual process of "dehospitalization." He explained this term meant that once a *murid* had said the *shahadah,* he was fully accepted by the Prophet and was under the Prophet's protection.

> So naturally, when anyone came, he doesn't want that person to lose that opportunity with the permission that is coming these days from the *awliya*. Now when Mawlana gives the *bayah,* these people are not firm in their Islamic knowledge, so what happens is, because they are still in a process of hospitalization and rehabilitation, if you go to them and ask them questions, he or she might give you answers from their very limited if any Islamic knowledge. Therefore, this is what you must be aware of.[290]

I then replied to Shaykh Hisham, "I agree everyone is in a state of hospitalization at one point or another. However, I am more concerned with how the shaykh deals with the hospitalization. Granted, once we accept that the *murid* is in the hospital, how does the shaykh get them out of the hospital?"

Shaykh Hisham paused briefly to reflect, and then very softly, with a most charming smile, said, "Oh, that's when the shaykh gives them his pills—nice pills, red pills, white pills, blue pills—and that's how they get them out." Everyone laughed at his answer, as it was delivered with such perfect timing and just the right dose of irony. Nevertheless, behind the humor was an extremely serious reply. So I interjected, "Maybe you could talk about how they get them out." Shaykh Hisham took a long look at me and smiled like a Cheshire cat.

Diagnosis: *Bayah* and Beyond

"Oh, I have to give you one of those pills, then." Everyone laughed and I too laughed, as the expression on his face was that of a young child who has just been caught with his hand in the cookie jar. The atmosphere reminded me of an old family reunion. I felt

[290] Kabbani, Hisham. Interview in Saddle River, N.J., by Andrew Vidich, interview, June 26, 1999.

unhesitatingly comfortable despite the fact that I had known Shaykh Hisham for fewer than two days. As I looked around the room, I sensed everyone was enjoying this special *suhbat* as much as I was. Shaykh Hisham continued to explain what happens after the seeker comes to the shaykh:

> So when they come to the Shaykh—the Prophet said, "Realize that when you come to a *mumin* [believer], that *mumin* can see completely because he can see by the *nur* of Allah (light of God) [*hadith*].[291] So when the Prophet says, "I am seeing you and you are seeing me, what is the difference between the two?" Therefore, why did the Prophet say, "Be aware, because a *mumin* can see by the Light of Allah?" *Mumins* have a special kind of vision. We describe them as saints. "*They are the saints of Allah, and no one can harm them, nor do they grieve.*" (10: 62) So these are the *mumins*. They can see far beyond what everyone else can see. This is how they differ. So if they look, they can see even behind the walls. So with that power, when someone comes in front of them, they can analyze their personality just like a psychoanalyst.

> After the murid takes *bayah* or the pledge [initiation] to his shaykh, the shaykh has the authority by order of the Prophet to begin to work on the *murid*. The shaykh then, through his spiritual powers of discernment, begins to analyze the condition of the seeker. In the same sense that a psychologist makes a diagnosis based on the observable behavioral symptoms and extensive interviews, the shaykh conducts an "innerview" of the condition of the seeker as if he were a transparent jar. Whatever is inside, whether it is sour or sweet, is known at a mere glance. Furthermore, if the shaykh is of the highest level, not only is the present condition known, but also the seeker's entire history from pre-eternity to post-eternity.

Treatment and Healing

Shaykh Hisham continued:

---

[291] *Hadith* of the Prophet.

> The shaykh, for example, knows that this person is suffering from a complexion of fear. Therefore, he has to give him something to raise his courage and to change that complex. Therefore, when the shaykh gives him that special pill, immediately he changes. In spirituality, we know that every person has a weakness, like the point or center of gravity. That center of gravity is like a car going up or down a hill. If you go down and the slope is not quite correct, or if it is a little bit tilted and you go fast, you will lose your center of gravity, and the car will flip over, because the center of gravity depends upon the alignment of the car with the earth, which, for example, might be in the middle of the car. Therefore, they built the car so that when you change the center of gravity by increasing the velocity of the car, what happens? The car flips immediately. So *awliya*, they look at your weakest point, which is the center of gravity of your personality or your self! When they look at that person, they direct their vision, that light [*nur Allah*] to the center point of your personality, and you flip. When you flip, you become a surrendering patient.[292]

As I hear these words, I am struck by the direct correlation to the concept of the nine points outlined in Naqshbandi methodology. These nine points represent the weak point in the personality of the seeker; or alternatively, the point where the ego is most clearly bound or attached. The authentic shaykh can, through his spiritual vision, detect the weak point and use it to his advantage in transforming the *murid*. To have access to this information is the secret to the methodology. Without it, the shaykh would be no different from any other *murid*. Paradoxically, the shaykh also begins the work of transformation using a principle akin to homeopathic medicine, in

---

[292] The weakest point in the personality is the point where the ego (*nafs*) is most firmly entrenched. There is a vast amount of literature now available on the theory and practice of the enneagram; see the work of Oscar Ichazo, Helen Palmer, and David Russo for a more detailed discussion. See Don Richard Riso and Russ Hudson's *Personality Types: Using the Enneagram for Self-discovery* (New York: Houghton Mifflin, 1996); see also J.G. Bennett's *Enneagram Studies* (York Beach, Me.: Samuel Weiser, 1983) and Dorothy DeChristopher's article reprinted from *The Movement Newspaper*, May 1981 in *Interviews with Oscar Ichazo* (New York: Arica Institute Press, 1982).

which the patient receives a smaller dose of the sickness he already has until his constitution is strengthened. After his personality is strengthened, the *murid* is ready to die to his own attributes and come to the zero point. This is the point where the inward and outward faces collapse, where *zahir* and *batin* disappear into unity. Finally, in dying to one's own attributes, the *murid* affirms the transcendent reality of the *shahadah*, "There is no god but God."[293]

> At that time, they begin to give you what you need to rehabilitate yourself. You then can begin to face your problem and overcome your difficulties. So this is their methodology. This is their candy. They know your weakest point, and they hit on it. When they hit on it, it catches you. When they catch you, you are finished. You now feel that this man did something to change your life, and you believe and trust him. When you trust him, then you become like the Sahaba or companions of the prophets, who trusted the Prophet. Because of their trust in the Prophet, whatever the Prophet said, they believed. The sahaba were believers. So whenever you trust someone, you know he is not cheating you. That is why the Prophet said, "If a judge was looking into a case, and he gave the exact and correct opinion and hit the truth, he is rewarded twice." If the judge did not hit the truth, he gave his judgment, and he was mistaken, he still gets one reward. Why? Because he did not have it in his heart to cheat anyone. He tried his best to give the correct opinion. However, what can he do? He is a man, he is human being, and he made a mistake. And mistakes are forgivable.[294]

One significant feature I observed of both Shaykh Hisham's and Shaykh Nazim's teaching style was the general principle of "demonstrating the unknown by that which is called 'known' by the

---

[293] Rumi makes a similar point when he says, "The Ocean's water brings the corpse to the surface, but if a man is alive, how can he escape its depths? When you have died to human attributes, the Ocean of mysteries will bring you up to a place of elevation" Chittick, W. *The Sufi Path of love* (Albany, N.Y.: State University of New York Press, 1983) p. 183).

[294] Kabbani, Hisham. Interview in Saddle River, N.J., by Andrew Vidich, June 27, 1999.

audience." This fundamental method is repeatedly applied, during both more formal *suhbats* and informal conversations with *murids*. The example of the judge mentioned above illustrates the underlying principle of trust in a way that can be grasped by people from this particular society to which we belong.

Since judges are considered trustworthy, the comparison with the Prophet and hence the shaykh can be understood without difficulty by the listener. This use of analogies and metaphors not only enhances the interest of the listener but tends to create a "point of relevance" for the listener and a shared "reference system" that acts as a mechanism to internalize knowledge.[295]

Treatment and Application

Explaining the nature of this application, Shaykh Hisham continued:

> The shaykh wants to build you up and bring you up. Therefore, the shaykh, when he looks at his followers, he is instilling them with his own life impulse. For example, if you see a danger coming toward you, what do you do? Immediately all your hormones begin to change in your body. Different glands secrete different types of hormones to build up a defense against that danger in order that you are able to resist that danger. We are so completely under stress, that is why danger can struggle with us, because you feel that if you are not building up a power against the danger, the danger might overcome you. Therefore, the shaykh strengthens you spiritually in your spiritual body, which is not this physical body...
>
> So any mass is composed of two components, the mass, or what is called the "regular mass," and the "energy." Each

---

[295] Afzal Iqbal, in his analysis of Rumi's *Mathnawi,* makes a similar point. The successful story does not at first point out to the reader the moral implied in it. On the contrary, it only becomes evident when the storyteller points it out. There is a vast difference between conveying an idea and conveying an experience, according to Iqbal: "There is an enormous difference between giving expression to an experience and giving experience to an idea, and this difference is the difference between Rumi and the systematic thinkers." Iqbal, A., *The Life and Work of Jalaluddin Rumi* (New York: Oxford University Press, 1956) p.258).

> atom must also have energy. A mass without energy does not function, and energy without mass cannot be utilized. You need a mass for it like a laser. For example, we have light in this room here, but you cannot use it, unless you have some kind of instrument. Similarly, there is electricity in the air, there are magnetic fields everywhere, but if there is no wire to carry that electricity, it is not usable. This *dunya* [world] needs energy because it is physical. Therefore, this body needs the physical dimension; but without the spiritual dimension, it is dead.
>
> When Allah created Adam, of course there was no decay, like here. He was standing without movement for many years until the spirit came. [Shaykh Hisham recites the verse from the Quran in Arabic, then gives the English translation.] "We have blown into him from Our spirit. Allah, gave us our Light. When He said and ordered he moved." So every atom needs energy, or it will not function. This is also true in the spiritual dimension...
>
> So the shaykh slowly begins to build up that spirituality within us. As this happens, it begins to change all our hormones inside our body. Every day he sends exciting visions, exciting dreams, exciting experiences, exciting *dhikr*, or exciting lectures. Therefore, he moves you spiritually from inside to get a bigger picture. That builds back up what was lost, and gradually the balance is restored between the body and energy [body and spirit].

Shaykh Hisham continued along these lines, using various analogies to make his point. Later in our discussion I asked him if he might relate some of his own spiritual experiences for the benefit of seekers that might illustrate some of the powers of the shaykh. He declined, saying that in his book, The Naqshbandi Sufi Way, he had told several stories, and that if I liked them, I could use them. I was interested in having him explain the exact nature of the transmission process of how a shaykh creates the spiritual power in the *murid*. He then reiterated the very strict injunction forbidding *murids* from revealing their inner experiences without authorization—a point which we have discussed earlier but bears mentioning again. He suggested:

> These people who write about their experiences with angels and other inner experiences are yet at the level of children. Because when you tell a story [about your experiences], ego is in it. But this is not the way of a spiritual person or someone who has been lifted up into the divine presence. When these people start speaking about their experiences, they cannot control themselves. If they continue in this way, their progress will stop. When they begin to speak about their experiences, it keeps them at that level, in that prison, in that shell.[296]

The conversation continued along these lines for a short while, until suddenly he suggested that I could in fact record some of the experiences *murids* had in becoming disciples in the Naqshbandi *tariqah*. I was at first surprised, as it seemed to contradict his earlier remarks. However, his approval granted a temporary immunity from the general rule of the order. My assumption was that a *murid* might discuss his or her experiences only with the permission of the shaykh. His remarks opened the door to anyone who wanted to share their experiences of how they were attracted and eventually took bay'at. At first, there was a deep silence, and no one volunteered. Then I said, "Shaykh Hisham, they won't speak unless you give them permission." Shaykh Hisham looked around the room and said, "Everyone is welcome to speak." A few moments passed, and then someone raised his hand and offered to relate his story. For the next hour or so, six *murids* from various cultural and religious backgrounds shared their "conversion experiences."[297] ...Generally, they reflected the rule of being drawn by the "charismatic presence" of Shaykh Nazim or Shaykh Hisham. As soon as the last *murid* had

---

[296] Kabbani, Hisham. Interview in Saddle River, N.J., by Andrew Vidich, June 27, 1999.

[297] For a fuller discussion of Naqshbandi conversion experiences, see the work of Ali Kose, "Conversion to Islam: A Study of British Converts," Ph.D. thesis, University of London, 1994, now published as *Conversion to Islam: A Study of British Converts to Islam,* London: Curzon Press, 1999.

finished, Shaykh Hisham looked around the room and reemphasized that despite the validity of these experiences of Shaykh Nazim, they were still only a fragmentary and incomplete picture:

> Whatever these *murids* are saying about how they have come to me, or to anyone who speaks on behalf of Mawlana Shaykh (either they had a real appointment or they are the appointed *khalifah* of the shaykh, whatever is the case), it is still a drop from the ocean. All of us, including my brother and I, who is now in the Middle East—and we have been appointed by Grandshaykh and Mawlana Shaykh Nazim as his *khalifahs* to Mawlana Shaykh—whatever other thousands of people who are his deputies, we are all of us not even a drop of the ocean of Mawlana...
>
> Once Mawlana said to me, "This is my turban, and all my murids are different jewels in the turban. The uniqueness of the turban is to have all the jewels in place. If even one jewel is missing, it looks like something is wrong whatever you are carrying." The big one or the small one must be complete, because human nature always looks at that one that is missing. Always the attention looks at the negative aspect in life. That is why Mawlana is so careful to have everything in its place. For that reason, in this *tariqah* we care so much for every person even if they come only once. One time is very important, in other words, to keep his place on the turban of Mawlana Shaykh, because if even one jewel drops away from the turban, it does not look beautiful. Similarly, if one color of the rainbow is missing, it is no longer a rainbow. So one needs all the colors.[298]

Training the *Murid* in the Relativism of All Knowledge

Shaykh Hisham continued to explain one of the special features of what can be referred to as "absolute relativism in relation to spiritual

[298] Kabbani, Hisham. Interview in Saddle River, N.J., by Andrew Vidich, June 21, 1999.

experience."[299] ...One aspect of this methodology bears careful consideration. In relationship to the training of the *murid*, Naqshbandi methodology continually underscores the state of *ayn al-jam*, that all knowledge is relative and therefore passing. The seeker must avoid at every step the temptation to become identified or attached to any form of knowledge or spiritual experience.[300] The moment the seeker identifies himself with the experience, he stops ascending and his progress comes to a halt. Shaykh Hisham explains:

> There are people who spiritually, when they reach a certain level, are afraid to lose that level. So what happens is that seeker stops ascending, and they are stopped because they are trying to keep it. These seekers believe if they let it loose, they will lose the experience and lose everything. In the Naqshbandi *tariqah*, this is false. You have to leave it in order to go higher and higher.[301]

Shaykh Hisham indicated that the tendency of the seeker to become attached to his condition is extremely dangerous and is countered with the technique of removing the veils from the top down. Shaykh Hisham explained this at considerable length:

> We know that there are 70,000 veils. And every veil has to be removed. And as it is removed, you move closer and closer in ascending degrees to your goal. Therefore, when you reach the tenth level or thirtieth or seventieth level, you are happy there. The seeker begins to perceive things. As soon as you begin to experience things, you also want to cling and do not want to let them go. Then your forward progress is stopped. However,

---

[299] For a fuller discussion of this concept, see Sviri, Sara, *The taste of things hidden*. Inverness, Calif.: Golden Sufi Center, 1997. The aspirant is constantly cautioned to refrain from identifying "with any state or stage, with any object or person, with any project or aspiration, be it blameworthy or praiseworthy. When viewed from the heart of hearts, from 'secret of secrets,' from the state of *'ayan al-jam,'* all is connected to the source of Total Being" (Sviri, 1997, p. 163).

[300] If there was one consistent theme of which every murid was conscious from the very beginning of discipleship, it was the passing nature of spiritual experience. This manifested in a lack of concern or interest in these temporary phenomena. As one disciple said, "Why try and analyze a dream within a greater dream?" (private interview, May 20, 1999).

[301] Kabbani, Hisham. Interview in Saddle River, N.J., by Andrew Vidich, June 26, 1999.

> the Naqshbandi *tariqah* does not do that. Your shaykh does not open the veils from the beginning. He keeps the first veil on you because he does not want your ego to play with you and get this kind of excitement and expecting that you are moving up. When that happens you begin to see yourself, "Oh, I am a shaykh, I am a *khalifah*, I am a deputy." ...All of this is imagination. All of this is hallucination. There is no such thing. The *tariqah* is what grandshaykh passed to grandshaykh who passed to grandshaykh who passed to grandshaykh, and it has to be obvious to everyone. Everyone must be able to see and know about it. You cannot hide it. Something has to be documented, both written physically and spiritually.[302]

It may take an entire lifetime for all these veils to be removed. However, the entire training of the *murid* is to reach this level. He continued:

> So this is the beginning of your training in seclusion, in *awrad*, in *dhikr*, and you begin to be lifted up.[303] When you reach the second level, then the first veil is removed from the other side. When you reach here, then he removes the last veil. Immediately you find yourself in the circle of saints. Because there is no ego to play with you. The shaykh has done his work from the other side.

I asked Shaykh Hisham at this point, "So do you see anything in the middle stages, or do you go straight to the goal?" Shaykh Hisham replied:

> All what they are observing is not yet anything to do with the ascending in the real meaning of spirituality. Because there are

---

[302] Kabbani, Hisham. Interview in Saddle River, N.J., by Andrew Vidich, June 26, 1999.

[303] According to Buehler, in addition to these practices, "the new disciple would learn the Mujaddidi methods of activating the subtle centers (*lataif*) and perform the guided meditations (*muraqabah*)." Buehler, A., *Sufi heirs of the Prophet: The Indian Naqshbandiyya order and the rise of the mediating Sufi Shaykh* (Columbia, S.C.: University of South Carolina Press, 1998) p. 96. From my observations and interviews, I found that some *murids* receive the higher training in activating the subtle centers, but they are a select few (private interview, August 16, 1999). In this sense, the order never reveals itself completely, nor would it be advisable, as some would make use of it for selfish purposes.

> five levels—*qalb* [heart], *ruh* [spirit], sirr [mystery], *khafa* [arcanum], *akhfa* [superarcanum]. The first level ends with the heart, where everything is there, even Satan goes there. This first level relates to everything in this worldly life. In this first level your prayers, your worship, your dealing with business, meeting with your shaykh, loving the shaykh, seeing the shaykh in your dreams, all your sinning and your repentance, all of this is called *maqam i-qalb*. Then there is the second level, which is *maqam i-ruh*. This level is only for the saints. They enter you via the second level. At the third level of *sirr*, they see the secrets of reality. They know what kinds of secrets Allah (glory be to him) has put in your heart; this is the level of *sirr*. Moreover, when they want to guide you, they look at that level. They guide their followers from this level.

At this point Shaykh Hisham became emphatic. His voice became very animated and high pitched. He wanted to make sure there was not the least bit of doubt concerning the levels of sainthood. According to Shaykh Hisham, the attainment of this level is a very rare achievement. Hundreds of people may claim they are shaykhs, deputies, or *khalifahs*, but from the Naqshbandi perspective this is all illusion. Even within the Naqshbandi *tariqah* of Shaykh Nazim, some claim this special status. Shaykh Hisham put this speculation to rest:

> Many people think they are speaking from the Divine Presence. They claim they reach the Prophet's presence and they claim they have reached Mawlana Shaykh's presence as well. Moreover, some, they even make as if they are equal to Shaykh Nazim. They are not even dust. We will be very happy if we are the dust of the feet of Mawlana Shaykh. So this second level [*maqam i-ruh*] is reserved only for saints.[304]

Beyond this lies the level of *sirr*, or the secret, which is reserved for a higher category of saints. These saints are even rarer than the previous category. Shaykh Hisham continued:

---

[304] Kabbani, Hisham. Interview in Saddle River, N.J., by Andrew Vidich, June 26, 1999.

> The third level, which is the *sirr*, or secret, is not accessed by even these saints. There are 124,000 saints, and only 7,007 of these 124,000 saints reach that secret. These *awliya* know more than the previous *awliya* and both are *awliya*. Both of them are saints. But the latter are at a higher level.

It is only after reaching the third level that the seeker is free from his or her ego. Until he reaches the level of secret, he is still subject to temptations of the ego. If this is the case, then the first-level saints are not completely free from the subtle and finer aspects of their own egos. Before I could ask Shaykh Hisham to explain this further, he did so himself. It was an important point, because it implied that only at the higher level of sainthood, or the realm of *maqam al-wilayat*, was the saint truly free. Again, Shaykh Hisham continued:

> The fourth level or *khafa* is reserved for the Prophet, upon whom be peace. And the last level, *akhfa*, is for Allah and even the Prophet does not know what is in that state. And all these five states are in the heart of man. That is why Allah said, "*I am nearer to you than your own jugular vein*" (1:16). Allah knows in that level what even the Prophet does not know. Therefore, that is real *tawhid*... The real *tawhid* no one can imagine; even Muhammad cannot reach that—impossible. Otherwise there would be no relationship between God, creator, and servant.[305]

I was somewhat surprised by this revelation, as nowhere else had I come across this particular point. I thought perhaps I had missed it in the writings of Shaykh Nazim; however, the only indication was in the cosmology of Ahmad Sirhindi, who posits the "reality of pure servanthood" above the "reality of Muhammad" and the "reality of Ahmad" as a co-equal stage attained from the path taken by the saints. Shaykh Hisham explained the difference between the second and third stages via a Sufi teaching story. It was not unusual, in fact it was quite common, for both Shaykh Hisham and Shaykh Nazim to present many of the Sufi ideas via the vehicle of a story. This method is a long-standing tradition that dates back to the Prophet and is "almost

---

[305] Kabbani, Hisham. Interview in Saddle River, N.J., by Andrew Vidich, June 26, 1999.

unknown outside the ranks of the initiates of the Way."[306] The teaching story, sometimes called "diagrammatic of impression tales," helps prepare the *murid* intellectually to receive the higher teaching by appealing directly to the heart. Correctly told by a competent teaching master at the right time and place, these tales prepare the mind of the *murid* for the higher teaching. This method, according to Sufi teaching, "can yield enlightenment to the individual in accordance with his capacity to understand."[307]

The following story made clear to me that the disciple is unable to perceive his own faults. The ego is so subtle that it can disguise itself in myriad ways. In fact, every action the shaykh takes is somewhat like a chess game against the *murid*'s ego. At some point during the telling, I became aware of how deeply affected I was by the story. Whether Shaykh Hisham intended to elicit that response, I do not know.

Overcoming the Ego and Levels of Sainthood

> One time there was a very big and well-known shaykh with his followers in Baghdad. They were all talking along the river Euphrates near Baghdad. As they were walking behind the shaykh, the shaykh suddenly pushed one *murid* into the river, which was a great distance down. Just as the *murid* was reaching the river, the shaykh appeared and caught him.
>
> When the shaykh had pushed the murid, he was actually testing him. Is he loving me and surrendering to me

---

[306] Shah, Idries, *Learning how to learn: Psychology and spirituality in the Sufi way*. San Francisco: Harper and Row. 1978, p. 197.

[307] *Op. cit*, p. 198. Idries Shah, in his book *Learning How to Learn: Psychology and Spirituality in the Sufi Way,* explicitly states that one of the intentions of the Sufi tale is that "its construction is such as to permit the presentation to the mind of a design or series of relationships. When the reader's mind is familiar with this structure, he can understand concepts and experiences which have a similar structure, but which operate on a higher level of perception. It could be called the relationship of the blueprint to the finished apparatus." Shah further adds that these teaching stories each contain or "imprison a priceless secret" which is "released by the power of a teaching master." Hence, to analyze these tales deprives them of their instrumental value. The secret lies in the hands of a competent teaching master to enable the disciple to experience them aright. (Shah, I., *Learning How to Learn: Psychology and Spirituality in the Sufi Way* New York: Dutton, 1978, p. 198).

completely, or not? So as the *murid* was falling down he was completely accepting, completely agreeing and accepting his shaykh's actions. So it means he was surrendered. He pushed him to check him, to test him. Because he passed the test, the shaykh raised him up to the first level of sainthood.

In the mind of the shaykh, there was no doubt in that *murid*'s heart about his shaykh and about all the other *murids*. He perceived the *murid* loved everyone and his worship was good. At that moment when he was being tested and he was seen to be worthy of the trust, he was raised up and given his trust. However, there was another shaykh watching all of this from a second level (*sirr as-sirr*), and at that moment this wali from the 7,007 asked the shaykh, "How did you give him this trust?" The shaykh replied, "I detected there was nothing." Then he said, "Yes, from the first level there was nothing, but from our level we detected something different." Like satellites from one galaxy or from one dome to another, the capability of the satellite depends on how big the satellite is. The bigger it is, the better it can detect what is happening millions of miles away.

Today we have satellites and telescopes that can detect stars thousands of light-years away. So the second shaykh said, "We detected something. When you pushed the *murid*, and gave him the trust, it had not yet reached from the first level to the second level. It was coming, but you didn't give it a chance to reach. When you pushed him, he didn't object while you pushed him; he surrendered. However, at our level we detected his heart saying, 'What was the wisdom that my shaykh pushed me?'" So the *murid* was questioning. With what wisdom? he wants to know. He was saying, "With what wisdom?" In other words, he was thinking to himself, "What am I going to gain or get [from this]?" [Everyone laughs.] So from their higher level, they saw there was something in his ego still playing with him. So the shaykh said, "From our level, we would not have given him the trust. But from the lower level it could not be detected."

I then responded, "So the intellect has to be completely killed." Shaykh Hisham replied, "Of course, yes. However, not intellectuality, it is egoism that has to be completely killed in you—not the good ego, [only] the bad desires. It has to be completely erased. We do not say killed but subdued, so it is not able to play with you or cheat you."

The whole notion of the ego and the role it plays in the development of the *murid* is not as simple as has been portrayed by many popular writers. The ego, according to Naqshbandi theology, is both an obstacle and the vehicle to perceive the higher reality. In other words, it is necessary. The ego is like a mirror, which shows us our face but is also not our face. It is merely a reflection of our true face. If one wants to see one's true face, or the "face of reality," one has to turn one's attention away from the mirror or bring the mirror inside oneself. So long as one is looking at oneself in the mirror, one cannot see the divine presence. By breaking the mirror, one can then turn one's attention toward the Divine Presence.

Not long after this portion of our discussion, Shaykh Hisham explained the actual techniques the shaykh's use to transform the hearts of their *murids*. I was particularly fascinated by his explanation because it seemed to answer specifically how a shaykh influences the *murids*. The discussion was prefaced by his explanation of how Islam was able to spread so quickly to many areas in the world where people knew neither the language nor anything about Islam.

"So how did they change the people to Islam? They did not know Chinese. How did they bring Islam there? Have the Muslim scholars of today asked this question?" I replied, "Because it was a living order." Shaykh Hisham continued, "Because it was a living light. There is attraction from the living light." He paused for a second and then quickly said six words in Arabic, which I did not catch. He then said, "This is very important." I asked him to repeat them and explain them in detail. He nodded yes.

The Six Realities of the Saints

> There are six realities in the heart of every human. They are *haqiqat al-jazbah*, or the reality of attraction; *haqiqat al-fayd*, or

the reality of inspiration; *haqiqat al-tawassul,* or the reality of intercession; *haqiqat al-tawajjuh,* or the reality of sending light; *haqiqat al-tai,* or the reality of moving in space by just saying *bismillah ir-rahman ir-rahim,* and you are able to move from one place to another; and *haqiqat al-irshad,* or the reality of guidance.[308]

These realities are in the heart of every *murid,* but you need a special code to open them. If you do not have that special code, you cannot open those doors. So when you have they six realities and they are evolving inside you and going up with that energy, you do not need to speak. All you need to do is send one of these realities, and you can go everywhere. And that is why the sahaba were able to reach everywhere with these realties that the Prophet gave them.

Why does the Prophet appear in the dreams of people? That is *haqiqat at-tawajjuh.* The shaykh can send dreams or visions anywhere. The saints (*awliya*) are given visions, while regular people get dreams. The Sahaba, they were using these powers that the Prophet trained them with. Moreover, they were attracting people without even talking. It might be in the dreams that he comes to someone in China. Therefore, you do not need any language. It is a spiritual language, or, as you say, the language of love. This spiritual relationship moves the masses. They may go to a leader of a tribe, they reach him, and then that leader changes the whole tribe. They do not need any language.

Why is the Naqshbandi order attracting people from east to west and from north to south without any media, literature, without rocket fuel, money, and without satellites? It is because there is a real relationship and lineage through

---

[308] Shaykh Hisham gives a slightly different version in his book *Mercy Oceans' Safety Shores* (Fenton, Michigan: Haqqani Islamic Trust, 1993) pp. 85 ff. See also Shaykh Nazim's *Mercy Oceans' Lovestreams* (Konya: Sebat Press, 1986) pp. 103-110. *Haqiqat ut-tayy* for *haqiqat al-tai,* which is the power to travel at will, and *haqiqat ul-fayd* for *haqiqat al-tufail,* which is the power of emanation of the divine presence to the murid.

> Grandshaykh to the Prophet ﷺ. There is a direct relationship. That shows that this *tariqah* and any other *tariqahs* like this that are growing have a direct relationship. In addition, there are other orders—the Rifai, Chishti, Qadiri, and others.[309]
>
> The Naqshbandi order is "giving light throughout the world" because it has a direct connection to the heart of Muhammad ﷺ, a direct connection to the prophetic heart. It is a direct lineage. So when that light comes, it is not disturbed or broken. [310] It is like a laser moving everywhere without hindrance and attracting people into the Naqshbandi order and into Islam.[311]

This is, in fact, the first reality mentioned by Shaykh Hisham, the reality of attraction (*jazbah*). The shaykh sets up these power stations, and then light is given to people everywhere. He referred to them as "attraction stations." Once these stations are set up, that light will connect them to the main line or main power source through the agency of the acting deputy of the shaykh.

Tawajjuh, or the Spiritual Transmission of the Shaykh

Once the *murid* is connected to the main power source by taking *bayah*, then the shaykh begins to send them dreams and visions using the power called the *haqiqat at-tawajjuh*, or the reality of visions or spiritual emanation.[312] This power, indeed all the six realities or powers, are the special province of the perfect shaykh, and as such the shaykhs were

---

[309] Kabbani, Hisham. Interview in Saddle River, N.J., by Andrew Vidich, June 26, 1999.

[310] Buehler notes, "Such a perfect shaykh, *sahib-i qal wa-hal*, represents one having an inner connection to Muhammad through the oral transmission (*qal*) of knowledge, e.g., Hadith study, and a person whose inner connection to Muhammad manifests itself outwardly in a spiritual state (*hal*). According to Muhammad Ibrahim Qusuri, the 'effect of a pir's spiritual energy (*tawajjuh*) should override all other considerations except *Shariah*-mindedness'" (1998, p. 153). This quotation helps support the centrality of the living shaykh as the sine qua non for the success of every order based upon the shaykh's inner connection to Muhammad. However, it goes a step further, stating that the litmus test for a shaykh is the "spiritual emanations of the shaykh" (*fayd*).

[311] Kabbani, Hisham. Interview in Saddle River, N.J., by Andrew Vidich, June 22, 1999.

[312] This is discussed at length in chapter 2.

referred to by Ibn Arabi as "red sulfur" (*kibrit ahmar*) or precious human being.

Tawajjuh is the concentrated spiritual attention radiating directly from the presence of an authentic shaykh that may or may not be directed to anyone in specific.[313] It may have its roots in the outward act of turning toward the *qiblah*[314] (*istiqbal*) and confronting it (*tawajjuh*). Thus, as Padwick notes, "the outward and inward acts are to go together"[315] It differs from visualization in that it is a gift from the shaykh, and receiving it involves no special effort on the part of the *murid*. The shaykh by means of his singular concentration (*tawajjuh*) can impart mystical experience directly to the *murid*.

This intentional flow of divine energy coming from the shaykh called *tawajjuh, tasarruf,* or *himmah* has the power not only to hasten the disciple's inner progress but also transport the disciple's soul directly to higher stations on the path. The degree of purification the *murid* has achieved and his capacity to receive the shaykh's transmission (*fayd*) usually condition such divine gifts. However, such gifts may also be given gratuitously as foretastes of the spiritual path to hasten the *murid*'s longing for the higher realities. In short, it is in the hand of the living shaykh to dispense as he sees fit.

While many Naqshbandi texts indicate the shaykh's *tawajjuh* could be transmitted through lectures and discussions, it could also be done through a handshake, touching the forehead, or placing a hand on the *murid*'s chest.[316] However, as in the above example, distance is

---

[313] An example of undirected *tawajjuh* is given in Jalal-ud-din Rumi's *Fiha ma fihi,* (In it What is in it) in which he cites the wordless transmission of the third Caliph, Uthman.

[314] The direction of Mecca, toward which Muslims orient themselves in prayer.

[315] Padwick notes, "A Turkish Naqshbandi worshipper about to recite his *silsila* of connection with the Prophet is given the following directions: 'First the faithful must free his heart as much as in him lies from all evil thoughts, must face the *qiblah* and sit in the proper posture for prayer, must close his eyes, and direct all his senses to the side of the fir-cone (*sanabar*, stone-pine) shaped heart. Then he must confront (*mutawajjuh*) God as present in all His greatness and love" (manuscript prayer book bought from a street hawker in Istanbul). Padwick, *Muslim Devotions* (Rockport, Mass.: One World Publications, 1996) p. 60.

[316] Buehler, A., *Sufi heirs of the Prophet: The Indian Naqshbandiyya order and the rise of the mediating Sufi Shaykh*. Columbia, S.C.: University of South Carolina Press, 1998, p. 133.

irrelevant if the spiritual connection between the *murid* and shaykh[317] is close. In the higher stages of this practice, Sirhindi writes that *rabitah* can be so close "that during his performance of the prayer the novice experiences his shaykh to be the person for whom he bows."[318] In this case, the bond or connection between the shaykh has been established and the disciple experiences "disappearance in the shaykh" or *fana fi-sh-shaykh*.

On the Reality of *Suhbah*

[One] night Shaykh Nazim gave what would be my final *suhbah*. I sensed something special was in store for me, but I did not know exactly what. He began his *suhbah* as usual with a physical survey of the room, like a surgeon reviewing patients before surgery. He appeared to review who would receive anesthesia, who needed special bandages, who required medication, and who was ready for surgery.

I was sitting as close as I could to him this night, perhaps less than a few feet away. I did not expect to be drawn so closely to Shaykh Nazim, as this "intimacy" seems more appropriately reserved for other murids. Nevertheless, I decided to make full use of the opportunity to observe Shaykh Nazim in this environment. As he began, I placed my recorder near his feet.

> Our Imam of the most distinguished Naqshbandi order, Bahauddin Naqshband, has said we are achieving perfection by our association with a shaykh. The shaykh has such a power that he may give you power. Working from the inside,

---

While the practice of *tawajjuh* does not receive a great deal of attention in Sufism other than in the Naqshbandi *tariqah*, there is ample evidence that it is widely practiced in many other traditions. See the work of C.P. Purdom, *God Man: The Life and Journeys and Work of Meher Baba with an Interpretation of His Silence and Spiritual Teaching* (Crescent Beach, S.C.: Sheriar Press, Inc., 1964) pp. 294-342.

[317] Buehler mentions that Birbali used to touch the chest to activate a disciple's subtle energy entities. M. Birbali, *Inqilab al-haqiqat*, 2nd ed. (Lahore: Aftab-i Alam Press, 1980) pp. 50-53; cited in Buehler, A., Sufi *heirs of the Prophet: The Indian Naqshbandiyya order and the rise of the mediating Sufi Shaykh* (Columbia, S.C.: University of South Carolina Press, 1998) p. 133.

[318] Haar, J.G.J., *Follower and heir of the Prophet: Shaykh Ahmad Sirhindi (1564-1624) as mystic* (Leiden, Netherlands: Hetoosters Instituut, 1992) p. 84.

a real shaykh through his association is able to make you perfect.

During winter, particularly during the morning time, some cars are not able to move or to start. People are saying that the battery is dead. What should we do in this situation when our car is not moving? What is the way to make that car work? The way they are saying is to bring a living car to make a contact. This battery is like a dead body. You must make a transfer from a living body to a dead body.

So they bring cables, put the cables on the dead battery, and then attach the other side of the cables to the living battery. Then they charge the battery, and in five, ten, or fifteen minutes they say, Now the battery is fine. You are OK. I am never hearing anything, only I am seeing that we hooked up the dead battery to the charger and within a short time they say, Now it is enough, and they start the car. That is the silent power of the living battery coming into contact with the dead battery, and it is now starting. This is no problem for everyone to accept. Everyone agrees it is fine. We put wires from one battery to a second battery and from the outside, both are looking identical to one another. Moreover, you are not seeing any special sounds coming from one battery or the other. Just silence. You are not learning anything. Everyone is accepting this event.

If we are saying, a shaykh may send from his heart a power, that he may give someone or his followers that power to their heart, "Oh," the people say, "They are like so many donkeys. Oh, what is that, it can't be." They are saying it is impossible for a man to give something from his heart to another person's heart. They are denying that power. People are becoming like dogs. They are never accepting spirituality. They are never accepting the special powers, the sacred powers of the shaykh. Shah Naqshband is saying this is the special meaning about the association with a shaykh. The shaykh may sit, and he has a power, *haqiqat al-tawajjuh*—which means he is capable of

> changing their mind. He is able to change their hearts. He may be able to change their will. He is able to change your thoughts. Even he has the power to change your destination from bad to good and from good to best. And that is the meaning of who is a shaykh in the *tariqat*. The shaykh may use his spiritual power on his followers, and he may give from himself his spiritual power. He brings his spirituality over your physical being so that you may be able to follow him. In addition, even if you are like a dead body, it does not matter. Therefore it is said in the Holy Qur'an about Jesus Christ that he was giving life to dead ones from his powerful spirituality, giving and sending life from his spirituality.
>
> People believe that a glass of water is giving life. A person may be about to die, and one single glass of water gives him life here. His willpower is turning, making this the reason why he is able to live. He, the Almighty, is giving that water the power to give life. If he is not going to put his will through that water, you may drink an ocean and you are not going to live. Moreover, the shaykh is that authorized person who can give life to the servants of the Lord Almighty Allah. They are authorized—that means their words are going to give you a special kind of power. That power is the power to have control over your physical being. Now your soul is riding on your material body and sending it towards its Lord.
>
> This is the method of the most distinguished Naqshbandi order and the description of the work of the *tariqah*. It is the description of the meaning of the shaykh and the description of the true meaning of association with a shaykh. Our brother was just asking today to give something for his book. I think it is OK for you to make a book out of this.[319]

As soon as Shaykh Nazim finished, all the murids burst forth in the concluding song of praise with voices attuned to each other and with renewed praise for their shaykh.

---

[319] **Vidich, *Op. cit.,* p. 403.**

I realized that Shaykh Nazim had indeed given me the essential core or "seed" of Naqshbandi methodology. It was clear that everything rests in the power of the shaykh, who is the authorized conduit through which the divine *barakah* flows. The path begins and ends in the shaykh.[320] As important as all the spiritual practices are, they are secondary, because only through the shaykh who gives from his own power is the *murid* really able to perform even the rudiments of the *Shariah*. Without this initial boost from the shaykh, the *murids* would not have the will to perform any of the spiritual practices. In the end, according to Shaykh Nazim, the shaykh's charging or spiritual life attracts, sustains, inspires, and guides the *murid*. The shaykh's unseen hand works gradually to change the *murid*'s will, thought patterns, and ultimately his or her destination. However, it is not a unilateral action. With each spiritual boost given by the shaykh, the *murid* must reciprocate with further action. Each correct effort on the part of the *murid* is in turn rewarded with further grace from the shaykh. In this way, grace and effort are mutually supportive of one another and co-dependent, each cycle of effort and grace completing a tiny portion of the arch of the wheel of Naqshbandi life.[321]

Once the *murid* begins to have various spiritual experiences, he or she then, according to the new *tajalliyyat*, learns the *Shariah* according to his or her capacity, including the refinement of character (*akhlaq*), correct manners (*adab*), and the various prayers. Following this, and to the

---

[320] In one of my interviews with Shaykh Hisham, he went to the extent of saying that the "*tariqah* is what Grandshaykh passed to Grandshaykh, who passed it to Grandshaykh. It is a tightly held secret" Kabbani, Hisham. Interview in Saddle River, N.J., by Andrew Vidich, June 27, 1999. This utterance of the centrality of the role of the shaykh in fact equates, at a fundamental level, the shaykh with the *tariqah* itself. No other *tariqah* of which I am aware has been so far-reaching in this claim and so insistent in its practice than the Naqshbandiyya. In contradistinction, many orders have even played down the role of the shaykh in both theology and methodology. In this regard, I am thinking of both the Jerrahi Halveti order and the Chishti order. The work of Francis Trix also suggests significant differences in the role that the shaykh plays in the Bektashi order. I am not suggesting that the shaykh is not important and critical in these orders, but certainly not to the degree that the Naqshbandi Haqqani order has implied. I also do not want to suggest that this holds true for all Naqshbandi orders. To the contrary, I would suggest that the living shaykh alone determines the extent of his role and influence, rather th at the reverse.

[321] **Vidich, *Op. cit.*, p. 409.**

degree the *murid* is able to "carry" more, the shaykh instructs the *murid* in the special practices of the order, including the order's litany (*awrad*), *dhikr*, and mystical exercises (*ashghal*); and through the companionship with the mentor (*suhbat*), a special relationship with the teacher is established (*rabitah*).

Through this relationship, the shaykh is able to change the course of the *murid*'s thoughts, emotions, and personality by using the reality of inspiration or *haqiqat al-fayd*.[322] This is followed by the shaykh's ability to intercede directly on behalf of the disciple by mitigating or changing his circumstances. The shaykh does so through continued testing (*bala*) of the *murid* under varied circumstances. The shaykh does this by using his extensive powers to appear anywhere at any time by moving in space, or *haqiqat al-tai*. In fact, Shaykh Nazim is said to "visit" each of his *murids* at least once every 24 hours. Those who are receptive to his visit will feel a special bliss or peace during those times as the shaykh's *tawajjuh* or *fayd* descends into their hearts. At this point, the *murid* must make the appropriate efforts to abide by the will of the shaykh in all the *murid*'s affairs.

The exalted nature and status of saints

The exalted nature and status of the saints was the one universal connecting theme throughout my associations with both Shaykh Hisham and Shaykh Nazim. In the concluding section, Shaykh Hisham explains something of the special powers the *awliya* have been given as a justification for their exalted status—a point few other *tariqahs* have emphasized with such insistence and historical support. However, his comments were also a profound reminder of the insignificance of man in relation to God.

---

[322] One interesting example of *haqiqat al-tufail* is found in the *Fawaid al-Fuad* of Nizamud din Awliya, where he describes the levels of progressive effect as the inspiration of the shaykh descends on the murid: "The happiness that one derives from *tilawat* (Quran recitation) and *Sama* is of three kinds, it is *anwar* (lights) or *ahwal* (spiritual states) or *athar* (sublime impressions). And these descend respectively on the soul, heart and on the limbs (of the body) from three *alams* (worlds). The world of God's dominion, the world of His Angels and the world of Almightiness which is in between the two." (*Fawaid al-Fuad: Morals of the Heart,* trans. by Bruce Lawrence, New York: Paulist Press, 1992, p. 122).

Awliya, when they read Quran, they not only understand what they are reading, but they go into the Quranic Word. Because the Holy Quran is His Word. And we call it the ancient word. We cannot say His created word. The Quran is not created. It is coming out of His attributes. Because it is Allah's Word. Allah's Word is one of his Attributes.

I asked, "Is that what is meant by 'the original light'?"

It is a form of spiritual light that gives or turns into the word. Now technology has made it easy. You see now they are reading the news; before when they were reading the news, they were bulbs coming into letters. Now it is not bulbs, it is a new technology. It appears on a big computer screen and the one who is speaking the news can read it.

So *awliya*, when they read the Quran, manifestations come into their heart. This knowledge comes into their hearts. Allah's creatures' words are limited because we are created, and everything created has a limit. But anything not created has no limit. Allah's Words are not created.

How many letters are contained in the Quran? More than 1 million. Every word is made up of certain letters. If you add all these words in the Holy Quran, it adds up to more than 500,000. So every letter *awliya* can read. The *awliya* can read or bring out knowledge into their heart just as you are reading on the computer; a vision comes, and it brings you knowledge. This is how the *awliya* wrote about Sufism and *tasawwuf*. This kind of level they have reached. They were able to get this knowledge from Allah's Word, which is the Holy Quran.

So every letter gives a light—and from that light, information comes. Grandshaykh said every letter of the Quran contains more than twelve thousand oceans of knowledge. In addition, each successive ocean is bigger than the preceding one. It means they can take infinite oceans of knowledge from them.

It means, as Allah said in the Holy Quran, "*Above every knower there is a greater knower.*" (12:76) At that point, they can take infinite knowledge from the Quran. But beyond that infinite knowledge, there is yet another infinite ocean of knowledge. Still further, beyond that infinite knowledge, there is again another infinite ocean of knowledge. And all this knowledge is like a drop in an ocean. Furthermore, the knowledge the *awliya* are bringing is but a drop of the Prophet's knowledge. In addition, if you take all the knowledge of all the scholars and activists, it is no more than a drop in the ocean of the *awliyas'* knowledge. Finally, if you take all the scholars, all the *awliyas'*, and the Prophet's knowledge, it is nothing but a drop in the infinite ocean of God's knowledge, and there is no end. What are we then? We are nothing.[323]

[323] Kabbani, Hisham. Interview in Saddle River, N.J., by Andrew Vidich, June 26, 1999.

Doctrinal Foundations of the Spiritual Path

Tazkiyyat an-Nafs (Purifying the Self) an Essential Sufi Principle

The Sufi teachers of old spread Islam across the Indian Subcontinent, throughout Central and Southeast Asia, in Africa, and even some parts of Russia—just as contemporary Sufi teachers are spreading the faith through Europe and America today. But where did the Sufis originate? When did they first appear? And what was the position of the schools of Islamic jurisprudence and the scholars of the Community regarding Sufism, or *tasawwuf?*[324]

Today, Islam is taught only with words by people who do not care to practice it purely nor to purify themselves in practice. This unfortunate devolution was foreseen in many *ahadith* that state, for example, "*They will order people and not heed their own warning, and they are the worst of people.*"[325] Similarly, the Prophet ﷺ said, "*I do not fear for you only the anti-Christ." They asked, "Then who else are you afraid of?" He said, "The misguided scholars.*"[326] The Prophet ﷺ also said, "*What I fear most for my nation is a hypocrite who has a scholarly tongue.*"[327] Such was not the way of the Companions, including the People of the Bench (*Ahl as-Suffa*), concerning whom the following verse was revealed:

> *And restrain thyself with those who call upon their Lord at morning and evening, desiring His countenance, and let not thine eyes turn away from them, desiring the adornment of the present life; and obey not him whose heart We have made neglectful of Our remembrance so that he follows his own lust, and his affair has become all excess.* (18:28)

---

[324] The footnotes in the following sections are more detailed in order to assist those students of the Way that wish to conduct further research into the topics discussed in these pages.

[325] Reported on the authority of Umar, Ali, Ibn Abbas, and others. These were collected by Abu Talib al-Makki in the chapter entitled "The Difference between the scholars of the world and those of the hereafter" in his *Qut al-qulub fi muamalat al-mahbub* (Cairo: Matbaat al-maymuniyya, 1310/1893) pp. 1:140-141.

[326] Ahmad narrated it in his *Musnad*.

[327] Ahmad narrated it in his *Musnad* with a good chain.

Nor was this the way of Abu Bakr as-Siddiq ﵁, about whom the Prophet ﷺ said, *"Abu Bakr does not precede you for praying much or fasting much, but because of a secret that has taken root in his heart."*[328] Nor was this the way of the Successors (*tabieen*) such as Hasan al-Basri, Sufyan al-Thawri, and others of the later generations of Sufis who looked back to them for models. Al-Qushayri relates that al-Junayd said, "*Tasawwuf* is not the profusion of prayer and fasting, but wholeness of the breast and selflessness."[329]

Nor was this the way of the Four Imams who emphasized doing-without (*zuhd*) and true god-fear (*wara*), above the mere satisfaction of obligations. Imam Ahmad ibn Hanbal composed two books with those two qualities as their respective titles. He placed the knowledge of saints above the knowledge of scholars, as is shown by the following report by his student, Abu Bakr al-Marwazi:

> I heard Fath ibn Abi al-Fath saying to Abu Abd Allah (Imam Ahmad) during his last illness, "Invoke God for us that He will give us a good successor to succeed you." He continued, "Who shall we ask for knowledge after you?" Ahmad replied, "Ask Abd al-Wahhab." Someone who was present there related to me that he said, "But he does not have much learning." Abu Abd Allah replied, "He is a saintly man, and such as he is granted success in speaking the truth."[330]

In a celebrated *fatwa* (legal ruling), the Shafii scholar al-Izz ibn Abd al-Salam gives the same priority to the gnostics, or Knowers of God (*arifin*), over the jurists. Imam Malik places the same emphasis on inner perfection in his saying, "Religion does not consist in the knowledge of many narrations, but in a light which God places in the breast." Ibn Ata Allah quoted Ibn Arabi as saying, "Certainty does not derive from the evidences of the mind but pours out from the depths of the heart."

This is why many of the imams of religion cautioned against the mere thirst for knowledge at the expense of the training of the ego. Imam Ghazali left the halls of learning in the midst of a prestigious career in order to

---

[328] Related by Ahmad with a sound chain in *Kitab fadail al-Sahaba*, ed. Wasi Allah ibn Muhammad Abbas (Makkah: Muassasat al-risala, 1983) 1:141 (#118).

[329] al-Qushayri, *Risalat kitab al-sama* in *al-Rasail al-qushayriyya* (Sidon and Beirut: al-maktaba al-asriyya, 1970) p. 60.

[330] Ahmad, *Kitab al-wara* (Beirut: Dar al-kitab al-arabi, 1409/ 1988) p. 10.

devote himself to self-purification. At its outset, he wrote his magisterial *Revival of the Religious Sciences* (*Ihya ulum al-din*), which begins with a warning to those who consider religion to consist merely of *fiqh*, or jurisprudence.

One of the early Sufis and the greatest of the *huffaz*, or *hadith* masters, of his time, Sufyan al-Thawri, sounded the same warning. He addressed those who use the narration of *hadith* for religion, when he said, "If *hadith* was a good it would have vanished just as goodness has vanished. Pursuing the study of *hadith* is not part of the preparation for death, but a disease that preoccupies people."

Dhahabi comments:

> By God he has spoken the truth. Today, in our time, the quest for knowledge and *hadith* no longer means for the *hadith* scholar the obligation of living up to it, which is the goal of *hadith*. He is right in what he said because pursuing the study of *hadith* is other than the *hadith* itself.[331]

It is for "the *hadith* itself," for the purpose of living up to the *Sunnah* of the Prophet ﷺ and the Holy Quran, that the great masters of self-purification forsook the pursuit of science as a worldly allurement, and placed above it the acquisition of *ihsan*, or perfect character. This is in accordance with the well-known *hadith* of Aisha ﵂ concerning the disposition of the Prophet ﷺ.[332] An example is Abu Nasr Bishr al-Hafi, who considered the study of *hadith* a conjectural science in comparison to the certitude in belief imparted by visiting Fudayl ibn al-Iyad.[333] Both *ihsan* and the process that leads to it are known as *tasawwuf*, as illustrated in the following pages.

---

[331] Dhahabi, as cited in Sakhawi, al-*Jawahir wa al-durar fi tarjamat shaykh al-Islam Ibn Hajar* (al-Asqalani), ed. Hamid Abd al-Majid and Taha al-Zaini (Cairo: wizarat al-awqaf, al-majlis al-ala li al-shuun al-islamiyya, lajnah ihya al-turath al-islami, 1986) p. 21-22.

[332] When asked about the Prophet's ﷺ character, Aisha ﵂ said, "His character was the Quran."

[333] See Ibn Sad, *Tabaqat* (ed. Sachau) 7(2):83; al-Arusi, *Nataij al-afkar al-qudsiyya* (Bulaq, 1920/1873); and Abd al-Wahhab al-Sharawi, *al-Tabaqat al-kubra* 1:57.

Sufism: Definitions, Terminology, and Historical Overview

Tasawwuf among the Pious Predecessors

As is made clear in the *hadith* narrated by Sayyidina Umar ؓ about Jibril's ؑ meeting with the Prophet ﷺ,[334] belonging to *Ahl as-Sunnah wal-Jamaah* (the People of the Tradition and the Majority, also known as "the Saved Group") cannot stop at the rules of faith. It involves the adoption of principles that lead to *ihsan*, or the perfection of belief and practice. Hence, the Saved Group follows one of the many schools of *suluk* (personal discipline in ethics and conduct), in accordance with the guidelines of the *Shariah* and the *azaim* (strict applications) of the *Sunnah*. These practices are collectively known as the science of *tasawwuf*, or "purification of the self."

In the first century after the Hijra, renunciation of the world (*zuhd*) grew as a reaction against worldliness in the society. This reaction was inspired by God's order to His Righteous Apostle ﷺ to purify people:

> *A Messenger who shall instruct them in Scripture and Wisdom, and sanctify them.* (2:129)

> *We have sent among you a Messenger of your own, rehearsing Our Signs, and purifying you, and instructing you in Scripture and Wisdom.* (2:151)

> *A Messenger from among themselves, rehearsing unto them the Signs of God, sanctifying them, and instructing them in Scripture and Wisdom.* (3:164)

> *Purify and sanctify them; and pray on their behalf, verily thy prayers are a source of security for them.* (9:103)

> *A Messenger from among themselves, to rehearse to them His Signs, to sanctify them, and to instruct them in Scripture and Wisdom.* (62:2)

The adherents to this way held firmly to the Prophetic way of life, as it was reflected in the lives of his Companions and their Successors, in the

---

[334] In Bukhari and Muslim through various chains. Nawawi included it in his collection of forty *ahadith* (#2).

ways they purified their hearts and character of bad manners, and in the ways they impressed on themselves and those around them the manners and upright moral stature of the Prophet ﷺ. Examples of these one-man schools of purification are listed by Abu Nuaym and others as "The Eight Ascetics," and include: Amir ibn Abd Qays, Abu Muslim al-Khawlani, Uways al-Qarani, al-Rabi ibn Khuthaym, al-Aswad ibn Yazid, Masruq, Sufyan al-Thawri, and Hasan al-Basri, among many others.

The Prophet ﷺ himself attested to the power of such saints and their benefit to people, as witnessed by the many *ahadith* related about Uways al-Qarani ؓ.[335] In the following *hadith*, the Prophet ﷺ orders the people, if they meet Uways ؓ, to have him ask forgiveness on their behalf, and declares that Uways' ؓ intercession will earn entry into Paradise for large numbers of people:

> *The Prophet ﷺ said, "Uways ibn Amir will dawn upon you with the assistance (imdad) of the people of Yemen from the tribe of Murad and Qaran. He was a leper and was healed except in a tiny spot. He has a mother whose rights he keeps scrupulously. If he took an oath by God, God would fulfill it. If you are able to let him ask forgiveness for you, do it. More people will enter Paradise through the intercession of a certain man from my Community than there are people in the tribes of Rabia and Mudar." Al-Hasan al-Basri said, "That is Uways al-Qarani."*[336]

Through slow evolution, and as a reaction against the increasing worldliness of the social environment, Muslims flocked to saints and their followers until their regimens became schools of practical thought and moral action, each with its own structure of rules and principles. This became the basis used by Sufi scholars to direct people on the Right Path. The world soon witnessed the development of a variety of schools of purification of the ego (*tazkiyat an-nafs*). Sufi thought, as it spread everywhere, served as a dynamic force behind the growth of Islamic education. These advances occurred from the first century after the Hijra to the seventh, and paralleled the developments of the foundations of *fiqh* (Law and Jurisprudence) through the Four Imams; the development of the foundation of *Aqida* (Doctrine) through al-Ashari and others; the

---

[335] Imam Ahmad reports some of them in his book entitled *al-Zuhd*.

[336] Ahmad, *al-Zuhd* (Beirut: dar al-kutub al-ilmiyya, 1414/ 1993) p. 416, 414.

development of the sciences of *hadith* (Traditions of the Prophet ﷺ); and the arts of *nahw* and *balagha* (speaking and writing Arabic).

Tariqah: The Spiritual Path

Tariqah, or "path," is a term derived from the Quranic verse:

> *Had they kept straight on the path (tariqah), We would have made them drink of a most limpid water.* (72:16)

The meaning of "path" in this verse is elucidated by the *hadith* of the Prophet ﷺ, related by Bukhari and Muslim, ordering his followers to follow his *Sunnah* and the *Sunnah* of his successors. Like *tariqah* in the verse, the meaning of "*sunnah*" in the *hadith* is "path" or "way." *Tariqah* thus came to be a term applied to groups of individuals belonging to the school of thought led by a particular scholar, or "shaykh," as such a person was often called.

Although the shaykhs applied different methods in training their followers, the core of each one's program was identical. The situation was not unlike what happens in faculties of medicine and law today. The approaches of the various universities may be different, but the body of law and the practice of medicine remain essentially the same. When students graduate from either of these faculties, each bears the stamp of the institution he attended, but no student is considered any less a lawyer or doctor because his training was different.

In a similar way, the student of a particular shaykh will bear the stamp of that shaykh's teaching and character. Accordingly, the names given to the various schools of Sufi thought differ according to the names and perspectives of their founders. This variation manifests itself in a more concrete fashion in the different supererogatory devotions, known as *awrad*, *ahzab*, or *adhkar*, that are used as the practical methodology of spiritual formation. Such differences, however, have nothing to do with religious principles. In basic principle, the Sufi schools are essentially the same, just as the differences in names among *madhahib*, or schools of law, refer to methods and not to the essence of religion, which is uniform.

The Sufi regimen under which individuals undertook the path to God was a finely-honed itinerary that charted the course of inward and outward progress in religious faith and practice. Following the tradition of the Companions of the Prophet ﷺ who frequented his company, the *Ahl as-Suffa*

("People of the Bench"), the practitioners of this regimen lived a communal life. Their dwelling-places were the alcove-schools (*zawiya*), border fort-schools (*ribat*), and guest-houses (*khaniqah*) where they gathered together on a regular basis and on specific occasions dedicated to the traditional festivals of the Islamic calendar. These structures often evolved into celebrated educational institutions.

Sufis also gathered in informal assemblies around the shaykh, called *suhbah*, to invoke the names of God and recite the *adhkar* (plural of *dhikr*, "remembrance") inherited from the Prophetic Tradition. Yet another reason for their gathering was to hear inspired preaching and moral exhortations (*wiaz*). The shaykhs instructed their students to actively respond to God and His Messenger ﷺ, to cleanse their hearts and purify their souls from the more base desires prompted by the ego, and to establish authentic doctrine. This was accomplished by firm adherence to the Prophetic *Sunnah*. The methods of remembering God that they instilled in their students were the very same methods passed down from the Prophet ﷺ. In this way, the shaykhs promoted upright behavior, through both word and deed, and encouraged believers to devote themselves to God wholeheartedly. The aim of their endeavor was nothing less than obtaining God's satisfaction and inspiring love for His Prophet ﷺ. In short, they aimed for a state where God was pleased with them, even as they were pleased with Him.

Sufi Leaders Who Established Thriving Communities

History books are filled with the names of wise, effective Sufis who devoted their lives to the spread of traditional, moderate Islam which enfused their communities with social justice, religious tolerance, and gender equity. Their amazing stories are too numerous to list in the span of a single book; suffice it to mention a few examples from modern history, as cited by the author of *The Reliance of the Traveller*:

> Among the Sufis whose missionary work Islamized entire regions are such men as the founder of the Sanusiyya Order, Muhammad Ali Sanusi, whose efforts from 1807 to 1859 consolidated Islam as the religion of peoples from the Libyan Desert of sub-Saharan Africa; the Shadhili shaykh Muhammad Maruf and Qadiri shaykh Uways al-Barawi, whose efforts spread Islam westward and inland from the East African Coast; and the hundreds of anonymous Naqshbandi shaykhs [including some of the Masters of the Golden Chain] who taught and

preserved Islam among the peoples of what is now the southern Soviet Union, and who still serve the religion there despite official pressure. It is plain from the example of these and similar men that the attachment of the heart to God, which is the main emphasis of Sufism, does not hinder spiritual works of any kind, but may rather provide a real basis for them. And God alone gives success.[337]

The reader is also referred to Benningsen's *Mystics and Commissars* for the role of Sufis in preserving Islam in the Soviet Union, and *Lion of Daghestan* for their struggle against the Tsars before that. Let it also be added that it was the Naqshbandis who preserved Islam in China, both in the past and in the darkest days of Mao Tse-tung's "Cultural Revolution."

Though some opponents of *tasawwuf* have accused the Sufis of focusing on spirituality to the detriment of their societal responsibilities, the above examples provide ample evidence that *tasawwuf*, far from encouraging escapism or the sort of quietism that impedes social progress, upheld the highest values of social consciousness and action—as well as religious inquiry and spiritual science. In fact, the Sufis were unremitting protagonists in the struggles against social injustice and social inaction that took place over centuries.

Contemporary Misconceptions

It is well-known in our time that some people have misunderstood the notion of *tasawwuf*. Some people believe it is against Islam, while others say they can find no mention of it in the *Shariah*, Quran, or *Sunnah*. However, the followers of the four Imams accepted *tasawwuf*, because they knew the reality of the term's meaning was more important than its age. Even scholars such as Ibn Taymiyya and Ibn Qayyim al-Jawziyya—despite their having opposed the doctrine of *Ahl as-Sunnah* in so many respects—accepted *tasawwuf*, precisely because they knew its roots were deep in the Quran, the *Sunnah*, and the *Shariah*.

It is true that the term *tasawwuf* was not known in the time of the Prophet ﷺ. However, while its name was of later derivation, its essence is part and parcel of the religion and cannot be separated from it.

---

[337] *Reliance of the Traveller*, p. 863.

Another factor that has contributed to the misunderstanding of *tasawwuf* in the modern era is the appropriation of some of its terms and teachings by non-Muslims. Today, we find some people mixing true *tasawwuf* with pseudo-*tasawwuf*, which denies the necessity of the *Shariah* and makes up its own rules, claiming for itself an amorphous authority that is not rooted in any precedent. Such people are neither Sufis nor *mutasawwif*, but *mustaswifa* or "pseudo-Sufis," in the words of the great master Ali al-Hujwiri.[338] Enemies of *tasawwuf*, however, often blur the difference between Sufis and *mustaswifa* (those who are busy purifying themselves) in their references to *tasawwuf* in order to be rid of both, as they have known Sufis to stand against their false teachings.

An example is the Mutazila sect's aversion to Sufis, which led them to deny the *karamat* (miracles of saints), as they never saw this sign of truth among themselves. Nowadays, there are people like the Mutazila, who want to create their own definition of Islam, to decide what fits into it and what does not, mixing right with wrong. They do this so that they might rid themselves of the essence of true Islamic teaching that exposes the incompleteness and error of what they have inherited.

The purpose of *tasawwuf* is first to purify the heart of bad desires and inclinations, and of the dirtiness that accumulates due to sin and wrongdoing. The purpose of *tasawwuf* is then to remove these bad manners and sins, to clean the self, and adorn and decorate the heart with the good behavior and good manners that are demanded by the Holy Quran and the Holy *Sunnah* of the Prophet ﷺ. Its ultimate purpose is to help the believer to reach the state of *ihsan*, or perfection of character, which was the state of the Prophet ﷺ and the state that each of his Companions strove to achieve.

Development of Islamic Sciences after the Time of the Prophet ﷺ

The science of *tasawwuf* was not the only one that developed after the time of the Prophet ﷺ. For example, in the time of the Prophet ﷺ, a child in the cradle of Islam, raised in the land of Hijaz, could read a poem or Arabic text without any need for diacritical marks (*tashkil*). It came naturally, as they were raised knowing the proper pronunciation. Later, however, when many non-Arabs entered Islam and Quran was being read incorrectly, it

---

[338] Al-Hujwiri, *Kashf al-mahjub*, trans. R.A. Nicholson (Karachi: *dar al-ishaat*, 1990) p. 35.

became necessary to create disciplines to assist new Muslims in reading Quran, so grammar was developed and diacritical marks were established.

The state of perfection (*ihsan*), the state of austerity (*zuhd*), the state of great fear of God (*wara*), and the state of godwariness (*taqwa*) were naturally practiced by the Companions, because they were in company of the Prophet ﷺ and those states were a direct result of their association with him. It is for this reason that they are called Companions, because they were the associates of the Prophet ﷺ, and it was their association with him that allowed them to be purified.

Just as the entrance of converts from other regions into the fold of Islam necessitated the development of *ilm al-nahu* (science of Arabic language), development of the science of self-purification was necessitated by the passing of the Prophet ﷺ and his Companions. Without them to teach the true path of Islam by way of example, it became necessary to establish schools that would develop the spiritual disciplines to perfect belief and practice. These matters were combined under the main discipline of *ilm al-tasawwuf* (science of spiritual perfection).

Far from being an innovation, as some of its detractors contend, the science of *tasawwuf* represents the logical and necessary evolution of teachings and practices that go to the very heart of the religion of Islam. Nor are the Orientalists correct who attempt to apply the term "superstition" (*shawaza*) to the science of *tasawwuf.*

The term *tasawwuf,* which refers to the method of cleansing the heart, denotes the same thing as *tazkiyat al-nafs* in the Quran. Both have the same subject matter as the sciences of "doing-without" (*zuhd*) and perfection of character (*ihsan*). The terms *zuhd, tazkiya,* and *ihsan* were all used in the time of the Prophet ﷺ. Later, these terms were defined with extensive detail, and refined according to the guidelines of the Quran and the *hadith,* as were the other Islamic sciences.

Of course, any term may be used to name a science, and one is free to define or use any term one wishes. It is dearly hoped that no one will be prevented or forbidden from learning this important science due to prejudice against the term *tasawwuf.* If the term is problematic to someone, let him give it a different name, but let him learn the science, by whatever name he wishes to call it.

Linguistic Roots of the Term *Tasawwuf*

There are four roots given to the word *tasawwuf*. The first is from the Arabic word *safa* or *safw*, which means "purity" and "limpidity." The Prophet ﷺ compared the world to a little rain water on a mountain plateau of which the *safw* had already been drunk and from which only the *kadar*, or dregs, remained.[339] He called Sham (Damascus) God's purest of lands (*safwat Allah min biladih*).[340] Ibn al-Athir defines the word in his dictionary *al-Nihaya* as "the best of any matter, its quintessence, and purest part."[341]

Another root is derived from *Ahl as-Suffa,* (the People of the Bench), who were those who lived in the Mosque of the Prophet ﷺ during his life and who were mentioned in the Quran in the following verse:

> *(O Muhammad,) keep yourself content with those who call on their Lord" morning and evening seeking His Face; and let not your eyes pass beyond them, seeking the pomp and glitter of this life; nor obey any whose heart We have permitted to neglect the Remembrance of Us, the one who follows his own desires, whose case has gone beyond all bounds.* (18:28)

This verse emphasizes how much the believers have to keep themselves in the state of *dhikr*, or recollection of God on the tongue, in the mind, and through the heart. This root is sometimes compared to *ahl al-suff,* or "the People of the Rank," in the sense of "first rank," as the first rank is blessed and the Sufis are the elite of the Community.

The third of these roots is *al-suf* or wool, as it was the manner of the pious people of Kufa to wear it. The fourth linguistic root is from *suffat al-kaffa,* or soft sponge, in reference to the Sufi whose heart is very soft due to its purity.

The Primacy of the Heart over All Other Organs

The heart is the seat of sincerity in a person, without which none of his actions are accepted. The Prophet ﷺ said, as Bukhari narrated, "*Surely there is in the body a small piece of flesh; if it is good the whole body is good and if it is*

---

[339] In Ibn Asakir from Ibn Masud. Al-Qushayri and al-Hujwiri mention it in their chapters on *tasawwuf,* respectively in *Kashf al-mahjub* (Nicholson trans. p.) and *al-Risala*: B.R. Von Schlegell trans., Principles of Sufism (Berkeley, Mizan Press, 1990) p. 301.

[340] Tabarani related it and Haythami authenticated the chain through *Irbad ibn Sariya in Majma al-zawaid,* chapter on the merits of Syria.

[341] Ibn al-Athir, *al-Nihaya,* s.v. *s-f-w.*

corrupted the whole body is corrupted and that is the heart." He said in two other *ahadith* narrated by Muslim, *"Surely God does not look at your bodies nor at your faces but He looks at your hearts,"* and *"No one will enter Paradise who has even an atom of pride in his heart."*

Many other *ahadith* explicitly state the primacy of the heart. Abu Hurayra ☙ narrates:

> *I said, O Messenger of God! Who will be the foremost people in gaining your intercession on the Day of Resurrection? God's Messenger ﷺ said, "O Abu Hurayra! I knew that no one would ask me about this before you because of your longing for the knowledge of hadith. The foremost of people in gaining my intercession on the Day of Resurrection is he who said, 'There is no deity but God' purely and sincerely from his heart (qalb) or his soul (nafs)."*[342]

Ibn Hajar said in his commentary on Bukhari:

> The Prophet ﷺ mentioned the heart for emphasis, as God said of the sinner, *"Verily his heart is sinful."* (2:283) "Foremost" alludes to their different order of entry into Paradise as distinct from their different ranks of sincerity, the latter being emphasized by his saying "from his heart" although it is clear that the seat of sincerity is the heart. However, the attribution of the action to that organ affects more emphasis.[343]

One of the Companions named Wabisa ☙ relates that all the people asked the Prophet ﷺ about the good things, but he resolved to ask him about the evil things. When he came to him, the Prophet ﷺ poked him in the chest with his fingers and said three times, *"O Wabisa, fear of God is here."* Then he said, *"Ask for your heart's decision, no matter the decision this one and that one gives you."*[344]

From Ibn Umar ☙:

> *The Prophet ﷺ said, "Everything has a polish, and the polish of hearts is dhikr of God. Nothing saves one from God's punishment more than dhikr of God."*

---

[342] Bukhari related it (English 1:79).

[343] Ibn Hajar, *Fath al-bari* (1989 ed.) 1:258 and 11:541.

[344] Related in Ahmad, Tabarani, Abu Yala, and Abu Nuaym.

They said, "Not even jihad for God's sake?" He said, "Not even if you strike with your sword until it breaks."[345]

Ibn Umar ﵁ relates:

I was sitting with the Prophet ﷺ when Harmala ibn Zayd al-Ansari of the Banu Haritha tribe came to him. He sat in front of God's Messenger ﷺ and said, "O Messenger of God, belief is here"—and he pointed to his tongue—"and hypocrisy is here"—and he pointed to his heart—"and I don't make dhikr of God except little." God's Messenger remained silent. Harmala repeated his words, whereupon the Prophet ﷺ seized Harmala's tongue by its extremity and said, "O God, give him a truthful tongue and a thankful heart, and grant him to love me and to love those who love me, and turn his affairs towards good." Harmala said, "O Messenger of God, I have two brothers who are hypocrites; I was with them just now. Shall I not point them out to you (so you will pray for them)?" The Prophet ﷺ said, "(Yes,) whoever comes to us in the way you have come, we shall ask forgiveness for them as we asked forgiveness for you; and whoever keeps to this path, God becomes his protector."[346]

From Ibn Umar ﵁ also:

The Prophet ﷺ said, "Do not speak much rather than make dhikr of God; speaking much without dhikr of God hardens the heart, and no-one is farther from God than the hard-hearted."[347]

It is clear, therefore, that the Prophet ﷺ tied everything to the good condition of the heart. When one leaves bad manners and takes on good manners, then he will have a perfect and healthy heart. That is what God mentioned in the Quran:

The Day wherein neither wealth nor sons will avail, but only he will prosper who brings to God a sound heart. (26:88-89)

---

[345] Bayhaqi relates it in *Shuab al-iman* 1:396 #522; al-Mundhiri in *al-Targhib* 2:396; and Ibn Abi al-Dunya.

[346] Al-hafiz Abu Nuaym narrated it in *Hilyat al-awliya*. Ibn Hajar said in *al-Isaba* (2:2 #1659): "Its chain of transmission is acceptable and Ibn Mindah also extracted it. We have narrated the same through Abu al-Darda in the *Fawaid* of Hisham ibn Ammar." Al-Tabarani also narrated through Abu al-Darda. Haythami said of that chain: "It contains one unknown narrator, but the rest are trustworthy."

[347] Tirmidhi related it and said: a rare *hadith* (*gharib*); also Bayhaqi in the *Shuab* 4:245 #4951.

God mentioned the hearts of His true knowers *(ulama)* when He said:

> *Know here are signs self-evident in the hearts of those who have been endowed with knowledge, and none but the unjust reject our signs.* (29:49)

What are the diseases of the heart? Imam Suyuti said in his book on the Shadhili Order, "The science of hearts, the knowledge of its diseases such as jealousy, arrogance, and pride, and leaving them is an obligation on every Muslim."[348] The exegetes have said that jealousy (*hasad*), ostentation (*riya*), hypocrisy (*nifaq*), and hatred (*hiqd*) are the most common bad manners, to which God referred when He said:

> *Say, the things that my Lord has indeed forbidden are: shameful deeds whether open or secret.* (7:33)

God's mentioning "whether open or secret" is the evidence for the need to not merely make the exterior actions correct, but to cleanse that which is hidden in a person's heart and is known only to his Lord.

Tasawwuf is the science and knowledge whereby one learns to purify the self of the ego's bad desires, such as jealousy, cheating, ostentation, love of praise, pride, arrogance, anger, greed, stinginess, respect for the rich, and disregard of the poor. Similarly, one must purify the external self. The science of *tasawwuf* teaches one to look at oneself, to purify oneself according to the Holy Quran and the *Sunnah* of the Prophet ﷺ, and to dress oneself with the perfect attributes (*al-sifat al-kamila*). These include repentance (*tawba*), godwariness (*taqwa*), keeping to the straight way (*istiqama*), truthfulness (*sidq*), sincerity (*ikhlas*), abstention (*zuhd*), great piety (*wara*), reliance on God (*tawakkul*), contentment with the Decree (*rida*), surrender to God (*taslim*), good manners (*adab*), love (*mahabba*), remembrance (*dhikr*), watchfulness (*muraqabah*), and other qualities too numerous to mention here.

Just as the science of *hadith* has dozens of classifications for *hadith*, the science of *tasawwuf* has numerous classifications for both the good characteristics (*akhlaq hasana*), which are obligatory for the believer to develop, and the bad ones (*akhlaq dhamima*), which it is necessary to eliminate to attain the state of *ihsan*. Through the science of *tasawwuf*, the heart, precious essence, and lifeblood of Islam are made manifest to us. For

---

348 Suyuti, *Tayid al-haqiqa al-aliyya wa-tashyid al-tariqa al-shadhiliyya,* ed. Abd Allah ibn Muhammad ibn al-Siddiq al-Ghumari al-Hasani (Cairo: *al-matbaa al-islamiyya,* 1934), p. 56.

Islam is not only an external practice, but also has an internal life. This is as God says:

Leave the outwardness of sin and its inwardness. (6:120)

Among the Believers are men who have been true to their Covenant with God. (33:23)

This means that not all believers are included in the group of those who "*kept their Covenant with God*" (33:23). It means a person can be a believer, but not among those who have kept their Covenant until he has reached a state of cleanliness: the state of *ihsan*, perfection of behavior, which the Prophet ﷺ mentioned in the *hadith*. This, as has now been made clear, is what became known later as the science of *tasawwuf*.

Evidence from the Quran

GOD DESCRIBES SELF-PURIFICATION AS A DUTY OF THE PROPHET ﷺ

As mentioned previously, the evidence for *tasawwuf* from the Quran is the same as the evidence for self-purification (*tazkiyat al-nafs*), which we have established above as the definition of *tasawwuf*. God says:

He is the One Who raised among the people of Makkah a Messenger from among themselves who recites to them His communications and purifies them, and teaches them the Book and the Wisdom, although they were before certainly in clear error. (62:2)

The term used here is *wa yuzakkihim* (purifies them). The various root meanings of the word *tazkiya* in Arabic are:

- *zaka:* he cleansed; he was clean
- *yuzakki*: to clean; to be purified
- *tazkiya:* purification
- *zakat:* Islamic poor-tax; charity; purity
- *azka*: the purest
- *zaki:* pure; innocent

In another verse:

By the soul and the proportion and order given to it, and its inspiration as to its wrong and its right; Truly he succeeds who purifies it, and he fails that corrupts it. (91:7-10)

This verse states the necessity of purifying and cleaning the ego (*nafs*) in order to succeed in this life and the next. This is precisely the goal of *tasawwuf.*

GOD PROMISES TO GUIDE THE BELIEVERS

In the Quran we find this command:

> *O Believers, be wary of God and find a means to approach Him and strive in His Way that perhaps you may be of the successful.* (5:35)

This verse means that a person must strive in God's way, not in the ego's way, nor towards the ego and its desires, if he wishes to be successful. It indicates the necessity of following the footsteps of the Prophet ﷺ as the means to approaching God and of taking him and those who know him as guides. God also says:

> *O ye who believe, fear God and keep company with those who are truthful.* (9:119)

This verse substantiates the need to accompany and associate with the best of God's servants. The *Sadiqin* are the ones who reached one of the highest stations of faith according to the verse, already mentioned:

> *Among the Believers are men who have been true to their Covenant with God and of them some have died and some still wait but they have never changed their determination (in the least).* (33:23)

This means that in every era there are people who hold fast to the Covenant of God. These are the friends of God mentioned in other verses, including:

> *Nay, they are the Friends of God; no fear shall come upon them, neither shall they grieve.* (10:62)

One of the Friends of God is al-Khidr عليه السلام, whom the Prophet Moses عليه السلام was ordered to accompany and learn from. God says:

> *Those who are striving in Our Way, We will guide them to Our paths, for verily God is with those who do good.* (29:69)

AL-KHIDR عليه السلام: ONE WHO LEARNED DIRECTLY FROM GOD'S PRESENCE

God describes the meeting of Moses عليه السلام with Al-Khidr عليه السلام eloquently:

> *So they found one of Our servants on whom We had bestowed mercy from Ourselves and whom We had taught knowledge from Our Own Presence. Moses said to him, "May I follow you on the condition that you teach me something of the Higher Truth which you have been taught?" The other said, "Surely you will not be able to have patience with me."* (18:65-67)

From these two verses, it is clear that even though Moses عليه السلام was a prophet, and the only prophet to speak with God directly (*kalimullah*), Khidr عليه السلام possessed knowledge that Moses عليه السلام did not have. Moses عليه السلام sought to obtain this knowledge from him, because he knew Khidr عليه السلام was receiving knowledge directly from the Presence of God (*ilm ladunni*) as one of God's Friends. God also says:

> *Follow the way of those who turn to Me.* (31:15)

Yusuf Ali correctly comments on this verse saying, "That is the way of those who love God." The state of love is related to the heart, not to the mind. Three of the many proofs that believers should follow a guide, or "teacher of upbringing" (*shaykh al-tarbiya*) in technical terms, are found in the verses of Moses' عليه السلام encounter with al-Khidr عليه السلام, and in the order to follow the path of God's true Lovers.

The Superiority of Love in Worship

Ibn Qayyim al-Jawziyya compiled some of the sayings of the great Sufis regarding love and its priority in sound worship:[349]

Junayd said:

> I heard al-Harith al-Muhasibi say, "Love is when you incline completely towards something; and then the preference of that thing over yourself, and your soul, and your possessions; then the compliance with that inwardly and outwardly; then your knowing of your shortcoming in your love to Him."

Abd Allah ibn al-Mubarak said:

> Whoever is given a portion of love and he has not been given an equivalent amount of awe, has been cheated.

Yahya bin al-Muadh al-Razi said:

---

[349] Ibn Qayyim, *Rawdat al-muhibbin wa nuzhat al-mushtaqin* (Beirut: Dar al-kutub al-ilmiyya, 1983) p. 406-409.

An atom's weight of love is more beloved to me than to worship seventy years without love.

Abu Bakrah al-Qattani said:

There was a discussion about love in Makkah during the Pilgrimage season and the shaykhs were speaking about it. Junayd was the youngest of them in age and they said, "Say what you have, O Iraqi." He lowered his head in deference and his eyes filled with tears then he said, "A slave taking leave of himself, connected with the remembrance of his Lord, standing with the fulfillment of his duties, looking at Him with his heart, whose heart is burned by the light of His Essence; his drink is clear from the cup of His love; and if he talks, it is by God; and if he utters, it is from God; and if he moves, it is by the order of God; and if he is silent, he is with God; and he is by God, he is for God, he is with God (*fa huwa billahi wa lillahi wa ma allahi*)." The shaykhs cried out and said, "There is nothing above that, may God strengthen you, crown of the Knowers!"

Junayd's words are related to those found in one of the foundational texts that provides evidence for the miracles of the saints, the following *hadith qudsi* (holy Tradition) related by Bukhari:

On the authority of Abu Hurayra ﷺ, the Messenger of God ﷺ said that God said: "Whosoever shows enmity to someone devoted to Me, I shall be at war with him. My servant draws not near to Me with anything more loved by Me than the religious duties I have enjoined upon him, and My servant continues to draw near to Me with supererogatory works so that I shall love him. When I love him I am his hearing with which he hears, his seeing with which he sees, his hand with which he strikes, and his foot with which he walks. Were he to ask something of Me, I would surely give it to him, and were he to ask refuge in Me, I would surely grant him it . . . "

Love was mentioned to Dhun Nun and he said, "Enough, do not discuss this question, as the ego (*nafs*) will hear it and take its claim in it." He continued, "For the disobedient one, fear and sorrow are better! Love is for the one who already has fear and is pure of all filth."

Dhun Nun also said:

> For everything there is punishment, and the punishment of the knower of God is the cutting from him of his remembrance of God *(dhikr Allah)*.

Junayd referred to this distinction of levels in his reply when he was told, "Over there are a people who say, they are definitely reaching the station of goodness by the leaving of deeds." He said:

> Are they talking about the cancellation of (obligatory and other) deeds? Nay, whoever commits adultery and steals is in a better condition than the one who says such a thing. For certainly God's knowers *(al arifina billah)* took the deeds from God and returned with these deeds to Him, and if I had lived a thousand years I would never decrease from the good deeds the least bit.

Junayd also said:

> The knower of God is not considered a knower until he becomes like the earth; it is the same to him whether the good person or the bad person steps on him; or like the rain, he gives without discrimination to those whom he likes and those he dislikes.

Sumnun said:

> The lovers of God have gained the honor of both the world and the hereafter. The Prophet ﷺ said, *"The human being is with the one he loves."* They are with God in the *dunya* and the next life.

Yahya ibn Muadh said:

> He is not a truthful one who pretends he loves Him and trespasses His boundaries.

He also said:

> The knower of God leaves this worldly life and he does not have enough of two things: crying over his own self, and his longing for his Lord.

Another seeker of self-purification said:

> The knower of God does not become a knower until, if he has been given the treasures of Sulayman عليه السلام, it will not busy him with other than God for the blink of an eye.

Classical Teachings on Purifying the Ego

Some of the verses referring to purification and self-purification in the Quran have already been mentioned. God says:

> *(A Messenger) who shall rehearse Your signs to them, instruct them in the Book and wisdom and purify them.* (2:129)

> *A similar (favor have you already received), in that we have sent among you a Messenger of your own, rehearsing to you Our signs, and purifying you . . .* (2:151)

> *Those will prosper who Purify themselves and glorify the Name of their Lord and pray.* (87:14)

> *And whoever Purifies himself does so to his own soul's benefit; and to God is the Journeying.* (35:18)

In all of these verses, God refers to the characteristics of the *mutassawif*, or those who are busy purifying themselves. They are always remembering their Lord, by recalling His Names and Attributes, and they are attentive to their prayers. This is the essence of *tasawwuf*, and also the essence of Islam. The reader is reminded again that this is only a technical term, and can be replaced by any synonym.

If someone claims to follow or practice Islam, this struggle to purify the self is incumbent upon him, as it is so clearly ordered in these verses. Indeed, it is meaningless to claim that there could be any surrender to God without the pursuit of self-purification. That is why some scholars, among them Imam Ghazali and Imam Suyuti, have considered *tasawwuf* a religious obligation (*wajib*).[350] Whether one is successful or not in this pursuit is in God's hands, but its necessity is incumbent on every Muslim, man or woman.

Classical Teachings on the State of Perfected Character (*Ihsan*)

Let us now turn to quote some verses that address the state of *ihsan* (excellence). God said:

> *For the Mercy of God is near to those who are good (*muhsinin*).* (7:56)

> *For God is with those who restrain themselves and who are good.* (16:128)

---

[350] Ghazali's opinion is cited in *The Reliance of the Traveller*, p. 12. For Suyuti, see below, section on the sayings of the scholars.

*Is there any reward for Excellence (*ihsan*) other than Excellence?* (55:60)

And He rewards those who do good with what is best. (53:31)

*God commands justice, the doing of good (*ihsan*), giving to kith and kin, and He forbids all indecent deeds and evil and rebellion: He instructs you that you may receive admonition*. (16:90)

Nay, whoever submits his whole self to God and is a muhsin (in the state of ihsan*), his reward is with his Lord, on those shall be no fear nor shall they grieve*. (2:112)

Whoever submits his whole self to God and is in a state of ihsan *has grasped indeed the firmest handhold, and to God will all things return*. (31:21)

Who can be better in religion than one who submits his whole self to God, and does good, and follows the way of Abraham . . . (4:125)

Verses about the state of *ihsan* are numerous, but what has been quoted is sufficient. The meaning of *ihsan*, as the Prophet ﷺ defined it, is praying with humility and submission (*khudu* and *khushu*), as if the believer is seeing God and is aware that He is seeing him. In his *Book of Definitions* (*Kitab al-tarifat*) al-Jurjani said:

Al-ihsan: verbal noun denoting what one ought to do in the way of good. In *Shariah* it means to worship God as if you see Him, and if you do not see Him, He sees you. It is the attainment of true worship-in-servanthood predicated on the sight of the Divine Lordship with the light of spiritual sight. That is: the sight of God as He is described by His Attributes and through His very Attribute, so that one will see Him with certitude, not literally (*fa huwa yarahu yaqinan wa la yarahu haqiqatan*). That is why the Prophet ﷺ said, "As if you were seeing Him." For one sees Him from behind the veil of His Attributes.[351]

The word *ihsan* and its derivatives have the following meanings in the dictionary:

- *hasuna* حَسُنَ : to become; to seem; to make excellent; beautiful
- *Ihsanan* إحسانا : to do excellently
- *Ahsana* أحسن: he did a great good

[351] Al-Sharif Ali ibn Muhammad al-Jurjani, *Kitab al-tarifat* (Beirut: *dar al-kutub al-ilmiyya,* 1408/1988) p. 12.

- *Ihsan* إحسان: kindness
- *Husna* حُسْنَى: reward
- *Hasan* حَسَنْ*:* excellent; beautiful
- *Hisanun* حِسانٌ *:* beautiful ones

"To become beautiful" in the first of these examples means to decorate oneself with good attributes; to beautify inwardly and outwardly. When used as an adjective, it means kindness as a trait or an internal attitude, as well as composure.

It should be clear by now that the state of *ihsan* mentioned in the Holy Quran is a very high state, one which the archangel Gabriel ﷺ showed to be an intrinsic part of the religion, and which he placed at the same level as the states of Islam and *iman*. The religion consists of three states: Islam, *iman* and *ihsan,* each of which has its own definition. That is why it is mentioned in the Holy Quran in so many places, and why the Prophet ﷺ, when asked about it by Gabriel ﷺ, gave it the same importance as he gave to Islam and *iman*.

The *Hadith* of Gabriel ﷺ

Muslim narrated:

Umar ﷺ also said: "While we were sitting with God's Messenger ﷺ one day, all of a sudden a man came up to us. He wore exceedingly white clothes. His hair was jet-black. There was no sign of travel on his person. None of us knew him. He went to sit near the Prophet ﷺ leaning his knees against the knees of the Prophet and placing his hands on his thighs.

"He said, 'O Muhammad! Tell me about submission.' God's Messenger ﷺ said, 'Submission is to bear witness that There is no god but God, and that Muhammad is the Messenger of God; to perform the prayer; to pay the poor-tax; to fast during Ramadan; and to make the pilgrimage to the House if you are able to go there.'

"The man said, 'You have spoken the truth.' We wondered at him; how could he be asking the Prophet ﷺ and confirming him at the same time? Then he said, 'Tell me about belief.' The Prophet ﷺ said, 'Belief is to believe in God, His angels, His books, His messengers, and the Last Day; and to believe in what-has-been-decreed, both its good and its evil.' The man said, 'You have spoken the truth. Now tell me about excellence.' The Prophet ﷺ replied, 'Excellence is

to worship God as if you see Him, for if you do not see Him, He certainly sees you.'

"The man said, 'Now tell me about the Hour.' The Prophet ﷺ replied, 'The one who is being asked knows no more about it than the questioner.' He said, 'Then tell me about its signs.' He replied, 'The slave-girl will give birth to her mistress, and you will see the barefoot, naked, destitute herdsmen outdo each other in building tall structures.' Then he left and time passed. Later he said to me, 'O Umar, do you know who that was asking questions?' I said, 'God and His Messenger know best.' He said, 'He was none other than Gabriel. He came to you to teach you your religion.'"

THE SOURCE OF ALL TRADITIONS

As said before, the term *tasawwuf* is a technical term that originated in the various meanings quoted in the first and second answers. It has deep roots in the *Sunnah* of the Prophet ﷺ, since its origin is *ihsan*, the state of Excellence that is mentioned in the *hadith* of archangel Gabriel ﵇ which is known to all scholars as the "Source of the *Sunnah* and of all *hadith*" *(umm al-sunnah wa umm al-ahadith).*

In this *hadith*, Gabriel ﵇ has divided religion into categories or main branches from which all religion, all *hadith*, and all *Sunnah* flow. He emphasized each branch by asking each question separate from the other. The first branch was related to his question, "What is Islam?" The second was related to the question, "What is *iman*?" The third is related to the question, "What is *ihsan*?" It cannot be said that religion is only Islam, or only *iman*, or only *ihsan*. Each of these branches is essential to the religion, and none can be left out. The Prophet ﷺ, in his answers to these questions, confirmed this and said to his Companions after Gabriel ﵇ left, "Gabriel came to teach you your religion."

Islam, *iman*, and *ihsan* may be called three pillars of religion. The first pillar represents the practical side of the religion, including worship, deeds, and other obligations. That pillar is the external side of the self, and is related to the body and the Community. Scholars call it the first pillar of *Shariah*. Scholars learned to specialize in this, and it was called "the Science of Jurisprudence" (*ilm al-fiqh*). The second pillar represents belief in the mind and heart: belief in God, His Messengers, His Books, the Angels, the

Last Day, and Destiny. This became known to the scholars as "the Science of Divine Oneness" (*ilm al-tawhid*). The third pillar represents *tasawwuf*.

THE THIRD COMPONENT OF ISLAM: *IHSAN*

The third aspect of the religion is known as the spiritual aspect of the heart. It is intended to make one aware when combining the first and second pillars, and to remind that one is always in the Presence of God, and that one should consider this in all thoughts and actions. If one cannot see Him—and, indeed, no one can see God in this life—then one must keep the continuous awareness of God's Presence in the heart. One must know that He is aware of every moment and detail in one's worship and one's belief. By doing these things, one will attain a state of excellence, a state of high quality, and will taste the spiritual pleasure and light of knowledge that God will direct to one's heart. That is what scholars have termed the Science of Truth or *ilm al-haqiqa,* known in the time of the Companions, as *al-siddiqiyya,* or the Path of the truthful saints. Only later did it become known by the name of *tasawwuf.*

In summary, Islam prescribes the behavior of a Muslim, *iman* relates to the beliefs and defines them, and *ihsan* refers to the state of the heart that determines whether one's Islam and *ihsan* will bear fruit in this life and the next. This is supported by the *hadith* in Bukhari mentioned earlier:

> *Verily there is in the body a small piece of flesh; if it is good the whole body is good and if it is corrupted the whole body is corrupted and that is the heart.*

Ihsan is divided into many parts, including all the good traits of a believer, such as *taqwa* (piety), *wara* (scrupulous fear of God), *zuhd* (abstention), *khushu* (reverence), *khudu* (humility), *sabr* (patience), *sidq* (truthfulness), *tawakkul* (reliance), *adab* (good character), *tawba* (repentence), *inaba* (turning to God), *hilm* (forbearance), *rahma* (compassion), *karam* (generosity), *tawadu* (humility), *haya* (modesty), *shajaa* (courage), etc.

All of these are the qualities of the Prophet ﷺ and, "His character was the Quran," according to Aisha ؓ.[352] The Prophet ﷺ, in turn, impressed these qualities on all his Companions, so that they became perfect and shining examples of how human beings should exist: in perfect harmony with the Creator and with each other.

---

[352] Muslim; Ahmad, *Musnad* 6:91, 163, and others.

In his explanation of the *hadith* of Gabriel عليه السلام, Imam Nawawi refers to *ihsan* in terms of the Station of Witnessing (*maqam al-mushahada*) and the Station of the Most Truthful Saints (*maqam al-siddiqeen*), which are two of the branches of *tasawwuf*. The following is the complete text of Nawawi's commentary on the *hadith* of Gabriel عليه السلام.

IMAM NAWAWI'S COMMENTARY ON THE HADITH OF GABRIEL عليه السلام

[Gabriel عليه السلام told the Prophet ﷺ,] "Tell me about belief (iman)."

Iman, lexically, means conviction of a general nature. Legally it is an expression for a specific conviction in the belief in God, His angels, His books, His messengers, the Last Day, and whatever is decreed, both its good and its evil. Islam is a word signifying the performance of the legal obligations. These are the external actions that one applies oneself to do.

God the Exalted has differentiated belief (*iman*) from submission (Islam) and this is also in the *hadith*. He said: *"The Arabs say: 'We believe.' Say: 'You do not believe, but say 'We submit.'"* (49:14) This is because the hypocrites prayed, fasted, and paid alms while denying everything in their hearts. When they claimed belief, God declared their claim a lie because of the denial in their hearts, but He confirmed their claim of submission because of their performance of the duties entailed by it.

God says: *"If the hypocrites come to you and say: 'We bear witness that you truly are God's Messenger,' God knows better than they that you are indeed His Messenger, and God witnesses that the hypocrites are liars."* (63:1) They are liars in their claim of bearing witness to the Message while their hearts are denying it. The words of their mouths do not match the contents of their hearts, whereas the condition of bearing witness to the Message is that the tongue confirms the heart. When they lied in their claim, God exposed their lie.

Since belief is also a condition for the validity of submission, God the Exalted distinguishes the submitter (Muslim) from the believer (*mumin*) by saying:

We brought out the believers who dwelled in it and found none left in it but one house of submitters. (51:35-36)

This distinction links belief and submission in the way of a condition and its fulfillment. Lastly, God named prayer by the name of "belief" when He said:

It was not God's purpose that your belief should be in vain. (2:143)

You knew not what the Book was nor what the Faith. (42:52)

[the Prophet ﷺ told Gabriel ﷺ,] "And to believe in what has been decreed, both its good and its evil."

The word ("decree") is pronounced both *qadar* and *qadr*. The way of the People of Truth (i.e. *Ahl as-Sunnah wal-Jamaah*) is to firmly believe in God's Decree. The meaning of this is that God—the Glorified and Exalted—has decreed matters from pre-Eternity, and that He knows that they shall take place at times known to Him and at places known to Him; and they do occur exactly according to what He has decreed—Glorified and Exalted is He!

[Gabriel ﷺ told the Prophet ﷺ,] "Tell me about ihsan.*" He said: "*Ihsan *is to worship God as if you saw Him."*

This is the Station of True Vision (*maqam al-mushahada*). Whoever is able to directly see the King shies away from turning to other than Him in prayer and busying his heart with other than Him.

The Station of *ihsan* is the Station of the Most Truthful Saints (*maqam al-siddiqeen*) to which we have referred in our commentary on the *hadith* of intention.[353]

---

[353] al-Muhasibi said, "Truthfulness (*sidq*) as an attribute of a servant of God, means evenness in the private and the public person, in visible and hidden behavior. Truthfulness is realized after the realization of all the stations (*maqamat*) and states (*ahwal*). Even sincerity (*ikhlas*) is in need of truthfulness, whereas truthfulness needs nothing, because although real sincerity is to seek God through obedience, one might seek Allah by praying and yet be heedless and absent in his heart while praying. Truthfulness, then, is to seek God Almighty by worshipping with complete presence of heart before Him. For every truthful one (*sadiq*) is sincere (*mukhlis*), while not every sincere one is truthful. That is the meaning of connection (*ittisal*) and disconnection (*infisal*): the truthful one has disconnected himself from all that is other than God (*ma siwa Allah*) and he has fastened himself to the presence before God (*al-hudur billah*). That is also the meaning of renunciation (*takhalli*) of all that is other than God and self-adornment (*tahalli*) with presence before God, the Glorified, the Exalted."

[the Prophet ﷺ told Gabriel عليه السلام,] "He certainly sees you."

He sees your heedlessness if you are heedless in prayer and chatting to your self.

[Gabriel عليه السلام told the Prophet ﷺ,] "Tell me about the Hour." He replied: "The one who is being asked knows no more about it than the questioner."

This answer indicates that the Prophet ﷺ did not know the Hour. Knowledge of the Hour is among the matters whose knowledge God has reserved for Himself. He said:

God has with Him the knowledge of the Hour. (31:34)

It is heavy in the heavens and the earth. It comes not to you save unawares. (7:187)

What can convey its knowledge unto thee (How canst thou know)? It may be that the Hour is nigh. (34:63, 42:17)

As for he who claims that the age of the world is 70,000 years and that 63,000 years remain, it is a false statement reported by al-Tawkhi in the "Causes of Revelation" from certain astrologers and mathematicians. Moreover, whoever claims that the term of the world is 7,000 years makes a bold affirmation concerning the Unknown, and it is not permitted to believe it.

[Gabriel عليه السلام told the Prophet ﷺ,] "Tell me about its signs." He replied: "The slave-girl will give birth to her mistress."

Another report has: "to her master." Most commentators say that this is a sign of the multiplicity of slave-girls and their offspring. A child by the slave-girl's master is like her master, because the owner's possessions go to his children. Some say that the meaning refers to slave-girls giving birth to kings. The mother would then fall under her child's sovereignty. Another meaning is that a person may have a son from his slave-girl before selling her away; then the son grows up and buys his own mother. That is one of the conditions of the Hour.

[the Prophet ﷺ told Gabriel عليه السلام,] "You will see the barefoot, naked, destitute herdsmen outdo each other in building tall structures."

It means the Bedouins who live in the desert and their like from among the needy and the poor will become experts in erecting tall structures. The world will become bountiful for them, and they will end up vying in luxury with their buildings.

[Umar ؓ said,] *"And he (the Prophet ﷺ) waited a long time."*

The reports also say: "I waited (*labithtu*) a long time." Both are sound. In Abu Dawud and Tirmidhi's narrations Umar ؓ says: "After three days," and in Baghawi's *Sharh al-tanbih*: "After three days or more," which apparently means after three nights had passed. All this apparently contradicts Abu Hurayra's statement in his narration (in Bukhari): "The man turned around and left, after which God's Messenger ﷺ said, 'Bring that man back to me,' and they looked to bring him back, but they found no one. Then he ﷺ said, 'That was Gabriel.'"

It is possible to reconcile the two versions of the event by considering that Umar ؓ may not have been present at the time of the Prophet's ﷺ disclosure, but that he had already risen and left the gathering by that time. So the Prophet ﷺ spoke on the spot to those who were present, and they in turn told Umar after three days, since he had not been present at the time the rest of the Companions had been informed.

[the Prophet ﷺ told Umar ؓ,] *"That was Gabriel. He came to you to teach you (the prescriptions of) your religion."*

There is an indication in that statement that Islam, *iman*, and *ihsan* are all named "religion" (*din*).

The *hadith* also provides a proof that belief in God's Decree is an obligation, that one should avoid probing matters, and that contentment with what comes to pass is an obligation.

A man came up to Ahmad ibn Hanbal and said: "Admonish me." He answered him:

If God, the Exalted, has taken upon Himself the provision of all sustenance, why do you fret? If indeed compensation for all things belongs to God, why be stingy? If indeed there is a Paradise, why rest now? If indeed there is a Fire, why disobey? If the questioning of

Munkar and Nakir is true, what good is human company?[354] If the world is bound for extinction, what peace of mind is there in it? If indeed there is a Reckoning, what good are possessions? And if all things are decreed to pass and measured out, what good is fear?

Behind the Prophet's House: The People of the Bench (*Ahl as-Suffa*)

The People of the Bench (*Ahl as-Suffa*) represent the prototype of the school of perfection and purification which the Prophet Muhammad ﷺ established in his blessed mosque in Madinah, after the Emigration. In this school, the true devotees flocked earnestly seeking nothing but God's good pleasure with them and the pleasure of the Prophet ﷺ. The People of the Bench and the methods of training they received under the direct discipline of the Prophet ﷺ became a precedent for the later generations.

Here we will relate some of the authentic narrations regarding the People of the Bench, their asceticism, and their isolation under the training of the Prophet ﷺ. The character and devotion of this extraordinary group of believers was spoken of in the Quran and protected by heavenly decrees. Such attestations by the Lord of creation were given to make clear the rank, faith, spirituality, and true devotion of these Companions of the Prophet ﷺ.

These were men whom *"neither business nor trading can divert them from the remembrance of God."* (24:37) They rejected the material comforts of this life, in favor of the eternal one. And God helped them in this by keeping from them wealth and power, both of which have proven snares in leading people to committing injustice and tyranny. They refused to feel despondent for the portion of this worldly life they were not granted, and accepted poverty in the way of God as their lot. Instead, they considered it insignificant and passing for their utmost happiness was to be engaged in worship of their Lord.

It is said that the following verse of Quran was revealed regarding the People of the Bench:

> *And keep yourself content with those who call on their Lord in the morning and the evening, seeking His face, and let not thine eyes pass beyond them, seeking the pomp and glitter of this life. Nor obey any whose heart We have*

---

[354] The sufi shaykh Ibn Ata Allah said, "When God alienates you from the company of His creatures, know that He wishes to open for you the door of His own intimacy." *Kitab al-hikam* #93.

permitted to neglect the remembrance of God one who follows his own desires, and his affair has become all excess. (18:28)

The People of the Bench, used to sit morning and evening behind the house of Prophet ﷺ reciting Quran and praising the Prophet ﷺ and making *dhikr*. Abd Allah ibn Masud related:

> A group from among the Quraysh passed by the Messenger of God ﷺ while Suhayb, Bilal, Ammar, Khabab and other poor Muslims were with him. They said to the Prophet ﷺ, "O Messenger of God, have you chosen this class of people from among your entire followers for your closest ones? Do you want us to follow such people? Are these the ones whom God has chosen from among all of us for His utmost favors? Get rid of them and perhaps if you do that we may follow you.
>
> It is then that God revealed, *"Send not away those who call on their Lord morning and evening, seeking His face. In naught art thou accountable for them, and in naught are they accountable for thee, that thou shouldst turn them away, and thus be (one) of the unjust. Thus did We try some of them by comparison with others, that they should say: 'Is it these then that God hath favoured from amongst us?' Doth not God know best those who are grateful?"* (6:52-53)

The Hafiz Abu Nuaym al-Isfahani in his commentaries about the People of the Bench said:

> God, the Lord of Majesty and Glory, moved their focus away from the world. He made the world look insignificant and small in their eyes. Furthermore, He restricted their access to it in order to protect them against its lures and to help them eschew transgression and injustices against their own souls or others. Hence, He kept them guarded under the shield of His protection, He lightened their burdens, and guarded their focus against aberrations, so that no wealth in this world could inhibit their concentration and dedication to worship Him, and nothing could lure their hearts or drive them to abandon their stations.[355]

Jafar bin Muhammad bin Amr narrated that Abi Saeed al-Khudri ☙ said:

---

[355] Abu Nuaym al-Isfahani, *Hilyat al-awliya The Beauty of the Righteous and Accounts of the Elite*, translation by Shaykh Muhammad al-Akili, p 373.

We were a group of poor Muslims who lived under the canopy of the Prophet's ﷺ Mosque, and we spent our time studying the Quran at the hand of a man from among us who also regularly prayed to God on our behalf. Once, the Messenger of God ﷺ came by us, and he saw our condition. I assumed that God's Messenger ﷺ did not know any of the people present by name, and when the people saw him coming, they felt extreme reverence for him; some even tried to hide behind the others to cover up some shame they felt about their torn rags. God's Messenger ﷺ then pointed out and invited the people to form a circle around him, and when they did, he asked them, "What were you studying?" They replied, "This man was reading the Quran for us and he also prays for us." God's Messenger ﷺ sat there for a moment, and then said, "All praise is to God, Who made among my followers a group with whom I am commanded to constrain myself and to keep my soul content in their company." (c.f. 18:28). He ﷺ then added, "Let the poor ones among the believers hearken to the glad tiding that they will enter the heavenly paradise 500 years before the rich. The poor will be enjoying its blessings while the rich will be facing their reckoning."[356]

Abu Bakr al-Talhi narrated that Khabab ibn al-Art ؓ once spoke in reference to the Quranic verse, "*Send not away those who call on their Lord morning and evening, seeking His face . . .*" (6:52) and he spoke of two people, al-Aqra bin Habis and Uyaina bin Hisn al-Fazari, who once harbored hypocrisy and often fought and betrayed the believers, and who primarily embraced Islam for ambitious selfish reasons, but later, and by the grace of Almighty God, they were guided to true Islam after they repented to God, the Magnificent Lord, and Who in His Divine Compassion, called in another verse *al-muallafit qulubuhum* (those whose hearts have been recently reconciled to the truth).

Khabab ibn al-Art ؓ said:

Al-Aqra bin Habis and Uyaina bin Hisn al-Fazari, once came to the mosque, and the found God's Messenger ﷺ sitting in the company of Bilal, Ammar, Suhayb, and Khabab (himself), along with other believers from among the poor and the meek who were known as the

---

[356] *Op. cit.*, p. 958.

People of the Bench. When al-Aqra and Uyaina saw that, they despised the group, and they requested a private audience with God's Messenger ﷺ, and they initially spoke to him with utter disrespect regarding the class of his company, indicating, "We want you to grant us a special set of rules concerning who sits with you when we come here. Make that a rank which will become recognized by the dignitaries among the various delegations of Arab tribes, besides others, who come to see you, so that they would recognize our status in this city. In fact, delegations of various noble tribes come regularly to see you, and we feel ashamed that they should see these paupers and slaves sitting in our company! Hence, when we come to see you, ask these people to leave, and when we take off and get back to our businesses, then you may sit with them as much as you want!" The Prophet of God ﷺ replied, "Let it be so!" the two men delighted in their condition was accepted and they hastily demanded, "Then write down your promise and make it an official decree!"

We were all sitting there observing the ramification when the Prophet of God ﷺ asked Ali ؓ to bring a paper to write on, but suddently the archangel Gabriel descended bringing the divine revelation, *"Do not segregate or evict (from God's House) those who call on their Lord morning and evening, seeking His countenance. You are not accountable for them, nor are they accountable for you, and should you turn them away, you would have committed an extreme injustice."* (6:52)

In His revelation, God, Glorious and Exalted, then mentioned al-Aqra bin Habis and Uyaina bin Hisn al-Fazari, saying *"And thus We put to trial (the faith and character of) some people versus others (to frustrate their vainness), so that they will come to (hear themselves) say, 'Are these the people whom God chose to favor over us?' Alas, does not God know best those who are truly grateful (from those who are not)? Therefore, when those who believe in Our signs come to see you, say 'Peace be upon you. Your Lord has decreed upon Himself to favor you with His mercy and that should any of you commit a wrongdoing out of ignorance, and then repents and amends his act, he will surely find God oft-forgiving and most compassionate.'"* (6:53-54).

God's Messenger ﷺ immediately discarded the paper Ali ؓ had just brought, as he called us to himself, and he kept on looking at us, and he greeted us cheerfully, "Peace be upon you, peace be upon you." Hence we happily drew closer and nestled by him, and we blithesomely sat so tightly close to him to the point that our knees touched his.

From that day on, God's Messenger ﷺ kept us in his proximity and under his direct watch; he regularly sat with us, and whenever he needed to attend to his other duties, he simply left us. This joyous privilege went on until the day when God, the Lord of Majesty and Glory, revealed His command, "*And keep thy soul content with those who call on their Lord morning and evening, seeking His Face; and let not thine eyes pass beyond them, seeking the pomp and glitter of this Life; nor obey any whose heart We have permitted to neglect the remembrance of Us, one who follows his own desires, whose case has gone beyond all bounds.*" (18:28)

The above verse refers to al-Aqra bin Habis and Uyaina bin Hisn al-Fazari. Almighty God then spoke of the parable of two men and their quest for the world, and He directed His blessed Messenger ﷺ to reply, "*Say, 'The truth comes from your Lord.' Let whosoever wants to believe in it, believe in it, and let whosoever wants to reject it, reject it . . . As to those who believe (in Our message) and who do righteous deeds, We surely do not leave unrewarded the work of someone who does good. Such ones will be rewarded with gardens beneath which rivers flow . . .* " (18:29-31)[357]

Abd Allah bin Muhammad bin Jafar narrated that Abu Hurayra ؓ said:

Among the People of the Bench there were at least seventy men who were extremely poor and did not have even a single large enough robe to cover themselves.[358]

Abd Allah bin Wahab narrated that Abu Hurayra ؓ said, "I stayed with the People of the Bench for some time . . . "[359]

Abu Hurayra ؓ also said:

The People of the Bench are the guests of Islam, they had no home or family to go to, nor did they have any money or possessions. Whenever God's Messenger received a collection of charities, he never took

[357] *Op. cit.*, p. 961.

[358] *Op. cit.*, p. 948.

[359] *Op. cit.*, p. 949.

anything for himself; instead, he immediately sent them in their entrety to the People of the Bench. However, whenever he received a gift, he took a small share of it for his family, and he sent the balance to them.[360]

The school of which these Companions partook did not die with the passing of the Prophet ﷺ. On the contrary, his methods and knowledge were turned over to his Companions, and each of them, in turn, became a school from which the Community learned the Prophet's ﷺ methods and knowledge. Over time, these schools developed and formalized their methods, and created the distinct science of *tasawwuf*.

The Relationship Between One's Deeds and Spiritual Evolution

The name "science of reality," or *ilm al-haqiqah*, is sometimes given to *tasawwuf*. Imam Ahmad said, upon hearing al-Harith al-Muhasibi speak, "I never heard on the science of realities (*ilm al-haqaiq*) such words as those uttered by that man."[361] The meaning of this expression is that the reality of the servant's worship addresses the spiritual condition of his heart, while the performance of his worship satisfies his external obligations. The second is the object of *Shariah*, and its exponents are many, while the first is the object of *haqiqah*, and its exponents are few.

An example of the fulfillment of both *Shariah* and *haqiqah* is prayer. It is obligatory to offer *salat*, or prayer, with all the required movements and details according to the *Shariah*. This is known as *jasad al-salat*, or the "body of the prayer." On the other hand, one of the essentials of prayer is to keep the heart in God's Divine Presence and know that He is looking at you throughout the *salat*. Such is the reality and essence of prayer. During the practice of *salat*, people may carry out the outward obligations of the prayer, but their hearts may not be involved. To pray from the heart is to strive for the state of *ihsan*; to keep the heart pure and clean of bad manners, and to remain immune to the distractions of the *dunya*. The Prophet ﷺ prayed this way, because he said he came to take people away from the attractions and distractions of the *dunya*, and he cursed these in many of his *ahadith*.

---

[360] *Op. cit.*, p. 944.

[361] Related with a sound chain by al-Khatib al-Baghdadi in his *Tarikh Baghdad* 8:214, and by al-Dhahabi in *Mizan al-itidal* 1:430.

By analogy, the external form of *salat* is its body, and humility (*khudu*) and self-effacement (*khushu*), its soul. What is the benefit of a body without a soul? If *salat* is movement without presence, then it is to move like a robot. As the soul needs the body to sustain it, so too does the body need the soul to give it life. The relationship between the *Shariah* and the *Haqiqa* is like the relationship of body and soul. The perfect believer who has reached a state of *ihsan* is the one who can join the two.

The Prophet ﷺ also expressed this distinction, in his *hadith*:

> *Knowledge is of two kinds: knowledge established in the heart and knowledge on the tongue.*[362]

Al-Izz ibn Abd al-Salam al-Maqdisi (not shaykh al-Islam as-Sulami) explained this to refer respectively to *Haqiqa* and *Shariah*:

Knowledge is of two kinds: knowledge of the external (*ilm al-zahir*) which applies to *Shariah*, and knowledge of the internal (*ilm al-batin*) which applies to *Haqiqah*. "[363]

Imam al-Shafii alluded to the same distinction in his saying, "Knowledge is of two kinds: knowledge of beliefs and knowledge of bodies." Suyuti related it in the introduction to his book *Prophetic Medicine* (*al-Tibb al-nabawi*).[364]

Therefore, the essential understanding of *tasawwuf* is to combine *Shariah* and *Haqiqah*, soul and body, externals and internals. Due to the immense difficulty of fulfilling *tasawwuf*, its methods are sometimes called spiritual warfare or *jihad an-nafs*.

Jihad an-Nafs: The Greater Struggle Is against the Ego

God declares in the Quran that He accepts acts of worship only from those who purify themselves, *"Truly he succeeds that purifies it,"* (91:9), achieve soundness of the heart *"But only he (will prosper) that brings to God a sound heart"* (26:89), and show a humble spirit *"and truly it is hard save for the humble-minded."* (2:45) Together, these are generally called "purification of the intention." That is why the great scholars like Bukhari, Shafii, Nawawi,

---

362 Narrated by Ibn Abd al-Barr, *Jami bayan al-ilm wa fadlih* 1:190; al-Mundhiri, al-Targhib 1:103; al-Khatib al-Baghdadi, *Tarikh Baghdad* 4:346; and others.

363 Al-Izz ibn Abd al-Salam, *Bayn al-sharia wa al-haqiqa aw hall al-rumuz wa mafatih al-kunuz* (Cairo: *matbaat nur al-amal*, n.d.) p. 11.

364 As mentioned by al-Ajluni in *Kashf al-khafa* 2:89 (#1765).

and others, began their books of *fiqh* (jurisprudence) with the *hadith*, "Actions are judged according to intention."

An act that is outwardly considered worship, but that is performed without pure intention, is not considered worship—even fighting and dying in defense of Muslims. The Prophet ﷺ said of one such warrior, "He is a companion of the Fire." In *Shariah*, they are called *shahid al-fasad* (corrupt martyr). Purification of intention is extremely necessary in all five pillars of Islam. It is for this reason that the term *jihad al-akbar* (the greatest jihad) is commonly understood as reference to the jihad of self-purification.

Ibn Qayyim al-Jawziyya writes in *al-Fawaid*:

> God said, *"Those who have striven for Our sake, We guide them to Our ways."* (29:69) He has thereby made guidance dependent on jihad. Therefore, the most perfect of people are those of them who struggle the most for His sake, and the most obligatory of jihads *(afrad al-jihad)* are the jihad against the ego, the jihad against desires, the jihad against the devil, and the jihad against the lower world *(jihad al-nafs wa jihad al-hawa wa jihad al-shaytan wa jihad al-dunya)*. Whoever struggles against these four, God will guide him to the ways of His good pleasure which lead to His Paradise, and whoever leaves jihad, then he leaves guidance in proportion to his leaving jihad.

Al-Junayd said:

> Those who have striven against their desires and repented for our sake, we shall guide them to the ways of sincerity, and one cannot struggle against his enemy outwardly (i.e. with the sword) except he who struggles against these enemies inwardly. Then whoever is given victory over them will be victorious over his enemy. Whoever is defeated by them, his enemy defeats him.[365]

Competition and rivalry are allowed to encourage excellence in worship. God established levels among the believers, as is written in His book, and as is clear from countless *ahadith*. The reward of the lesser, or military, jihad is immense, as attested to by the Prophet ﷺ in the *hadith* where he says, if he could, he would ask God to bring him back to life so that he could go back and die as a *shahid* (martyr) many times over. Yet,

---

[365] Ibn Qayyim al-Jawziyya, *al-Fawaid*, ed. Muhammad Ali Qutb (Alexandria: dar al-dawa, 1412/1992) p. 50.

with respect to *tasawwuf,* those who remember God, including perfect scholars who truly know God, are superior to the *mujahidin* (warriors, who make jihad). For example, although Zayd ibn Haritha and Khalid ibn Walid were great generals, their demise was less serious for Islam, than that of Abu Musa al-Ashari or Ibn Abbas ﷺ. For this reason, the Prophet ﷺ explicitly declared the superiority of those who remember God, in the following authentic *hadith*:

> *The Prophet ﷺ said, "Shall I tell you something that is the best of all deeds, constitutes the best act of piety in the eyes of your Lord, elevates your rank in the hereafter, and carries more virtue than the spending of gold and silver in the service of God, or taking part in jihad and slaying or being slain in the path of God?" They said, "Yes!" He said, "Remembrance of God."*[366]

Traditions on the Jihad against the Ego

The *hadith* master Mulla Ali al-Qari relates in his book *al-Mawduat al-kubra,* also known as *al-Asrar al-marfua* that as-Suyuti said:

> Al-Khatib al-Baghdadi relates in his work *History,* on the authority of Jabir, that the Prophet ﷺ came back from one of his campaigns saying, "You have come forth in the best way of coming forth; you have come from the smaller jihad to the greater jihad." They said, "And what is the greater jihad?" He replied, "The striving *(mujahadat)* of God's servants against their idle desires." [367]

The *hafiz* Ibn Abu Jamra al-Azdi al-Andalusi says in his commentary on Bukhari, entitled *Bahjat al-nufus*:

> Umar narrated that a man came to the Prophet ﷺ asking for permission to go to jihad. The Prophet ﷺ asked, "Are your parents alive?" He said that they were. The Prophet ﷺ replied, "Then struggle to keep their rights" (*fihima fa jahid*). There is in this *hadith* evidence that the *Sunnah* for entering the path and undertaking self-discipline is to act under the

---

[366]Related on the authority of Abu al-Darda by Ahmad, Tirmidhi, Ibn Majah, Ibn Abi al-Dunya, al-Hakim who declared it sound, and Dhahabi confirmed him, Bayhaqi, Suyuti in *al-Jami al-saghir*, and Ahmad also related it from Muadh ibn Jabal.

[367]Ibn Hajar al-Asqalani said in *Tasdid al-qaws:*"This saying is widespread and it is a saying by Ibrahim ibn Ablah according to Nisai in *al-Kuna.* Ghazali mentions it in the *Ihya* and al-Iraqi said that Bayhaqi related it on the authority of Jabir and said: 'There is weakness in its chain of transmission.'" Ali al-Qari, *al-Asrar al-marfua* (Beirut 1985 ed.) p. 127.

expert guidance, so that he may be shown the way that is best for him to follow, and the soundest for the particular wayfarer. For when that Companion wished to go out to jihad, he did not content himself with his own opinion in the matter, but sought advice from one more knowledgeable than him and more expert. If this is the case in the Lesser Jihad, then what about the Greater Jihad?[368]

The Prophet ﷺ said in the Farewell Pilgrimage:

"...the mujahid is he who makes jihad against himself (jahada nafsah) *for the sake of obeying God."*[369]

Another version relates:

The strong one is not the one who overcomes people, the strong one is he who overcomes his ego (ghalaba nafsah). [370]

---

[368] Ibn Abu Jamra, *Bahjat al-nufus sharh mukhtasar sahih al-bukhari* 3:146.

[369] Ibn Hibban relates in his *Sahih* from Fadala ibn Ubayd, Tirmidhi, Ahmad, Tabarani, Ibn Majah, al-Hakim, and Qudai also relate it. The contemporary *hadith* scholar Shuayb al-Arnaut confirmed that its chain of transmission is sound in his edition of Ibn Hibban, Sahih 11:203 (#4862).

[370] Related by Al-Haythami, who declared it sound in his *Majma al-zawaid* in the chapter on *Jihad al-nafs.*

Scholarly Opinions on the Precedence of Internal Knowledge

al-Hasan al-Basri (d. 110 AH/ 732 CE)

Al-Hasan al-Basri was one of the early Sufis in both the general and the literal sense, as he wore a cloak of wool (*suf*) all his life. The son of a freedwoman (by Umm Salama ☙, the Prophet's ﷺ wife) and a freedman (by Zayd ibn Thabit ☙, the Prophet's ﷺ stepson), this great imam of Basra was a leader of saints and scholars in his day. He was widely known for his strict and encompassing embodiment of the *Sunnah* of the Prophet ﷺ. He was also famous for his vast knowledge, his austerity and asceticism, his fearless protests against the authorities, and his appeal both in discourse and appearance.

Ibn al-Jawzi wrote a 100-page book on his life and manners entitled, *Adab al-shaykh al-Hasan ibn Abi al-Hasan al-Basri*. He mentions a report that, when he died, al-Hasan left behind a white, wool cloak (*jubba*) that he had worn exclusively for twenty years, winter and summer, and that was still in a state of immaculate beauty, cleanliness, and quality.[371]

In a book he devoted to the sayings and the deeds of Sufis, Ibn Qayyim relates, "A group of women went out on the day of Eid and went about looking at people. They were asked, 'Who is the most handsome person you have seen today?' They replied, 'It is a shaykh wearing a black turban.' They meant Hasan al-Basri."[372]

The *hadith* master Abu Nuaym al-Isfahani mentions that it is al-Hasan's student, Abd al-Wahid ibn Zayd, who was the first person to build a Sufi *khaniqah*, or guest-house, and school at Abadan, on the present-day border of Iran with Iraq.[373]

---

[371] Ibn al-Jawzi, *Sifat al-safwa* 2(4):10 (#570).
[372] Ibn al-Qayyim, *Rawdat al-muhibbin wa nuzhat al-mushtaqin* (The Garden of Lovers and the Excursion of the Longing Ones) p. 225.
[373] Abu Nuaym al-Isfahani, *Hilyat al-awliya* 6:155.

It was on the basis of Hasan al-Basri and his students' fame as Sufis that Ibn Taymiyya stated, "*Tasawwuf's* place of origin is Basra."[374] This is a misleading assertion. Rather, Basra was chief among the places renowned for the formal development of the schools of purification that became known as *tasawwuf,* and whose principles were none other than the Quran and the *Sunnah*, as already demonstrated at length.

On the topic of *jihad al-nafs,* Ghazali relates that Hasan al-Basri said:[375]

> Two thoughts roam over the soul, one from God, one from the enemy. God shows mercy on a servant who settles at the thought that comes from Him. He embraces the thought that comes from God, while he fights against the one from his enemy. To illustrate the heart's mutual attraction between these two powers the Prophet ﷺ said, "*The heart of a believer lies between two fingers of the Merciful.*"
>
> The fingers stand for upheaval and hesitation in the heart. If man follows the dictates of anger and appetite, the dominion of Satan appears in him through idle passions (*hawa*) and his heart becomes the nesting-place and container of Satan, who feeds on passions. If he does battle with his passions and does not let them dominate his *nafs,* imitating in this the character of the angels, at that time his heart becomes the resting-place of angels, and they alight upon it.

A measure of the extent of Hasan al-Basri's extreme godwariness and scrupulousness (*wara*) is offered by his following statement, also quoted by Ghazali:

> Forgetfulness and hope are two mighty blessings upon the progeny of Adam; but for them the Muslims would not walk in the streets.[376]

Imam Abu Hanifa (81-150 AH/700-767 CE)

Imam Abu Hanifa said:

> If it were not for two years, I would have perished. For two years I accompanied Jafar as-Sadiq ﵁ and I acquired the spiritual knowledge

---

[374] Ibn Taymiyya, *al-Sufiyya wa al-faqara al-Tasawwuf* in *Majmua al-fatawa al-kubra* 11:16.

[375] In the section of his renowned *Ihya* entitled *Kitab riyadat al-nafs wa tahdhib al-akhlaq wa mualajat amrad al-qalb* (Book of the Training of the Ego, and the Disciplining of Manners and the Healing of the Heart's Diseases).

[376] In Ghazali, trans. T.J. Winter, *The Remembrance of Death* p. 18.

that made me a knower in the Way.[377]

The book *Ad-Durr al-Mukhtar* mentions that Ibn Abidin said:

Abu Ali Dakkak, one of the Sufi saints, received his path from Abul Qasim an-Nasarabadi, who received it from Shibli, who received it from Sari as-Saqati, who received it from Maruf al-Karkhi, who received it from Dawud at-Tai, who received the knowledge, both the external and the internal, from Imam Abu Hanifa, who supported the Sufi spiritual path.[378]

Sufyan al-Thawri (d. 161 AH/ 783 CE)

Ibn Qayyim al-Jawziyya and Ibn al-Jawzi relate that Sufyan al-Thawri said:

If it were not for Abu Hashim al-Sufi, I would have never perceived the presence of the subtlest forms of hypocrisy in the self... Among the best of people is the Sufi learned in jurisprudence. [379]

Ibn al-Jawzi also narrates the following:

Abu Hashim al-Sufi said, "God has stamped alienation upon the world in order that the friendly company of the seekers (*muridin*) consists solely in being with Him and not with the world, and in order that those who obey Him come to Him by means of avoiding the world. The People of Knowledge of God *(ahl al-marifa billah)* are strangers in the world and long for the hereafter."[380]

Imam Malik (94-179 AH/716-795 CE)

Imam Malik said:

Whoever studies jurisprudence and does not study Sufism will be corrupted. Whoever studies Sufism and does not study jurisprudence will become a heretic. Whoever combines both will reach the Truth.[381]

---

[377] *Ad-Durr al-mukhtar*, vol. 1, p. 43.

[378] See Ali al-Adawi with explanation by Imam Abul Hasan, vol. 2, p. 195.

[379] Ibn Qayyim, *Madarij al-salikin;* Ibn al-Jawzi, *Sifat al-safwa* (Beirut: dar al-kutub al-ilmiyya, 1403/1989) 1 (2):203 (#254); Abu Nuaym, *Hilyat al-awliya*, s.v. "Abu Hashim al-Sufi."

[380] Ibn al-Jawzi, *Op. cit.*

[381] Imam Adjluni, *Kashf al*-khafa *wa Muzid al-albas*, vol. 1, p. 341.

Imam Shafii (150-205 AH/767-820 CE)

Imam Shafii said:

> I accompanied the Sufi people, and I received from them three kinds of knowledge: they taught me how to speak; they taught me how to treat people with leniency and a soft heart; they guided me in the ways of Sufism.[382]

Imam Ahmad ibn Hanbal (164-241 AH/780-855 CE)

Imam Ahmad, advising his son, said:

> O my son, you have to sit with the Sufis, because they are like a fountain of knowledge. They recite the remembrance of God in their hearts. They are the ascetics, and they have the most spiritual power.[383]

He also said about the Sufis:

> I do not know any people better than them.[384]

Imam al-Muhasibi (d. 243 AH/857 CE)

The Prophet ﷺ said, *"My Community is going to split into seventy-three divisions. Only one of them will be in the group of salvation."* And God knows best that the group is the people of Sufism.[385]

al-Qasim ibn Uthman al-Jui (d. 248 AH/ 870 CE)

He is one of the great saints of Damascus who took *hadith* from Sufyan ibn Uyayna. Ibn al-Jawzi relates in *Sifat al-safwa* that al-Qasim ibn Uthman al-Jui explained that he got the name al-Jui ("of the hunger") because God had strengthened him against physical hunger by means of spiritual hunger. He said:

> Even if I was left one month without food I would not care. O God, you have done this with me. Therefore complete it for me![386]

---

[382] Shaykh Ain al-Kurdi, *Tanwir al-qulub*, p. 405.

[383] *Ghiza al-albab*, vol. 1, p. 120.

[384] *Op. cit.*

[385] Imam al-Muhasibi, *Kitab al-wasaya*, pp. 27-32.

[386] Ibn al-Jawzi, *Sifat al-safwa* 2(2):200 (#763).

In *Siyar alam al-nubala,* adh-Dhahabi calls him: "The Imam, the exemplar, the saint, the Muhaddith, the Shaykh of the Sufis and the friend of Ahmad ibn al-Hawari."

Ibn al-Jawzi also relates that Ibn Abu Hatim al-Razi said:

> I entered Damascus to see the transcribers of *hadith.* I passed by Qasim al-Jui's circle and saw a large crowd sitting around him as he spoke. I approached and heard him say:
>
> > Do without others in your life in five matters:
> > 1. If you are present among people, do not be known;
> > 2. If you are absent, do not be missed;
> > 3. If you know something, your advice is unsought;
> > 4. If you say something, your words are rejected;
> > 5. If you do something, you receive no credit for it.
> >
> > I advise you five other things as well:
> > 1. If you are wronged, do not reciprocate it;
> > 2. If you are praised, do not be glad;
> > 3. If you are blamed, do not be distraught;
> > 4. If you are called a liar, do not be angry;
> > 5. If you are betrayed, do not betray in return.

Ibn Abu Hatim said, "I made these words all the benefit I got from visiting Damascus."[387]

Imam al-Junayd al-Baghdadi (d. 297 AH/ 919 CE)

The Imam of the world in his time, al-Junayd al-Baghdadi, defining a Sufi said:[388]

> The Sufi is the one who wears wool on top of purity, follows the path of the Prophet ﷺ, endures bodily strains, and leaves behind all that pertains to the world.[389]

---

[387] *Op. cit.*

[388] al-Junayd, *Kitab dawa al-arwah,* ed. & trans. A.J. Arberry in Journal of the Royal Asiatic Society (1937).

[389] A saying by Abu Ali al-Rudhabari (d. 322), narrated by Suyuti in his book on *tasawwuf* entitled *Tayid al-haqiqa al-aliyya* (Cairo: al-matbaa al-islamiyya, 1352/1934) p. 15.

al-Hakim al-Tirmidhi (d. 320 AH/ 942 CE)

Abu Abd Allah Muhammad ibn Ali al-Hakim al-Tirmidhi al-Hanafi, was a *faqih* and *muhaddith* of Khorasan, and one of the great early authors of *tasawwuf* who is quoted extensively by Ibn Arabi. He wrote many books, of which the following have been published:

- *al-Masail al-maknuna*: The Concealed Matters
- *Adab al-nafs*: The Discipline of the Ego
- *Adab al-muridin*: Ethics of the Seekers of God, or Ethics of Sufi Students
- *al-amthal min al-kitab wa al-sunnah*: Examples from the Quran and the Sunnah
- *Asrar mujahadat al-nafs*: The Secrets of the Struggle against the Ego
- *Ilm al-awliya*: The Knowledge of the Saints
- *Khatm al-wilaya*: The Seal of Sainthood
- *Shifa al-ilal*: The Healing of Defects
- *Kitab manazil al-ibad min al-ibadah, aw, Manazil al-qasidin ila Allah*: The Book of the Positions of Worshippers in Relation to Worship, or: The Positions of the Travelers to God
- *Kitab marifat al-asrar*: Book of the Knowledge of Secrets
- *Kitab al-Ada wa-al-nafs; wa al-aql wa al-hawa*: The Book of the Enemies, the Ego, the Mind, and Vain Desires
- *al-Manhiyyat*: The Prohibitions
- *Nawadir al-usul fi marifat ahadith al-Rasul*: The Rare Sources of the Religion Concerning the Knowledge of the Prophet's Sayings
- *Tabai al-nufus: wa-huwa al-kitab al-musamma bi al-akyas wa al-mughtarrin*: The Different Characters of Souls, or: The Book of the Clever Ones and the Deluded Ones
- *al-Kalam ala mana la ilaha illa Allah*: Discourse on the Meaning of "There is no god but God"

Imam al-Qushayri (d. 465 AH/1072 CE)

Imam al-Qushayri said about Sufism:

> God made this group the best of His saints. He honored them above all of His servants after His messengers and prophets. He made their hearts the secrets of His Divine Presence. He chose them from among the Community to receive His Lights. They are the means of humanity. He purified them from all connections to this world. He lifted them to

> the highest states of vision. He unveiled to them the Realities of His Unique Oneness. He made them observe His Will operating in them. He made them shine in His Existence and appear as lights of His Lights.[390]

Imam Ghazali (450-505 AH/1058-1111 CE)

Imam Ghazali, the "Proof of Islam," said about Sufism:

> I know to be true that the Sufis are the seekers in God's Way. Their conduct is the best conduct. Their way is the best way. Their manners are the most sanctified. They have purified their hearts from other than God and they have made them as pathways for rivers to run receiving knowledge of the Divine Presence.[391]

Imam Fakhr ad-Din Ar-Razi (544-606 AH/1149-1209 CE)

Imam Fakhr ad-Din al-Razi said:

> The way the Sufis seek knowledge is to disconnect themselves from this worldly life, and keep themselves constantly busy in their mind and in their heart with *dhikr Allah* during all their actions and behaviours.[392]

Imam Nawawi (620-676 AH/1223-1278 CE)

Imam Nawawi said, in his *al-Maqasid*:

The specifications of the Way of the Sufis are five:

1. To keep the Presence of God in your heart in public and in private.
2. To follow the *Sunnah* of the Prophet ﷺ by actions and speech.
3. To keep away from dependence on people.
4. To be happy with what God gives you, even if it is little.
5. To always refer your matters to God, Almighty and Exalted.[393]

Ibn Taymiyya (661-728 AH/1263-1328 CE)

In his *Majmua fatawa*, Ibn Taymiyya says:

---

[390] Imam al-Qushayri, *ar-Risalat al-Qushayriyya*, p. 2.

[391] Imam Ghazali, *al-Munqidh min ad-dalal*, p. 131.

[392] Imam Fakhr ad-Din ar-Razi, *Itiqadat furaq al-muslimin*, pp. 72-73.

[393] Imam Nawawi, *Maqasid at-tawhid*, p. 20.

> You have to know that the rightly guided shaykhs must be taken as guides and examples in the faith, as they follow in the footsteps of the prophets and messengers. The Way of those shaykhs is to call people to God's Divine Presence and obedience to the Prophet ﷺ... The shaykhs whom we need to take as guides are our examples, and we have to follow them. As when on the prescribed pilgrimage, one needs a guide to reach the Kabah, these shaykhs are our guide to God and our Prophet ﷺ.[394]

Ibn Taymiyya quotes from Bayazid al-Bistami:

> The great Sufi shaykh, Bayazid al-Bistami, and the famous story of when he saw God in a vision and said to Him, "O God, what is the way to You?" And God responded, "Leave yourself and come to Me."
>
> I shed my self as a snake sheds its skin.[395]

Implicit in this quotation is an indication of the need for self-denial or abstention from worldly life, as that was the path followed by Bayazid al-Bistami. So we see from the above quotes that Ibn Taymiyya accepted many shaykhs by quoting them and urging people to follow guides to show the way, to obey God and to obey the Prophet ﷺ.

IBN TAYMIYYA DEFINES THE TERM "SUFISM"

What Ibn Taymiyya said about the definition of Sufism:

> Praise belongs to God, the use of the word Sufism has been thoroughly discussed. This is a term that was given to those who were dealing with that branch of knowledge.[396]
>
> Sufism is the science of realities and states of experience. The Sufi is that one who purifies himself from everything which distracts him from the remembrance of God. (The Sufi) is so filled with knowledge of the heart and knowledge of the mind that the value of gold and stones will be equal to him. Sufism safeguards the precious meanings and leaves behind the call to fame and vanity to reach the state of truthfulness. The best of humans after the prophets are the truthful

---

[394] *Majmua fatawa Ibn Taymiyya*, vol. 11 (Book of Tasawwuf), p. 497.

[395] *Op. cit.*, p. 499.

[396] *Op. cit.*, vol. 10, (Book of *Ilm as-suluk*), p. 510.

ones, as God mentioned them in the Quran, *"All who obey God and the Messenger are in the company of those on whom is the grace of God: the prophets, the sincere lovers of truth (siddiqeen), the martyrs and the righteous. Ah! What a beautiful fellowship"* (4:69) . . . (Sufis) strive to be obedient to God. Among them you will find the foremost in nearness by virtue of their striving, and some of them are among the People of the Right Hand . . . [397]

IBN TAYMIYYA ON SAINTS AND SAINTHOOD

A servant of God, Almighty and Exalted, cannot be considered a saint unless he is a true believer. God mentions in the Quran:

> *Now surely, on the friends of God there is no fear, nor shall they grieve; those who believe and guard against evil.* (10:62-63)

He then quotes the famous Tradition from Bukhari:

> *My servant draws not near to Me with anything more loved by Me than the religious duties I have enjoined upon him, and My servant continues to draw near to Me with supererogatory works so that I shall love him. When I love him I am his hearing with which he hears, his seeing with which he sees, his hand with which he strikes, and his foot with which he walks. Were he to ask (something) of Me, I would surely give it to him, and were he to ask Me for refuge, I would surely grant him it. I do not hesitate about anything as much as I hesitate about (seizing) the soul of My faithful servant: he hates death and I hate hurting him.*[398]

He explains the phrase, *"Whoever comes against one of My saints is challenging Me to fight"* thus:

> It means that God is expressing: "I will seek revenge against anyone who comes against My saints like an aggressive lion."[399]

IBN TAYMIYYA ON MIRACLES OF SAINTS

Ibn Taymiyya continues in the same book:

> What is considered as a miracle for a saint is that sometimes the saint might hear something that others do not hear or see something that

[397] *Op. cit.*, vol. 11, p. 497.

[398] *Op. cit.*, p. 190.

[399] *Op. cit.*, p. 314.

> others do not see, not while asleep, but in a wakened state of vision. He can know something, through revelation or inspiration, that others cannot know.[400]

In another book, he writes:

> The miracles of saints are absolutely true and correct, and acknowledged by all Muslim scholars. The Quran has pointed to it in different places, and the Traditions of the Prophet ﷺ have mentioned it. Whoever denies the miraculous power of saints are innovators or following innovators.[401]

He continues quoting the Prophet's ﷺ saying about the saints:

> You are the witnesses of God on earth.

IBN TAYMIYYA ON THE UNVEILING OF APPEARANCES

God Almighty will unveil to his saints states that have never been unveiled before. He will give them support without measure. If that saint begins to speak from the things of the unseen, past or present or future, it is considered miraculous knowledge. Anything that a saint does for people or for listeners, which is from the unseen, of healing, or teaching knowledge is accepted, and we must thank God for it. [402]

IBN TAYMIYYA CITES SOME GREAT SUFI SHAYKHS

In the volume entitled *Ilm as-suluk*, he says:

> The great Sufi shaykhs are well known and accepted, such as Bayazid al-Bistami, Shaykh Abd al-Qadir Gilani, Junayd ibn Muhammad, Hasan al-Basri, al-Fudayl ibn al-Ayyad, Ibrahim bin al-Adham, Abi Sulayman ad-Darani, Maruf al-Karkhi, Sari as-Saqati, Shaykh Hammad and Shaykh Abul Bayan… Those great Sufis were the leaders of humanity. They call to what is right and forbid what is wrong.[403]

---

400 *Op. cit.*

401 *Mukhtasar al-fatawa al-masriyya*, p. 603.

402 *Majmua fatawa Ibn Taymiyya*, vol. 11, p. 313.

403 *Op. cit.*, vol. 10, p. 516.

IBN TAYMIYYA'S QADIRI LINEAGE AS A SUFI SHAYKH

At present, we are in a position to go much further than saying that Ibn Taymiyya simply praised Sufism. We can say with definitiveness that he was an aspirant in the Sufi Way, primarily in the Qadiri Order, of Shaykh Abd al-Qadir Gilani.

In a unique manuscript of the Hanbali Yusuf ibn Abd al-Hadi (d. 909 AH/1503 CE), entitled *Bad al-ulqa bi labs al khirqa,* Ibn Taymiyya is listed in a Sufi spiritual genealogy with other well-known Hanbali scholars. The links in this genealogy are, in descending order from Abd al-Qadir Gilani:

- Shaykh Abd al-Qadir Gilani (d. 561 AH/1165 CE)
- Abu Umar ibn Qudama (d. 607 AH/1210 CE)
- Muwaffaq ad-Din ibn Qadama (d. 620 AH/1223 CE)
- Ibn Ali ibn Qudama (d. 682 AH/1283 CE)
- Ibn Taymiyya (d. 728 AH/1328 CE)
- Ibn Qayyim al-Jawziyya (d. 751 AH/1350 CE)
- Ibn Rajab (d. 795 AH/1393 CE)[404]

Furthermore, there is another unique manuscript of the work of Ibn Taymiyya himself. Here are Ibn Taymiyya's own words, as quoted from a work of his, *al-Masala at-Tabriziyya,*

> I wore the blessed Sufi cloak of my Shaykh Abd al-Qadir Gilani, there being between him and me two Sufi shaykhs.[405]

In another manuscript he said:

> I have worn the Sufi cloak of a number of Sufi shaykhs, belonging to various Ways, among them Abd al-Qadir Gilani, whose Way is the greatest of the well-known ones, may God have mercy on him.

After him the lineage continues on to his student, Ibn Qayyim al-Jawziyya and then to his student, Ibn Rajab.

THE SUFI CLOAK

Before proceeding to Imam Ibn Qayyim, it may be useful to say something about the wearing of the Sufi cloak. In the view of the

---

404 *Bad al-ulqa bi labs al-khirqa,* fol. 171b-172a.

405 Jamal al-din al-Talyani. *Targhib al-mutahabbin fi labs khirqaat al-mutamayyazin,* quoting from Ibn Taymiyya, *al-Masala at-tabriziyya,* fol. 67a.

trustworthy, there are three categories of shaykhs: the shaykh of the cloak; the shaykh of the *dhikr*; the shaykh of guidance.

The first two categories (the shaykh of the cloak and the shaykh of the *dhikr*) are really deputies of a shaykh, representing the reality of the shaykh of the Way through the intermediary of either the cloak or the *dhikr*. The shaykh of the cloak depends on the power of the cloak to act on the disciple. The disciple takes his support from the cloak, which a fully realized shaykh of guidance has imbued with his blessings.

The disciple of the shaykh of *dhikr* is supported by the *dhikr*, not directly by the shaykh. In these two cases, the shaykh becomes the symbol, because the real support of the disciple is the cloak or the *dhikr*.

The highest of the three categories is the shaykh of guidance. He is the one who supports the disciple without any intermediary, directly from himself to the disciple. He is the real shaykh because, without any means, he supports and directs the disciple directly through his heart. That is why Ahmad al-Faruqi said, "In our Path, the shaykh guides the disciple directly, unlike other Sufi orders which use the cloak and other means to lift up their disciples."

In the Naqshbandi Order only one shaykh, the shaykh of guidance, is therefore accepted as possessing real authority. When that shaykh passes away, the disciples must renew their initiation with his successor, to whom he has transmitted all his secrets and his inheritance from the Prophet ﷺ and all his predecessors in the Golden Chain.

Ibn Qayyim (691-751 AH/1292-1350 CE)

Ibn Qayyim stated:

> We can witness the greatness of the people of Sufism in the eyes of the earliest generations of Muslims by what has been mentioned by Sufyan al-Thawri (d. 161 AH/777 CE), one of the greatest imams in the second century and one of the foremost legal scholars. He said, "If it had not been for Abu Hisham al-Sufi (d. 115 AH/733 CE), I would never have perceived the action of the subtlest forms of hypocrisy in the self... Among the best of people is the Sufi learned in jurisprudence."[406]

[406] *Manazil as-sairin.*

Ibn Khaldun (733-808 AH/1332-1406 CE)

Ibn Khaldun said:

> The way of the Sufis is the way of our predecessors from the scholars among the Companions, their followers, and their successors. Its basis is to worship God and to leave the ornaments of this world and its pleasures.[407]

Tajuddin As-Subki (727-771 AH/1327-1370 CE)

Tajuddin as-Subki mentioned in his book *Muid an-naam,* under the chapter entitled Sufism:

> May God praise them and greet them. May God cause us to be with them in Paradise. Too many things have been said about them and too many ignorant people have said things which have no relation to them. The truth is that they have left this world and are busy with worship… They are the people of God, whose supplications and prescribed prayers God accepts, and by means of whom, God supports human beings.[408]

Jalaluddin as-Suyuti (849-911 AH/1445-1505 CE)

He said in his book *Tayid al-haqiqat al-aliyya*:

> Sufism, in itself, is the best and most honorable knowledge. It explains how to follow the *Sunnah* of the Prophet ﷺ and to put aside innovation.[409]

Abd Allah ibn Muhammad ibn Abd al-Wahhab (1115-1201 AH/1703-1787 CE)

The following is a quotation from a book by Muhammad Mansur Numani:

> Shaykh Abd Allah, the son of Shaykh Muhammad ibn Abd al-Wahhab, said about Sufism, "My father and I do not deny or criticize the science of Sufism, but on the contrary we support it because it purifies the external and the internal of the hidden sins which are related to the

---

[407] Ibn Khaldun, *Muqaddiman Ibn Khaldun,* p. 328.

[408] Tajuddin as-Subki, *Muid an-niam,* p. 190.

[409] Jalaluddin as-Suyuti, *Tayid al-haqiqat al-aliyya,* p. 57.

heart and the outward form. Even though the individual might externally be on the right way, internally he might be on the wrong way. Sufism is necessary to correct it."[410]

In the fifth volume of the collection of letters by Muhammad ibn Abd al-Wahhab, he states:

I never accused Ibn Arabi or Ibn al-Farid of unbelief for their Sufi interpretations.[411]

Ibn Abidin (1198-1252 AH/1784-1836 CE)

The great scholar, Ibn Abidin states:

The seekers in this Way do not hear except from the Divine Presence. They do not love any but Him. If they remember Him, they cry. If they thank Him, they are happy. If they find Him, they are awake. If they see Him, they will be relaxed. If they walk in His Divine Presence, they melt. They are drunk with His Blessings. May God bless them.[412]

Shaykh Muhammad Abduh (1265-1323 AH/1849-1905 CE)

Sufism appeared in the first century of Islam and it received a tremendous honor. It purified the self, straightened the conduct and gave knowledge to people from the wisdom and secrets of the Divine Presence.[413]

Shaykh Rashid Rida (1282-1354 AH/1865-1935 CE)

Sufism was a unique pillar from the pillars of the religion. Its purpose was to purify the self and to take account of one's daily behavior and to raise the people to a high station of spirituality.[414]

---

410 Muhammad Manzur Numani. *Ad-Diaat al-mukaththafa did ash-shaykh Muhammad ibn Abdul Wahhab*, p. 85.

411 *Ar-Rasail ash-shakhsiyya* (Letters by Muhammad ibn Abdul Wahhab), pp. 12, 61, 64.

412 Ibn Abidin, *Rasail ibn Abidin*, pp. 172-173.

413 *Majallat al-muslim*, p. 24.

414 *Op. cit.*, p. 726.

Mawlana Abul Hasan Ali an-Nadwi (B. 1331 AH/1913 CE)

Mawlana Abul Hasan Ali an-Nadwi is a member of the Islamic-Arabic Society of India and Muslim countries. He said in his book, *Muslims in India,* written some years ago:

> These Sufis initiate people in Oneness and sincerity in following the *Sunnah* of the Prophet ﷺ, in repentance from their sins and in avoidance of every disobedience to God, Almighty and Exalted. Their guides encourage them to move in the way of perfect Love of God.[415]

> In Calcutta, India, everyday more than a thousand people are being initiated into Sufism. Thanks to the influence of Sufi people, thousands and hundreds of thousands in India found their Lord and reached a state of perfection through the Islamic religion. [416]

Abul Ala Mawdudi (1321-1399 AH/1903-1979 CE)

Mawdudi said in his book *Mabadi al-Islam*:

> Sufism is a reality whose signs are the love of God and the love of the Prophet ﷺ, where one absents oneself for their sake and one is annihilated from anything other than them. It instructs how to follow in the footsteps of the Prophet ﷺ.

> Sufism searched for sincerity of heart, purity of intention, and trustworthiness of obedience in all of an individual's actions. The Divine Law and Sufism: what is the similitude of the two? They are like the body and the soul. The body is the external knowledge, the Divine Law, and the spirit is the internal knowledge.[417]

Conclusion

In summary, Sufism, in the present as in the past, is the effective means for spreading the reality of Islam, extending the knowledge and understanding of spirituality, and fostering happiness and peace. With it, human beings can find themselves, and in so doing, find their Lord. With it, human beings can improve, transform, and elevate themselves and find salvation from the ignorance of this world and the misguided pursuit of

---

[415] *Muslims in India,* pp. 140-146.

[416] *Op. cit.*

[417] *Mabadi al-islam,* p. 17.

some materialistic fantasy. And God knows best what He intends for His servants.

The crucible itself tells you, when you are strained,
Whether you are gold or gold-plated copper.
(*Sanai*)[418]

It is said that, after the Seal of Prophets ﷺ,
revelation does not descend upon anyone else.
Why not?
In fact it does, but then it is not called "revelation."
It is what the Prophet ﷺ referred to when he said,
"The believer sees with the Light of God."
When the believer looks with God's Light,
he sees all things:
the first and the last,
the present and the absent.
For how can anything be hidden from God's Light?
And if something is hidden,
then that is not the Light of God.
Therefore the meaning of revelation exists,
even if it is not called revelation.
(Rumi's *Fihi ma fihi*[419])

[418] Jalaluddin Rumi, *Signs of the Unseen: The Discourses of Jalaluddin Rumi* (*Fihi ma Fihi*), translated by W.M. Thackston., p. 156.
[419] Jalaluddin Rumi, *Mathnavi*, translated by William Chittick, p. 120.

Dhikr: Remembrance of God

Before we speak about the Naqshbandi method of *dhikr* and specific practices, we would like to clarify the principles of *dhikr*, or remembrance of God. In this chapter, we provide clear evidence that *dhikr* is Islamic, that it provides countless benefits, and that it was observed by the Prophet ﷺ and Companions.

Dhikr is the Greatest Obligation and a Divine Command

Dhikr, or remembrance of God (*Allah*), is the most excellent act of God's servants, and is stressed over a hundred times in the Holy Quran. It is the most praiseworthy practice to earn God's pleasure, the most effective weapon to overcome the enemy, and the deed most deserving of reward. It is the flag of Islam, the polished heart, the essence of the science of faith, the immunization against hypocrisy, the foremost worship, and the key of all success.

There are no restrictions on the method, frequency, or timing of *dhikr* whatsoever. Any restrictions on method pertain to certain specific obligatory acts that are not the issue here, such as *salat*. The *Shariah* is clear and everyone is aware of these obligations. Indeed, the Prophet ﷺ said that the People of Paradise will regret only one thing, not having made enough *dhikr* in the world!

God says in His Holy Book:

O Believers, make abundant mention of God! (33:41)

He also says His servants are *"those who remember their Lord standing, sitting, and lying on their sides."* (3:191) ; in other words, those who remember Him at all times of the day and night.

God said:

> *The creation of heaven and earth and the changes of night and day are signs for people who have wisdom—those who remember God standing up, sitting, and lying on their sides . . .* (3:190-191)

Aisha ؓ said, as narrated by Muslim, that the Prophet ﷺ remembered God at all times of the day and night.

The Prophet ﷺ said:

If your hearts were always in the state that they are in during dhikr, the angels would come to see you to the point that they would greet you in the middle of the road.[420]

Imam Nawawi commented on this *hadith* saying, "This kind of sight is shown to someone who persists in meditation (*muraqabah*), reflection (*fikr*), and anticipation (*iqbal*) of the next world."[421]

Muadh ibn Jabal said that the Prophet ﷺ also said:

The People of Paradise will not regret except one thing alone: the hour that passed them by and in which they made no remembrance of God.[422]

God placed His remembrance above prayer in value by making prayer the means and remembrance the goal. He said:

Lo! Worship guards one from lewdness and iniquity, but verily, remembrance of God is greatest. (29:45)

He is successful who purifies himself, and remembers the name of his Lord, and so prays. (87:14-15)

So establish prayer for My remembrance. (20:14)

Qadi Abu Bakr ibn al-Arabi explains that no good deed is valid without *dhikr*, and whoever does not remember God in his heart at the time of his charity or fasting, for example, has left that deed is incomplete. Therefore, *dhikr* may be seen as the best of deeds.[423]

In fact, all creation does *dhikr*, because God said that all creation praises Him constantly, and *tasbih* is a kind of *dhikr*. God said of the Prophet Jonah (Yunus) ﷺ, when the whale swallowed him:

Had he not been one of My glorifiers (musabbihin), he would have remained inside the whale's stomach until Judgment Day. (37:143-144)

---

[420] Muslim narrated it.

[421] Nawawi, *Sharh sahih muslim*

[422] Narrated by Bayhaqi in *Shuab al-iman* (1:392 #512-513) and by Tabarani. Haythami in *Majma al-zawaid* (10:74) said that its narrators are all trustworthy *(thiqat)*, while Suyuti declared it *hasan* in his *Jami al-saghir* (#7701).

[423] Related by Ibn Hajar in his *Fath al-bari* (1989 ed. 11:251).

Dhikr is something of tremendous importance. Abu Hurayra ﷺ said that the Prophet ﷺ said:

> *The earth and everything in it is cursed, except for dhikr and what attends dhikr, and the teacher, and the student.*[424]

By the words *"the world and everything in it,"* the Prophet ﷺ refers to all that which claims status or existence apart from God. This *hadith* also stresses the importance of following a teacher of knowledge, so as not to incur curse instead of blessing. This is what Abu Yazid al-Bistami meant when he said, "Whoever has no shaykh, his shaykh is Satan." This is confirmed by two other *ahadith* of the Prophet ﷺ:

> *Abu Bakrah ﷺ said: I heard the Prophet ﷺ say, "Become a learned person (alim), or a student of knowledge (mutallim), or an auditor of knowledge (mustami), or an amateur of knowledge (muhibb), but do not be the fifth one for you will perish."*[425]

> Sakhawi said:
>
> Ibn Abd al-Barr said, "The fifth one is one who shows enmity towards the scholars and contempt of them, and whoever does not love them shows contempt for them or is on the brink of having contempt for them, and there lies destruction."[426]

The Prophet ﷺ said: *"Blessing is with your elders."*[427] Another narration has:

> *When the young teach the old, then blessing has been lifted.*[428]

---

[424] Narrated by Tirmidhi who said it is *hasan*, Ibn Majah who said the same, Bayhaqi, and others. Suyuti cites it in *al-Jami al-saghir* from al-Bazzar's similar narration from Ibn Masud and he declared it *sahih*. Tabarani also narrated it in *al-Awsat* from Abu al-Darda.

[425] Al-Haythami said in *Majma al-zawaid* (1:122): "Tabarani narrated it in *al-Mujam al-saghir* (2:9), *al-Mujam al-awsat*, and *al-Mujam al-kabir*, also al-Bazzar (in his *Musnad*), and its narrators are considered trustworthy." It is also narrated by Abu Nuaym in *Hilyat al-awliya* (7:237) and al-Khatib in *Tarikh Baghdad* (12:295).

[426] Sakhawi, *al-Maqasid al-hasana* (p. 88 #134). See Ibn Abd al-Barr's *Jami bayan al-ilm wa fadlih* (1:30).

[427] Narrated by Ibn Hibban in his *Sahih*, al-Hakim who said it is *sahih*, and Ibn Daqiq al-Eid confirmed him.

[428] See Sakhawi's *al-Maqasid al-hasana* (p. 158-159 #290).

The one who engages in *dhikr* has the highest rank of all before God. The people who call on God without distraction have been mentioned in Quran. The effect that calling has on their hearts has also been mentioned:

In houses which God has permitted to be exalted and that His name may be remembered in them; there glorify Him therein in the mornings and the evenings, Men whom neither merchandise nor selling diverts from the remembrance of God . . . (24:36-37)

Those who believe, and whose hearts find their rest in the remembrance of God—for, verily, in the remembrance of God hearts do find their rest. (13:28)

A *hadith* states:

During the Night Journey and Ascension, the Prophet ﷺ was taken up to a point where he heard the screeching of the Pens, which signifies the writing of the divine Decree. He saw a man who had disappeared into the light of the Throne. The Prophet ﷺ said, "Who is this? Is this an angel?" It was said to him, "No." He said, "Is it a Prophet?" Again the answer was no. He said, "Who is it then?" The answer was, "This is a man whose tongue was moist with God's remembrance in the world, and his heart was attached to the mosques, and he never incurred the curse of his father and mother."[429]

In another *hadith*, it is reported:

A man came to the Prophet ﷺ and said, "O Prophet of God, the laws and conditions of Islam have become too many for me. Tell me something that I can always keep." The Prophet ﷺ said, "Keep your tongue always moist with the dhikr of God."[430]

In other words, the man wanted something particular, as opposed to the many rules and conditions that must be kept in general. He wanted something that he would be sure to uphold.

It is well-known in Islam that the best work in the path of God is jihad. Yet the Prophet ﷺ placed *dhikr* even above jihad in the following authentic *ahadith*.

Abu ad-Darda ؓ narrates:

---

[429] Shaykh Muhammad Alawi al-Maliki cited it in his collated text of the sound narrations on that topic entitled *al-Anwar al-bahiyya min Isra wa miraj khayr al-bariyya*.

[430] Ahmad, Tirmidhi, Ibn Majah, and Ibn Hibban declared that this *hadith* is fair *(hasan)*.

The Prophet ﷺ once asked his companions, "Shall I tell you about the best of all deeds, the best act of piety in the eyes of your Lord, which will elevate your status in the Hereafter, and carries more virtue than the spending of gold and silver in the service of God or taking part in jihad and slaying or being slain in the path of God? The dhikr of God."[431]

Abu Saeed narrates:

The Prophet ﷺ was asked, "Which of the servants of God is best in rank before God on the Day of Resurrection?" He said, "The ones who remember him much." I said, "O Messenger of God, what about the fighter in the way of God?" He answered, ". . . truly those who do dhikr are better than him in rank."[432]

Abd Allah ibn Umar ؓ said that the Prophet ﷺ said:

Everything has a polish, and the polish of hearts is dhikr of God. Nothing is more calculated to rescue from God's punishment than dhikr of God. He was asked whether this did not apply also to jihad in God's path, and he replied, "Not even if one should ply his sword until it breaks."[433]

Meanings of *Dhikr*

The word *dhikr* has various meanings: the Book of God and its recitation, prayer, learning, and teaching: The author of *Fiqh al-sunnah* said in his chapter on *dhikr*:

> Said ibn Jubayr said, "Anyone engaged in obeying God is in fact engaged in the remembrance of God." Some of the earlier scholars tied it to some more specified form. Aata said, "The gatherings of *dhikr* are the gatherings where the lawful and the prohibited things are discussed, for instance, selling, buying, prayers, fasting, marriage, divorce, and pilgrimage."

Qurtubi said:

---

[431] Related in Malik's *Muwatta*, the *Musnad* of Ahmad, the *Sunan* of Tirmidhi, Ibn Majah, and the *Mustadrak* of Hakim. Al-Bayhaqi, Hakim and others declared it *sahih*.

[432] Related in Ahmad, Tirmidhi, and Bayhaqi.

[433] Bayhaqi narrated it in *Kitab al-daawat al-kabir* as well as in his *Shuab al-iman* (1:396 #522), also al-Mundhiri in *al-Targhib* (2:396) and Tibrizi mentions it in *Mishkat al-masabih*, at the end of the book of Supplications.

Gatherings of *dhikr* are the gatherings for knowledge and admonition, those in which the Word of God and the *Sunnah* of His Messenger ﷺ, accounts of our righteous predecessors, and sayings of the righteous scholars are learned and practiced without any addition or innovation, and without any ulterior motives or greed.

Dhikr can also mean: invocation of God with the tongue, according to one of the formulas taught by the Prophet ﷺ, or any other formula, and remembrance of God in the heart, or with both the heart and the tongue.

The present text is concerned with the last two meanings: that of the mentioning of God, as in the verse, "*The believers are those who, when they hear God mentioned, their hearts tremble*" (8:2); and the Prophet's ﷺ saying, "The best *dhikr* is *la ilaha illallah*."[434] The Prophet ﷺ did not say, "the best *dhikr* is giving a lecture," or "giving advice," or "raising funds."

The present text is also concerned with the meaning of remembrance through the heart, as exemplified by the verse: "*The men and women who remember God abundantly*" (33:35). The Prophet ﷺ both praised and explained the verse when he said, "The single-hearted are foremost."[435] When asked, "O Messenger of God, who are the single-hearted?" he replied, "The men and women who remember God abundantly."

The Prophet ﷺ further clarified the role of the heart in effecting such remembrance of God when he said to Abu Hurayra ؓ:

> *Go with these two sandals of mine and whoever you meet behind this wall that witnesses that there is no god except God with certitude in his heart, give him glad tidings that he will enter Paradise.*[436]

Dhikr may sometimes mean both inner remembrance and outward mention, as in the verse, "*Remember Me, and I shall remember you*" (2:152), when it is read in light of the *hadith qudsi*:

> *Those that remember Me in their heart, I remember them in My heart; and those that remember Me in a gathering (i.e. that make mention of Me), I remember them (i.e. make mention of them) in a gathering better than theirs.*

This important *hadith* will be explained in greater detail later.

---

434 In Tirmidhi and Ibn Majah from Ibn Jubayr.

435 Related in Muslim.

436 Narrated by Muslim.

Broadly speaking, there are three types of *dhikr*: that of the heart, that of the tongue, and that of the two together.

Ibn Hajar explained that, according to Abu ad-Darda's ﷺ narration of the primacy of *dhikr* over jihad, what is meant by *dhikr* is the complete *dhikr* and consciousness of God's greatness, whereby one becomes better, for example, than those who battle the disbelievers without such recollection.[437]

In another *hadith* narrated by Bukhari, the Prophet ﷺ compared those who make *dhikr* among those who do not, to those who are alive among the dead.[438]

Ibn Hajar comments:

> What is meant by *dhikr* here is the utterance of the expressions which we have been encouraged to say, and say abundantly, such as the enduring good deeds (*al-baqiyat al-salihat*), and they are: "*subhanallah,*" "*Alhamdulillah,*" "*la ilaha illallah,*" "*allahu akbar,*" and all that is related to them such as the *hawqala* ("*la hawla wa la quwwata illa billah*"), the *basmala* ("*bismillah al-rahman al-rahim*"), the *hasbala* ("*hasbunallahu wa nima al-wakil*"), *istighfar,* and the like, as well as invocations for the good of this world and the next.

Dhikr also applies to diligence in obligatory or praiseworthy acts, such as the recitation of Quran, the reading of *hadith,* the study of the sciences of Islam, and supererogatory prayers.

Dhikr can take place with the tongue, for which the one who utters it receives reward—and it is not necessary for this that he understand or recall its meaning, on condition that he not mean other than its meaning by its utterance. If, in addition to its utterance, there is *dhikr* in the heart, then it is more complete. If there is, added to that, the recollection of the meaning of the *dhikr* and what it entails, such as magnifying God and exalting Him above defect or need, it is even more complete. If all this takes place inside a good deed, whether an obligatory prayer or other than that, it is even more complete. If one perfects one's turning to God and purifies one's sincerity towards Him, then that is the farthest perfection.

---

[437] Ibn Hajar, *Fath al-Bari* (1989 ed. 11:251)

[438] Book of *daawat* ch. 66 "The merit of *dhikr Allah.*"

Fakhr ad-Din al-Razi said:

What is meant by the *dhikr* of the tongue is the expressions that stand for *tasbih* (exaltation), *tahmid* (praise), and *tamjid* (glorification). As for the *dhikr* of the heart, it consists in reflection on the proof-texts that point to God's essence and His attributes, on those of the obligations, including what is enjoined and what is forbidden, so that one may examine the rulings that pertain to them, and on the secrets of God's creation.

As for *dhikr* of the limbs, it consists in their being immersed in obedience, and that is why God named prayer "*dhikr*" when He said, "*When the call is proclaimed on Friday, hasten earnestly to the remembrance of God.*" (62:9)

It is reported from some of the Knowers of God that *dhikr* has seven aspects:

❖ *Dhikr* of the eyes, which consists in weeping (*buka*);
❖ *Dhikr* of the ears, which consists in listening (*isgha*);
❖ *Dhikr* of the tongue, which consists in praise (*thana*);
❖ *Dhikr* of the hands, which consists in giving (*ata*);
❖ *Dhikr* of the body, which consists in loyalty (*wafa*);
❖ *Dhikr* of the heart, which consists in fear and hope (*khawf wa raja*);
❖ *Dhikr* of the spirit, which consists of utter submission and acceptance (*taslim wa rida*)."[439]

Loudness in *Dhikr*

The Prophet ﷺ praised a man who was *awwah* (literally: one who says, "ah, ah!"); that is, loud in his *dhikr*, even when others censured him. Ahmad narrated with a good chain from Uqba ibn Amir:

The Prophet ﷺ said of a man named Dhu al-Bijadayn, "He is a man who frequently says 'ah.'" He was a man abundant in dhikr Allah, with Quran recitation, and he raised his voice high when supplicating.[440]

God said of the Prophet Abraham ﷺ:

Verily, Abraham was most tender-hearted, forbearing. (9:114, 11:75)

---

[439] Ibn Hajar, *Fath al-Bari* (1989 ed. 11:250).

[440] Ahmad, *Musnad* (4:159).

That is, according to *Tafsir al-jalalayn*, "Crying out and suffering much, out of fear and dread of his Lord." The Prophet ﷺ prayed to be *awwah* in the following invocation, "O God, make me one who often cries out 'ah' to you (*rabbi ijalni ilayka awwahan*)." This is narrated by Tirmidhi,[441] Ibn Majah,[442] and Ahmad[443] with a strong chain in the following words:

> *The Prophet ﷺ supplicated thus, "O my Lord! help me and do not cause me to face difficulty; grant me victory and do not grant anyone victory over me; devise for me and not against me; guide me and facilitate guidance for me; make me overcome whoever rebels against me; O my Lord! make me abundantly thankful to You, abundantly mindful of You, abundantly devoted to You, perfectly obedient to You, lowly and humble before You, always crying out and turning back to You!"*

Gatherings of Collective, Loud *Dhikr*

The previously quoted *hadith qudsi*, beginning "*Those that remember Me in a gathering,*" presents gatherings of collective, loud *dhikr* as the gateway to realizing God's promise "*Remember Me, and I shall remember you.* " It is no wonder that such gatherings receive the highest praise and blessing from God and His Prophet ﷺ, as narrated in many authentic *ahadith*.

According to Bukhari and Muslim:

> *The Prophet ﷺ said that God has angels roaming the roads to find the people of dhikr [and in another version of Imam Muslim, majalis, or "gatherings" of dhikr]. When they find a group of people (qawm) reciting dhikr [in a version of Imam Muslim, they sit with them], and they call each other and encompass them in layers reaching up to the first heaven.*[444] *God asks His angels, and He knows already,*[445] *"What are My servants saying?"*[446] *The angels say, "They are praising You (tasbih) and magnifying Your Name (takbir), and glorifying*

---

[441] Tirmidhi, book of *daawat* #102, *hasan sahih.*

[442] Ibn Majah, *Dua* #2.

[443] Ahmad, *Musnad* 1:227.

[444] This is to say, an unlimited number of angels are going to be over that group. He did not say, "when they find one person." Therefore it is a must to be in a group to get this particular reward.

[445] He asks in order to place emphasis on what His servants are doing and to facilitate our understanding.

[446] He did not say "servant," but *ibadi*, "servants" in the plural.

> *You (tahmid), and giving You the best Attributes (tamjid). God says, "Have they seen Me?" The angels answer, "O our Lord! They did not see You . . . " He says, "What if they see Me?" The angels answer, "O our Lord, if they saw You they would be even more fervent in their worship, glorification, and praise." He says, "What are they asking?" The angels say, "They are asking Your Paradise!" He says, "Did they see Paradise?" They say, "O our Lord, no, they have not seen it." He says, "And how will they be if they see it?" They say, "If they see Paradise, they are going to be more attached and attracted to it!" He says, "What are they fearing and running away from?"*[447] *They say, "They are fearing and running away from Hellfire." He says, "And have they seen Hellfire?" They say, "O our Lord, no, they did not see Hellfire." He says, "And how will they be if they see Fire and Hell?" They say, "If they see Your Fire, they are going to be running from it and be even more afraid of it." And God says, "I am making you witness*[448] *that I have forgiven them."*[449] *One of the angels says, "O my Lord, someone was there who did not belong to that group, but came for some other need."*[450] *God says, "Those are such a group that anyone who sits with them that person will also have his sins forgiven."*

The late Imam Ahmad Mashhur al-Haddad (d. 1416/1995) said in his book *Miftah al-janna*:

> This *hadith* indicates what merit lies in gathering for *dhikr*, and in everyone present doing it aloud and in unison, because of the phrases, "They are invoking You" in the plural, and "They are the people who sit," meaning those who assemble for remembrance and do it in unison, something which can only be done aloud, since someone whose *dhikr* is silent has no need to seek out a session in someone else's company.
>
> This is further indicated by the *hadith qudsi*:

---

[447] When one says, "*Ya Ghaffar* (O Forgiver), *Ya Sattar* (O Concealer)," it means one fears Him because of his or her sins. One is asking Him to hide his or her sins and forgive him or her.

[448] God needs no witness since He said, "*God is sufficient as witness*" (4:79, 4:166, 10:29, 13:43, 29:52). "*Making you witness*" here means, "Assuring you."

[449] God has forgiven them because, as the beginning of the *hadith* states, they are a group of people reciting the Names of God and remembering Him with His *dhikr*.

[450] That person came for some other purpose than *dhikr*, to ask someone for something.

God says, I am to My servant as he expects of Me, I am with him when he remembers Me. If he remembers Me in his heart, I remember him to Myself, and if he remembers Me in an assembly, I mention him in an assembly better than his...[451]

Thus, silent *dhikr* is differentiated from *dhikr* said out loud by His saying: *"remembers Me within himself,"* meaning silently, and *"in an assembly,"* meaning aloud.

Dhikr in a gathering can only be done aloud and in unison. The above *hadith* thus constitutes proof that *dhikr* done out loud in a gathering is an exalted kind of *dhikr*, which is mentioned in the Highest Assembly by our Majestic Lord and the angels who are near to Him, who extol Him night and day, and never tire. (21:20)

The affinity is clearly evident between those who do *dhikr* in the transcendent world, who have been created with an inherently obedient and remembering nature—namely, the angels—and those who do *dhikr* in the dense world, whose natures contain lassitude and distraction—namely, human beings. The reward of the latter for their *dhikr* is that they be elevated to a rank similar to that of the Highest Assembly, which is a sufficient honor and favor for anyone.[452]

God has bestowed a special distinction upon those who remember Him. Abu Hurayra ؓ said:

While on the road to Makkah the Prophet ﷺ passed on top of a mountain called Jumdan (frozen in its place), at which time he said, "Move on! Here is Jumdan Mountain, and the single-minded (al-mufarridun) are foremost." They said, "Who are the single-minded, O Messenger of God?" He said, "The men and women who remember God."[453]

In other words, the mountain has overtaken the people because the mountain is reciting *dhikr* also. Ibn Qayyim al-Jawziyya explains that the term *mufarridun* has two meanings here: either the *muwahhidun*, the people engaged in *tawhid* who declare God's Oneness as a group (i.e., not

---

[451] Narrated by both Bukhari and Muslim.
[452] Imam Ahmad Mashhur al-Haddad, *Miftah al-janna*, translated by Mostafa Badawi in *Key to the Garden*, Quilliam Press p. 107-108.
[453] Narrated by Tirmidhi and Muslim, in his *Sahih*, beginning of the book of *Dhikr*.

necessarily alone), or those whom he calls *ahad furada,* those engaged in *tawhid* individually, while sitting alone.[454]

From this example it is evident that in Ibn al-Qayyim al-Jawziyya's explanation, sittings of *dhikr* can be in a group or alone. In another explanation of *mufarridun,* also cited by Ibn Qayyim, the reference is to "those that tremble from reciting *dhikr Allah,* entranced with it perpetually, not caring what people say or do about them." This is because the Prophet ﷺ said:

> *Remember and mention God as much as you want, until people say that you are crazy and foolish.*[455]

The *mufarridun* are the people who are really alive. Abu Musa ؓ reported, "The likeness of the one who remembers his Lord and the one who does not remember Him is like comparing a living to a dead person."[456]

Ibn Umar ؓ reported:

> *The Prophet ﷺ said, "When you pass by the gardens of Paradise, avail yourselves of them." The Companions asked, "What are the gardens of Paradise, O Messenger of God?" He replied, "The circles of dhikr. There are roaming angels of God who go about looking for the circles of dhikr, and when they find them they surround them closely."*[457]

Abu Saeed al-Khudri and Abu Hurayra ؓ reported that the Prophet ﷺ said:

> *When any group of men remembers God, angels surround them and mercy covers them, tranquility descends upon them, and God mentions them to those who are with Him.*[458]

Muslim, Ahmad, and Tirmidhi narrate from Muawiya ؓ:

> *The Prophet ﷺ went out to a circle of his Companions and asked, "What made you sit here?" They said, "We are sitting here in order to remember and mention God (nadhkurullaha) and to glorify Him (nahmaduhu) because He*

---

454 Ibn Qayyim al-Jawziyya, *Madarij al-salikin.*

455 Narrated by Ahmad in his *Musnad,* Ibn Hibban in his *Sahih,* and al-Hakim who declared it *sahih.*

456 Bukhari.

457 Tirmidhi narrated it *(hasan gharib)* and Ahmad.

458 Narrated by Muslim, Tirmidhi, Ahmad, Ibn Majah, and Bayhaqi.

guided us to the path of Islam, and he conferred favors upon us." Thereupon he adjured them by God and asked if that was the only purpose of their sitting there. They said, *"By God, we are sitting here for this purpose only."* At this the Prophet ﷺ said, *"I am not asking you to take an oath because of any misapprehension against you, but only because Gabriel came to me and informed me that God, the Exalted and Glorious, was telling the angels that He is proud of you!*

Note that the *hadith* used the term *jalasna*, or "we sat," in the plural, not singular. It referred to an association of people in a group, not one person.

Shahr ibn Hawshab relates:

> One day Abu ad-Darda ؓ entered the Masjid of Bayt al-Maqdis (Jerusalem) and saw people gathered around their admonisher (*mudhakkir*) who was reminding them, and they were raising their voices, weeping, and making invocations. Abu ad-Darda said, "My father's life and my mother's be sacrificed for those who moan over their state before the Day of Moaning!" Then he said, "O Ibn Hawshab, let us hurry and sit with those people. I heard the Prophet say, 'If you see the groves of Paradise, graze in them.' And we said, 'O Messenger of God, what are the groves of Paradise?' He said, 'The circles of remembrance, by the One in Whose hand is my soul, no people gather for the remembrance of God Almighty except the angels surround them closely, and mercy covers them, and God mentions them in His presence, and when they desire to get up and leave, a herald calls them saying, Rise forgiven, your evil deeds have been changed into good deeds!'" Then Abu ad-Darda made towards them and sat with them eagerly.[459]

The above shows evidence for the permissibility of loud *dhikr*, group *dhikr*, and the understanding of *dhikr* as including admonishment and the recounting of stories that benefit the soul.

Types and Frequency of *Dhikr*

Because *dhikr* is the life of the heart, Ibn Taymiyya is quoted by his student, Ibn Qayyim, as saying that *dhikr* is as necessary for the heart as

---

[459] The *hafiz* Ibn al-Jawzi relates it with his chain of transmission in the chapter entitled: "Mention of those of the elite who used to attend the gatherings of story-tellers" of his book *al-Qussas wa al-mudhakkirin* (The Storytellers and the Admonishers) ed. Muhammad Basyuni Zaghlul (Beirut: dar al-kutub al-ilmiyya, 1406/1986) p. 31.

water for the fish. Ibn Qayyim himself wrote a book, *al-Wabil al-sayyib*, on the virtues of *dhikr*, where he lists more than one hundred such virtues, among them: [460]

- ❖ It induces love for God. He who seeks access to the love of Almighty God should make *dhikr* profusely. Just as reading and repetition is the door of knowledge, so *dhikr* of God is the gateway to His love.
- ❖ *Dhikr* involves *muraqabah* (watchfulness, meditation), through which one reaches the state of *ihsan* (excellence), wherein a person worships God as if he is actually seeing Him.
- ❖ The gatherings for *dhikr* are gatherings of angels, and gatherings without *dhikr* are gatherings of Satan.
- ❖ By virtue of *dhikr*, the person doing *dhikr* is blessed, as also the person sitting next to him.
- ❖ In spite of the fact that *dhikr* is the easiest form of worship (the movement of the tongue being easier than the movement of any other part of the body), it is the most virtuous form.

Dhikr is also a form of *sadaqah* (charity).

Abu Dharr al-Ghifari ❀ said:

The Messenger of God ❀ said, "Sadaqah is for every person every day the sun rises." I said, "O Messenger of God, from what do we give sadaqah if we do not possess property?" He said, "The doors of charity (sadaqah) are takbir (i.e. to say, "Allahu Akbar," or God is Greatest); Subhanallah (God is exalted high); alhamdulillah (all praise is for God); La ilaha illallah (there is no god other than God); Astaghfirullah (I seek forgiveness from God); enjoining good; forbidding evil. These are all the doors of charity (sadaqah) from you which is prescribed for you, and there is a reward for you even in sex with your wife." [461]

All words of praise and glory to God, extolling His Perfect Attributes of Power and Majesty, Beauty and Sublimity, whether one utters them by tongue or says them silently in one's heart, are known as *dhikr*, or

---

[460] Quoted in Maulana M. Zakariyya Kandhalvi, *Virtues of Dhikr* (Lahore: Kutub Khana Faizi, n.d.) p. 74-76

[461] Narrated by Ahmad and Ibn Hibban, and there is something of similar effect in Muslim.

remembrance of God. He has commanded us to remember Him at all times. God says:

> O you who believe! Celebrate the praises of God, and do so often; and glorify Him morning and evening. (33:41-42)

> Remember me, I shall remember you. (2:152)

Remembrance of God is the foundation of good deeds. Whoever succeeds in it is blessed with the close friendship of God. That is why the Prophet ﷺ was in a state of remembrance of God at all times. When a man complained, "The laws of Islam are too heavy for me, so tell me something that I can easily follow," the Prophet ﷺ told him, "Let your tongue be always busy with the remembrance of God."[462]

Remembrance of God is also a means of deliverance from Hellfire. Muadh ؓ reported:

> "The Prophet ﷺ said, 'No other act of man is a more effective means for his deliverance from the chastisement of God than the remembrance of God.'"[463]

Ahmad also reports that the Prophet ﷺ said:

> All that you say in celebration of God's Glory, Majesty, and Oneness, and all your words of Praise for Him gather around the Throne of God. These words resound like the buzzing of bees, and call attention to the person who uttered them to God. Do you not wish to have someone there in the presence of God who would call attention to you?

Meditate as Often as Possible

God ordered that He should be remembered abundantly. Describing the wise men and women who reflect on His signs, the Quran mentions:

> Those who remember God standing, sitting, and lying on their sides. (3:191)

> Those men and women who engage much in God's praise, for them has God prepared forgiveness and a great reward. (33:35)

The author of *Fiqh al-sunnah* says that Mujahid explained, "A person cannot be one of *'those men and women who engage much in God's praise,'* as

---

[462] Narrated by Ahmad with two sound chains, also by Tirmidhi and Ibn Majah through other chains, and Ibn Hibban who declared it *sahih* as well as al-Hakim.

[463] Narrated by Ahmad.

mentioned in the above verse of the Quran, unless he or she remembers God at all times, standing, sitting, or lying in bed." He also says that when asked how much *dhikr* one should do to be considered one of *"those who remember God much,"* that Ibn as-Salah said that "much" is "when one is constant in supplicating, in the morning, and evening, and in other parts of the day and the night as reported from the Prophet ﷺ."

Concerning the above Quranic verses, Ibn Abbas ؓ said:

> All obligations imposed on man by God are clearly marked (by conditions of fulfillment) and one is exempted from them only when one completes them. The only thing that is never considered to have been completed is *dhikr*, for God has set no specific limits for it, and under no circumstances is one allowed to be negligent of it. God imposed obligations on mankind, and whoever fulfils their conditions does his duty. Whoever prayed at the specified times fulfilling its conditions, completed the obligation of prayer; whoever fasted Ramadan did his duty and completed it; and whoever made the pilgrimage fulfilled that obligation. The exception to this condition is *dhikr*: God did not want to limit it, rather He said in Quran, *"O you who believe! Remember God with much remembrance"* (33:41) and, thus, He did not assign it a limit nor a condition of completion.

It is clear through the above evidence that there is no such thing as too much *dhikr*. The Prophet ﷺ said, "He who loves something mentions it much."[464] Those who love God and His Prophet ﷺ mention God and His Prophet ﷺ. No one will limit this practice except those who do not feel such love.

Imam Ghazali said:[465]

> It is man's soul and spirit that constitute his real nature. Upon death, his state changes in two ways. First, he is now deprived of his eyes, ears and tongue, his hand, his feet, and all his parts, just as he is deprived of family, children, relatives, and all the people he knew, and of his horses and other riding-beasts, his servant-boys, his houses and

---

[464] Narrated by Abu Nuaym in the *Hilya* and Daylami in *Musnad al-firdaws*. Sakhawi cites it in *al-Maqasid al-hasana* p. 393 #1050 and does not comment upon it.

[465] Imam Ghazali, in the fortieth book of his *Ihya* entitled *The Remembrance of Death and The Afterlife* (p. 124 in the translation of T.J. Winter).

property, and all that he once owned. There is no distinction to be drawn between his being taken from these things and these things being taken from him, for it is the separation itself that causes pain.

If there was anything in the world in which he had found consolation and peace, then he will greatly lament for it after he dies, and feel the greatest sorrow over losing it. His heart will turn to thoughts of everything he owned, of his power and estates, even, for example, to a shirt he wore and took pleasure from.

However, had he taken pleasure only in the remembrance of God, and consoled himself with Him alone, then his will be great bliss and perfect happiness. For the barriers that lay between him and his Beloved will now be removed, and he will be free of the obstacles and cares of the world, all of which had distracted him from the remembrance of God. This is one of the aspects of the difference between the states of life and death.

On the same topic Imam Habib al-Haddad said:[466]

> Time and days are a man's capital, while his inclinations, desires, and various ambitions are the highway robbers. The way in which one profits on this journey lies in succeeding in coming to God and in attaining everlasting happiness, while one loses by being veiled from God, and being consigned to the painful torment of the Fire.

For this reason the intelligent believer transforms his breathing into acts of obedience, and interrupts them only with the *dhikr* of God.

The Importance of Silent Remembrance

The author of *Fiqh al-sunnah* writes: The purpose of *dhikr* is to purify hearts and souls and awaken the human conscience. The Quran says:

> *And establish regular prayer, for prayer restrains from shameful and unjust deeds, and remembrance of God is the greatest thing in life, without doubt.* (29:45)

In other words, the remembrance of God has a greater impact in restraining one from shameful and unjust deeds than just the regular, formal prayer. This is so because when a servant opens up his soul to his Lord, extolling His praise, God strengthens him with His light, increasing

---

[466] Imam Habib al-Haddad, *Key to the Garden* p. 104.

thereby his faith and conviction, and reassuring his mind and heart. This refers to:

> *Those who believe, and whose hearts find their rest in the remembrance of God—for, verily, in the remembrance of God hearts do find their rest.* (13:28)

And when hearts are satisfied with the Truth, they turn to the highest ideals without being deflected by impulses of desire or lust. This underscores the importance of *dhikr* in man's life. Obviously it would be unreasonable to expect these results just by uttering certain words, for words of the tongue unsupported by a willing heart are of no consequence. God Himself has taught us the manner in which a person should remember Him, saying:

> *And do bring your Lord to remembrance in your very soul, with humility and in reverence, without loudness in words, in the mornings and evening, and be not of those who are unheedful.* (7:205)

This verse indicates that doing *dhikr* in silence and without raising one's voice is better. Once during a journey the Prophet heard a group of Muslims supplicating aloud. Thereupon the Prophet ﷺ said:

> *Give yourselves a respite, you are not calling upon someone deaf or absent. Surely He Whom you are calling upon is near you and He listens to all. He is nearer to you than the neck of your mount.*[467]

This *hadith* underlines the love and awe a person should feel while engaged in *dhikr*. It is related from Saad ؓ that the Prophet ﷺ said,

> *The best dhikr is the hidden dhikr, and the best money is what suffices.*[468]

Ibn Hajar said, in response to an inquiry regarding Nawawi's saying, "*Dhikr* of the tongue with presence of the heart is preferable to *dhikr* of the heart (without):"[469]

> It is not because *dhikr* of the heart is an established worship in the lexical sense (i.e. consisting in specific formulae) that it is preferable,

---

[467] Muslim.

[468] Ahmad narrates it in his *Musnad,* Ibn Hibban in his *Sahih,* and Bayhaqi in *Shuab al-iman.* Nawawi said the *hadith* was not firmly established.

[469] Nawawi, at the end of the chapter entitled "*Dhikr* Gatherings" in his Commentary on *Sahih Muslim.*

but because, through it, one intently means in his heart to exalt and magnify God above all else. That is the meaning both of the aforementioned saying of Nawawi and of the saying of some that "There is no reward in *dhikr* of the heart." By denying there is a reward in it, one means "There is no reward in the words, which are not uttered"; and by establishing that there is reward in it, one means "in the fact that the heart is present," as we have just said. Consider this, for it is important. And God knows best. [470]

Shaykh Muhammad Bahauddin Shah Naqshband, from whom this Order takes its name, said, "There are two methods of *dhikr*; one is silent and one is loud. I chose the silent one because it is stronger and, therefore, more preferable."

Shaykh Amin al-Kurdi said:[471]

Know that there are two kinds of *dhikr*: "by heart" (*qalbi*) and "by tongue" (*lisani*). Each has its legal proofs in the Quran and the *Sunnah*. The *dhikr* by tongue, which combines sounds and letters, is not easy to perform at all times, because buying, and selling, and other such activities altogether divert one's attention from such *dhikr*. The contrary is true of the *dhikr* by heart, which is named that way in order to signify its freedom from letters and sounds. In that way, nothing distracts one from his *dhikr*: with the heart remember God, secretly from creation, wordlessly, and speechlessly. That remembrance is best of all: out of it flowed the sayings of the saints.

That is why many scholars following the way of Shah Naqshband have chosen the *dhikr* of the heart. Moreover, the heart is the place where the Forgiver casts his gaze, the seat of belief, the receptacle of secrets, and the source of lights. If it is sound, the whole body is sound, and if it is unsound, the whole body is unsound, as was made clear for us by the Chosen Prophet ﷺ.

Something confirming this was narrated on the authority of Aisha ؓ:

God favors dhikr above dhikr seventy-fold (meaning, silent dhikr over loud dhikr). On the Day of Resurrection, God will bring back human beings to His account, and the Recording Angels will bring what they have recorded and

[470] Ibn Hajar al-Asqalani, quoted in the *Fatawa hadithiyya* of al-Haytami (p. 48).

[471] Shaykh Amin al-Kurdi, *Tanwir al-qulub* (Enlightenment of Hearts) p. 522.

written, and God the Almighty, will say, "See if something that belongs to My servant was left out." The angels will say, "We left nothing out concerning what we have learnt and recorded, except that we have assessed it and written it." God will say, "O my servant, I have something good of yours for which I alone will reward you, it is your hidden remembrance of Me."[472]

Also on the authority of Aisha ؅ it is said:

The dhikr not heard by the Recording Angels equals seventy times the one they hear.[473]

Spiritual Retreat, or Seclusion (*khalwah, uzla*)

Silent *dhikr* is the *dhikr* of the servant who secludes himself away from people. Abu Saeed al-Khudri ؅ narrated:

A Bedouin came to the Prophet ؅ and said, "O God's Apostle! Who is the best of mankind?" The Prophet said, "A man who strives for God's Cause with his life and property, and also a man who lives (all alone) in a mountain path among the mountain paths to worship his Lord and save the people from his evil."[474]

Abu Saeed al-Khudri ؅ said:

I heard the Prophet ؅ say, "There will come a time upon the people when the best property of a Muslim man will be his sheep which he will take to the tops of mountains and to the places of rainfall to run away with his Religion far from trials.[475]

Muslim and Tirmidhi narrate:

Abu Hurayra said, "While on the road to Makkah the Prophet ؅ passed on top of a mountain called Jumdan (frozen in its place), at which time he said: 'Move on! Here is Jumdan Mountain, and the single-minded (al-mufarridun) are foremost.' They said, 'Who are the single-minded, O Messenger of God?' He said, 'The men and women who remember God unceasingly.'"[476]

The version in Tirmidhi reads:

---

[472] Bayhaqi narrated it.
[473] Bayhaqi narrated it.
[474] Bukhari (English translation), Volume 8, Book 76, Number 501.
[475] Bukhari (English translation), Volume 8, Book 76, Number 502.
[476] Muslim related it in his *Sahih*, beginning of the book of *Dhikr*.

The Prophet ﷺ said, "The single-minded (al-mufarridun) are foremost." They said, "Who are the single-minded?" He said, "Those who dote on the remembrance of God and are ridiculed because of it, and whose burdens the dhikr removes from them, so that they come to God fluttering."

Nawawi writes:

Some pronounced it *mufridun* (those who isolate themselves). Ibn Qutayba and others said, "The original meaning of this is those whose relatives have died and they have become single (in the world) with regard to their passing from them, so they have remained remembering God the Glorious and Exalted." Another narration has, "*They are those who are moved at the mention or remembrance of God,*" that is, they have become fervently devoted and attached to His remembrance. Ibn Arabi said, "It is said that a man becomes single *(farada al-rajul)* when he becomes learned, isolates himself, and concerns himself exclusively with the observance of God's orders and prohibitions."[477]

Al-Mundhiri said:

These are the ones who are fired up with the remembrance of God.[478]

Dhikr in isolation or seclusion (*khalwa*) is corroborated by the *hadith* in Bukhari, beginning, "*Seven people will be shaded by God . . .* " The seventh person mentioned is, "A person who remembers God in seclusion, and his eyes get flooded with tears."

According to Tirmidhi:

Aisha — relates: "In the beginnings of the Messenger of God's Prophethood ﷺ, at the time God desired to bestow honor upon him and mercy upon His servants through him, he would not have any vision except it came to pass as surely as the sun rises. He continued like this for as long as God wished. Most beloved to him was seclusion (al-khalwa), and there was nothing he loved more than to be alone in seclusion."[479]

---

[477] Nawawi, *Sharh Sahih Muslim*, Bk. 48, Ch. 1, *Hadith* 4.

[478] Al-Mundhiri, *al-Targhib wa al-tarhib* (The Encouragement to Good and the Discouragement from Evil).

[479] Tirmidhi narrates it and said: *hasan sahih gharib*. Bukhari and Muslim narrate something very similar through different chains and the word *khala* is used instead of *khalwa*.

Ibn Hajar said in his commentary on Bukhari:[480]

Ibn al-Mubarak relates in *Kitab al-raqaiq* from Shuba, from Khubayb ibn Abd al-Rahman, from Hafs ibn Asim, that Umar ؓ said, "Take your part of fortune from seclusion." And what a good saying is al-Junayd's (may God grant us the benefit of his blessings) saying: "Undergoing the difficulty of seclusion is easier than mixing with society unscathed." Al-Khattabi said in his *Book of Seclusion* (*Kitab al-uzla*), "If there were not in seclusion other than safety from backbiting and the sight of what is forbidden but cannot be eliminated, it would have been enough of an immense good." Bukhari's title ("Chapter on Seclusion As Rest From Keeping Company Towards Evil") refers to the *hadith* cited by al-Hakim from Abu Dharr from the Prophet ﷺ with a fair (*hasan*) chain, "Isolation is better than to be sociable in committing evil." However, what is usually retained is that it is a saying of Abu Dharr ؓ or Abu ad-Darda ؓ. Ibn Abi Asim cited it.

Al-Qushayri said in his *Risalah*:

The method of the one who enters seclusion is that he must have the belief that he is keeping people from his evil, not the reverse, for the former presupposes belittlement of himself, which is the attribute of the humble, while the latter indicates that he considers himself better than others, which is the attribute of the arrogant.

Abu Bakr ibn al-Arabi writes:

If it is said that the times have become so corrupt that there is nothing better than isolating oneself, we say one isolates oneself from people in one's actions, while he keeps mixing with them with his physical body; however, if he cannot succeed, then at that time he isolates himself from them physically, but without entering into monasticism (*yataziluhum bi badanihi wa la yadkhulu fi al-rahbaniyya*) which is condemned and rejected by the *Sunnah*.[481]

Empowering *Dhikr* with the Divine Name "Allah"

God said in the Quran:

---

[480] Ibn Hajar, *Fath al-Bari* in the commentary on Bukhari's chapter on seclusion.
[481] Abu Bakr ibn al-Arabi, *Aridat al-ahwadhi sharh sahih al-Tirmidhi*, Book 45 (*daawat*), Ch. 4.

And mention the name of your Lord and devote yourself to Him with a complete devotion. (73:8)

Qadi Thanaullah Panipati said, "Know that this verse points to the repetition of the name of the Essence (*ism al-dhat*); that is, '*Allah*.'"[482] The same meaning is intimated also by the following verse:

. . . *Say, "Allah." Then leave them to their play and vain wrangling.* (6:91)

According to one *hadith*, the Prophet ﷺ said:

The Hour will not rise before "Allah, Allah" is no longer said on earth.

According to another chain he said:

The Hour will not rise on anyone saying, "Allah, Allah."[483]

Imam Nawawi said, in his commentary on this chapter, "Know that the narrations of this *hadith* are unanimous in the repetition of the name of God, the Exalted, for both versions, and that is the way it is found in all the authoritative books."[484]

Imam Muslim placed the *hadith* under the chapter-heading, "Disappearance of Belief (*iman*) at the End of Times," although there is no mention of belief in the *hadith*. This shows that saying "*Allah, Allah*" indicates belief. Those who say it show belief, while those who do not say it, do not show belief. Therefore, those who fight those who say it are actually worse than those who merely lack belief and do not say "*Allah, Allah*."

Nawawi highlights the authenticity of the form's repetition to establish that the repetition of the words "*Allah, Allah*" is a *sunnah mathura*, or practice inherited from the Prophet ﷺ and the Companions. Ibn Taymiyya's insistence that the words must not be used alone, but only with a vocative form (i.e., "*Ya Allah*"), therefore contradicts the *Sunnah*.

It is noteworthy that the Siddiqi translation of *Sahih Muslim* mistranslates the first narration cited above as, "The Hour (Resurrection) would not come so long as God is supplicated in the world," and the second as "The Hour (Resurrection) would not come upon anyone so long as he supplicates God." This is wrong as a translation, but accepted as a

---

482 Qadi Thanullah Panipati, *Tafsir Mazhari* (10:111).

483 Muslim narrated both in his *Sahih*, Book of Iman (Belief), chapter 66 entitled: *dhahab al-iman akhir al-zaman* "The Disappearance of Belief at the End of Times."

484 Nawawi, *Sharh Sahih Muslim*, Dar al-Qalam, Beirut ed. vol. 1/2 p. 537.

commentary, since saying "*Allah, Allah*" is supplicating Him. This is true of all worship, according to the *hadith* of the Prophet ﷺ, "*Supplication; that is what worship is.*"[485] However, for the translation to be accurate, the word form highlighted by Nawawi must be retained in any explanation of this *hadith*. It is not merely "supplicating God;" it is saying, "*Allah, Allah*" according to the Prophet's ﷺ own words.

One who knows that the *dhikr* "*Allah, Allah*" has been mentioned by the Prophet ﷺ himself is not at liberty to debate whether or not it was used by the Companions in order to establish its validity. Its validity is sufficiently established in confirming that the Prophet ﷺ said it. Yet, it is established that, while undergoing torture, Bilal often recited the *dhikr* "*Ahad, Ahad*." Ibn Hisham says in his *Sira*:

Ibn Ishaq narrates (with his chain of transmission) saying:

> *Bilal was a faithful Muslim, pure of heart. Umayya ibn Khalaf often brought him out in the hottest part of the day and would throw him on his back in the open valley and have a great rock put on his chest; then he would say to him, "You will stay here until you die or deny Muhammad and worship al-Lat and al-Uzza." He said while he was enduring this, "Ahad, Ahad"—"One, One!"*[486]

***Dhikr* with "*Hu*," "*Hayy*," and "*Haqq*"**

One who knows that "*Allah, Allah*" is a *dhikr* used by the Prophet ﷺ is also not at liberty to object to similar forms of *dhikr*, such as "*Hu*," or "*Hayy*," or "*Haqq*."

"*Hu*" is a pronoun of God Almighty, and "*Hayy*" is His Name, according to the Verse of the Throne (*ayat al-Kursi*):

> *Allah! There is no god except He (Hu) the Living (al-Hayy), the Self-Subsistent (Allahu la ilaha illa Hu al-Hayy al-Qayyum).* (2:255)

"*Haqq*" is one of the names listed in the *hadith* that enumerates the ninety-nine Names of God, in Bukhari and Muslim.[487] Furthermore, the Prophet ﷺ prayed to God with the following invocations:

❖ "At your command, O God of Truth (*Labbayka ilah al-Haqq*)."[488]

---

485 Tirmidhi and others narrate it.

486 Ibn Hajar cites it in *al-Isaba* (1:171 #732).

487 see below

❖ "You are Truth (*Anta al-Haqq*)."[489]

God said:

To God belong the Most beautiful Names, so call Him with them. (7:180)

These names are not confined to ninety-nine, as Nawawi explicitly stated in his commentary on the *hadith* whereby the Prophet ﷺ said:

There are ninety-nine names which belong to God, one hundred less one; whoever memorizes (or recites) them enters Paradise.[490]

Nawawi and others showed that the meaning of this *hadith* is not, "There are only ninety-nine names," but "There are ninety-nine well-known names," or "There are ninety-nine names that suffice to enter Paradise if memorized."

The Prophet ﷺ called God by *all* His Names, as is clear from the following *hadith*:

O God, I invoke You with all of Your beautiful Names.[491]

Dhikr in Dimly lit Surroundings

God said to the Prophet ﷺ:

And some part of the night awake for it, a largess for thee. (17:79)

Lo! the vigil of the night is a time when impression is more keen and speech more certain. (73:6)

The superiority of prayer at night is known in all books of *hadith* and *fiqh* because of the elimination of worldly distractions at that time. That is why Imam Ghazali wrote on that topic:

The root of thought is the eye. He whose *niyyat* (intention) is fine and who aims high cannot be diverted by what occurs in front of him, but he who is weak falls prey to it. The medicine is to cut off the roots of these distractions and to shut up the eyes, to pray in a dark room, not to keep anything in front which may attract attention and not to pray in

[488] It is narrated in the book of *Hajj* in al-Nasai's *Sunan*, and in the book of *Manasik* in Ibn Majah's.

[489] Bukhari and Muslim.

[490] Bukhari and Muslim

[491] Arabic: *Allahumma inni aduka bi asmaika al-husna kulliha*. Narrated by Ibn Majah, book of *Dua*; and by Imam Malik in his *Muwatta, Kitab al-Shir*.

a decorated place. For this reason, the saints worshipped in dark, narrow and unspacious rooms.[492]

Movement During *Dhikr*

In reference to the *hadith* of Muslim whereby the Prophet ﷺ praised the *mufarridun*, or those who are single-minded in their remembrance of God, Nawawi said:

> They are those who shake or are moved at the mention or remembrance of God, that is, they have become fervently devoted and attached to His remembrance.

> Imam Habib al-Haddad said:
> *Dhikr* returns from the outward feature, which is the tongue, to the inward, which is the heart, where it becomes solidly rooted, so that it takes firm hold of its members. The sweetness of this is tasted by the one who has taken to *dhikr* with the whole of himself, so that his skin and heart are softened. As God said, *"Then their skins and their hearts soften to the remembrance of God."* (39:23)[493]

The "softening of the heart" consists in the sensitivity and timidity that occur as a result of nearness and *tajalli* (manifestation of one or more Divine Attributes). Sufficient is it to have God as one's Intimate Companion!

As for the "softening of the skin" this is the ecstasy and swaying from side to side which result from intimacy and manifestation, or from fear and awe. No blame is attached to someone who has reached this rank if he sways and chants, for in the painful throes of love and passion, he finds something which arouses the highest yearning.

The exhortation provided by fear and awe brings forth tears and forces one to tremble and be humble. These are the states of the righteous believers (*abrar*) when they hear the Speech and *dhikr* of God, the Exalted. *"Their skins shiver,"* and then soften with their hearts and incline to *dhikr* of Him, as they are covered in serenity and dignity, so that they are neither frivolous, pretentious, noisy, or ostentatious. God, the Exalted, has not described them as people whose sense of reason has departed, who faint, dance, or jump about.

---

[492] Imam Ghazali, *Ihya Ulum al-Din*, Book of *Salat*.

[493] Imam Habib al-Haddad, in *Key to the Garden* (p. 116).

More Traditions on the Virtues of *Dhikr*

Abu Hurayra reported that the Prophet said:

When a servant of God utters the words "la ilaha illallah" (there is no god except God) sincerely, the doors of heaven open up for these words until they reach the Throne of God, so long as its utterer keeps away from the major sins.[494]

Abu Hurayra also reported:

The Prophet said, "Renew your faith." "How can we renew our faith?" they asked. The Prophet replied, "Say always, 'la ilaha illallah.'"[495]

Jabir reported that the Prophet said:

The best remembrance of God is to repeat "la ilaha illallah" and the best invocation (dua) is al-hamdulillah (all praise belongs to God).[496]

Abu Hurayra reported that the Prophet said:

There are two phrases that are light on the tongue, but heavy on the scale of rewards and are dear to the Gracious One. These are: "Glorified is God with all praise to Him," and, "Glorified is God, the Great."[497]

Abu Hurayra also reported that the Prophet said:

I love repeating, "Glorified is God, and Praise be to God, and There is no God but God, and God is most Great," more than all that the sun shines upon.[498]

Abu Dharr reported:

The Prophet said, "Shall I tell you the words that God loves the most?" I said, "Yes, tell me, O Messenger of God." He said, "The words dearest to God are, "Glorified is God with all praise to Him."[499]

In Tirmidhi's version, the following is also found:

---

[494] Narrated by Tirmidhi, who says it is *hasan gharib*. Al-Mundhiri included in *al-Targhib* 2:414.

[495] Narrated by Ahmad with a fair chain of authorities.

[496] Narrated by Nasai, Ibn Majah, and Hakim who declared its chain sound.

[497] Arabic: "*Subhanallah wa bi hamdihi,*" and "*Subhanallah al-azim.*" Narrated by Bukhari, Muslim, and Tirmidhi.

[498] Arabic: "*Subhanallah, wa alhamdulillah, wa la ilaha illallah, wallahu akbar.*" Narrated by Muslim and Tirmidhi.

[499] Arabic: "*Subhanallah wa bi hamdihi.*" Narrated by Muslim and Tirmidhi.

The words most dear to God which He has chosen for His angels are, "Glorified is my Lord with all praise to Him, Glorified is my Lord with all praise to Him!"[500]

Jabir ؓ reported that the Prophet ﷺ said:

Whoever says, "Glorified is God, the Great, with all praise to Him," will have a palm tree planted for him in Paradise.[501]

Abu Saeed ؓ reported:

The Prophet ﷺ said, "Perform the enduring goods deeds (al-baqiyat al-salihat) more frequently." They asked, "What are these enduring good deeds?" The Prophet ﷺ replied: Takbir ("allahu akbar"), Tahlil ("la ilaha illallah"), Tasbih ("subhanallah"), "alhamdulillah," and "la hawla wa la quwwata illa billah."[502]

Abd Allah ibn Masud ؓ reported that the Prophet ﷺ said:

During the Night Journey I met Abraham who said to me, O Muhammad, convey my greetings to your Community, and tell them that the Paradise is of pure land, its water is sweet, and its expanse is vast, spacious, and even. And its seedlings are:

- Glory to God (*subhanallah*)
- Praise to God (*walhamdulillah*)
- There is no god but God (*wa la ilaha illallah*)
- God is greatest (*wallahu akbar*)[503]

Samura ibn Jundub ؓ reported:

The Prophet ﷺ said: "The dearest phrases to God are four: 'Glorified is God, and Praise be to God, and There is no God but God, and God is most Great,'[504] There is no harm in beginning them in any order you choose while remembering God."[505]

Ibn Masud ؓ reported that the Prophet ﷺ said:

---

[500] Arabic: "*Subhana rabbi wa bi hamdihi subhana rabbi wa bi hamdihi.*"
[501] Narrated by Tirmidhi, who said it is *hasan*.
[502] Narrated by Nasai and Hakim, who said its chain is authentic.
[503] Narrated by Tirmidhi and Tabarani whose version adds, "There is no power nor strength save through God."
[504] Arabic: *subhanallah, wa al-hamdulillah, wa la ilaha illallah, wallahu akbar.*
[505] Narrated by Muslim.

If anyone recites the last two verses of Surat al-Baqara at night (2:285-286), they will suffice for him.[506]

That is, these two verses will bring him a reward equivalent to that of a night prayer, and will safeguard him from any hurt during that night.

Abu Saeed al-Khudri ﵁ narrated:

The Prophet ﷺ asked, "Can anyone of you recite a third of the Quran during the night?" The Companions considered this difficult and they said: "Who among us can do so, O Prophet of God?" Thereupon the Prophet ﷺ said: "God, the One, the Eternally-Besought (i.e., Surat al-Ikhlas) is a third of the Quran."[507]

Abu Hurayra ﵁ reported that the Prophet ﷺ said:

Whoever says, "There is no god but God, alone, without partner. His is the sovereignty, and His the praise, and He has power over everything,"[508] *a hundred times a day will have a reward equivalent to the reward for freeing ten slaves. In addition, a hundred good deeds will be recorded for him and a hundred bad deeds of his will be wiped off, and it will be a safeguard for him from Satan that day until evening, and no one will be better in deeds than such a person except he who does more than that.*[509]

In the version of Muslim, Tirmidhi, and Nasai, it is added:

Whoever says, "Glorified is God with all praise to Him,"[510] *a hundred times during a day, will have all his sins wiped off even if they were as numerous as the foam on the surface of the sea.*

Istighfar—Asking God's Forgiveness

Anas ﵁ reported that he heard the Prophet ﷺ saying that God says:

O son of Adam, whatever you asked Me and expect from Me I forgave—respecting that which you owed to Me—and I do not care (how great this

---

[506] Narrated by Bukhari and Muslim, Ibn Khuzayma in his *Sahih* mentioned it under the chapter "The Recitation of the Quran Equivalent in Reward to a Night Prayer."

[507] Narrated by Bukhari and Muslim.

[508] Arabic: *la ilaha illallahu wahdahu la sharika lah, lahul-mulku wa lahul-hamd, wa huwa ala kulli shayin qadir.*

[509] Narrated by Bukhari, Muslim, Tirmidhi, Nasai and Ibn Majah.

[510] Arabic: *subhanallah wa bi hamdihi.*

was). O Son of Adam, even if your sins pile up to the sky and then you seek My forgiveness I will forgive you, and O son of Adam, even if you have an earthful of sins, but you meet Me without associating any other thing with Me, I will forgive you.[511]

Abd Allah ibn Abbas ﷺ said:

If one supplicates without fail for forgiveness from God, He finds a way out for him to get out of every distress and difficulty, and gives him sustenance through ways utterly not thought of.[512]

Juwayriyya bint al-Harith ﷺ, one of the wives of the Prophet ﷺ, reported that one day the Prophet ﷺ left her apartment in the morning as she was busy observing her dawn prayer in her place of worship. He came back in the forenoon and she was still sitting there. The Prophet ﷺ said to her, "You have been in the same place since I left you?" She said: "Yes." Thereupon the Prophet ﷺ said:

I recited some words three times after I left you and if these are to be weighed against what you have recited since morning these would outweigh them, and these words are: "Glory to God and praise to Him to the number of His creation, and to the extent of His pleasure, and to the extent of the weight of His Throne, and to the extent of ink used in recording words for His Praise."[513]

Ibn Umar ﷺ reported that the Prophet ﷺ told them:

A servant of God said, "My Lord! All praise belongs to You as much as befits Your Glory and Sublime Majesty."[514] *This was too much for the two angels to record. They did not know how to record it. So they soared to the heaven and said, "Our Lord! Your servant has said something which we do not know how to record." God asked them—and, of course, He knew what the servant had said—"What did My servant say?" They said, "He said, 'My Lord! All praise belongs to You as much as befits Your Glory and Sublime Majesty.'" God said*

---

511 Narrated by Tirmidhi who said it is *hasan sahih.*

512 Narrated by Abu Dawud, Nasai, Ibn Majah, and Hakim, who said its chain of authorities is sound.

513 Arabic: *Subhanallahi wa bi hamdihi adada khalqihi wa rida nafsihi wa zinata arshihi wa midada kalimatihi.* Narrated by Muslim and Abu Dawud.

514 Arabic: *Ya rabbi laka al-hamdu kama yanbaghi li jalali wajhika wa li azimi sultanik.*

to them, "Write it down as My servant has said until he should meet Me and I reward him for it."[515]

Abd Allah ibn Amr ibn al-As ❧ said:

I saw the Prophet counting the glorifications of God on his right hand's fingers.[516]

Yusayra bint Yasir ❧ reported that the Prophet ﷺ commanded them (the Emigrant women) to be regular in remembering God by saying *tahlil* *("la ilaha illallah")* and *tasbih ("subhanallah")* and *takbir ("allahu akbar")*, and never to be forgetful of God and His Mercy, and to count them on their fingers, for the fingers will be questioned and will speak.[517]

Use of *Dhikr* Beads (*Masbaha, Sibha, Tasbih*)

Saad ibn Abi Waqqas ❧ reported:

Once the Prophet ﷺ saw a woman who had some date-stones or pebbles which she was using as beads to glorify God. The Prophet ﷺ said to her, "Let me tell you something that would be easier or more excellent for you than that." So he told her to say instead:

- ❖ "Glory be to God as many times as the number of what He has created in Heaven,"
- ❖ "Glory be to God as many times as the number of what He has created on Earth,"
- ❖ "Glory be to God as many times as the number of what He has created between them,"
- ❖ "Glory be to God as many times as the number of that which He is creating."

And then repeat all of the above four times but substituting "Glory be to God" with:

- ❖ "God is the most great" in the first repetition,
- ❖ "Praise be to God" in the second repetition,
- ❖ "There is no god but God" in the third repetition, and

---

[515] Narrated by Ibn Majah.

[516] Narrated by Tirmidhi who said *hasan gharib*, Nasai, Abu Dawud, and Ahmad.

[517] Narrated by Ahmad, Tirmidhi who said it is *gharib*, Abu Dawud, and al-Hakim. Shawkani in *Nayl al-awtar* 2:316 said that Suyuti declared sound *(sahih)* its chain of transmission.

- "There is no change and no power except with God" in the fourth repetition.

Safiyya bint Huyayy ﵂ the Prophet's ﷺ wife said:

The Prophet ﷺ came in to see me and in front of me there were 4,000 date-stones with which I was making tasbih (counting "subhanallah"). He said, "You make tasbih with so many! Shall I teach you what surpasses your number of tasbih?" She said, "Teach me!" He said, "Say: Glory to God the number of His creation."[518]

God says in His Holy Book, addressing His Holy Prophet ﷺ:

Remind people, for reminding benefits them. (51:55)

Reminder has various forms, public and private. A public form of reminder is the *adhan*. The *masbaha*—or *sibha, tasbih*, or *dhikr* beads—has had, since the earliest Companions, the function of private reminder. It is for that reason that the *tasbih* was called by them *mudhakkir* or *mudhakkira* (reminder). There is a narration traced to the Prophet ﷺ whereby he said, *"What a good reminder are the* dhikr *beads!"*[519]

The statement that counting *dhikr* on beads is an innovation is undoubtedly false. The use of beads for counting *dhikr* was definitely allowed by the Prophet ﷺ and was a *Sunnah* of the Companions. This is proven by the *sahih hadith* of Saad ibn Abi Waqqas ﵁, who related that the Prophet ﷺ once saw a woman using some date-stones or pebbles to count *dhikr,* and did not prohibit her use of them.[520] Another *sahih hadith* to that effect was related by Safiyya ﵂, who was seen by her husband the Prophet ﷺ counting "*Subhanallah*" with four thousand date stones.[521]

---

[518] Arabic: *Subhanallah adada khalqihi.* Narrated by Tirmidhi who said it is *gharib,* and both al-Hakim and Suyuti declared it *sahih.*

[519] Arabic: *nima al-mudhakkir al-sibha.* Shawkani narrates it from Ali ibn Abi Talib as evidence for the usefulness of *dhikr*-beads in *Nayl al-awtar* (2:317) from Daylami's narration in *Musnad al-firdaws* with his chain, and Suyuti cites it in his *fatwa* on *dhikr*-beads in *al-Hawi li al-fatawi* (2:38).

[520] This *hadith* is found in Abu Dawud, Tirmidhi, Nisai, Ibn Maja, Ibn Hibban, and Hakim. Dhahabi declared it *sahih.*

[521] This *hadith* is found in Tirmidhi, Hakim, and Tabarani, and was confirmed as *sahih* by Suyuti.

Shawkani said:

The Prophet ﷺ justified the counting of *dhikr* on the fingers by the fact that the fingers will be questioned and will speak; that is, they will witness to that effect. It follows that counting *tasbih* on them, because of this, is better than using *dhikr* beads or pebbles. However, the two other *ahadith* (of Saad ibn Abi Waqqas ؓ and Safiyya bint Huyayy ؓ) indicate the permissibility of counting *tasbih* with date-stones and pebbles, and with *dhikr* beads, because there is no distinguishing factor among them in the Prophet's stipulation to the two women, and no disapproval of it. As for directing to what is better, this does not negate permissibility. There are reports to that effect.

It is related in Hilal al-Haffar's monograph, through Mutamar ibn Sulayman, from Abu Safiyya ؓ, the Prophet's freedman, that a mat would be spread for him (Abu Safiyya) and a basket made of palm leaves brought which was filled with pebbles with which he would make *tasbih* until mid-day. Then it would be taken away, and then brought back after he had prayed, and he would make *tasbih* again until evening. Imam Ahmad narrates it in *Kitab al-zuhd* (with his chain).

Ahmad also narrates from al-Qasim ibn Abd al-Rahman ؓ that Abu ad-Darda ؓ had a bag filled with date-stones and that whenever he prayed the noon prayer he would bring them out one by one and make *tasbih* on them until they were finished.

Ibn Saad in his *Tabaqat* narrates (with his chains) that Saad ibn Abi Waqqas ؓ counted *tasbih* on pebbles, and that Fatimah bint al-Husayn ibn Ali ibn Abi Talib ؓ said *tasbih* with a thread stringed with knots, and that Abu Hurayra ؓ made *tasbih* with a string of pebbles (*al-nawa al-majmu*).

Abd Allah, the son of Imam Ahmad, narrated in *Zawaid al-zuhd* that Abu Hurayra ؓ had a thread stringed with one thousand knots and that he would not sleep until he had counted *tasbih* on them.

Ad-Daylami narrates, in *Musnad al-firdaws* through Zainab bint Sulayman ibn Ali, and from Umm al-Hasan bint Jafar, from her father, from her grandfather, from Ali ؓ, and it is traced back to the Prophet ﷺ, *"What a good reminder are the* dhikr *beads!"*

Suyuti related reports with their chains in his monograph on the subject entitled *al-Minha fi al-sibha*, and it is part of his collected *fatwas*. He says towards the end of it, "It is not related from any one of the Predecessors (*salaf*) nor the later scholars (*khalaf*) that it is forbidden to count *tasbih* on the *sibha* (*dhikr* beads). On the contrary, most of them counted *tasbih* on it, and they did not consider it disliked."[522]

The Indian *hadith* scholar, Zakariyya al-Khandlawi, relates that Abu Hurayra ☙ said, "I recite *istighfar* (the formula for asking forgiveness) 12,000 times daily." He also relates that, according to Abu Hurayra's grandson, he had a piece of thread with 1,000 knots and would not go to sleep until he had said "Glory to God" (*subhanallah*) on all of these knots.[523] According to her grand-daughter, through Imam al-Husayn ☙, Fatimah ☙ also counted her *dhikr* on a thread with knots.

Mawlana Zakariyya continues:

It is well-known that many other Companions of the Prophet ☙ used beads in their private devotions, such as Saad ibn Abi Waqqas ☙ himself; Abu Safiyya, the slave of the Prophet ☙; Abu Saad ☙; Abu ad-Darda ☙; and Fatima ☙. Stringing, or not stringing, the beads together does not make any difference.

It is well established that counting *dhikr* is a *Sunnah* of the Prophet ☙. He himself advised his wives, Ali ☙, and Fatimah ☙ to count *tasbih*, *tahmid*, and *takbir* thirty-three times each before going to bed at night. Ibn Amr ☙ relates that he saw the Prophet ☙ count the times he said *"subhanallah"* on his right hand. This does not mean that it is not allowed to use the left also, as the Prophet ☙ simply said, "Count (the *dhikr*) on your fingers."

Imam Suyuti recounted, in one of his *fatwas*, the story of Ikrima, who asked his teacher, Umar al-Maliki, about *dhikr* beads.[524] Umar answered that he had also asked his teacher, Hasan al-Basri, about it and was told, "Something we have used at the beginning of the road we are not desirous to leave at the end. I love to remember God with my heart, my hand, and my tongue." Suyuti comments, "And how should it be otherwise, when the *dhikr* beads remind one of God, the Exalted, and a person seldom sees *dhikr*

---

[522] Shawkani, *Nayl al-awtar* (2:316-317).

[523] Zakariyya al-Khandlawi, *Hayat al-sahaba*.

[524] Suyuti, *al-Minha fi al-sibha* (The profit derived from using *dhikr*-beads).

beads except he remembers God, which is among the greatest of its benefits."

As for Albani's statements against *dhikr* beads, his rejection of the *hadith* "*What a good reminder are the* dhikr *beads!*"[525] and his astounding claim that whoever carries *dhikr* beads in his hand to remember God is misguided and innovating, let the reader be directed to their refutation in Mahmud Said's *Wusul al-tahani bi ithbat sunniyyat al-sibha wa al-radd ala al-albani* (The Alighting of Mutual Benefit, and the Confirmation That the *Dhikr* Beads Are a *Sunnah,* and the Refutation of Albani).

The spurious claim that *dhikr* beads come from Buddhism or Christianity is not supported by the scholars but may simply be dismissed as just one more of the scholar Ignaz Goldziher's dubious legacies to orientalist literature.

Weak Report on Collective *Dhikr* in Darimi's *Sunan*

The following weak narration is sometimes used by the uninformed in their attacks against collective *dhikr*:

Al-Darimi narrates the following from from al-Hakam ibn al-Mubarak, who narrates from Amr ibn Salima al-Hamadani:[526]

> *We sat by the door of Abd Allah ibn Masud ﷺ before the morning prayer, so that when he came out we would walk with him to the mosque. (One day) Abu Musa al-Ashari ﷺ came to us and said, "Has Abu Abd al-Rahman come out yet?" We replied, "No." So he sat down with us until he came out. When he came out, we all stood along with him, so Abu Musa said to him, "O Abu Abd al-Rahman! I have just seen something in the mosque which I considered wrong, but all praise is for God, I did not see anything except good in it." He inquired, "What is it?"*
>
> *Abu Musa replied, "If you live, you will see it. I saw in the mosque people sitting in circles awaiting the Prayer. In each circle they had pebbles in their hands and a man would say, 'Repeat allahu akbar a hundred times.' So they would repeat it a hundred times. Then he would say, 'Say la ilaha ill-Allah a hundred times.' So they would say it a hundred times. Then he would say, 'Say subhanallah a hundred times.' So they would say it a hundred times." Ibn*

---

[525] See Albani's *Silsila daifa* #83.

[526] Al-Darimi, *Muqaddima* of his *Sunan*.

> *Masud asked, "What did you say to them?" Abu Musa said, "I did not say anything to them. Instead I waited to hear your view on it." Ibn Masud replied, "Would that you had ordered them to count their evil deeds and assured them that their good deeds would not be lost!" Then we went along with him until he came to one of these circles whereby he stood and said, "What is this I see you doing?"*
>
> *They replied, "O Abu Abd al-Rahman! These are pebbles upon which we are counting takbir, tahlil and tasbih." He said, "Count your evil deeds instead. I assure you that none of your good deeds will be lost. Woe to you, O Ummah of Muhammad ﷺ, how quickly you go to destruction! Here are your Prophet's Companions available in abundance (mutawafirun). And there are his clothes which have not yet decayed and his bowl which is unbroken. By Him in Whose Hand is my soul! Either you are following a Religion that is better guided than the Religion of Muhammad ﷺ or you are opening a door of misguidance."*
>
> *They said, "O Abu Abd al-Rahman! By God, we only intend good!" He said, "How many are there who intend good but do not achieve it. Indeed, God's Messenger said to us, 'A people will recite the Quran but it will not pass beyond their throats.' By God! I do not know, but perhaps most of them are from among you." Then he left them. Amr ibn Salima said, "We saw most of those people fighting against us on the day of Nahrawan, on the side of the Khawarij."*

The chain of the above report is unacceptable because it includes the name of Amr ibn Yahya al-Hamadani, Amr ibn Salima's grandson, and he is considered *daif*, or "weak."[527] A single weak report can never overrule something that is established by many sound reports, as cited in relation to each of the issues discussed above.

Even if the report were not weak, it would not be enough to support the stance against collective gatherings of *dhikr*, against gathering for *dhikr* in a circle, against counting *dhikr* by the hundreds, or against using pebbles for counting *dhikr*. All the above shows that the report narrated by Darimi

---

[527] Ibn Main saw him and said, "his narrations are worth nothing." Ibn Kharrash said, "he is not accepted." Dhahabi listed him among those who are weak and whose *hadith* is not retained in *al-Duafa wa al-matrukin* (p. 212 #3229), *Mizan al-itidal* (3:293), and *al-Mughni fi al-duafa* (2:491). and al-Haythami declared him weak (*daif*) in *Majma al-zawaid,* chapter entitled *Bab al-ummal ala al-sadaqa*

can never be used to contest the lawfulness of gathering for *dhikr*, sitting in a *dhikr* circle, counting *dhikr*, or using pebbles to count *dhikr*; whoever says it does is clearly unaware of the *Sunnah* on this issue. If the *hadith* is authentic, then the key to Darimi's report lies in the context of the following passages:

- Abu Musa al-Ashari's ﷺ words: "I have just seen something in the mosque which I considered wrong, but I did not see anything except good in it."
- Ibn Masud's ﷺ words: "Here are your Prophet's Companions available in abundance."
- Ibn Masud's ﷺ words: "God's Messenger said to us, 'A people will recite the Quran but it will not pass beyond their throats.' By God! I do not know, but perhaps most of them are from among you."
- Amr ibn Salima's words, "We saw most of those people fighting against us on the day of Nahrawan, on the side of the Khawarij."

It is clear that Abu Musa's ﷺ reaction was mixed because, on the one hand, he disapproved of the people themselves, but not of their *dhikr*. The reason for the disapproval is left unsaid, while Ibn Masud alludes to it by blaming the people in question for their isolationist stance away from the Companions. This is confirmed by Ibn Masud's citing of one of the most famous *ahadith* concerning the Khawarij, or Separatists, about whom it is known that they considered themselves more pious than all other Muslims, and better than even the Companions. This is again confirmed, beyond the shadow of a doubt, by Amr ibn Salima's explicit identification of the people in question as allies of the Khawarij on the day of Nahrawan.

This demonstrates that Abu Musa's view and Ibn Masud's condemnation are directed against the fact that the people in question were Separatists, not that they were making *dhikr*. The shamefulness of separating oneself from the Companions is underlined by Ibn Masud's exclamation, "Here are your Prophet's Companions available in abundance." The *hadith* master Abu Zura al-Razi said, "At the time the Prophet's ﷺ soul was taken back, the Companions who had narrated from and/or heard him directly (including his tacit presence) numbered 114,000."[528]

---

[528] This is related by the *hadith* master Ibn Jamaa in his book *al-Manhal al-rawi fi mukhtasar ulum al-hadith al-nabawi* (The quenching spring: Abridged manual of the sciences of the prophetic *hadith*), 3rd ed., ed. Muhyiddin Abd al-Rahman *Ramadan* (Damascus: Dar al-fikr, 1406/1986) p. 113.

The Khawarij are from among the tribes of Banu Hanifa, Banu Tamim, and Wail in the Najd area of Eastern Arabia. They committed *baghi* (or rebellion) against Prince of the Believers, our master Ali ﵁, and opposed the larger group of Muslims. They declared both Ali ﵁ and Muawiya ﵁ disbelievers, and declared licit their blood and property as well as the blood and property of those who accompanied them. The Khawarij made their land a land of war and declared their own land an abode of faith.

They accepted from the Prophet's *Sunnah* only what agreed with their own doctrine, and drew evidence for their beliefs from seemingly ambiguous verses in the Quran. They were known to apply Quranic verses meant to refer to unbelievers to the believers, as predicted by the Prophet.[529] Ibn Abbas ﵄ debated them until four thousand returned to the truth. They were the first to separate from the Congregation of Muslims. The Prophet ﷺ referred to them as "The dogs of the people in Hell,"[530] and he gave the order to fight and kill them by saying, "They will pass through Islam like an arrow passes through its quarry. Wherever you meet them, kill them!"[531]

As a final note on the descendents of the Khawarij of our time, Imam Muhammad ibn Abidin (d. 1252/1836) said:

> The name of *Khawarij* is applied to those who part ways with Muslims and declare them disbelievers, as took place in our time with the followers of Ibn Abd al-Wahhab, who came out of Najd and attacked the Two Noble Sanctuaries (Makkah and Madina). They (Wahhabis) claimed to follow the Hanbali school, but their belief was such that, in their view, they alone are Muslims and everyone else is a *mushrik* (polytheist). Under this guise, they said that killing *Ahl al-Sunnah* and their scholars was permissible, until God, the Exalted, destroyed them in the year 1233/1818 at the hands of the Muslim army.[532]

Benefit of Invoking Blessings on the Prophet ﷺ

Sakhawi says Abd Allah ibn Amr ibn al-As ﵄ said that he heard the Prophet ﷺ say:

---

[529] See *Sahih Bukhari*, English ed. 9:50.

[530] A sound narration related through various chains by Ibn Majah, and Ahmad.

[531] *Sahih Bukhari* and *Sahih Muslim*.

[532] Imam Muhuammad ibn Abidin, *Hashiyat radd al-muhtar ala al-durr al-mukhtar* (3:309), Chapter entitled *Bab al-Bughat* (Chapter on Rebels).

> *When you hear the* muadhdhin, *repeat his words after him, then invoke blessings upon me. Whoever invokes blessings upon me once, God bestows blessings upon him ten times. Then ask God for the* wasila *to be granted to me. It is a position in Paradise that may not be granted to any but one of God's servants, and I dearly hope that I will be that servant. Whoever asks God the* wasila *for me, my intercession is guaranteed for him.*[533]

It has already been expounded that there is no such thing as invoking too much *salawat* on the Prophet ﷺ. Further evidence on this topic is mentioned here only by way of a reminder.

Abu Hurayra ؓ narrated that the Prophet ﷺ said:

> *Dust for the face of the one before whom I am mentioned, and he does not invoke blessings upon me.*[534]

Abu Hurayra ؓ also reported that the Prophet ﷺ said:

> *If people sit in an assembly in which they do not remember God nor invoke a blessing on the Prophet, it will be a cause of grief for them on the Day of Judgment.*[535]

The author of *Fath al-allam* said:

> This *hadith* proves that it is incumbent on one to remember God and invoke blessings on the Prophet ﷺ while sitting in an assembly, for whether we take the words "cause of grief" to mean torment of fire or any other chastisement, obviously a punishment is incurred only when an obligatory act is neglected, or a forbidden act is committed. Here it is both the remembrance of God and the invoking of blessings on His Prophet ﷺ that are apparently incumbent.

Ibn Rajab al-Hanbali said in his book on love of God and love of the Prophet ﷺ:

> Love for the Prophet ﷺ is on two levels: The first level is obligatory. This is the love that requires one to accept whatever the Prophet ﷺ brought from God and to receive it with love, pleasure, esteem, and

---

[533] Sakhawi, *al-Qawl al-badi* (p. 179), chapter on the *salawat* after *adhan*. He continues: "It is narrated by Muslim and the Four (Tirmidhi, Abu Dawud, Ibn Majah, Nasai) except Ibn Majah, and also by Bayhaqi, Ibn Zanjawayh, and others."

[534] A sound *hadith* narrated by Tirmidhi (*hasan gharib*) and al-Hakim.

[535] Narrated by Tirmidhi, who graded it *hasan*.

> submission, without seeking guidance from any other source whatsoever.
>
> The second level is superior. This type of love requires following his example in an excellent way and fulfilling the following of his *Sunnah* with respect to his behavior, manners, voluntary deeds, superogatory actions, eating, drinking, dressing, excellent behavior with his wives, and other aspects of his perfect manners and pure behavior. It also includes learning about his life and days. It also includes the heart trembling when mentioning him, saying prayers and blessings upon him often out of what resides in the heart of love for him, esteem for him, and respect for him. It also includes loving to listen to his words and preferring them over the words of the rest of creation. And one of the greatest aspects of this love is to follow him in his abstinence of this world, to suffice with little, and to desire and pine after the everlasting Hereafter.[536]

Specific Benefits of *Salawat*

Here again are the principal benefits obtained by invoking blessings on the Prophet ﷺ (*salawat*) as compiled by Hafiz as-Sakhawi in his book devoted to the topic:

> Among the rewards of one who performs *salawat* upon God's Messenger ﷺ are the following:
>
> - The *salawat*—blessing—of God, His angels, and His Prophet ﷺ on that person;
> - The expiation of his faults;
> - The purification of his works;
> - The exaltation of his rank;
> - The forgiveness of his sins;
> - The asking of forgiveness for him by his own *salat*;
> - The recording of rewards, the like of Mount Uhud, for him and his repayment in superabundant measure;
> - The comfort of his world and his hereafter if he devotes his entire *salat* to invoking blessings upon him;

---

536 Ibn Rajab al-Hanbali, *Istinshaq nasim al-uns min nafahat riyad al-quds* (Inhaling the Breeze of Intimacy from the Whiffs of the Gardens of Sanctity).

- The obliteration of more faults than that effected by the manumission of a slave;
- His deliverance from affliction because of it;
- The witnessing of the Prophet ﷺ himself to it;
- The guarantee of the Prophet's ﷺ intercession for him;
- God's pleasure, mercy, and safety from His anger;
- Admission under the shade of the Throne for him;
- Preponderance of his good deeds in the Balance;
- His admission to drink from the Prophet's ﷺ Pond;
- His safety from thirst and deliverance from the Fire;
- His ability to cross the Bridge swiftly;
- The sight of his seat in Paradise before he dies;
- The preponderance of his prayers over more than twenty military conquests;
- Its equivalency to giving alms to the needy;
- Its being *zakat* and purification for him;
- His wealth will increase because of its blessing;
- More than one hundred of his needs will be fulfilled through it;
- It constitutes worship;
- It is the most beloved of all deeds to God;
- It beautifies meetings;
- It cancels out poverty and material duress;
- It lets him expect and find goodness everywhere;
- It makes him the most deserving of goodness;
- He benefits from it as well as his children and theirs, as well as those to whom its reward is gifted in the register of his good deeds;
- It brings him near to God and to His Prophet ﷺ;
- It is a light that helps him against his enemies;
- It cleans his heart of hypocrisy and rust;
- It commands the love of people and the sight of the Prophet ﷺ in dreams;
- It forbids slander (*ghiba*) against him.

In summary, it is among the most blessed, most meritorious, most useful of deeds in religion and in the life of the world, and carries desirable rewards other than all this for those who are clever and eager to acquire the deeds that constitute treasures for them, and harvest the most flourishing and glowing of hopes. They do this by focusing on the deed that includes all these tremendous merits, noble qualities, manifold and all-encompassing benefits which are not found together in any other.[537]

Excerpts on the Remembrance of God

Abd al-Rahman al-Sufuri wrote in his book *Nuzhat al-majalis wa muntakhab al-nafais* (The Pleasant Gatherings and the Select Precious Matters):

God, the Exalted, said, *"Verily in the remembrance of God do hearts find rest!"* (13:28) If it is asked, how is the meaning of this verse reconciled with that of His saying, *"They only are the true believers whose hearts feel fear ("wajilat,"* to tremble or shake*) when God is mentioned"* (8:2); it is answered that in the latter, the purpose of God's mention is to bring to mind His greatness and the intensity of His vengeance against those who disobey Him. This verse was revealed at a time when the Companions had a disagreement concerning the spoils of the Battle of Badr. Therefore, the mention or the remembrance of what is fearsome became appropriate. As for the former verse, it concerns whoever God guided and who has turned to God with love. Therefore, the mention of God's mercy became appropriate.

The two meanings of fearsomeness and mercy are reunited in *Surat al-Zumar*:

God hath now revealed the fairest of statements, a Scripture consistent, wherein promises of reward are paired with threats of punishment, whereat doth creep the flesh of those who fear their Lord, so that ("thumma," and then*) their flesh and their hearts soften to God's reminder (or, to the celebration of God's praises; or, to God's remembrance; meaning, to God's mercy and generosity).* (39:23)

The Prophet ﷺ said:

He who remembers God much, God loves him. The night that I was enraptured to my Lord I passed by a man extinguished within the light of God's Throne. I asked, "Who is this, and is he an angel?" I was told "No," and

---

[537] al-Sakhawi, *al-Qawl al-badi fi al-salat ala al-habib al-shafi* (The Radiant Discourse Concerning the Invocation of Blessings on the Beloved Iintercessor). p. 98.

I asked again, "Is it a Prophet?" I was told "No," and I said, "Who then?" It was said, "This is a man who, while he was in the world, his tongue was constantly moist with the mention of God, and his heart was attached to the mosques."

On the authority of Muadh ibn Jabal ﷺ, the Prophet ﷺ said that God said:

No servant of Mine mentions Me in himself, except I mention him in an assembly of My angels, and he does not mention Me in an assembly, except I mention him in the Highest Company.

On the authority of Abu Hurayra ﷺ, who said that, while on the road to Makkah, the Prophet ﷺ passed on top of a mountain called Jumdan, at which time he said, *"Move on, for here is Jumdan which has overtaken the single-minded."* They said, "What are the single-minded (*mufarridun*)?" He said, *"The men and women who remember God abundantly"* (33:35).[538]

Tirmidhi stated:

It was said, "And what are the single-minded?" He replied, "Those who dote on the remembrance of God and are ridiculed because of it, whose burden the dhikr removes from them, so that they come to God fluttering!"

Al-Mundhiri said:

The single-minded and those who dote on the *dhikr* and are ridiculed for it; these are the ones set afire with the remembrance of God.[539]

The Prophet ﷺ said:

The one who mentions or remembers God among those who forget Him is like a green tree in the midst of dry ones.

The one who mentions or remembers God among those who forget Him, God shows him his seat in Paradise during his life.

The one who mentions or remembers God among those who forget Him is like the fighter behind those who run away.

The one who mentions or remembers God among those who forget Him, God looks at him with a look after which He will never punish him.

---

538 Muslim related it.

539 Al-Mundhiri, in *al-Targhib wa al-tarhib*

> *The one who mentions or remembers God among those who forget Him is like a light inside a dark house.*
>
> *The one who mentions or remembers God among those who forget Him, God forgives him his sins to the amount of every eloquent and dumb speaker (that is, animals and human beings).*
>
> *The one who mentions or remembers God in the marketplace will have light in every hair of his on the Day of Resurrection.*

The Sufis say *dhikr* has a beginning, which is a truthful application;[540] it has a middle, which is a light that strikes; it has an end, which is a piercing difficulty; it has a principle, which is purity; it has a branch, which is loyalty; it has a condition, which is presence; it has a carpet, which is righteous action; it has a peculiar characteristic, which is the Manifest Opening (cf. Quran 48:1).

Abu Saeed al-Kharraz said:

> When God desires to befriend a servant of His, He opens the door of *dhikr* for that servant. After the latter takes pleasure in *dhikr*, He opens the door of proximity for him. After that, He raises him to the meetings of intimacy, and after that, He makes him sit on a throne of Oneness.
>
> Then He removes the veils from him, and He makes him enter the abode of Singleness, and unveils Majesty and Sublimity to him. When the servant beholds Majesty and Sublimity, he remains without "he." He becomes extinguished, immune to the claims and pretensions of his ego, and protected for God's sake.[541]

Another seeker of Divine Truth said:

---

[540] Truthfulness should not be confused with sincerity, since it is possible to act with sincerity but not to reach truthfulness, as Nawawi explained in his commentary to the second of his "forty *ahadith*" (*ahadith* about *islam, iman,* and *ihsan*) entitled *Sharh al-arbain hadith*. Ibn al-Jawzi relates in *Sifat al-Safwa* (4:98) that Mansur said he heard Musa ibn Isa say he heard his uncle say: "I heard Aba Yazid (al-Bistami) say: 'If once I could utter purely *"la ilaha illallah"* (there is no god except God alone), I would not care about anything after that.'"

[541] T.J. Winter: Ahmad ibn Isa Abu Said al-Kharraz (d. 277/890-1) was an important Sufi who, according to Huwjiri, was "the first to explain the doctrine of annihilation (*fana*) and subsistence (*baqa*)." He was the close companion of Dhul-Nun, Bishr al-Hafi, and al-Sari al-Saqati, and was renowned for the emphasis he placed on *ishq*, the passionate love of Allah, and upon the scrupulous observance of the Law. Sources: Sulami, *Tabaqat al-Sufiyya* 223-228; Qushayri, *al-Risala* 1:161-162; Brockelmann, 1:646.

> *Dhikr* is the medicine ("*tiryaq*," literally treacle; antidote for poison) of the sinners, the familiarity of the estranged, the treasure of those who practice reliance, the repast of those who possess certitude, the adornment of those who are connected, the starting-point of knowers, the carpet of those brought near Him, and the intoxicant of lovers.

> The Prophet ﷺ also said:

> *Remembrance of God is firm knowledge of one's belief, immunity from hypocrisy, a fortress against Satan, and a guarded refuge from the Fire.* [542]

Ibn al-Salah was asked about the measure by which the servant is estimated to be among "*those who remember God much.*" (33:35) He said, "If he perseveres in the forms of *dhikr* inherited in the *Sunnah* morning and evening and in the various times and occasions, then he is of those who remember God much."

Moses ﷺ said, "O my Lord! Are You near, so that I may speak to You intimately, or are You far, so that I may call out to You?" God inspired to him, "I am sitting next to the one who remembers Me." He said, "O my Lord, we are sometimes in a state of major impurity, and we hold You in too high regard to dare remember You at that time." He replied, "Remember me in every state."[543]

Abd al-Rahim ibn al-Hasan al-Isnawi (al-Shafii) said in his *Alghaz* (Riddles):

> A man in a state of minor impurity is forbidden from certain forms of *dhikr*, as illustrated by the nullification of the act of worship incurred when entering such a state during the Friday sermon, because ritual purity is a condition for its validity.

On the *Dhikr* of Inanimate Objects

> *The seven heavens and the earth and all that is therein praise Him, and there is not a thing but sings His praise; but ye understand not their praise. Lo! He is ever Clement, Forgiving.* (17:44)

Ibrahim al-Nakhai said concerning God's saying, "*There is not a thing but sings His praise*" (17:44): "Everything praises Him, including the door

[542] Mentioned by al-Layth al-Samarqandi.

[543] Ghazali mentioned it in the *Ihya*.

when it squeaks."[544] It has also been said, "The verse is general, and it applies particularly to the one endowed with speech, as in God's saying, 'Everything was destroyed,' [545] whereas the houses of Ad were not destroyed, and in His saying concerning Sheba (Balqis), '*And she has been given from all things*' (27:23) whereas she had not been given anything from Solomon's (Sulayman's) ﷺ kingdom."

It was also said that the verse has a universal meaning, whereby the one endowed with speech glorifies God by word, while the silent one glorifies through his state. This is by virtue of his being in existence; he testifies to His Maker through having been made.

In Taj al-Din ibn al-Subki's *Tabaqat al-Shafiiyya al-kubra,* the interpretation favored by the Shafii *madhdhab* is that all things make glorification through actual utterance, because such a thing is not impossible and is indicated by many proof-texts. God, the Exalted, said:

> *We have placed the mountains under His dominion; they praise God at nightfall and at sunrise.* (38:18)

The mountains' glorification through actual utterance does not necessitate that we hear it. In *al-Wujuh al-musfira an ittisa al-maghfira* (The Faces Made Radiant by the Vastness of Mercy) is related the following commentary:

> It is more likely that they literally glorify, except that this phenomenon is hidden from the people and is not perceived except through the rupture of natural laws. The Companions heard the glorification of food and other objects placed before the Prophet ﷺ.

Concerning God's saying at the end of the verse, "*Lo! He is ever Clement, Forgiving*" (17:44), it applies to the state of those addressed by the verse in three ways. First, in the vast majority of cases, people are distracted from glorifying God, the Exalted—unlike the heavens, and the earth, and all that

---

544 T.J. Winter: I. ibn Yazid al-Nakhai was a devout and learned scholar of Kufa who opposed the writing of a*hadith* as an unjustified innovation. He studied under al-Hasan al-Basri and Anas ibn Malik, and taught Abu Hanifa, who may have been influenced by his extensive use of personal judgment (*ray*) in matters of jurisprudence. Sources: Ibn Hibban, *Mashahir ulama al-amsar* 101; M.M. Azami, *Studies in Early Hadith Literature* 65-66; Ibn al-Jazari, *Ghayat al-nihaya* 1:29.

545 "*Destroying all things by commandment of its Lord. And morning found them so that naught could be seen save their dwellings. Thus do we reward the guilty folk.*" (46:25)

is therein. These distracted ones become in need of clemency and forgiveness. Second, they do not understand the praise of all these objects, and this may be because they do not sufficiently contemplate and reflect upon them; they then become in need of clemency and forgiveness. Third, the fact that they do not hear the praises may cause them to feel contempt towards these objects and drive them to deny the rights of creation; they again become in need of clemency and forgiveness.

Without doubt he who beholds with full understanding the glorification of things in existence honors and magnifies them in respect to this glorification, even if the Lawgiver ordered him to disdain them in another respect.

The author of *al-Wujuh al-musfira* cited the following story:

> One of God's servants sought to perform the purification from defecation by using stones to clean himself. He took one stone, and God removed the veil from his hearing so that he was now able to hear the stone's praise. Out of shame he left it and took another one, but he heard that one praising God also. And every time he took another stone he heard it glorifying God. Seeing this, at last he turned to God so that He would veil from him their praise to enable him to purify himself. God then veiled him from hearing them. He proceeded to purify himself despite his knowledge that the stones were making *tasbih*, because the one who reported about their *tasbih* is the same Lawgiver who ordered to use them for purification. Therefore, in the concealment of *tasbih* there is a far-reaching wisdom.

This is true, and in Fakhr ad-Din al-Razi's *Tafsir* it is said that what the scholars have agreed upon is that whoever is not alive is not empowered with speech, and it has been firmly established that inanimate objects praise God through the medium of their state. And God knows best.

Six Benefits of Remembrance of God

1. THE RANKS OF *DHIKR*

One of the commentators of Quran said concerning God's saying, "*But among them are some who wrong themselves and among them are some who are lukewarm, and among them are some who outstrip others through good deeds, by*

God's leave" (35:32), that they are respectively the rememberer by tongue, the rememberer by heart, and the one who never forgets his Lord.

Ibn Ata Allah said:

> The one who utters the Word of Oneness needs three lights: the light of guidance, the light of sufficiency, and the light of Divine help. Whoever God graces with the first light, he is immune (*masum*) from associating a partner to God. Whoever God graces with the second light, he is immune from committing great sins and indecencies; and whoever God graces with the third light, he is protected (*mahfuz*) from the corrupt thoughts and motions that typify those given to heedless actions. The first light belongs to "the ones who wrong themselves," the second to "those that are lukewarm," and the third to "the ones who outstrip others through good deeds."[546]

Al-Wasiti was asked about the remembrance of God.[547] He said:

> It is the exiting from the battlefield of heedlessness into the outer space of direct vision (*mushahada*) on the mount of victory over fear and intensity of love.

One of the special attributes of the remembrance of God is that it has been placed in direct correspondence with God's own remembrance of us. God Mighty and Exalted said, "*Remember Me, and I shall remember you*"

---

[546] Nuh Keller, Victor Danner: Abu al-Fadl Ibn Ata Allah (d. 709/1309) of Alexandria, Egypt: One of the great Sufi imams and a Maliki jurist, author of the *Hikam* (Aphorisms), *Miftah al-falah* (The Key to Success), *al-Qasd al-mujarrad fi marifat al-ism al-mufrad* (The Pure Goal Concerning Knowledge of the Unique Name), *Taj al-arus al-hawi li tadhhib al-nufus* (The Bride's Crown Containing the Discipline of Souls), *Unwan al-tawfiq fi adab al-tariq* (The Sign of Success Concerning the Discipline of the Path), the biographical *al-Lataif fi manaqib Abi al-Abbas al-Mursi wa shaykhihi Abi al-Hassan* (The Subtle Blessings in the Saintly Lives of Abu al-Abbas al-Mursi and His Master Abu al-Hasan), and others, five of which were transmitted with their chains by the *hadith* master and historian al-Sakhawi (d. 902/1497) to the Shadhili commentator Ahmad Zarruq (d. 899/1493). Ibn Ata Allah was the student of Abu al-Abbas al-Mursi (d. 686/1288), the second successor of Imam Abu al-Hasan al-Shadhili, and the shaykh of the Shafii imam Taqi al-Din al-Subki. He related from al-Shadhili the following saying: "This path is not monasticism, eating barley and bran, or the garrulousness of affectation, but rather perseverance in the divine commands and certainty in the divine guidance." Some sources: al-Zirikly, *al-Alam* 1:221; Asqalani, *al-Durar al-kamina* 1:273; Subki, *Tabaqat al-shafiiyya* 9:23.

[547] T.J. Winter: Muhammad ibn Musa al-Wasiti (d. 320/932): A Sufi who associated with al-Junayd and al-Nuri in Baghdad and who later moved to Merv where he died. He was also an authority on *fiqh*. Sources: Qushayri, *Risala* 1:174; Sulami, *Tabaqat* 302-307.

(2:152). Musa said, peace be upon him, "O my Lord, where do you dwell?" He replied, "In the heart of my believing servant."[548] The meaning of this is the heart's rest brought about by His remembrance.

Muhammad ibn al-Hanafiyya ؓ said:

Verily the angels lower their gaze in the presence of the rememberer of God, just as the people lower their gaze before lightning.[549]

2. REMITTANCE OF SINS THROUGH *DHIKR*

It is related that a servant of God will join the gatherings of *dhikr* with sins the like of mountains and then rise and leave one such gathering with nothing left of them to his name. This is why the Prophet ﷺ called it one of the groves of Paradise when he said, "If you pass by the groves of Paradise, be sure to graze in them," and someone said, "What are the groves of Paradise?" to which he replied, "The circles of *dhikr*."

Aata ؓ said:

Whoever sits in a gathering in which God is remembered, God will remit for him ten evil gatherings of his.

Abu Yazid al-Bistami, "I have entrusted you with a secret for which you shall render Me an account under the Tree of Bliss (*shajarat tuba*)." He said, "We are under that tree as long as we remain in the remembrance of God."

---

[548] Ibn Majah narrates from Abu Anbasa, and Tabarani from Abu Utba that the Prophet ﷺ said: "God has vessels from among the people of the earth *(lillahi aniyatun min ahli al-ard)*, and the vessels of your Lord are the hearts of His righteous servants, and the most beloved of those to Him are the softest and the most sensitive." Al-Jarrahi said in *Kashf al-khafa* that this was the basis of the saying attributed to the Prophet ﷺ: "The heart of the believer is the house of God" al-Qari said that the latter, though not a saying of the Prophet ﷺ, was correct in meaning. Imam Ahmad narrates in his *Kitab al-zuhd* from Wahb ibn Munabbih: God opened the heavens to Ezekiel ؑ until he beheld the very Throne, whereupon he said: "Glory to Thee, what greatness is Thine, O my Lord!" God said: "Verily the heavens and the earth are unable to encompass Me, and the devoted, soft heart of My faithful servant is able to encompass Me." Imam Ghazali mentioned it in his *Ihya Ulum al-din*.

[549] Abu al-Qasim Muhammad ibn Ali ibn Abi Talib ؓ, named ibn al-Hanafiyya: A saintly son of Sayyidina Ali ؓ. He took *hadith* from him and from several other Companions including Jabir ibn Abd Allah ؓ, the last of the Companions who died in Madina. Sources: Ibn Adi, *al-Kamil* 2:113b; Ibn Hajar, *Tahdhib al-tahdhib* 9:354 (M.M. Azami). The Prophet ﷺ gave Ali ؓ special permission to name him both Abu al-Qasim and Muhammad, which he otherwise forbade: Tirmidhi (#2846) and Abu Dawud (*Adab* #4967).

It is related on Ali's ﷺ authority that God manifests Himself (*yatajalla*) to the rememberers during *dhikr* and the recitation of Quran.

The Prophet ﷺ said:

No group gathers and remembers God seeking nothing other than Him except a caller from Heaven calls out to them: Arise forgiven, for your bad deeds have been turned into good ones!

Abu ad-Darda ﷺ said:

The Prophet ﷺ said, "God verily will raise on the Day of Resurrection people bearing light in their faces, carried aloft on pulpits of pearl, whom the people will envy. They are neither prophets nor martyrs." Upon hearing this a Bedouin Arab fell to his knees and said, "Show them to us (ajlihim), O Prophet of God!;" that is, "describe them for us." He replied, "They are those who love one another for God's sake alone. They come from many different tribes, countries, and cities. They gather together for the remembrance of God the Exalted, remembering Him."

Someone said concerning God's saying with reference to Solomon ﷺ, *"Verily, I will punish him with hard punishment"* (27:21) that it means, "Verily I shall drive him far from the gatherings of *dhikr*." Al-Junayd concerning God's saying, *"And (He is the One) Who causeth me to die, then giveth me life again"* (26:81), said that this means, "He causes me to die with heedlessness (of Him), then He causes me to live with remembrance (of Him)." Al-Hasan al-Basri said, "No people sit remembering God, the Exalted, with one of the people of Paradise in their midst except God grants him to intercede for all of them."

3. *DHIKR* OF THE FROGS

The Prophet David (Dawud) ﷺ said, "I shall praise God with a kind of praise that none among his creatures ever used before." Thereupon a frog called out to him, "Do you pride yourself before God for your praise, while for seventy years my tongue has been moist from remembering Him, and I have eaten nothing in the past ten nights because I kept busy uttering two words?" David ﷺ said, "What are these two words?" The frog replied, "O Praiser of Thyself with every tongue, O Remembered One in every place!"

It is related in *Nuzhat al-nufus wa al-afkar* (The Recreation of Minds and Thoughts) that an angel once said to David ﷺ, "O David, understand what the frog is saying!" whereupon he heard it saying, "Glory and praise to You to the farthest boundary of Your knowledge!" David ﷺ said, "By the One Who made me a prophet, verily I shall sing my Lord's praise in this way." The commentators have said that the frogs' words were: "Glory to the King, the Holy One!" *(subhan al-malik al-quddus)* while al-Baghawi has, "Glory to my Lord Most Holy!" *(subhana rabbi al-quddus)*, and Ali ﷺ uses the words, "Glory to the One Who is worshipped in the abysses of the sea!"

4. *DHIKR* OF THE PROPHET JONAH

Ali ﷺ said:

In the time of Jonah (Yunus) ﷺ, there was a frog which had lived past the age of 4,000 years. It never rested from glorifying God. One day it said, "O my Lord, no one glorifies You like I do!" Jonah ﷺ said, "O my Lord, I say what it says!" and he said, "Glory to You by the number of times each of your creatures says 'Glory to You,' and glory to You by the number of times each of Your creatures does not say 'Glory to You,' and glory to You according to the expanse of Your knowledge, and the light of Your countenance, and the adornment of Your throne, and the reach of Your words!"

5. LENGTHENING THE PRONUNCIATION OF *LA ILAHA ILL-ALLAH*

Ibn Abbas and his father ؄, narrated the Prophet ﷺ said:

The day God created the heavens and the earth He created an angel and ordered him to say, "There is no god except God alone" (la ilaha ill-Allah). The angel lengthens his delivery as he utters it and will not rest from this until the Trumpet is blown.

One of the Companions said that whoever says, "No god except God" and lengthens his pronunciation intending thereby to magnify God, God will remit 4,000 grave sins for him, and if he did not commit 4,000, God will remit the difference for his family and neighbors. It is related in the *hadith*, "Whoever says 'No god except God' and lengthens his pronunciation intending thereby to magnify God, 4,000 of his sins are struck thereby from the register of his sins." Hence it is praiseworthy to lengthen one's pronunciation upon uttering it, as Nawawi said.

The Prophet ﷺ also said:

Whoever lengthens his pronunciation upon saying "No god except God," God will make him dwell in Paradise in the Abode of Majesty by which he has named Himself when He said: "There remaineth but the countenance of thy Lord of Might and Glory" (55:27), and God will grant him to behold His Gracious Countenance.

Anas ibn Malik ﷺ narrated from the Prophet ﷺ:

O human beings! Whoever says "No god except God" in astonishment at something, God creates from each letter of his utterance a tree with as many leaves as the days of this world, each leaf asking forgiveness for him and praising God on his behalf until the Day of Judgment . . .

It has been related that this phrase has on the side of Iblis (Satan) the effect that a gangrenous sore would have on the side of a human being. Qadi Iyad relates in the *Shifa* from Ibn Abbas ﷺ that written on the door of Paradise is the inscription, "There is no god but God alone, Muhammad is the Messenger of God; Whoever says this, I shall not punish him." [550]

The following account is part of the explanation of God's saying, "*And speak (O Moses and Aaron) unto him (Pharaoh) a gentle word*" (20:44). Moses ﷺ said, "O Lord, how can a word be gentle?" God replied, "Say to him, 'Would you like a good compromise? You have followed your own self for four hundred and fifty years; follow our intent but for one year, and God will forgive you all your sins. If not one year, then one month; if not, one week; if not, one single day; if not, one single hour. If you do not (wish to humor us) for all of an hour, then say in a single breath, "There is no god but God" so that I may bring peace to you.'"

After Moses ﷺ conveyed the message, Pharaoh gathered his armies and said to them, "*I am your Most High Lord!*" (79:24) At this the heavens and the earth shook and pleaded before God the Glorious and Exalted that Pharaoh be put to death. God said, "*He is like the dog: only the stick is good for him. O Moses, cast your staff.*" (cf., 7:117, 27:10, 28:31) Moses ﷺ cast his staff

---

[550] Abu al-Fadl Iyad ibn Musa al-Yahsubi al-Maliki of Andalusia and Fes, Morocco. The imam of his time in the sciences of *hadith*, and a scholar of *tafsir*, *fiqh*, Arabic grammar and language, and Arab genealogy. He wrote many books including a commentary on the *Sahih* of Muslim which Nawawi used in his own great commentary. Ibn Farhun in *Dibaj al-dhahab* says of his book *al-Shifa*: "No one disputes the fact that it is totally unique nor denies him the honor of being the first to compose such a book. Everyone relies on it and writes about its usefulness and encourages others to read and study it. Copies of it have spread East and West." (Qadi Iyad, *Muhammad Messenger of Allah: Al-shifa of Qadi Iyad*, trans. Aisha Abdarrahman Bewley (Granada, Spain: Madinah Press, 1991) p. 511.

(which became a huge snake or dragon) and the magicians of Pharaoh's court immediately submitted. Pharaoh fled to his bedchamber. Moses ﷺ said, "If you do not come out, I shall order it to enter where you are." Pharaoh said, "Give me a little respite." Moses ﷺ answered, "I have no permission to respite you." But God, the Exalted, inspired to him, "Respite him, for verily I am the Clement, I do not hasten to punish."

Pharaoh began to relieve himself forty times a day while previously he would relieve himself only once every forty days. Moses ﷺ gave him a respite. When the day came, Pharaoh exceeded his bounds and rebelled. God therefore *"seized him and made him an example for the afterlife and the former"* (79:25); that is, He punished him with drowning because of his former word ("I am your Most High Lord"), and He punished him with Hell because he said, *"I know not that ye have a god other than me."* (28:38) Ibn Abbas ؓ said, "This is the former word, while the other came later, and between them lay forty years."

It is mentioned in the book *Zumrat al-ulum wa zuhrat al-nujum* (The Array of the Sciences and the Brightness of Stars) that the Prophet ﷺ said:

> Gabriel told me, "I stood in wait before God at the time Pharaoh said: 'And what is the Lord of the Worlds?' (26:23) whereupon I outstretched two of my wings to smite him with punishment, but God, the Exalted, said, 'Wait, O Gabriel! He hastens to punish who fears the lapse of time.'"

It was also mentioned in that book that when Pharaoh said, *"I am your Lord the Most High"* (79:24) Gabriel wanted to shake the earth from under his feet, but when he sought permission from his Lord, the Exalted, He did not give it to him and ordered him to ignore Pharaoh instead.

Al-Alai said in his explanation of the *surah* of the Story (*al-qasas*) that Iblis entered Pharaoh's presence as the latter was in the bath and said, "O Pharaoh, I enticed you with every transgression, but I never told you to claim absolute Lordship!" Then he gave him forty lashes and left him in anger. Pharaoh said to him, "O Iblis, should I take back this claim?" He replied, "It would not be right for you to take it back after making it."[551]

A group of the disbelievers of Quraysh gathered among the Pharaoh of their community, Abu Jahl, at Abu Talib's house during the latter's last illness. Abu Jahl said to him, "You know what has taken place between us

---

[551] Author of a massive commentary on Bukhari's *"Sahih"* entitled *Umdat al-Qari*.

and your brother's son. Therefore obtain what is rightfully ours from him and what is rightfully his from us before you die." Abu Talib called the Prophet ﷺ and said, "O my nephew, these are the nobility of your people, so leave them be, and they shall leave you be." He replied, "Do they agree to obey me if I ask them to say but one word?" Abu Jahl said, "Nay, we shall obey you if you ask us to say ten!" The Prophet ﷺ then said, "Say, *La ilaha ill-Allah*," whereupon they said, "Are you asking us to reduce all our gods to only one? Truly you are asking us for the strangest thing!" and they dispersed. Abu Talib said, "O Muhammad, you have asked them for nothing excessive." That is, "You have not asked them for anything difficult."

Concerning God's saying, "*Judge aright between us and be not unjust (lit. do not exceed the proper bounds)*" (38:22); that is, "Do not swerve in your judgment," the Prophet ﷺ hoped that his uncle would profess Islam, so he said to him, "Say it (the phrase: There is no god but God alone), so that I will be permitted to intercede for you on the Day of the Rising." Abu Talib replied, "Were it not that people—that is, the Quraysh—might think that I said it out of fear (of death), indeed I would say it."

Al-Razi said in his explanation of the *surah* of the Cattle (al-Anam):

> Abu Talib said, "Ask me to say other than this because your people hate it." The Prophet ﷺ replied, "I will never say other than this even if they were to dislodge the sun from its place and put it in my hand." They said, "Then stop cursing our gods, otherwise we will curse you and Him Who orders you to do this," whereupon God's saying was revealed, "*Revile not those unto whom they pray beside God lest they wrongfully revile God through ignorance.*" (6:108)

If it is said, "To curse the idols is among the most meritorious acts of obedience to God; why then did God forbid it?" The answer is, God forbade it because cursing them might lead to the gravest of transgressions—exalted is God far above the saying of wrong-doers—namely cursing God and His Messenger ﷺ, and it is an obligation to take precautions against it.

6. GOD'S SIMILES FOR THE "PHRASE OF ONENESS"

God compared the Phrase of Declaring Oneness *(kalimat al-tawhid)* to the following:

- Water, because water cleanses; similarly, this phrase cleanses from sins;
- Soil, because the soil gives forth much in exchange for a single seed; similarly, this phrase multiplies its return;
- Fire, because fire burns, and this phrase burns sins;
- The Sun, because the latter sheds light on the worlds, and this phrase illumines even the grave;
- The Moon, because it dispels the darkness of night, and this phrase sheds light with the same certainty;
- Stars, because they are guides for travelers, and this phrase is a guide for the people of misguidance to follow the right way;
- Date palms, when He said, "*A goodly tree, its root set firm, its branches reaching into heaven, giving its fruit at every season by permission of its Lord*" (14:24-25);
- The date palm does not grow in every land; similarly, this phrase does not grow in every heart;
- The date palm is the tallest fruit tree; similarly, the root of this phrase is in the heart and the top of its branches are under the Throne;
- The value of the fruit does not diminish because of the pit; similarly, the value of the believer does not diminish despite the disobedience lodged between himself and God the Exalted; and,
- The bottom of the date palm is thorns while its top is moist dates; similarly, the initial stages of this phrase are duties, and whoever fulfills them reaches the fruit which is to behold God the Exalted.

The Phrase of Oneness is the key to the Garden of Paradise: "Every key must have teeth,"[552] and its teeth are to forsake all that is forbidden and do what is ordained. God, the Exalted, says, "*Therefore know that there is no god but God alone*" (47:19) and the Prophet ﷺ said, "*Whoever said, 'There is no god but God alone,' taking care that it is unalloyed (*mukhlisan bihi*) and from the heart, enters Paradise.*" It was asked in what being-unalloyed (*ikhlas*) consisted. He said, *"In barring one from what God, the Exalted, has declared forbidden."*

---

[552] A saying by Wahb ibn Munabbih, reported by *Bukhari* in the title of the first chapter of the Book of Funeral Prayers *(Janaiz)*.

The Prophet ﷺ also said:

O Abu Hurayra! Every good deed on your part shall be weighed on the Day of Rising except the Witnessing that there is no god but God alone, for verily it can never be placed in the Balance.

Guidebook of the Saints of the Golden Chain

The Naqshbandi Way of *Dhikr*

Among the readers of this book may be some Sufi aspirants who have been practicing one or several of the other Sufi paths or their branches other than the Naqshbandi Path. If you are one of these people you may be wondering what difference there is between the Naqshbandi and the other Sufi ways.

It is axiomatic that all Sufi paths lead to the Divine Presence. The Prophet ﷺ said, *"The ways to God are as numerous as the breaths of human beings."* The differences lie mostly in the realm of style and taste, and reflect the need to accommodate the variety of types among the aspirants. Differences also stem from the unique individualities of the great luminaries who imprinted each of the Sufi orders—may God be pleased with all of them!

There are also some differences of approach. Most Sufi paths offer aspirants a gradual unveiling of the heart's eye, accomplished through the practice of *dhikr*, the remembrance of God. This spiritual exercise may contain repetition of various of God's Holy Names. Some forms of *dhikr* involve practices designed to break the spell of mundane consciousness and propel the practitioner into a state of altered awareness. Such practices may include repetition of many thousands of holy phrases, sometimes connecting with breathing exercises and often with physical movements. Without a doubt, through the steadfast and dedicated practice of these methods, the aspirant may experience spiritual states and attain stations unimaginable in a normal state of consciousness. The aspirant may feel himself to be flying towards the heavenly goals, beholding the wonders of the mysterious and hidden aspects of creation.

If your eyes have been thus opened, and if you are greatly enamored of the wide vistas you have beheld, then be warned. Should you embark upon the Naqshbandi Path, your colorful plumage will be clipped and replaced with the humble cloak of obscurity. For the main difference between the Naqshbandi Way and others is that, while they are giving, we are taking away. Everything must go, even your separate existence. First you will be without anything, then you will be nothing. Only those who are prepared to take such a step can be real Naqshbandi disciples. As long as a drop is falling from the heavens, it may be called a drop. When it falls into the ocean, it is no longer a drop; it is the ocean.

If anyone is interested in spiritual stations and powers, he may attain them through following any of the forty Sufi paths, as these ways are quite efficacious. Through the recitation of the most beautiful Names of God everyone receives bountifully in accordance with his intention. In the end, however, the sincere seeker will be struck with remorse if he becomes fixated at the stage of stations and states. One day, he will perceive how he has fallen victim to distraction and say: "O my Lord, I have been wasting myself and my efforts on something other than You."

Should a seeker's life end while he is in those states, he will regret that they distracted him from seeking the Divine Countenance of his Lord. Therefore, grandshaykhs have been ordered to strip their followers of their spiritual adornments, so that they may be presented to their Lord in perfect lowliness: "This is your servant, oh our Lord; accept him. He is lost to himself and exists only for You." This is their top priority, and helping their followers attain such a reality is their duty.

It is understood by all orders that strange and enchanting experiences are the scenery of the journey, not the goal. The goal is to reach the Divine Presence by the attraction of the Beloved Himself. The Holy Prophet Muhammad ﷺ is the guide and example. On His miraculous Night Journey, in which he was conducted by the angel Gabriel عليه السلام first from Makkah to Jerusalem and then up to the seven heavens and into the Divine Presence, he passed through the whole universe. God Almighty informs us in the Holy Quran that the Prophet's ﷺ vision *"neither swerved nor wavered"* (53:2). In other words, he looked and beheld but never let those sights distract him from ascending towards his most exalted destination. The Holy Prophet ﷺ was able to behold those sights without being distracted because his heart was only for his Lord. He is the Beloved of God. As for ourselves, we are vulnerable and weak-willed. Those experiences and attainments may accord with our ego's desires, whereas annihilation is never an attractive proposition for the ego.

Therefore, in order to provide maximum protection, the Naqshbandi masters take a different approach to the unveiling of the heart's eye. There are 70,000 veils between us and the station of the Prophet ﷺ. A Naqshbandi master rends these veils in descending order, starting with those closest to the Divine Presence and then successively downwards towards the level of the disciple. This process continues throughout the training of the disciple until there is but one veil, the veil of humanity, restraining the disciple's vision from contemplation of the Divine Reality. In order to protect the disciple from attraction to something other than his Lord, however, the shaykh does not rend that last veil until the disciple reaches the highest state of perfection or until his final seven breaths on his deathbed.

If the veils are removed from the bottom up by means of mystical practices, the disciple beholds a succession of new panoramas. That very vision may keep him from progressing. Those who attain such stations during this life may discover that they have become powerful and famous among people. This is also a danger. Power and recognition are conditions conducive to worldliness. The ego will never neglect such an opportunity to demand its share of the excitement and admiration, and by doing so taint the whole process of spiritual endeavor.

The Sufi aspirant must seek his Lord, not fame. Look at history's most renowned holy woman, the Virgin Mary ﷺ, who once prayed, *"Would that I had been a thing forgotten and out of sight!"* (19:23). She has taught all humanity to seek only obscurity in the sight of the world and not to look for recognition. The striving for power and fame is a heavy burden. The Sufi seeks rather to be forgotten in the ocean of Unity of God Almighty.

The Naqshbandi Sufi shaykhs say that whoever works according to the following series of recommendations, and acts on it, will attain the exalted stations, especially the station of nearness to God, Who is Powerful and Sublime, on the Day of Resurrection. The faithful and diligent application of these practices is certain to temper the influence of the lower elements which exist in every human being: the ego, worldliness, vain desires, and Satan. A person who manages to keep these principles of the Naqshbandi Order will achieve the light of his shaykh, who will lift him to the Presence of the supreme teacher, the Prophet ﷺ, who in his turn, will lift him up to the station of annihilation in God.

God, Almighty and Exalted, taught Prophet Muhammad ﷺ good manners, for which reason the Holy Prophet ﷺ said, *"My Lord taught me good manners and perfected His teaching."* The best of manners is to keep the orders of God, and the seeker must follow the example of the Prophet ﷺ in keeping the obligations of His Lord and in following the spiritual path. He must be persistent in keeping to the conduct of the Order, until he attains the knowledge of the Divine Law and the Way.

The beginner must always begin at the beginning. He should recognize the difference between the Divine Law and the Way. The Divine Law is a reality that is obligatory for every believing man and woman. Concretely speaking, the Divine Law consists of practicing that which God has ordered and avoiding that which He has forbidden. The believer relies on guides to indicate clearly to him what to discard and what to follow. The Quran and *Sunnah* are the foundation of all guidance. The schools of the Divine Law, the writing of the scholars, and their living inheritors relay and explain the guidance. Whoever keeps to this guidance will be on the Straight Path.

The Way is the firm intention of the Divine Law. It does not exist outside the Divine Law. It is the resolution to follow the *Sunnah* of the Prophet ﷺ as completely as possible in every aspect, both external and internal, exposed and hidden, exoteric and esoteric, physical and spiritual. To follow the Way, the disciple puts his trust in the judgment of the shaykh for the correct understanding and application of the guidance of the Quran and the *Sunnah*. The disciple places his hand in the hand of an authorized, living shaykh and must proceed as indicated by him. He must be ready at all times to receive the orders of his shaykh, just as the Prophet ﷺ awaited the coming of Gabriel عليه السلام with revelation from God, Almighty and Exalted. In the same way, he must follow the shaykh's orders, carrying them out to the letter. He must have the "conduct of anticipation," which means that he must constantly await the orders of his guide. He must adopt the attitude of a hunter to its prey, being oblivious to all other directions. His sight, hearing, existence, and thoughts should be ready to receive orders, and he should always be ready to carry out some new order. Such a person will be a master of the proper conduct of the Exalted Naqshbandi Order, and this manifestation will become apparent in him.

The disciple should keep to his daily *dhikr* and should obey the order of his shaykh without veering to the right or to the left. Grandshaykh, Shaykh Abd Allah ad-Daghestani, said, "My tongue is the tongue of the secret of the Divine Law and of the secret of the Quran." Then he asked a question saying, "Who are the bearers and protectors of the Quran?" and answered himself: "The bearers and protectors of the Quran are the ones who set foot in all the exalted stations and know them with true understanding. And is it not right, my children, that I should indicate to you that you should follow this path so that you may reach and discover these stations?"

Shaykh Abd Allah ad-Daghestani continued saying, "Whoever receives the keys to the five stations: heart, secret, secret of the secret, hidden, and most hidden is the one who takes care to conduct himself properly and perform the spiritual practices in their correct manner. This enables him to reach the station of Bayazid al-Bistami, in which he said, "I am also the Real (*al-Haqq*)." Whoever wishes to enter the station of the two Attributes of the Real, Almighty and Exalted, the Attribute of Beauty and that of Majesty, must follow this Way.

The Spiritual Practices

The spiritual practices of seekers are of three kinds: for Initiates, for the Prepared, and for the People of Determination.[553]

Daily Spiritual Practices for Initiates

ADAB				ادب
Practice	Dhikr	Arabic	Meaning	Repeat
Bear witness - shahāda	ash-hadu an lā ilāha ill-Allāh wa ash-hadu anna Muḥammadan ʻabduhū wa rasūluh	أَشْهَدُ أَنْ لا إله إلا الله وأَشْهَدُ أَنَّ مُحَمَّدًا عَبْدُهُ ورَسُولُهُ	I testify that there is no god but God, and I testify that Muhammad is the Servant and Messenger of God.	3
Seek forgiveness – istighfār	Astaghfirullāh	أستغفر الله	God forgive me.	70
Seek blessings	Sūratu 'l-Fātiḥa	الفاتحة الشريفة		1
	Āman ar-rasūlu (Quran 2:285-6)	See Page 726		1
	Sūratu 'l-Ikhlāṣ	سورة الإخلاص		11
	Sūratu 'l-Inshirāḥ	سورة الانشراح		7
	Sūratu 'l-Falaq	سورة الفلق		1

553 To facilitate proper pronunciation for non-Arab speakers, text in the following sections are rendered in a special diacritical font using the system of Arabic transliteration adopted by the Library of Congress in the United States.

	Sūratu 'n-Nās	سورة الناس		1
kalimah	Lā ilāha illa-llāh	لا إله إلا الله		9
	Lā ilāha illa-llāh Muḥammadun Rasūl Allāh	لا إله إلا الله مُحَمَّدًا رَسُول الله	There is no god but God, and Muhammad is the Servant and Messenger of God.	1
Prayers on the Prophet - ṣalawāt	Allāhumma ṣalli 'alā Muḥammadin wa 'alā āli Muḥammadin wa sallim	اللهمَّ صلِّ على مُحَمَّد وعلى آل مُحَمَّد وسلِّم	O God send blessings and peace upon Muhammad and the family of Muhammad.	10
Gift the reward - Ihdā	See page 729	إهداء		1
Recitation	Sūratu 'l-Fātiḥa	الفاتحة الشريفة		1
WIRD				ورد
Practice	Dhikr	Arabic	Meaning	Repeat
Remember God- dhikr	Allāh, Allāh	ذكرُ الجلالة: الله الله الله	God, God.	1500
Prayers on the Prophet- ṣalawāt	Allāhumma ṣalli 'alā Muḥammadin wa 'alā āli Muḥammadin wa sallim	اللهمَّ صلِّ على مُحَمَّد وعلى آل مُحَمَّد وسلِّم	O God send blessings and peace upon Muhammad and the family of Muhammad.	100
Recitation of Qur'ān	One juz' (1/30) of the Qur'ān -or- Sūratu 'l-Ikhlāṣ	جزء من القرآن او اخلاص الشريفة		1 -or- 100

Prayers on the Prophet-Ṣalawāt	One chapter of Dalā'il al-Khayrāt -or- Allāhumma ṣalli 'alā Muḥammadin wa 'alā āli Muḥammadin wa sallim	دلائل الخيرات او اللهمّ صل على مُحَمّد وعلى آل مُحَمّد وسلم	O God send blessings and peace upon Muhammad and the family of Muhammad	1 -or- 100

Spiritual Practices for the Prepared

The *adab* and *wird* for the Prepared (*musta'id*) seeker is identical to that of the Initiate (*muḥib*), with the following additions:

Increase the number of repetitions of God's name from 1,500 to 2,500 by tongue and add another 2,500 by heart, meditating upon it.

Increase the number of *ṣalawāt* from 100 to 300 on all days except Monday, Thursday, and Friday when it is done 500 times.

Spiritual Practices for People of Determination

The *adab* and *wird* for the People of Determination are similar to that of the Prepared (*musta'id*), with the following additions:

❖ *Sayyid aṣ-ṣalawāt* (chief of the Prayers on the Prophet) is recited before the *Ihdā* (see page 729).
❖ After the *Sūratu 'l-Fātiḥa* of the *Ihdā,* the seeker repeats *Allāh Hū Allāh Hū Allāh Hū Ḥaqq* three times, imagining himself between the Hands of his Lord.
❖ There is an increase in the number of repetitions of God's name from 2,500 to 5,000 each by tongue and by heart, and an increase in the number of *ṣalawāt* from 300 to 1,000 on all days except Monday, Thursday, and Friday, when it is done 2,000 times.

Notes to the Spiritual Practices

Prayers

The essence of the practices of the Naqshbandī shaykhs is built on the pillar (*rukn*) of prayer (*ṣalāḥ*) and on remembrance of God (*dhikrullāh*). For those desiring high stations and distinguished ranks, the observance of prayer is the key. The seekers must strive to imitate their shaykhs in the observance of not only the obligatory prayers, but the supererogatory *sunan* and *nawāfil* prayers that the shaykhs maintain as a constant daily practices. You will find the following practices are based around the five obligatory prayers, in addition to the night vigil, which consists of *ṣalātu 'n-najāt, Ṣalātu 'sh-shukr, Ṣalātu 't-tasbīh,* and *ṣalātu 't-tahajjud.*

Thus, it is incumbent on the seeker—before attempting the large number of voluntary forms of prayer described in this book—to learn and practice the fundamental principles of the prescribed prayers (*Ṣalāt*) correctly, based on the prescription of a recognized school (*madhhab*) of Islamic jurisprudence (*fiqh*). These include purification from greater or lesser impurities (*ṭahārah*) consisting of the greater ablution (*ghusl*) or the lesser (*wuḍu*); proper intention (*nīyyat*); facing the *qiblah* determined according to the principles of the madhhab; and, where possible, praying in congregation. Additionally, the integrals of the prayers should be observed correctly, including the proper movements, for the Prophet ﷺ said, "*There is no* ṣalāh *for one who does not straighten his back in bowing* (ruku') *and prostration* (sujūd)." Thus the new seeker in this Way, if not already acquainted and familiar with these fundamentals, must seek out an authorized teacher and learn them.

Testification of Faith

The Testification of Faith (*shahādah*) is pronounced three times. The first testification is for one's self, bringing to mind the Presence of the Prophet ﷺ and saying in one's heart, "O my master; O Prophet of God! You are my witness; God is my witness; all angels are my witness; all the Companions are my witness; all the prophets are my witness; everyone in creation is my witness; and my shaykh is my witness," then pronounce the testification, for you are renewing your Islam. Then pronounce the second testification on behalf of yourself, your parents, your children, your family, your brothers and sisters, your relations, your friends and neighbors, and all Muslim people. The third testification is said on behalf of unbelievers with the intention that they become believers.

Allahu Allahu Allahu Haqq

Sit on the knees, meditating on the connection (*rābiṭah*) to your shaykh, from your shaykh to the Prophet ﷺ, and from the Prophet ﷺ to the Divine Presence.

The Verse "*The Messenger believeth...*" (2:285-286)

ĀYAT ĀMAN AR-RASŪLU (2:285-286) — آمَنَ الرَّسُولُ

Āmana ar-rasūlu bimā unzila ilayhi min rabbihi wa 'l-mu'minūn. kullun āmana billāhi wa malā'ikatihi wa kutubihi wa rusulihi lā nufarriqu bayna āhadin min rusulihi wa qālū sam'inā wa aṭanā ghufrānaka rabbanā wa ilaykal maṣīr. Lā yukallif-ullāhu nafsan illa wus'ahā. lahā mā kasabat wa 'alayhā māktasabat. Rabbanā lā tū'ākhidhnā in nasīnā aw akhṭānā. Rabbanā wa lā taḥmil 'alaynā iṣran kamā ḥamaltahu 'alā alladhīnā min qablinā. Rabbanā wa lā tuḥamilnā mā lā ṭāqata lanā bihi w'afu 'anā waghfir lanā warḥamnā Anta mawlānā f'anṣurnā 'alā l-qawmi 'l-kāfirīn.

آمَنَ الرَّسُولُ بِمَا أُنزِلَ إِلَيْهِ مِن رَّبِّهِ وَالْمُؤْمِنُونَ كُلٌّ آمَنَ
بِاللَّهِ وَمَلَائِكَتِهِ وَكُتُبِهِ وَرُسُلِهِ لَا نُفَرِّقُ بَيْنَ أَحَدٍ مِّن
رُّسُلِهِ وَقَالُوا سَمِعْنَا وَأَطَعْنَا غُفْرَانَكَ رَبَّنَا وَإِلَيْكَ
الْمَصِيرُ لَا يُكَلِّفُ اللَّهُ نَفْسًا إِلَّا وُسْعَهَا لَهَا مَا كَسَبَتْ
وَعَلَيْهَا مَا اكْتَسَبَتْ رَبَّنَا لَا تُؤَاخِذْنَا إِن نَّسِينَا أَوْ
أَخْطَأْنَا رَبَّنَا وَلَا تَحْمِلْ عَلَيْنَا إِصْرًا كَمَا حَمَلْتَهُ عَلَى
الَّذِينَ مِن قَبْلِنَا رَبَّنَا وَلَا تُحَمِّلْنَا مَا لَا طَاقَةَ لَنَا بِهِ
وَاعْفُ عَنَّا وَاغْفِرْ لَنَا وَارْحَمْنَا أَنتَ مَوْلَانَا فَانصُرْنَا
عَلَى الْقَوْمِ الْكَافِرِينَ

The Messenger believeth in what hath been revealed to him from his Lord, as do the men of faith. Each one (of them) believeth in God, His angels, His books, and His apostles. "We make no distinction (they say) between one and another of His apostles." And they say: "We hear, and we obey: (We seek) Thy forgiveness, our Lord, and to Thee is the end of all journeys." On no soul doth God place a burden greater than it can bear. It gets every good that it earns, and it suffers every ill that it earns. (Pray:) "Our Lord! Condemn us not if we forget or fall into error; our Lord! Lay not on us a burden Like that which Thou didst lay on those before us; Our Lord!

Lay not on us a burden greater than we have strength to bear. Blot out our sins, and grant us forgiveness. Have mercy on us. Thou art our Protector; Help us against those who stand against faith."

Whoever recites this verse will attain a high rank and a great position. He will receive the station of safety in this world and the next. He will enter the circle of security in the Presence of God, Almighty and Exalted. He will reach all the stations of the most distinguished Naqshbandi Order. He will be an inheritor of the secret of the Prophet ﷺ and of the saints, and will arrive at the stage of Bāyazīd al-Bisṭāmī, the Īmām of the Order, who said, "I am also the Real (*al-Ḥaqq*)." This is the magnificent manifestation which belongs to this verse, and to other verses also. Grandshaykh Khālid al-Baghdādī received the vision and the secret of this verse, through which God made him special for his time.

Suratu-l-Fatiha (1)

The first time Sūratu 'l-Fātiḥa is recited, it is with the intention of participating in the blessings sent down with it when it was revealed in Makkah. The second time it is recited should be with the intention of sharing in the Divine Grace which was sent down when it was revealed the second time in Madinah. Grandshaykh said, "If someone recites Sūratu 'l-Fātiḥa, he will not leave this world without attaining those Divine Blessings that are hidden behind the meaning of Sūratu 'l-Fātiḥa which enable him to reach a state of submission to God, Almighty and Exalted."

The blessings that God has sent down with Sūratu 'l-Fātiḥa when it was revealed to the Prophet ﷺ will never cease, and will last forever with the one who recites Sūratu 'l-Fātiḥa. No one is able to know how much blessings there are except God and His Messenger ﷺ. Whoever recites it without this intention receives general Divine Favors, while whoever recites Sūratu 'l-Fātiḥa, with the intention of sharing in the Divine Grace, will attain a high position and a great rank. This Sūrah possesses innumerable and limitless stations in the Sight of God, Who is Powerful and Sublime.

Chief of prayers on the Prophet

SAYYID AṢ-ṢALAWĀT

سيّد الصلاة الشريفة المأثورة

ʻAlā ashrafi ʼl-ʻālamīna Sayyidinā Muḥammadini ʼṣ-ṣalawāt ṣalla-llāhū ʻalayhi wa sallam. ʻAlā afḍali ʼl-ʻālamīna Sayyidinā Muḥammadini ʼṣ-ṣalawāt ṣalla-llāhū ʻalayhi wa sallam. ʻAlā akmali ʼl-ʻālamīna Sayyidinā Muḥammadini ʼṣ-ṣalawāt ṣalla-llāhū ʻalayhi wa sallam.

على أشْرَف العالَمينَ سَيّدنا مُحَمَّد الصَلَوات.
على أفْضَل العالَمينَ سَيّدنا مُحَمَّد الصَلَوات.
على أكْمَل العالَمينَ سَيّدنا مُحَمَّد الصَلَوات.

Upon the Noblest of all Creation, our Master Muhammad, blessings.

Upon the most Preferred of all Creation, our Master Muhammad, blessings.

Upon the most Perfect of all Creation, our Master Muhammad, blessings.

Ṣalawātullāhi taʻalā wa malāʼikatihi wa anbīyāʼihi wa rusulihi wa jamīʻi khalqihi ʻalā Muḥammadin wa ʻalā āli Muḥammad, ʻalayhi wa ʻalayhimu ʼs-salām wa raḥmatullāhi taʻalā wa barakātuhu, wa raḍī-Allāhū tabāraka wa taʻalā ʻan sādātinā aṣḥābi Rasūlillāhi ajmaʻīn, wa ʻani ʼt-tabiʻīna bihim bi iḥsān, wa ʻani ʼl-aʼimmati ʼl-mujtahidīni ʼl-māḍīn, wa ʻani ʼl-ʻulamā il-muttaqqīn, wa ʻani ʼl-awlīyā ʼiṣ-ṣāliḥīn, wa ʻām-mashayikhinā fi ʼṭ-ṭarīqati ʼn-Naqshbandīyyati ʼl-ʻalīyyah, qaddas-Allāhū taʻalā arwāḥahumu ʼz-zakīyya, wa nawwar Allāhū taʻalā aḍriḥatahumu ʼl-mubāraka, wa aʻād-Allāhū taʻalā ʻalaynā min barakātihim wa fuyūḍātihim dāʼiman wa ʼl-ḥamdulillāhi Rabb il-ʻālamīn, al-Fātiḥā.

صَلَواتُ الله تعالى ومَلائكته وأنبيائه ورسُله وجَميع
خَلْقه على مُحَمّد وعلى آل مُحَمّد، عليه وعليهمْ
السّلامُ ورَحْمَةُ الله تَعالى وبَرَكاتُهُ ورَضيَ اللهُ تَبارَك
وتَعالى عَنْ سادَتنا أصْحاب رَسُول الله أجْمَعين
وعَن التّابعينَ بهم بإحْسان وعَن الأئمّة المُجْتَهدين
الماضين وعَن العُلماء المتّقين وعَن الأوْلياء الصالحين
وعَن مَشايخنا في الطَريقة النَقْشْبَنْديّة العَليّة، قدّسَ
الله تعالى أرْواحَهُمُ الزَكيّة ونَوّر الله تعالى أضْرحَتَهُم
المُبارَكة وأعادَ الله تعالى علينا من بَرَكاتهم
وفُيوضاتهم دائمًا والحَمدُ لله رَبّ العالمين – الفاتحة

Blessings of God (Exalted is He!), of His angels, of His prophets, of His Emissaries, and of all creation be upon Muhammad and the family of Muhammad; may the peace and mercy of God (Exalted is He!) and His blessings be upon him and upon them. May God, the Blessed and Most High, be pleased with every one of our Masters, the Companions of the Emissary of God, and with those who followed them in excellence, and with the early masters of juristic reasoning, and with the pious scholars, and the righteous saints and with our Shaykhs in the exalted Naqshbandi Order. May God (Exalted is He!) sanctify their pure souls, and illuminate their blessed graves. May God (Exalted is He!) return to us of their blessings and overflowing bounty, always. Praise belongs to God, the Lord of the worlds, al-Fātiḥa.

Dedication

IHDĀ	إهْداء
Allāhumma balligh thawāba mā qarā'nāhū wa nūra mā talawnāhū hadīyyatan wāṣilatan minnā ila rūḥi Nabīyyīnā Sayyidinā wa Mawlānā Muḥammadin ṣalla-llāhū 'alayhi wa sallam. Wa ilā arwāḥi ikhwānihi min al-anbiyā'i wa 'l-mursalīn wa khudamā'i sharā'ihim wa ila arwāḥi 'l-a'immati 'l-arba'ah wa ila arwāḥi mashāyikhinā fi 'ṭ-ṭarīqati 'n-naqshbandīyyati 'l-'aliyyah khāṣṣatan ila rūḥi Imāmi 'ṭ-ṭarīqati wa ghawthi 'l-khalīqati Khwājā Baḥā'uddīn an-Naqshband Muḥammad al-Uwaisī 'l-Bukhārī wa ḥaḍarati Mawlanā Sulṭānu 'l-awlīyā ash-Shaykh 'Abd Allāh al-Fā'iz ad-Dāghestanī wa sayyidunā ash-Shaykh Muḥammad Nāẓim al-Ḥaqqānī Mu'ayyad ad-dīn wa sa'iri sādātinā waṣ-ṣiddiqīna al-Fātiḥā.	اللّهُمَّ بَلّغْ ثوابَ ما قَرأناهُ ونورَ ما تلَوْناهُ هَديّةً واصلةً منّاإلى رُوحِ نبيّنا مُحَمَّد (صلّى الله عليه وسلّم) وإلى أرواحِ إخوانه من الأنْبياء والمُرسَلينَ وخُدَماء شَرائعهم وإلى أرواح الأئمّة الأربعة وإلى أرْواح مَشايخنا في الطرِيقة النَقشْبنْديّة العَليّة، خاصةً إلى روح إمام الطَّرِيقة وغَوْث الخَليقة خَواجه بَهاءُ الدين النقْشبند مُحَمَّد الأوْيسى البُخاري وإلى حضرة مَوْلانا سُلْطان الأوْلياء الشَيْخ عَبْدُ الله الفائز الداغَسْتَانى وإلى مولانا سيدنا الشيخ محمّد ناظم الحقّانى مؤيد الدين وإلى سائر ساداتنا والصدّيقين الفاتحة

O God! Grant that the merit of what we have read, and the light of what we have recited, are (considered) an offering and gift from us to the soul of our Prophet Muhammad, and to the souls of the prophets, and the saints; in particular the soul of the Imām of the ṭarīqat and arch-Intercessor of the created world, Khwaja Bahauddin an-Naqshband Muhammad al-Uwaisi al-Bukhari, and our venerable teacher and master, the Sultan of Saints, our Shaykh Abd Allah ad-Daghestani, and our master Shaykh Muhammad Nazim al-Haqqani Mu'ayyad ad-din, and to all our masters and to the righteous ... al-Fātiḥa.

This presents the reward of the preceding recitations to the Prophet ﷺ and to the shaykhs of the Naqshbandi Order.

Suratu-l-Ikhlas (112)

Whoever recites this Sūrah should obtain the Divine Grace of the two Names of Glory, al-Aḥad (the One), and as-Ṣamad (the Eternal). Anyone who reads it must receive a portion of this.

Suratu-l-Inshirah (94)

On each letter and on each verse of the Quran there is a Divine manifestation, which is different from that on any other. Whoever recites a verse or letter of the Quran, will attain the Divine Grace that is particular to that verse or letter. If anyone recites this Sūrah of the Quran, he will receive that Divine Grace and those virtues. Whoever wishes to obtain these virtues, must keep these spiritual practices daily along with his obligations. Then he will gain true and eternal life.

Suratu-l-Falaq (113) and Suratu-n-Nas (114)

The reality of the secret and the perfect wholeness of God's Greatest Name are connected with these two chapters. Since they mark the end of the Quran, they are linked with the completion of the Divine Grace. By means of these spiritual practices, the masters of the most distinguished Naqshbandi Order became oceans of knowledge and gnosis. Grandshaykh Abd Allah ad-Daghestani said:

> You have now reached the beginning, where each verse, letter and Surah of the Quran has its own special manifestation which does not resemble any other. For that reason the Messenger of God ﷺ said, *"I left three things with my Community—death which makes them afraid, true dreams which give them good tidings, and the Quran which speaks to them."* By means of the Quran, God will open up the gates of Divine Grace in the Last Times, as it came down in the time of the Holy Prophet ﷺ and the Companions, and in the times of the caliphs, and in the time of the saints.

These stations and continuous Divine Graces are closely bound together and they cannot be separated, so any deficiency in the spiritual practices will automatically create a deficiency in the Divine Grace being sent down. As an example, if we want to wash our hands, we may wait in front of the tap for water to come out. If the pipes are disconnected so that the water escapes before reaching the tap, then no matter how long we wait, the water will not flow out. So we must not let any deficiency enter our *dhikr* until we obtain the Divine Grace.

These spiritual practices for the three different levels of followers must be performed once every twenty-four hours, together with all other obligations, according to the Divine Law. Everything which the Prophet ﷺ brought was founded on these spiritual practices. It is the way that the servant reaches the key of Nearness to God, the All-Powerful, the Sublime. It was by means of it that the prophets, messengers, and saints reached their Creator, and it is by means of these spiritual practices that we reach all these stations of the most distinguished Order.

The masters of the most distinguished Naqshbandi Order say that whoever claims that he is affiliated with one of the other orders or with the most distinguished Naqshbandi Order, but nevertheless has not entered seclusion even once in his life, then such a person should be ashamed of connecting himself with the people of the path.

In our time, Grandshaykh Abd Allah ad-Daghestani said:

> Whoever of the people of the end of time wishes to attain a high rank and an exalted state and receive what a disciple normally receives by means of seclusion and spiritual exercises must continuously perform these spiritual practices and remembrances of God. With these as the foundation, we have set the way for the higher stations which are built on this foundation. The disciple ought to know that if he fails to attain an exalted station and high grade in this world because of his lack of effort, then he shall not be separated from this world, but that the shaykhs make him reach it, and reveal for him his station, either during his lifetime, or at the time of the seven last breaths during the agonies of death.

If anyone performs these spiritual practices and then performs an action which is forbidden, he will be like the one who builds his house on the side of a cliff, and then his house collapses down the side of the cliff. So we should always be aware of our actions, gauging them to see if they are permitted or forbidden, if God is going to be angry with our actions or not. And we need to think about every action so much that ultimately we do not do any unlawful thing which might weaken our foundation. As the Prophet ﷺ said in his Tradition, *"One hour's contemplation is better than seventy years of worship."* We should perform our actions in the perfectly correct way, that is to say without any prohibited deeds intervening.

On this basis, God has divided the day into three parts: eight hours for worship, eight hours for earning a living, and eight hours for sleeping. Anyone who does not accept and follow this division of energies will exemplify the Tradition, *"He who is erratic will be erratic in the Hellfire."* He who goes according to his own will and reasoning does not progress, and he who wishes to obtain exalted stations, levels, and stages which previous generations earned by means of retreats and other spiritual exercises must remember God throughout the course of the day.

He who makes a regular practice of these spiritual exercises shall attain the Water of True Life, with which he will perform ablution. He will bathe in it, and drink it, and by means of it he shall reach his goal. There may be a person who claims that he has been in the Order for thirty years and as yet has not seen anything and not attained anything. That person should look at his actions over the past years. How many deficient actions has he performed? When he sees the deficiency he should quickly avoid it, then he will reach God, Who is Powerful and Sublime. When the disciple forsakes the daily duties which the shaykhs have told him to perform, then he will be absolutely incapable of making further progress, and he will be unable to keep any state he had previously attained. No prophet ever attained prophethood, nor did any saint ever attain sainthood, nor did any believer ever attain the stage of faith without utilizing his time for his daily *dhikr*.

Muhasabah **– Accounting**

Al-Hasan ibn Ali ibn Abi Talib ﷺ said:

> A believer polices his own self; he criticises and appraises it for the sake of God. The Final Accounting (*hisab*) may turn out to be mild on some people simply because they were wont to appraise themselves in this life; and the Final Accounting on the Day of Judgment may turn out to be rigorous on a people who took this life with levity, and thought they would not be called to account.

In our way, in order to eliminate the darkness of the heart, it is necessary for the seeker to take a notebook and write down the bad characteristics of one's ego. Everyone is able to document at least 200 bad manners; to write them down is the key to dissolving them. Whoever has not done it must do it. Among these bad characteristics are stealing, lying and anger. One of the worst of bad characters is anger. If you are angry with someone restrain yourself for forty days.

Shaykh Nazim wrote for himself over one hundred bad manners so we are not above blame. When you observe the bad characteristics of your ego you will be disgusted: This process will demolish the inciteful ego (*an-nafs al-ammara*). If you write what is coming to your heart with the spiritual support of your Shaykh your ego will become afraid. If anyone finds your notebook, let them look for it is better to feel ashamed in this life than on Judgment Day.

In addition the seeker must pause at the end of each day to take account of himself: what has he done and why has he done it? What has he omitted and why? Who has he harmed and whom has he helped? Then take one's *tasbih* and seek God's forgiveness (*istighfar*) for each wrong act of commission or omission.

Dhikr in Congregation: Khatmu-l-Khwajagan

In the Naqshbandi Order, the daily spiritual exercises and the weekly congregational *dhikr*, known as *Khatmu 'l-Khwājagān*, are important practices which the disciple must not leave. The *Khatmu 'l-Khwājagān* is done sitting with the shaykh in congregation. This is held once a week, preferably on Thursday night or Friday, two hours before sunset. The *Khatmu 'l-Khwājagān* is of two categories: the long *khatm* and the short *khatm.*

The Long Khatm — خَتْمُ الخَواجَكانِ الكبيرِ

1. Distribute 79 of the smaller pebbles among the attendees and the shaykh, dividing them as evenly as possible based on the number of those present. The Imam retains 21 of the pebbles, along with the 7 larger stones and one big stone.

2. The shaykh begins the Khatm, which is performed silently:

Intention: Niyyatu ādā' al-khatm ibtighā' riḍwān Allāhi ta'la	نِيةُ أداءِ الخَتْمِ أبْتِغاءِ رِضْوانِ اللهِ تعالى
Intention to perform the Khatm seeking the pleasure of God the most High.	
Shahāda (3 times): Ash-hadu an lā ilāha ill-Allāh wa ash-hadu anna Muḥammadan 'abduhu wa rasūluh I testify that there is no god but God, and I testify that Muhammad is the Servant and Messenger of God.	كَلمةُ الشَّهادتين (3 مرات) أشْهَدُ أنْ لا إله إلا الله وأشْهَدُ أنَّ مُحَمَّدًا عَبْدُهُ ورَسُولُهُ
Istighfār (70 times): Astaghfirullāh God forgive me.	إستغفار: 70 مرة أستغفر الله
Astaghfirullāhi 'l-'Aẓīm alladhī lā ilāha illa Hū al-Ḥayyu 'l-Qayyūm wa atūbu ilayh innahu hūwa 't-tawābu 'r-raḥīm min kulli dhanbin wa ma'ṣīyatin wa min kulli mā yukhālifu dīn al-Islām, yā arḥam ar-	يتلو الإمام: اسْتَغْفر اللهَ العَظيم الذي لا إله إلا هُوَ الحيُّ القَيُّوم وأتُوبُ إليْه إنَّهُ هو التَّوابُ الرَحيم. من كُلِّ ذَنْبٍ ومَعْصيّةٍ ومن كُلِّ ما يُخالِفُ دينَ الإسْلام

Rāḥimīn, min kulli mā yukhālifu 'sh-sharī'at, min kulli mā yukhālifu 'ṭ-ṭarīqata, min kulli mā yukhālifu 'l-ma'rifata, min-kulli mā yukhālifu 'l-ḥaqīqata, min kulli mā yukhālifu 'l-'azīmata, yā arḥam ar-rāḥīmin.

ومن كُلّ ما يُخالفُ الشَرِيعة ومن كُلّ ما يُخالفُ الطَرِيقة ومن كُلّ ما يُخالفُ المَعْرفة ومن كُلّ ما يُخالفُ الحَقيقة ومن كُلّ ما يُخالفُ العَزِيمة يا أَرْحَمَ الراحمين

I ask forgiveness from God Almighty, there is no god but He, the Living, the Self-Subsisting, and I turn in repentance to Him, verily He is the Forgiver, the Merciful, from every sin and disobedience and from all that opposes the religion of Islam, from all that opposes the Divine Law, from all that opposes the Path, from all that opposes Spiritual Realization, from all that opposes Reality, from all that opposes firm Intention, O most Merciful of the Merciful.

The shaykh recites the following supplication:

يَتلو الإمامُ:

Allāhumma yā Musabbib al-asbāb, yā Mufattiḥ al-abwāb, yā Muqallib al-qulūbi wa 'l-abṣār, yā Dalīl al-mutaḥayyirīn, yā Ghiyāth al-mustaghīthīn, yā Ḥayyu, yā Qayyūm, yā Dhal-Jalāli wa 'l-Ikrām! Wa ufawwiḍu amrī ilā-Allāh, inna-llāha baṣīrun bil-'ibād.

اللّهمَ يا مُسَبّبَ الأسباب ويا مُفَتّح الأبواب. يا مُقَلّبُ القُلوب والأبصار. يا دَليل المُتَحَيّرين يا غياث المُسْتَغيثين يا حيُّ يا قَيُّوم. يا ذا الجلال والإكْرام. وأُفَوّضُ أمْري إلى الله. إنَّ اللهَ بَصيرٌ بالعباد

O Bestower! O Bestower! O Bestower! O Originator of causes! O Opener of doors! O Tuner (Changer) of hearts and eyes! O Guide of the perplexed! O Succor for those who seek Your aid! O Living! O Self-Subsisting One! O (You who are) possessed of Majesty and Bounty! I entrust my affair unto God. Truly, God is aware of His servants.

Rābiṭat ash-sharīfā.

الرابطة الشَرِيفة

Connect your heart to the heart of the shaykh, from him to the heart of the Prophet, from the Prophet to the Divine Presence;

3. The shaykh then distributes 7 of the larger stones, keeping 1 for himself and passing the other 6 among the attendees to his right. Those who receive a large stone recite the Fātiḥā. The larger stones are then returned to the shaykh.

Sūratu 'l-Fātiḥa (7 times)

سورة الفاتحة (7 مَرات)

4. The shaykh then asks the group to recite As-Ṣalawātu 'sh-Sharīfah. Each person recites it one time for each pebble that he holds in his hand. The Imam completes the recitation by counting on the 21 pebbles he reserved.

Ṣalawāt (100 times):

صلوات: 100 مرة

Allāhumma ṣalli 'alā Muḥammadin wa 'alā āli Muḥammadin wa sallim.

اللّهُمَّ صلّ على مُحَمّد وعلى آل مُحَمّد وسلّم

5. The shaykh then asks the group to recite Sūratu 'l-Inshirāḥ, following the same methodology.

Sūratu 'l-Inshirāḥ (79 times) — سُورةُ الانشراح (79 مرة)

6. The shaykh then distributes the remaining 21 pebbles among the attendees as evenly as possible.

7. Then the shaykh asks the group to recite Sūratu 'l-Ikhlāṣ, with the Basmalah. Each one recites according to the number of pebbles in his hand. This is repeated 10 times. After completing the tenth round of recitation, the shaykh takes the big stone and reads Ikhlāṣ on it, making for 1,001 recitations of this surah.

Sūratu 'l-Ikhlāṣ (1,001 times) — سُورةُ الإخلاص (1001 مرّة)

8. The shaykh again distributes 7 of the larger stones, keeping one for himself and passing the other 6 to the attendees to his left. Once again, those who receive a large stone recite the Fātiḥā and the stones are then returned to the shaykh.

Sūratu 'l-Fātiḥā (7 times) — سُورةُ الفاتحة (7 مرّات)

9. The shaykh again asks the group to recite aṣ-Ṣalawātu 'sh-Sharīfah, each according to the number of pebbles in his hand.

Ṣalawāt (100 times): — صَلوات 100 مرة

Allāhumma ṣalli 'alā Muḥammadin wa 'alā āli Muḥammadin wa sallim.

اللّهمّ صلّ على مُحمّدٍ وعلى آلِ مُحمّدٍ وسلّم

O God send blessings and peace upon Muḥammad and the family of Muhammad.

10. The shaykh, or a person designated by him, then recites Chapter 12, Verse 101 (12:101) of the Holy Quran.

Rabbi qad ātaytanī min al-mulki wa 'allamtanī min ta'wīlil aḥādīth fāṭira as-samāwāti wa 'l-arḍi anta waliyyī fī ad-dunyā wa 'l-ākhirati tawaffanī musliman wa alḥiqnī biṣ-ṣāliḥīn; Āmantu billāhi sadaq-Allāhul 'Aẓīm. Subḥāna rabbika rabb al-'izzati 'amā yaṣifūn wa salāmun 'alā 'l-mursalīn wa 'lḥamdulillāhi rabbi l-'alamīn.

يتلو الإمامُ:
أعُوذُ بِاللهِ من الشَيْطانِ الرَّجيم. بِسْمِ اللهِ الرَّحْمنِ الرَّحيم. رَبِّ قدْ آتَيْتَني من المُلكِ وعَلَّمْتَني من تأويل الأحاديث فاطِرَ السَماوات والأرْض أنتَ وليّ في الدُنيا والآخرة. تَوَفَّني مُسْلِمًا وألْحِقْني بِالصالحين.

O my Lord! You have indeed bestowed on me some power, and taught me something of the interpretation of dreams and events. Creator of the Heavens and the Earth! You are my Protector in this world and in the Hereafter. Take my soul (at death) as one submitting to Your Will (as a Muslim), and unite me with the righteous.

11. The shaykh reads the dedication.

Ihdā: (see page 729)	إهْداء

12. The shaykh then proceeds with the loud portion of the dhikr.

Loud Part	
F'alam annahū: Lā ilāhā ill-Allāh (100 times)	فَاعْلَمْ أَنَّهُ: لا إله إلا الله (100 مرّة)
There is no god but God.	
Ila sharaf in-Nabī ṣalla-llāhū 'alayhi wa sallam wa ālihi wa ṣaḥbih, wa ila arwāḥi sā'iri sādātinā waṣ-ṣīddiqīn, al-Fātiḥa.	إلى شَرَف النَبي صلى الله عليه وسلم وإلى آله وصَحْبه وإلى أَرْواح مشائحنا وسائر ساداتنا والصدّيقين الفاتحة
For the honor of the Prophet ﷺ and to the souls of the prophets and the veracious ones ... al-Fātiḥa.	
Present the reward of the preceding recitations to the Prophet ﷺ and to the shaykhs of the Naqshbandi Order.	
Dhikr al-Jālāla:	ذِكْرُ الجَلالة
Allāh, Allāh (100 times)	الله الله (حوالي 100 مرّة)
God, God	
Ḥasbun-Allāh wa ni'm al-wakīl, ni'm al-Mawlā wa ni'm an-Naṣīr, lā ḥawla wa lā quwwata illa billāh il-'Alīyy il-'Aẓīm.	الإمام: حَسبنا الله ونعم الوكيل نعْمَ المولى ونعم المصير ولا حَوْل ولا قُوَّة إلا بِالله العَليّ العَظيم
God is sufficient for us and the Best of Protectors, the Best Patron, and the Best of Helpers; there is no power and no might except in God, the High, the Exalted.	
Hū, Hū (33 times)	هُو. هُو. هُو. (حوالي 33 مرّة)
He, the Absolute Unknown One.	
Ḥasbun-Allāh wa ni'm al-wakīl, ni'm al-Mawlā wa ni'm an-Naṣīr, lā ḥawla wa lā quwwata illa billāh il-'Alīyy il-'Aẓīm.	الإمام: حَسبنا الله ونعْمَ الوكيل نعْمَ المولى ونعم المصير ولا حَوْل ولا قُوَّة إلا بِالله العَليّ العَظيم
God is sufficient for us and the Best of Protectors, the Best Patron, and the Best of Helpers; there is no power and no might except in God, the High, the Exalted.	
Ḥaqq, Ḥaqq (33 times)	حَق. حَق. حَق. (حوالي 33 مرّة)
The Ultimate Reality.	
Ḥasbun-Allāh wa ni'm al-wakīl, ni'm al-Mawlā wa ni'm an-Naṣīr, lā ḥawla wa Lā quwwata illa billāh il-'Alīyy il-'Aẓīm.	الإمام: حَسبنا الله ونعْمَ الوكيل نعْمَ المولى ونعم المصير ولا حَوْل ولا قُوَّة إلا بِالله العَليّ العَظيم

God is sufficient for us and the Best of Protectors, the Best Patron, and the Best of Helpers; there is no power and no might except in God, the High, the Exalted.	
Ḥayy, Ḥayy (33 times) Ever-living One.	حَيّ. حَيّ. حَيّ.(حوالي 33 مرّة)
Ḥasbun-Allāh wa ni'm al-wakīl, ni'm al-Mawlā wa ni'm an-Naṣīr, lā ḥawla wa lā quwwata illa billāh il-'Alīyy il-'Aẓīm.	الإمام: حَسبنا الله ونِعْمَ الوكيل ولا حَوْلَ ولا قُوَّة إلا بالله العَلِيّ العَظيم
God is sufficient for us and the Best of Protectors, the Best Patron, and the Best of Helpers; there is no power and no might except in God, the High, the Exalted.	
Allāh Hū, Allāh Ḥaqq (10-12 times) God is He the Absolute Unknown One, God is the Ultimate Reality.	الله هُو الله حَقّ الله هُو لله حَقّ (10 أو 12 مرّة)
Allāh Hū, Allāh Ḥayy (10-12 times) God is He the Absolute Unknown One, God is Ever-living	الله هُو الله حَيّ . الله هُو الله حَيّ (10 أو 12 مرّة)
Allāh Ḥayy Yā Qayyūm (10-12 times) God Ever-living, O Self-sufficient One	الله حَيّ يا قَيُّوم الله حَيّ يا قَيُّوم (10 أو 12 مرّة)
Ḥasbun-Allāh wa ni'm al-wakīl, ni'm al-Mawlā wa ni'm an-Naṣīr, lā ḥawla wa lā quwwata illa billāh il-'Alīyy il-'Aẓīm.	الإمام: حَسبنا الله ونِعْمَ الوكيل ولا حَوْلَ ولا قُوَّة إلا بالله العَلِيّ العَظيم
God is sufficient for us and the Best of Protectors, the Best Patron, and the Best of Helpers; there is no power and no might except in God, the High, the Exalted.	
Yā Hū, Yā Hū, Yā Dā'im (3 times); Allāh Yā Hū, Yā Dā'im (1 time) O Absolute Unknown One, O Eternal One, God is He the Absolute Unknown One, O Eternal One.	الإمام: يا هُو يا هُو يا دائم (3 مرّة)، الله يا هو يا دائم
Yā Dā'im x3, Yā Allāh (2 times) O Eternal One x3, O God	يا دائم. يا دائم. يا دائم يا الله (مرّتان)
Yā Ḥalīm x3, Yā Allāh (2 times) O Clement One, x3, O God	يا حَليم. يا حَليم. يا حَليم يا الله (مرّتان)
Yā Ḥafī· x3 Yā Allāh (2 times) O Preserver x3, O God	يا حَفيظ. يا حَفيظ. يا حَفيظ يا الله (مرّتان)
Yā Laṭīf x3, Yā Allāh (2 times) O Subtle One x3, O God	يا لَطيف. يا لَطيف. يا لَطيف يا الله (مرّتان)
Yā Ghaffār x3, Yā Allāh (2 times)	يا غَفّار. يا غَفّار. يا غفّار يا الل (مرّتان)

O Forgiver x3, O God	
Yā Sattār x3 Yā Allāh (2 times) O Concealer x3, O God	يا سَتَّار . يا سَتَّار . يا سَتَّار يا الله (مَرَّتان)
Yā Fattāḥ x3, Yā Allāh (2 times) O Opener x3, O God	يا فَتَّاح . يا فَتَّاح . يا فَتَّاح يا الله . (مَرَّتان)
Yā Mujīb x3, Yā Allāh (2 times) O Answerer of Prayers x3, O God	يا مُجيب . يا مُجيب . يا مُجيب يا الله . (مَرَّتان)
Yā Muʿiz x3, Yā Allāh (2 times) O Honorer x 3, O God	يا مُعز . يا مُعز . يا مُعز يا الله . (مَرَّتان)
Yā Muʿīn x3, Yā Allāh (2 times) O Giver of Aid, x 3, O God	يا مُعين . يا مُعين . يا مُعين يا الله . (مَرَّتان)
Yā Wadūd x3, Yā Allāh (2 times) O Most Loving x3, O God	يا وَدود . يا وَدود . يا وَدود يا الله . (مَرَّتان)
Yā Raḥmān x3, Yā Allāh (2 times) O Most Compassionate x3, O God	يا رَحْمن . يا رَحْمن . يا رَحْمن يا الله . (مَرَّتان)
Yā Raḥīm x3, Yā Allāh (2 times) O Most Merciful x3, O God	يا رَحيم . يا رَحيم . يا رَحيم يا الله . (مَرَّتان)
Yā Ḥannān x3, Yā Allāh (2 times) O Most Caring x3, O God	يا حَنَّان . يا حَنَّان . يا حَنَّان . يا الله . (مَرَّتان)
Yā Mannān x3, Yā Allāh (2 times) O Beneficent x3, O God	يا مَنَّان . يا مَنَّان . يا مَنَّان . يا الله . (مَرَّتان)
Yā Dayyān x3, Yā Allāh (2 times) O Most Just x3, O God	يا دَيَّان . يا دَيَّان . يا دَيَّان . يا الله . (مَرَّتان)
Yā Subḥān x3 , Yā Allāh (2 times) O Most Glorious One x3, O God	يا سُبْحان . يا سُبْحان . يا سُبْحان . يا الله . (مَرَّتان)
Yā Sulṭān x3, Yā Allāh (2 times) O Supreme Ruler x3, O God	يا سُلْطان . يا سُلْطان . يا سُلْطان . يا الله . . (مَرَّتان)
Yā Amān x3, Yā Allāh (2 times) O Giver of Safety x3, O God	يا أمان . يا أمان . يا أمان . يا الله . (مَرَّتان)
Yā Allāh x3, Yā Allāh (2 times) O God x 4	يا الله . يا الله . يا الله . . . . (مَرَّتان)

The Shaykh may add more of God's Beautiful Names as he is inspired.

Ḥasbun-Allāh wa niʿm al-wakīl, niʿm al-	الإمام: حَسبنا الله ونعْم الوكيل ولا حَوْل ولا قُوَّة إلا

Mawlā wa ni'm an-Naṣīr, lā ḥawla wa lā quwwata illa billāh il-'Alīyy il-'Aẓīm.	بالله العَليّ العَظيم

God is sufficient for us and the Best of Protectors, the Best Patron, and the Best of Helpers; there is no power and no might except in God, the High, the Exalted.

Inna-Allāha wa malā'ikatahū yuṣalluna 'alā an-Nabī, yā ayyuh-alladhīnā āmanū, ṣallū 'alayhi wa sallimū taslīmā. (Ṣadaq-Allāhu 'l-'Aẓīm)	إنَّ اللهَ ومَلائكتَهُ يُصَلُّونَ على النَّبي يا أيُّها الذين آمَنُوا صَلّوا عليه وسَلِّموا تَسْليمًا

God and His angels send blessings on the Prophet: O you who believe! Send blessings on him and greet him with all respect. (God speaks the Truth).

Ṣalawāt (10 times): Allāhumma ṣalli 'alā Muḥammadin wa 'alā āli Muḥammadin wa sallim	صلوات: 10 مرات – اللّهُمَّ صلّ على مُحَمَّد وعلى آل مُحَمَّد وسلّم

O God send blessings and peace upon Muhammad and the family of Muhammad.

The shaykh then makes invocation as he is inspired.

The shaykh then recites the Chief of Prayers (see page 728)	الصلاة الشريفة المأثورة
The shaykh then recites the Ihdā (see page 729).	إهداء

Short Khatm (Aloud) — خَتْمُ الخَواجَكانِ الصغير – جهر

The Short Khatm is identical to the Long Khatm except that it is recited aloud in its entirety, and has the following differences in number of repetitions in the Adab.

Sūratu 'l-Fātiḥā (7 times)	الفاتحة (7 مَرات)
Prayers on the Prophet ﷺ (ṣalawāt) (10 times): Allāhumma ṣalli 'alā Muḥammadin wa 'alā āli Muḥammadin wa sallim	صَلوات (10 مرات) صل على مُحَمّد وعلى آل مُحَمّد وسلّم

O God send blessings and peace upon Muhammad and the family of Muhammad.

Sūratu 'l-Inshiraḥ (7 times)	سُورةُ الانشراح (7 مَرات)
Sūratu 'l-Ikhlāṣ (11 times)	سُورةُ الإخْلاص (11 مَرّة)

Sūratu 'l-Fātiḥā (7 times)	سُورةُ الفَاتِحَة (7 مَرَات)
Ṣalawāt (10 times): Allāhumma ṣalli ʿalā Muḥammadin wa ʿalā āli Muḥammadin wa sallim	صَلَوات (10 مَرات) أَللّٰهُمَّ صلّ على مُحَمَّد وعلى آل مُحَمَّد وسلِّم
O God send blessings and peace upon Muhammad and the family of Muhammad.	

The remainder of the Khatm is identical to the Long Khatm (section 10) from the point the shaykh assigns someone to recite from the Qur'ān (12:101) (see page 736).

Invoking the Masters

Our Grandshaykh, Shaykh Abd Allah ad-Daghestani, called on the Prophet ﷺ through the shaykhs of the Order in the manner described below when asking for their intercession. This formulation was transmitted to him by his shaykh who received it through the Golden Chain, each shaykh passing it from one to another. It begins with a prayer and then each of the saints of the Golden Chain is invoked.

Yā sayyid as-sādāt wa nūr al-mawjudāt, yā man hū al-malja'u liman massahu ḍaymun wa ghammun wa alam. Yā aqrab al-wasā'ili ilā-Allāhi ta'alā wa yā aqwā'l-mustanad, attawasalu ila janābīk al-'a·am bi-hādhihi's-sādāti, wa āhlillāh, wa āhli baitika al-kirām, li-daf'i ḍurrin lā yudfa'u illā bi wāsiṭatik, wa raf'i ḍaymin lā yurfa'u illā bi-dalālatika bi Sayyidī wa Mawlāy, yā Rasūl Allāh, yā Raḥmatan lil-'ālamīn:	يا سَيِّدَ السّادات ويا نورَ المَوْجُودات، يا من هُوَ المَلْجأ لمنْ مَسَّهُ ضَيْمٌ وغَمٌّ وأَلَمٌ، يا أقْرَبَ الوَسائل إلى الله تعالى ويا أقْوى المُسْتَنَد، أتَوَسَّلُ إلى جنابكَ الأعْظم بهَؤُلاء السّادات وأهْل الله وأهْل بيْتكَ الكرام لدَفْع ضرٌ لا يُدْفَعُ إلا بوَسيلتكَ ورَفْع ضيْم لا يُرْفَعُ إلا بدَلالَتكَ بسَيّدي ومَوْلاي يا سَيّدي يا رَسُولَ الله يا من أرسله الله رَحْمَةً للعالمين
Nabī	نَبِيٌّ
Ṣiddīq	الصدّيق
Salmān	سلمان
Qāsim	قاسمُ
J'afar	جعفر
Ṭayfūr	طيفور
Abu 'l-Ḥasan	ابو الحسن
Abū 'Alī	ابو علی
Yūsuf	يُوسف
Abu 'l-'Abbās	أبو العباس
'Abd al-Khāliq	عبد الخالق
'Arif	عارفُ
Maḥmūd	محمود
'Alī	على
Muḥammad Bābā as-Samāsī	محمد بابا السماسي

Sayyid Amīr Kulālī	سيد أمير كلالي
Khwājā Bahā'uddīn Naqshband	خواجه بهاء الدين النقشبند
'Alā'uddīn	علاء الدين
Ya'qūb	يعقوب
'Ubayd Allāh	عبيد الله
Muḥammad Zāhid	مُحَمَّد زاهد
Darwīsh Muḥammad	درويش مُحَمَّد
Khwājā Amkanākī	خواجه الامكناكي
Muḥammad al-Bāqī	مُحَمَّد الباقى
Aḥmad al-Fārūqī	أحمد الفاروقى
Muḥammad Ma'ṣūm	مُحَمَّد معصوم
Sayfuddīn	سيف الدين
Nūr Muḥammad	نور مُحَمَّد
Ḥabībullāh	حبيب الله
'Abd Allāh	عبد الله
Shaykh Khālid	الشيخ خالد
Shaykh Ismā'īl	الشيخ إسماعيل
Khāṣ Muḥammad	خاص مُحَمَّد
Shaykh Muḥammad Effendi al-Yarāghī	الشيخ محمد أفندي اليراغى
Sayyid Jamāluddīn al-Ghumūqī al-Ḥusaynī	سيد جمال الدين الغموقى الحسينى
Abū Aḥmad aṣ-Ṣughūrī	ابو أحمد الصغوري
Abū Muḥammad al-Madanī	ابو مُحَمَّد المدنى
Shaykh Sharafuddīn ad-Dāghestānī	الشيخ شرف الدين الدغستانى
Shaykh 'Abd Allāh al-Fā'iz ad-Dāghestānī	الشيخ عبد الله الفائز الدغستانى
Shaykh Muḥammad Nāẓim 'Adil al-Ḥaqqānī	الشيخ مُحَمَّد ناظم الحقاني

Invocation of Imam al-Mahdi and His Deputies

Today, many no longer believe in the coming of the al-Mahdi al-Muntadhar ﷵ (the Awaited Savior). In their ignorance, some claim that the concept of al-Mahdi ﷵ is a Shiite one. However, belief in al-Mahdi ﷵ is part of both the Sunni and Shiite doctrines, and his reality is firmly established by many authentic Traditions. For example, the Prophet ﷺ said:

> *If this world has just one day remaining, God will extend that day until a man comes. He is from me (or "from my family"). His name is like my name (i.e., Muhammad) and his father's name is like my father's name (i.e., Abd Allah). He fills the earth with equality and justice, as it has been filled with injustice and oppression.*[554]

The advent of al-Mahdi ﷵ has long been awaited by the saints, for it heralds the return of the Prophet Jesus (Isa) ﷵ and the restoration of justice and peace in the world. The Prophetic Traditions also make it clear that al-Mahdi ﷵ will be accompanied by seven ministers. Their names were sought by the saints of the Golden Chain, including Shaykh Abd Allah ad-Daghestani, through their visions, leading to the formulation of this invocation:

Sāḥib az-Zamān Imāmu 'l-Mahdī	صاحبُ الزَمان الإمام مُحَمَّد المَهْدي عليه السلام
Shahāmatu 'l-Fardānī	شهامة الفرداني
Yūsuf as-Ṣiddīq	يُوسف الصدّيق
'Abdur-Ra'uf al-Yamānī	عَبْدُ الرَؤوف اليَماني
Imāmu 'l-'Ārifīn Amānu 'l-Ḥaqq	إمامُ العارفين أمان الحَقّ
Lisānu 'l-Mutakallimīn 'Awnullāh as-Sakhāwī	لِسانُ المُتَكَلِّمين عَوْن اللهِ السَخاوي

---

[554] It is related from Ibn Masud, Abu Dawud recorded it in his ***Sunan***. Al-Hafiz as-Suyuti recorded it both in his *Jami* and his *Tafsir*, Ibn Abi Shaybah and Ahmad in his *Musnad*, some with different wording.

'Ārifu 't-ṭayyār al-Mā'rūf bi Mulḥān	عارفُ الطيّار المَعْرُوف بمُلْحان
Burhānu 'l-Kuramā' Ghawth il-Anām	بُرْهان الكُرَماء غَوْثُ الأنام
Yā Ṣāḥib z-Zamān, yā Ṣāḥib al-'Unṣur.	يا صاحبُ الزَمان، يا صاحبُ العُنْصُر
Yā rijāl-Allāh āa'lā Allāhu ta'alā darajātihim dā'iman wa amadnā bi-maddadihim wa-nafa'anā bi-barakātihim wa anfāsihim al-qudsīyya, bi-ḥurmati man lā Nabīyya ba'dah, bi sirri Sūratu 'l-Fātiḥa.	يا رجالَ الله أعلى اللهُ تعالى دَرَجاتهم دائماً وأمدنا بمددهم ونفّعنا بِبَرَكات أَنْفاسَهُم القُدُسيَّة بِحُرْمة من لا نَبَيَّ بَعْدَهُ وبسرِّ سُورة الفاتحة

O Master of the Period, O one of high pedigree, O men of God. May God (Exalted is He!) raise their stations always, support us with their support and benefit us through the blessings of their holy breath. By the sanctity of the one after whom there is no other prophet, and by the secret of ... al-Fātiḥa.

صَلاةُ المغرب

Salatu-l-Maghrib

Adhan (call to prayer)	الآذان
Allāhu akbar (4 times) God is Greatest	الله أكْبر، الله أكْبر، الله أكْبر، الله أكْبر
Ash-hadu an lā ilāha ill-Allāh (2 times) I bear witness that there is no god but God	اشْهَدُ أنْ لا إلَهَ إلاَّ الله اشْهَدُ أنْ لا إلَهَ إلاَّ الله
Ash-hadu anna Muḥammadan Rasūlullāh (2 times) I bear witness that Muhammad is the Messenger of God.	اشْهَدُ أنَّ محمداً رسول الله – اشْهَدُ أنَّ محمداً رسول الله
Ḥayya ʻalā ʼṣ-ṣalāh (2 times) Hasten to the prayer	حيَّ عَلى الصَلاة حيَّ عَلى الصَلاة
Ḥayyā ʻāla ʼl-falāḥ (2 times) Hasten to salvation	حيَّ عَلى الفَلاح حيَّ عَلى الفَلاح
Aṣ-ṣalātu khayrun min an-nawm (2 times, only before Fajr) Prayer is better than sleep	الصلاة خير من النوم الصلاة خير من النوم
Allāhu akbar (2 times) God is Greatest	اللهُ أكْبَراللهُ أكْبَر
Lā ilāha illa-Allāh There is no god but God	لا إله إلاَّ الله

AṢ-ṢALĀTU WAS-SALĀM

الصلاة والسلام

(to be made aloud by the muadhdhin):

Aṣ-ṣalātu was-salāmu 'alayk, yā man arsalahullāhu ta'alā raḥmatan lil-'ālamīn.

Aṣ-ṣalātu was-salāmu 'alayk, wa 'alā ālika wa aṣḥābika ajma'īn.

Aṣ-ṣalātu was-salāmu 'alaykum, yā anbiyā'Allāḥ.

الصلاة والسلام عليك يا من أرسله الله تعالى رحمة للعالمين

الصلاة والسلام عليك وعلى آلك وأصحابك أجمعين الصلاة والسلام عليكم، يا أنبياء الله

Blessings and peace be upon you, whom God Most High sent as mercy to the Worlds.

Blessings and peace be upon you, and upon all your family and your Companions.

Blessings and peace be upon you, O Prophet of God.

INVOCATION (DU'A):

دُعاءُ:

(to be made silently by all who hear the adhān):

Allāhumma rabba hādhihī 'd-da'wat it-tāmma waṣ-ṣalāt il-qā'ima, āti Sayyidinā Muḥammadan al-wasīlata wa 'l-faḍīlata wa 'd-darajati 'r-raf'īati 'l-'alīyya wab'athhu Rabbī al-maqām al-maḥmūd alladhī w'adtahu, warzuqnā shaf'atahu yawm al-qīyāma. Innaka lā tukhlifu 'l-mī'ad.

اللَّهُمَّ رَبَّ هَذه الدعْوة التّامّة والصَّلاة القائمة آت مُحَمَّداً الوَسيلة والفَضيلة والدَرَجة الرَفيعة العالية وأبعَثه رَبّى المقام المَحْمُودَ الذي وَعَدْتَه وارْزقنا شَفاعَتَهُ يَوْمَ القيامةإنكَ لا تُخْلفُ الميعاد (وزوّجْنا من الحُور العِين)

O God! Lord of this perfect supplication and of this established prayer, grant Muhammad the Means (of nearness to You) and the excellence of the sublime and supreme rank. Raise him, O my Lord, to the Praiseworthy Station, which You promised him, and grant us his intercession on the Day of Judgment, for You do not fail Your promise.

2 RAK'ATS SUNNAH

رَكعَتَين سُنَّة

performed After Adhān.

IQAMATU 'Ṣ-ṢALĀT

إقامة الصَلاة

Identical to Adhān with the insertion after Ḥayyā 'āla 'l-falāḥ of:

Qad qāmati 'ṣ-Ṣalāt (2 times)

The prayer is beginning

مثل الآذان ولكن مع إدخال قد قامت الصلاة قد قامت الصلاة – بعد حى على الفلاح (على المذهب الحنفي)

3 RAK'ATS FARḌ

ثلاثُ ركْعات فرْض

After the final salām:

Recite:

بعد التسليم

lā ilāha ill-Allāh Muḥammadur Rasūlullāh (3 times)

لا إلَهَ إلاّ الله (ثَلاثُ مرّات) مُحَمّد رَسُولُ الله

Astaghfirullāh 3 times

I ask God's forgiveness

إسْتِغْفار (ثَلاثُ مرّات)

Astaghfirullāh al-'A·īm alladhī lā ilāha illa Hū al-Ḥayyu 'l-Qayyūm wa atūbu ilayḥ

I ask forgiveness from God Almighty, there is no god but He, the Living, the Self-Subsisting, and I turn in repentance to Him.

أَسْتَغْفِرُ اللهَ العَظِيم الذي لا إله إلا هُوَ الحيُّ القَيُّوم وأَتُوبُ إليْه

أَوْ أَسْتَغْفِرُ الله. أَسْتَغْفِرُ الله. أَسْتَغْفِرُ الله

INVOCATION (DU'A):

دُعاءُ:

Allāhumma anta 's-Salām wa minka 's-salām tabārakta wa ta'ālayta yā Dhal-jalāli wa 'l-ikrām. Lā ilāha ill-Allāhu wāḥdahu lā sharīka lah, lahu 'l-mulku wa lahu 'l-ḥamd, wa Hūwa 'alā kulli shay'in qadīr. Sami'nā wa aṭa'nā, ghufrānaka, Rabbanā, wa ilayk al-maṣīr.

اللَّهُمَّ أنتَ السَّلامُ ومنكَ السَّلام تبارَكْتَ وتعاليت يا ذا الجلال والإكْرام. لا إلَهَ إلاَّ الله وَحْدَهُ لا شَرِيكَ لَهُ، لَهُ المُلْكُ ولَهُ الحَمْدُ يحى ويميت وهُوَ على كُلِّ شَيْءٍ قدير. سَمِعْنا وأَطَعْنا غُفْرانَكَ رَبّنا وإليْكَ المصير

O God! You are Peace and from You comes Peace. Blessed and lofty are You, O Lord of Majesty and Bounty. There is no god but God, He is One, no partner has He. His is the Kingdom and His is all praise, and He is over all things Powerful. We have heard and obeyed. Your forgiveness, O our Lord! And to Thee is the end of all journeys.

2 RAK'ATS SUNNAH

ركعَتَيْن سُنّة

'Alā Rasūlinā 'ṣ-ṣalawāt. Astaghfirullāh, subḥānallāh wa 'l-ḥamdulillāh, wa lā ilāha ill-Allāh w-Allāhū akbar, wa lā ḥawla wa lā quwwata illa billāhi 'l-'Alīyy il-'Āẓīm.

على رَسُولنا الصَّلَوات. أَسْتَغْفِرُ الله. أَسْتَغْفِرُ الله. أَسْتَغْفِرُ اللهَ سُبْحانَ الله والحَمْدُ لله ولا إلَهَ إلاّ الله والله أَكْبَر ولا حَوْلَ ولا قُوَّةَ إلا بالله العَلِيُّ العَظِيم

Blessings upon our Prophet. I ask God's forgiveness. Glory be to God! Praise be to God! There is no god but God and God is Greatest. There is no power and no strength save in God, All-High and Almighty.

CHAPTER 2: VERSE 163

البقرة، 163

A'udhū billāhi min ash-shayṭān ir-rajīm. Bismillāhi 'r-Raḥmāni 'r-Raḥīm.

Wa ilāhukum ilāhun wāḥidun, lā ilāha illa Hū ar-Raḥmānu 'r-Raḥīm.

أعُوذُ بالله من الشَّيْطان الرَّجيم

بِسْم الله الرَّحْمن الرَّحيم

وإلهكم إلهٌ واحدٌ لا إلهَ إلاّ هُوَ الرَّحْمن الرَّحيم

I seek refuge with God from Satan, the Cursed. In the name of God, the All-Beneficent, the All-Merciful. Your God is One God; there is no god but He, the All-Merciful, the All-Compassionate.

ĀYATU 'L-KURSĪ (THRONE VERSE)

آيَةُ الكُرْسي

Allāhū lā ilāha illa Hūwa 'l-Ḥayyu 'l-Qayyūm, lā tākhudhuhū 's-sinatun wa lā nawm, lahū mā fis-samāwāti wa mā fil-arḍ. Man dhā-ladhī yashfa'u 'indahū illā bi idhniḥ ya'lamu mā bayna aydīhim wa mā khalfahum wa lā yuḥīṭunā bi-shay'im min 'ilmihi illā bimā shā'. Wasi'a kursīyyuhu 's-samāwāti wa 'l-arḍa, wa lā ya'uduhū ḥifẓuhuma, wa Hūwa al-'Alīyyu 'l-'Aẓīm.

Ṣadaq-Allāhu 'l-'Aẓīm.

اللهُ لا إلهَ إلا هُوَ الحيُّ القَيُّوم لا تَأخُذُهُ سِنَةٌ ولا نَوْمٌ لَهُ ما في السماوات وما في والأرْض من ذا الذي يَشْفَعُ عِنْدَهُ إلا بإذنه يَعْلَمُ ما بَيْنَ أيديهم وما خَلفَهُم ولا يُحيطونَ بِشَيْءٍ من علمه إلا بما شاء وَسِعَ كُرْسِيُّه السماوات والأرْضَ ولا يَؤُدُهُ حفظُهما وهُوَ العَليُّ العَظيمُ – صَدَقَ الله العَظيم

God, there is no god but He, the Living, the Everlasting. Slumber seizes Him not, neither sleep; to Him belongs all that is in the heavens and the earth. Who is there that shall intercede with Him save by His leave? He knows what lies before them, and they comprehend not anything of His knowledge save such as He wills. His Throne comprises the heavens and the earth; the preserving of them oppresses Him not; He is the All-High, the Almighty.

God spoke the Truth.

TASBĪḤ

تَسبيح

Subḥānak yā 'Aẓīm subḥānallāh, subḥānallāh (33 times)

سُبحانَكَ يا عَظيم: سُبْحانُ الله (33 مَرّة)

Glory be to You, O Almighty! Glory be to God.

'Alā n'imat il-Islām wa sharaf al-īmān dā'iman alḥamdulillāh, alḥamdulillāh (33 times)

على نعمة الإسْلام وشَرَف الإيمان دائماً: الحَمْدُ لله (33 مَرّة)

For the gift of Islam, the nobility of faith, always, praise be to God.

Ta'alā shā'nuhū wa lā ilāha ghayruhū, Allāhū akbar, Allāhū akbar (33 times)

تعالى شأنُهُ ولا إله غيرُهُ: اللهُ أكبر(33 مرّة)

Exalted is His Affair, and there is no god but He, God is Greatest.

Allāhū akbaru kabīran wa 'lḥamdulillāhi kathīran wa subḥānallāhi bukratan wa aṣīla. Lā ilāha illa-llāh wāḥdahū lā sharīka lah, lahul-mulku wa lahul-ḥamd yuḥīy wa yumīt wa Hūwa 'alā kulli shay'in qadīr. Subḥāna Rabbīu 'l-'Alīyyu 'l-'āla 'l-Wahhāb.

اللهُ أكبرُ كبيرًا والحَمْدُ لله كثيرًا وسُبْحانَكَ اللهم بُكرةً وأصيلاً لا إله إلا اللهُ وَحْدَهُ لا شَريكَ له، له المُلكُ وله الحَمْدُ يُحي ويُميت وهُوَ على كلِّ شيءٍ قَديرٍ سُبْحانَ رَبّي العَليّ الأعلى الوهّاب

God is most Great in His Greatness and much praise be to God. Glory be to God, early and late. There is no god but God. He is One, no partner has He. His is the Kingdom and all praise. He brings to life and makes to die, and He is over all things Powerful. Glory be to my Lord, All-High, Supreme, Most Munificent.

SUPPLICATION (DU'A)

دُعاء (شخصي)

Recite a personal invocation as one is inspired.

AL-FĀṬIHA

الفاتحة

Allāhumma ṣalli 'alā Muḥammadin wa 'alā āli Muḥammadin wa sallim.

اللّهُمَّ صَلِّ على مُحَمَّدٍ وعلى آلِ مُحَمَّدٍ وسلّم

Then pray (the funeral prayer)

Salatu-l-Janazah

ṢALĀT AL-JANĀZATU 'ALĀ AL-GHĀ'IB

صلاةُ الغائب

Funeral Prayer in Absentia

F'ātabiru yā ulil-abṣār la'allakum tufliḥun. Inna lillāhi wa inna īlayhi rāji'un. Ṣalātu 'l-janāza 'an il-ghā'ibīn alladhīna antaqalu ilā raḥmatillāhi min ummati Muḥammad ṣalla-llāhū 'alayhi wa sallam.

فَاعْتَبِرُوا يا أولي الأبصار لعلكم تفلحون. إنّا لله وإنّا إليه راجعون. صلاةُ الجَنازة عَن الغائبينَ الذين أنتَقلوا إلى رَحْمة الله من أمّة مُحَمّد (صلى اللهُ عليه وسلّم)

Therefore, take heed, you who can see. Surely we belong to God and to Him we return. This is the funeral prayer for the deceased who have parted to the mercy of

God of the nation of Muhammad ﷺ.

AT-TAKBĪRATU 'L-ŪLĀ (FIRST TAKBĪR)

التَكْبيرة الأولى:

Allāhū akbar.

God is Greatest!

الله أكْبر

Subḥānaka Allāhumma wa bi ḥamdika, wa tabāraka ismuka wa ta'alā jadduka, wa jalla thāna'uka, wa lā ilāha ghayruka. (In Shāfi'ī madhab: Recite al-Fātiḥa)

سُبْحانَكَ اللّهمَّ وبحَمْدِك، وتَبارَكَ اسْمُكَ وتعالى جَدُّكَ وجَلَّ ثنائك ولا إله غَيْرُكَ

Glory and praise be to You, O my God. Great is Your Praise, and there is not god but You. (In the Shāfi'ī Madhhab: Recite al-Fātiḥa).

AT-TAKBĪRATU 'TH-THĀNĪYA (SECOND TAKBĪR)

التَكْبيرة الثانية :

Allāhū akbar.

God is Greatest!

الله أكْبر

Allāhumma ṣalli 'alā Muḥammadin wa 'alā āli Muḥammadin, kama ṣallayta 'alā Ibrāḥīma wa 'alā āli Ibrāḥīma innaka ḥamīdun majīdun. Allāhumma bārik 'alā Muḥammadin wa 'alā āli Muḥammadin, kamā bārakta 'alā Ibrāhīm wa 'alā āli Ibrāhīma, innaka ḥamīdun majīdun.

اللّهمَّ صَلّ على مُحَمَّد وعلى آل مُحَمَّد كما صَلّيْتَ على إبراهيم وعلى آل إبراهيم إنكَ حَميدٌ مَجيدٌ. اللّهمَّ بارِكْ على مُحَمَّد وعلى آل مُحَمَّد كما بارَكْتَ على إبراهيم وعلى آل إبراهيم إنكَ حَميدٌ مَجيدٌ.

O God! Exalt Muhammad and the family of Muhammad, as You have exalted Abraham and the family of Abraham. Truly, You are All-Laudable, All-Glorious. O God! Bless Muhammad and the family of Muhammad, as You have blessed Abraham and the family of Abraham. Truly, You are All-Laudable, All-Glorious.

AT-TAKBĪRATU TH-THĀLITHA (THIRD TAKBĪR)

التَكْبيرة الثالثة:

Allāhū akbar.

God is Greatest!

الله أكْبر

Allāhumma 'ghfir li ḥayyinā wa mayyitinā wa shāhidinā wa ghā'ibinā wa ṣaghīrinā wa kabīrinā wa dhakarinā wa unthānā. Allāhumma man aḥyaytahū minna fa aḥyihi 'alā al-Islām wa man tawaffaytahū minnā fa tawaffahū 'alā al-īmān. Allāhumma 'ghfir lahum wa 'rḥamhum. Allāhumma lā taḥrimnā ajrahum wa lā

اللّهمَّ اغفِرْ لحَيّنا ومَيّتنا وشاهدنا وغائبنا وصَغيرنَا وكَبيرنَا ذَكَرنا وأنثانا . اللّهمَّ من أحْيَيْتَهُ منّا فَأحْيه على الإسْلام ومن تَوَفَيْتَهُ منّا فتَوَفَهُ على الإيمان. اللّهمَّ اغفِرْ لَهم وارْحَمْهم اللّهمَّ لا تَحرِمْنا أجْرَهُم ولا تَفتِنّا بَعْدهُم

taftinā b'ādahum.

O God! Forgive our living and our dead, those present and absent, our young and our old, male and female. O God! To those of us whom You have given life, make them live according to the religion of Islam, and whosoever dies, make him die in faith. O God! Forgive them and have mercy on them. O God! Do not deny us their reward (and) do not lead us astray after them (i.e. after their death).

AT-TAKBĪRATU R-RĀBI'A (FOURTH TAKBĪR)

التَّكْبِيرة الرَّابِعةُ:

Allāhū akbar.

اللهُ أَكْبَرُ

God is Greatest!

اللهم لا تحرمنا أجرهم ولا تفتنا بعدهم واغفر لنا ولهم

TASLĪM

تسليم

(To the right) as-salāmu 'alaykum wa raḥmatullāḥ

إلى اليمين: السَّلامُ عَلَيْكم ورَحْمَةُ الله

Peace be upon you and the mercy of God.

(To the left) as-salāmu 'alaykum wa raḥmatullāḥ

إلى اليَسار: السَّلامُ عَلَيْكم ورَحْمَةُ الله

Peace be upon you and the mercy of God.

DU'A (SUPPLICATION)

دُعاء

Allāhumma 'ghfir li aḥyā'inā wa 'rḥam mawtānā washf'i marḍānā bi ḥurmat il-Fātiḥā.

اللَّهُمَّ اغفِرْ لأَحْيائنا وارْحَمْ مَوْتانا واشْفِ مَرْضانا وانصر سلطاننا بحُرْمَةِ من أرسلته رحمة للعالمين وبسر سورة الفاتحة

O God! Forgive the living and have mercy on our dead, and cure our sick, by the sanctity of al-Fātiḥā.

Ṣalātu 'l-Janaza is then followed by six rak 'ats of Ṣalātu 'l-Awwābīn.

Salatu-l-Awwabin

صلاة الأوابين

6 rak 'ats (3 sets of 2 Rak'āts).

(ست ركعات)

KALIMATU SH-SHAHĀDA (3 TIMES)

كَلمةُ الشَهادة (3 مرّات):

Ash-hadu an lā ilāha ill-Allāh wa ash-hadu anna Muḥammadan 'abduhu wa rasūluh.

أشْهَدُ أن لا إله إلا الله وأشْهَدُ أنّ مُحَمّداً عَبْدُهُ ورَسُولُهُ

I bear witness that there is no god but God, and Muhammad is His Servant and Messenger.

ISTIGHFĀR (100 TIMES) | اسْتغفار (100 مرّة)

Astaghfirullāh | أَسْتَغْفِرُ الله

I ask God's forgiveness.

DU'A (SUPPLICATION) | دُعاء

Astaghfirullāh min kulli dhanbin wa ma'ṣīyatin wa min kulli mā yukhālifu dīn al-Islām, yā arḥam ar-Rāḥimīn.

أَسْتَغْفِرُ اللهَ من كُلّ ذنب ومَعْصيّة ومن كُلّ ما يُخالِفُ دينَ الإسْلام يا أَرْحَمَ الراحمين

I ask God's forgiveness for every sin and desobedience and from all that opposes the religion of Islam, O most Merciful of Merciful.

SŪRATU S-SAJDA (PROSTRATION) | سُورةُ السَجْدة

A'udhūbillāhi min ash-shayṭān ir-rajīm. Bismillāhi 'r-Raḥmāni 'r-Raḥīm.

أَعُوذُ بالله من الشّيْطان الرَّجيم. بِسْم الله الرَّحْمن الرَّحيم

I seek refuge with God from Satan, the Cursed. In the Name of God, the Most Merciful, the Most Compassionate (This will be omitted hereafter, but must be read before any Quran reading). Then, read Sūratu 'l-Fātiḥa, followed by Sūratu 's-Sajda.

SŪRATU 'L-IKHLĀṢ (SINCERITY) (3 TIMES) | سُورةُ الإخْلاص (3 مرات)

SŪRATU 'L-FALAQ (DAYBREAK) ONCE | سُورةُ الفَلَق

SŪRATU 'N-NĀS (MANKIND) ONCE | سُورةُ الناس

TAHLĪL (10 TIMES) | تهليل:

Lā ilāha ill-Allāh

There is no god but God.

(After the tenth)

Muḥammadur Rasūlullāh ﷺ.

Muhammad is the Messenger of God ﷺ.

لا إله إلا الله (10 مرات)

(بَعْدَ العاشرة) مُحَمَّدٌ رَسُولُ الله صلّى اللهُ عليه وسلّم

ṢALAWĀT (10 TIMES)

Allāhumma ṣalli 'alā Muḥammadin wa 'alā āli Muḥammadin wa sallim.

صلوات:

اللَّهُمَّ صَلِّ على مُحَمَّدٍ وعلى آلِ مُحَمَّدٍ وسلم (10 مَرَّة)

Blessings and peace be upon Muhammad and the family of Muhammad.

DU'A (INVOCATION)

Ṣalli, yā Rabbī, wa sallim 'alā jamī'i il-anbīyā'i wa 'l-mursalīn, wa ālin kullin ajma'īn wa 'l-ḥamdulillāhi Rabb il-'ālamīn.

دعاء

صلِّ يا ربّي وسلِّم على جَميعِ الأنبياءِ والمُرسَلينَ وآلِ كُلٍّ أجمَعينَ والحَمْدُ لله ربِّ العالمينَ

Blessings, O my Lord, and peace be upon all the prophets and messegers, and on the family of every one of them. Praise belongs to God, the Lord of the worlds.

CHIEF OF THE PRAYERS ON PROPHET
(see page 728)

الصلاة الشريفة المأثورة

DEDICATION

Recite the Ihdā (see page 729)

إهْداء

صلاةُ العشاء

Salatu-l-Isha

Performed in the same manner as Ṣalātu 'l-Maghrib with the following changes:

4 RAK'ATS SUNNAH	4 رَكْعات سُنّة: رَكْعَتَيْنِ سُنّة ورَكْعَتَيْنِ نافلة بِتَسْليم واحِد أو بِتَسليمين
4 RAK'ATS FARḌ	4 رَكْعات فَرْض
4 RAK'ATS SUNNAH	4 رَكْعات سنة: رَكْعَتَيْنِ سُنّة ورَكْعَتَيْنِ نافلة بِتَسْليم واحِد أو بِتَسليمين
ṢALATUL-WITR (3 RAK'ATS)	صَلاة الوِتْرِ (ثَلاثُ رَكْعات)
Before the ruku', or bowing, in the third rak'at, recite:	
QUNŪT PRAYER (SEE NOTES) Allāhu akbar. Allāhumma innā nasta'īnuka wa nastahdīka; wa nastaghfiruka wa natūbu ilayk wa nu'minu bika, wa natawakkalu 'alayk, wa nuthnī 'alayk al-khayr kullahā wa nashkuruka, wa lā nakfuruka, wa nakhla'u wa natruku man yafjuruka. Allāhumma iyyāka na'budu wa laka nuṣalli wa nasjudu wa ilayka nas'ā wa naḥfiḍu wa	دعاء القُنوت (في الرَّكْعة الثالثة قبل الركوع) اللهُ أَكْبَر. اللَّهُمَّ إنَّ نَسْتَعينُكَ ونَسْتَهْدِيكَ ونَسْتَغْفِرُكَ ونَتُوبُ إليك ونُؤْمِنُ بكَ ونَتَوَكَّلُ عليك ونُثْني عليكَ الخَيْر كلَّه نَشْكُرُكَ ولا نَكْفُرُ ونَخْلَعُ ونَتْرُكُ من يَفْجُرُكَ. اللَّهُمَّ إياكَ نَعْبُدُ ولك نُصَلِّي ونَسْجُدُ إليك نَسْعى

ونَحْفِدُ ونَرْجو رَحْمَتَكَ ونَخْشَى عَذابَكَ إنَّ
عَذابَكَ الجِدَّ بالكُفَّار مُلحَقٌ وصلّى اللهُ على النَبى
وآله وسلّم

narju raḥmataka, wa nakhshā ʿadhābak, inna ʿadhābak al-jidda bil-kuffāri mulḥaq, wa ṣalla-llāhū ʿalā an-Nabī wa ʿalā ālihi wa sallam. Allāhu akbar!

God is Greatest! O God! To You alone we pray for succour, for guidance, and for forgiveness. And to You we return in repentance; We believe in You, and trust in You, and praise You by all that is good. We thank You and are not ungrateful. We remove and leave those who sin against You. O God! We serve only You, and to You we pray and prostrate, and towards You we strive. We hope for your mercy and fear Your chastisement, for truly, Your severe punishment will befall the disbelievers. God's blessings and peace be upon the Prophet and upon his family. God is Greatest!

Go into rukʿū.

Ṣalātu ʾl-Witr is followed by the customary tasbīḥ and waẓīfā (see Ṣalātu ʾl-Maghrib) reciting Sūratu ʾl-Mulk in place of Sūratu ʾs-Sajda, followed by the customary adhkār.

صَلاةُ الفَجرِ

Salatu-l-Fajr

The adab of Ṣalātu 'l-Fajr is presented in its entirety because it differs greatly from the other prayers. For common elements, such as the adhān, see Ṣalātu 'l-Maghrib.

ADHĀN	اذان
2 RAK'ATS SUNNAH	2 رَكْعتان سنة

KALIMATU SH-SHAHĀDA (3 TIMES)

كلمة الشَهادة:

Ash-hadu an lā ilāha ill-Allāh, wa ash-hadu anna Muḥammadan 'abduhū wa rasūluḥ.

أَشْهدُ أنْ لا إله إلا الله وأشْهدُ أنَّ مُحَمَّدًا عَبْدُهُ ورَسُولُهُ (3 مَرّات)

I bear witness that there is no god but God, and Muhammad is His servant and Messenger.

Iqāmat 'uṣ-ṣalāt wa ītāu 'z-zakāt wa ṣawmu ramaḍān, wa Ḥajju 'l-bayti Ḥaqq. Āmantu billāhi wa malā'ikatihi wa kutubihi wa rusulihi wa 'l-yawm il-āhkiri wa bil-qadari khayrihi wa sharrihi min Allāhi ta'alā. Awda'nā hātayni 'l-kalimatayni 'sh-shahādatayn 'indaka yā Rasūlullāh wa hīya lanā wadī'atun yawma 'l-qiyāmati ya man arsalahullāhū ta'alā raḥmatan li 'l-'ālamīn.

إقامةُ الصَلاة وإيتاءُ الزكاة وصَوْمُ رَمَضانَ وحَجُّ البيْت حَقٌّ آمَنْتُ بالله ومَلائكه وكُتُبه ورُسُله وباليَوْم الآخر وبالقَدَر خَيْره وشَرِّه. أَوْدَعْنا هاتَيْن الشَهادَتَيْن عنْدَكَ يا سيدي يا رَسُول الله وهى لنا وَديعَة يَوْمَ القِيامة يا من أَرْسَلَهُ اللهُ رَحْمةً للعالَمينَ.

The performance of prayer, the payment of alms, the fast in Ramadān, and the Pilgrimage to the House, are true. I declare my belief in God, His Angels, His Books, His messengers, the Day of Judgment, and in Destiny—both its good and evil being from God (Exalted is He!). May the truth of what I say be accepted, O Lord.

We have commended these two testimonials to your safekeeping, O Messenger of God. They are for us a trust on the Day of Judgment, O you who were sent by God (Exalted is He!) as a mercy to the worlds.

Subḥānallāh wa bi ḥamdhihi subḥānallāh il-'Azīm Astaghfirullāh (100 times)

سُبحانَ اللهِ وبِحَمْدِه. سُبْحانَ اللهِ العَظيم أَسْتَغْفِرُ اللهَ – 100 مرة

Glory be to God, and to Him be praise. Glory be to God Almighty. I ask God's forgiveness.

(after the 100th time)

بَعْدَ المِئَة:

Astaghfirullāh al-'Aẓīm alladhī lā ilāha illa Hū al-Ḥayyu 'l-Qayyūm wa atūbu ilayḥ innahu hū at-tawābu 'r-raḥīm min kulli dhanbin wa ma'ṣīyatin wa min kulli mā yukhālifu dīn al-Islām, yā arḥam ar-Rāḥimīn, min kulli mā yukhālif ush-sharī'at, min kulli mā yukhālif uṭ-ṭarīqata, min kulli mā yukhālifu 'l-ma'rifata, min-kulli mā yukhālifu 'l-ḥaqīqata, min kulli mā yukhālifu 'l-'azīmata, yā arḥam ar-rāḥīmin.

أَسْتَغْفِرُ اللهَ العَظيمَ الذي لا إله إلا هُوَ الحيُّ القَيُّوم وأَتوبُ إليه إنَّهُ هو التَّوابُ الرَّحيم، من كُلِّ ذَنْبٍ ومَعْصِيَةٍ ومن كُلِّ ما يُخالفُ دينَ الإسْلام ومن كُلِّ ما يُخالفُ الشَّريعة ومن كُلِّ ما يُخالفُ الطَّريقة ومن كُلِّ ما يُخالفُ المَعْرِفة ومن كُلِّ ما يُخالفُ الحَقيقة ومن كُلِّ ما يُخالفُ العَزيمة يا أَرْحَمَ الراحمين.

I ask forgiveness from God Almighty, there is no god but He, the Living, the Self-Subsisting, and I turn in repentance to Him, verily He is the Forgiver, the Merciful, from every sin and disobedience and from all that opposes the religion of Islam, from all that opposes the Divine Law, from all that opposes the Path, from all that opposes Spiritual Realization, from all that opposes Reality, from all that opposes firm Intention, O most Merciful of the Merciful.

Astaghfirullāhu 'l-'Aẓīm, wa atūbu ilayh (100 times)

أَسْتَغْفِرُ اللهَ العَظيمَ وأَتوبُ إليه – 100 مرة

I ask forgiveness from God Almighty and I turn to Him in repentance.

(after the 100th time)

Tawbatan 'abdin ẓālimin li nafsihi, lā yamliku li nafsihi mawtan wa lā ḥayātan wa lā nushūrā.

Allāhumma anta Rabbī, lā ilāha illa Ant. Khalaqtanī wa anā 'abduka wa anā 'alā 'ahdika wa wa'dika ma 'staṭa't. A'udhū bika min sharri mā ṣan'āt, abū'u laka bi ni'matika 'alayya, wa abū'u bi dhanbī faghfir lī fa innahū lā yaghfir udh-dhunūba illa Anta Yā Allāḥ.

تَوْبَةَ عَبْدٍ ظالِمٍ لِنَفْسِه لا يَمْلِكُ لِنَفْسِه مَوْتًا ولا حَياةً ولا نُشُورًا اللَّهُمَّ رَبِّي لا إله إلا أَنْتَ خَلَقْتَني وأنا عَبْدُكَ وأنا على عَهْدِكَ ووَعْدِكَ ما اسْتَطَعْتُ أَعُوذُ بِكَ من شَرِّ ما صَنَعْتُ وأَبُوءُ لَكَ بِنِعْمَتِكَ عَلَيَّ وأَبُوءُ بِذَنْبِي فاغْفِرْ لِي فإنَّهُ لا يَغْفِرُ الذُّنوبَ إلا أَنْتَ يا الله.

The repentance of a slave who has oppressed himself, who neither has power over his death, nor his life, nor his resurrection.

O God! You are my Lord. There is no god but You. You have created me. I am Your slave, and I hold fast to Your convenant and Your promise (as much as I am able). I take refuge in You from the evil I have done, and testify that Your Grace is upon me, and profess my sin. Forgive me, for there is none who forgives sins except You, O God!

CHAPTER 3, VERSE 8

سُورَةُ آل عمْران آية 8

Rabbanā lā tuzigh qulūbanā ba'da idh hadaytanā wa hab lanā min ladunka raḥmatan innaka Anta' l-Wahhāb.

رَبَّنا لا تزِغْ قلوبنا بَعْدَ إذْ هَدَيْتَنا وهَبْ لنا من لَدُنْكَ رَحْمةً إنكَ أنتَ الوَهّاب.

Our Lord, make not our hearts to swerve after You have guided us, and give us Your Mercy; You are the Bestower.

Yā Wahhāb. Yā Wahhāb. Yā Wahhāb. Yā Musabbib al-asbāb, yā Mufattiḥu 'l-abwāb, yā Muqallibu 'l-qulūbi wa 'l-abṣār, yā Dalīl al-mutaḥayyirīn, yā Ghiyāth al-mustaghīthīn, yā Ḥayyu, yā Qayyūm, yā Dhal-Jalāli wa 'l-Ikrām! Wa ufawwiḍu amrī ila-Allāh, inna-llāha baṣīrun bi 'l-'ibād.

يا وَهّاب يا وَهّاب يا وَهّاب، يا مُسَبِّبَ الأسباب. ويا مُفَتِّحُ الأبواب. يا مُقَلِّبُ القُلوب والأبصار. يا دَليل المُتَحَيِّرين يا غياثَ المُسْتَغيثين يا حيٌّ يا قَيُّوم. يا ذا الجلال والإكرام. وأُفَوِّضُ أمْري إلى الله. إنَّ الله بَصيرٌ بالعباد.

O Bestower! O Bestower! O Bestower! O Originator of causes! O Opener of doors! O Tuner (Changer) of hearts and eyes! O Guide of the perplexed! O Succour for those who seek Your aid! O Living! O Self-Subsisting One! O (You who are) possessed of Majesty and Bounty! I entrust my affair unto God. Truly, God is aware of His servants.

DU'Ā

دُعاء

Yā man lā maljā'a minhu illa ilayhi fa lā tukhayyib rajā'anā, yā Qadīm al-iḥsān. lā taqnaṭu min raḥmati-llāh, inna-llāha yaghfir udh-dhūnuba jamī'an, innahū Hū al-Ghafūru 'r-Raḥīm.

Allāhumma innā nas'aluka 'l-'afwa wal 'āfiyata fi 'd-dīni wad-dunyā wa 'l-ākhira.

Allahumma 'sturnā bi satrik al-jamīl.

Allāhumm 'ustur 'awratī, wa āmin raw'atī, waqḍi lī daynī. Allāhumma inna nā'ūdhū bika min jahdil-balā'i, wa darki 'sh-shaqā'i, wa sūi 'l-qaḍā'i, wa shamātati 'l-a'dā'i, bi ḥurmati man arsaltahū raḥmatan li 'l-'ālamīn.

يا من لا ملجأ منه إلا إليه فلا تُخَيِّبْ رَجاءَنا يا قَديمَ الإحْسان لا تَقْنَطوا من رَحْمة الله إنَّ الله يَغفِرُ الذنوبَ جَميعًا إنَّهُ هو الغفور الرَّحيم

اللَّهُمَّ إنّا نَسْألُكَ العَفْوَ والعافيةَ في الدين والدُنيا والآخرةَ اللَّهُمَّ اسْتُرْنا بِسَتْرِكَ الجَميل. اللَّهُمَّ اسْتُرْ عَوْرَتي وآمِنْ رَوْعَتي واقضِ دَيْني. اللَّهُمَّ إنّا نَعوذُ بك من جَهْد البَلاء ودَرك الشَّقاء وسُوء القَضاء وشَماتة الأعْداء بِحُرْمة من أرْسَلْتَهُ رَحْمةً للعالَمينَ.

O From whom there is no refuge except in Him, do not disappoint our hopes, O Eternally Beneficent. Do not despair of the mercy of God, for God forgives every sin. Truly, He is the All-Forgiving, All-Merciful. O God! We ask Your pardon, and ask for strength in religion, in this life and the Hereafter.

O God! Veil us with Your Beautiful Veil.

O God! Veil my imperfection and set me rest when I fear, and settle my debts.

O God! We take refuge in You from the pangs of tribulations, from being overtaken by misfortune, and from an evil destiny, and from the gloating of mine enemies. By the sanctity of the one whom you sent as a mercy to the worlds (Sayyidinā Muhammad ﷺ).

Salatu munajiyyah صلاة المنجية

Allāhumma ṣalli ʿalā Muḥammadin ṣalātan tunjīnā bihā min jamīʿi ʾl-ahwāli wa ʾl-āfāt, wa taqḍī lanā bihā min jamīʿi ʾl-ḥājāt, wa tuṭahhirunā bihā min jamīʿi ʾs-sayyiʾāt, wa tarfaʿunā bihā ʿindaka ʿalā ʾd-darajāt, wa tuballighunā bihā aqṣā ʾl-ghāyāt min jamīʿi ʾl-khayrāti fi ʾl-ḥayāt wa baʿd al-mamāt.

اللَّهُمَّ صلِّ على سيِّدنا مُحَمَّد صلاةً تنجينا بها من جميع الأهوال والآفات وتَقْضى لنا بها جميعَ الحاجات وتطهِّرنا بها من جميع السيِّئات وترفعُنا بها عندَكَ أعلى الدرجات وتبلِّغنا بها أقصى الغايات من جميع الخَيْرات في الحَياة وبَعْدَ المَمات

O God! Blessings upon Muhammad. May they be blessings that delivers us from every fear. And appoint for us the fulfillment of every need. May we be cleansed by them (the blessings) from every sin, and by them may we be raised to the highest stations. And by them make us attain the furthest degrees in all that is good in this life and the life and after death.

Allāhumma ʾsliḥ ummata Muḥammad. اللَّهُمَّ أصْلِحْ أمَّة مُحَمَّد

O God! Reconcile the nation of Muhammad.

Allāhumma ʾrḥam ummata Muḥammad. اللَّهُمَّ ارْحمْ أمَّة مُحَمَّد

O God! Have mercy on the nation of Muhammad.

Allāhūmma ʾstur ummata Muḥammad. اللَّهُمَّ اسْتُرْ أمَّة مُحَمَّد

O God! Veil the imperfection of the nation of Muhammad.

Allāhūmm ʾghfir li ummati Muḥammad. اللَّهُمَّ اغفِرْ لأمَّة مُحَمَّد

O God! Forgive the nation of Muhammad.

Allāhūmm ʾaḥfaẓ ummata Muḥammad. اللَّهُمَّ احْفَظْ أمَّة مُحَمَّد

O God! Preserve the nation of Muhammad.

Allāhūmma 'nṣur ummata Muḥammad.	اللهمَّ أنصرْ أمّةَ مُحَمّد

O God! Succour the nation of Muhammad.

Yā arḥam ar-Rāḥīmīn arḥamnā. Yā arḥam ar-Rāḥīmīn fa'fu 'annā. Yā arḥam ar-Raḥīmīn, yā Ghaffār adh-dhūnub, Yā Sattār al-'uyūb, Yā Fattāḥ al-qulūb.	يا أرْحَمَ الراحمين ارْحَمْنا . يا أرْحَمَ الراحمين اعْفُ عَنّا . يا أرْحَمَ الراحمين يا غفّارَ الذنوبَ يا ستّارَ العُيُوبَ يا فتّاحَ القُلوب

O Most Merciful of the Merciful! Have mercy on us. O Most Merciful of the Merciful! Forgive us. O Most Merciful of the Merciful! O Pardoner of sins! O Veiler of our shortcomings! O Opener of hearts!

Allāhumma 'sqinā l-ghaytha suqyā raḥmatan wa lā taj'alnā min al-qāniṭīn. Āmīn. Āmīn. Āmīn.	اللهمَّ اسْقِنا الغيثَ سُقْيَة رَحْمَةً ولا تجْعَلْنا من القانطينَ رب اغفر وارحم وأنتَ خيرُ الرّاحمين. آمين آمين آمين

My Lord, pardon and forgive, for You are the best of those who forgive. Āmīn. Āmīn. Āmīn.

Wa salāmun 'alā l-mursalīn, wa 'lḥamdu-lillāhi Rabb il-'alamīn.	وسَلامٌ على المُرْسَلينَ والحَمْدُ لله رَبّ العالمينَ .

Peace be upon the messengers and praise be to God, the Lord of the worlds.

SŪRATU 'L-IKHLĀṢ (CHAPTER 112) (3 TIMES)

سُورةُ الإخْلاص – 3 مرات

CHAPTER 37: VERSE 180

سورة الصافات 180

Subḥāna Rabbika Rabbi 'l-'izzati 'ammā yaṣifūn wa salāmun 'ala 'l-mursalīn wa 'l-ḥamdulillāhi Rabbi 'l-'ālamīn.	سُبْحانَ ربّك رَبّ العزّة عمّا يَصفونَ وسَلامٌ على المُرْسَلينَ والحَمْدُ لله رَبّ العالمينَ

Glory be to Your Lord, the Lord of Power, above what they describe! And peace be upon the Emissaries. Praise belongs to God, the Lord of the Worlds.

Lā ilāhā ill-Allāh, wāḥdahū lā sharīka lah, lahu 'l-mulku wa lahu 'l-ḥamd, yuḥī wa yumīt, wa Hūwa Ḥāyyun dā'imun, lā yamūt, bi yadihi 'l-khayr, wa Hūwa 'alā kulli shay'in qadīr.	لا إله إلا الله وَحْدَهُ لا شَريكَ له، له المُلكُ وله الحَمْدُ يُحي ويُميت وهُوَ حيٌّ دائمٌ لا يَموتُ بيده الخَيْرُ وهُوَ على كُلِّ شَيْءٍ قَديرٌ .

There is no god but God. He is One, no partner has He. His is the Kingdom, and His is all praise, He brings to life and causes to die. He is forever Living, never dying. In His Hands is (all) good, and He is over all things Powerful.

DEDICATION

إهْداء

Ila sharaf in-Nabī ṣall-Allāhū ʻalayhi wa sallama wa ālihi wa ṣaḥbih, wa ilā arwāḥi ikhwānihi min al-anbiyā'i wa 'l-mursalīn wa khudamā'i sharā'ihim wa ila arwāḥi 'l-a'immati 'l-arba'ah wa ila arwāḥi mashāyikhinā fi 'ṭ-ṭarīqati 'n-naqshbandīyyati 'l-'aliyyah khāṣṣatan ila rūḥi Imāmi 'ṭ-ṭarīqati wa ghawthi 'l-khalīqati Khwājā Baḥā'uddīn an-Naqshband Muḥammad al-Uwaisī 'l-Bukhārī wa ḥaḍarati Mawlanā Sulṭānu 'l-awlīyā ash-Shaykh 'Abd Allāh al-Fā'iz ad-Dāghestanī wa sayyidunā ash-Shaykh Muḥammad Nāẓim al-Ḥaqqānī wa sa'iri sādātinā waṣ-ṣiddiqīna al-Fātiḥā

إلى شَرَف النبي وآله وصحْبه، وإلى أرْواح إخْوانه من الأنبياء والمُرسَلين وخُدَماء شَرائعهم وإلى أرْواح الأئمَّة الأرْبَعة، وإلى أرْواح مَشايخنا في الطَرِيقة النَقْشْبَنْدِيّة العَلَيّة خاصَةَ إلى رُوح إمام الطَريقة وغَوْث الخَليقة خواجه بَهاءُ الدّين النَقْشْبَنْد مُحَمَّدُ الأُوْيسى البُخاري وإلى حَضْرَة مولانا سلطان الأولياء الشيخ عبد الله الدغستاني ومولانا الشيخ محمد ناظم الحقاني وإلى سائر ساداتنا والصدّيقين. الفاتحَة

Honor be to the Prophet ﷺ, and his family, and his distinguished Companions, and to our honored Shaykhs and to our Master, Sulṭānu 'l-awlīyā Shaykh 'Abd Allāh al-Fā'izi 'd-Daghestanī and our Master ash-Shaykh Muḥammad Nāẓim al-Ḥaqqānī and to all our masters, and (those who are) the righteous ... al-Fātiḥa.

(LIE DOWN ON RIGHT SIDE RECITING CHAPTER 20: VERSE 55)

اسْتَرِحْ على جَنْبكَ الأيمن:

Minhā khalaqnākum, wa fīhā nu'īdukum, wa minhā nukhrijukum tāratan ukhrā.

سورة طه 55

منها خَلَقْناكم وفيها نُعيدُكم ومنها نُخْرِجُكم تارةً أخْرى

CHAPTER 2: 156

Wa innā lillāhi wa innā ilayhi rāji'ūn.

سورة البقرة 156

إنّا لله وإنّا إليه راجعُونَ

CHAPTER 40: 12

Fal-ḥukmu lillāh il-'Alīyyi il-Kabīr. Allāhumma thabbitnā 'alā al-īmān.

سورة غافر 12

فالحُكْمُ لله العَلىّ الكبير
اللّهمَّ ثبّتنا على الإيمان

Thereof (earth) We created you, and we shall return you unto it, and bring you forth from it a second time. And truly we belong to God and to Him we return. And the decree belongs to God, Most High, Most Great. O God! Keep us steadfast in faith.

IQĀMATU ṢALĀT (AS IN ṢALĀTUL-MAGHRIB)	إقامة الصلاة
2 RAK'ATS FARḌ	رَكْعتَان فَرْض

QUNŪT PRAYER (SEE NOTES) — دعاء القُنُوت

Allāhumma 'hdinā bi-faḍlika fī man hadayt, wa 'āfinā fī-man 'āfayt, wa tawallanā fī-man tawallayt, wa bārik lanā fī-mā a'ṭayt, wa qinā w'aṣrif 'annā sharra mā qaḍayt [palms turned down from wa qinā to qaḍayt]. Fa innaka taqḍī wa lā yuqḍā 'alayk, wa innahū lā yadhillu man wālayt, wa lā ya'izzu man 'ādayt. Tabārakta Rabbanā wa ta'ālayt, wa laka 'l-ḥamdu 'alā mā qaḍayt. Nastaghfiruk 'allāhumma wa natūbu ilayk, wa ṣalla-llāhu 'alā 'n-Nabī il-ummīyy wa 'alā ālihi wa ṣaḥbihi wa sallam.

بعد سمع الله لمن حمده:
اللَّهُمَّ اهْدنا بفضلك فيمَنْ هَدَيْتَ، وَعَافنا فى مَنْ عَافَيْتَ، وَتولَّنا فى مَنْ تَوَلَّيْتَ، وَبَارك لنا فيما أَعْطَيْتَ، وَقنا شَرَّ مَا قَضَيْتَ، فَإنكَ تَقْضى بالحقّ، وَلا يُقْضى عَلَيْكَ، وإنّه لا يَذل مَنْ وَاليتَ، وَلا يَعزُّ مَن عَادَيْتَ تَبَارَكْتَ رَبَّنا وَتَعَالَيْتَ فلَكَ الحَمْدُ على ما قَضَيْتَ نَسْتَغْفرُكَ اللَّهُمَّ من كل الذنوب ونَتُوبُ إليكَ وصَلّى اللهُ على النَّبى الأمّى وعلى آله وصَحْبه وسَلّم

O God! Guide us, by Your favor, to those whom You guided, and pardon us with those whom You have pardoned. Bring us close to those whom You have brought nigh (befriended), and bless us in all that You gave us. Protect us and turn away from us the evil of what You have decreed. For it is You that decrees and there is no decree upon You. You do not humiliate the one whom You have befriended and do not increase (empower) the one whom You have taken as an enemy. Blessed and Exalted are You, our Lord. To You is all praise for what You have decreed. We ask Your forgiveness, O God, and turn in repentance to You; God's blessings and peace be upon the unlettered Prophet and on his family and his Companions.

Allāhumma 'k-ashif 'anā minal-balāya mā lā yakshifuhu ghayruk — اللَّهُمَّ اكْشِفْ عنّا من البَلايا ما لا يَكْشِفُهُ غَيْرُك

O God! Lift from us trials which no one but You can lift.

Allāhumma 'sqina 'l-ghaytha suqyā raḥmatin wa lā taj'alna min al-qāniṭīn. Rabbi 'ghfir warḥam wa Anta khayru 'r-rāḥimīn. — اللَّهُمَّ اسْقنا الغيثَ سُقْياً رَحْمةً ولا تَجْعَلْنا من القانطينَ ربِّ اغْفرْ وارْحَمْ وأنتَ خَيْرُ الراحمين

O God! Give us to drink from the rain of Your Mercy and let us not be of the despondent; Lord, forgive and have mercy, for You are (Most) Merciful.

Allāhumma 'ftaḥ lanā fatḥan mubīnan wa — اللَّهُمَّ افْتَحْ لنا فتحاً مُبِينًا وأنتَ خَيْرُ الفاتحين

Anta khayru 'l-fātiḥīn

O God! Open for us a manifest opening for You are the best of Openers.

CHAPTER 6: VERSE 45

سورة الأنعام 45

Fa-quṭi'a dābiru 'l-qawm illadhīna ẓalamū wa 'l-ḥamdulillāhi Rabbi 'l-'ālamīn. (Then go to prostration without wiping face nor chest with hands.)

فقطع دابرُ القوم الذين ظلموا والحمد لله رب العالمين

So the last remnant of the people who did evil was cut off. Praise be to God, Lord of the Worlds. God is Greatest.

بعد التسليم من الصلاة

(AFTER THE SALUTATIONS)

لا إلَهَ إلاَ الله محمد رسول الله – 3 مرات

Lā ilāhā ill-Allāh (3 times)

Muḥammadur-Rasūlullāḥ

There is no god except God, Muhammad is the Prophet of God.

ISTIGHFĀR

استغفار (3 مرّة)

Astaghfirullāh (3 times)

I ask God's forgiveness.

DU'A (INVOCATION)

دُعاء

Allāhumma Anta 's-Salām wa minka 's-salām wa ilayka ya'ūdu 's-salām, fa ḥayyinā Rabbanā bis-salām, wa 'dkhiln'al-Jannata bi luṭfika wa karamika wa jūdika dāraka, dār as-salām. Tabārakta Rabbanā wa tā'alayta, yā Dhal-Jalāli wa 'l-Jamāli wa 'l-Baqā'i wa 'l-'Aẓamati wa 'l-Ikrām. Yā Rabbanā, Yā Rabbi 'ghfir warḥam wa Anta Khayru 'r-Raḥīmīn.

اللهم أنتَ السلام ومنك السلام وإليك يعود السلام فحينا ربنا بالسلام وادخلنا الجنة بلطفك وكرمك وجودك دارك دار السلام. تباركت ربنا وتعاليت يا ذا الجلال والجمال والبقاء والعظمة الإكرام. يا ربنا يا رب اغفر وارحم وأنتَ خير الراحمين.

O God! You are Peace and from You comes Peace and to You returns Peace; Make us live in peace, our Lord. Enter us into the Garden by Your Grace and Generosity and Presence. And Your Abode is the Abode of Peace. Blessed and lofty are You, O Lord of Majesty, and Beauty, and Everlastingness, and Greatness, and Bounty. O our Lord! O Lord forgive and have mercy, for Yours is the best of Mercy.

Lā ilāhā ill-Allāh, wāḥdahū lā sharīka lah, lahul-mulku wa lahul-ḥamd, yuḥī wa yūmīt, wa Hūwa 'alā kulli shay'in qadīr. (9 times).

لا إلَهَ إلاَّ الله وَحْدَهُ لا شَرِيكَ لَهُ، لَهُ المُلْكُ ولَهُ الحَمْدُ وُيحْي وُيميتُ وهُوَ على كُلّ شَيْء قدير (9 مرّات).

There is no god but God. He is One, no partner has He. His is the Kingdom and His is all praise, He gives life and gives death, and He is over all things Powerful.

Lā ilāhā ill-Allāh, wāḥdahū lā sharīka lah, lahu 'l-mulku wa lahu 'l-ḥamd, yuḥī wa yumīt, wa Hūwa Ḥāyyun dā'imun, lā yamūt, bi yadihi 'l-khayr, wa Hūwa 'alā kulli shay'in qadīr.	لا إله إلا الله وَحْدَهُ لا شَرِيكَ له، له المُلكُ وله الحَمْدُ يُحي ويُميت وهُوَ حيٌّ دائمٌ لا يَموتُ بيده الخَيْرُ وهُوَ على كُلِّ شَيْءٍ قدير.

There is no god but God. He is One, no partner has He. His is the Kingdom, and His is all praise, He brings to life and causes to die. He is forever Living, never dying. In His Hands is (all) good, and He is over all things Powerful.

Sam'inā wa ata'nā, ghufrānaka Rabbanā wa ilayk al-maṣīr	سَمِعْنا وأطَعْنا غفْرانكَ رَبّنا وإليْكَ المَصير

We have heard and obeyed, O our Lord! Yours is our destiny.

'Alā Rasūlinā 'ṣ-ṣalawāt (in a low voice): Allāhūma ṣalli 'alā sayyidinā Muḥammad	على رَسُولنا الصَّلَوات

On the Prophet of God, prayers. O God, bless our master Muhammad.

Astaghfirullāh, subḥānallāh wa 'l-ḥamdulillāh, wa lā ilāha ill-Allāh w'Allāhū akbar, wa lā ḥawla wa lā quwwata illa billāhi 'l-'Alīyy il-'Āẓīm.	أستَغْفِرُ الله. أستَغْفِرُ الله. أستَغْفِرُ الله سُبْحانَ الله والحَمْدُ لله ولا إلَهَ إلا الله والله أكْبَرُ ولا حَوْلَ ولا قوَّةَ إلا بالله العَلِيِّ العَظيم

I ask God's forgiveness. Glory be to God! Praise be to God! There is no god but God and God is Greatest. There is no power and no strengh save in God, All-High and Almighty.

CHAPTER 2, VERSE 163	البقرة 163
A'udhū billāhi min ash-shayṭān ir-rajīm. Bismillāhi 'r-Raḥmāni 'r-Raḥīm. Wa ilāhukum ilāhun wāḥidun, lā ilāha illa Hūwa 'r-Raḥmānu 'r-Raḥīm.	أعُوذُ بالله من الشَّيْطان الرَّجيم. بِسْمِ الله الرَّحْمن الرَّحيم. وإلَهُكُم إلهٌ واحدٌ لا إلَهَ إلاّ هُوَ الرَّحْمن الرَّحيم.

I seek refuge with God from Satan, the Cursed. In the name of God, the All-Beneficent, the All-Merciful. Your God is One God; there is no god but He, the All-Merciful, the All-Compassionate.

ĀYATU 'L-KURSĪ (THE VERSE OF THE THRONE)

آيَةُ الكُرْسي

اللهُ لا إلهَ إلا هُوَ الحيُّ القَيُّوم لا تَأْخُذُهُ سِنَةٌ ولا نَوْمٌ لَهُ
ما في السَماوات والأَرْض من ذا الذي يَشْفَعُ عِنْدَهُ
إلا بإِذْنه يَعْلَمُ ما في بيْنَ أيدبهم وما خَلَفَهُم ولا
يُحيطُونَ بشَىْء من علْمه إلا بما شاء وَسعُ كُرْسيُّهُ
السَماوات والأَرْضَ ولا يَؤُدُهُ حفظُهُما وهُوَ العَليُّ
العَظيمُ. صَدَقَ اللهِ العَظيم

Allāhū lā ilāha illa Hūwa 'l-Ḥayyu 'l-Qayyūm, lā tākhudhuhū 's-sinatun wa lā nawm, lahū mā fis-samāwāti wa mā fil-arḍ. Man dhā-ladhī yashfa'u 'indahū illā bi idhniḥ ya'lamu mā bayna aydīhim wa mā khalfahum wa lā yuḥīṭunā bi-shay'im min 'ilmihi illā bimā shā'. Wasi'a kursīyyuhu 's-samāwāti wa 'l-arḍa, wa lā ya'uduhū ḥifẓuhuma, wa Hūwa al-'Alīyyu 'l-'Aẓīm.

Ṣadaq-Allāhu 'l-'Aẓīm.

God, there is no god but He, the Living, the Everlasting. Slumber seizes Him not, neither sleep; to Him belongs all that is in the heavens and the earth. Who is there that shall intercede with Him save by His leave? He knows what lies before them, and they comprehend not anything of His knowledge save such as He wills. His Throne comprises the heavens and the earth; the preserving of them oppresses Him not; He is the All-High, the Almighty.

CHAPTER 3, VERSE 18-19

سورة آل عمران 18–19

شَهد اللهُ أَنَّهُ لا إله إلا هُوَ والمَلائكةُ وأُولُو العلْم قائمًا
بالقسْط لا إله إلا هُوَ العَزيزُ الحَكيمُ إنَّ الدبن عنْدَ الله
الإسْلام

Shahid-Allāhu annahū lā ilāha illa Hū. Wa 'l-malā'ikatu wa ūlu 'l-'ilmi qā'iman bi 'l-qisṭ. Lā ilāha illa Hūwa 'l-'Azīzu 'l-Ḥakīm. Inna 'd-dīna 'ind Allāhi 'l-islām.

God bears witness that there is no god but He—and the angels and men of knowledge—upholding justice; there is no god but He, the All-Mighty, the All-Wise. The religion with God is Islam.

CHAPTER 3, VERSE 26-27

سورة آل عمران 26–27

قل اللَّهُمَّ مالكُ المُلْك تؤْتى المُلْكَ من تشاء وتَنْزع
المُلْكَ ممَّن تشاء وتُعزُ من تشاء وتُذل من تشاءُ
بيَدكَ الخَيْرَ إنكَ على كُلِّ شىء قدبر تُولجُ اللَّيْل في
النَهار وتُولجُ النهارَ في اللَّيل وتُخْرجُ الحىَّ من الميّت
وتُخْرجُ الميّتَ من الحىّ وتَرْزُقُ من تَشاءُ بغَيْر
حسابٍ

Qul 'illāhumma Mālik al-mulki. Tu'tī 'l-mulka man tasha'u wa tanzi'u 'l-mulka mimman tashā'u wa tu'izzu man tashā'u wa tudhillu man tashā'u, bi yadik al-khayr, innaka 'alā kulli shay'in qadīr. Tūliju 'l-layla fi 'n-nahāri wa tūliju 'n-nahāra fi 'l-layl, wa tukhriju 'l-ḥāyya min al-mayyiti, wa tukhriju 'l-mayyita min al-ḥāyy, wa tarzuqu man tashā'u bi ghayri ḥisāb.

Say: O God, Master of the Kingdom, Thou givest the Kingdom to whom Thou wilt, and seizest the Kingdom from whom Thou wilt, Thou exaltest whom Thou wilt, and

Thou abasest whom Thou wilt; in Thy hand is the good; Thou art over all things Powerful. Thou makest the night to enter into the day, and Thou makest the day to enter into the night, Thou bringest forth the living from the dead, and Thou bringest forth the dead from the living, and Thou providest for whomsoever Thou wilt without reckoning.

Allāhumma lā māni'a limā āa'ṭaytu, wa lā mu'ṭīya limā man'ata wa lā rādda limā qaḍayta, wa lā yanfa'u dhāl-jaddi minka 'l-jadd. Rabbī wa lā ḥawla wa lā quwwata illa billāhi 'l-'Alīyy il-'Aẓīm.

اللّهمَّ لا مانع لما أعْطَيْتَ ولا مُعْطى لما مَنَعْتَ ولا رادَّ لما قَضَيْتَ ولا يَنفعُ ذا الجدّ منك الجَدُّ ربّى لا حَوْلَ ولا قوّةَ إلا بالله العَليّ العَظيم

O God! No one can disallow the one to whom You are giving, and there is no giver to the one whom You have denied. And there is no refusing Your decree. Riches and good fortune will not profit the possessor thereof with You (for nothing will profit him but acting in obedience to You). My Lord, there is no power and no strengh save in God, All-High and Almighty.

CHAPTER 57, VERSE 3

سورة الحديد 3

Hūwa 'l-Awwalu wa 'l-Ākhiru, waẓ-Ẓāhiru wa 'l-Bāṭin, wa Hūwa bi kulli shay'in 'alīm.

هو الأول والآخر والظاهر والباطن وهو بكل شيء عليم

He is the First and the Last, the Outward and the Inward; He has knowledge of everything.

SŪRATU 'L-FĀTIḤĀ — سورة الفاتحة

SŪRATU 'L-IKHLĀṢ — سورة الإخْلاص

SŪRATU 'L-FALAQ — سورةُ الفلَق

SŪRATU 'N-NĀS — سُورةُ الناس

TASBĪḤ

تَسْبيح

Yā rabbi dhul-Jalāli wa 'l-Ikrām, Subḥānaka yā 'Aẓīm subḥānallāh, subḥānallāh (33 times)

يا ربّىَ ذا الجلال والكمال سُبحانَكَ يا عَظيم: سُبْحان الله (33 مرّة)

O my Lord, Possessor of Glory and Perfection, Glory be to You, O Almighty One! Glory be to God.

'alā n'imat il-Islām wa sharaf al-īmān dā'iman alḥamdulillāh, alḥamdulillāh (33 times)	على نعمة الإسلام وشَرَف الإيمان دائمًا: الحَمْدُ لله (33 مرّة)

For the gift of Islam, the nobility of faith, always, praise be to God.

Ta'alā shā'nuhū wa lā ilāha ghayruhū, Allāhū akbar, Allāhū akbar (33 times)	تَعالَى شأنُهُ ولا إله غيرُهُ: اللهُ أكْبر (33 مرّة)

Exalted is His Affair, and there is no god but He, God is Greatest.

Allāhū akbaru kabīran wa 'lḥamdulillāhi kathīran wa subḥānallāhi bukratan wa aṣīla. Lā ilāha illa-Allāh wāḥdahū lā sharīka lah, lahu 'l-mulku wa lahu 'l-ḥamd yuḥīy wa yumīt wa Hūwa 'alā kulli shay'in qadīr. Subḥāna Rabbīu 'l-'Alīyyu 'l-'āla 'l-Wahhāb.	اللهُ أكْبَرُ كَبيرًا والحَمْدُ لله كَثيرًا وسُبْحانَكَ اللهم وبحمده بُكرَةً وأصيلاً لا إله إلا اللهُ وَحْدَهُ لا شَرِيكَ له، له المُلكُ وله الحَمْدُ يُحي ويُميت وهُوَ على كُلِّ شيءٍ قَدير. سُبْحانَ رَبّي العَليّ الأعلى الوهّاب

God is most Great in His Greatness and much praise be to God. Glory be to God, early and late. There is no god but God. He is One, no partner has He. His is the Kingdom and all praise. He brings to life and makes to die, and He is over all things Powerful. Glory be to my Lord, All-High, Supreme, Most Munificent.

CHAPTER 33, VERSE 56	سورة الأحزاب, 56
Inna-Allāha wa malā'ikatahū yuṣallūna 'alā an-Nabī, yā ayyuh-alladhīnā āmanū, ṣallū 'alayhi wa sallimū taslīmā. (Ṣadaq-Allāhu 'l-'Aẓīm)	إنَّ اللهَ ومَلائكتَهُ يُصَلّونَ على النبي، يا أيها الذينَ آمَنوا صَلّوا عليه وسلّموا تَسْليمًا

God and His angels send blessings on the Prophet: O you who believe! Send blessings on him and greet him with all respect. (God speaks the Truth).

ṢALAWĀT (3 TIMES)	صلوات
Allāhumma ṣalli 'alā Sayyidinā Muḥammadin wa 'alā āli Sayyidinā Muḥammad. Bi 'adadi kulli dā'in wa dawā'in wa bārik wa sallim 'alayhi wa 'alayhim kathīrā.	اللهُمَّ صلِّ على سَيِّدنا مُحَمَّد وعلى آلِ سَيِّدنا مُحَمَّد بعَدَدِ كُلِّ داء ودَواء وبارِكْ وسَلِّمْ عليه وعليهم كَثيرًا
(AFTER THE 3RD TIME)	في المَرّةِ الثالثة كَثيرًا كَثيرًا
kathīran kathīra, wa 'l-ḥamdulillāhi Rabbi 'l-'ālamīn.	

O God! Upon Muhammad and the family of Muhammad be blessings, according to the number of every illness and cure. Bless and grant peace to him and them, many times, endlessly. And praise belongs to God, the Lord of the worlds.

TAHLĪL

تهليل:

F'ālam annahū: lā ilāha illa-llāh, lā ilāha illa-llāh (100 times).

Know that: There is no god but God.

فاعْلَمْ أَنَّهُ

لا إله إلا الله (100 مرّة)

ṢALAWĀT (10 TIMES)

صَلوات (10 مرات)

Allāhumma ṣalli 'alā Muḥammadin wa 'alā āli Muḥammadin wa sallim.

اللّهمّ صلّ على مُحَمَّدٍ وعلى آل مُحَمَّد وسلّم

O God send blessings and peace upon Muhammad and the family of Muhammad.

DU'A (INVOCATION)

دُعاء

Ṣalli, yā Rabbī, wa sallim 'alā jamī'i il-anbīyā'i wa 'l-mursalīn, wa ālin kullin ajma'īn wa 'l-ḥamdulillāhi Rabb il-'ālamīn

صلّ يا رَبّي وسلّم على جَميع الأَنْبياء والمُرْسَلينَ وآل كُلٍّ أَجْمَعينَ والحَمْدُ لله رَبّ العالَمينَ

Blessings, O my Lord, and peace be upon all the prophets and Emissaries, and on the family of every one of them. Praise belongs to God, the Lord of the worlds.

CHIEF OF PRAYERS ON THE PROPHET (SEE PAGE 728)

الصلاة الشريفة المأثورة

Subḥāna Rabbīu 'l-'Alīyyu 'l-'Ala 'l-Wahhāb.

سُبْحانَ رَبِّي العَلِيِّ الأَعْلى الوَهّاب

Glory be to my Lord, All-High, Supreme, Most Munificent.

PERSONAL DU'A (INVOCATION)

دعاء شخصي

followed by:

ثم تقرأ:

CHAPTER 59, VERSE 22-24

سورة الحشر 22-24

A'udhūbillāhi min ash-shayṭān ir-rajīm. Bismillāhi 'r-Raḥmāni 'r-Raḥīm. Hūwa Allāhu 'lladhī lā ilāha illa Hū. 'Ālimu 'l-ghaybi wa 'sh-shahādati, Hūwa 'r-Raḥmānu 'r-Raḥīm. Hūwa Allāh 'ulladhī lā ilāha illa Hūw al-Maliku 'l-Quddusu 's-Salāmu 'l-Mu'minu 'l-Muhayminu 'l-'Azīzu 'l-Jabbāru 'l-Mutakabbir.

أَعُوذُ بالله من الشَّيْطان الرَّجيم. بِسْمِ اللهِ الرَّحْمنِ الرَّحيم. هُوَ اللهُ الذي لا إله إلا هُوَ عالمُ الغَيْبِ والشَّهادة هُوَ الرَّحْمنُ الرَّحيمُ هُوَ اللهُ الذي لا إله إلا هُوَ المَلِكُ القُدُّوسُ السَّلامُ المُؤْمِنُ المُهَيْمِنُ العَزيزُ الجَبّارُ المُتَكَبِّرُ، سُبْحانَ اللهِ عَمّا يُشْرِكون.

Subḥānallāhi 'ammā yushrikūn. Hūw 'Allāh 'ul-Khāliqu 'l-Barī'u 'l-Musawwiru lahu 'l-asmā'u 'l-ḥusnā. Yusabbiḥu lahū mā fi 's-samāwāti wa 'l-arḍ, wa Hūwa 'l-'Azīzu 'l-Ḥakīm.	هُوَ اللهُ الخالقُ البارئُ المُصوّرُ له الأسْماءُ الحُسْنى يُسَبّحُ له ما في السّماوات والأرْض وهُوَ العَزيزُ الحَكيمُ

He is God; there is no god but He. He is the Knower of the Unseen and Visible; He is the All-Merciful, the All-Compassionate. He is God; there is no god but He. He is the King, the All-Holy, the All-Peacable, the All-Faithful, the All-Preserver, the All-Mighty, the All-Compeller, the All-Sublime. Glory be to God, above what they associate! He is God, the Creator, the Maker, the Shaper. To Him belong the Names Most Beautiful. All that is in the heavens and the earth magnifies Him; He is the All-Mighty, the All-Wise.

CHAPTER 57, VERSE 3	سورة الحديد 3
Hūwa 'l-Āwwalu wa 'l-ākhiru waẓ-Ẓāhiru wa 'l-Bāṭin, wa Hūwa bi kulli shay'in 'Alīm. Ṣadaq-Allāhu 'l-'Aẓīm.	هُوَ الأوّلُ الآخرُ والظّاهرُ والباطنُ وهُوَ على كلّ شيْءٍ عليم. صدَقَ اللهُ العظيم

He is the First and the Last, the Outward and the Inward; He has knowledge of everything. (God speaks the Truth).

DU'A (INVOCATION)	دُعاءٌ :
Rabbanā taqabbal minna, wa'fu 'annā, waghfir lanā, warḥamnā, wa tub 'ālaynā, wasqinā, wasliḥ shā'nanā wa shā'n al-Muslimīn, fanṣurna 'alā al-qawm il-mufsidīn, bi ḥurmati man anzalta 'alayhi Sūratu 'l-Fātiḥa.	ربّنا تَقَبّل منّا واعْفُ عنّا واغفرْ لنا وارْحَمْنا وتُبْ علينا واهْدنا واسْقنا واصْلحْ شأننا وشأنَ المُسْلمينَ وانْصُرْنا على القوم الكافرين بحُرْمَة من أُنزلتَ عليه سُورةُ الفاتحة

O our Lord! Accept (this) from us and absolve us. Forgive us and have mercy on us. Accept our repentance and guide us. Quench (our thirst), and improve our condition and the condition of the Muslims. Give us success over those who falsify the Truth, by the sanctity of the one to whom You revealed Sūrat al-Fātiḥa.

KALIMATU 'SH-SHAHĀDA (3 TIMES)	كلمة الشّهَدُاْ
Ash-hadu an lā ilāha ill-Allāh, wa ash-hadu anna Muḥammadan 'abduhū wa rasūluḥ.	أشْهَدُ أنْ لا إله إلا الله وأشْهَدُ أنَّ مُحَمّدًا رَسُولُ الله (3 مرّات) (بصَوْت خفى) صلّى اللهُ عليه وسلّم

I bear witness that there is no god but God, and Muhammad is His servant and Messenger.

ISTIGHFĀR

اسْتِغفار:

Astaghfirullāh (100 times)

أسْتَغْفِرُ الله (100 مَرّة)

I ask God's forgiveness.

Astaghfirullāh min kulli dhanbin wa ma'ṣīyatin wa min kulli mā yukhālifu dīn al-Islām, yā arḥama 'r-Rāḥimīn.

أسْتَغْفِرُ الله من كُلّ ذَنْب ومَعْصيّة ومن كُلّ ما يُخالفُ دينَ الإسْلام يا أرْحَمَ الراحمين

I ask God's forgiveness for every sin and disobedience and from all that opposes the religion of Islam. O Merciful of the Merciful.

SŪRATU 'L-FĀTIḤĀ

الفاتحة

SŪRAT YĀ SĪN (CHAPTER 36)

سُورة يس

CHAPTER 28, VERSE 88

سورة القصص 88

Kullu shay'in hālikun illa Wajhah, lahu 'l-ḥukmu wa ilayhi turja'ūn.

ثم تنتهي: كُلُّ شَيْء هالكٌ إلا وَجْهه له الحُكْمُ واليه تُرْجَعُون

All things perish except His Face. His is the Judgment, and unto Him you shall be returned.

99 Beautiful Names of God

أسْماءُ الله الحسنى

(Asmā'ullah)

A'udhūbillāhi min ash-shayṭān ir-rajīm. Bismillāhi 'r-Raḥmāni 'r-Raḥīm. Hūwa Allāhu 'lladhī lā ilāha illa Hū. 'Ālimu 'l-ghaybi wa 'sh-shahādati, Hūwa 'r-Raḥmānu 'r-Raḥīm (Jalla Jallāluhū). Hūwa Allāh 'ulladhī lā ilāha illa Hūw al-Maliku 'l-Quddusu 's-Salāmu 'l-Mu'minu 'l-Muhayminu 'l-'Azīzu 'l-Jabbāru 'l-Mutakabbir (Jalla Jallāluhū). Al-Khāliqu 'l-Bāri'u 'l-Musawwiru 'l-Ghaffāru 'l-Qahhāru 'l-Wahhābu 'r-Razzāqu 'l-Fattāḥu 'l-'Alīm (Jalla Jallāluhū), al-Qābiḍu 'l-Bāsiṭu 'l-Khāfiḍu 'r-Rāf'iu 'l-Mu'izzu 'l-Mudhillu 's-Samī'u 'l-Baṣīr, (Jalla

أعُوذُ بالله من الشَيْطان الرَّجيم. بِسْم الله الرَّحْمن الرَّحيم.

هُوَ اللهُ الذي لا إلهَ إلّا هُوَ، الرَّحْمَنُ، الرَّحيمُ، المَلكُ، القُدُّوسُ، السَّلامُ، المؤمنُ، المُهَيْمنُ، العَزيزُ، الجَبّارُ، المتَكَبِّرُ، الخالقُ، البارِئُ، المُصوّرُ، الغفارُ، القَهّارُ، الوَهّابُ، الرَّزاقُ، الفَتّاحُ، العَليمُ، الباسطُ، الخافضُ، الرّافعُ، المعزُّ، المُذلُّ، السَّميعُ، البَصيرُ، الحَكَمُ، العَدْلُ، اللّطيفُ، الخَبيرُ، الحَليمُ، العَظيمُ، الغفورُ، الشَّكورُ، العَليُّ، الكَبيرُ، المُغيثُ، الحَسيبُ، الجَليلُ، الكَريمُ، الرَّقيبُ، المُجيبُ، الواسعُ، الحَكيمُ، الوَدودُ،

Jallāluhū), al-Ḥakamu 'l-'Adlu 'l-Laṭīfu 'l-Khabīru 'l-Ḥalīmu 'l-'Aẓīmu 'l-Ghafūr ush-Shakūru 'l-'Aliyyu 'l-Kabīr, (Jalla Jallāluhū), al-Ḥafīẓu 'l-Muqītu 'l-Ḥasību 'l-Jalīlu 'l-Karīmu 'r-Raqību 'l-Mujību 'l-Wās'iu 'l-Ḥakīmu 'l-Wadūdu 'l-Majīd, (Jalla Jallāluhū), al-Bā'ith ush-Shahīdu 'l-Ḥaqqu 'l-Wakīlu 'l-Qawīyyu 'l-Matīnu 'l-Walīyyu 'l-Ḥamīdu 'l-Muḥsīyu 'l-Mubd'īu 'l-Mu'īdu 'l-Muḥīyyu 'l-Mumītu 'l-Ḥāyyu 'l-Qayyūm (Jalla Jallāluhū), al-Wājidu 'l-Mājidu 'l-Wāḥidu 'l-Āḥad uṣ-Ṣamadu 'l-Qādiru 'l-Muqtadir (Jalla Jallāluhū), al-Muqaddimu 'l-Mu'akhkhiru 'l-Awwalu 'l-Ākhir uẓ-Ẓāhiru 'l-Bāṭinu 'l-Wālīyu 'l-Muta'ālu 'l-Barru 't-Tawwāb (Jalla Jallāluhū), al-Muntaqimu 'l-'Afuwwu 'r-Ra'uf Māliku 'l-mulki dhul-Jalāli wa 'l-Ikrām (Jalla Jallāluhū), al-Muqsiṭu 'l-Jāmi'u 'l-Ghanīyyu 'l-Mughnīyyu 'l-Mu'ṭīu 'l-Māni'u 'd-Ḍārr un-Nāfi' un-Nūr (Jalla Jallāluhū), al-Hādīyu 'l-Bad'īu 'l-Bāqīyu 'l-Wārithu 'r-Rashīd uṣ-Ṣabur.

Jalla Jallāluhū wa jallat 'āẓamatahū wa lā ilāha ghayruhu 'lladhī lam yalid wa lam yūlad wa lam yakun lahū kufuwan āḥad

المَجيدُ، الباعثُ، الشَهيدُ، الحَقُّ، الوَكيل، القويُّ، المَتينُ، الوَليُّ، الحَميدُ، المُحْصى، المُبْدىءُ، المعيدُ، المُحْيى، المُميتُ، الحَىُّ، القَيّومُ، الوَاجدُ، المَاجدُ، الوَاحدُ، الصَمَدُ، القادرُ، المقْتدرُ، المقدّمُ، المؤَخرُ، الأوّلُ، الآخرُ، الظَاهرُ، البَاطنُ، الوَالي، المتَعال، البَرُّ، التّوَابُ، المُنْتَقمُ، العَفوُّ، الرَّؤُوف، مالكُ المُلك، ذو الجَلال وَالإكْرَام، المقْسط، الجامعُ، الغَنيُّ، المُغْنى، المَانعُ، الضار، النَافعُ، النُورُ، الهَادي، البَديعُ، الباقى، الوَارثُ، الرَشيدُ، الصَبُور

جل جلاله و جلّت عظمته و لا إله غيره الّذي لَمْ يَلِدْ وَلَمْ يُولَدْ وَلَمْ يَكُن لَّهُ كُفُواً أَحَدٌ

In the Name of God, the Most Merciful, the Most Compassionate. May He be Glorified and Exalted! He is God; there is no god but He. He is the Knower of the Unseen and Visible; He is the All-Merciful, the All-Compassionate, (His Greatness has become manifest). The King, the All-Holy, the Source of Peace, the All-Faithful, the the Guardian, the Mighty, the Compeller, the Greatest, (His Greatness has become manifest). The Creator, the Maker, the Fashioner, the All-Forgiver, the Irrestible, the All-Bounteous, the Provider, the Opener, the Omniscient, (His Greatness has become manifest). The Contracter, the Expander, the Abaser, the Exalter, the Bestower of Honor, the Humiliator, the All-Hearing, the All-Seeing, (His Greatness has become manifest). The Supreme Arbiter, the Just, the Subtle, the All-Cognizant, the Forbearing, the Magnificent, the Most Forgiving, the Appreciative, the Most High, the Grand, (His Greatness has become manifest). The Preserver, the Nourisher, the Reckoner, the Sublime, the Generous, the Ever-Watchful, the Responsive, the Limitless, the All-Wise, the Loving, the Glorious, (His Greatness has become manifest). The Resurrector, the Witness, the Ultimate Truth, the Trustee, the Most Strong, the Firm, the Protecting Friend, the Praiseworthy, the Reckoner, the

Originator, the Restorer, the Granter of Life, the Bringer of Death, the Ever-Living, the Self-Subsisting, (His Greatness has become manifest). The Founder Who has no needs, the Glorified, the Unique, the Eternally Besought, the All-Powerful, the Bestower of Power, (His Greatness has become manifest). The Advancer, the Delayer, the First, the Last, the Manifest, the Hidden, the Governor, the Highly Exalted, the Beneficent, the Accepter of Repentance, (His Greatness has become manifest). The Avenger, the Eraser of Sin, the Most Compassionate, the Lord of All Dominion, the Possessor of Majesty and Bounty, (His Greatness has become manifest). The Upholder of Equity, the Gatherer, the All-Wealthy, the Enricher, the Giver, the Preventer, the Distresser, the Creator of Good, the Light, (His Greatness has become manifest). The Guider, the Originator, the Everlasting, the Inheritor, the Guide, the Patient, (His Greatness has become manifest).

His Greatness has become manifest, and there is no god but He, Who has not begotten and has not been begotten, and equal to Him is not any one.

Yā Āḥad, Yā Ṣamad, ṣalli 'alā Muḥammad (3 times).

يا أحَد . يا صَمَد صل على محمد (3 مرات)

O Unique One! O Eternally Besought! Bless Muhammad.

SŪRATU 'L-IKHLĀṢ (CHAPTER 112) (11 TIMES)

سُورةُ الإخْلاص (11 مرة)

SŪRATU 'L-FALAQ (CHAPTER 113) (ONCE)

سُورةُ الفَلَق

SŪRATU 'N-NĀS (CHAPTER 114) (ONCE)

سُورةُ الناس

TAHLĪL WITH ṢALAWĀT (10 TIMES)

تهليل:

Lā ilāhā ill-Allāh Muḥammadur Rasūlullāh, Ṣalla-llāhū ta'alā 'alayhi wa 'alā ālihi wa ṣaḥbihi wa sallam.

لا إله إلا الله مُحَمَّدٌ رَسُولُ الله صلّى الله تعالى عليه وعلى آله وصحبه وسلم (10 مرات)

There is no god but God. Muhammad is the Messenger of God, blessings and peace of God (Exalted is He!) be upon him, his family, and his Companions.

ṢALAWĀT (10 TIMES)

الصَلَوات الشريفة (10مرّات)

Allāhumma ṣalli 'alā Muḥammadin wa 'alā āli Muḥammadin wa sallim.

اللّهمّ صلّ على مُحَمَّد وعلى آل مُحَمَّد وسلم

Blessings and peace be upon Muhammad and the family of Muhammad.

DU'A (INVOCATION)	دُعاء
Ṣalli, yā Rabbī, wa sallim 'alā jamī'i il-anbīyā'i wa 'l-mursalīn, wa ālin kullin ajma'īn wa 'l-ḥamdulillāhi Rabb il-'ālamīn	صلِّ يا ربِّي وسلِّم على جميع الأنبياء والمُرسَلينَ وآلِ كُلٍّ أجْمَعينَ والحَمْدُ لله ربِّ العالمينَ
Blessings, O my Lord, and peace be upon all the prophets and emissaries, and on the family of every one of them. Praise belongs to God, the Lord of the worlds.	
CHIEF OF PRAYERS ON PROPHET (PAGE 728)	الصلوات الشريفة المأثورة
IHDĀ (SEE PAGE 729)	إهْداء

صَلاةُ الظُهرِ

Salatu-z-Zuhr

Ṣalātu 'ẓ-Ẓuhr is performed in the same sequence as Ṣalātu 'l-'Ishā, from the Adhān to the end, with the exception of Ṣalātu 'l-Witr, which is omitted.

4 RAK'ATS SUNNAH	4 ركْعات: ركْعَتَيْن سُنّة وركْعَتَيْن نافلة بتَسْليم واحد أو بتسليمين
4 RAK'ATS FARḌ	أرْبَعُ ركْعات فرَض
4 RAK'ATS SUNNAH	أرْبَعُ ركْعات سُنّة
SŪRATU 'L-MULK (CHAPTER 67)	سُورةُ المُلك

At the end of Sūratu 'l-Mulk add: Allāhu ta'alā Rabbunā wa Rabbu 'alamīn. Then continue with the same practices as in Ṣalātul-'Ishā with the exception of Ṣalātu 'l-Witr.

صلاةُ العصر

Salatu-l-Asr

Ṣalātu 'l-'Asr is performed exactly in the same way a Ṣalātu 'l-'Ishā, with the exception of the final 4 rak'āts Sunnah prayer and Ṣalātu 'l-Witr.

4 RAK'ATS SUNNAH	4 ركْعات سُنّة ركْعَتَيْن سُنّة وركْعَتَيْن نافلة بتَسْليم واحد أو بتسليمين
4 RAK'ATS FARḌ	4 ركْعات فرَض
SŪRATU 'N-NABĀ(CHAPTER 78)	سُورةُ النبأ
Continue reading with Chapter 89, Verses 24-30 Fa yawmaydhin lā yu'adhibu 'adhābahu āḥadun wa lā yuthiqu wathāqahu āḥad. Yā ayyatuhā 'n-nafsu 'l-muṭma'innatu 'rji'ī ilā rabbika rāḍīyyatan marḍīyyah. f'adkhulī fī 'ibādī w'adkhulī jannatī. Then add: Razzaqanā Allāhu, yā Allāḥ, Āmannā billāhi. Ṣadaqa-Allāhu 'l-'Aẓīm.	فَيَوْمَئذ لَّا يُعَذّبُ عَذَابَهُ أَحَدٌ . وَلَا يُوثِقُ وَثَاقَهُ أَحَدٌ يَا أَيَّتُهَا النَّفْسُ الْمُطْمَئنَّةُ ارْجعى إِلَى رَبّك رَاضيَةً مَّرْضيَّةً فَادْخُلى فى عبَادي وَادْخُلى جَنَّتى رزقنا الله يا الله. آمَنّا بالله. صدق الله العظيم

Then continue the recitation to the end as in Ṣalātu 'l-'Ishā.

Practices During Rajab, Shaban and Ramadan

Practice of the Month of Rajab

ادب شهر رجب

This Adab is performed on the day before Rajab begins between Ṣalātu 'l-'Asr and Ṣalātu 'l-Maghrib and is repeated as the daily practice of the seeker every day, beginning before Ṣalātu 'l-Fajr by an hour and a half but without the Grand Transmitted Invocation of Grandshaykh (Ad-du'āu 'l-māthūr li Sulṭān al-Awliyā on page 793) which is done only the first night.

BATHING OF PURIFICATION

غُسل

When the month of Rajab is entered, the murīd begins its night between Ṣalātu 'l-'Asr and Ṣalātu 'l-Maghrib receiving the month of Rajab. One performs the major ritual purification (ghusl, or shower).

إذا دخل شهر رجب بادر المريد في ليلة ابتدائه للغسل ما بين العصر والمغرب.

One dresses in the best clothes and (for a man) puts on a nice scent, then prays 2 rak'ats sunnat al-wuḍū'.

ثم يلبس أفضل الثياب واطهرها يتطيب ويستقبل القبلة ثم يصلى ركعتين سنة الوضوء
ثم يقرأ:

Recite: Yā Rabb al-'izzati wa 'l-'aẓamati wa 'l-jabbarūt

يا رب العزة والعظيمة الجبروت

O Lord of Honor and Greatness, Imposer of Thy Will.

The murīd takes three steps in the direction of the Qiblah in his place of worship.

و يتقرب في محرابه ثلاثة اقدام نحو القبلة

NĪYYAT

النية:

Nawaytu 'l-arbā'īn, nawaytu 'l-'itikāf, nawaytu 'l-khalwa, nawaytu 'l-'uzla, nawaytu 'r-riyāda, nawaytu 's-sulūk, lillāhi ta'ala fī hādhā 'l-masjid (or fī hādha al-jāmi')

نَوَيتُ الأربعين، نَوَيتُ الاعتكاف نَوَيتُ الخَلوَة نَوَيتُ العُزلَة، نَوَيتُ الرياضَة نَوَيتُ السلوك، لله تعالى في هَذا المسجد

INTENTION:

I intend the forty (days of seclusion); I intend seclusion in the mosque; I intend seclusion; I intend isolation; I intend discipline (of the ego); I intend to travel in God's Path; I intend to fast for the sake of God in this mosque.

100 times Yā Ḥalīm (for removing anger).

يا حَليم. يا حَليم. يا حَليم (100 مَرَّة)

O Clement One!

100 times Yā Ḥafīẓ (for removing affliction).

يا حَفيظ. يا حَفيظ. يا حَفيظ (100 مَرَّة)

O Guardian!

Imagine yourself in the blessed Garden (al-Rawḍa) in front of the maqām of the Prophet ﷺ facing God's Messenger ﷺ and saying:

ṢALAWĀT

صَلَوات —100 مرة

100 times Allāhumma ṣalli 'alā Sayyidina Muḥammadin wa 'alā āli Muḥammadin wa sallim.

اللَّهُمَّ صَلِّ على مُحَمَّد وعلى آل مُحَمَّد وسلِّم

O God, pray on our master Muhammad and on his family and greet them with peace. Make the intention that God makes you to be in the spiritual Presence of God's Messenger ﷺ, Imām al-Mahdī ؏, and our shaykhs.

NĪYYAT:

النية:

Yā Rabbī innanī nawaytu an ataqaddama nahwa baḥri waḥdanīyyatika ilā maqāmi 'l-fanā'i fīka. Falā tarudanī yā Rabbi, yā Allāh khā'iban ḥatta tuwaṣṣilanī ila dhāk al-maqām al-maqāmu 'l-fardānī.

يا ربي إنني نويت ان أتقدم نحو بحر واحدانيتك إلى مقام الفناء فيك فلا تردني يا ربي يا الله خائبا حتى توصلني إلى ذاك المقام — المقام الفرداني.

INTENTION:

O my Lord, I am moving and stepping forward for the Station of Annihilation in the Divine Presence. O God—glory be to You, the Most High—I am asking you to cause me to vanish before Your Existence and, O my Lord, I am moving toward your Ocean of Unity. O my Lord, do not reject me until I reach the Unique Station.

Yā Rabbī, yā Allāh ḥaithu hādha ash-shahru hūwa shahruka, ji'tuka ḍa'ifan wa nāwī'an an 'amala 'amalan bidūn 'iwaḍun aw an yakūna fīhi ṭālaban lil-faḍīlati qāṣidan iyyāka Ilāhī anta

يا ربي يا الله حيث هذا الشهر هو شهرك جئتك ضيفا وناويا ان أعمل عملا بدون عوض أو ان يكون فيه طلبا للفضيلة. قاصدا اياك الهي أنت مقصودي ورضاك

maqsūdī wa riḍāka maṭlūbi.

مطلوبى

O my Lord, O God, since this month is your month, I came to you as a weak guest and intending to worship You without asking anything in return. My God, You are my aim, and Your good pleasure is what I seek, and that is why I am coming. Please do not reject me.

Yā Rabbī, kullu ʿumrī qad amḍaytuhu fī 'l–maʿāsī wash-shirkil-khafī. Wa innanī uqirru bi-annanī lam āʾti ilā bābika bi-ʿamalin maqbūlin ʿindaka anta-Allāhu 'lladhī lā yāʾtī āḥad ilā bābika bi ʿamalihi bal bi-faḍlika wa jūdika wa karamika wa iḥsānika. Anta-Allāhu 'lladhī la taruddu ʿabdan jāʾa ilā bābika falā taruddanī yā Allāh.

يا ربى كل عمري قد امضيته في المعاصى والشرك الخفى
وانى اقر بأنى لم أئت إلى بابك بعمل مقبول عندك أنتَ
الله الذي لا يأتى احد إلى بابك بعمله بل بفضلك وجودك
وكرمك واحسانك أنتَ الله الذي لا ترد عبدا جاء إلى
بابك فلا تردني يا الله،

O my Lord, I say out of abject humility that it as if I spent all my life in unbelief, polytheism, and bad behavior, and I am declaring wholeheartedly that I did not do any deed that is accepted by You. You are God, Who never threw away anyone that came to Your door. You are God, and no one came to Your door by his deeds, but (only) by Your grant and reward.

Yā Rabbī, kullu umūrī fawwaḍtuhā ilayka, ḥayātī wa mamātī wa bʿada mamāti, wa yawmu 'l-ḥashr. Kullu umūri ḥawwaltuhā ʿindaka. Wa fawwaḍtu amrī ilayka, lā amliku min amri nafsī shay-an. Lā nafʿan, wa lā ḍarran, wa lā mawtan, wa lā ḥayātan, wa lā nushūran. Kullu umūri wa ḥisābī wa suʾālī wa jawābī ḥawwaltuhu ʿindaka yā Rabbī yā Allāḥ. Nāṣīyatī bi-yadika wa anā ʿājizun ʿan il-jawābi wa law mithqāla dharratin.

يا ربى كل اموري فوضتها إليك حياتى ومماتى وبعد مماتى
ويوم الحشر كل اموري حولتها عندك وفوضت أمري إليك
لا املك من امر نفسى شيئًا لا نفعا ولا ضرا ولا موتا ولا
حياة ولا نشور . كل اموري وحسابى وسؤالي وجوابى
حولته عندك يا ربى يا الله، ناصيتى بيدك وانا عاجز عن
الجواب ولو مثقال ذرة

O my Lord, I have given everything into Your hands—my life, my death, my afterlife, and Judgment Day. All my things I have transferred to You, and You are the One Who controls me. O my Lord, I do not possess anything with my ego and my soul. I cannot give good to myself, or bad to myself, or life to myself, or death to myself, but I have transferred all my accounts, and all Your judgment on me, and all your questions to me, and all my answers I have transferred to You. Whatever You want to do with me, You do. My neck is in Your hand. I am helpless in answering Your questions; even the smallest answer I cannot give. With all this weakness, and helplessness, and hopelessness, I am coming to Your door.

law kāna laka yā Rabbī bābayni āḥadahumā mukhaṣaṣṣun lit-tā'ibīna min 'ibādika al-mu'minīn wa 'l-ākharu lit-tā'ibīna min 'ibādika al-'aṣīn. Ji'tuka yā Allāh naḥwu bābik alladhī yaḥtāju an yadkhula minhu 'ibāduka al-'aāṣīn. Wa innanī uqirru wa āa'tarif annahu yajibu an ujaddida islāmī wa īmānī min hādhal-bāb li-iẓhāri 'l-'ajzi.	لو كان لك يا ربي بابين احدهما مخصص للتائبين من عبادك المؤمنين والأخر للتائبين من عبادك العاصين ، جئتك يا الله نحو بابك الذي يحتاج ان يدخل منه عبادك العاصين وانني اقر واعترف انه يجب ان اجدد إسلامي وإيماني من هذا الباب لاظهار العجز.

O my Lord, if you had two doors for Your servant to enter through—one for the believers from Your servants and one for the unbelievers from Your servants—I am coming to You from the door that the unbeliever needs to come through, and I am declaring my belief that this is the only door for me to come through. I am saying to you that I have to renew my faith and my testimony of faith from this door to show humility and helplessness.

Wa hādhā al-'amalu hūwa āwwalu 'amalin lī b'ada mā shahidtu bi 'l-islāmi ḥaqqan. Yā Rabbī wa Anta wakīlī yā Wakīl ḥaithu naqūlu Allāha 'alā mā naqūlu Wakīl wa Shahīd.	و هذا العمل هو اول عمل لي بعد ما شهدت بالإسلام حقا يا ربي وأنتَ وكيلي يا وكيل حيث نقول الله على ما نقول وكيل وشهيد.

This deed and this Shahāda is the first deed for me after I am pronouncing the Shahāda and entering Islam, and You are my Protector from whence we say: God is the Protector and Witness over what we say.

3 times Shahādah.	ثم تبدأ بكلمتي الشهادة (3 مرات)

Iqāmu 'ṣ-ṣalāti wa ītāu 'z-zakāt wa ṣawmu ramaḍāna, wa Ḥajju 'l-bayt.	تجديد اركان الإسلام: اقام الصلاة وايتاء الزكاة وصوم رمضان وحج البيت

Re-affirmation of Islam's five pillars:

I believe in the establishment of prayer, paying the poor-due, fasting Ramadan, and the Pilgrimage to the House of God.

Āmantu billāhi wa malā'ikatihi wa kutubihi wa rusulihi wa 'l-yawmi 'l-ākhiri wa bi 'l-qadari khayrihi wa sharrihi min Allāhi ta'alā.	تجديد الإيمان: آمنت بالله وملائكته وكتبه ورسله وباليوم الاخر وبالقدر خيره وشره.

Re-affirmation of the pillars of faith:

I believe in God, His Angels, His books, His Messengers, the Last Day, and that the Destiny—its good and its bad—is from God, the Most High.

Yā Rabbī, yā Allāhu, kam ẓahara minnī min adh-dhunūbi wa 'l-ma'āṣīyy ẓāhiran wa bāṭinan wa sirran	يا ربي يا الله كم ظهر مني من الذنوب والمعاصي ظاهرا وباطنا وسرا من عهد ايجاد ذرتي وروحي ودخول

min ʿahdiījādi dharratī wa rūḥī, wa dukhūli rūḥī ilā jismī wa ẓuhūrī min al-ʿadami ilā ʾl-wujūdi wa ẓuhūrī fī ʿālami ʾd-dunyā ilā yawminā hādha, rajʿatu ʿani ʾl-jamīʿi ilayka bi ʾt-tawbati wa ʾl-istighfār.	روحى إلى جسمى وظهوري من العدم إلى الوجود وظهوري في عالم الدنيا إلى بومنا هذا، رجعت عن الجميع اليك بالتوبة والإستغفار

O my Lord, from the Day of Promises, whatever there was of promise from Me to You, I accept and promise to do it all. O my Lord, O God, from the day You created my atom, my essence, and from the day You brought up my soul, and from the day my soul came from the absolute abstract to existence, until our day, how much of disobedience has appeared from me and my essence, and from my soul and my body, spiritually and physically! I am regretting it all, and regretting what I did, and coming back to You asking forgiveness and repentance.

Wa innanī qad dakhaltu wa salaktu fī raḥmāti shahrika hādha ʾl-mubārak falā taruddnī yā Rabbī, ʿan bābika wa lā tatruknī li-aḥwāli nafsī wa law li-laḥzah wa anā astaghfiruka.	و انني قد دخلت وسلكت في رحمات شهرك هذا المبارك فلا تردني يا ربى عن بابك ولا تتركني لاحوال نفسي ولو لحظة، وانا استغفرك

O my Lord, I entered and I moved into the ocean of blessings of Your praised month. O my Lord, do not reject me from Your door, and do not leave me to my ego for the blink of an eye, and I am asking forgiveness of You.

ISTIGHFĀR	أستغفار
100 times Astaghfirullāh I ask God's forgiveness	أستغفر الله (100 مرات)

Continue with the remainder of the Naqshbandi *Adab* from the verse Āmanar-Rasūl until its end.	اية آمن الرسول. . . . .إلى الأخر

In the case of the daily practice of Rajab, continue to the Adhkār al-yawmi, the daily recitation of the wird, including "Allah, Allah" and ṣalawāt, at the level of the People of Determination (see page 724)

500 TIMES YĀ ṢAMAD	يا صمد .(500 مرّة)

With the intention to eliminate the bad aspects of the ego.

500 TIMES ASTAGHFIRULLĀH	أستغفر الله (500 مرة)

Recite with the intention of asking God to forgive your sins, from the day of creation of your soul to the present day.

500 TIMES ASTAGHFIRULLĀH   أَسْتَغْفِرُ الله (500 مرة)

Recite with the intention that, from the present day to the last day on earth, God will protect you against sins.

500 TIMES ALḤAMDULILLĀH   الْحَمدُ لله (500 مَرة).

Out of gratitude that God did not create you from the nation of other prophets.

500 TIMES ALḤAMDULILLĀH   الْحَمدُ لله (500 مَرة).

Out of gratitude that God has created you from the nation of the Prophet Muḥammad ﷺ and honored you by Sayyidina Abū Bakr aṣ-Ṣiddīq ؓ, 'Abd al-Khāliq al-Ghujdawānī, Shaykh Sayyid Sharafuddīn ad-Daghestānī, and honored you by Grandshaykh Shaykh 'Abd Allāh al-Fā'iz ad-Daghestānī, and honored you by making you a follower of Mawlana Shaykh Muhammad Nā·im al-Ḥaqqānī.

THE GRAND TRANSMITTED INVOCATION (AD-DU'AU 'L-MĀTHŪR) OF SULṬĀN AL-AWLIYĀ   الدعاء المأثور عن سلطان الأولياء

(see page 793)

Daily Practices Between Maghrib and Isha in Rajab

ادب رجب اليومي بين المغرب والعشاء

1. Avoid the company of people and perform the Naqshbandi Adab in the last third of the night until sunrise, and/or between Ṣalātu 'l-'Asr and Ṣalātu 'l-Maghrib and/or between Ṣalātu 'l-Maghrib and Ṣalātu 'l-'Ishā.

المحافظة على الإعتكاف عن الخلق من الثلث الأخير من الليل وإلى طلوع الشمس، وما بين العصر والمغرب ، وما بين المغرب والعشاء .الأدب بعاد كل يوم في الثلث الأخير من الليل أو بين المغرب والعشاء

NĪYYAT:

النية:

Nawaytu 'l-arbā'īn, nawaytu 'l-'itikāf, nawaytu 'l-khalwa, nawaytu 'l-'uzla, nawaytu 'r-riyāda, nawaytu 's-sulūk, lillāhi ta'ala fī hādhā 'l-masjid (or fī hādha al-jāmi').

نَوَيتُ الأربَعين، نَوَيتُ الاعتكاف نَوَيتُ الخَلْوَة نَوَيتُ العُزلَة، نَوَيتُ الرياضَة نَوَيتُ السُلوك، لله تَعالى في هَذا المسجد

INTENTION:

I intend the forty (days of seclusion); I intend seclusion in the mosque; I intend seclusion; I intend isolation; I intend discipline (of the ego); I intend to travel in God's Path; I intend to fast for the sake of God in this mosque.

SŪRATU 'L-AN'AM

سورة الأنعام كل يوم (إذا امكن)

Recite each day if possible.

One juz' of Quran everyday (as part of daily wird)

جزء من القرآن كل يوم

DALĀ'ILU 'L-KHAYRĀT

دلائل الخيرات

(as part of daily wird)

DAILY WIRD

الأوراد اليومية

FASTING

الصيام

Increase in fasting, particularly on Monday and Thursday, as well as on Raghā'ib the 7th, the middle of Rajab, and the 27th.

الإكثار من الصيام ، وخاصة صيام يوم الإثنين والخميس ونهار ليلة الرغائب. اي السابع من رجب ونصف شهر رجب ويوم السابع العشرين

Invocation of Rajab

دعاء رجب

Bismillāhi 'r-Raḥmāni 'r-Raḥīm

Allāhuma innī istāghfiruka min kulli mā tubtu 'anhu ilayka thumma 'udtu fīh. Wa istāghfiruka min kulli mā 'aradtu bihi wajhika fa-khālatanī fīhi mā laysa fīhi riḍā'uk. Wa istāghfiruka li 'n-ni'am allatī taqawwaytu bihā 'alā ma'sīyatik. Wa istāghfiruka min adh-dhunūb allatī lā ya'lamuhā ghayruka wa lā yaṭṭali'u 'alayhā āḥadun siwāk wa lā yas'uha illa raḥmatika wa lā tunjī minhā illa maghfiratuka wa ḥilmuka. Lā ilāha illa-Anta, subhānak! Innī kuntu min aẓ-ẓālimīn.

اللهم انى استغفرك من كل ما تبت عنه اليك ثم عدت فيه، استغفرك من كل ما اردت به وجهك فخالطنى فيه ما ليس فيه رضائك. واستغفرك للنعم التى تقويت بها على معصيتك، واستغفرك من الذنوب التى لا يعلمها غيرك ولا يطلع عليها احد سواك ولا تسعها الا رحمتك ولا تنجى منها الا مغفرتك وحلمك لا اله الا أنتَ سبحانك انى كنت من الظالمين.

In the name of Allah, the All-Beneficent, the All-Merciful

O Allah, I ask forgiveness of You for everything for which I repented to You then returned to. And I ask forgiveness of You for everything I displeased You with and all that concerns me with which You are displeased. And I ask forgiveness of You for the favors which I used for increasing my disobedience towards You. And I ask forgiveness of You for the sins which no one knows except You and no one sees except You and nothing encompasses except Your Mercy and nothing delivers from except Your forgiveness and clemency. There is no god except You alone. Glory be to You! Indeed I was an oppressor to myself.

Allāhuma innī istaghfiruka min kulli ẓulmin ẓalamtu bihi 'ibādak. Fa ayyumā 'abdin min 'ibādika aw 'amatin min 'imā'ika ẓalamtu fī badanihi aw 'irdihi aw mālihi fa-ā'atihi min khazā'iniki 'llatī lā tanquṣ. Wa as'aluka an tukrimanī bi-raḥmatiki 'llatī wasi'at kulla shay'in wa lā tuhīnanī bi-'adhābika wa tu'ṭīyyanī mā as'aluka fa-innī ḥaqīqun bi-raḥmatika ya arḥamu 'r-Rāhimīn. Wa ṣalla-Allāhu 'alā Sayyidinā Muḥammadin wa 'alā ālihi wa ṣāḥbihi ajm'aīn. Wa lā ḥawla wa lā quwatta illa billāh il-'Alīyyi 'l-'Āẓīm.

اللهم انى استغفرك من كل ظلم ظلمت به عبادك فايما عبد من عبادك أو امة من امائك ظلمت في بدنه أو عرضه أو ماله فأعطه من خزائنك التى لا تنقص وأسألك ان تكرمنى برحمتك التى وسعت كل شىء ولا تهيننى بعذابك وتعطينى ما أسألك فانى حقيق برحمتك يا ارحم الراحمين. وصلى الله على سيدنا محمد وآله وصحبه أجمعين، ولا حول ولا قوة الا بالله العلى العظيم.

O Allah, I ask forgiveness of You for the injustice I committed against Your servants. Whatever of Your male or female servants whom I have hurt, physically or in their dignity or in their property give them of Your bounty which lacks nothing. And I ask You to honor me with Your mercy which encompasses all things. Do not humble me with Your punishment but give me what I ask of You, for I am in great need of Your mercy, O Most Merciful of the merciful. May Allah send blessings upon Muhammad and upon all his companions. There is no power and no might except in Allah the High, the Exalted.

Practices on the Blessed Night of Desires	ادب ليلة الرغائب
To be done after Ṣalātu 'l-'Ishā on the night of the first Thursday of the month of Rajab, considered by scholars to be the night in which the light of the Prophet ﷺ passed from his father 'Abd Allah ibn 'Abd al-Muṭṭalib ؓ to the womb of his mother Āmina bint Wahb ؓ.	بعد صلاة العشاء
NĪYYAT:	النية:
Nawaytu 'l-arbā'īn, nawaytu 'l-'itikāf, nawaytu 'l-khalwa, nawaytu 'l-'uzla, nawaytu 'r-riyāda, nawaytu 's-sulūk, lillāhi ta'ala fī hādhā 'l-masjid (or fī hādha al-jāmi').	نَوَيتُ الأربَعين، نَوَيتُ الاعتكاف نَوَيتُ الخَلوَة نَوَيتُ العُزلَة، نَوَيتُ الرياضَة نَوَيتُ السُلوك، لله تعالى في هَذا المسجد

INTENTION:

I intend the forty (days of seclusion); I intend seclusion in the mosque; I intend seclusion; I intend isolation; I intend discipline (of the ego); I intend to travel in God's Path; I intend to fast for the sake of God in this mosque.

ADABU 'Ṭ-ṬARĪQAH	ادب الطريقة
THE GRAND TRANSMITTED INVOCATION (AD-DU'AU 'L-MĀTHŪR) OF SULṬĀN AL-AWLIYĀ (see page 793)	الدعاء المأثور عن سلطان الأولياء
KHATMU 'L-KHWAJAGĀN (see page 734)	ختم الخواجكان مع الذكر
MAWLID	قراءة المولد الشريف
ṢALĀTU 'Ṭ-ṬASĀBĪḤ	صلاة التسابيح اربع ركعات
Fasting its day (and it is desired to present a sacrifice to God).	صيام نهاره (يستحب تقديم القرابين شكرا لله)

Practices on Night of Ascension

ادب ليلة الإسراء والمعراج

On the night preceding the 27th day of Rajab (Laylat al-Isrā' wa 'l-Mi'rāj), considered by many to be the night in which the Prophet ﷺ was invited to the Divine Presence, observe the following:

NĪYYAT:

Nawaytu 'l-arbā'īn, nawaytu 'l-'itikāf, nawaytu 'l-khalwa, nawaytu 'l-'uzla, nawaytu 'r-riyāda, nawaytu 's-sulūk, lillāhi ta'ala fī hādhā 'l-masjid (or fī hādha al-jāmi').

النية:

نَوَيْتُ الأَرْبَعين، نَوَيْتُ الاعتكاف نَوَيتُ الخَلْوَة نَوَيتُ العُزْلَة، نَوَيْتُ الرياضَة نَوَيتُ السُلوك، لله تَعالى في هَذا المسجد

INTENTION:

I intend the forty (days of seclusion); I intend seclusion in the mosque; I intend seclusion; I intend isolation; I intend discipline (of the ego); I intend to travel in God's Path; I intend to fast for the sake of God in this mosque.

ADABU 'Ṭ-ṬARĪQAH

ادب الطريقة

THE GRAND TRANSMITTED INVOCATION (AD-DU'AU 'L-MĀTHŪR) OF SULṬĀN AL-AWLIYĀ

الدعاء المأثور عن سلطان الأولياء

(see page 793)

KHATMU 'L-KHWAJAGĀN

ختم الخواجكان مع الذكر

(see page 734)

MAWLID

قراءة المولد الشريف

ṢALĀTU 'Ṭ-ṬASĀBĪḤ	صلاة التسابيح اربع ركعات
ṢALĀTU 'SH-SHUKR & QUNŪT INVOCATION	صلاة الشكر ركعتين مع دعاء القنوت
IHDĀ (SEE PAGE 729)	الإهداء
DU'A AND AL-FĀTIḤĀ	الدعاء الفاتحة
It is desired to fast the 27th and to make a sacrifice in thankfulness to God and to fast on the last day of Rajab.	و يستحب صيام اليوم 27 وان يستحب تقديم القرابين شكرا لله. وصيام آخر يوم من شهر رجب

Daily Practice Between Maghrib and Isha in Shaban

ادب الاوراد اليومية

When the crescent appears for the month of Sha'bān, the murīd makes ghusl and greets the month with two rak'ats of Ṣalātu 'l-wuḍu. Then he stands facing the Qiblah and completes 100 ṣalawāts on the Prophet. And he repeats this every day until the end of the month.

اذا هل هلال شهر شعبان على المرِيد ان يغتسل وسِتقبل شهر شعبان بِركعتين سنة الوضوء ثم يقف على القبلة وِيكمل مائة صلوات شرِيفة ويهديها على النبي ﷺ ويكرر هذا الادب كل يوم حتى نهاية الشهر

DAILY AWRĀD WITH INTENTION:

Nawaytu 'l-arbā'īn, nawaytu 'l-'itikāf, nawaytu 'l-khalwa, nawaytu 'l-'uzla, nawaytu 'r-riyāda, nawaytu 's-sulūk, lillāhi ta'ala fī hādhā 'l-masjid (or fī hādha al-jāmi').

ادب الاوراد اليومية مع المحافظة على النية التى سبق ذكرها اي :

نويت نَوَيْتُ الأَرْبَعين، نَوَيْتُ الاعتكاف نَوَيتُ الخَلْوَة نَوَيتُ العُزْلَة، نَوَيْتُ الرياضَة نَوَيْتُ السُلوك، لله تعَالى في هَذَا المسجد

I intend the forty (days of seclusion); I intend seclusion in the mosque;

I intend seclusion; I intend isolation; I intend discipline (of the ego);

I intend to travel in God's Path for the sake of God in this mosque.

Avoid the company of people and perform the Naqshbandi Adab in the last third of the night until sunrise, and/or between Ṣalātu 'l-'Asr and Ṣalātu 'l-Maghrib and/or between Ṣalātu 'l-Maghrib and Ṣalātu 'l-'Ishā.

المحافظة على الاوقات الثلاثة من الثلث الاخير على طلوع الشمس ما بين العصر والمغرب والعشاء

SŪRATU 'L-AN'AM

سورة الأنعام كل يوم (إذا امكن)

DALĀ'ILU 'L-KHAYRĀT (as part of daily wird)	دلائل الخيرات
SALAWĀT (2000 TIMES) This is in addition to that of the daily awrād.	الفين صلوات شريفة هدية للنبي صلى الله عليه وسلم غير الأوراد
SALAWĀT (100 TIMES) Performed while standing in the direction of the Qiblah and donating it to the Prophet.	مائة صلوات شريفة وقوفا نحو القبلة بنهيها بالصيغة الصلوات المأثورة ويهديها للنبي صلى الله عليه وسلم
DAILY AWRĀD.	يكمل اوراده اليومية
FASTING.	الصيام

Practices of the 15th of Shaban

(nisf Sha'bān)

ادب ليلة النصف من شهر شعبان

Adab aṭ-Ṭarīqah

ادب الطريقة

Reading of Sūrah Yasīn three times; first with the intention of long life in Islam and faith (imān), second with the intention to ward off affliction from one's self and from the nation of Muhammad ﷺ; and the third time with the intention of receiving one's sustenance without reliance on men.

قراءة يس ثلاث مرات، المرة الاولى بنية طول العمر بالإسلام والإيمان، والمرة الثانية بنية دفع البلاء عنه وعن الامة المحمدية ، والمرة الثلاثة بنية الرزق والإستغناء عن الناس

After every reading recite:

Allāhumma yā Dhāl-Manni lā yamannu 'alayhi aḥad, yā Dhāl-Jalāli wa 'l-Ikrām yā Dhāṭ-Ṭūli wa 'l-An'ām. Lā ilāha illa Anta. Ṭaharal-Aji'īn wa Jāru 'l-mutaji'īn wa Amānu 'l-khā'ifīn. Allāhumma in kunta katabtanī 'indaka fī ummi 'l-Kitābi shaqīyan aw maḥrūman aw maṭrūdan aw muqataran 'alayya min ar-rizq famḥu-llāhumma bi-faḍlika shaqāwatī wa ḥurmāni wa ṭurdī wa iqtāra rizqī wa thabitnī 'indaka fī ummi 'l-kitābi sa'īdan wa marzūqan li 'l-khayrāti fa-innaka qulta wa qawluku 'l-ḥaqq fī kitābik al-munzal 'ala lisāni nabīyyika 'l-mursal: yamḥullāhu mā yashā'u wa yuthbitu wa 'indahu Ummu 'l-Kitāb. Ilāhī bi 't-tajallī al-ā'aẓami fī lalayti 'n-niṣfi min shahri sha'bāni 'l-mu'aẓami 'l-mukarrami 'llatī yufraqu fīhā kullu amrin ḥakīmin wa yubram, an takshifa 'annā min al-balā'i mā na'lamu wa mā lā na'lamu wa mā Anta bihi ā'alamu innaka Anta al-A'azzu 'l-Akram. Wa ṣalla-Allāhu 'alā sayyidinā Muḥammadin wa 'alā ālihi wa ṣāḥbihi wa sallam.

و بعد كل مرة تدعوا بهذا الدعاء:

اللهم يا ذا المن لا يمن عليه احد يا ذا الجلال والإكرام يا ذا الطول والأنعام، لا إله إلا أنتَ ظهر اللاجئين وجار المستجيرين وامان الخائفين اللهم ان كنت كتبتني عندك في ام الكتاب شقيا أو محروما أو مطرودا أو مقترا عليّ من الرزق فامح اللهم بفضلك شقاوتي وحرماني وطردي واقتار رزقي وثبتني عندك في ام الكتاب سعيدا ومرزوقا للخيرات فانكَ قلت وقولك الحق في كتابك المنزل على لسان نبيك المرسل يمحوا الله ما يشاء ويثبت وعنده ام الكتاب. إلهي بالتجلي الأعظم في ليلة النصف من شهر شعبان المعظم المكرم التي يفرق فيها كل امر حكيم ويبرم ان تكشف عنا من البلاء ما نعلم وما لا نعلم وما أنتَ به اعلم إنكَ أنتَ الأعز الأكرم. وصلى الله على سيدنا محمد وعلى آله وصحبه وسلم.

O God, Tireless Owner of Bounty. O Owner of Sublimity, Honor, Power, and Blessings. There is no god except You, the Support of refugees and Neighbor of those who seek nearness, Guardian of the fearful. O God, if you have written in Your Book that I be abject, deprived, banished, and tight-fisted, then erase O God, through

Your bounty, my misery, deprivation, banishment, and stinginess and establish me with you as happy, provided with blessings in the Mother of Books, for surely Your Promise in Your Revealed Book on the tongue of Your Messenger is true. God blots out or confirms what He pleases, and with Him is the Mother of Books. My God, by the Great Manifestation of the Night of the middle of the Noble Month of Sha'bān in which every affair of wisdom is made distinct and authorized, remove from us calamities—those we know and those we do not know, and Thou knowest best—for surely You are the Most Mighty, the Most Generous. May God bless Muhammad and his Family and Companions.

One then invokes God with the Grand Transmitted Supplication of Sulṭan al-'Awliyā (see page 793) if it is easy, after each recitation, or if not, one time after the three recitations.

وتدعو بالدعاء الأعظم المأثور عن سلطان الأولياء اذا تيسر بعد كل مرة، وإلا تدعو به مرة واحدة بعد القراءة الثالثة

KHATMU 'L-KHWAJAGĀN

ختم الخواجكان مع الذكر

(see page 734)

ṢALĀTU 'Ṭ-ṬASĀBĪḤ

صلاة التسابيح اربع ركعات

ṢALĀTU 'SH-SHUKR

صلاة الشكر ركعتين مع دعاء القنوت

two rakats with Qunūt.

ṢALĀTU 'T-TAHAJJUD

صلاة تجتهد

After 'Ishā, complete 100 raka'ts of Ṣalāt at-Tahajjud. In the first raka'h after the Fātiḥa recite Sūrat al-Ikhlāṣ twice and in the second, once.

ثم بعد صلاة العشاء تجتهد ان تكمل 100 ركعة تقرأ في الركعة الأولى بعد الفاتحة سورة الاخلاص مرتين تقرأ في الركعة الثانية بعد الفاتحة اخلاص الشريفة مرة

FASTING

الصيام

You are to fast its day and make a sacrifice to Allāh as a ransom for yourself and your family and distribute it to the needy.

ثم تصوم نهارها وتقدم قربان إلى الله فداء عنك وعن أهلك وتوزعه على الفقراء المساكين

The Grand Transmitted Supplication

From Sulṭan al-'Awliyā, Mawlānā ash-Shaykh 'Abd-Allāh al-Fā'iz ad-Dāghestānī, may God sanctify his secret.

الدعاء الأعظم المأثور
لسلطان الأولياء مولانا الشيخ عبد الله الفائز الدغستاني

Bismillāhi 'r-Raḥmāni 'r-Raḥīm.

Allāhumma ṣalli 'alā Muḥammadin an-Nabī il-mukhtār 'adada man ṣalla 'alayhi min al-akhyār, wa 'adada man lam yuṣalli 'alayhi min al-ashrār, wa 'adada qaṭarāti 'l-amṭār, wa 'adada amwāji 'l-biḥār, wa 'adada 'r-rimāli wa 'l-qifār, wa 'adadu awrāqi 'l-ashjār, wa 'adada anfāsi 'l-mustaghfirīna bi 'l-ashār, wa 'adada akmāmi 'l-athmār, wa 'adada mā kāna wa mā yakūnu ila yawmi 'l-ḥashri wa 'l-qarār, wa ṣalli 'alayhi mā ta'āqabu 'l-laylu wa 'n-nahāru wa ṣalli 'alayhi mā 'khtalafu 'l-malawān wa ta'āqabu 'l-'asrān wa karrara 'l-jadīdān wa 'staqbal al-farqadān, wa balligh rūḥahu wa arwāhi āhli baytihi minnā taḥīyyatan wat-taslīm wa 'alā jamī'i 'l-anbīyā'i wa 'l-mursalīn wa 'l-ḥamdu lillāhi Rabbi 'l-'alamīn.

بسم الله الرحمن الرحيم

اللهم صل على محمد النبي المختار عدد من صلى عليه من الاخيار ، وعدد من لم يصل عليه من الاشرار، وعدد قطرات الامطار، وعدد امواج البحار، وعدد الرمال والقفار، وعدد اوراق الاشجار ، وعدد انفاس المستغفرين بالاسحار، وعدد اكمام الاثمار، وعدد ما كان وما يكون إلى يوم الحشر والقرار، وصل عليه ما تعاقب الليل والنهار، وصل عليه ما اختلف الملوان وتعاقب العصران وكرر الجديدان واستقبل الفرقدان، وبلغ روحه وأرواح أهل بيته منا تحية وتسليم وعلى جميع الأنبياء والمرسلين والحمد لله رب العالمين.

In the name of God, the Beneficent, the Merciful.

God, bless Muḥammad, the Chosen Prophet on the number of those who pray on him among the righteous and on the number of those who did not pray on him among the wicked; and on the number of the drops of the rain and on the number of waves of the oceans and on the number of the grains of sand and the wastelands, on the number of the leaves of the trees and on the number of the breaths of those who seek Your forgiveness by morning and on the number of the rinds of fruit and on the number of what was and what is until the Day of Gathering and Verdict. And Bless him (O God), as the turning of nights and days and bless him as long as the colors alternate and with the changing of time, and with the return of things renewed and with the constancy of diversity. And convey from us to his soul and the soul of his family, greetings and salutations and on all the prophets and messengers. And all Praise is due to God.

Allāhumma ṣalli ʻalā Muḥammad wa ʻalā āli Muḥammadin bi ʻadadi kulli dharratin alfa alfa marrah. Allāhumma ṣalli ʻalā Muḥammadin wa ʻalā āli Muḥammadin wa ṣaḥbihi wa sallim. Subūḥun quddūsun rabbunā wa rabbu ʼl-malāʻikati wa ʼr-Rūḥ, Rabbighfir wa ʼrḥam wa tawājaz ʻamma tʻalamu innaka Anta ʼl-Aʻazzu ʼl-Akram.

اللهم صل على محمد وعلى آل محمد بعدد كل ذرة الف الف مرة. اللهم صل على محمد وعلى آله وصحبه وسلم، سبوح قدوس ربنا ورب الملائكة والروح، رب اغفر وارحم وتجاوز عما تعلم إنكَ أنتَ الأعز الأكرم.

O God bless Muḥammad and the Family of Muḥammad of the number of the atom a thousand times over. O God bless Muḥammad and the Family of Muḥammad and His Companions and grant them peace. Glory and Holiness belongs to our Lord, Lord of the angels and the Holy Spirit. O our Lord forgive and have mercy and pardon of what You know (best), for You are surely the Most Mighty, Most Honorable.

Bismillāhi ʼr-Raḥmāni ʼr-Raḥīm.

Allāhumma innī astaghfiruka min kulli mā tubtu ʻanhu ilayka thumma ʻudtu fīhi. Wa astaghfiruka min kulli mā āradtu bihi wajhaka fakhālaṭani fīhi la laysa fīhi raḍāʻuk. Wa astaghfiruka li ʼn-niʻam ʼillatī taqawwaytu bihā ʻalā mʻaṣīyatik. Wa astaghfiruka min adh-dhunūb ʼillati lā yʻalamuhā ghayruka, wa lā yaṭaliʻu ʻalayhā aḥadun siwāk wa lā tasaʻūhā illa raḥmatika, wa lā tunjī minhā illa maghfiratuka wa ḥilmuka. Lā ilāha illa Anta subḥānaka innī kuntu min aẓ-ẓālimīn.

بسم الله الرحمن الرحيم

اللهم انى استغفرك من كل ما تبت عنه اليك ثم عدت فيه، واستغفرك من كل ما اردت به وجهك فخالطنى فيه ما ليس فيه رضائك. واستغفرك للنعم التى تقوت بها على معصيتك، واستغفرك من الذنوب التى لا يعلمها غيرك ولا يطلع عليها احد سواك ولا تسعها الا رحمتك ولا تنجى منها الا مغفرتك وحلمك لا اله الا أنتَ سبحانك اني كنت من الظالمين.

In the name of Allah, the All-Beneficent, the All-Merciful

O Allah, I ask forgiveness of You for everything for which I repented to You then returned to. And I ask forgiveness of You for everything I displeased You with and all that concerns me with which You are displeased. And I ask forgiveness of You for the favors which I used for increasing my disobedience towards You. And I ask forgiveness of You for the sins which no one knows except You and no one sees except You and nothing encompasses except Your Mercy and nothing delivers from except Your forgiveness and clemency. There is no god except You alone. Glory be to You! Indeed I was an oppressor to myself.

Allāhumma innī astaghfiruka min kulli ẓulmin ẓalamtu bihi ʻībāduka fa ayyamā ʻabdan min ʻibādika aw ʼamatin min

اللهم انى استغفرك من كل ظلم ظلمت به عبادك فايما عبد من عبادك أو أمة من امائك ظلمت في بدنه أو

عرضه أو ماله فأعطه من خزائنك التى لا تنقص وأسألك ان تكرمنى برحمتك التى وسعت كل شىء ولا تهيننى بعذابك وتعطينى ما أسألك فانى حقيق برحمتك يا ارحم الراحمين. وصلى الله على سيدنا محمد وآله وصحبه أجمعين، ولا حول ولا قوة الا بالله العلي العظيم .

imā'ika ẓalamtu fī badanihi aw 'irdhihi aw mālihi f'āṭihi min khazā'inak 'illati lā tanquṣ, wa as'aluka an tukrimanī bi raḥmatik 'illati wasi'at kulla shay'in wa lā tuhīnanī bi 'adhābika wa t'uṭianī mā as'aluka fa innī ḥaqīqun bi-raḥmatika ya Arḥam ar-rāḥimīn. Wa ṣalla-Allāhu 'alā sayyidinā Muḥammadin wa ālihi wa ṣāḥbihi ajmā'īn wa lā ḥawla wa lā quwwata illa billāhi 'l-'Aliyyi 'l-'Aẓīm.

O God, I ask forgiveness of You for the injustice I committed against Your servants. Whatever of Your male or female servants whom I have hurt, physically or in their dignity or in their property give them of Your bounty which lacks nothing. And I ask You to honor me with Your mercy which encompasses all things. Do not humble me with Your punishment but give me what I ask of You, for I am in great need of Your mercy, O Most Merciful of the merciful. May God send blessings upon Muḥammad and upon all his companions. And there is no power and no might except in God the Most High, the Exalted.

بسم الله الرحمن الرحيم

بسم الله النور، نور على نور والحمد لله الذي خلق السموات والارض وجعل الظلمات والنور وانزل التوراة على جبل الطور في كتاب مسطور ، والحمد لله الذي هو بالغنى مذكور بالعز والجلال مشهور، والحمد لله الذي خلق السموات والارض وجعل الظلمات والنور ثم الذين كفروا بربهم يعدلون، كهيعص حمعسق اياك نعبد واياك نستعين يا حي يا قيوم، الله لطيف بعباده يرزق من يشاء وهو القوي العزيز، يا كافي كل شيء اكفنى واصرف عنى كل شيء إنكَ قادر على كل شيء بيدك الخير إنكَ على كل شيء قدير

Bismillāhi 'r-Raḥmāni 'r-Raḥīm.

Bismillāhi 'n-Nūr, nūrun 'alā nūr, alḥamdulillāhi 'lladhī khalaq as-samawāti wa 'l-arḍ wa ja'ala aẓ-ẓulumāti wa 'n-nūr wa anzala at-tawrāta 'alā jabali 'ṭ-Ṭūri fī kitābin masṭūr.

Wa 'l-ḥamdulillāhi 'lladhī hūwa bil-Ghanī madhkūr wa bi 'l-'izzi wa 'l-Jalāl mashhūr, w' alḥamdulillāhi 'lladhī khalaq as-samāwāti wa 'l-arḍ wa ja'ala 'ẓ-zulumāti wa 'n-nūr thumma 'lladhīna kafarū bi-rabbihim ya'dilūn. Kāf, Hā, 'Ayn, Ṣād. Ḥā, Mīm, 'Ayn, Sīn, Qāf. Īyāka n'abudu wa Īyāka nasta'īn. Yā Ḥayyu Yā Qayyūm. Allāhu laṭīfun bi 'ibādihi yarzuqū man yashā'u wa Hūwa 'l-Qawiyyu 'l-'Azīz. Yā Kāfī kulla shay'in ikfinī waṣrif 'anī kulla shay'in innaka Qādirun 'alā kulli shay'in bi-yadik al-khayr innaka 'alā kulli shay'in Qadīr.

In the name of God, the All-Beneficent, the All-Merciful.

In the name of God, the Source of Light, Light upon Light. All praise is due to God who hath created the heavens and the earth. He created the darkness and the light and hath revealed the Torah on Mount Tūr in a Composed Book. All praise is due to God who created the heavens and the earth and created the darkness and the light.

"Yet those who reject Faith hold (others) as equal, with their Guardian-Lord." (6:1)

Kāf, Hā, 'Ayn, Ṣād. Ḥā, Mīm, Sīn, Qāf. "You alone do we worship and You alone do ask for help." (1:4) O Ever-Living One, O Self-subsisting One.

"Gracious is Allah to His servants: He gives Sustenance to whom He pleases: and He has power and can carry out His Will." (42:19)

O Giver of all, provide me and turn from me everything that harms me. Surely You are capable over all things. In Your hands is all good and You have power over all things.

Allāhumma ya Kathīr an-nawāli wa yā Dā'im al-wiṣāli wa yā Ḥusna 'l-fi'āli wa yā Razzāq al-'ibādi 'alā kulli ḥāl.

اللهم يا كثير النوال ويا دائم الوصال ويا حسن الفعال ويا رازق العباد على كل حال.

O God, the One who Grants plenty, O One of the Abiding Connection, O Doer of Good, O Provider of Your servants in every state.

Allāhumma in dakhala ash-shak fī īmānī bika wa lam ā'alam bihi tubtu 'anhu wa aqūlu lā ilāha ill-Allāh Muḥammadur-Rasūlullāh ﷺ.

االلهم إن دخل الشك في إمانى بك ولم أعلم به تبت عنه وأقول لا إله إلا الله محمد رسول الله ﷺ.

O God, if doubt has entered my belief in You, and of which I was unaware, I repent from it and say: There is no god except God, Muḥammad ﷺ is the Prophet of God.

Allāhumma in dakhal ash-shakka wa 'l-kufr fī tawḥīdī īyāka wa lam ā'alam bihi tubtu 'anhu wa aqūlu lā ilāha ill-Allāh Muḥammadur-Rasūlullāh ﷺ.

اللهم إن دخل الشك والكفر في توحيدي اياك ولم أعلم به تبت عنه وأقول لا إله إلا الله محمد رسول الله ﷺ.

O God, if doubt and disbelief entered my affirmation of Your Oneness, and of which I was unaware, I repent from it and say: There is no god except God, Muḥammad ﷺ is the Prophet of God.

Allāhumma in dakhala ash-shubhata fī m'arifati īyāka wa lam ā'alam bihi tubtu 'anhu wa aqūlu lā ilāha ill-Allāh Muḥammadur-Rasūlullāh ﷺ.

اللهم إن دخلت الشبهة في معرفتي اياك ولم أعلم به تبت عنه وأقول لا إله إلا الله محمد رسول الله (ص).

O God, if doubt enters my realization of You, and of which I was unaware, I repent from it and say: There is no god except God, Muḥammad ﷺ is the Prophet of God.

Allāhumma in dakhal al-'ujb wa 'r-riyā' wa 'l-kibrīyā wa 's-sum'atu fī 'ilmī wa lam ā'alam bihi tubtu 'anhu wa aqūlu lā ilāha ill-Allāh Muḥammadur-Rasūlullāh ﷺ.

اللهم إن دخل العجب والرياء والكبرياء والسمعة في علمى ولم أعلم به تبت عنه وأقول لا إله إلا الله محمد رسول الله (ص).

O God, if vanity, affected piety, arrogance and infamy affected me and of which I was unaware, I repent from it and say: There is no god except God, Muḥammad ﷺ is the Prophet of God.

Allāhumma in jara 'l-kadhiba 'alā lisānī wa lam ā'alam bihi tubtu 'anhu wa aqūlu lā ilāha ill-Allāh Muḥammadur-Rasūlullāh ﷺ.

اللهم إن جرى الكذب على لساني ولم أعلم به تبت عنه وأقول لا إله إلا الله محمد رسول الله (ص) .

O God, if lies run upon my tongue, of which I was unaware, I repent from it and say: There is no god except God, Muḥammad ﷺ is the Prophet of God.

Allāhumma in dakhala an-nifāq fī qalbī min adh-dhunūbi 's-saghā'iri wa 'l-kabā'iri wa lam ā'alam bihi tubtu 'anhu wa aqūlu lā ilāha ill-Allāh Muḥammadur-Rasūlullāh ﷺ.

اللهم إن دخل النفاق في قلبي من الذنوب الصغائر والكبائر ولم أعلم به تبت عنه وأقول لا إله إلا الله محمد رسول الله (ص)

O God, if hypocrisy entered my heart from the minor and major sins, and of which I was unaware, I repent from it and say: There is no god except God, Muḥammad ﷺ is the Prophet of God.

Allāhumma mā asdayta ilayya min khayrin wa lam ashkuruka wa lam ā'alam bihi tubtu 'anhu wa aqūlu lā ilāha ill-Allāh Muḥammadur-Rasūlullāh ﷺ.

اللهم ما اسديت إليّ من خير ولم أشكرك ولم أعلم به تبت عنه وأقول لا إله إلا الله محمد رسول الله (ص) .

O Allāh, from what You have granted me of all that is good and for which I had not thanked You, and I was unaware of it, I repent from it and say: There is no god except God, Muḥammad ﷺ is the Prophet of God.

Allāhumma mā qadarta lī min amrin wa lam arḍāhu wa lam ā'alam bihi tubtu 'anhu wa aqūlu lā ilāha ill-Allāh Muḥammadur-Rasūlullāh ﷺ.

اللهم ما قدرت لي من أمر ولم أرضه ولم أعلم به تبت عنه وأقول لا إله إلا الله محمد رسول الله (ص) .

O God, whatever You have destined for me in matters which I did not accept, and of which I was unaware, I repent from it and say: There is no god except God, Muḥammad ﷺ is the Prophet of God.

Allāhumma mā an'amta 'alayya min n'imatin fa-'aṣaytuka wa ghafaltu 'an shukrika wa lam ā'alam bihi tubtu 'anhu wa aqūlu lā ilāha ill-Allāh Muḥammadur-Rasūlullāh ﷺ.

اللهم ما انعمت من نعمة فعصيتك وغفلت عن شكرك ولم أعلم به تبت عنه وأقول لا إله إلا الله محمد رسول الله (ص) .

O God, from what You had conferred upon me of bounty for which I neglected to thank You, and of which I was unaware, I repent from it and say: There is no god except God, Muḥammad ﷺ is the Prophet of God.

Allāhumma mā mananta bihi 'alayya min khayrin fa lam āḥmaduka 'alayhi wa lam ā'alam bihi tubtu 'anhu wa aqūlu lā ilāha ill-Allāh Muḥammadur-Rasūlullāh ﷺ.

اللهم ما مننت به على من خير فلم أحمدك عليه ولم أعلم به تبت عنه وأقول لا إله إلا الله محمد رسول الله (ص).

O God, whatever You have bestowed on me of goodness and I did not praise You for it, and of which I was unaware, I repent from it and say: There is no god except God, Muḥammad ﷺ is the Prophet of God.

Allāhumma ma ḍayyatu min 'umrī wa lam tarḍa bihi tubtu 'anhu wa aqūlu lā ilāha ill-Allāh Muḥammadur-Rasūlullāh ﷺ.

اللهم ما ضيعت من عمري ولم ترض به وتبت عنه وأقول لا إله إلا الله محمد رسول الله (ص).

O God, whatever I have wasted from my allotted lifetime which You were not pleased, I repent from it and say: There is no god except God, Muḥammad ﷺ is the Prophet of God.

Allāhumma bimā awjabta 'alayya min al-naẓari min maṣnū'ātika fa-ghafaltu 'anhu wa lam ā'alam bihi tubtu 'anhu wa aqūlu lā ilāha ill-Allāh Muḥammadur-Rasūlullāh ﷺ.

اللهم بما اوجبت عليّ من النظر في مصنوعاتك فغفلت عنه ولم أعلم به تبت عنه وأقول لا إله إلا الله محمد رسول الله (ص).

O God, of what You have imposed upon me in the observation of the creation of Your design and of which I was heedless, and I was unaware of it, I repent from it and say: There is no god except God, Muḥammad ﷺ is the Prophet of God.

Allāhumma mā qaṣartu 'anhu āmālī fī rajā'ika wa lam ā'alam bihi tubtu 'anhu wa aqūlu lā ilāha ill-Allāh Muḥammadur-Rasūlullāh ﷺ.

اللهم ما قصرت عنه آمالي في رجائك ولم أعلم به تبت عنه وأقول لا إله إلا الله محمد رسول الله (ص).

O God, from whatever fell short of my hope in my turning to You, and of which I was unaware, I repent from it and say: There is no god except God, Muḥammad ﷺ is the Prophet of God.

Allāhumma mā'tamadtu 'alā aḥadin siwāka fī 'sh-shadā'idi wa lam ā'alamu bihi tubtu 'anhu wa aqūlu lā ilāha ill-Allāh Muḥammadur-Rasūlullāh ﷺ.

اللهم ما اعتمدت على احد سواك في الشدائد ولم أعلم به تبت عنه وأقول لا إله إلا الله محمد رسول الله (ص).

O God, from placing dependence on other than You in the face of calamities, and of which I was unaware, I repent from it and say: There is no god except God, Muḥammad ﷺ is the Prophet of God.

Allāhumma mā astana'tu li-ghayrika fi'sh-shadā'idi wa 'n-nawā'ibi wa lam ā'alam bihi tubtu 'anhu wa aqūlu lā ilāha

اللهم ما استعنت بغيرك في الشدائد والنوائب ولم أعلم به تبت عنه وأقول لا إله إلا الله محمد رسول الله

ill-Allāh Muḥammadur-Rasūlullāh ﷺ.

(ص) .

O God, in what I had sought assistance from other than You in calamities and misfortune, and of which I was unaware, I repent from it and say: There is no god except God, Muḥammad ﷺ is the Prophet of God.

Allāhumma in zalla lisānī bis-su'āli li-ghayrika wa lam ā'alam bihi tubtu 'anhu wa aqūlu lā ilāha ill-Allāh Muḥammadur-Rasūlullāh ﷺ.

اللهم إن زلّ لسانى بالسؤال لغيرك ولم أعلم به تبت عنه وأقول لا إله إلا الله محمد رسول الله (ص) .

O God, if my tongue has slipped by askng other than You and I was unaware of it, I repent from it and say: There is no god except God, Muḥammad ﷺ is the Prophet of God.

Allāhumma mā ṣaluḥa min shānī bi-faḍlika farā'ituhu min ghayrika wa lam ā'alam bihi tubtu 'anhu wa aqūlu lā ilāha ill-Allāh Muḥammadur-Rasūlullāh ﷺ.

اللهم ما صَلُح من شأنى بفضلك فرأيته من غيرك ولم أعلم به تبت عنه وأقول لا إله إلا الله محمد رسول الله (ص) .

O God, whatever was rectified in my affairs through Your Grace and I saw it coming from other than You, and I was unaware of it, I repent from it and say: There is no god except God, Muḥammad ﷺ is the Prophet of God.

Allāhumma bi-ḥaqqi lā ilāha ill-Allāh wa bi-'izzatih

اللهم بحق لا إله إلا الله وبعزته

O God, by the right of lā ilāha ill-Allāh and its Might;

Wa bi-ḥaqqi 'l-'arshi wa 'aẓamatihih

و بحق العرش وعظمته

And by the right of the Throne and its grandeur;

Wa bi-ḥaqqi 'l-kursī wa sa'atih

و بحق الكرسي وسعته

And by the right of the Chair and its vastness;

Wa bi-ḥaqqi 'l-qalami wa jariyatihi

و بحق القلم وجَرَيته

And by the right of the Pen and its motion;

Wa bi-ḥaqqi 'l-lawḥi wa ḥafaẓatih

و بحق اللوح وحفظته

And by the right of the Tablet and its preservation;

Wa bi-ḥaqqi 'l-mīzāni wa khifatih

و بحق الميزان وخفته

And by the right of the Scale and its accuracy;

Wa bi-ḥaqqi 'ṣ-Ṣirāṭi wa riqqatihi

و بحق الصراط ورقته

And by the right of the Bridge and it narrowness;

Wa bi-ḥaqqi Jibrīl wa amānatihi

و بحق جبريل وامانَته

And by the right of Jibrīl and his trust;

Wa bi-ḥaqqi Riḍwān wa jannatih — و بحق رضوان وجنته

And by the right of Riḍwān and his paradise;

Wa bi-ḥaqqi Mālik wa zabānīyatih — و بحق مالك وزبانيته

And by the right of Mālik and his angels of punishment;

Wa bi-ḥaqqi Mīkā'īl wa shafqatih — و بحق ميكائيل وشفقته

And by the right of Mīkā'īl and his compassion;

Wa bi-ḥaqqi Isrāfīl wa nafkhatih — و بحق اسرافيل ونفخته

And by the right of Isrāfīl and his blowing (of the Trumpet);

Wa bi-ḥaqqi 'Azrā'īl wa qabḍatih — و بحق عزرائيل وقبضته

And by the right of 'Azrā'īl and his seizing (of the soul in death);

Wa bi-ḥaqqi Ādam wa ṣafwatih — و بحق آدم وصفوته

And by the right of Ādam and his purity;

Wa bi-ḥaqqi Shu'ayb wa nubūwwatih — و بحق شعيب ونبوته

And by the right of Shu'ayb and his prophethood;

Wa bi-ḥaqqi Nūḥ wa safīnatih — و بحق نوح وسفينته

And by the right of Nūḥ and his vessel;

Wa bi-ḥaqqi Ibrāhīm wa khullatih — و بحق ابراهيم وخلته

And by the right of Ibrāhīm and his Friendship (to God);

Wa bi-ḥaqqi Isḥāq wa dīyānatih — و بحق اسحاق وديأنَته

And by the right of Isḥaq and his belief;

Wa bi-ḥaqqi Ismā'īl wa fidyatih — و بحق اسماعيل وفديته

And by the right of Ismā'īl and his ransom;

Wa bi-ḥaqqi Yūsuf wa ghurbatih — و بحق يوسف وغربته

And by the right of Yūsuf and his estrangement;

Wa bi-ḥaqqi Mūsā wa āyātih — و بحق موسى وآياته

And by the right of Mūsa and his signs;

Wa bi-ḥaqqi Hārūn wa ḥurmatih — و بحق هارون وحرمته

And by the right of Hārūn and his sanctity;

Wa bi-ḥaqqi Hūd wa haybatih And by the right of Hūd and his Veneration;	و بحق هود وهيبته
Wa bi-ḥaqqi Ṣāliḥ wa nāqatih And by the right of Ṣāliḥ and his she-camel;	و بحق صالح وناقته
Wa bi-ḥaqqi Lūṭ wa jīratih And by the right of Lūṭ and his guests;	و بحق لوط وجيرته
Wa bi-ḥaqqi Yūnus wa da'watih And by the right of Yūnus and his invocation;	و بحق يونس ودعوته
Wa bi-ḥaqqi Dānyāl wa karāmatih And by the right of Danyāl and his miracles;	و بحق دنيال وكرامته
Wa bi-ḥaqqi Zakariyā wa ṭahāratih And by the right of Zakariyā and his purity;	و بحق زكريا وطهارته
Wa bi-ḥaqqi 'Isā wa sīyāḥatih And by the right of 'Isa and his wandering;	و بحق عيسى وسياحته
Wa bi-ḥaqqi sayyidinā Muḥammadin ﷺ wa shafā'atih And by the right of Our Master Muḥammad and his Intercession;	و بحق سيدنا محمد(ص) وشفاعته
An taghfir lanā wa li-wālidīynā wa li-'ulamā'inā wa an tākhudha bi-yadī wa t'utīyanī su'āli wa tubalighanī āmālī wa an taṣrifa 'anī kulla man 'aādānī bi-raḥmatika yā Arḥamu 'r-Rāhimīn, wa taḥfaẓnī min kulli sū'in, lā ilāha illa Anta, subḥānaka innī kuntu min aẓ-ẓālimīn. That You forgive us, our parents and our scholars. And to take me by the hand and to grant me my asking and deliver me to my goals. And fend off all those who harm me, by Your mercy, O the Most Merciful of those who give mercy. And to protect me from every vice. There is no god except You, Glory be to You! Surely I have been a wrong-doer.	ان تغفر لنا ولوالدينا ولعلمائنا وان تأخذ بيدى وتعطينى سؤالي وتبلغنى آمالي وان تصرف عنى كل من عادانى برحمتك يا ارحم الراحمين وتحفظنى من كل سوء لا إله إلا أنتَ سبحانك إني كنت من الظالمين
Yā Ḥayyu, yā Qayyūm. Lā ilāha illa Anta, yā Allāh, astāghfiruka wa atūbu ilayk. Fastajabnā lahu wa najaynāhu min al-ghamm wa kadhālika nanjī al-mu'minīn wa ḥasbuna-llāhu wa n'ima 'l-wakīl ḥasbī Allāhu lā ilāha illa hūwa 'alayhi	يا حى يا قيوم لا إله إلا أنتَ يا الله استغفر ك واتوب إليك فاستجبنا له ونجيناه من الغم وكذلك ننجى المؤمنين. وحسبنا الله ونعم الوكيل حسبى الله لا إله إلا هو عليه توكلت وهو رب العرش العظيم ولا حول ولا

tawakkaltu wa Hūwa rabbu 'l-'Arshi 'l-'Aẓīm wa lā ḥawlah wa lā quwwata illa billāhi 'l-'Aẓīm.

قوة إلا بالله العلي العظيم

O Living, O Eternal there is no god except You. O Allāḥ, I seek forgiveness in You and I turn to You, So We listened to him: and We delivered him from distress: and thus do We deliver those who have faith. God is enough for us, the best Disposer of affairs; God sufficeth me: there is no god but He: On Him is my trust,- He the Lord of the Throne (of Glory) Supreme!" And there is no strength, nor power except by God, The High, The Mighty.

Wa ṣalla-Allāhu 'alā sayyidinā Muḥammad wa 'alā ālihi wa ṣāḥbihi wa sallim ajmā'īn. subḥānā rabbika rabbi 'l-'Izzati 'amā yaṣifūn wa salāmun 'alā 'l-mursalīn wa 'l-ḥamdulillāhi rabbi 'l-'ālamīn.

و صلى الله على سيدنا محمد وعلى آله وصحبه وسلم أجمعين. سبحان ربك رب العزة عما يصفون وسلام على المرسلين والحمد لله رب العالمين.

May God bless our master Muḥammad, His Family and Companions altogether. Glory to Allah, the Lord of the Throne: (High is He) above what they attribute to Him! And Peace on the Messengers and all Praise is due to the Lord of the worlds.

Bismillāhi 'r-Raḥmāni 'r-Raḥīm.

بسم الله الرحمن الرحيم.

Allāhumma innī as'aluka bi mushāhadati asrāri 'l-muḥibbīn wa bi 'l-khalwati 'llatī khaṣaṣta bihā sayyid al-mursalīn ḥīna asrayta bihi laylat as-sāb'i wa 'l-'ishrīn an tarḥam qalbī al-ḥazīn wa tujīb d'awatī yā Akram al-Akramīn yā Arḥamar-Rāḥimīn. Wa ṣalla-Allāhu 'alā sayyidinā Muḥammadin wa 'alā ālihi wa ṣāḥbihi wa sallim ajmā'īn.

ثم نقول اللهم انى أسألك بمشاهدة اسرار المحبين وبالخلوة التى خصصت بها سيد المرسلين حين اسريت به ليلة السابع والعشرين ان ترحم قلبي الحزين وتجيب دعوتي يا أكرم الأكرمين يا ارحم الراحمين وصلى الله على سيدنا محمد وآله وصحبه أجمعين.

In the name of God, the Beneficent, the Merciful.

O God, surely I beseech You by the witnessing of the secrets of the Lovers and the reclusion which you hath specified with the Master of Messengers when You raised Him on the Night of the 27th. And to pity by depressed heart and to answer my plea, O Most Generous of those who show generosity, O Most Merciful of those who show mercy. May God bless our master Muḥammad, His Family and all his Companions and greet them with peace.

Bismillāhi 'r-Raḥmāni 'r-Raḥīm.

بسم الله الرحمن الرحيم

Lā illāha ill-Allāh Muḥammadu Rasūlullāh yā Raḥmān yā Raḥīm yā Musta'an yā Allāh yā Muḥammad ṣalla-Allāhu 'alayhi wa sallam. Yā Abā Bakr,

لا إله إلا الله محمد رسول الله يا رحمن يا رحيم يا مستعان بالله يا محمد صلى الله عليه وسلم، يا أبا بكر يا عمر يا عثمان يا علي يا حسن يا حسين يا يحي يا

yā 'Umar, yā 'Uthmān, yā 'Alī, yā Ḥasan, yā Ḥusayn, yā Yahyā; yā Ḥalīm, yā Allāh, wa lā ḥawlah wa lā quwwata illa billāhi 'l-'Aliyyi 'l-'Aẓīm.	حليم يا الله ولا حول ولا قوة إلا بالله العلي العظيم.

In the name of God, the Beneficent, the Merciful.

There is no god except God, Muḥammad is the Messenger of God; O Merciful, O Beneficent One, O Musta'ān, O God; O Muḥammad peace and blessings be upon him. O Abū Bakr; O 'Umar; O 'Uthmān; O 'Alī; O Ḥasan; O Ḥusayn; O Yaḥyā; O Forbearing One, O God. There is no power and no strength save in God, All-High and Almighty.

Astaghfirullāh dhul-jalāli wa 'l-Ikrām min jamī'i 'dh-dhunūb wa 'l-āthām.	استغفر الله ذو الجلال والإكرام من جميع الذنوب والآثام
Āmīn.	آمين.

I seek forgiveness in God, the Possessor of Majesty and Honor, from every sin and transgression. Amen.

Ramadan Salatu-t-Tarawih	التراويح في رمضان
2 OR 4 RAK'ATS SUNNAH	صلاة السنة 2 أو 4 ركعات
4 RAK'ATS FARḌ 'ISHĀ	صلاة العشاء
2 RAK'ATS SUNNAH	وبعدها ركعتين السنة البعدية
INTENTION	ينوي الصيام
Intend to fast the obligatory fast of the next day, then intend Ṣalāt at-Tarāwīḥ (20 rak'ats).	ثم ينوي لصلاة التراويح قائلا: نويت ان اصلى 20 ركعات صلاة التراويح لله تعالى رب العالمين
After each four rak 'ats sit and read 3 times Sūratu 'l-Ikhlāṣ, followed by the following: liqā'ullāh yurjā fīṣ-ṣīyām wa nūru qalbī fī 'l-qīyām, ta'al-Allāh dhul 'arshi'l majīd aṣ-Ṣalātu jāmi'a Ṣalātu't-tarāwīḥ athāb akumullāh. An-nabī yashfa'u liman yuṣalli 'alayh. Allāhumma ṣalli 'alā Muḥammadin wa 'alā Muhammdin wa sallam. Allāhumma innā nas'aluka'l-jannata wa na'udhu bika min an-nār.	و بعد كل 4 ركعات اقرأ سورة الاخلاص 3 مرات أو قل: لقاء الله يرجى في الصيام ونور قلبي في القيام تعالى الله ذو العرش المجيد، الصلاة الجامعة صلاة التاروبح أثابكم الله، النبى يشفع لمن يصلى عليه. اللهم صل على سيدنا محمد وعلى آل سيدنا محمد . اللهم إنا نسألك الجنّة ونعوذ بك من النار
ṢALĀTU 'T-TARĀWĪH. (20 RAK'ATS)	صلاة التراويح (20 ركعات)
ṢALĀTU 'L-WITR (3 RAK'ATS)	صلاة الوتر (3 ركعات)
Then recite: 'alā Rasūlinā 'ṣ-ṣalawāt Then continue with the normal recitations following Ṣalāt al-'Ishā.	على رسولنا الصلوات
ĀMAN AR-RASŪLU (see page 726) 2:285- 286	آمَنَ الرَّسُولُ
SŪRATU 'L-FĀTIHĀ	الفاتحة

Notes to the Guidebook

These notes address unusual or special practices. All the practices, however, are based on the Sunnah of the Prophet ﷺ and explanations of their special benefits can be found in the traditional references.

The following notes are meant to clarify some of the practices which occur in the preceding pages. The perfection of them has come to us from our Master Shaykh Muhammad Nazim al-Haqqani al-Naqshbandi (may God continually raise his station). If there is any imperfection in this text, however, it comes from us, and may God be Merciful with us and forgive us.

Note: The Shaykh uses the *miswāk* (natural toothstick) before every ritual action, and before every Qur'ān reading.

Salatu-l-Maghrib

The two rak'ats sunnah prayer before the obligatory (*farḍ*) prayer are a "non-emphasized Sunnah" (*sunnah ghayr mu'akkada*). They were quickly prayed by the Sahaba ؓ of the Prophet ﷺ after hearing the *adhān* of Ṣalāt al-Maghrib. We find hadith on this practice in some of the traditional hadith collections, and referenced by Imam Suyuti. The Prophet ﷺ never prevented the Companions from doing this and, therefore, it is considered a *Sunnah*, based on what the Prophet ﷺ did, what the Prophet ﷺ said, and what the Prophet ﷺ approved of (i.e., did not specifically forbid). It is mentioned that many of the great Sufi shaykhs maintained this practice, including Imam Ghazali.

Salatu-l-Janazah

The funeral prayer for those absent persons who have died without anyone praying over them is a daily fard kifāya, a practice which only one member of the community has to perform. Like the two *Sunnah* rak'ats before Ṣalāt al-Maghrib, we know that the great shaykhs made this a daily practice. The prayer is performed standing, facing the *Qiblah*.

Salatu-l-Awabin

The 2-2-2 rak'at Ṣalātu 'l-Awābīn refers to those who turn frequently in prayer to their Lord. They constitute six rak'ats of two rak'ats each with a *taslīm* (*a*s-salām 'alaykum wa ra*ḥ*matullāh to the right and left, at the end), between every two rak'ats.

Salatu-l-Witr

The *qunūt* prayer is inserted in the third rak'at after reading al-Fātiḥa and a sūra from the Qur'ān (the Shaykh usually reads Sūrat al-Ikhlāṣ), and before the *ruk'u,* or bowing. After you have finished reading, raise your hands to your ears—as you would to begin the prayer—and say the *takbīr, Allāhu akbar* and continue with the *du'ā* (supplication) indicated in the text. After reciting the *du'ā,* go into *ruk'u,* then continue as in a normal prayer sequence.

Salatu-l-Fajr

The congregational morning prayer is a major pillar of the daily devotions. One should try to stay awake until the actual rising of the sun and then perform the two *Sunnah* rak'ats of *Ishrāq* five to ten minutes after it has risen.

While reading Sūrat YāSīn Mawlana Shaykh Nazim pauses to recite the words *Ṣalla-Allāhu 'alayhi wa sallam,* as "YāSīn" is one the names of the Prophet ﷺ.

After reciting Verse 36:58, he says, r*azaqanā Allāh* (God grant it to us!).

After reciting Verse 36:59, he says, *a'ādhanā Allāh* (God protect us!).

The pauses in the recitation of the 99 names of God are not fixed. The Shaykh frequently changes the places of these pauses in his recitations.

Explanations and Procedures

In the following prayers, to keep track of any given number of recitations, it is permitted to lightly press one finger of each hand in turn, in whatever position they are (i.e., crossed or hanging at the sides). However, the *an-Najāt* and *Tasbīḥ* prayers are for the People of Determination and the Prepared; these prayers are not for beginners.

Salatu-n-Najat

One should get up at least one hour before Fajr since it is at this time that the gate of the Mercy of God, Who is Powerful and Sublime, is opened and the time when the great shaykhs look at their murīds. One should get up and perform ablution and perform two rak'ats of *Taḥīyyatu 'l-wuḍu* and then stand up, facing the *Qiblah* and ask that God, Exalted and Glorious, to purify oneself from the anger of one's *nafs* and, with this intention, one should then recite *Yā Ḥalīm* 100 times, and then one should seek protection from one's external and internal enemies, and from both heavenly and earthly misfortune, reciting *Yā Ḥafīẓ* 100 times.

Whoever wishes to reach the station of the People of Determination must keep up these practices. Our shaykhs tell us about the importance of this time and its virtues, saying: "If a person gets up one hour before Fajr and does nothing, not even praying, not even making *tasbīḥ*, but gets up to drink something, such as coffee or tea, or eat a morsel of food, then he must also be raised with the vigilant people (*ahlu 's-sahar*)."

Ṣalātu 'n-Najāt, the Prayer of Salvation, is prayed according to the following steps:

In the first rak'at read Sūratu 'l-Fātiḥa as usual.	الفاتحة الشريفة
This is followed by reading the Verse of the Throne (2:255) and (3:18-19), and (3:26-27).	

ĀYATU 'L-KURSĪ (THE VERSE OF THE THRONE)

آيةُ الكُرْسي

CHAPTER 2, VERSE 255

البقرة 2

Allāhū lā ilāha illa Hūwa 'l-Ḥayyu 'l-Qayyūm, lā tākhudhuhū 's-sinatun wa lā nawm, lahū mā fis-samāwāti wa mā fil-arḍ. Man dhā-ladhī yashfa'u 'indahū illā bi idhniḥ ya'lamu mā bayna aydīhim wa mā khalfahum wa lā yuḥīṭunā bi-shay'im min 'ilmihi illā bimā shā'. Wasi'a kursīyyuhu 's-samāwāti wa 'l-arḍa, wa lā ya'uduhū ḥifẓuhuma, wa Hūwa 'l-'Alīyyu 'l-'Aẓīm.

الله لا إلهَ إلا هُوَ الحيُّ القيّوم لا تأخُذهُ سنةٌ ولا نومٌ لهُ
ما في السّماوات والأرْض من ذا الذي يَشفَعُ عندَهُ إلا
بإذنه يَعْلَمُ ما في بينَ أيديهم وما خَلفَهُم ولا يُحيطونَ
بشَيْءٍ من علمه إلا بما شاء وَسعُ كُرْسيهُ السّماوات
والأرْضَ ولا يَؤدُهُ حفْظهُما وهُوَ العَليُّ العَظيم

Ṣadaq-Allāhu 'l-'Aẓīm.

God, there is no god but He, the Living, the Everlasting. Slumber seizes Him not, neither sleep; to Him belongs all that is in the heavens and the earth. Who is there that shall intercede with Him save by His leave? He knows what lies before them, and they comprehend not anything of His knowledge save such as He wills. His Throne comprises the heavens and the earth; the preserving of them oppresses Him not; He is the All-High, the Almighty.

CHAPTER 3, VERSE 18-19

سورة آل عمران 18–19

Shahid-Allāhu annahū lā ilāha illa Hū. Wa 'l-malā'ikatu wa ūlu 'l-'ilmi qā'iman bil-qisṭ. Lā ilāha illa Hū al-'Azīzu 'l-Ḥakīm. Inna 'd-dīna 'ind Allāhi 'l-islām.

شَهد الله أنَّهُ لا إله إلا هُوَ والملائكة وأولو العلْم قائمًا
بالقسْط لا إله إلا هُوَ العزيزُ الحكيمُ إنَّ الدين عندَ الله
الإسْلام

God bears witness that there is no god but He—and the angels and men of knowledge—upholding justice; there is no god but He, the All-Mighty, the All-Wise. The religion with God is Islam.

CHAPTER 3, VERSE 26-27

سورة آل عمران 26-27

Qul 'illāhumma Mālik al-mulki. Tu'tī 'l-mulka man tasha'u wa tanzi'u 'l-mulka mimman tashā'u wa tu'izzu man tashā'u wa tudhillu man tashā'u, bi yadika 'l-khayr, innaka 'alā kulli shay'in qadīr. Tūliju 'l-layla fī 'n-nahāri wa tūliju nahāra fī 'l-layl, wa tukhriju 'l-ḥāyya min al-mayyiti, wa tukhriju 'l-mayyita min al-ḥāyy, wa tarzuqu man tashā'u bi ghayri ḥisāb.

قل اللَّهُمَّ مالكُ المُلك تؤتى المُلكَ من تشاء وتَنزع المُلكَ ممَّن تشاء وتعزُ من تشاء وتذل من تشاءُ بيدكَ الخَيْرإنكَ على كُل شىء قدير تولجُ اللّيلَ في النهار وتُولجُ النهارَ في الليْل وتُخرجُ الحىَ من الميّت وتخرجُ الميّتَ من الحيّ وترْزُقُ من تشاءُ بغيْرِ حساب

Say: O God, Master of the Kingdom, Thou givest the Kingdom to whom Thou wilt, and seizest the Kingdom from whom Thou wilt, Thou exaltest whom Thou wilt, and Thou abasest whom Thou wilt; in Thy hand is the good; Thou art over all things Powerful. Thou makest the night to enter into the day, and Thou makest the day to enter into the night, Thou bringest forth the living from the dead, and Thou bringest forth the dead from the living, and Thou providest for whomsoever Thou wilt without reckoning.

In the second rak'at, read the Fātiḥa.

تقرأ في الركعة الثانية بعد الفاتحة الشريفة

THEN SŪRATU 'L-IKHLĀṢ (11 TIMES).

سورة الاخلاص (11 مرات)

After completing the taslīm (final salām right and left), go into prostration with the intention of asking God to rid your heart of all envy.

بعد التسليم من الصلاة
تدعوا بهذا الدعاء:

DU'A

دعاء:

Yā Rabbī, kamā tākul un-nāru 'l-ḥataba hākadha yākulu 'amalīyy jamī'an al-ḥasadu mu'tasila fīyya fa khalliṣnī minh yā Rabbī wa khalliṣnī ayḍan 'an il-ghadab an-nafsānī wa 'an nafs iṭ-ṭifl il-madhmuma, wa 'an il-akhlāq idh-dhamīma wa baddil yā Rabbī akhlāqī jamī'an ila akhlāqin ḥamīdatin wa af'ālin ḥasana.

يا ربّى كما تأكُلُ النارُ الحطَبَ هكذا الحسَدُ المتأصّل فيّ يأكل جميع أعمالي. يا ربّى خلّصْنى منه ومنَ الغضَب النفسانى ومن نفْس الطفْل المذْمُومة ومن الأخْلاق الذميمة ويا ربّى بَدّلْ كُلَّ أخْلاقى إلى أخْلاق حميدة وأفعال حسَنة

O my Lord! Just as fire consumes firewood, in the same way the envy which is rooted in me consumes all my actions. Purify me, O my Lord, from it and purify me, too, from the anger of my ego. Rid me as well, O my Lord, of the blameworthy ego of the child and reprehensible manners. And, O my Lord, change all my manners to laudable manners and into good actions.

Salatu-t-Tasabih

These are four rak'ats prayed with a taslīm between them. This prayer can be done in two ways, but we have included only the one the Shaykh uses (with the taslīm at the end of the fourth rak'at). The tasbīḥ which is recited during this prayer is:

Subḥānallāhi wa 'l-ḥamdulillāhi wa lā illāha ill-Allāh wallāhu akbar.

سبحان الله والحمد لله ولا إله إلا الله والله أكبر

Glory be to God! Praise be to God! There is no god but God, and God is Greatest.

At the end of every set of 10 or 15 tasbīḥs the Shaykh adds: wa lā ḥawla wa lā quwwata illa billāhi 'l-'Alīyyi 'l-'Āẓīm.

و لا حول ولا قوة إلا بالله العليّ العظيم

There is no power and no strength save in God, All-High and Almighty.

The total number of tasbīḥs recited is 300, with 75 in each rak'at. Also, the tasbīḥs is added to the regular parts of the prayer. We have observed the Shaykh using the following method:

WHEN TASBIḤ IS RECITED	NUMBER OF TIMES
After reciting the Thanā', before Sūratu 'l-Fātiḥa	15
After reciting Sūratu 'l-Fātiḥa and two Sūratu 'l-Ikhlāṣ	10
In ruk'u, (bowing position)	10
In qiyām (standing position), after the ruk'u	10
In the first sajda (prostration)	10
In jalsa (sitting position), after the first sajda	10
In the second sajda	10
Sub-total for first rak'at	75
The second rak'at is performed as above (no tasbīḥs is recited in the final jalsa, only tashahhud)	75
The third rak'at is performed as above	75
The fourth rak'at is performed as above (no tasbīḥs are recited in the final jalsa, only tashahhud)	75

Conduct of Pilgrimage - Hajj

God says:

And complete the Ḥajj or 'Umrah in the service of Allah. But if ye are prevented (From completing it), send an offering for sacrifice, such as ye may find, and do not shave your heads until the offering reaches the place of sacrifice. And if any of you is ill, or has an ailment in his scalp, (Necessitating shaving), (He should) in compensation either fast, or feed the poor, or offer sacrifice; and when ye are in peaceful conditions (again), if any one wishes to continue the 'umrah on to the Ḥajj, He must make an offering, such as he can afford, but if he cannot afford it, He should fast three days during the Ḥajj and seven days on his return, Making ten days in all. This is for those whose household is not in (the precincts of) the Sacred Mosque. And fear Allah, and know that Allah Is strict in punishment. For Ḥajj are the months well known. If any one undertakes that duty therein, Let there be no obscenity, nor wickedness, nor wrangling in the Ḥajj. And whatever good ye do, (be sure) Allah knoweth it. And take a provision (With you) for the journey, but the best of provisions is right conduct. So fear Me, o ye that are wise. (2:196-197).

And proclaim the Pilgrimage among men: they will come to thee on foot and (mounted) on every kind of camel, lean on account of journeys through deep and distant mountain highways; That they may witness the benefits (provided) for them, and celebrate the name of God, through the Days appointed, over the cattle which He has provided for them (for sacrifice): then eat ye thereof and feed the distressed ones in want. (22:27-38)

This section contains a summarized version of the Ḥajj/Umrah rites. The intent here behind this section is not to detail each aspect of the Ḥajj/'Umrah, but is to present the spiritual aspects of the niyyah and recitations at various point in the pilgrimage. However, to observe the Ḥajj correctly it is essential to follow the instructions and details that your Ḥajj guide directs you to do.

Obligations of Hajj According to the Four Schools

ḤANAFĪ	SHAFI'Ī	MĀLIKĪ	ḤANBALĪ
Iḥrām.	Iḥrām.	Iḥrām.	Iḥrām.
Spending a day at 'Arafah	Spending a day at 'Arafah.	Spending a day at 'Arafah.	Spending a day at 'Arafah.
Sa'ī between Ṣafā and Marwah.	Sa'ī between Ṣafā and Marwah.	Sa'ī between Ṣafā and Marwah.	Sa'ī between Ṣafā and Marwah.
Circumambulation. Ṭawāf al-Ifāḍah which is done at the Yawm an-Naḥr - the day of sacrifice - on returning from Minā. (Iḥrām is a prerequisite for the validity of Ṭawāf.)	Circumambu-lation. Ṭawāf al-Ifāḍah which involves seven rounds of the Ka'bah.	Circumambu-lation. Ṭawāf al-Ifāḍah which involves seven rounds of the Ka'bah.	Circumambu-lation. Ṭawāf al-Ifāḍah which involves seven rounds of the Ka'bah.
	Clipping some of the pilgrim's hair or shaving it all.		
	Close sequence of most rites of Ḥajj, e.g. Iḥrām must proceed all other rites and standing at 'Arafah must proceed Ṭawāf .		

Restrictions of *Ihram*

Sexual intercourse and all matters leading to it such as kissing, caresses or talking with one's spouse about intercourse or related sexual matters.
Violating the limits ordained by Allah and disobeying His orders.

Disputing, arguing or fighting with servants, companions or others.

Wearing any sewn clothes which fit the body

It is forbidden for the Muḥrim to wear clothes dyed with a scented material that lingers with him wherever he goes. He is forbidden from using perfume on body, clothes or hair.

Abū Ḥanīfa and ath-Thawrī held that a Muḥrim may contract a marriage but he is forbidden to consummate it.

There is a consensus among the scholars that, in the state of Iḥrām, the Muḥrim is forbidden to clip his nails without any genuine excuse.

It is forbidden for a Muḥrim to cover his head with any normal headcover.

There is consensus among the scholars that hunting is forbidden to the Muḥrim even if he does not actually slaughter the animal

Summarized Steps of Hajj

On the pre-noon of the eighth Dhul-Ḥijjah enter into Iḥrām from your place and perform ghusl (total washing) if it is possible and put on the Iḥrām cloths and repeat the Talbīyah

Set out and stay at Minā to pray Ẓuhr, 'Aṣr, Maghrib, 'Isha and Fajr prayers. Every prayer comprising of four rak'ats is to be shortened to two rak'ats only.

At 'Arafah perform Ẓuhr and 'Aṣr obligatory prayers in combination for travelers; each prayer shortened to two rak'ats. Stay there until sunset and implore God frequently facing the Qiblah.

When the sun sets, march from 'Arafah to Muzdalifah. Once at Muzdalifah you should pray Maghrib, Isha and Fajr prayers. Stay there to implore God until sunrise. If you are weak and are not able to walk and mingle with the crowd, you may go to Minā at late night. However the 49 stones must be collected by you or someone on your behalf.

When the sun is about to rise, walk from Muzdalifah to Minā; when you arrive at Minā, do the following:

A: Stone Jamarat al-'Aqabah which is the Stoning Site located nearest to Makkah. You have to throw seven pebbles, one by one, pronouncing Takbīr (Allāhu Akbar!) at every throw and say:

raghman li 'sh-Shaytan riḍan li 'r-Raḥmān 3 times, bismillāh Allāhu akbar! رغماً للشيطان رضاً للرحمن 3 مرات بسم الله الله أكبر.

In opposition to Satan, seeking God's good pleasure and satisfaction; God is greater!

B: Slaughter a sacrificial animal, eat from its meat and distribute the rest to the poor. The slaughtering of a sacrificial animal is obligatory on the one doing Ḥajj Tamattu' or Ḥajj Qirān (combined 'Umrah and Ḥajj).

C: Shave or shorten the hair of your head. Shaving is recommended (women should shorten their hair equal to a fingertip length). The order of the three above-mentioned acts is: first, throwing the pebbles, second, slaughtering the sacrificial animal and third to shave or shorten the hair of the head. There is no harm if the order is interchanged. After completion of the above mentioned three acts, you can put on your normal clothes and do all the acts prohibited during the Ḥajj with the exception of sexual intercourse.

Then go to Makkah with the intention to perform Ṭawāf al-Ifāḍah (Ṭawāf al-Ḥajj) and to perform Sa'ī between Ṣafā and Marwah (Sa'ī al-Ḥajj).

When you reach Makkah, do circumambulation (Ṭawāf) of the Ka'bah seven times starting from the corner of Ḥajaru 'l-Aswad (the Black Stone) and finishing by it. One then prays two rak'ats behind Maqām Ibrahīm, if possible.

After the performance of two rak'ats, go to the hillock of Ṣafā to perform Sa'ī seven times commencing from Ṣafā and ending at Marwah.

After completion of Ṭawāf and Sa'ī, go back to Minā in order to spend the two nights of 11th and 12th of Dhul-Ḥijjah. By completion of Ṭawāf al-Ifāḍah, every act prohibited for the pilgrim during the Ḥajj time now becomes lawful including sexual intercourse.

On the days of 11th and 12th of Dhul-Ḥijjah, after the sun declines, throw the pebbles at the three Stoning Sites (Jamarahs). Start with the furthest from Makkah and then the middle one and finally Jamarat al-'Aqabah. Throw seven pebbles at each Stoning Site and pronounce the Takbīr every time a stone is thrown. After throwing at the first and the middle Stoning Site, implore God facing the Qiblah; it is a must that throwing of the stones in these two days (i.e. 11th and 12th) be after zawāl (noon).

When you complete throwing the pebbles on the 12th of Dhul-Ḥijjah, you may go out of Minā before sunset. If you want to delay going out it is better to spend the night of the 13th of Dhul-Ḥijjah at Minā and repeat throwing pebbles at the three Stoning Sites after the sun reaches its noon peak (zawāl) as before.

If you want to go back home, you have to perform a Farewell Circumambulation (Ṭawāf al-Wida') (seven turns around the Ka'bah). There is no Ṭawāf al-Wida' enjoined on a woman in the post-partum state or one in her menses.

Umrah – Summary of Steps

'Umrah technically means paying a visit to Ka'bah, performing circumambulation (Ṭawāf) around it, walking between Ṣafā and Marwah seven times (Sā'ī). A performer of 'Umrah puts off his Iḥrām by having his hair shaved or cut.

If you want to perform 'Umrah, make the intention (niyyah) for 'Umrah, first perform ghusl (shower). Next put on the Iḥrām clothes. Pray two rakats Sunnatu 'l-Iḥrām. Then pronounce the Talbīyah.

When you reach Makkah, do circumambulation (Ṭawāf) of the Ka'bah seven times for 'Umrah starting from the corner of Ḥajar al-Aswad (the Black Stone) and finishing by it. One then prays two rak'ats behind Maqām Ibrahīm, if possible.

After the performance of two rak'ats, go to the hillock of Ṣafā to perform Sa'ī seven times commencing from Ṣafā and ending at Marwah.

After completion of Sa'ī you may shorten your hair. By this, your 'Umrah is complete and you may disengage from Iḥrām clothes and put on normal clothes.

Hajj and *Umrah* - Detailed Steps

Here we present details of some but not all aspects of the rites of Ḥajj and 'Umrah for which the shaykhs of the Naqshbandi Way have given particular recitations and or methodologies, to be observed in addition to all the normal steps performed by the pilgrim in following his or her particular madhhab and the guide assigned to his or her group.

PREPARATION FOR ḤAJJ

Imam Nawawī said according to the consensus of scholars it is from the *adab* of Ḥajj, that the essential intention of Ḥajj is to repent. Such repentance has the following conditions:

1. to leave all manner of sins;

2. to never return to these sins;

3. to regret the sins you have committed;

4. to ask forgiveness of anyone you have harmed, upset or made angry. If you owe someone money but you are unable pay them back at the time, you should inform them of your intention to make Ḥajj and give them a faithful promise to repay them in the future.

5. to write a will, since one does not knows if he will return from Ḥajj alive;

6. to use only money from licit means (ḥalāl) to go for Ḥajj, as God said:

> *O ye who believe! Give of the good things which ye have (honourably) earned, and of the fruits of the earth which We have produced for you, and do not even aim at getting anything which is bad, in order that out of it ye may give away something, when ye yourselves would not receive it except with closed eyes.* (2:267)

Abu Hurayra reported God's Messenger as saying:

> O people, God is Good and He therefore, accepts only that which is good. And God commanded the believers as He commanded the Messengers by saying: *"O Messengers, eat of the good things, and do good deeds; verily I am aware of what you do."* (23:51). And He said, *"O those who believe, eat of the good things that We gave you."* (2:172) He then made a mention of a person who travels far and wide, his hair dishevelled and covered with dust. He lifts his hand towards the sky (to makes supplication), "O Lord, O Lord," whereas his diet is unlawful, his drink is unlawful, and his clothes are unlawful and his nourishment is unlawful. How then can his supplication be accepted?

The meaning of this is that when going for Ḥajj, you must only use only licit means and leave all that is forbidden and repent from it, as God ordered: *"O ye who believe! Turn to God with sincere repentance."* (66: 8).

The pilgrim visits his family, neighbors and friends, informs them he is leaving and asks them to pray for him.

One states the intention to go for Ḥajj before the 8th of Dhul-Ḥijjah, or before arriving at the location (al-mīqāt) for dressing in the Iḥrām, whichever comes first. Intention should normally be made before starting one's trip, or at least one hour by plane from arrival at Jeddah. If coming by land from outside the Ḥijāz, it is recommended to make intention before setting out.

Before you enter into travel, take a shower and pray two rak'ats niyyatu 'l-Ḥajj, according to the Prophet ﷺ who said, "The best that a servant can put behind him when he travels to take care of his family, are two rak'ats that he prays before he sets forth on his travel; they which will be like his deputy during his absence [calipha]."[555]

If more than two are travelling together should choose one among them as a leader, according to the hadith, "If three are travelling let them choose one as leader."[556]

Make intention to undertake a great deal of supplication (du'a) and to give generously in the way of God for the poor, for the Prophet ﷺ said, "Spending (on others) in Ḥajj is like giving in the way of God: one dirham is rewarded seven hundred-fold."[557]

Ihram

Types of *Iḥrām*

For men, Iḥrām consists of two pieces of white, un-sewn and plain cloth; for women no special form of dress is required.

There are three types of Iḥrām:

1. Ifrād (single)

One intends only the Ḥajj and maintains Iḥrām up to the Day of Sacrifice. No offering is required from the mufrid.

2. Qirān (combined)

One intends the Ḥajj and 'Umrah combined. 'Umrah is done and Ḥajj is followed immediately in the same Iḥrām. Only after pelting the Jamrah of al-'Aqabah, and shaving the hair for men or trimming the hair (men and women) can the pilgrim take

[555] Ibn Abi Shaybah from Miqdad (*mursal*).

[556] Ibn Majah from Abu Hurayrah.

[557] Narrated by Ahmad from Ibn Buraydah.

off Iḥrām. The condition is to slaughter an animal, or if one is unable, to fast three days during Ḥajj and seven upon returning home.

3. Tamattu' (interrupted)

One intends 'Umrah and Ḥajj separately. One performs 'Umrah in Iḥrām, then return to a normal state and dress and remains like that until the Yawm al-tarwīyya, which is the 8th of Dhul-Ḥijjah, when he again dresses in Iḥrām from the mīqāt with the intention of Ḥajj and performs the Ḥajj. After fulfilling the Ḥajj rituals, one should offer a sacrificial animal.

INTENTION

Correct intention is crucial when putting on Iḥrām for Ḥajj or 'Umrah. The intention is made based on the type of Ḥajj/'Umrah being performed.

1. ***Ḥajj Ifrād***

نية الحج:

One says:

اللهم إني نَوَيْتُ الحج فيسره لي وتقبله مني

Allāhuma innī nawaytu al-Ḥajja, fa-yassirhu lī wa taqabalhu minnī.

O God I intend to make the pilgrimage so make it easy for me and accept it from me.

2. ***'Umrah***

نية العمرة:

For 'Umrah alone one says:

اللهم إني نويتُ العمرة فيسرها لي وتقبلها مني

Allāhuma innī nawaytu al-'Umrata, fa-yassirhā lī wa taqabalhā minnī.

O God I intend to make the lesser pilgrimage so make it easy for me and accept it from me.

3. ***Qirān***

نية الحج والعمرة:

For Ḥajj and 'Umrah combined one says:

اللهم إني نويتُ الحج والعمرة فيسرهما لي وتقبلهما مني

Allāhuma innī nawaytu al-'umrata wal-Ḥajja, fa-yassirhumā lī wa taqabalhumā minnī.

O God I intend to make both the lesser pilgrimage and the greater pilgrimage so make them both easy for me and accept them both from me.

One then says:

نَويتُ الأربعين، نويتُ

Nawaytu 'l-arbā'īn, nawaytu 'l-'itikāf, nawaytu 'l-khalwah, nawaytu 'l-'uzlah, nawaytu 'r-riyāda, nawaytu 's-sulūk, lillāhi ta'alā al-'Adhīm.

الاعتكاف نويتُ الخلوة نَويتُ العُزْلة، نويتُ الرياضة نويتُ السُلوك، لله تعالى

For the sake of blessing (barakah) I intend the forty (days of seclusion); I intend isolation; I intend discipline (of the ego); I intend to travel in God's Path; for the sake of God, the Exalted.

I am intending to perform Ḥajj on behalf of myself and my family and on behalf of the entire Nation of the Prophet ﷺ. If God with His Favor, honors me by accepting my Ḥajj, I gift the rewards of this worship (faḍīlat), to the Prophet ﷺ, to all 124,000 prophets and messengers, to the Sahabah, to the saints, to Imam Mahdi and to my Shaykh. I am sharing all the rewards that He is granting me in His Mercy with the entire Nation of the Prophet ﷺ, without leaving one person behind.

TALBĪYAH

التلبية

Recite three times:

Labaik allāhumma labaik, labaika lā sharīka laka labaik. Inna al-ḥamda w'an-ni'mata laka wal-mulk, lā sharīka laka labaik.

لبيك اللهم لبيك لبيك لا شريك لك لبيك، إن الحمد والنعمة لك، والملك لا شريك لك

At Your service O my God, at your service. At Your service, there is no partner to You, at Your service. Verily all praise, and all bounty belongs to You, as does the Kingdom. There is no partner to You, at Your service.

Then sit and recite the Naqshbandi Adab up to the first Ihdā. (see page 722)

ABANDONING ANGER AND SMOKING

Then from that time onwards, do not speak unnecessarily. Two things must be avoided at all costs during Ḥajj: anger and smoking. Anger must be abandoned completely. Know that that there will be a lot of testing to see if you have truly eliminated anger. Know that God, His Angels, the Prophet ﷺ and the inheritors of the Prophet ﷺ the awliya and the Abdāl are observing you. Even on the last moment of your pilgrimage, you might face a disliked situation that incites your anger, so you must be careful. If your anger emerges; if you complain or fight, your Ḥajj will be brought to nought, so beware of anger.

Anger in Ḥajj is utterly unacceptable. If you sense that you are likely to get angry, do not go for Ḥajj, but rather work to eliminate this bad characteristic from your self.

Avoid smoking.

CONDUCT OF TRAVEL

ادب السفر

As soon as you enter the vehicle of travel recite:

100x Bismillāhi 'r-Raḥmāni 'r-Raḥīm. Dhālika taqdīru 'l-'Azīzi 'l-'Alīm (36:38)

بِسْمِ اللهِ الرَّحْمٰنِ الرَّحِيمِ.
ذٰلِكَ تَقْدِيرُ الْعَزِيزِ الْعَلِيمِ

In the name of God the Beneficent, the Merciful. That is the decree of (Him), the Exalted in Might, the All-Knowing.

From that time on, occupy the time on your journey with whatever comes to your heart of dhikr, praise of the Prophet ﷺ, reading Quran, reading Dalā'il al-Khayrāt or making any kind of glorification (tasbīḥ) until you reach your destination.

When one approaches Madīnah (if flying, this is about an hour and a half before arriving at Jeddah), you pay respect towards the Prophet ﷺ by praising and seeking his intercession to accept you to be from his Ummah, and to facilitate your Ḥajj and your Visitation (ziyārah) to him. Then call upon the Men of God (rijālullāh) of Makkah and Madīnah to support you in that intention, as mentioned in the hadith that the Prophet said:

> *If one of you loses something or seeks help or a helper (ghawth), and he is in a land where there is no-one to befriend, let him say: "O servants of God, help me! (yā 'ibād Allāh, aghithūnī), for verily God has servants whom he does not see.*[558]

Praise the Prophet ﷺ excessively one hour before landing, five hundred or one thousand times continuously until you reach your first entry point or destination in Ḥijāz.

When you reach the entry point (the airport at Jeddah or the border, if coming by

---

[558] Abu Yala, Ibn al-Sani, and Tabarani in *al-Mujam al-kabir*. Al-Haythami said in *Majma al-zawaid* (10:132): "The men in its chain of transmission have been declared reliable despite weakness in one of them."

land), you will go through some formalities after which your guide will take you to either Makkah or Madīnah depending on your date of arrival.

CONDUCT OF ARRIVAL IN MAKKAH

When you arrive in Makkah, proceed directly to the accommodations assigned to you, whether it be a hotel room, a room in a house or any other form of lodging. Do not fight with other members of your Ḥajj group by demanding special treatment or accommodations, but rather go directly to whatever accommodations have been assigned to you or is available.

If you are tired rest. Then shower (ghusl), pray two rak'ats, then proceed to Masjid al-Ḥarām for making 'Umrah, if you are doing Ḥajj tamattu'. Intend to make your 'Umrah immediately after you enter Masjid al-Ḥarām.

Before entering the Sanctuary (ḥaram), recite a greeting for the Ka'bah:

GREETING KA'BAH

تحية الكعبة:

Allāhumma anta 's-Salām wa minka 's-salām wa ilayka yā'ūdu 's-salām, fa ḥayyinā Rabbanā bi 's-salām, wa adkhilnā 'l-Jannata bi luṭfika wa karamika wa jūdika dāraka, dār as-salām. Tabārakta Rabbanā wa tā'alayta, yā Dhal-Jalāli wa 'l-Jamāli wal-Baqā'i wa 'l-'Aẓamati wa 'l-Ikrām. Kulluna laka 'abdun. Wa aḥaqqu mā yaqūl al-'abd Allāhumma lā māni'a limā āa'ṭayta, wa lā mu'ṭiya limā man'ata wa lā rādda limā qaḍayta, wa lā yanfa'u dhāl-jaddi minka al-jaddu. Rabbī lā ḥawla wa lā quwwata illa billāhi 'l-'Alīyyi 'l-'Aẓīm.

اللهم أنت السلام ومنك السلام وإليك يعود السلام فحينا ربنا بالسلام وادخلنا الجنة بلطفك وكرمك وجودك دارك دار السلام. تباركت ربنا وتعاليت يا ذا الجلال والجمال والبقاء والعظمة الإكرام. كلنا لك عبد, واحق ما يقول العبد اللهمَّ لا مانع لما أعطيتَ ولا مُعْطي لما مَنَعْتَ ولا رادَّ لما قَضيتَ ولا يَنْفعُ ذا الجدّ منك الجَدُّ ربّي لا حَوْلَ ولا قوّةَ إلا بالله العَليّ العَظيم.

O God! You are Peace and from You comes Peace. Blessed and lofty are You, O Lord of Majesty and Bounty. There is no god but God, He is One, no partner has He. His is the Kingdom and His is all praise, and He is over all things Powerful. We have heard and obeyed. Your forgiveness, O our Lord! And to Thee is the end of all journeys. All of us are servants to You, and the most true of what a servant may say is: O God! No one can disallow the one to whom You are giving, and there is no giver, to the one whom You have denied. And there is no refusing Your decree. Riches and good fortune will not profit the possessor thereof with You (for nothing will profit him but acting in obedience to You). My Lord, there is no power and no strength save in God, All-High and Almighty.

That is greeting for Makkah and the Ka'bah. You ask the spiritual servants of God, His angels and the inheritors of the Prophet ﷺ to direct you as you perform your ¤ajj/ 'Umrah. When you enter, it is recommended to enter from the Bāb us-salām – the Gate of Peace. Bāb us-salām is below where adhān is called, as you enter the Ḥaram, there is a line of sight direct to the Ka'bah where you recite greetings to the Ka'bah, raising your two hands towards the Ḥajar al-Aswad or if it is possible to approach it without scuffling, one should do so and kiss it, otherwise raise both hands towards it and say:

Face the Ḥajar al-Aswad and say:

بسم الله الله اكبر (3 مرات)

Bismillāh Allāhu Akbar (3 times)

السلام عليك يا كعبة الله

As-salāmu 'alayki yā Ka'batallāh

Peace be upon you, O Ka'bah of God.

السلام عليك يا بيت الله

As-salāmu 'alayka yā Baytallāh

Peace be upon you, O House of God.

If God wants, you will hear the Ka'bah return the greeting to you, as many saints hear. If you have not yet reached that level, the Ka'bah will return your greeting but you will not hear anything.

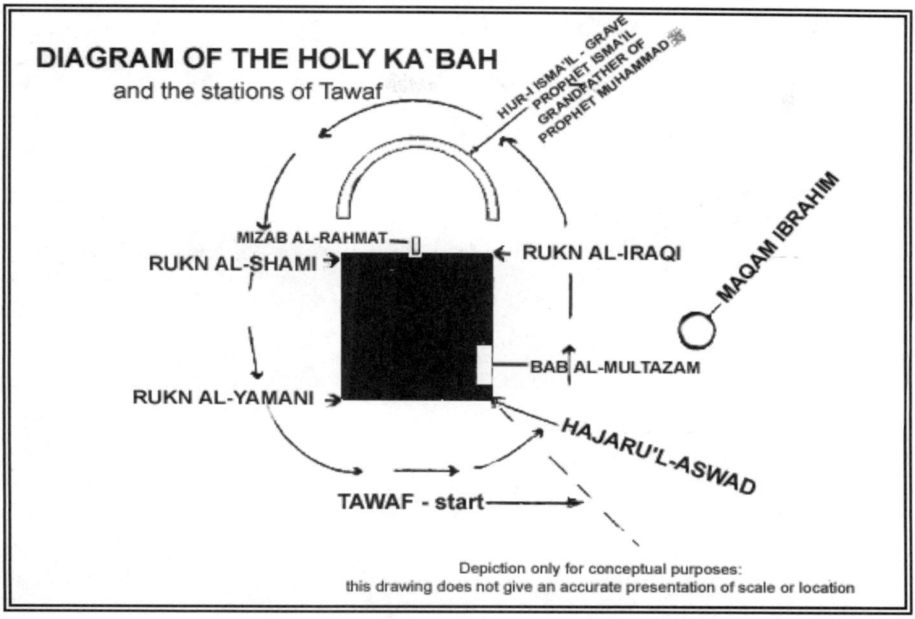

Tawaf al-Qudum

Before ʿUmrah or Ḥajj, the Ṭawāf al-qudūm is required (wājib).

First make intention, depending on whether doing Ḥajj or ʿUmrah:

Intention (Ḥajj) نَوَيتُ طوف القدوم

Nawaitu Ṭawāf al qudūm.

I intend the preliminary circumambulation.

Intention (*ʿUmrah*) نَوَيتُ طواف العمرة

Nawaitu Ṭawāf al ʿumrāh.

I intend the circumambulation of the lesser pilgrimage.

Raise hands towards the Black Stone and say: بسم الله الله أكْبر (3 مرات)

Bismillāh, Allāhu Akbar three times.

During circumambulation talbīyah is not done, until after complete sāʿī.

When in front of the door of the Ka'bah say:

Allāhumma innal bayta baytuk, wal-ḥaramu ḥaramuk, wal-amnu amnuk wa hadhā maqāmu 'l-'ā'idha bika min an-nār.

امام باب الكعبة:

اللهم إنّ البيت بيتك والحرم حرمك والأمن أمنك وهذا مقام العائذ بك من النار

O God, this house is Thy house, this sacred territory is Thy sacred territory, this security is Thy security, and this is the place for one who seeks protection with Thee against the hell fire.

(ii) At the corner of the second wall by the opening of the ḥijr (semi-circular wall):

Allāhumma innī 'aūdhu bika min ash-shakki wa 'sh-shirki wa 'sh-shiqāqi wa 'n-nifāqi wa sū 'il-akhlāqi wa sū 'il-munqalabi fil āhli wal-māli wal-walad.

(ب) امام باقى الجدار من باب الكعبة:

اللهم أعوذ بك من الشك والشرك والشقاق والنفاق وسوء الأخلاق وسوء المنقلب في الأهل والمال والولد.

O God I ask Thy protection against doubt, polytheism, schism, hypocrisy, bad morality, and ill-return in the family, property and children.

(iii) While passing the second wall, in front of the drainspout of Mercy (mīzāb ar-raḥmah): Allāhumma aẓillanī fee ẓillika yauma lā ẓilla illā ẓilla 'arshik. Wasqinī bi-kā'si sayyidinā Muḥammadin sallallāhu 'alaihi wa sallam, sharbatan hanī'atan ma-rī'atan lā azmā'u b'adahā abadan yā dhal jalāli wal-ikrām.

(ج) عند الجدار الثانى:

اللهم أظلنى في ظلك يوم لا ظل إلا ظل عرشك واسقنى بكأس سيدنا محمد صلى الله عليه وسلم شربة هنيئة مريئة لا أظمأ بعدها أبدا، يا ذا الجلال والإكرام.

O God, put me under Thy shadow on the day when there will be no shadow except the shadow of Thy Throne and give me to drink from the cup of our master Muhammad a delicious and sating drink after which I shall never get thirsty, O Thou full of Majesty and Bounty.

(iv) When crossing the third wall between the third corner and the Yamānī corner (and according to whether it is during the Ḥajj or the 'Umrah):

Allāhum 'aj'alhu Ḥajjan mabrūrā/ (aj'alhā

(د) عند الجدار الثالث حسب الحج او العمرة:

اللهم اجعله حجا مبرورا (أو عمرة مبرورة) وذنبا مغفورا وسعيا مشكورا وتجارة لن تبور

'umratam-mabrūra) wa dhanban maghfūran wa sā'īyan mashkūrān wa tijāratan lan tabūra yā 'Azīzu yā Ghafūr.

يا عزيز يا غفور

O God, make that this be a Ḥajj /'Umrah which is accepted, with (my) sin which is pardoned, an accepted work, a commerce which is not lost, O Thou the Powerful, the Forgiving.

When one reaches the Yamānī corner do not kiss it, but touch it if possible and then kiss one's hand.

(v) While crossing the fourth wall:

(ه) عند الجدار الرابع:

Rabbanā ātinā fid-dunyā ḥasanatan wa fī 'l-ākhirati ḥasanatan wa qinā 'adhāb an-nār.

ربنا آتنا في الدنيا حسنة وفي الآخرة حسنة وقنا عذاب النار.

O our Lord, give us good in this world and good in the Hereafter, and protect us from the punishment of the hell fire.

Once one reaches the Black Stone a single round (ṭawāf) has been completed. It is Sunnah for men to trot in the first three rounds and to bare their right shoulders, except in the Farewell Ṭawāf. However if this means leaving any women without menfolk to accompany, this should not be done, or some men should remain with the women.

After completing the circumambulation until you finish seven turns (ṭawāf), reciting what you are able of the above invocations then you go to Bāb al-Multazam and make du'a there. If it is difficult due to crowds, do not fight, but step back and go to Maqām Ibrāhīm and from far away make the invocation. Then pray two raka'at at Maqām Ibrāhīm. It is often not possible for ladies to pray there, so they should pray two raka'ats in the ladies section.

Sai

Then you go to do Sa'ī. At this portion of 'Umrah/Ḥajj one should keep in mind the struggle of Lady Hajar, searching desperately for water for her baby, the Prophet Isma'īl.

CONDUCT OF SA'Ī

ادب السعي

Begin saying:

بِسْمِ اللهِ الرَّحْمٰنِ الرَّحِيمِ

Bismillāhi 'r-Raḥmāni 'r-Raḥīm

In the name of God the Beneficent, the Merciful.

Then invoke God (du'a):

Ya Rabbī, Ya Allāh, I am making Sa'ī I am seeking the means of support through the Prophet ﷺ and the inheritors of his spiritual states, the saints. O God, if You favor me by accepting my 'Umrah/Ḥajj, all the rewards that I receive I will share with all your servants on this earth.

After completing Sa'ī, present your 'Umrah, or Ḥajj to the Presence of the Prophet ﷺ, by saying, "Ya Rasulullāh, I performed that 'Umrah/Ḥajj by trying to follow your footsteps, I am requesting that it be accepted and be changed from imitational to real worship and that you O Prophet of God, present it to the Presence of God."

You then ask from God whatever you want for this life and the hereafter.

You return to your lodging if you are making 'Umrah.

In the case of Ḥajj at-Tamattu', after completing the 'Umrah, the pilgrim trims his or her hair, showers, and changes into everyday clothes.

These steps complete the 'Umrah portion of the Ḥajj at-Tamattu'. All restrictions of the Iḥrām are temporarily lifted. The pilgrim waits until the 8th of Dhul-Ḥijjah to start the rites of Ḥajj and return to Iḥrām.

INTENTION AND *IḤRĀM* FOR ḤAJJ *TAMATTU'*

If doing Ḥajj at-Tamattu', on the 8th of Dhul-Ḥijjah, the pilgrim pronounces a new intention (nīyyah) at the place to perform Ḥajj. There is no need to go to the mīqāt for this. The pilgrim changes into Iḥrām in the prescribed manner and proceeds to Minā soon after the Fajr Prayers.

Then perform the rites of Ḥajj, by going to 'Arafah, Minā and Muzdalifa and Minā and observing all the details following one's Ḥajj guide.

Standing at Arafah

It is no crime in you if ye seek of the bounty of your Lord (during pilgrimage). Then when ye pour down from (Mount) Arafah, celebrate the praises of God at the Sacred Monument, and celebrate His praises as He has directed you, even though, before this, ye went astray. (2:198).

There is consensus among Muslim scholars that spending the Day of 'Arafah is the most important part of Ḥajj.

'Abd ar-Raḥmān bin Ya'mur reported that the Prophet ﷺ ordered an announcer to proclaim, "Ḥajj is 'Arafah...."

Standing as much as possible is very much recommended, especially around the plains of Jabal ar-Raḥmah (Mount of Mercy) where the Prophet ﷺ delivered his last sermon.

In another hadith, Jābir reported that the Prophet said:

> *....And there is no day better in the sight of Allah than the Day of 'Arafah. On this day Allah, the Almighty and the Exalted, descends to the nearest heaven, and He is proud of His slaves on the earth, and says to those in Heaven, "Look at My servants. They have come from far and near, with hair dishevelled and faces covered with dust, to seek My mercy, even though they have not seen My chastisement." Far more people are freed from the Hell-fire on the Day of 'Arafah than on any other day.*

On that day the pilgrims should spend most of their time reading the Qur'an, making remembrance of God (dhikr), supplication (du'a), praising the Prophet (ṣalawāt) ﷺ, and most importantly asking Allah for forgiveness.

Stoning the *Jamarat*

One pelts the Stoning Sites on the four days of Eid. On the first day you throw seven stones at the Jamarat al-'Aqabah only. On the remaining three days you must throw 21 stones altogether each day, seven at each Jamarah, one-by-one pronouncing the formula below. Some people take the stones and throw them altogether - this is not accepted. Similarly, it is unacceptable to use your slippers or other objects to stone the sites.

Ladies can appoint someone to throw stones for them if the Stoning Sites are very crowded.

CONDUCT OF STONING

ادب الرجم

Take one pebble at a time and with each one say:

رغماً للشيطان رضاً للرحمن 3 مرات، للرحمن،بسم الله، الله أكبر.

Raghman li 'sh-shaiṭān, riḍan li 'r-Rahman, 3 times, Bismillāh, Allāhu Akbar.

And then throw it at the Jamarah.

In opposition to Satan, seeking God's good pleasure and satisfaction; In opposition to Satan, seeking God's good pleasure and satisfaction.; God is greater!

Stay at Mina

During one's stay at Minā, the pilgrim should engage in much remembrance (dhikr, tasbiīḥ), praise of the Prophet ﷺ (ṣalawāt), recitation of Qur'an, invocation (du'a) and supererogatory prayers, for God said:

> *Then pass on at a quick pace from the place whence it is usual for the multitude so to do, and ask for Allah's forgiveness. For Allah is Oft-forgiving, Most Merciful. So when ye have accomplished your holy rites, celebrate the praises of Allah, as ye used to celebrate the praises of your fathers,- yea, with far more Heart and soul. (2:199-200)*

And:

> *Celebrate the praises of Allah during the Appointed Days. But if any one hastens to leave in two days, there is no blame on him, and if any one stays on, there is no blame on him, if his aim is to do right. Then fear Allah, and know that ye will surely be gathered unto Him.* (2:203)

And:

> *O you who believe! Remember Allah with much remembrance. And glorify His praises morning and evening.* (33:41-42).

ṬAWĀF AL-WADA'

This is the Ṭawāf of farewell, which is unrelated to either the 'Umrah or Ḥajj. One makes this before leaving with the intention not to return.

This conclues the essential conduct of Ḥajj. Keep in mind this contains only a summarized version of the Ḥajj rites. The main intent here is to present the spiritual aspects of the intention and recitations at various point in the pilgrimage. However, to observe the Ḥajj correctly it is essential to follow the instructions and details that your Ḥajj guide directs you to do.

Zamzam

It is recommended to do much of drinking the water of the well of Zamzam for whatever intention one wishes, religious or other-worldly, as the Prophet ﷺ said, "The water of Zamzam is for whatever it is drunk for."[559]

It is Sunnah to face the Ka'bah standing while drinking, to breathe three times and say, "Bismillāh" each time one drinks and "alḥamdulillāh," drinking one's fill of it. People often take bottles of Zamzam water home from pilgrimage to share as a blessing (barakah) with family and friends. The same adab is observed when drinking it.

The Prophet ﷺ is reported to have said that the Earthly Ka'bah is the diametrically opposite of the mosque of the angels underneath the Throne of God, (and so exactly so that if one were to throw a stone from there, it would fall on the top of the Ka'bah on earth).[560] The scholar Ibn Kathīr reports that there is a particular Ka'bah at each of the seven heavens, each for the use of the inhabitants of that heaven.[561] He adds the name of the Ka'bah at the seventh heaven is Bait al-Ma'mūr, the Celebrated House, and that the earthly Ka'bah is at exactly the point below this heavenly Ka'bah.[562]

The Bait al-Ma'mūr was originally in the place where the Ka'bah stands today, sent down from Paradise by God, and built as the first house by Adam with the help of angels.[563] God ordered Adam to circumambulate it, as the angels turn about the Throne of the Merciful. At the time of Noah's flood, the House was raised up to the heavens, and the Prophet ﷺ saw the angels circumambulating it when he was taken to the heavens on the Night of Ascension.[564]

The Prophet Abraham was ordered by God to rebuild the Ka'bah with the help of his son, Prophet Ismail, and the archangel Gabriel brought out the only remaining stone

[559] Keller, *Reliance of the Traveler*, j11.6 (3), p. 349.

[560] *Bukhari*.

[561] Ibn Kathir, *Al-Bidayah wa al-nihayah*, 1, 163.

[562] Ibn Kathir, *Tafsir*, on surah 52, verse 4.

[563] Al-Kisai, Muhammad ibn Abdullah, *Qisas al-anbiya: Tales of the Prophets* (Kazi, 1997) p. 62.

[564] Adil, Hajjah Amina, *Lore of Light*, volume 1, p. 167.

from the original Ka'bah, the Black Stone, which had been ensconced within Mount Abu Qubais above Makkah since the time of the flood.[565]

It is recommended to look at the Ka'bah, for it is the locus of the Divine Gaze, and it is said that God sends down one hundred and twenty mercies day and night upon the House of God: sixty for those circumambulating; forty for those praying there and twenty for those looking at it.[566]

Significance of the Black Stone

The Black Stone - Ḥajaru 'l-Aswad - was sent down from heaven and the angels put it in the Ka'bah in the time of Adam, before he made the first circumambulation.[567] On the Day of Judgement it will bear witness for all those who have performed Ḥajj or *'Umrah.*

When you say Allāhu Akbar 3x, each time you make Ṭawāf, remember that the maqām of the Black Stone (Ḥajaru 'l-aswad) is a sacred place. That stone has life and it greets those visiting it, so greet it with full reverence. For that reason the Prophet ﷺ kissed the Black Stone.

It is reported that when 'Umar ibn al-Khaṭṭāb ؓ performed pilgrimage and embraced the (Black) Stone, he said, "I know by God that you are a stone which neither harms nor benefits, and had I not seen God's Messenger embrace you, I would not have embraced you."

However, 'Alī ibn Abī Ṭālib ؓ said to him, "Abū Hafs, do not say this, for God's Messenger ﷺ did not embrace it (the Black Stone) save for wisdom he knew,... It has two eyes and two lips and possesses a keen tongue that testifies for those who fulfill their obligations to it."[568]

An authentic narration states that the Black Stone shall appear with two eyes and a tongue on the Day of Resurrection.[569]

---

565 Adil, Hajjah Amina, *Lore of Light*, volume 1, p. 22, 23.

566 Keller, *Reliance of the Traveler*, j11.6 (2), p. 349.

567 Adil, Hajjah Amina, *Lore of Light*, volume 1, p. 22.

568 Reported by Imam Ghazali, *Ihya ulum ad-din*, and, Hajjah Amina Adil, *Lore of Light*, volume 1, p.24, with additional wording.

569 Narrated by Tirmidhi, Ibn Majah, Ahmad, al-Darimi, Ibn Hibban (#3711-3712), and others.

Significance of *Sai*

The story is related in *Qiṣas al-Anbīyā* that Prophet Abraham ﷺ took Lady Hagar (Hājar) and the baby Ishmael to the Sacred valley at Bakkah (now Makkah), near the Ka'bah of Adam ﷺ, which had been destroyed by the Flood of Noah ﷺ. Prophet Abraham told Lady Hagar, "Remain here with my child, for thus I have been commanded." "Upon whom shall I rely?" asked Lady Hagar. "Upon your Lord," answered Prophet Abraham, who then turned to the right and the left, but seeing no one called upon God:

> *O our Lord! I have made some of my offspring to dwell in a valley without cultivation, by Thy Sacred House; in order, O our Lord, that they may establish regular Prayer: so fill the hearts of some among men with love towards them, and feed them with fruits: so that they may give thanks.* (14:37)

When the heat became unbearable, Lady Hagar saw a tree where the Well of Zamzam was destined to be, over which she suspended a robe to shade them from the heat of the sun. as they had finished the water in the jug they had with them and were thirsty, Hagar did not know what to do. First she ran in the direction of the hillock Ṣafā in search of water, and then towards the hillock Marwāh, crying, "Our God, do not destroy us by thirst!"

Then [archangel] Gabriel ﷺ descended to them bearing tidings of relief, whereupon she went to Ishmael, who was scratching the earth with his finger; there the well of Zamzam sprang up, and she fell down prostrate in thanks to God. Lady Hagar said, "It is abundant water [Zamzam in her language]," from which the well took its name. Then she gathered stones around the spring lest it the water flow away. Prophet Muhammad ﷺ explained that had she not done that, the water would have flowed across the face of the earth from east to west.

Later a caravan approached from Yemen headed for Syria. When they saw birds hovering above Lady Hagar and the child, they were perplexed and said, "Birds hover only over water and inhabited places." Drawing near, they found Hagar and baby Isma'īl beside a well of sweet water. After some discussion, Lady Hagar gave them permission to draw water and they came with their flocks and people and settled there, and eventually Isma'īl married a noble woman from their tribe. Lady Hagar died and it is said she was buried by the Ka'bah, in the semi-circular area known as Hijr - Isma'īl, where the Prophet Ishmael ﷺ was later buried as well.570

In one narration Lady Hagar, when she was running in search of water between Ṣafā and Marwāh, heard a voice and called out: "O you whose voice you have made me hear! If there is a ghawth (help/helper) with you (then help me)!" and an angel appeared at the spot of the spring of Zamzam."571

DAILY ṬAWĀF

When you enter the Sacred Mosque, it is preferred to make a Ṭawāf as it is the greeting for the Ka'bah (Taḥīyyatul Ka'bah). Use the same steps mentioned above, leaving out the wording "al-qudūm" from the intention. If it is not possible to do the Ṭawāf, pray first, and when it is less crowded make Ṭawāf if you are able.

When you leave the Sacred Mosque, it is not necessary to make Ṭawāf.

SHOPPING AND DAILY ACTIVITY

During pilgrimage it is permitted to shop, but one should not spend excessive time doing so. Similarly, excessive time should not be spent in restaurants and coffee shops. Rather, keep oneself busy in praying, remembrance (dhikr) and praise of the Prophet (ṣalawāt) ﷺ.

Holy Places of Visitation in Makkah

JANNAT AL-MU'ALLA

Also known as al-Hājūn, this is a general cemetery in existence from before the time of the Prophet ﷺ and in which his first wife, the Mother of the Believers (Umm al-mu'minīn) Sayyida Khadījat al-kubrā is buried. Buried there too are many member of the Family of the Prophet ﷺ, his Companions, Successors, Successors of the Successors, saints and scholars. The Prophet ﷺ used to visit it frequently. It is the second holiest graveyard after al-Baqi' in Madīnah.

Those buried here include:

Grave of 'Abd Manāf: Great, great-grandfather of the Holy Prophet ﷺ

Grave of Hāshim: Great-grandfather of the Holy Prophet ﷺ

Grave of 'Abd al-Muṭṭalib: Grandfather of the Holy Prophet ﷺ, who raised him in

---

570 Al-Kisai, Muhammad ibn Abdullah, *Qisas al-anbiya: Tales of the Prophets*, (Kazi, 1997) p. 152.

571 *Bukhari.*

his early childhood.

Grave of Sayyidah Āmina bint Wahb: Mother of the Holy Prophet ﷺ who died when he was only 5 years old. According to another source, Sayyidah Āmina is buried in Abwā (between Makkah and Madīna)

Grave of Sayyidinā 'Abd Allāh ibn 'Abd al-Muṭṭalib: The blessed father of our Holy Prophet ﷺ, who died and was buried in Madīna. Later his body was disinterred and found to be intact. It was transferred to Makkah and buried in Jannat al-Mu'alla.

Grave of Abū Ṭālib: The uncle of the Prophet ﷺ who raised him after the passing of his grandfather 'Abd al-Muṭṭalib. He was father of 'Alī ibn Abī Ṭālib, Ja'far and 'Aqīl.

Grave of Khadīja: First wife of the Holy Prophet ﷺ and mother of his daughters.

Grave of Qāsim: son of the Holy Prophet ﷺ who died in his infancy.

MASJID AL-JINN

A group of Jinn were passing by, when they heard the Prophet ﷺ reciting the Holy Quran. They were so moved that they came to the Prophet ﷺ, repented and accepted Islam. A masjid was later built at the location and named Masjid al-Jinn.

CAVE OF THAWR

During the Hijrah the Prophet ﷺ stayed here for three days during the Migration from Makkah. The miraculous incident took place here, in which a spider spun a web and a pigeon laid eggs at the mouth of this cave causing the trackers sparing the Prophet ﷺ and his companion Abū Bakr aṣ-Ṣiddīq from being found and harmed by the pursuing Makkans. (see page 78 for more details of this blessed event).

CAVE OF HIRĀ

The cave in which the Prophet ﷺ used to seclude himself before the first revelation, and in which the first revelation, the Surah "The Clot" was revealed to him by the archangel Gabriel.

MOUNT OF MERCY (JABAL RAḤMAH)

This is a mountain in the plain of 'Arafah. It is highly recommended to pray two rak'at Prayer of Need (ḥājah) here.

MUZDALIFAH

Pilgrims on Ḥajj are required to spend the night here. It is here they collect 70 pebbles for lapidating the pillars representing Satan in Minā.

MINĀ

This is a city that comes to existence for three days during the year. All pilgrims are required to spend the night in Minā, to stone the three pillars representing Satan each day and to sacrifice an animal for the sake of God, whose meat is distributed to the indigent. Men must shave their heads or cut their hair, while women are required only to cut the hair.

MASJID KHAYF

It is highly recommended to pray six rak'at of prayer in this Masjid in Minā and that has great reward as it is said that many prophets of God prayed here.

MASJID HUDAYBĪYYAH

This is the location where the Prophet ﷺ gave a special initiation (baya') to the Companions that were with him seeking to make pilgrimage, after Quraysh captured our master 'Uthmān ibn 'Affān and held him.

Visiting Madinat al-Munawwarah

The merits of Madīnah, of prayer in Madīnah, of visiting the Masjid al-Nabawī, of living in Madīnah, of not cutting trees there, etc. are all based on the fact that the Prophet ﷺ is there.

Thus in Madīnah, you must keep even more respect than in Makkah, because there you are in the presence of the Prophet ﷺ. Make continuous ṣalawāt in your heart, in unison with fellow pilgrims if you are on a bus, until you reach Madīnah. Whether you enter Madīnah by bus or by plane, after you clear the checkpoints, you will travel four or five miles before you begin to see the Sanctuary of the Prophet's Holy Mosque (ḥaram) in the distance. When you do, ask permission from the Prophet ﷺ to enter into his territory.

Significance of the Prophet's Mosque and Grave

In Islam, the Prophet's Mosque is second in rank with regard to merit and status in God's sight. The same applies to the reward for the worshipers and those heading there.

The Prophet ﷺ said:

Do not undertake a journey, but to one of the three Mosques: the Sacred Mosque, this Mosque of mine, and Al-Aqsā Mosque.[572]

It has been narrated that performing prayers in the Prophet's Mosque is of great merit and reward when the Prophet ﷺ said, "A prayer in this Mosque of mine is a thousand times more excellent than a prayer in any other mosque except the Sacred Mosque (in Mecca)."[573]

The Prophet ﷺ said:

Between my Grave and my Pulpit lies a grove from the groves of Paradise.[574]

The Blessed Grove of Paradise, known as Rawḍatu 'sh-Sharīfah, is the space in the

---

[572] Bukhari, Muslim,Tirmidhi, al-Nasai, Abu Dawud, Ibn Majah, Ahmad, al-Darimi.

[573] al-Bazzar authentic (*sahih*).

[574] Bukhari and Muslim.

mosque which lies between the pulpit and the Room in which the Prophet ﷺ is buried.

On the authority of Abū Hurayrah ؓ the Prophet ﷺ said: "My Pulpit (minbar) overlooks my Pool."

Al-Khaṭṭābī said that the meaning of this hadith is that "He who keeps the prayers at my Pulpit shall be given water from the Prophet's Pool on the Day of Judgment.[575]

Ibn 'Umar ؓ related that the Prophet ﷺ said:

> *Whoever comes to me as a visitor, with nothing in his heart except the intention to visit me, it is an obligation on me to be his intercessor on Judgment Day.*[576]

Anas ؓ narrates: God's Messenger ﷺ said:

> *He who visits me in Madīna counting on his visit to me (muḥtasiban), I will be his witness and intercessor on the Day of Judgment.*[577]

It is written in large script on the Rawḍah the famous hadith:

> *Whoever visits my grave, my intercession is obligatory for him.*[578]

The Prophet ﷺ said:

> *Whoever invokes blessings on me at my grave, I hear him, and whoever invokes blessings on me from afar, I am informed about it.*[579]

Abū Hurayrah ؓ said, "I heard the Prophet ﷺ say:

---

575 Bukhari and Muslim.

576 Tabarani in *al-Awsat* and *al-Kabir* with a chain containing Maslama ibn Salim, and by al-Daraqutni in his *Amali* and by Ibn al-Sakan in his *Sunan al-Sihah* as stated by al-Shirbini in *Mughni al-Muhtaj* (1:512).

577 Mentioned by Ibn al-Jawzi in *Muthir Al-Gharam Al-Sakin Ila Ashraf Al-Amakin*

578 Arabic: ***man zāra qabrī wajabat lahu shafaatī.*** Narrated from Ibn Umar by al-Daraqutni in his *Sunan* (2:278 #194), Abu Dawud al-Tayalisi in his *Musnad* (2:12), al-Dulabi in *al-Kuna wa al-Asma* (2:64), al-Khatib in *Talkhis al-Mutashabih fi al-Rasm* (1:581), Ibn al-Dubaythi in *al-Dhayl ala al-Tarikh* (2:170), Ibn Abi al-Dunya in *Kitab al-Qubur*, al-Bayhaqi in *Shuab al-Iman* (3:490), al-Hakim al-Tirmidhi in *Nawadir al-Usul* (p. 148), al-Haythami (4:2), al-Subki in *Shifa al-Siqam* (p. 12-14), Abu al-Shaykh, Ibn Adi in *al-Kamil* (6:235, 6:351), al-Uqayli in *al-Duafa* (4:170), and Ibn Hajar who indicated its grade of *hasan* in *Talkhis al-Habir* (2:266) as it is strengthened by other hadiths which both he and al-Haythami mention.

579 Abu al-Shaykh cites it in *Kitab al-Salat ala al-nabi* (Jala al-afham p. 22), and Ibn Hajar says in *Fath al-Bari* (6:379): "Abu al-Shaykh cites it with a good chain (*sanad jayyid*)." Bayhaqi mentions it in *Hayat al-anbiya* and *Shuab al-iman* (2:218 #1583) with ublightuhu in the end.

Jesus ﷺ will descend as an arbitrator and just judge and sincere Imam and he will follow the pilgrimage or the one with 'Umrah, or with intention to do both, and he will come to my grave, reciting greetings on me and I will respond to him."[580]

So it is very important to stand before the door of the grave of the Prophet ﷺ with utmost reverence, feeling the greatness of the Seal of Messengers, invoking God with whatever words come to the heart, keeping in mind the verse:

We sent not a messenger, but to be obeyed, in accordance with the will of God. If they had only, when they were unjust to themselves, come unto thee and asked God's forgiveness, and the Messenger had asked forgiveness for them, they would have found God indeed Oft-returning, Most Merciful. (4:64)

One must keep in mind the hadith from Abū Hurayrah ﷺ where the Prophet ﷺ said:

No one greets me except God has returned my soul to me so that I can return his greetings.[581]

And 'Abd Allāh ibn Mas'ud ﷺ said: God's Messenger ﷺ said, "God has angels that roam the earth bringing me the greetings of my nation."

The eminent scholar Imām aṣ-Ṣuyūti said that what is meant here by returned my soul is permanently, and not temporarily.[582] In other words, God does not return the Prophet's ﷺ soul and take it back, then return it again and then take it back again, but He has returned it to him permanently. Thus the Prophet ﷺ is alive permanently without interruption or lapse. Consider this, at every moment there is someone sending him greetings to the Prophet ﷺ, so there is no time in which his soul is absent.

HOW THE OTTOMAN SULTAN WOULD CLEAN THE RAWḌAH

Our master Shaykh Nazim relates that in the time of the Ottomans, the Sultan would come from Anatolia himself during the time of Hajj. Approaching the Blessed

---

580 Al-Hakim narrated it and graded it authentic (595/2), and al-Dhahabi concurred.

581 Abu Hurayra in Abu Dawud (Manasik #2039) with a sound chain; Ibn Asakir, *Mukhtasar Tarikh Dimashq* 2:407; Ahmad, *Musnad* 2:527; Abu Nuaym, *Akhbar Asbahan* 2:353; Ibn al-Najjar, *Akhbar al-Madina* p. 145; Bayhaqi, *Shuab al-iman* #4161; Haythami, *Majma al-zawaid* 10:162; Ibn Kathir, *Tafsir* 6:464; al-Mundhiri, *al-Targhib wa al-tarhib* 2:499; *Talkhis al-habir* 2:267.

582 in *Anba al-adhkiya bi hayat al-anbiya*

Hujratu 'sh-Sharifah crawling he would await the sign of his acceptance: the doors of the Hujrah would open of themselves. Still crawling, he would enter with perfect manners and proceed to dust and clean the room. Then, with fresh rose oil from roses grown especially for this purpose in Isparta, he would wash the surface of the grave and its floor. For the Ottoman sultans, this was the highest honor, and for their honoring the God's Messenger, God honored them with steadfast rule, respect and dignity before the world for over 500 years. Today the Blessed Rawḍah has not been cleaned in many years and the dust has been left to accumulate inside the *maqām*.

Etiquette in the *Rawdah*

A visitor should not raise his voice in the Mosque as a sign of politeness with the Messenger of God's ﷺ. Lowering one's voice is also a sign of obedience to the words of the Almighty God:

> *O ye who believe! Raise not your voices above the voice of the Prophet, nor speak aloud to him in talk, as ye may speak aloud to one another, lest your deeds become vain and ye perceive not. Of those who lower their voices in the presence of God's Messenger, their hearts has God tested for piety: for them is forgiveness and a great reward.* (49:2-3)

This is a warning to those who raise their voices in the presence of God's Messenger, that God will render their deeds vain and void and will not reward them.

It has been narrated that Abū Bakr aṣ-Ṣiddīq ؓ used to say, "There should be no raising of voices in the presence of a prophet, whether dead or alive."

Hearing the sound of a tent peg or a nail being hammered in the neighboring houses, 'A'ishah ؓ dispatched them a messenger saying, "Do not hurt God's Messenger ﷺ."

'Umar bin al-Khaṭṭāb ؓ heard two men raising their voices in the Mosque of the Prophet ﷺ. At this he asked them, "Where do you come from?" They answered, "From Ṭāif." Thereupon he said, "Had you been from Madīnah, I would have punished you. No voice should be raised in this Mosque of ours."

Qāḍī 'Iyād expresses the consensus of Muslims that the site of the Prophet's grave is the holiest site on earth.[583] Thus the visitation to the Prophet ﷺ (*ziyārah*) is of crucial importance to every believer, and to pray in the masjid of the Prophet ﷺ is also very important. The Prophet ﷺ said, "Between my grave and my pulpit lies a grove from

---

[583] in *al-Shifa*, in the chapter on visiting the Prophet.

the groves of Paradise."[584]

CONDUCT OF ENTERING THE MOSQUE OF THE HOLY PROPHET ﷺ

When you enter al-Ḥaram ash-Sharīf, take your miswāk and make Sunnat al-istiyāk saying, Allāhumma ṭāhir qalbī min ash-shirki wa 'n-nifāq (O God, purify my heart from the lesser association with You and from hypocrisy). For men it is preferred to enter from Bāb ar-Rahmah (Door of Mercy), the door of Sayyidinā Abū Bakr ؓ, Bāb as-Salām (Door of Peace), Bāb Jibrīl ؑ (Door of Archangel Gabriel), Bāb Fāṭimata 'z-Zahrah ؓ (Door of Fāṭima, daughter of the Prophet ﷺ). For women there is no choice, they have to enter through one special door. Before entering stand still and recite greetings on the Prophet ﷺ and his caliphs, his children, the Sahaba of the Prophet ﷺ and on awlīyāullāh, especially your shaykh, in the following manner:

Aṣ-ṣālatu was-salāmu 'alayka yā Sayyidī yā Rasūlullāh — الصلوة والسلام عليك يا رسول الله

Blessings and peace be upon you, O Prophet of God.

Aṣ-ṣālatu was-salāmu 'alayka yā Ḥabīballāh — الصلوة والسلام عليك يا حبيب الله

Blessings and peace be upon you, O Beloved of God.

As-salāmu 'alayka yā Sayyidinā Abā Bakr aṣ-Ṣiddīq — السلام عليك يا سيدنا أبا بكر الصديق

Peace be upon you, O our master Abū Bakr aṣ-Ṣiddīq.

As-salāmu 'alayka yā Sayyidinā 'Umar al-Fārūq — السلام عليك يا سيدنا عمر الفاروق

Peace be upon you, O our master 'Umar al-Fārūq.

As-salāmu 'alayka yā Sayyidinā 'Uthman wa yā Sayyidinā 'Alī — السلام عليك يا سيدنا عثمان وسيدنا علي

Peace be upon you, O our master 'Uthman and our master 'Alī.

As-salāmu 'alayki yā Sayyidatinā Fāṭimat az-Zahrah — السلام عليك يا سيدتنا فاطمة الزهرة

Peace be upon you, O our Lady Fāṭimat az-Zahrah.

---

[584] Bukhari and Muslim.

As-salāmu 'alaykum yā Āhla-Jannati 'l-Baq'i	السلام عليكم يا يا اهل جنة البقيع
Peace be upon you, O inhabitants of the Garden of Baq'i.	
As-salāmu 'alayka yā Sayyidinā Ḥamzah	السلام عليك يا سيدنا حمزة
Peace be upon you, O our master Ḥamzah.	
As-salāmu 'alaykum yā Shuhadā Uḥud.	السلام عليكم يا شهداء احُد
Peace be upon you, O martyrs of Uḥud.	
You then enter the Prophet's Mosque with your right foot saying: A'udhū billāhi 'l-'Aẓīm wa wajhihi 'l-karīm wa sulṭānahu 'l-qadīm min ash-shayṭāni 'r-rajīm. Allāhuma 'ftaḥ abwāba raḥmatik. I seek refuge with the Mighty God. I seek protection in His Generous Countenance and His Everlasting Authority against the cursed Devil. In the Name of God. O God! Bless Muhammad and his family. O God! Forgive my sins, and open the gates of Your mercy to me.[585]	إذا وصلت إلى المسجد النبوي فقدم رجلك اليمين عند دخوله وقل أعوذ بالله العظيم ووجهه الكريم وسلطانه القديم من الشيطان الرجيم اللهم افتح لي أبواب رحمتك .
One then says: Nawaitu 'l-arbā'īn, nawaytu 'l-'itikāf, nawaytu 'l-khalwah, nawaytu 'l-'uzlah, nawaytu 'r-riyāda, nawaytu 's-sulūk, lillāhi ta'alā al-'Adhīm fī ḥarami 'n-Nabi ﷺ. Then enter the Mosque.	نويتُ الأربعين، نويتُ الاعتكاف، نَويتُ الخَلْوَة نَوَيتُ العُزْلة، نويتُ الرياضة نويتُ السلوك لله تَعالى في حَرَم النبى صلى الله عليه وسلم

For the sake of blessings (*barakah*) I intend the forty (days of seclusion); I intend isolation; I intend discipline (of the ego); I intend to travel in God's Path; for the sake of God, the Exalted in the Holy Place of the Prophet ﷺ.

[585] Ibn Majah, Tirmidhi, Ahmad.

If it is not possible to visit the Prophet ﷺ immediately because it is crowded, or it is time for congregational prayer, then pray two rak'at greeting the Mosque (taḥiyyat al-masjid). However, if you are able to do so, go directly to make your visit. When you visit the Prophet ﷺ, try to enter from the door of Sayyidinā Abū Bakr ؓ or Bāb as-Salām, opposite the grave. Move all the way across the space to arrive at the Prophet's ﷺ Muwājihatu 'sh-Sharīfah. If you are coming at the time of prayer, enter the Mosque from any door, pray first with the congregation, then make your visit to the Prophet ﷺ after finishing the prayers.

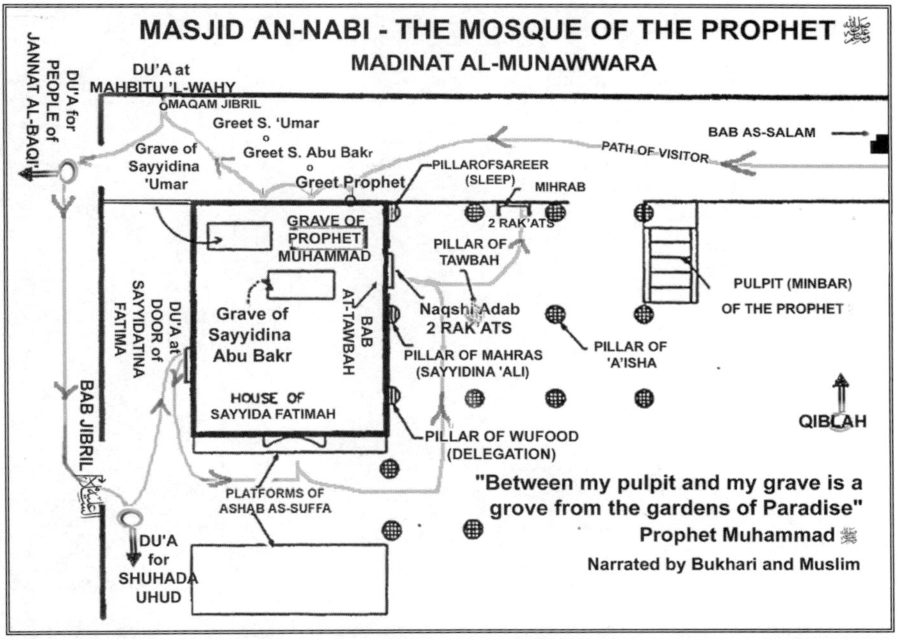

CONDUCT OF ZĪYĀRAH

At the Muwājihatu 'sh-Sharīfah face the holy grave of the Prophet ﷺ. Be careful, as many people mistakenly think that the first door with a hole is the door of the Prophet ﷺ. The first two doors, with two small holes, contain nothing. The one in the middle which has a large hole and two small holes is the grave of Sayyidinā Muhammad ﷺ and directly behind his grave, at his feet is the grave of Sayyidinā Abu Bakr ؓ; Sayyidinā Umar ؓ is buried at the feet of Sayyidinā Abu Bakr ؓ.

Greeting the Prophet ﷺ

Stand in front of the middle door a bit far away behind where there are two pillars, and say:

O Prophet of God, I came to your presence, please accept me.

Aṣ-ṣālatu was-salāmu 'alayka yā Sayyidī yā Rasūlullāh

السلام عليك يا سيدنا أبا بكر الصديق

Blessings and Peace be upon you, O Prophet of God.

Aṣ-ṣālatu was-salāmu 'alayka yā Ḥabīballāh

السلام عليك يا سيدنا عمر الفاروق

Blessings and Peace be upon you, O Beloved of God.

Aṣ-ṣālatu was-salāmu 'alayka yā Shāfi'an li 'l-muslimīn

الصلوة والسلام عليك يا شافعاً للمسلمين

Blessings and Peace be upon you, O Intercessor of the Muslims.

Aṣ-ṣālatu was-salāmu 'alayka yā Rasūla rabbi' l-'alamin

الصلوة والسلام عليك يا رسول رب العالمين

Blessings and Peace be upon you, O Messenger of the Lord of the Worlds.

Then add to that whatever comes to your heart of greetings to the Prophet ﷺ.

Testification of Faith (Shahāda)

كلمة الشّهادتين (3 مرات)

3 times: ash-hadu an lā ilāha illa-Allāh wa ash-hadu anna Muḥammadan 'abduhu wa rasūluh;

أَشْهَدُ أَنْ لا إله إلا الله وأَشْهَدُ أَنَّ مُحَمَّدًا عَبْدُهُ وَرَسُولُهُ

I testify that there is no god but God and I testify that Muḥmmad is His Servant and Messenger.

The first Testification of Faith (Shahādah) is for one's self, bringing to mind the Presence of the Prophet ﷺ and saying in one's heart, "Yā Sayyidī Yā Rasūlullāh, you are my witness; Allah is my witness; all angels are my witness; all Ṣaḥābah are my witness; all Prophets are my witness; everyone in creation is my witness; and my Shaykh is my witness," then pronounce the Shahādah, for you are renewing your

Islam. Then pronounce the second Shahādah on behalf of yourself, your parents, your children, your family, your brothers and sisters, your relations, friends and neighbors and all Muslim people. The third Shahādah is on behalf of unbelievers with the intention that they become believers.

Istighfār: 3x Istighfārullāh

أستغفر الله (3 مرات)

I ask forgiveness of God.

The first Istighfār is for yourself; the second is for your family and for whoever asked you to pray (make du'ā) for them and the third is for the Community of the Prophet ﷺ.

Yā Rabbī, yā Allāh, kam ẓahara minnī min adh-dhunūbi wa 'l-ma'āṣīyy ẓāhiran wa bāṭinan wa sirran min ẓuhūrī fī 'ālami 'd-dunyā ilā yawminā hādha, raj'atu 'ani 'l-jamī'i bi 't-tawbati wa 'l-istighfār wa as'aluka an taghfira lī bi-jāhi Nabīyyika Muḥammad.

يا ربي يا الله، كم ظهر مني من الذنوب والمعاصي
ظاهرا وباطنا وسرا من عهد ايجاد ذرتي
وروحي ودخول روحي إلى جسمي وظهوري من
العدم إلى الوجود وظهوري في عالم الدنيا إلى يومنا
هذا، رجعت عن الجميع اليك بالتوبة والإستغفار
وأسألك ان تغفر لي يا الله بجاه نبيّك

O My Lord, O God, from the day of my appearance in creation until our day, how much of disobedience has appeared from me spiritually or physically - I am regretting them all coming and asking forgiveness and repentance, and I am asking you to forgive me for the sake of the Prophet.

Kamā qāl Allāhu ta'ala fil-Qur'ān:

wa mā arsalnā min rasūlin illā liyuṭā'a bi-idhnillāhi wa law annahum idh dhalamū anfusahum jā'ūka fastaghfarū'llāha wastaghfara lahumu 'r-rasūlu la-wajadū'llāha tawwāban rahīmān.

كما قال الله تعالى في القرآن:
وَمَا أَرْسَلْنَا مِن رَّسُولٍ إِلَّا لِيُطَاعَ بِإِذْنِ اللَّهِ وَلَوْ أَنَّهُمْ
إِذ ظَّلَمُوا أَنفُسَهُمْ جَاءُوكَ فَاسْتَغْفَرُوا اللَّهَ وَاسْتَغْفَرَ
لَهُمُ الرَّسُولُ لَوَجَدُوا اللَّهَ تَوَّابًا رَّحِيمًا

As God said in the Holy Quran:

> *We sent not a messenger, but to be obeyed, in accordance with the will of God. If they had only, when they were unjust to themselves, come unto thee and asked God's forgiveness, and the Messenger had asked forgiveness for them, they would have found God indeed Oft-returning, Most Merciful.* (4:64)

Then you invoke God, asking for whatever you need or desire, seeking a good life for yourself, your family and for your Shaykh, for the Muslims in general, and mercy and peace for all mankind.

Then you move on (it is not necessary to move physically) to give greetings to Sayyidinā Abu Bakr as-Siddiq ﷺ. Follow the same adab as with the Prophet ﷺ. Then move on to give greetings to Sayyidinā 'Umar ﷺ, again following the same adab.

Then, before leaving, give greetings in your heart to to Sayyidinā 'Uthman ﷺ, Sayyidinā 'Alī ﷺ, all the Companions, all 124,000 prophets and messengers, all 124,000 saints because their souls too, have a spiritual presence in that holy place. Finally, send greetings to Sayyidinā al-Ḥasan ﷺ and Sayyidinā al-Ḥusain ﷺ.

As-salāmu 'alayka yā Sayyidinā Abā Bakr aṣ-Ṣiddīq — السلام عليك يا سيدنا أبا بكر الصديق

Peace be upon you, O our master Abā Bakr aṣ-Ṣiddīq.

As-salāmu 'alayka yā Sayyidinā 'Umar al-Fārūq — السلام عليك يا سيدنا عمر الفاروق

Peace be upon you, O our master 'Umar al-Fārūq.

As-salāmu 'alayka yā Sayyidinā 'Uthmān wa yā Sayyidinā 'Alī — السلام عليك يا سيدنا عثمان وسيدنا علي

Peace be upon you, O our master 'Uthmān and our master 'Alī.

As-salāmu 'alaykum yā asḥāb an-Nabī — السلام عليكم يا اصحاب النبي

Peace be upon you, O Companions of the Prophet.

As-salāmu 'alaykum yā awlīyā'ullāh. — السلام عليكم يا أولياء الله

Peace be upon you, O saints of God.

Then, on the right side before the exit door is a large wall covered with ceramic ornamention/calligraphy. There is the Maḥbitu 'l-waḥī, where Gabriel ﷺ used to come to bring revelation to the Prophet. In the past, one could make a turn inside, but it is now blocked with a fence, so you have to go outside. But before you go outside, make du'ā at the Maḥbitu 'l-waḥī. From this station, you face Qiblah and say:

Ya Rabbi' l-'izzati wa 'l-'aẓamati wa 'l- — يا رب العزة والعظيمة الجبروت

jabarūt.

O Lord of Honor and Greatness, Imposer of Thy Will.

As-salāmu 'alayka yā Sayyidinā Jibrīl. Peace be upon you, O our master Gabriel.	السلام عليك يا سيدنا جبريل
As-salāmu 'alayka yā Sayyidinā Mikā'īl. Peace be upon you, O our master Michael.	السلام عليك يا سيدنا ميكائيل
As-salāmu 'alayka yā Sayyidinā Izrā'īl. Peace be upon you, O our master Izra'īl.	السلام عليك يا سيدنا عزرائيل
As-salāmu 'alayka yā Sayyidinā Isrāfīl. Peace be upon you, O our master Isrāfīl.	السلام عليك يا سيدنا اسرافيل
As-salāmu 'alayka yā Sayyidinā Riḍwān. Peace be upon you, O our master Riḍwān.	السلام عليك يا سيدنا رضوان
As-salāmu 'alayka yā Sayyidina Mālik. Peace be upon you, O our master Mālik.	السلام عليك يا سيدنا مالك
As-salāmu 'alaykum yā Malāi'kati 's-samāwati al-'aẓīm. Peace be upon you, O Angels of the Tremendous Heavens.	السلام عليكم يا ملائكة السموات والأرض
As-salāmu 'alaykum yā Malā'ikati 'l-karībiyyūn. Peace be upon you, O Cherubim.	السلام عليكم يا ملائكة الكربيون
As-salāmu 'alaykum yā Ḥamalat ul-'Arsh. Peace be upon you, O our master O Bearers of the Throne.	السلام عليكم يا حملة العرش
As-salāmu 'alaykum yā Malā'ikati Anwārillāh Peace be upon you, O Angels of God's Light.	السلام عليكم يا ملائكة انوار الله

You beseech God there saying: 'Yā Rabbī for the sake of the Prophet ﷺ, for the sake of his Sahaba and his caliphs; for the sake of Mahdī and for the sake of all saints, Yā

Rabbī Yā Allāh…", and then invoke God in du'a for whatever you like.

And then after reciting these greetings to the angels you make whatever *du'a* you like, and then pray two rak'at. You exit from that door, at which point you will be facing Jannat al-Baq'i. You make a Fatiha for all who are buried there. You go left and go down, then enter the door of Sayyidatina Fāṭimatu 'z-Zahrā ﷺ and go left in there to an empty area, just before reaching the Platforms of Aṣḥāb aṣ-Ṣuffah. It is reported historically that the angels have transferred Sayyidatina Fāṭimat az-Zahra ﷺ from Jannat al-Baq'i to this grave. So you approach the grave and say:

As-salāmu 'alaykī ya Sayyidatanā Fāṭimata 'z-zahrā.	السلام عليك يا سيدتنا فاطمة الزهرة

Peace be upon you, O our Lady ā Fāṭimata 'z-zahrā.

As-salāmu 'alaykī yā Umi 'l-Ḥasani wa 'l-Ḥusain	السلام عليك يا سيدتنا أم الحسن والحسين

Peace be upon you, O mother of al-Ḥasan and al-Ḥusain.

As-salāmu 'alaykī yā Sayyidata nisā'i āhli 'l-jannah.	لسلام عليك يا سيدة نساء أهل الجنة

Peace be upon you, O Noble Chief of the ladies of the People of Paradise.

You then go around and come to the Blessed Garden (Rawḍat ash-Sharīfah) if you are able. If you are not able to, you come anywhere adjacent to Rawḍat ash-Sharīfah. There is Bāb at-Tawbah which is the last closet of Quran's, near the Rawḍah. Try to reach there, but if you cannot stand at a distance, face the Qiblah and say:

Law kāna laka yā Rabbī bābayni āḥadahumā mukhaṣaṣṣun lit-tā'ibīna min 'ibādika al-mu'minīn wal-ākharu lit-tā'ibīna min 'ibādika al-mudhinibīn. Ji'tuka yā Allāh naḥwu bābik alladhī yaḥtāju an yadkhula minhu 'ibāduka al-mudhinibīn. Wa innanī uqirru wa āa'tarif annahu yajibu an ujaddida islāmī wa īmānī min hādha 'l-bāb iẓhāran li 'l-'ajzi.	لو كان لك باربى بابين احدهما مخصص للتائبين من عبادك المؤمنين والأخر للتائبين من عبادك المذنبين، جئتك يا الله نحو بابك الذي يحتاج ان يدخل منه عبادك المذنبين واننى اقر واعترف انه يجب ان اجدد إسلامى وإيمانى من هذا الباب إظهاراً للعجز.

O my Lord, O God, I am coming to your door, the door of repentance. Yā Rabbi, if you had two doors for Your servant to enter through; one for the believers from

Your servants and one for the sinner from Your servants, I am coming to You from the door that the sinner needs to come through and I am declaring that believing that this is the only door for me to come through. I am saying to you that I have to renew my faith from this door to show humility and helplessness.

Recite Shahādah three times and the remainder of the adab of the Naqshbandi Order, leaving out the dhikr. This will take from ten minutes. Following the adab pray two rak'at, and then to invoke God seeking whatever you like.

DAILY CONDUCT

It was the custom of Mawlana Shaykh Nazim to perform these devotions a half-hour after Fajr prayer, when it would be less crowded. During the Ḥajj season, however, it is always crowded. Still, there are some times that are better than others. One of these is the period after Duḥā (mid-day), until the time of Ẓuhr prayer (9 a.m. to noon). The other is the period between Ẓuhr and 'Aṣr prayers, because people then go to eat and take an afternoon nap. During that time, ladies—but not men—can enter the Rawḍah, so this is the best time for them to perform these devotions.

It is recommended to visit the Prophet ﷺ every day as long as you are staying in Madīnah. For those with a higher level of aspiration, it is strongly advised to make one ziyārah of Prophet ﷺ in the morning and one in the evening.

The murīd should try to hold fast to as much as of the above aspects of adab as possible, but should not worry if some parts of it are missed.

Finally keep in mind you must control your ego as much as possible. If you get angry quickly take a shower and ask forgiveness from God and seek the Prophet's ﷺ asking forgiveness on your behalf.

FAREWELL VISITATION

When the time comes for you to leave Madīnah, on your last day in the city, you make ziyārah and you ask permission from the Prophet ﷺ to travel.

Perform the Farewell Visitation of the Prophet ﷺ (ziyāratu 'l-wada') and then you set forth.

Holy Places of Visitation in Madinah

SEEKING BLESSINGS BY MEANS OF PLACES THE PROPHET ﷺ VISITED (*TABARRUK*)

Abū Burdā ؓ narrated:

When I came to Madīnah, I met 'Abd Allāh bin Salām. He said, "Will you come to me so that I may serve you with sawiq (i.e. powdered barley) and dates, and let you enter a (blessed) house in which the Prophet entered?. . ."

Thus to visit any location where the Prophet's ﷺ blessed feet touched the earth, was touched by his holy hand or his breath entered is to take blessings. For that reason, the entire earth of Madīnah, its air and its water are blessed.

The Prophet of God ﷺ, invoked:

> *O God! Make us love Madīnah as much as we love Mecca or even more. Make it sound and bless us in its sa' and its mudd (units of measure used in Madīnah). . .*[586]

As the Prophet ﷺ asked God's Blessings on the city and its fruits, then Madīnah must be full of blessing, as his supplication is an or answered prayer (du'a mustajāb). Therefore, it is common practice for pilgrims to purchase dates from Madīnah for the blessings, and to bring them back home to share among those who could not make the pilgrimage. It is said that there remain living some of the date palms planted by the Holy Prophet ﷺ himself ﷺ.

THE GRAVEYARD BAQI' AL-GHARQAD

The term Baqi' signifies soft land void of stones. This is the sort of land in which graves are commonly dug. Madīnah has several places of that sort, such as: Baqi' of al-Zubair, Baqi' of al-Khail, and others.

> *God's Messenger ﷺ went out frequently at night to visit Baqi' al-Gharqad and to pray for its dwellers. He used to say, "Peace be upon you, O abode of Believers" or "Peace be upon the believing men and women dwelling here. May Allah grant mercy to those from among us who passed away and those who are to come after us. Certainly, Allah willing, we will join you."*[587]

---

[586] Muwatta, Book 45, Number 45.4.14.

[587] Muslim, An-Nasai, Ahmad, Ibn Majah.

It has been narrated that the Prophet ﷺ said:

> *I am the first person for whom the earth will split asunder on the Day of Judgment. This means that I am the first to be resurrected. Then, I, Abū Bakr and 'Umar will head for the people of Baqi' who will be resurrected and followed by the people of Mecca. Thereupon, I will be resurrected between the Two Mosques.*[588]

About ten thousand Companions have been buried in Madīnah ﷺ.

It is desirable that one go daily to the cemetery of Baqi', but particularly on Friday; before the visit, one should first pronounce greetings on the Prophet ﷺ.

When one arrives at Baqi', say:

as-Salāmu 'alaykum dāra qawmin mu'minīna wa innā inshā-Allāhu bikum lāhiqūn, Allāhumma ighfir li āhli Baqi' al-gharqad, Allāhumma ighfir lanā wa lahum.

السَّلَامُ عَلَيْكُمْ دَارَ قَوْمٍ مُؤْمِنِينَ وَإِنَّا إِنْ شَاءَ اللَّهُ بِكُمْ لَلَاحِقُونَ اللَّهُمَّ اغْفِرْ لِأَهْلِ بَقِيعِ الْغَرْقَدِ اللَّهُمَّ اغْفِرْ لَنَا وَلَهُمْ

Peace be upon ye, abode of the believing folk. And indeed we will soon be meeting with ye. O God forgive the people of Baqi' al-gharqad, O God forgive us and them.

Then he visits the visible graves there, such as that of Ībrahīm, 'Uthmān, al-'Abbās, al-Ḥasan the son of 'Alī, 'Alī the son of al-Ḥusayn, Muḥammad ibn 'Alī, Ja'far ibn Muḥammad, and others ﷺ. The last stop would be the grave of Safīyya ﷺ, the Aunt of God's Messenger ﷺ;. It has been established in numerous sound hadiths that there is merit in the graves of the Baqi' and in visiting them.

THE QUBĀ MOSQUE

It was the first mosque to be built in Madīnah. God praised this Mosque and those who maintained it:

> *There is a Mosque whose foundation was laid from the first day on Piety; it is more worthy of thy standing forth [for Prayer] therein. In it are men who love to be purified, and God loveth those who make themselves pure.* (9:108)

> *Thereupon, the Prophet ﷺ said to them, "What is the good thing you are performing in this Mosque that Allah has so highly praised you?" They said, "We use both stone and water for purification."*[589]

[588] Tirmidhi.

[589] Tirmidhi, Abu Dawud, Ibn Majah, Ahmad.

It has been narrated that the Prophet ﷺ used to ride his camel and visit Qubā every Saturday and Monday. The Prophet ﷺ said, "Whoever performs ablution at home, then comes to Qubā Mosque to perform Prayer therein, will get the reward as for 'Umrah."[590]

It has also been reported that the Prophet ﷺ said, "Whoever prays in Qubā Mosque on Monday and Thursday is given the reward as for 'Umrah."[591]

It is recommended to visit the well of Ārīs, which is located by the mosque of Qubā, and drink from its water and perform ablution with it.

It is desirable that one visit all the sites of significance in Islam. There are approximately thirty such places, and they are known to the inhabitants of Madīnah. The pilgrim should visit as many as he can.

SEVEN MOSQUES

Masjid Qiblatain: In this mosque, God directed Prophet Muhammad ﷺ, who was in the middle of prayers along with his Companions, to turn his face from Islam's first Qiblah (Baitu 'l-Maqdis) towards the Ka'bah in Masjid al-Ḥarām in the verse:

"Verily! We have seen the turning of your face towards the heaven. Surely, We shall turn you to a Qiblah that shall please you, so turn your face in the direction of al-Masjid al-Ḥarām...." (2:144).

That is why this mosque is known as a mosque with two Qiblas.

Masjid Jum'ah: This mosque was built at a place where the Prophet offered his first Jum'ah prayer in Madīnah.

Masjid Ghamāmah: This mosque is not far from Masjid an-Nabī. The Prophet ﷺ used to offer his the prayers of the two Eids here. Once the Prophet ﷺ led prayer for rain (istasqā) in it and suddenly clouds appeared and it started raining, hence the name ghamāma (clouds).

Masjid Abū Bakr, Masjid Umar Farūq and Masjid 'Alī: These three mosques are near Masjid Ghamāmah.

---

[590] Bukhari and Muslim.

[591] Tirmidhi, Ibn Majah, Ahmad.

BADR

The plain and dune of Badr is 32 kilometers southwest of Madīnah where the first battle between 313 Muslims and 1,000 Quraish of Makkah took place in 624 A.D. The Muslims had 70 camels and two horses whereas the Quraish had a cavalry of 200 horses and 700 camels. They were superior in weapons as well, but Muslims were victorious because they were strong in morale and strategy due to the of the Holy Prophet's leadership.

UḤUD MOUNTAIN

About seven kilometers to the north of Madīnah, the famous battle of Uḥud was fought here. Sayyidina Hamza ؄, the Holy Prophet's uncle and other companions are buried at the foot of the mountain.

It is reported that the Prophet ﷺ said, "Uḥud is a mountain which loves us and we love it."[592]

SALA'A MOUNTAIN

This is the site for the battle of the Trench was fought in 5 A.H. Now there are six mosques at this location.

WATER-WELLS OF THE PROPHET ﷺ

It is a blessing to visit the wells where the Prophet ﷺ used to perform ablution and wash. There are seven such wells.

Additionally the visitor can ask the muṭawaf to assist you in Madīnah to visit the seven mosques, the many cemeteries, wells and other locations of historical significance.

---

[592] Muslim.

Conclusion

Conclusion

We are honored to be Almighty God's servants. We know of no rank higher than the rank of being His servant. There is no greater honor to attain, no finer position to occupy. We were all in the Divine Presence on the day of the covenant in the world of souls. The real servants are the real saints and the real inheritors of Divine Knowledge of God Almighty. They know the covenant they made with their Lord. Without boasting, I may say that the grandshaykhs of the Naqshbandi Order and the shaykhs of other orders are among the true servants. Whoever would like to reach the glory of the Divine Presence may follow them. There are many guides, but it is enough for us to take only one. You must recognize him as your guide, and act according to his commands. Then it is his obligation and his duty to lift you up to the heart of the Divine Presence, which is the real secret of the hidden Essence.

The activity of Sufism is the purification of the self. Its aim is the attainment of eternal felicity and blessedness. The Holy Prophet ﷺ said, *"Speak to each in accordance with his understanding."* This is especially important in introducing the Sufi reality to the one who yearns to become intimate with Sufism. Do not suffocate him with factual details as you can harm him or threaten him if his capacity to understand is faulty or wrongly trained. It is always best to first know the state of the one who seeks Sufi knowledge and tell him only what will be useful to him. The steady accrual of knowledge of the Sufi reality, supervised by the shaykh, will gradually and steadily lift the seeker on the Sufi Path. It is not mere information, but the connection to the heart of a humble and enlightened knower, that can lead the sincere seeker to reach the states that God has prepared for him in His Divine Presence.

Those who would like to be raised with the generous prophets, the magnificent saints, and the people of the Way, must forsake the enmity which they harbor. They must cultivate love. It is for this reason that the pride of all creation, on whom be the best of prayers and peace, said, "He who has good thoughts about people will not come to a bad end." No matter how much he sins, if he thinks generous thoughts, he will be raised with the people of God. He who only thinks badly of the people, however, will not have such a good ending, and the station of Divine Love will elude him.

It is essential to acknowledge that the grandshaykhs of the Naqshbandi Order and all other orders advised us to turn a blind eye to the wrongdoing of others. We must look always to what is good in them. We must cherish calm and abandon anger. We must do our best to be of service to everyone. This is the way of all prophets and saints whose kindness and good humor, gentleness and ease, made them of benefit to all they touched. These characteristics are the true indication of Divine Knowledge and are the heart of the Islamic teaching. We must remember, therefore, what has been presented to us, so that we may earn the blessings of Eternal Love and God's Divine Mercy. And from God is all success.

Bibliography

Abū Zahra, Muḥammad. *Tārīkh al-madhāahib al-islāmīyya*. Beirut: Dar al-Fikr, 1989.

al-'Ajlūnī. *Kashf al-Khafā*. Cairo, 1351 AH.

al-Alawi, Shaykh. *Knowledge of God*. Norwich: Diwan Press, 1981.

al-Asbahānī, Abū Na'īm. *H.ilyat al-awlīyā*. Beirut, 1980.

al-'Asqalānī, Imām. *Iṣāba fī tamyīz aṣ-ṣaḥāba*. Beirut: Dar al-Fikr.

al-Fārābī, Abū Nasr (Richard Walzer, trans.). *On the Perfect State (Mabādi' ārā' al-madīnat al-fādilah)*. Chicago, IL: Kazi Publ., revised ed., 1998.

al-Ghazālī, Abū Hāmid Muhammad (Richard Joseph McCarthy, trans.). *Deliverance from Error—Five Key Texts, Including His Spiritual Autobiography, al-Munqidh min al-Dalal*. Louisville, KY: Fons Vitae, 2nd ed., 2000.

_____ (T.J. Winter, trans.). *Al-Ghazālī on Disciplining the Soul & on Breaking the Two Desires: Books XII and XIII of the Revival of the Religious Sciences*. Cambridge, UK: The Islamic Texts Society, 1995.

_____ *Iḥyā 'ulum id-dīn*. Beirut: Dar an-Nadwa.

_____ *Ayyuha 'l –walad*. Beirut, 1969.

_____ (David B. Burrell, trans.). *On Faith in Divine Unity and and Trust in Divine Providence*. Louisville, KY: Fons Vitae, 2001.

_____ (Michael E. Marmura, trans.). *The Incoherence of the Philosophers*. Provo, UT: Brigham Young University Press, 2000.

_____ (Asaad F. Shaker, trans.). *Al-Ghazālī on Intention, Sincerity and Truthfulness: Book XXXVII of the Revival of the Religious Sciences*. Cambridge, UK: The Islamic Texts Society, 2002.

_____ (Kojiro Nakamura, trans.). *Al-Ghazālī on Invocations and Supplications: Book IX of the Revival of the Religious Sciences*. Cambridge, UK: The Islamic Texts Society, 1990.

_____ (Muhammad Abul Quasem, trans.). *The Jewels of the Qur'ān*. London: Kegan Paul Int'l., 1984.

_____ (Denys Johnson-Davies, trans.). *Al-Ghazālī on the Manners Relating to Eating: Book XI of the Revival of the Religious Sciences*. Cambridge, UK: The Islamic Texts Society, 2000.

_____ (David B. Burrell and Nazih Daher, trans.). *Al-Ghazālī on the Ninety-nine Beautiful Names of God*. Cambridge, UK: The Islamic Texts Society, 1992.

_____ (Henry T. Littlejohn, trans.). *Al-Ghazālī on Patience and Thankfulness: Book XXXIII of the Revival of the Religious Sciences*. Cambridge, UK: The Islamic Texts Society, 2002.

_____ (Asaad F. Shaker, trans.). *Al-Ghazālī on Poverty and Abstinence: Book XXXIV of the Revival of the Religious Sciences.* Cambridge, UK: The Islamic Texts Society, 2002.

_____ (T.J. Winter, trans.). *Al-Ghazālī on the Remembrance of Death and the Afterlife: Book XL of the Revival of the Religious Sciences.* Cambridge, UK: The Islamic Texts Society, 1989.

Gianotti, Timothy J. *Al-Ghazālī's Unspeakable Doctrine of the Soul: Unveiling the Esoteric Psychology and Eschatology of the Ihyā.'* Leiden: E.J. Brill, 2001.

al-Haythamī, Ibn Ḥajar. *Fatāwa al—ḥadithīyya*. Beirut.

_____ *Sawā'iq al-muhriqā*, as. Istanbul: Dar ash-Shafaqa, 1990.

al-Hujwiri, *The Kashf al-Mahjub, the Oldest Persian Treatise on Sufism*, London, Luzac Press, 1959.

al-Khānī, *Bahjat as-Saniyya fi ādab an-naqshbandīyya*, Istanbul: Dar ash-Shafaqa. 1992.

al-Khānī, Muḥammad. *al-Ḥadā'iq al-wirdīyya fi ḥaqā'iq ajillā an-naqshbandīyya*. Cairo, 1306 AH.

al-Kisai, Muhammad ibn Abdullah, *Qisas al-anbiya* (Tales of the Prophets), Kazi, 1997.

al-Kurdī, Shaykh Amīn. *Tanwīr al-qulūb*. Egypt: Matba'at as-Sa'ada.

al-Misri, Ahmad Naqib, . (Nuh HM Keller, transl.) *'Umdat al-salik wa 'uddat al-nasik* (Reliance of the Traveler and Tools of the Worshipper), pp., Sunna Books, 1991.

al-Mundhirī. *al-Targhīb wat-tarhīb*. Beirut: Dar Iḥya Turath al-'Arabi, 1388 AH.

al-Nawawi, Yahia bin Sharaf al-Din (Nuh Ha Mim Keller, trans.) *Al-Nawawi's Manual of Islam.* Cambridge, UK: The Islamic Texts Society, 1996.

al-Qashani, Abd al-Razzaq, *A Glossary of Sufi Technical Terms*, London, Octagon Press, 1991.

al-Qushayrī, Īmām. *Risālat al-Qushayrīyya*. Egypt: Dar al-Kitab al-Hadith.

al-Ṣarrāj, Abū Naṣr. *Kitāb al-luma'*. Ed. By R. Nicholson, 1911.

al-Sha'rāni, 'Abd al-Wahhāb. *Ṭabaqāt al-kubrā*. Beirut: al-Maktabat ash-Sha'biyya.

al-Suhrawardi, Abu al-Najib, *A Sufi Rule for Novices*, Cambridge, MA, Harvard University Press, 1975.

al-Zahawi, Jamal Effendi al Iraqi al-Sidqi, (Shaykh Muhammad Hisham Kabbani trans.), *Al-Fajr as-sadiq fi al-radd ala munkari al-tawassul wa al-khawariq*, (The Doctrine of Ahl-Sunna Versus the "Salafi" Movement A Complete Refutation and Translation in English with Introduction and Notes), Chicago: As-Sunnah Foundation of America, 1996.

Ali, Abdullah Yusuf. *The Holy Qur'an: Text, Translation and Commentary.* Washington, DC: Amanah, 1989.

Adil, Hajjah Amina, *Lore of Light*, volume 1-3, Cyprus,1988.

Amuli Sayyid Haydar, *Inner Secrets of the Path*, Longmead, Element Books, 1989.

an-Nadwī, Abul Ḥasan. *al-Muslimun fil-hind*, al. Damascus 1962.

The Koran Interpreted. (Arthur J. Arberry, trans.), New York: Macmillan, 1955.

Arberry, Arthur John, trans. The Doctrine of the Sufis (translation of Kalābādhī's Kitāb al-ta'arruf). Cambridge, UK: Cambridge University Press, 1977.

Arberry, Arthur John. Discourses of Rumi. London: John Murray, 1961.

Arberry, Arthur John. Mystical Poems of Rūmī. Chicago, IL: University of Chicago Press, 1968.

As'ad, Ṣāhib. *Bughiat al-wājib fī maktubat Khālid*. Damascus, 1334 AH.

Badawī, Abdar Raḥmān. *Shaṭaḥāt aṣ-ṣufiyya*. Kuwait: Wikalat al-Matbu'at, 1978.

Baddeley, John F. *The Russian Conquest of the Caucasus*. London: Longmans, Green and Co., Ltd, 1908.

Bakhtiar, L. *Sufi Expression of the Mystic Quest*. New York: Thames and Hudson,1976.

_____ *God's Will be Done*, vols. 1-3. Chicago: Kazi Publications, 1994.

Baljon, J.M.S. *Religion and Thought of Shah Wali Allah Dihlawi, 1730-1762*. Leiden, Netherlands: E.J. Brill, 1986.

Begg, W.D. *The Holy Biography of Hazrat Khwaja Muinuddin Chishti*. Tucson, Ariz.: Chisti Sufi Mission of America, 1977.

Bennett, John. *Concerning Subud*. NY: Hodder and Stoughton, 1958.

_____ *Witness*. Tucson, AZ: Omen Press, 1974.

Blanch, Leslie. *Sabres of Paradise*. NY: Carrol and Graf Publishers, 1984.

Buehler, A. *Sufi heirs of the Prophet: The Indian Naqshbandiyya order and the rise of the mediating Sufi Shaykh*. Columbia, S.C.: University of South Carolina Press, 1998.

_____ "The Naqshbandiyya in Timurid India: The central Asian legacy," Journal of Islamic Studies 7(2):208-228, 1972.

Bukharī, Īmām. *Saḥīḥ Bukhārī*. Beirut: Dar al-Qalam, 1407 AH.

Burckhardt, T. *Mystical Astrology According to ibn 'Arabi*. Bulent Rauf, trans. Cheltenham, England: Beshara Publications, 1997.

_____ and Angela Culme-Seymour. *The Wisdom of the Prophets* (*Fusus al—Ḥikam*). Gloucestershire, UK: Beshara Publications, 1975.

_____ *An Introduction to Sufism*, Aquarian Press, 1990.

Chisti, H.M. *The Sufi Book of Healing*. New York: Inner Traditions Press, 1985.

Chittick, William. *Khwaja Khurd's Light of Oneness in God is Beautiful and He Loves Beauty*. Festschrift in honor of Annemarie Schimmel. Bern: Peter Lang, 1992.

_____ *Sufi Path of Love: The Spiritual Teachings of Rumi*. Albany: SUNY Press, 1983.

_____ Chittick, William C., *Faith and Practice of Islam: Three Thirteenth-Century Sufi Texts*, Albany, State University of New York Press, 1992.

Chodkiewicz, Michel. *Le Sceau des saints: Prophétie et sainteté dans la doctrine d'Ibn 'Arabi*. Paris: Gallimard, 1986.

_____ *Seal of the Saints: Prophethood and Sainthood in the Doctrine of ibn Arabi*. L. Sherrard, trans. Cambridge, England: Islamic Texts Society, 1994.

Corbin, H. *The man of Light in Iranian Sufism*. N. Person, trans. Boulder, Colo.: Shambhala Publications.1978.

_____ *Alone with the Alone: Creative Imagination in the Sufism of ibn 'Arabi.* Mythos ed. Bollingen series 91. Princeton, N.J.: Princeton University Press, 1997.

Cornell, Vincent J. *Realm of the Saint: Power and Authority in Moroccan Sufism.* Austin, TX: University of Texas Press, 1998.

_____ "The logic and analogy and role of the Sufi shaykh in post-Marind Morocco," International Journal of Middle Eastern Studies 15:67-93, 1983.

_____ *The Way of Abu Madyan.* Cambridge, UK: The Islamic Texts Society, 1996.

Cragg, Kenneth. *The Wisdom of the Sufis.* New York: W.W. Norton, 1976.

Darqawi, Mulay al-Arabi. *Letters of a Sufi Master.* Bedford: Perennial Books, 1969.

Dawood, N.J. *The Koran.* Harmondsworth: Penguin, 1956.Dermenghem, Emile. *Vie des saints musulmans.* Paris: Sinbad, 1981.

Draper, I.K.B. "A case study of a Sufi order in Britain." Master's thesis, University of Birmingham, 1985.

el-Sakkakini, Widad. *First Among Sufis: The Life and Thought of Rabia al-Adawiyya, the Woman Saint of Basra.* London: Octagon Press, 1982.

Ernst, C.W. *Sufism: An Essential Introduction to the Philosophy and Practice of the Mystical Tradition of Islam.* Boston: Shambhala, 1997.

_____ *Ruzbihan Baqli, the Unveiling of Secrets: The Diary of a Sufi master.* C.W. Ernst, trans. Chapel Hill, N.C.: Parvardigar Press, 1997.

_____ *Ruzbihan Baqli: Mysticism and the Rhetoric of Sainthood in Persian Sufism.* Surrey, England: Curson Press, 1996.

Ewing, K.P. "The pir or saint in Pakistani Islam. Dissertation", University of Chicago, Illinois, 1980.

_____ *Arguing sainthood: Modernity, Psychoanalysis and Islam.* London: Duke University Press. 1997.

Faruqi, B.A. *The Mujaddid's Conception of Tauhid.* Lohore: Sh. Muhammad Ashraf Publications, 1979.

Fārūqī, Rabbāni Aḥmad. *al-Maktūbāt.* Turkey: Sharakat Sonmaz.

Faruqi, Z.H. (ed.). *Fawa'id al-Fu'ad: Spiritual and Literary Discourses of Shaikh Nizamuddin Awliya.* New Delhi, India: D.K. Printworld, 1995.

Fu'ād, 'Abdul-Bāqī. *Mu'jam al-mufahras, al.* Cairo, 1378 AH.

Friedmann, Y. *Shaykh Ahmad Sirhindi: An Outline of His Thought and a Study of His Image in the Eyes of Posterity.* Montreal and London: McGill Queens University Press, 1971.

Fusfeld, W. "The Shaping of Sufi leadership in Delhi: The Naqshbandi Mujaddidiyya, 1750 to 1920. " Ph.D. dissertation, University of Pennsylvania, 1986.

_____ "Naqshbandi Sufism and Reformist Islam," Journal of Asian and African Studies 18(July/October) 1983.

Gaborieau, M., Popovic, A., Zarcone, T. *Naqshbandis: Chimenements et situation actuelle d'un ordre mystique Musulman.* Istanbul and Paris: Editions Isis, 1990.

Galip, S. "Un Gorou Naqshbandi: Seyh Nazim Kibrisi." In Marc Gaborieau, Alexandre Popovic, and Thierry Zarcone, eds., *Naqshbandis: Chimenements et situation actuelle d'un ordre mystique Musulman.* Istanbul and Paris: Editions Isis. 1990.

Gammer, Moshe. *Muslim Resistance to the Tsar: Shamil and the Conquest of Chechnia and Daghestan*. Portland, OR: Frank Cass, 1994.

Gīlāni, 'Abd al-Qādir. *The Endowment of Grace*. Philadelphia, PA: Pearl Publishers, 1992.

Guillaume, Alfred. *The Life of Muhammad: A Translation of Ibn Ishaq's Sirat Rasul Allah.* London: Oxford University Press, 1955.

Ḥaddād, Ḥabīb A ḥmad Mashhur. *Key to the Garden*. Translated by Mos ṭafa al-Badawī. London: Quilliam Press, 1990.

Haeri, Shaykh Fadhlalla, *Living Islam East and West*, Longmead/Dorset, Element Books Limited, 1989.

Haeri, Shaykh Fadhlalla, *The Journey of the Self: A Sufi Guide to Personality*, San Francisco, Harper, 1989.

Hafiz, *Teachings of Hafiz translated by Gertrude Lowthian*, London, Octagon Press Press for the Sufi Trust, 1979.

Ibn 'Abbad of Ronda, *Letters on the Sufi Path*, NYC, Paulist Press, 1986.

Ibn 'Ajība. *Futuḥāt al-ilāhīyya*. Matba'a Jamaliya.

Ibn 'Arabi, Muhyiuddin, *Sufis of Andalusia*, London, Austin, 1971.

_____ *The Bezels of Wisdom*, NYC, Paulist Press, 1980.

_____ *Futuḥāt al-makkīyya*. Beirut: Dar as-Sadr.

_____ *Tarjumān al-ashwāq*. Beirut, 1961.

_____ (Barak and R. Harris, trans.), *What the Seeker Nneeds: Essays on Spiritual Practice, Oneness, Majesty and Beauty*, Chestnut Ridge, N.Y.: Threshold Sufi Classics, 1992.

_____ (Charles Kingsley trans.), *Quest for Red Sulfur: The Life of Ibn Arabi*, Claude Addas, Cambridge: Islamic texts, 1993.

_____ (T. Burckhardt, trans.), *The Wisdom of the Prophets: Fusus al-Hikam*. Gloucestershire, England: Beshara Publications, 1975.

_____ (M. Holland, trans.), *Journey to the Lord of Power*. New York: Inner Traditions, 1990.

_____ *Kernel of the kernel*, I.H. Bursevi, trans. Gloucester, England: Beshara Publications.

_____ (R. Bulent, trans.), *Mystical astrology according to ibn 'Arabi*. Cheltenham, England: Beshara Publications, 1997.

Ibn 'Ata'illāh, (Victor Danner trans.), *Sufi Aphorisms*. Leiden: E.J. Brill, 1984.

Ibn Ḥanbal, Āḥmad. *Musnad*. Beirut: Dar Sadir, 1389 AH.

Ibn Hishām. *Sīrat an-nabawīyya*. Beirut: Dar al-Qalam.

Ibn Kathīr. *Bidāya wan-nihāya, al*. Beirut.

Ibn Qayyim al-Jawzīyya. *Madārij as-sālikīn*, Beirut.

Ibn Taymīyya. *al-Fatāwi al-kubrā*. Egypt: Dar ar-Rahmat.

Jami, 'Abd al-Rahman. *The Nafahat al-Ons min Hadarat al-Qods, or the Lives of the Soofies by Mawlana Noor al-Din*. Calcutta, 1859.

Kabbani, M.H. *Encyclopedia of Islamic Doctrine*, vol. 1-7. Mountain View, Calif.: As Sunnah Foundation of America. 1998.

_____ *The Doctrine of Ahl al-Sunnah versus the "Salafi" movement*. Mountain View, Calif.: As Sunnah Foundation of America, 1996.

_____ *Mercy Oceans' Shore of Safety*. Fenton, Mich.: Haqqani Islamic Trust, 1993.

_____ *Angels Unveiled: A Sufi Perspective*. Chicago: Kazi Publications, 1995.

_____ *The Naqshbandi Sufi Way: History and Guidebook of the Saints of the Golden Chain*. Chicago: Kazi Publications, 1995.

_____ *Salafis Unveiled*. Mountain View, Calif.: As Sunnah Foundation of America. 1998.

_____ *The Approach of Armageddon? An Islamic Perspective*. Washington, DC: Islamic Supreme Council of America, 2003.

_____ *Pearls and Coral*. Washington, DC: Islamic Supreme Council of America, 1995.

Kandhlavī, Mawlana Muḥammad Zakarīyya. *The Virtues of Zikr*. Lahore: Kutub Khana.

_____ *Ḥayāt aṣ—ṣaḥāba*. India: Dairat il-Ma'arif al-Usmaniyya, 1379 AH.

Khādimi, Abu Sa'īd al-, *al-Barīqat sharḥ aṭ-ṭarīqat*. Istanbul: Sharikat al-Usmaniyya, 1325 AH.

Khan, H. I. *The Mysticism of Sound: The Sufi Teaching of Hazrat Inayat Khan*. Rev. ed. Boston: Shambhala, 1996.

_____ *The Inner life: Three Classic Essays on the Spiritual life by the Beloved Teacher who Brought Sufism to the West*. Boston: Shambhala, 1997.

_____ *The Message in our time: The Life and Teachings of the Sufi Master Pir-O-Murshid Inayat Khan*. New York: Harper Collins, 1978.

Le Gall, D. "The Ottoman Naqshbandiyya in the pre-Mujaddidi phase: A study of Islamic Religious Culture and its Transmission." Ph.D dissertation, Princeton University, 1992.

Lifchez, Raymond (ed.), *The Dervish lodge : architecture, art, and Sufism in Ottoman Turkey*, Berkeley, University of California Press, 1992.

Lings, Martin. *Muhammad: his life based on the earliest sources*. New York: Inner Traditions

International, 1983.

_____ *What is Sufism?*, Berkeley, CA, University of California Press, 1977.

_____ *A Sufi Saint of the Twentieth century: Shaykh Ahmad Al-Alawi, his Spiritual Heritage and Legacy*. Golden Palm Series. Cambridge: Islamic Texts Society, 1994.

Malamud, M. "Gender and spiritual self-fashioning: The master-disciple relationship in classical Sufism," Journal of the American Academy of Religion 64(1):89-117, 1994.

Maneri, Sharafuddin, *The Hundred Letters*, NYC, Paulist Press, 1980.
Massignon, L. *Hallaj: Mystic and Martyr*. H. Mason, trans. Princeton, N.J.: Princeton University Press, 1994.
Meier, Fritz. *Meister und Schüler im Orden der Naqshbandiyya: Vorgetragen am 10.* Heidelberg: Universitötsverlag C. Winter, 1995.
Metcalf, B. *Moral Conduct and Authority: The Place of Adab in South Asian Islam*. Los Angeles: University of California Press, 1983.
Michon, J. "The spiritual practices of Islam." In Seyyed Hossein Nasr, ed., Islamic Spirituality: Foundations. New York: Crossroads, 1987.
Munawī, 'Abd ar-Ra'uf. *Fayḍ al-qadīr*. Cairo: Mustafa Muhammad, 1356 AH.
Murata, Sachiko and William C. Chittick. *The Vision of Islam*. New York: Paragon House, 1994.
Muslim, Īmām. *Ṣaḥīḥ Muslim*. Egypt: Dar at-Taba'a, 1329.
Nabahānī, Yusuf an. *Jāmi' karāmāt al-awlīyā*. Beirut: al-Maktabat ath-Thaqafiyya, 1988.
Naqshband, Īmām Muḥammad Bahā'uddīn. *al-Awrād an-naqshbandīyya*. Istanbul.
_____ *Hadiyyat as-sālikīn wa tuḥfat aṭ-ṭālibīn*. Istanbul.
_____ *Tanbīh al-ghāfilīn*. Istanbul.
Naqshbandis, Cheminement et Situation actuelle d'un ordre mystique musulman. Paris/Istanbul: l'Institut Francais d'Etudes Anatoliennes d'Istanbul, 1990.
Nawawī, Īmām. *al-Adhkār*. Saudi Arabia: al-Maktabat at-Tijariyya, 1412 AH.
_____ *Sharḥ an-Nawawī Ṣaḥīḥ Muslim*. Beirut: Dar al-Fikr, 1403.
Nasr, Seyyed Hossein. *Muhammad: Man of God*. Chicago, IL: Kazi Publ., 1995.
_____ *Sufi Essays*. New York: State University of New York Press, 1991.
_____ *Ideals and Realities of Islam*. London: Allen & Unwin, 1966.
_____ *Three Muslim sages: Avicenna-Suhrawardi-Ibn Arabi*. New York, 1964.
_____ ed. *Foundations of Islamic spirituality*. New York: Crossroads, 1987.
_____ ed. *Islamic Spirituality Manifestations*. New York: Crossroads, 1987.
Nazim, Shaykh M.. *The Divine Kingdom*. Los Altos, Calif.: Haqqani Islamic Trust for New Muslims, 1994.
_____ *Mystical Secrets of the Last Days*. Los Altos, Calif.: Haqqani Islamic Trust for New Muslims, 1994.
_____ *Mercy Oceans, Endless Horizons*. Konya: Sebat Offset Printers, 1982.
_____ *Mercy Oceans, Pink Pearls*, Konya, 1982.
_____ *Mercy Oceans, Divine Sources* (summer lectures; 1983 winter lectures). Konya, 1984.
_____ *Toward the Divine Presence*. Karachi, Pakistan: Jamil Wahab (Trust) Foundation, 1984.
_____ *Mercy Oceans, Rising Sun*. Konya: Sebat Offset Printers, 1986.
_____ *Mercy OceanLovestreams*. Konya, 1986.
_____ *The Secrets behind the Secrets behind the Secrets*, 2nd ed. Birmingham: Berlin, 1988.

_____ *Oceans of Unity*. Konya: Sebat Offset Printers.

_____ *Mercy Oceans' Hidden Treasures*. Konya: Sebat Offset Printers, 1987.

_____ *The Fruit of Perfect Practicing and Real Beliefs is Peace*. Birmingham: Zero Productions, 1988.

_____ *Islam: A Shelter for Mankind Forever*. Birmingham: Zero Productions, 1988.

_____ *Don't Waste*. Sri Lanka: Zero Productions, 1989.

_____ *Hakkani*. Cyprus 1987, London 1987: Lefke, 1991.

_____ *Mercy Oceans: Secrets of the Heart*. Fenton: Haqqani Press, 1992.

_____ *Power Oceans of Love*. London: Zero Productions, 1993.

_____ *Keys to Paradise: Ramadan Talks*, 1993. London: Zero Productions, 1994.

_____ *When will Peace come to Earth?* England: Redwood Books, 1995.

_____ *Power Oceans of Light: London Talks, 1994; Italy talks, 1994*. London: Zero Productions, 1994.

_____ *Star from Heaven: England, Italy, Switzerland and Germany talks, 1995*. London: Healing Arts/Zero Productions, 1996.

_____ *Islam: The Freedom to Serve*. Schwarzwald, Germany: Gorski and Spohr, 1997.

_____ *Defending Truth: Associations with a Sufi Master of Our Time*. London: Zero Productions, 1997.

_____ *Secret Desires: England and Germany Talks, 1996*. London: Zero Productions, 1997.

_____ *Pure Hearts*. London: Healing Arts/Zero Productions, 1998.

_____ *The Naqshbandi Handbook of Daily Practices*.

_____ *In the Mystic Footsteps of the Saints*, vol. 1 & 2, Washington, DC: Islamic Supreme Council of America, 2003.

_____ *Liberating the Soul*, vol. 1 & 2, Washington, DC: Islamic Supreme Council of America, 2003.

_____ *Misterios Tras los Misterios Detras de los Misterios*, Granada, Spain: Haqqani Espana, 2000.

Newby, Gordon. *The Making of the Last Prophet: A Reconstruction of the Earliest Biography of Muhammad*. Columbia, SC: University of South Carolina Press, 1989.

Nicholson, Reynold. *Sufiyya fil-Islām, al-*. Cairo, 1951.

_____ *The Idea of Personality in Sufism*. Cambridge, UK: Cambridge University Press, 1923.

_____ *Studies in Islamic Mysticism*. Cambridge, UK: Cambridge University Press, 1921.

_____ ed. and trans. *Mathnawi of Jalaluddin Rumi*. London: E.J.W. Gibb Memorial Trust/Luzac & Co., 1977.

Nurbaksh, J. "Sufism: Fear and hope, contraction and expansion, gathering and dispersion," W. Chittick, trans., Journal of Sufism, vol. 2., 1992.

Ozelsel, M. *Forty days: The Diary of a Traditional Solitary Sufi Retreat*. A. Gaus, trans. Brattleboro, Vt.: Threshold, 1996.

Padwick, C.E. *Muslim Devotions: A Study of Prayer-manuals in Common Use*. Oxford, England: One World Publications, 1996.

Pinto, D, *The Piri-murid Relationship: A Study of the Nizamuddin Dergah*. New Delhi: Ajay Kumar Jain Publishers, 1995.

Rakhāwī, Muḥammad. *Anwār al-qudsīyya fī manāqib as-sādāt al-naqshbandīyya, al-*. Cairo, 1344 AH.

Renard, J. *Seven Doors to Islam: Spirituality and the Religious Life of Muslims*. Berkeley and Los Angeles: University of California Press, 1996.

Rizvi, A.A. *The History of Sufism in India*. 2 vols. Delhi, England: Munshiram Manoharlo, 1983.

Robinson, Francis. *Atlas of the Islamic World since 1500*. New York: Facts on File, 1982.

Rumi Jalal-ad-din. *Mystical Poems of Rumi*. A.J. Arberry, trans. Chicago: University of Chicago Press, 1968.

_____ *Fīhī mā fīhī*. Translated by William Thackson, [*Signs of the Unseen: The Discourses of Rumi*]. Putney, VT: Threshold Books, 1994.

_____ *Discourses of Rumi*, London, Allen and Unwin Ltd, 1961.

Schimmel, Annemarie. *And Muhammad is His Messenger: The Veneration of the Prophet in Islamic Piety*. Chapel Hill, NC: University of North Carolina Press, 1985.

_____ *Mystical Dimensions of Islam*. Chapel Hill, N.C.: University of North Carolina Press, 1975, 1986.

_____ *As Through a Veil*. New York: Columbia University Press, 1982.

_____ *Islam: An Introduction*, Albany, NY, State University of New York Press, 1992.

_____ *Sufi literature*, New York, Afghanistan Council of the Asia Society, 1975.

_____ *The Triumphal Sun: A Study of the Works of Jalaludin Rumi*, Albany, NY, State University of New York Press, 1993.

_____ *I am wind, you are fire : the life and work of Rumi*, Boston, Shambhala, 1992.

_____ *Mystical dimensions of Islam*, Chapel Hill, University of North Carolina Press, 1975.

_____ *Pain and grace : a study of two mystical writers of eighteenth-century Muslim India*, Leiden, E. J. Brill, 1976.

_____ As through a veil : mystical poetry in Islam, *Annemarie Schimmel*, New York, Columbia University Press, 1982.

Sāfī, 'Alī ibn Ḥusain. *Rashahāt 'ayn al-hayāt*. Turkey: al-Maktabat al-Islamiyya.

_____, *Rashaḥāt 'ain al-ḥāyāt* Beads of Dew from the Source of Life (trans. M. Holland), Ft. Lauderdale, Fl.: Al-Baz Publishing, 2001.

Schuon, F. *Sufism: Veil and Quintessence*. W. Stoddart, trans. Bloomington, Ind.: World Wisdom Books, 1981.

_____. *Understanding Islam*. Rev. ed. Bloomington, Ind.: World Wisdom Books, 1998.

Sells, Michael. *Approaching the Qur'an: The Early Revelations*. Ashland, OR: White Cloud Press, 1999.

_____ ed. *Early Islamic Mysticism: Sufi, Qur'an, Mi'raj, Poetic and Theological Writings*. New York: Paulist Press.

Shabrawi-Al, A. Al-K. *The Degrees of the Soul*. M. Al-Badawi, trans. London: Quilliam Press, 1997.

Shah, I. Tales *of the Dervishes: Teaching Stories of the Sufi masters over the Past Thousand Years*. New York: E.P. Dutton, 1970.

_____ *Learning How to Learn: Psychology and Spirituality in the Sufi way*. San Francisco: Harper and Row, 1978.

Shah, O. *The Course of the Seeker*. Los Angeles: Tale Weaver Publishing, 1988.

Shah. S.I.A. (1979). *Islamic Sufism*. Reprint. Delhi, India: Idarah-i Adabiyat-i Delli.

Shakoor, M. *The Writing on the Water: Chronicles of a Seeker on the Islamic Sufi path*. England: Element Limited, 1988.

Shushud, H.L. *Masters of Central Asian wisdom*. Muhtar Holland, trans. Reprint of 1958 ed., Turkey. Oxford: Coobe Springs Press, 1983.

Siraj Ad-Din, Abu Bakr, *The Book of Certainty*, NYC, Samuel Weiser Inc, 1970.

Smith, Margaret, *RABI'A The Life and Work of Rabi'a and other Women Mystics in Islam*, Oxford, Oneworld Publications, 1994.

_____ *Muslim Women Mystics: The Life and Work of Rabi'a and Other Women Mystics in Islam*. Oxford, England: Oneworld, 2001.

Suhrawardi, S. *The Mystical and Visionary Treatises of Suhrawardi*. England: Octagon Press, 1982.

_____ *The Shape of Light*, interpreted by Tosun Bayrak al Jerrahi a-Halveti. Louisville, Ky.: Fons Vitae, 1998.

Sulami, H. *The Book of Sufi Chivalry*. T. Bayrak, trans. New York: Inner Traditions International, 1983.

Sulaymān, Muḥammad. *al-Ḥadīqa an-nadīyya fī ādāb an-naqshbandīyya*. Cairo, 1313 AH.

Suyūṭī, Jalāluddīn. *Tārīkh al-khulafā*. Cairo: Matba'at al-Madani, 1383 AH.

Tarjumana, Ab, R. The *Darqawi way: Letters from the Shaykh to the Fuqara by Mawlay al-'Arabi ad-Darqawi*. England: Diwan Press, 1979.

Ter Haar, Johan. "The Importance of the Spiritual Guide in the Naqshbandi Order." In *The Legacy of Mediaeval Persian Sufism*, pp. 311-322. Edited by Leonard Lewisohn. London: Khaniqahi Nimatullahi Publications, 1992.

Trimingham, S.J. *The Sufi Orders in Islam*. 3rd ed. Oxford, England: Oxford University Press, 1998.

Trix, F. *Spiritual Discourse: Learning with an Islamic Master*. Conduct and Communication series. Philadelphia: University of Philadelphia Press, 1995.

Tweedie, Irene. *The Chasm of Fire: A Woman's Experience of Liberation through the Teaching of a Sufi Master*. England: Element Books, 1979.

Webb, G. "Tradition and innovation in contemporary American Islamic spirituality: The Bawa Muhaiyaddeen fellowship." In Haddad Smith and Jane Smith, eds., *Muslim communities in North America*. Albany, N.Y.: State University of New York Press, 1994, pp. 75-108.

Walbridge, J. *The Science of Mystic Lights: Qutb al-din Shirazi and the Illuminationist Tradition in Islamic Philosophy*. Cambridge, Mass.: Harvard University Press, 1992.

Werbner, P. "Stamping the earth in the name of Allah: Zikr and the sacralizing of space among British Muslims." In B.D. Metcalf, ed., *Making Muslim Space in North America and Europe.* Berkeley: University of California Press, 1996, pp. 167-185.

Weismann, Itzchak. *Taste of Modernity: Sufism, Salafiyya, & Arabism in Late Ottoman Damascus*, Brill, 2002.

Yagan, M. *I came from behind Kaf mountain: The Spiritual Autobiography of Murat Yagan.* Vernon, British Columbia: Kebzeh Publications, 1997.

Zarrūq, Āḥmad. *Qawā'id at-taṣawwuf*. Tunisia: Matabi' al-Muwahhada, 1407 AH.

Arabic-English Glossary

A

abdāl: substitute saints who are able to substitute for spiritual pole

adab: code of good conduct

adhkār, (sing.) *dhikr*: invocations, remembrance of God

'adm: void

aḥadīth, (sing.) *ḥadith*: sayings of Prophet ﷺ

aḥadīyya: Oneness of God

Āhl al-Bayt: the people of the Household of the Prophet ﷺ

Āhl aṣ-ṣuffa: people of the bench or porch

Āhl as-Sunnah wa 'l-Jamā'ah: People of the way of the Prophet ﷺ; the People of the Tradition and the Majority

akhfa: most hidden

ākhir az-zamān: the end time, the Last Days

ākhirah: the hereafter

'alam al-ajsām: material plane

'alam al-arwāḥ: world of spirits

'alim: religious scholar

anṣār: helpers

anwār adh-dhāt al-Āḥadīyya: light of the Unique Essence

'aqīdah: system of belief

aqṭāb (sing.) *quṭb*: spiritual poles

'arif kāmil: perfect knower

'arif: knower

'arsh: throne

'asr: mid-afternoon prayer

asrār (sing.) *sirr*: secrets

awlīyā-ullah, awlīya: Friends of God, saints

awqāf (sing.) *waqf*: religious endowments

awrād (sing). Wird, aḥzāb (sing. *) ḥizb* or *adhkār* (sing.) *dhikr*: devotions, spiritual practices

awtād: pillar saints, main supports of the spiritual pole

ayāt (sing.) *ayah*: signs, verses of the Quran

'ayn al-yaqīn: vision of certainty

'azīmah: strictest modes of worship

B

bāb al-'ilm al-khāriq: miraculous knowledge

band: bond

baqa': subsistence

Baqi', al-: cemetery of the Companions

barakah: blessing

bāṭil: falsehood

bay'ah: initiation, pledge

bayt al-ma'mūr: Ka'bah of the heavens

baytu 'l-māl: public treasury

bāz gasht: returning

bid'ah: innovation

burdah: cloak

burqā': veil

D

dalīl: guide

da'wah: calling to religion

dhawq: taste

dhikr: remembrance of God

dhāt al-baht: God's Absolute Unknowable Essence

dhul janaḥayn: shaykhs of the two wings
dīn: religious faith and practice
du'a: supplication
duḥa: late morning prayer
dunyā: lower world, worldliness

F

fajr: dawn prayer
fanā: annihilation, self-effacement
fanā fi 'sh-shaykh: annihilation in the presence of the shaykh
fanā fi 'sh-shaykh: annihilation in the presence of the Prophet ﷺ
fanā fillāh: annihilation in the Divine Presence
faqih: jurisprudent
fatāwa, (sing.) *fatwa*: legal decisions
fayḍ: transmission of divine bounty
fiqh: jurisprudence
fuqarā, al—(sing.) *faqīr*: poor, impoverished

G

ghayb: unseen
ghawth: Arch-Intercessor
ghayba: state of self-effacement

H

ḥajaru 'l-aswad: the Black Stone
ḥajj: pilgrimage
ḥaqā'iq al-mumkināt: reality of receiving heavenly inspiration
ḥaqīqat al-irshād: reality of guidance
ḥaqīqat al-jadhbah: reality of attraction
ḥaqīqat al-Muḥammadīyya: reality of the Prophet ﷺ
ḥaqīqat at-tayy: reality of folding space
ḥaqīqat at-tawajjuh: reality of directing the heart's power to someone
ḥaqīqat at-tawassul: reality of intercession
ḥaqq ul-yaqīn: reality of certainty
Ḥaqq, al: the real
ḥarām: unlawful
hawā: vain desires
hidāyatullāh: guidance of God
hijāb al-basharīyya: veil of humanity
hosh dar dam: conscious breathing
ḥulūl: incarnation
Hūwa: He, the Name of God in His Absolute Unknowable Essence

I

'īd: festival
iḥsan: perfect, good character
'ijāza: permission
ijtihād: striving for God
'ilm al-bāṭin: hidden knowledge
'ilm al yaqīn: knowledge of certainty
'ilm as-sulūk: science of traveling the way to God
'ilmu 'l-ladunni: heavenly knowledge
'ilmu 'l-wājib: necessary knowledge
īmām: religious leader
irāḍah: desire
irshād: guidance
'īsawī: Living One; on the path of the Prophet Jesus ﷺ
'isha: night prayer
ishrāq: sunrise *sunnah* prayer
ism al-jalāla: most Majestic Name
istighfār: seeking forgiveness
istikhāra: spiritual consultation
ithnā 'asharī: twelve imams
izār: waist cloth

J

jalāl: sublimeness and glory
jamāl: beauty
janāza: funeral prayer
jihād: struggle
jihād an-nafs: self-struggle
jubba, habra: robe
juz': one thirtieth of the Quran

K

Ka'bah: House of God's worship in Makkah
kalīmullah: the station of one to whom God speaks
kamāl: perfect wholeness
karāmat: miraculous powers
kashf: unveiling, vision
khafā: hidden
khalīqa: creation
khalwat dar anjumān: solitude in the crowd
khalwah: seclusion
khāniqah: guest houses, retreats
khāṣṣ: special One
Khatmu 'l-Khwājagān: recitation of the Masters
khawāṣ, al—: preferred people
khuff: leather socks
Khwājagān: masters of Central Asia
kufr: unbelief
kursī: chair

L

lā ilāha ill-Allāh Muḥammadun Rasūl Allāh: declaration of Oneness of God
laṭā'if: subtle things.
lawḥ al-maḥfūdh: Preserved Tablet

M

mā lā yā'nī: needless actions
ma'rifat: perfect knowledge
mabādi' ta'ayyunāt al a'lām: origin of the well-springs of the created universes
madad: support
majdhūb: person lost in the Divine Love
madrasah: traditional center of learning
maghrib: sunset prayer
majlis: meeting
mandūb: preferred
maqām an-nubūwwa: Prophetic station
maqām aṣ-ṣiddīqīyya: truthful station
maqām at-talwīn: stations of colors and changes
maqām: station, tomb of a saint
maqāmāt: stations
marja': reference
mashrab: drinking-well
mazhar: features
minbar: place for sitting or standing to give a sermon
mubālagha: emphasis
mubtadi': initiate
muḥaqqiqīn: verifiers
muḥāsaba: reckoning
mujaddid: reviver of religion
mujāhadah: striving
mujāhidīn: those who struggle against enemies of the faith

mujtahid muṭlaq: capable of independent legal reasoning
mujtahid: qualified to give legal decisions
mukāshafa: unveiling
munāzala: descent
muqarrabīn: close ones
murād: sought
murīd: seeker
murāqabah: contemplation of the heart, meditation
murīd: disciple, person of determination
murshid: initiator
mushāhadah: vision
mushāhid: witness
musha'wazīn: charlatans
musta'idd: those who are prepared

N

nafs: ego
naqsh: engraving
nawāfil: supererogatory worship
nazar bar qadam: watch your step
nigāh dasht: attentiveness
nīyyah: intention
nūrullāh: Light of God

Q

qaḍā mubram: fixed destiny
qaḍā mu'allaq: suspended or mutable destiny, foreordained things
qalb: heart
qiblah: focus of attention
qudrah: power
qurb: station of closeness
quṭb: spiritual pole

R

Rabb, ar-: the Sustainer
rabiṭah: heart's connection
rāhib: hermit
raḥmah: mercy
ribāt: border forts
rijāl: saints (lit. "men"), those who attained spiritual maturity; (singular: *rajul*)
rūḥānīyya: spiritual presence
rutbah: rank

S

ṣadaqa: charity
ṣādiq: trustworthy
ṣādiqīn: truthful believers
ṣadr: chest
ṣafā'a: purify
safar dar waṭan: journey homeward
saḥāb: clouds
ṣaḥāba, aṣḥāb: Companions
ṣāliḥīn: the righteous
sayyid: descendant of the Holy Prophet ﷺ
sharī'ah: Divine Law, Islamic Law
shayṭān: devil, Satan
shirk: worshipping God together with other than Him, polytheism
shuhadā: martyrs
shuhūd at-tanzīh: exalted witnessing
ṣiddīqīn: truthful, trustworthy persons (sing.) *Ṣiddīq*
sidratu'l-muntahā: Furthermost Limit
ṣifāt: Attributes, Divine
silsila: chain
sirr as-sirr: secret of the secret
sīrah: life story, biography
ṣirāṭ al-mustaqīm: Straight Path
sirr: secret
ṣuḥbah: associations

ṣuḥbah: companionship
sulṭān adh-dhikr: greatest remembrance
sulūk: wayfaring
Sunnah: custom or practice of the Prophet ﷺ, the Way
ṣūrat al-mushāhada fil qalb: vision of the Divine Presencein the heart

T

tadḥīya: selflessness
tafsīr: exegesis
tahajjud: night prayer
taḥmīd: praising God
tajalli-l-jalāl: manifestation of Divine Majesty
tajalli 'l-jamāl: manifestation
tajwīd: recitation
takbīr: exalting God
talqīn adh-dhikr: recitation
tamkīn, at-: firmness and constancy
taqwā: God-consciousness
ta'rīf: identification
ṭarīqah: path
tasbīḥ: glorifying God
tawāf: circumambulation
tawakkul: dependence
tawbah: repentance
tawḥīd: knowledge of Oneness of God, monotheism
ṭayy, at-: folding time and space
tazkīyat an-nafs: purification of the ego

U

'ūd: sandalwood
'ulama: scholars
Umm al-kitāb: Mother of the Book
ummah: community
Ummatu-d-da'wah: everyone who came after the Prophet ﷺ
Ummatu-l-ijāba: those who accepted the message
Ummatu-l-mutāba'a: those who accepted the message and followed in the footsteps of the Prophet ﷺ
uns: intimacy
'urwat ul wuthqā: unbreakable bond; firm handhold
uwaysī: spiritual connection
'uzlah: isolation

W

waḥdanīyya: Unique Oneness*walī*: saint
waḥdat al-wujūd: unity of creation
waḥdat ash-shuhūd: unity of appearances
wasīlah: means
waẓīfa: daily duty
wi'aẓ: moral exhortations
wilāyat: friendship of God
wird: devotion
wuqūf qalbī: awareness of the heart
wuqūf zamānī: awareness of time

Y

yad kard: essential remembrance
yad dasht: recollection
yadullāh: Hand of God
yaqīn: certainty

Z

zāḥid: ascetic
zakāt: poor-due
zawāyā: monasteries (sing.) *zawīyā*
zuḥd: renunciation of the world, self-denial
Ẓuhr: noon prayer

English-Arabic Glossary

A

annihilation: *fanā'*

Arch-Intercessor: *ghawth*

ascetic: *zāhid*

association: *ṣuḥbah*

attentiveness: *nīgāh dasht*

attributes, Divine: *ṣifāt*

authority: *mujtahid*

awareness of the heart: *wuqūf qalbī*

awareness of time: *wuqūf zamānī*

B

beauty: *jamāl*

Black Stone: *ḥajaru l-aswad*

blessing: *barakah*

bond: *band*

bond, unbreakable: *'urwat ul wuthqa*

border forts: *ribāṭ*

C

calling to religion: *da'wah*

capable of independent legal reasoning: *mujtahid muṭlaq*

cemetery of the companions: *Baqi', al-*

certainty: *yaqīn*

certainty, knowledge of: *'ilm al-yaqīn*

certainty, Reality of: *ḥaqq al-yaqīn*

certainty, vision of: *'ayn al-yaqīn*

chain: *silsila*

chair: *kursī*

charity: *ṣaḍaqa*

charlatans: *musha'wazīn*

chest: *ṣadr*

circumambulation: *ṭawāf*

cloak: *burda*

close ones: *muqarrabīn*

closeness, station of: *qurb*

clouds: *saḥāb*

colors and changes, station of: *maqām al-talwīn*

Community: *ummah*

Community of the way of the Prophet ﷺ: *Āhl as-Sunnah wa 'l-Jama'ah*

companions: *ṣaḥāba, aṣḥāb* (sing.) *ṣaḥābi* (fem.) *saḥābīa*

companionship: *ṣuḥbah*

conduct, code of: *adab*

conscious breathing: *hosh dar dam*

contemplation of the heart: *murāqabah*

creation: *khalīqa*

D

daily duty: *wazīfa*

dawn prayer: *fajr*

dependence on God: *tawakkul*

descendants of the Holy Prophet ﷺ: *sayyid*

descent: *munāzala*

desire: *irāda*

destiny, fixed: *qaḍā' mubram*

devil: *shayṭān*

devotion: *wird*

devotions: awrad, *aḥzāb or adhkār*

direction of prayer: *qiblah*

disciple: *murīd*

Divine Law: *Sharīah*
drinking well: *mashrab*

E

ego: *nafs*
emphasis: *mubālagha*
endowments, religious: *awqāf*
engraving: *naqsh*
erasure, state of: *ghayba*
essential remembrance: *yad kard*
etiquette; protocol: *adab*
everyone who came after the Prophet ﷺ: *Ummatu-d-da'wah*
exalted witnessing: *shuhūd at-tanzīh*
exalting God: *takbīr*
exegesis: *tafsīr*

F

falsehood: *bāṭil*
features: *mazhar*
festival: *'Eid*
firm handhold: *'urwati-l-wuthqā*
firmness and constancy: *at-tamkīn*
focus of attention: *qiblah*
foreordained things: *qaḍā'*
forgiveness, seeking: *istighfār*
friends of God: *awlīyā-ullāh*
friendship of God: *wilāyat*
funeral prayer: *janāza*
furthermost Limit: *sidratu'l-muntaha*

G

gatherings: *suḥbah*
glorifying God: *tasbīḥ*
God: Allāh
God-consciousness: *taqwā*
God's Absolute Unknowable Essence: *dhāt al-baht*
good character, perfect: *iḥsān*
guest houses: *khāniqah*
guidance: *irshād*
guidance of God: *hidāyatullāh*
guide: *dalīl*

H

hand of God: *yadullāh*
He (God's Absolute Unknowable Essence): *Hūwa*
heart: *qalb*
heart's connection: *rābiṭah*
heavenly knowledge: *'ilmu 'l-ladunni*
helpers: *anṣār*
hereafter, the: *ākhirah*
hermit: *rāhib*
hidden: *khafā*
hidden, most: *akhfā*
House of God's worship in Makkah: *Ka'bah*

I

identification: *ta'rīf*
incarnation: *ḥulūl*
initiates: *mubtadi'*
initiation: *bay'ah*
initiator: *murshid*
innovation: *bid'a*
intention: *'aẓīmah, nīyyah*
intimacy: *uns*
Islamic Law: *sharī'a*
isolation: *'uzlah*

J

journey homeward: *safar dar waṭan*
jurisprudence: *fiqh*
jurisprudent: *faqīh*

K

Ka'bah of the heavens: *bayt al-ma'mūr*

knower: *'arif*

knowledge, heavenly: *'ilmu-l-ladunni*

knowledge, hidden: *'ilm al-bāṭin*

knowledge, miraculous: *bāb al-'ilm al-khāriq*

knowledge, perfect: *ma'rifat*

L

Last days: *ākhir az-zamān*

leather socks: *khuff*

legal decisions: *fatāwa*

legal decisions, qualified to give: *mujtahid*

life story: *sīrah*

Light of God: *nūrullāh*

Light of the Unique Essence: *anwār adh-dhāt al-Aḥadīyya*

Living One: *'īsawī*

M

manifestation of heavenly beauty: *tajalli-l-jamāl*

manifestation: *tajalli*

manifestation of Divine Majesty: *tajalli-l-jalāl*

martyrs: *shuhadā*

Masters of Central Asia: *Khwājagān*

material plane: *'alam al-ajsām*

means: *wasīlah*

meditation: *murāqabah*

meeting: *majlis*

mercy: *raḥmah*

miraculous powers: *karāmah*

monastery(ies): *zawīyā/zawāya*

monotheism: *tawḥīd*

(see Oneness of God)

moral exhortations: *wi'aẓ*

Most Majestic Name: *ism al-jalāla*

Mother of the Book: *umm al-kitāb*

N

necessary Knowledge: *'ilmu 'l-wājib*

needless actions: *mā lā yā'nī*

O

one who speaks with God, the station of: *kalīmullāh*

Oneness of God: *aḥadīyya*

Oneness of God: *tawḥid*

Oneness of God, phrase of: *lā ilāha ill-Allāh Muḥammadun Rasāl Allāh*

origin of the wellsprings of the created universes: *mabādi' ta'ayyunāt al-a'lām*

P

parts of the Quran: *juz'*

passage through time and space: *aṭ-ṭayy*

path: *ṭarīqah*

people of determination: *murīd*

People of the Bench or Porch: *ahl aṣ-ṣuffa*

People of the way of the Prophet (the People of the Tradition and the Majority) ﷺ: *Āhl as-Sunnah wa 'l-Jamā'ah*

people, preferred: *al-khawāṣ*

perfect knower: *'arif kāmil*

permission: *'ijāza*

person lost in the Divine Love: *majdhūb*

pilgrimage: *ḥajj*

pillar saints: *awtād*

pious people: *ṣālihīn*

place for sitting or standing to give a sermon: *minbar*

poor towards God: *faqīr*

poor, the: *al-fuqarā*
poor-due: *zakāt*
power: *qudrah*
praising God: *taḥmīd*
prayer, late morning: *duḥā*
prayer, late night: *tahajjud*
prayer, noon: *ẓuhr*
prayer, sunrise *Sunnah* prayer: *ishrāq*
preferred: *mandūb*
Preserved Tablets: *lawḥ al-maḥfūdh*
Prophetic station: *maqām an-nubūwwa*
public treasury: *baytu 'l-māl*
purification of the ego: *tazkīyyat an-nafs*
purify: *ṣafā'a*

R

rank: *rutbah*
real, the: *al-Ḥaqq*
reality: *haqīqah*
reality of all possible creation: *ḥaqā'iq al-mumkināt*
reality of attraction: *ḥaqīqat al-jadhbah*
reality of directing the hearts' power to someone: *ḥaqīqat at-tawajjuh*
reality of folding space: *ḥaqīqat at-tayy*
reality of guidance: *ḥaqīqat al-irshād*
reality of intercession: *ḥaqīqat at-tawassul*
reality of receiving inspiration: *ḥaqīqat al-fayḍ*
reality of the Prophet ﷺ: *al-ḥaqīqat al-Muḥammadīyya*
recitation: *tajwīd*
recitation: *talqīn adh-dhikr*Recitation of the Masters: *Khatmu 'l-Khwājagān*
reckoning: *muḥāsaba*
recollection: *yad dasht*
reference: *marja'*
religious faith and practice: *dīn*
religious leader: *īmām*
religious scholar: *'alim*
remembrance of God: *dhikr*
remembrance, greatest: *sulṭān adh-dhikr*
renewer: *mujaddid*
renunciation of the world: *zuḥd*
repentance: *tawba*
retreat: *khāniqah*
returning: *bāz gasht*
reviver of religion: *mujaddid*
righteous: *ṣāliḥīn*
robe: *jubba, habra*

S

saint: *walī*
saints: *awlīyā, rijāl* (lit. "men")
sandalwood: *'ūd*
satan: *shayṭān*
sayings of the Prophet ﷺ: *aḥādīth;* (sing.) *ḥadīth*
scholars: *'ulama'*
seclusion: *khalwat*
secret: *sirr*
secret of the secret: *sirr as-sirr*
secrets: *asrār*
seeker: *murīd*
self-denial: *zuḥd*
self-effacement: *fana', ghayba*
self-struggle: *jihād an-nafs*
shaykh of the two wings: *dhul janaḥayn*
signs: *ayāt;* (sing.) *ayah*
solitude in the crowd: *khalwat dar anjumān*
sought: *murād*
special one: *khāṣṣ*
spirits, world of: *'alam al-arwāḥ*

spiritual connection: *Uwaysī*
spiritual consultation: *istikhāra*
Spiritual Pole: *quṭb;* (pl.) *aqṭāb*
spiritual practices: *awrād*
spiritual presence: *ruḥāniyya*
station: *maqām*
stations: *maqāmāt*
Straight Path: *ṣirāṭ al-mustaqīm*
striving: *mujāhadah*
striving for understanding: *ijtihād*
struggle: *jihād*
struggle, people who: *mujāhidīn*
student: *ṭālib;* (fem.) *ṭāliba*
Sublimeness and Glory: *Jalāl*
subsistence: *baqā*
substitute saints: *abdal*
subtle things: *laṭā'if;* (sing.) *laṭīfa*
supererogatory worship: *nawāfil*
supplication: *du'a*
support: *madad*
suspended or mutable destiny: *qaḍā' mu'allaq*
Sustainer, the: *ar-Rabb*
system of belief: *'aqīdah*

T

taste: *dhawq*
those who accepted the message: *Ummatu-l-ijāba*
those who accepted the message and followed in the footsteps of the Prophet ﷺ: *Ummatu-l-mutāba'a*
those who are prepared: *musta'idd*
throne: *'arsh*
tomb: *maqām*
traditional center of learning: *madrasah*
transmission of divine bounty: *fayḍ*
traveling the way to God, science of: *'ilm as-sulūk*
trustworthy: *ṣādiq*
trustworthy and truthful: *ṣiddiqīn* (sing.) *ṣiddīq*
truthful believers: *ṣadiqīn*
truthful station: *maqām aṣ-ṣiddīqiyya*
truthfulness, the station of: *maqām as-ṣidq*
twelve imams: *ithnā 'ashari*

U

unbelief: *kufr*
Unique Oneness: *waḥdānīyya*
unity of creation: *waḥdat al-wujūd:*
unity of appearances: *waḥdat ash-shuhūd:*
unlawful: *ḥarām*
unseen: *ghayb*
unveiling: *kashf, mukāshafa*

V

vain desires: *hawā*
veil: *burqā*
veil of humanity: *ḥijāb al-basharīyya*
verifiers: *muḥaqqiqīn*
vision: *kashf, mushāhada*
vision of the Divine Presence in the heart: *ṣūrat al-mushāhada fi 'l-qalb*
void: *'adm*

W

waist-cloth: *izār*
watch your step: *nazar bar qadam*
way: *sunnah*
Way of Prophet Muhammad ﷺ: *Sunnah*
wayfaring: *sulūk*
wholeness, perfect: *kamāl*
witness: *mushāhid*
world, lower, worldliness: *dunyā*

world, next: *ākhirāh*

worship, strictest modes of worship: *'azīmah*

worshipping other than God, polytheism: *shirk*

Islamic Months and Holy Days

NAME	TRANSLITERATION	HOLY DAYS
مُحَرَّمٌ	Muḥarram	1st Islamic New Year; 9th-11th days of fasting; 10th 'Ashūrah.
صَفَرٌ	Ṣafar	
رَبِيعُ أَوَّلٌ	Rabi' al-Āwwal	12th Prophet Muhammad's birthday, known as *mawlid*, *milād*, *mawlud*; celebrated globally.
رَبِيعُ ثَانٍ	Rabi' ath-Thānī	
جُمَادَى أَوَّلٌ	Jumādā al-Āwwal	
جُمَادَى ثَانٍ	Jumādā ath-Thānī	
رَجَبٌ	Rajab	According to the Traditions, the month of God. 7th Laylat ar-Raghā'ib (see page 783). 27th Mi'raj an-Nabī (see page 786). Superogatory fasting and prayers.
شَعْبَانٌ	Sha'bān	According to the Traditions, the month of the Prophet. 15th Nisf Shaban (see page 787). Superogatory fasting and prayers.
رَمَضَانٌ	Ramaḍān	According to the Traditions, the month of the Nation. The month of fasting. (see page 804).
شَوَّالٌ	Shawwāl	1st-3rd Eid al-Fitr, celebration marking the end of Ramadan, of two or three days duration.
ذُوالقَعْدَةِ	Dhul-Qi'dah	
ذُوالحِجَّةِ	Dhul-Ḥijjah	The month of Hajj. 9th Standing at Mount 'Arafah; 10th Eid al-Adha the celebration commemorating Hajj (see page 811).

Index of Quranic Verses

A

A goodly tree, its root set firm, its branches reaching into heaven (14:24-25).......713
A Messenger from among themselves, rehearsing unto them the Signs of God (3:164).......607
A Messenger from among themselves, to rehearse to them His Signs, to sanctify them, and to instruct them in Scripture and Wisdom. (62:2).......607
A Messenger who shall instruct them in Scripture and Wisdom, and sanctify them. (2:129).......607
A similar (favor have you already received), in that we have sent among you a Messenger of your own... (2:151).......623
Above every knower there is a greater knower (12:76).......140
Above every knower there is a greater knower. (12:76).......599
Again and again will those who disbelieve (15:2).......136
All who obey God and the Messenger (4:69).......651
Allah! There is no god except He, the Living, the Self-Subsistent........682
Am I not your Lord?.......169, 170
Am I not your Lord? (7:171.......536
Among the Believers are men who have been true to their Covenant with God. (33:23).......618, 619
And (away from the fire) shall be kept (92:17-21).......90
And (He is the One) Who causeth me to die (26:81).......708
And establish regular prayer, for prayer restrains from shameful and unjust deeds... (29:45).......675
And few of My servants are thankful (34:13).......237
And for him who fears to stand before his Lord there are two gardens. (55:46).......91
And fulfill the Covenant of God when you have made it...(16:91).......36
And fulfill the covenant, for the covenant shall be questioned about. (17:34).......36
O you who believe! Celebrate the praises of God, and do so often.......673
And He (God) has sent him (Muhammad) (62:3).......103
And He rewards those who do good with what is best. (53:31).......624
And he said to his companion (9:40).......91
And landmarks, and by the stars they find a way. (16:16).......456
And leave the one who turns away 53:29).......237
And mention the name of your Lord and devote yourself to Him with a complete devotion. (73:8).......681
And remember thy Lord in thyself (7:205).......47
And remember We appointed (2:51).......50
And restrain thyself with those who call upon their Lord at morning and evening (18:28).......603
And she has been given from all things (27:23).......704
And some part of the night awake for it, a largess for thee. (17:79),.......683
And speak (O Moses and Aaron XE "Aaron") unto him (Pharaoh) a gentle word (20:44).......710
And We have set a barrier (36:9).......396
And We have taught him from Our heavenly knowledge. (18:65).......130
And what is the Lord of the Worlds? (26:23).......711

And whoever Purifies himself does so to his own soul's benefit; and to God is the Journeying. (35:18).......623
Apply yourself with patience to remain in the company of those who call upon their Lord (18:28).......614, 632, 636
As for him who gives and keeps his duty, we facilitate for him the way to ease. (92:5-7).......90

B

Be with the trustworthy ones (9:119).......238
Betake yourself to the cave (18:16).......51, 407
But among them are some who wrong themselves (35:32),.......706
But His command, when He intends a thing, is only that he says unto it Be! and it is. (36:82).......448
But only he (will prosper) that brings to God a sound heart (26:89).......638
By the soul and the proportion and order given to it, (91:7-10).......618

C

Call unto your Sustainer (7:55).......146

D

Do not segregate or evict (from God's House) those who call on their Lord morning and evening (6:52)........635

E

Enjoin the right and forbid the wrong (3:110, 114).......191
Every day (moment) He manifests Himself (55:29).......239
Every time that Zachariah entered.......363

F

Fear God and keep company with those who are truthful. (9:119).......31, 619
Follow the way of those who turn to Me. (31:15).......620
For God is with those who restrain themselves and who are good. (16:128).......623
For the Mercy of God is near to those who are good (muhsinin). (7:56).......623

G

God and His angels bless the Holy Prophet. (33:56).......90
God blots out or confirms what He pleases (13:39).......412
God commands justice, the doing of good (16:90).......624
God has set a seal (2:7).......159
God has with Him the knowledge of the Hour. (31:34).......630
God hath now revealed the fairest of statements, a Scripture consistent,...(39:23).......700
God is the best Protector (12:64).......397
God wants ease for you (2:185;20:2).......84

H

Had they kept straight on the path (72:16).......ix, 609
He begets not nor was begotten. (112:3).......448
He is successful who purifies himself, and remembers the name of his Lord,. (87:14-15).......660
He is the One Who raised among the people of Makkah a Messenger from among themselves (62:2).......618
He it is who sends His blessings (33:43).......90
He said to his friend, 'Grieve not, for verily God is with us.' (9:40).......78
He was the second of two in the cave (9:40).......26

I

I am about to place a viceroy (khalifa) in the earth (2:30).......451
I am nearer to you than your own jugular vein (1:16).......587
I am your Lord the Most High (79:24).......711
I did not create jinn and mankind except to worship me. (51:56).......223
I know not that ye have a god other than me. (28:38).......711

I verily will punish him with hard punishment (27:21).......708
If anyone slew a person (5:32).......71
If the hypocrites come to you and say (63:1).......628
If they had only, when they were unjust to themselves, come unto thee (4:64).......71
If you are thankful, God will increase for you. (14:7).......114
If you want to love God, then follow me. (3:31).......200
In houses which God has allowed to be raised to honor. (24:36-37).......662
Is there any reward for Excellence (ihsan) other than Excellence? (55:60).......624
It is He who removes it and lifts up the coverings. (50:22).......159
It is heavy in the heavens and the earth. It comes not to you save unawares. (7:187).......630
It was not God's purpose that your belief should be in vain. (2:143).......629

J

Judge aright between us and be not unjust (38:22).......712

K

Know here are signs self-evident (29:49).......617

L

Leave the outwardness of sin and its inwardness. (6:120).......618
Lo! He is ever Clement, Forgiving (17:44).......704
Lo! the vigil of the night is a time when impression is more keen and speech more certain. (73:6).......683
Lo! Worship guards one from lewdness and iniquity, but verily, (29:45).......660

M

Men who remember God much.......42

N

Nay, they are the Friends of God; no fear shall come upon them, neither shall they grieve. (10:62).......577, 619
Nay, whoever who submits his whole self to God (2:112).......624
Now surely, on the friends of God there is no fear, nor shall they grieve; those who believe and guard against evil. (10:62-63).......651

O

O Believers, be wary of God and find a means to approach Him (5:35).......619
O Believers, make abundant mention of God! (33:41).......659
O Believers, repent to God with a pure repentance (66:8).......168
O fire, be cool and safe for Abraham. (21:69).......203
O my Lord! Truly am I in need of any good that Thou dost send me! (28:24).......142
O soul in complete rest and satisfaction! Come back to thy Lord (89: 27-30).......319
O ye who believe! Obey God, obey the Prophet and those in authority among you, (4:59).......315
O you who believe! Remember God with much remembrance; and glorify Him morning and evening. (33:41-42).......42
O you who believe, Believe! (4:136).......238
Obey God, obey the Prophet and those in authority among you. (4:59).......415

P

Peace! A Word (of salutation) from a Lord Most Merciful. (36:58).......404
People whom neither business nor profit distract from the remembrance of God. (24:37).......154, 273
Praise belongs to God, Lord of the Worlds. (1:2).......237
Purify and sanctify them; and pray on their behalf, verily thy prayers are a

source of security for them. (9:103).......607

R

Recite, in the name of your Lord (96:1-5).......73

Remember God excessively. (33:41).......169

Remember Me, and I shall remember you (2:152).......42, 664, 667, 673, 707

Remember your Lord much.......42

Remind people, for reminding benefits them. (51:55).......690

S

Say (O Prophet): O humanity! I am a Messenger to you all from God, to Whom belongs the kingdom of the heavens and the earth. (7:158).......61

Say 'The truth comes from your Lord' (18:29-31).......636

Say, the things that my Lord has indeed forbidden are: shameful deeds . (7:33).......617

Seek forgiveness of your Lord, certainly Your Lord is oft-Forgiving. (11:52).......114

So establish prayer for My remembrance. (20:14).......660

So her Lord accepted her with a gracious acceptance, and caused her to grow an excellent growth, and made Zachariah her guardian. (3:37).......51

So remember the name of thy Lord, and devote thyself to Him with full devotion. (73:8).......51

So they found one of Our servants on whom We had bestowed mercy from Ourselves (18:66-67).......620

T

The Arabs say: 'We believe.' Say: 'You do not believe, but say 'We submit.' (49:14.......628

The creation of heaven and earth and the changes of night and day are signs for people who have wisdom. (3:190-191).......659

The Day wherein neither wealth nor sons will avail but only he will prosper who brings to God a sound heart. (26:88-89).......616

The distance of two bows' length (53:9).......52, 75, 395, 396, 529

The men and women who remember God abundantly (33:35)........664, 701

The second of two when they were in the cave. (9:40).......89

The seven heavens and the earth and all that is therein praise Him (17:44).......703

Their skins shiver (39:23).......684

Then their skins and their hearts soften to the remembrance of God. (39:23).......684

There is no change and no power except with God, (18:39).......114

There is not a thing but sings His praise (17:44).......703

There is nothing for man but what he strives to acquire. (53:39).......314

T

There remaineth but the countenance of thy Lord of Might and Glory (55:27).......710

Therefore know that there is no god but God alone (47:19).......713

They only are the true believers whose hearts feel fear when God is mentioned (8:2).......700

Those are the Ones who have been guided by God, so follow their guidance. (6:90).......228

Those men and women who engage much in God's praise, for them has God prepared forgiveness and a great reward. (3:191, 33:35).......673

Those who are striving in Our Way, We will guide them to Our paths(29:69).......619

Those who believe, and whose hearts find their rest in the remembrance of God—for, verily, in the remembrance of God

hearts do find their rest. (13:28).......42, 662, 676
Those who have striven for Our sake, We guide them to Our ways. (29:96).......639
Those who remember God much. (33:35).......674, 703
Those who remember God while standing, sitting, and lying on their sides (3:191).......42, 659, 673
Those will prosper who Purify themselves and glorify the Name of their Lord and pray. (87:14).......623
Thus did he (Pharaoh) make fools of his people, and they obeyed him. Lo! they were a wanton folk. (43:54).......455
To God belong the Most beautiful Names, so call Him with them. (7:180).......683
To God we belong, and to Him is our return. (2:156).......401
To Whom belongs the kingdom of the heavens and the earth. (7:158).......61
To whom belongs the Kingdom on this day? (40:16).......170, 238
Truly he succeeds that purifies it (91:9).......638
Truly it is hard save for the humble-minded (2:45).......638
Truly you are of a sublime nature. (68:4).......82, 114
Truly, they are alive with their Lord, receiving sustenance." (3:169).......234

V

Verily his heart is sinful. (2:283).......615
Verily in the remembrance of God do hearts find rest! (13:28).......700
Verily those who swear allegiance to thee indeed swear allegiance to God. (48:10).......36
Verily We have honored the children of Adam. (17:70).......448
Verily, Abraham was most tender-hearted, forbearing. (9:114, 11:75).......666

W

We brought out the believers who dwelled in it. (51:35-36).......628
We have enjoined on the human being kindness to his parents (45:15-16).......91
We have honored the children of Adam. (17:70).......450, 452
We have placed the mountains under His dominion; they praise God at nightfall and at sunrise. (38:18).......704
We have revealed the dhikr, and we are the One to protect that dhikr in you. (15:9).......413
We have sent among you a Messenger of your own, rehearsing Our Signs, and purifying you, and instructing you in Scripture and Wisdom. (2:151).......607
We made you nations and tribes that you might know one another. (49:13).......472
We will tell you stories of the prophets who came before you, to make your heart firm. (11:120).......350
What can convey its knowledge unto thee (How canst thou know)? It may be that the Hour is nigh. (34:63, 42:17).......630
Whatever the Prophet gives you, take it, and whatever he withholds from you, leave it. (59:7).......273
When the call is proclaimed on Friday, hasten earnestly to the remembrance of God. (62:9).......666
Who can be better in religion than one who submits his whole self to God (4:125).......624
who shall rehearse Your signs to them, instruct them in the Book and wisdom and purify them. (2:129).......623
Whoever disbelieves in idols and believes in God has grasped the Firm Handhold. (2:256).......206
Whoever submits his whole self to God (31:21).......624
Without doubt, I am He that forgives again and again, (20:82).......328
Would that I had been a thing forgotten and out of sight! (19:23).......719

Y

You knew not what the Book was nor what the Faith. (42:52).......629
You see them looking at you but without clear vision. (7:198).......127
You shall return to us alone, as We created you the first time. (6:94).......124
Your creation and your resurrection is in no wise but as an individual soul. (31:28).......71

Index of Hadith

A

A man who strives for God's Cause with his life and property.......678
A people will recite the Quran but it will not pass beyond their throats.......695
A servant of God said, 'My Lord! All praise belongs to You'.......688
Abu Bakr does not precede you.......92, 604
Abu Bakr was the only person.......93
Abu Bakr, you will be the first.......97
Abu Hurayra said, "While on the road to Makkah the Prophet.......678
All of creation is a servant of God........87
All that you say in celebration of God's Glory, Majesty, and Oneness.......673
All your actions are shown to me.......71
among whom was the Pharaoh of this Community, Abu Jahl.......711
And take counsel with them.......91
As long as you say, 'There is no god but God,' it will lift God's punishment from you and change you for the good........87
Ask God forgiveness and health.......87
At the beginning of every century, God will send someone by whom the religion will be revived........270

B

Be austere in this lower world.......86
Be in this world as a stranger.......86
Be merciful and God will be merciful towards you........87
Be near the poor.......86
Beware of the lower world.......87
Beware of the vision of the believer.......198
Blessing is with your elders........661

C

Close all doors which face my mosque except the door of Abu Bakr.......239
Close your eyes and listen to me.......46

D

Die before you die.......33
Do not speak much rather than make dhikr.......616
Do you want me to tell you of your best deeds.......44
During the Night Journey I met Abraham.......686
Dust for the face of the one.......697

E

Each is facilitated for that for which he was created........453
Every good deed on your part shall be weighed.......714
Everything has a polish.......44, 615
Excellence is to worship God as if you see Him........29, 49, 626
Expect death always and live accordingly.......97

F

Forgive others and God will forgive you........87

G

Gabriel came to me and ordered me.......46
Gabriel told me, I stood in wait before God.......711
Give me your pledge.......37
Glory to God and praise to Him to the number of His creation.......688
Go with these two sandals of mine.......664
God favors dhikr.......48, 677
God has expanded my breast to receive what He has expanded the breast of Abu Bakr.......26
God is One and He likes the odd number........228

God rewards people according to what they achieve........86
God said, 'O Son of Adam.......86
God verily will raise on the Day of Resurrection people bearing light.......708
God will show His glory.......91
God, Almighty and Exalted, has angels who seek the people of dhikr.......43
God, Almighty and Exalted, put a limit on all the obligations.......44
God's Attributes are as numerous as the breaths of human beings.......152
God's saints are under His domes........86

H

Had he not been one of My glorifiers.......660
He heard the screeching of the Pens.......662
He who has good thoughts about people.......855
He who remembers God much, God loves him.......700
Here is Jumdan which has overtaken the single-minded.......701
His character was the Quran.......627
How many people welcome a day.......86

I

I am as my servant thinks of Me.......44
I am going to my Lord from one state to a better state.......153
I am the City of Knowledge, and Ali is the Door........26, 61
I am with My servant when he remembers Me.......47
I am with the one who remembers Me.......199
I came to the Prophet with many people from the Helpers.......37
I do not fear for you only the anti-Christ........603
I had a vision that I was put on one side of the scale..........92
I have been ordered to speak with people.......220
I have two sides: one faces my Creator.......154
I love repeating, "Glorified is God".......685
I saw the Prophet counting the glorifications of God.......689
I saw the Prophet on a moonlit night.......84
I was a Prophet when Adam was between water and clay.......70
I was made to love seclusion.......52
If anyone recites the last two verses of Surat al-Baqara at night.......687
If faith were at the Pleiades.......103
If I had taken to myself a beloved friend.......26
If I were to take an intimate friend other than my Lord..........92
If My servant mentions Me.......46
If people sit in an assembly in which they do not remember God nor invoke a blessing on the Prophet.......697
If you pass by the gardens of paradise.......43
If you pass by the groves of Paradise.......707
If you sit with the People of Truth.......228
If your hearts were always in the state that they are in during dhikr.......660
In all my life, he never asked me once,.......84
In the beginnings of the Messenger of God's Prophethood.......679
In the time of the Prophet ...we did not recognize anyone higher than Abu Bakr as-Siddiq.........92
In the time of the Prophet the people raised their voices in dhikr........46
In this Way, you have no more.......139

K

Keep God and He will keep you.......86
Keep what you are doing secret.......87
Khidr (the Green Man) was so named.......140
Knowledge is of two kinds..........638

L

Let your tongue be always busy with the remembrance of God.......673

M

Make everything easy.......86
Make your dying ones say.......169
My Community will never agree on error.......203
My intercession is for the sinners of my Community........204
My Lord taught me good manners.......719
My servant draws not near to Me with anything more loved by Me.......621

N

Neither My heaven nor My earth could contain Me.......254
Never has the sun risen or set on a person..........91
Never was anything revealed to me..........92
No group gathers and remembers God seeking nothing other than Him.......708
No one was dearer to me than the Holy Prophet.......83
No one will enter Paradise who has even an atom of pride.......615
No servant of Mine mentions Me in himself except I mention him.......701
Nothing but supplication averts the decree.......101
Nothing puts fear in my heart except the fear of God.......399
Nothing saves you from God's punishment except dhikr.......44

O

O Ali, the best of what I and all prophets before me said.......46
O Ali, you have to continuously recite dhikr.......46
O Commander of the Faithful tell us about Abu Bakr.......92
O God, do not leave me to my ego for the blink of an eye........360
O Lord, my Community, my Community!'.......95
O Messenger of God! Who will be the foremost people in gaining your intercession.......615
O Messenger of God, belief is here.......616
O my Lord! help me and do not cause me to face difficulty.......667
O people, are you not ashamed.......87
O Salman, did you see.......101
O son of Adam whatever you asked Me.......687
O Umar, your religion is your flesh and blood.......35
O Wabisa, fear of God is here.......615
On the day of resurrection the sun will come near created beings.......379
On the Day of Resurrection, the people will surge.......95

P

Part of faith.......197
Prayer is the ascension of the believer.......204
Prophet has poured into my heart.......73

R

Raise your hand and repeat after me.......47
Remember and mention God as much as you want.......670
Remembrance of God is firm knowledge of one's belief.......703

S

Salman has spoken the truth.......103
Satan moves freely in the veins.......146
Say it (the phrase: There is no god but God alone), so that I will be permitted to intercede for you.......712
Send prayers for me wherever you are.......220
Seven people will be shaded by God.......679
Shall I tell you something that is the best of all deeds.......640

Shall I tell you the words that God loves the most?.......685
Speak the truth.......86
Speak to each in accordance with his understanding........855
Speak to people at a level they can understand.......40
Surely God does not look at your bodies.......615
Surely there is in the body a small piece of flesh.......614

T

The believer sees with the Light of God........658
The best deed is when people will be safe from your tongue and your hand........87
The best remembrance of God is to repeat "la ilaha illallah".......685
The day God created the heavens and the earth He created an angel.......709
The dhikr not heard by the Recording Angels.......48, 678
The difference between one who recites dhikr and one who does not recite dhikr.......43
The dogs of the people in Hell.......696
The fast is for Me.......199
The heart of a believer.......644
The master of a people is the one who serves them........41
The men and women who remember God unceasingly.......678
The most sinful person is the one whose tongue is always lying........87
The one under the heaviest punishment.......87
The one who has the most perfect mind.......86
The one who knows God.......231
The one who mentions or remembers God among those who forget.......701
The people of dhikr are the people of My Presence.......41
The People of Paradise will not regret except one thing alone.......660
The Phrase of Oneness is the key to the Garden of Paradise.......713
The portion of my Community destined for the hellfire.......203
The Prophet came in to see me and in front of me there were four thousand date-stones.......690
The Prophet loved to seclude himself.......51
the Prophet poured into my heart.......395
the Prophet remembered God at all times of the day and night........659
The Prophet said that God has angels roaming the roads to find the people of dhikr.......667
The Prophet went out to a circle of his Companions.......670
The single-hearted are foremost.......664
The single-minded (al-mufarridun) are foremost.......679
The ways to God are as numerous.......717
The womb of a mother is composed of........56
The words most dear to God.......686
There are ninety-nine names which belong to God.......683
There are roaming angels of God.......670
There are seven who will be kept under God's Shadow.......54
There are two phrases that are light on the tongue.......685
There is no one to whom I am obligated..........92
There will be among my Community.......267
There will come a time upon the people when the best property of a Muslim man will be his sheep.......678
They will pass through Islam like an arrow passes through its quarry........696
Those that remember Me in their heart.......664
To the limit that you can bear.......37

V

Verily there is in the body a small piece of flesh.......627

W

We did not remember You as You deserve.......157
Were it not for him I would not have.......70
What a good reminder are the dhikr beads.......690
What do you think of two when God is their third.......78
What have you left for your family.......34
What I fear most for my nation is a hypocrite who has a scholarly tongue.......603
Whatever God poured into my breast.......26
Whatever God poured into my heart.......61, 75, 78
When a servant of God utters the words 'la ilaha illallah'.......685
When God loves someone.......87
When God wants good for His servant.......87
When I heard the dhikr, I would know that the congregational prayer had ended.......46
When the young teach the old, then blessing has been lifted.......661
When you hear the muadhdhin, repeat his words after him,.......697
When you pass by the gardens of Paradise, avail yourselves of them.......670
Whenever God's saints are mentioned, His mercy descends on that group.......184
Whenever I offered Islam to anyone.......93
Whenever the servant says the testimony of faith.......449
Which of the servants of God is best in rank before God.......663
While on the road to Makkah the Prophet passed on top of a mountain called Jumdan.......669
While we were sitting with God's Messenger.......625
Who is the best person after God's Apostle?.......92
Who will be the foremost people in gaining your intercession.......615
Whoever comes against one of My saints.......86, 368, 651
whoever comes to us in the way you have come.......616
Whoever imitates a group of people.......37, 157
Whoever knows himself knows His Lord.......157
Whoever lengthens his pronunciation upon saying "No god except God," God will make him dwell in Paradise.......709
Whoever loves me, I will burden him........197
Whoever said, There is no god but God alone.......713
Whoever says "No god except God" in astonishment at something, God creates from each letter..........710
Whoever says, "Glorified is God with all praise to Him.......687
Whoever says, "There is no god but God, alone, without partner.......687
Whoever sees Me sees the Truth.......304
Whoever sees me, has seen Reality.......131
Whoever sees the face of a knower of God.......131
Worship God as if you see Him.......33
written on the door of Paradise is the inscription.......710

Y

You are the witnesses of God on earth.......652
You have to follow my way and the way of my caliphs after me.......249
Your Lord is Munificent and Generous.......101

Main Index

A

Aaron.......710
Aata.......112, 663, 707
Abah Anom.......464
Abbas ibn Abd al-Muttalib.......88
Abbasids.......38
Abd al-Ahad.......266, 267, 291
Abd al-Aziz Uyun as-Sud.......429
Abd al-Hamid.......376
Abd al-Jalil Murad.......429
Abd al-Jamil.......146
Abd al-Karim al-Barzinji.......308
Abd al-Karim Jili.......331
Abd al-Khaliq al-Ghujdawani.......26, 28, 57, 58, 80, 137, 139, 145, 146, 147, 149, 150, 151, 158, 169, 184, 190, 191, 193, 229, 304, 329, 440, 509
Abd Allah ad-Daghestani.......512
Abd Allah ad-Dahlawi.......296, 297, 298, 306, 310, 311, 312, 322, 325
Abd Allah al-Faiz ad-Daghestani.......xv, 54, 57, 58, 342, 344, 371, 383, 387, 388, 389, 390, 391, 392, 395, 405, 409, 426, 429, 435, 437, 447, 455, 457, 471, 720, 721
Abd Allah al-Fardi.......312
Abd Allah al-Khani.......463
Abd Allah bin Muhammad bin Jafar.......636
Abd Allah bin Wahab.......636
Abd Allah Ghuwayni.......134
Abd Allah Gymnastiar.......464
Abd Allah ibn Abbas.......37, 44, 46, 85, 90, 91, 640, 674, 688, 696, 709, 710
Abd Allah ibn al-Mubarak.......620
Abd Allah ibn Amr ibn al-As.......696
Abd Allah ibn Jafar.......37
Abd Allah ibn Masud.......686, 693
Abd Allah ibn Muhammad ibn Abd al-Wahhab.......655
Abd Allah ibn Umar.......37, 92, 615, 616, 663, 670, 688
Abd Allah Kazgan.......210
Abd Allah Mirza.......243
Abd al-Muttalib ibn Hashim.......71
Abd al-Qadir al-Jili al-Madani Qadiri.......453
Abd al-Qadir Gilani.......38, 39, 52, 58, 135, 253, 268, 269, 299, 311, 410, 427, 436, 437, 438, 443, 652, 653
Abd al-Rahim ibn al-Hasan al-Isnawi.......703
Abd al-Rahman al-Sufuri.......700
Abd al-Rahman Jami.......v
Abd al-Wahhab ash-Shaarani.......215
Abd al-Wahid ibn Zayd.......643
Abd an-Nur.......404
Abd ar-Rahim al-Barzinji.......308
Abd ar-Rahman ad-Daghestani.......322, 328
Abd ar-Rahman ibn Abi Zannad.......106
Abd ar-Rahman ibn Yahya.......123
Abd ar-Rauf al-Munawi.......290
Abd ar-Rauf al-Yamani.......422
Abd as-Salam.......262
Abdurrahman Wahid.......463
Abi al-Bakhtari.......104
Abi Bakr al-Kaffal.......233
ablution.......42, 81, 85, 187, 204, 219, 305, 318, 329, 362, 387, 395, 732
Abraham, Prophet.......71, 95, 100, 140, 199, 203, 277, 290, 296, 312, 354, 406, 566, 666, 686
Absolute Light.......232
Absolute Nothingness.......i, 232
Abu ad-Darda.......44, 103, 662, 665, 671, 680, 691, 692

Abu Ahmad as-Sughuri.......357, 359, 360, 361, 363, 364, 366, 367, 373, 377, 378, 379
Abu Ali al-Farmadi.......128, 129, 130, 229
Abu Ali Dakkak.......645
Abu Ayyub al-Ansari.......81
Abu Bakr al-Marwazi.......604
Abu Bakr al-Qittani.......157
Abu Bakr al-Talhi.......634
Abu Bakr as-Siddiq.......xix, 25, 26, 27, 34, 37, 57, 58, 61, 73, 74, 75, 78, 79, 80, 82, 88, 89, 90, 91, 92, 94, 97, 104, 106, 107, 112, 185, 197, 229, 239, 271, 278, 290, 293, 304, 348, 410, 420, 431, 432, 437, 512, 513, 604, 661
Abu Bakr ibn al-Arabi.......660, 680
Abu Bakrah al-Qattani.......621
Abu Dawud.......37, 46, 270, 631
Abu Dharr al-Ghifari.......672, 680, 685
Abu Hafs an-Nishaburi.......40
Abu Hanifa, Imam.......113, 241, 272, 302, 644, 645
Abu Hashim al-Sufi.......645, 654
Abu Hurayra.......43, 47, 636, 661, 669, 670, 685, 687, 692, 697, 701
Abu Ishaq ash-Shirazi.......134
Abu Jahl.......127, 711
Abu Juhayfa.......103
Abu Mabad.......46
Abu Madian.......174
Abu Muhammad al-Madani.......364, 365, 366, 367, 368, 370, 373, 376, 378, 380, 397
Abu Musa al-Ashari.......43, 640, 693
Abu Muslim al-Khawlani.......608
Abu Nasr Bishr al-Hafi.......605
Abu Nuaym al-Isfahani.......107, 633, 643
Abu Saad.......692
Abu Saad al-Awbahi.......237
Abu Saeed.......328
Abu Saeed Abd Allah ibn Abi Asrun.......134
Abu Saeed al-Kharraz.......702
Abu Saeed al-Khudri.......663, 670, 678, 686, 687
Abu Saeed, King.......242, 243
Abu Safiyya.......691, 692
Abu Saud.......51
Abu Taher Madani.......292
Abu Talhah Zayd ibn Sahl.......88
Abu Talib.......71, 74, 711, 712
Abu Turab an-Naqshabi.......209
Abu Umar ibn Qudama.......653
Abu Zannad.......106
Abu Zura al-Razi.......695
Abul Hasan al-Ashari, Imam.......ix
Abul Hasan Ali Nadwi.......38
Abul Hasan al-Kharqani.......57, 58, 124, 125, 126, 128, 157, 209, 229
Abul Hasan an-Nuri.......183, 297, 337
Abul Hasan ash-Shadhili.......53, 206
Abul Hasan Sumnun.......163, 347, 391
Abul Qasim al-Qushayri.......45
adab.......509, 526
Adam.......ii, 70, 95, 146, 281, 354, 405, 448, 450, 464, 581, 644, 688
Adam, Prophet.......566
ad-Daylami.......123, 691
adhan.......81
adh-Dhahabi.......120, 121, 647
Adil, Hajjah Amina.......482
Adnan Kabbani.......471, 485
Adnan Menderes.......434
adultery.......287
advice.......41
ahl al-saff.......614
Ahl as-Suffa.......603, 609, 614, 632
Ahl as-Sunnah wal-Jamaah.......467, 607
Ahmad al-Faruqi as-Sirhindi.......57, 153, 203, 262, 263, 265, 266, 276, 281, 290, 311, 312, 410, 413, 456, 513, 524, 531, 568, 587, 654
Ahmad al-Jami.......267
Ahmad al-Kashghari.......190
Ahmad al-Rifai.......308, 452
Ahmad al-Yasawi.......243

Ahmad an-Namiqi al-Jami.......310
Ahmad as-Siddiq.......158
Ahmad Chishti.......312
Ahmad ibn al-Hawari.......647
Ahmad ibn Hanbal, Imam.......25, 37, 41, 46, 47, 303, 305, 334, 335, 604, 631, 637, 646, 666, 667, 673, 691
Ahmad Koftaro.......460
Ahmad Mashhur al-Haddad.......668
Ahmad Syahid.......463
Ahmad Yar.......305
Ahzab, Battle of.......27
Aisha.......48, 51, 52, 53, 87, 88, 94
akhfa.......586, 587
akhlaq.......597
akhlaq dhamima.......617
akhlaq hasana.......617
al-Abbas ibn Hamza.......124
al-Albani.......693
al-Ansari al-Harawi.......321
al-Aqra bin Habis.......634, 635
al-Aswad ibn Anas.......85
al-Aswad ibn Yazid.......608
Alauddin al-Bukhari al-Attar.......197, 202, 210, 215, 217, 218, 226, 229, 235, 269, 329
Alauddin al-Ghujdawani.......235
al-Azhar.......487
al-dhat al-baht.......447
al-Fatiha.......190, 243
al-Fawaid.......639
al-Ghalayini, Ibrahim.......484
al-Ghawth.......436
al-Hakam ibn al-Mubarak.......693
al-Hakim Attar.......194
al-Harith al-Muhasibi.......620, 637
al-Hasan ibn Ali ibn Abi Talib.......37
al-Husayn ibn Ali ibn Abi Talib.......37
Al-Husayn ibn Zayd.......454
Ali al-Hujwiri.......438, 612
Ali ar-Ramitani.......165, 167, 168, 176
Ali Damman.......214
Ali ibn Abi Talib.......xviii, xix, 25, 32, 40, 46, 58, 73, 78, 106, 112, 269, 311, 348, 420, 431, 512
Ali Ramitani.......190, 229
Ali Rida.......310
alimun amil.......314
al-Izz ibn Abd al-Salam.......604, 638
al-Jurjani.......624
al-Khatib al-Baghdadi.......640
Allahu akbar.......46, 124
al-Midani, Abul Khayr.......484
al-Mundhiri.......679, 701
al-Qahhar.......134
al-Qasim ibn Abd al-Rahman.......691
al-Qasim ibn Uthman al-Jui.......646
al-Qattan.......113
al-Rabi ibn Khuthaym.......608
al-Tawkhi.......630
al-Wasiti.......706
amber.......83, 420
Amin Abidin.......319
Amin al-Kurdi.......48, 677
Amina Adil.......434
Amina, mother of Abd Allah ad-Daghestani.......393
Amina, mother of the Prophet.......71, 147
Amir ibn Abd Qays.......608
Amir Kulal.......28
Ammar.......633, 634
Amr ibn al-As.......83, 689
Amr ibn Salima.......694
Amr ibn Salima al-Hamadani.......693
Amr ibn Yahya al-Hamadani.......694
Anas ibn Malik.......43, 84, 95, 96, 290, 687, 710
Andrew Vidich.......507
anesthesia.......594
angels.......43, 278, 441, 582, 644, 698
anger.......xvii, 84, 208, 352, 386, 447, 617, 644, 699, 711, 807, 809, 856
animals.......255
annihilation.......36, 49, 75, 119, 127, 199, 220, 223, 238, 239, 258, 263, 268, 273, 279, 295, 296, 303, 360, 361, 432, 718, 719
anti-Christ.......603
Anwar ash-Shirwani.......322
apologize.......41
Arabic.......viii, ix, 21, 72, 79, 114, 146, 311, 317, 348, 354, 428, 433, 434, 455, 609, 612, 613, 614, 618, 657
Arabs.......421
Arch-Intercessor.......38, 77, 125, 133, 135, 136, 147, 184, 253, 266, 268, 269, 391, 436, 437, 438, 441

Arif ad-Din Karrani.......194
Arif ar-Riwakri.......158, 159, 160, 161, 190, 229
ark.......142
Arlar Khan.......349
army.......85, 101, 102, 243, 244, 245, 325, 354, 362, 363, 369, 392, 397, 402, 696
arrow.......84, 114, 201, 696
Ascension.......75, 77, 89, 176, 278, 279, 303, 406
ascetic.......126, 134, 235, 298, 359
asceticism.......53, 145, 290, 308
Ashur ad-Daya.......443
Asim ibn Umar ibn Qatada.......100
Asiya.......393
as-Saib.......46
as-Sakhawi.......661, 696, 698
as-Samad.......447
as-Saqqa.......192
as-Sari as-Saqati.......311
as-Siddiqiyya.......57
as-Simnani.......130
Association of Muslim Scholars of Lebanon.......xv
as-Sulami.......27
astrologers.......630
Ataturk.......376, 389
atheism.......459
at-Tabari.......85, 101, 113
attack.......41
at-Tayfuriyya.......57
Attentiveness.......157
at-Turki.......192
awareness of numbers.......229, 399
awareness of time.......201, 202
awe.......620
awliya.......599, See saints
Awliya al-Kabir.......150, 158
awrad.......509
Aws Khazraji.......88
axe.......101
Ayyub as-Saqityani.......107
Azizan.......168, 173, 174, 192, 193, 195, 201, 226

B

backbite.......37, 123, 302
backbiting.......40
bad manners.......54
Bahira.......71
Bakr ibn Abd Allah.......604
Balagha.......609
Balance.......46, 699, 714
Balkan War.......371
band.......27
Bani Nadhir.......81
Banu Hanifa.......696
Banu Tamim.......696
barakah.......481, 513, 597
batin.......579
battery.......595
battle.......81, 82, 93, 94, 100, 343, 400, 402, 423, 468, 644, 665, 700
bayah.......528, 546, See initiation, See initiation
Bayazid al-Bistami.......26, 27, 57, 115, 117, 157, 229, 241, 447, 521, 650, 707, 721
Baydawi.......308
baz gasht.......157
beach.......569
beads.......692
beauty.......72, 75, 190, 198, 269, 276, 290, 367, 431, 643, 672, 721
beauty mark.......83
beggar.......557
Bektashi.......544
believers.......x, 78, 84, 90, 93, 150, 160, 610, 614, 618, 620, 628, 639, 684, 696, 700
Beloved of God.......70
Bible.......54
Bilal al-Habashi.......xviii, 93, 430, 633, 634, 682
Bill Gates.......481
black.......189
Black Stone.......72, 109
blacksmith.......123
blessing.......562
boat.......142
bond.......27, 29, 56, 103
Bottcher, Annabelle.......479
bow.......84, 91, 114, 201, 210, 220, 233, 452
boy.......142
bread.......191
bridge.......200, 699
Buddhism.......693
Buddhists.......459, 468
Bukhari, Imam.......36, 40, 43, 49, 51, 92, 140, 271
bullet.......400
Buraq.......74, 395
Busayri.......69

C

calendar.......x, 21, 610
caliph.......25, 85, 90, 92, 93, 94, 107, 136, 158, 165, 191, 240, 266, 267, 287, 298, 299, 308, 312, 323, 325, 342, 376, 387, 389
caliphate.......450
calling to religion.......303
camel.......81, 84
capable of independent legal reasoning.......226
cat.......317, 418
cave.......26, 50, 51, 52, 72, 78, 79, 80, 81, 91, 327, 398, 399, 407

center of gravity…....578
certainty…....96, 179, 191, 196, 232, 297, 298, 331, 333, 405, 408, 445, 713
Chair…....137
Chapter of Humanity…....xviii
Chapter of Sincerity…....xviii
Chapter of the Dawn…....xviii
charcoal…....340
charisma…....542
charismatic…....582
charity…....84, 107, 208, 297, 302, 387, 618, 672
charlatans…....xi, 150
chemistry…....485
chess…....588
chest…....58, 82, 198, 204, 221, 363, 406, 615, 682
chicken…....55
children…....36, 42, 441, 699
Chishti…....266, 272, 274, 292, 298, 299, 312, 366, 378, 592
Christian…....21, 100, 136, 418, 489
Christianity…....v, 693
Christians…....459, 468
church…....435, 547
circumambulation…....105, 444
City of Knowledge…....61
Clear Book…....413
cloak…....59, 84, 85, 113, 122, 189, 190, 191, 192, 193, 195, 258, 267, 328, 356, 360, 426, 435, 438, 643, 653, 654, 717
clothes…....59
clouds…....72, 85, 293, 306, 323, 367
CNN…....481
coal…....352
Coca-Cola…....482
code of conduct…....xi, 28
coins…....438
college…....502
Communism…....423
Communist…....29
Community…....viii, x, xvii, xix, 61, 62, 71, 73, 77, 79, 83, 92, 95, 96, 160, 203, 249, 267, 385, 392, 403, 608, 614, 646, 648, 686, 711
Community of the Prophet…....viii
Companions…....ii, vii, viii, x, xv, xvii, xviii, 21, 25, 30, 32, 36, 37, 38, 46, 47, 51, 69, 74, 77, 78, 80, 83, 85, 88, 90, 91, 96, 100, 102, 106, 169, 191, 193, 206, 209, 271, 290, 296, 303, 356, 379, 395, 409, 420, 427, 603, 607, 609, 612, 613, 615, 626, 627, 631, 637, 641, 655, 659, 670, 681, 682, 684, 687, 690, 692, 694, 695, 700, 704, 709, 730, 773
companionship…....See conduct of anticipation…....528
constellations…....89
contemplation…....72, 83, 133, 155, 198, 204, 221, 237, 286, 294, 295, 301, 719
conversion…....582
copper…....44
crown…....184, 210, 279, 392
crown of the Knowers…....621
crows…....243
crying…....622
crystal…....154
culture…....497

D

Daghestaniyya…....57
Dalail al-Khayrat…....309, 463
dance…....519
Darimi…....694
Darwish Muhammad…....253, 254, 255
data…....494
date palm…....713
David, Prophet…....708, 709
dawah…....482, 483, 485
dawn…....xviii, 52, 59, 129, 137, 149, 173, 183, 187, 192, 223, 229, 234, 296, 318, 343, 362, 396, 400, 418, 608, 688
dawn prayer…....xviii, 59, 187, 192, 234, 296, 301, 343, 362, 396, 400, 404, 428, 431, 438, 440, 441
Day of Promises…....169, 185, 218
Day of Resurrection…....48, 702
death…....160
Decree…....74, 371, 617, 629, 631, 662
deer…....85, 255, 352
defects…....32
dependence…....121, 649
deputies…....586
Derbent…....467
dergah…....551, 555, 564, 569
descent…....269, 382
destiny…....412
devil…....333, 639
devils…....152, 441
devotion…....xiv, 51, 80, 187, 352
devotions…....x, 609, 692, 806

dhikr.......v, xii, 44, 45, 46, 47, 48, 49, 50, 53, 57, 72, 80, 102, 108, 150, 154, 155, 156, 157, 164, 168, 169, 175, 181, 193, 201, 203, 228, 235, 238, 254, 255, 263, 271, 299, 300, 302, 303, 309, 319, 324, 333, 334, 339, 350, 366, 372, 378, 381, 383, 389, 399, 413, 418, 427, 438, 449, 456, 460, 465, 469, 486, 509, 516, 527, 558, 562, 581, 610, 614, 616, 617, 622, 654, 659, 660, 663, 666, 667, 669, 670, 671, 672, 674, 675, 676, 677, 678, 679, 682, 684, 690, 691, 692, 693, 694, 695, 701, 702, 703, 707, 708, See Remembrance
dhikr of the heart.......47, 48, 49, 72, 146, 202, 666, 676
Dhu al-Bijadayn.......666
Dhu-Janahayn.......183
Dhul-Hijja.......108
Dhul-Qida.......317, 319, 322, 338
Dhun Nun al-Masri.......121, 621
Dhun Nun al-Misri.......121
dinar.......84, 107
dirham.......35, 84, 107
disciple.......38, 41, 201
disciples.......41
Divine attraction.......188
Divine Attributes.......33, 42, 134, 137, 239, 294, 376, 446, 447, 684
Divine Care.......189
Divine Essence.......i, 239, 321, 407, 444, 447
Divine guidance.......vii
Divine help.......706
Divine knowledge.......50
Divine Law.......ix, x, xv, 28, 32, 34, 39, 40, 45, 50, 106, 130, 136, 146, 164, 168, 180, 183, 191, 193, 196, 202, 214, 226, 243, 247, 275, 276, 282, 286, 298, 308, 309, 311, 332, 340, 366, 368, 376, 393, 394, 426, 428, 446, 456, 657, 720
Divine Light.......82
Divine Love.......i, xx, 25, 42, 58, 59, 75, 168, 180, 189, 202, 228, 338, 348, 376, 379, 392, 426, 444, 445, 856
Divine Name.......393, 447
Divine Names.......415
Divine Order.......142
Divine Reality.......223
Divine Secrets.......75, 204, 351, 392
Divine Truth.......702
Divine Unity.......239
doctor.......ix, 35, 39, 251, 296, 395, 419, 472, 609
dog.......113, 300, 527
donkey.......84, 565, 595
dunya.......581
dying.......59, 60, 61, 169, 401, 639, 761

E

earth.......46
egg.......55, 453
ego.......522, 590
Egyptian.......141, 142
elect.......49
electricity.......581
Elijah, Prophet.......148, 149
emanation.......See tajalli
Emigration.......80
Encyclopedia of the Age.......226
engraving.......27, 57, 174, 407
Eskici Ali Usta.......385, 387
Essence.......520
ethics.......107, 286
excavation.......101
excellence.......29, 33, 49, 73, 416, 623, 625, 627, 639, 672
exegesis.......27, 111, 146, 429
external knowledge.......28
eye surgery.......418
eyes.......46, 53, 54, 56, 60, 74, 82, 83, 108, 127, 131, 152, 156, 159, 217, 228, 240, 244, 250, 263, 271, 275, 278, 287, 289, 290, 295, 296, 318, 319, 322, 328, 329, 332, 334, 338, 339, 349, 351, 361, 376, 382, 383, 391, 402, 407, 419, 431, 432, 443, 446, 466, 603, 614, 621, 640, 654, 663, 666, 674, 679, 683, 717, 735, 759

F

face.......131
Fadl.......88
Fakhr ad-Din al-Razi.......51, 649, 666, 705
falsehood.......vii, 44, 218, 332, 359, 468
Family of the Prophet.......ii
fana.......570
fana fi-sh-shaykh.......533, 594
faqih.......124, 648
Fath ibn Abi al-Fath.......604
Fatimah bint al-Husayn ibn Ali ibn Abi Talib.......691
Fatimah bint Muhammad.......xvii, xviii, 692

fayd.......513, 545, 558, 563, 567, 593
fearsome.......700
feet.......152
fiqh.......487
Fire.......699
Firm Handhold.......206
firmness and constancy.......235
First to be created.......69
focus of attention.......125
follower.......33
foot.......78, 79, 85, 189, 218, 234, 276, 286, 322, 341, 353, 371, 433, 434, 447, 621, 651, 720
forbidden.......34, 455, 519, 523, 528, 666, 680, 692
foreordained things.......412
forgetfulness.......45
Forgiver, the.......48
fragrance.......520
French.......54
friends of God.......118, 137, 651
frog.......708
fruit.......54
Fudayl ibn al-Iyad.......312, 605, 652
funeral prayer.......123, 200, 271, 319, 390, 420, 805

G

Gabriel.......xviii, xix, 46, 52, 71, 73, 74, 75, 88, 137, 141, 199, 529, 671, 711, 718, 720
galaxy.......589
garden.......159
gardens of paradise.......43
gaze.......153
generosity.......569
Ghazali, Imam.......49, 129, 130, 131, 366, 604, 623, 640, 644, 649, 674, 683, 684, 703, 707
Ghazi Muhammad.......327, 342, 343, 344
gland.......580
glorification.......42
Gnostic.......41
God-consciousness.......36, 96, 456
God's Greatest Name.......416
godwariness.......644
gold.......44, 100, 640, 650, 658, 663
Golden Chain.......vii, xiv, xvii, 38, 57, 59, 69, 74, 77, 79, 80, 90, 110, 115, 124, 128, 131, 139, 146, 147, 158, 161, 177, 184, 185, 189, 190, 215, 223, 229, 232, 245, 255, 262, 274, 283, 288, 296, 298, 306, 311, 319, 329, 336, 343, 345, 357, 364, 390, 410, 423, 426, 463, 468, 511, 514, 610, 654
good conduct.......32, 39, 40, 41, 237, 286, 460, 466, See adab
Good conduct.......200
Gothic.......547
graves.......84, 124, 220, 318, 459
gravity.......578
Greek.......548
Greeks.......371, 548
gunfire.......411
gunpowder.......340
Gurdjieff.......403, 404

H

Habib al-Haddad.......675, 684
Hafiz ad-Din.......164
Hakim ibn al-Abbas al-Kalbi.......113
Halima.......409
Halima as-Saadiyya.......71
Hallaj.......35, 169, 205, 206, 239, 271
Hamiduddin ash-Shashi.......235
Hamza Bek ibn Ali al-Hutsali.......343
Hanafiya.......100
Hand of God.......36, 201
haqiqah.......571
haqiqat al-fayd.......590, 598
haqiqat al-irshad.......591
haqiqat al-jazbah.......590
haqiqat al-tai.......591, 598
haqiqat al-tawassul.......591
haqiqat at-tawajjuh.......591, 592
Haqqaniyya.......57
Harmala ibn Zayd al-Ansari.......616
Hasan Abu Saeed.......96
Hasan al-Basri.......200, 311, 312, 604, 608, 643, 644, 652, 692, 708
Hasan ibn Ali ibn Abi Talib.......732
Hasan Muhammad Effendi.......372
Hasan Simnani.......134
He who is erratic will be erratic in the hellfire.......732
Healing.......577
heart.......561
heart's connection.......242
heavenly.......399
heavenly knowledge.......26, 94, 130, 134, 146, 174, 184, 202, 206, 221, 247, 262, 269, 312, 322, 337, 351, 360
heavens.......46
heedlessness.......42, 45

hell…....28, 96, 118, 206, 383, 401, 668
hellfire…....43
helpers…....76
Helpers…....37, 78, 343
heretic…....324
hermit…....126
hijab…....538
Hilal al-Haffar…....691
himmah…....593
Hinduism…....v
Hindus…....468, 496
Holy Names…....717
Holy Spirit…....73, 88
homeopathic…....348
horse…....83, 84, 190, 193, 210, 211, 243, 276, 277, 308, 334, 371, 565
horseman…....192
hosh dar dam…....151
human being…....xix, 31, 44, 46, 48, 53, 55, 61, 70, 73, 77, 88, 141, 148, 152, 170, 177, 186, 220, 237, 269, 304, 324, 339, 351, 385, 392, 401, 440, 441, 445, 452, 459, 627, 655, 657, 669, 677, 702, 710, 717
humiliation…....445
humility…....41, 150, 559
hungry…....329
Husayn Ali…....410
Husayn ibn Ali ibn Abi Talib…....692
Huwa…....238
hypocrites…....84, 240, 324, 616, 628

I

I left three things with my Community…....730
Ibn Abd al-Barr…....661
Ibn Abi Asim…....680
Ibn Abi Atiq…....85
Ibn Abi Hatim…....91
Ibn Abidin…....645, 656
Ibn Abu Hatim al-Razi…....647
Ibn Abu Jamra al-Azdi al-Andalusi…....640
Ibn Ali ibn Qudama…....653
ibn Ali, Hafiz…....35
Ibn al-Jawzi…....645
Ibn al-Mubarak…....680
Ibn al-Salah…....703
Ibn Arabi…....679
Ibn as-Saqa…....134, 135, 136
Ibn Ata Allah…....105, 145, 604
Ibn Hajar al-Asqalani…....53, 308, 615, 665, 676
Ibn Hajar al-Haythami…....39, 40, 50, 134, 308
Ibn Ishaq…....100, 682
Ibn Khaldun…....655
Ibn Majah…....44
Ibn Qayyim al-Jawziyya…....44, 45, 49, 50, 611, 620, 639, 645, 653, 669, 670
Ibn Qutayba…....679
Ibn Rajab al-Hanbali…....653, 697
Ibn Saad…....691
Ibn Sireen…....200
Ibn Taymiyya…....119, 121, 611, 644, 649, 650, 651, 653, 671, 681
Ibrahim ash-Shashi…....233
Ibrahim ibn Ali ibn Yusuf al-Firuzabadi…....134
Ibrahim Khawwas…....121
identification…....695
Ignaz Goldziher…....693
Ihsan Ibrahim Pasha…....308
Ikrima…....692
illness…....324
Ilm as-suluk…....652
immigrants…....500, 503
incarnation…....258, 268, 448
Indo-Pakistan…....540
industrialists…....457
initiation…....34, 82, 528, 571, 577
ink…....86, 242, 688
innovation…....xi, 25, 28, 51, 118, 123, 150, 191, 276, 286, 465, 655, 664, 690
insan al-kamil…....175
intellect…....590
intention…....32, 41, 123, 135, 164, 180, 200, 202, 220, 243, 248, 317, 366, 369, 629, 638, 639, 657, 683, 718, 720, 725, 727, 807, 809
intercede…....708
intercession…....61, 71, 95, 96, 112, 122, 160, 180, 204, 267, 271, 303, 383, 385, 401, 440, 608, 615, 699
internal knowledge…....28
Internet…....485, 490
intimacy…....26, 72, 594, 684, 702
intoxicant…....703
irshad…....483
Islamic Law…....27, 118, 308, 470
Islamic sciences…....28
Ismail al-Kashi…....310
Ismail al-Madani…....301
Ismail ash-Shirwani…....57, 318, 319, 321, 322, 323, 324, 325, 329, 332, 335, 336, 342, 343, 345
isolation…....50, 112, 439, 679
Israfil…....71, 137
Izrail…....352
Izza bint Khayyil…....37

J

Jabir.......685, 686
Jabir ibn Hayyan.......27
Jacob.......219
jadhba.......316, 517
Jafar as-Sadiq.......26, 27, 58, 110, 112, 113, 115, 229, 311, 644
Jafar ibn Muhammad,.......454
Jalaluddin as-Suyuti.......26, 46, 47, 267, 308, 513, 617, 623, 638, 640, 655, 692, 805
Jalaluddin Rumi.......xvii, 58, 89, 133, 139, 159, 179, 257, 281, 359, 365, 425, 427, 443, 452, 557, 658
Jamaluddin al-Ghumuqi al-Husayni.......326, 329, 330, 342, 345, 347, 348, 349, 354, 356, 361, 379
Jamaluddin al-Lasuni.......428
Japan.......464
Jesus.......21, 51, 58, 95, 101, 140, 233, 354, 404, 406, 422, 423, 566
jewel.......xii, 279, 583
Jews.......459, 468
jinn.......79, 287
John G. Bennett.......416, 421, 452
John, Prophet.......566
Jonah, Prophet.......660, 709
Joseph, Prophet.......219
Judaism.......v
Judgment Day.......xix, 46, 106, 109, 117, 137, 149, 170, 180, 294, 383, 385, 440, 441, 660
Jumada al-Akhir.......97
Junayd al-Baghdadi.......34, 49, 199, 296, 311, 445, 604, 620, 621, 622, 639, 647, 652, 680, 708
jurisprudence.......ix, 28, 32, 85, 106, 111, 130, 134, 146, 150, 151, 168, 174, 308, 322, 338, 348, 376, 393, 428, 429, 575, 605, 639, 645, 654
jurisprudent.......124, 134
Juwayriyya bint al-Harith.......688

K

Kabah.......72, 81, 99, 105, 109, 136, 174, 271, 275, 278, 291, 309, 313, 355, 426, 431, 444, 650
Kabir al-Awliya.......190
Karaja Ahmad.......357
Khabab.......633
Khadija.......72, 74, 109
khafa.......406, 586, 587
Khalid al-Baghdadi.......57, 306, 307, 308, 312, 323, 325, 329, 456, 463
Khalid ibn Walid.......409, 640
Khalidiyya.......57, 323
khalifah.......485, 492, 585
Khalil Ghirani.......194
khalwah.......154
khalwat dar anjuman.......154, 541
Khalwati.......366, 378
Khan, Nuzrat Fatih Ali.......482
Khas Muhammad ash-Shirwani.......329, 330, 331, 332, 334, 335
khatm.......509
Khatm al-Khwajagan.......80, 389, 465
Khattabi.......680
Khawarij.......696
Khidr.......21, 58, 124, 130, 137, 139, 140, 141, 142, 143, 146, 147, 148, 149, 164, 229, 234, 255, 269, 298, 369, 619, 620
Khubayb ibn Abd al-Rahman.......680
Khwaja Khurd.......261
Khwaja Mahmud.......161, 163, 164
Khwajagan.......iv, 145, 164, 184
Khwajaganiyya.......57
king.......74, 84, 85, 101, 136, 146, 170, 194, 208, 210, 214, 232, 243, 272, 296, 301, 302, 409
King Faruq.......409
King Khata.......244
King of Kings.......70, 122, 279, 310
knees.......61, 237, 302, 379, 625, 708, 726
knots.......691
knowers.......703
knowledge of certainty.......333, 405, 408
Kubrawi.......298
Kuthum Shaykh.......194

L

la ilaha ill-Allah.......46, 47, 49, 70, 95, 147, 155, 156, 169, 190, 196, 221, 238, 254, 277, 377, 378, 407, 413, 418, 436
laser.......581
Last Days.......xiv
lataif.......405, 509
laugh.......150
Law-giver.......705
lawyer.......ix, 472, 609
Laylat al-Qadr.......186
Laylat al-Raghaib.......147
Layth ibn Saad.......27, 113
leather socks.......85

legal decisions…...27, 29, 111, 168, 226, 276
Leslie Blanch…...342, 354
letter…...599
letters…...28, 48, 152, 200, 301, 656, 677
Levis…...482
light…...232, 449, 577, 599, 706
Light of God…...49, 72, 118, 198, 200, 452, 577
Light of Lights…...i, 100
Light of Muhammad…...143
Light of Prophecy…...i
Light of the Unique Essence…...158
lineage…...512
lion…...113
literalist…...134
Living One…...233
living organism…...557
loud dhikr…...28
love…...vii, viii, x, xii, xiii, xvii, xix, 36, 39, 47, 52, 55, 75, 76, 79, 85, 86, 99, 112, 117, 118, 121, 122, 125, 127, 129, 131, 136, 150, 156, 164, 187, 189, 190, 194, 197, 199, 200, 201, 205, 206, 221, 222, 226, 227, 228, 236, 238, 239, 241, 249, 250, 251, 255, 273, 275, 278, 282, 294, 295, 318, 337, 338, 339, 379, 380, 383, 385, 391, 420, 423, 425, 432, 443, 445, 459, 468, 471, 572, 574, 610, 616, 617, 620, 621, 651, 656, 657, 661, 672, 674, 676, 684, 685, 692, 697, 698, 699, 700, 706, 708, 855
Love of God…...27
lower world…...150

M

Mabad ibn Hilal al-Anzi…...95
madhahib…...487
madhhab…...492
Madiha…...409, 410, 421
Madinah…...105
Mahdi…...79, 271, 318, 389, 404, 422, 423, 455
mahfuz…...706
Mahmud…...229
Mahmud Khan…...313
Mahmud Said…...693
Maimuna…...87
majesty…...198, 702
Makkah…...604
Malik bin Sinan al-Ansari…...149
Malik, Imam…...107, 113, 146, 604, 645
manners…...107
Mansur…...113
Mansur al-Hallaj…...217
Mao Tse-tung…...611
maqam at-talwin…...222
Marshall McLuhan…...543
martyrs…...xi, 401, 651, 708
Maruf al-Karkhi…...645, 652
Mary…...21, 51, 101, 719
Masjid al-Umari al-Kabir…...435
Masruq…...608
master…...32
Master of Masters…...70
Master of Messengers…...70
Masud al-Bukhari…...29
materialism…...55, 434
materialist…...446
mathematician…...348, 630
Mawlana Qasim…...251
mawlid…...539, 540
Maysara…...72
meat…...86, 327, 365, 372, 418
medicine…...ix, xv, 233, 324, 419, 578, 609, 683, 703
meditating…...56, 190, 232, 361, 428, 726
meditation…...51, 52, 72, 83, 190, 221, 235, 236, 286, 395, 429, 660
Mediterranean Sea…...450
men…...42
mercy…...137, 196, 459, 700
mercy oceans…...560
Mevlevi…...428
Michaela Ozelsel…...508
microscope…...viii
Miftah al-janna…...668
minbar…...85, 90, 267, 354
mines…...371
Miqdad ibn al-Aswad…...379, 380, 394
Mir Akbar Ali…...306
Mir Husamuddin…...267
miracles…...xiv, 85, 86, 148, 184, 209, 255, 279, 349, 360, 367, 389, 409, 426, 612, 621, 652
miraculous powers…...27, 72, 111, 114, 155, 174, 184, 198, 248, 290, 361, 378, 435
miraj…...521
mirror…...i, 44, 72, 123, 152, 154, 199, 223, 276, 291, 300, 326, 590
Mirza Aleg Beg…...213
Mirza Babar…...243
Mirza Rahim Allah Beg al-Maruf…...310
Monday…...71, 81, 88, 97, 170, 181, 214, 332
money…...34, 150

monotheism.......xi, 32, 70, 75
moon.......72, 74, 84, 85, 89, 126, 137, 189, 218, 257, 258, 286, 298, 308
moral goodness.......40
Moses, Prophet.......50, 73, 78, 95, 139, 140, 141, 142, 164, 185, 186, 265, 296, 354, 393, 399, 406, 566, 619, 620, 703, 710
mosque.......x, xviii, 29, 59, 62, 74, 81, 90, 137, 151, 165, 176, 190, 192, 193, 195, 215, 227, 228, 239, 244, 254, 272, 302, 305, 306, 311, 313, 319, 325, 327, 335, 339, 342, 343, 353, 371, 389, 394, 397, 402, 409, 410, 418, 420, 427, 428, 429, 433, 435, 436, 438, 457, 462, 467, 693, 695
moss.......341
most hidden.......405, 406, 432, 721
Most Majestic Name.......380
mother.......xi, 27, 51, 55, 56, 60, 71, 91, 106, 112, 142, 146, 147, 148, 149, 180, 186, 232, 233, 274, 298, 310, 327, 369, 377, 393, 397, 398, 400, 403, 411, 427, 608, 630, 662, 671
Mother of the Book.......412, 449
mountain.......72, 73, 109, 160, 222, 234, 325, 326, 384, 398, 399, 435, 614, 669, 678, 701
Muadh.......92
Muadh ibn Jabal.......44, 701
Muawiya.......37, 670
mufti.......429
Muhammad Abid.......291, 292
Muhammad ad-Darwish Abd al-Azim al-Abadi.......310
Muhammad Afdal.......291, 292
Muhammad Ahmad al-Mahi al-Bukhari.......453
Muhammad Alamagir.......282
Muhammad al-Baqi Billah.......261, 263, 266
Muhammad al-Baqir.......112, 115
Muhammad Ali Sanusi.......610
Muhammad Ali Uyun as-Sud.......429
Muhammad al-Kuzbari.......309
Muhammad al-Qasim as-Sanandaji.......309
Muhammad al-Yaraghi.......341
Muhammad as-Siddiq.......276
Muhammad as-Sirbili.......232
Muhammad at-Tawil.......370
Muhammad az-Zahid.......245, 247, 248, 254, 255
Muhammad az-Zubayr.......291
Muhammad Baba as-Samasi.......28, 171, 173, 174, 177, 180, 184, 187, 188, 190, 194, 229
Muhammad Effendi al-Yaraghi.......326, 329, 330, 336, 337, 338, 340, 341, 342, 343, 344, 345, 349, 366
Muhammad Hafiz Muhsin.......293
Muhammad Hisham Kabbani.......xiv, xv, 485, 487, 488, 513, 525, 535, 536, 537, 538, 539, 540, 542, 546, 570, 573, 576, 577, 579, 580, 581, 582, 583, 585, 586, 587, 588, 590, 592, 598
Muhammad ibn Abd al-Wahhab.......655, 656
Muhammad ibn Abidin.......696
Muhammad ibn al-Hanafiyya.......92
Muhammad Khwaja al-Amkanaki.......256, 257, 258, 259, 262, 267
Muhammad Mansur Numani.......655
Muhammad Masum.......274, 275, 276, 277, 279, 282, 287, 291
Muhammad Nazim Adil al-Haqqani.......2, 9, vii, xv, xix, 58, 75, 410, 414, 420, 421, 423, 425, 426, 433, 434, 449, 453, 455, 456, 458, 462, 463, 464, 465, 466, 467, 468, 469, 470, 471, 472, 477, 480, 482, 483, 484, 485, 489, 491, 492, 494, 500, 507, 508, 511, 512, 516, 517, 519, 520, 529, 531, 532, 535, 536, 547, 548, 549, 550, 552, 553, 554, 555, 556, 558, 560, 562, 564, 567, 568, 569, 570, 582, 586, 594, 598
Muhammad Parsa.......29, 150, 213, 214, 215, 219
Muhammad Sayfuddin.......281
Muhammad Yahya.......244
Muhammad Zahid.......210, 212

Muhammad Zubayr…....299
Muhammadun Rasul Allah…....70, 85, 147, 156, 184, 189, 196, 407
Muharram…....110, 348
Muhyi al-Din ibn Abi al-Wafa…....557
Muhyiddin ibn Arabi…....38, 99, 237, 271, 443, 604
Muhyiddin ibn Arabi Mosque…....420, 451
Mujaddidiyya…....57
mujahadah…....408
Mujahid…....673
Mukhtar Alayli…....435
Mulay al-Arabi ad-Darqawi…....45, 285
Mulla Ali al-Qari…....640
Mullah Abdur-Razzaq…....295
Mullah Muhammad Salih…....308
Mullah Nazim…....295
multiculturalism…....497
Munawi…....49
Munir al-Malek…....430, 432
muraqabah…....532, 617, 672, See meditation, See watchfulness
murder…....141
murid…....38, 538, 546, 556, 562, 569, 576, 579, 582, 584, 589, 597
Murid Wars…....326
murshid…....185
Musa al-Kazim…....311
mushaf…....94
mushahada…....706
music…....516
musk…....83, 420
Muslim, Imam…....35, 36, 49, 50, 226, 681, 687
Muslims…....vii, 459
Musnad…....25
Mustafa Alayli…....485
Mustafa al-Kurdi…....309
Mustafa Ceric…....459
Mustaliq…....81
Mutamar ibn Sulayman…....691
mutassawif…....623
Mutazila…....612
Muwaffaq ad-Din ibn Qadama…....653

N

Nafi…....113
Nahw…....609
Najmuddin al-Kubra…....151, 311
Names…....239
Names and Attributes…....i, 190, 456, 623
naqib al-ummah…....421
naqsh…....27, 57
Naqshband, Shah Bahauddin…....See Shah Bahauddin Naqshband
Nasai…....687
Nasir ad-Din al-Qadiri…....298
Nasir Chishti…....312
navel…....60, 82, 156, 351
Nawawi…....42, 47, 52, 628, 638, 649, 660, 676, 677, 679, 681, 682, 683, 684, 709
Naziha Muhammad Nazim Adil…....xiv, xvii, 485
needy…....418
negative attention…....558
New Age…....468
New Testament…....566
Night Journey…....78, 93, 395, 662, 686, 718
Night of Ascension…....52, 395
Night of Power…....186, 234
Nile…....142
Nimatullah…....248
nine points…....578
Nine Points…....58, 290, 404, 406, 407, 412
nine saints…....404, 412, 413
Nisai…....37
Nizamuddin al-Khamush…....232, 234
Noah, Prophet…....140, 405
Noble Sanctuaries…....696
Nor is there anything fresh or dry but it is inscribed in a clear Record. (6:59)…....413
notebook…....732
Nothingness…....232
nun…....114
Nur Muhammad al-Badawani…....283, 285, 286, 287, 290, 292
Nuridin ash-Shahid…....136

O

obligations…....40
obligatory…....34
ocean…....ii, 72, 117, 118, 119, 120, 127, 150, 159, 184, 196, 207, 262, 270, 291, 298, 311, 334, 348, 376, 388, 389, 392, 396, 405, 426, 448, 600, 718, 719
ocean of light…....196
Old Testament…....566
One hour's contemplation…....73 1
Oneness…....223, 702
Oneness of Existence…....451
Oneness of God…....xi, 27, 29, 32, 118, 156, 158, 190, 237, 382, 427

Opening Chapter.......See Fatiha
orientalist.......54
Origin of Origins.......i
Orkallisa Muhammad.......353, 354
orphan.......83, 487
Ottoman.......489
Ottoman Army.......400
Ottomans.......38, 460
oxen.......565
Oxford.......482
oxidation.......44

P

paper.......242
paradise.......28, 43, 47, 97, 114, 118, 120, 123, 205, 206, 215, 372, 383
passage through time and space.......268
patience.......xiii, 84, 96, 255, 296, 457, 620, 627
peace.......i, ii, viii, xiii, xv, 21, 41, 42, 52, 53, 76, 97, 153, 199, 244, 282, 334, 380, 404, 423, 426, 428, 437, 458, 469, 470, 471, 632, 657, 675, 707, 710, 741, 754, 768, 769, 773, 774, 855
pearl.......9, ii, 89
pen.......70, 86, 242, 248, 360, 362, 443
Pen.......i, 70, 73, 74
People of Determination.......72 2, 807
People of the Bench.......603, 614, 632, See Ahl as-Suffa
Perfect Human.......415
perfect human being.......69, 70, 269
perfect knower.......145, 276
perfect knowledge.......36, 223
perfection.......ii, 25, 33, 34, 41, 72, 75, 153, 155, 158, 160, 207, 210, 219, 222, 229, 237, 247, 273, 287, 290, 291, 292, 297, 303, 325, 337, 354, 361, 379, 381, 382, 446, 452, 604, 607, 612, 613, 618, 632, 657, 665, 719
perfume.......85
Persian.......101
Pharaoh.......710
PhD.......507
philosopher.......54, 249, 332, 448
Phrase of Oneness.......713
physician.......452
physiognomy.......453
pilgrimage.......29, 82, 107, 109, 113, 174, 214, 278, 309, 313, 336, 355, 425, 443, 625, 650, 663
pill.......576
pious people.......119, 134, 148, 220, 350, 614
Pir Mikail Chis Anchit.......308
Pledge of Loyalty.......82
poem.......310, 311, 426, 612
poets.......74, 94
poison.......86, 189, 449, 703
policymakers.......457
polish.......45
politics.......423
poor towards God.......142
poor-due.......29, 32, 94, 114, 302
porch.......x
post-Eternity.......ii
poverty.......699
power.......137, 220
praising.......42
praising God.......41, 42
prayer.......552
pre-eternity.......521
pre-Eternity.......ii, 70, 77, 114, 629
Presence of God.......39, 41
Presence of Intimacy.......137
Preserved Tablets.......392, 394, 412
princess.......146
prisoner.......362
prohibited.......273, 300, 663
Prophetic Presence.......31
Prophetic Station.......27, 112
prostration.......393
Psalms.......54
psychoanalyst.......577
public treasury.......94
pulse.......419
purify.......viii, x, 32, 61, 76, 77, 152, 175, 385, 446, 603, 607, 610, 612, 617, 623, 638, 656, 675, 705, 807, 809

Q

Qadi Iyad.......710
Qadiri.......266, 267, 269, 274, 292, 298, 299, 309, 311, 366, 378, 427, 428, 437, 438, 439, 467, 592, 610
Qadiriyah wa Naqshbandiya.......46 4
Qalam.......114
qalb.......405, 586
Qasim al-Jui.......647
Qasim at-Tabrizi.......235
Qasim bin Muhammad bin Abu Bakr as-Siddiq.......108, 109

Qasim ibn Muhammad ibn Abu Bakr.......112
Qasim ibn Muhammad ibn Abu Bakr as-Siddiq.......104, 105, 106, 229
Qastallani.......53
qiblah.......190, 191, 196, 258, 593
Quran.......509, 540, 581
Quranic Conference in Russia.......467
Quraysh.......633
Qurtubi.......663
Qushayri.......35, 130, 301, 447, 604, 648, 680
Qutada.......85
Qutb ad-Din.......208, 236
Quthum ibn al-Abbas.......88
Quthum ibn al-Abbas.......468

R

Rabi al-Awwal.......71, 81, 88, 137, 158, 165, 214, 244, 251, 279, 363, 373, 393
Rabia.......409, 410
Rabia al-Adawiyya.......109, 205, 393
rabitah.......242, 509, 530, 594, 598
Rafiq Tarar.......465
rainbow.......ii, 376, 583
raisins.......191
Raja Ashman Shah.......462
Rajab.......360, 434, 442
Ramadan.......53, 81, 106, 107, 112, 186, 209, 232, 272, 276, 317, 336, 372, 419, 420, 434, 442, 472, 625
rank.......26, 355, 403, 405, 410, 614, 640, 662, 663, 669, 684, 698, 727, 731, 855
Rawdat an-Nabi.......309
Realities.......120
Reality.......i, vii, 29, 45, 54, 76, 112, 121, 131, 137, 156, 158, 176, 180, 184, 189, 209, 219, 258, 262, 269, 276, 303, 313, 322, 333, 360, 405, 637, 719
reality of attraction.......353, 592
reality of certainty.......333, 408
reality of directing the heart's power to someone.......353
reality of guidance.......353
reality of intercession.......353
Reality of Muhammad.......406
Reality of Realities.......i
Reality of the Prophet.......176
recitation.......50, 80, 94, 156, 308, 382, 383, 394, 404, 429, 431, 663, 665, 666, 708, 718, 737, 806
reckoning.......198, 766, 809
recollection.......157, 614
red.......84, 278, 298, 324, 349, 391, 404, 406, 431, 432
Red Sulphur.......9, 455
reference.......27, 91, 120, 130, 134, 135, 168, 291, 338, 348, 614, 639, 670, 684
reference system.......545, 580
refugees.......487
relationship.......545
religious leader.......133
religious scholar.......133, 241
remembrance.......47, 48
remembrance of God.......xii, xiii, 28, 42, 50, 86, 126, 154, 208, 221, 237, 646, 650, 659, 717
renewer.......88, 180, 456
repentance.......44, 164, 168, 193, 247, 294, 354, 617, 657, 770
research.......568
respect.......40
retreat.......27, 55, 244, 277, 283, 464
revelation.......142
reverence.......52, 175, 204, 282, 452, 627, 676
reviver of religion.......184, 391
Rifai.......366, 378, 592
Risala Qudsiyya.......29, 215
robe.......60, 61, 73, 84, 113, 121, 179, 277, 278, 279, 338, 468
ruh.......586
rulings.......107
running.......44
Russian.......341, 362
Russian Army.......397
Russian Empire.......423

S

Saad ad-din al-Kashgari.......250
Saad ad-Din Jibawi.......410
Saad ibn Abi Waqqas.......101, 689, 690, 691, 692
Sadr-i Jahan.......557
Safar.......87, 230, 274, 306, 400
safar dar watan.......153
Safiyya bint Huyayy.......690, 691
Sahl at-Tustari.......124, 143
Said as-Suba'i.......429

Said ibn Jubayr.......663
Said Nursi.......387, 388
Said Pasha.......312
sainthood.......52, 148, 174, 186, 232, 268, 270, 293, 361, 648, 732
sajda.......520
Salafi.......480, 488
Salahuddin Aisha.......352
Salim ibn Abd Allah ibn Umar.......106
Salma bint Qays.......37
Salman al-Farsi.......26, 27, 97, 99, 100, 102, 103, 109, 229, 343
salutations.......42
Samura ibn Jundub.......686
Sanai.......658
sanctified.......33
sandalwood.......420
Sanusiyya.......610
Satan.......33, 122, 146, 208, 384, 441, 445, 450, 454, 586, 644, 672, 687, 703, 719, 765
satellite.......589
Sayfuddin al-Faruqi al-Mujaddidi.......279
Sayyid al-Amir Burhanuddin.......181
Sayyid al-Amir Hamza.......181
Sayyid al-Amir Shah.......181
Sayyid al-Amir Umar.......181
Sayyid al-Kharraz.......155
Sayyid Amir Kulal.......177, 179, 180, 181, 184, 188, 189, 190, 191, 192, 193, 229
scholar.......ix, xv, 27, 32, 38, 54, 56, 87, 108, 130, 134, 158, 169, 174, 185, 229, 233, 241, 274, 276, 298, 308, 309, 310, 338, 340, 348, 376, 463, 604, 605, 609, 656, 692, 693
Seal of Prophets.......70, 88, 658
seas.......86, 173
seashore.......569
seaside.......569
seclusion.......50, 51, 52, 53, 54, 55, 56, 59, 62, 72, 121, 150, 154, 155, 181, 188, 194, 220, 222, 232, 237, 308, 309, 325, 340, 361, 378, 379, 384, 398, 399, 400, 405, 410, 418, 436, 438, 439, 440, 441, 453, 679, 680, 731
secret.......88, 231
secret knowledge.......74, 251, 349, 350
Secret of All Secrets.......70
secret of the secret.......405, 406, 432, 721
seed.......41, 54, 55, 56, 96, 335, 713
seeker.......xii, xx, 32, 33, 35, 38, 39, 40, 47, 48, 49, 50, 119, 152, 153, 154, 155, 156, 157, 158, 169, 198, 199, 200, 202, 205, 220, 221, 222, 227, 232, 238, 239, 240, 241, 258, 262, 268, 273, 291, 295, 310, 316, 326, 332, 333, 338, 348, 383, 416, 426, 435, 446, 452, 458, 486, 507, 522, 525, 530, 573, 575, 577, 581, 584, 587, 622, 645, 649, 656, 702, 718, 719, 722, 724, 725, 733, 855, See murid
Seeker.......153
self-denial.......27, 29, 118, 121, 133, 181, 310, 650
self-effacement.......25, 33, 223, 229, 239, 249, 263, 286, 291, 303, 322, 351, 384, 428, 638
self-struggle.......130
Seljuks.......38
Selly Oaks Institute.......511
Serbians.......371
Shaban.......427, 434, 442
Shadhili.......366, 378, 610, 617
Shafii, Imam.......130, 134, 272, 308, 332, 375, 604, 638, 646, 704
Shah Abd ar-Rahim.......292
Shah Bahauddin Naqshband.......26, 28, 29, 57, 58, 150, 151, 153, 155, 181, 183, 184, 185, 186, 187, 188, 193, 197, 198, 199, 200, 201, 202, 203, 204, 205, 206, 207, 208, 209, 210, 211, 212, 213, 214, 215, 218, 219, 222, 223, 226, 229, 234, 235, 236, 242, 269, 270, 296, 299, 301, 303, 304, 305, 329, 383, 384, 385, 410, 413, 437, 446, 456, 468, 509, 594, 677
Shah Kalshan.......291
Shah Sakandar.......311
Shah Shawus.......338, 340
Shah Wali Allah.......v, 291
Shahr ibn Hawshab.......671
Shakran.......88
Shamil.......327, 342, 349, 362
Shams al-Halwani.......164
Shamsuddin al-Ambikuti.......191
Shamsuddin Habib Allah Jan-i-Janan al-Mazhar.......v, 288, 289, 290, 291, 292, 293,

294, 295, 296, 299, 304, 306
Sharafuddin ad-Daghestani…....58, 59, 107, 147, 184, 185, 356, 364, 371, 372, 373, 375, 376, 377, 379, 383, 384, 386, 387, 388, 389, 392, 393, 396, 413
Shariah…....iv, 315, 342, 497, 509, 517, 518, 519, 547, 554, 571, 575, 597, 607, 611, 624, 637, 638, 659
Sharif Abd Allah…....410
Sharif al-Jarjani…....29
Sharp Corporation…....464
Shawkani…....691
Shawwal…....317, 356
Shaykh al-Bakharazi…....228
shaykh at-tarbiyyah…....453
Shaykh Kallan…....250
Shaykh Mazdakhin…....190
Shaykh Sadruddin…....146
Shaykhs of the Two Wings…....58
Sheba…....704
sheep…....377
shepherd…....377
Shihabuddin ash-Shirwani…....226, 229
ship…....341, 370
shirk…....447
Shohibul Wafa Tadjul Arifin…....464
shoulders…....82, 149, 278
Sign of Oneness…....70
signs…....ii, 72, 100, 174, 233, 337, 371, 445, 617, 623, 626, 657, 659, 673
Sikhs…....468, 496
silent dhikr…....28
silsila…....513, 514
silver…....44, 640
sinners…....703
sins…....688, 707
Sirajuddin al-Birmisi…....234
sirr…....405, 568, 586, 587
sirr as-sirr…....406, 568
snake…....78, 79, 122, 379, 400, 650, 711
snow…....400
Sorbonne…....479
sore…....710
sounds…....48
spark…....101
special one…....365
spirit…....x, 35, 41, 47, 59, 95, 123, 137, 175, 185, 193, 200, 231, 257, 269, 300, 338, 361, 382, 384, 392, 638, 657, 666, 674
spiritual connection…....57, 58, 62, 291, 379
spiritual pole…....215, 234, 262, 266, 267, 269, 276, 291, 298, 310, 328, 348
spiritual practices…....x, xiii, 721, 730, 731
spiritual presence…....57, 120, 184, 185, 272, 329
spiritual vision…....72, 93, 131, 218, 274, 433
sponge…....614
stars…....26, 27, 61, 72, 77, 89, 177, 189, 227, 298, 392, 456
State Department…....488
state of erasure…....223, 258
states…....34
station of purity…....28
station of truthfulness…....38
storm…....399
Straight Path…....ix, xiv, 106, 291, 720
struggle…....xi, xiii, 25, 114, 134, 146, 199, 222, 235, 303, 311, 323, 341, 343, 611, 623, 639, 640, 648
student…....ix, xi, 27, 57, 134, 168, 173, 282, 349, 354, 428, 452, 463, 604, 609, 643, 653, 661, 671
sublimity…....702
subsistence…....127, 137, 239, 268, 273, 275, 279, 295, 361, 396
Successors…....vii, viii, 38, 106
Successors of the Successors…....38
suf…....614
suffat al-kaffa…....614
Sufi…....126
Sufyan al-Thawri…....113, 114, 302, 604, 605, 608, 645, 654
Sufyan bin Ayinah…....113
Sufyan ibn Uyayna…....646
Suhayb…....633, 634
suhbah…....517, 529, 594
Suhrawardi…....266, 272, 274, 292, 298, 311
Sulaiman al-Teemi…....103, 104
Sulayman Arzurumi…....428
sultan…....278
Sultan Abul Hamid…....370
Sultan adh-Dhikr…....413, 414
Sultan Ahmad…....244
Sultan Ahmad Mosque…....428
Sultan al-Arifeen…....183
Sultan al-Awliya…....124, 388, 390, 392

Sultan Mahmud al-Ghazni.......127
sultan of saints.......184
Sumnun.......622
Sunnah.......300, 509
sunrise.......52
supplication.......35, 53, 101, 106, 119, 149, 187, 195, 283, 305, 306, 323, 327, 328, 343, 354, 360, 377, 380, 439, 806
surgery.......594
sweat.......60, 61, 83, 204, 207, 235, 286, 379
sweetness.......559
sweets.......35
sword.......84, 94, 361, 453, 616, 639, 663

T

Tabarani.......37, 47, 92
Taj al-Din ibn al-Subki.......704
tajalliyyat.......447, 572, 597
Tajuddin al-Kawlaki.......227
takbir.......46
tariqah.......ix, 32, 342, 436, 477, 479, 480, 481, 486, 489, 490, 491, 492, 494, 495, 504, 510, 519, 539, 566, 567, 570, 572, 582, 585, 586, 592, 598
Tariqah.......609
tasarruf.......593
tasawwur.......510, 530, See muraqabah
tasbih.......558
taste.......vii, xii, 33, 34, 49, 53, 122, 176, 190, 258, 282, 299, 303, 405, 407, 458, 627, 717
tawajjuh.......316, 510, 569, 570, 593, 598
Tawajjuh.......593
Tawfiq al-Hibri.......410
tawhid.......587
Tawhid adh-dhat.......444
Tawhid al-afal.......445
Tawhid as-siffat.......444
tayammun.......81
Teacher.......160
tear.......78
technology.......456
teeth.......82, 156, 311, 713
telescope.......589
terror.......423, 468
terrorist.......469
Thabit al-Bunnani.......95
Thahir Bin Abd al-Fatah.......463
Thanaullah an-Naqshbandi.......311
Thanaullah Panipati.......681
thankfulness.......xix, 45
The Muslim Magazine.......535
the poor.......x, 84, 93, 94, 107, 131, 141, 199, 207, 208, 209, 311, 313, 318, 324, 327, 341, 368, 466, 472, 617, 625, 630
theology.......590
theory.......494
thesis.......507
thirsty.......329
throat.......73, 271, 279, 394
throne.......190, 196
Throne.......137, 279, 699
Thuayba.......71
Timur.......468
Tirmidhi.......26, 37, 43, 44, 46, 277, 306, 631, 648, 667, 670, 678, 679, 685, 687, 701
tolerance.......viii, xiii, xv, 195, 467, 610
tomb.......59, 137, 190, 195, 278, 409, 410, 430, 438
Torah.......54, 99
torture.......74
Treaty of Hudaybiyya.......82, 93
tree.......41, 55, 85, 86, 160, 210, 213, 255, 271, 286, 371, 378, 399, 686, 701, 707, 710, 713
Trumpet.......137
trustworthy.......31, 33, 72, 77, 333, 654
truth.......27, 45
truthful.......27, 31, 32, 72, 77, 158, 160, 210, 240, 276, 616, 619, 622, 627, 628, 650, 702
Truthful Station.......112
tsar.......341
turban.......84, 85, 227, 242, 435, 583, 643
Turkish army.......397
Turks.......548
Tutty Alawiyya.......463
Twelve Imams.......312
tyranny.......423
tyrant.......455

U

Ubada ibn Samit.......36, 47
Ubayd Allah al-Ahrar.......33, 57, 58, 151, 203, 229, 230, 231, 232, 243, 248, 250, 262, 526, 570
Uhud.......94
Ulum al-Hadith.......86
Umar ibn Abd al-Aziz.......107
Umar ibn al-Khattab.......xix, 26, 32, 34, 37, 60, 91, 97, 102, 197, 420, 435, 680
Umayyads.......38
Umm al-Hasan bint Jafar.......691
Umm Hiram.......427
Umm Salama.......643
Ummat ad-dawah.......203

Ummat al-ijaba……204
Ummat al-mutabaa……204
unbelief……xi, 123, 312, 361, 656
unbelievers……74, 78, 81, 83, 84, 85, 91, 120, 301, 343, 696
Unique Oneness……137, 197, 347, 350, 381, 382, 649, 877
Unique Oneness of the Actions……445
Unique Oneness of the Attributes……444
Unique Oneness of the Essence……444
Uniqueness of God……190
United Nations……464
United Nations Millennium Peace Summit……470
United States……485
universe……200
unlawful……123, 249, 282, 731
unseen……i, xi, 53, 129, 131, 137, 167, 173, 174, 184, 191, 194, 197, 198, 200, 225, 232, 249, 254, 321, 324, 382, 392, 652
Unseen Essence……151
unveiling……137, 181, 188, 211, 267, 273, 360, 361, 381, 440, 652, 717, 718
Urwa……112
Urwa ibn Adhina……111
Uthman ibn Affan……32, 37, 85, 197, 308, 318, 420, 543
Uways al-Barawi……610
Uways al-Qarani……58, 59, 60, 61, 196, 329, 608
Uwaysi……26, 28, 57, 58, 62, 184, 515
Uyaina bin Hisn al-Fazari……634, 635

V

vain desires……648, 719
Vatican……457
veil……84, 152, 187, 191, 205, 223, 261, 274, 376, 522, 624, 705, 719
veil of humanity……719
verifiers……262
vision of certainty……333, 408
vision of the Divine Presence in the heart……50
visions……233, 304, 305, 399, 437
void……120, 173, 185, 223, 294

W

Wabisa……615
Wahb……113
wahdat al-shuhud……524
wahdat al-wujud……447, 451, 524
Wahhabi……465, 467, 540, 696
Wahhabism……480
waist……61, 84
wakefulness……42
walking……44
Waraqah ibn Nawfal……73
Watchfulness……316
water……596
Way of God……45
way of knowers……52
wayfaring……191
wealth……34
whale……660
white……44, 73, 82, 85, 140, 277, 332, 338, 349, 364, 376, 383, 406, 431, 432, 625, 643
whose……467
widow……83
wilayat……518, 524
will……419
willpower……596
winter……595
wisdom……xi, 50, 53, 86, 122, 141, 164, 174, 175, 244, 324, 376, 392, 394, 396, 443, 453, 455, 456, 459, 623, 656, 659, 705
witnessing……123, 137, 205, 268, 296, 333, 334, 348, 353, 407, 699
wolf……85
womb……55
wool……614
world……52
World Conference on Religion and Peace……470
world of souls……79, 855
worldliness……viii, 607, 608, 719
worldly desires……154
worldly life……622
worms……97, 372
Wujud Haqqani……451

Y

Y2K……550
yad dasht……157
yad kard……155
Yahya bin al-Muadh al-Razi……620, 622
Yahya ibn Sayyid……107
Yaqub al-Charkhi……202, 223, 225, 226, 227, 229, 230, 235
YaSin……214, 404
yatajalla……708
Yathrib……71
Year of the Elephant……71
yellow……278, 406, 431

Yusayra bint Yasir.......689
Yusuf al-Hamadani.......131, 133, 134, 146, 147, 229
Yusuf Ali.......620

Z

Zachariah, Prophet.......566
zahir.......579
Zain al-Abidin.......112, 115, 311
Zainab bint Sulayman ibn Ali.......691
Zainuddin al-Khawafi.......229
Zainuddin at-Tibabi.......241
Zakariyya al-Khandlawi.......692
zakat.......699
zawiya.......326
Zayd ibn Haritha.......640
Zayd ibn Thabit.......643
Zia ul-Haq.......465
zodiac.......89
Zoroastrian.......27, 100, 118
Zuhri.......113

Index of Numbers

1

1 veil.......719
1,000 knots.......692
10 times 'la ilaha ill-Allah'.......xviii
10 times salawat.......xviii
10,000 times 'la ilaha ill-Allah'.......155
100,000 dinars.......107
100,000 warriors.......243
114 cases against Shaykh Nazim.......433
114,000 Companions who narrated or heard hadith.......695
12 days of Prophet's final illness.......88
12,000 knowledges.......186, 413
12,000 meanings on every letter of Quran.......413
12,000 specialties granted Shah Naqshband.......186
12,000 times asking forgiveness.......692
124,000 Companions.......395, 431, 441
124,000 prophets.......77, 79, 296, 431, 441
124,000 saints.......77, 354, 431, 587
124,000 salutations on the Prophet.......437
124,000 times 'la ilaha ill-Allah'.......437
124,000 white birds.......353
13 years in Makkah.......74
1400 years ago.......56
142 Traditions from Abu Bakr.......94
148,000 times 'Allah, Allah'.......398
19,999 times Sultan adh-Dhikr.......413

2

2 categories of travel.......153
2 Knowledges.......312
2 Suns.......312
2 Wings.......312
24,000 times salawat.......398
27 pilgrimages led by Shaykh Nazim.......434

3

3 bad human characteristics.......44 5
3 kinds of hearts.......160
3 lights.......706
30,000 troops commanded by Salman.......102
300 palm trees.......100
313 exalted saints.......76, 77, 429, 441
313 messengers.......59, 76, 429
313,000 times 'Allah, Allah'.......437
350 rakats daily practice of Shaykh Khas Muhammad.......334
363 times in 24 hours.......186
39 spiritual Ways other than the Naqshbandi.......269

4

4 Imams.......90, 604, 608
4 letters.......152
4 mistakes.......117
4,000 date stones.......690
4,000 grave sins forgiven on saying la ilaha ill-Allah.......709
4,000 year-old frog.......709
40 days avoiding anger.......733
40 days rain.......306
40 days seclusion.......50, 53, 410, 439
40 days snake wrapped around Shaykh Abd Allah ad-Daghestani.......400
40 days vision of the Prophet.......399
40 days without food.......300
40 saints.......77
40 years – age when Prophet Muhammad received first revelation.......72
400,000 people attended Shaykh Abd Allah's funeral.......420
450 years Pharoah's following his own self.......710
48,000 times 'Allah, Allah'.......381

5

5 greatest prophets.......140
5 spiritual poles.......77, 441
5 stages of Ascension.......75
5 stations of the heart.......405, 406
5 years seclusion of Shaykh Abd Allah ad-Daghestani.......398
5,000 times 'Allah, Allah'.......381
5,000 times 'la ilaha ill-Allah'.......155
50 prescribed prayers.......77
500 circumambulations of al-Qasim by the Kabah.......105
500 Traditions.......94
500,000 Traditions.......226

6

6 cold showers daily during seclusion.......398
600,000 letters in Quran.......413
63 years lifetime of Prophet.......88
63,000 years.......630

7

7 stages of Dhikr of Allah.......381
7 steps of the journey.......381
7 under God's Shadow.......54
7,000 deputies of Shaykh Muhammad Masum.......279
7,000 years.......630
7,007 Naqshbandi saints.......59, 76, 77, 79, 186, 187, 388, 431, 441, 587, 589
70,000 angels.......137
70,000 times God's Gaze was directed at the Light of Muhammad.......143
70,000 veils.......187, 584, 718
70,000 years.......630
777,777 times 'Allah, Allah'.......399

8

8 principles.......150

9

9 months and 10 days.......55
9 points.......58
9 saints.......58, 404, 413
9 times Sultan adh-Dhikr.......413
9,999 times Sultan adh-Dhikr.......413
900,000 people initiated by Shaykh Muhammad Masum.......279
99 Divine Names and Attributes.......131, 152, 381, 396, 683
99 times Sultan adh-Dhikr.......413
999 times Sultan adh-Dhikr.......413

Index of Places

A

Africa........502
Ajam........262
Aleppo........309, 409, 419, 429
Alexandria........409
al-Madain........27
al-Qudayd........107
Amad........325
Amasya........329
Ambikata........192
America........25, 423, 468, 471, 603
Amman........436
Anatolia........146
Ankara........457
Arafah........108, 109, 444
Armenia........326, 355, 387
ar-Raha........309
Asruniyya Souk........455
Aswan Dam........422
Australia........458, 472
Austria........458
Azarbaijan........355

B

Badr........81, 94, 100, 700
Baghdad........134, 135, 197, 308, 312, 410, 436, 438, 588
Bakshur........137
Balkh........227
Bandung........463
Banu Qurayzah........81
Barcelona........459
Basra........95, 643, 644
Bayazit........428
Bayt al-Mamur........431
Beirut........411, 419, 421, 435, 442
Belgium........458, 485
Bellapais........547
Berne........507
Birmingham........489
Bistam........120, 124, 128, 310
Bitala........298
Black Forest........482
Black Sea........369
Bonndorf........482
Bosnia........487, 502
Bosnia........459
Bosporus........356
Bostra........71
Brunei........461
Bukhara........28, 29, 134, 146, 147, 158, 160, 164, 165, 168, 170, 174, 180, 184, 188, 190, 192, 194, 204, 210, 211, 213, 215, 218, 219, 223, 227, 229, 234, 235, 242, 250, 258, 267, 368, 456, 467, 468
Bursa........366, 371, 378, 385, 390, 397, 422, 457
Buzanjird........134
Byzantium........136, 300

C

Cairo........422
Calcutta........657
California........486
Canada........458, 469, 485, 502
Cape Town........466
Caucasia........322, 323, 326, 338, 354, 369
Caucasus........491
Central Asia........29, 134, 145, 146, 174, 215, 380, 677
Charkh........226
Chechnya........335, 336, 341, 466
China........25, 422, 472, 591, 611
Cordoba........459
Cyprus........420, 421, 422, 433, 442, 547, 549

D

Daghestan........185, 323, 325, 326, 327, 332, 335, 336, 338, 340, 341, 342, 343, 344, 348, 349, 354, 355, 360, 362, 366, 367, 375, 378, 379, 380, 385, 386, 387, 392, 395, 396, 403, 410, 466, 467, 611
Damascus........28, 54, 71, 101, 124, 136, 146, 309, 313, 317, 318, 319, 323, 325, 336, 389, 409, 410, 417, 419, 428, 429, 430, 434, 435, 438, 455, 485, 614, 646, 647
Dar al-Arqam........74
Dardanelles........400
Delhi........262, 263, 282, 291, 299, 301, 306, 311, 322
Dome of the Rock........174, 176, 312, 395
Durban........466

E

Egypt........226, 229, 409, 434
England........421, 422, 481
Eskisehir........387, 390, 457
Ethiopia........74
Europe........25, 421, 422, 458, 459, 471, 472, 489, 491, 502, 603

F

Far East........393, 422, 461, 471
Farmad........131
Fatahabad........228
France........458
Freiburg........480

G

Ganep........376
Garnin........226
Germany........422, 458
Ghanib........366
Ghazikumuk........348, 349, 351
Ghaziut........208, 213
Ghujdawan........28, 146, 160
Granada........459
Grozny........467
Gunekoy........371, 373

H

Hadramaut........466
Hama........429
Hamadan........134
Hayy al-Maidan........430
Herat........137, 208, 211, 226, 227, 235, 248, 249, 250, 251, 310
Hijaz........100, 214, 301, 309, 312, 313, 362, 612
Hira........50, 51, 52, 72, 399
Holland........458
Homs........325, 409, 429, 430
Hulgatu........230
Hunayn........82

I

India........25, 262, 266, 267, 282, 286, 290, 302, 310, 312, 323, 466, 499, 657
Indonesia........502
Iran........124, 128, 310, 312, 499, 643
Iraq........211, 300, 308, 311, 312, 326, 643
Isfahan........27, 100, 134
Islamabad........465
Isparta........457
Istanbul........355, 356, 357, 366, 369, 370, 371, 378, 387, 390, 428, 429, 457, 547
Italy........458
Ivory Coast........499
Izmir........390

J

Jaganyan........223, 229
Jahanabad........262, 310, 311
Jam........310
Jannat al-Mualla........109
Jerusalem........74, 78, 81, 312, 317, 671, 718
Johannesburg........466
Jordan........410, 419, 434, 436
Jumdan........669, 701

K

Kabul........226, 262, 310
Kaman Kashan........244
Kandahar........226, 310
Karachi........465
Karada........308
Kawlak........227
Kazan........352, 354, 355, 368
Kenya........469
Khalil........312
Khandaq........81, 101, 343
Kharqan........128, 310
Khaybar........82
Khurasan........130, 137, 243, 300
Khwarazm........134, 170, 211
Kikunu........366, 368, 376
Kirsehir........457
Konya........457
Korean Peninsula........422
Kuala Lumpur........462
Kubu........348
Kufa........614
Kumama........312
Kuman........325
Kural........338
Kurdemir........322

L

Lahore........266, 311, 438, 465
Larnaca........427
Latakia........409
Lebanon........410, 421, 434, 435, 443, 444, 480, 490
Lefke........xiv, 480, 548
London........458, 462, 471, 472, 549
Los Altos........485
Lote-Tree of the Furthermost Boundary........61, 176

M

Madian........142
Madinah........27, 29, 71, 78, 81, 90, 91, 93, 100, 101, 106, 107, 110, 111, 113, 141, 278, 310, 356, 379, 394, 410, 439, 444, 453
Maidan District........409
Makkah........51, 71, 73, 74, 78, 81, 82, 90, 91, 93, 106, 108, 109, 110, 148, 309, 336, 355, 403, 434, 444, 618, 621, 669, 678, 696, 701, 718, 727
Malaysia........461, 472, 481, 499

Marja……..325, 436
Marmara……..378, 397
Menteng Pulo……..462
Merv……..29, 134, 137, 148, 211
Michigan……..485
Middle East……..28, 146, 456, 489, 502
Mina……..444
Morocco……..479, 499, 502
Moscow……..368, 369, 467
Mosul……..309
Mount Qasiyun……..451
Muta……..82

N

Nabdilkahand……..301
Nahrawan……..695
Najd……..696
Naskh……..192
New York City……..550
New Zealand……..472
Nishapur……..310
North America……..489, 491

O

Olympus……..422
Orhanghazi……..371, 390

P

Pakistan……..266, 438, 461, 465, 499, 502
Persia……..27, 71, 85, 118, 326, 338
Persian Gulf……..422
Peshawar……..310
Pleiades……..103
Punjab……..295, 298, 465

Q

Qasiyun……..317, 410, 435
Qasr al-Arifan……..28, 29, 174, 184, 188, 195, 213, 218
Qilit……..165
Quba……..81
Quds……..317

R

Ramitan……..168, 174
Ramta……..436
Rashadiya……..371, 397
Ray……..310
Riwakar……..160, 161

S

Safar Barlik……..400
Samar……..236
Samarqand……..134, 233, 234, 242, 243, 244, 248, 250, 251, 262, 266
Samas……..177, 181, 187
Sammas……..174
Sana……..85
Sanandaj……..308
Sarawak……..462
Saray……..211
Sartar……..368
Senegal……..499
Shadiman……..248
Sham……..72, 310, 312, 313, 325, 326, 453, 614
Shash……..232
Sheffield……..493
Shirwan……..322
Siberia……..369, 370, 371
Sihar Nidbasin……..266
Simnan……..211, 310
Sinai……..266
Sindh……..465
Singapore……..461, 472
Sirhind……..266, 267, 274, 283
South Africa……..465, 466, 603
South America……..458
Southeast Asia……..489
Southern Africa……..472
Soviet Union……..25, 611
Spain……..458, 459
Sri Lanka……..461, 464, 481
Sueileh……..436
Sughur……..360, 363
Sulaymaniyyah……..308, 309, 310
Syria……..100, 300, 312, 313, 438, 484, 499

T

Tabriz……..325
Tabuk……..82
Tanzania……..469
Tashkent……..233, 242, 243, 250, 468
Tehran……..310
Thawr……..78, 106
Tiflis……..325
Tigris……..101
Timurhansuro……..366
Trabzon……..369, 370
Transoxiana……..194, 210, 226, 300, 312
Tripoli, Lebanon……..421, 429, 430, 432, 443, 484
Turkestan……..244
Turkey……..59, 312, 326, 336, 338, 355, 356, 366, 369, 372, 378, 387, 389, 395, 396, 397, 403, 409, 423, 499, 502
Turkmenistan……..134
Tus……..131, 310

U

Uhud……..81, 93, 100, 698
United Kingdom……..458
United States……..458, 479
Uskudar……..356
Uzbekistan……..28, 146, 147, 467, 468

Notes

In keeping with the tradition of the classical Islamic style from times when books were copied by hand as a labor of love and service, we provide additional space here for the reader to use in writing notes and personal thoughts.